I'm wearing a mask shaped like this.

It's kind of futuristic!

I was sick a lot last year, especially during the second half. Actually, I have a cold as I'm writing this. This is what happens when all you do is create manga. And so my resolution for this year is to not catch a cold.

-Tite Kubo, 2010

BLEACH is author Tite Kubo's second title. Kubo made his debut with *ZOMBIEPOWDER.*, a four-volume series for *WEEKLY SHONEN JUMP*. To date, *BLEACH* has been translated into numerous languages and has also inspired an animated TV series that began airing in the U.S. in 2006. Beginning its serialization in 2001, *BLEACH* is still a mainstay in the pages of *WEEKLY SHONEN JUMP*. In 2005, *BLEACH* was awarded the prestigious Shogakukan Manga Award in the *shonen* (boys) category.

BLEACH
3-in-1 Edition

SHONEN JUMP Manga Omnibus Edition Volume 15
A compilation of the graphic novel volumes 43–45

STORY AND ART BY
TITE KUBO

English Adaptation/Lance Caselman
Translation/Joe Yamazaki
Touch-up Art & Lettering/Mark McMurray
Design - Manga Edition/Kam Li, Yukiko Whitley
Design - Omnibus Edition/Fawn Lau
Editor - Manga Edition/Alexis Kirsch
Editor - Omnibus Edition/Pancha Diaz

Printed in the U.S.A.

Published by VIZ Media, LLC
P.O. Box 77010
San Francisco, CA 94107

10 9 8 7 6 5 4 3 2
Omnibus edition first printing, May 2016
Second printing, November 2018

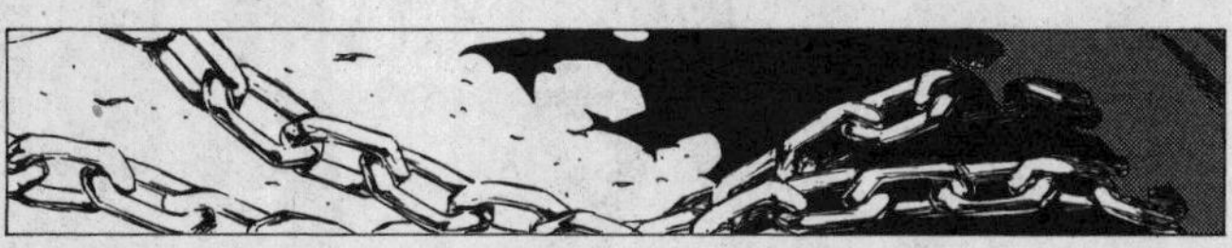

Decay is my friend
Night is my servant
I wait for you in a palace of elm
While I let the crows peck at my body

BLEACH 43 KINGDOM OF HOLLOWS

Shonen Jump Manga

STARS AND

有昭田鉢玄
Hachigen Ushoda

Love Aikawa

愛川羅武

砕蜂
Soi Fon

plot

When high school student Ichigo Kurosaki meets Soul Reaper Rukia Kuchiki his life is changed forever. Soon Ichigo is a soul-cleansing Soul Reaper too, and he finds himself having adventures, as well as problems, that he never would have imagined. Now Ichigo and his friends must stop renegade Soul Reaper Aizen and his army of Arrancars from destroying the Soul Society and wiping out Karakura as well.

While Ichigo defeats Ulquiorra in Hueco Mundo to save Orihime, the Thirteen Court Guard Companies battle it out with the Espadas in Karakura. But when Aizen himself appears on the battlefield, things look grim indeed for the Soul Reapers. Then a dangerous new element is introduced into this already explosive mix with the arrival of the Visoreds. And there's one question on everyone's mind—whose side are they on?

BLEACH ALL

Lilinette

Barragan

Stark

STORIES

BLEACH 43

KINGDOM OF HOLLOWS

Contents

368. The Fearless Child

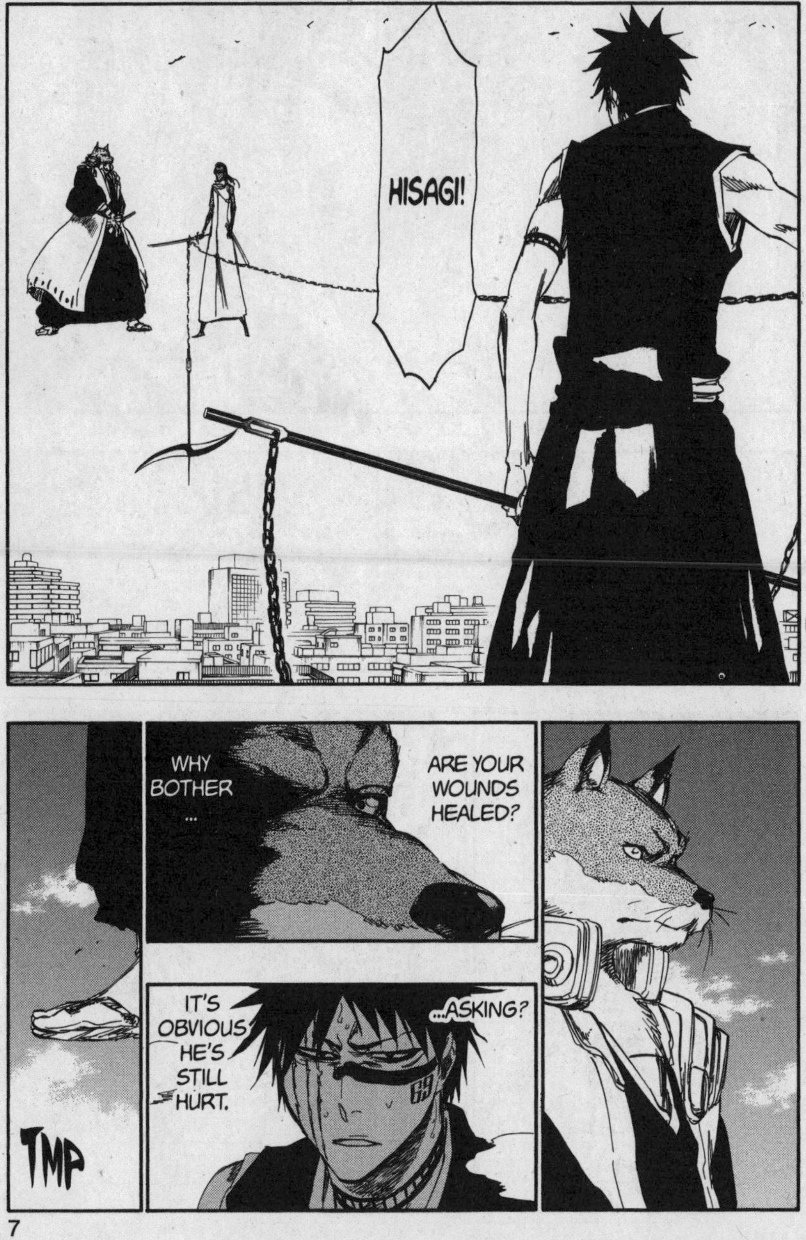

HISAGI!
ARE YOUR WOUNDS HEALED?
WHY BOTHER...
...ASKING?
IT'S OBVIOUS HE'S STILL HURT.
TMP

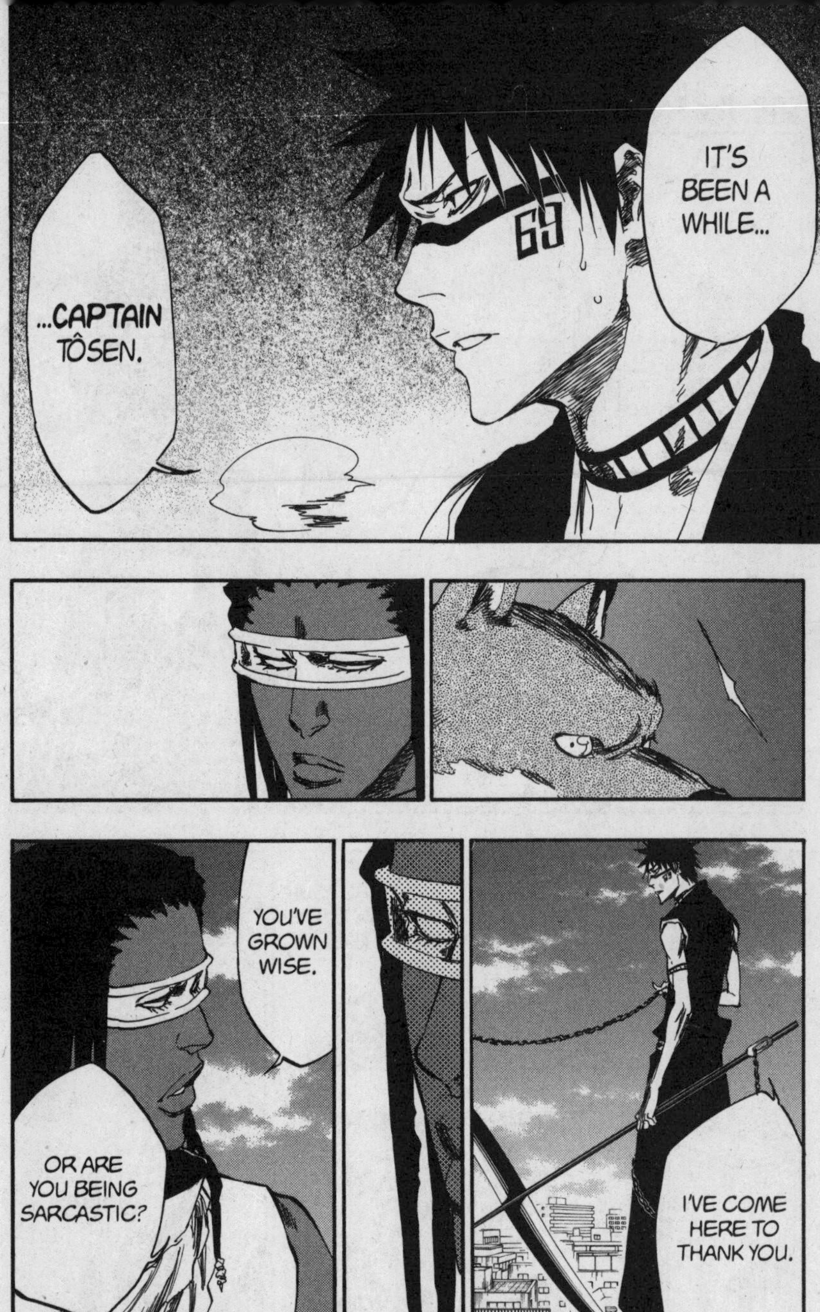
IT'S BEEN A WHILE...
...CAPTAIN TÔSEN.
I'VE COME HERE TO THANK YOU.
YOU'VE GROWN WISE.
OR ARE YOU BEING SARCASTIC?

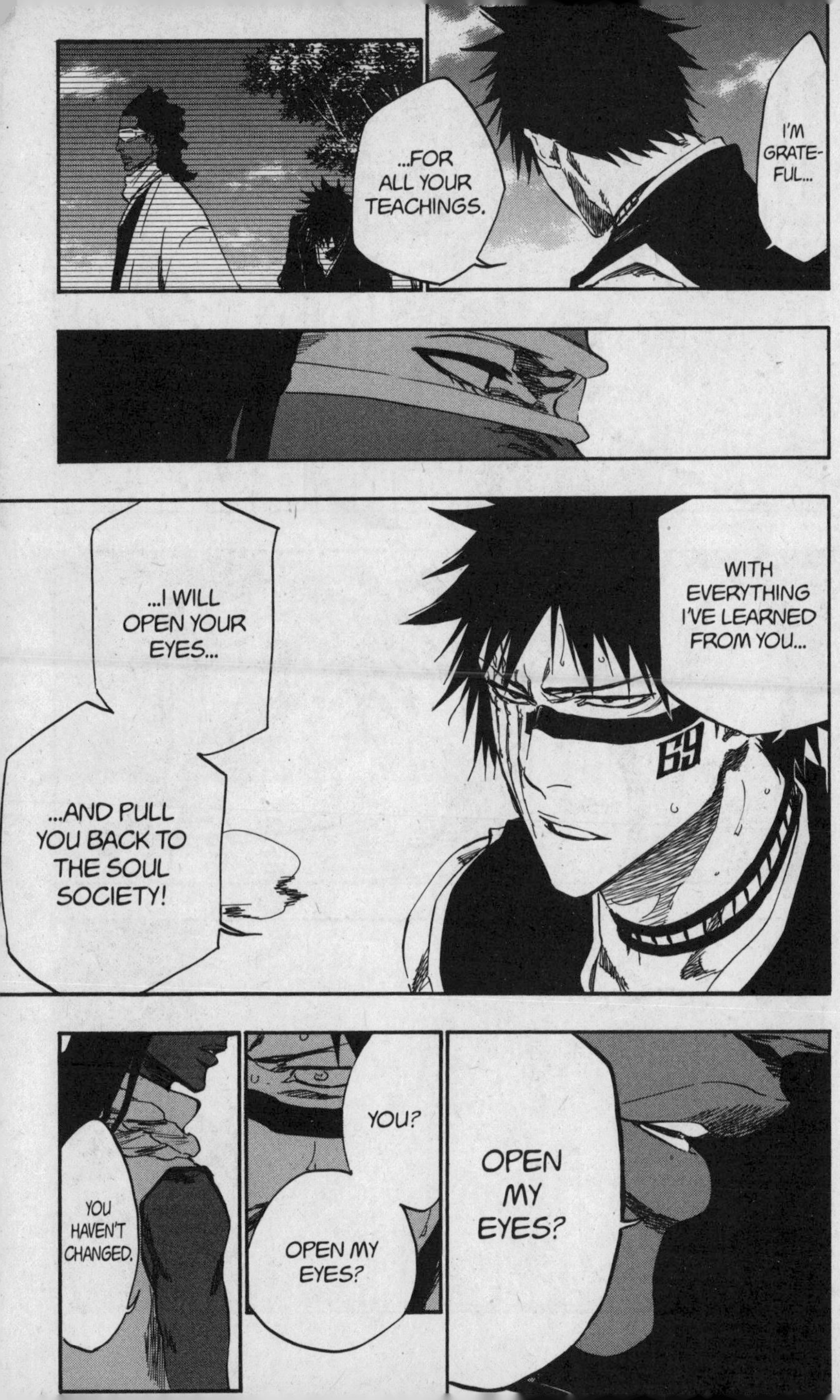
I'M GRATE-FUL...
...FOR ALL YOUR TEACHINGS.
WITH EVERYTHING I'VE LEARNED FROM YOU...
...I WILL OPEN YOUR EYES...
...AND PULL YOU BACK TO THE SOUL SOCIETY!
OPEN MY EYES?
YOU?
OPEN MY EYES?
YOU HAVEN'T CHANGED.

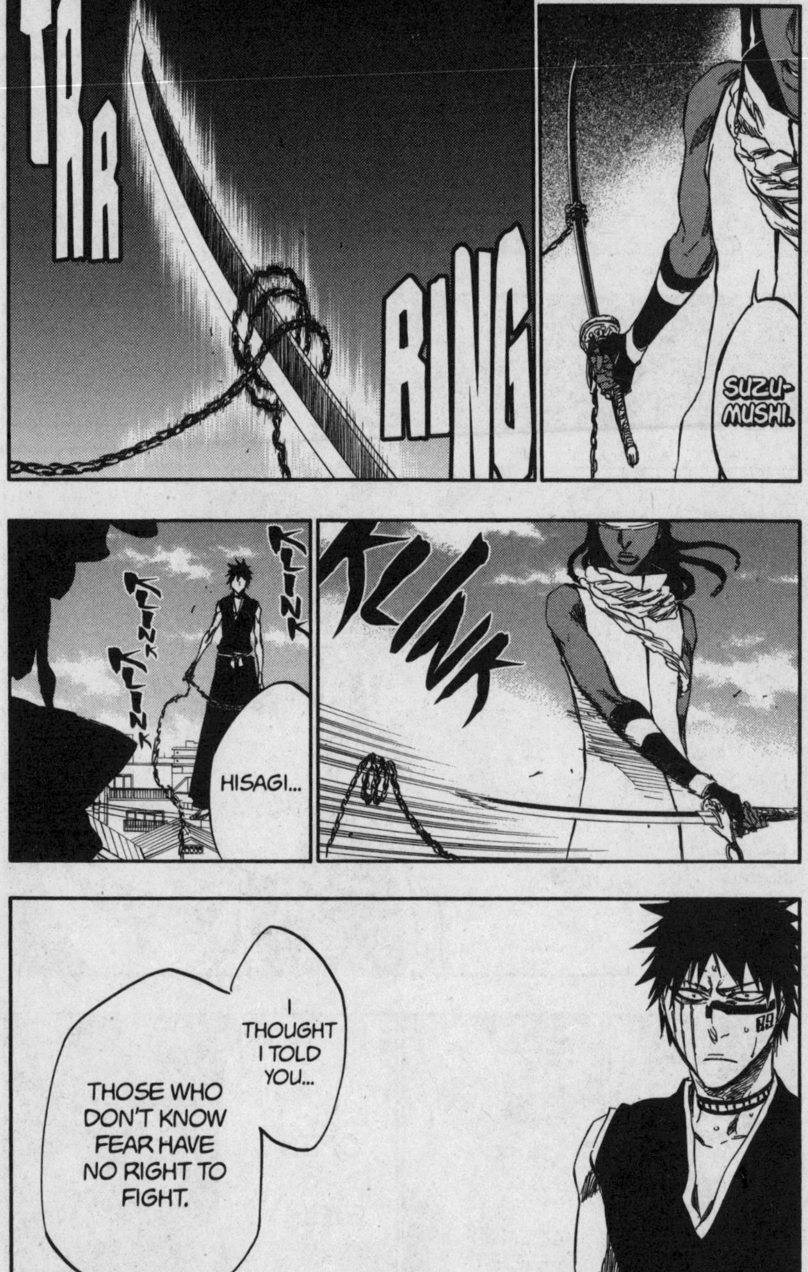
SUZU-MUSHI.
RING
TARR
KLINK
KLINK
KLINK KLINK
HISAGI...
I THOUGHT I TOLD YOU...
THOSE WHO DON'T KNOW FEAR HAVE NO RIGHT TO FIGHT.

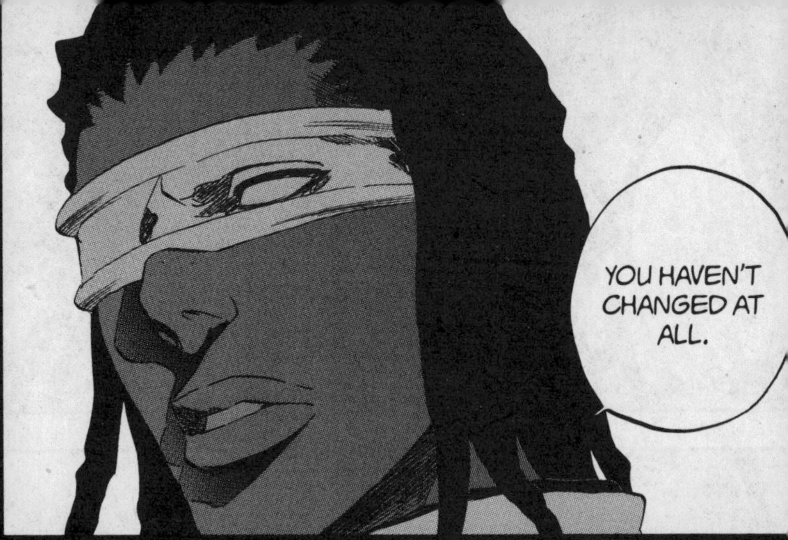
YOU HAVEN'T CHANGED AT ALL.

BLEACH

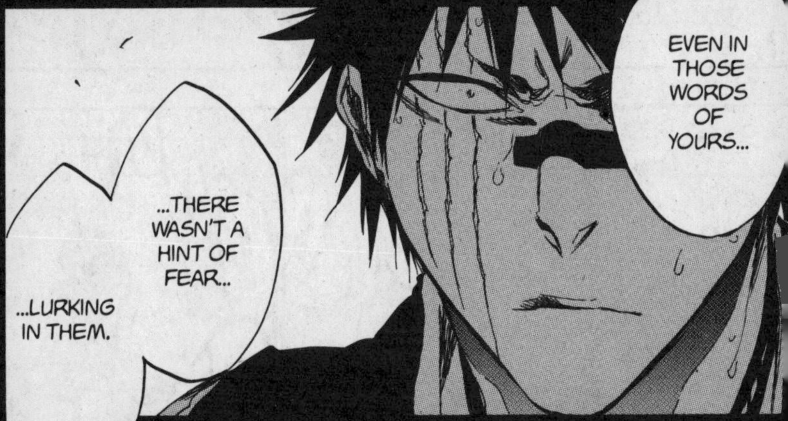
EVEN IN THOSE WORDS OF YOURS...
...THERE WASN'T A HINT OF FEAR...
...LURKING IN THEM.

368. The Fearless Child

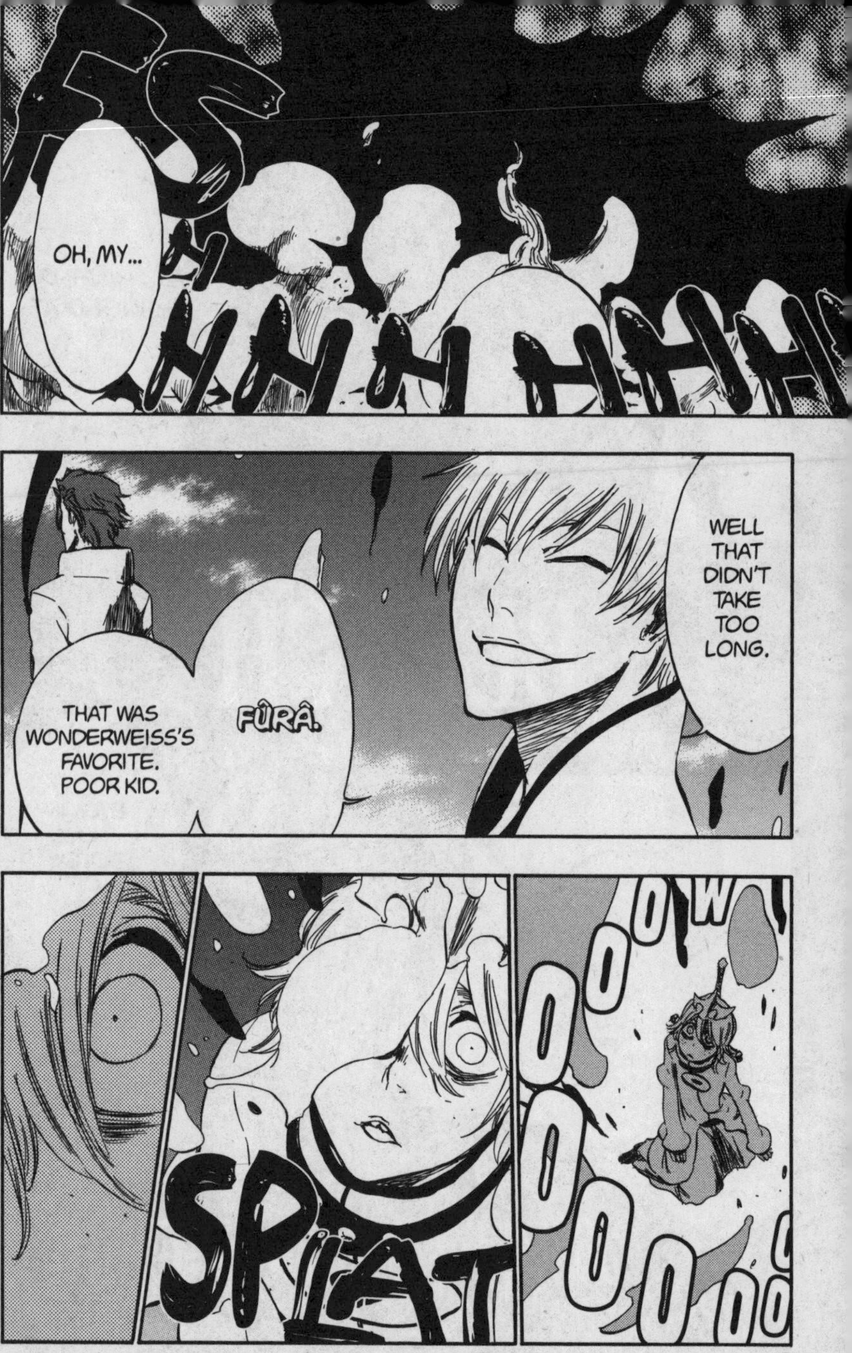
OH, MY...
WELL THAT DIDN'T TAKE TOO LONG.
FÛRÂ.
THAT WAS WONDERWEISS'S FAVORITE. POOR KID.
SPLAT

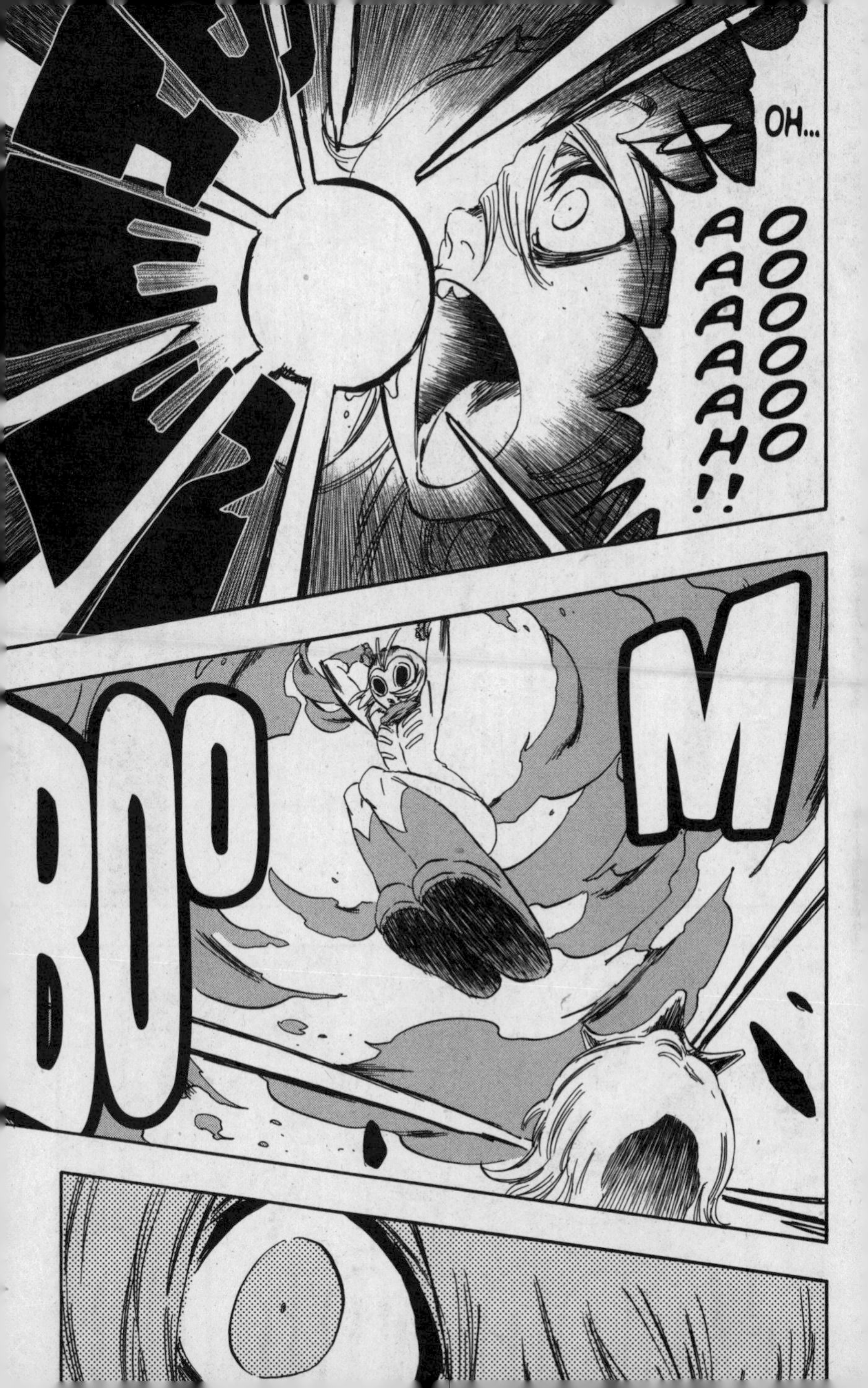
OH...
OOOOOOOAAAAAH!!
BOOM

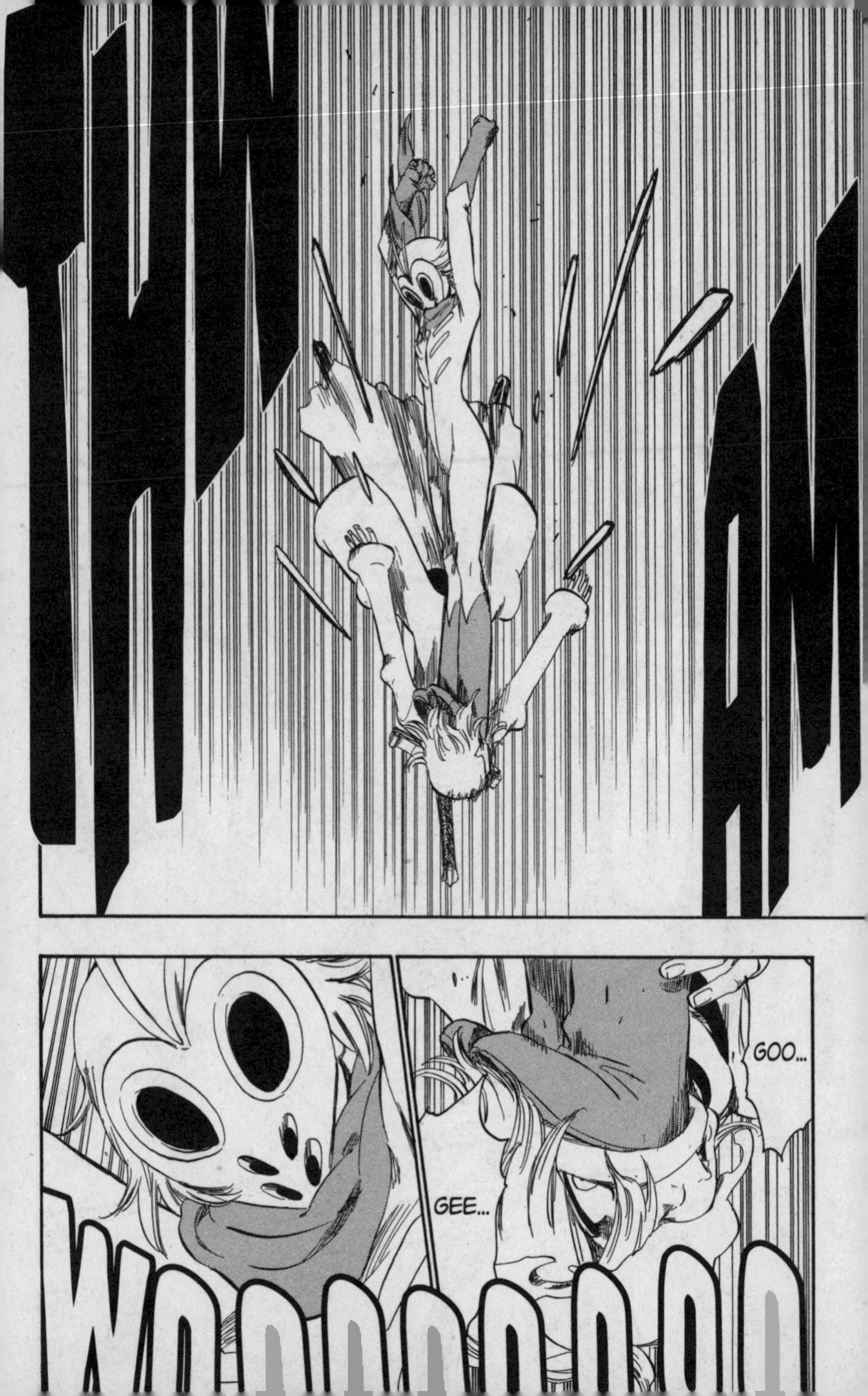
THWAM
!..
GOO...
GEE...

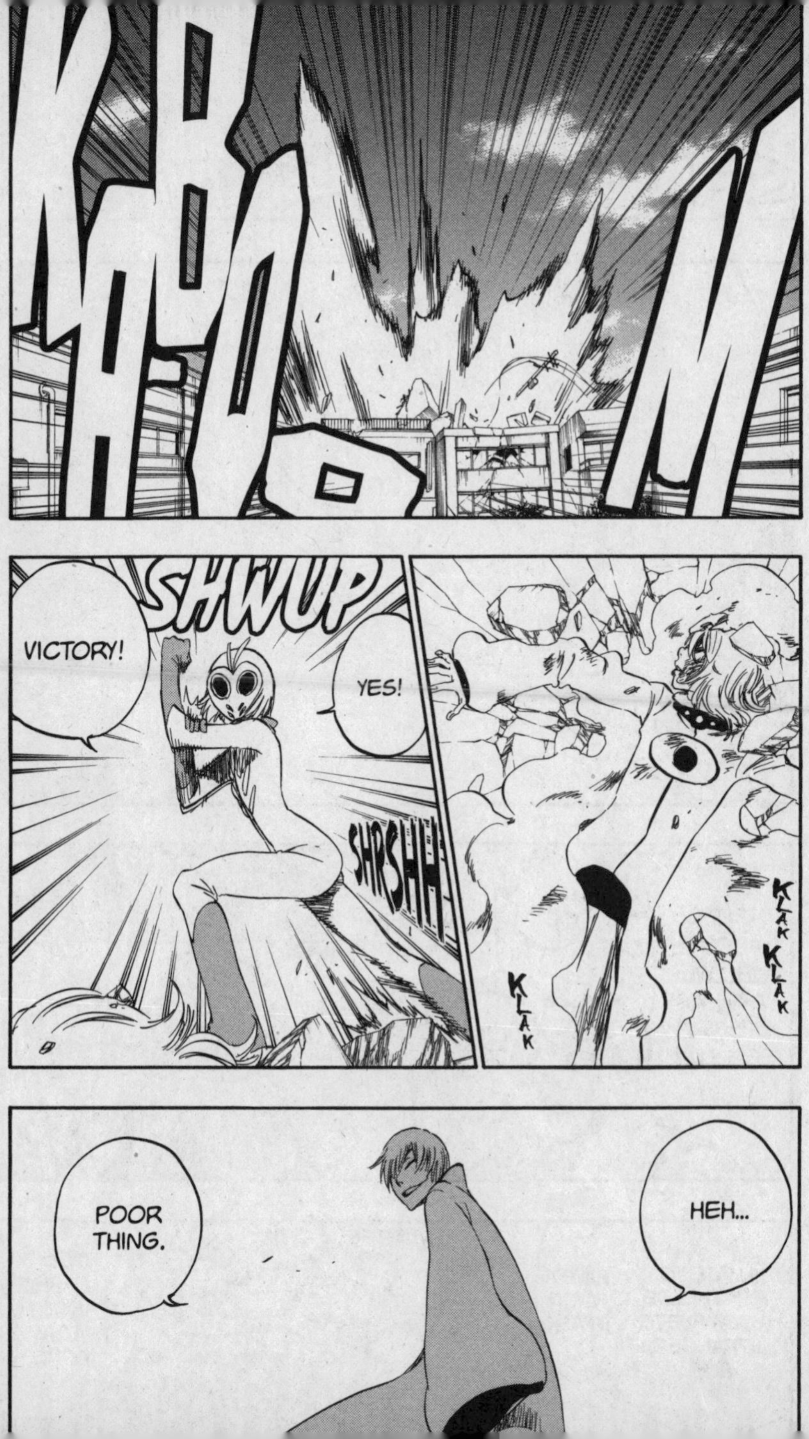
KABOOM
KLAK
KLAK
KLAK
SHWUP
YES!
VICTORY!
SHRSHH
HEH...
POOR THING.

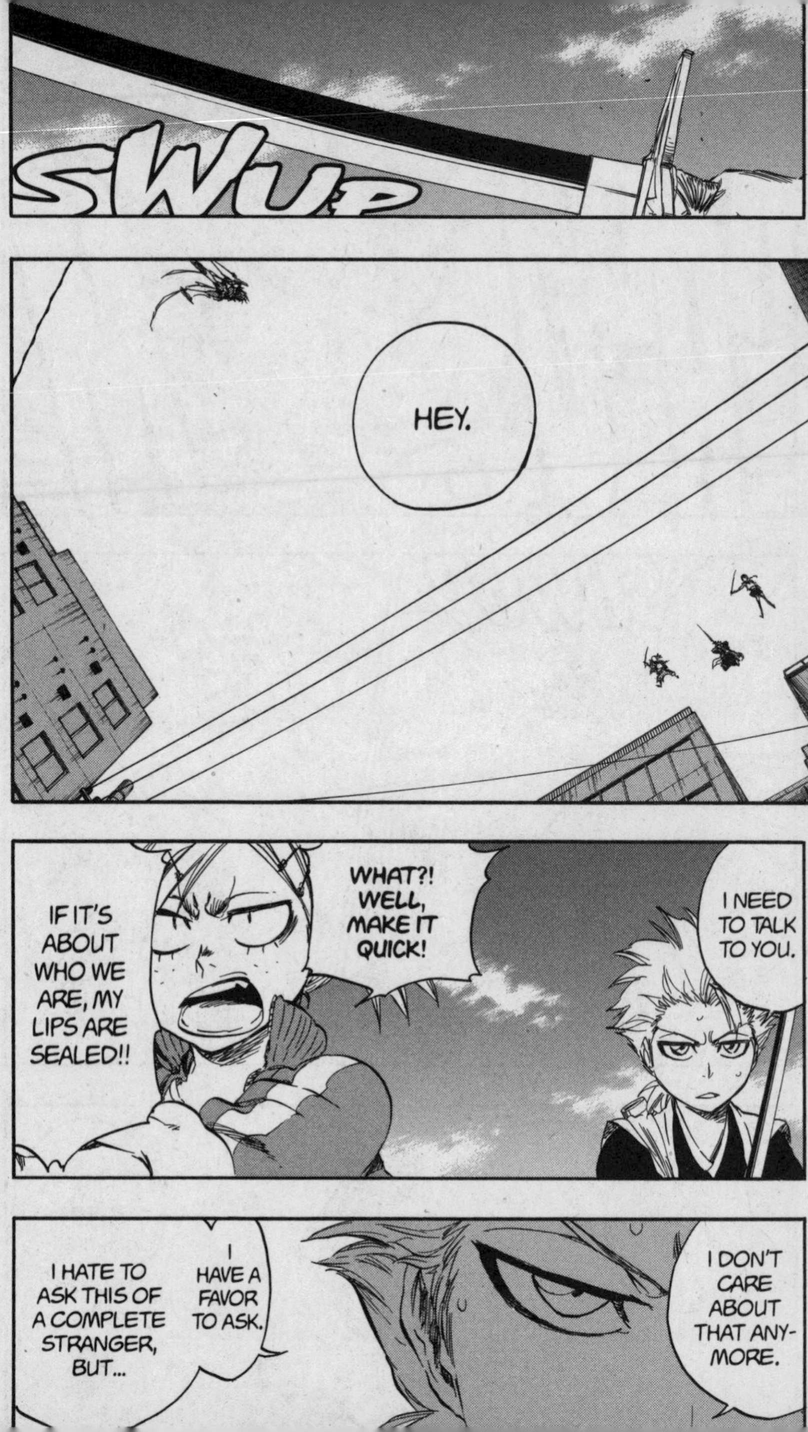
SWUP
HEY.
I NEED TO TALK TO YOU.
WHAT?! WELL, MAKE IT QUICK!
IF IT'S ABOUT WHO WE ARE, MY LIPS ARE SEALED!!
I DON'T CARE ABOUT THAT ANYMORE.
I HAVE A FAVOR TO ASK.
I HATE TO ASK THIS OF A COMPLETE STRANGER, BUT...

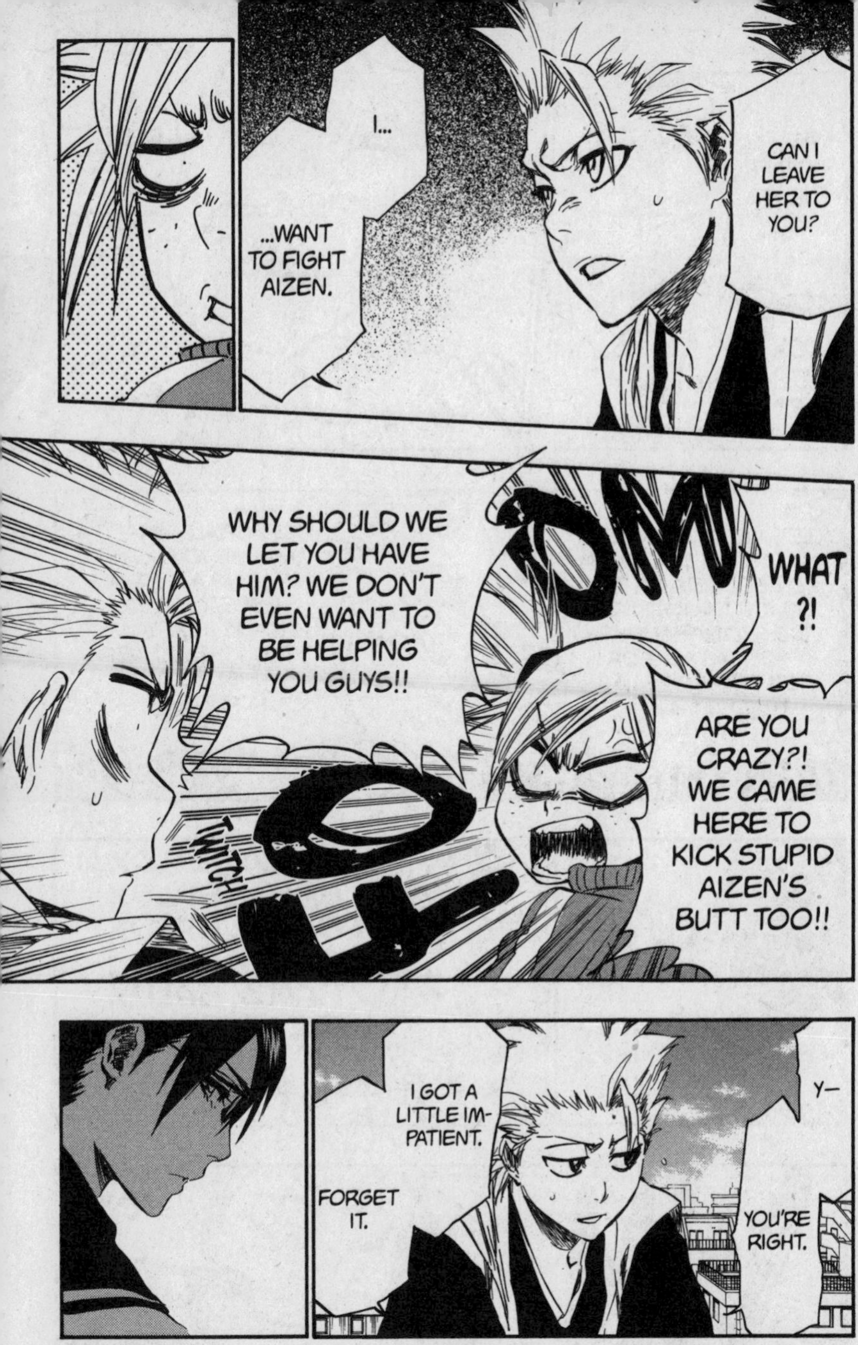
CAN I LEAVE HER TO YOU?
I...
...WANT TO FIGHT AIZEN.
WHAT?!
ARE YOU CRAZY?! WE CAME HERE TO KICK STUPID AIZEN'S BUTT TOO!!
WHY SHOULD WE LET YOU HAVE HIM? WE DON'T EVEN WANT TO BE HELPING YOU GUYS!!
TWITCH
Y—
YOU'RE RIGHT.
I GOT A LITTLE IM-PATIENT.
FORGET IT.

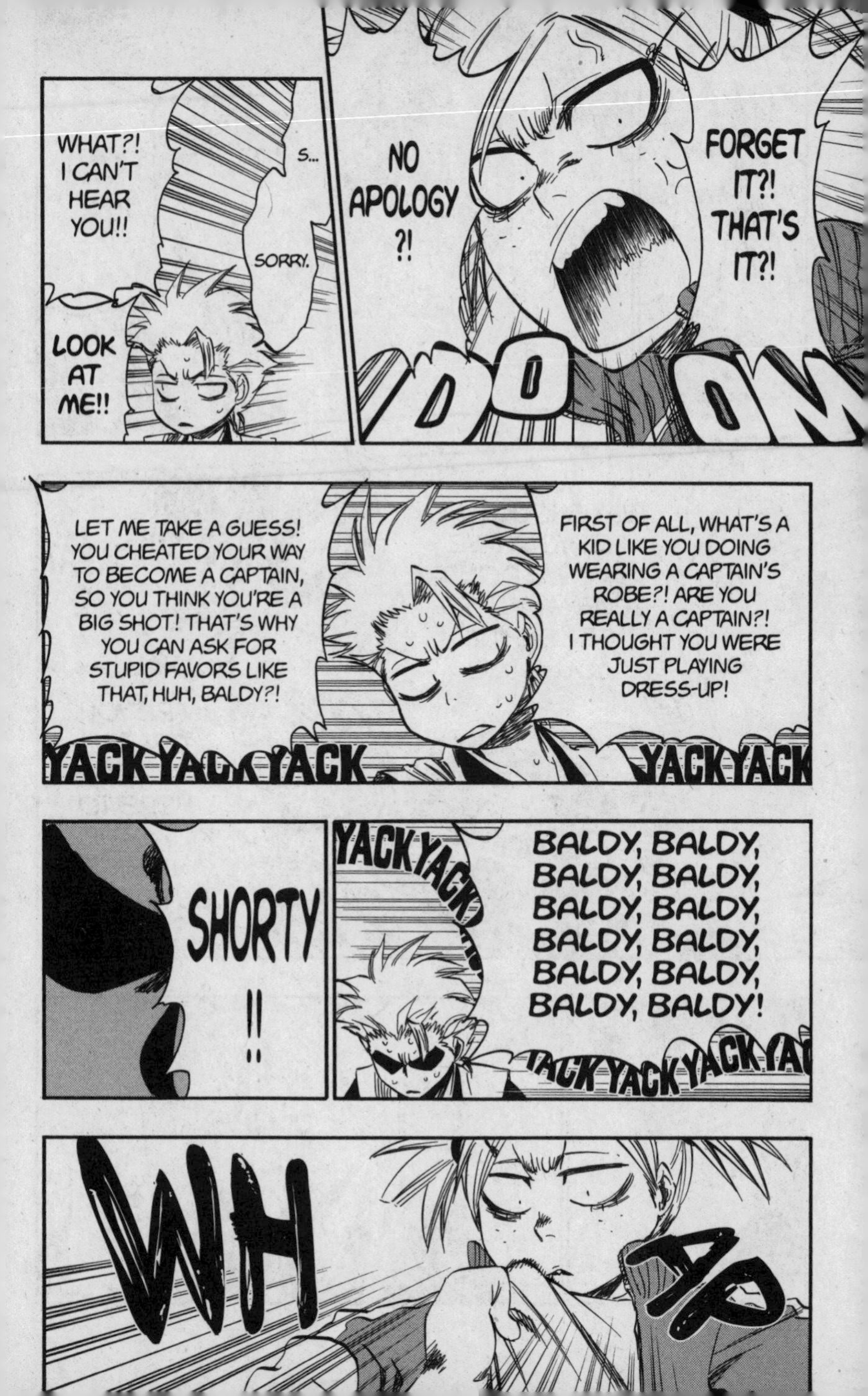
FORGET IT?! THAT'S IT?!
NO APOLOGY?!
DOOM
S...
SORRY.
WHAT?! I CAN'T HEAR YOU!!
LOOK AT ME!!
FIRST OF ALL, WHAT'S A KID LIKE YOU DOING WEARING A CAPTAIN'S ROBE?! ARE YOU REALLY A CAPTAIN?! I THOUGHT YOU WERE JUST PLAYING DRESS-UP!
LET ME TAKE A GUESS! YOU CHEATED YOUR WAY TO BECOME A CAPTAIN, SO YOU THINK YOU'RE A BIG SHOT! THAT'S WHY YOU CAN ASK FOR STUPID FAVORS LIKE THAT, HUH, BALDY?!
YACKYACK
YACK YACK YACK
BALDY, BALDY, BALDY, BALDY, BALDY, BALDY, BALDY, BALDY, BALDY, BALDY, BALDY, BALDY!
YACKYACK
YACK YACK YACK
SHORTY!!
WHAP

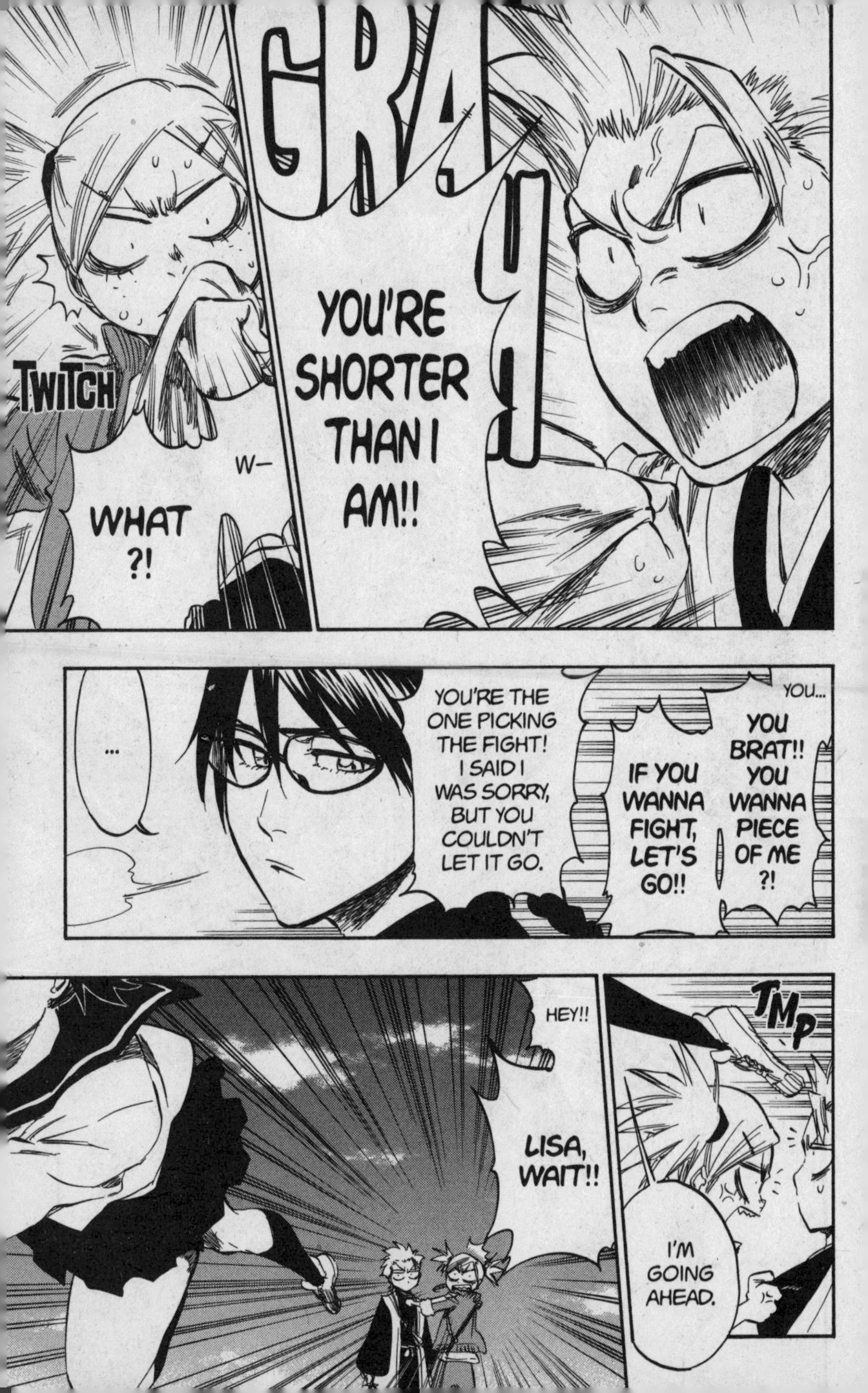
GRAB
YOU'RE SHORTER THAN I AM!!
TWITCH
W—
WHAT ?!
YOU...
YOU BRAT!! YOU WANNA PIECE OF ME ?!
IF YOU WANNA FIGHT, LET'S GO!!
YOU'RE THE ONE PICKING THE FIGHT! I SAID I WAS SORRY, BUT YOU COULDN'T LET IT GO.
...
TMP
I'M GOING AHEAD.
HEY!!
LISA, WAIT!!

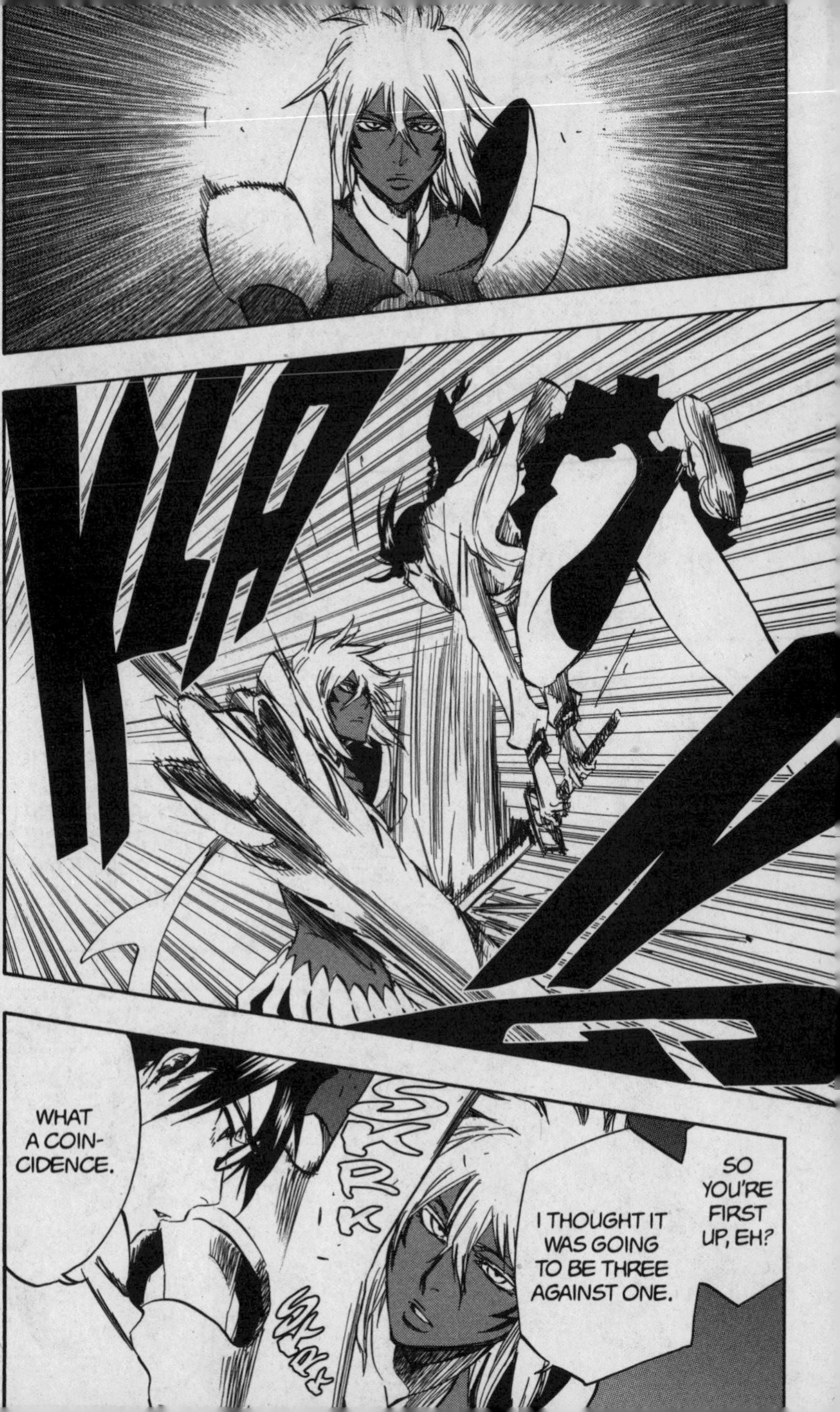
SO YOU'RE FIRST UP, EH?
I THOUGHT IT WAS GOING TO BE THREE AGAINST ONE.
SKRK
WHAT A COINCIDENCE.

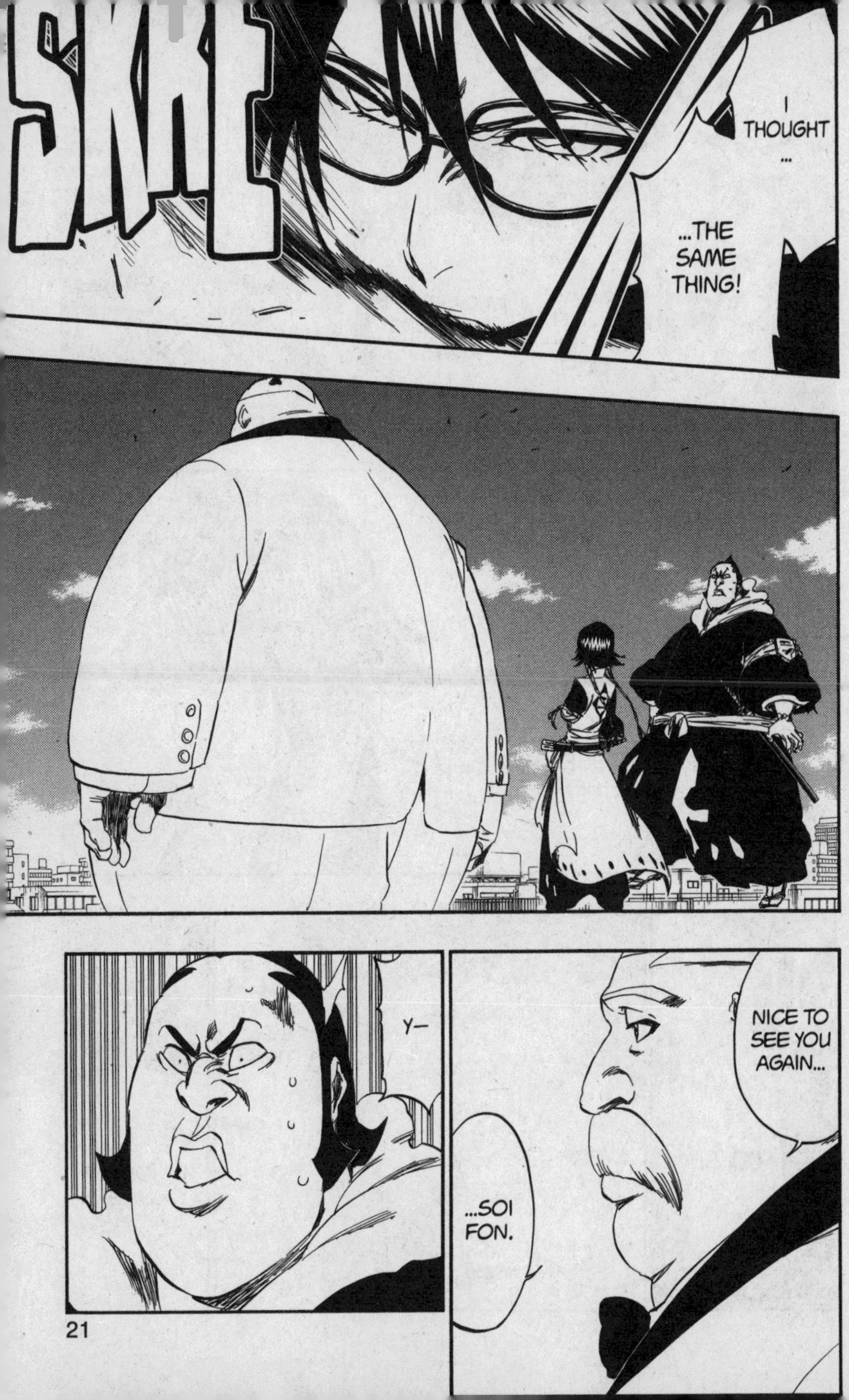
SKRE
I THOUGHT ...
...THE SAME THING!
NICE TO SEE YOU AGAIN...
...SOI FON.
Y—

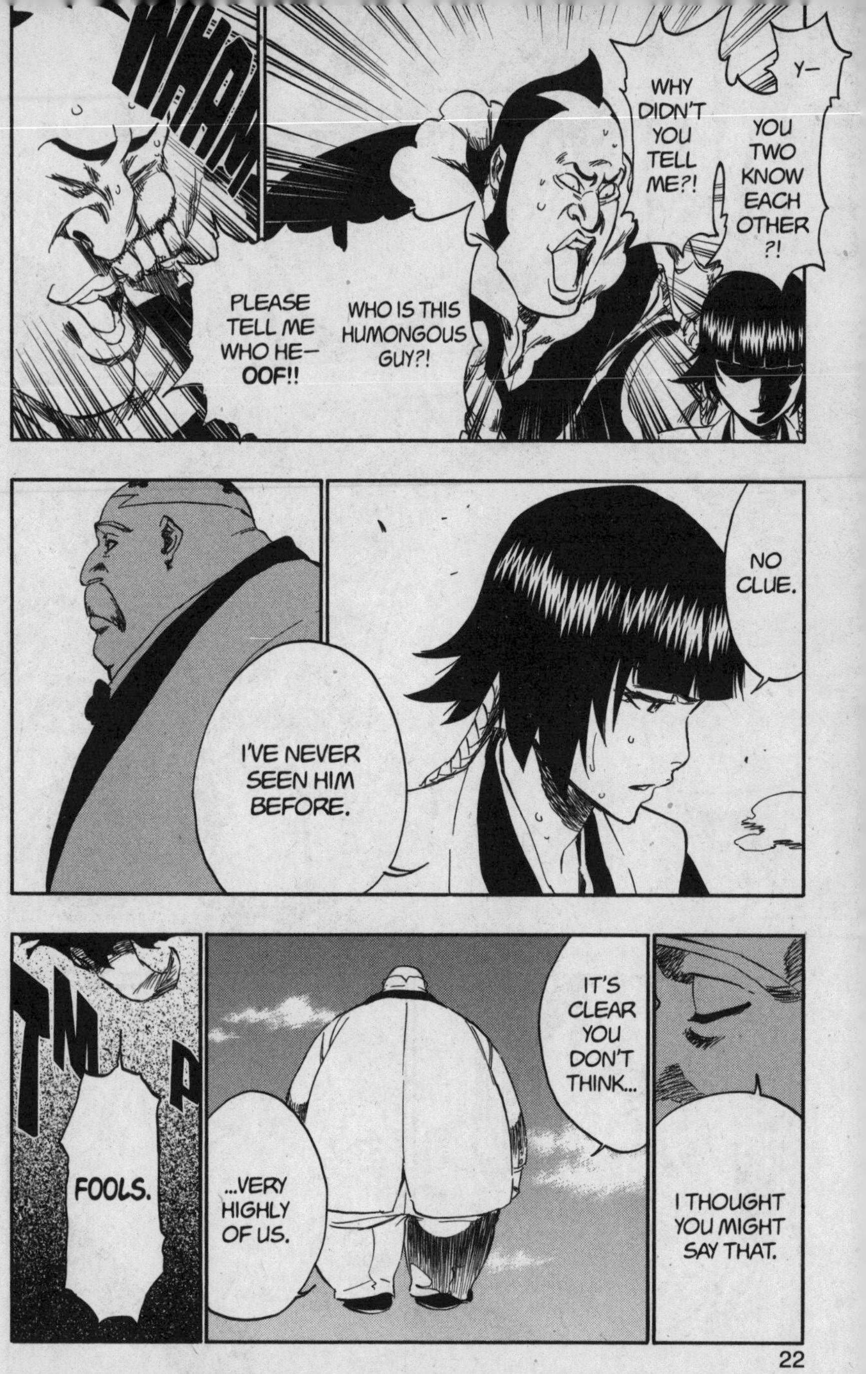
Y—
YOU TWO KNOW EACH OTHER?!
WHY DIDN'T YOU TELL ME?!
WHO IS THIS HUMONGOUS GUY?!
PLEASE TELL ME WHO HE— OOF!!
NO CLUE.
I'VE NEVER SEEN HIM BEFORE.
I THOUGHT YOU MIGHT SAY THAT.
IT'S CLEAR YOU DON'T THINK...
...VERY HIGHLY OF US.
FOOLS.

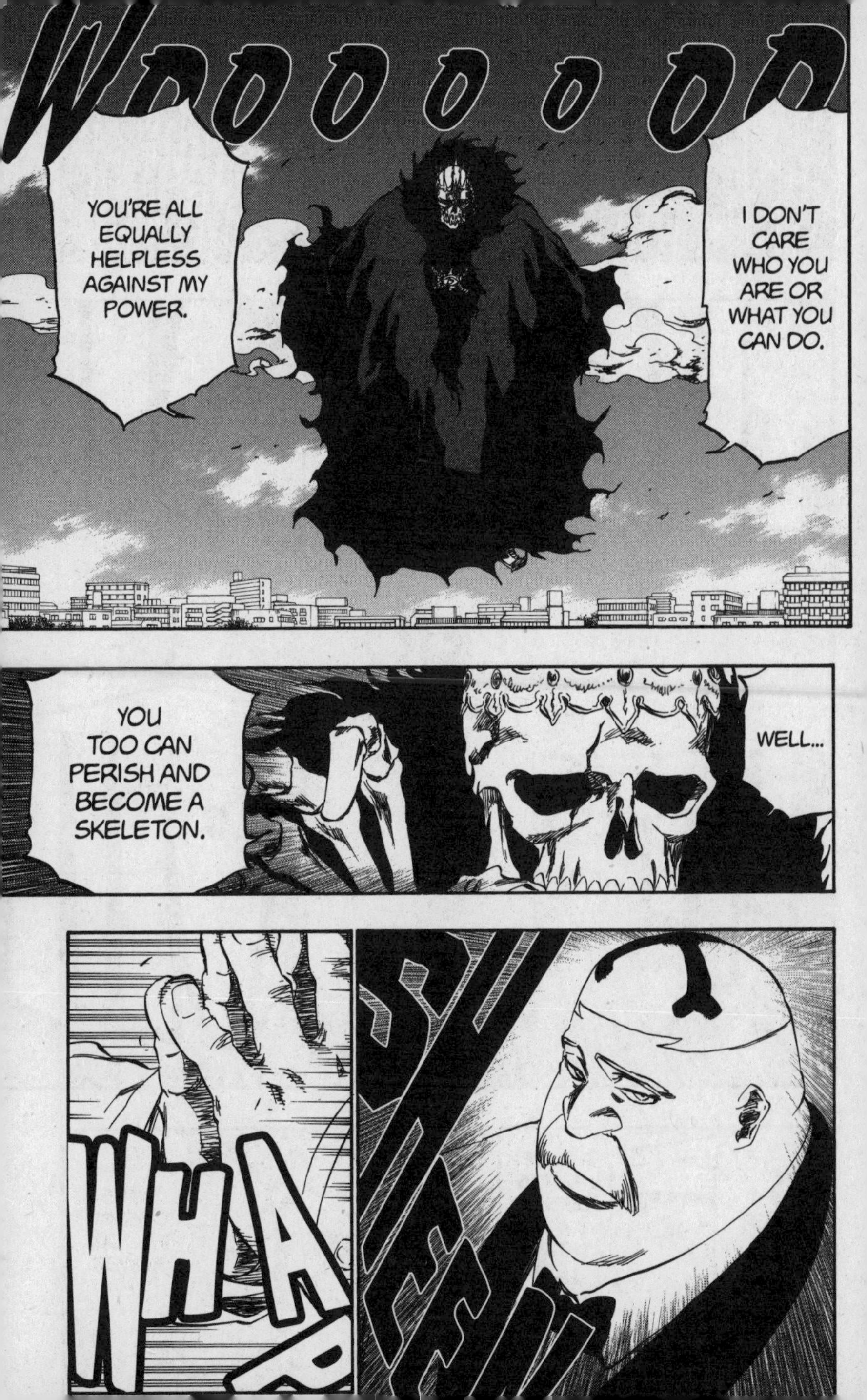
WOOOOOOO
I DON'T CARE WHO YOU ARE OR WHAT YOU CAN DO.
YOU'RE ALL EQUALLY HELPLESS AGAINST MY POWER.
WELL...
YOU TOO CAN PERISH AND BECOME A SKELETON.
WHAP

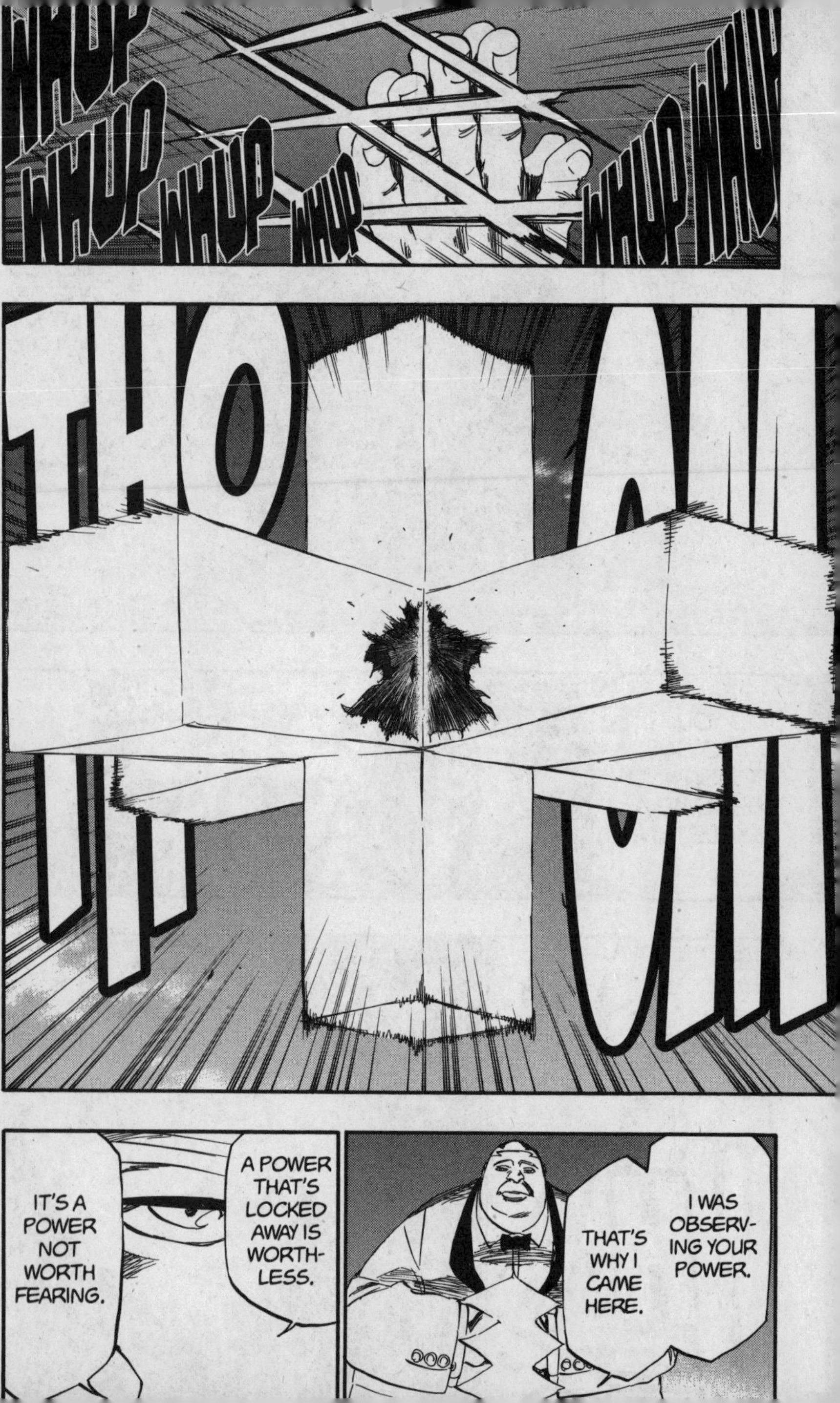
WHUP WHUP
WHUP
WHUP
WHUP
WHUP
WHUP
THOOM
I WAS OBSERV-ING YOUR POWER.
THAT'S WHY I CAME HERE.
A POWER THAT'S LOCKED AWAY IS WORTH-LESS.
IT'S A POWER NOT WORTH FEARING.

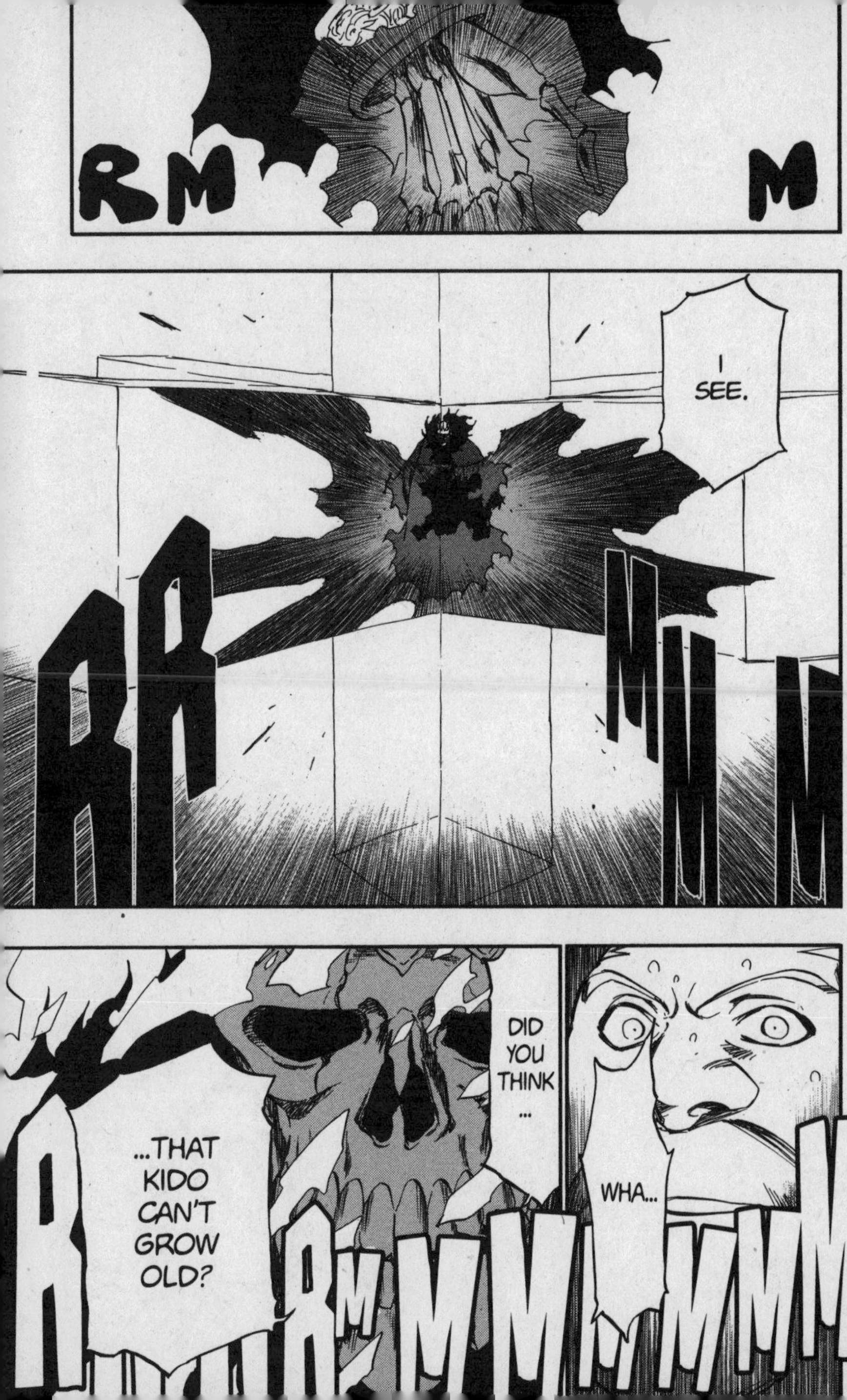
RM
M
I SEE.
RR
MMMM
WHA...
DID YOU THINK...
...THAT KIDO CAN'T GROW OLD?
RRMMMMMMMMM

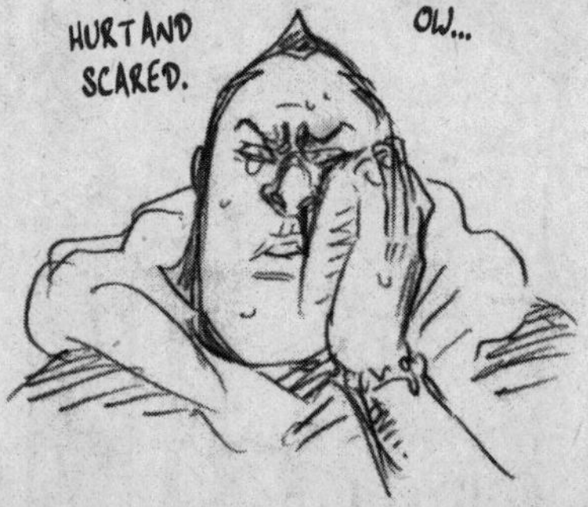
I'M HURT AND SCARED.
OW...

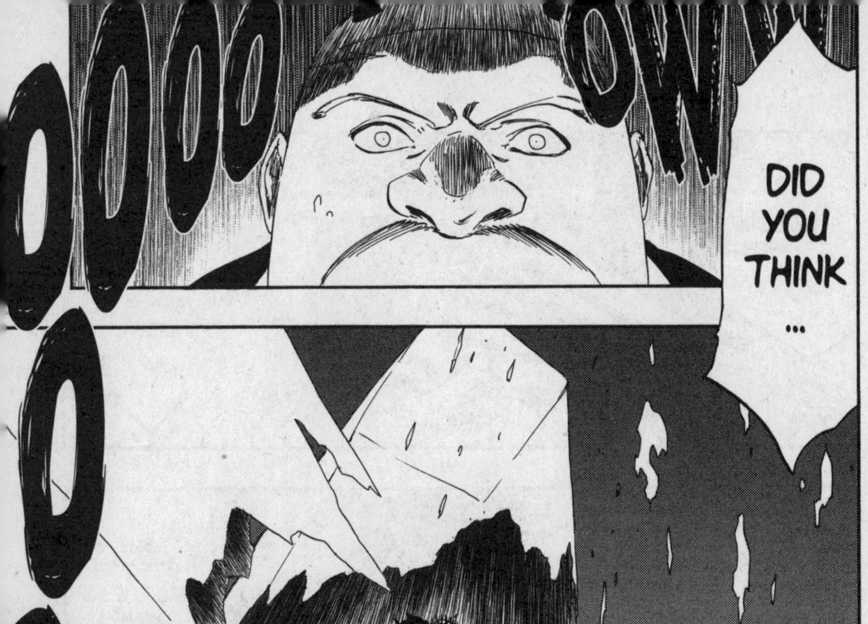
DID YOU THINK ...
...THAT KIDO CAN'T GROW OLD?

369. Spit on Your Own God

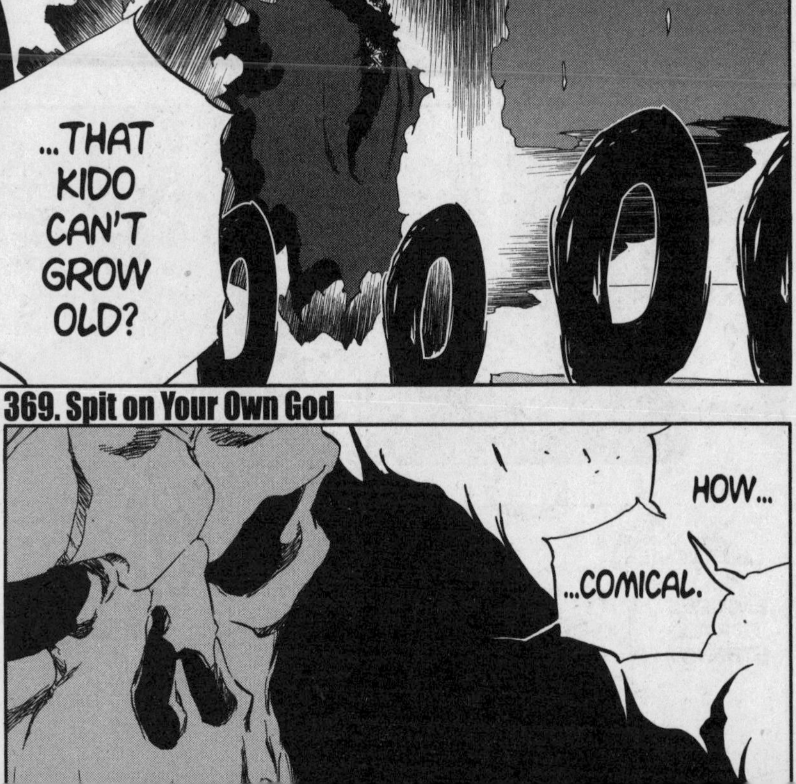
HOW...
...COMICAL.

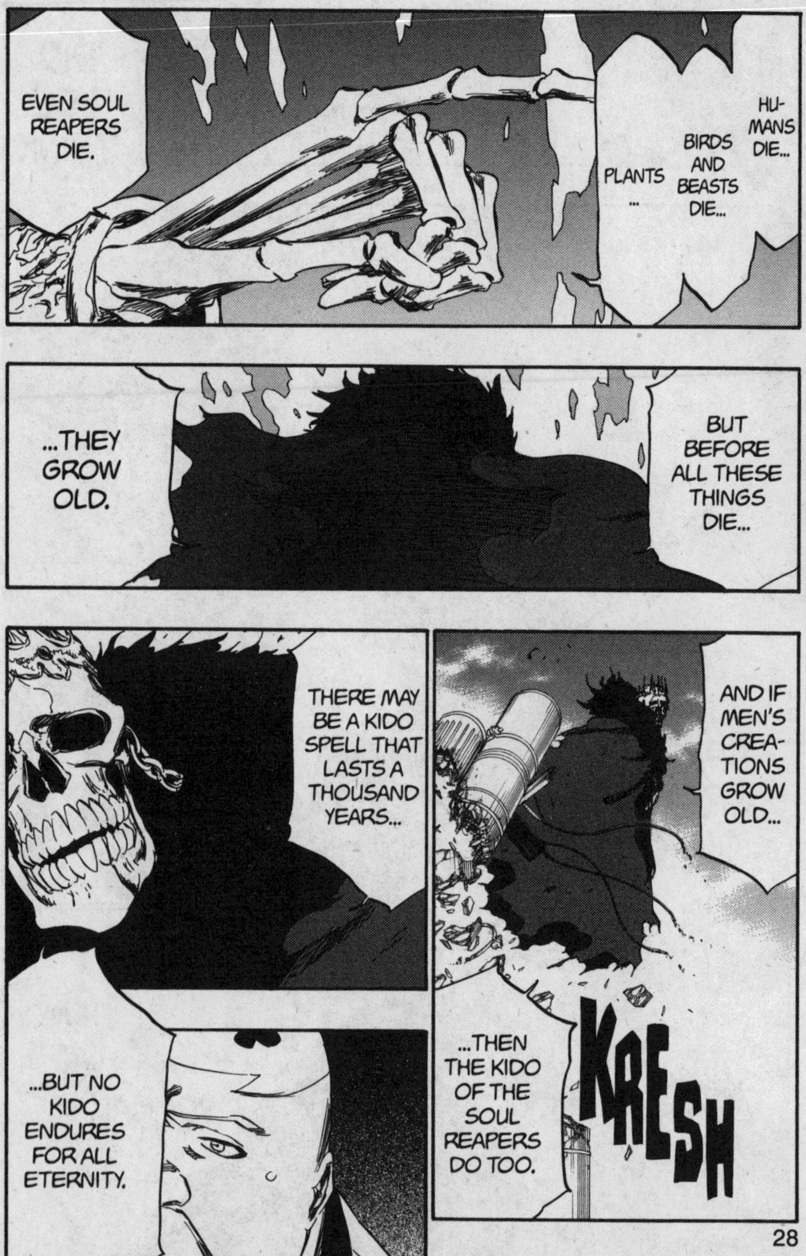
HUMANS DIE...
BIRDS AND BEASTS DIE...
PLANTS...
EVEN SOUL REAPERS DIE.
BUT BEFORE ALL THESE THINGS DIE...
...THEY GROW OLD.
AND IF MEN'S CREATIONS GROW OLD...
...THEN THE KIDO OF THE SOUL REAPERS DO TOO.
KRESH
THERE MAY BE A KIDO SPELL THAT LASTS A THOUSAND YEARS...
...BUT NO KIDO ENDURES FOR ALL ETERNITY.

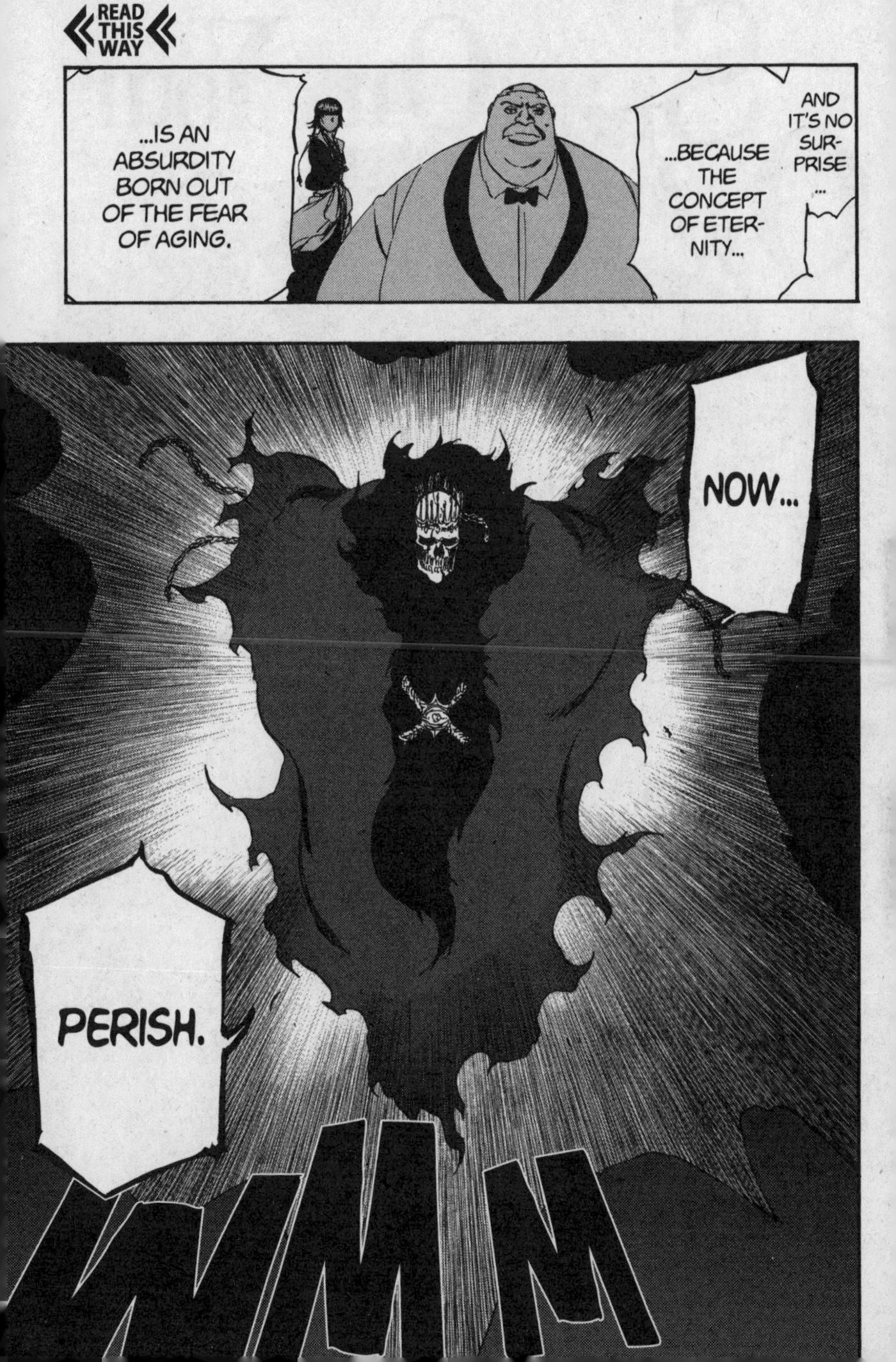
READ THIS WAY
AND IT'S NO SUR-PRISE...
...BECAUSE THE CONCEPT OF ETER-NITY...
...IS AN ABSURDITY BORN OUT OF THE FEAR OF AGING.
NOW...
PERISH.

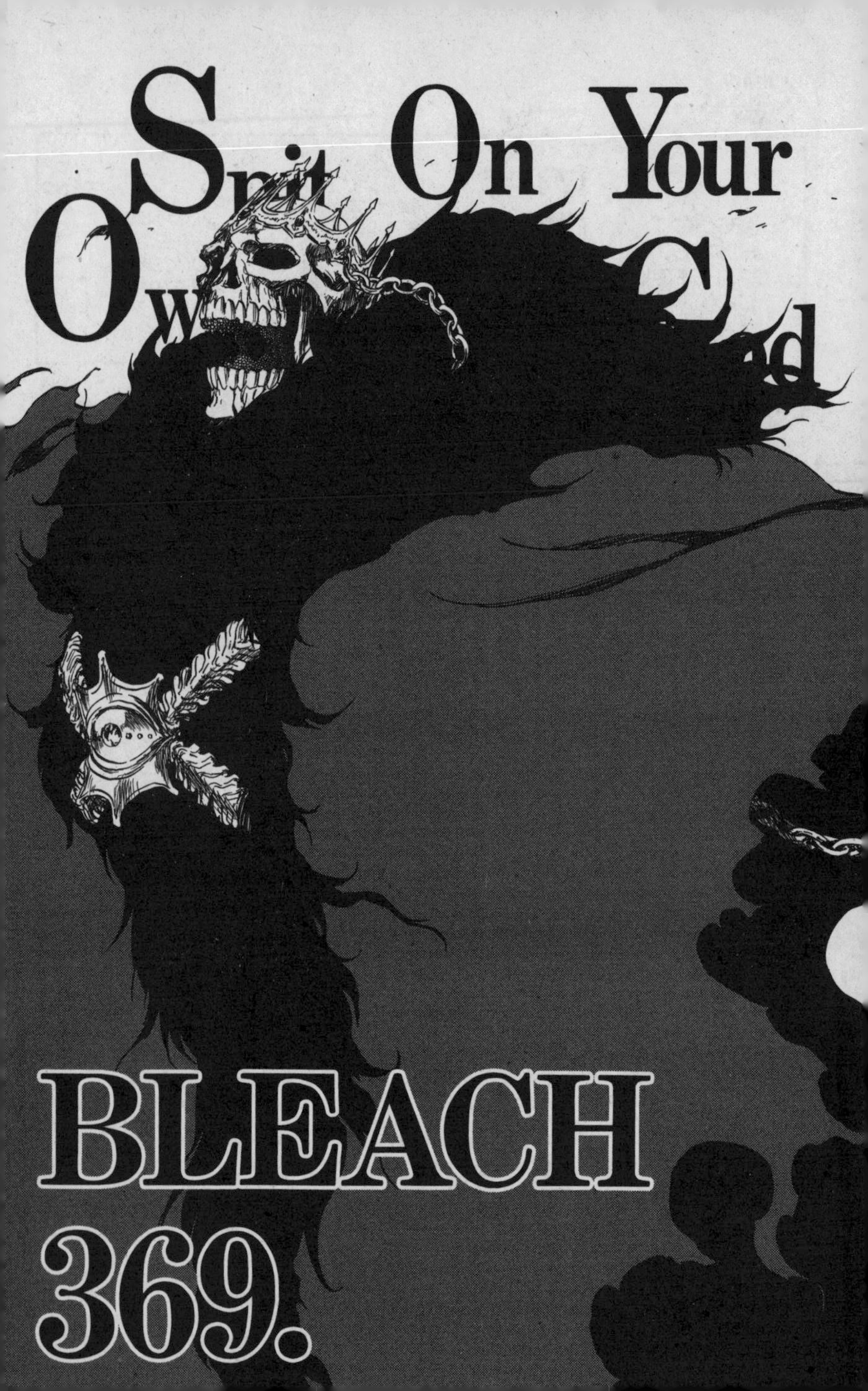
Spit On Your
BLEACH
369.

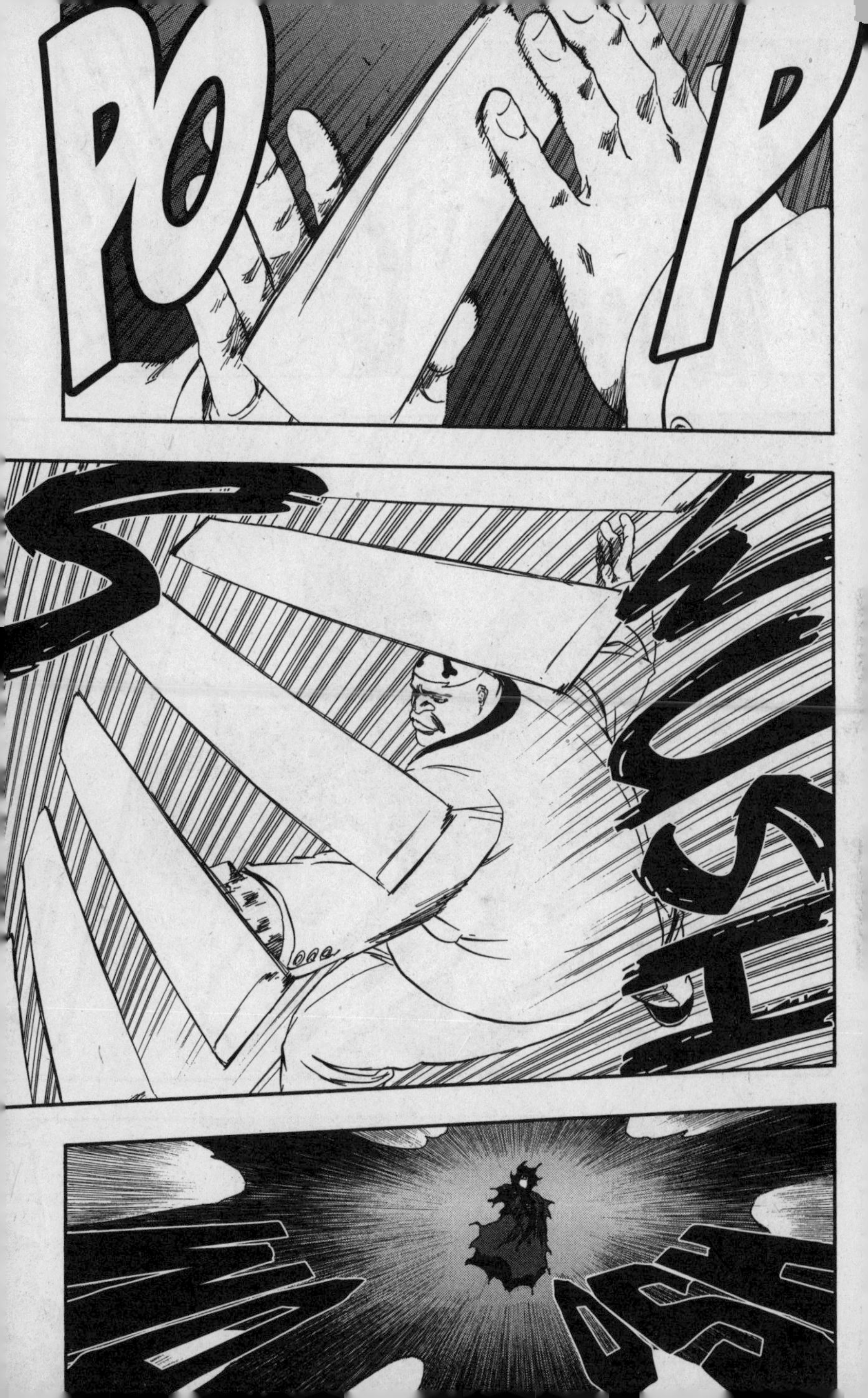
POP
SWUSH

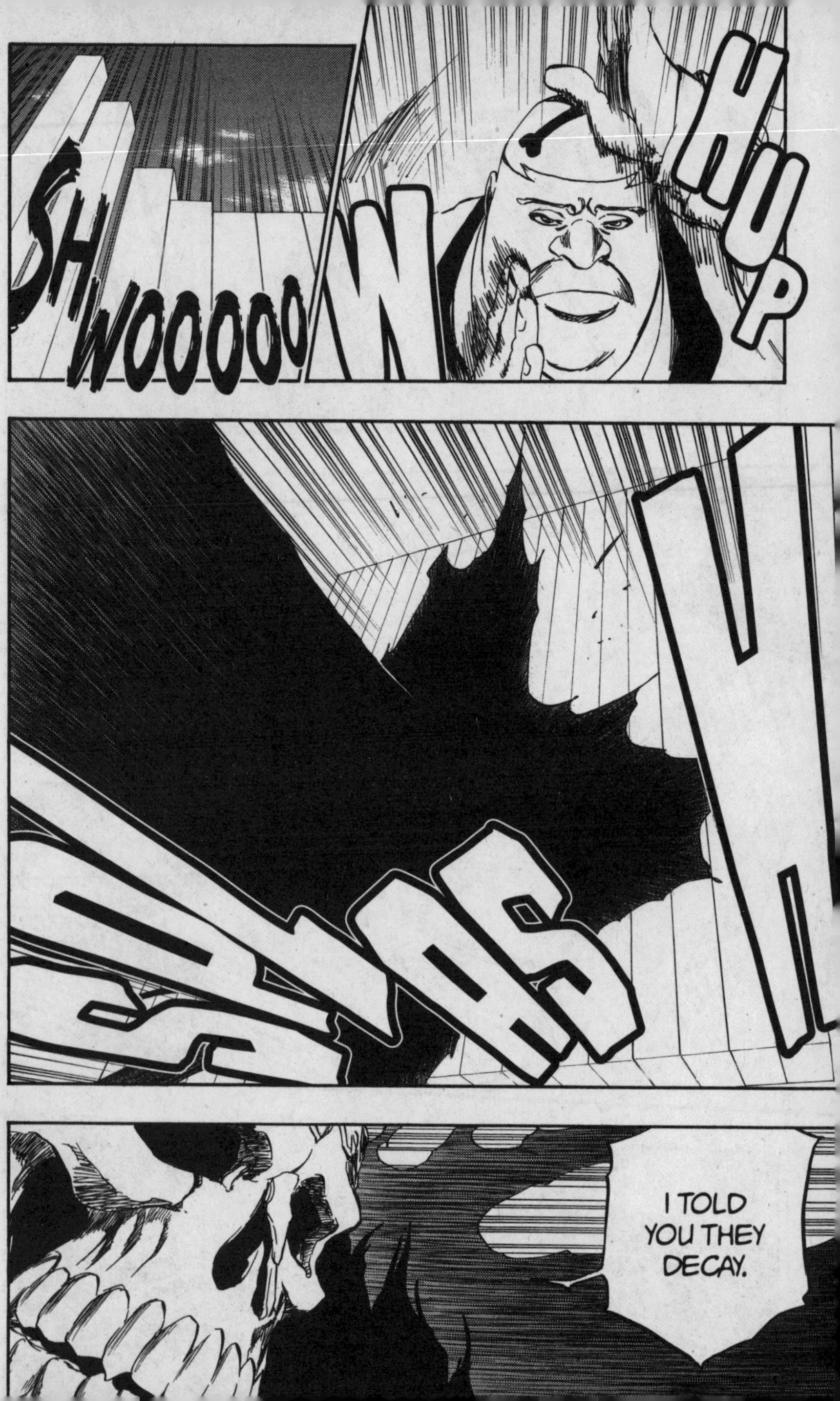
HUP
SHWOOOOON
I TOLD YOU THEY DECAY.

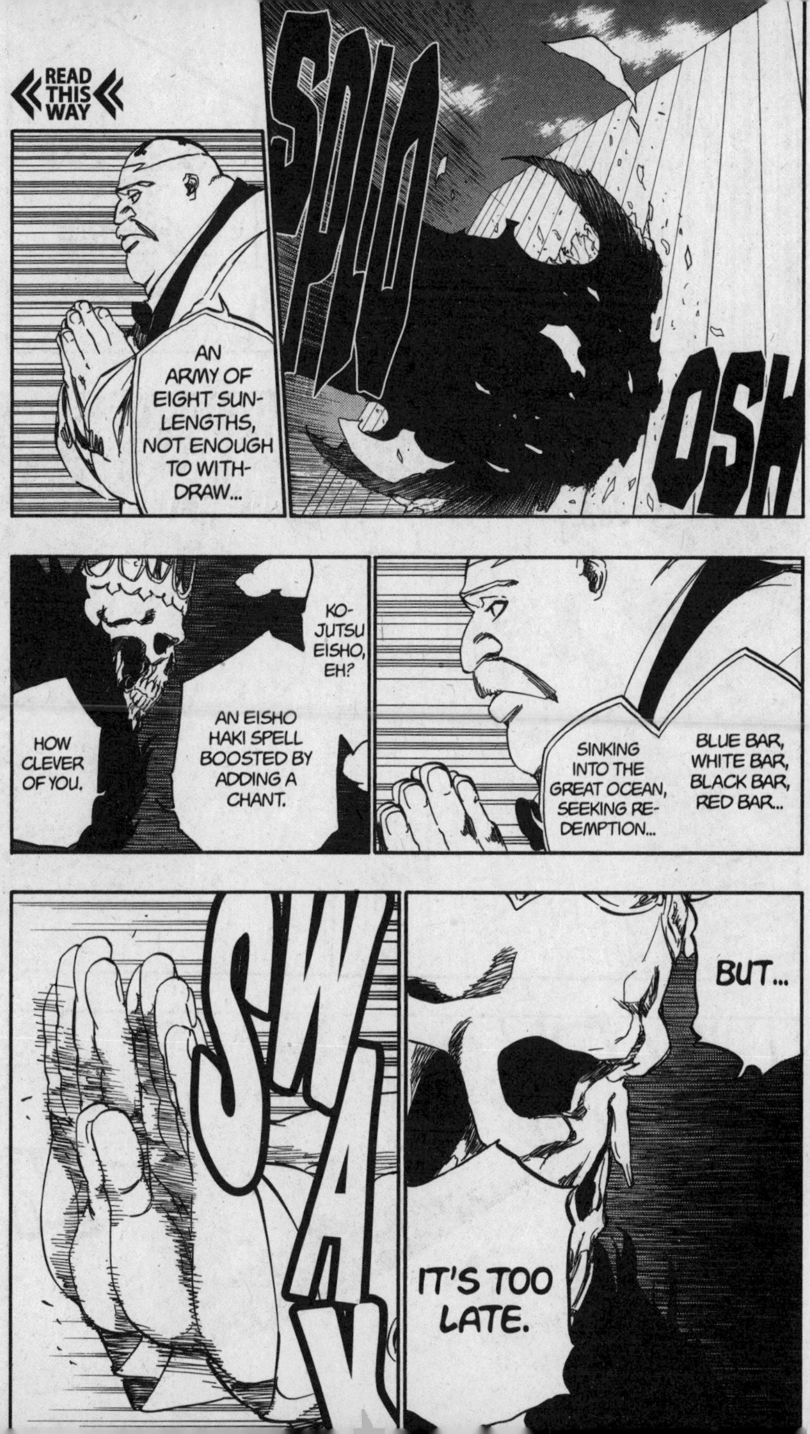
READ THIS WAY
OSH
AN ARMY OF EIGHT SUN-LENGTHS, NOT ENOUGH TO WITH-DRAW...
BLUE BAR, WHITE BAR, BLACK BAR, RED BAR...
SINKING INTO THE GREAT OCEAN, SEEKING RE-DEMPTION...
KO-JUTSU EISHO, EH?
AN EISHO HAKI SPELL BOOSTED BY ADDING A CHANT.
HOW CLEVER OF YOU.
BUT...
IT'S TOO LATE.

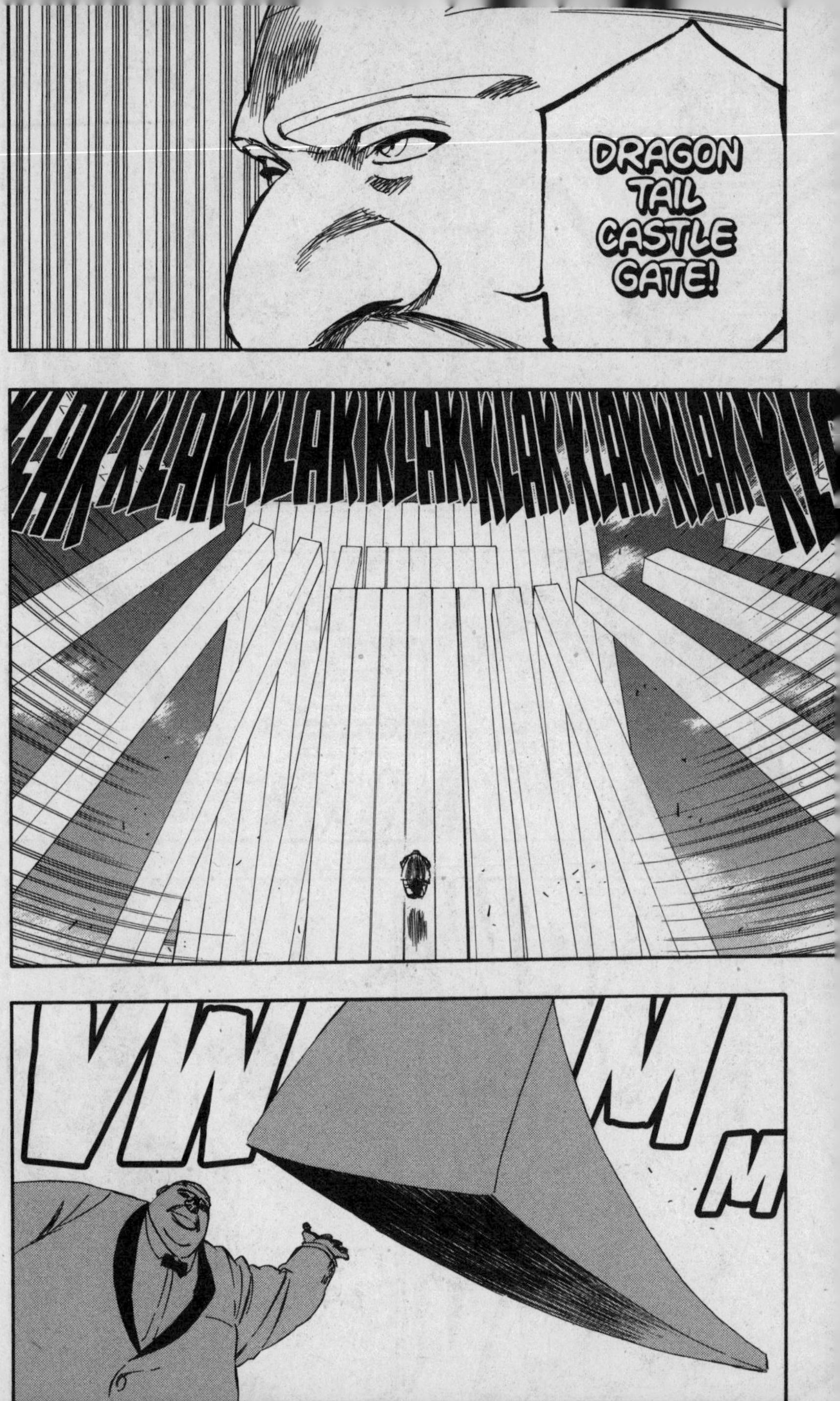
DRAGON TAIL CASTLE GATE!
KLAK KLAK KLAK KLAK KLAK KLAK KLAK KLAK
VWMMM

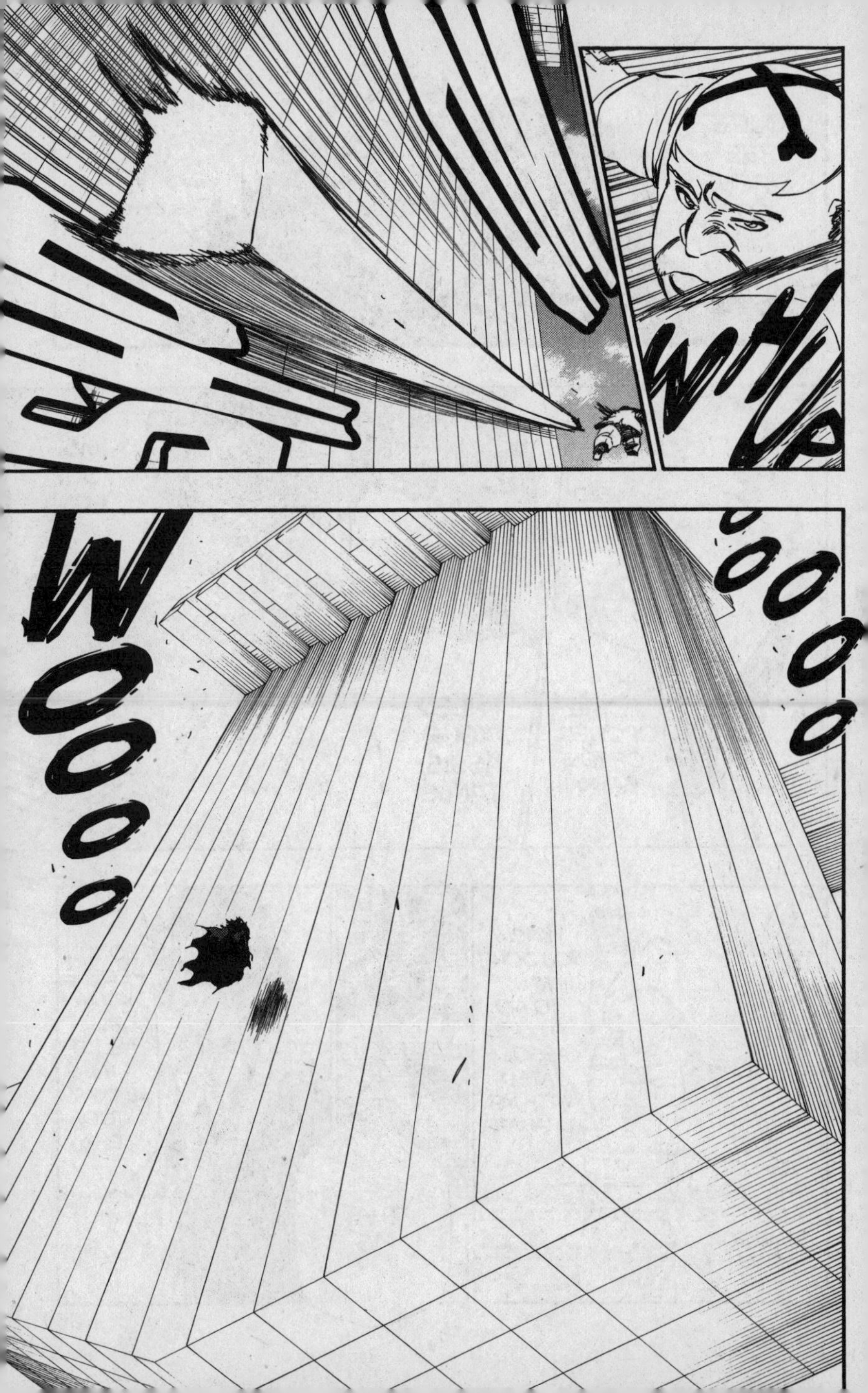
WHOOOOOO
WOOOO

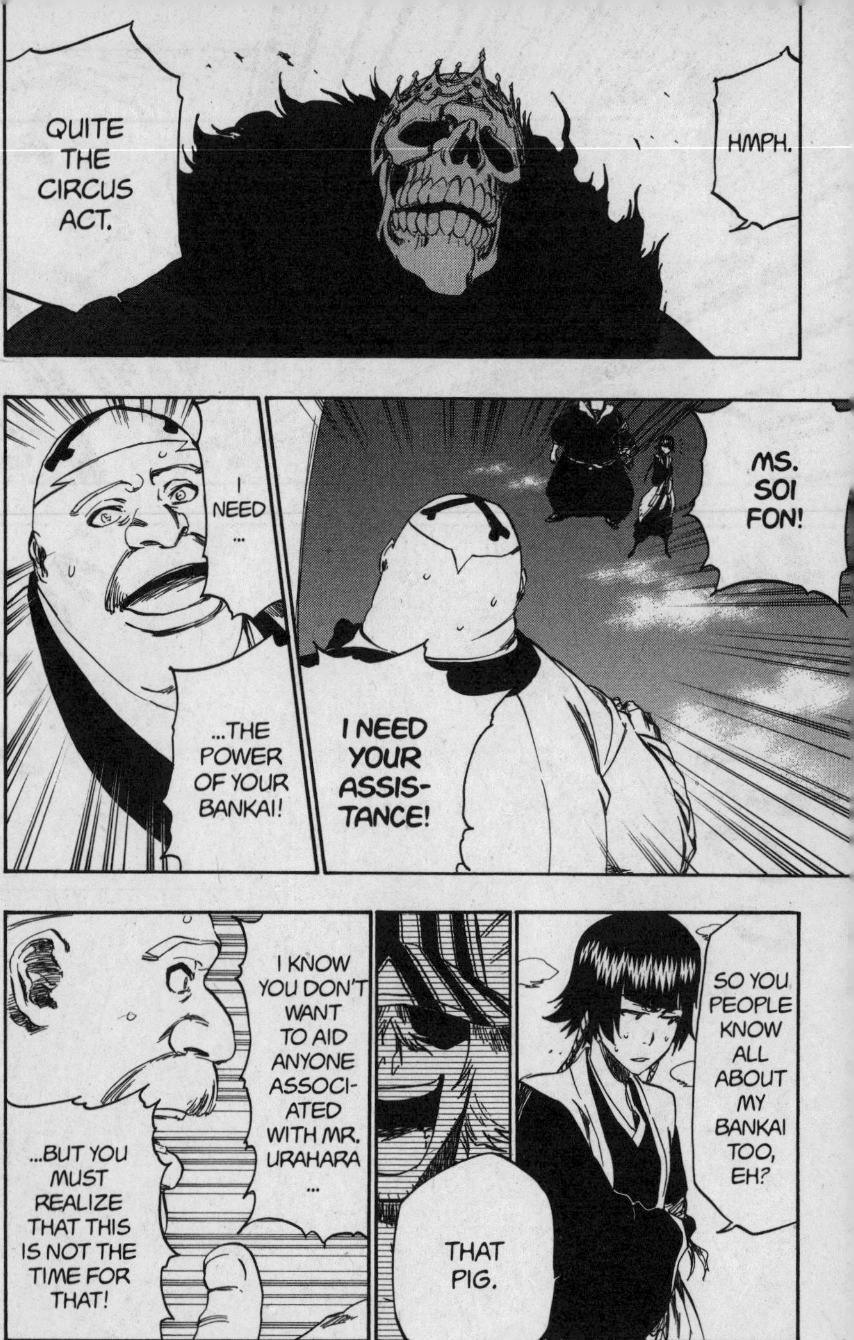
HMPH.
QUITE THE CIRCUS ACT.
MS. SOI FON!
I NEED YOUR ASSISTANCE!
I NEED ...
...THE POWER OF YOUR BANKAI!
SO YOU PEOPLE KNOW ALL ABOUT MY BANKAI TOO, EH?
THAT PIG.
I KNOW YOU DON'T WANT TO AID ANYONE ASSOCIATED WITH MR. URAHARA ...
...BUT YOU MUST REALIZE THAT THIS IS NOT THE TIME FOR THAT!

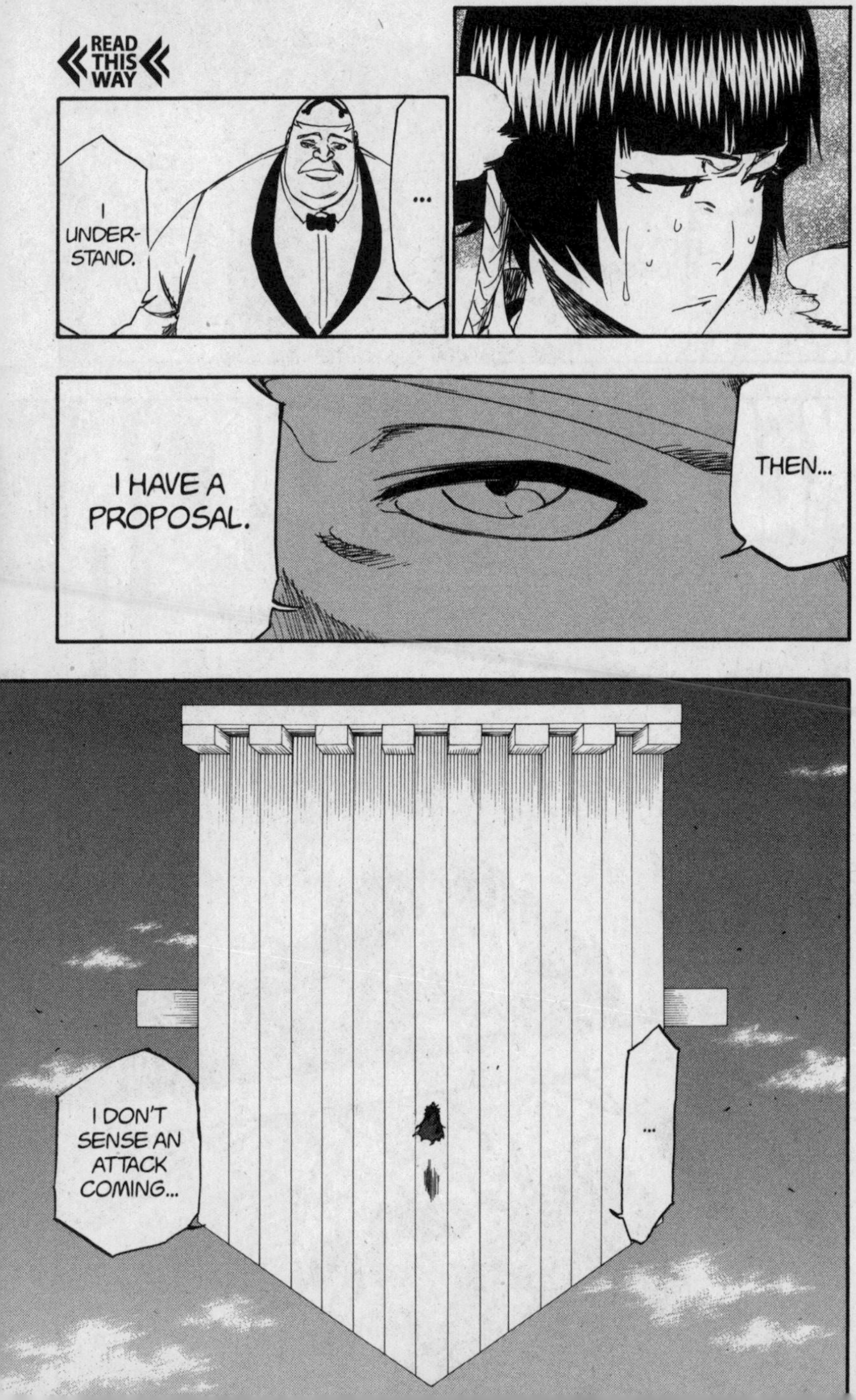
READ THIS WAY
...
I UNDER-STAND.
THEN...
I HAVE A PROPOSAL.
...
I DON'T SENSE AN ATTACK COMING...

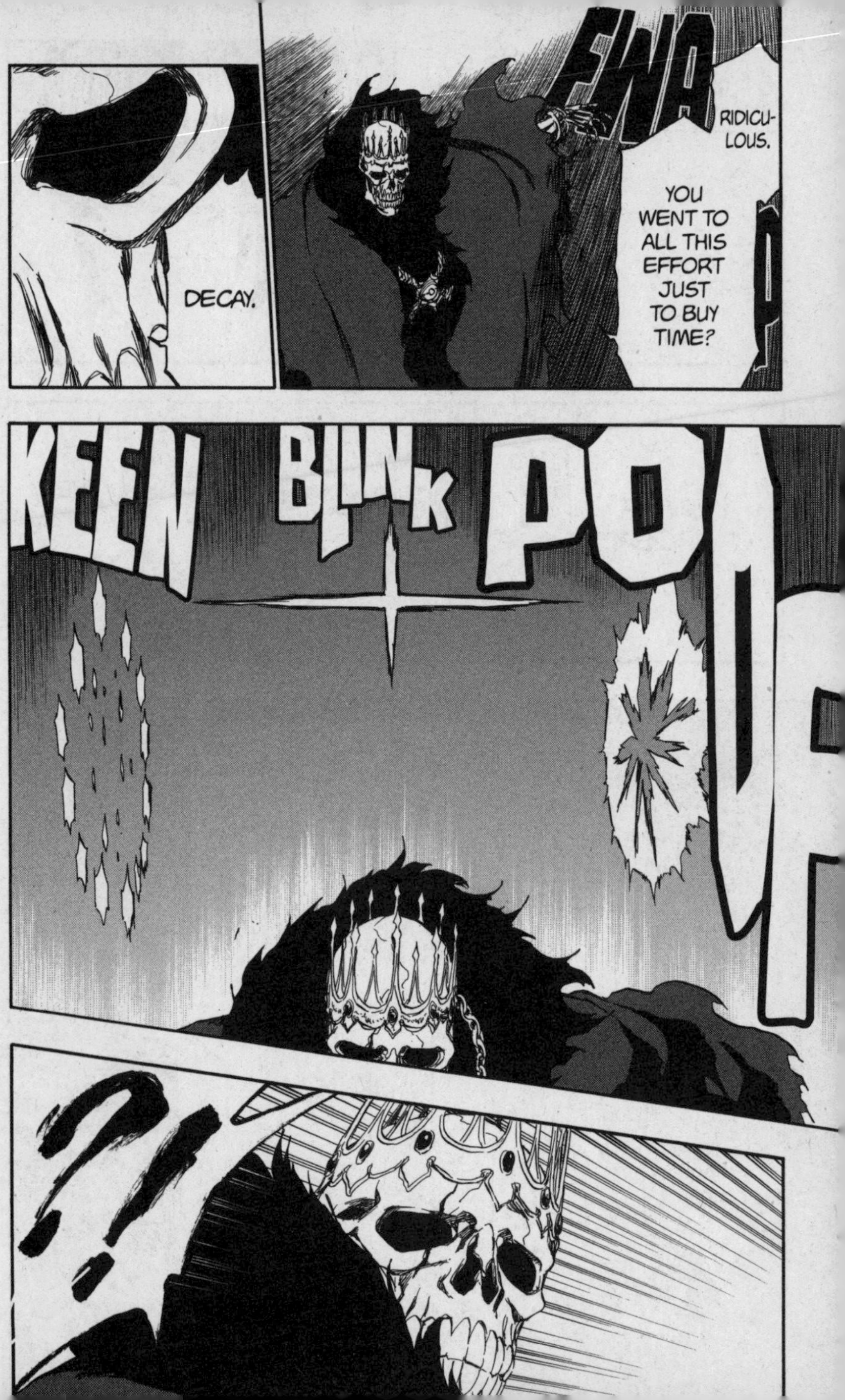
RIDICU-LOUS.
YOU WENT TO ALL THIS EFFORT JUST TO BUY TIME?
DECAY.
POP
BLINK
KEEN
?!

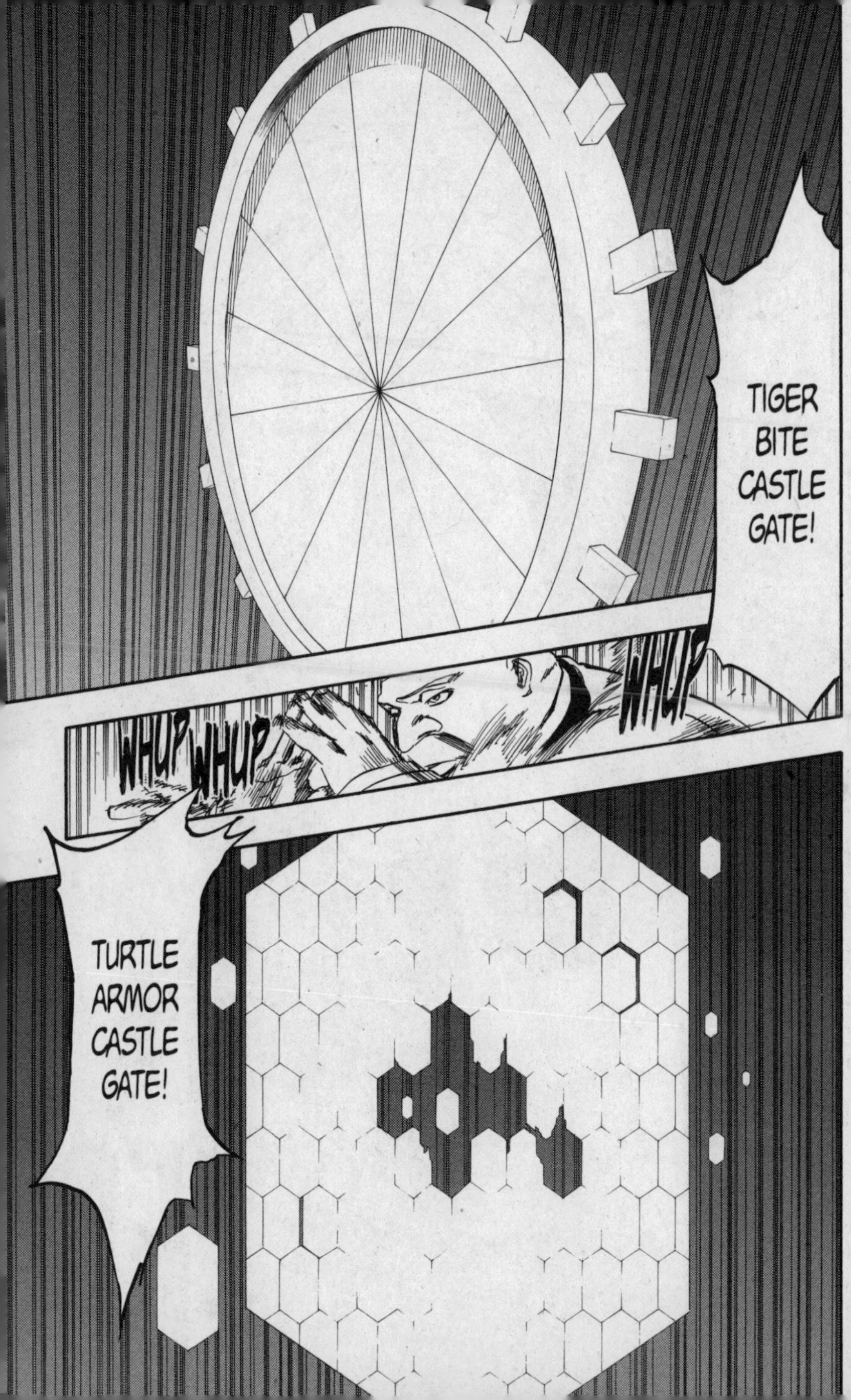
TIGER BITE CASTLE GATE!
WHUP
WHUP WHUP
TURTLE ARMOR CASTLE GATE!

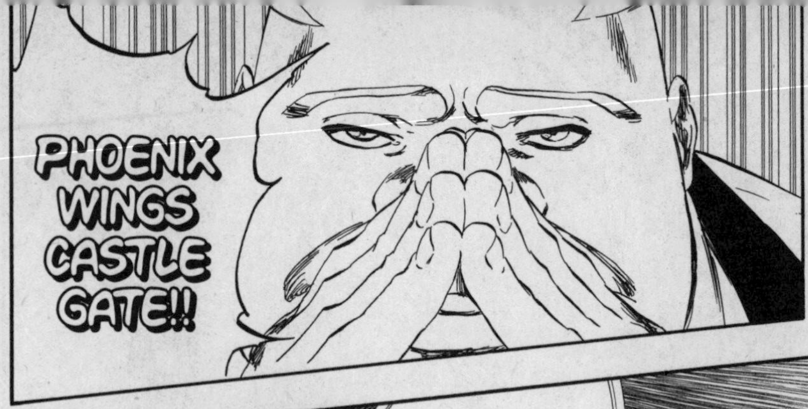
PHOENIX WINGS CASTLE GATE!!

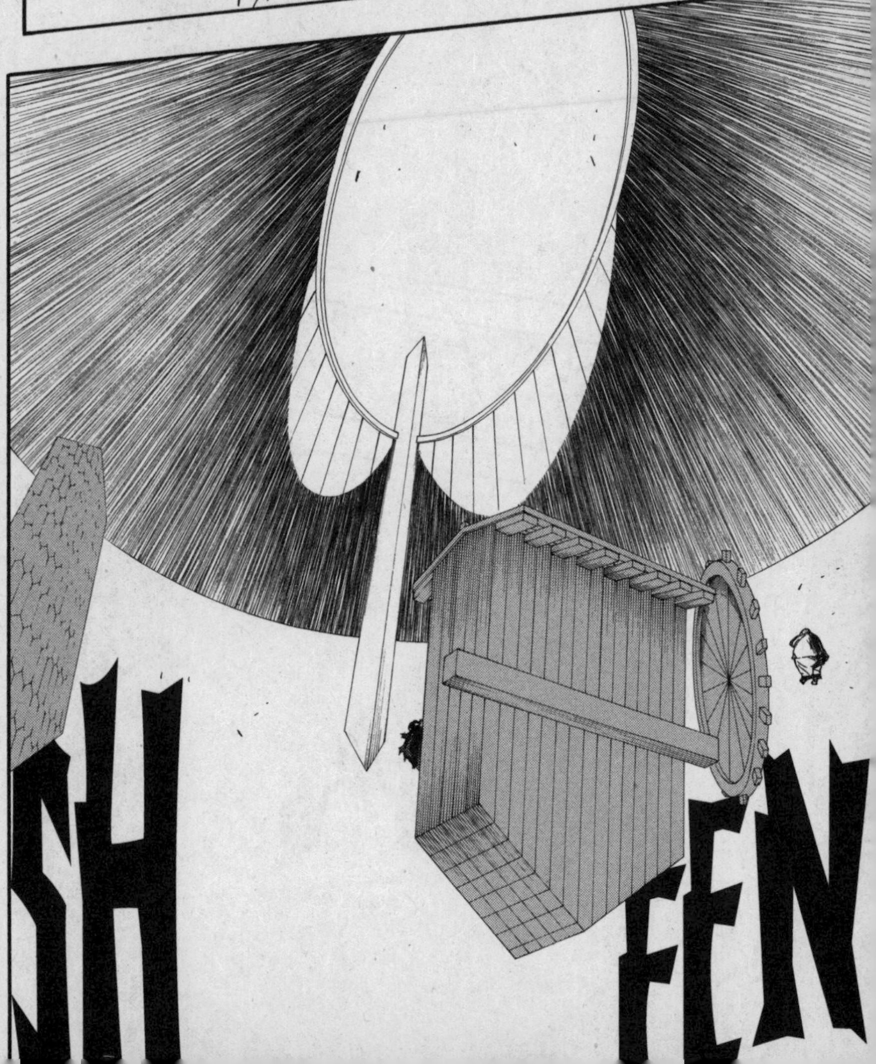
FEN
SH

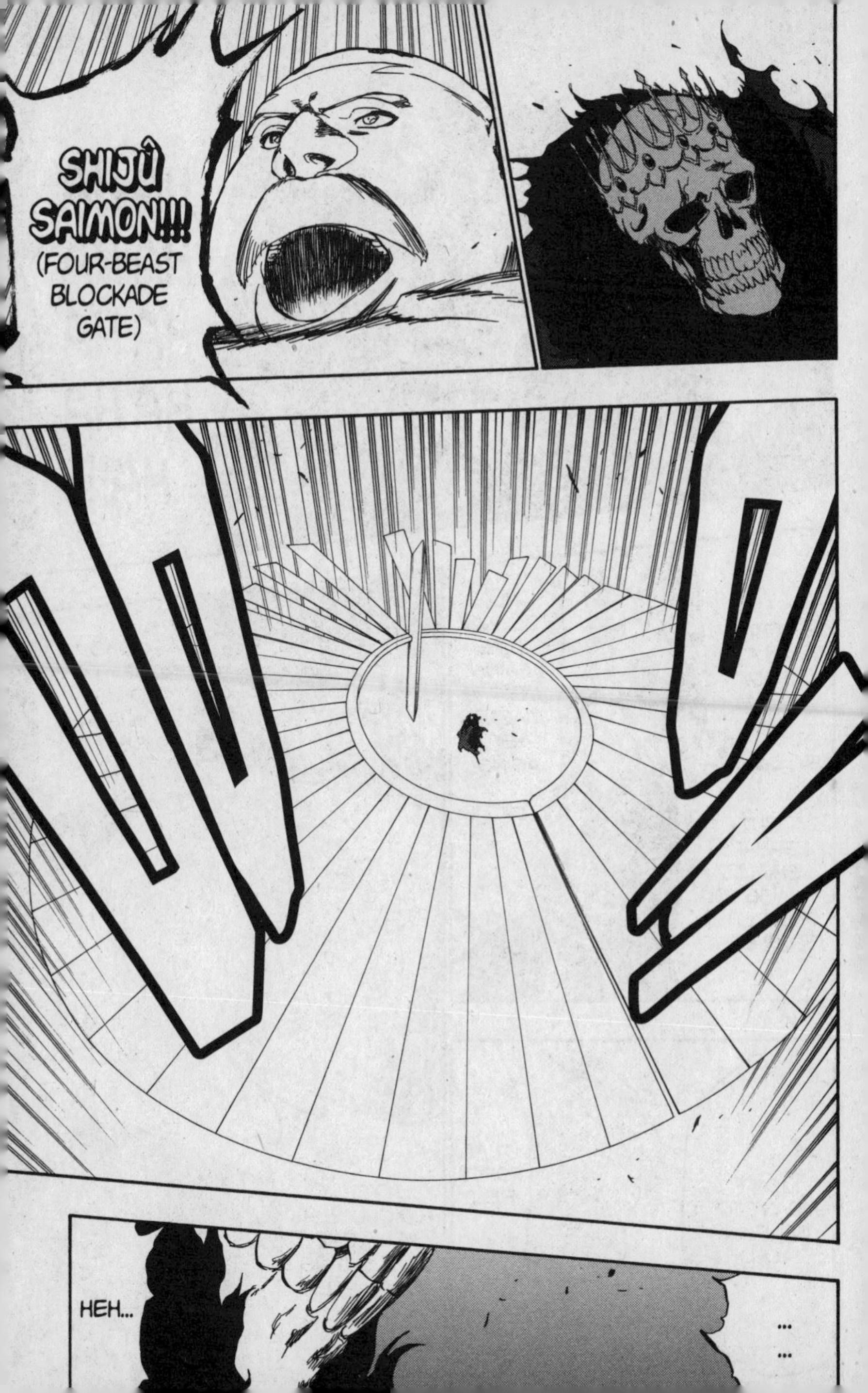
SHIJÛ SAIMON!!!
(FOUR-BEAST BLOCKADE GATE)
...
...
HEH...

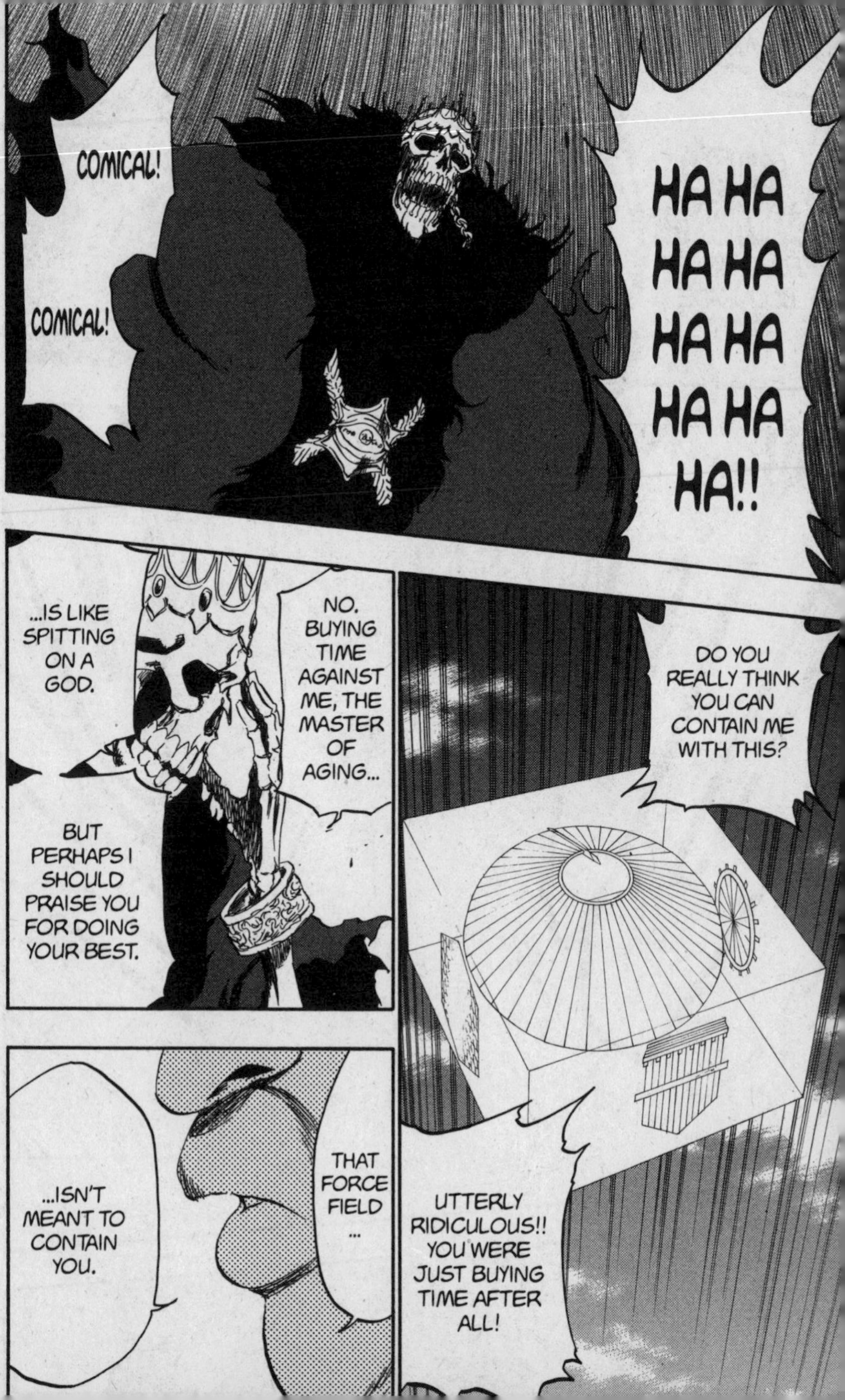
HA HA HA HA HA HA HA HA HA!!
COMICAL!
COMICAL!
DO YOU REALLY THINK YOU CAN CONTAIN ME WITH THIS?
UTTERLY RIDICULOUS!! YOU WERE JUST BUYING TIME AFTER ALL!
NO. BUYING TIME AGAINST ME, THE MASTER OF AGING...
...IS LIKE SPITTING ON A GOD.
BUT PERHAPS I SHOULD PRAISE YOU FOR DOING YOUR BEST.
THAT FORCE FIELD...
...ISN'T MEANT TO CONTAIN YOU.

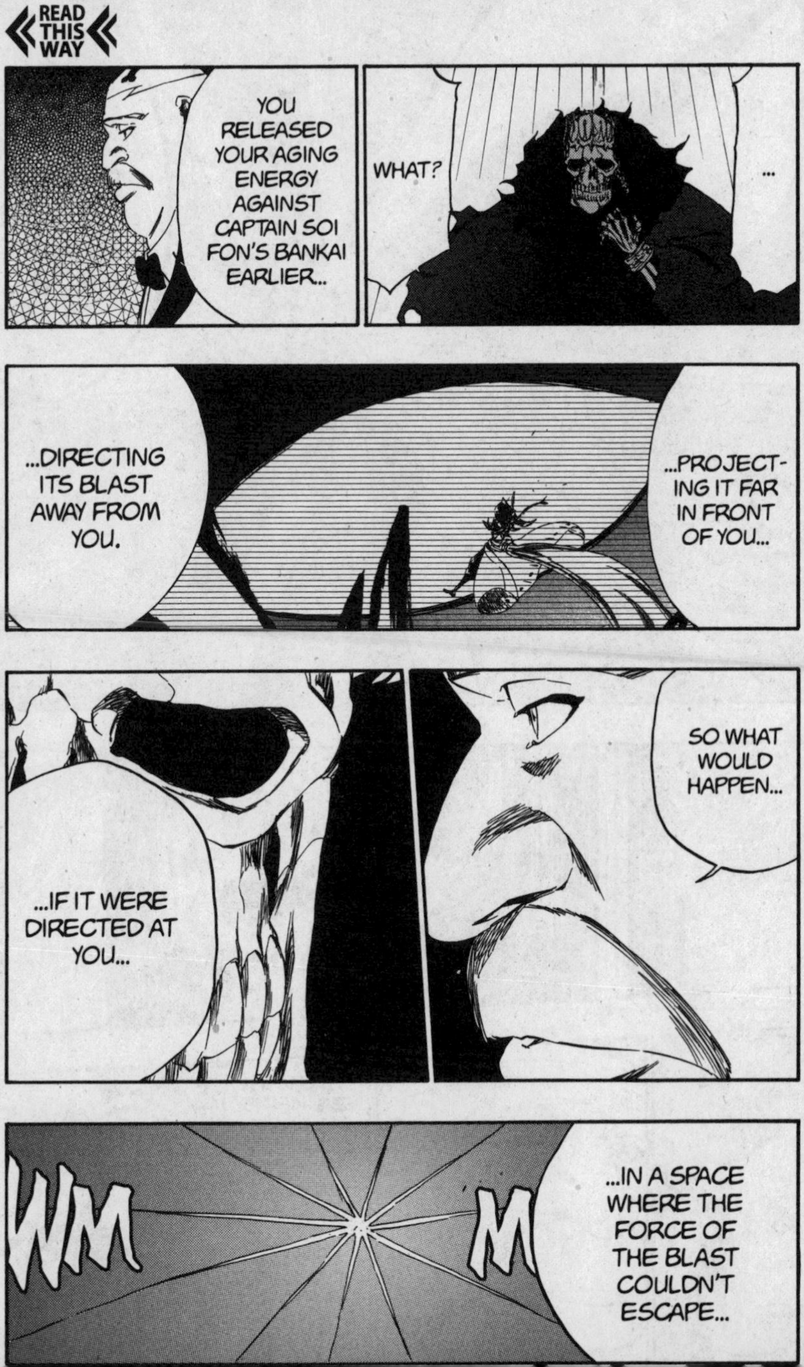
READ THIS WAY
...
WHAT?
YOU RELEASED YOUR AGING ENERGY AGAINST CAPTAIN SOI FON'S BANKAI EARLIER...
...PROJECTING IT FAR IN FRONT OF YOU...
...DIRECTING ITS BLAST AWAY FROM YOU.
SO WHAT WOULD HAPPEN...
...IF IT WERE DIRECTED AT YOU...
...IN A SPACE WHERE THE FORCE OF THE BLAST COULDN'T ESCAPE...
WM
M

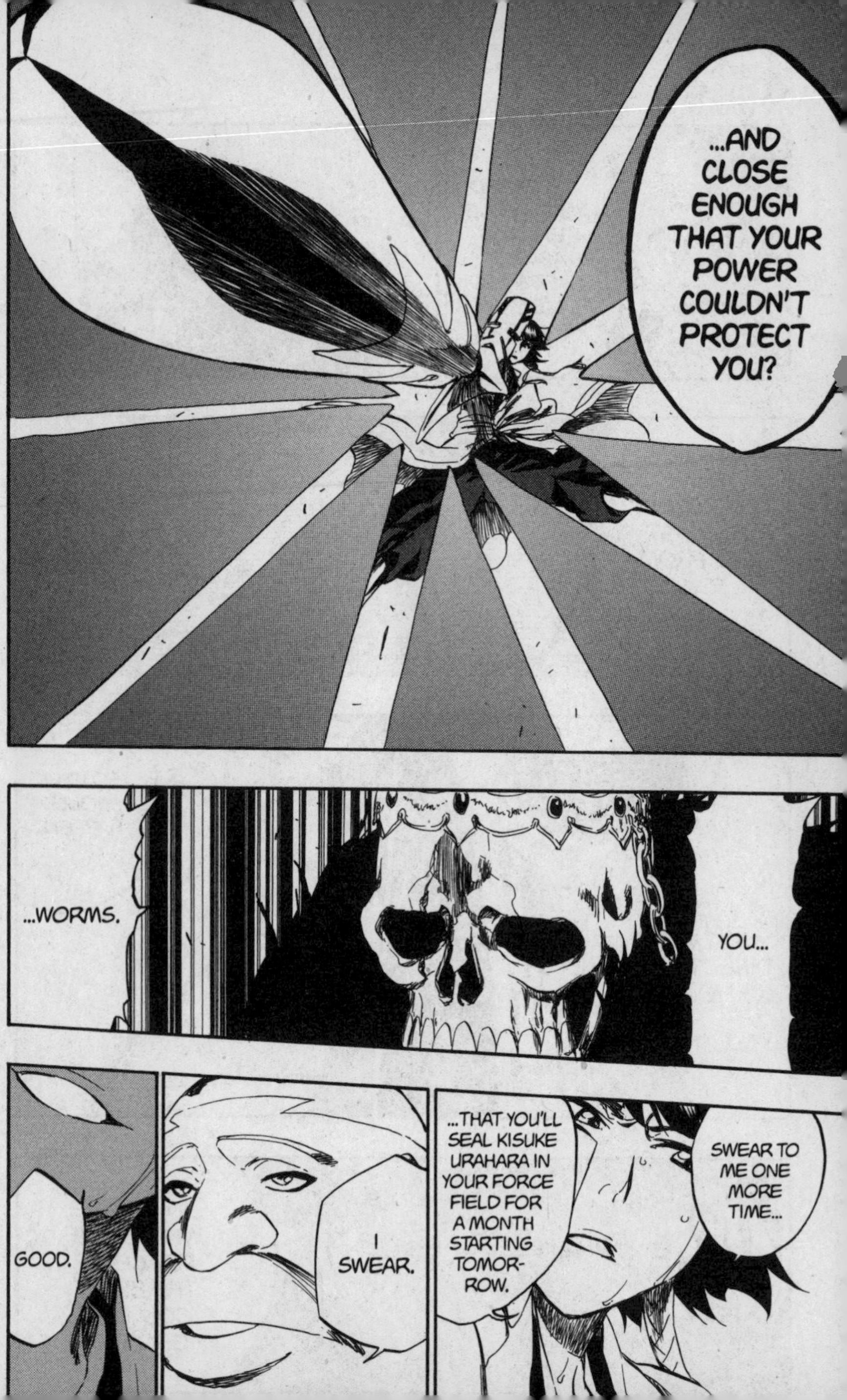
...AND CLOSE ENOUGH THAT YOUR POWER COULDN'T PROTECT YOU?
YOU...
...WORMS.
SWEAR TO ME ONE MORE TIME...
...THAT YOU'LL SEAL KISUKE URAHARA IN YOUR FORCE FIELD FOR A MONTH STARTING TOMOR-ROW.
I SWEAR.
GOOD.

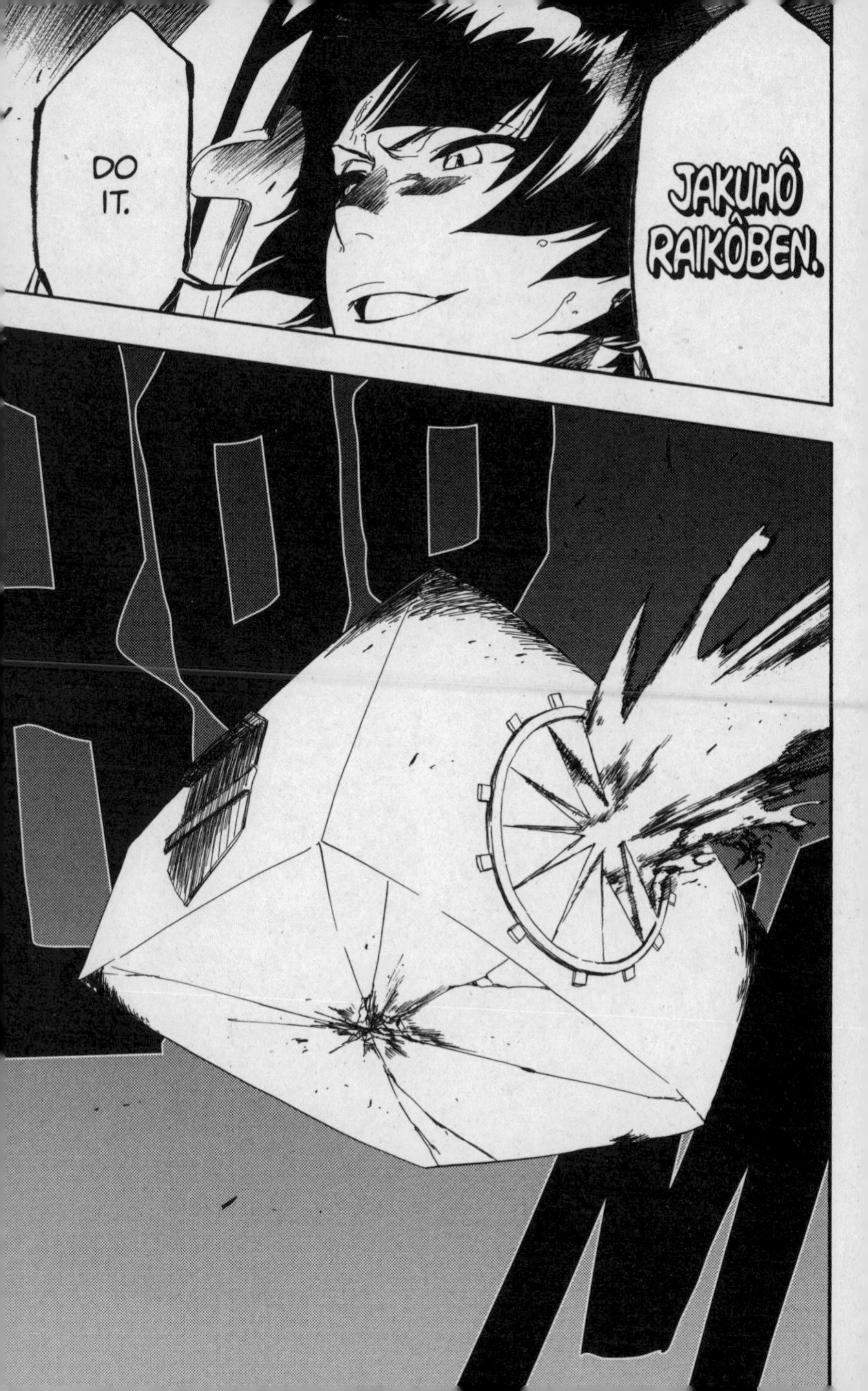
JAKUHÔ RAIKÔBEN.
DO IT.

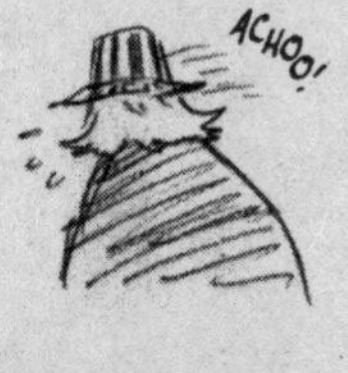
ACHOO!

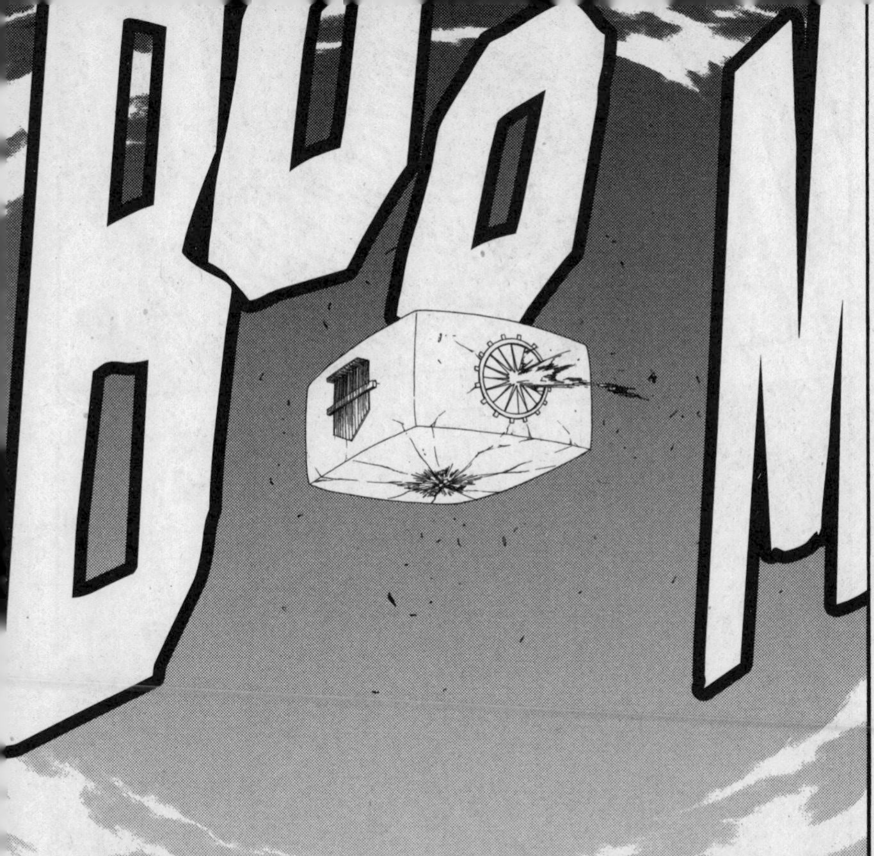
BOOM

370. Discussing Life from God's Perspective

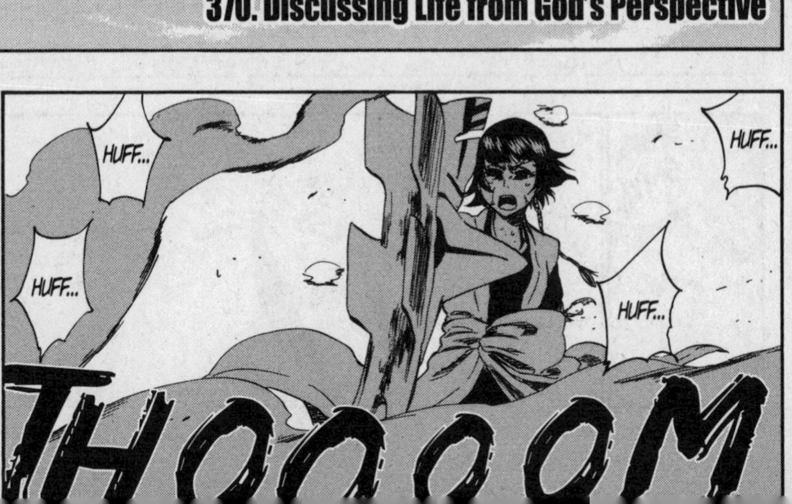
HUFF...
HUFF...
HUFF...
HUFF...
THOOOOM

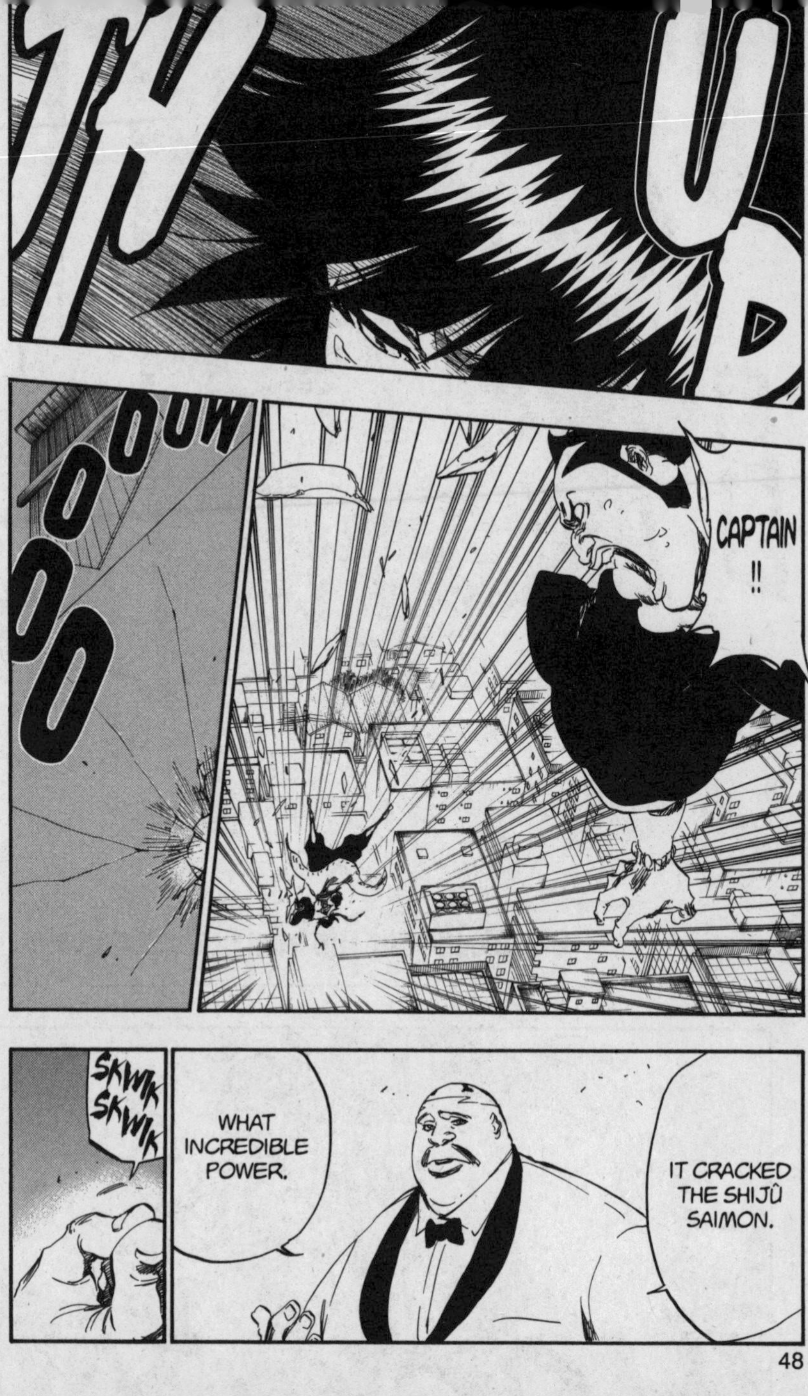
THUD
CAPTAIN !!
OOOOOUW
IT CRACKED THE SHIJÛ SAIMON.
WHAT INCREDIBLE POWER.
SKWIK SKWIK

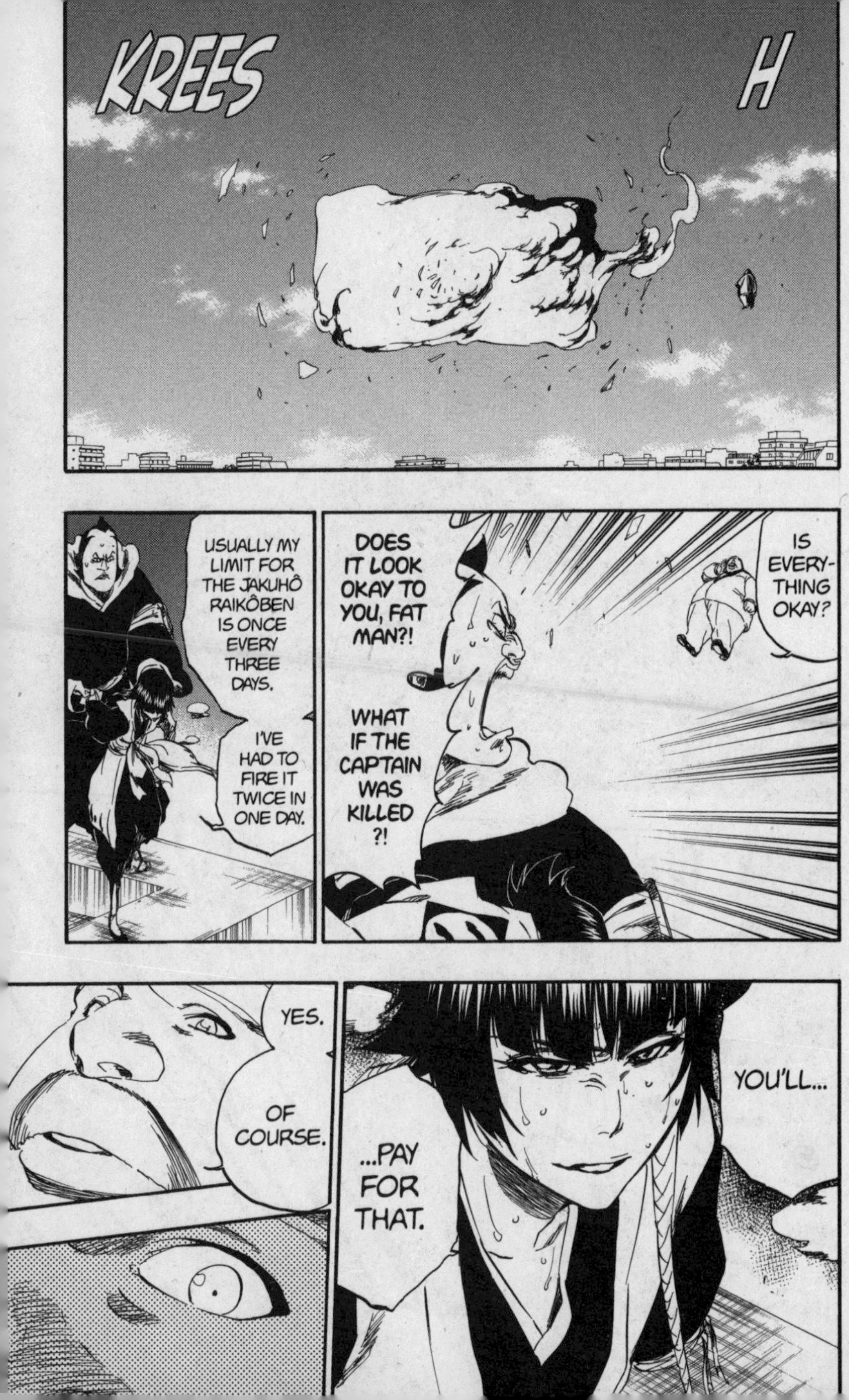
KREES H
IS EVERYTHING OKAY?
DOES IT LOOK OKAY TO YOU, FAT MAN?!
WHAT IF THE CAPTAIN WAS KILLED?!
USUALLY MY LIMIT FOR THE JAKUHÔ RAIKÔBEN IS ONCE EVERY THREE DAYS.
I'VE HAD TO FIRE IT TWICE IN ONE DAY.
YOU'LL...
...PAY FOR THAT.
YES.
OF COURSE.

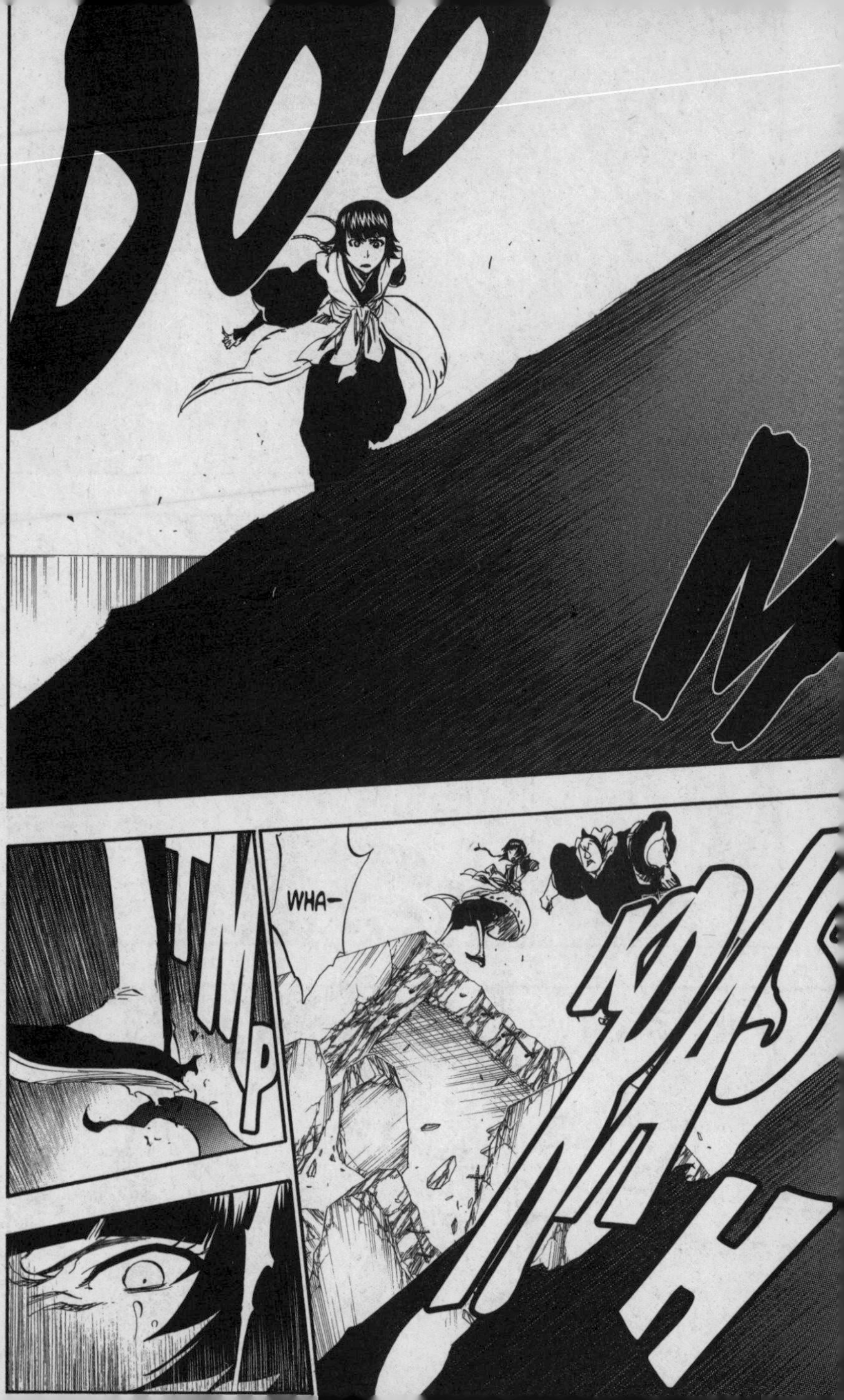
DOOM
WHA-
TMP

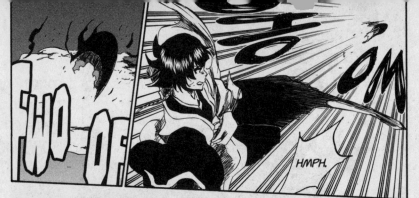

HMPH.
TWO OF
UNFOR-GIVABLE.
WOOOOOO
UNFOR-GIVABLE!
H—
HOW?
I'M BADLY INJURED.
YOU ANTS WON'T GET AWAY WITH THIS!

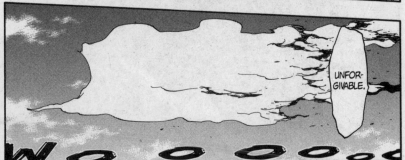

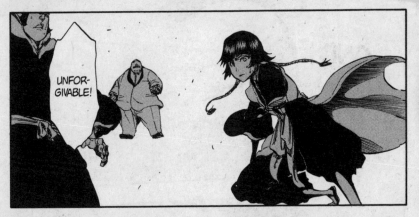

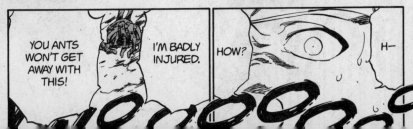

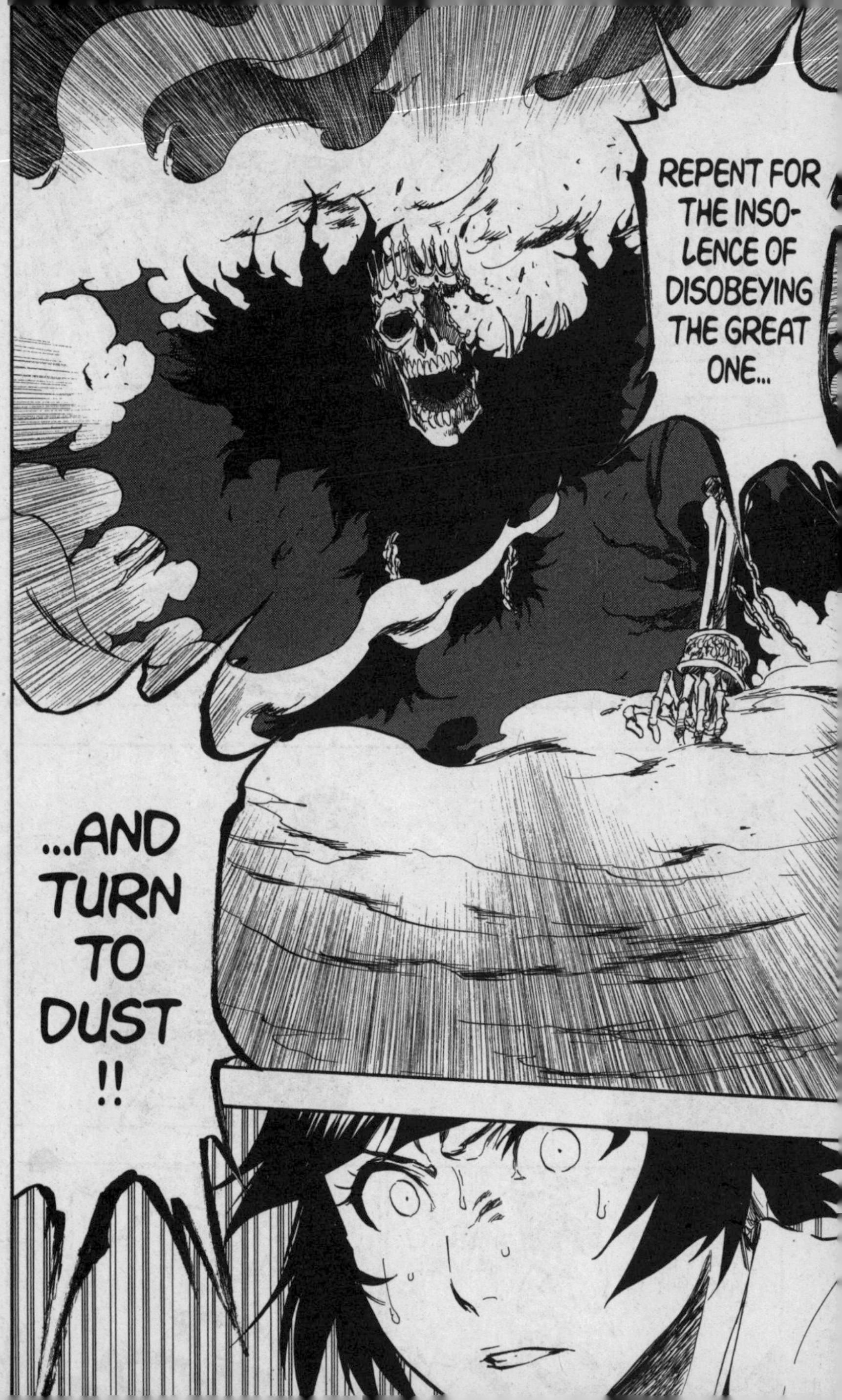
REPENT FOR THE INSOLENCE OF DISOBEYING THE GREAT ONE...
...AND TURN TO DUST!!

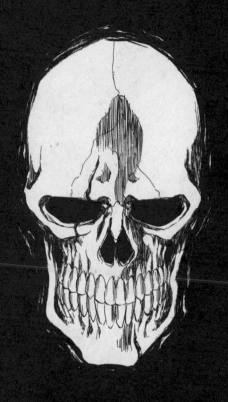

BLEACH370.

Discussing Life from God's Perspective

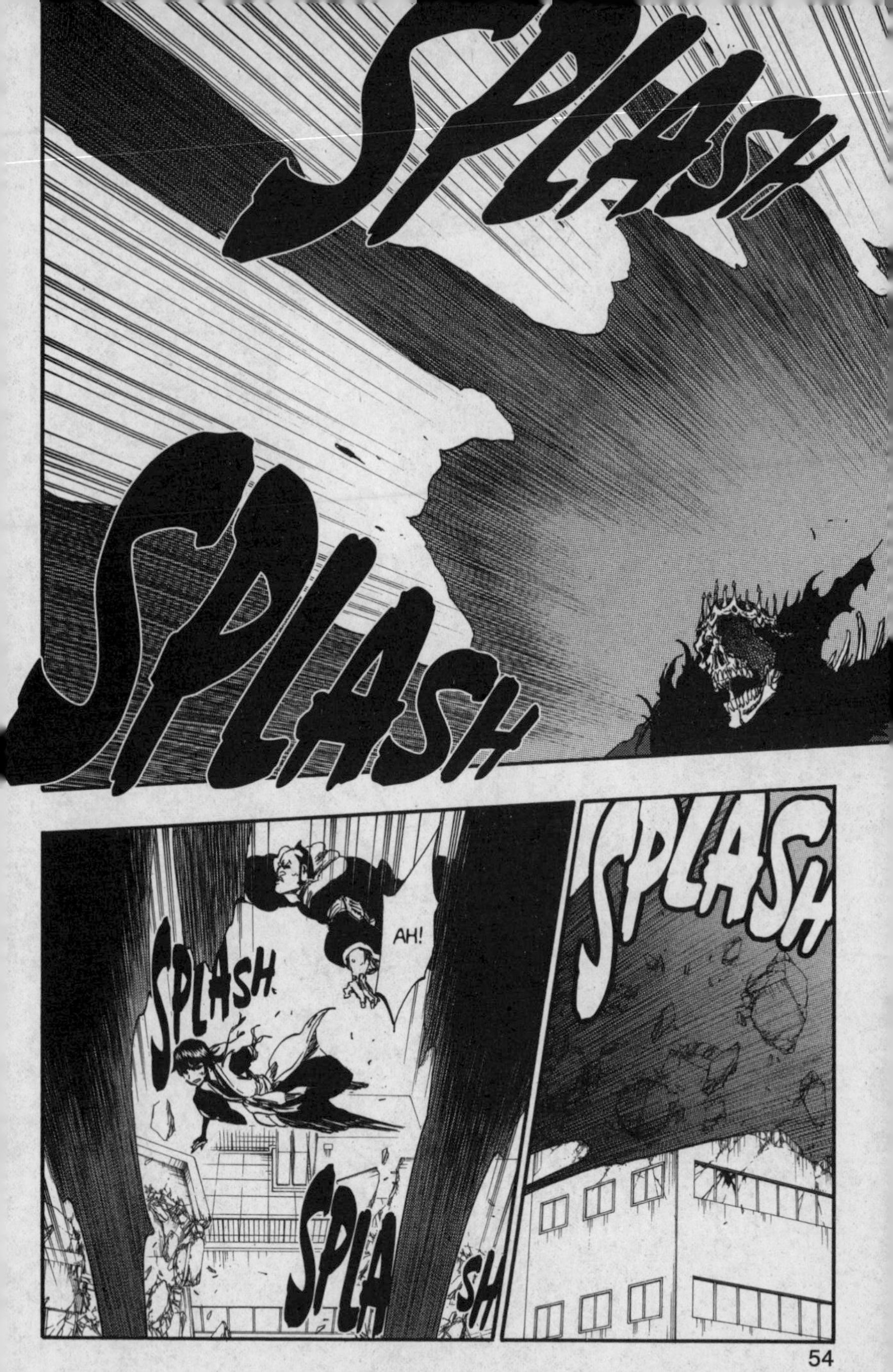
SPLASH
SPLASH
SPLASH
AH!
SPLASH
SPLASH

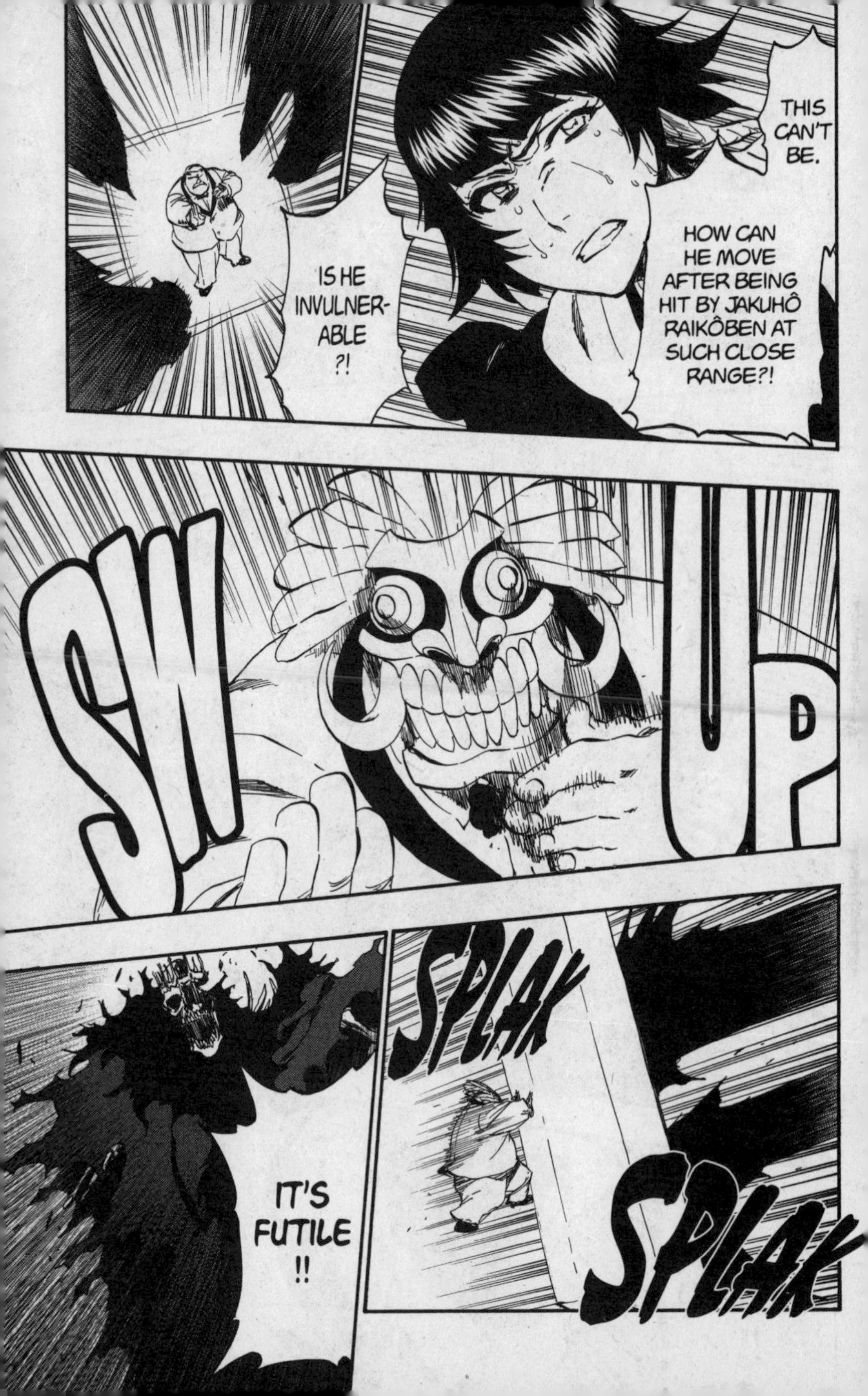
THIS CAN'T BE.
HOW CAN HE MOVE AFTER BEING HIT BY JAKUHÔ RAIKÔBEN AT SUCH CLOSE RANGE?!
IS HE INVULNER-ABLE ?!
SW
UP
SPLAK
SPLAK
IT'S FUTILE !!

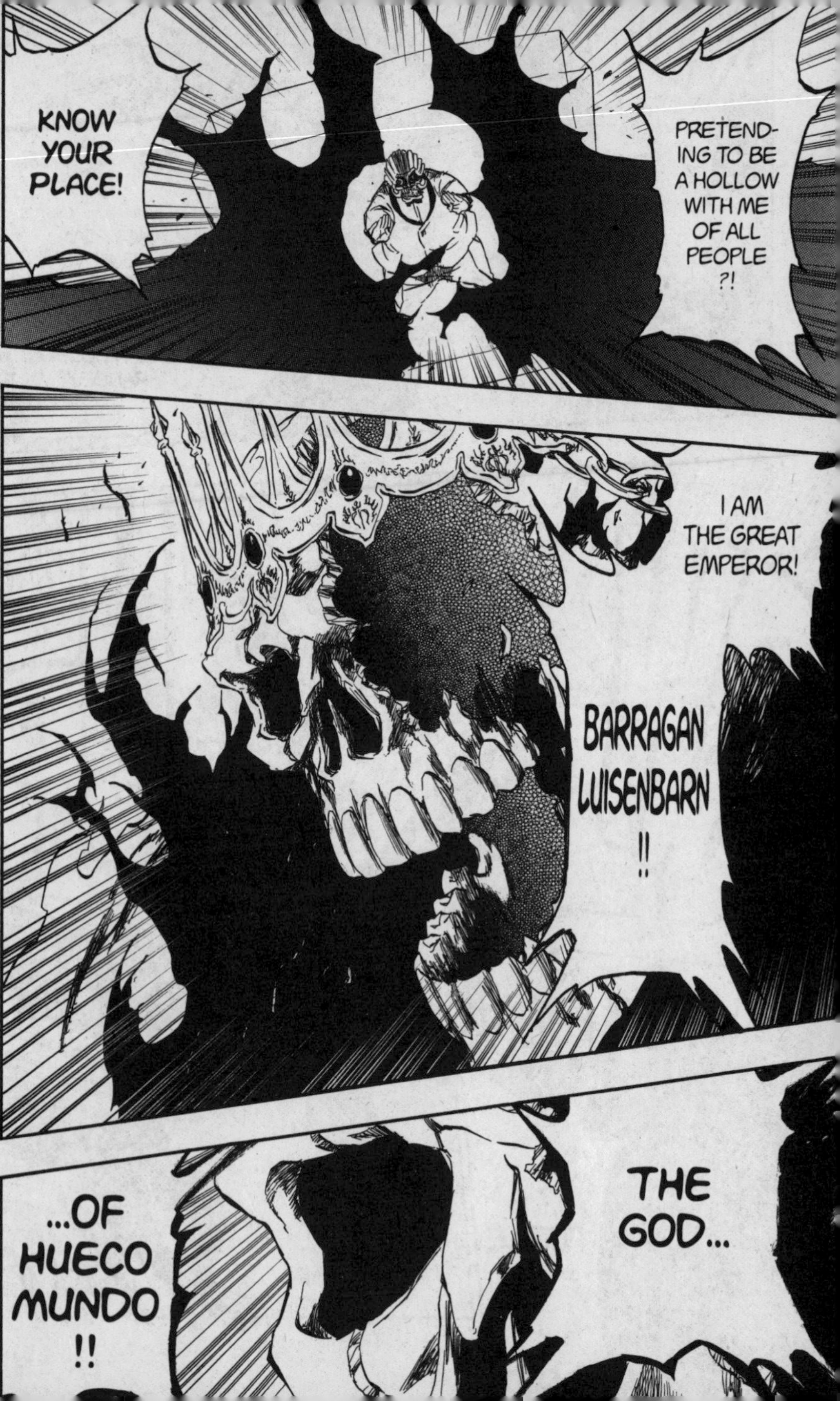
PRETEND-ING TO BE A HOLLOW WITH ME OF ALL PEOPLE ?!
KNOW YOUR PLACE!
I AM THE GREAT EMPEROR!
BARRAGAN LUISENBARN !!
THE GOD...
...OF HUECO MUNDO !!

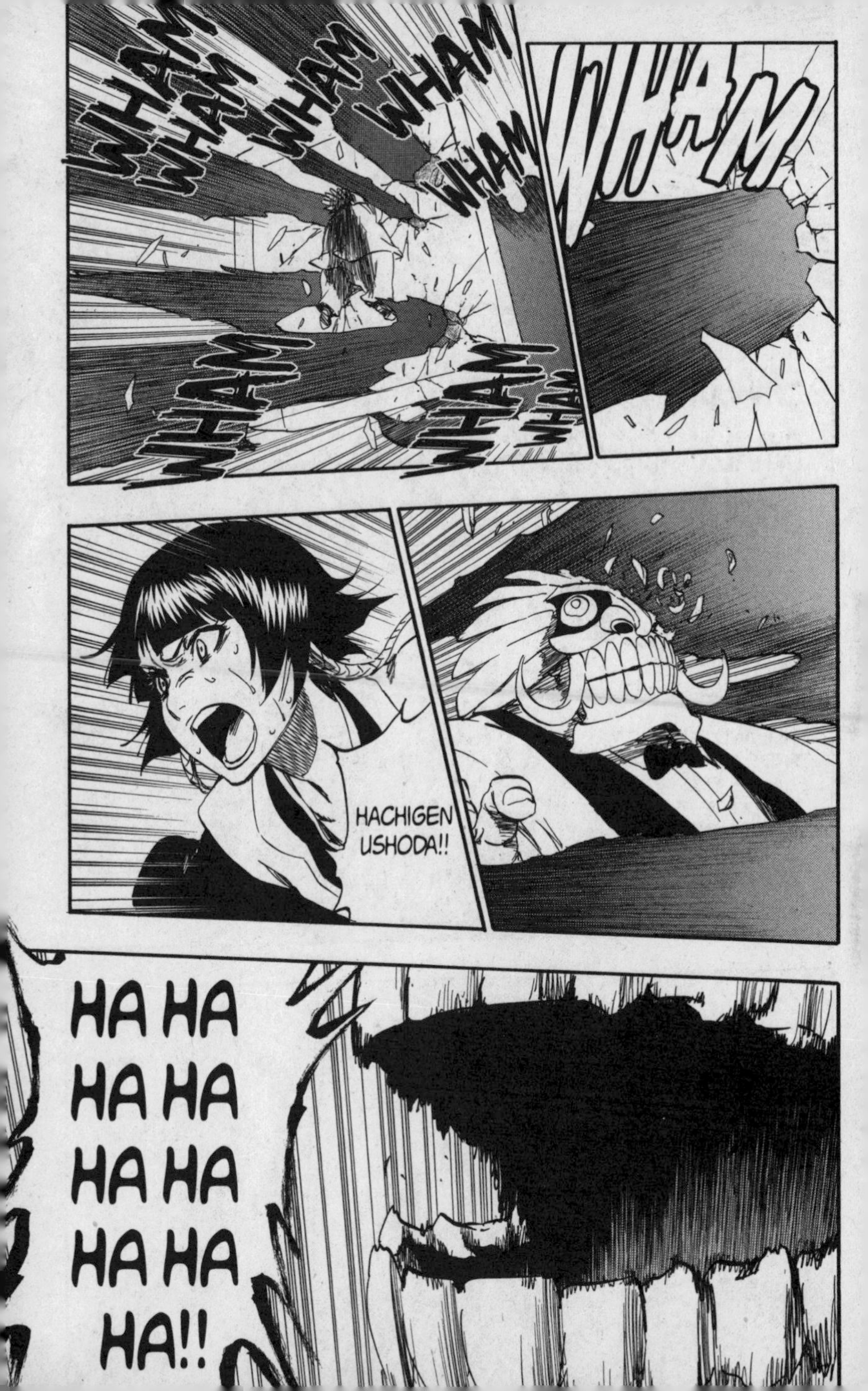
WHAM
WHAM
WHAM
WHAM
WHAM
WHAM
WHAM
WHAM
WHAM
WHAM
HACHIGEN USHODA!!
HA HA HA HA HA HA HA HA HA HA HA HA HA HA HA HA HA!!

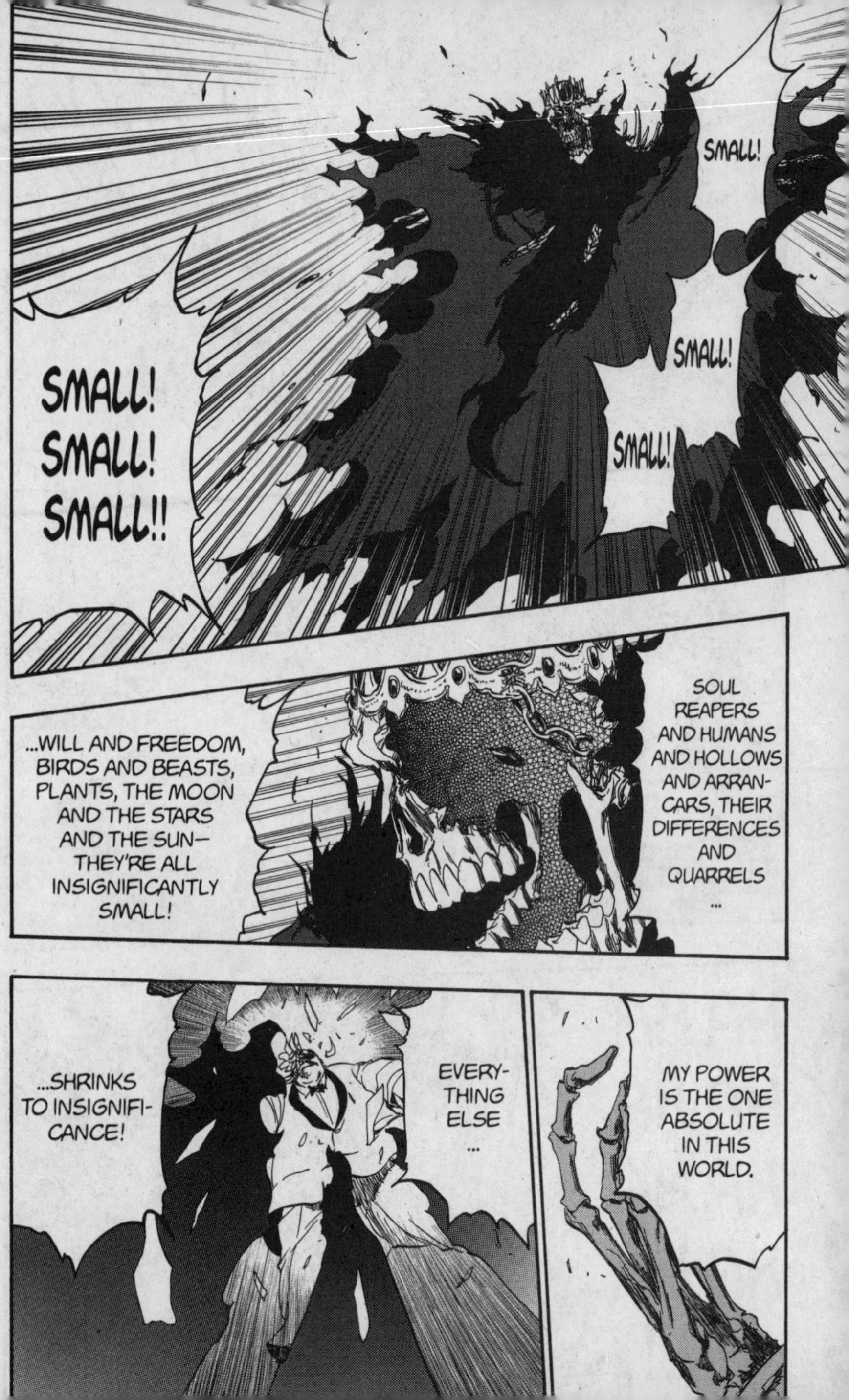
SMALL!
SMALL!
SMALL!
SMALL! SMALL! SMALL!!
SOUL REAPERS AND HUMANS AND HOLLOWS AND ARRANCARS, THEIR DIFFERENCES AND QUARRELS ...
...WILL AND FREEDOM, BIRDS AND BEASTS, PLANTS, THE MOON AND THE STARS AND THE SUN— THEY'RE ALL INSIGNIFICANTLY SMALL!
MY POWER IS THE ONE ABSOLUTE IN THIS WORLD.
EVERYTHING ELSE ...
...SHRINKS TO INSIGNIFICANCE!

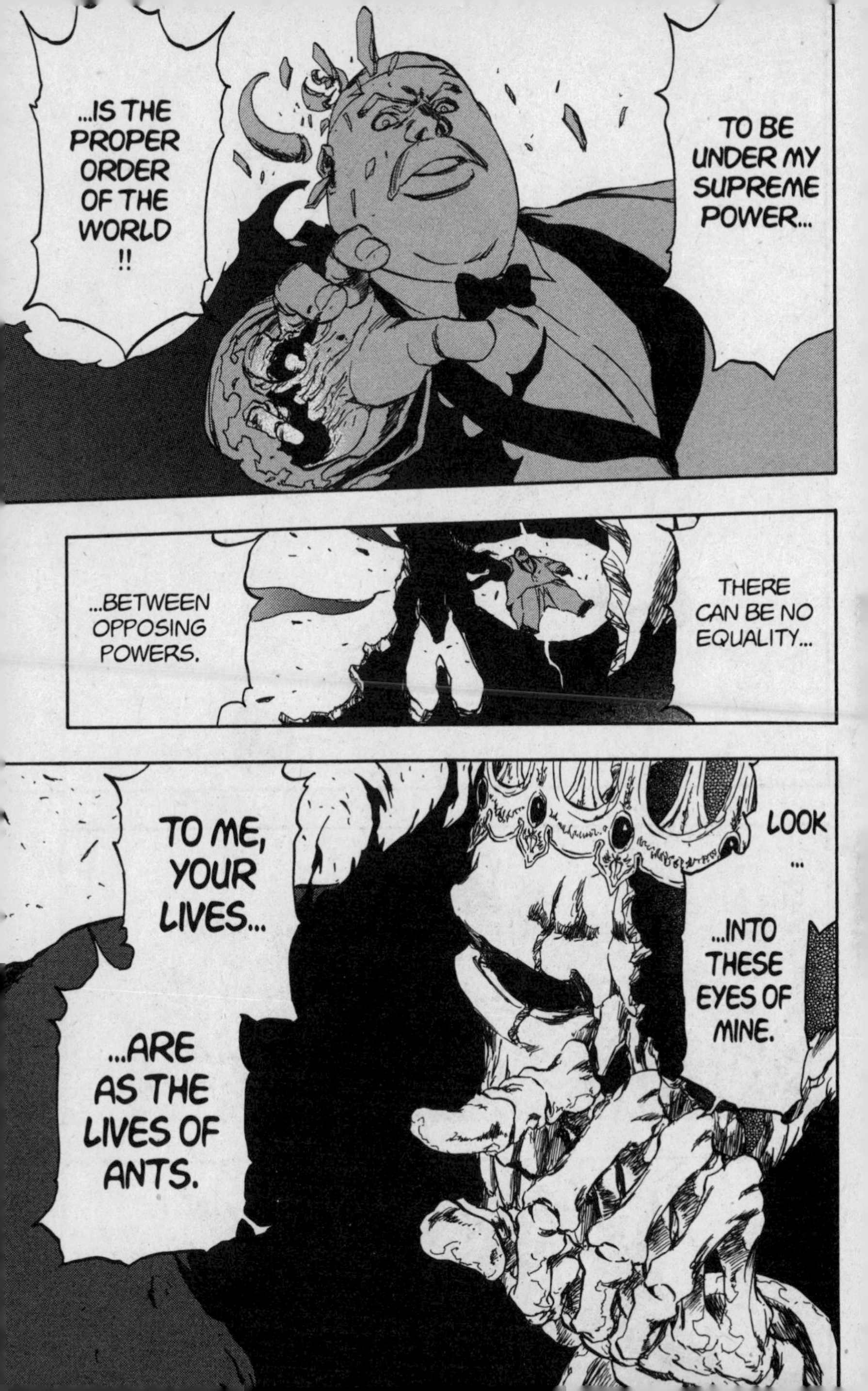
TO BE UNDER MY SUPREME POWER...
...IS THE PROPER ORDER OF THE WORLD !!
THERE CAN BE NO EQUALITY...
...BETWEEN OPPOSING POWERS.
LOOK ...
...INTO THESE EYES OF MINE.
TO ME, YOUR LIVES...
...ARE AS THE LIVES OF ANTS.

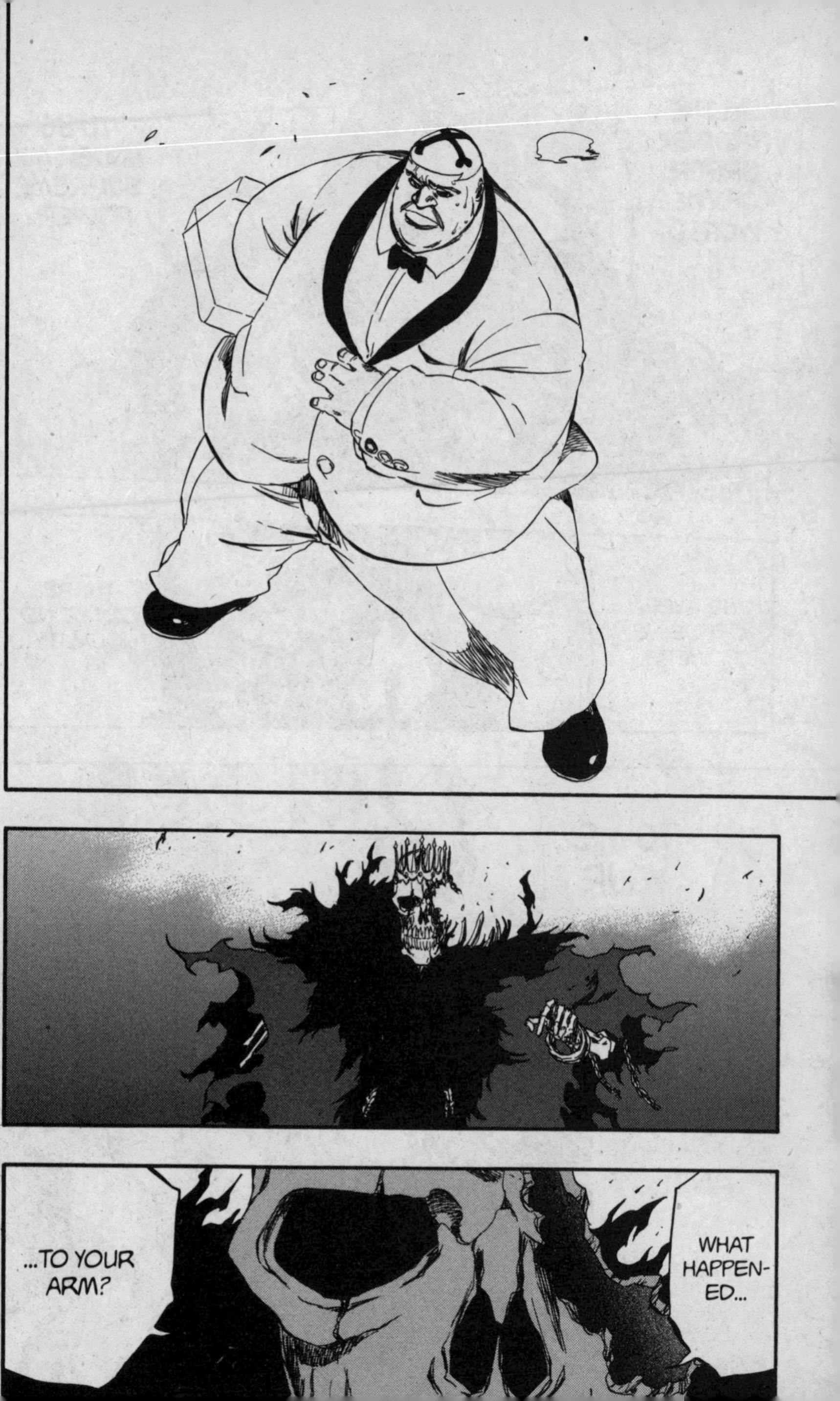
WHAT HAPPEN-ED...
...TO YOUR ARM?

READ THIS WAY

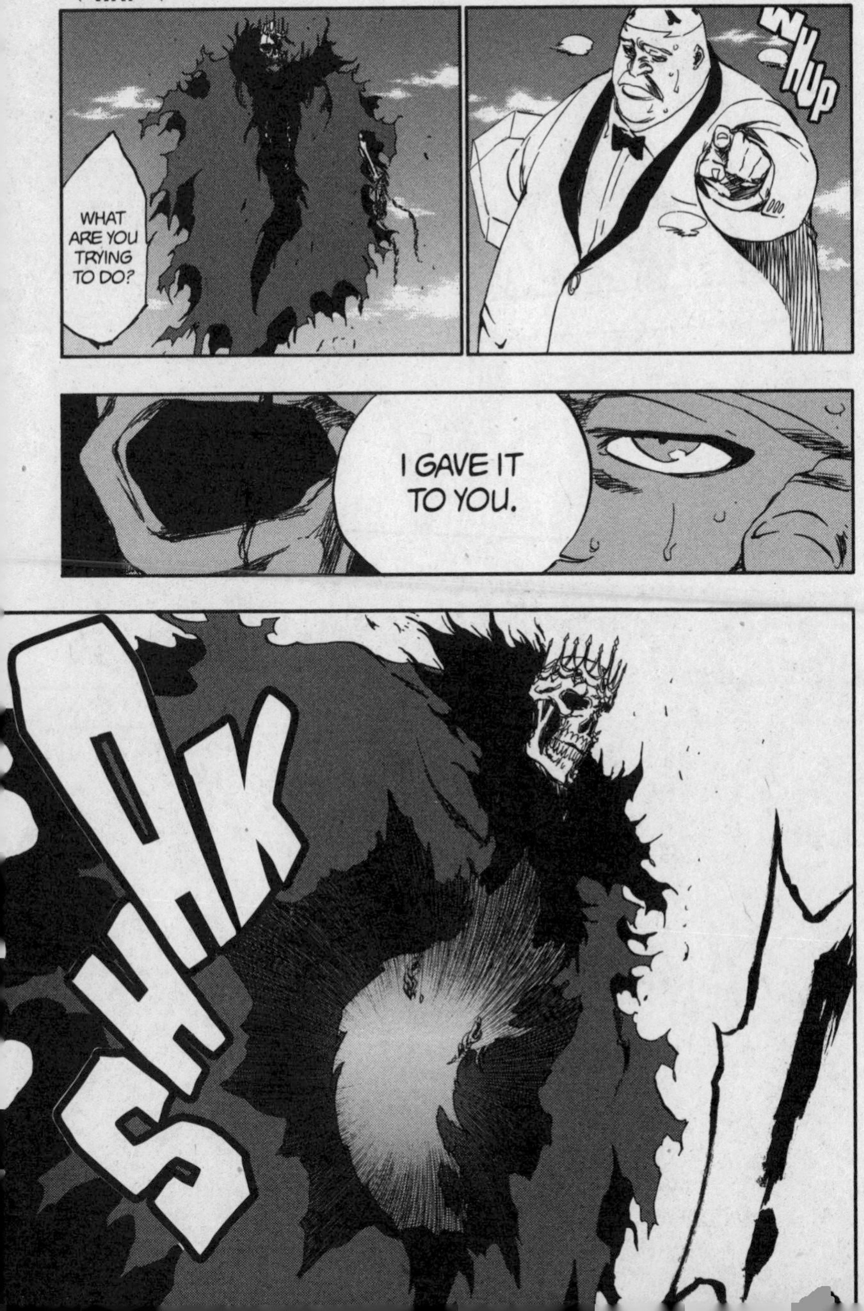
WHUP
WHAT ARE YOU TRYING TO DO?
I GAVE IT TO YOU.
SHAK

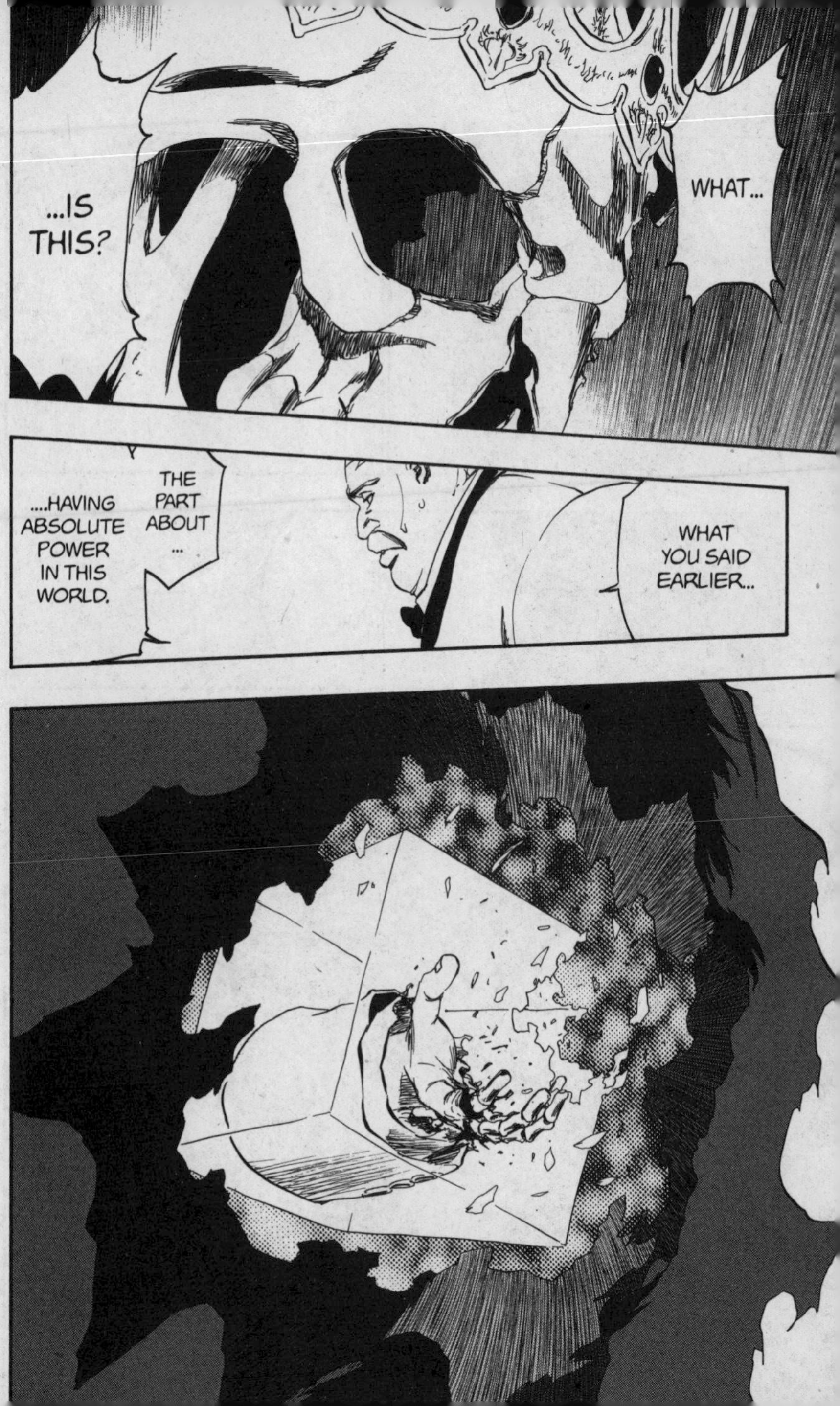
WHAT...
...IS THIS?
WHAT YOU SAID EARLIER...
THE PART ABOUT...
....HAVING ABSOLUTE POWER IN THIS WORLD.

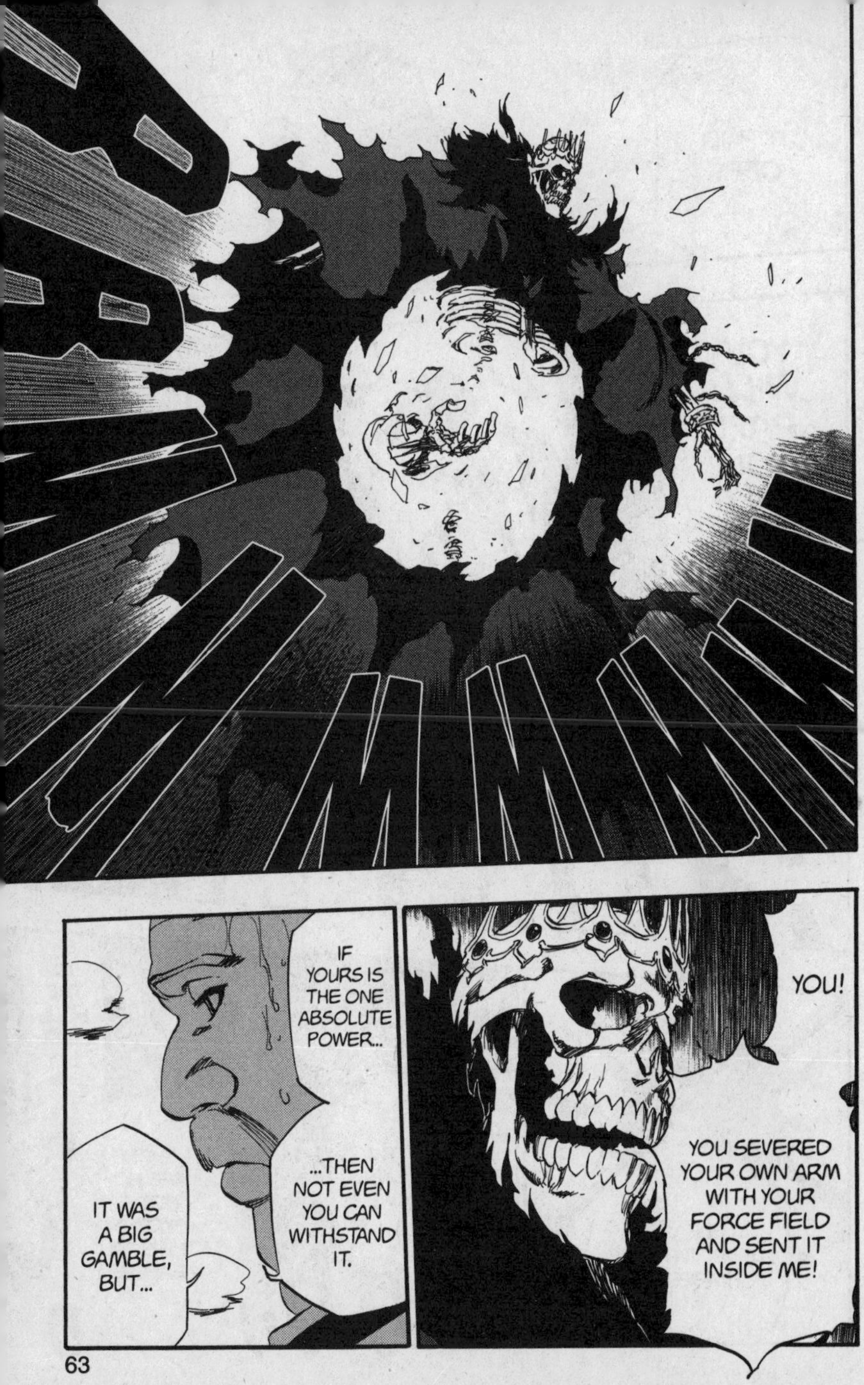
YOU!
YOU SEVERED YOUR OWN ARM WITH YOUR FORCE FIELD AND SENT IT INSIDE ME!
IF YOURS IS THE ONE ABSOLUTE POWER...
...THEN NOT EVEN YOU CAN WITHSTAND IT.
IT WAS A BIG GAMBLE, BUT...

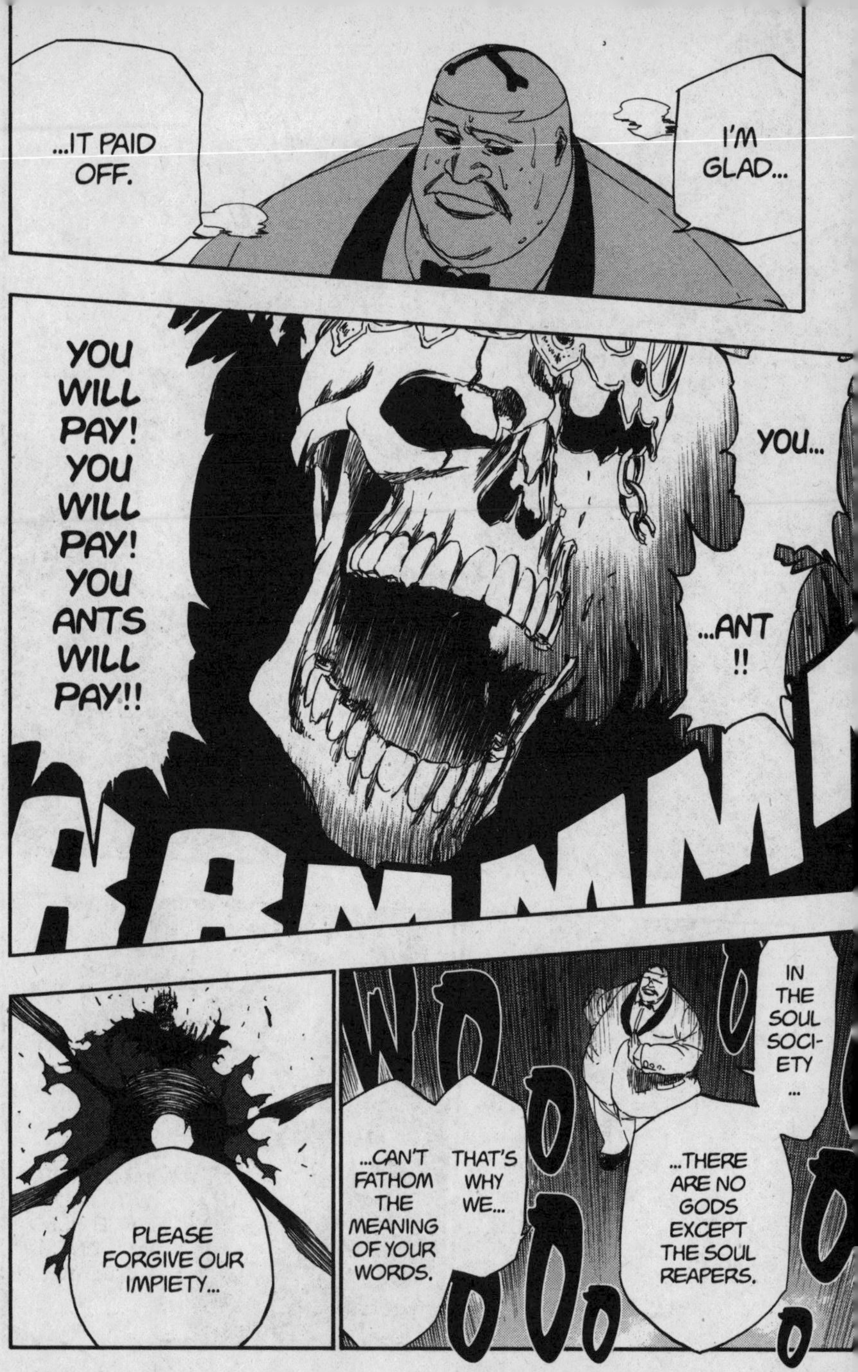
I'M GLAD...
...IT PAID OFF.
YOU...
...ANT !!
YOU WILL PAY! YOU WILL PAY! YOU ANTS WILL PAY!!
IN THE SOUL SOCI-ETY...
...THERE ARE NO GODS EXCEPT THE SOUL REAPERS.
THAT'S WHY WE...
...CAN'T FATHOM THE MEANING OF YOUR WORDS.
PLEASE FORGIVE OUR IMPIETY...

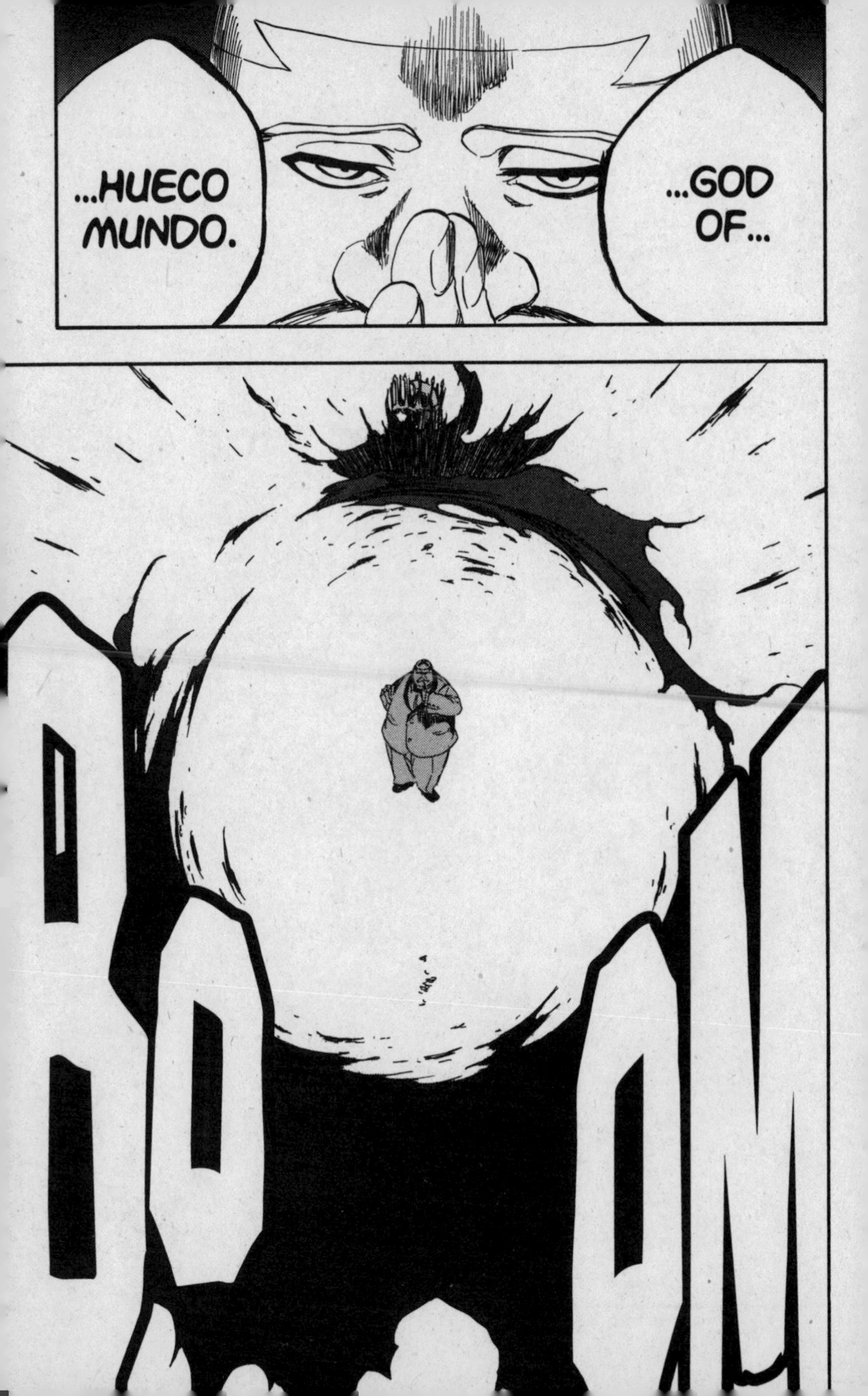
...GOD OF...
...HUECO MUNDO.
BOOM

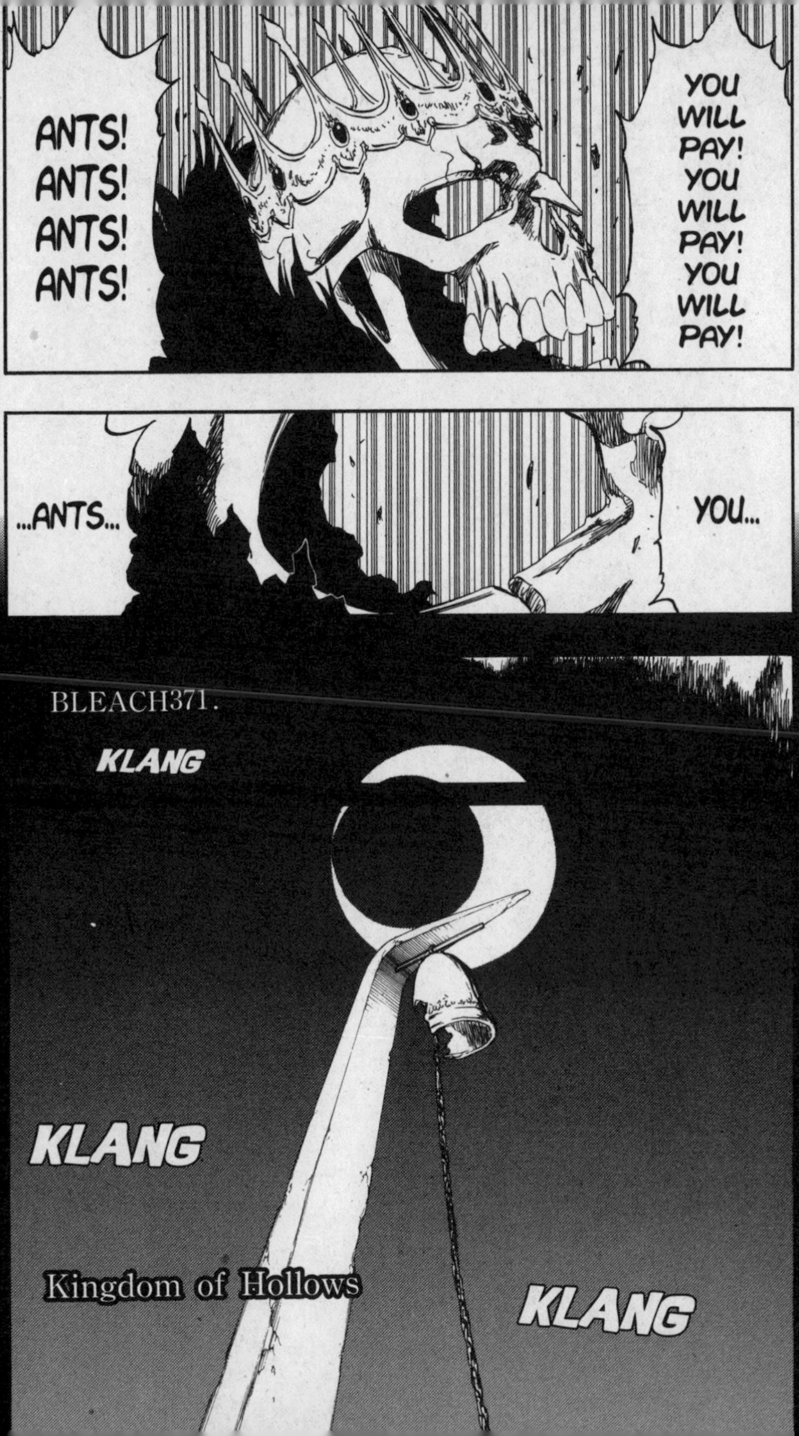
YOU WILL PAY! YOU WILL PAY! YOU WILL PAY!
ANTS! ANTS! ANTS! ANTS!
YOU...
...ANTS...
BLEACH371.
KLANG
KLANG
KLANG
Kingdom of Hollows

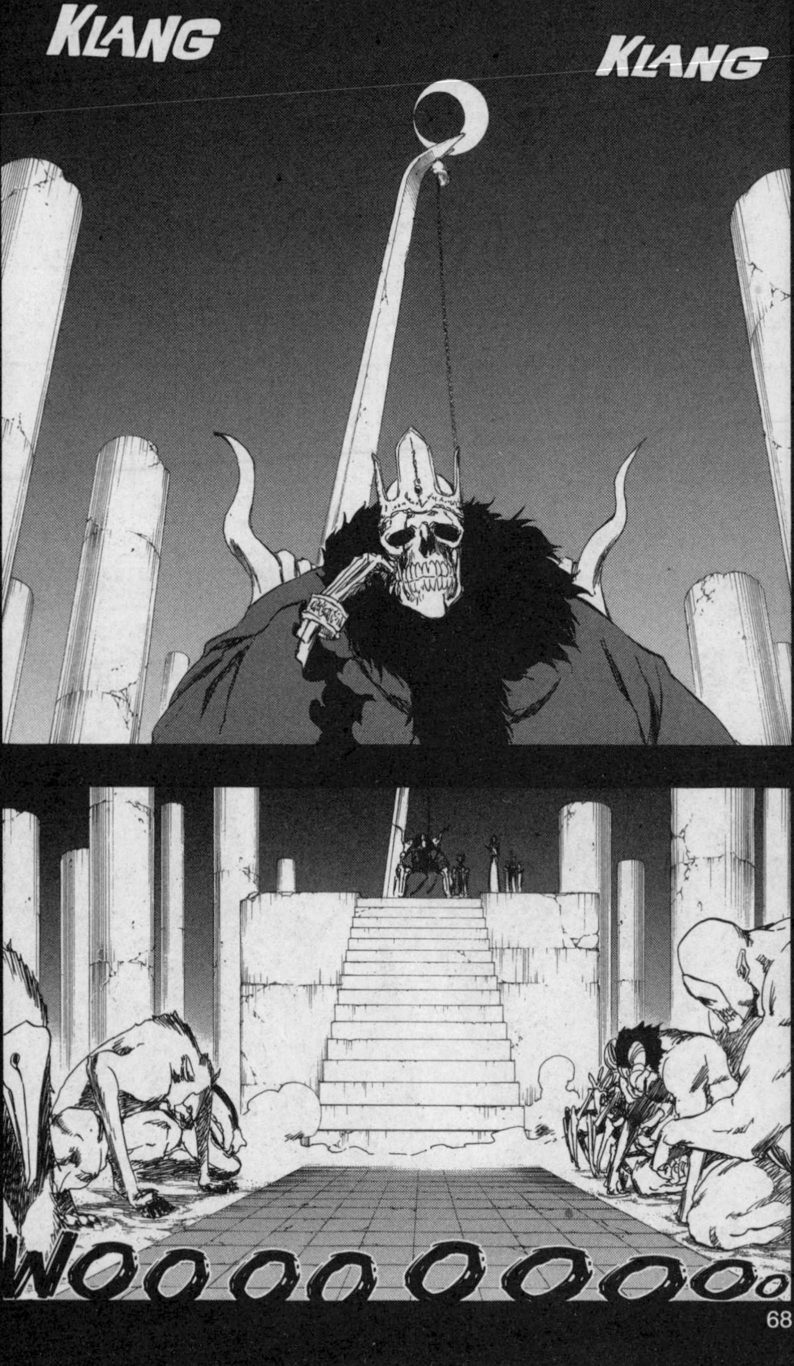
KLANG
KLANG
WOOOO OOOOO.

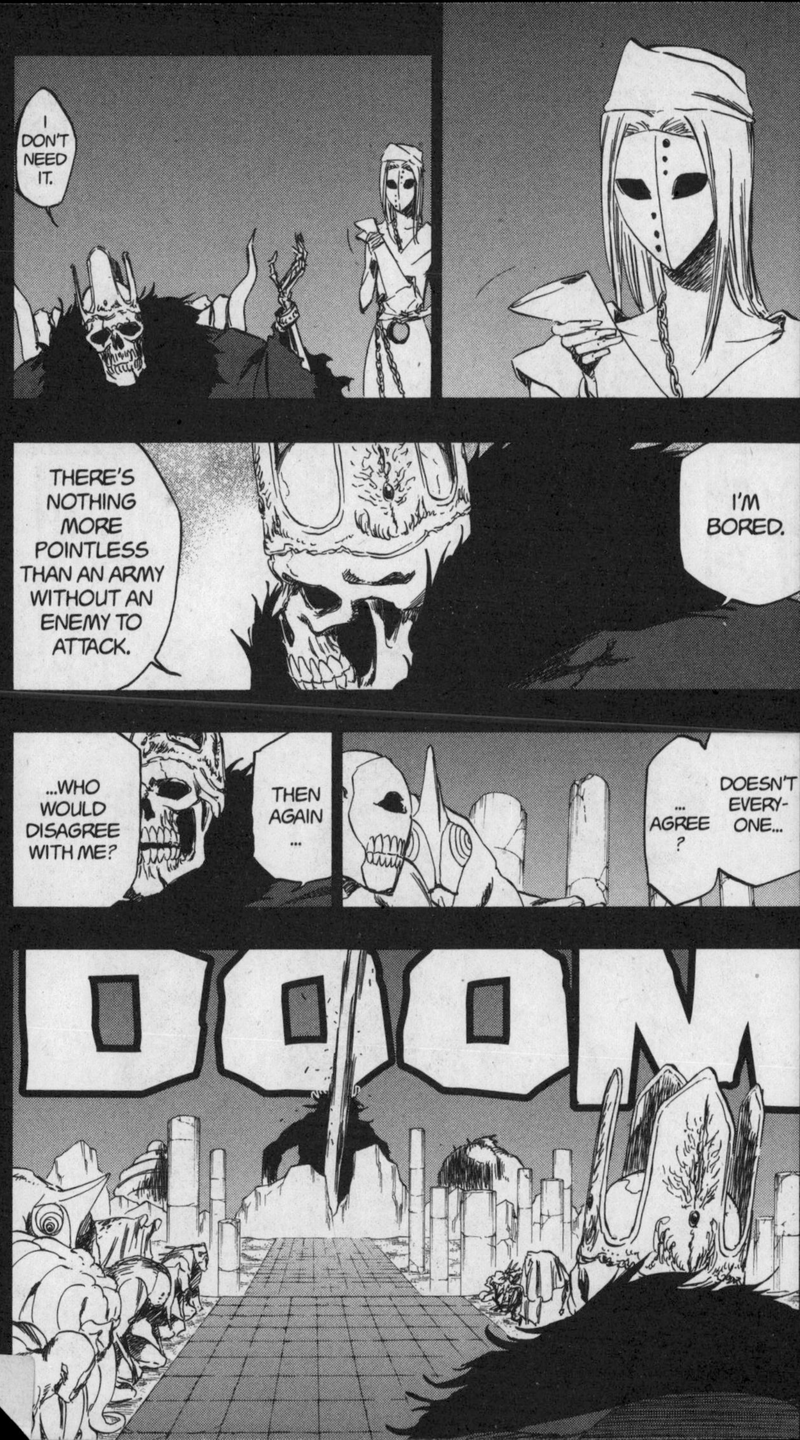
I DON'T NEED IT.
I'M BORED.
THERE'S NOTHING MORE POINTLESS THAN AN ARMY WITHOUT AN ENEMY TO ATTACK.
DOESN'T EVERY-ONE... ...AGREE?
THEN AGAIN...
...WHO WOULD DISAGREE WITH ME?
DOOM

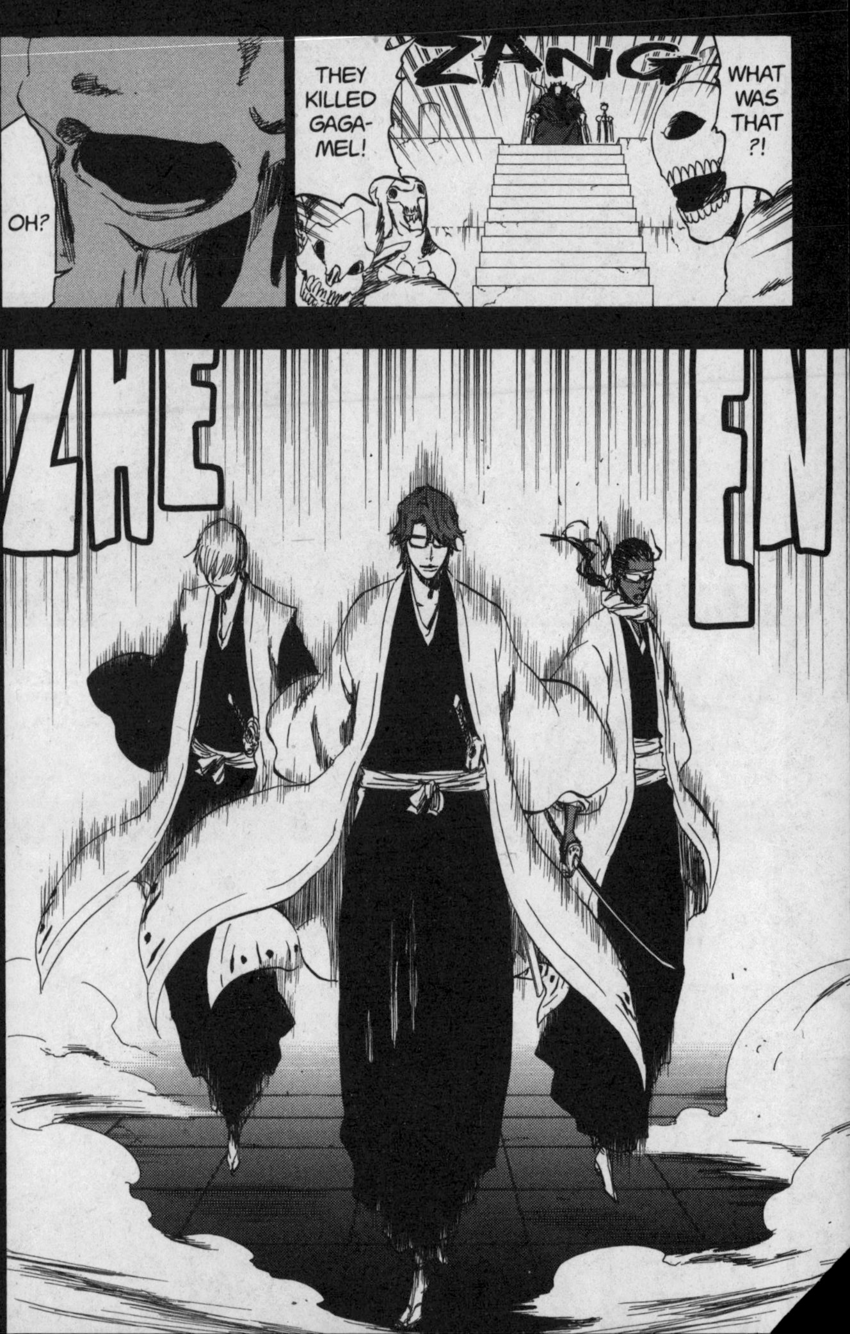
ZANG
WHAT WAS THAT ?!
THEY KILLED GAGA-MEL!
OH?
ZHE
EN

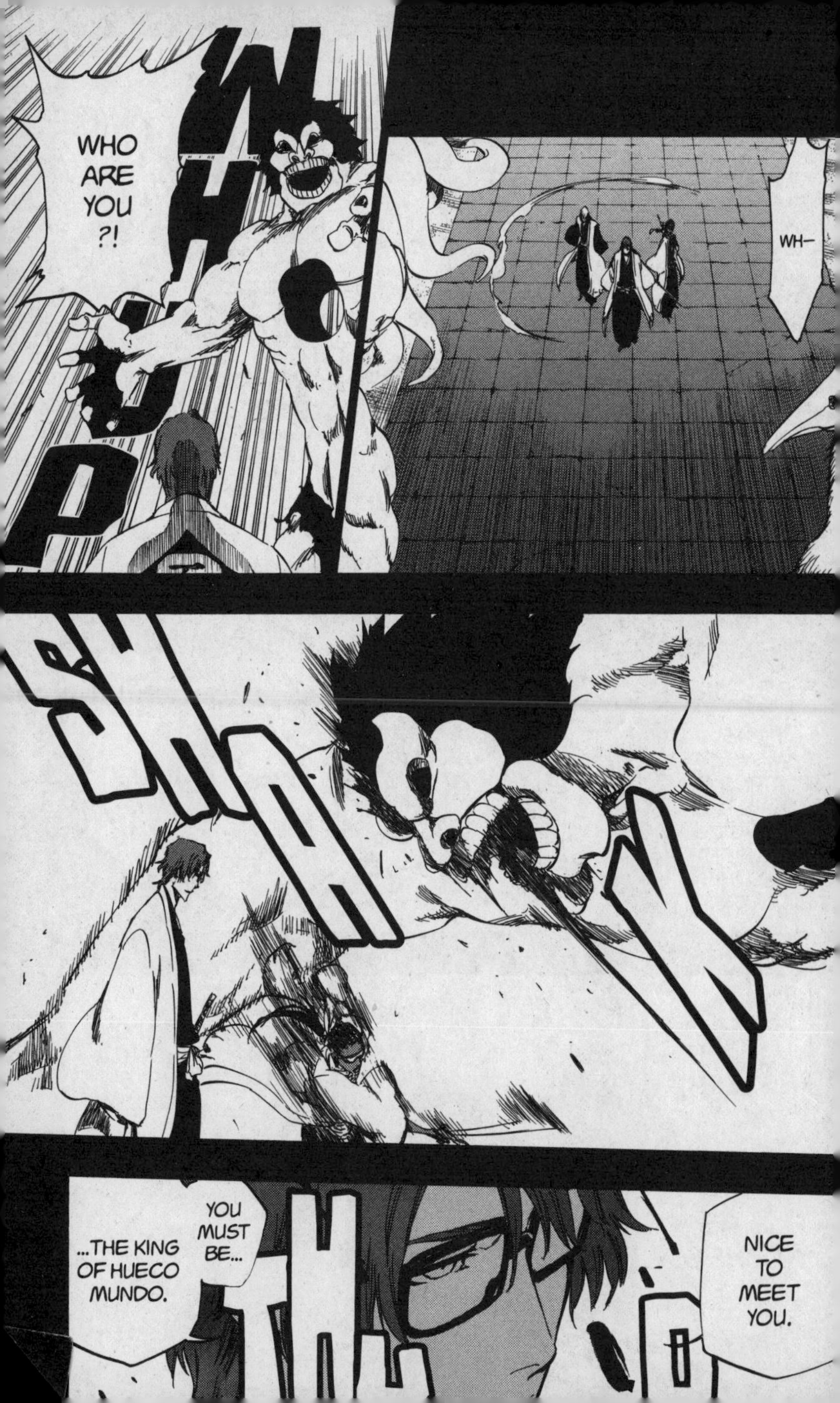
WH—
WHO ARE YOU ?!
NICE TO MEET YOU.
YOU MUST BE...
...THE KING OF HUECO MUNDO.

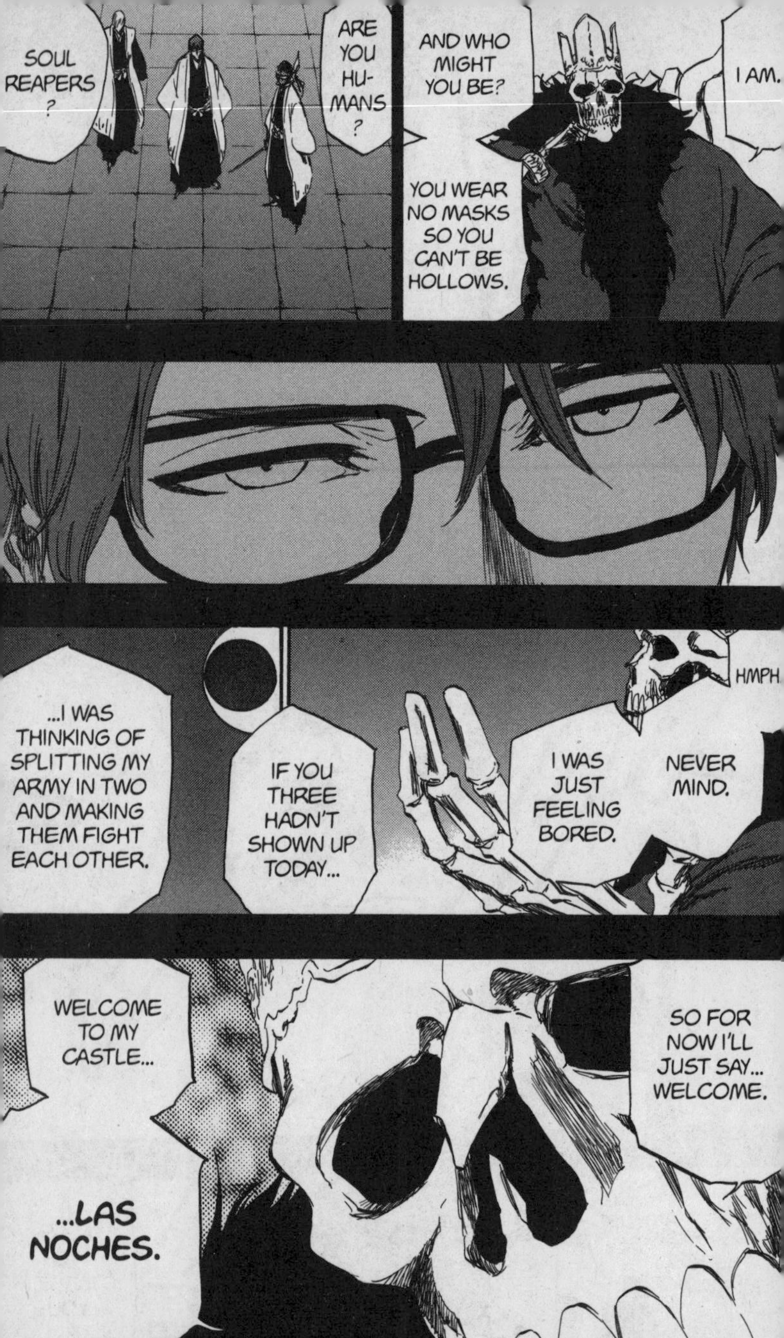
I AM.
AND WHO MIGHT YOU BE?
YOU WEAR NO MASKS SO YOU CAN'T BE HOLLOWS.
ARE YOU HU-MANS?
SOUL REAPERS?
HMPH
NEVER MIND.
I WAS JUST FEELING BORED.
IF YOU THREE HADN'T SHOWN UP TODAY...
...I WAS THINKING OF SPLITTING MY ARMY IN TWO AND MAKING THEM FIGHT EACH OTHER.
SO FOR NOW I'LL JUST SAY... WELCOME.
WELCOME TO MY CASTLE...
...LAS NOCHES.

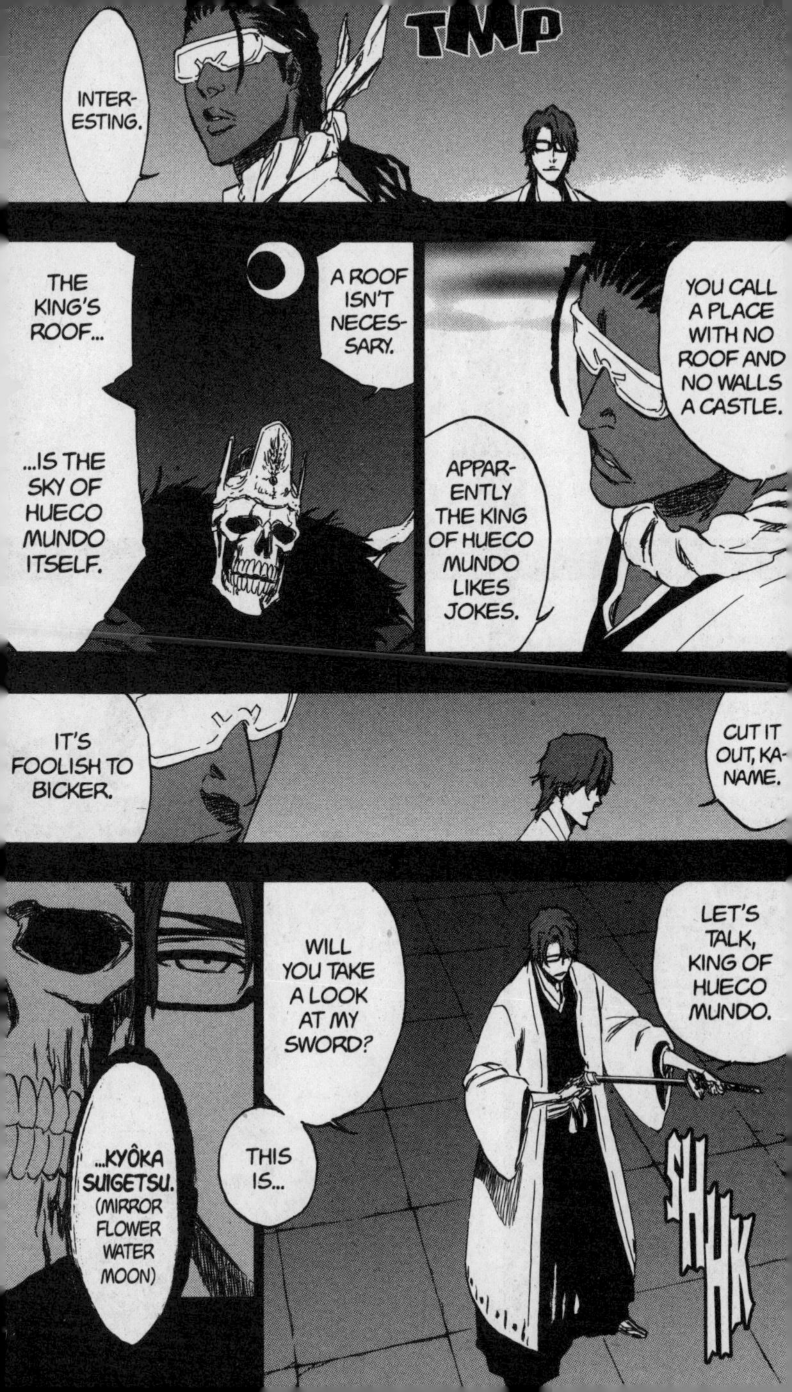
TMP
INTERESTING.
YOU CALL A PLACE WITH NO ROOF AND NO WALLS A CASTLE.
APPARENTLY THE KING OF HUECO MUNDO LIKES JOKES.
A ROOF ISN'T NECESSARY.
THE KING'S ROOF...
...IS THE SKY OF HUECO MUNDO ITSELF.
CUT IT OUT, KANAME.
IT'S FOOLISH TO BICKER.
LET'S TALK, KING OF HUECO MUNDO.
SHHK
WILL YOU TAKE A LOOK AT MY SWORD?
THIS IS...
...KYÔKA SUIGETSU. (MIRROR FLOWER WATER MOON)

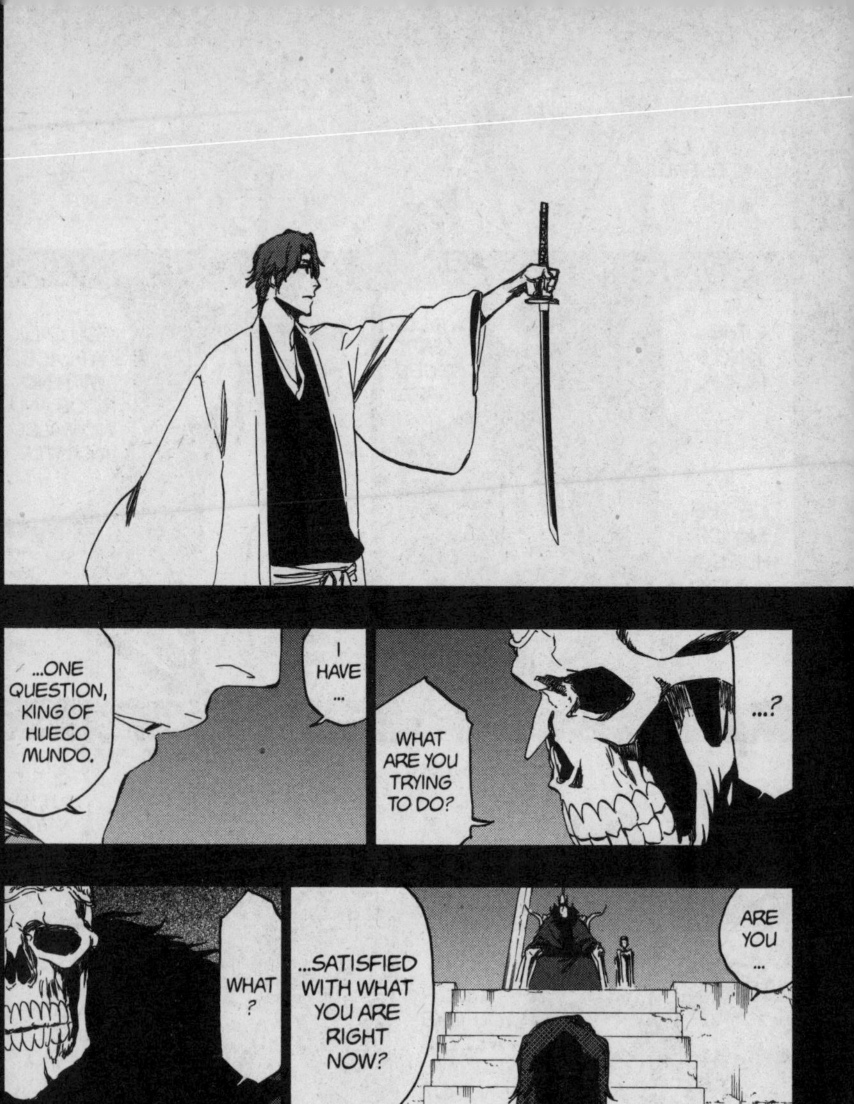
...?
WHAT ARE YOU TRYING TO DO?
I HAVE ...
...ONE QUESTION, KING OF HUECO MUNDO.
ARE YOU ...
...SATISFIED WITH WHAT YOU ARE RIGHT NOW?
WHAT ?

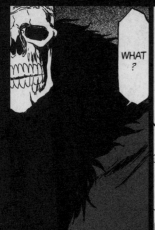

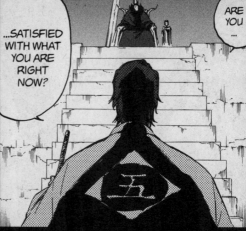

READ THIS WAY

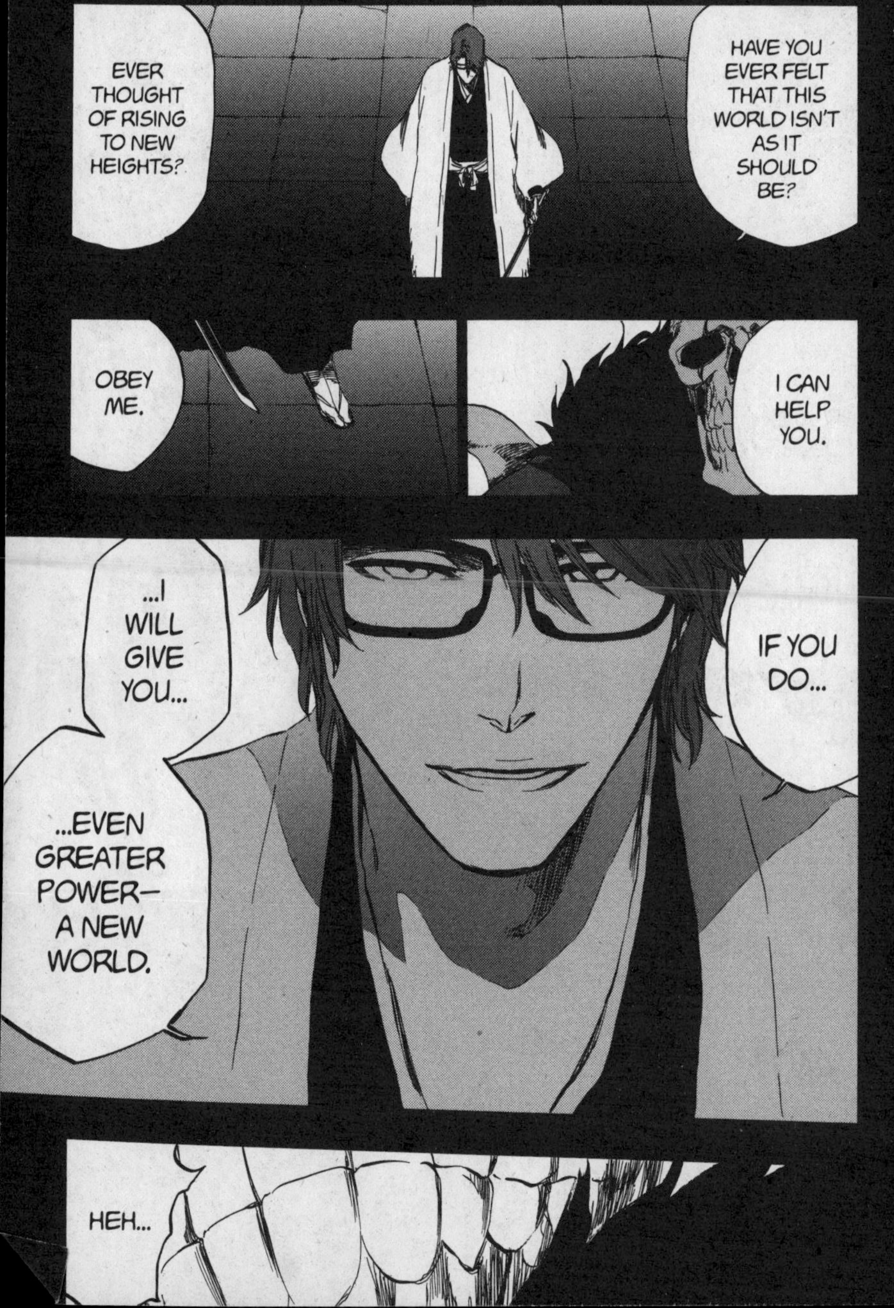

HAVE YOU EVER FELT THAT THIS WORLD ISN'T AS IT SHOULD BE?
EVER THOUGHT OF RISING TO NEW HEIGHTS?
I CAN HELP YOU.
OBEY ME.
IF YOU DO...
...I WILL GIVE YOU...
...EVEN GREATER POWER—A NEW WORLD.
HEH...

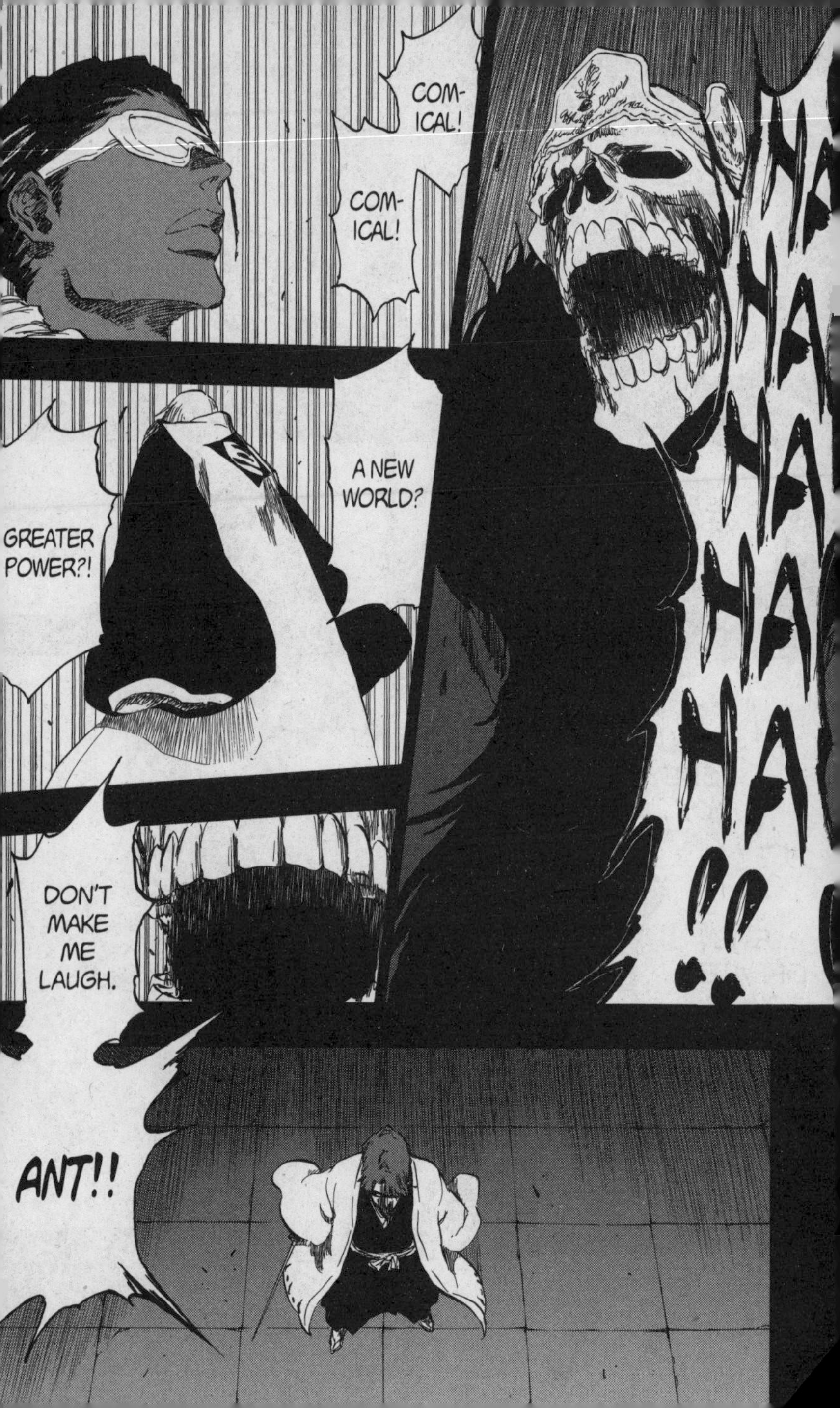
HA HA HA HA HA HA HA HA!!
COM-
ICAL!
COM-
ICAL!
A NEW
WORLD?
GREATER
POWER?!
DON'T
MAKE
ME
LAUGH.
ANT!!

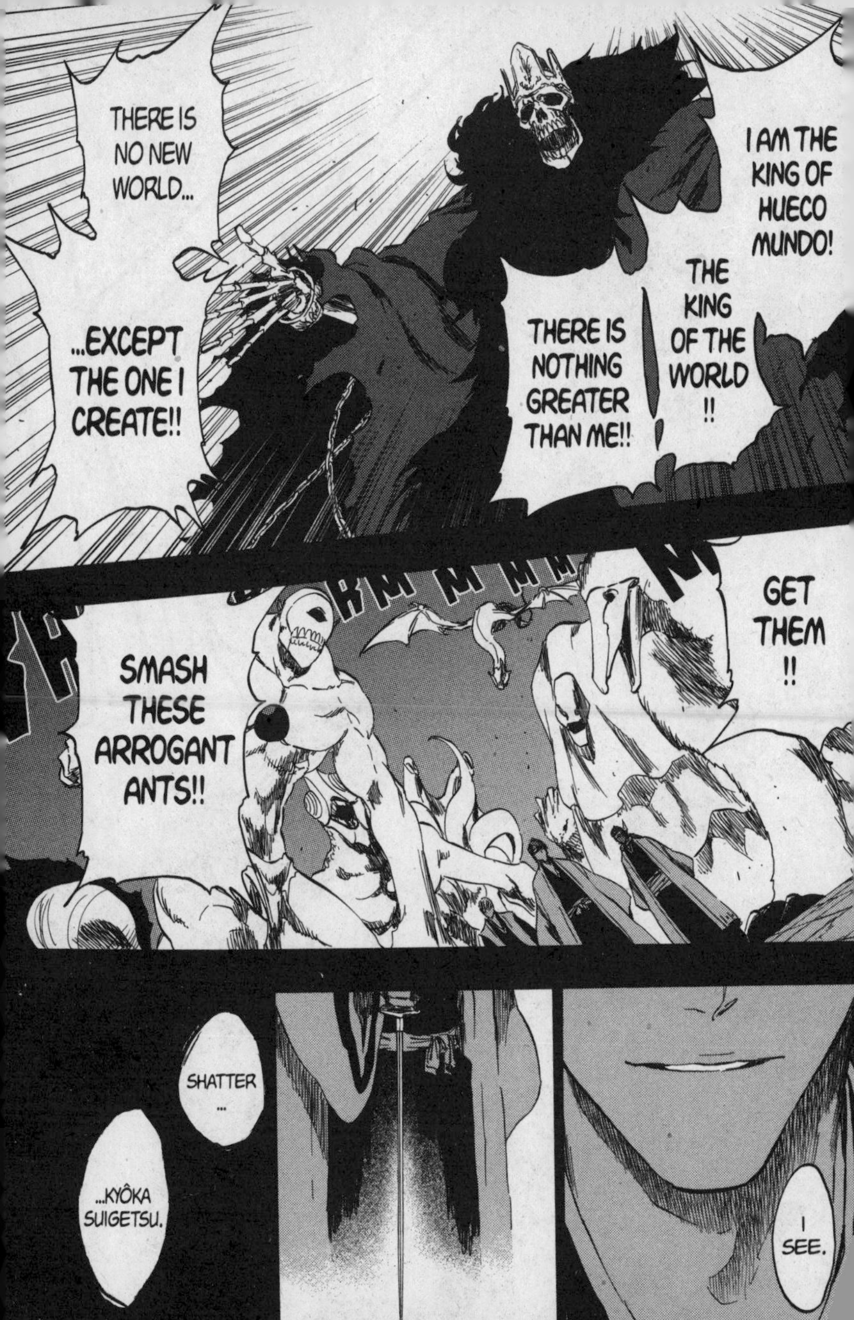
I AM THE KING OF HUECO MUNDO!
THE KING OF THE WORLD !!
THERE IS NOTHING GREATER THAN ME!!
THERE IS NO NEW WORLD...
...EXCEPT THE ONE I CREATE!!
GET THEM !!
SMASH THESE ARROGANT ANTS!!
I SEE.
SHATTER ...
...KYÔKA SUIGETSU.

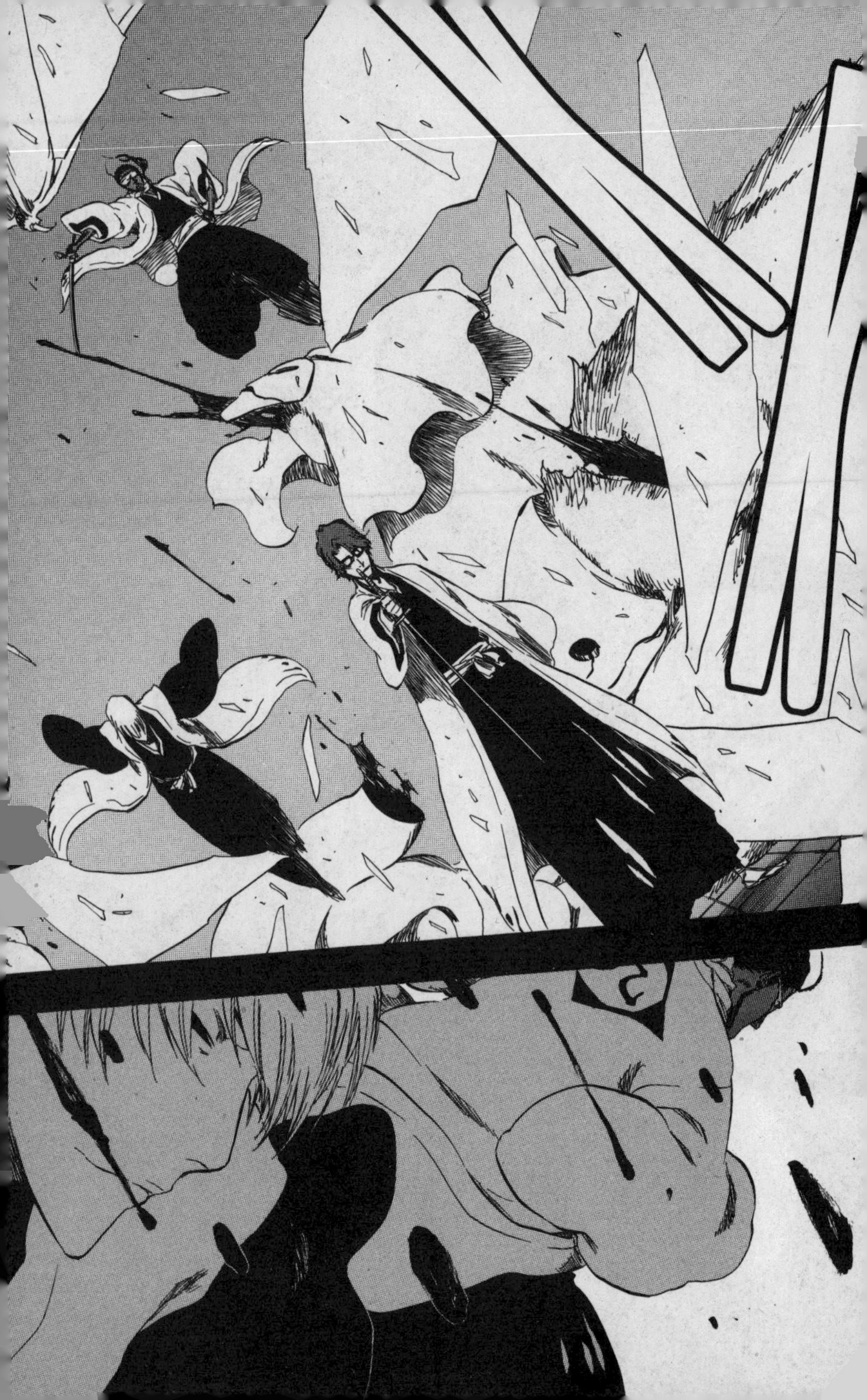

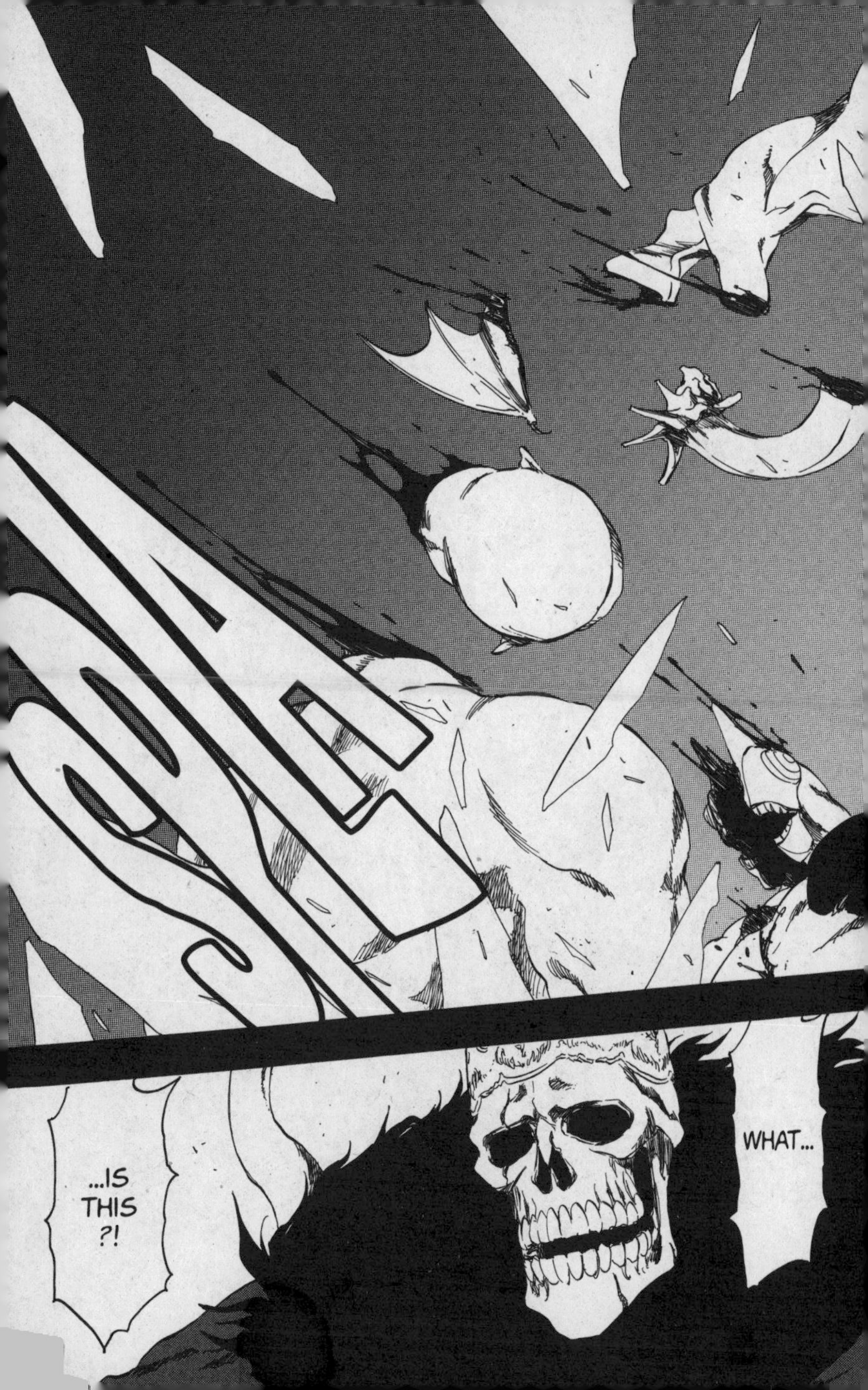
WHAT...
...IS THIS ?!

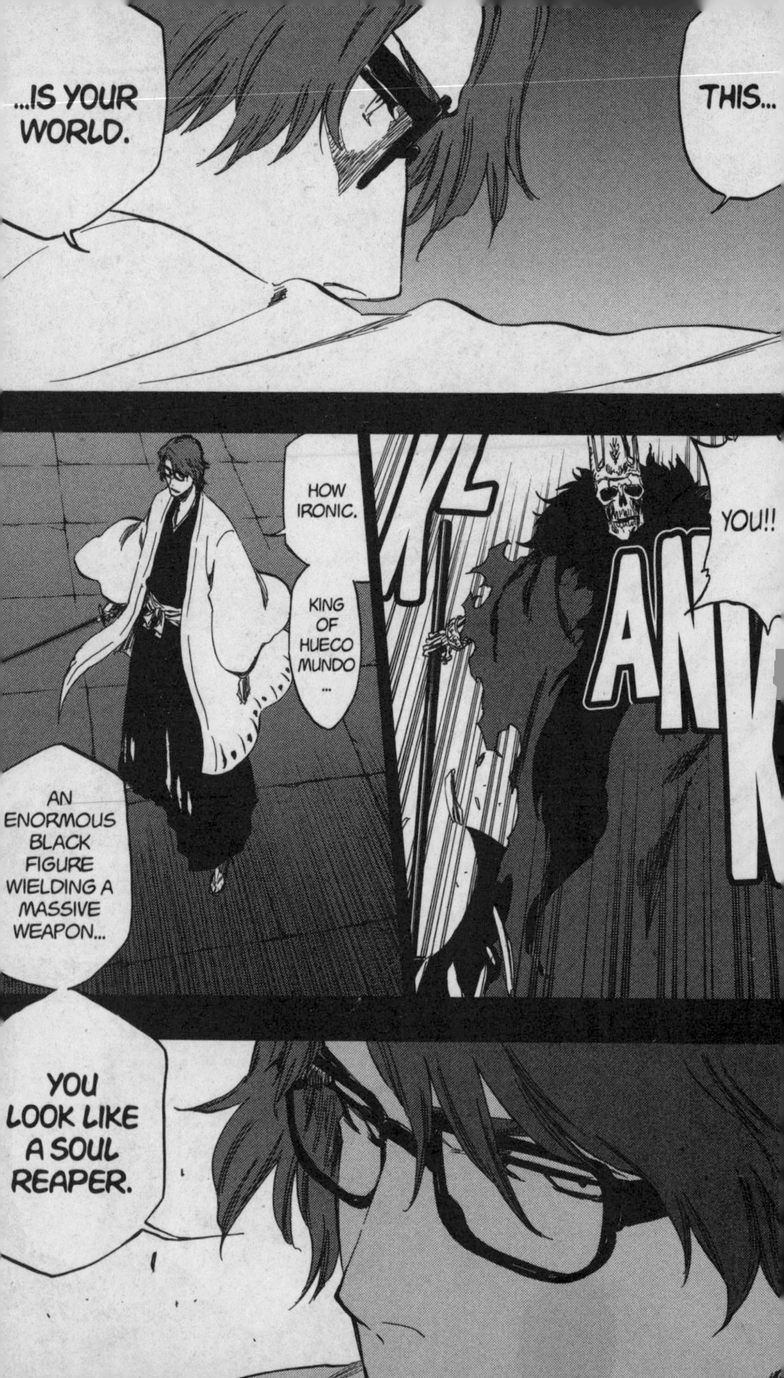
THIS...
...IS YOUR WORLD.
YOU!!
HOW IRONIC.
KING OF HUECO MUNDO...
AN ENORMOUS BLACK FIGURE WIELDING A MASSIVE WEAPON...
YOU LOOK LIKE A SOUL REAPER.

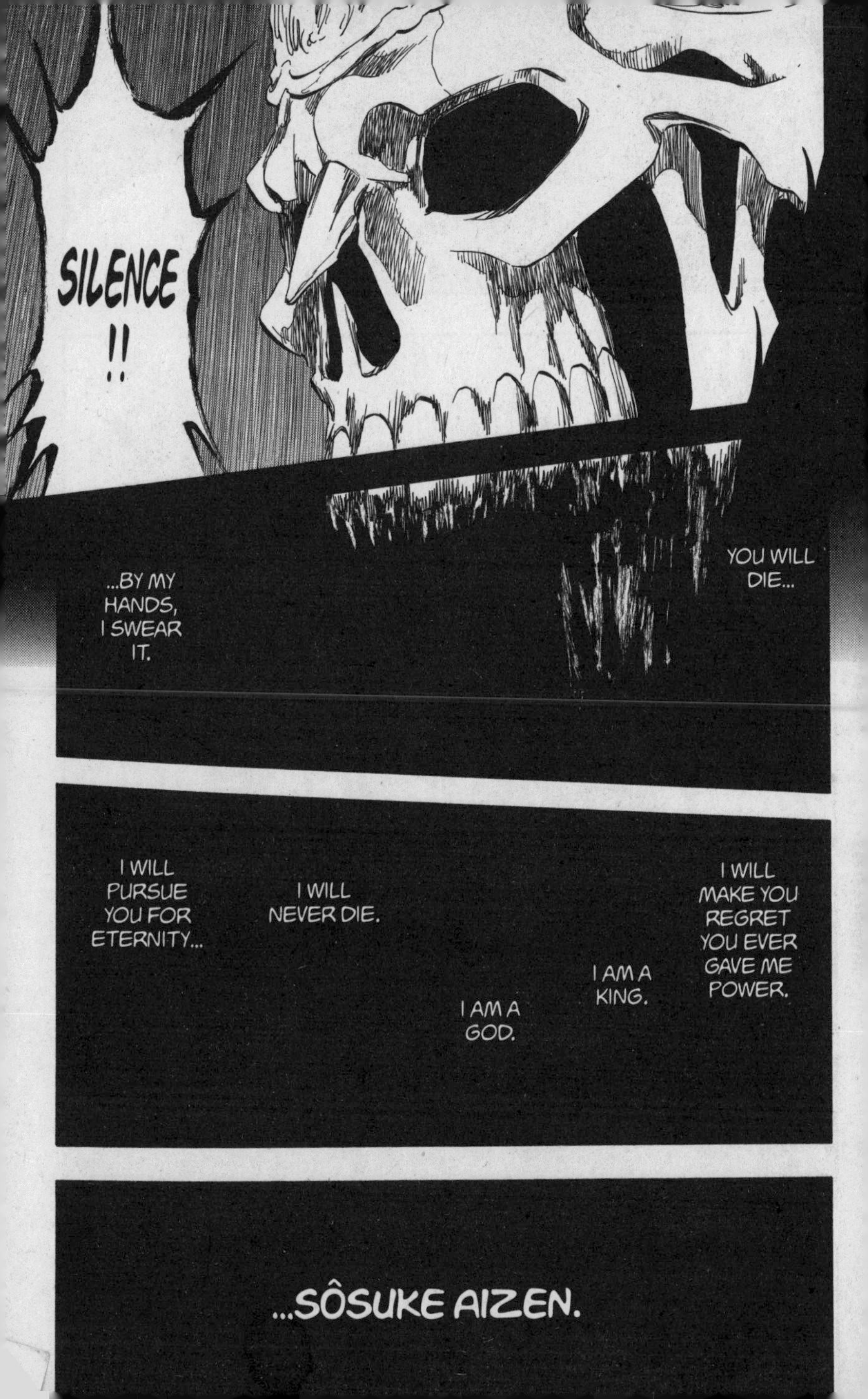
SILENCE !!
YOU WILL DIE...
...BY MY HANDS, I SWEAR IT.
I WILL MAKE YOU REGRET YOU EVER GAVE ME POWER.
I AM A KING.
I AM A GOD.
I WILL NEVER DIE.
I WILL PURSUE YOU FOR ETERNITY...
...SÔSUKE AIZEN.

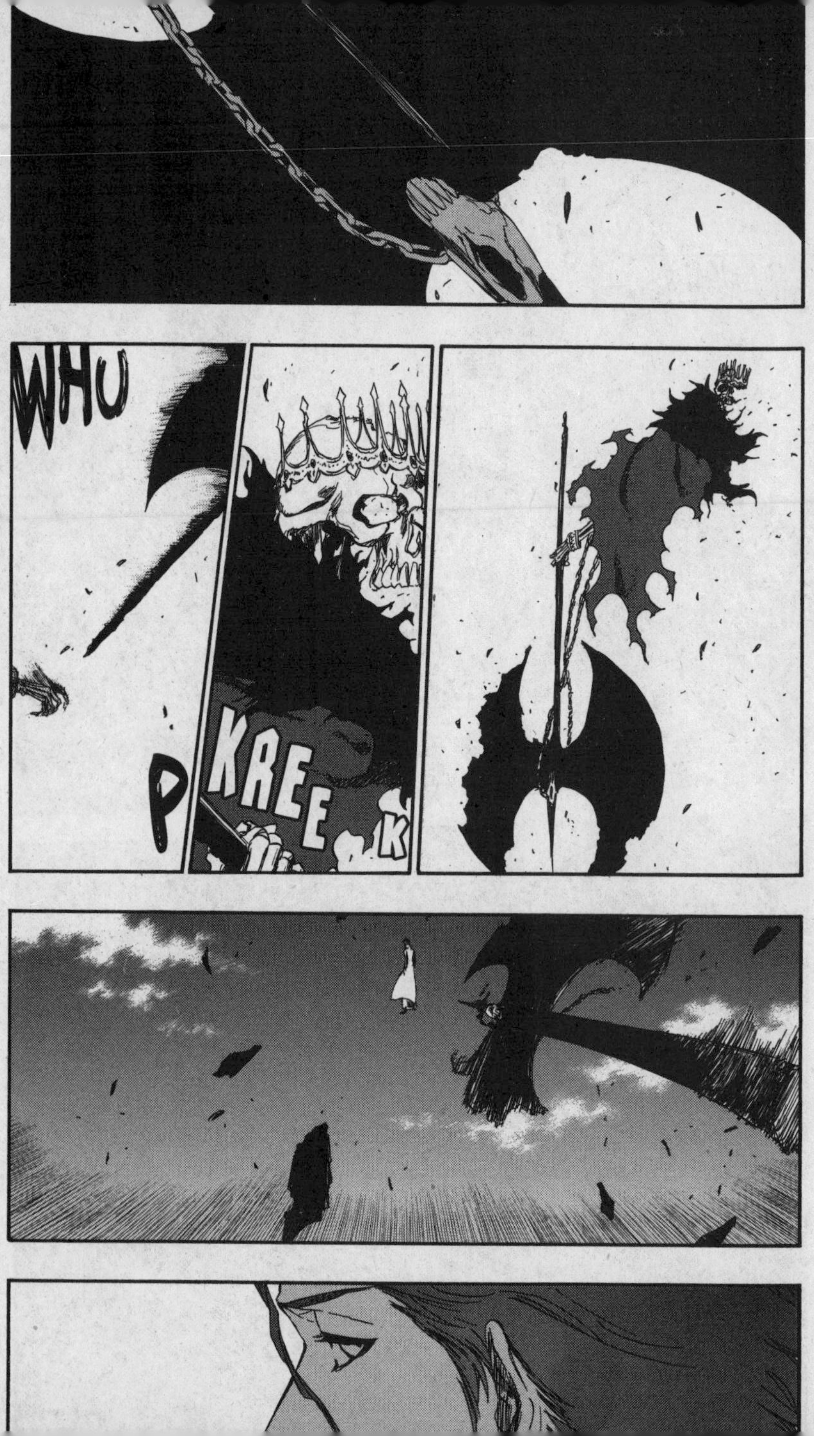
KREEK
WHU
P

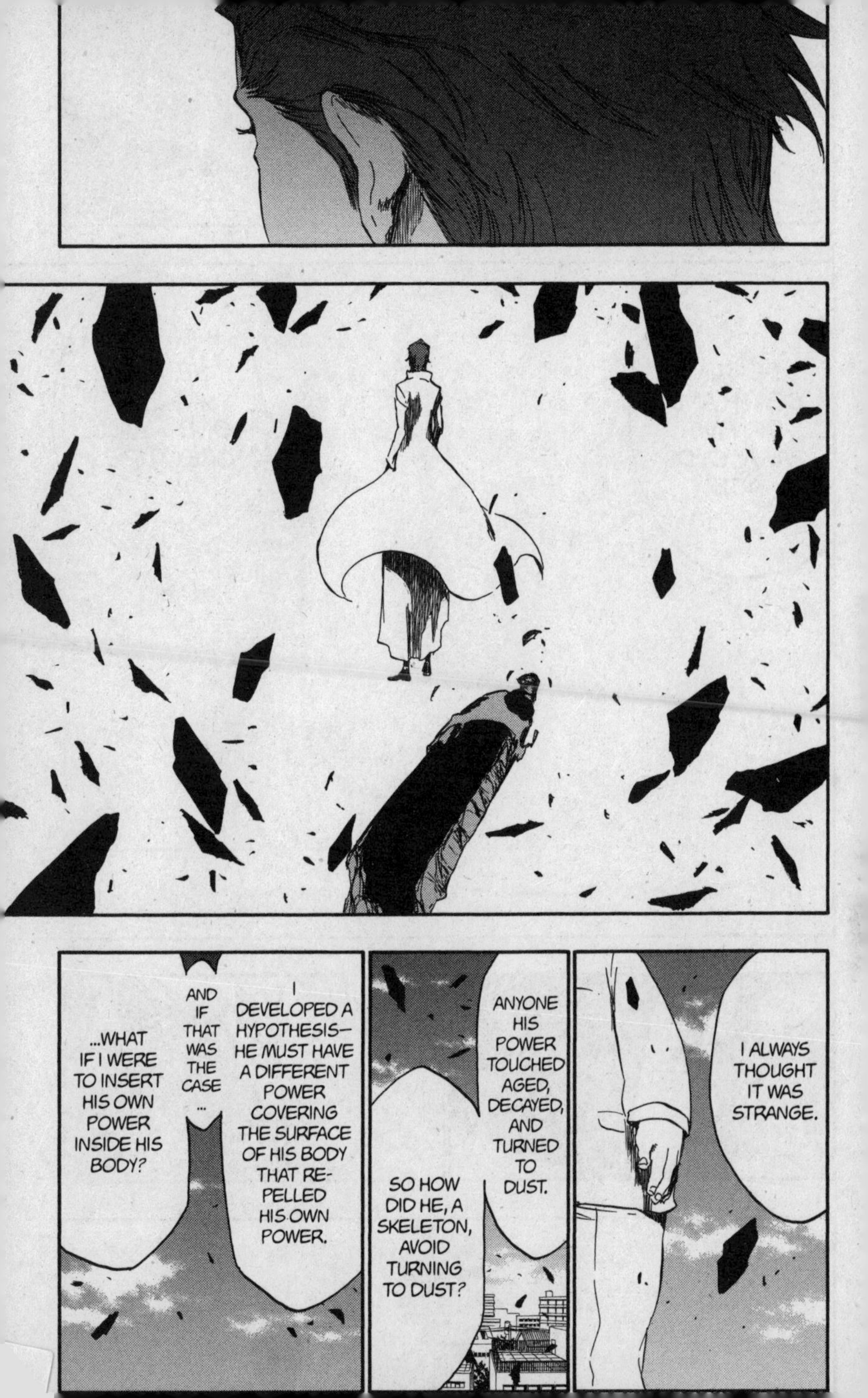
I ALWAYS THOUGHT IT WAS STRANGE.
ANYONE HIS POWER TOUCHED AGED, DECAYED, AND TURNED TO DUST.
SO HOW DID HE, A SKELETON, AVOID TURNING TO DUST?
I DEVELOPED A HYPOTHESIS—HE MUST HAVE A DIFFERENT POWER COVERING THE SURFACE OF HIS BODY THAT RE-PELLED HIS OWN POWER.
AND IF THAT WAS THE CASE...
...WHAT IF I WERE TO INSERT HIS OWN POWER INSIDE HIS BODY?

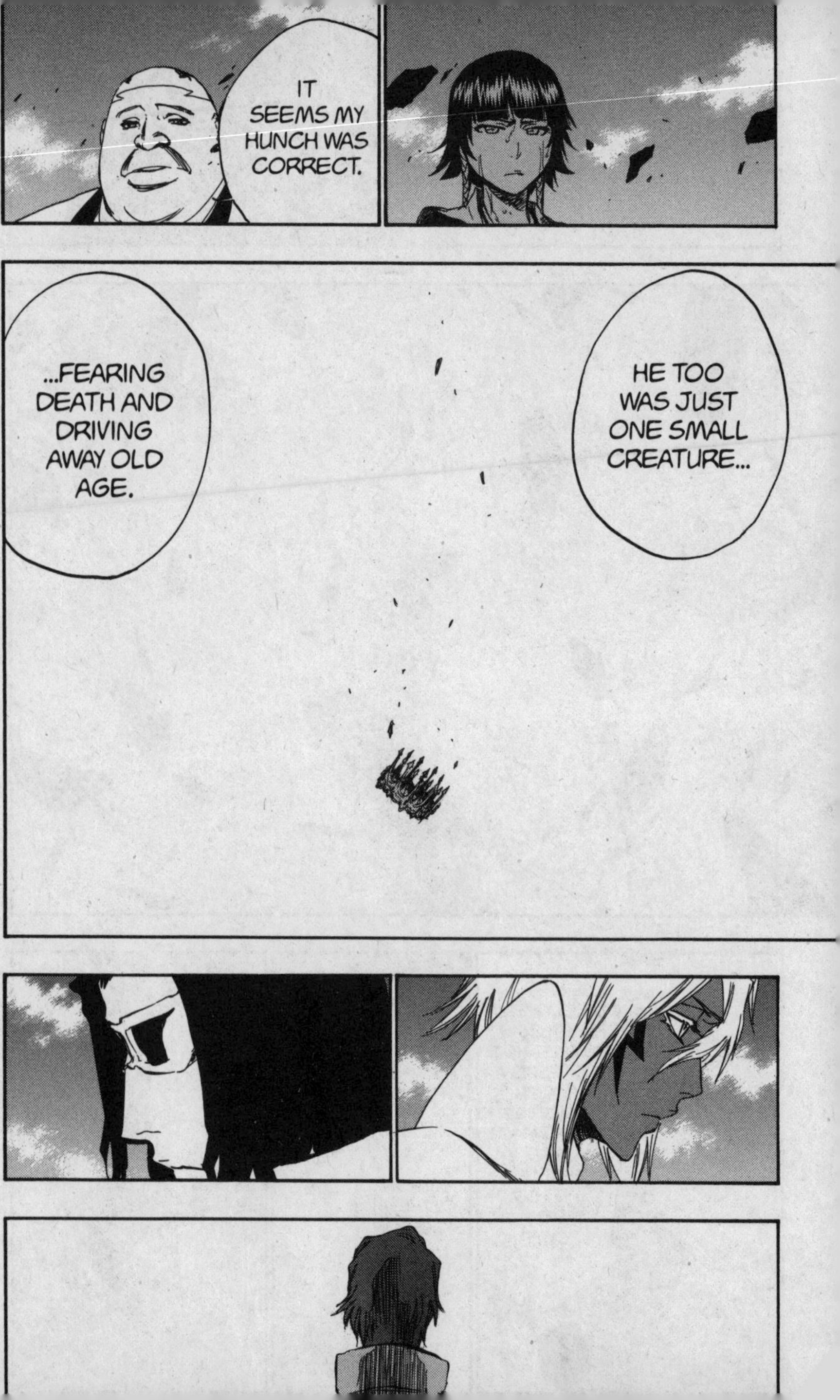
IT SEEMS MY HUNCH WAS CORRECT.
HE TOO WAS JUST ONE SMALL CREATURE...
...FEARING DEATH AND DRIVING AWAY OLD AGE.

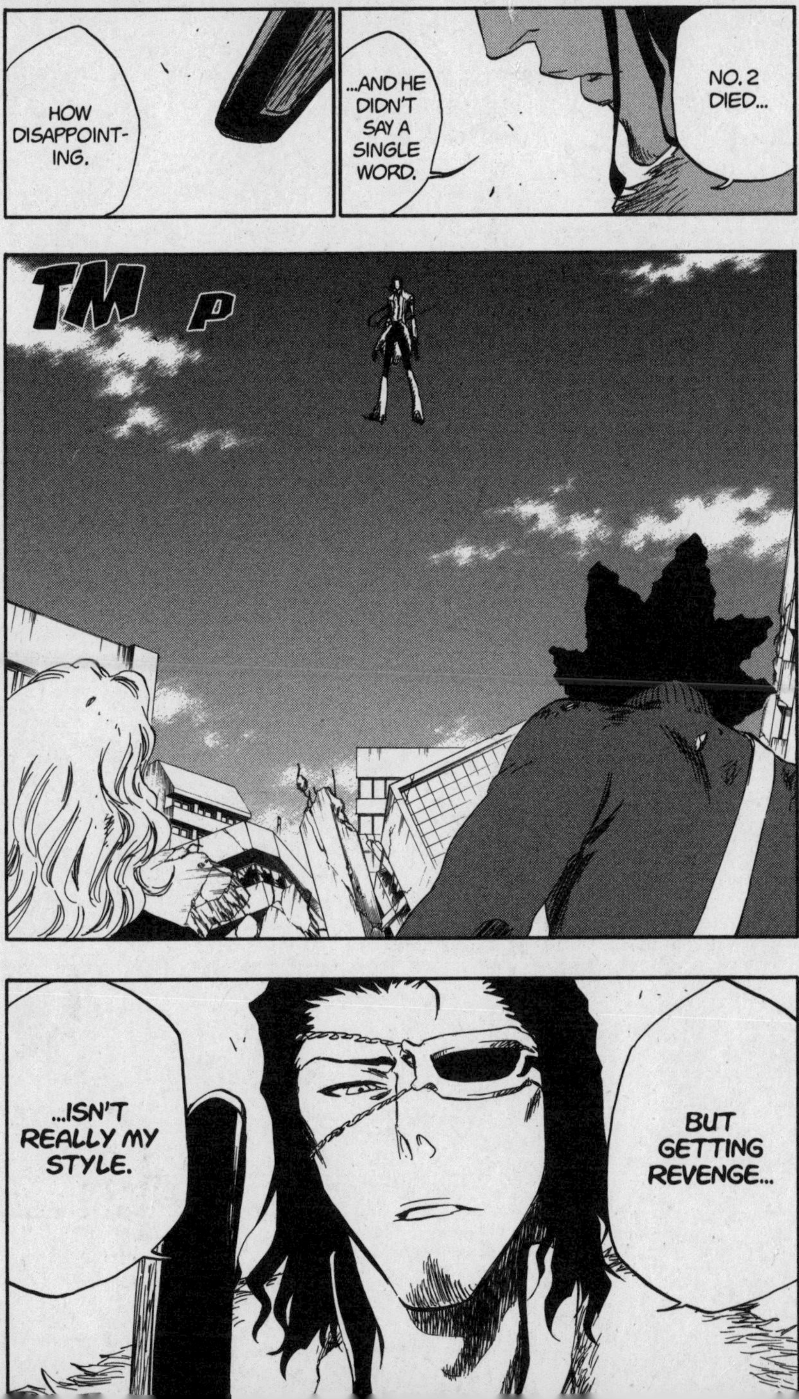
NO. 2 DIED...
...AND HE DIDN'T SAY A SINGLE WORD.
HOW DISAPPOINT-ING.
TMP
BUT GETTING REVENGE...
...ISN'T REALLY MY STYLE.

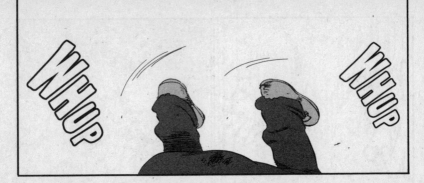

WHOP

WHOP

HACHI GOT HIM!

HEY!

COME ON OUT, ROSE!!

372. The Metal Cudgel Flinger

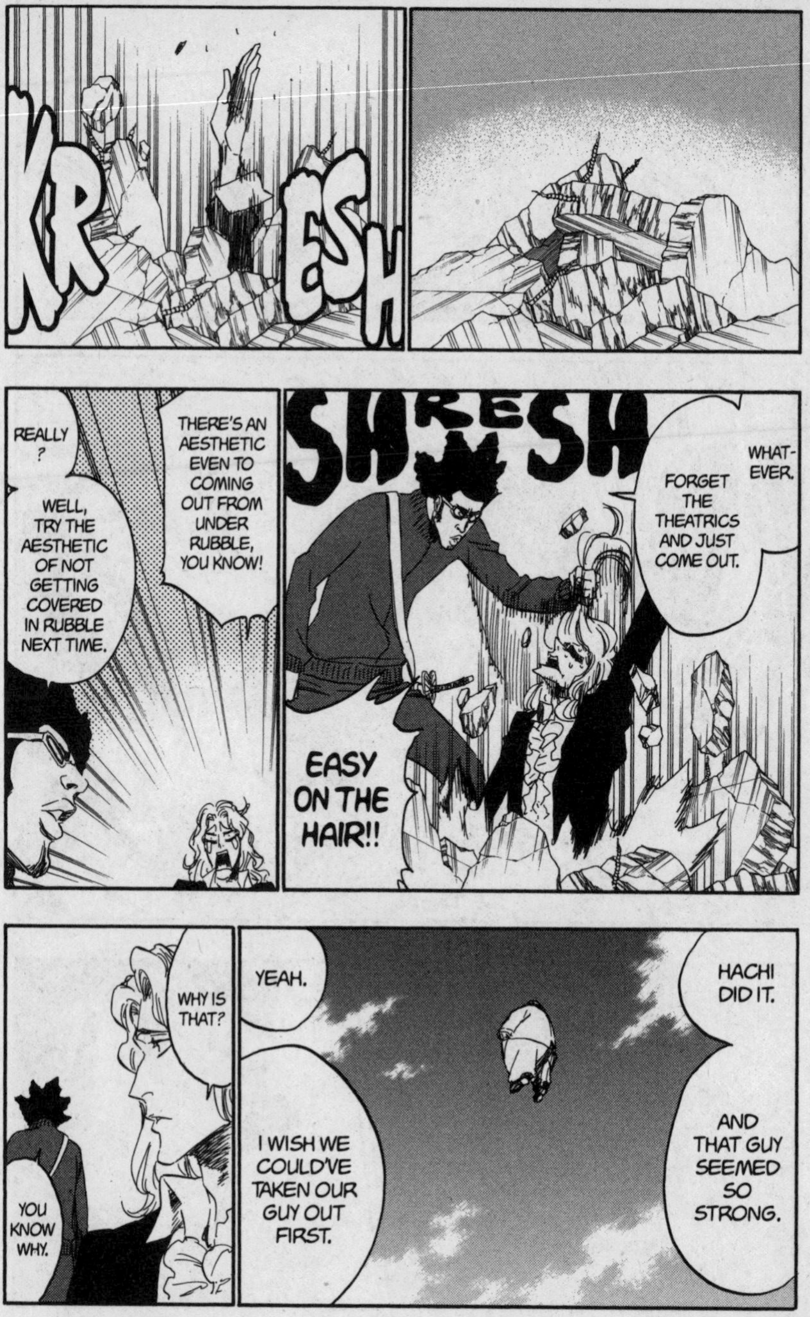
KRESH
WHAT-EVER.
FORGET THE THEATRICS AND JUST COME OUT.
SHRESH
EASY ON THE HAIR!!
THERE'S AN AESTHETIC EVEN TO COMING OUT FROM UNDER RUBBLE, YOU KNOW!
REALLY?
WELL, TRY THE AESTHETIC OF NOT GETTING COVERED IN RUBBLE NEXT TIME.
HACHI DID IT.
AND THAT GUY SEEMED SO STRONG.
YEAH.
I WISH WE COULD'VE TAKEN OUR GUY OUT FIRST.
WHY IS THAT?
YOU KNOW WHY.

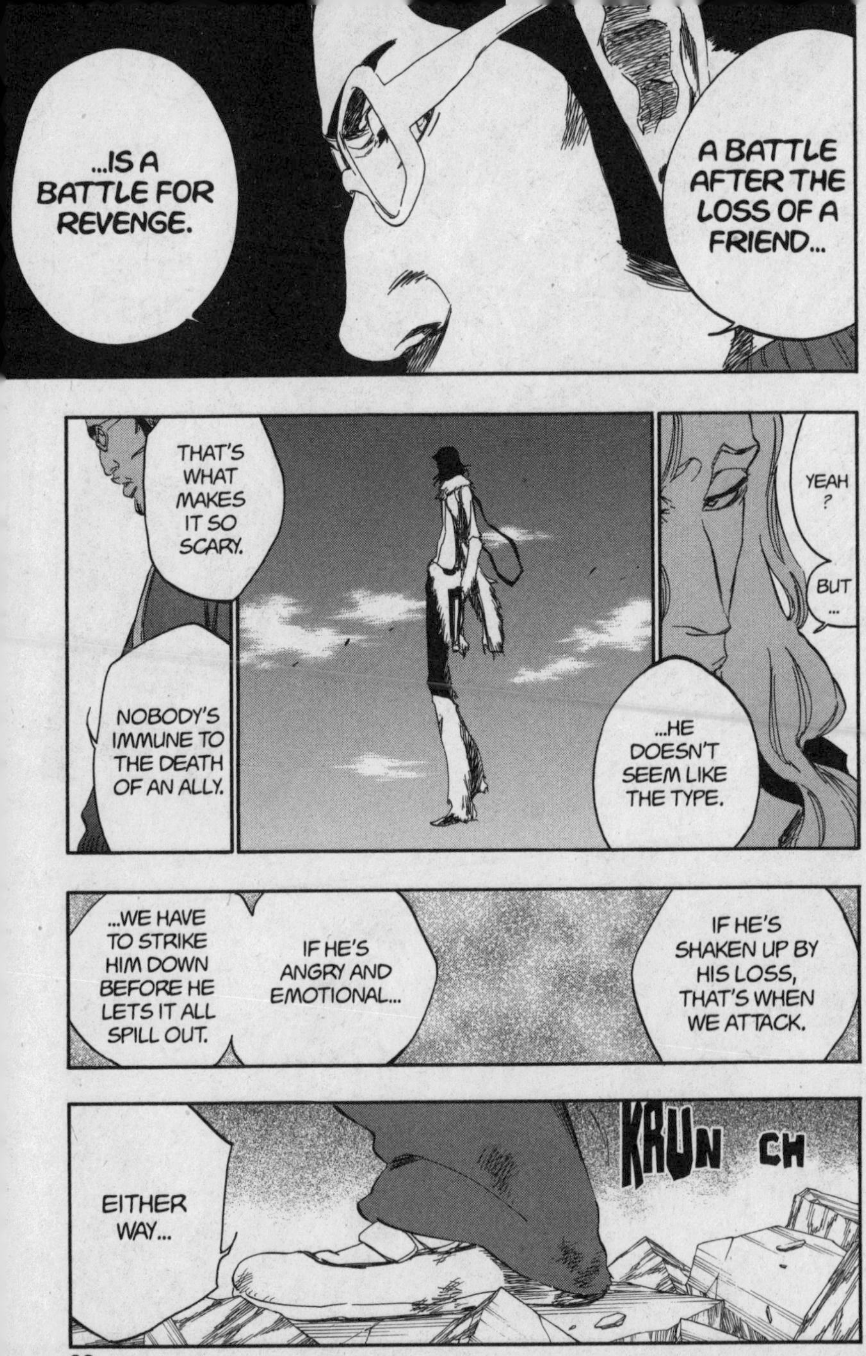
A BATTLE AFTER THE LOSS OF A FRIEND...
...IS A BATTLE FOR REVENGE.
YEAH?
BUT...
...HE DOESN'T SEEM LIKE THE TYPE.
THAT'S WHAT MAKES IT SO SCARY.
NOBODY'S IMMUNE TO THE DEATH OF AN ALLY.
IF HE'S SHAKEN UP BY HIS LOSS, THAT'S WHEN WE ATTACK.
IF HE'S ANGRY AND EMOTIONAL...
...WE HAVE TO STRIKE HIM DOWN BEFORE HE LETS IT ALL SPILL OUT.
KRUNCH
EITHER WAY...

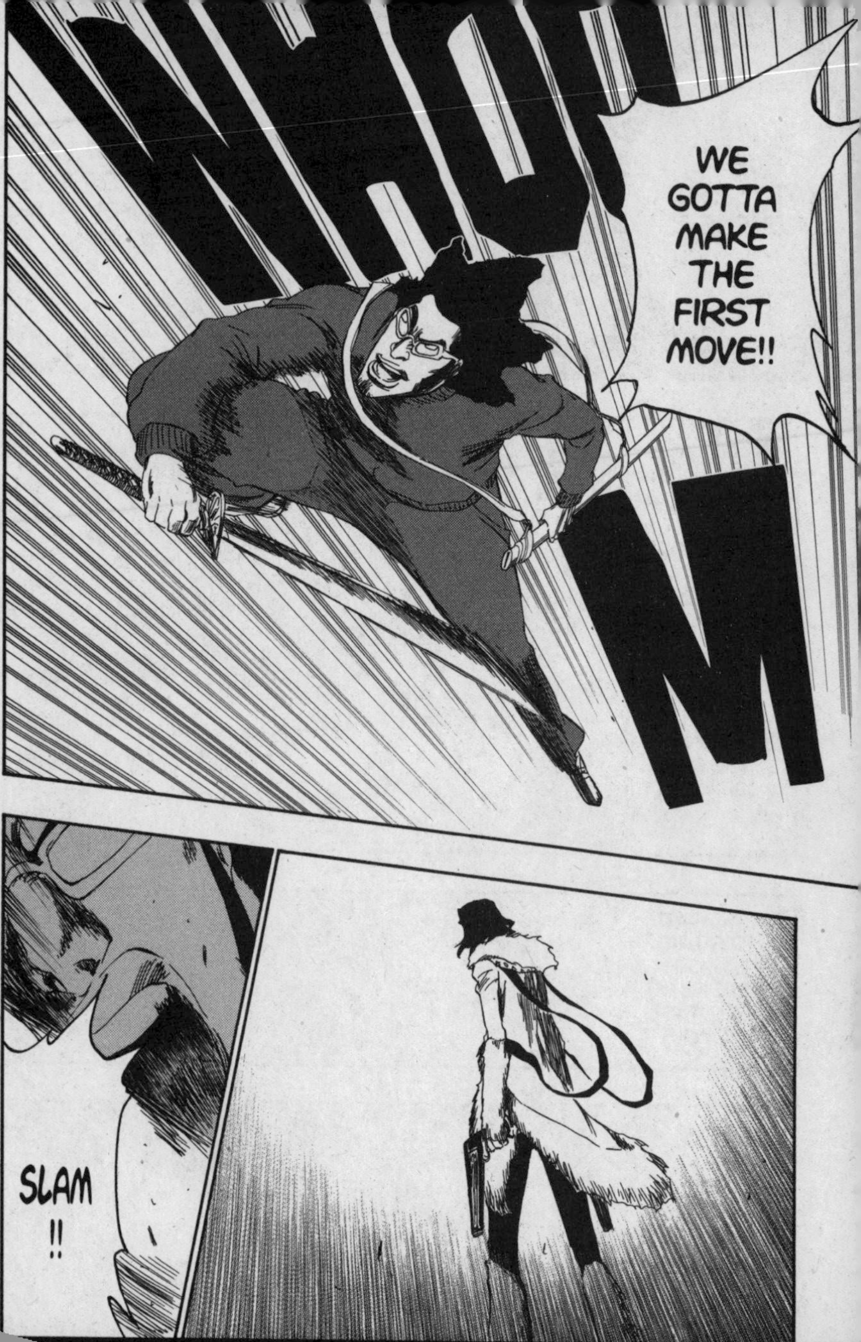
WE GOTTA MAKE THE FIRST MOVE!!
SLAM !!

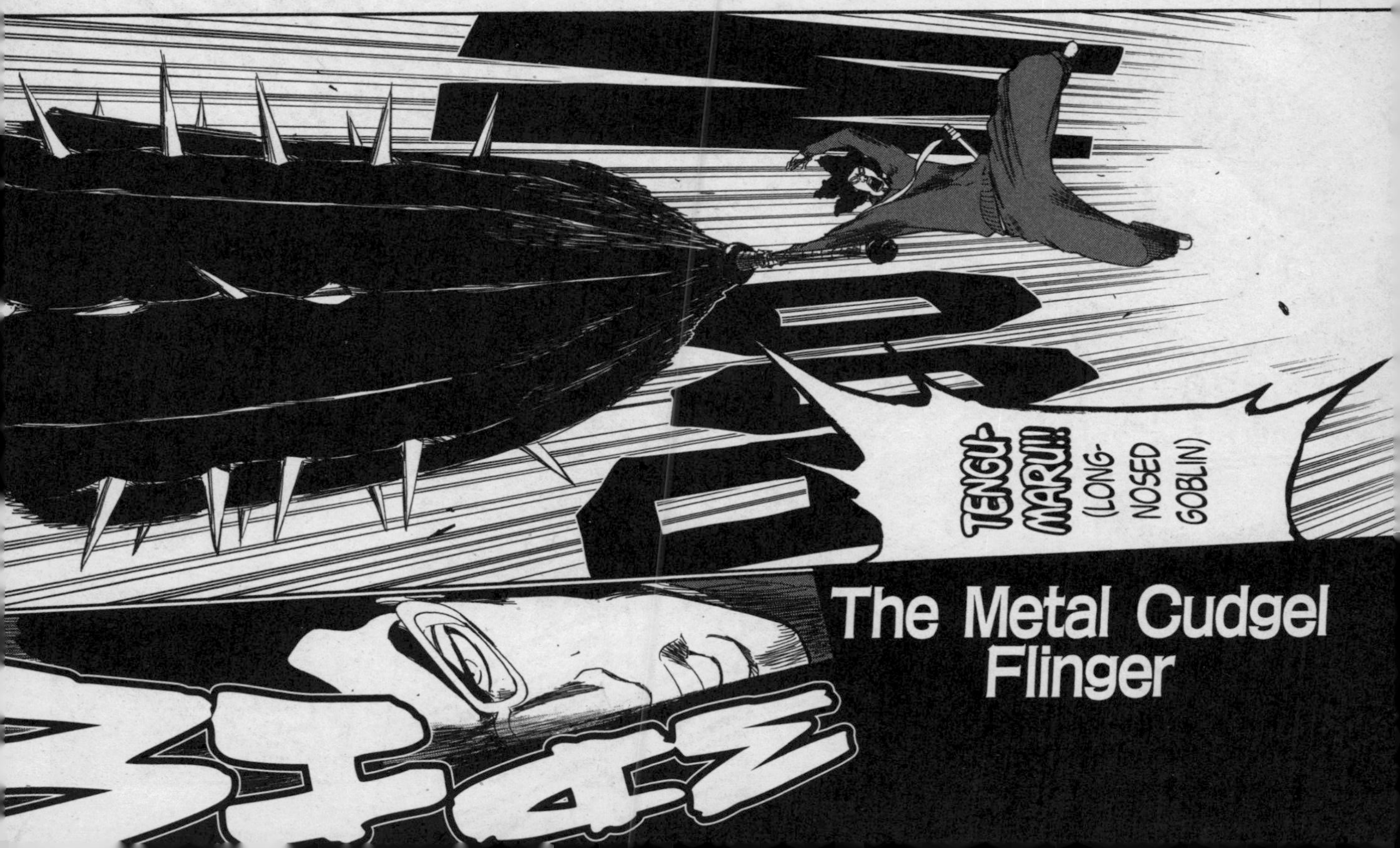
TENGU-MARU!!
(LONG-NOSED GOBLIN)
The Metal Cudgel Flinger
WHAM

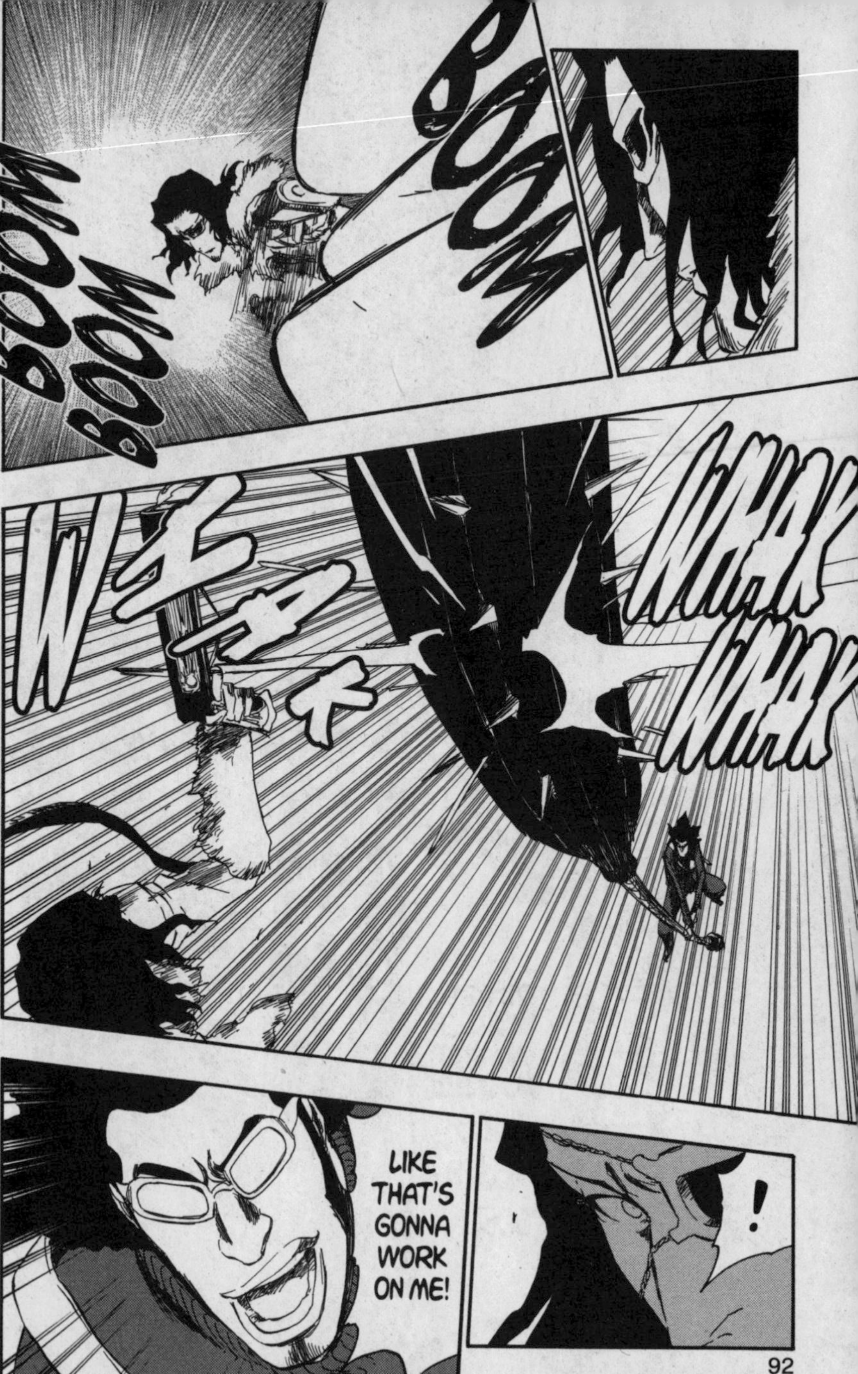
BOOM
BOOM
BOOM
WHAK
WHAK
!
LIKE THAT'S GONNA WORK ON ME!

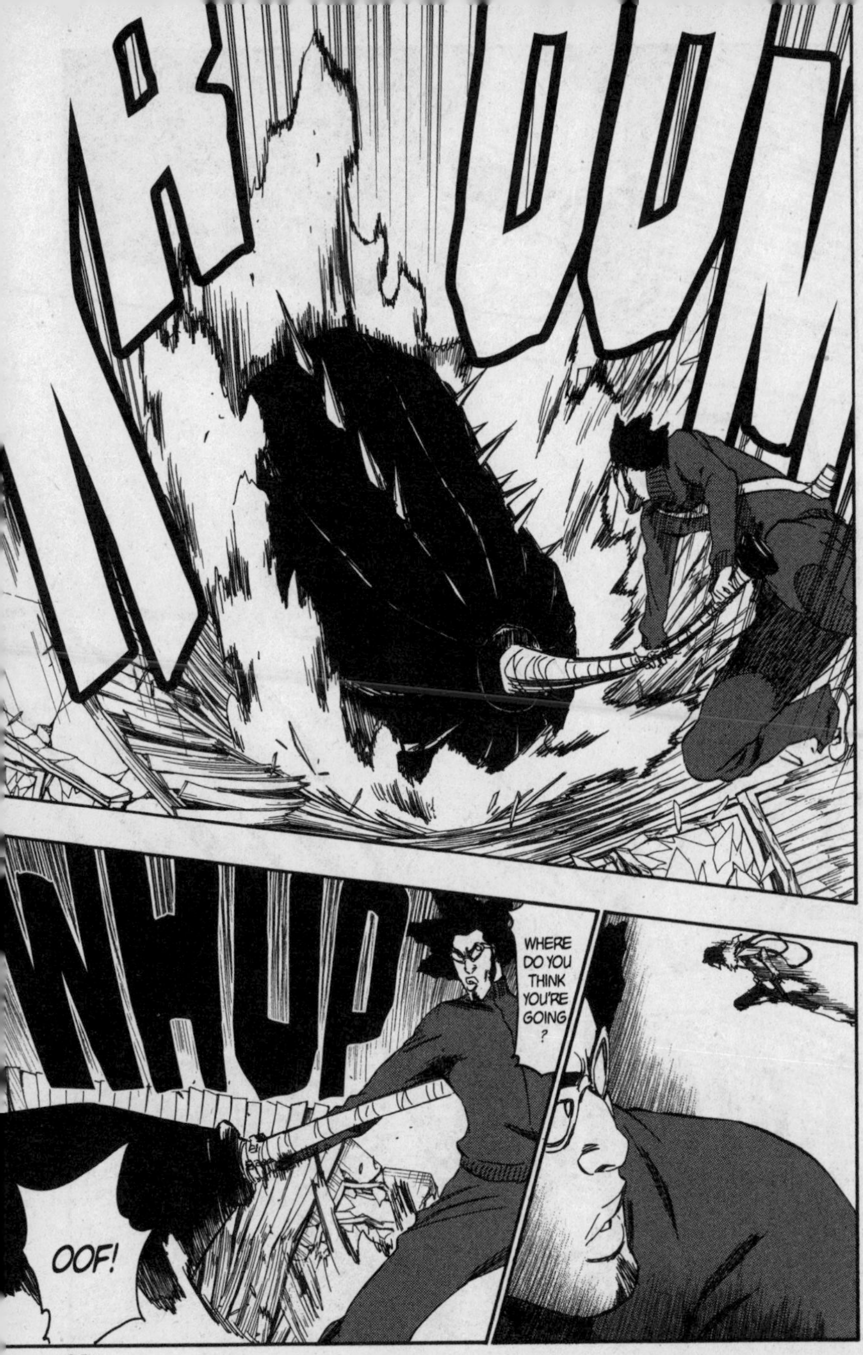
WHERE DO YOU THINK YOU'RE GOING?
OOF!

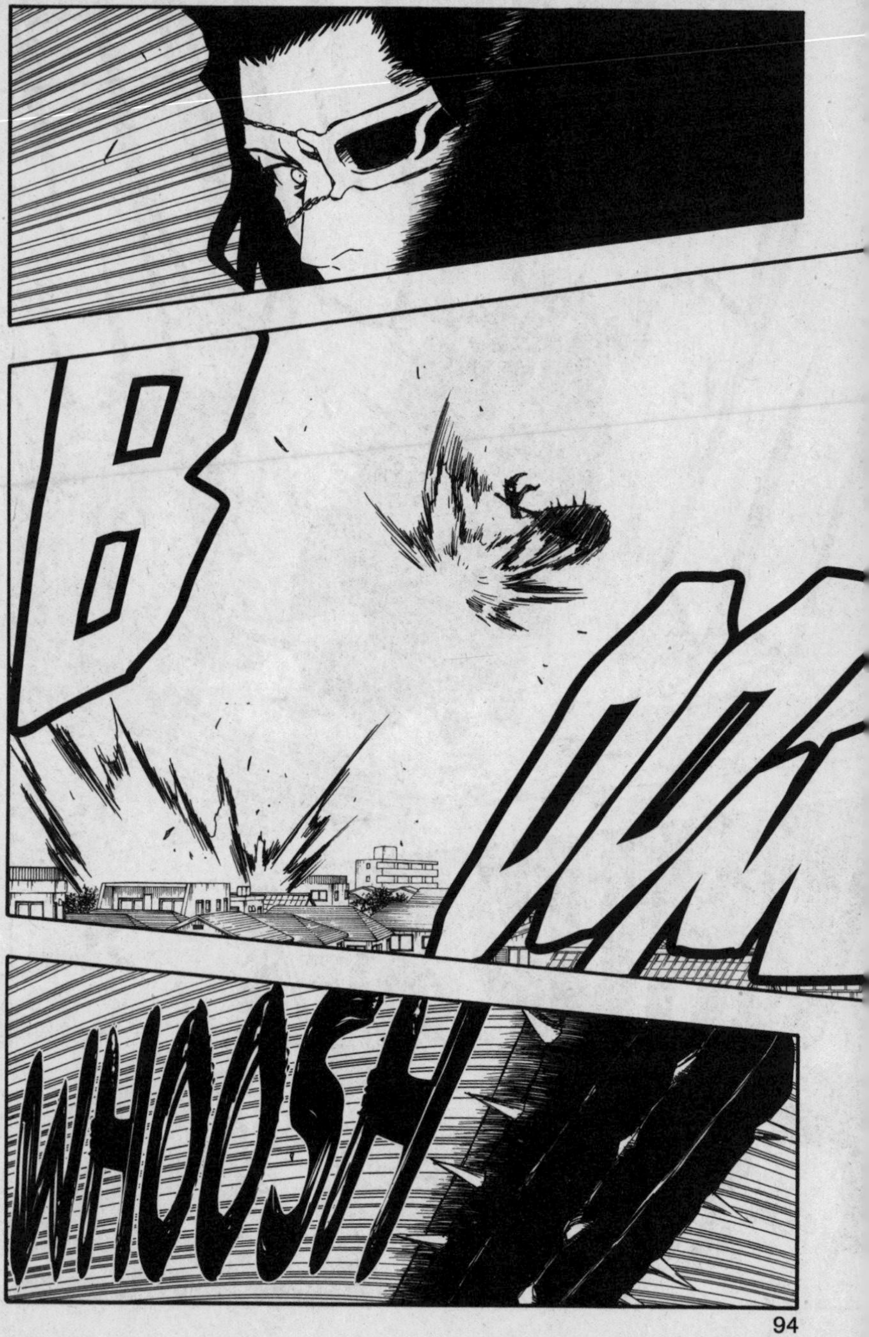
BOOM
WHOOSH

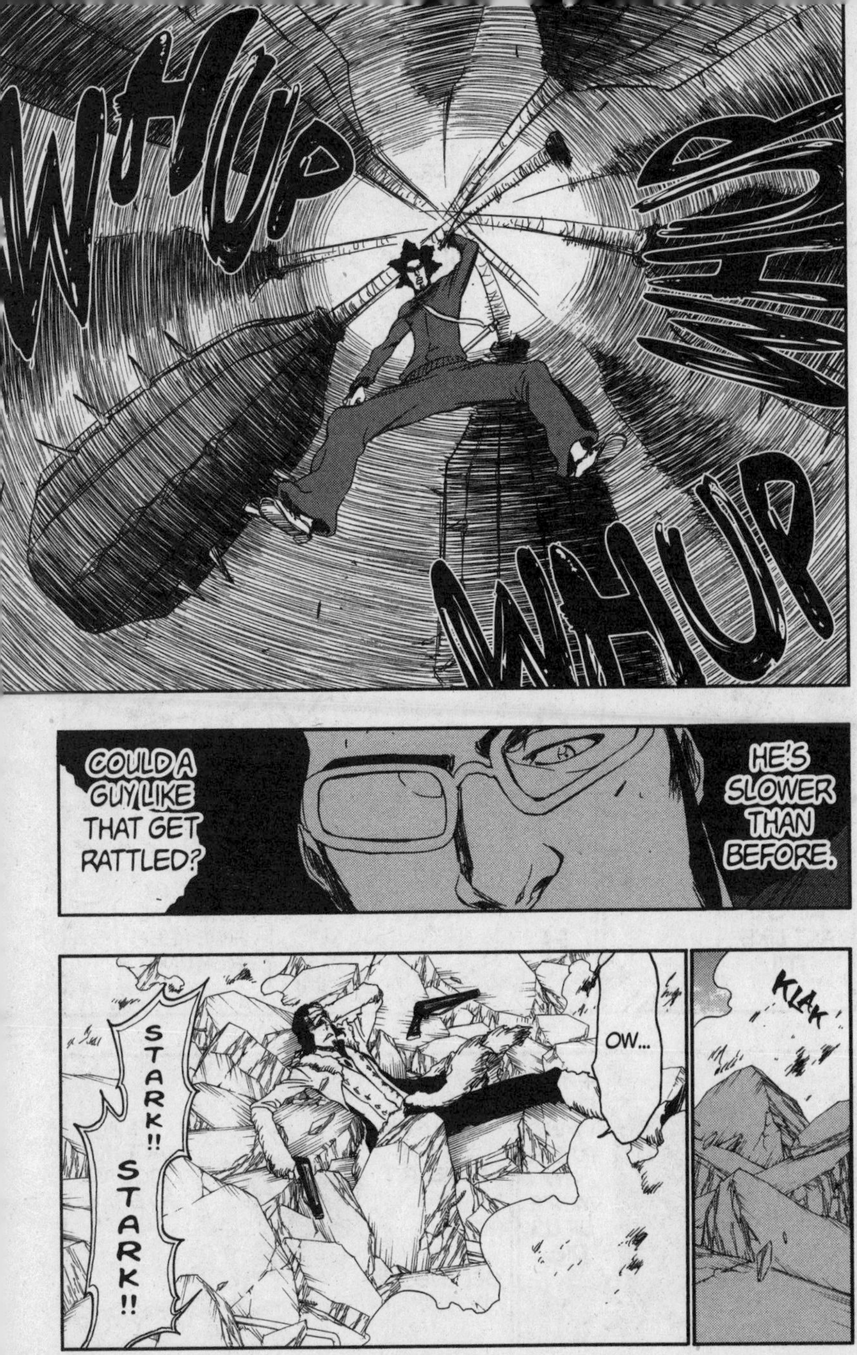
WHUP
WHUP
HE'S SLOWER THAN BEFORE.
COULD A GUY LIKE THAT GET RATTLED?
KLAK
OW...
STARK!! STARK!!

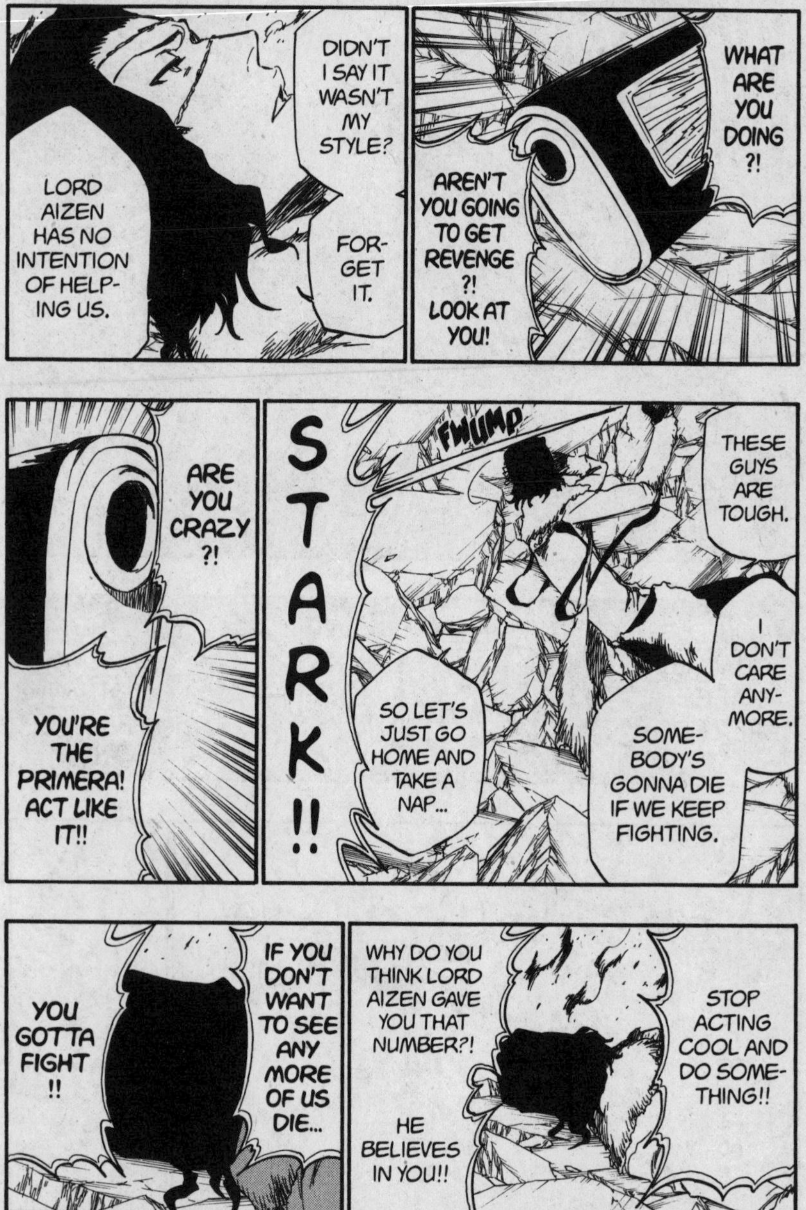
WHAT ARE YOU DOING?!
AREN'T YOU GOING TO GET REVENGE?! LOOK AT YOU!
DIDN'T I SAY IT WASN'T MY STYLE?
FOR-GET IT.
LORD AIZEN HAS NO INTENTION OF HELP-ING US.
FWUMP
THESE GUYS ARE TOUGH.
I DON'T CARE ANY-MORE.
SOME-BODY'S GONNA DIE IF WE KEEP FIGHTING.
SO LET'S JUST GO HOME AND TAKE A NAP...
STARK!!
ARE YOU CRAZY?!
YOU'RE THE PRIMERA! ACT LIKE IT!!
STOP ACTING COOL AND DO SOME-THING!!
WHY DO YOU THINK LORD AIZEN GAVE YOU THAT NUMBER?!
HE BELIEVES IN YOU!!
IF YOU DON'T WANT TO SEE ANY MORE OF US DIE...
YOU GOTTA FIGHT!!

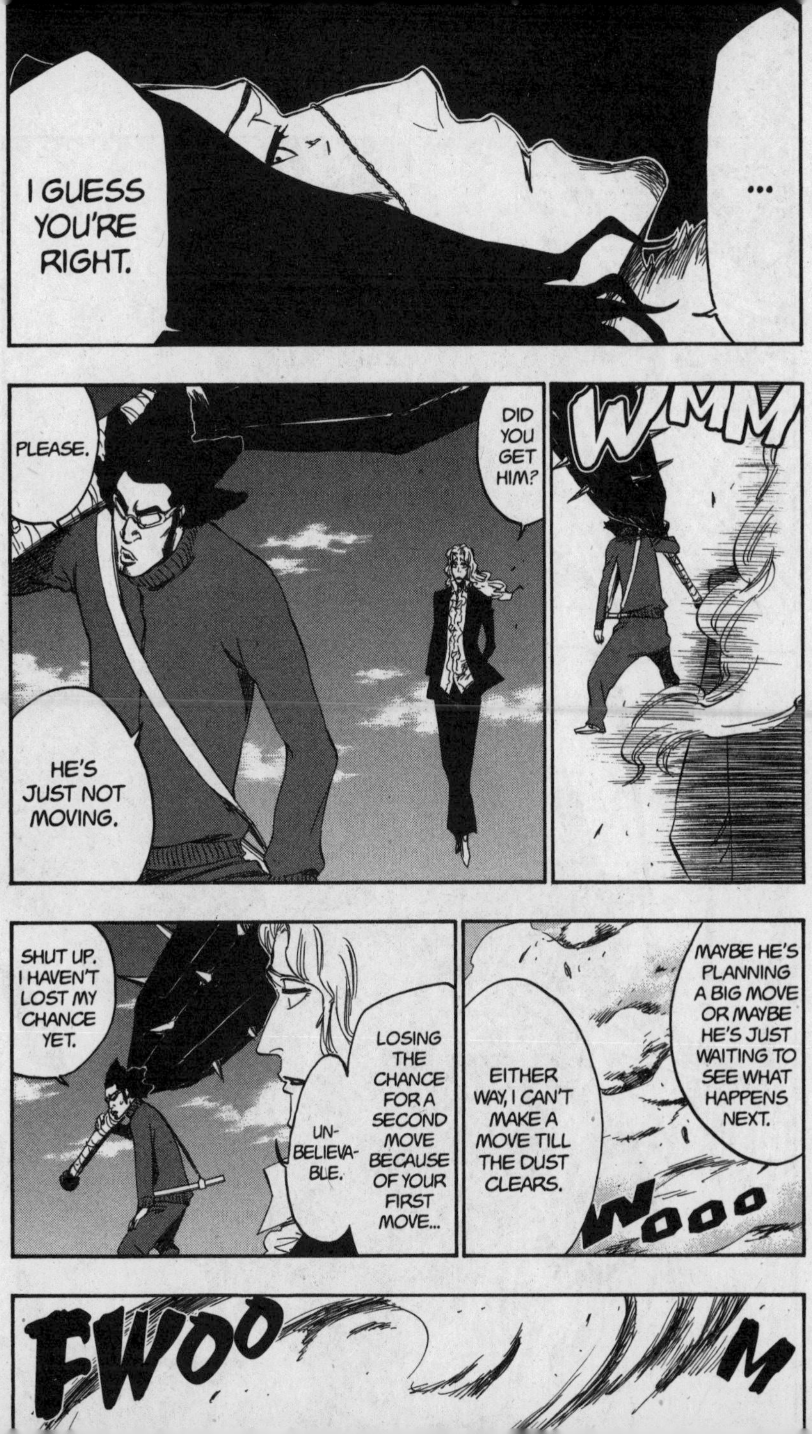
...
I GUESS YOU'RE RIGHT.
WMM
DID YOU GET HIM?
PLEASE.
HE'S JUST NOT MOVING.
MAYBE HE'S PLANNING A BIG MOVE OR MAYBE HE'S JUST WAITING TO SEE WHAT HAPPENS NEXT.
EITHER WAY, I CAN'T MAKE A MOVE TILL THE DUST CLEARS.
WOOO
LOSING THE CHANCE FOR A SECOND MOVE BECAUSE OF YOUR FIRST MOVE...
UN-BELIEVA-BLE.
SHUT UP. I HAVEN'T LOST MY CHANCE YET.
FWOOM

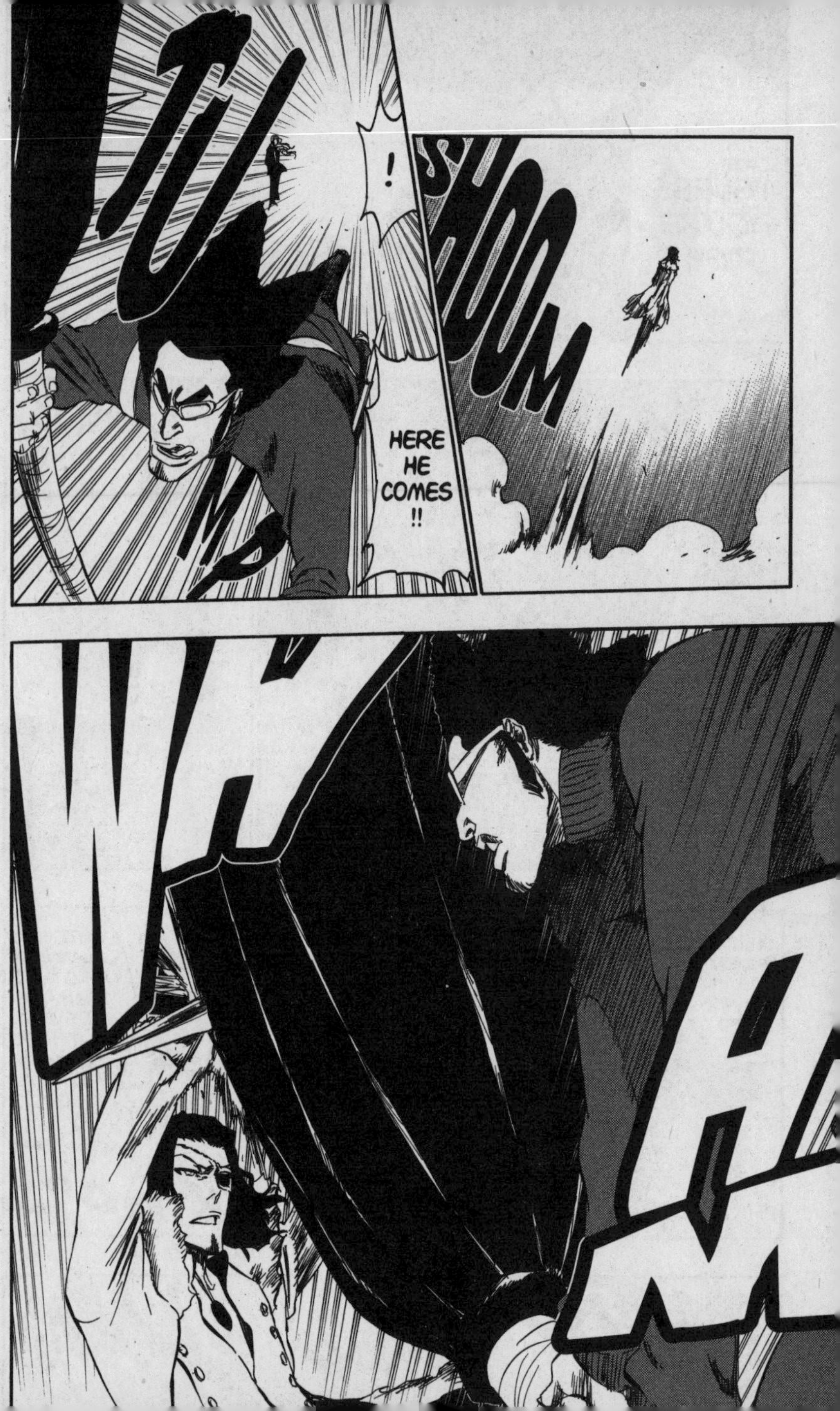
SHOOM
!
HERE HE COMES !!

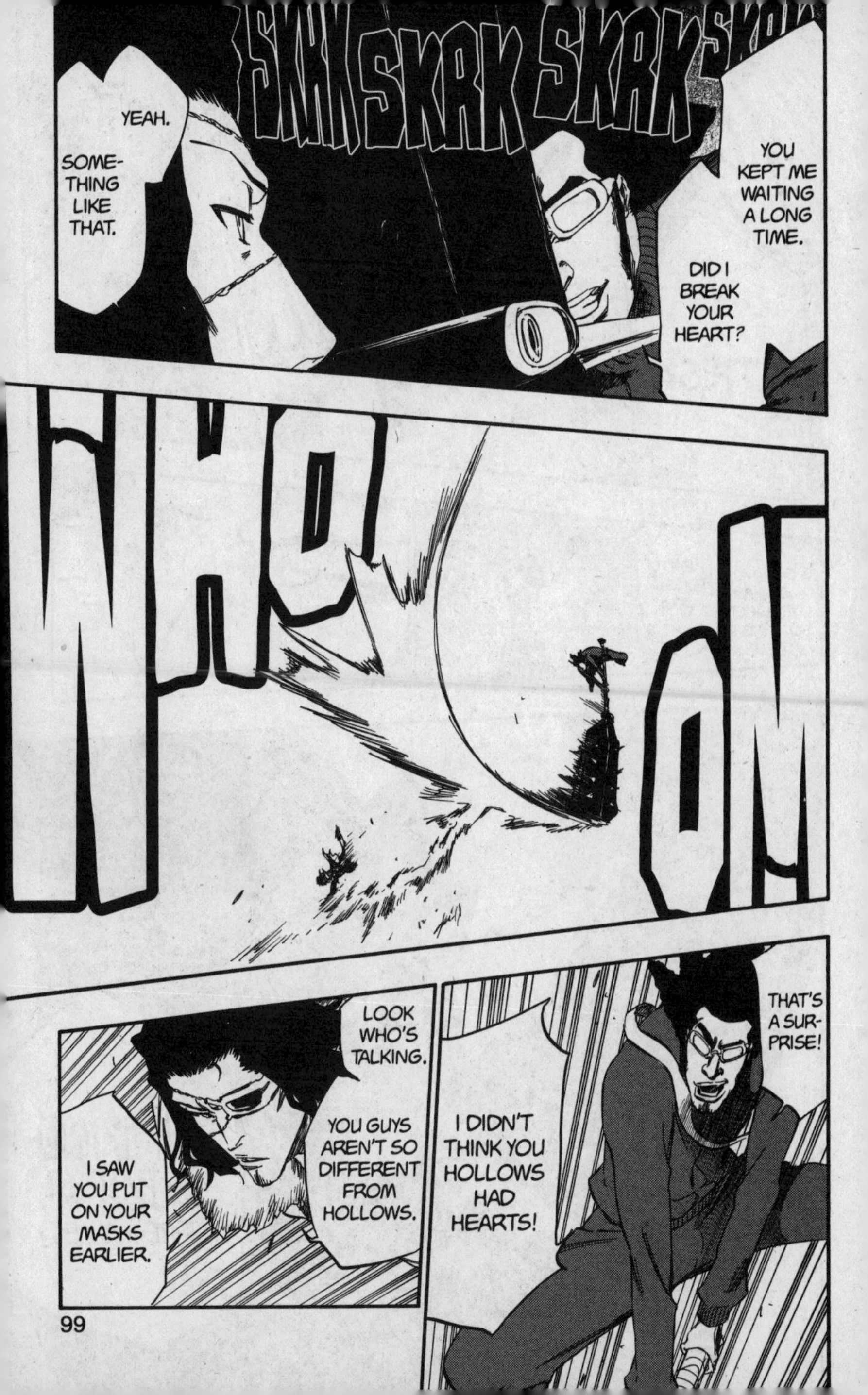
SKRK SKRK SKRK SKRK
YOU KEPT ME WAITING A LONG TIME.
DID I BREAK YOUR HEART?
YEAH.
SOMETHING LIKE THAT.
WHOOM
THAT'S A SURPRISE!
I DIDN'T THINK YOU HOLLOWS HAD HEARTS!
LOOK WHO'S TALKING.
YOU GUYS AREN'T SO DIFFERENT FROM HOLLOWS.
I SAW YOU PUT ON YOUR MASKS EARLIER.

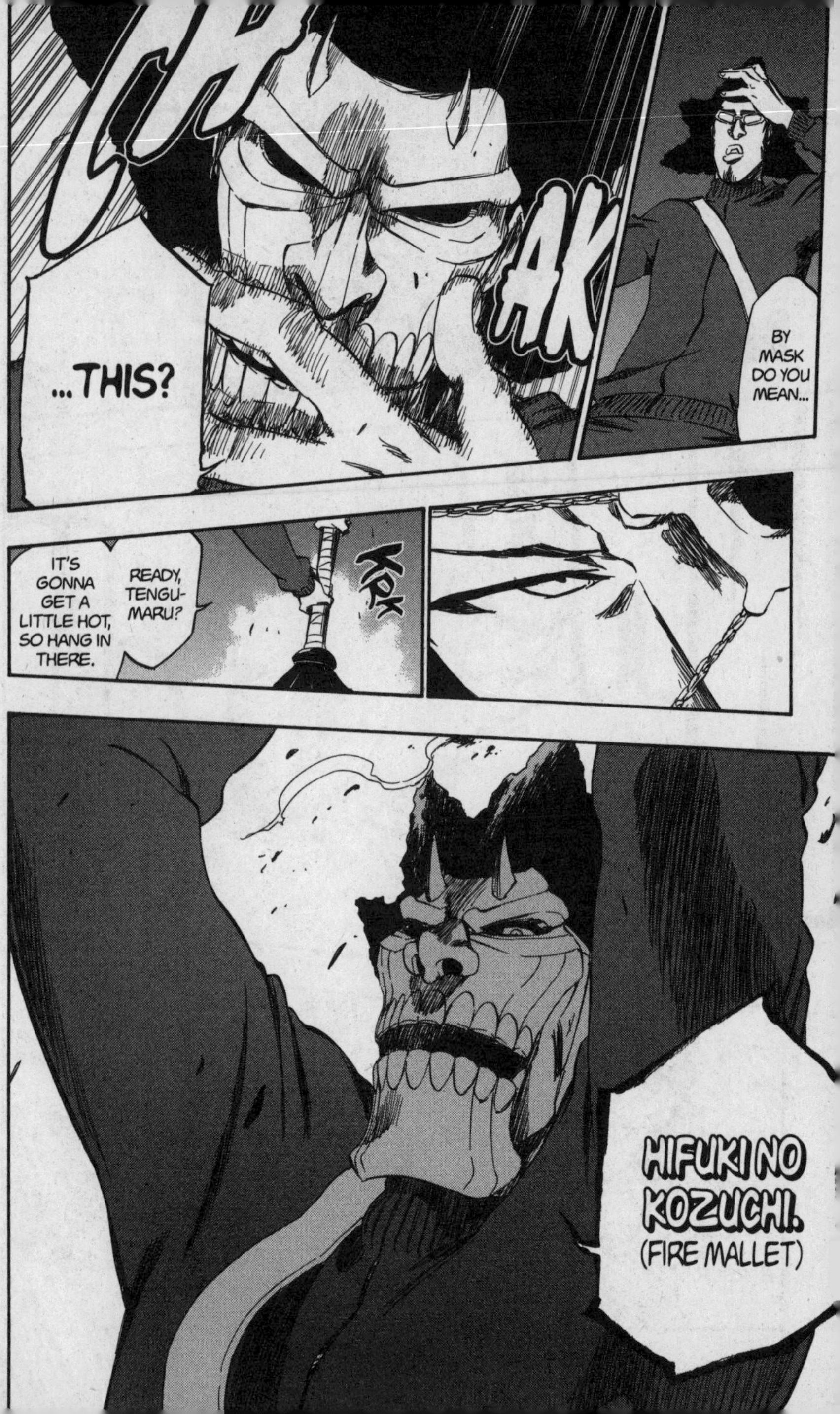
BY MASK DO YOU MEAN...
AK
...THIS?
READY, TENGU-MARU?
KRK
IT'S GONNA GET A LITTLE HOT, SO HANG IN THERE.
HIFUKI NO KOZUCHI.
(FIRE MALLET)

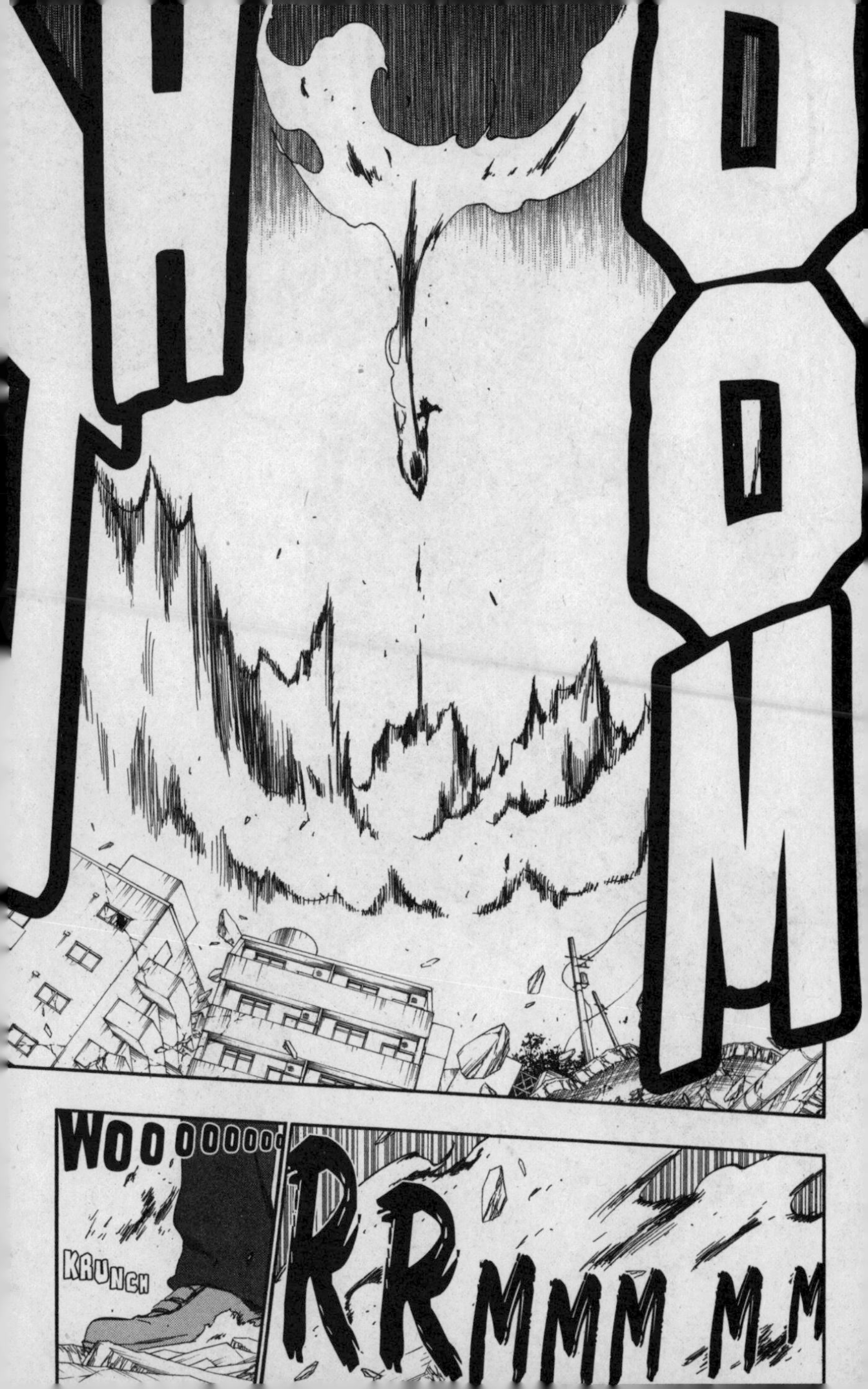
WHOOM
RRMMM MM
WOOOOOOO
KRUNCH

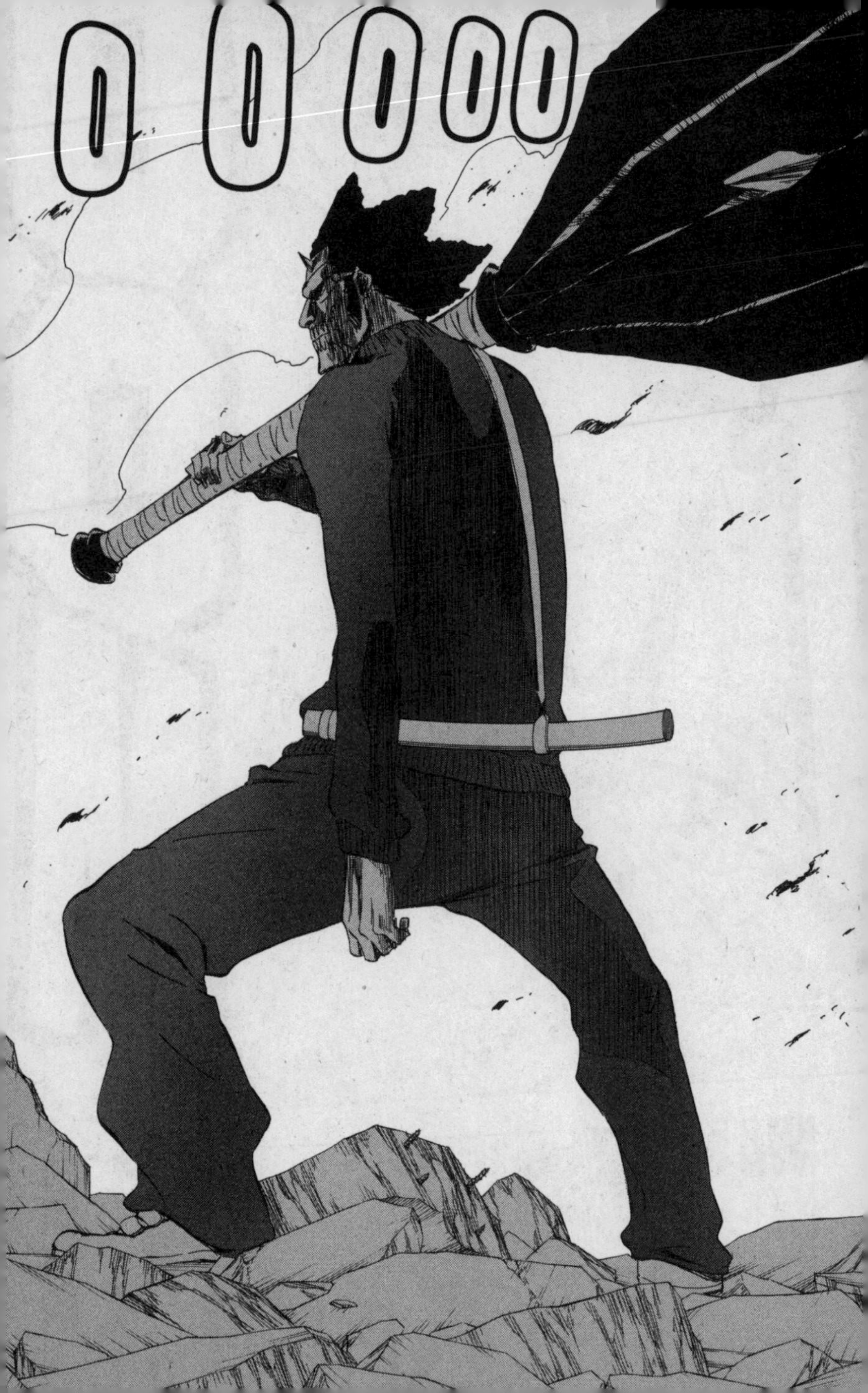
O O OOO

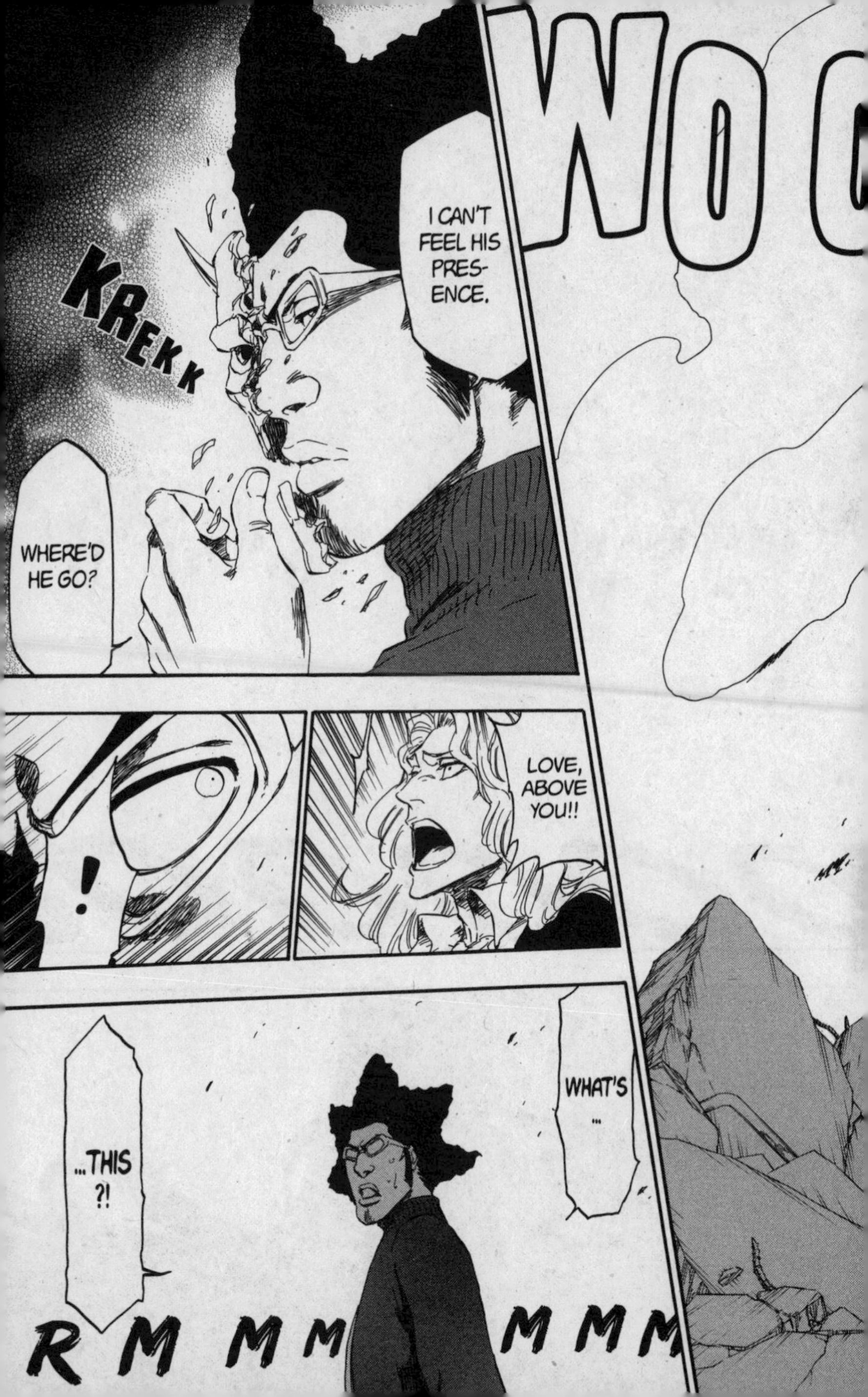
WOO
I CAN'T FEEL HIS PRES-ENCE.
KREKKK
WHERE'D HE GO?
LOVE, ABOVE YOU!!
!
WHAT'S ...
...THIS ?!
RMMMMMMM

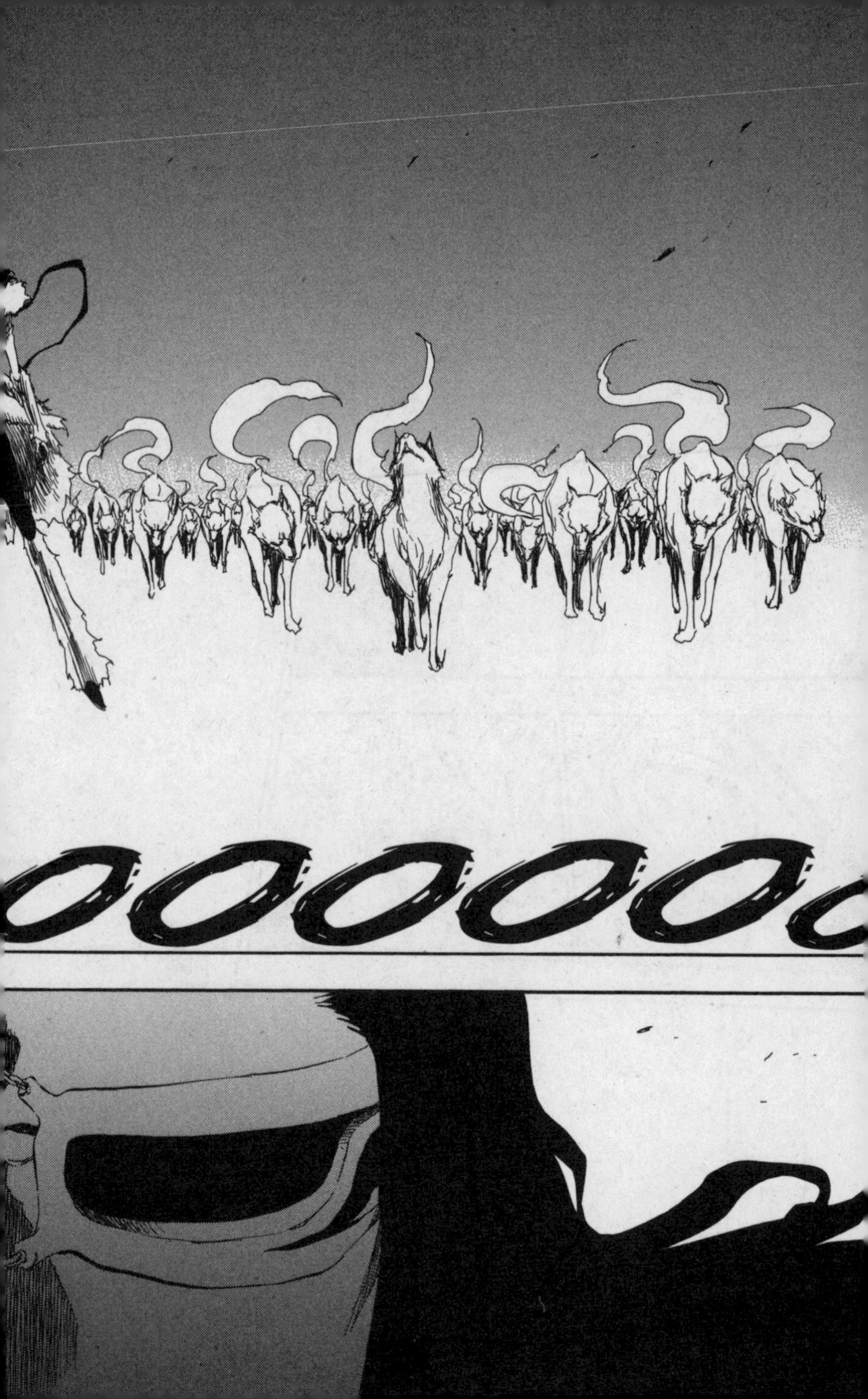

WOOOOO

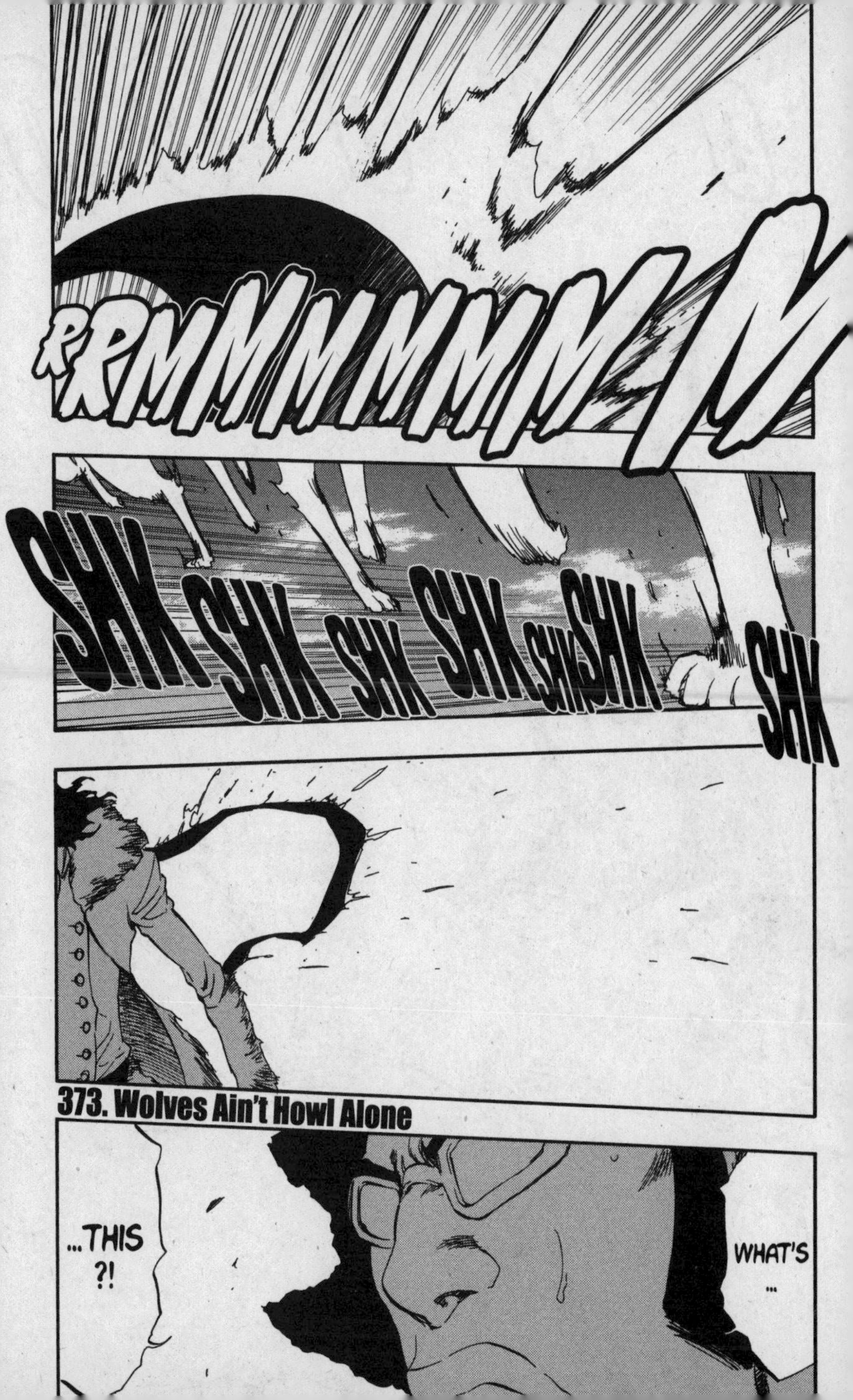
RRMMMMMMMMMM
SHK SHK SHK SHK SHK SHK SHK SHK
373. Wolves Ain't Howl Alone
WHAT'S ...
...THIS ?!

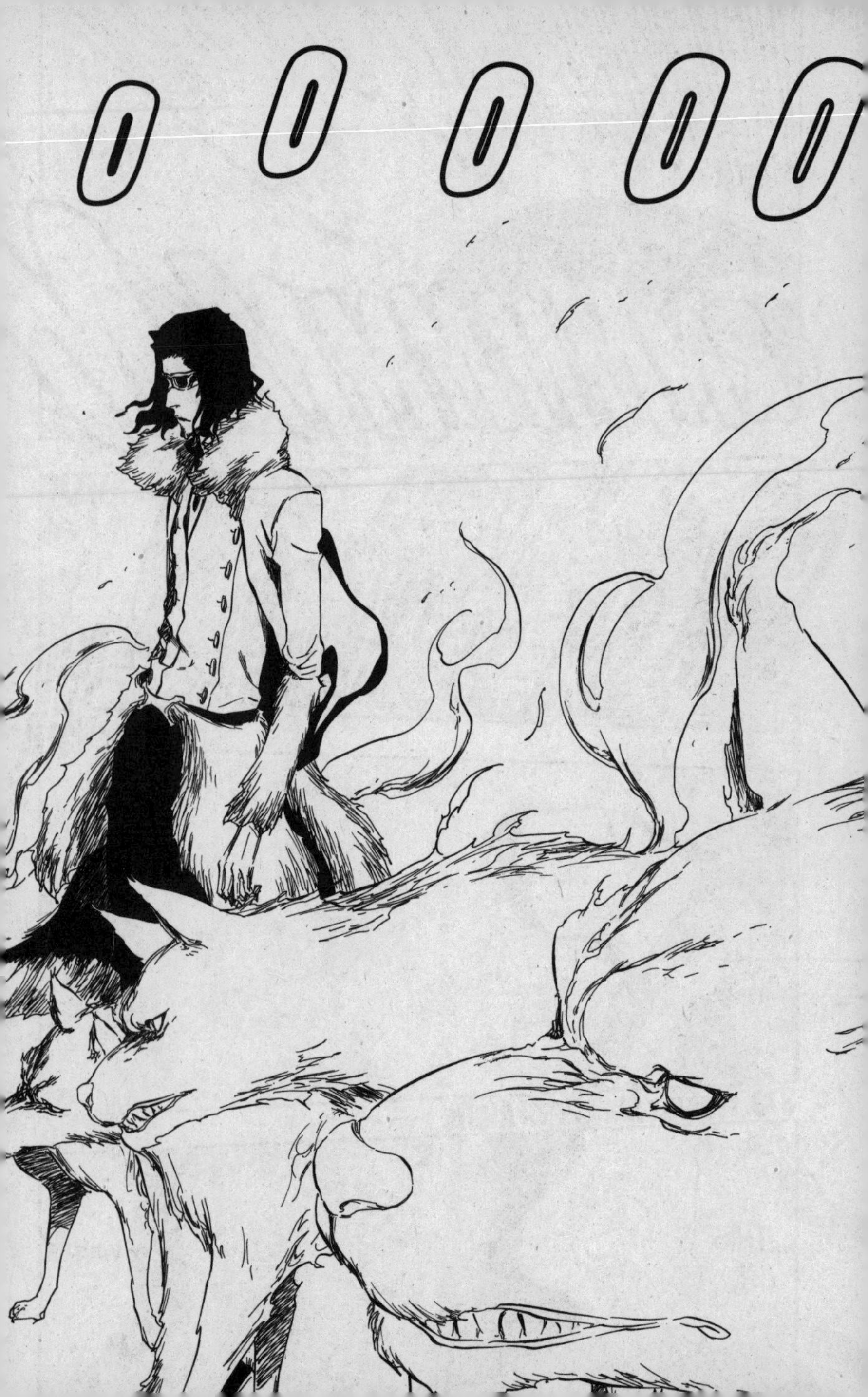
OOOOO

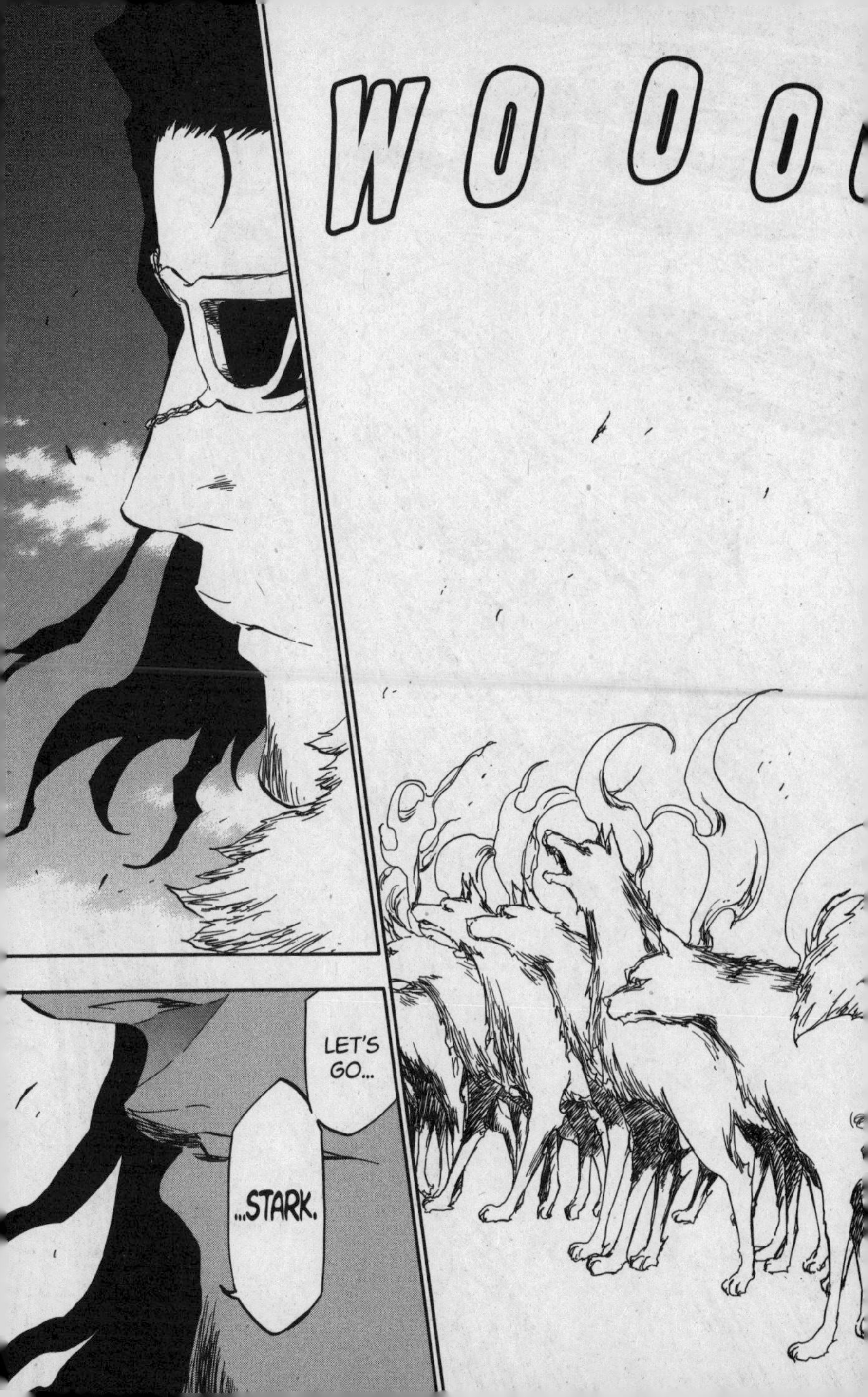
WOOOO
LET'S GO...
...STARK.

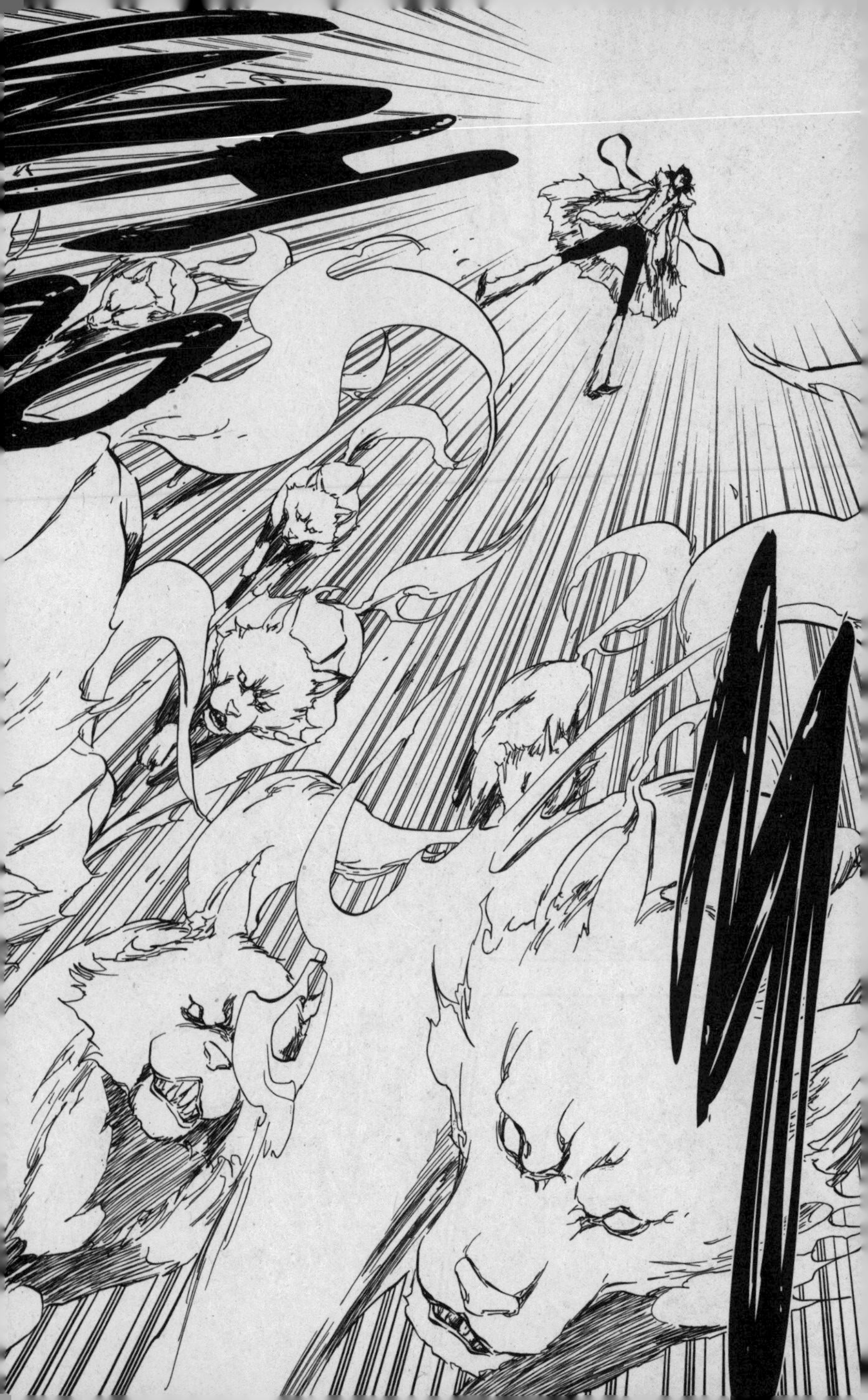

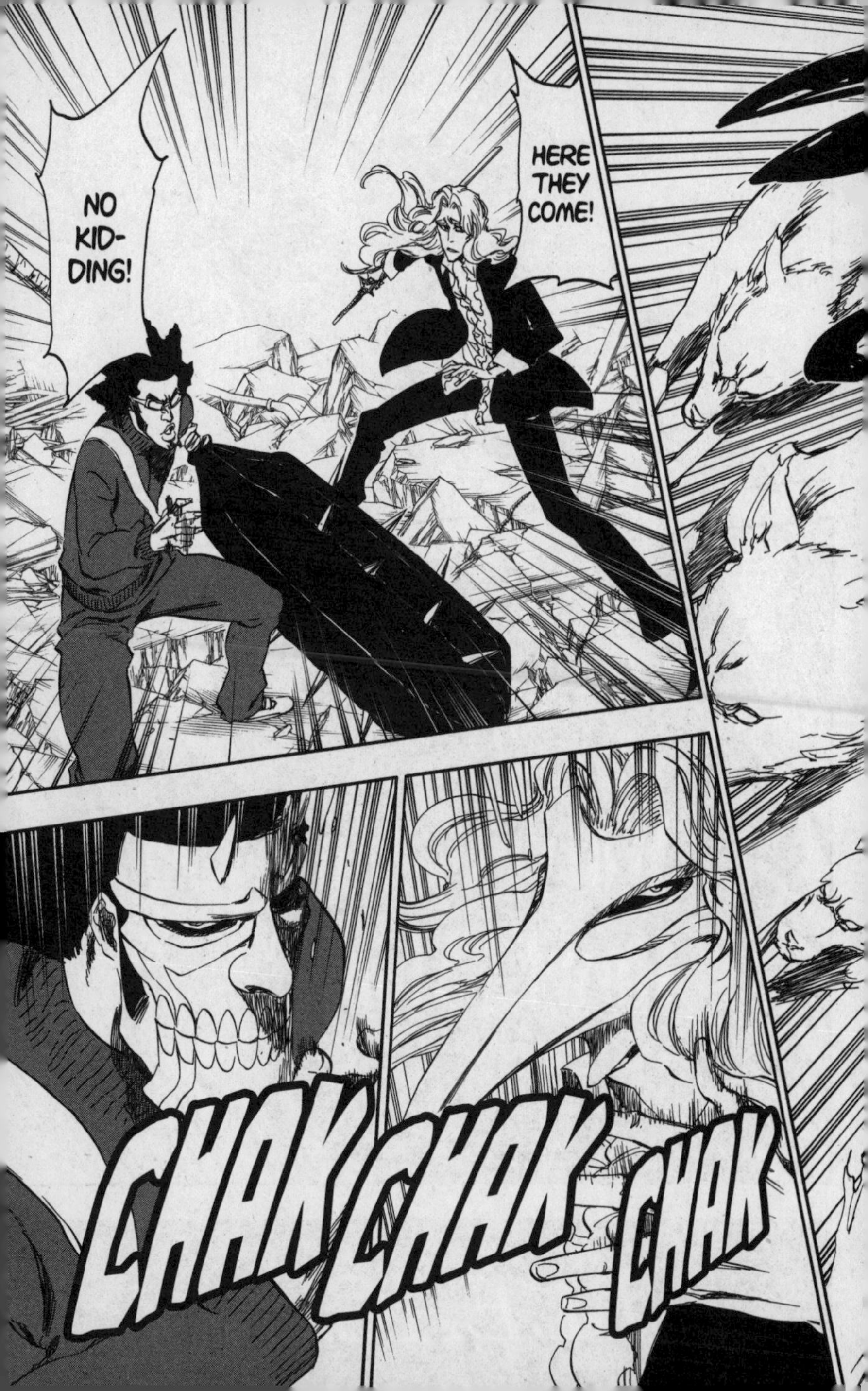
HERE THEY COME!
NO KID-DING!
CHAK CHAK CHAK

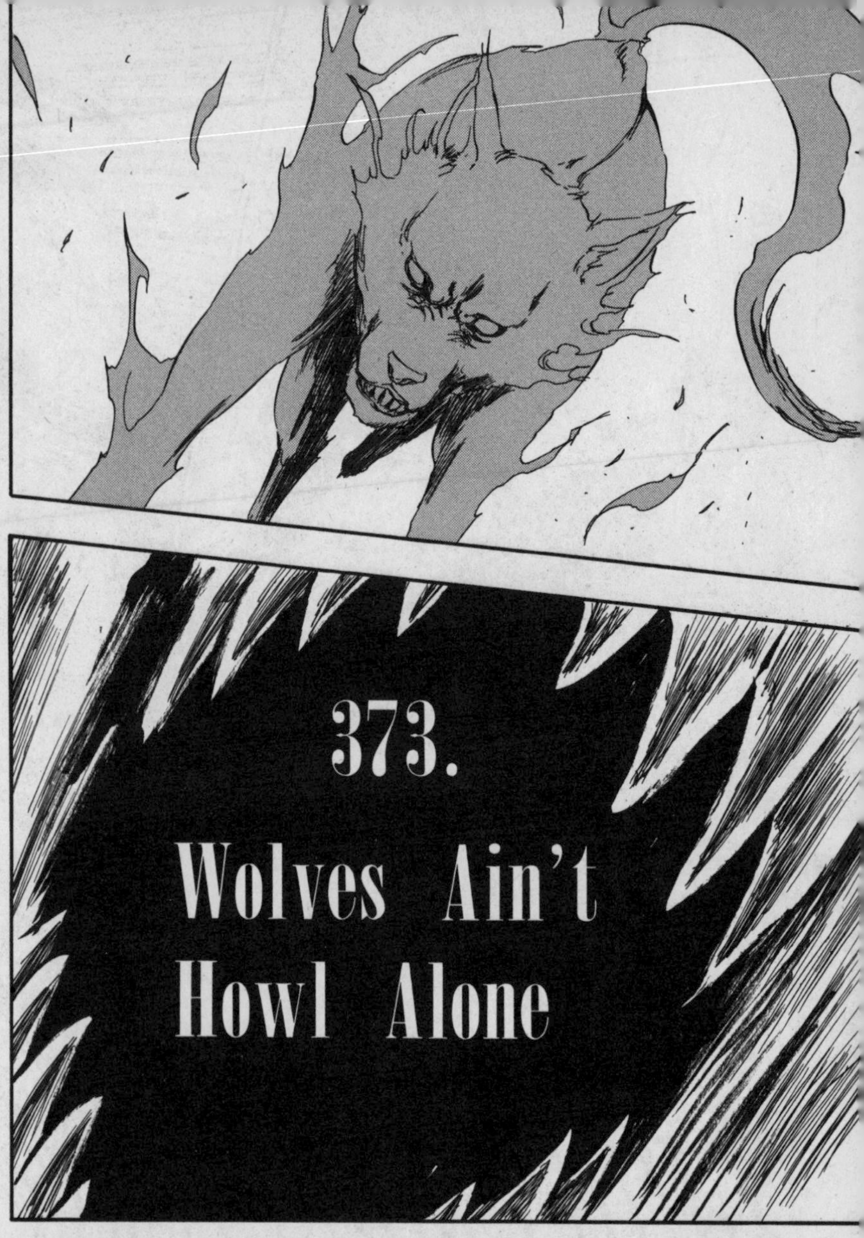
373.
Wolves Ain't Howl Alone

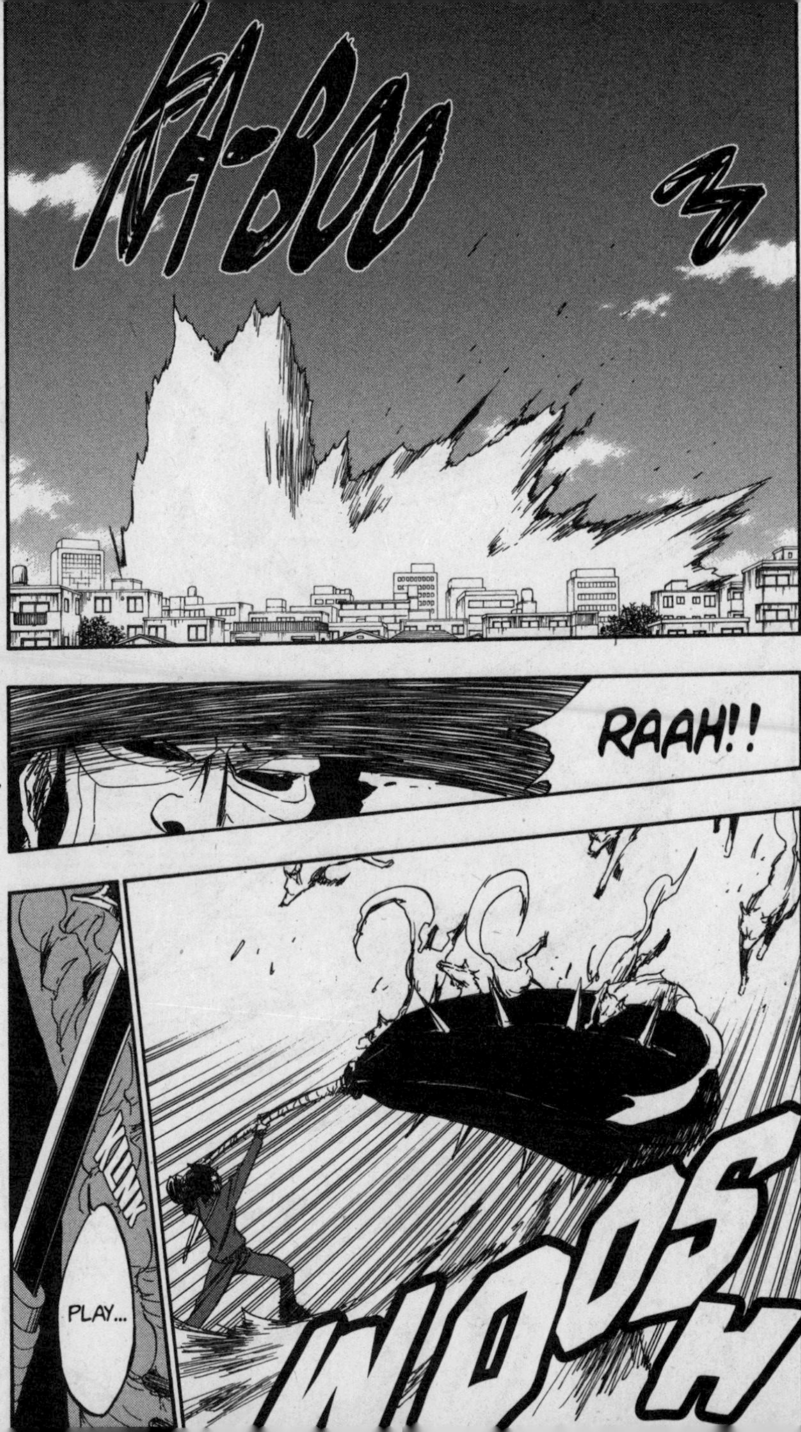
KA-BOOM
RAAH!!
KLINK
PLAY...

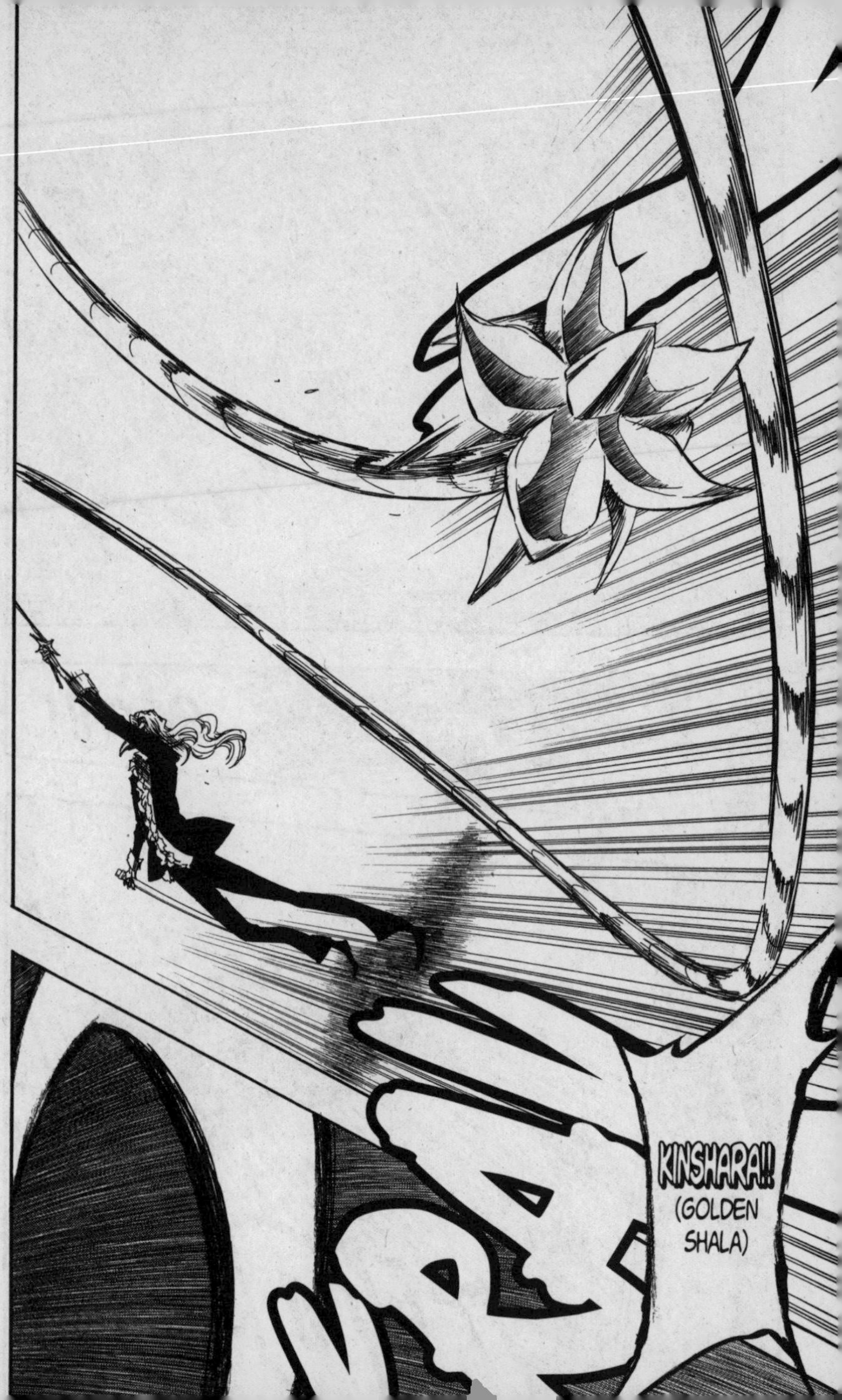
KINSHARA!!
(GOLDEN SHALA)

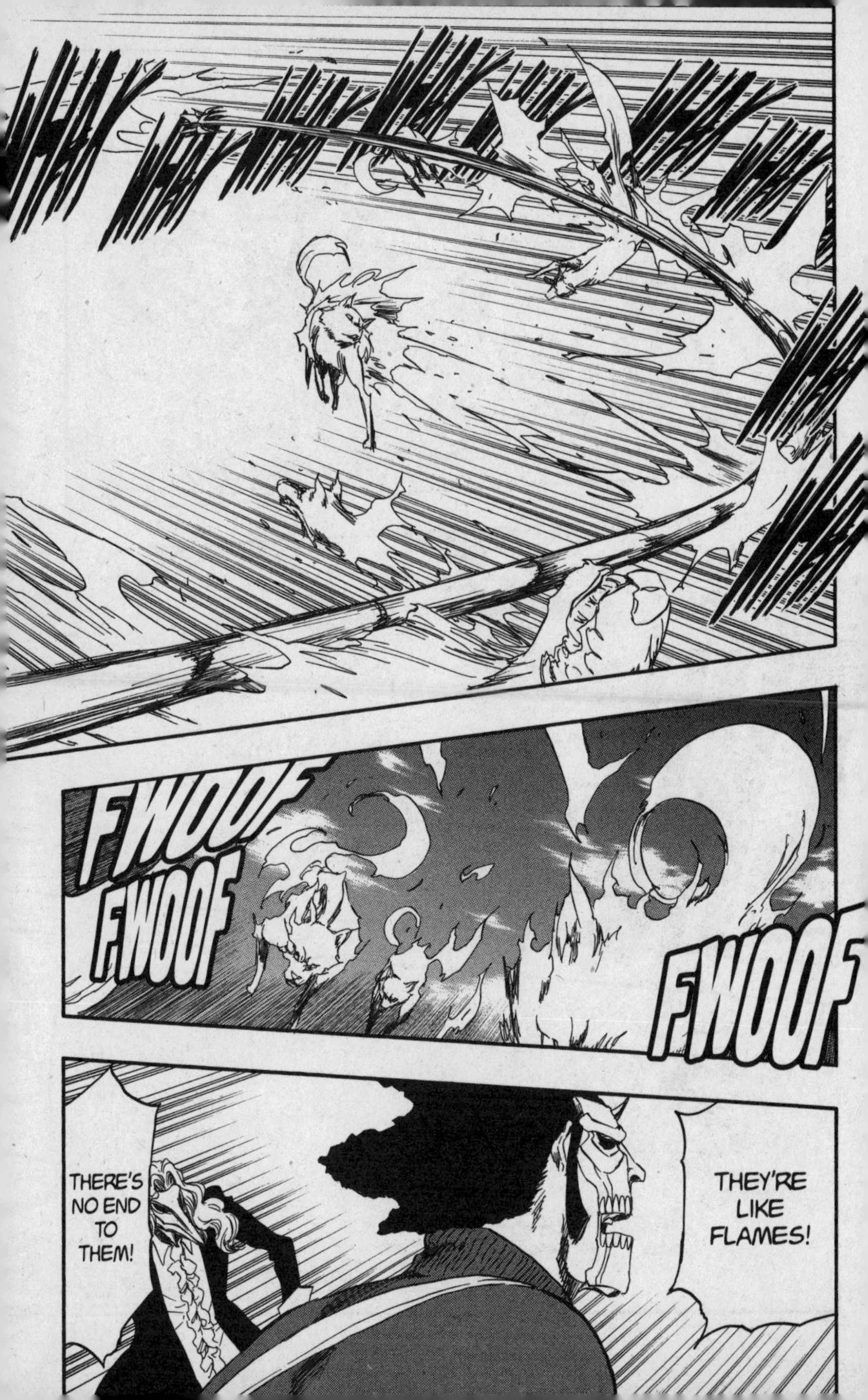
FWOOF
FWOOF
FWOOF
THEY'RE LIKE FLAMES!
THERE'S NO END TO THEM!

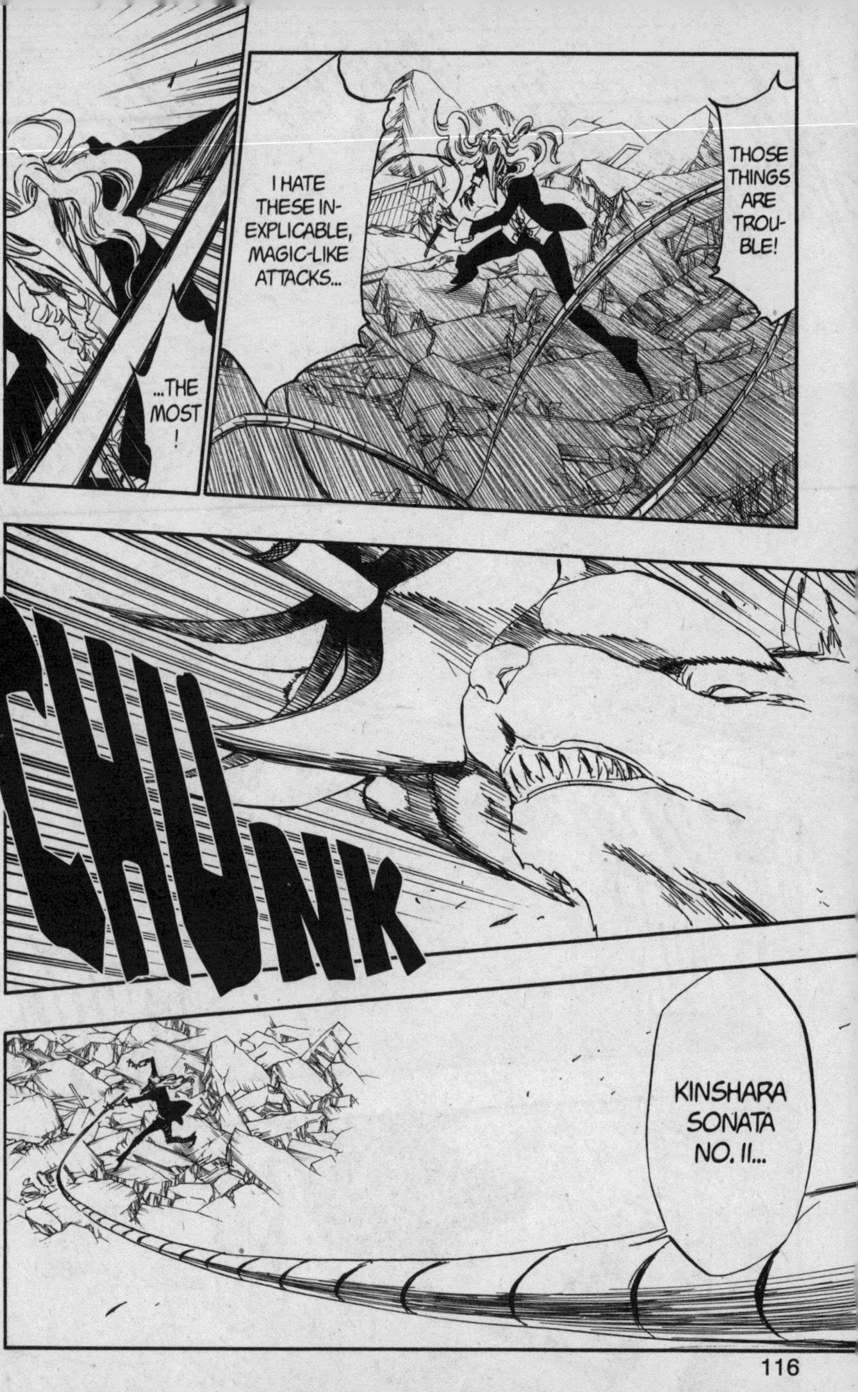
THOSE THINGS ARE TROUBLE!
I HATE THESE INEXPLICABLE, MAGIC-LIKE ATTACKS...
...THE MOST!
CHUNK
KINSHARA SONATA NO. 11...

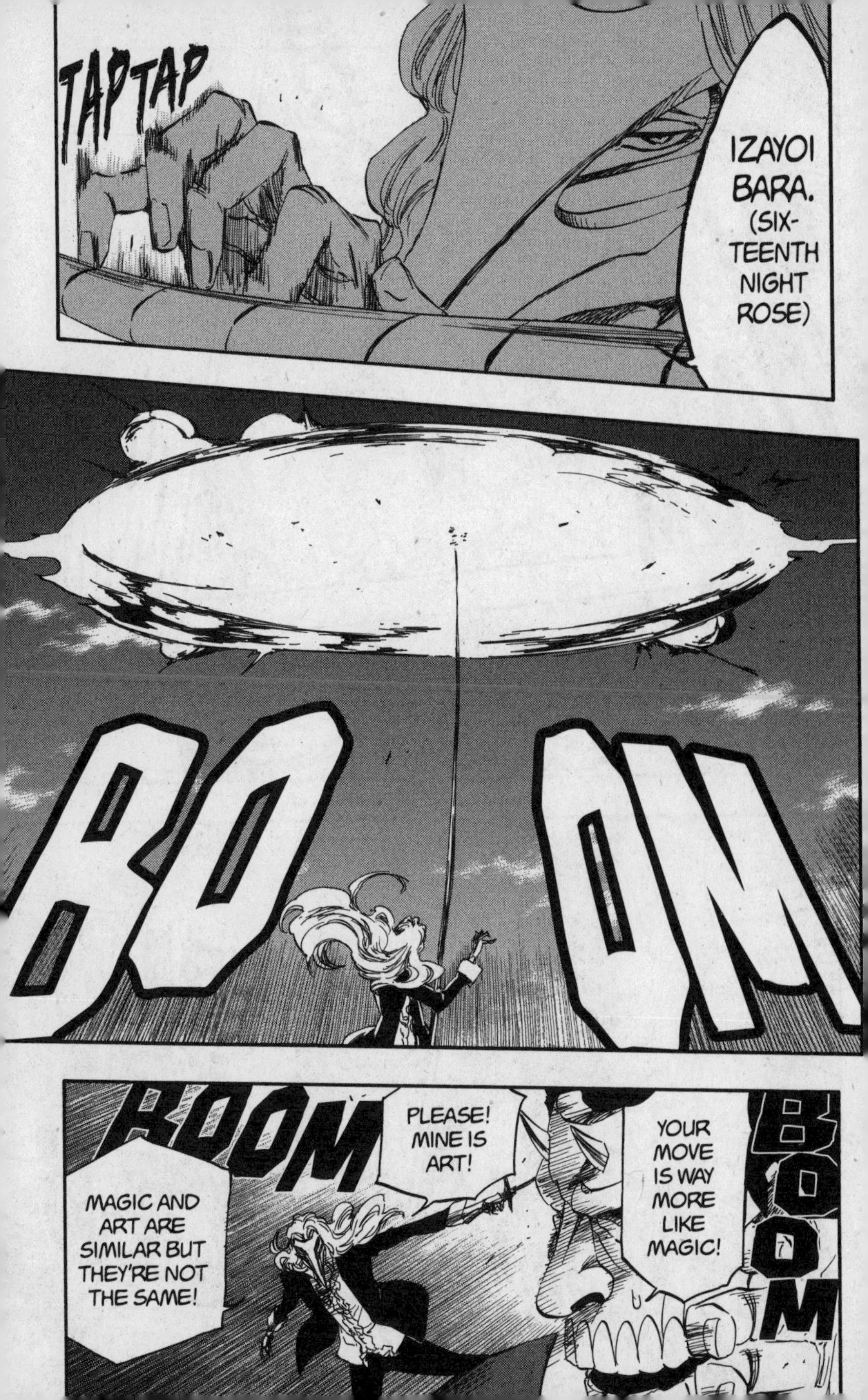
IZAYOI BARA. (SIXTEENTH NIGHT ROSE)
TAPTAP
BOOM
BOOM
YOUR MOVE IS WAY MORE LIKE MAGIC!
PLEASE! MINE IS ART!
BOOM
MAGIC AND ART ARE SIMILAR BUT THEY'RE NOT THE SAME!

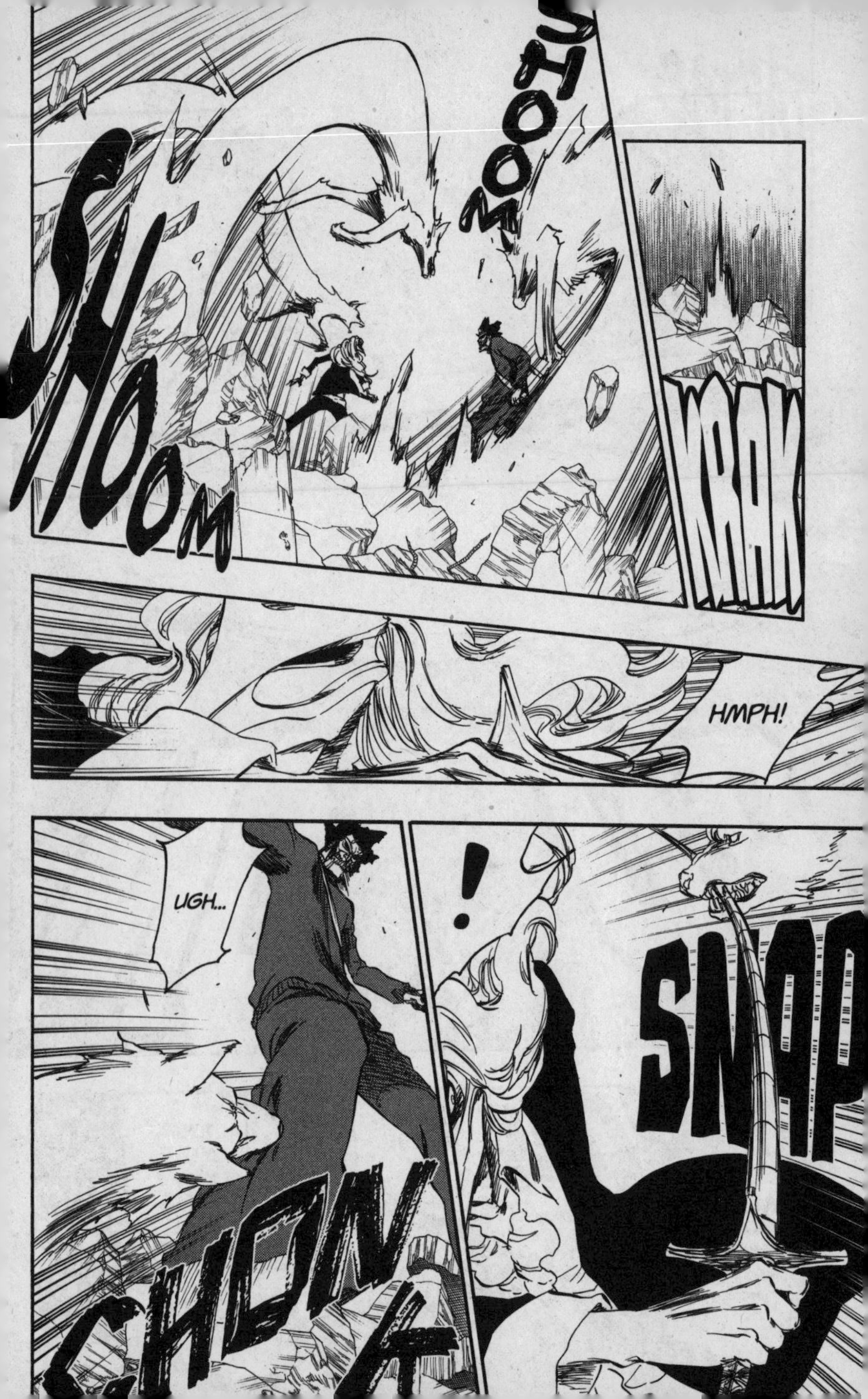
KRAK
SHOOM
SHOOM
HMPH!
!
SNAP
UGH...
CHONK

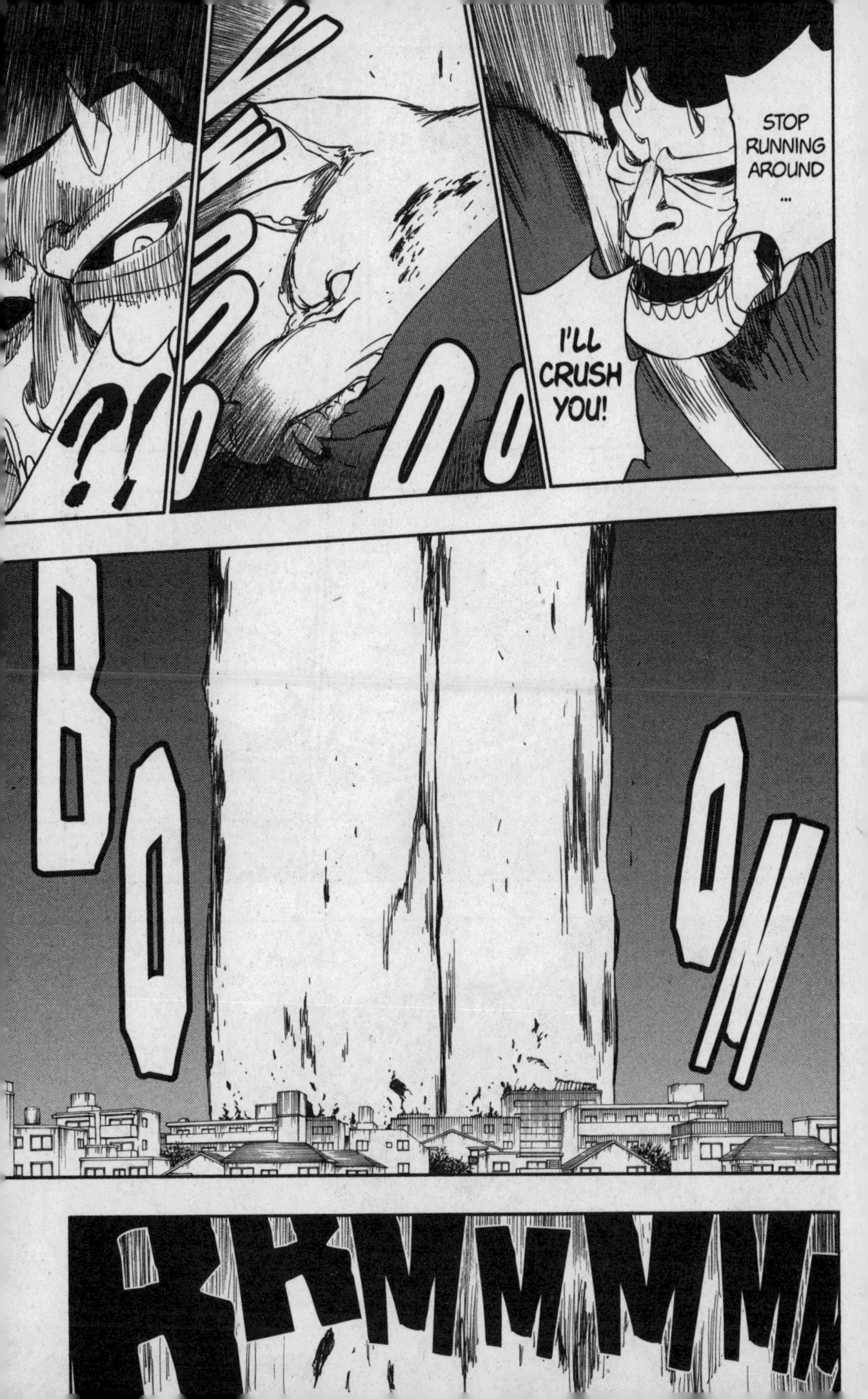
STOP RUNNING AROUND ...
I'LL CRUSH YOU!
?!
BOOOM

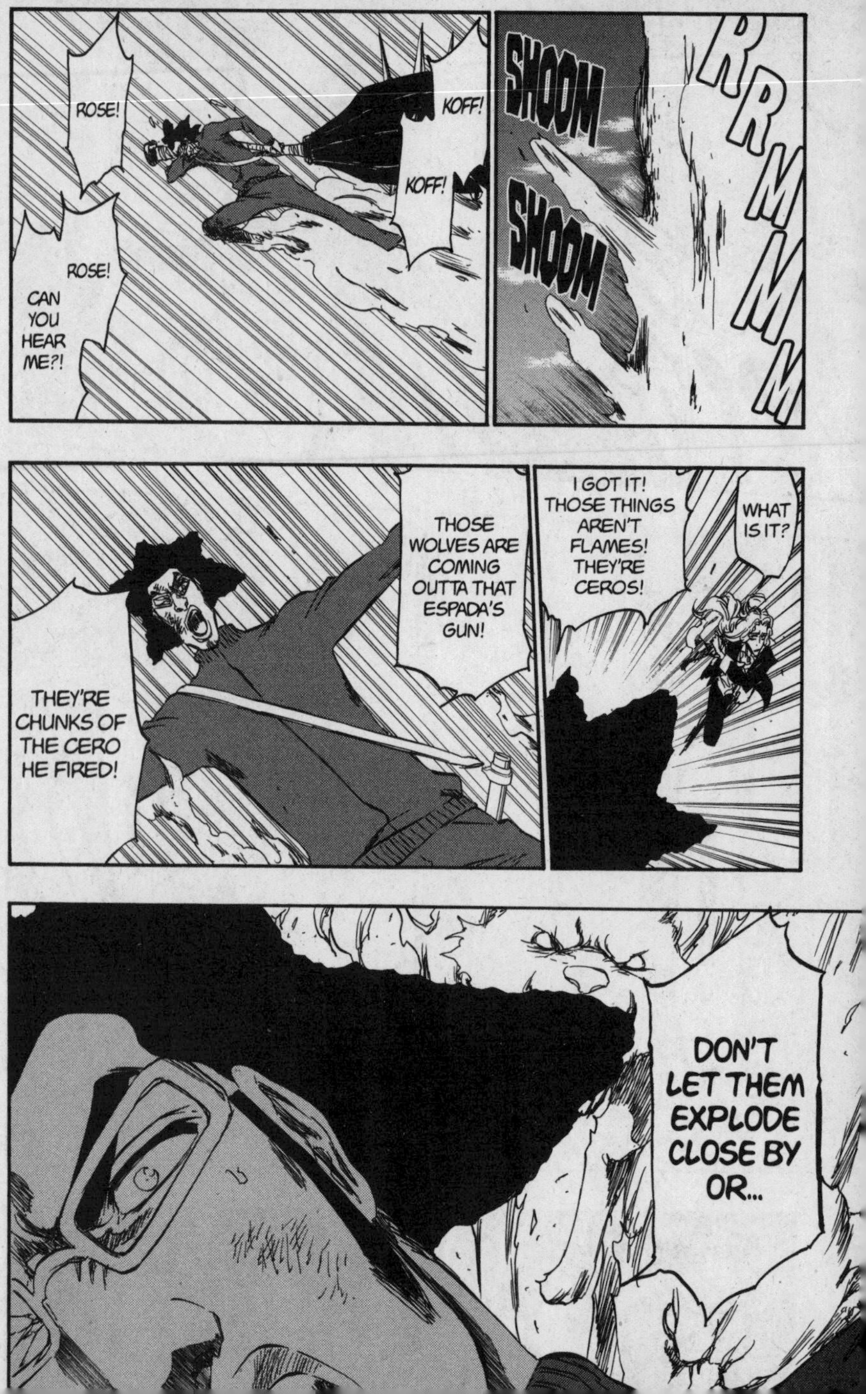
RRMMMM
SHOOM
SHOOM
KOFF!
KOFF!
ROSE!
ROSE!
CAN YOU HEAR ME?!
WHAT IS IT?
I GOT IT! THOSE THINGS AREN'T FLAMES! THEY'RE CEROS!
THOSE WOLVES ARE COMING OUTTA THAT ESPADA'S GUN!
THEY'RE CHUNKS OF THE CERO HE FIRED!
DON'T LET THEM EXPLODE CLOSE BY OR...

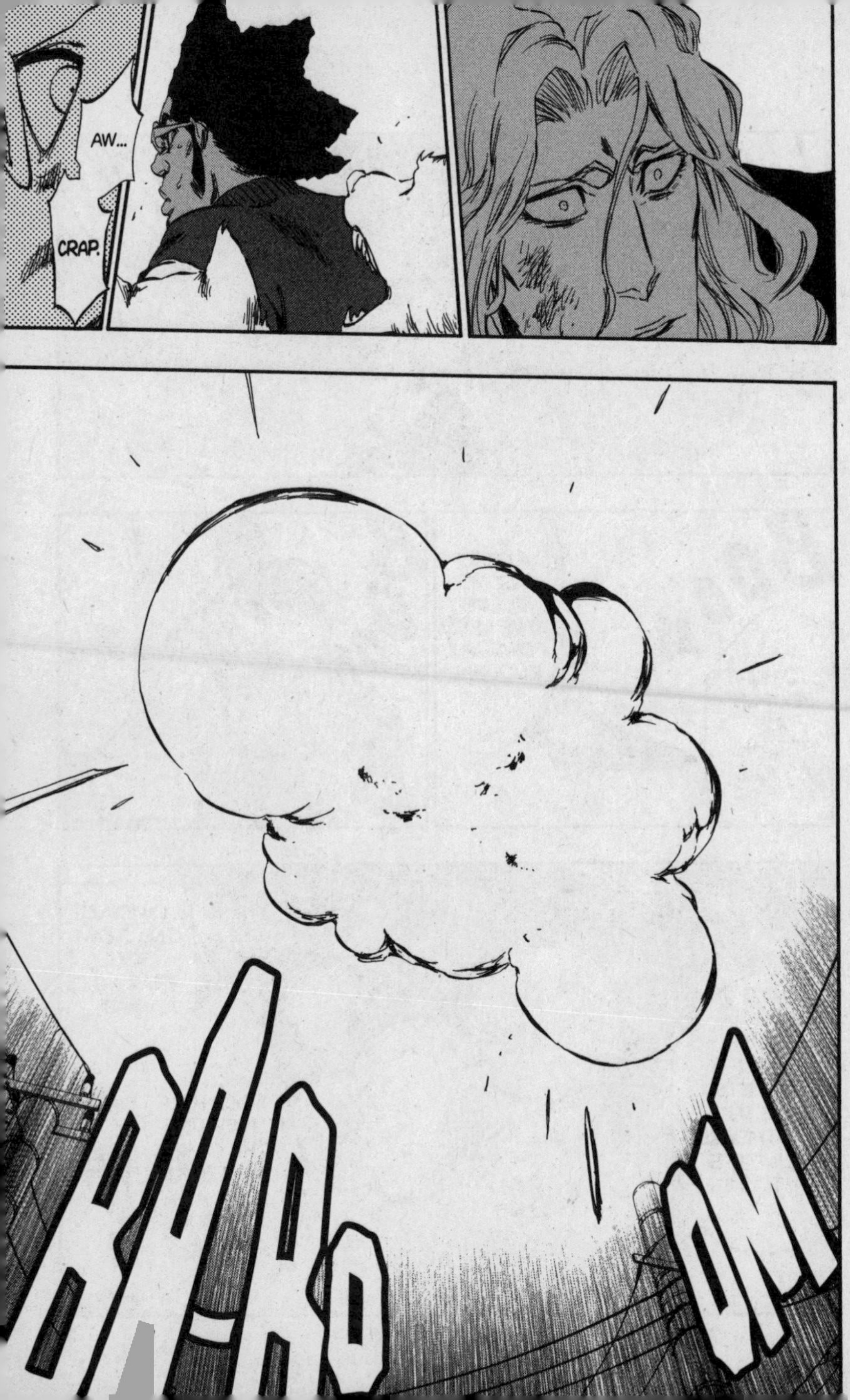
AW...
CRAP.
BA-ROOM

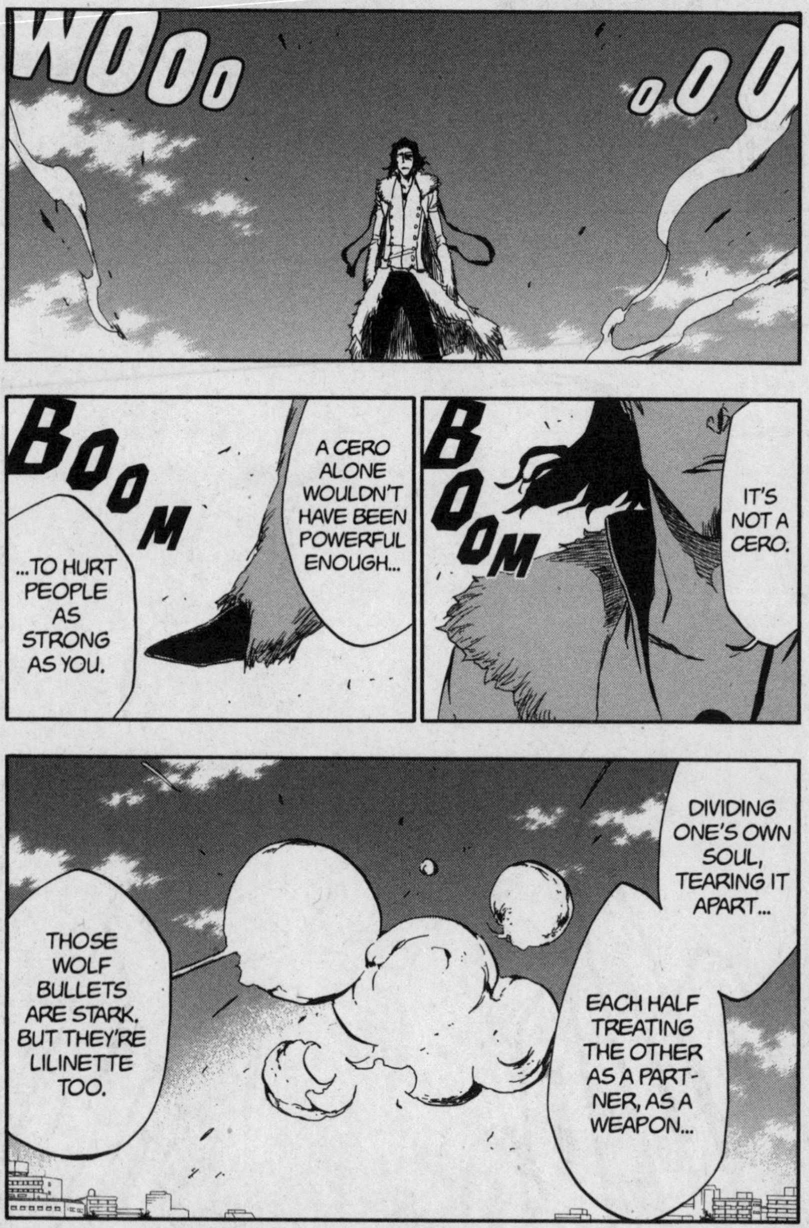
WOOO
OOO
BOOM
IT'S NOT A CERO.
BOOM
A CERO ALONE WOULDN'T HAVE BEEN POWERFUL ENOUGH...
...TO HURT PEOPLE AS STRONG AS YOU.
DIVIDING ONE'S OWN SOUL, TEARING IT APART...
EACH HALF TREATING THE OTHER AS A PART-NER, AS A WEAPON...
THOSE WOLF BULLETS ARE STARK. BUT THEY'RE LILINETTE TOO.

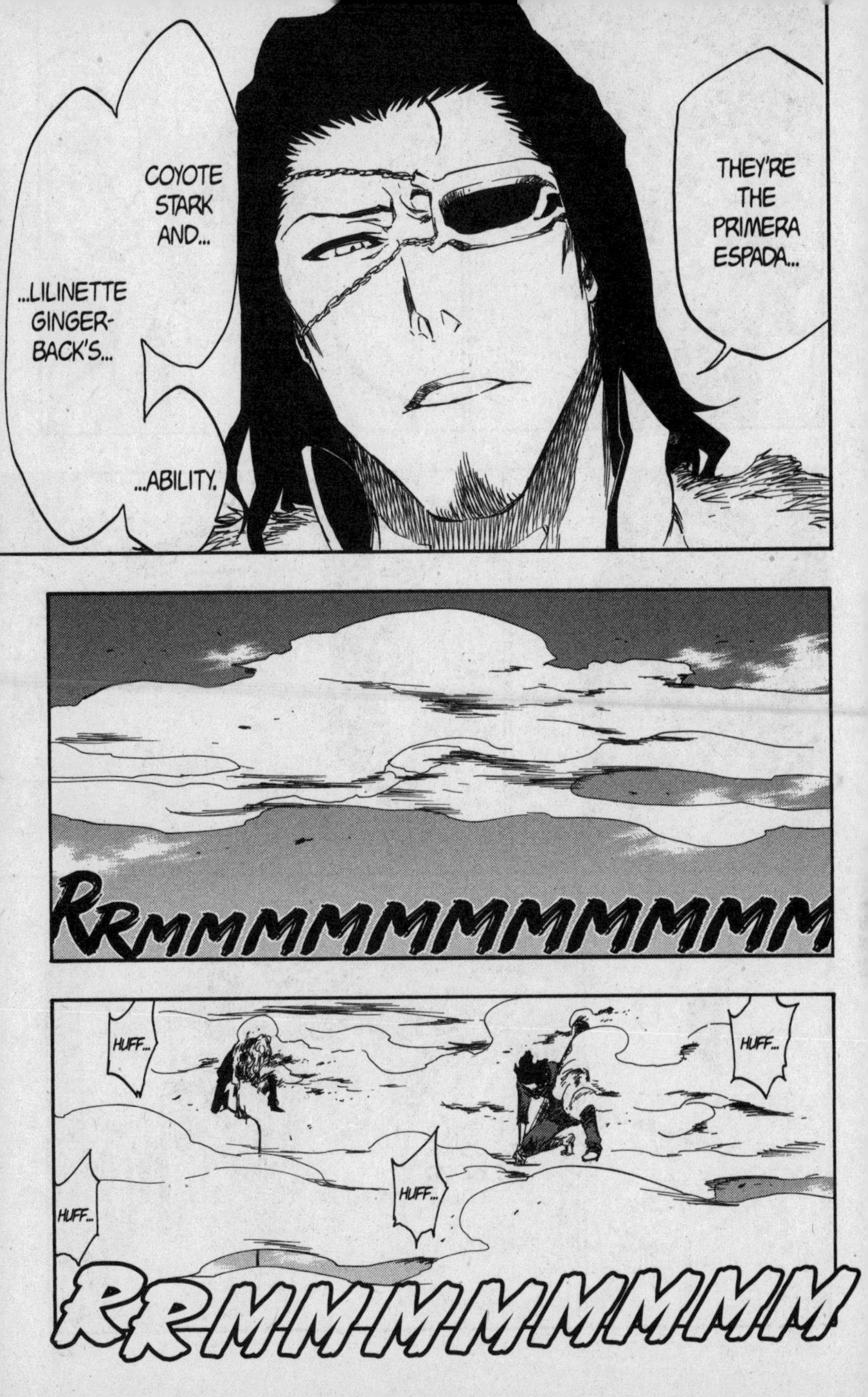
THEY'RE THE PRIMERA ESPADA...
COYOTE STARK AND...
...LILINETTE GINGER-BACK'S...
...ABILITY.
RRMMMMMMMMMMMMM
HUFF...
HUFF...
HUFF...
HUFF...
RRMMMMMMMMMM

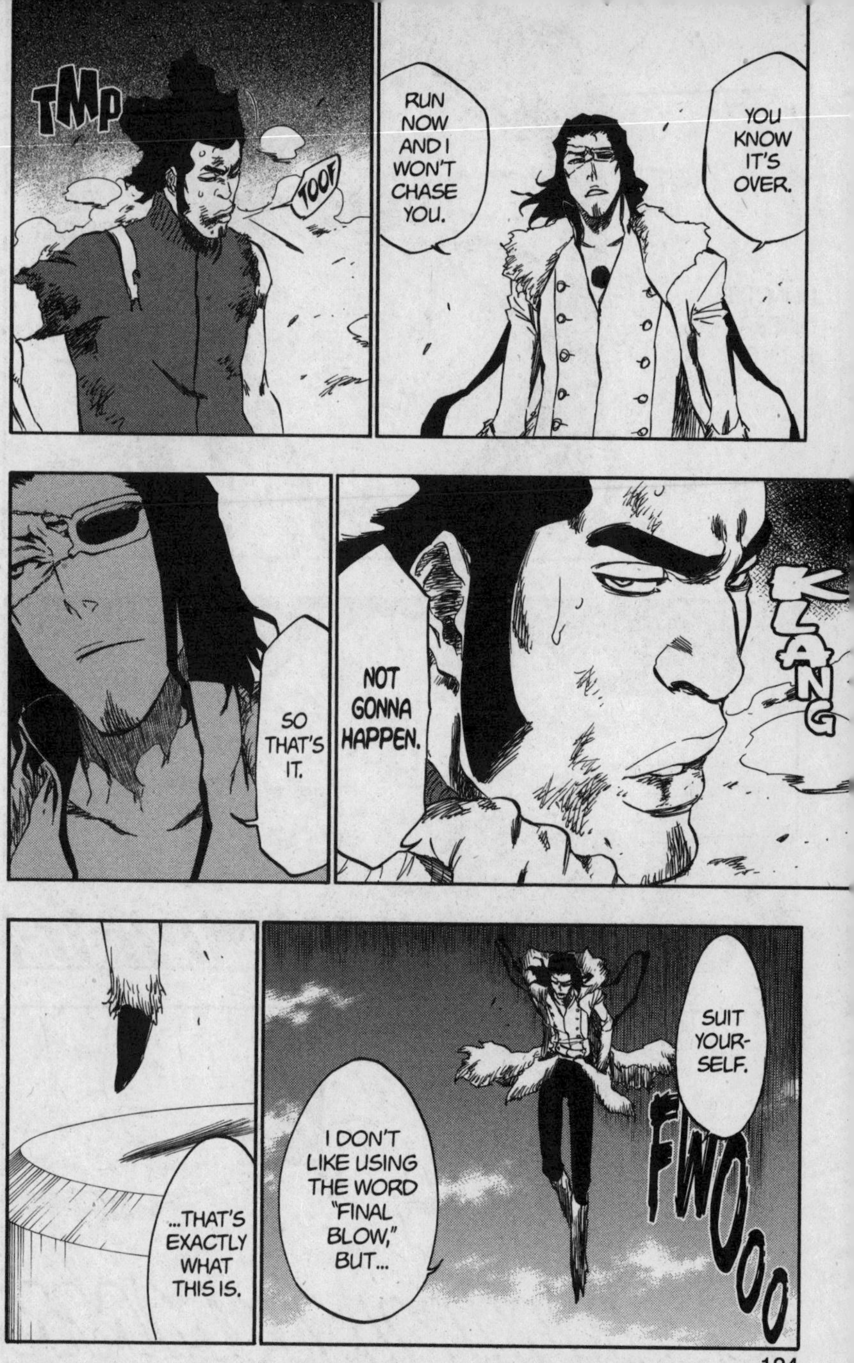
YOU KNOW IT'S OVER.
RUN NOW AND I WON'T CHASE YOU.
TMP
TOOF
KLANG
NOT GONNA HAPPEN.
SO THAT'S IT.
SUIT YOUR-SELF.
FWOOOO
I DON'T LIKE USING THE WORD "FINAL BLOW," BUT...
...THAT'S EXACTLY WHAT THIS IS.

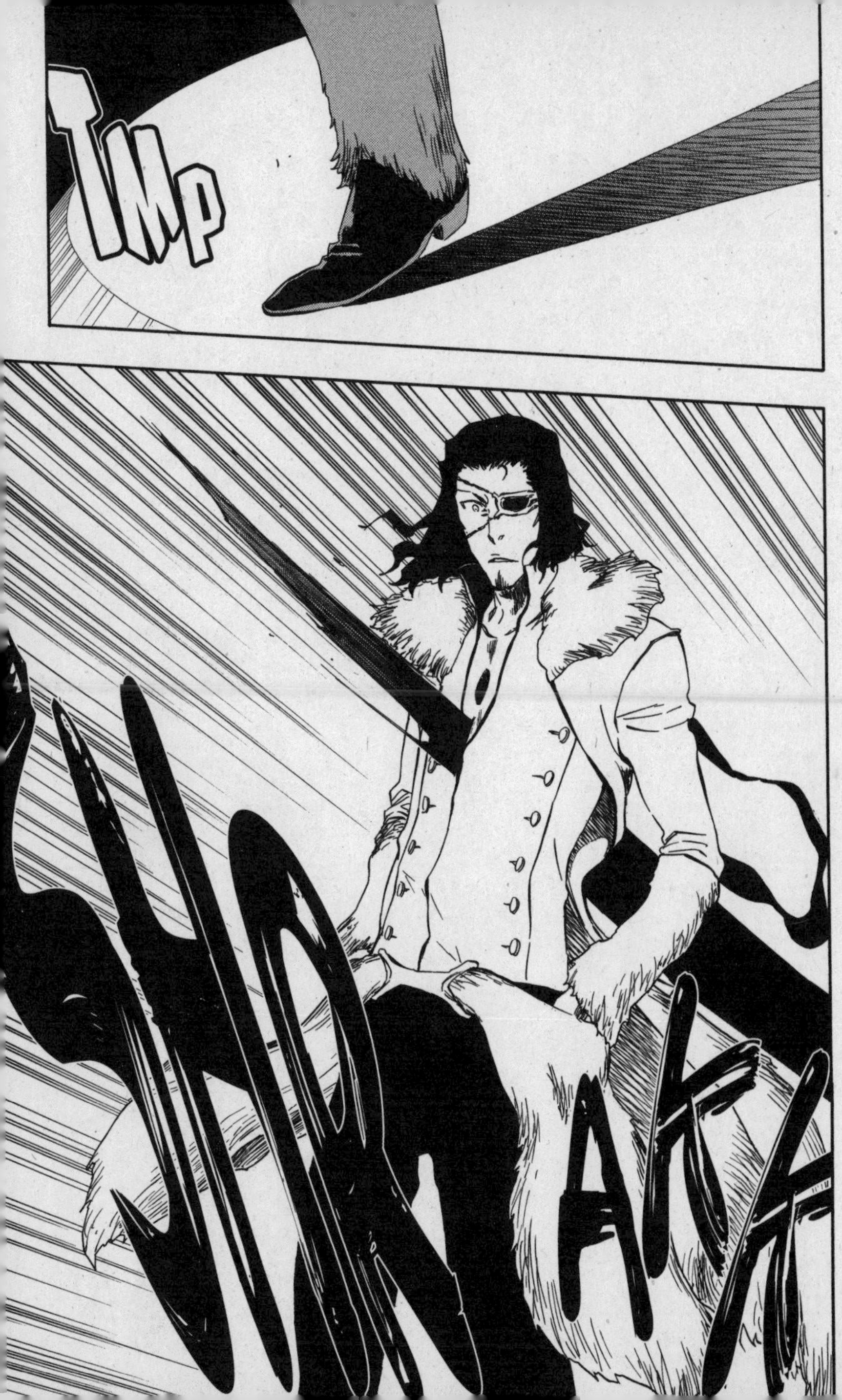
TMP

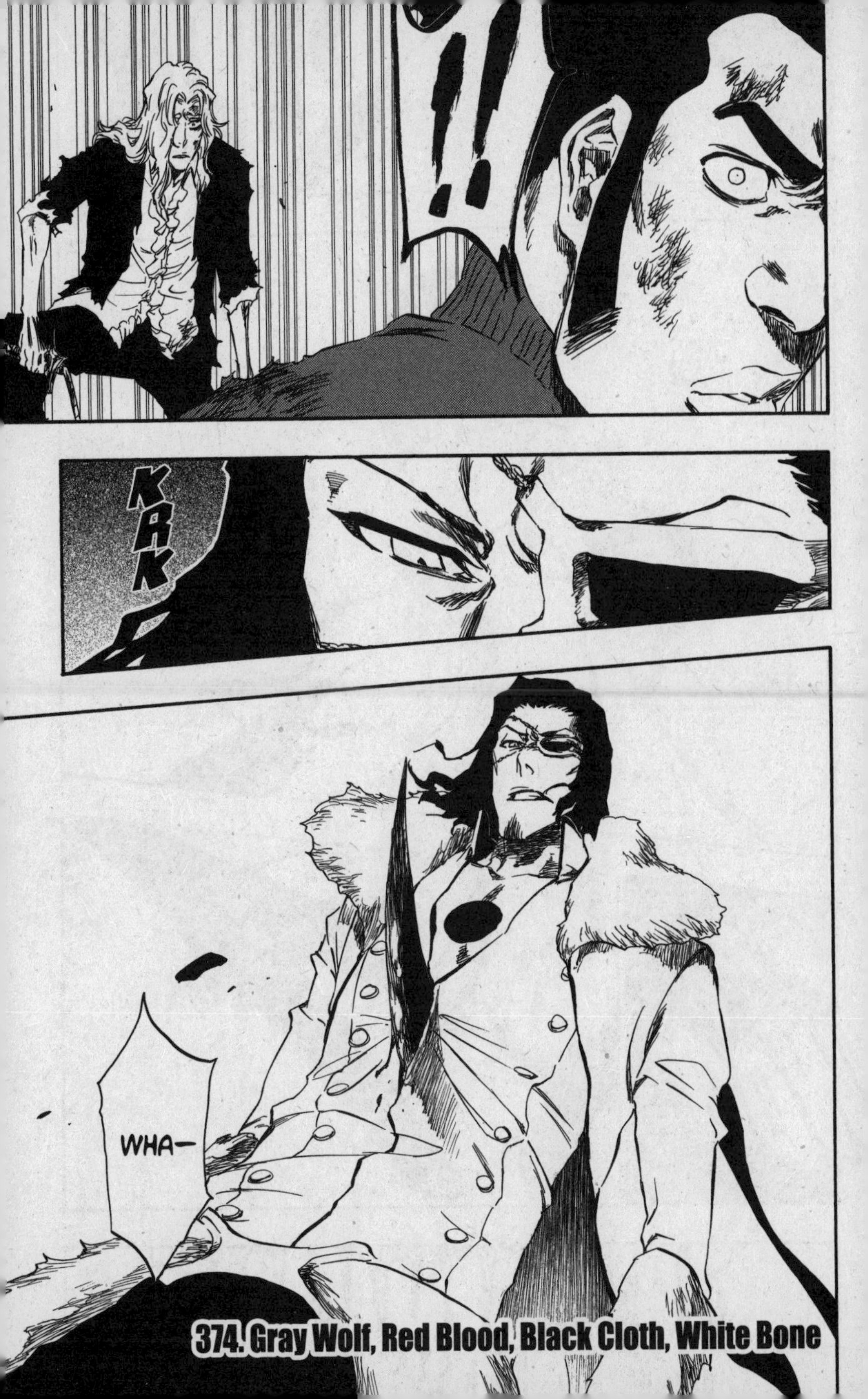
!!
KRK
WHA-
374. Gray Wolf, Red Blood, Black Cloth, White Bone

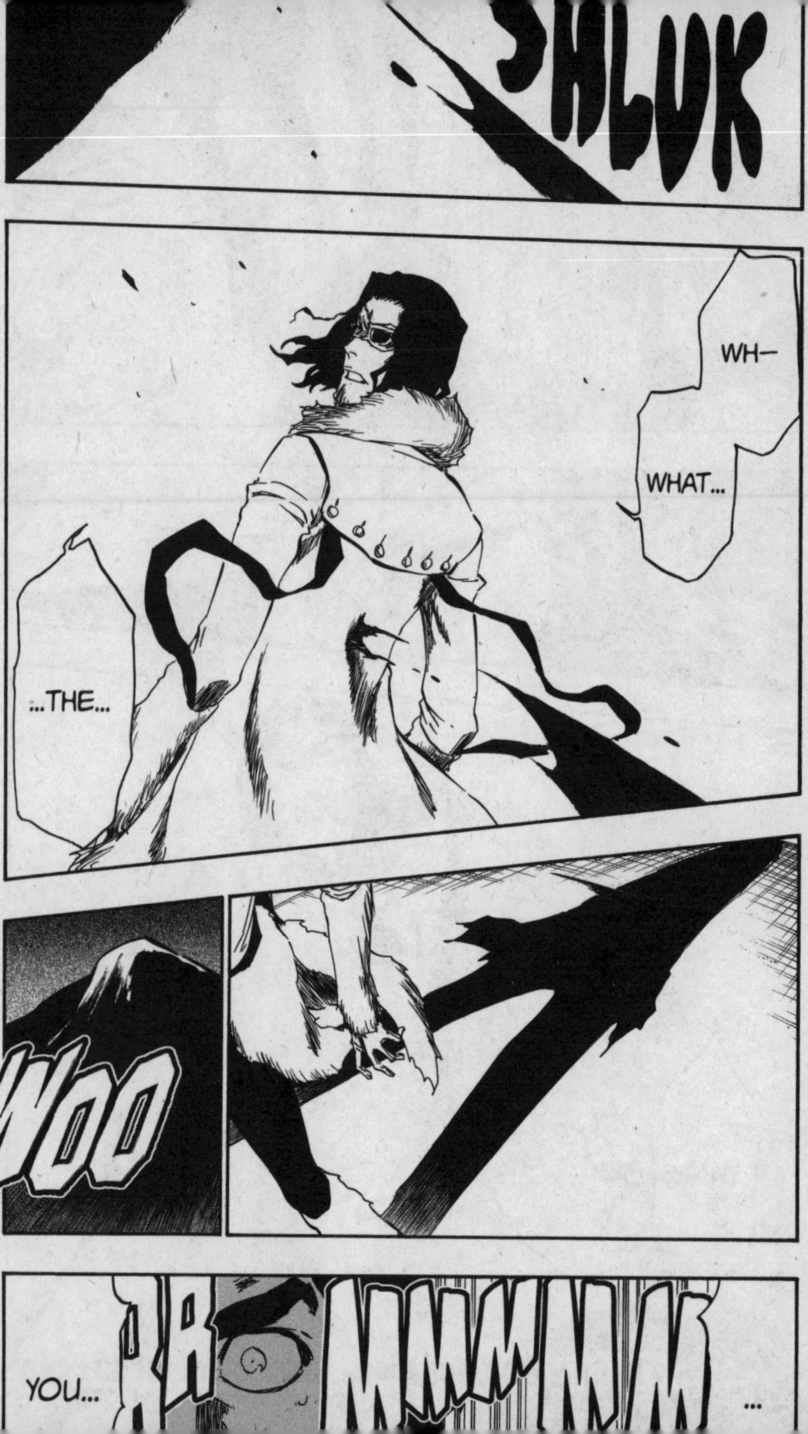
SHLUK
WH—
WHAT...
...THE...
WOO
...
RAMMMMMM
YOU...

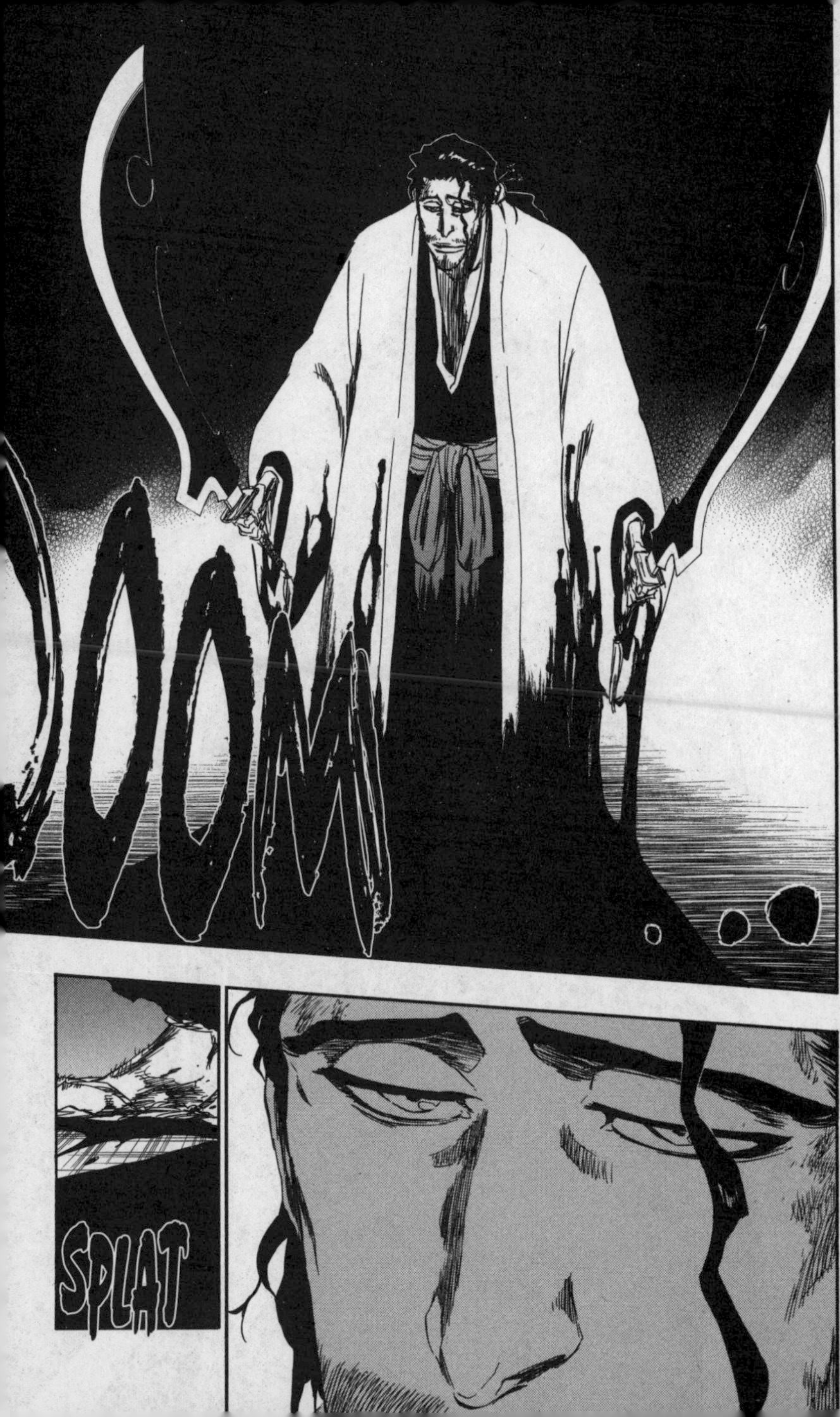
OOM...
SPLAT

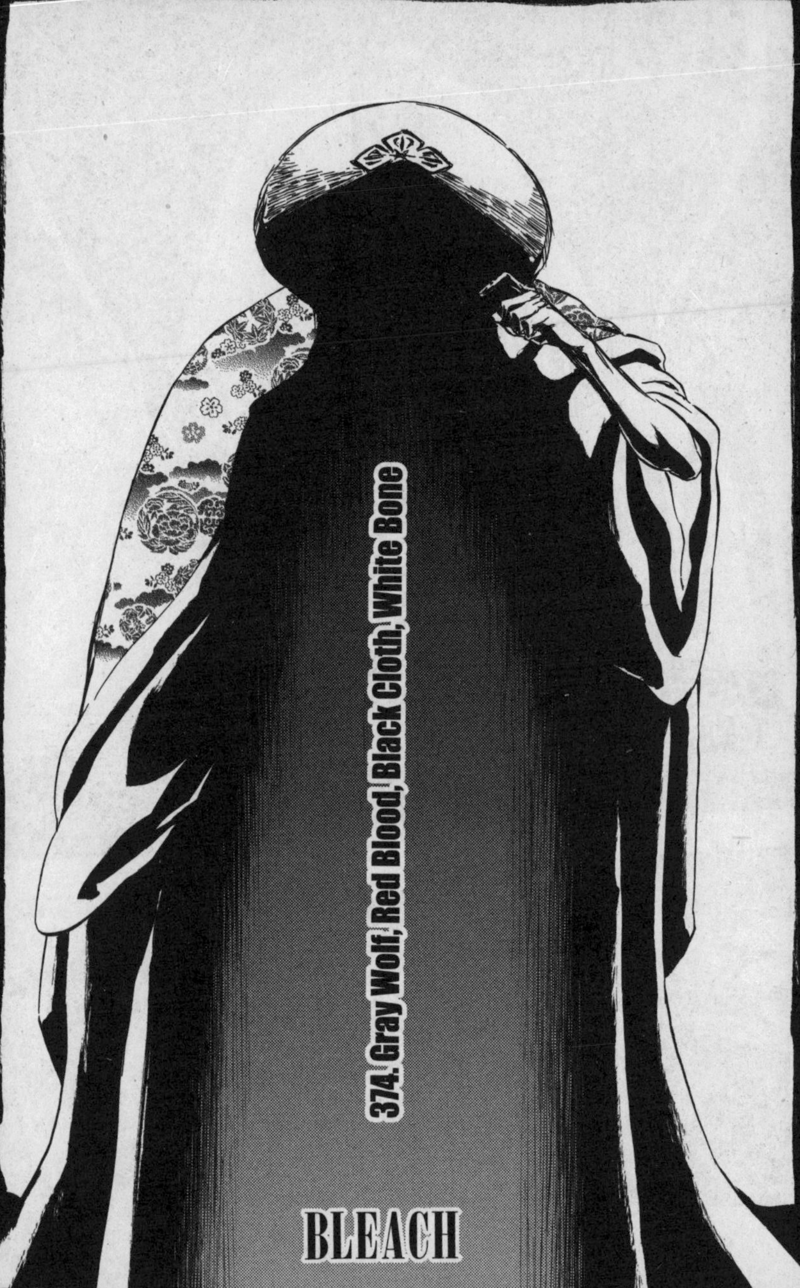
374. Gray Wolf, Red Blood, Black Cloth, White Bone
BLEACH

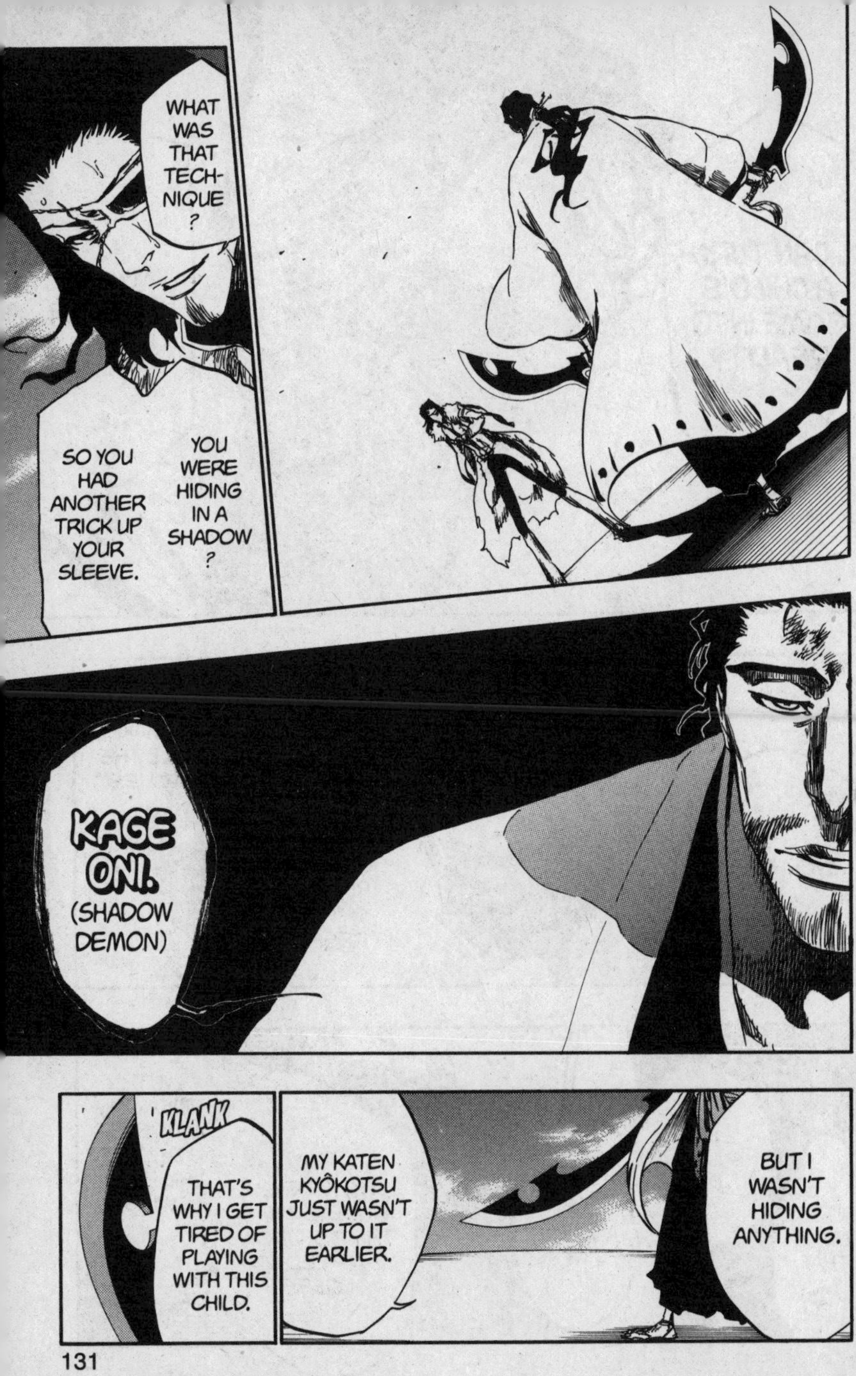
WHAT WAS THAT TECHNIQUE?
YOU WERE HIDING IN A SHADOW?
SO YOU HAD ANOTHER TRICK UP YOUR SLEEVE.
KAGE ONI. (SHADOW DEMON)
BUT I WASN'T HIDING ANYTHING.
MY KATEN KYÔKOTSU JUST WASN'T UP TO IT EARLIER.
KLANK
THAT'S WHY I GET TIRED OF PLAYING WITH THIS CHILD.

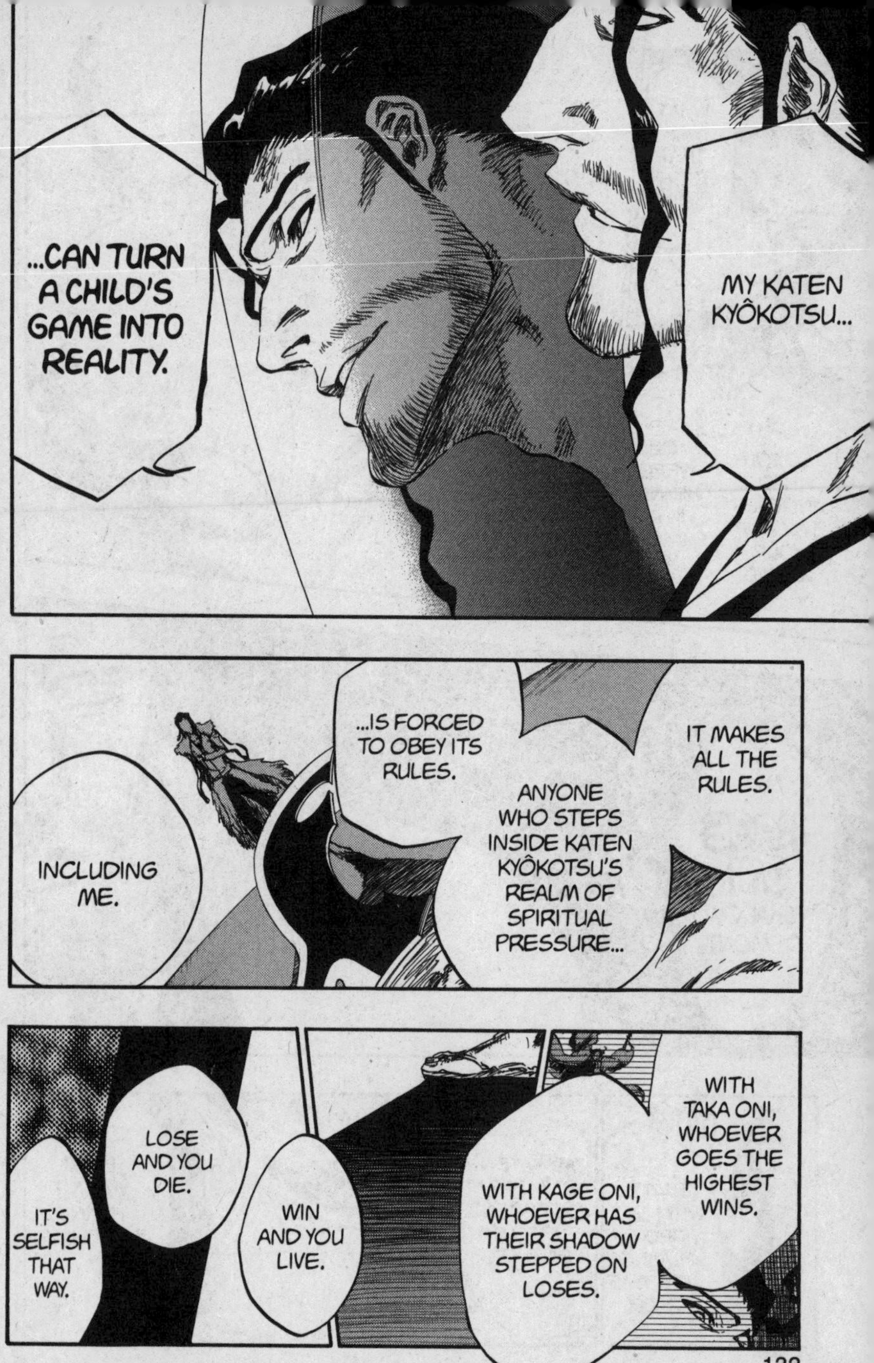
MY KATEN KYÔKOTSU...
...CAN TURN A CHILD'S GAME INTO REALITY.
IT MAKES ALL THE RULES.
ANYONE WHO STEPS INSIDE KATEN KYÔKOTSU'S REALM OF SPIRITUAL PRESSURE...
...IS FORCED TO OBEY ITS RULES.
INCLUDING ME.
WITH TAKA ONI, WHOEVER GOES THE HIGHEST WINS.
WITH KAGE ONI, WHOEVER HAS THEIR SHADOW STEPPED ON LOSES.
WIN AND YOU LIVE.
LOSE AND YOU DIE.
IT'S SELFISH THAT WAY.

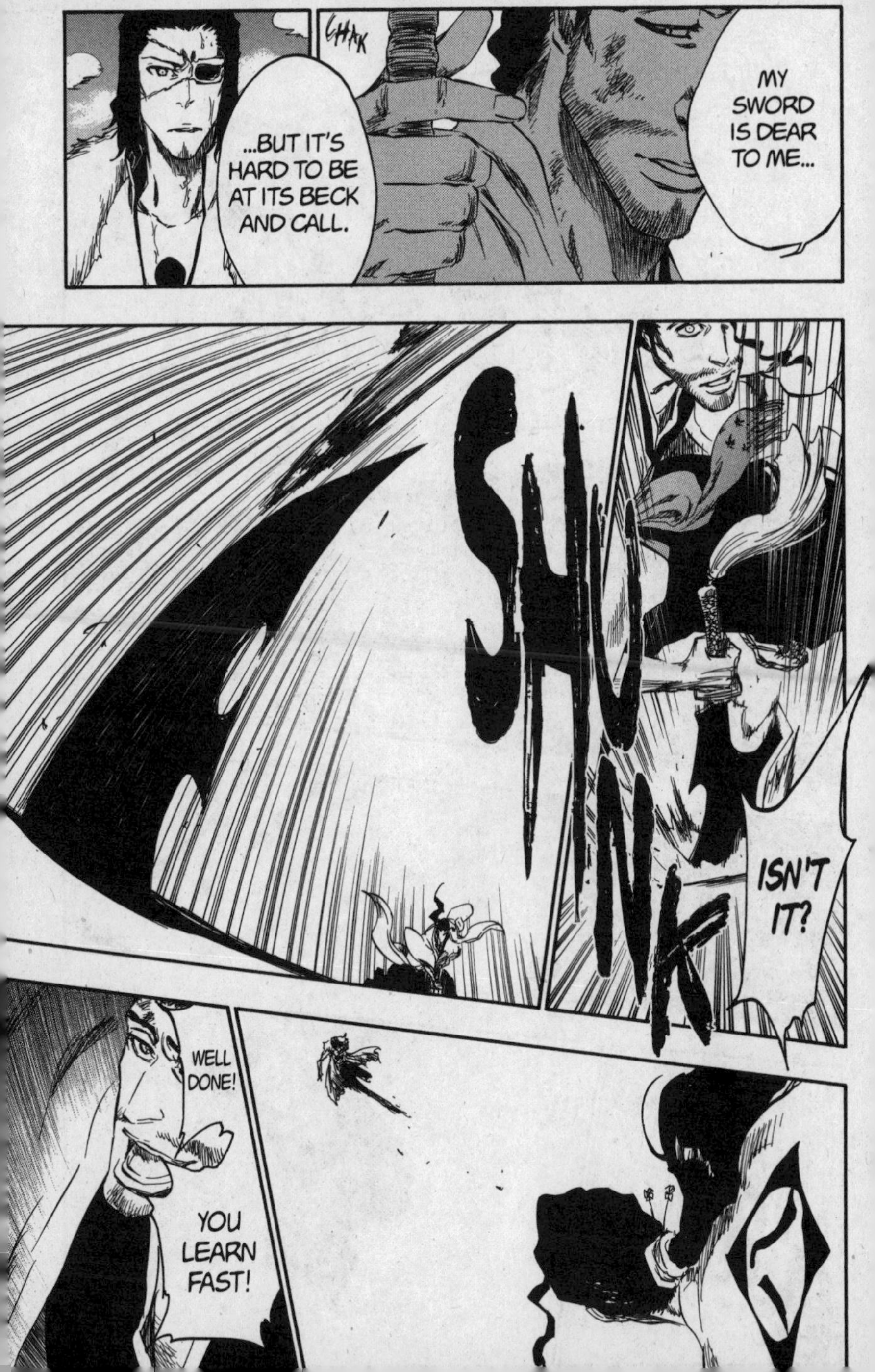
CHAK
MY SWORD IS DEAR TO ME...
...BUT IT'S HARD TO BE AT ITS BECK AND CALL.
ISN'T IT?
SHUNK
WELL DONE!
YOU LEARN FAST!

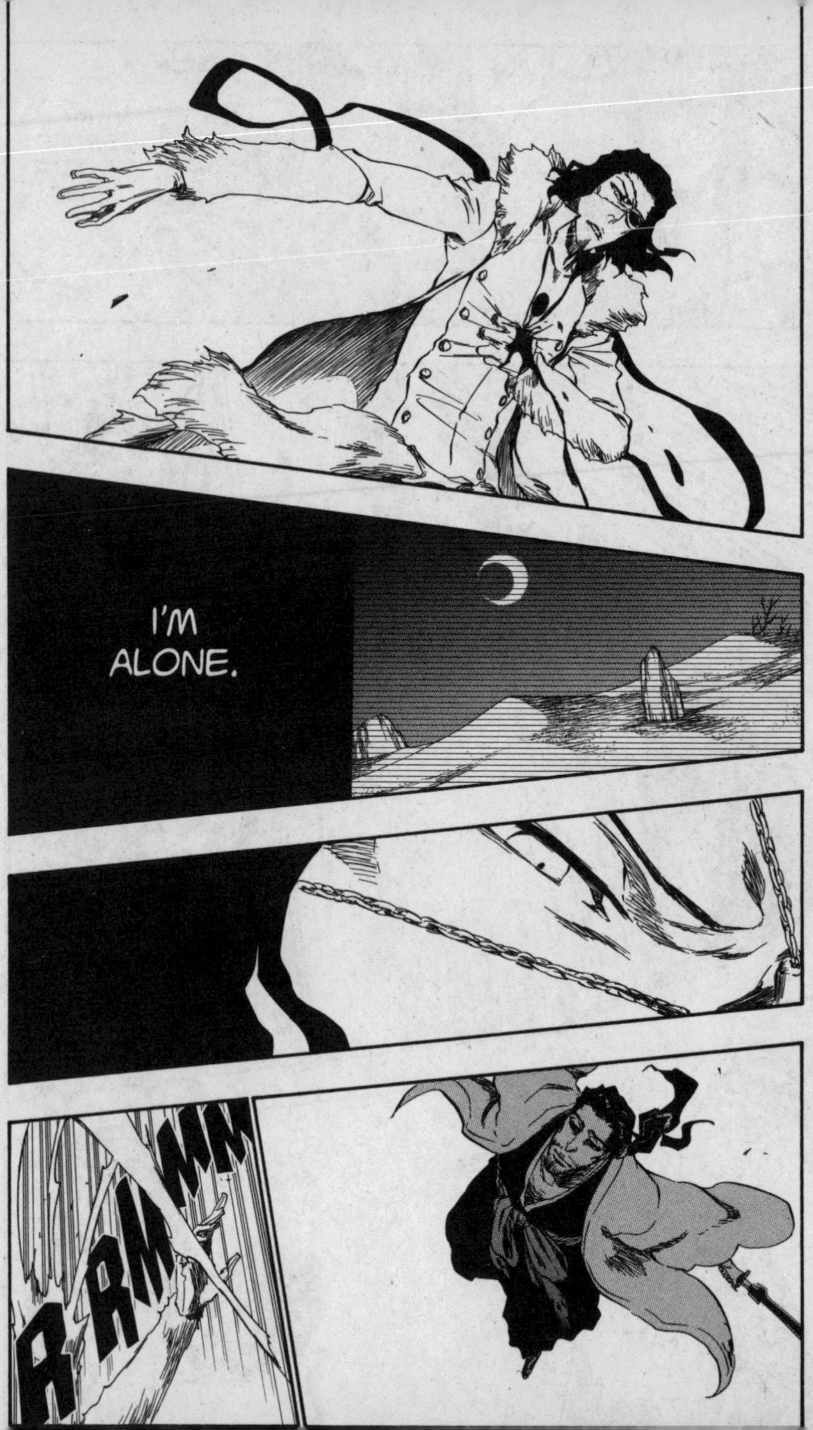
I'M ALONE.
RRMMMN

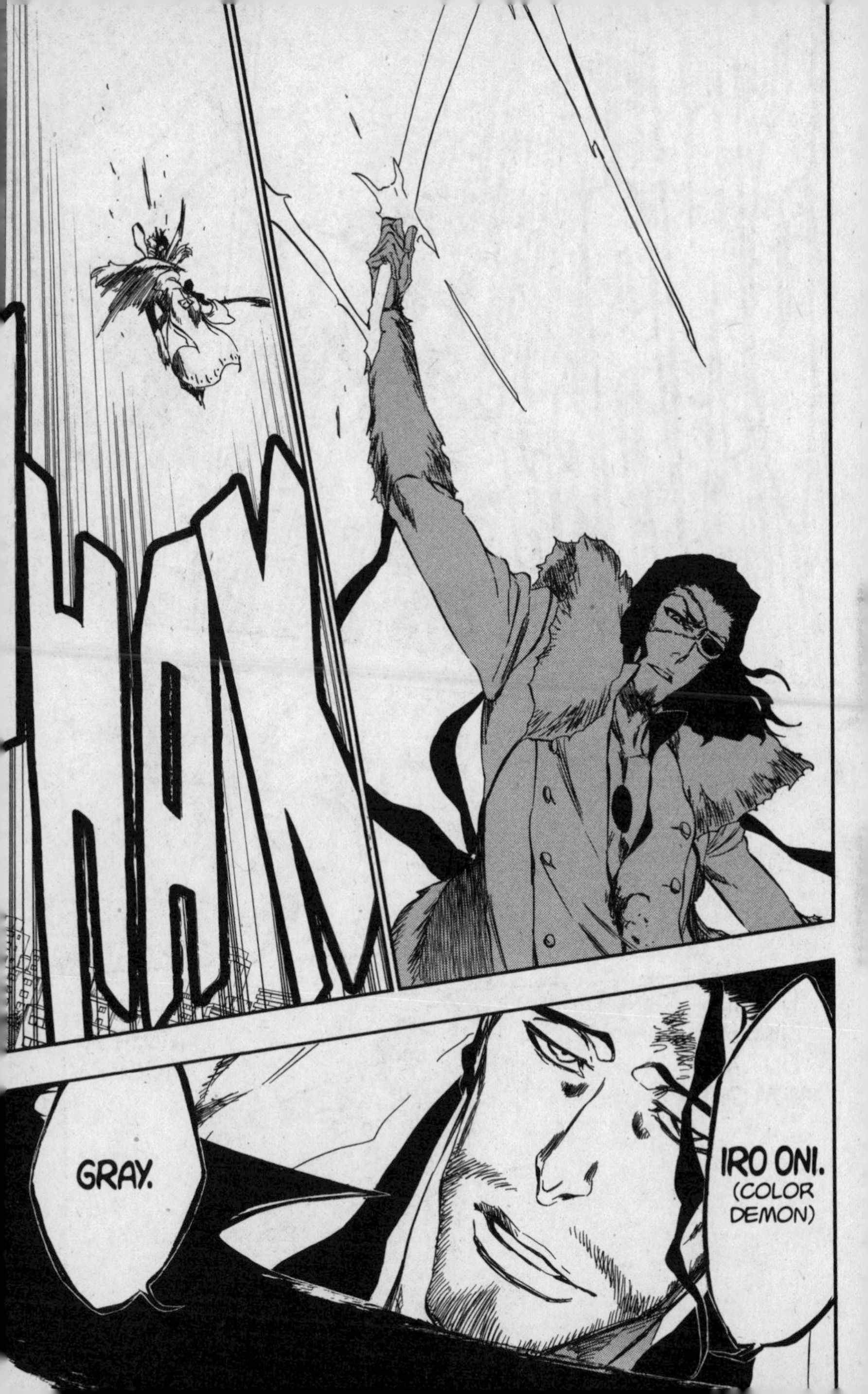
IRO ONI.
(COLOR
DEMON)
GRAY.

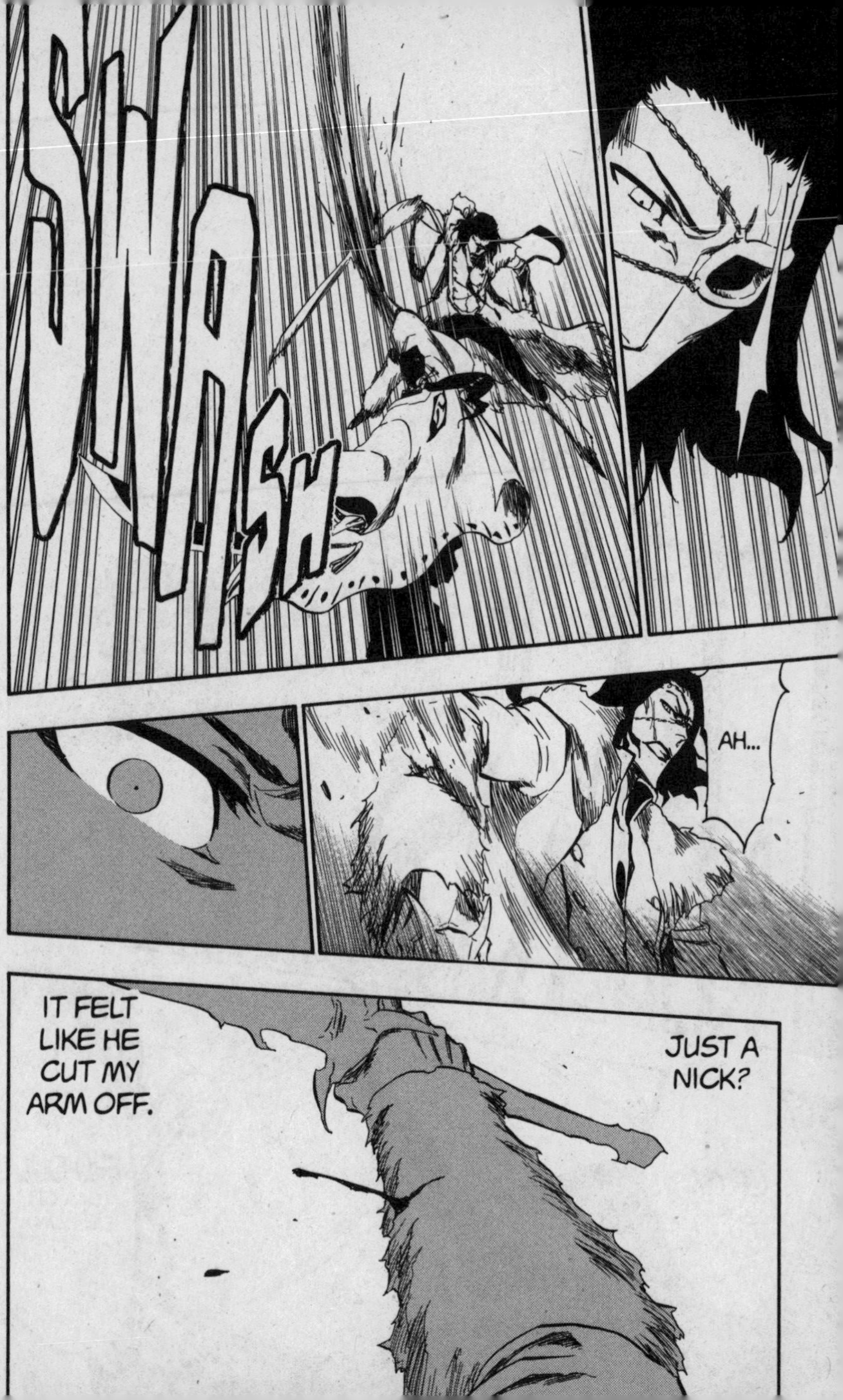
SWASH
AH...
JUST A NICK?
IT FELT LIKE HE CUT MY ARM OFF.

IRO
ONI

GRAY

THERE'S
NO GRAY
ON HIM.

MY ARM
IS GRAY.

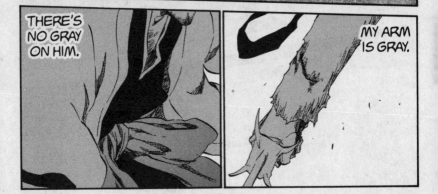

WHAT'S
WRONG?

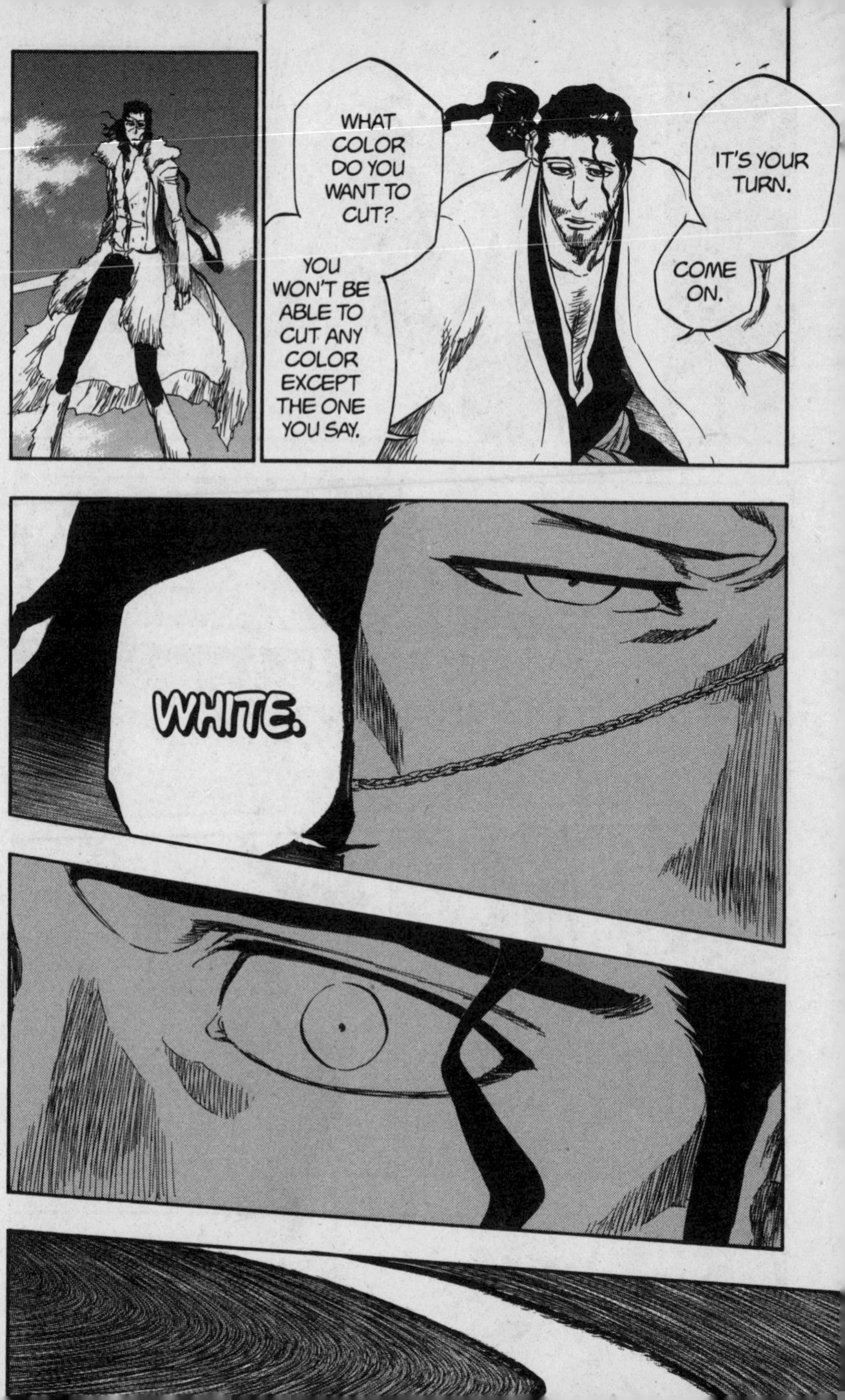
IT'S YOUR TURN.
COME ON.
WHAT COLOR DO YOU WANT TO CUT?
YOU WON'T BE ABLE TO CUT ANY COLOR EXCEPT THE ONE YOU SAY.
WHITE.

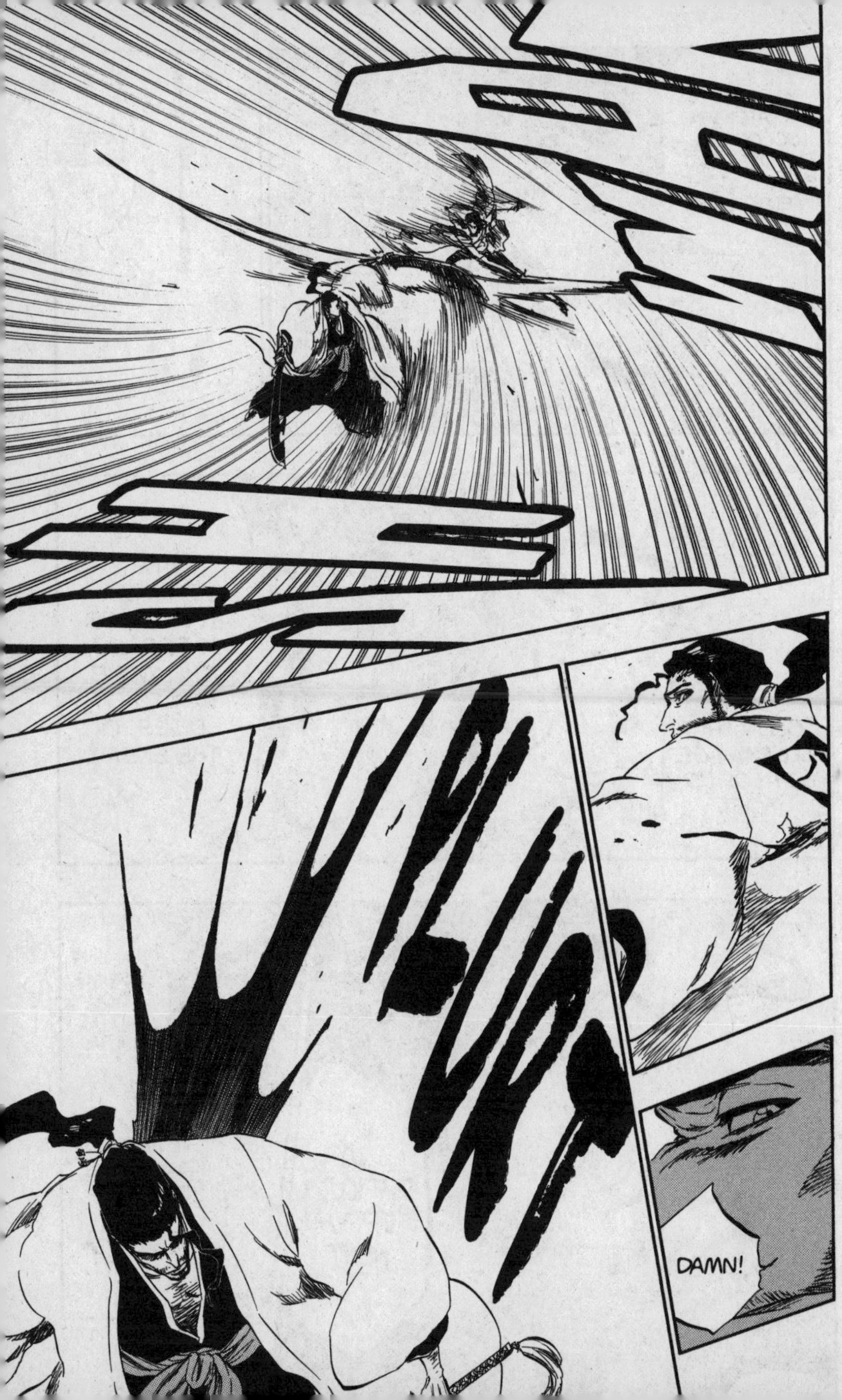
DAMN!

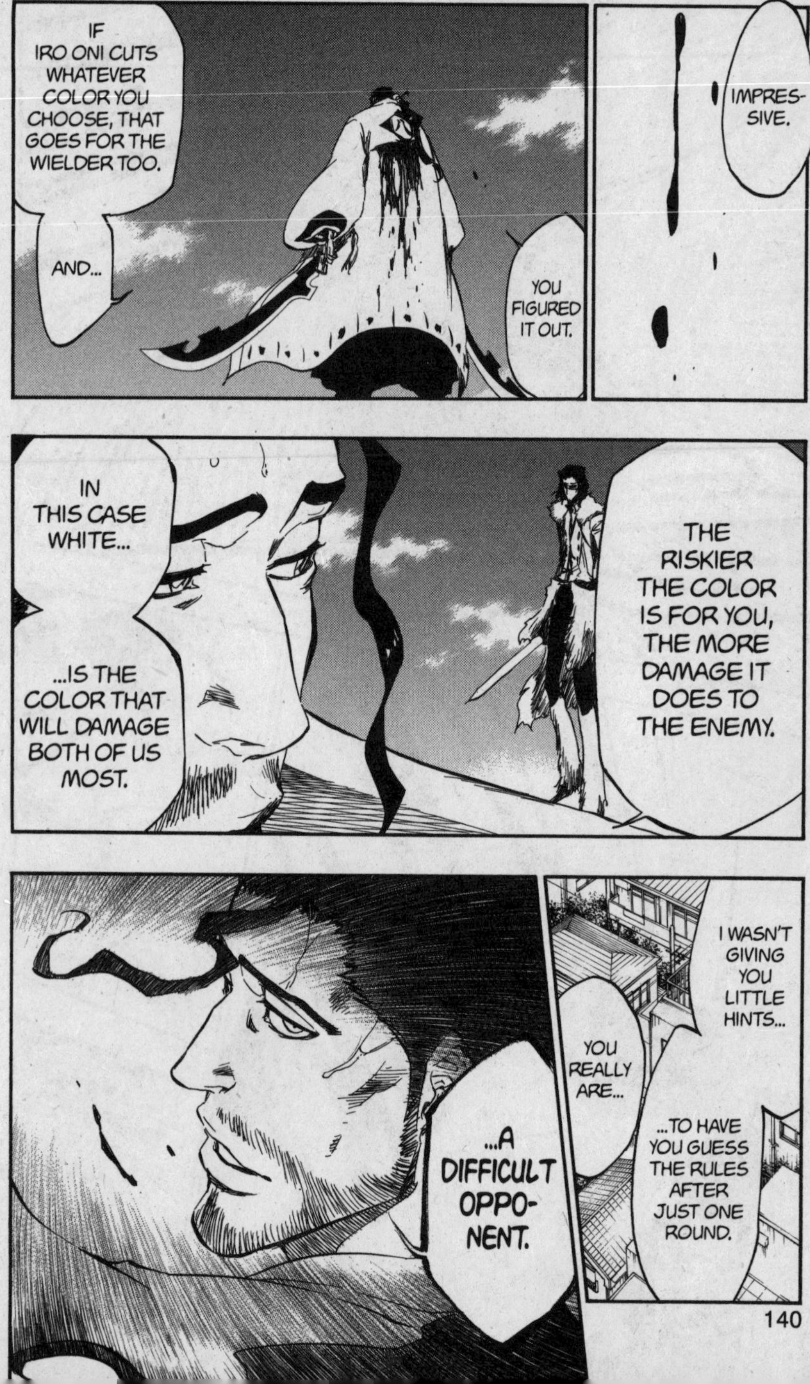
IMPRES-SIVE.
YOU FIGURED IT OUT.
IF IRO ONI CUTS WHATEVER COLOR YOU CHOOSE, THAT GOES FOR THE WIELDER TOO.
AND...
THE RISKIER THE COLOR IS FOR YOU, THE MORE DAMAGE IT DOES TO THE ENEMY.
IN THIS CASE WHITE...
...IS THE COLOR THAT WILL DAMAGE BOTH OF US MOST.
I WASN'T GIVING YOU LITTLE HINTS...
...TO HAVE YOU GUESS THE RULES AFTER JUST ONE ROUND.
YOU REALLY ARE...
...A DIFFICULT OPPO-NENT.

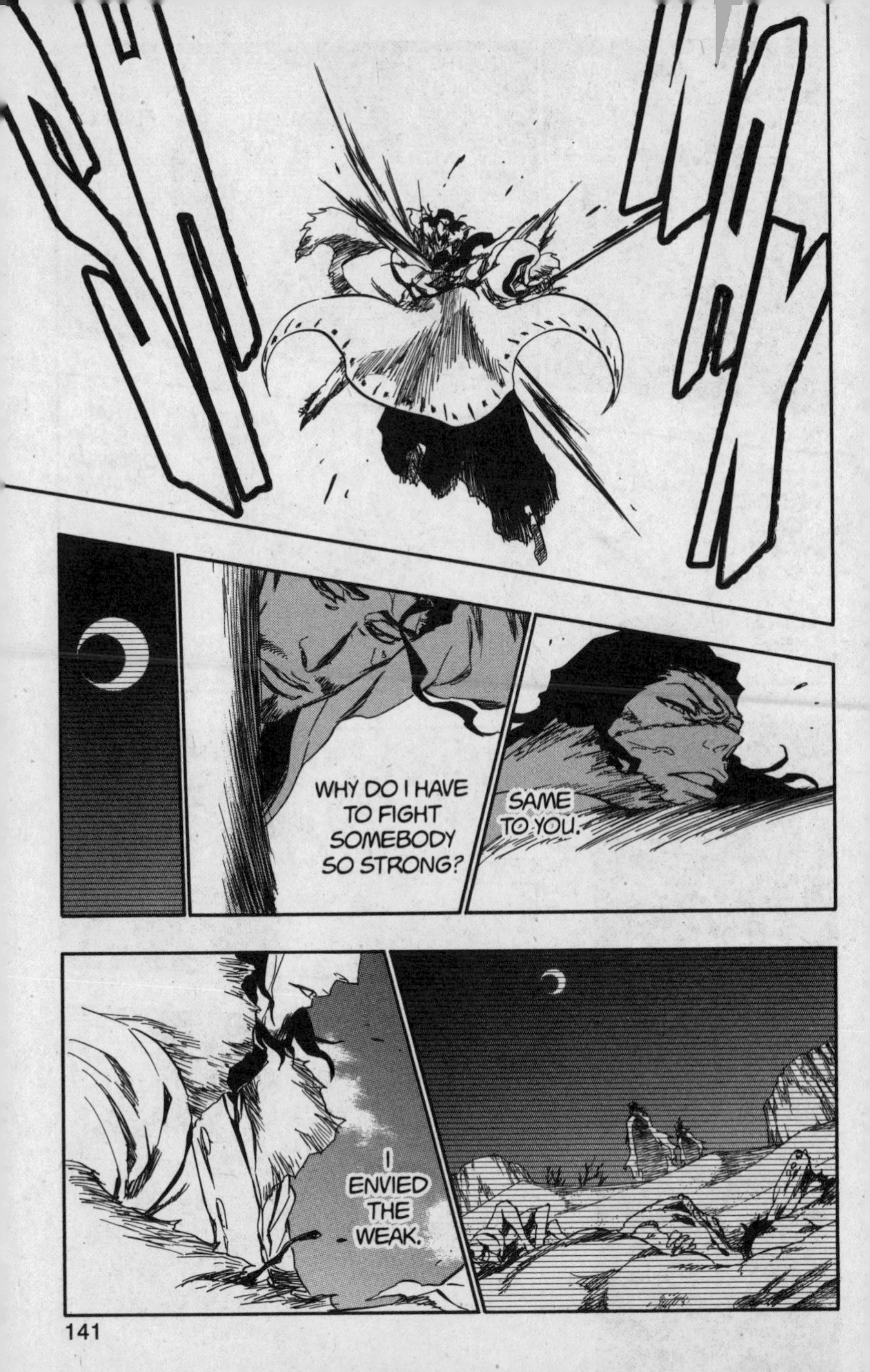
SAME TO YOU.
WHY DO I HAVE TO FIGHT SOMEBODY SO STRONG?
I ENVIED THE WEAK.

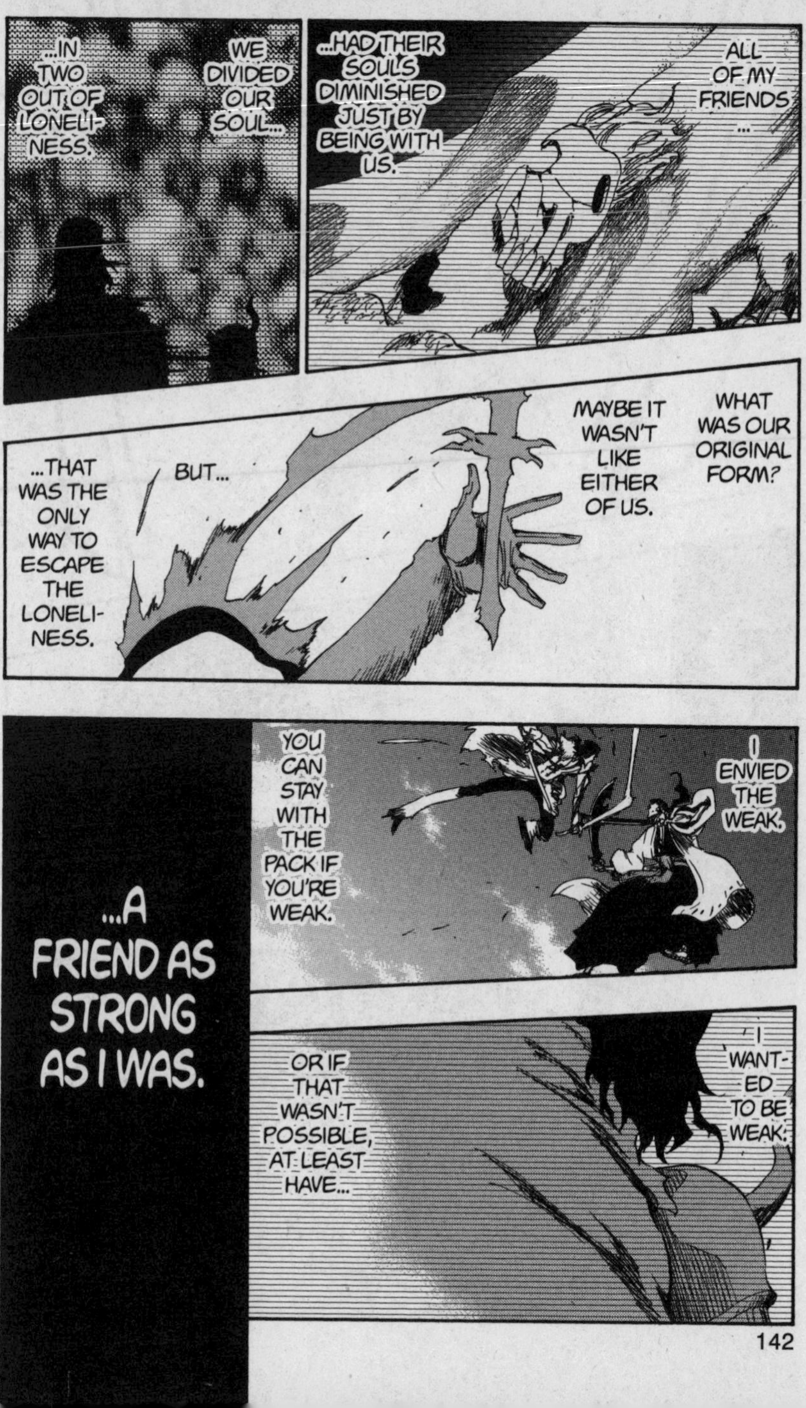
ALL OF MY FRIENDS ...
...HAD THEIR SOULS DIMINISHED JUST BY BEING WITH US.
WE DIVIDED OUR SOUL...
...IN TWO OUT OF LONELINESS.
WHAT WAS OUR ORIGINAL FORM?
MAYBE IT WASN'T LIKE EITHER OF US.
BUT...
...THAT WAS THE ONLY WAY TO ESCAPE THE LONELINESS.
I ENVIED THE WEAK.
YOU CAN STAY WITH THE PACK IF YOU'RE WEAK.
I WANTED TO BE WEAK.
OR IF THAT WASN'T POSSIBLE, AT LEAST HAVE...
...A FRIEND AS STRONG AS I WAS.

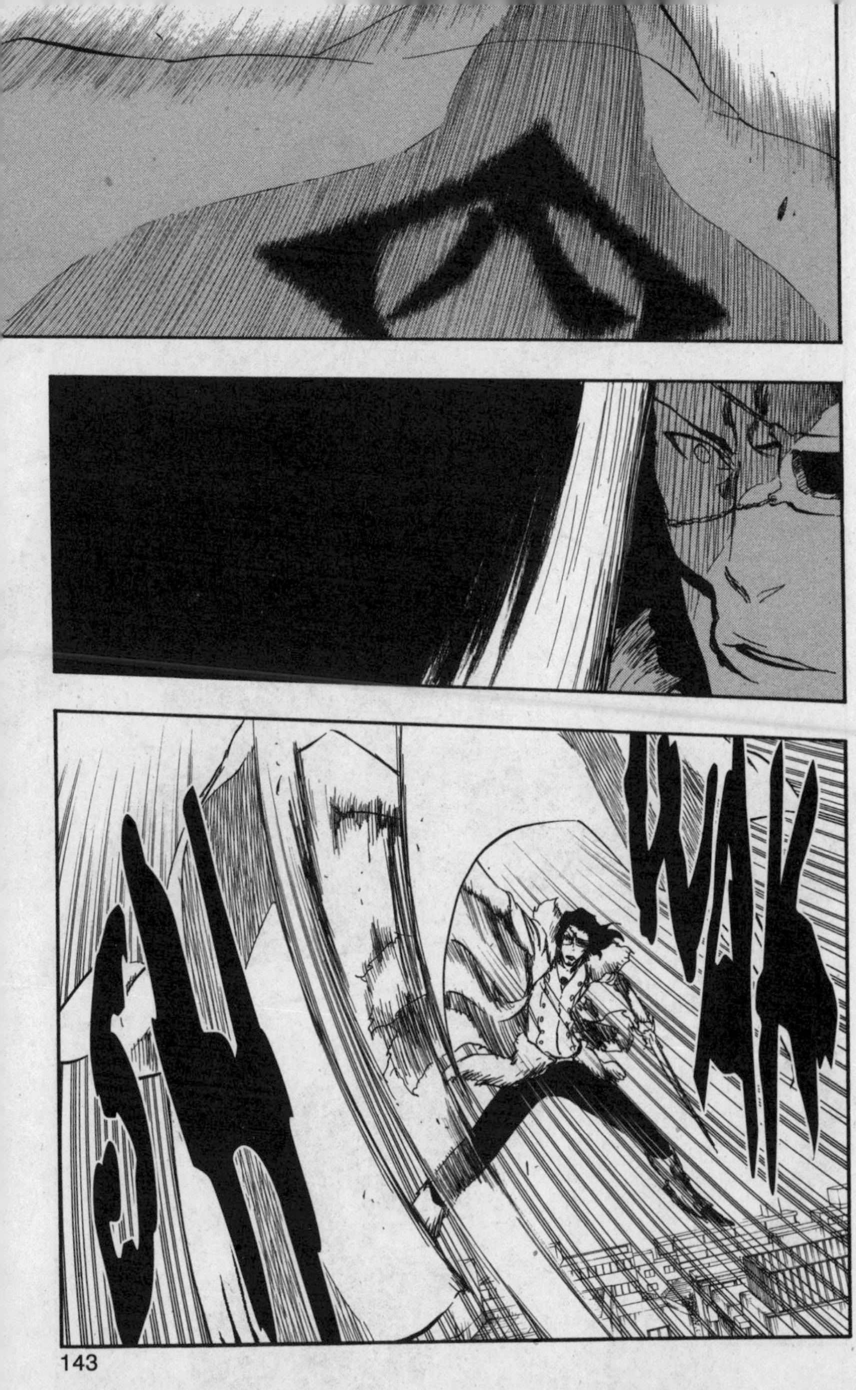
WAK

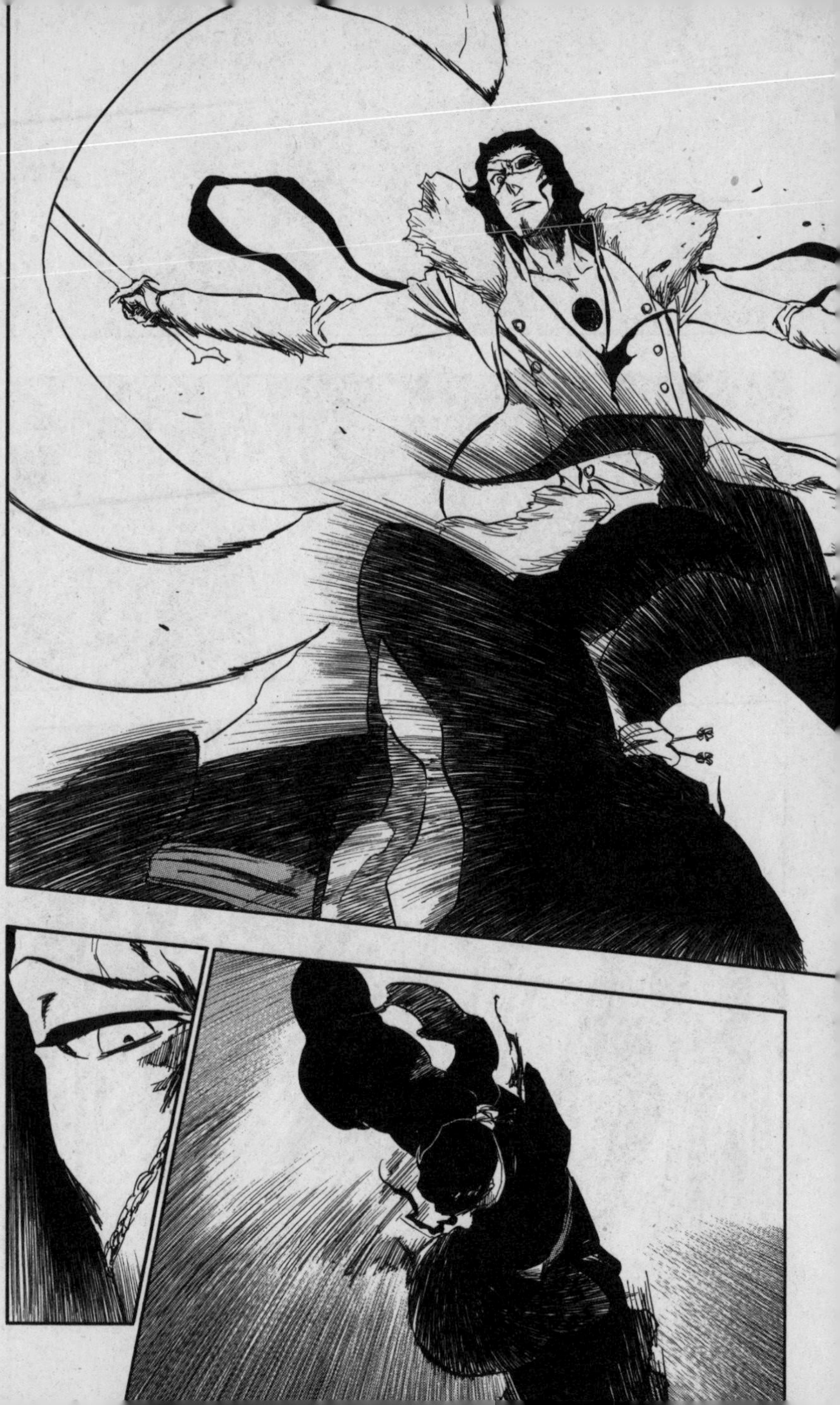

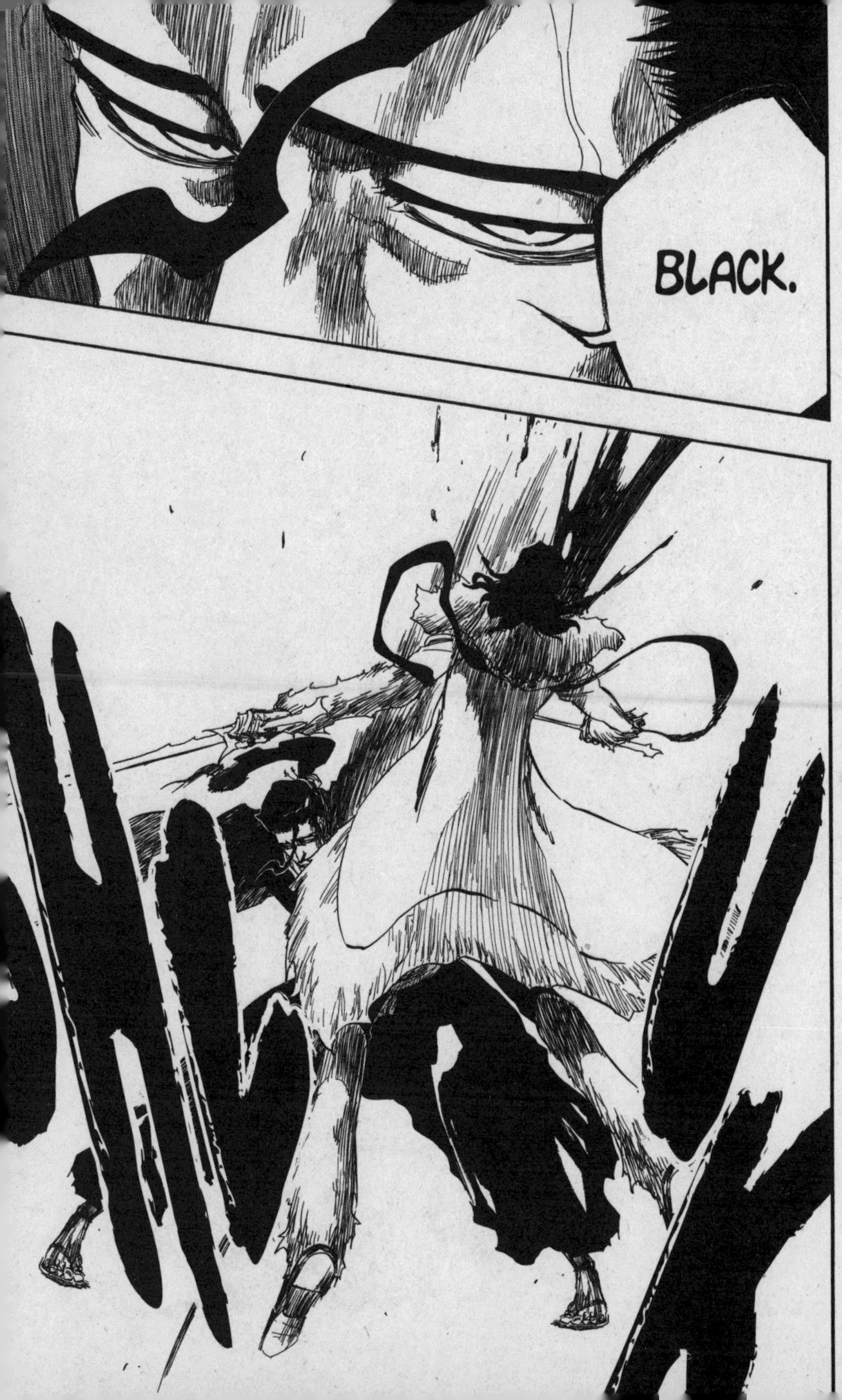
BLACK.

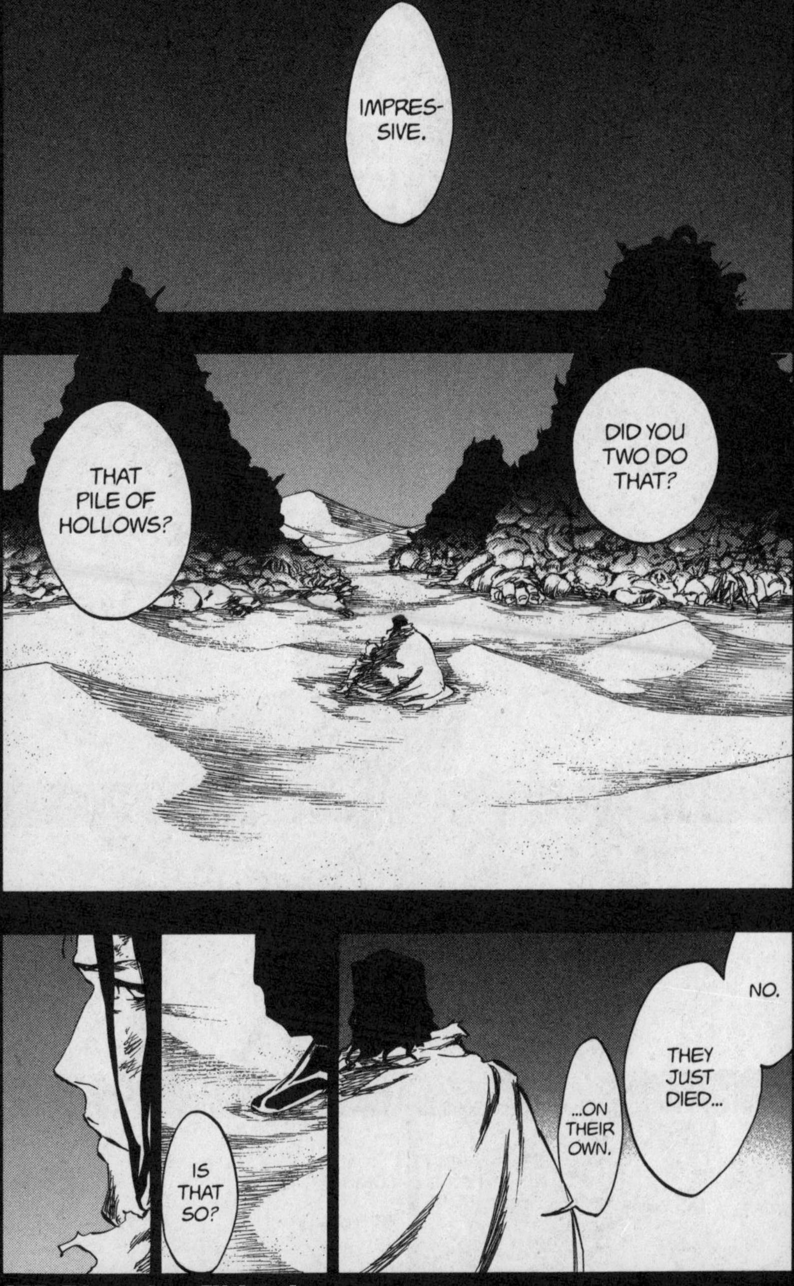
IMPRESSIVE.
DID YOU TWO DO THAT?
THAT PILE OF HOLLOWS?
NO.
THEY JUST DIED...
...ON THEIR OWN.
IS THAT SO?

375. EXecution, EXtinction

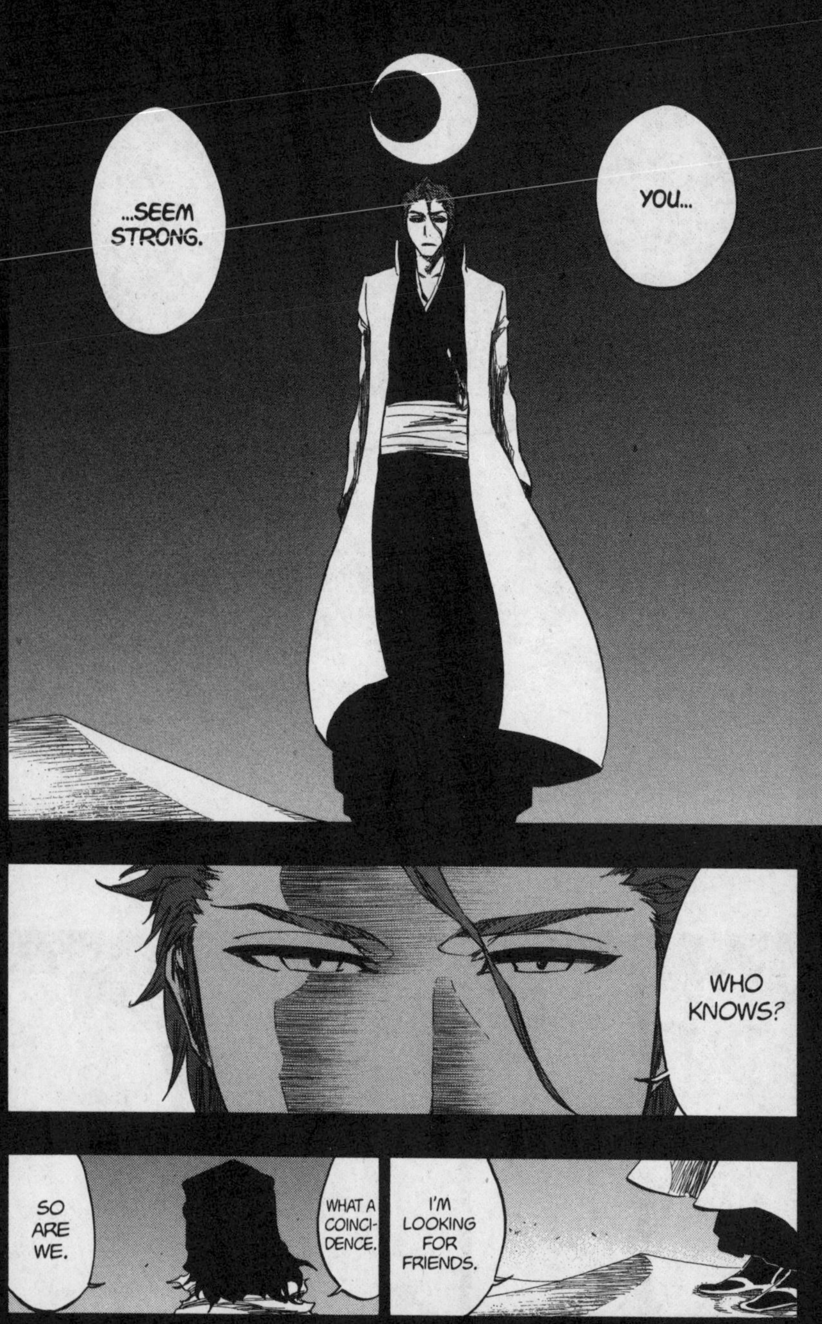
YOU...
...SEEM STRONG.
WHO KNOWS?
I'M LOOKING FOR FRIENDS.
WHAT A COINCI- DENCE.
SO ARE WE.

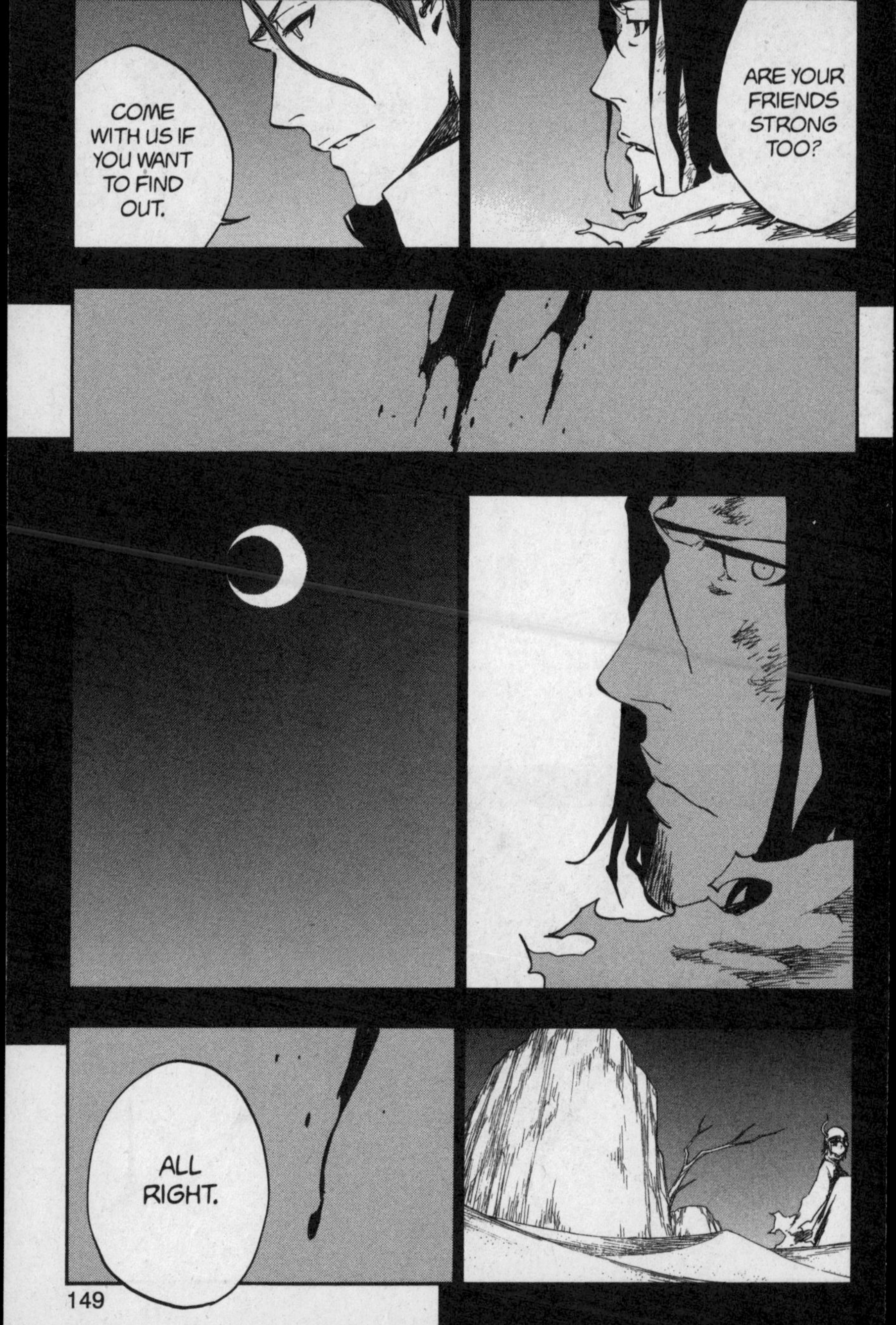
ARE YOUR FRIENDS STRONG TOO?
COME WITH US IF YOU WANT TO FIND OUT.
ALL RIGHT.

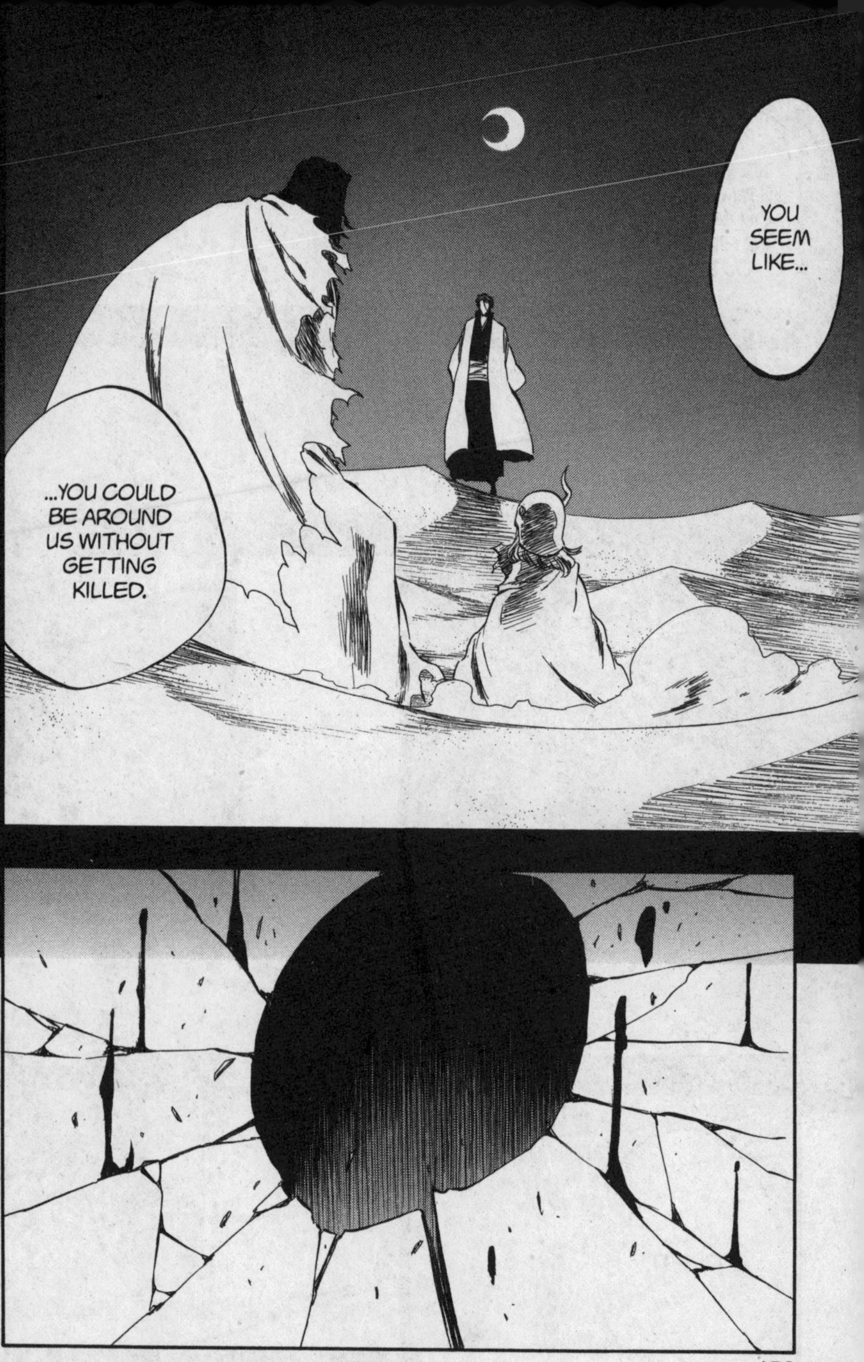
YOU SEEM LIKE...
...YOU COULD BE AROUND US WITHOUT GETTING KILLED.

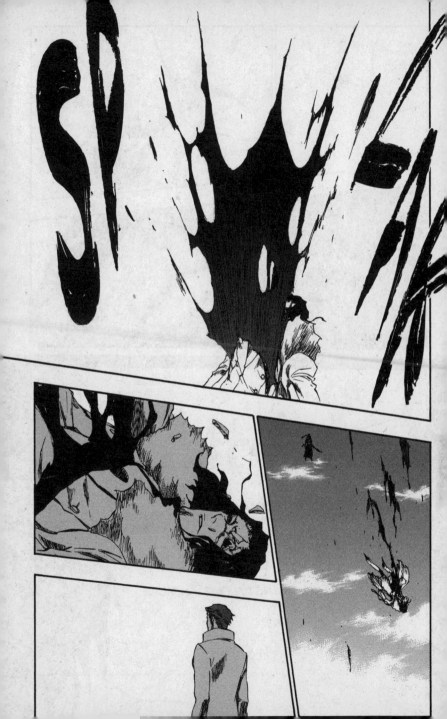

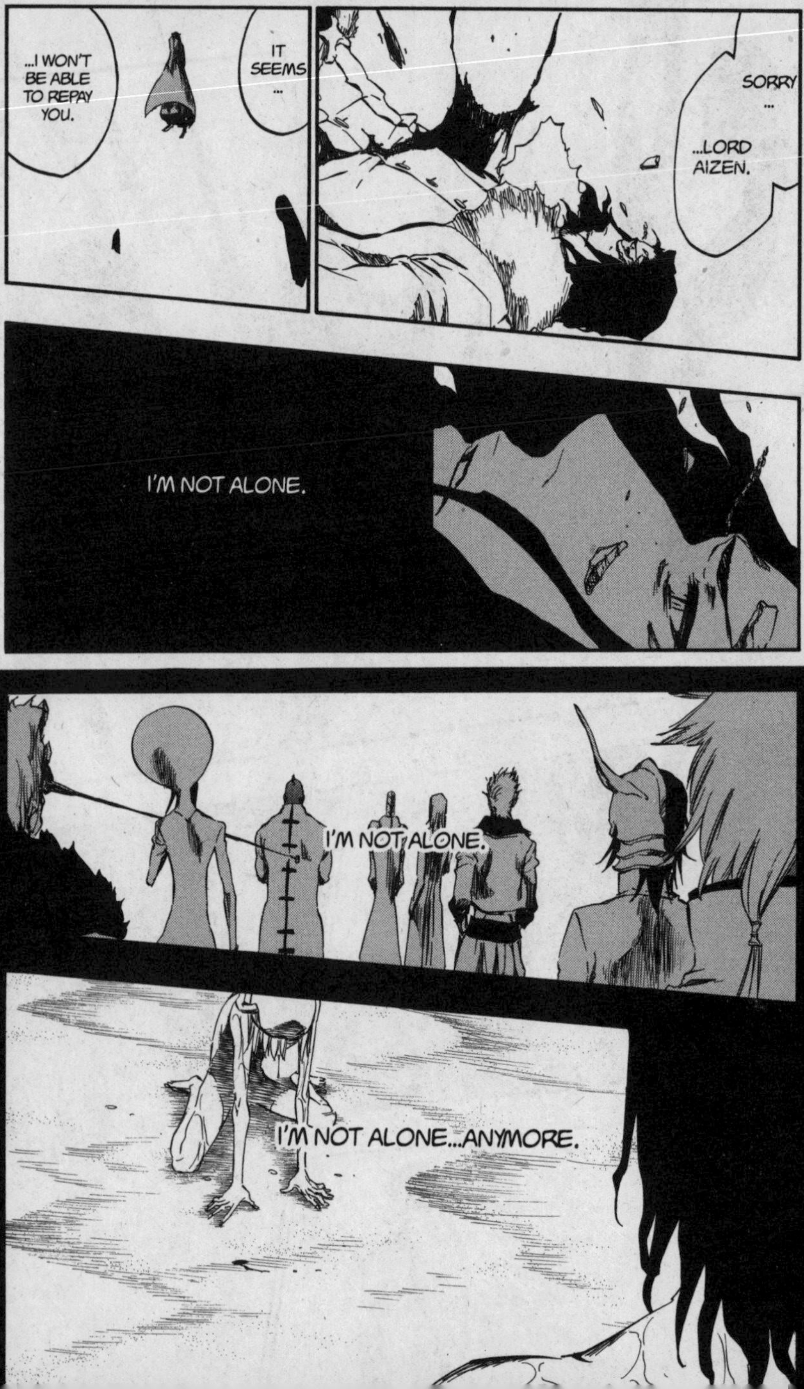
SORRY ... ...LORD AIZEN.
IT SEEMS ...
...I WON'T BE ABLE TO REPAY YOU.
I'M NOT ALONE.
I'M NOT ALONE.
I'M NOT ALONE...ANYMORE.

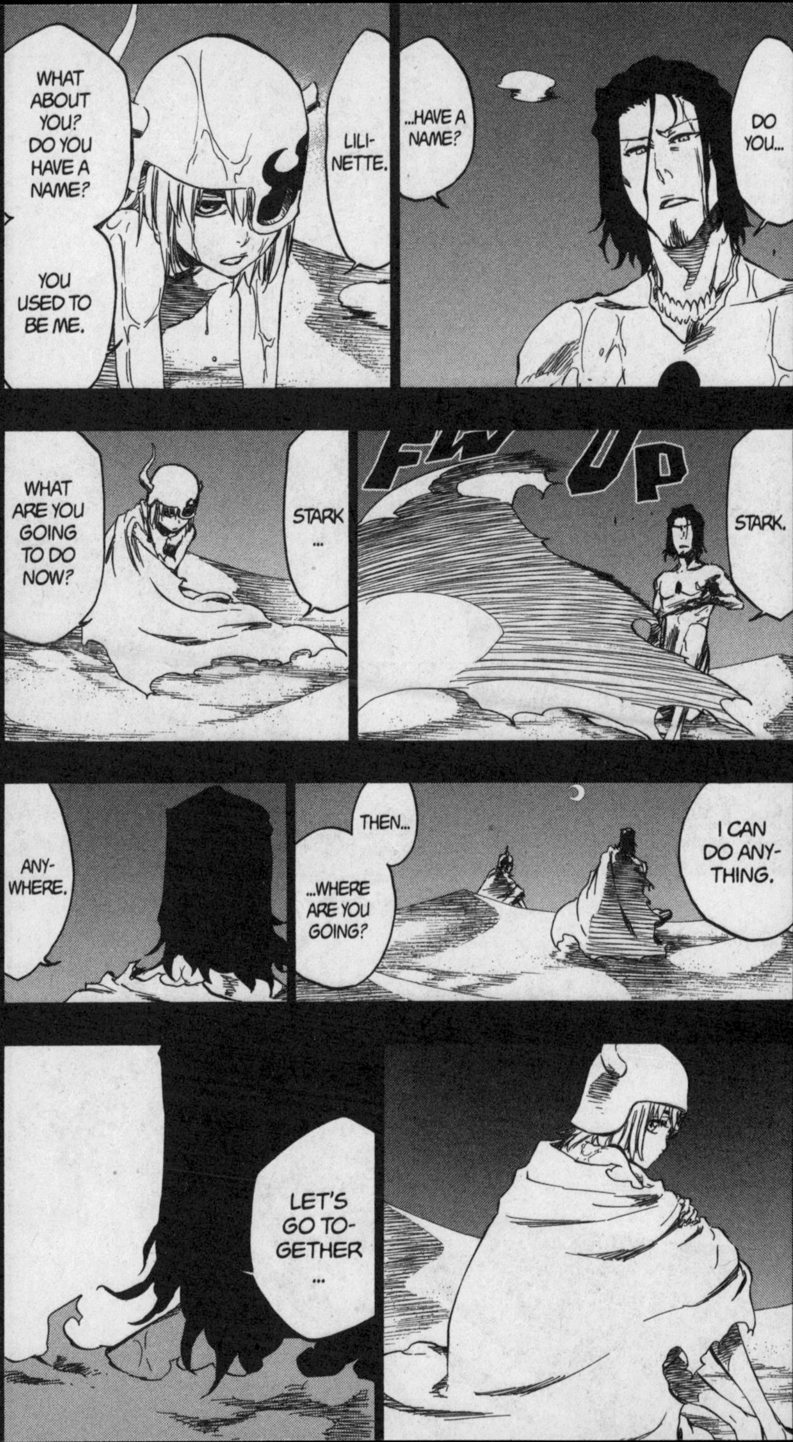
DO YOU...
...HAVE A NAME?
LILI-NETTE.
WHAT ABOUT YOU? DO YOU HAVE A NAME?
YOU USED TO BE ME.
STARK.
FW UP
STARK ...
WHAT ARE YOU GOING TO DO NOW?
I CAN DO ANY-THING.
THEN...
...WHERE ARE YOU GOING?
ANY-WHERE.
LET'S GO TO-GETHER ...

...FOREVER.

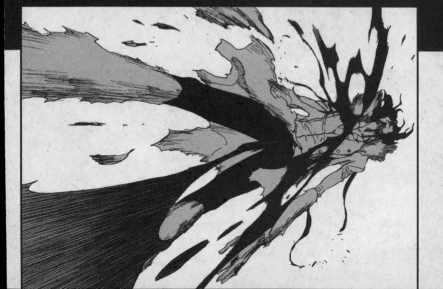

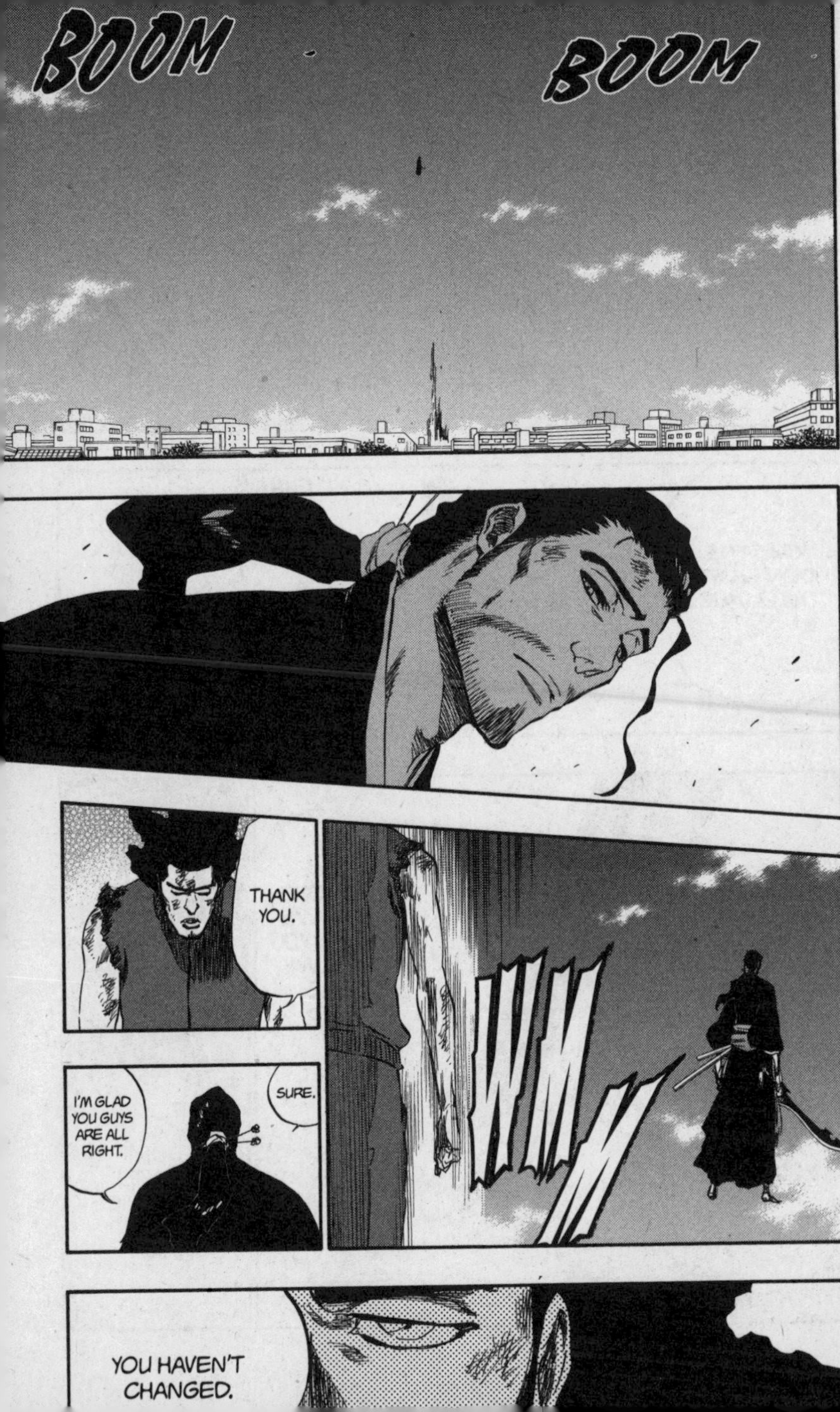
BOOM
BOOM
WMM
THANK YOU.
SURE.
I'M GLAD YOU GUYS ARE ALL RIGHT.
YOU HAVEN'T CHANGED.

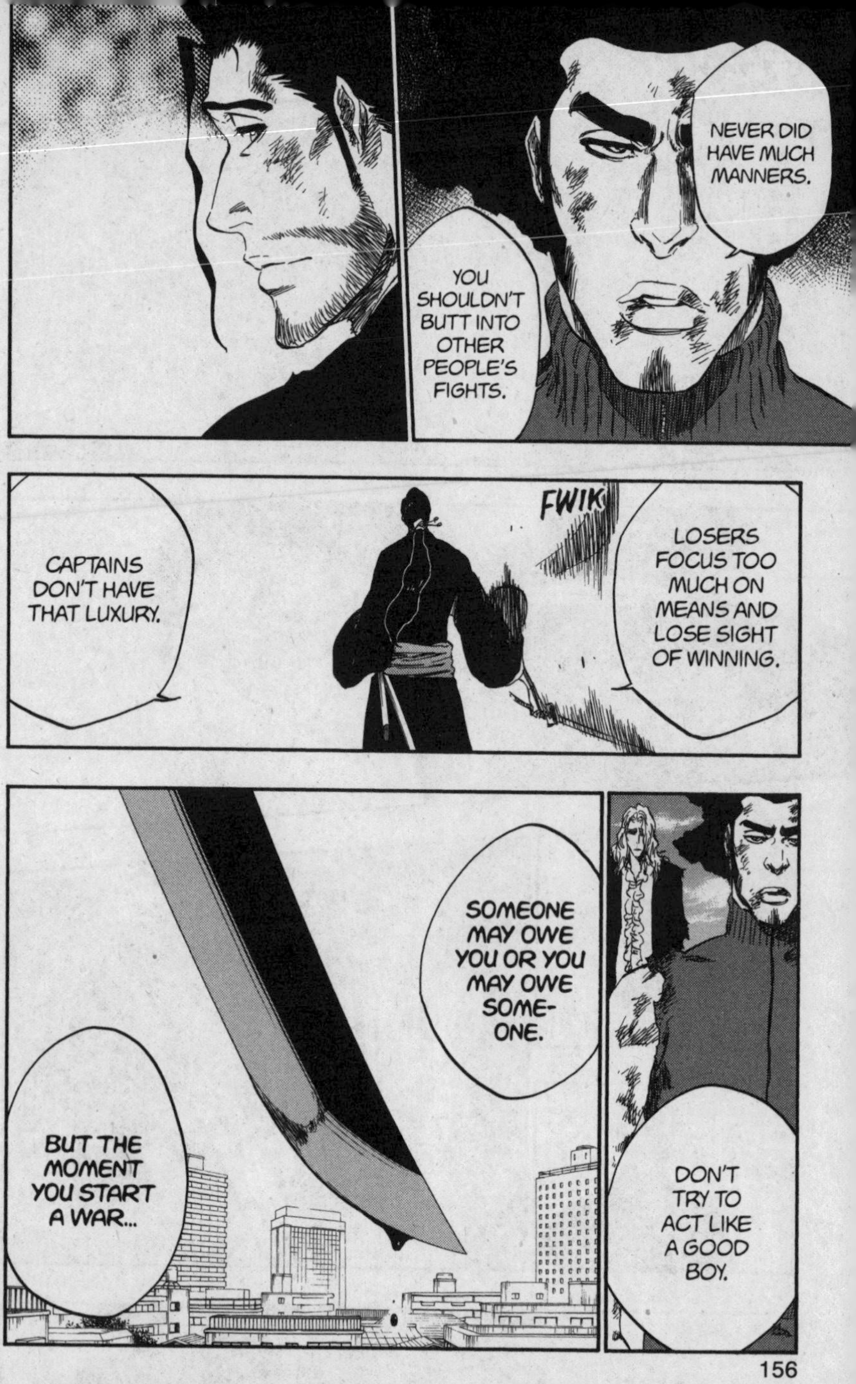
NEVER DID HAVE MUCH MANNERS.
YOU SHOULDN'T BUTT INTO OTHER PEOPLE'S FIGHTS.
FWIK
LOSERS FOCUS TOO MUCH ON MEANS AND LOSE SIGHT OF WINNING.
CAPTAINS DON'T HAVE THAT LUXURY.
DON'T TRY TO ACT LIKE A GOOD BOY.
SOMEONE MAY OWE YOU OR YOU MAY OWE SOME-ONE.
BUT THE MOMENT YOU START A WAR...

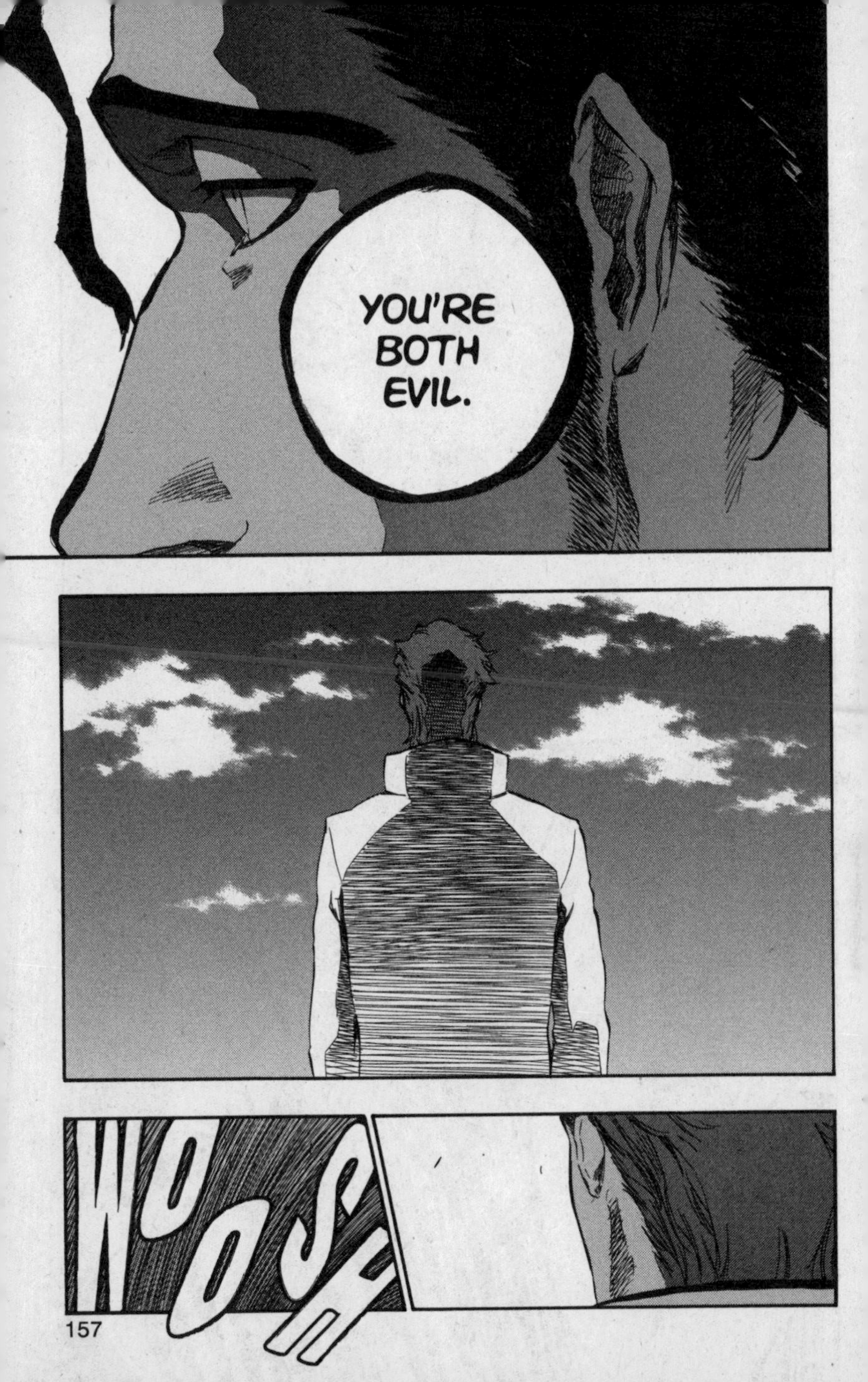
YOU'RE BOTH EVIL.
WHOOSH

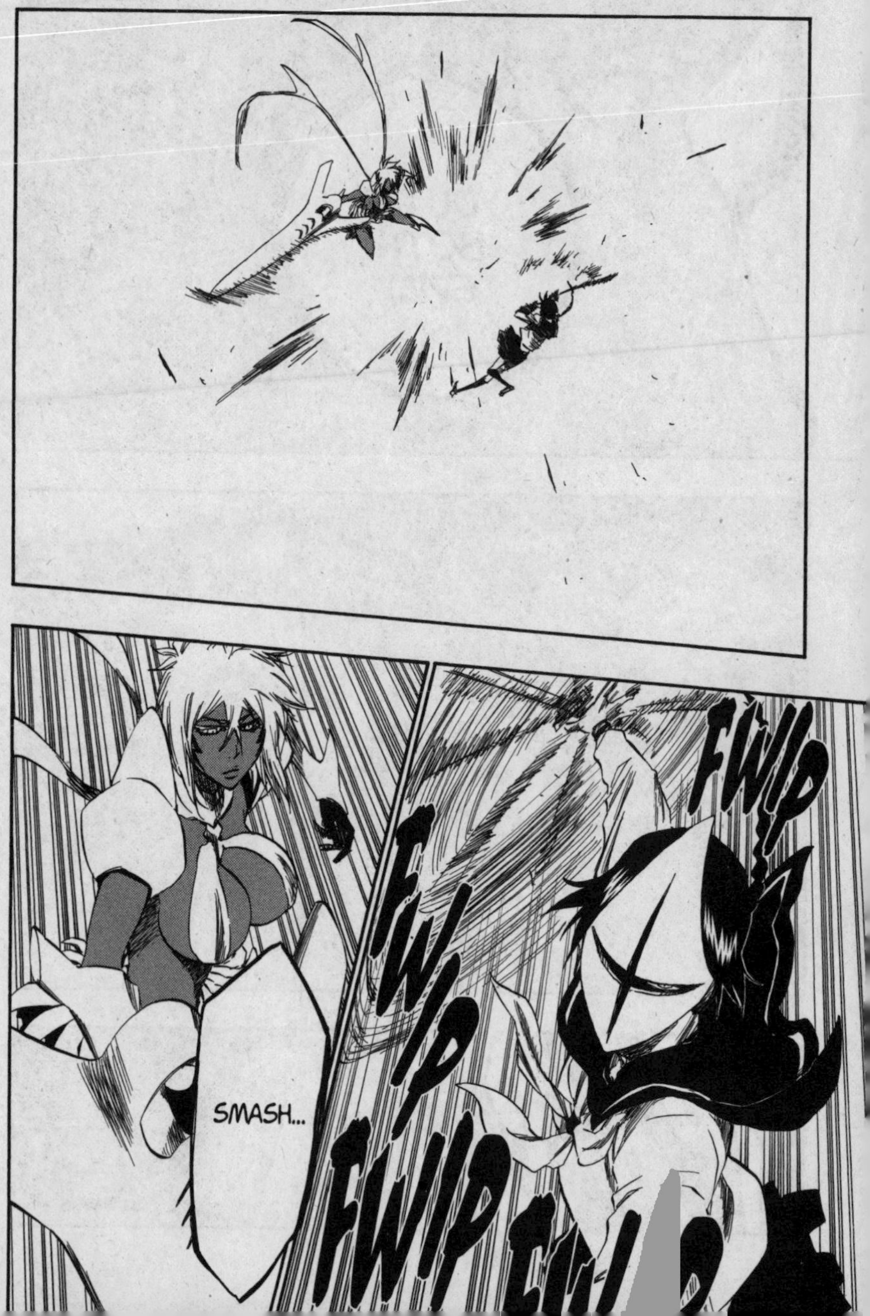
FWIP
FWIP
FWIP
SMASH...

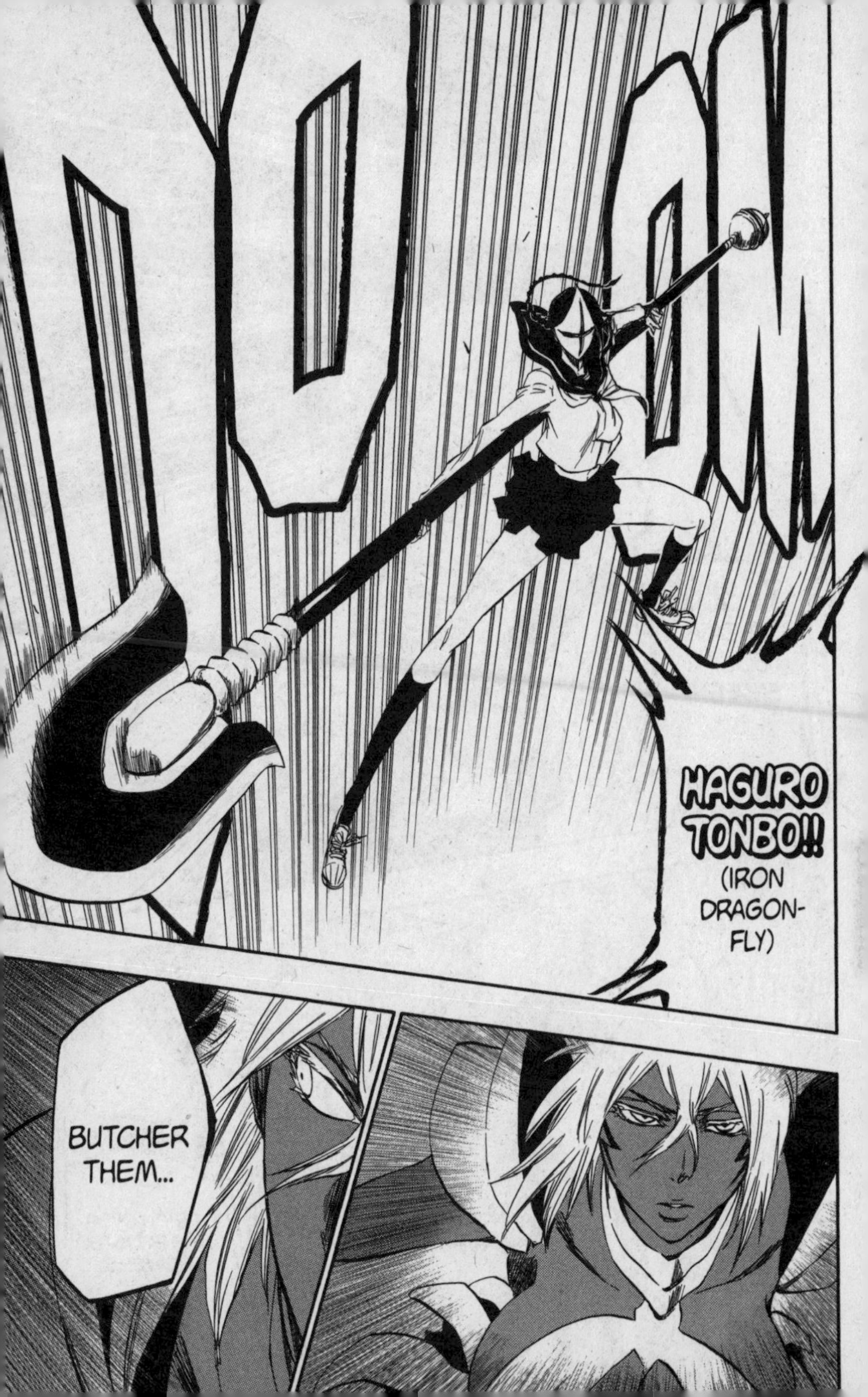
HAGURO TONBO!!
(IRON DRAGON-FLY)
BUTCHER THEM...

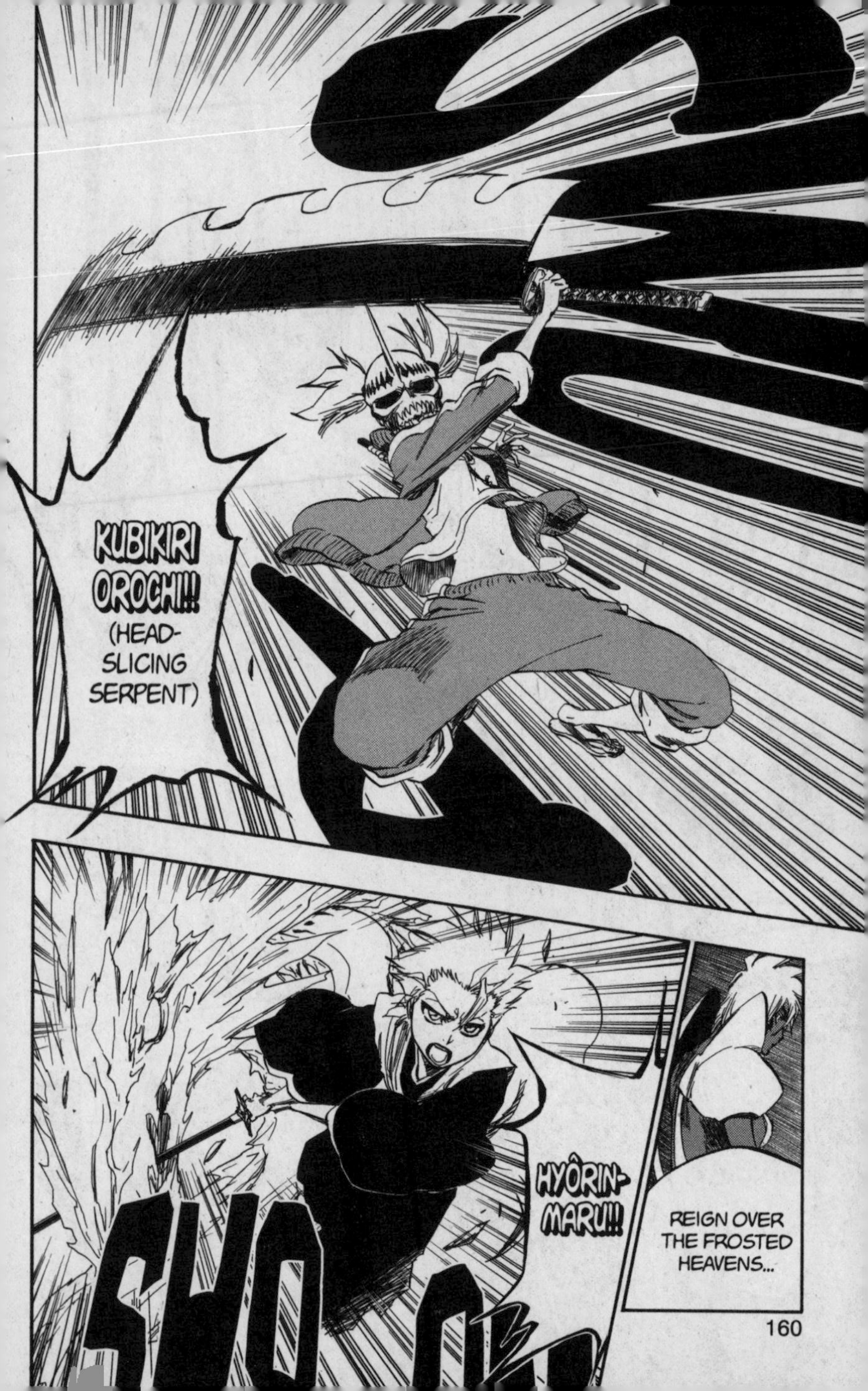
KUBIKIRI OROCHI!!! (HEAD-SLICING SERPENT)
REIGN OVER THE FROSTED HEAVENS...
HYÔRIN-MARU!!!

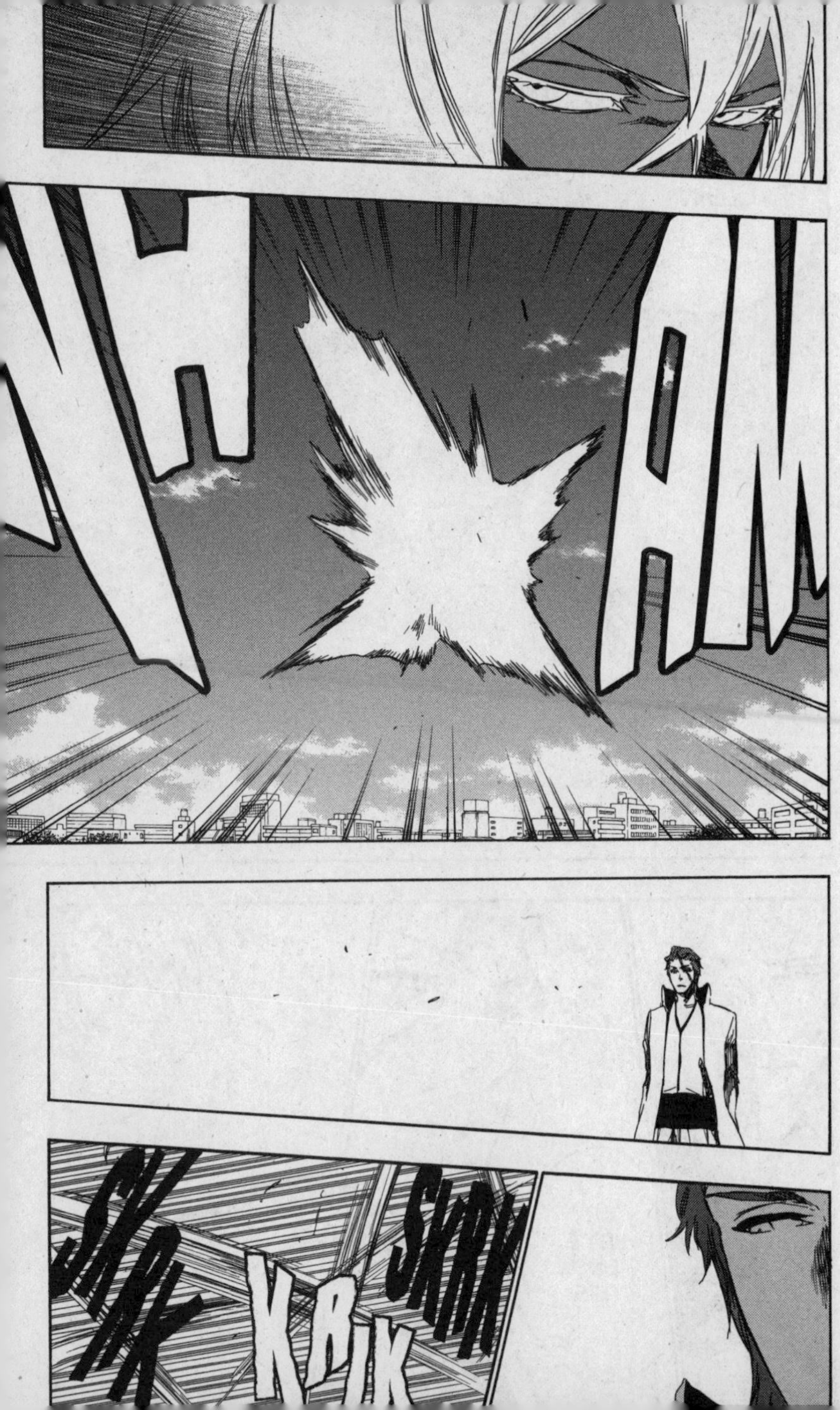
SKRK
KRIK
SKRK

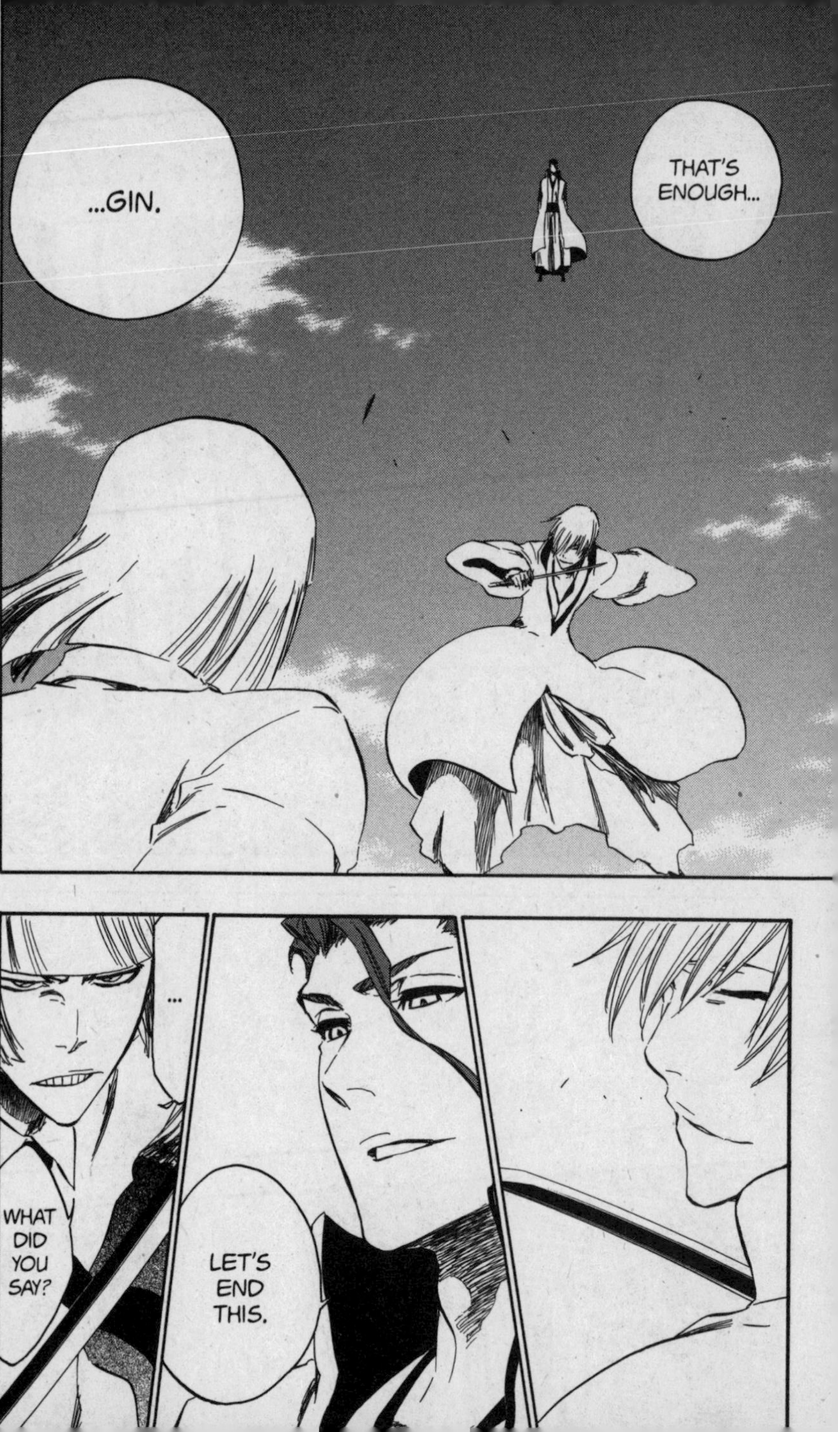
THAT'S ENOUGH...
...GIN.
LET'S END THIS.
...
WHAT DID YOU SAY?

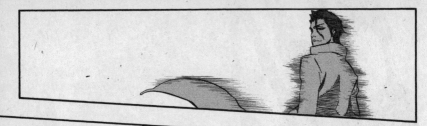

LORD
...

AIZEN
...

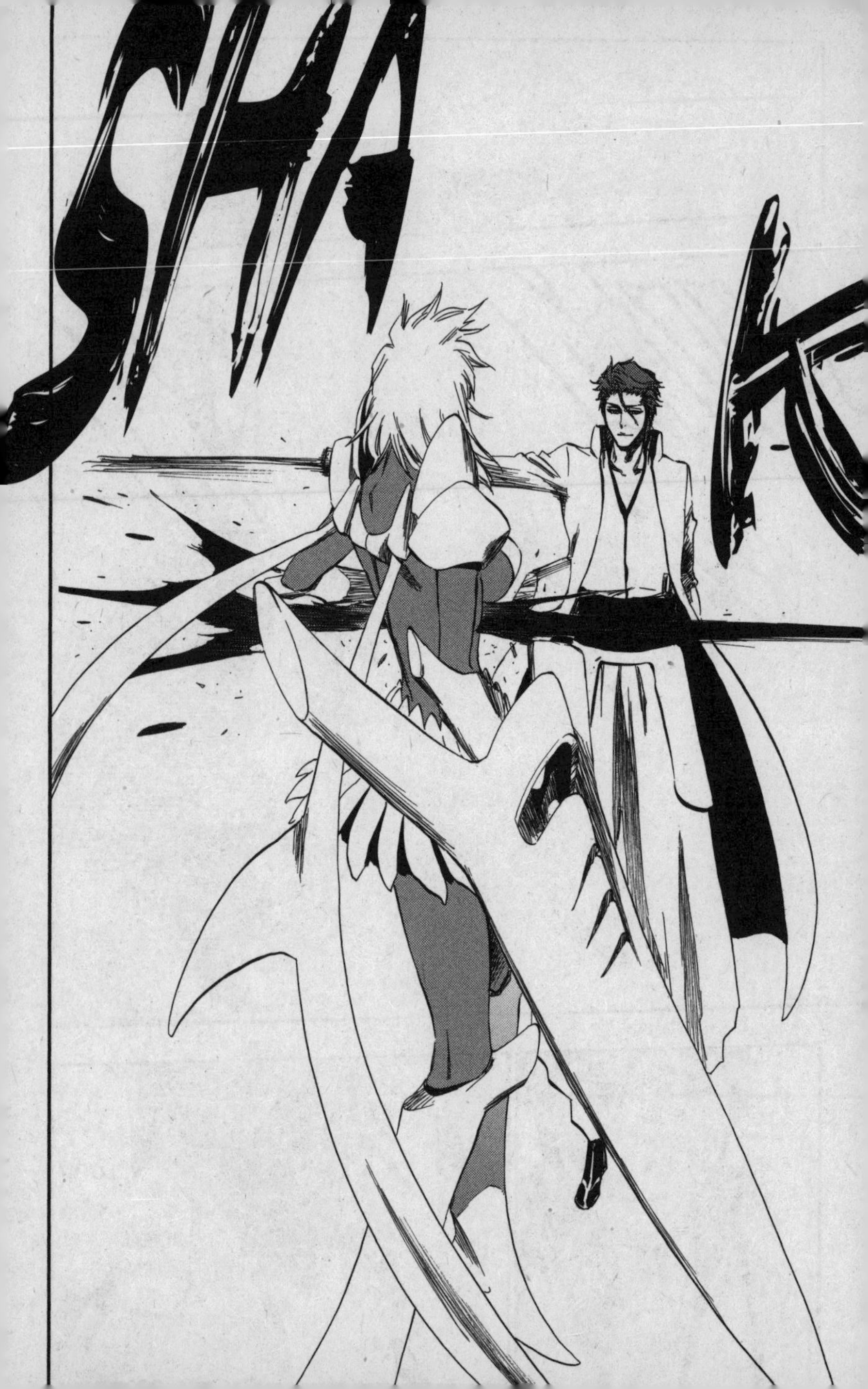
SHAK

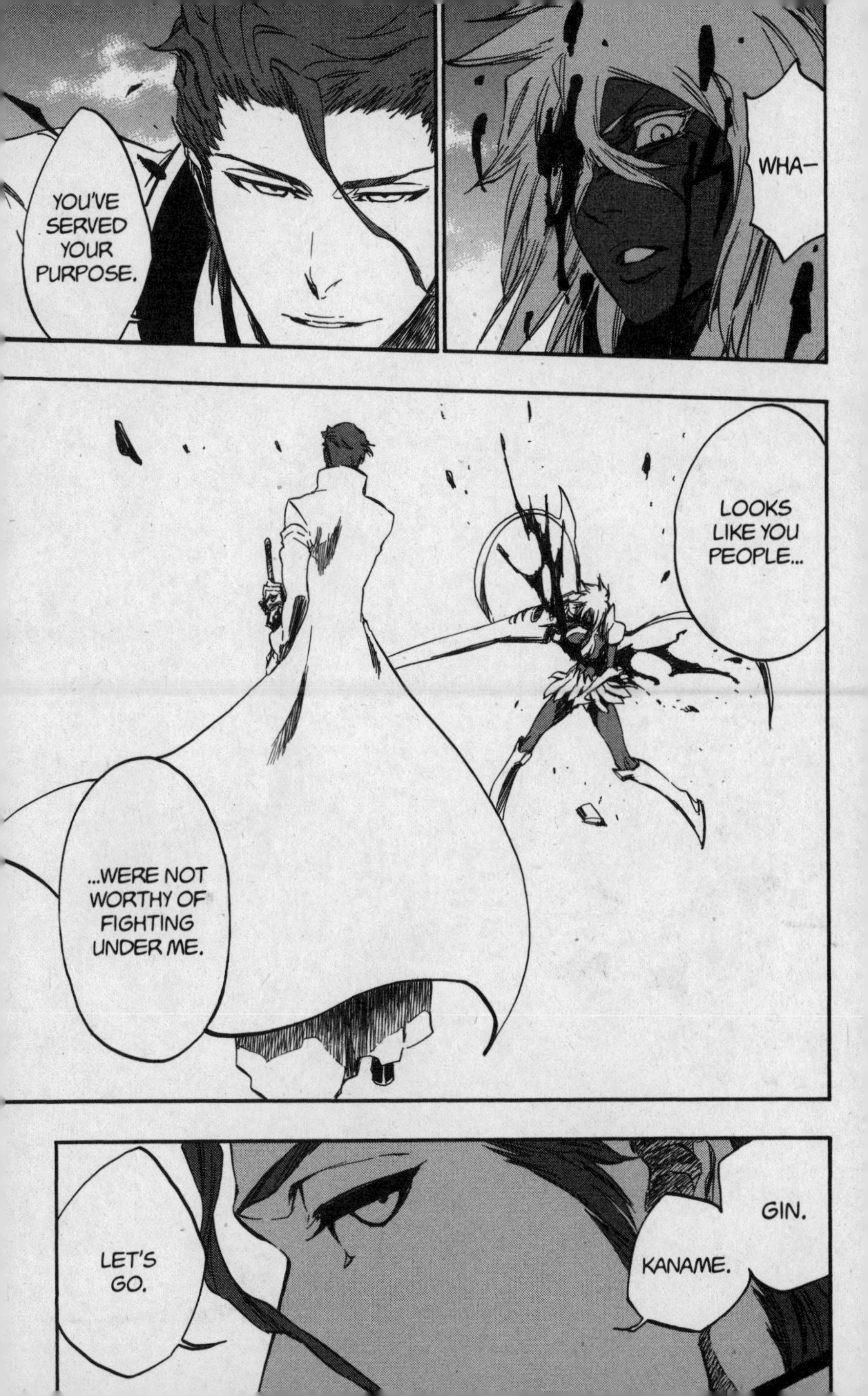
WHA—
YOU'VE SERVED YOUR PURPOSE.
LOOKS LIKE YOU PEOPLE...
...WERE NOT WORTHY OF FIGHTING UNDER ME.
GIN.
KANAME.
LET'S GO.

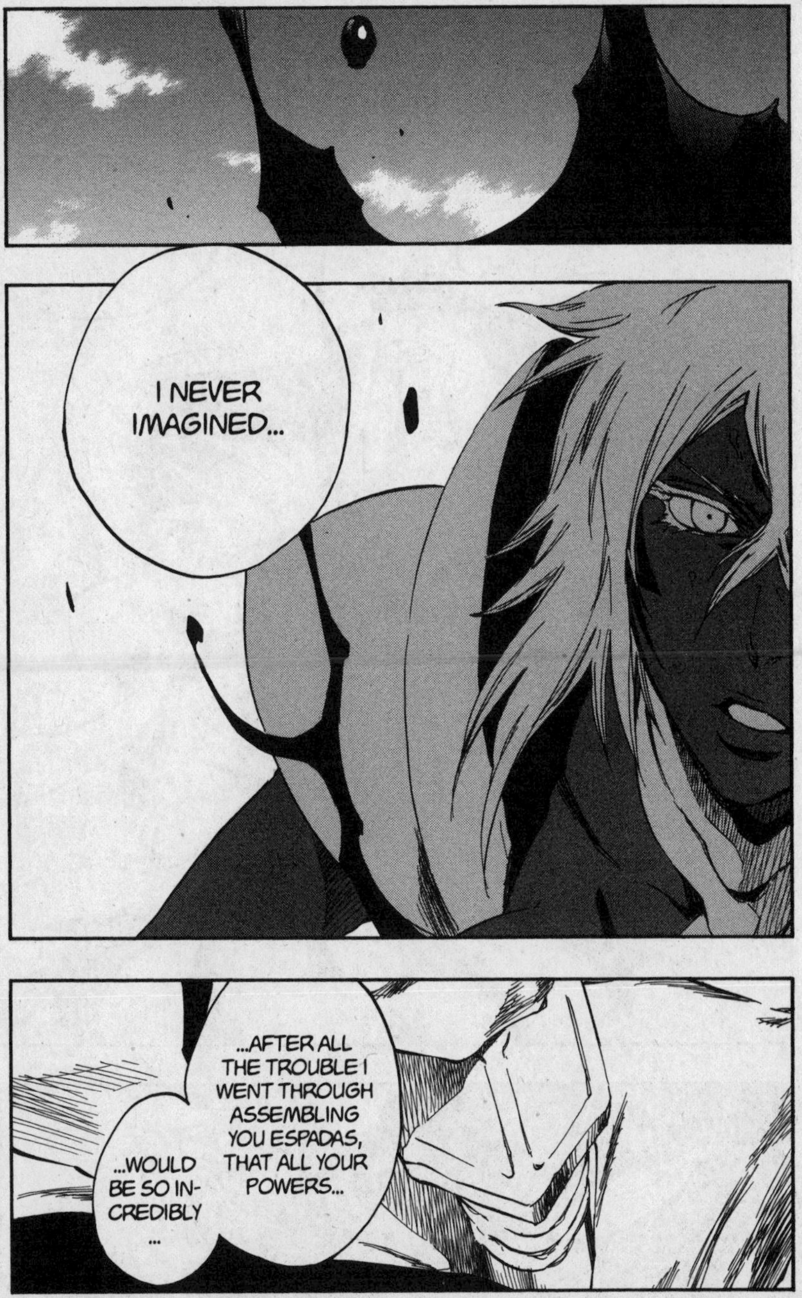
I NEVER IMAGINED...
...AFTER ALL THE TROUBLE I WENT THROUGH ASSEMBLING YOU ESPADAS, THAT ALL YOUR POWERS...
...WOULD BE SO IN-CREDIBLY ...

376. EXecution, EXtinction 2

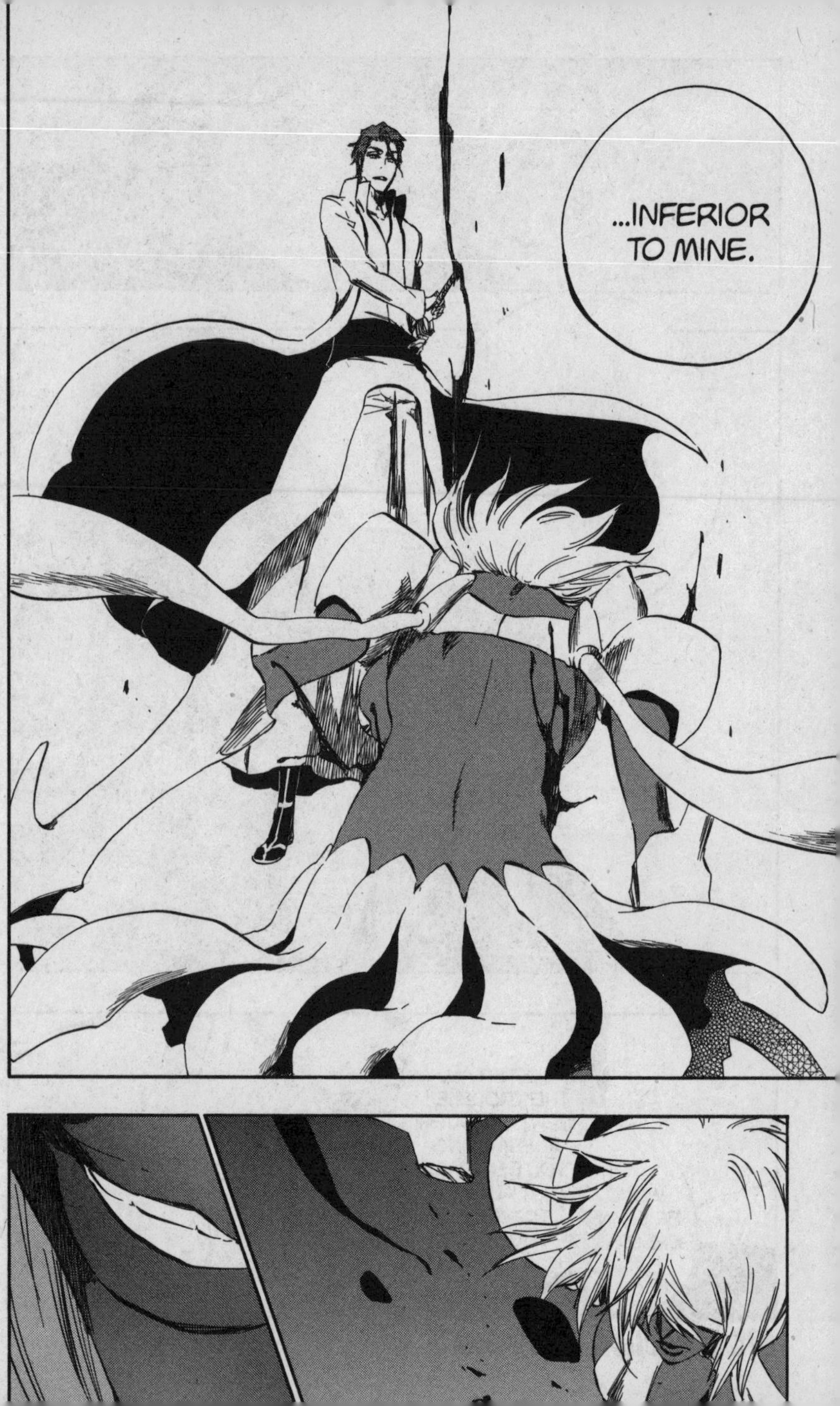
...INFERIOR TO MINE.

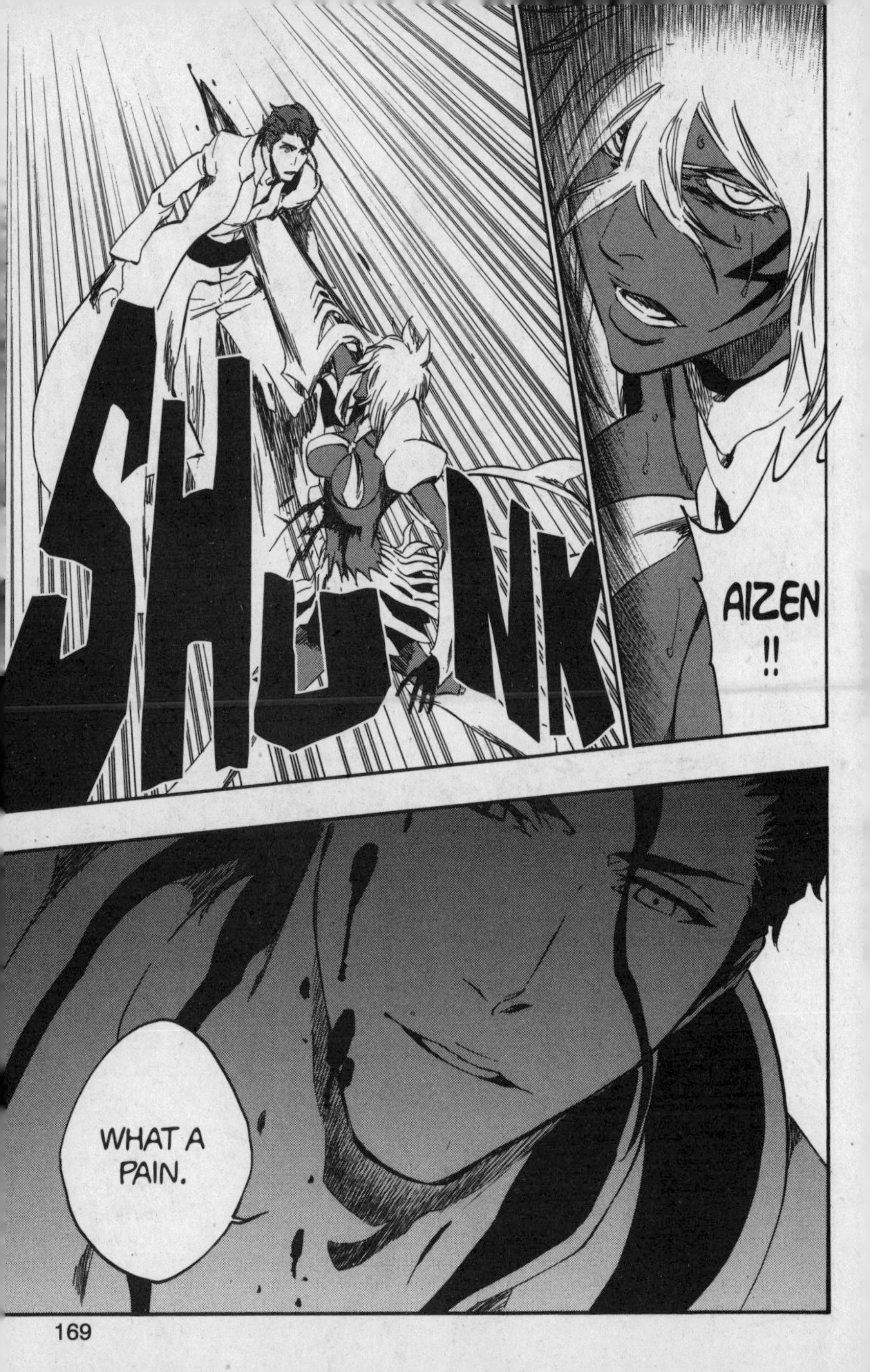
AIZEN !!
SHUNK
WHAT A PAIN.

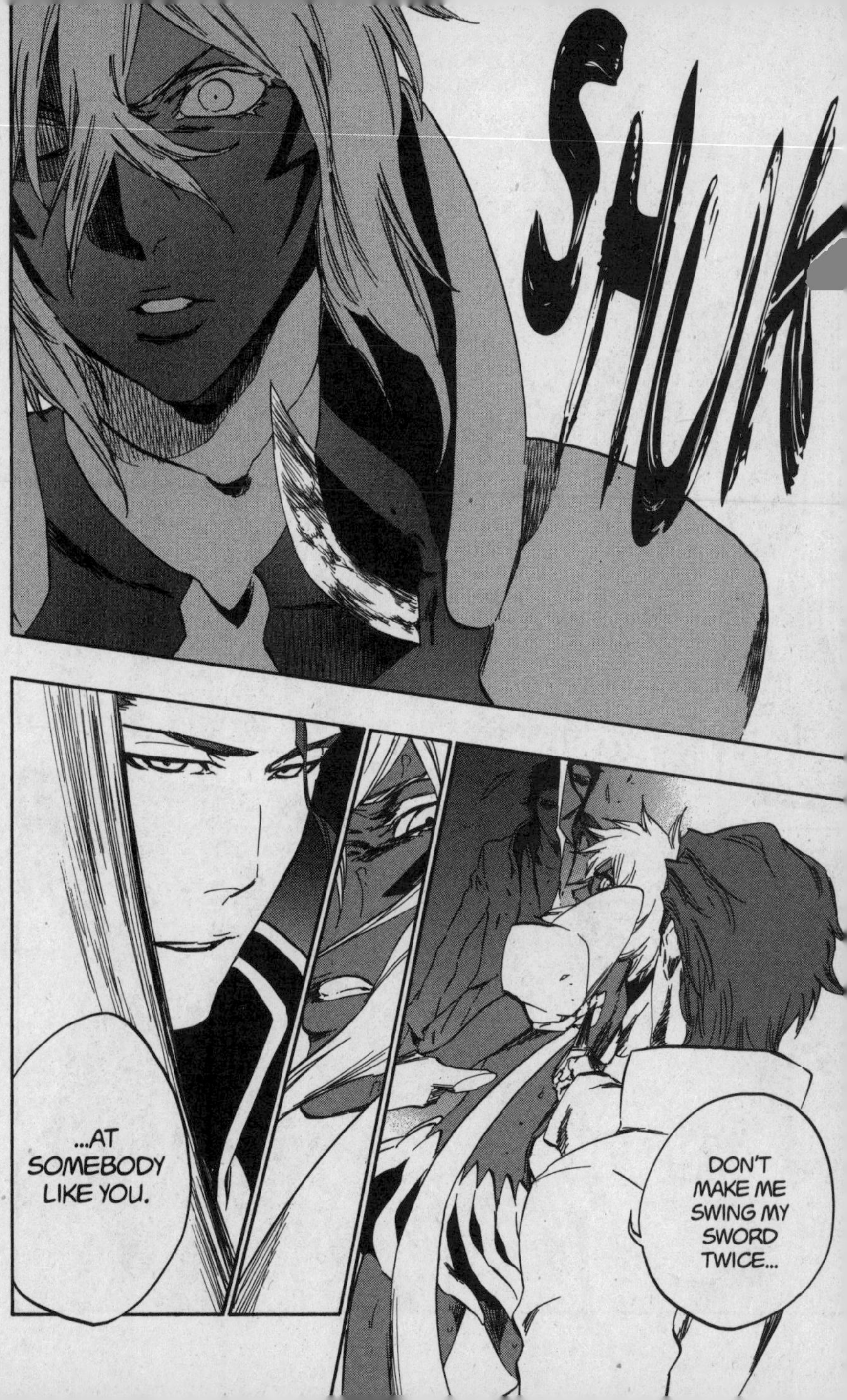
SHUK
DON'T MAKE ME SWING MY SWORD TWICE...
...AT SOMEBODY LIKE YOU.

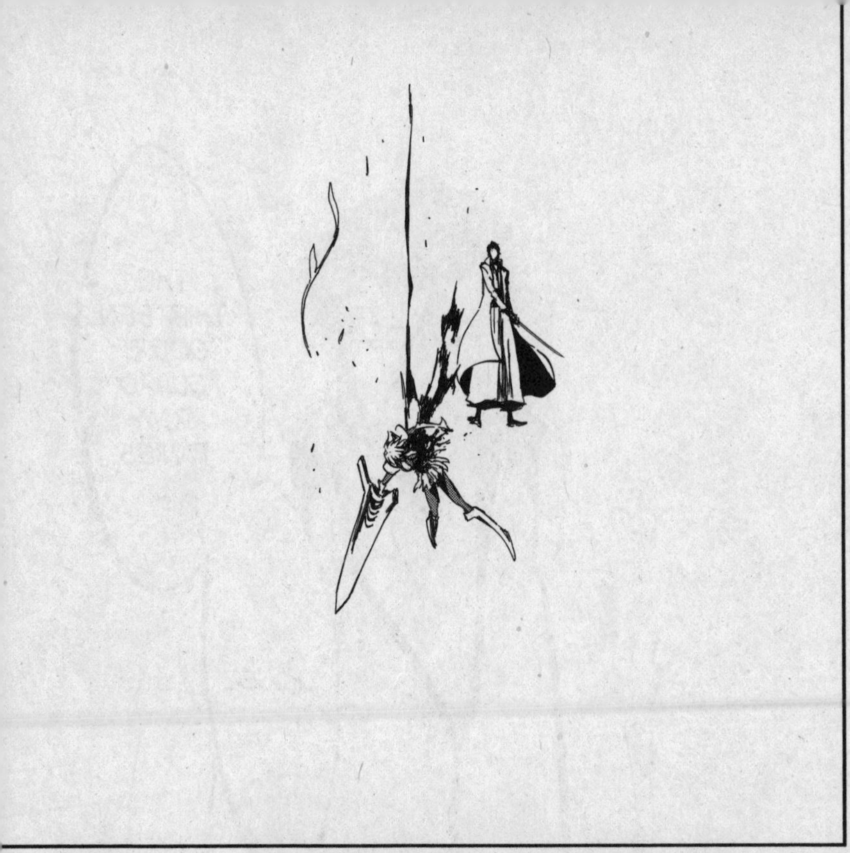

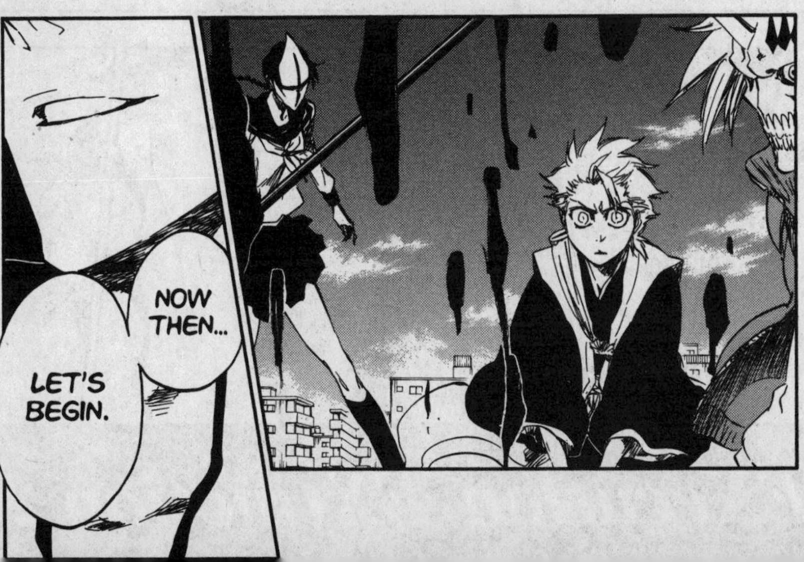
NOW THEN...
LET'S BEGIN.

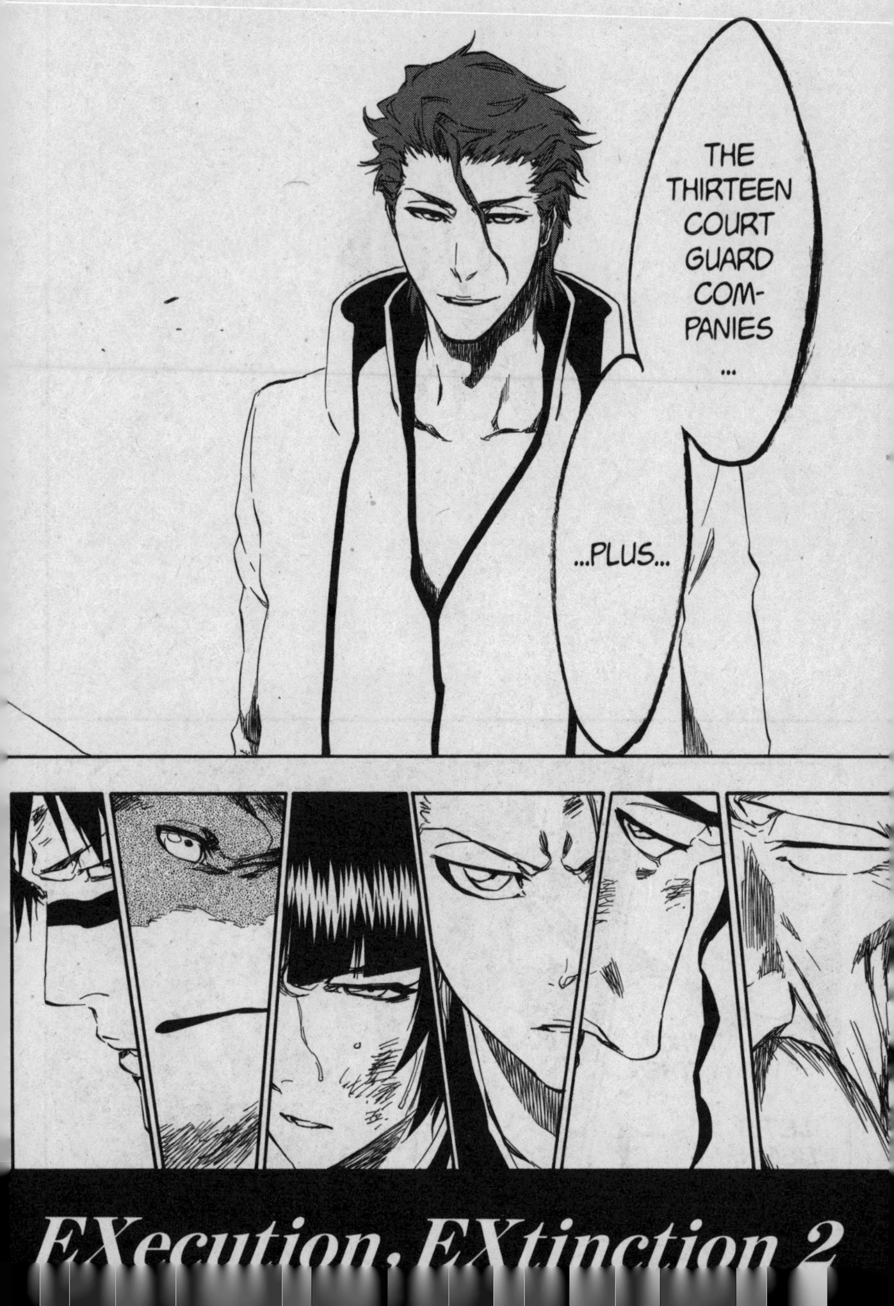
THE THIRTEEN COURT GUARD COM-PANIES ...
...PLUS...

EXecution, EXtinction 2

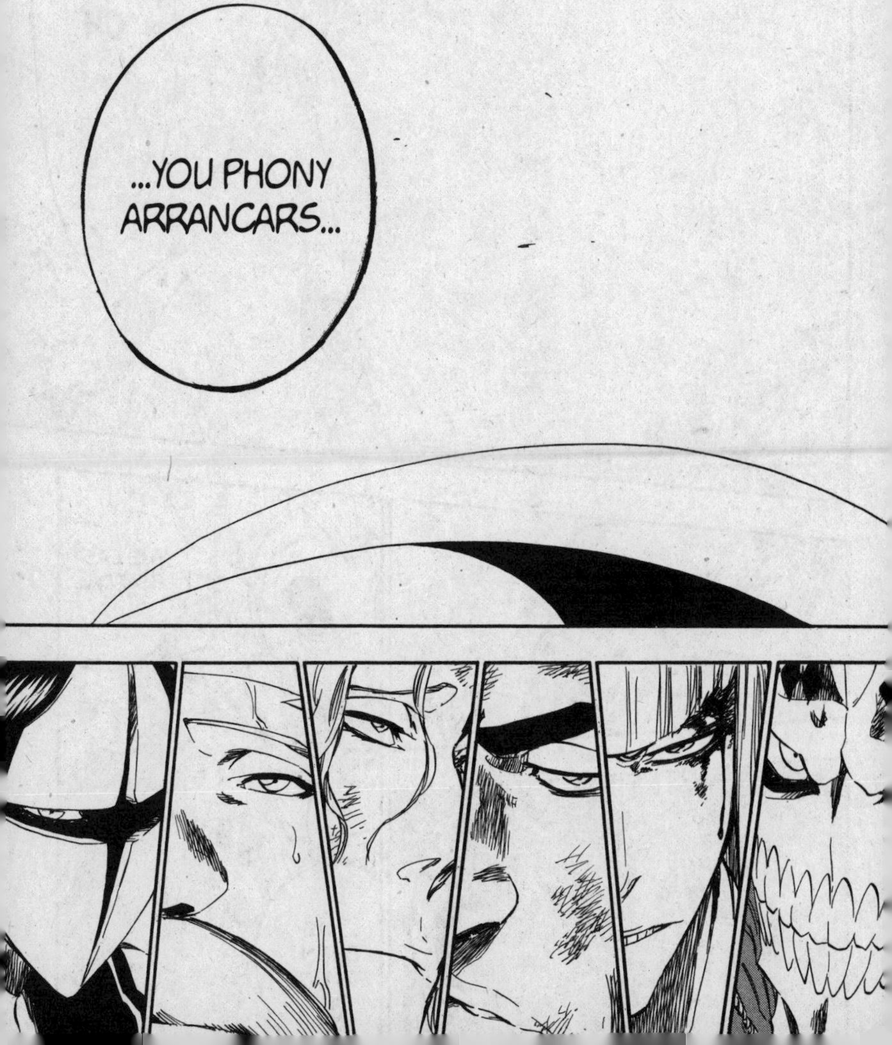
...YOU PHONY ARRANCARS...

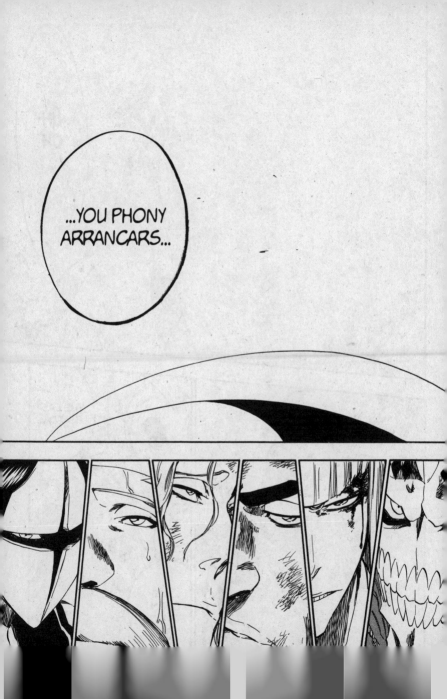

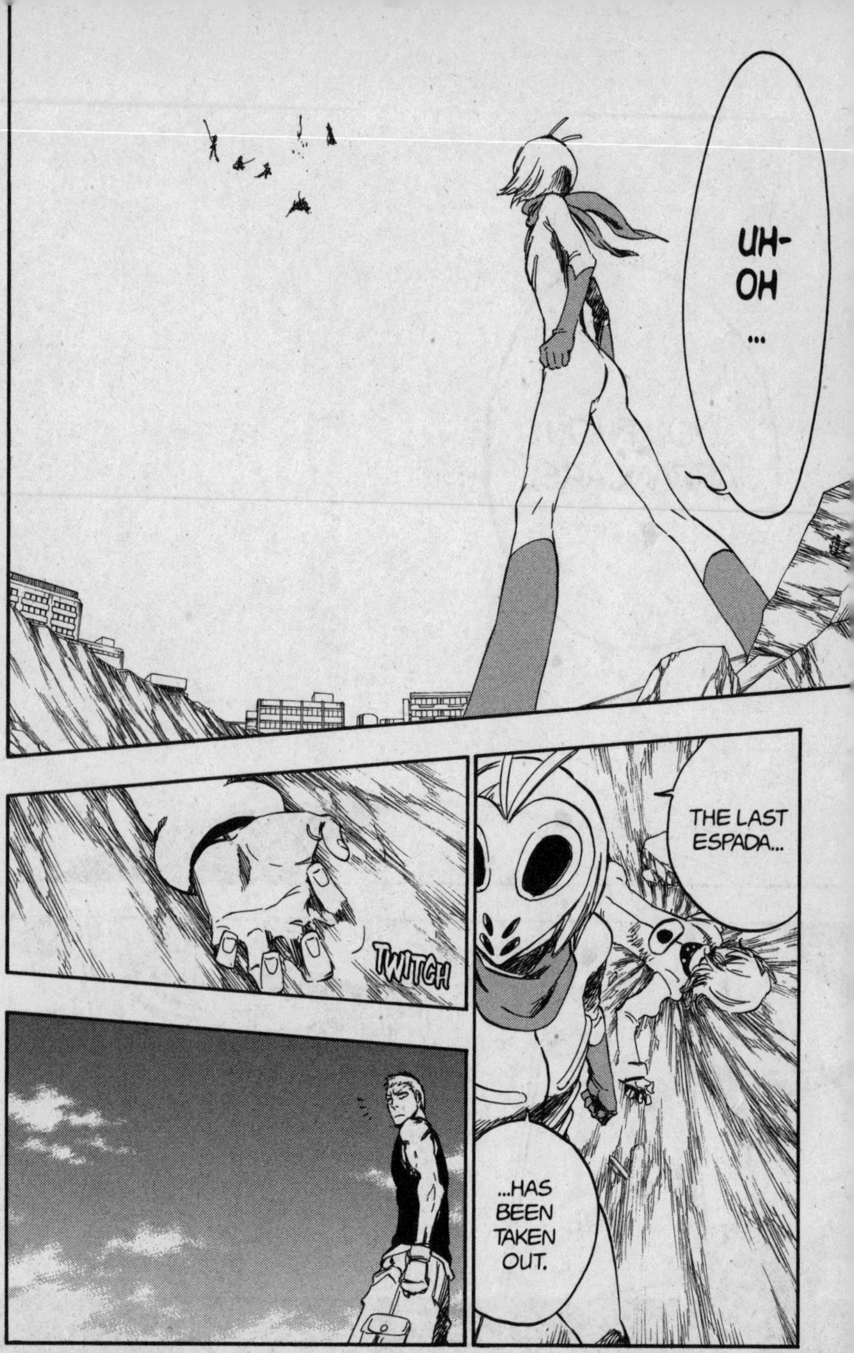
UH-OH ...
THE LAST ESPADA...
...HAS BEEN TAKEN OUT.
TWITCH

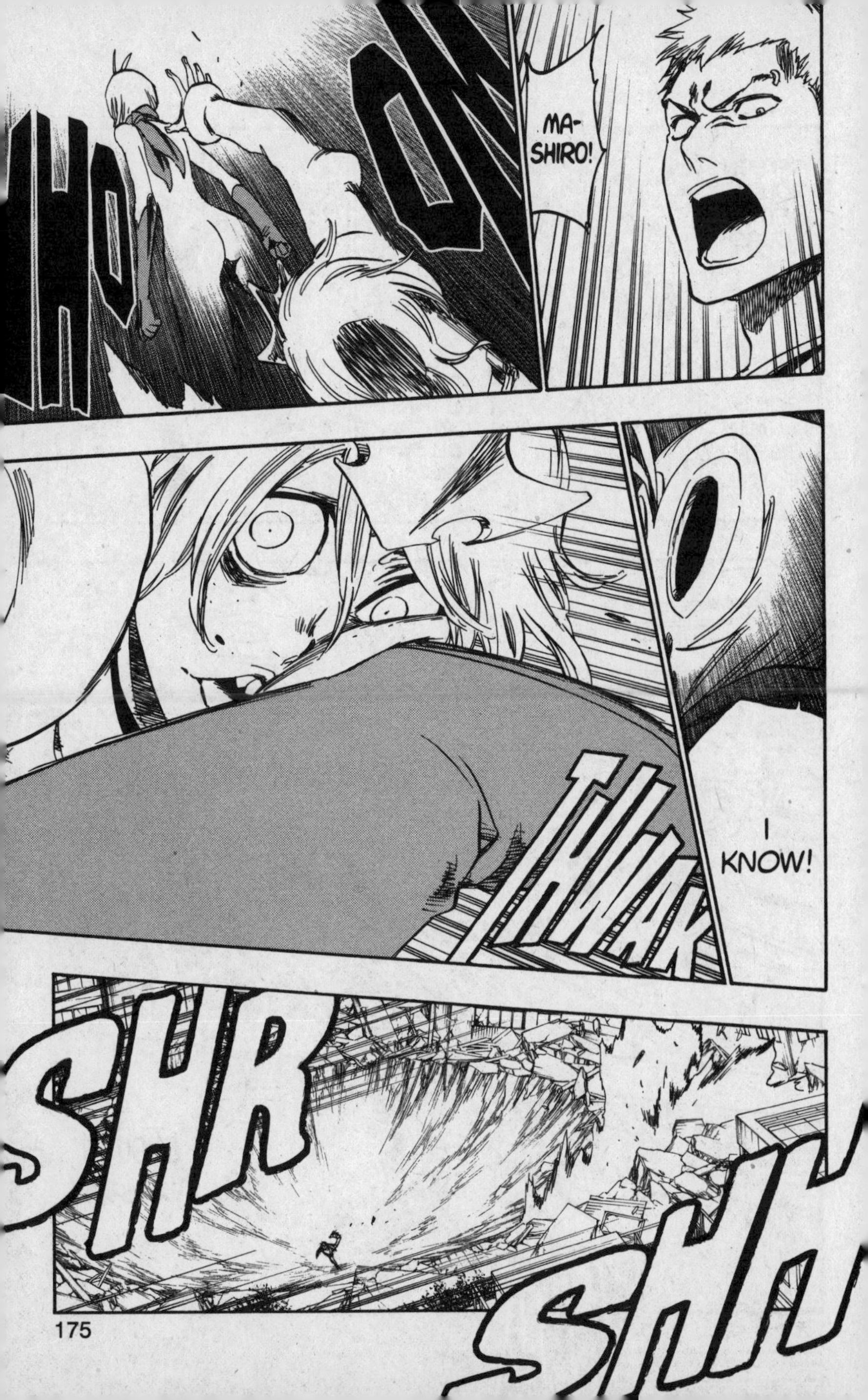
MA-SHIRO!
I KNOW!
THWAK
SHR
SHU

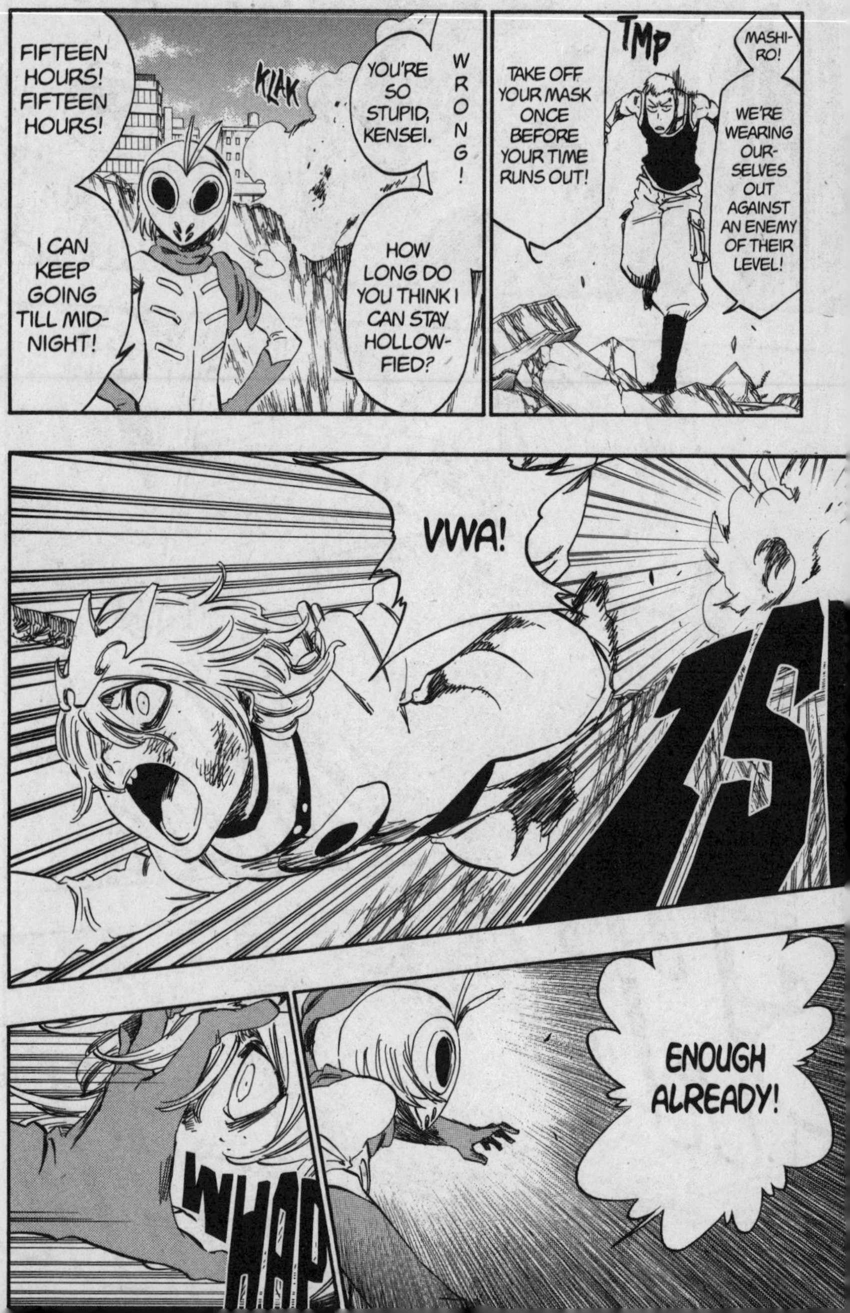
TMP
MASHIRO!
WE'RE WEARING OURSELVES OUT AGAINST AN ENEMY OF THEIR LEVEL!
TAKE OFF YOUR MASK ONCE BEFORE YOUR TIME RUNS OUT!
WRONG!
YOU'RE SO STUPID, KENSEI.
HOW LONG DO YOU THINK I CAN STAY HOLLOWFIED?
KLAK
FIFTEEN HOURS! FIFTEEN HOURS!
I CAN KEEP GOING TILL MIDNIGHT!
VWA!
ENOUGH ALREADY!
WHAP

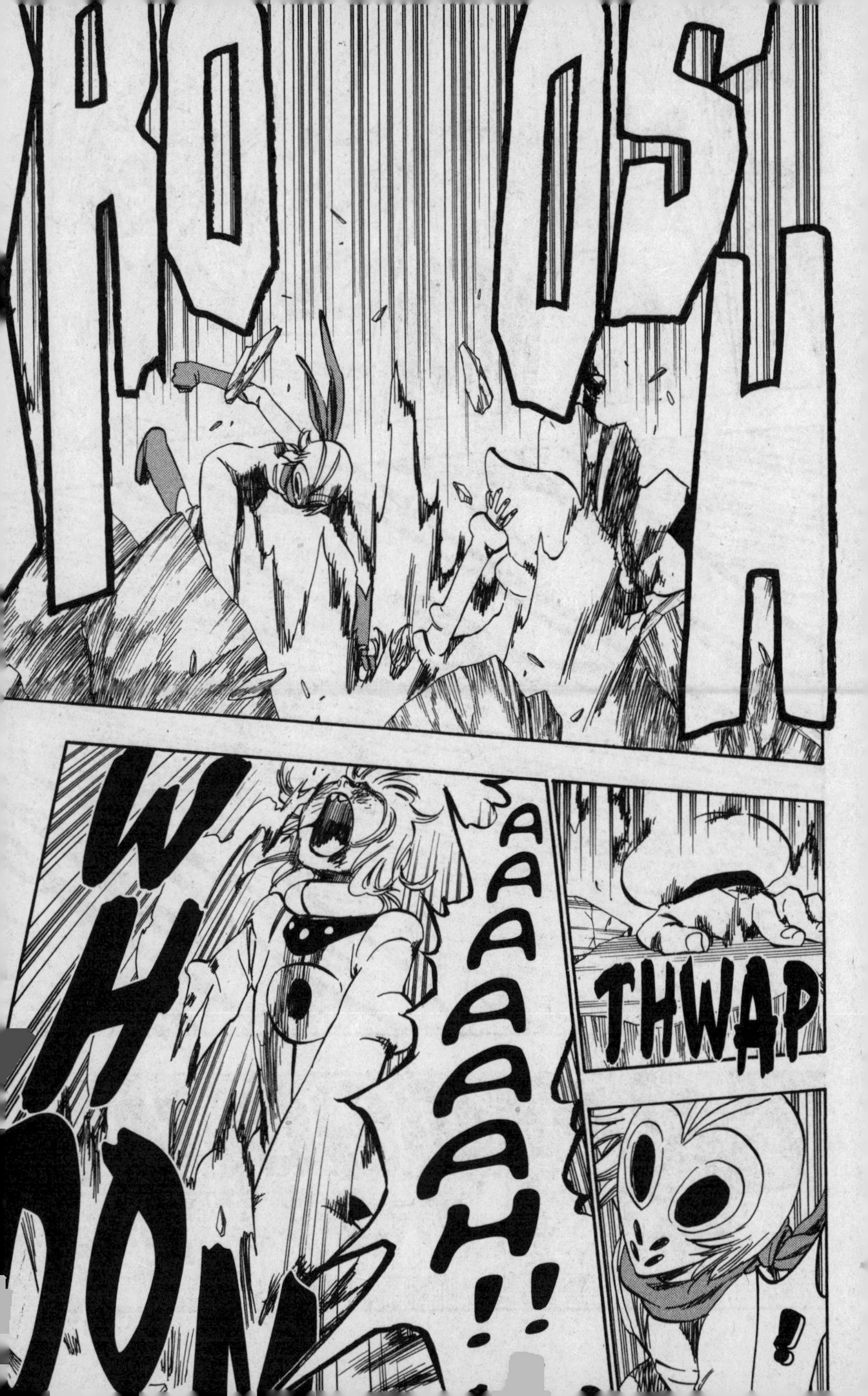
AAAAAAH!!
THWAP
!

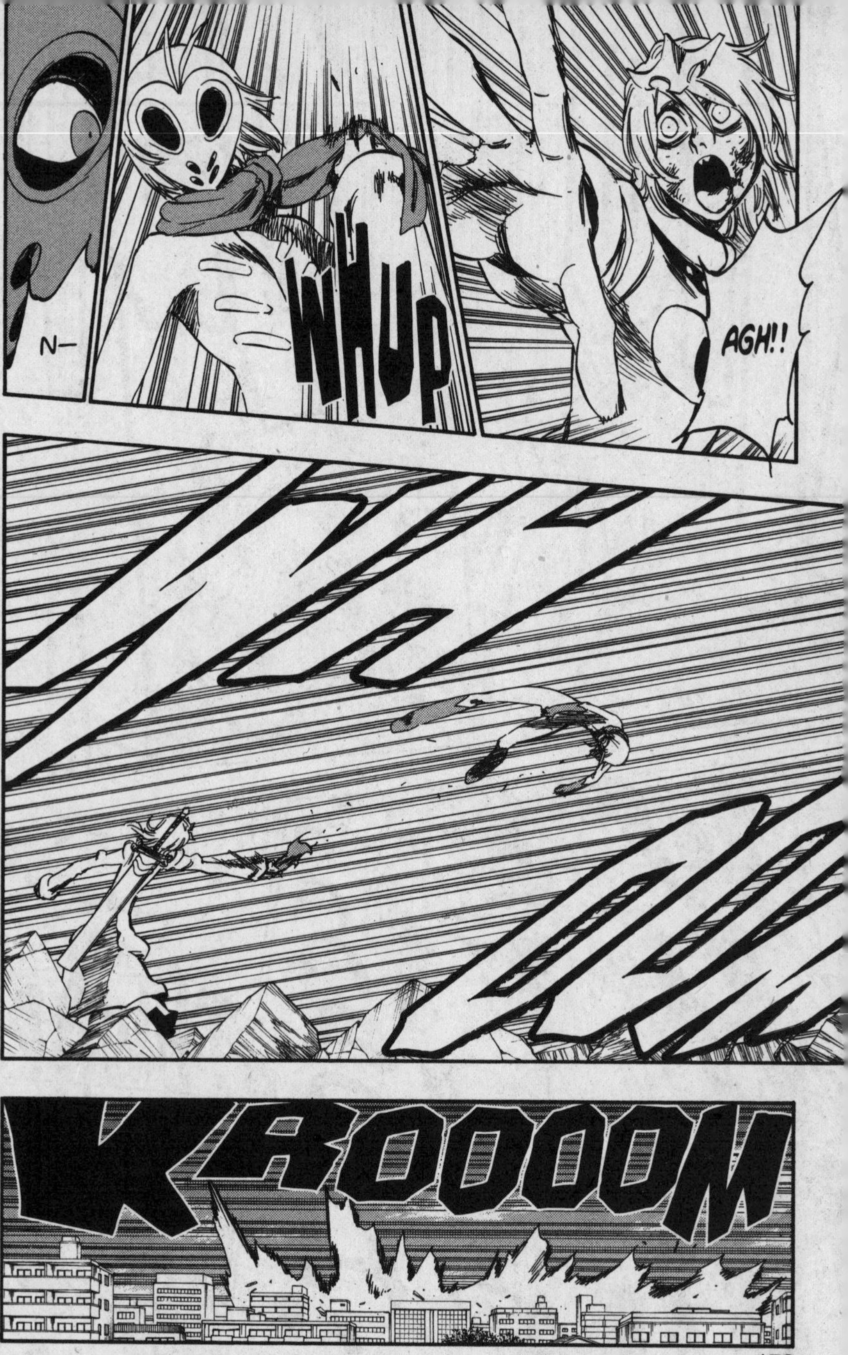
AGH!!
WHUP
N—
KROOOOM

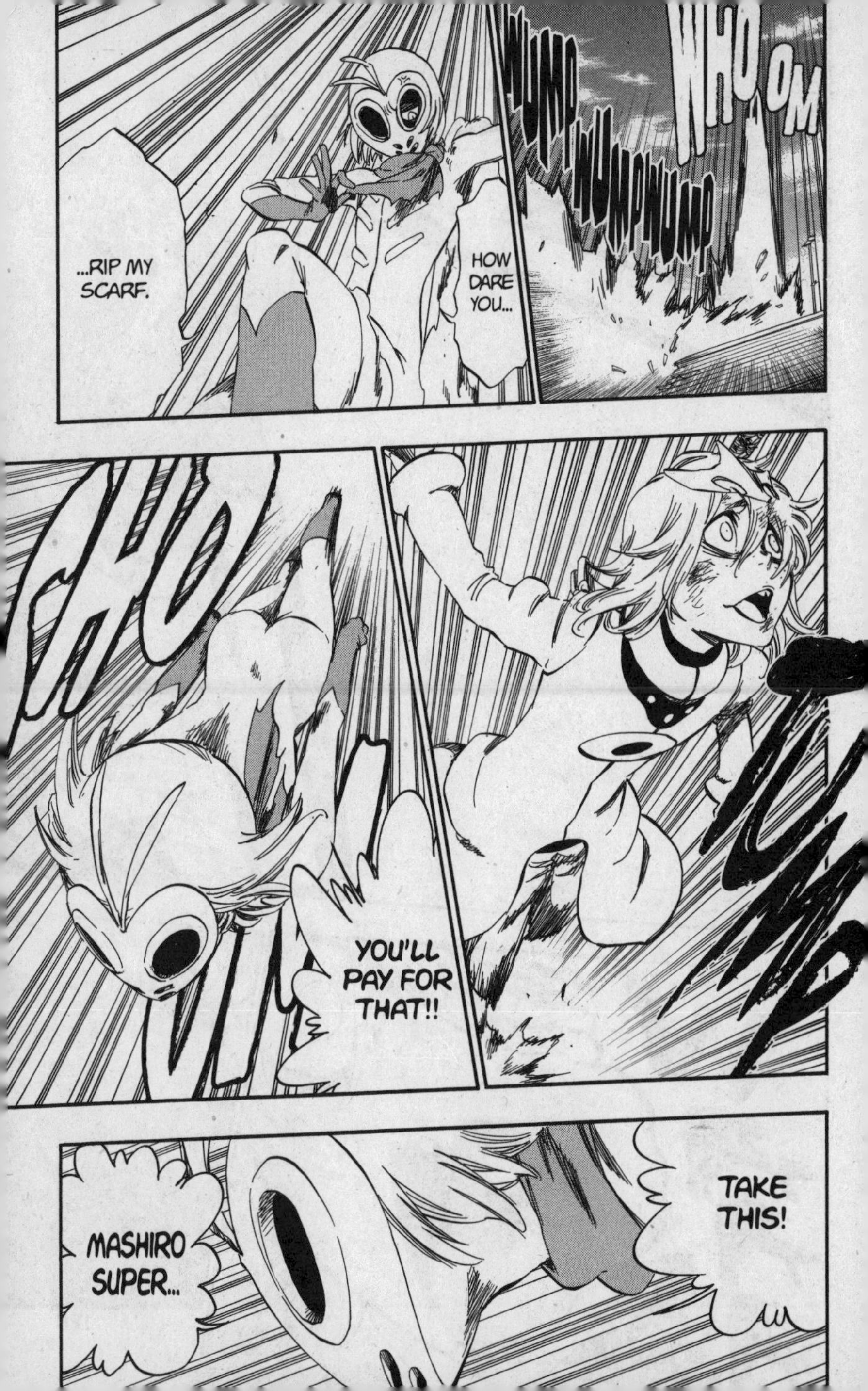
WHOOM
WUMP
WUMPWUMPWUMP
HOW DARE YOU...
...RIP MY SCARF.
YOU'LL PAY FOR THAT!!
TAKE THIS!
MASHIRO SUPER...

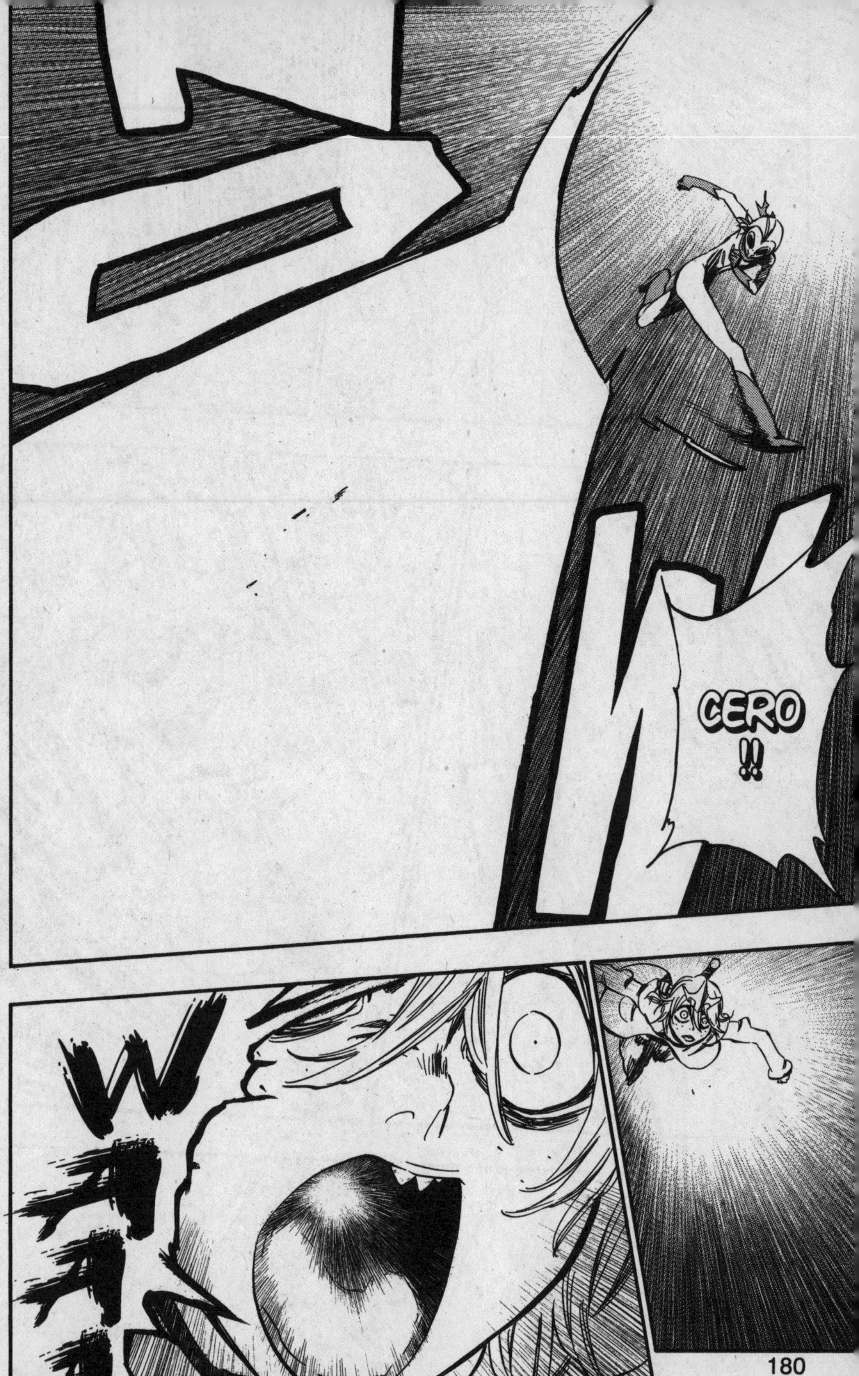
CERO !!

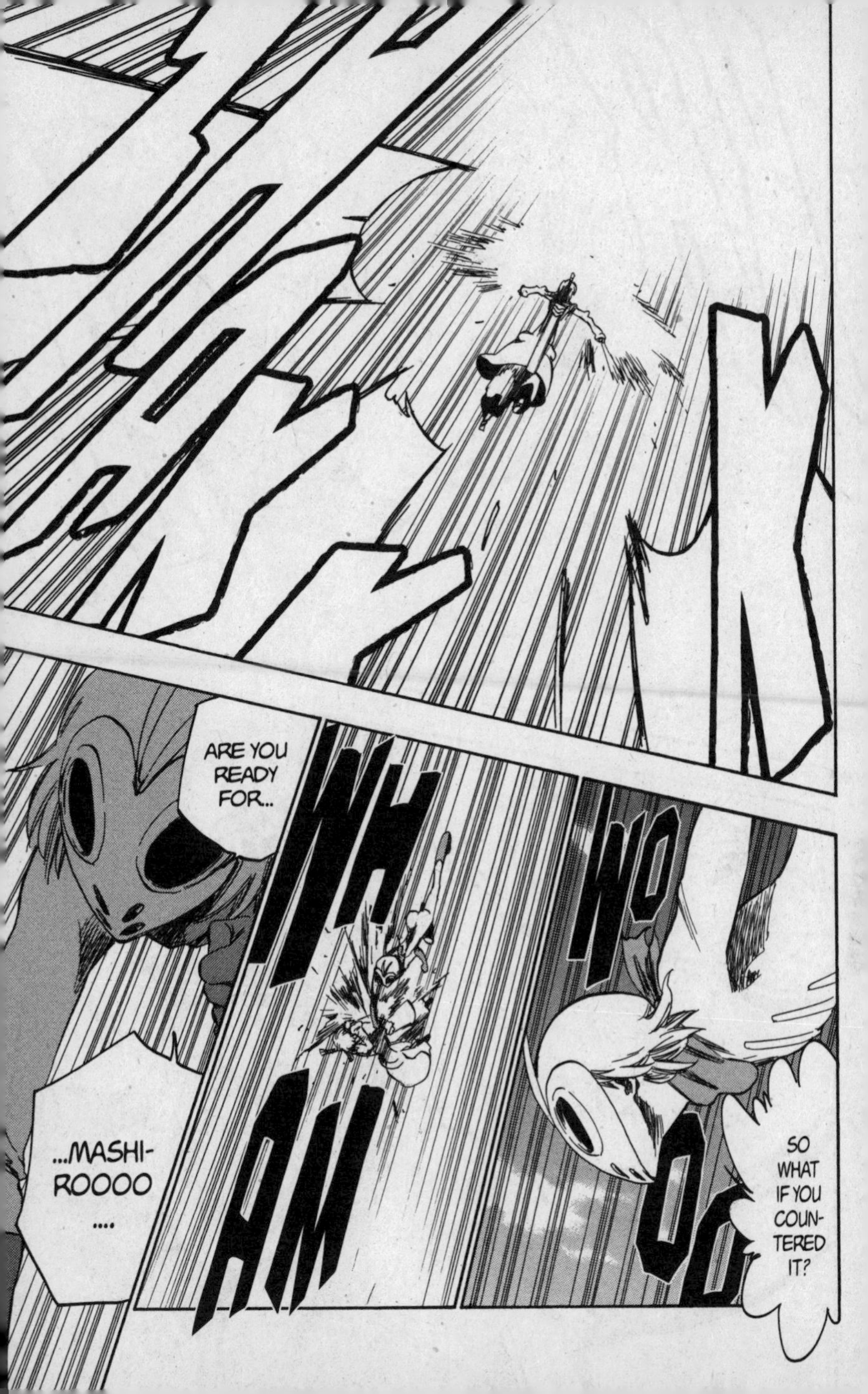
SO WHAT IF YOU COUN-TERED IT?
WHAM
ARE YOU READY FOR...
...MASHI-ROOOO ....

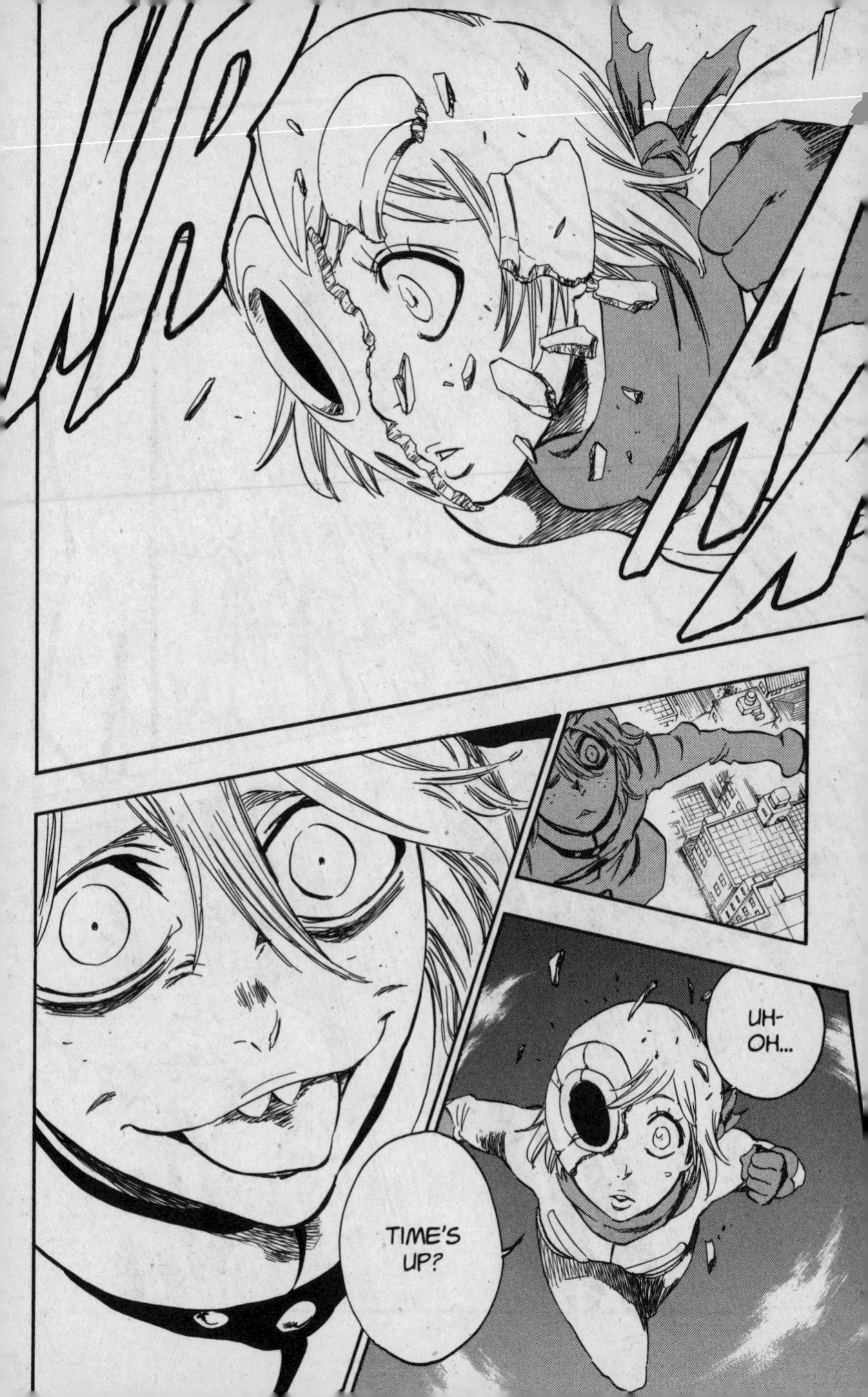
UH-OH...
TIME'S UP?

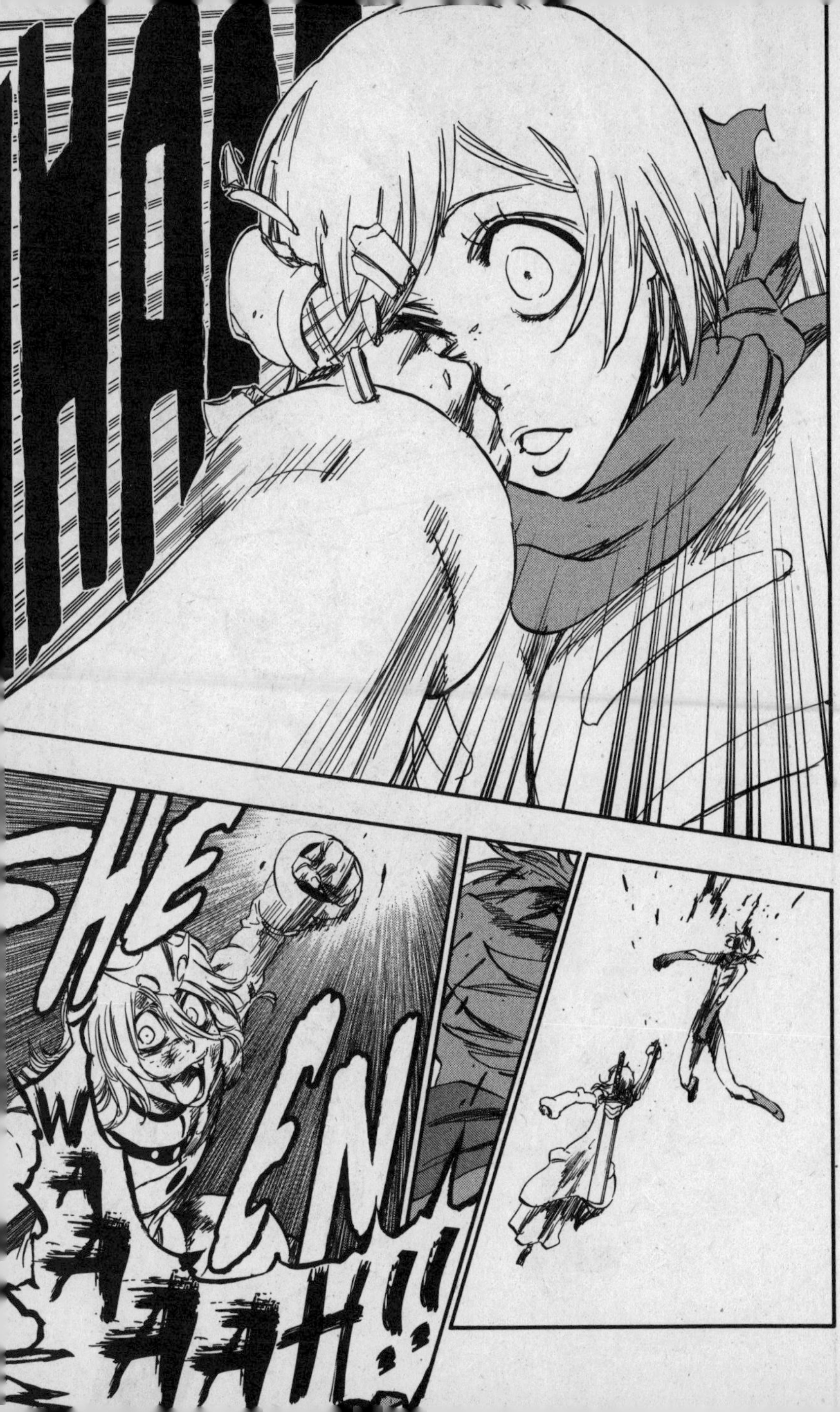
WAAAH!!

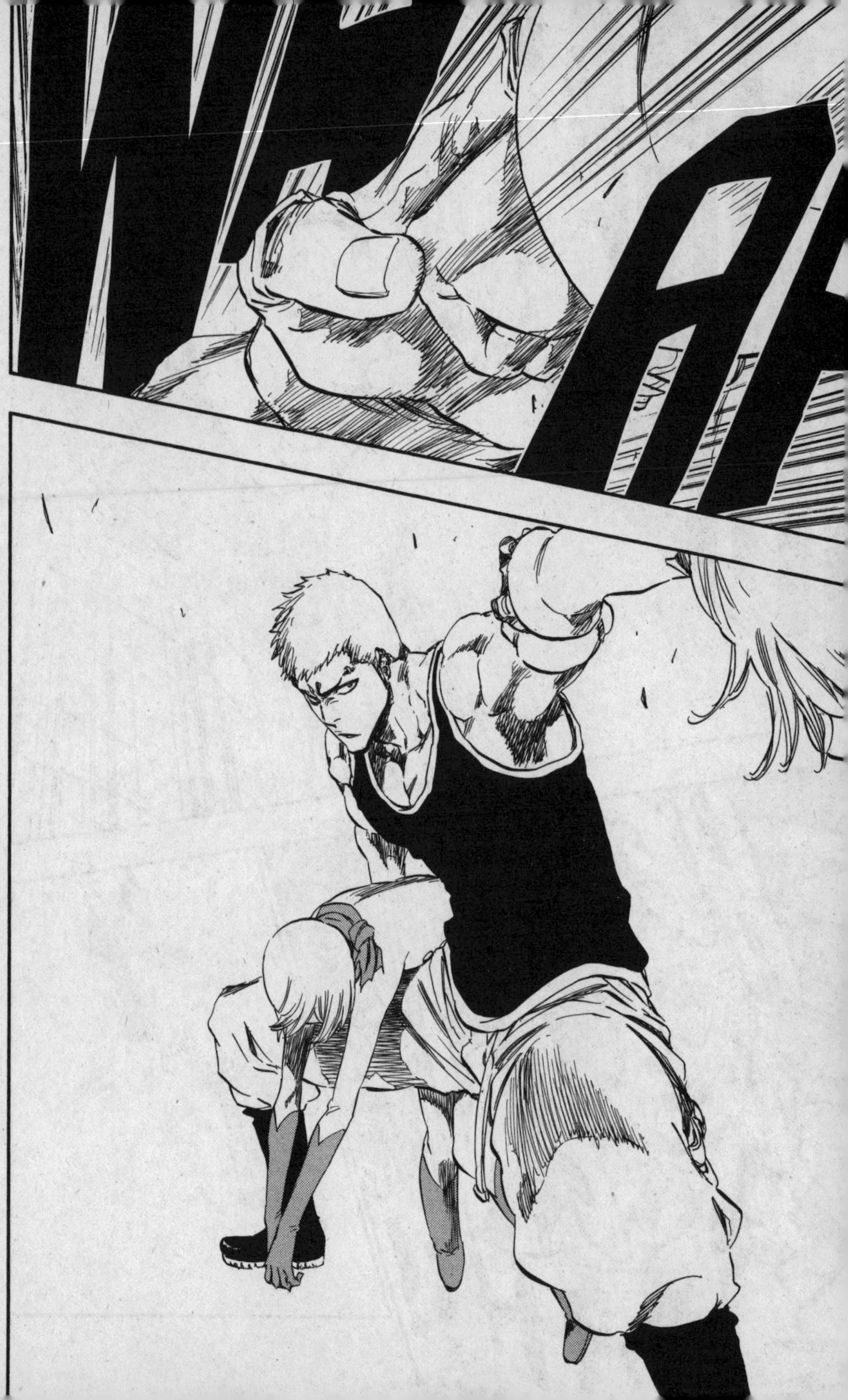

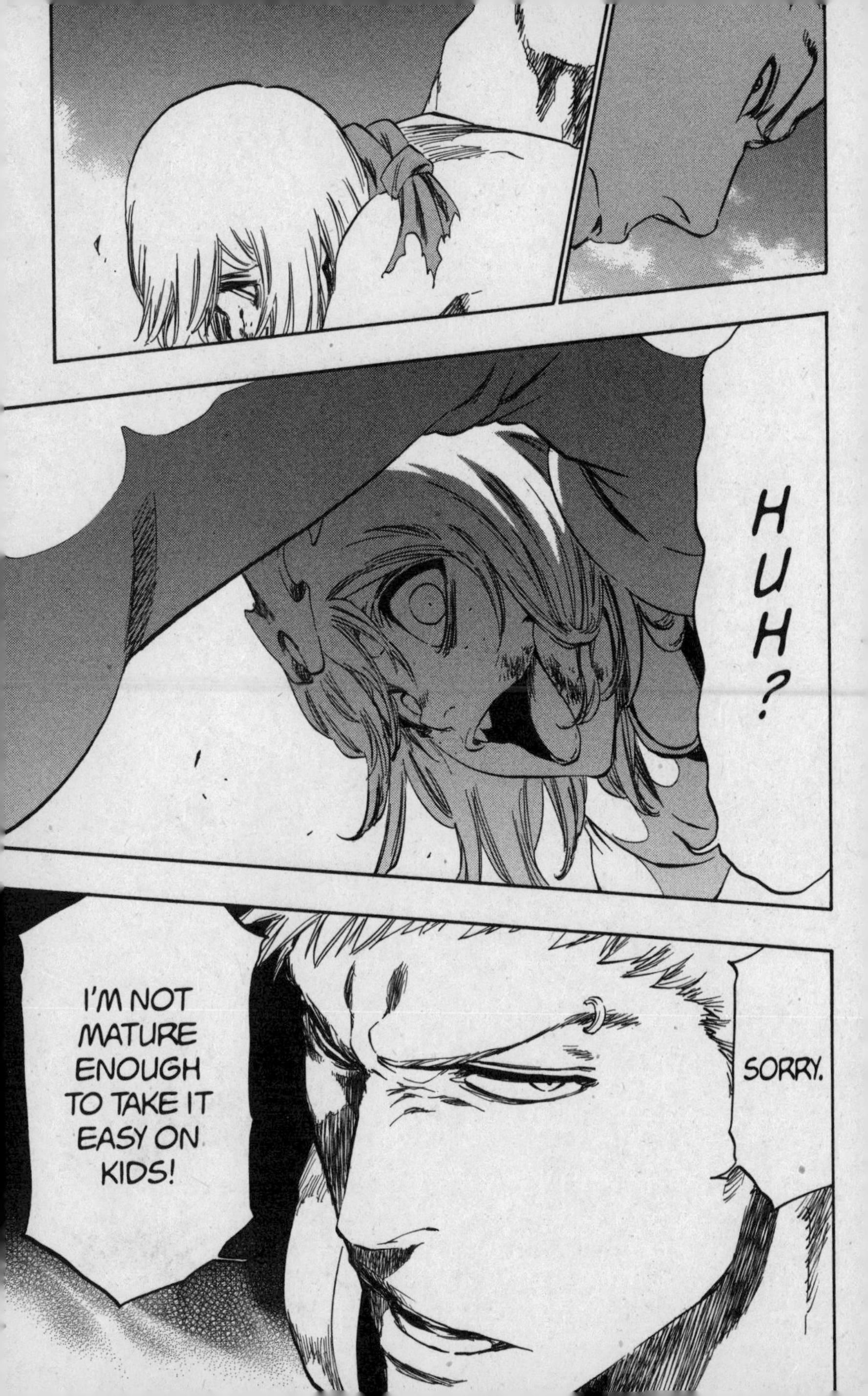
HUH?
SORRY.
I'M NOT MATURE ENOUGH TO TAKE IT EASY ON KIDS!

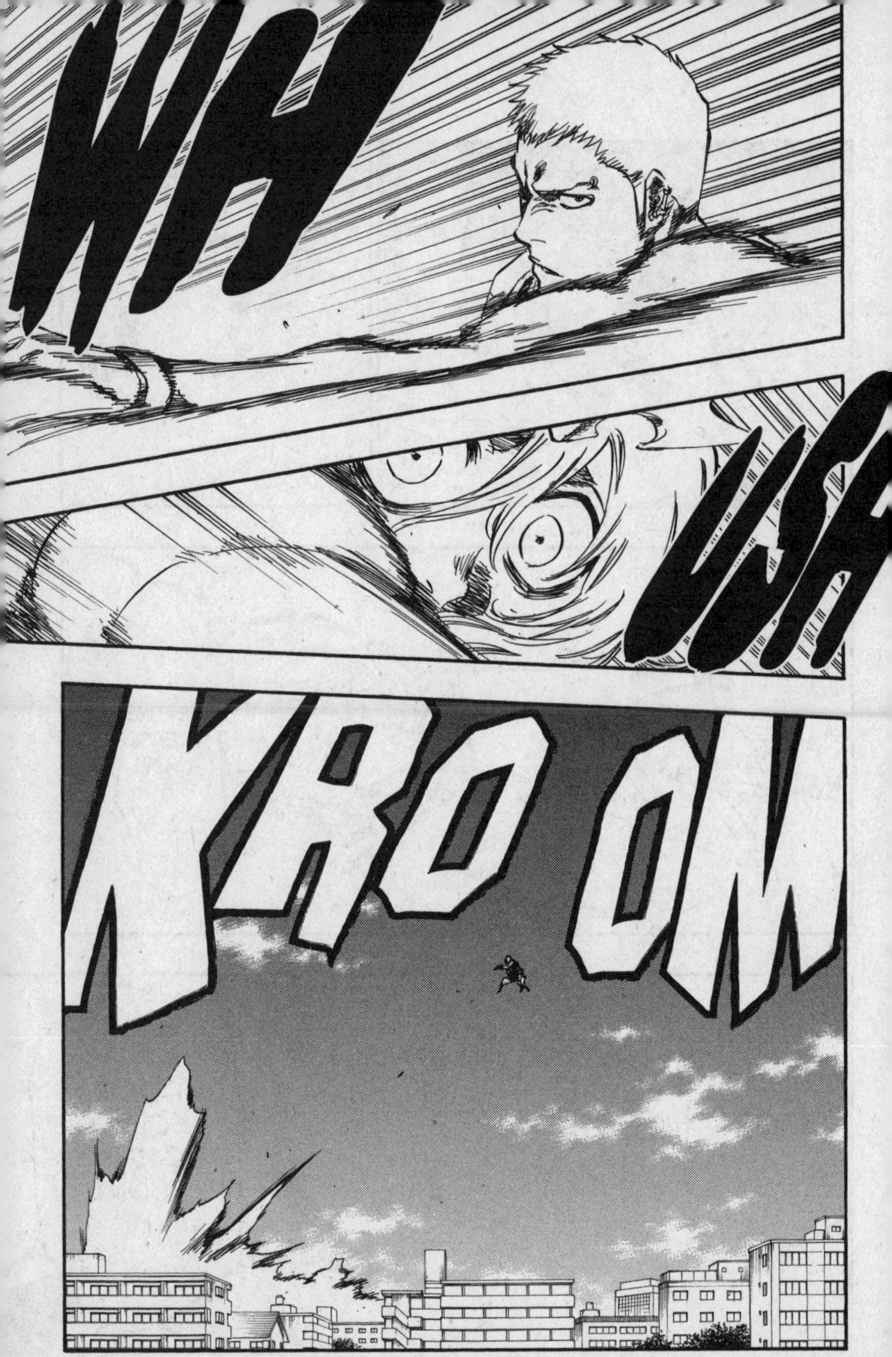
KROOM

377. Shout at the Dark

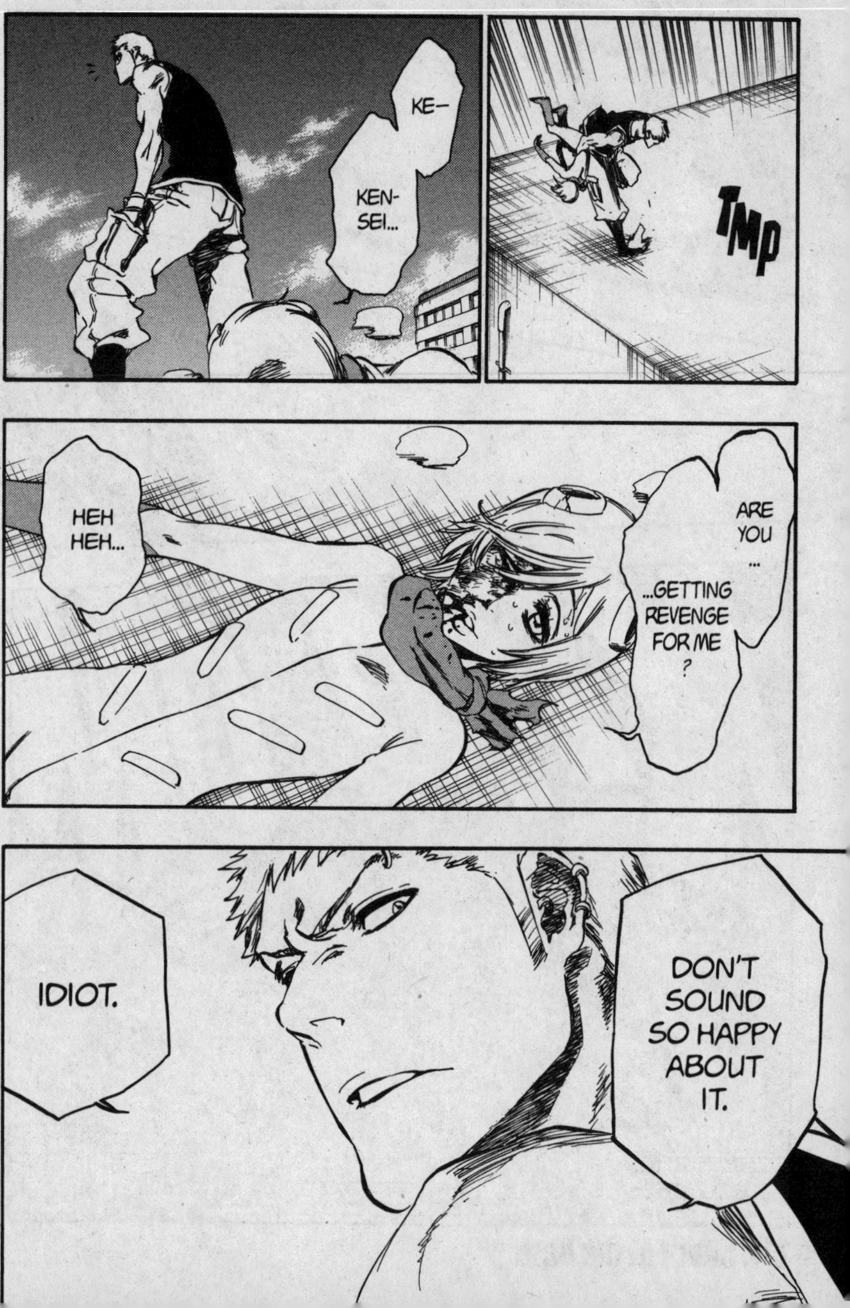
TMP
KE-
KEN-SEI...
ARE YOU ...
...GETTING REVENGE FOR ME?
HEH HEH...
DON'T SOUND SO HAPPY ABOUT IT.
IDIOT.

READ THIS WAY

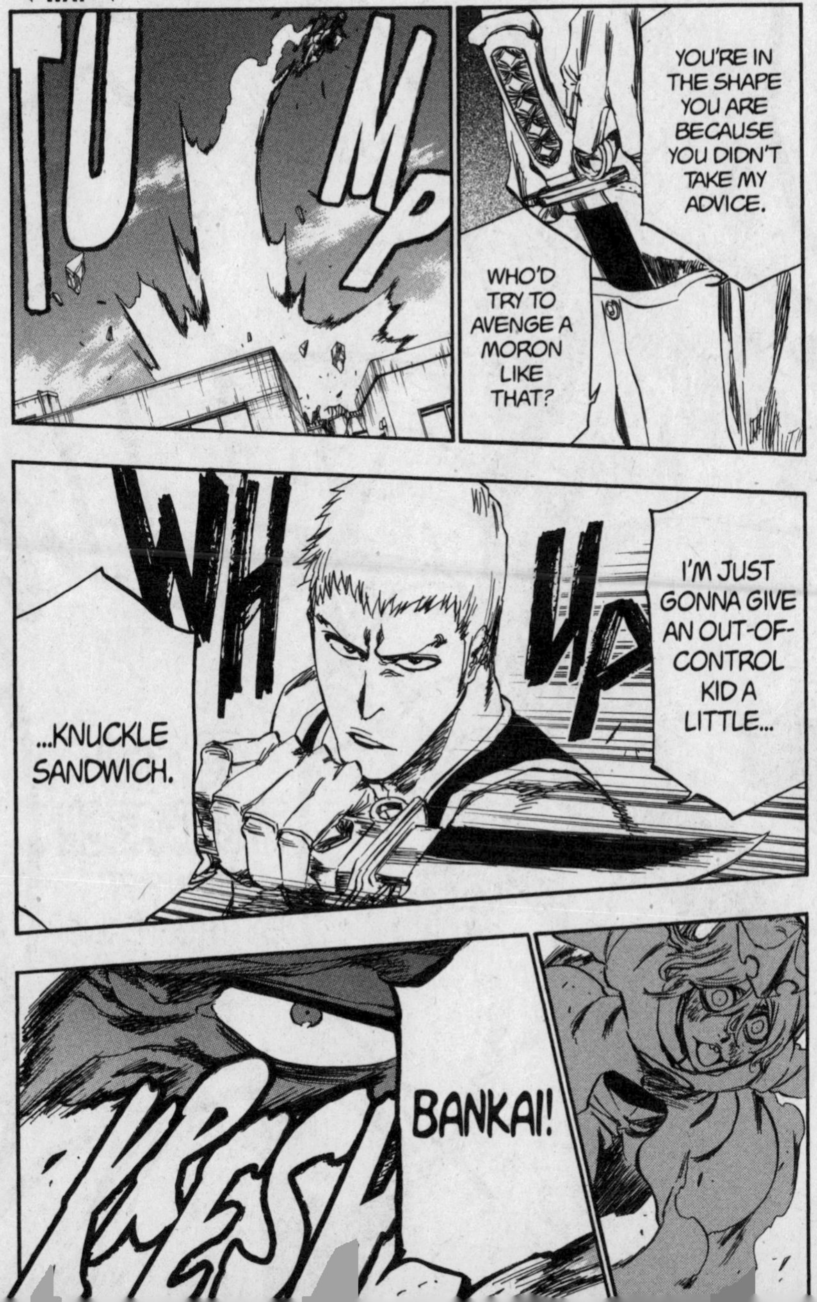

YOU'RE IN THE SHAPE YOU ARE BECAUSE YOU DIDN'T TAKE MY ADVICE.
WHO'D TRY TO AVENGE A MORON LIKE THAT?
TUMP
I'M JUST GONNA GIVE AN OUT-OF-CONTROL KID A LITTLE...
WHUP
...KNUCKLE SANDWICH.
BANKAI!

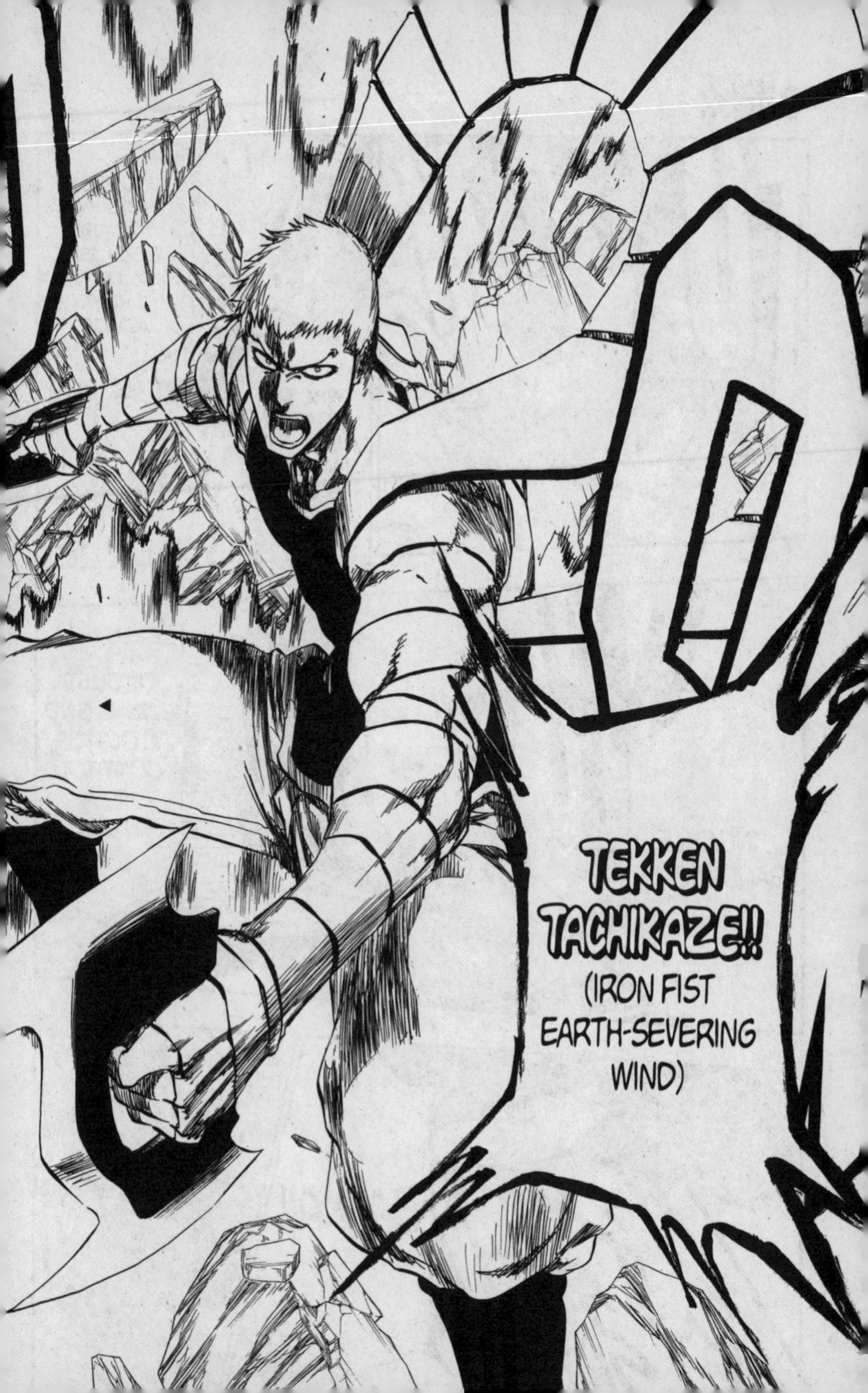
TEKKEN TACHIKAZE!!
(IRON FIST EARTH-SEVERING WIND)

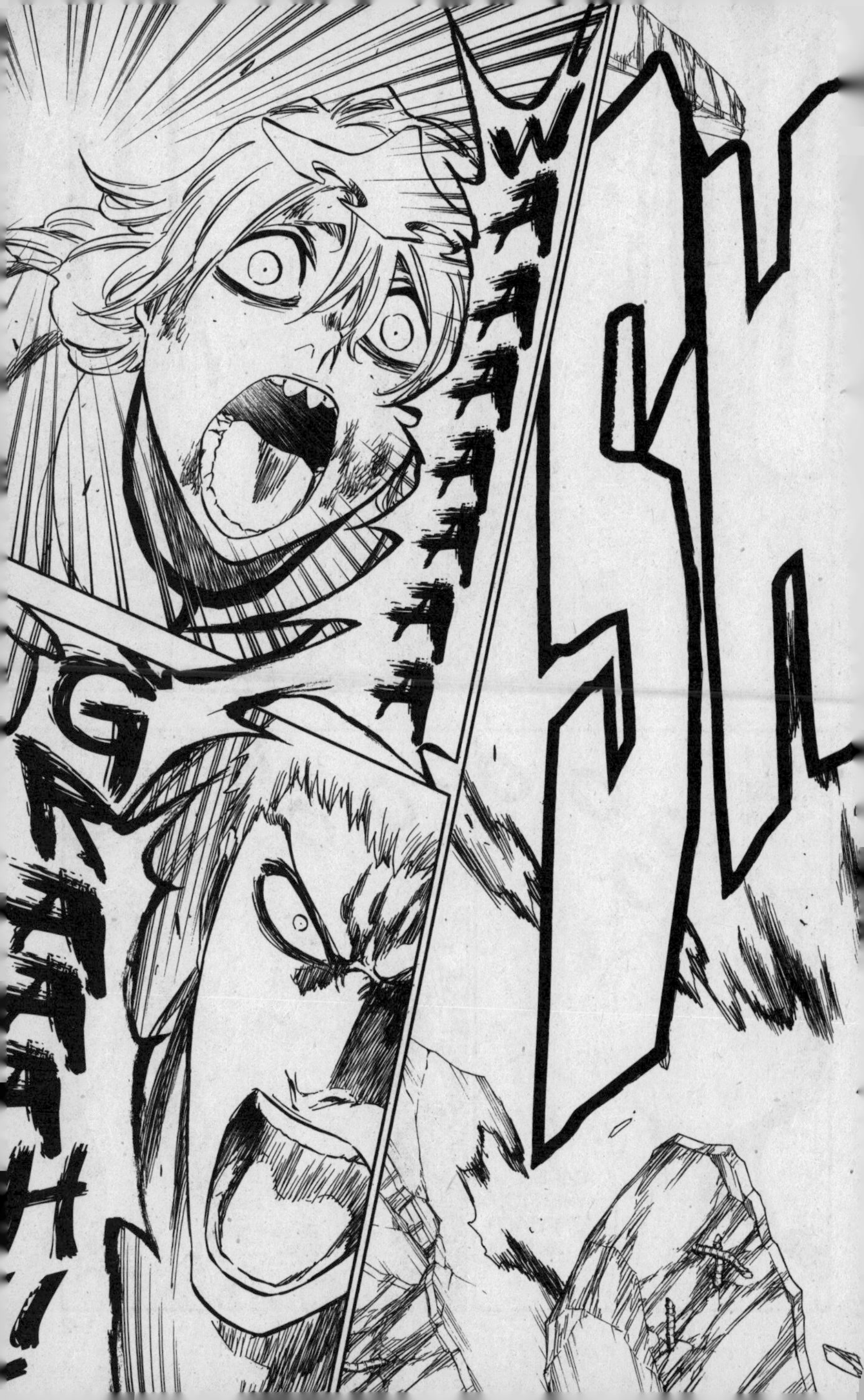
WAAAAAAAAA
GRAAAH!

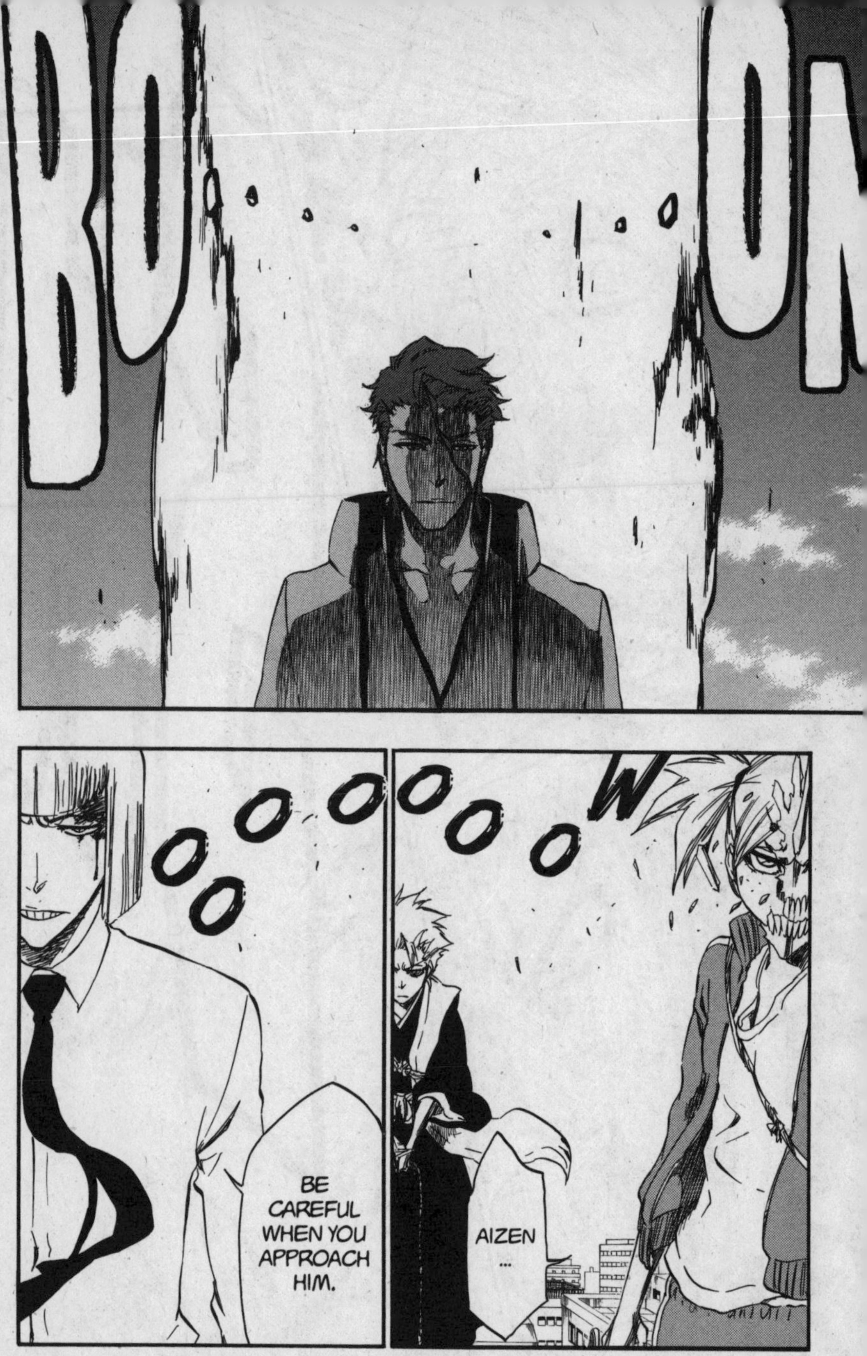
BO...ON
OOOOOOOW
AIZEN ...
BE CAREFUL WHEN YOU APPROACH HIM.

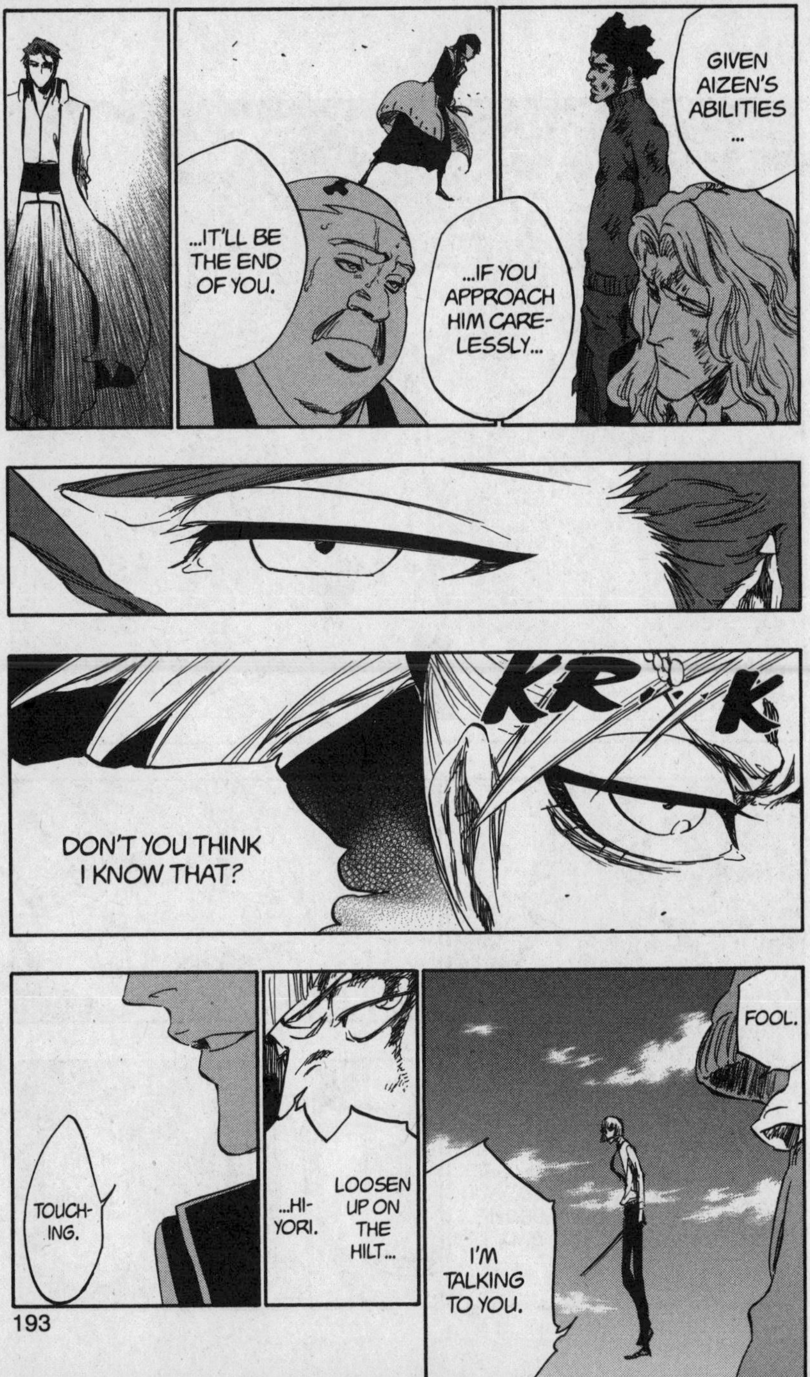
GIVEN AIZEN'S ABILITIES ...
...IF YOU APPROACH HIM CARELESSLY...
...IT'LL BE THE END OF YOU.
KR..K
DON'T YOU THINK I KNOW THAT?
FOOL.
I'M TALKING TO YOU.
LOOSEN UP ON THE HILT...
...HIYORI.
TOUCHING.

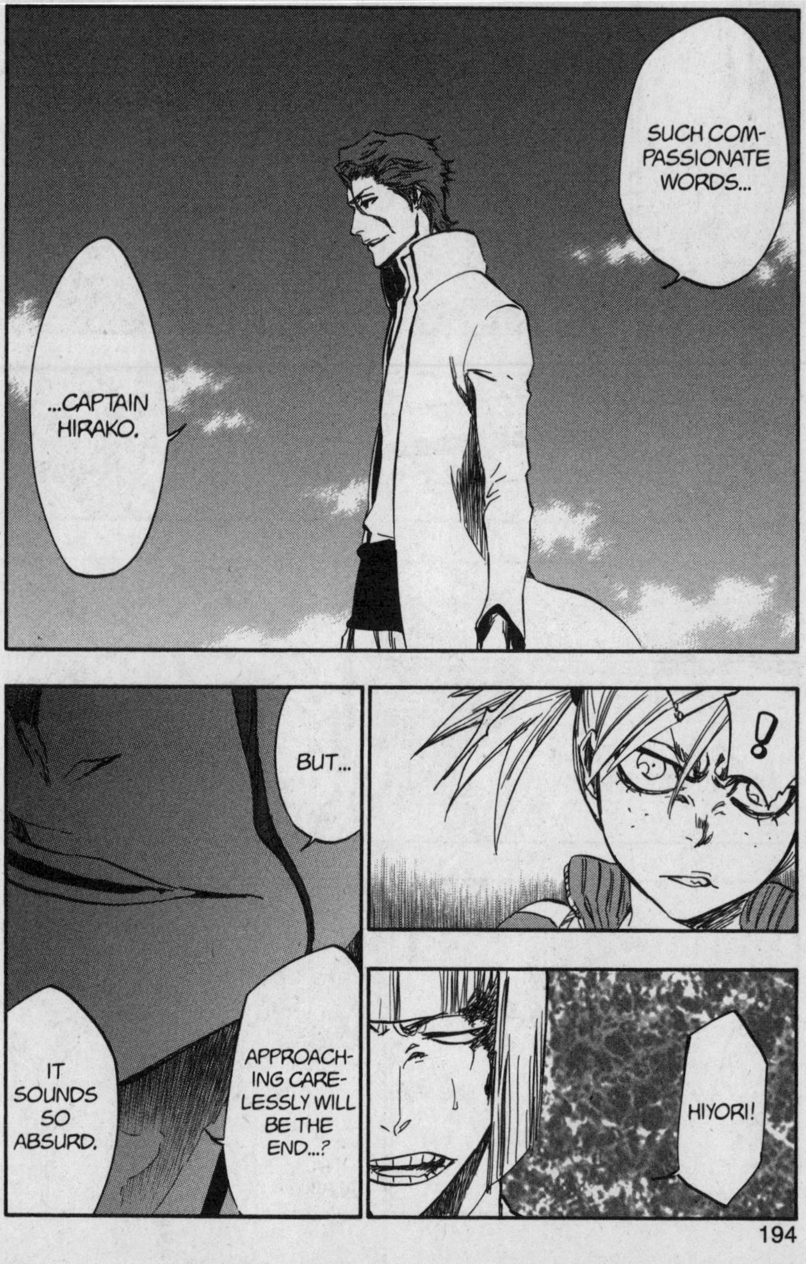
SUCH COM-
PASSIONATE
WORDS...
...CAPTAIN
HIRAKO.
!
HIYORI!
BUT...
APPROACH-
ING CARE-
LESSLY WILL
BE THE
END...?
IT
SOUNDS
SO
ABSURD.

READ THIS WAY

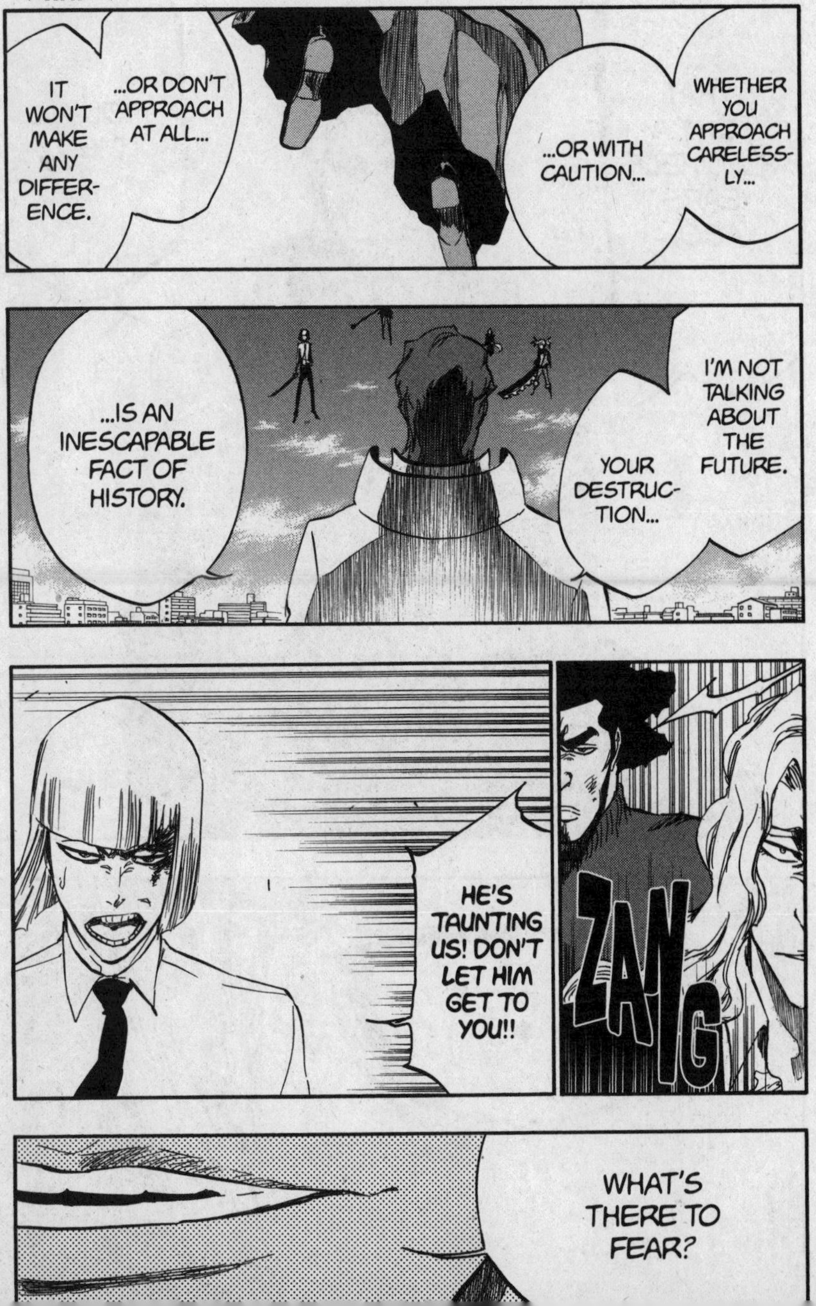
WHETHER YOU APPROACH CARELESS-LY...
...OR WITH CAUTION...
...OR DON'T APPROACH AT ALL...
IT WON'T MAKE ANY DIFFER-ENCE.
I'M NOT TALKING ABOUT THE FUTURE.
YOUR DESTRUC-TION...
...IS AN INESCAPABLE FACT OF HISTORY.
ZANG
HE'S TAUNTING US! DON'T LET HIM GET TO YOU!!
WHAT'S THERE TO FEAR?

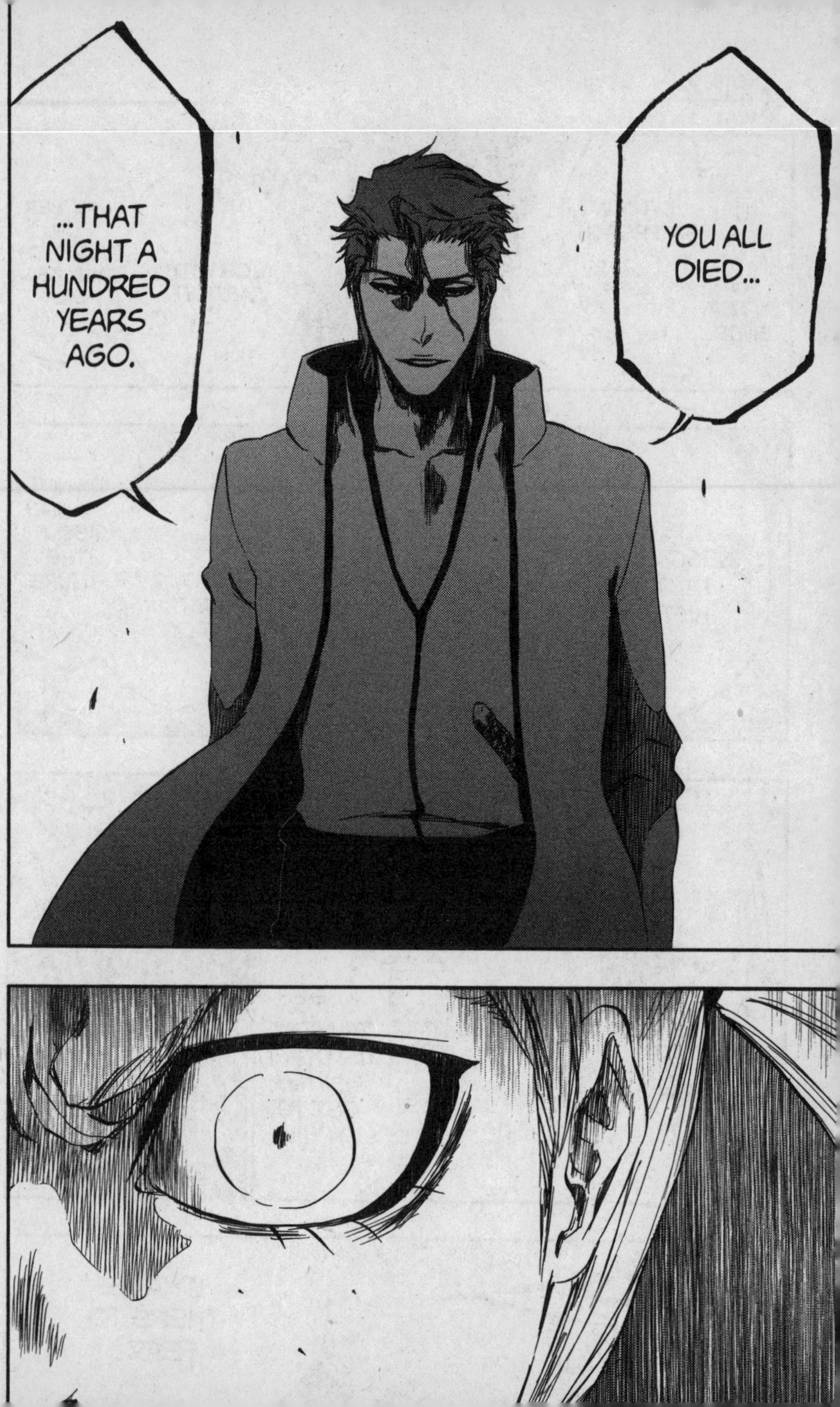
YOU ALL DIED...
...THAT NIGHT A HUNDRED YEARS AGO.

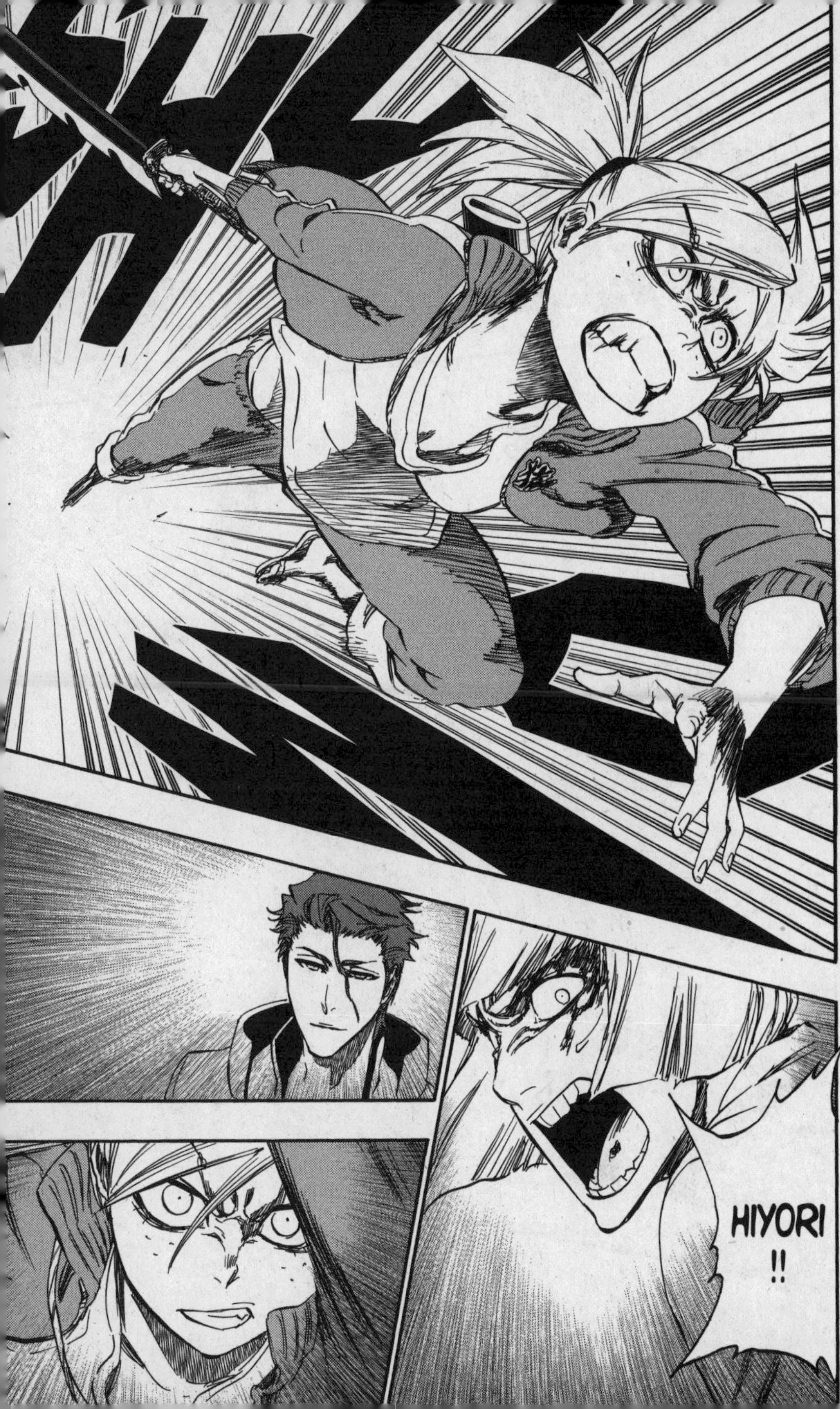
HIYORI
!!

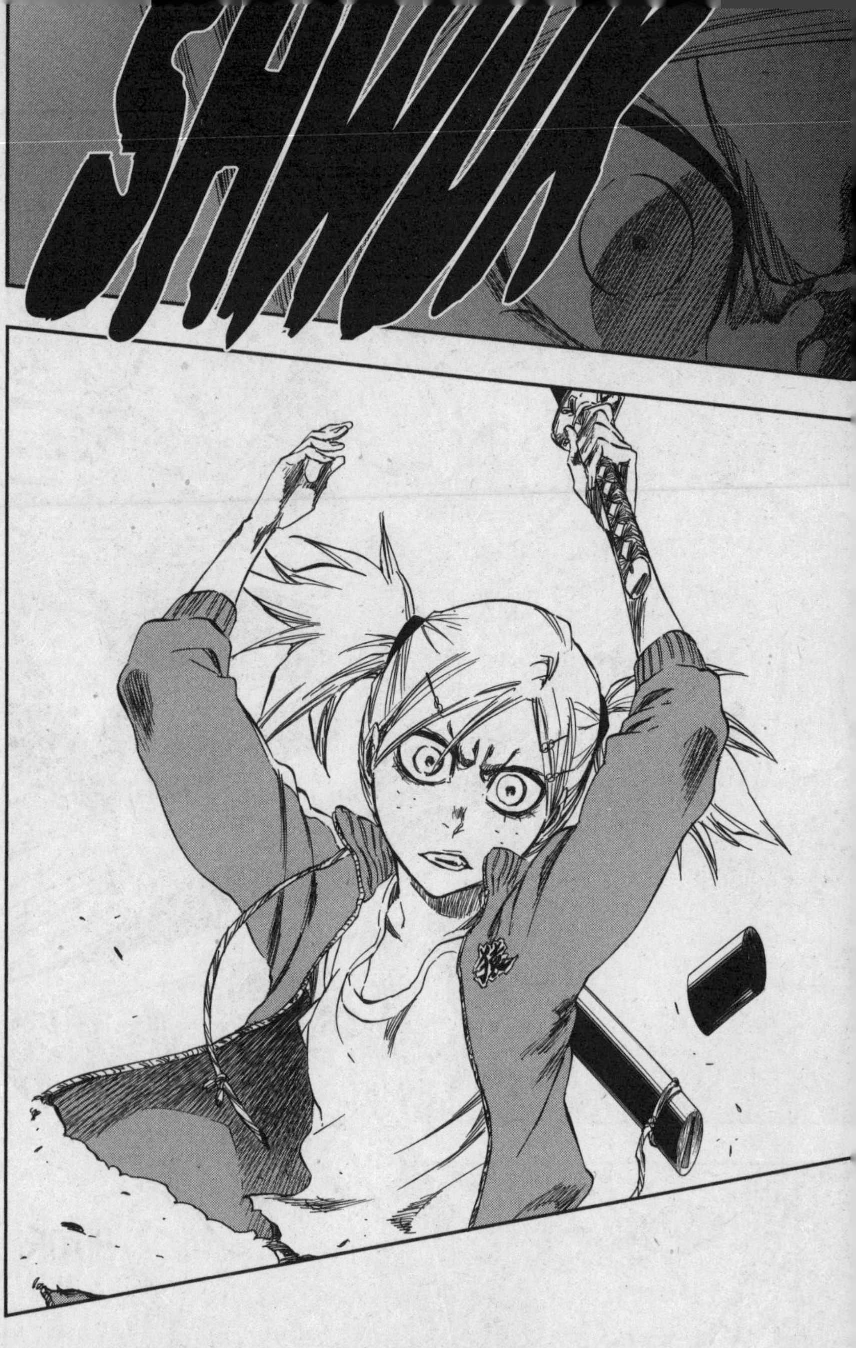
SHWUSH

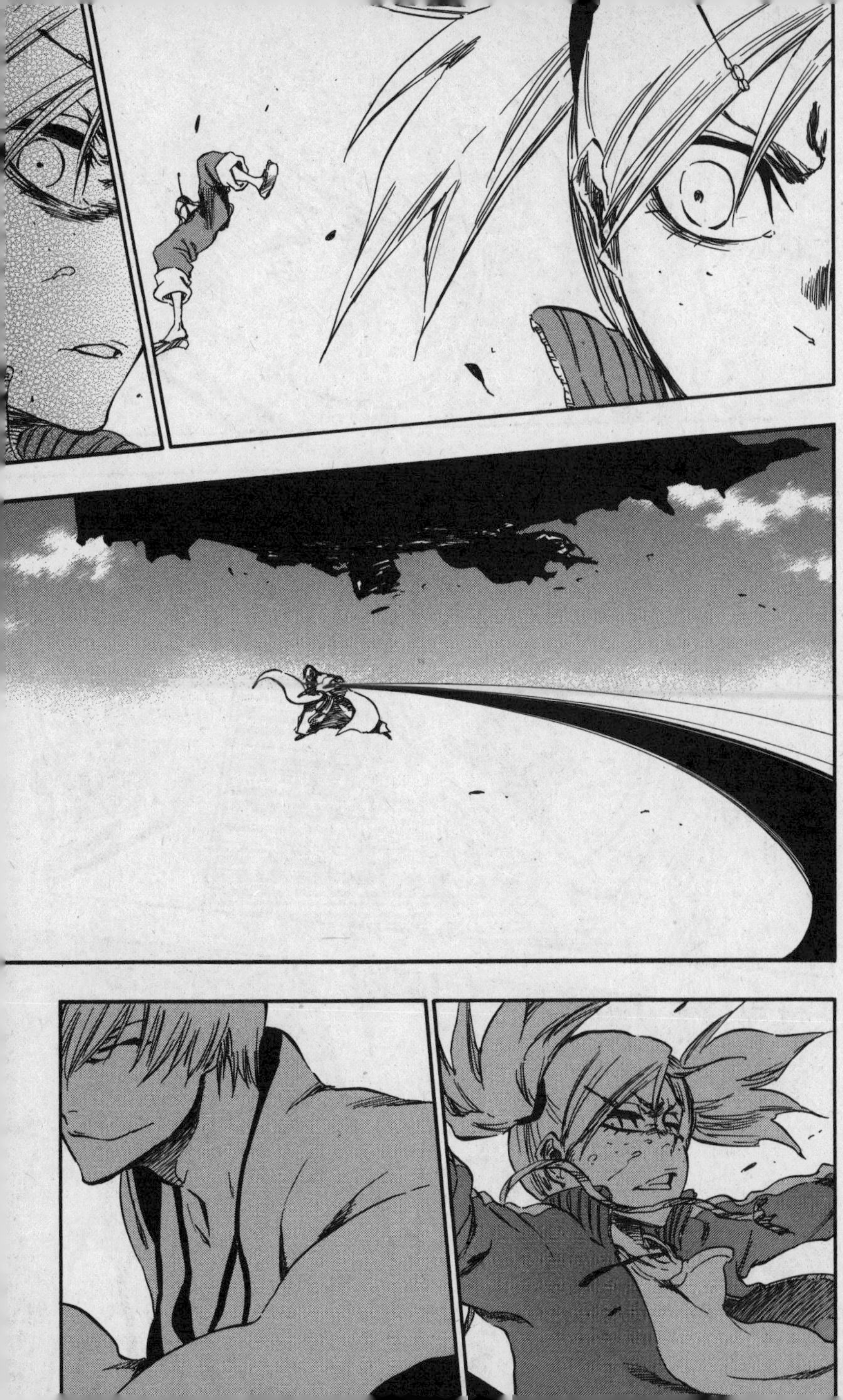

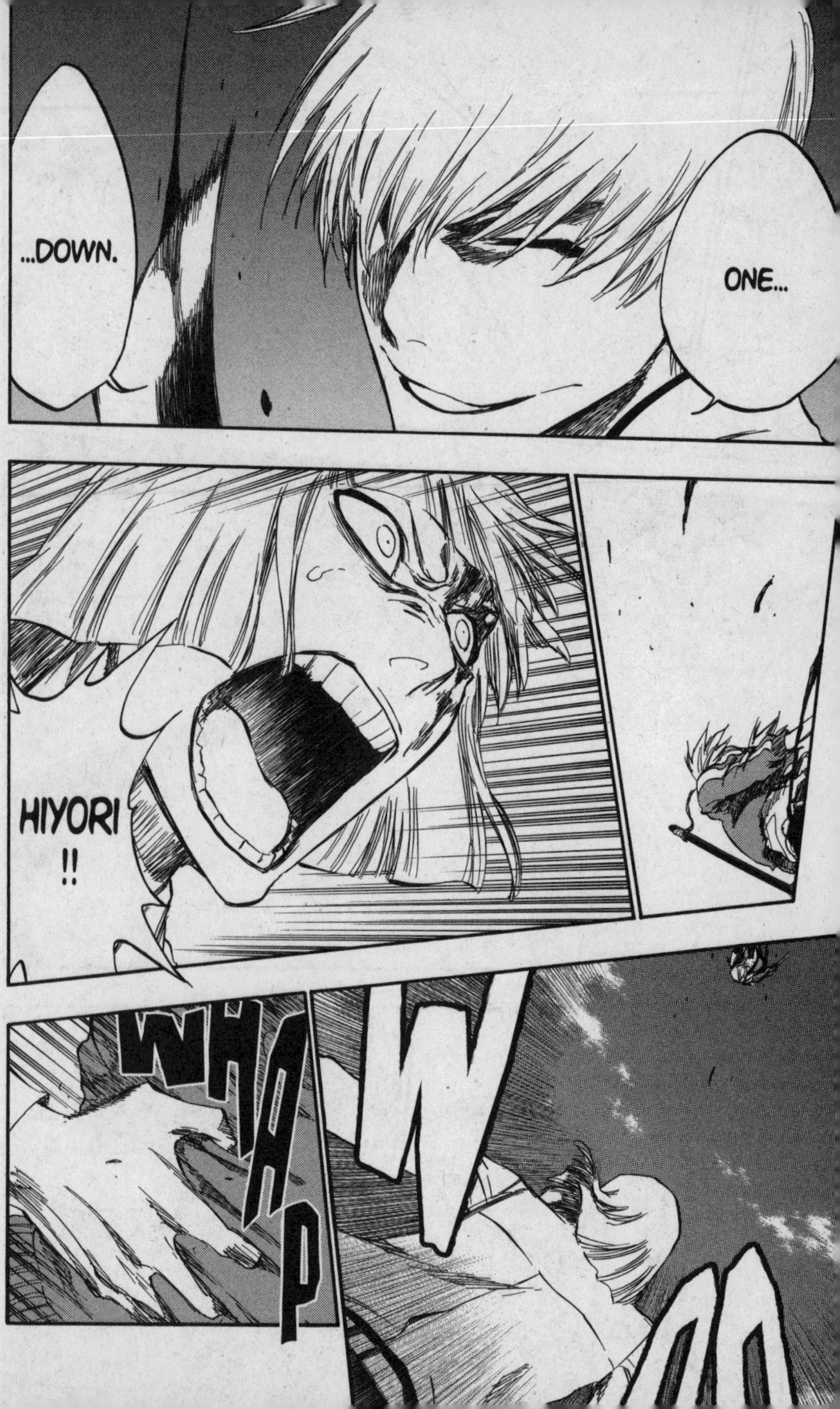
ONE...
...DOWN.
HIYORI !!
WHAAP

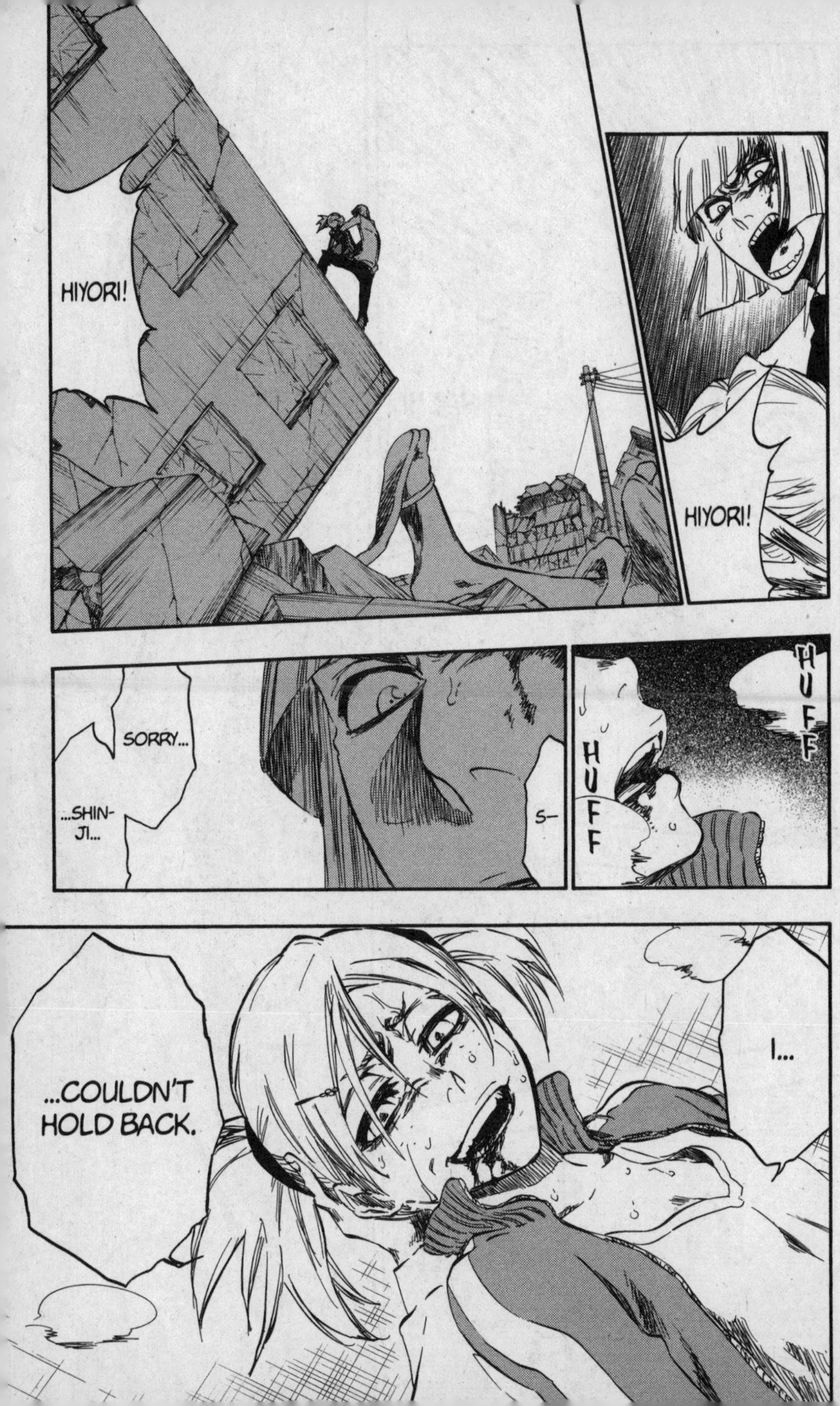
HIYORI!
HIYORI!
HUFF
HUFF
S—
SORRY...
...SHIN-JI...
I...
...COULDN'T HOLD BACK.

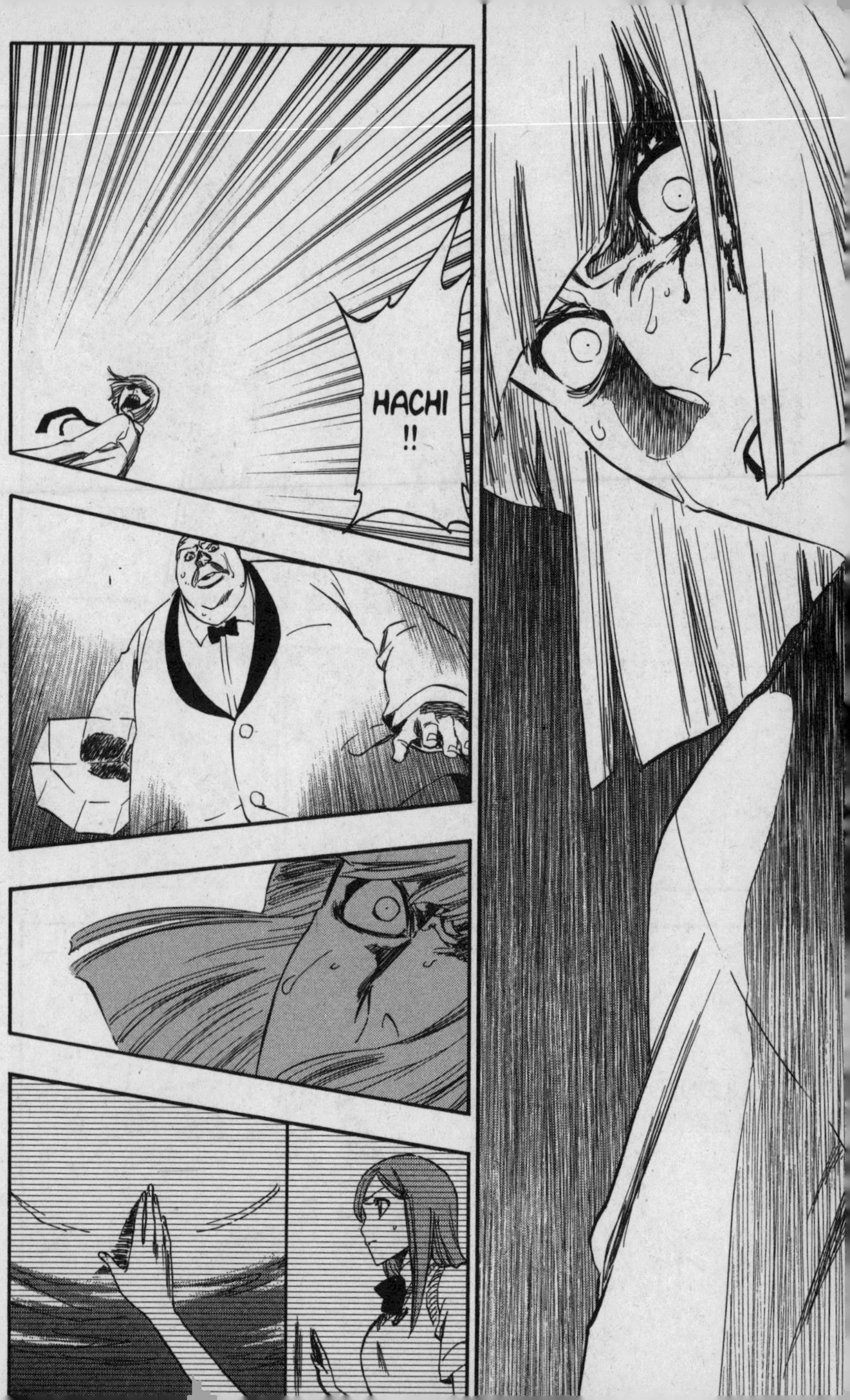
HACHI !!

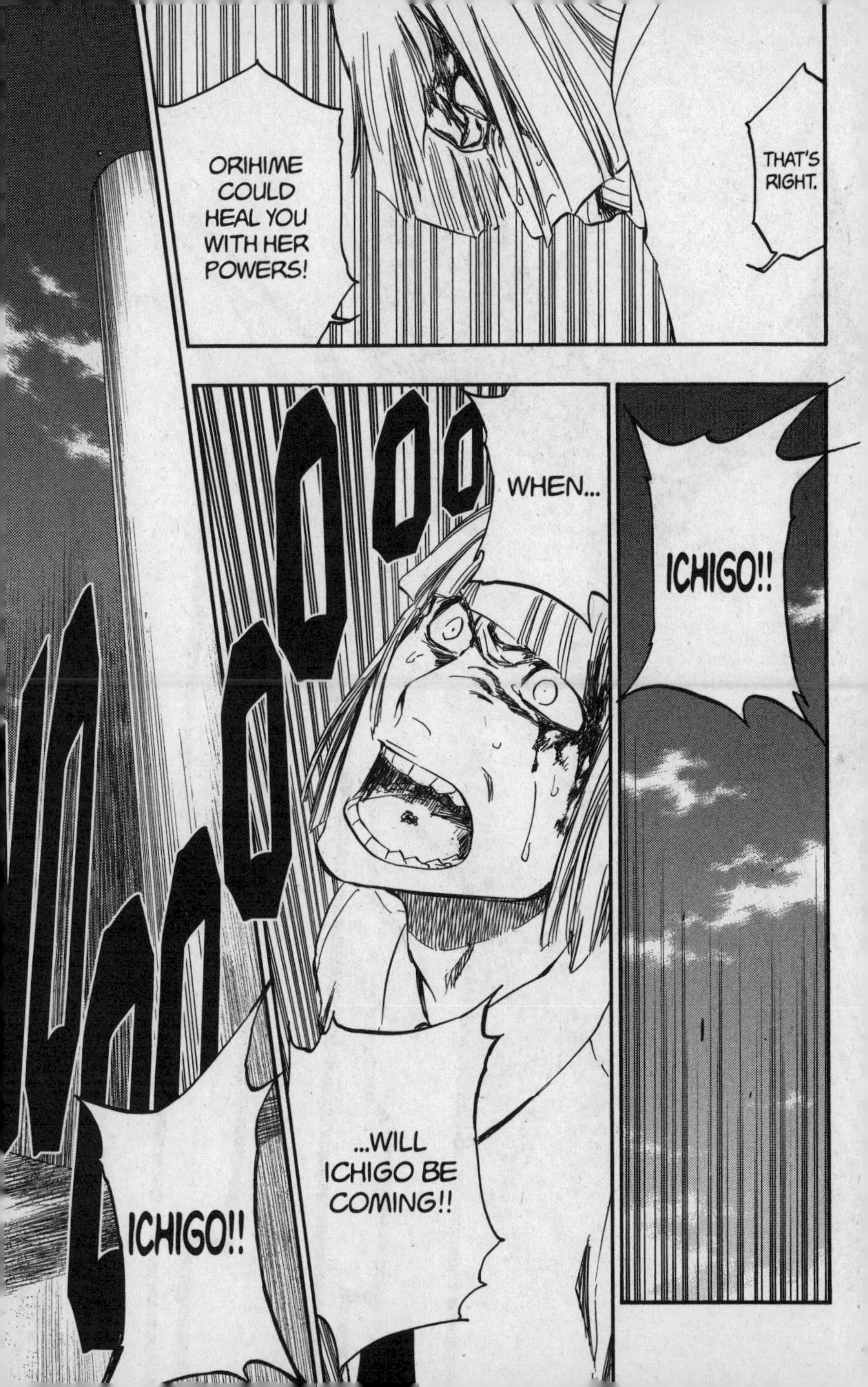
THAT'S RIGHT.
ORIHIME COULD HEAL YOU WITH HER POWERS!
ICHIGO!!
WHEN...
...WILL ICHIGO BE COMING!!
ICHIGO!!

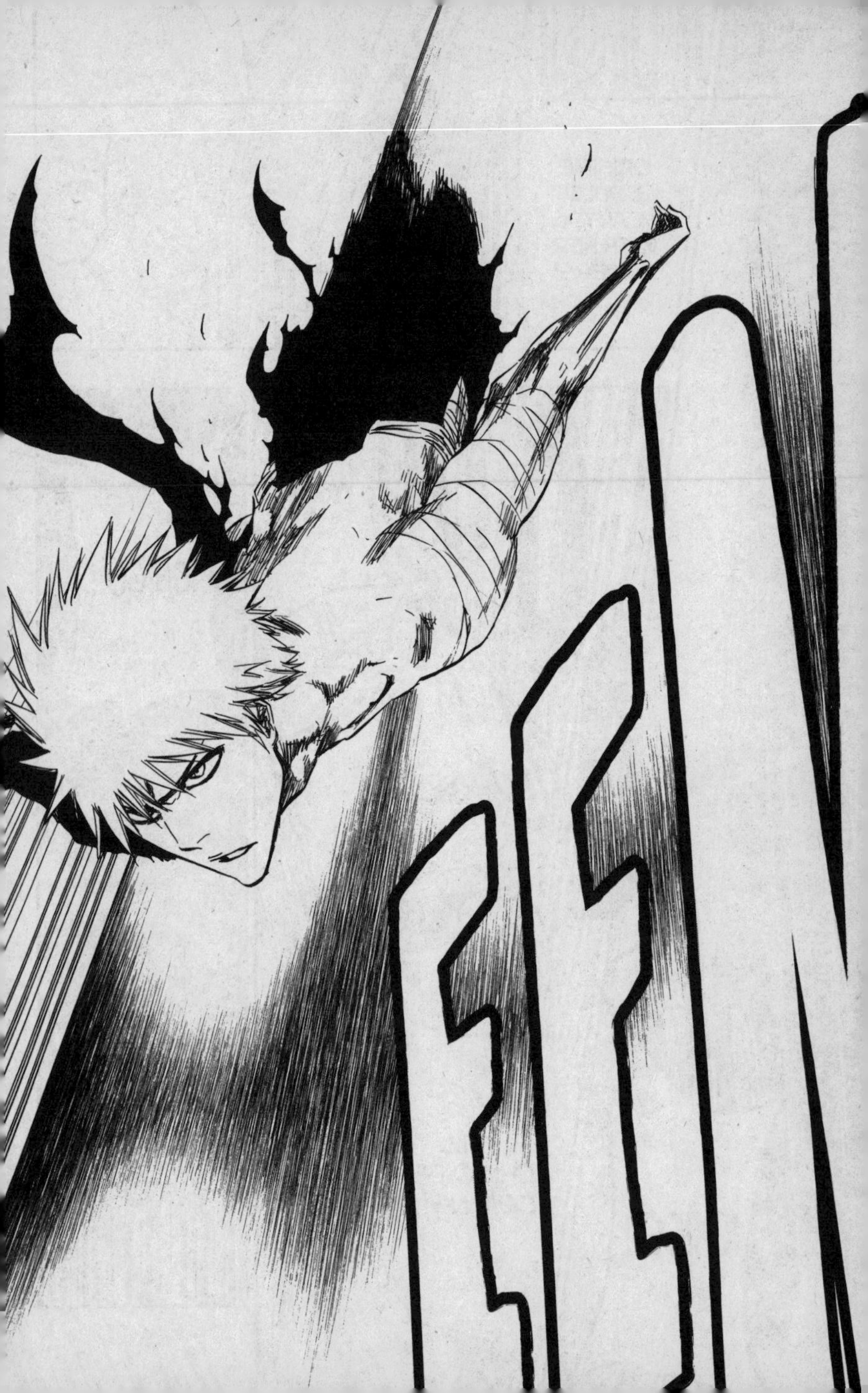

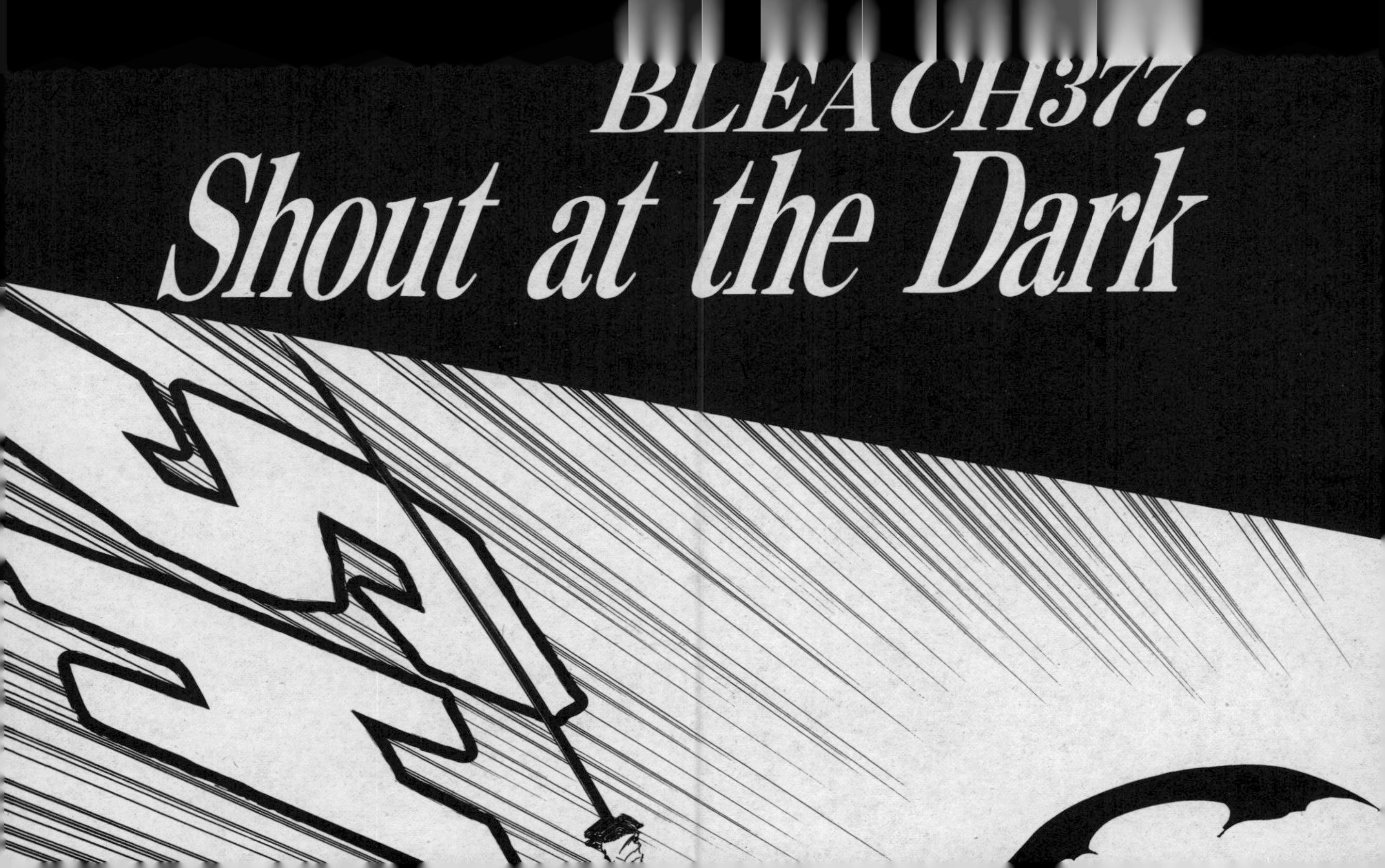
BLEACH377.
Shout at the Dark

BLEACH
ブリーチ

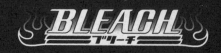

I'm making a new table as I prepare to move into my new place. It has lines of dialogue from Bleach in its transparent legs.

It looks like it's floating on English words.

I'm nuts about furniture.

I'm moving at the end of March. In other words, by the time this volume comes out in Japan, I should be in my new place.

Hey!
Will I be?!
I will be, right?!

-Tite Kubo, 2010

People are all evil.
In order to falsely believe yourself to be just
You must inevitably falsely believe
That someone else is more evil than you.

BLEACH44 VICE IT

STARS AND

Rukia Kuchiki

Yammy

Ichigo Kurosaki

plot

When high school student Ichigo Kurosaki meets Soul Reaper Rukia Kuchiki his life is changed forever. Soon Ichigo is a soul-cleansing Soul Reaper too, and he finds himself having adventures, as well as problems, that he never would have imagined. Now Ichigo and his friends must stop renegade Soul Reaper Aizen and his army of Arrancars from destroying the Soul Society and wiping out Karakura as well.

Ichigo reveals a new side of himself when he defeats Ulquiorra to rescue Orihime, and Rukia faces a Yammy who has transformed into a huge monster! Meanwhile, the Thirteen Court Guard Companies and the Visoreds face the Espadas in mortal combat. But will the tide of battle turn with the appearance of Aizen himself?

BLEACH ALL

狛村左陣

Sajin Komamura

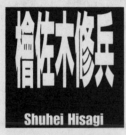

檜佐木修兵

Shuhei Hisagi

Kaname Tôsen

東仙要

69

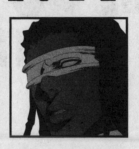

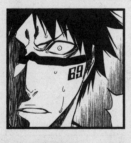

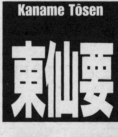

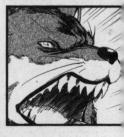

STORIES

BLEACH 44

VICE IT

Contents

378. Eyes of the Victor

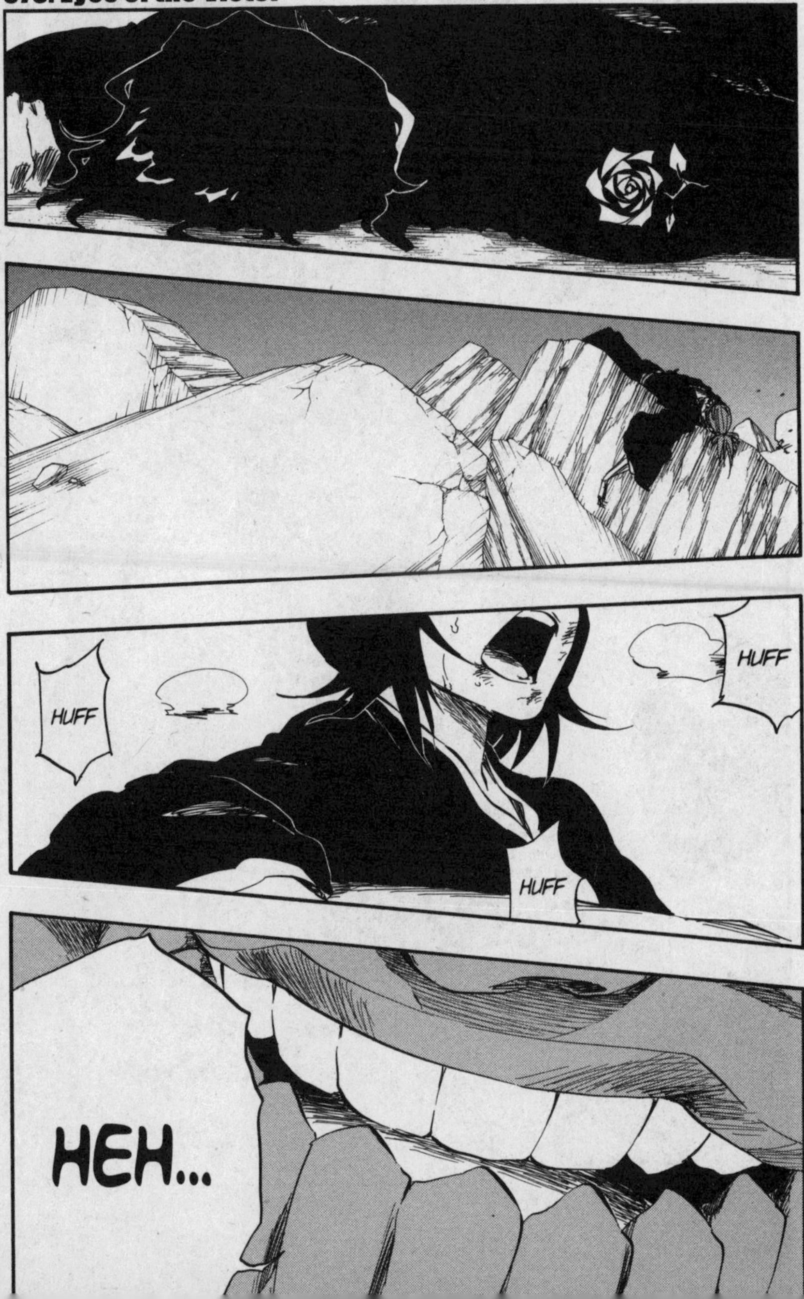
HUFF
HUFF
HUFF
HEH...

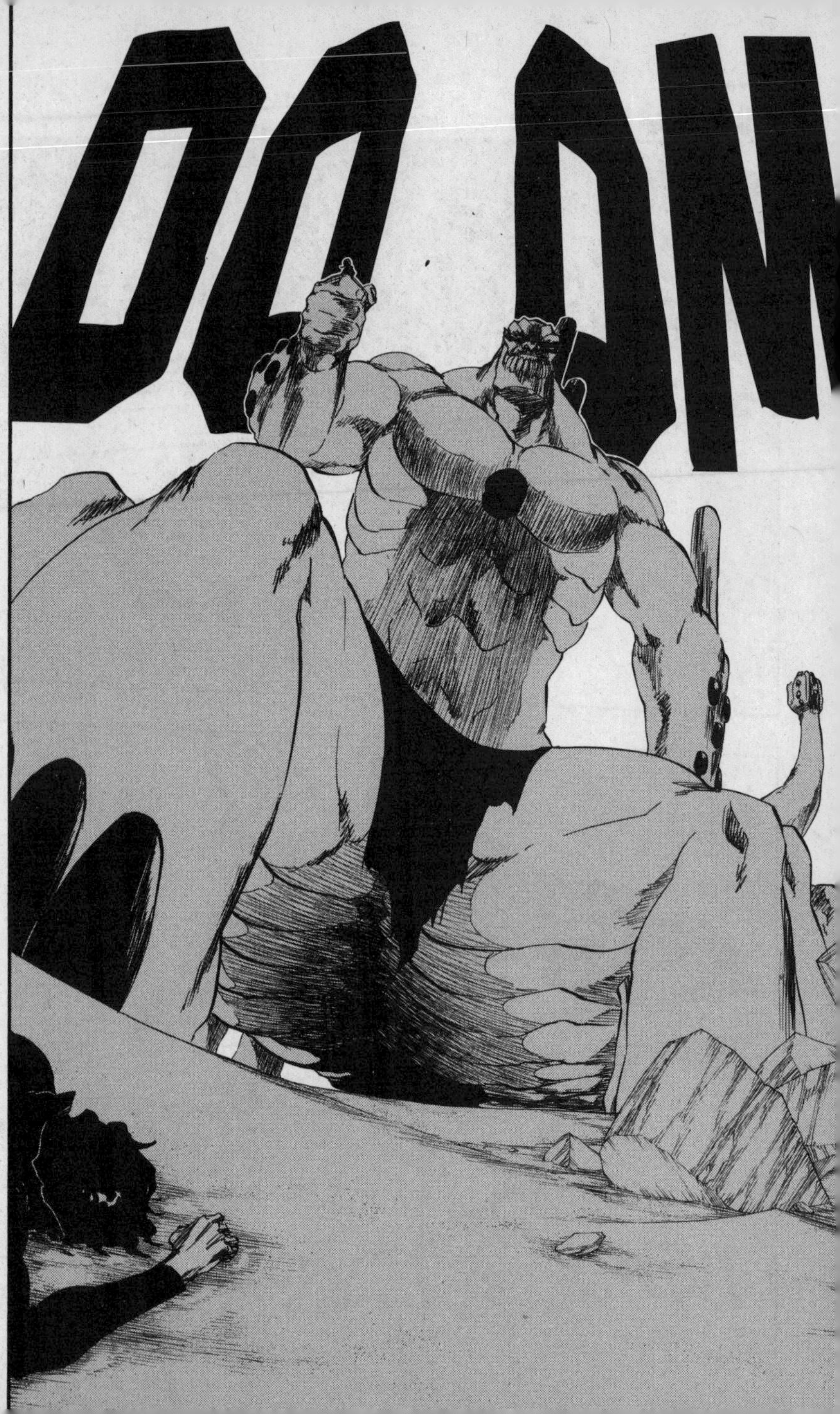
DOOM

READ THIS WAY

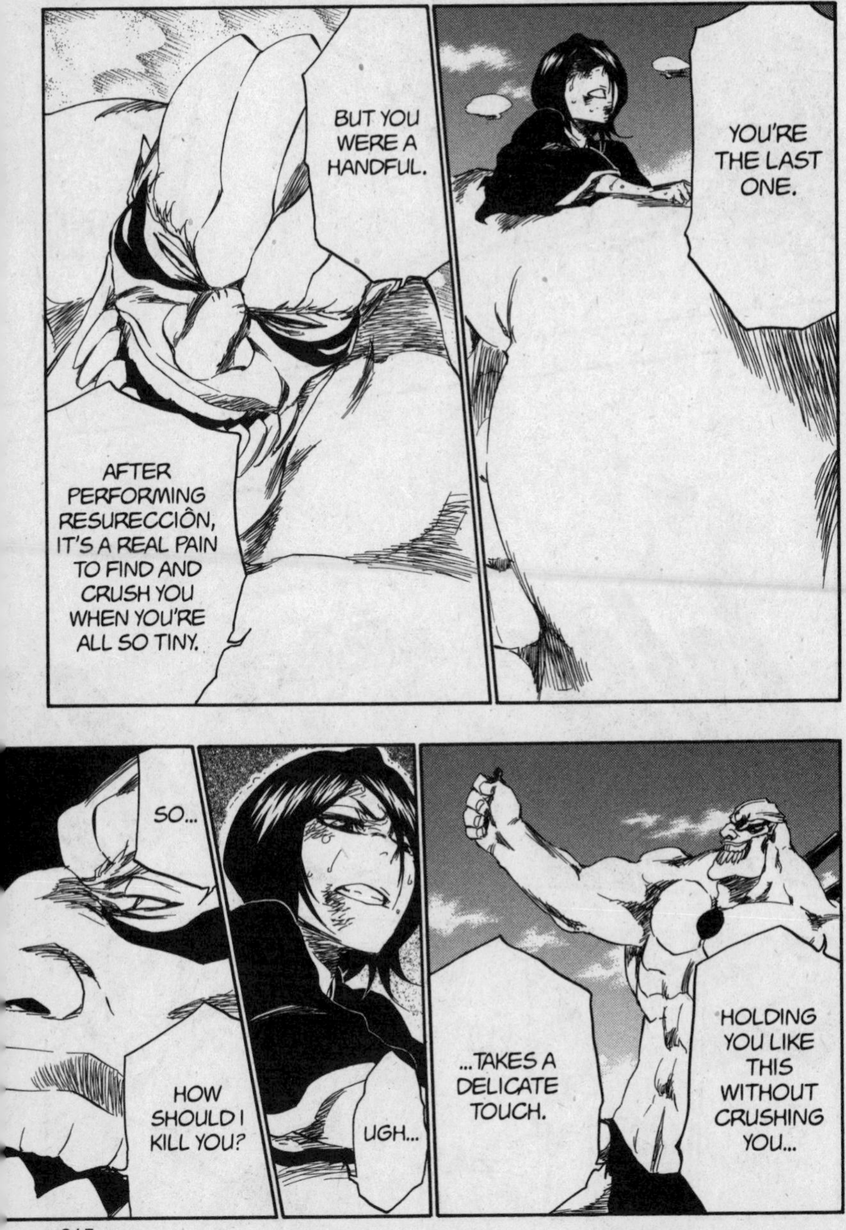

YOU'RE THE LAST ONE.
BUT YOU WERE A HANDFUL.
AFTER PERFORMING RESURECCIÔN, IT'S A REAL PAIN TO FIND AND CRUSH YOU WHEN YOU'RE ALL SO TINY.
HOLDING YOU LIKE THIS WITHOUT CRUSHING YOU...
...TAKES A DELICATE TOUCH.
UGH...
SO...
HOW SHOULD I KILL YOU?

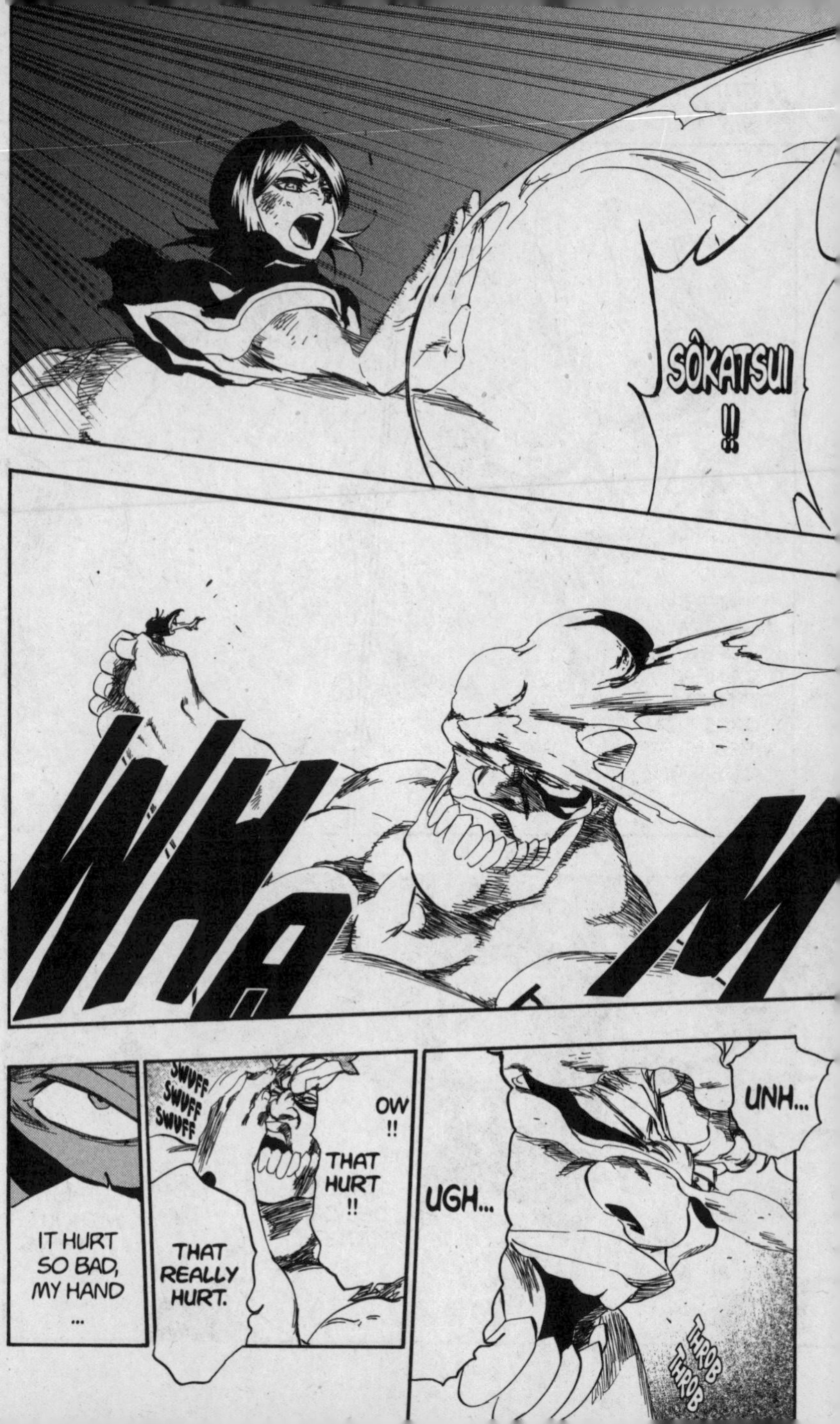

SÔKATSUI!!
WHAM
UNH...
UGH...
THROB THROB
OW!!
THAT HURT!!
SWUFF SWUFF SWUFF
THAT REALLY HURT.
IT HURT SO BAD, MY HAND...

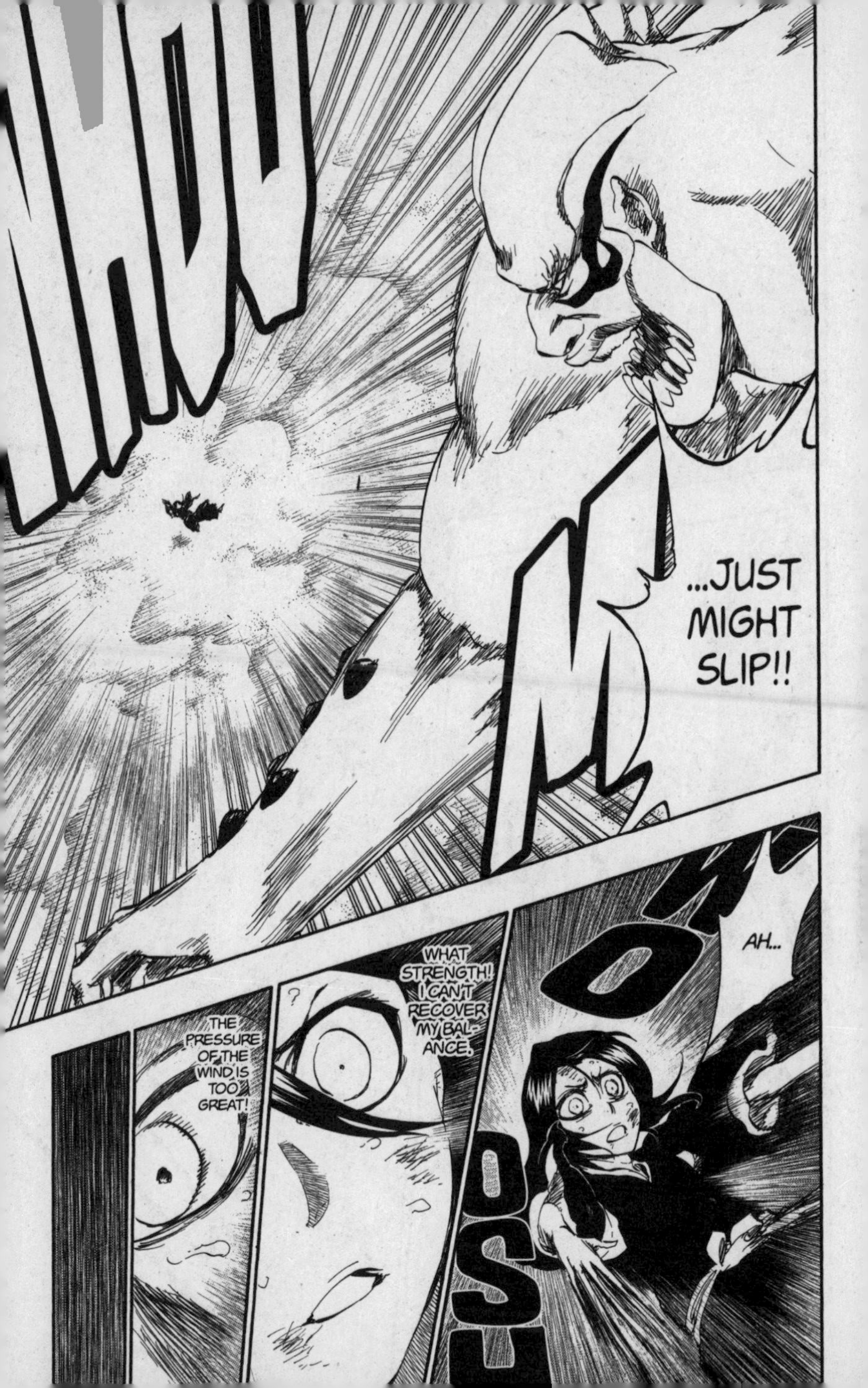
...JUST MIGHT SLIP!!
AH...
WHAT STRENGTH! I CAN'T RECOVER MY BAL-ANCE.
THE PRESSURE OF THE WIND IS TOO GREAT!

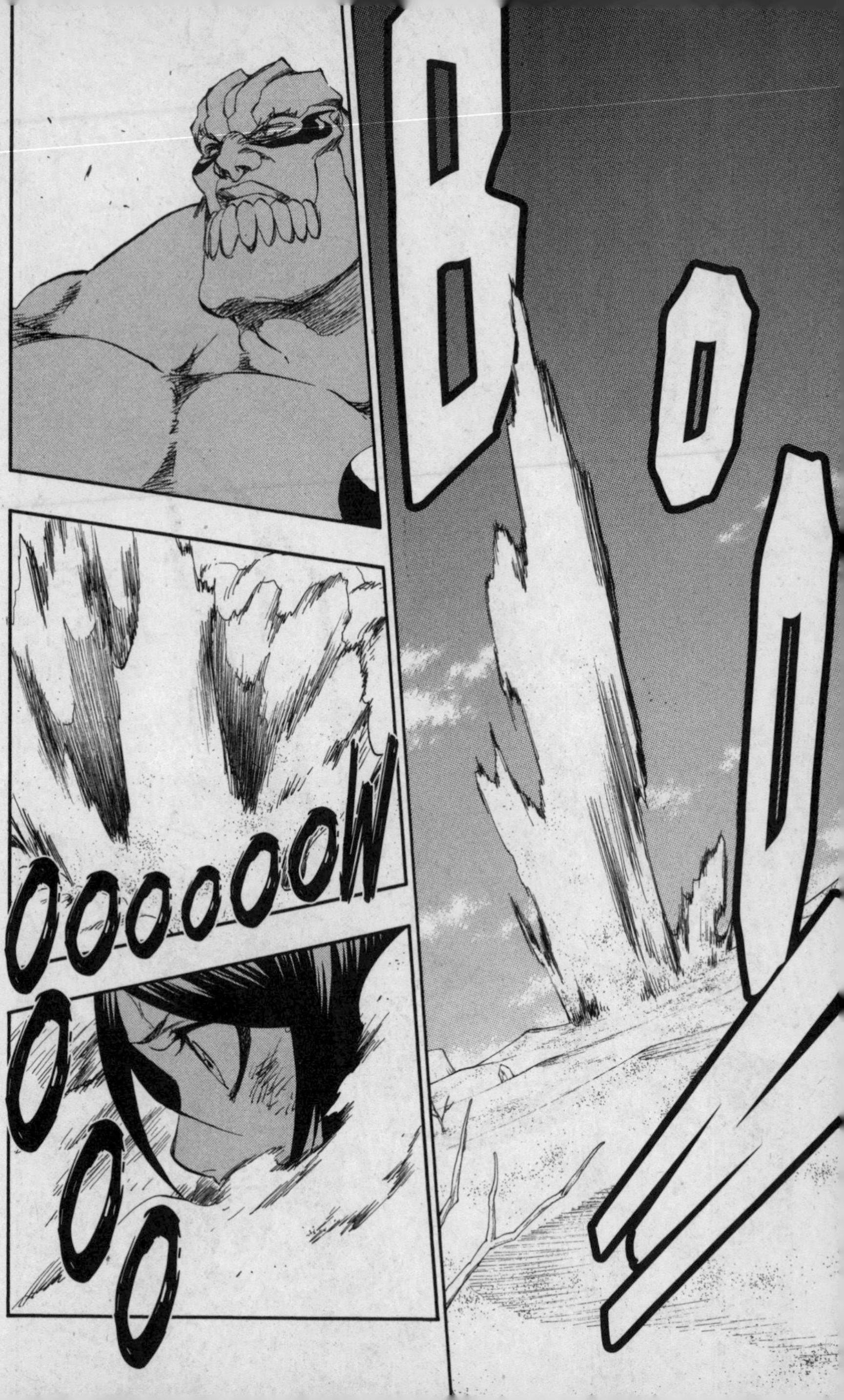
BOOO
OOOOOOOW
OOOO

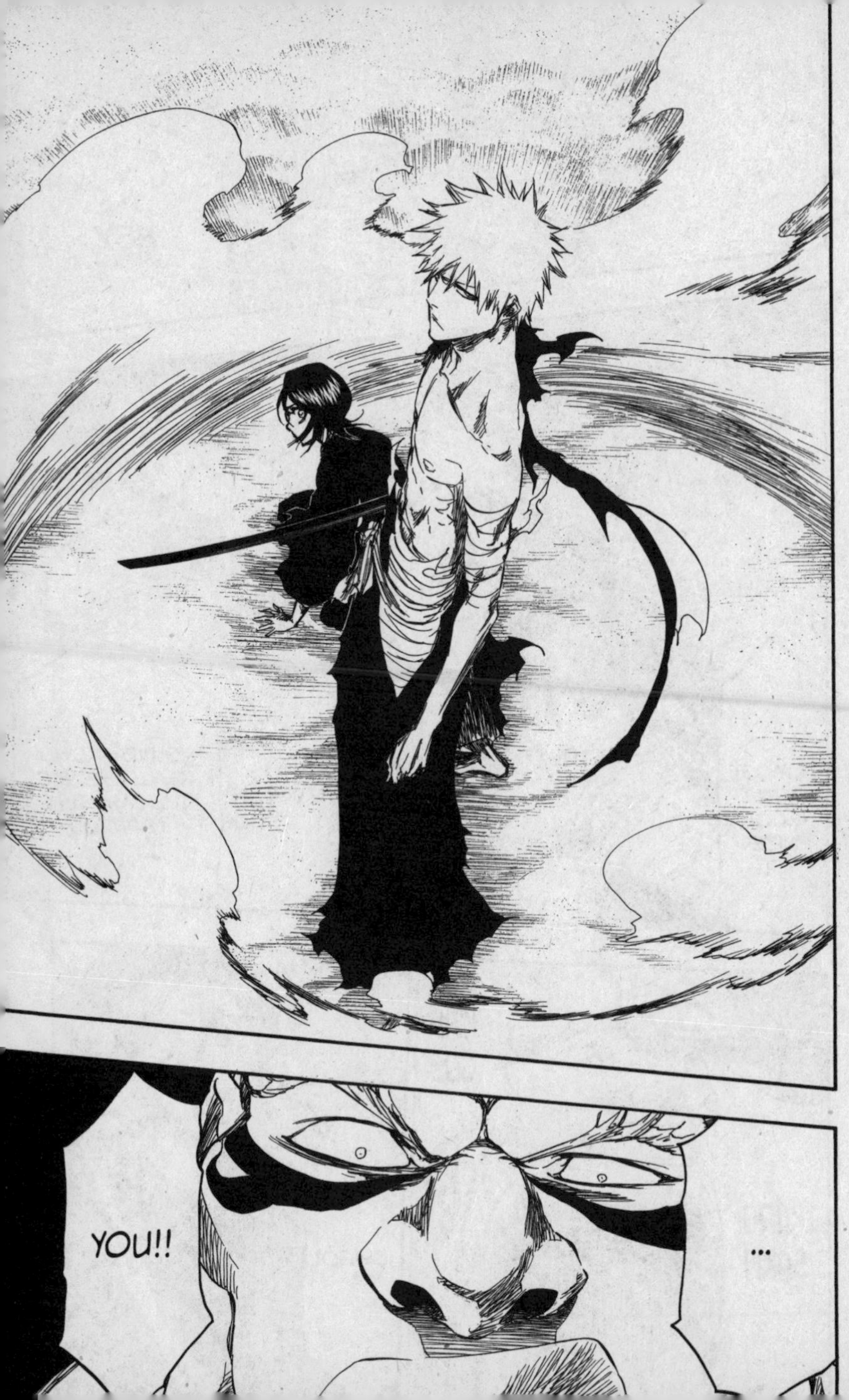
...
YOU!!

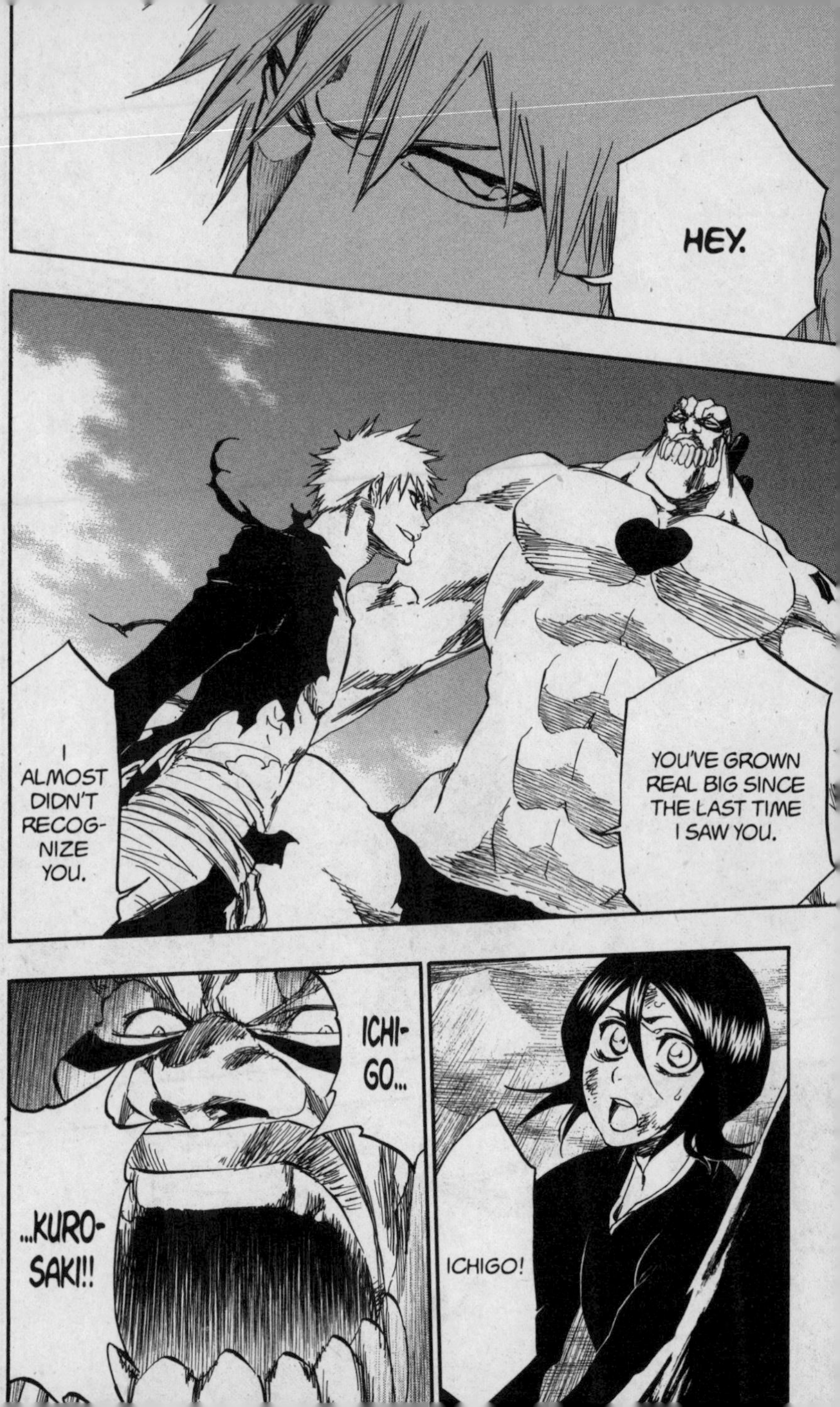
HEY.
YOU'VE GROWN REAL BIG SINCE THE LAST TIME I SAW YOU.
I ALMOST DIDN'T RECOG-NIZE YOU.
ICHIGO!
ICHI-GO...
...KURO-SAKI!!

BLEACH378. Eyes of the Victor

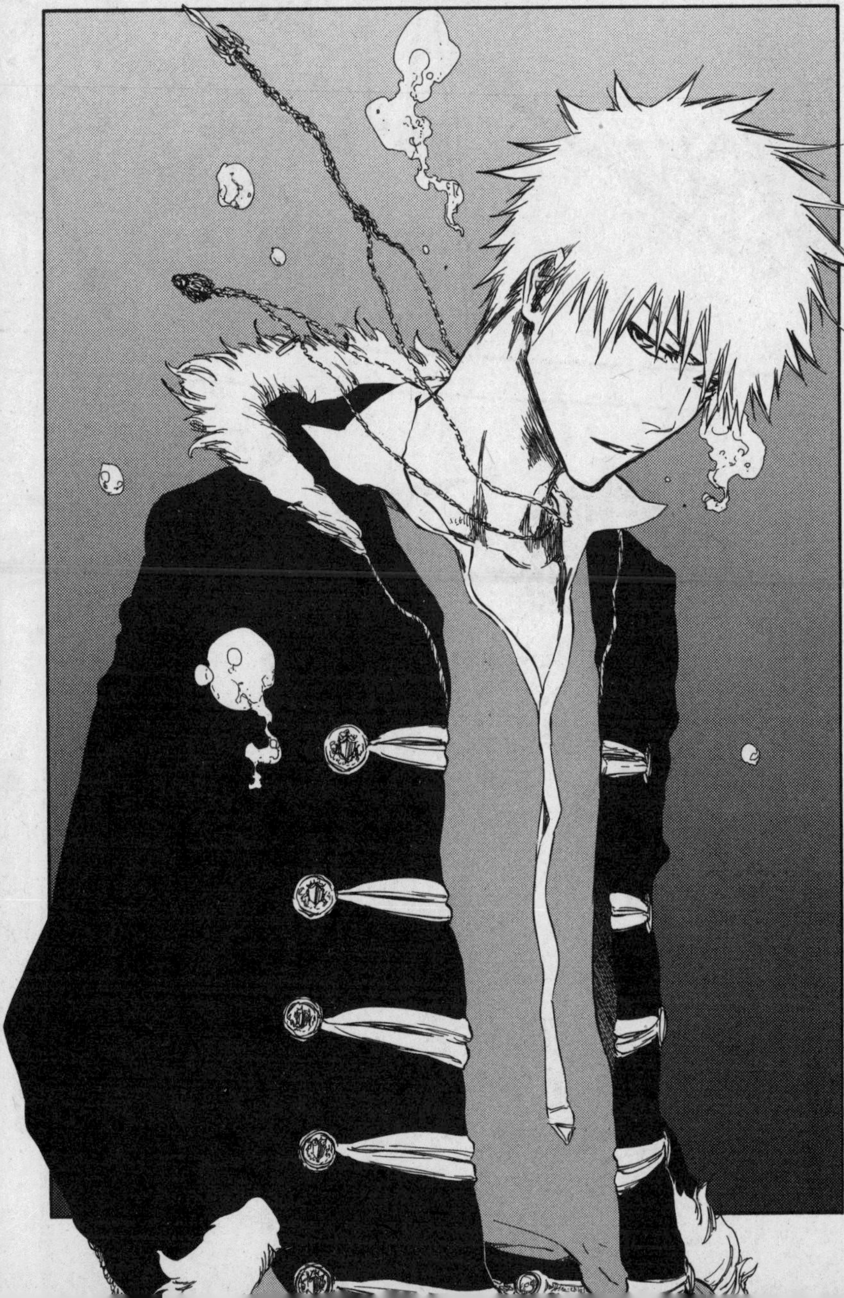

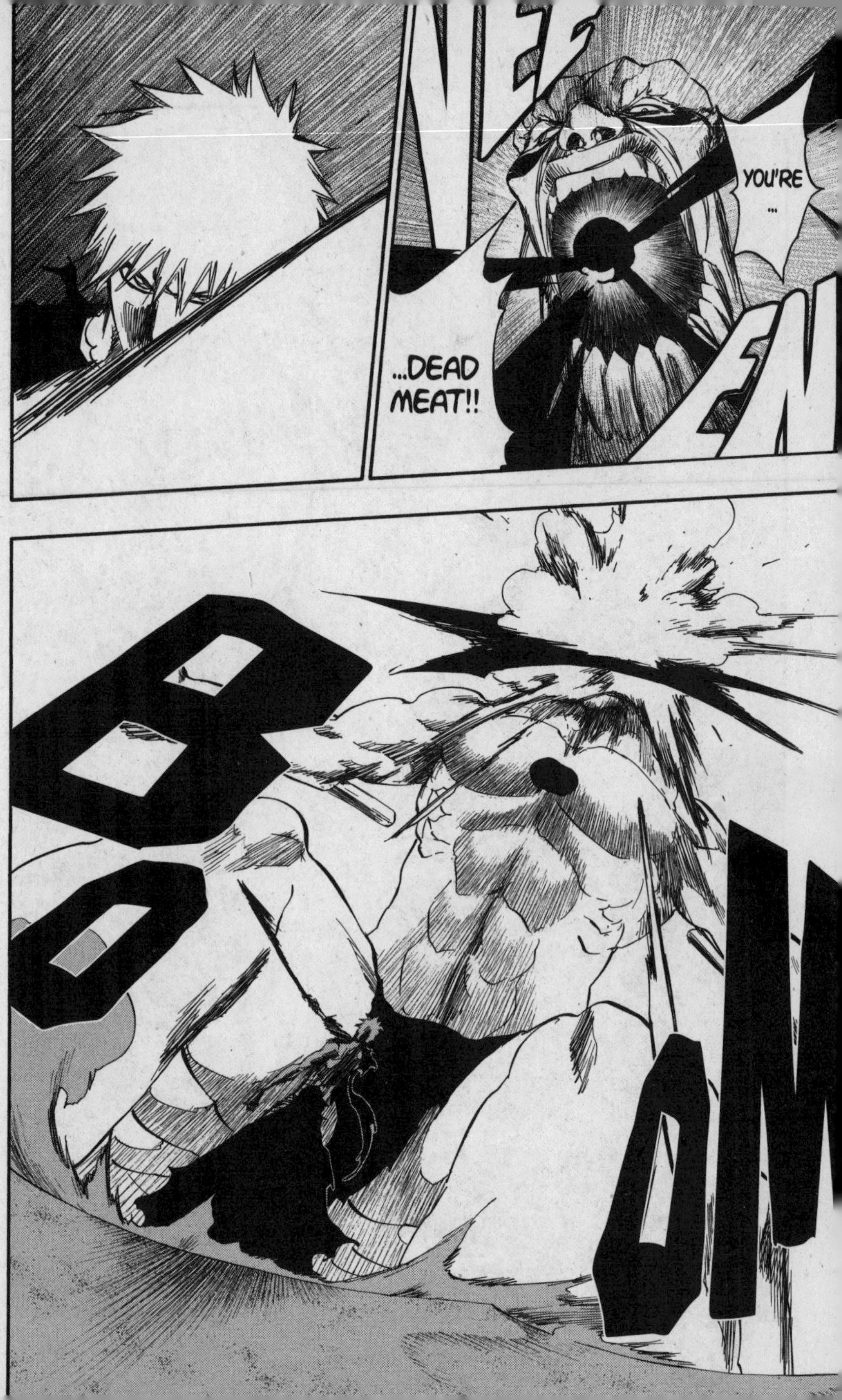
YOU'RE
...
...DEAD
MEAT!!

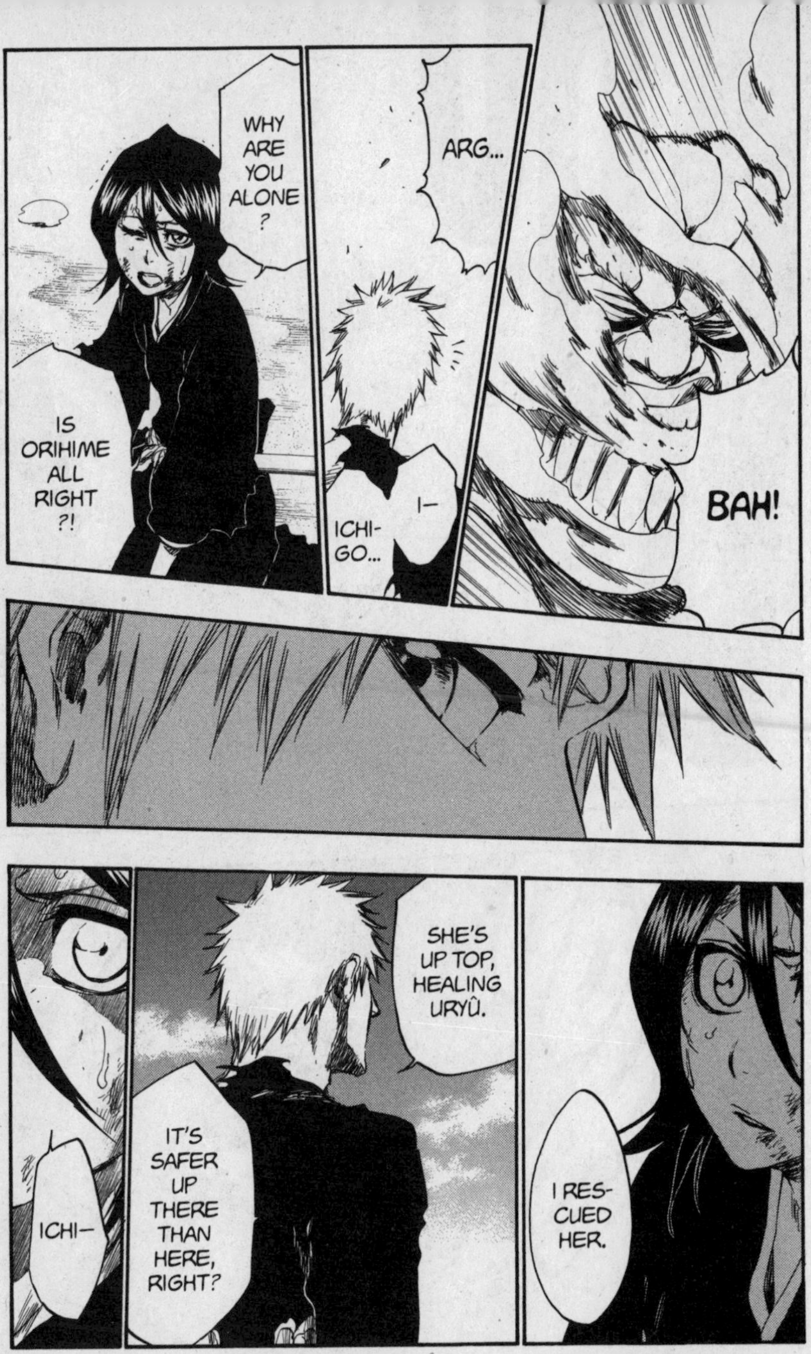
BAH!
ARG...
I— ICHI-GO...
WHY ARE YOU ALONE?
IS ORIHIME ALL RIGHT?!
I RES-CUED HER.
SHE'S UP TOP, HEALING URYÛ.
IT'S SAFER UP THERE THAN HERE, RIGHT?
ICHI—

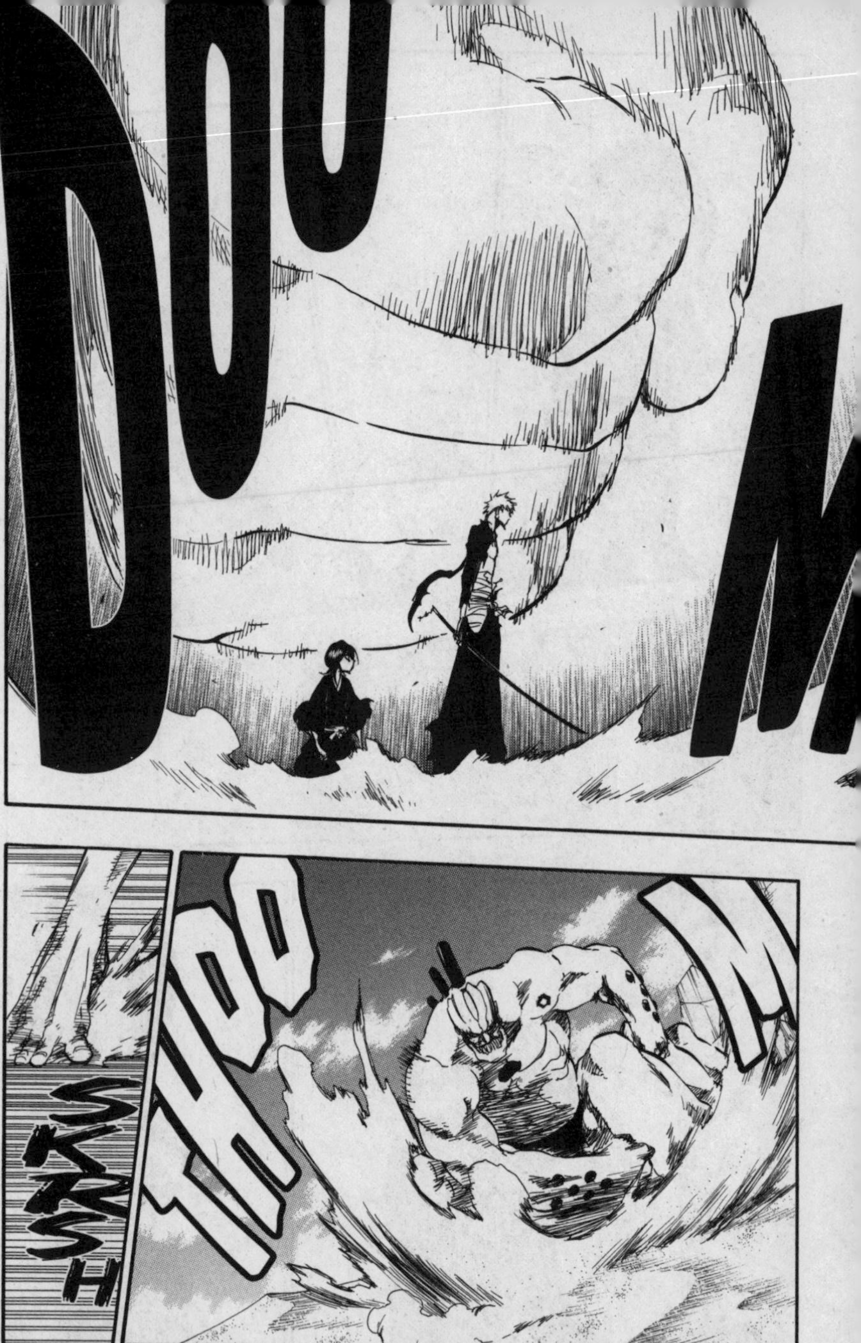
DOOM
THOOM
SKRSH

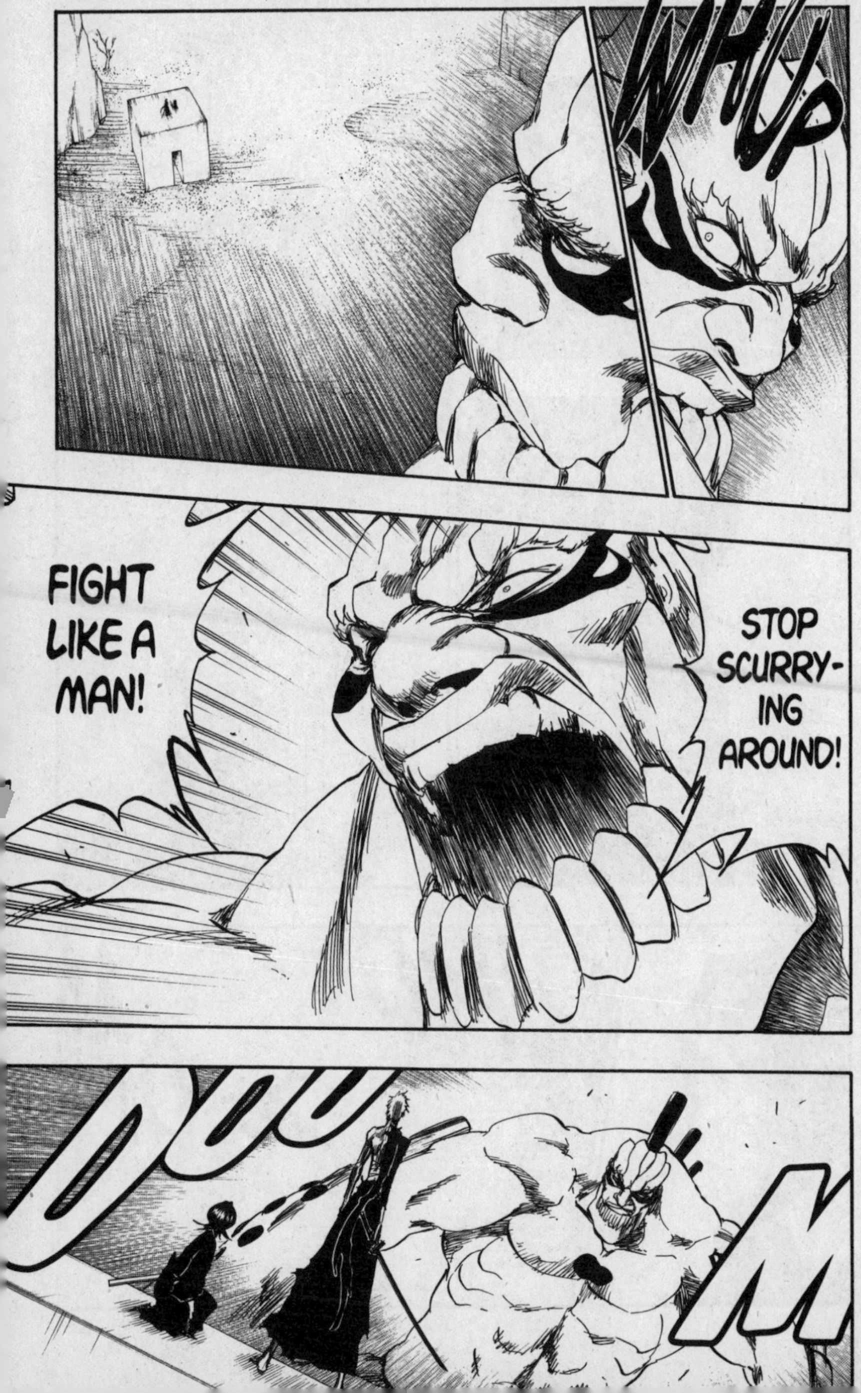
WHUP
STOP SCURRY-ING AROUND!
FIGHT LIKE A MAN!

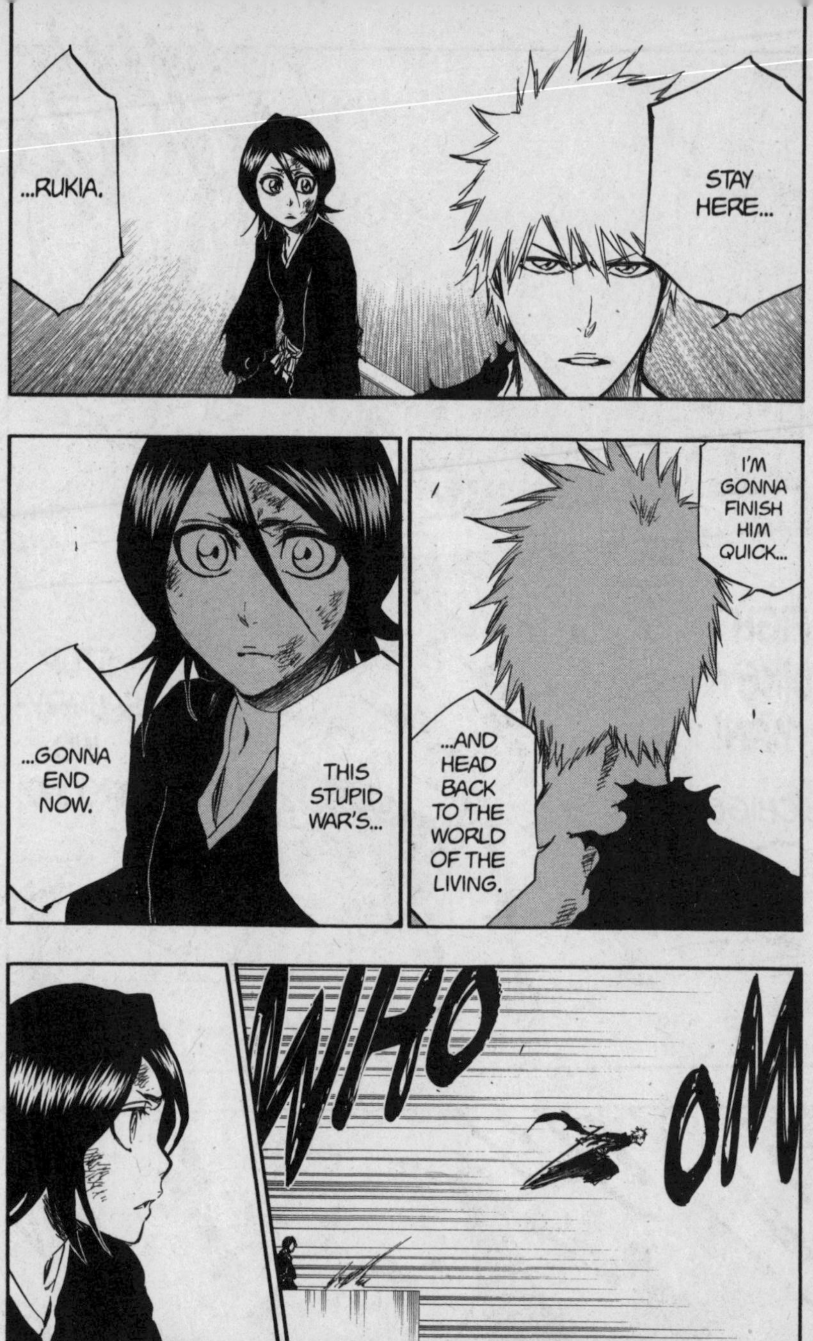
STAY HERE...
...RUKIA.
I'M GONNA FINISH HIM QUICK...
...AND HEAD BACK TO THE WORLD OF THE LIVING.
THIS STUPID WAR'S...
...GONNA END NOW.
WHOOM

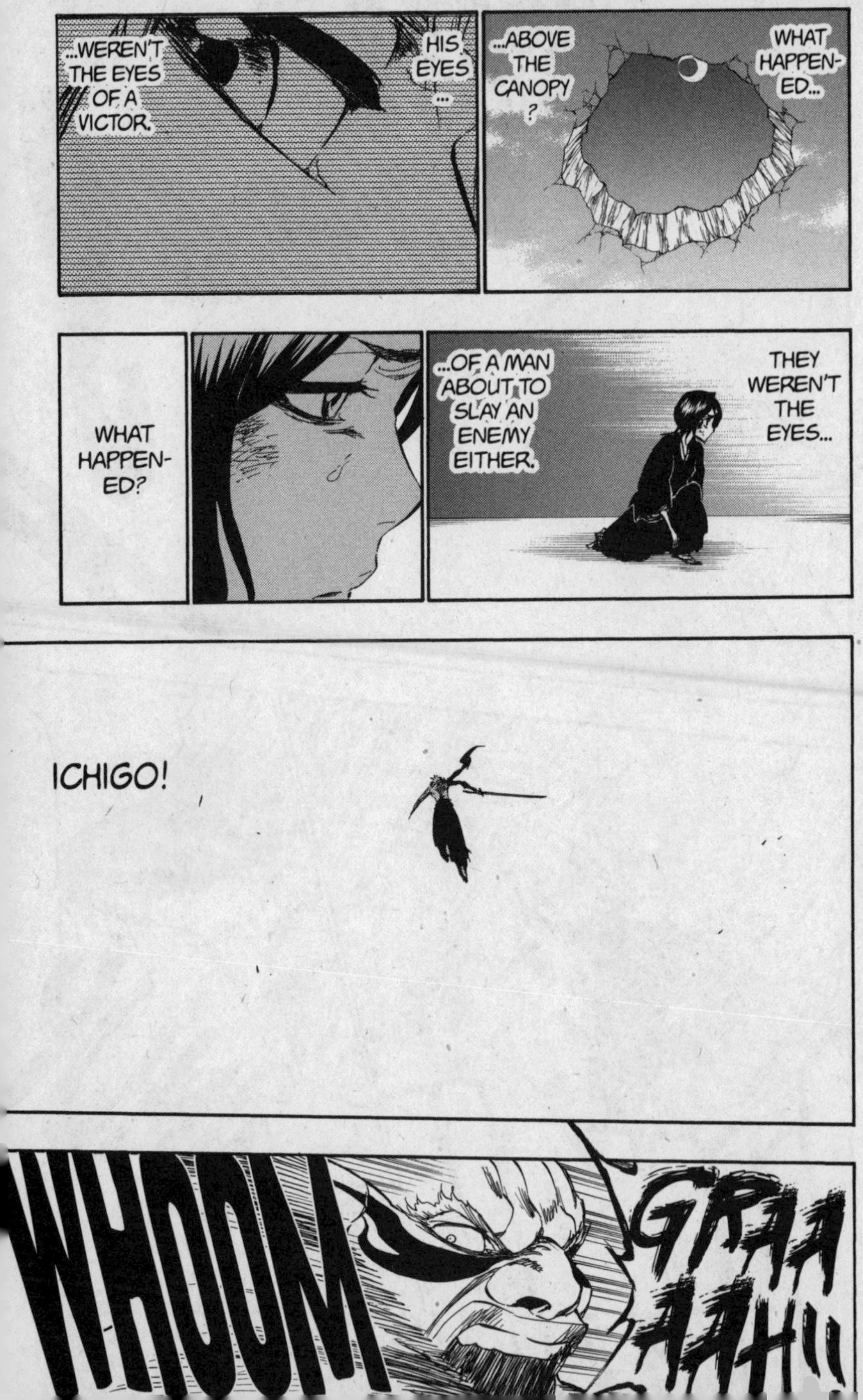
WHAT HAPPEN-ED...
...ABOVE THE CANOPY?
HIS EYES...
...WEREN'T THE EYES OF A VICTOR.
THEY WEREN'T THE EYES...
...OF A MAN ABOUT TO SLAY AN ENEMY EITHER.
WHAT HAPPEN-ED?
ICHIGO!
GRAA AAH!!
WHOOM

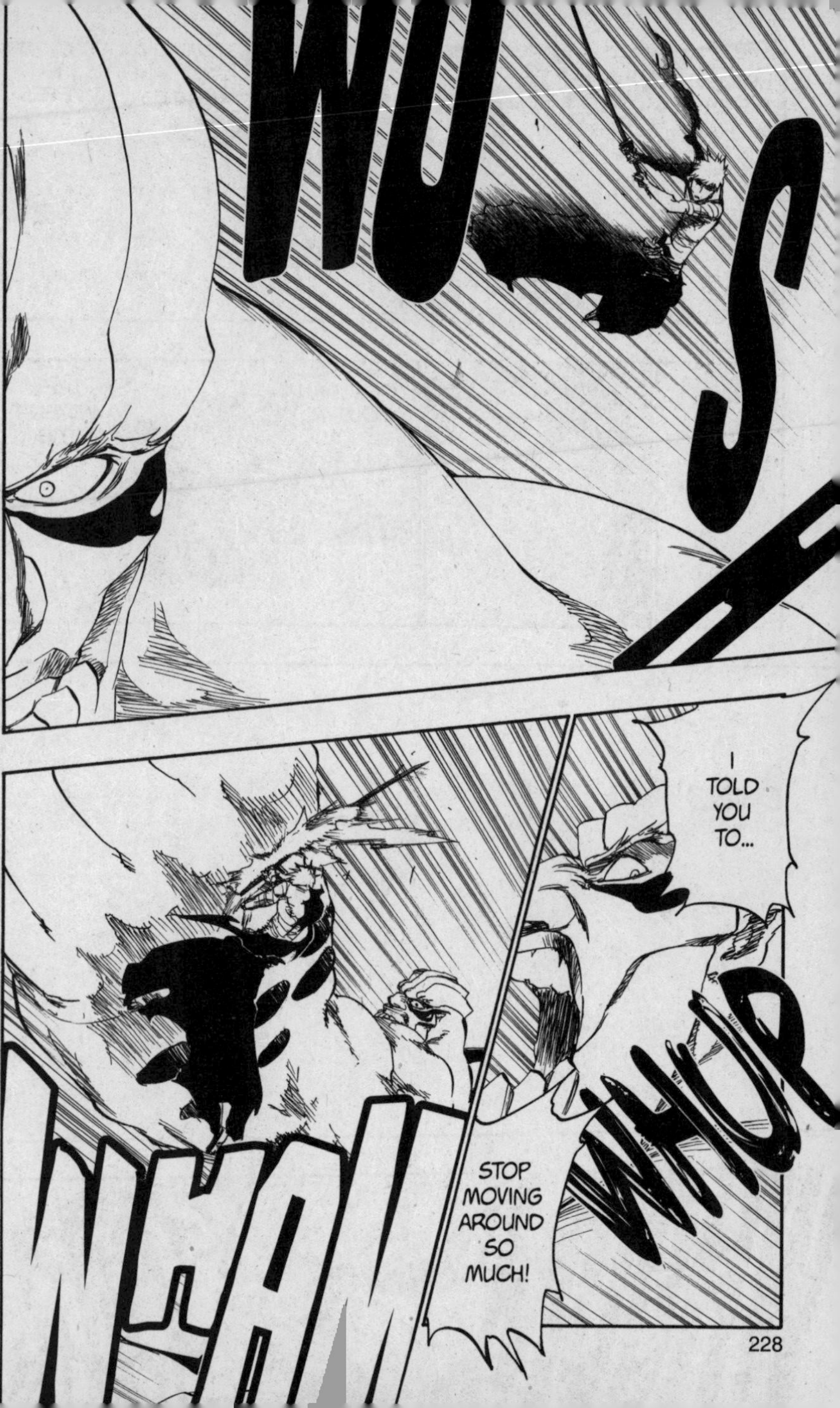
I TOLD YOU TO...
WHUP
STOP MOVING AROUND SO MUCH!
WHAM

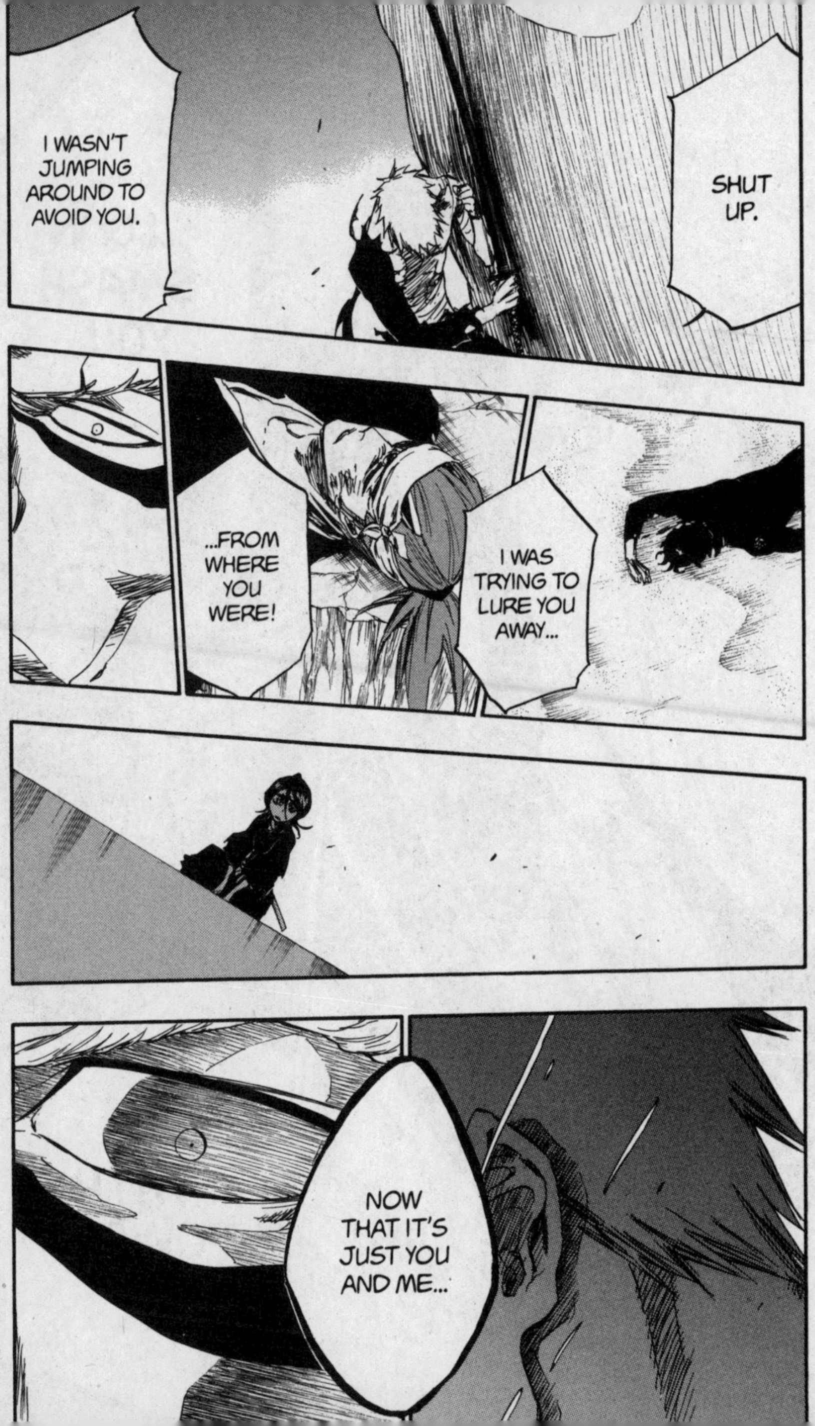
SHUT UP.
I WASN'T JUMPING AROUND TO AVOID YOU.
I WAS TRYING TO LURE YOU AWAY...
...FROM WHERE YOU WERE!
NOW THAT IT'S JUST YOU AND ME...

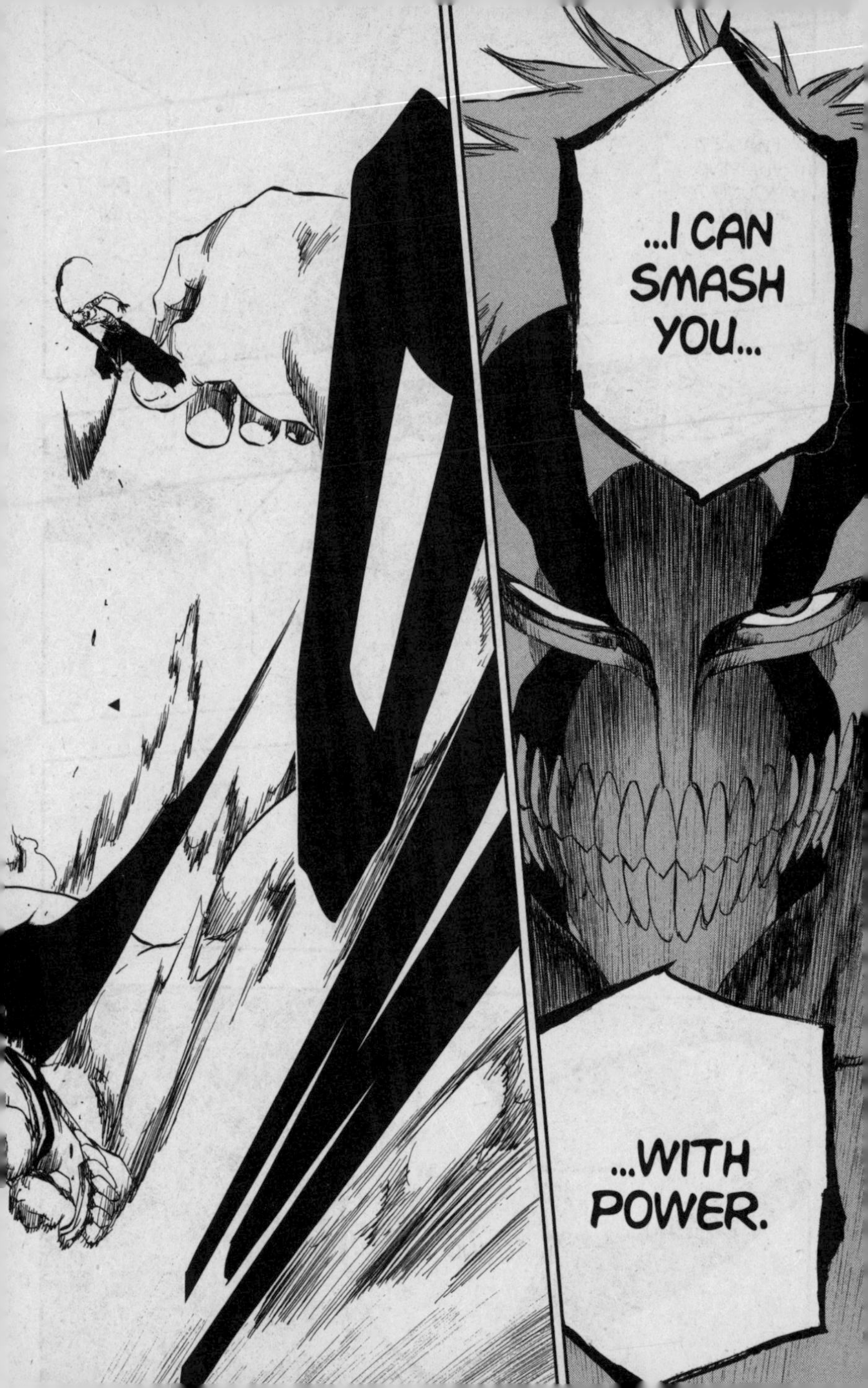
...I CAN SMASH YOU...
...WITH POWER.

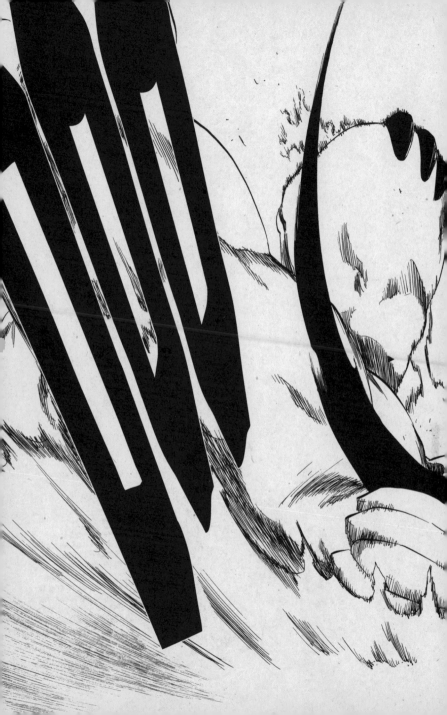

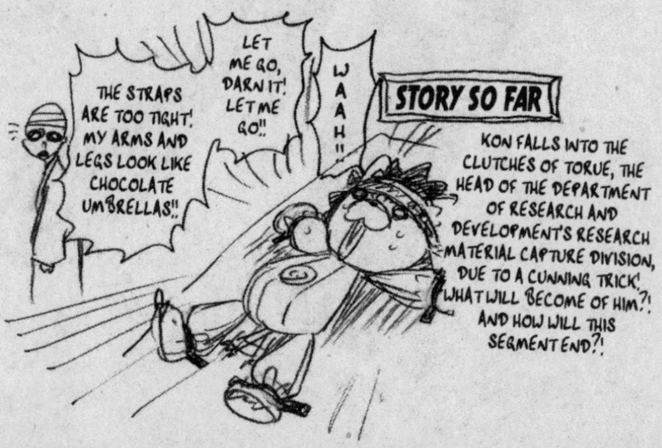
STORY SO FAR
KON FALLS INTO THE CLUTCHES OF TORUE, THE HEAD OF THE DEPARTMENT OF RESEARCH AND DEVELOPMENT'S RESEARCH MATERIAL CAPTURE DIVISION, DUE TO A CUNNING TRICK! WHAT WILL BECOME OF HIM?! AND HOW WILL THIS SEGMENT END?!
WAAAH!!
LET ME GO, DARN IT! LET ME GO!!
THE STRAPS ARE TOO TIGHT! MY ARMS AND LEGS LOOK LIKE CHOCOLATE UMBRELLAS!!

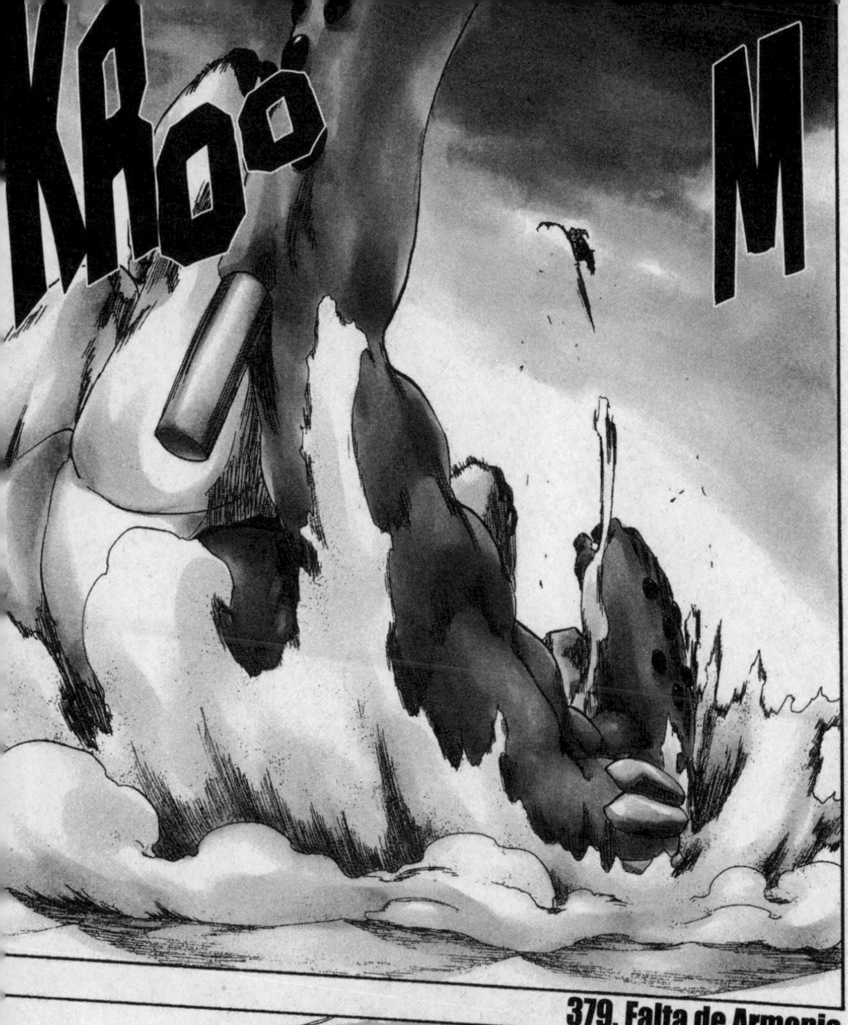
KRAOOOM

379. Falta de Armonia

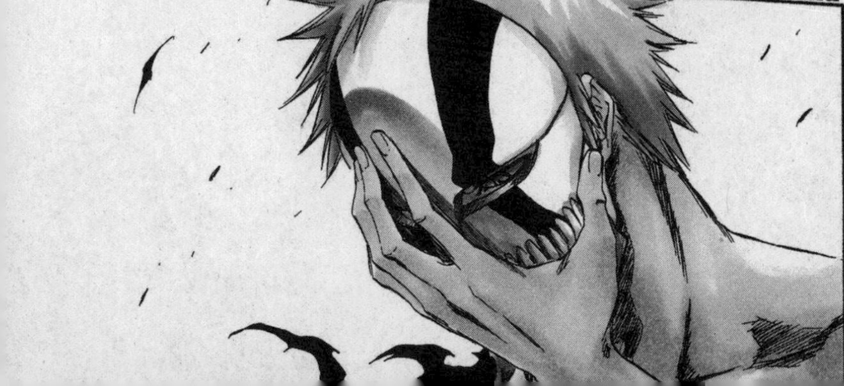

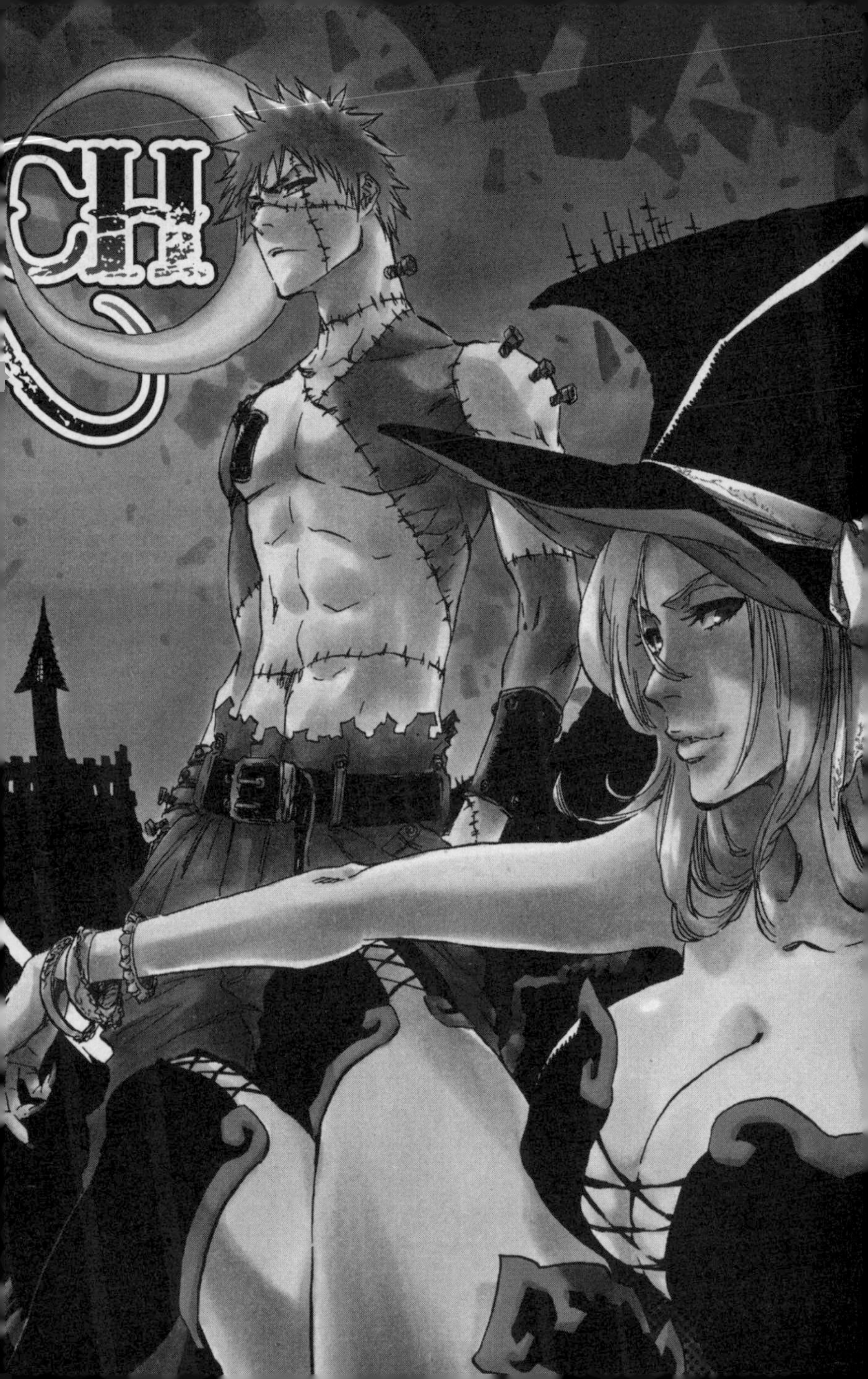
CHI

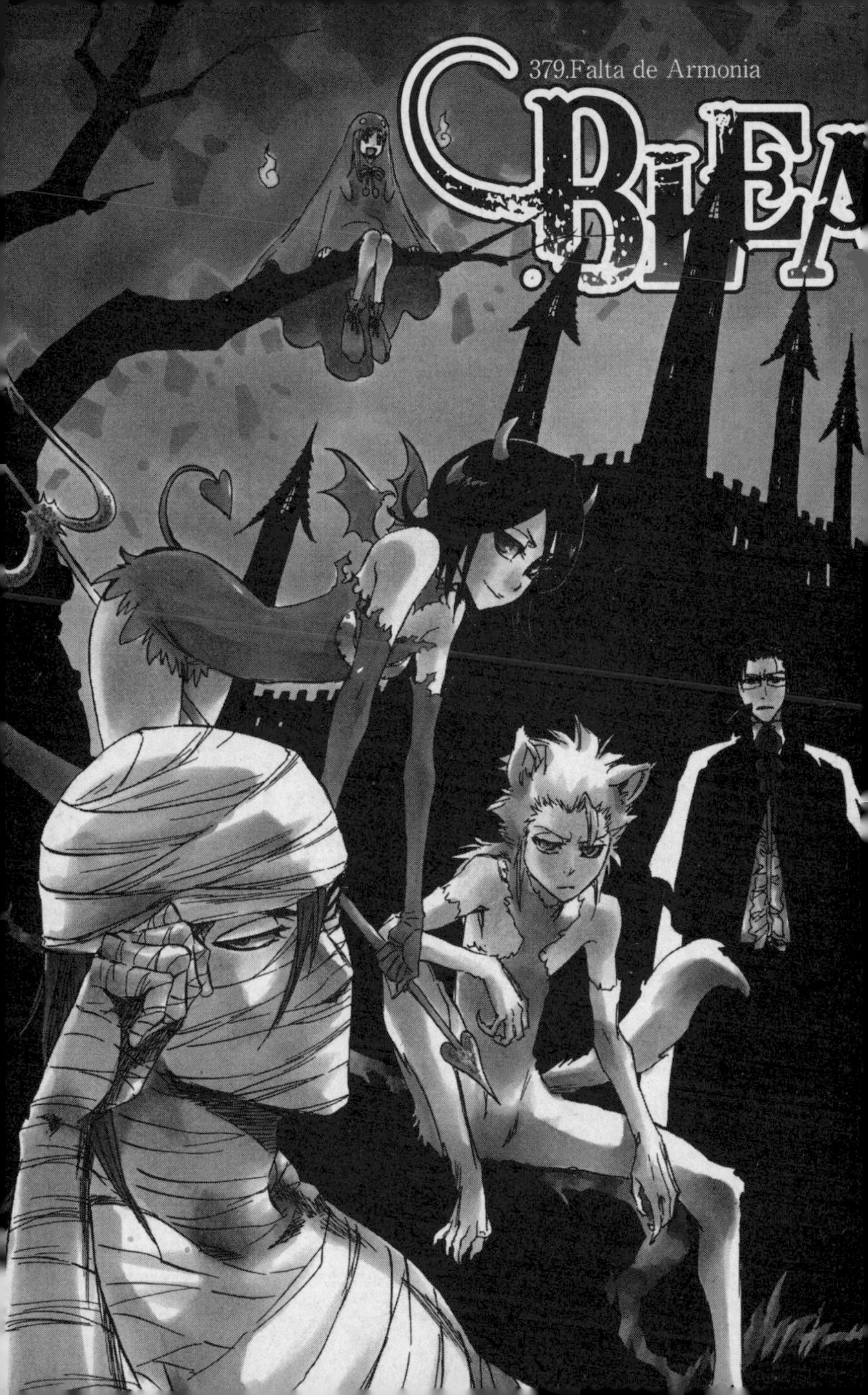
379.Falta de Armonia
BLEA

BLEACH
ブリーチ

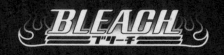

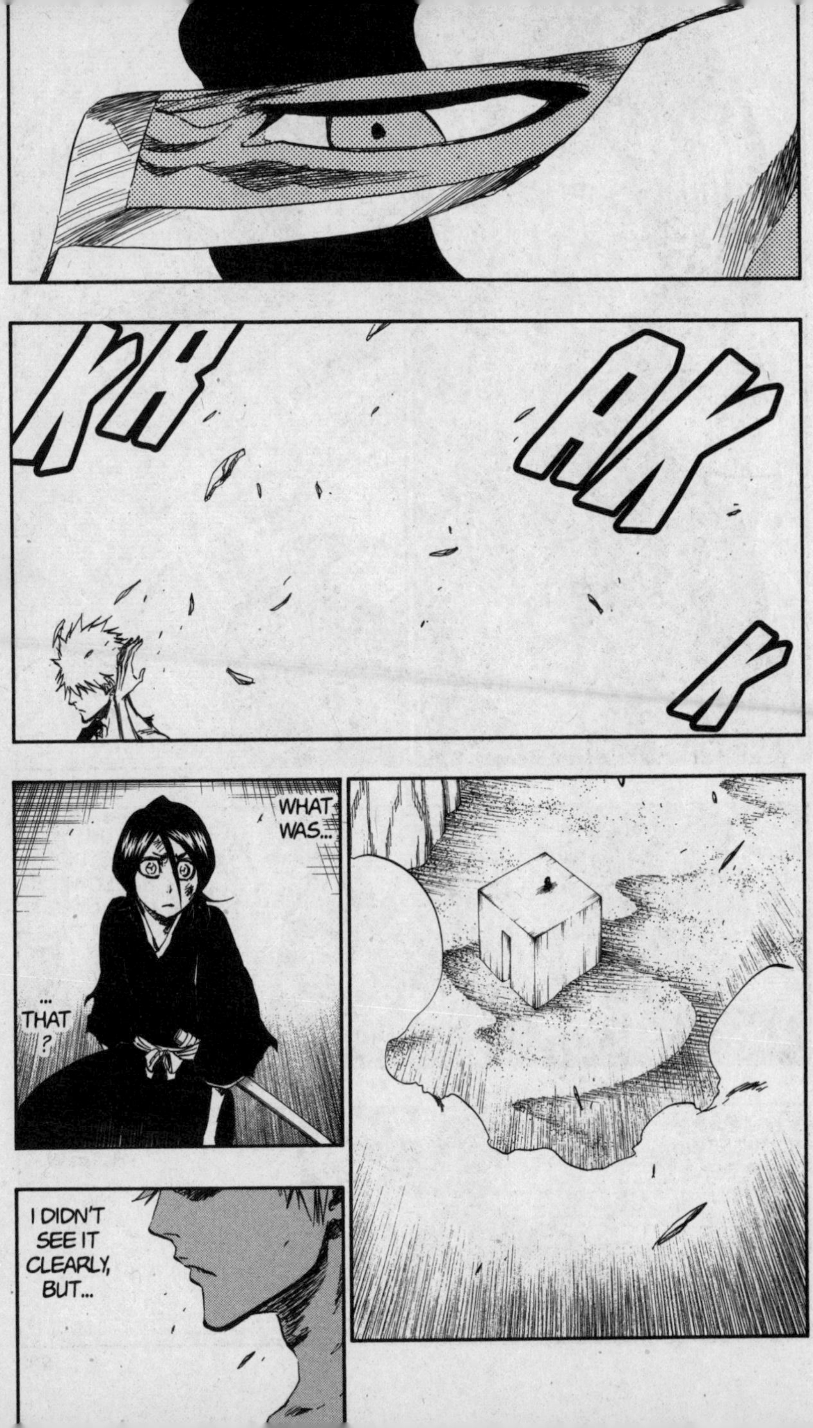
KRAKK
WHAT WAS...
...THAT?
I DIDN'T SEE IT CLEARLY, BUT...

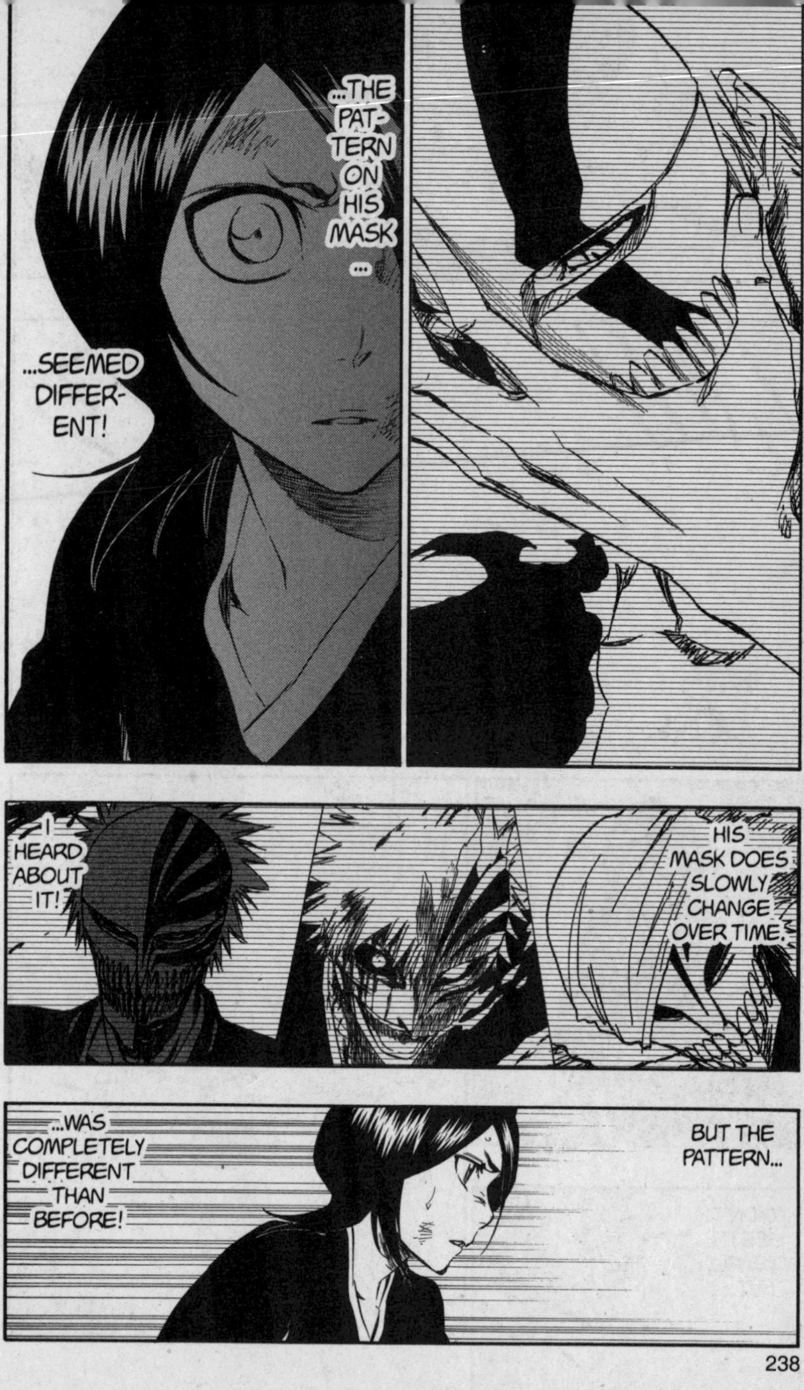
...THE PATTERN ON HIS MASK...
...SEEMED DIFFERENT!
HIS MASK DOES SLOWLY CHANGE OVER TIME.
I HEARD ABOUT IT!
BUT THE PATTERN...
...WAS COMPLETELY DIFFERENT THAN BEFORE!

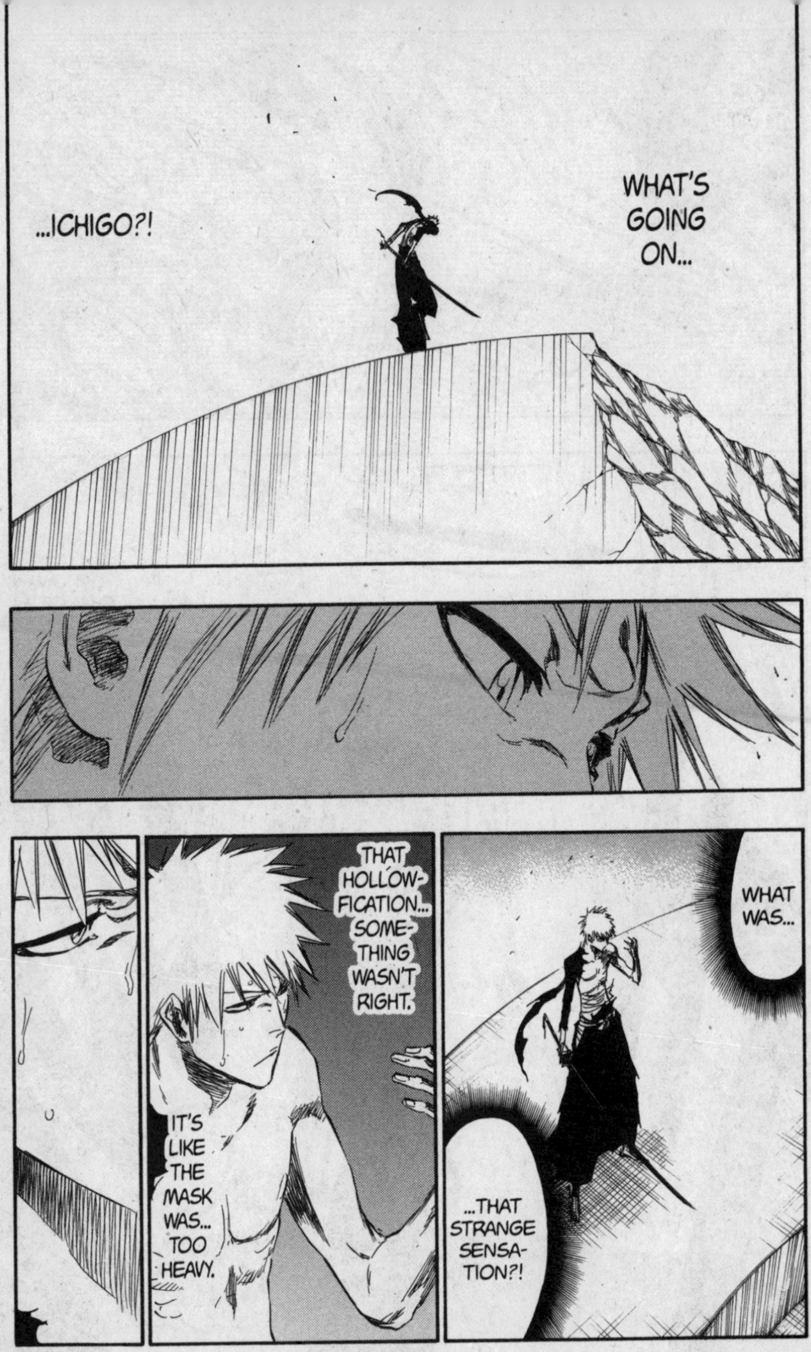
WHAT'S GOING ON...
...ICHIGO?!
WHAT WAS...
...THAT STRANGE SENSATION?!
THAT HOLLOW-FICATION... SOME-THING WASN'T RIGHT.
IT'S LIKE THE MASK WAS... TOO HEAVY.

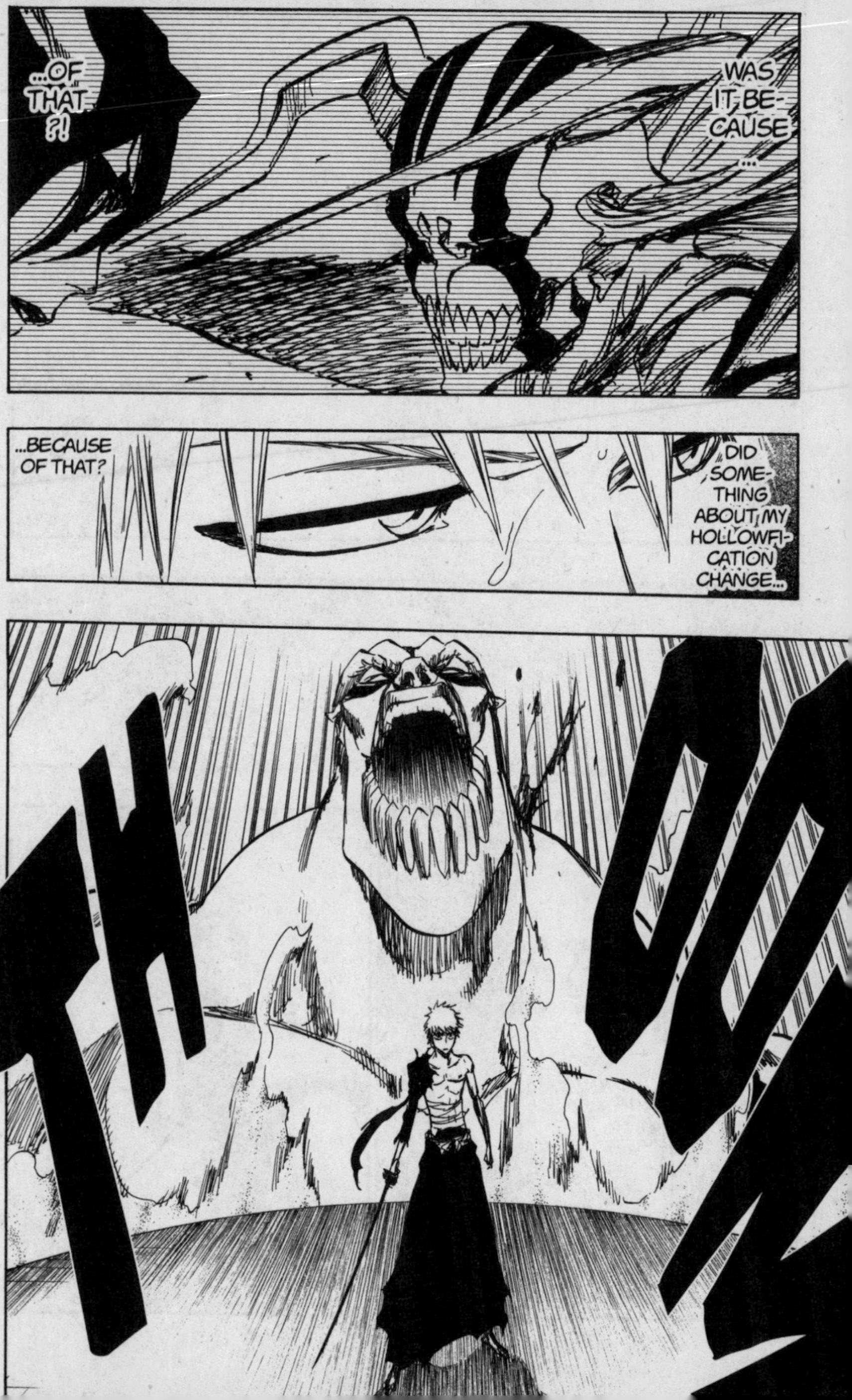
WAS IT BE-CAUSE...
...OF THAT?!
DID SOME-THING ABOUT MY HOLLOWFI-CATION CHANGE...
...BECAUSE OF THAT?
THOOM

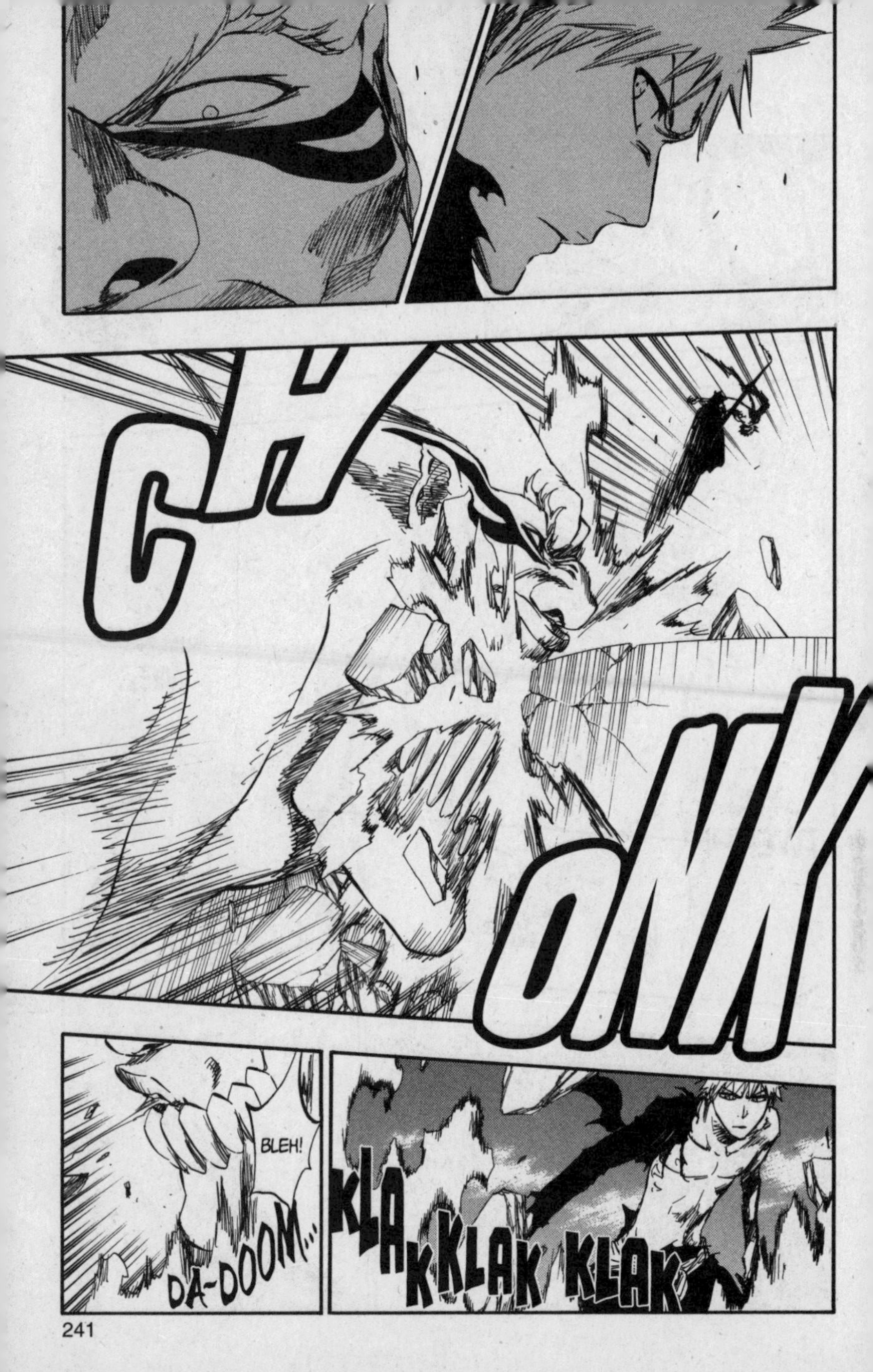

CH
ANK
KLAK KLAK KLAK
BLEH!
DA-DOOM...

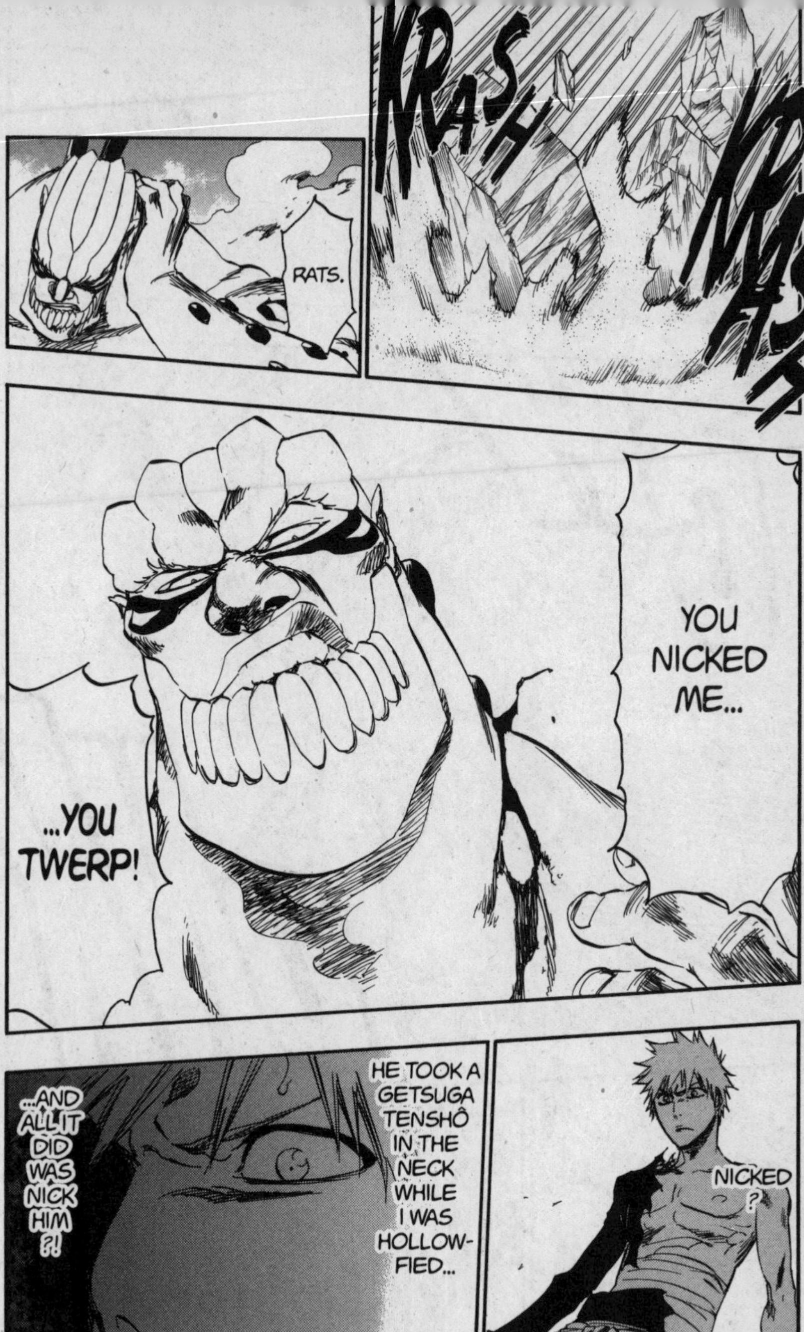
KRASH
KRASH
RATS.
YOU NICKED ME...
...YOU TWERP!
NICKED ?
HE TOOK A GETSUGA TENSHÔ IN THE NECK WHILE I WAS HOLLOW-FIED...
...AND ALL IT DID WAS NICK HIM ?!

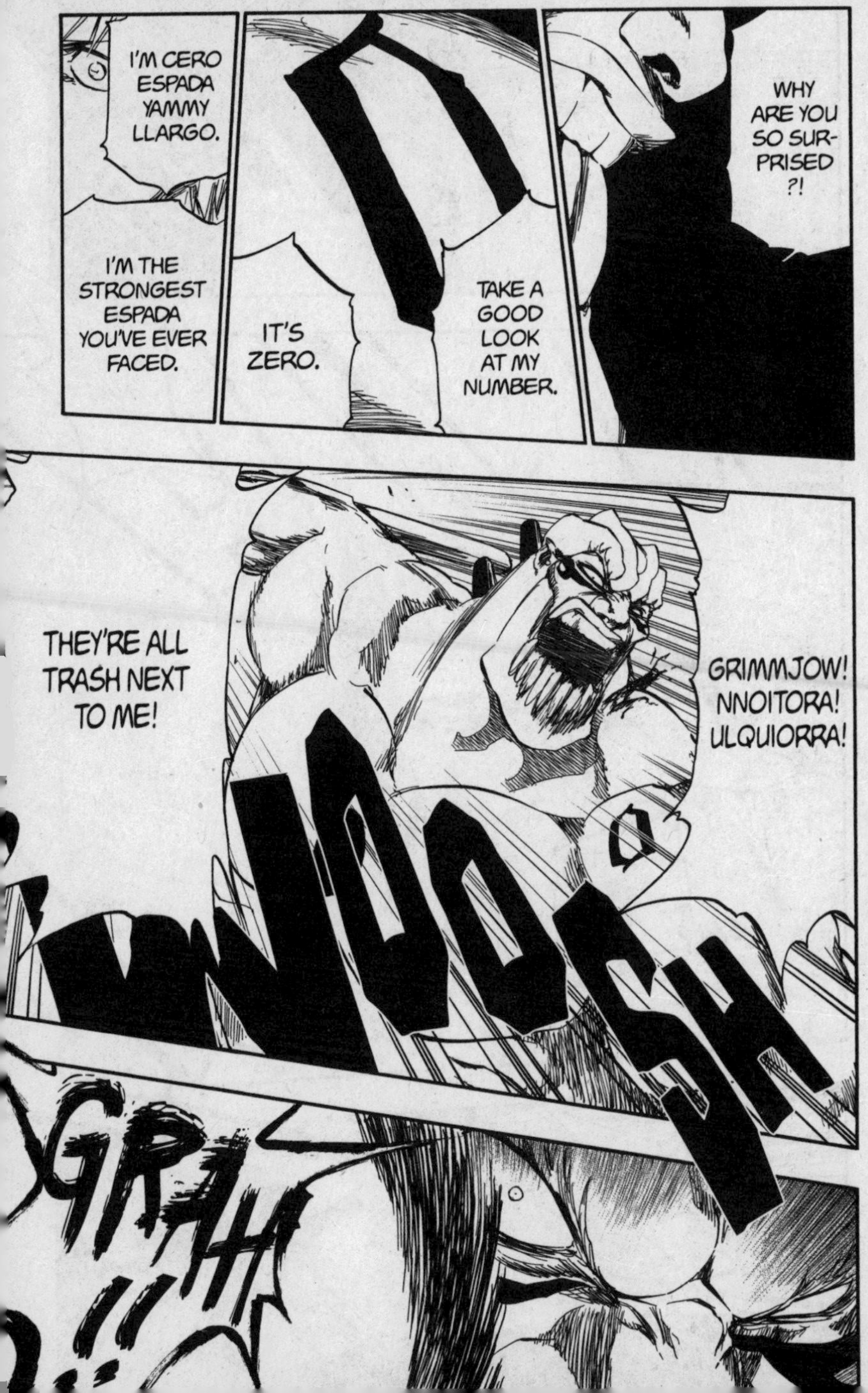
WHY ARE YOU SO SURPRISED?!
TAKE A GOOD LOOK AT MY NUMBER.
IT'S ZERO.
I'M CERO ESPADA YAMMY LLARGO.
I'M THE STRONGEST ESPADA YOU'VE EVER FACED.
GRIMMJOW! NNOITORA! ULQUIORRA!
THEY'RE ALL TRASH NEXT TO ME!
WHOOSH
GRAHH...!!

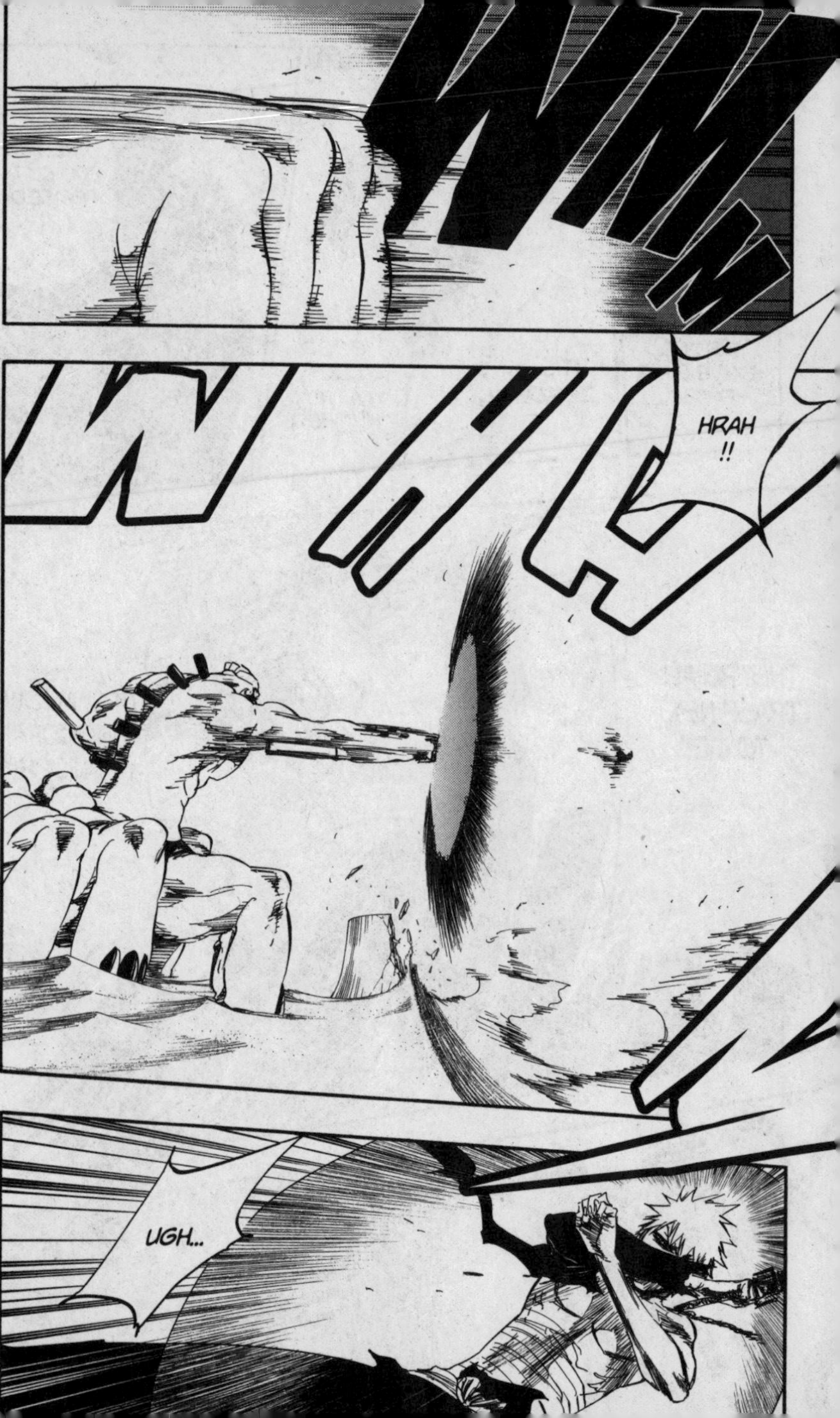
HRAH !!
UGH...

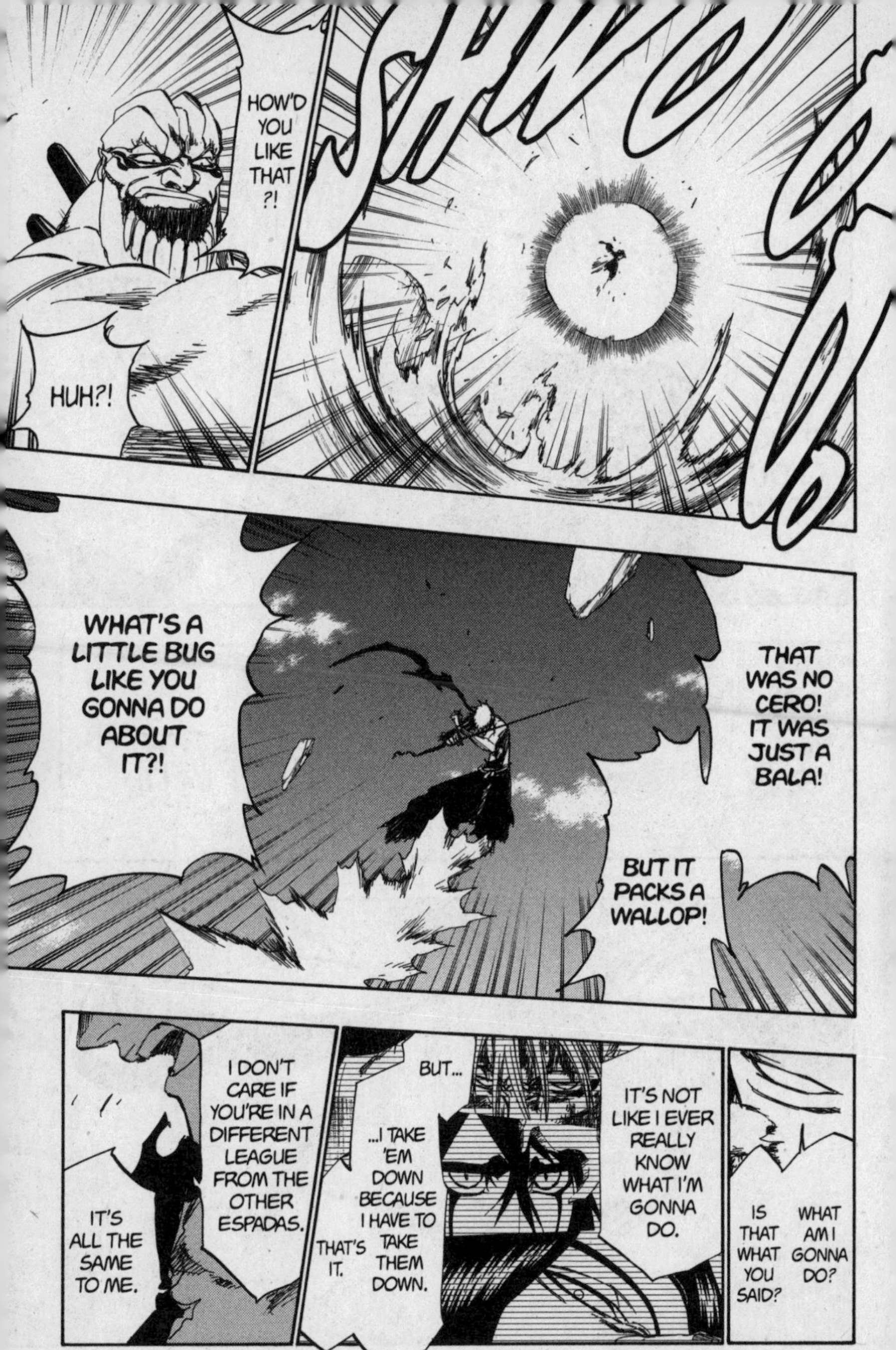
HOW'D YOU LIKE THAT?!
HUH?!
THAT WAS NO CERO! IT WAS JUST A BALA!
BUT IT PACKS A WALLOP!
WHAT'S A LITTLE BUG LIKE YOU GONNA DO ABOUT IT?!
WHAT AM I GONNA DO?
IS THAT WHAT YOU SAID?
IT'S NOT LIKE I EVER REALLY KNOW WHAT I'M GONNA DO.
BUT...
...I TAKE 'EM DOWN BECAUSE I HAVE TO TAKE THEM DOWN.
THAT'S IT.
I DON'T CARE IF YOU'RE IN A DIFFERENT LEAGUE FROM THE OTHER ESPADAS.
IT'S ALL THE SAME TO ME.

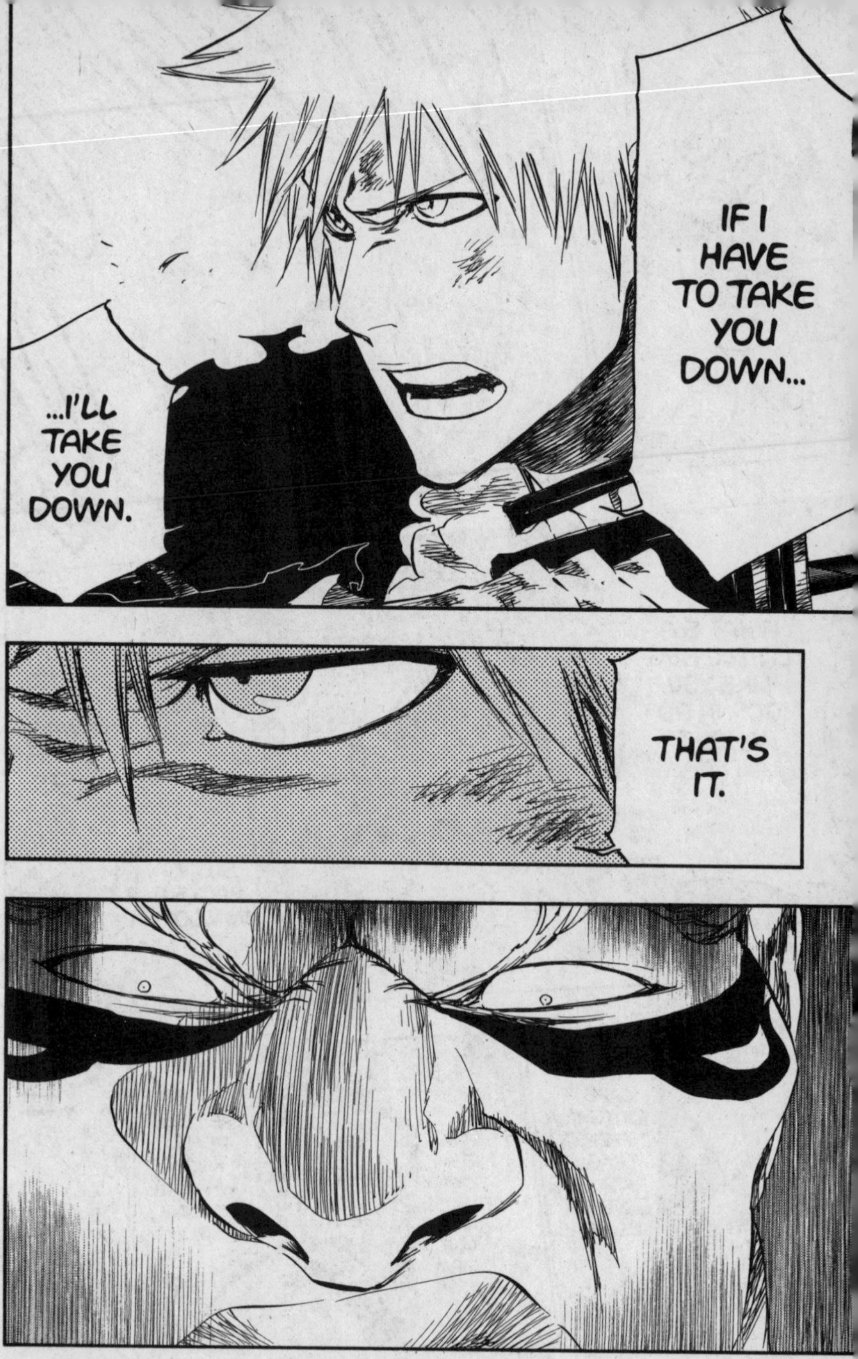
IF I HAVE TO TAKE YOU DOWN...
...I'LL TAKE YOU DOWN.
THAT'S IT.

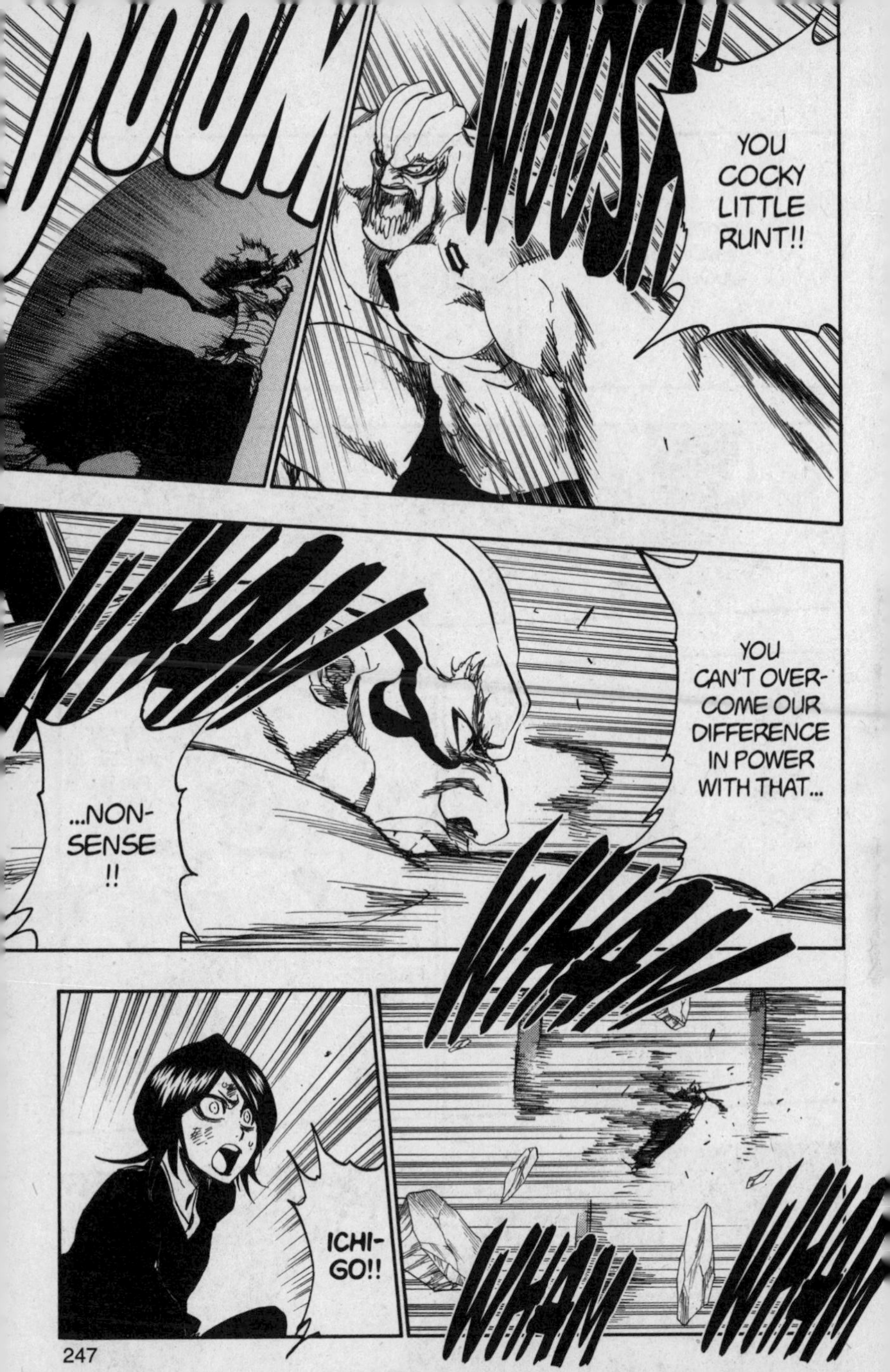
WOOSH
YOU COCKY LITTLE RUNT!!
DOOM
YOU CAN'T OVER-COME OUR DIFFERENCE IN POWER WITH THAT...
WHAM
...NON-SENSE !!
WHAM
WHAM
WHAM
ICHI-GO!!

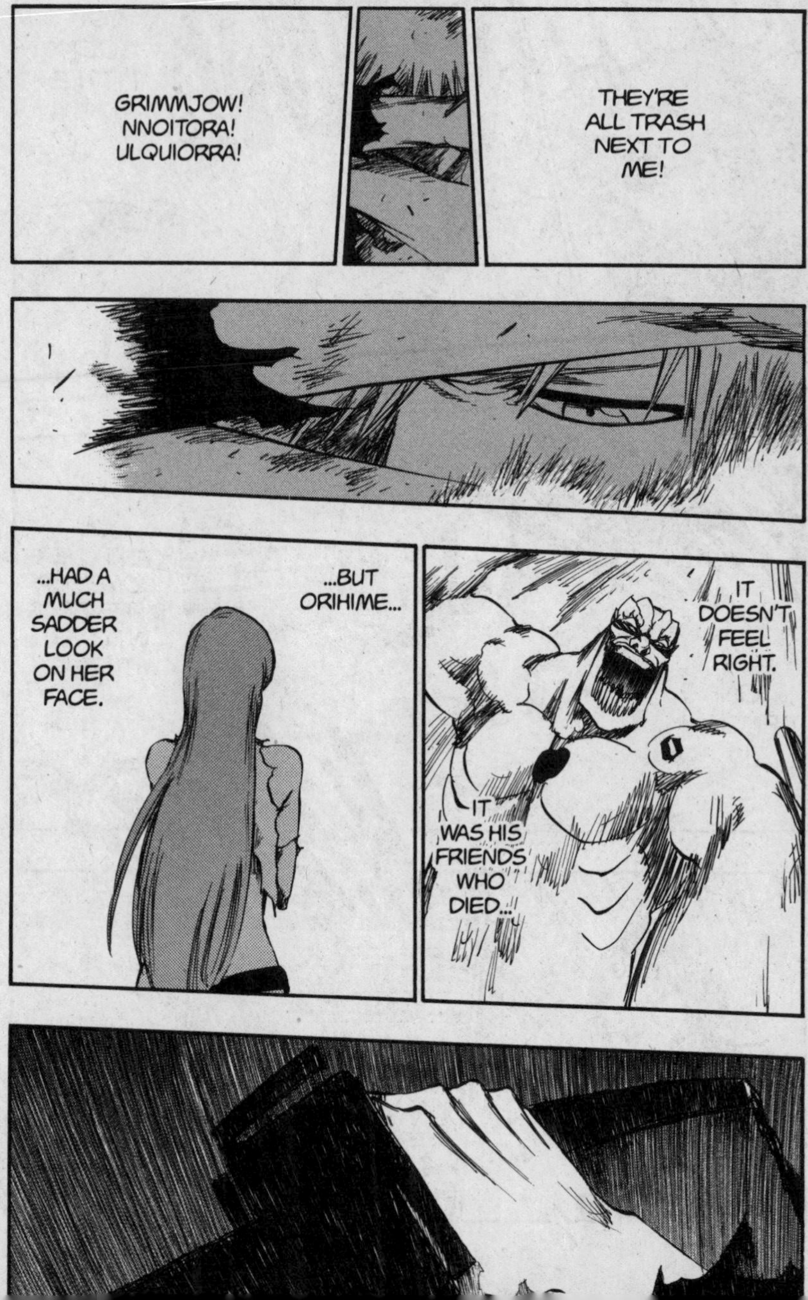
THEY'RE ALL TRASH NEXT TO ME!
GRIMMJOW! NNOITORA! ULQUIORRA!
IT DOESN'T FEEL RIGHT.
IT WAS HIS FRIENDS WHO DIED...
...BUT ORIHIME...
...HAD A MUCH SADDER LOOK ON HER FACE.

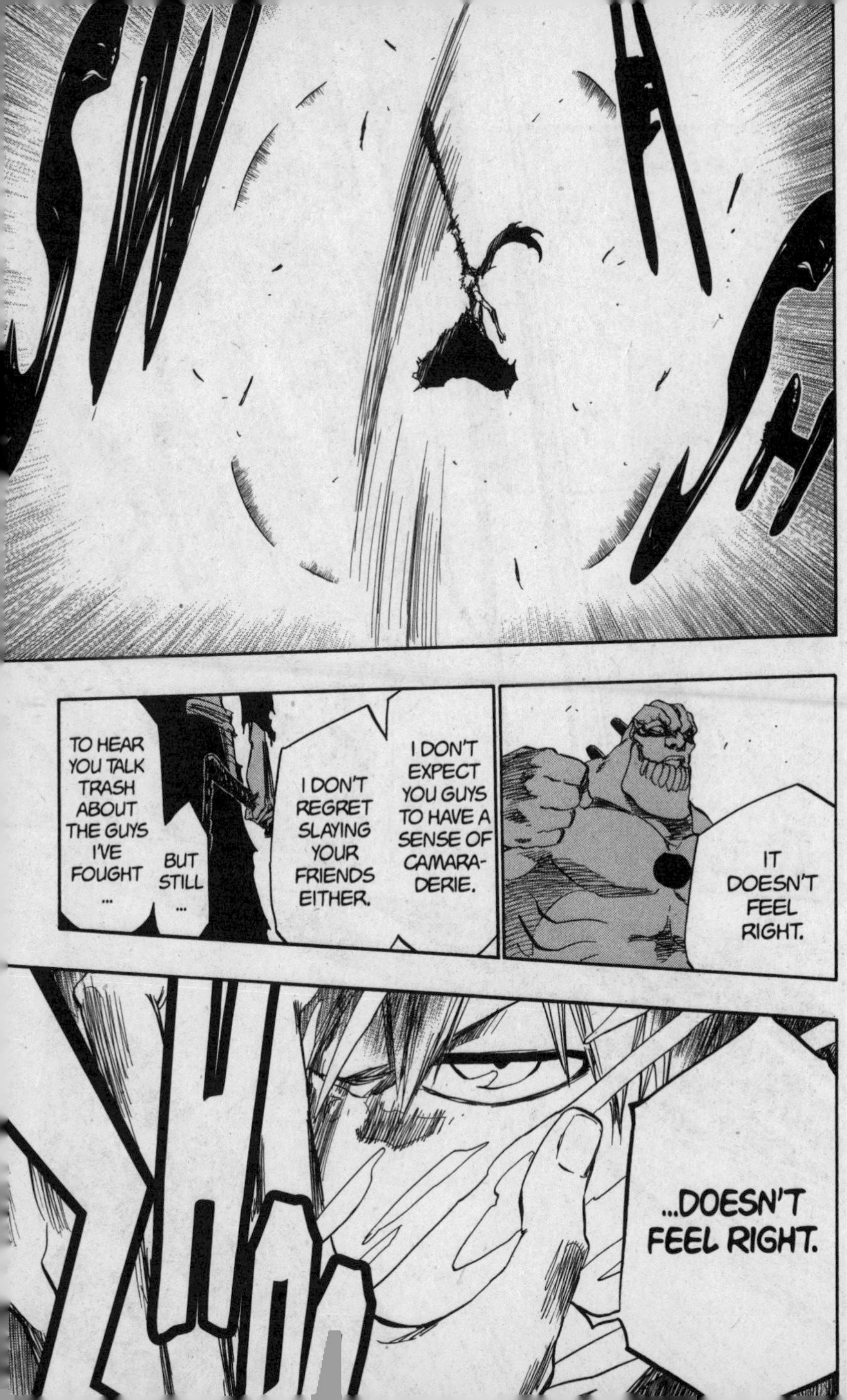
IT DOESN'T FEEL RIGHT.
I DON'T EXPECT YOU GUYS TO HAVE A SENSE OF CAMARA-DERIE.
I DON'T REGRET SLAYING YOUR FRIENDS EITHER.
BUT STILL ...
TO HEAR YOU TALK TRASH ABOUT THE GUYS I'VE FOUGHT ...
...DOESN'T FEEL RIGHT.

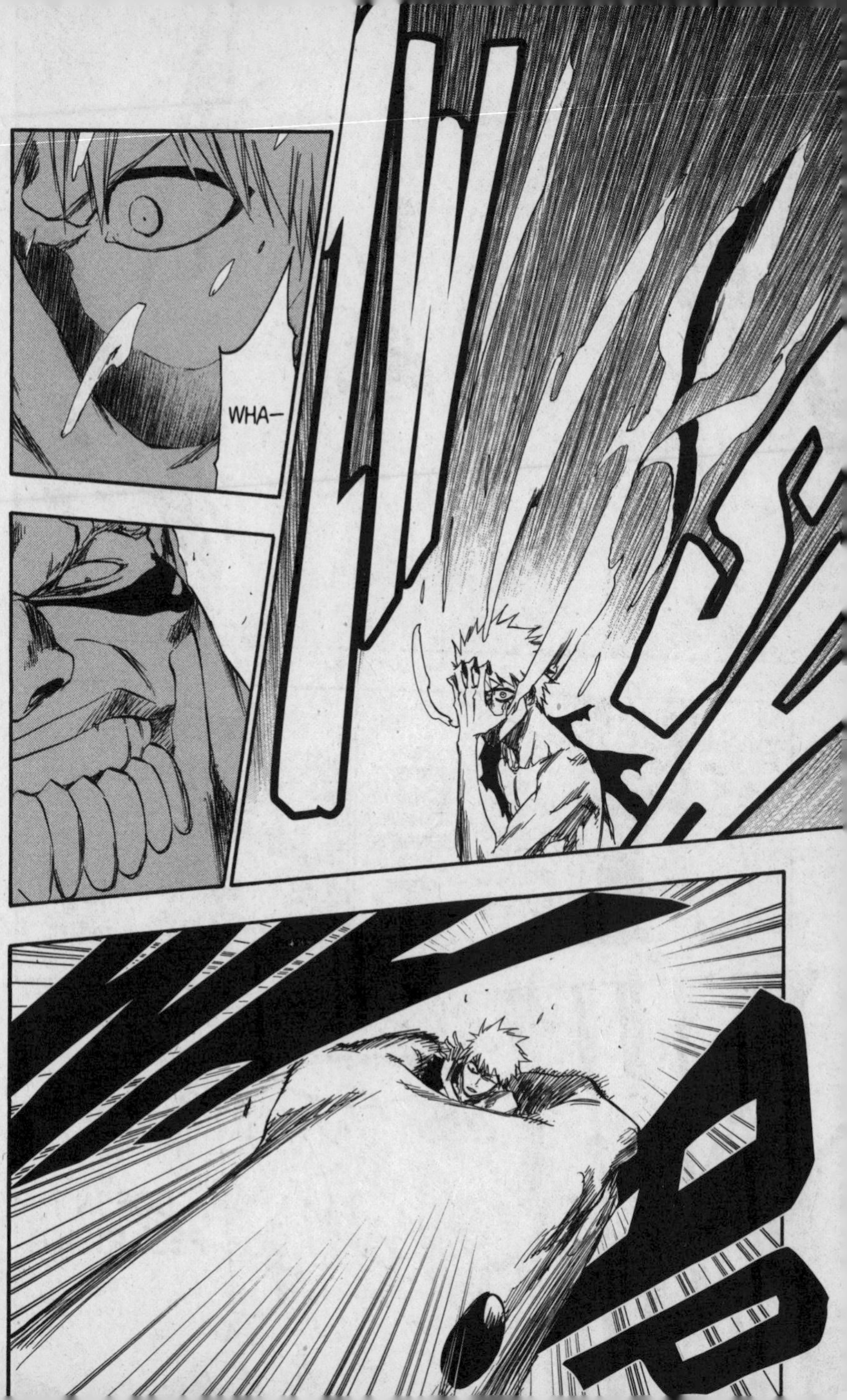
WHA–

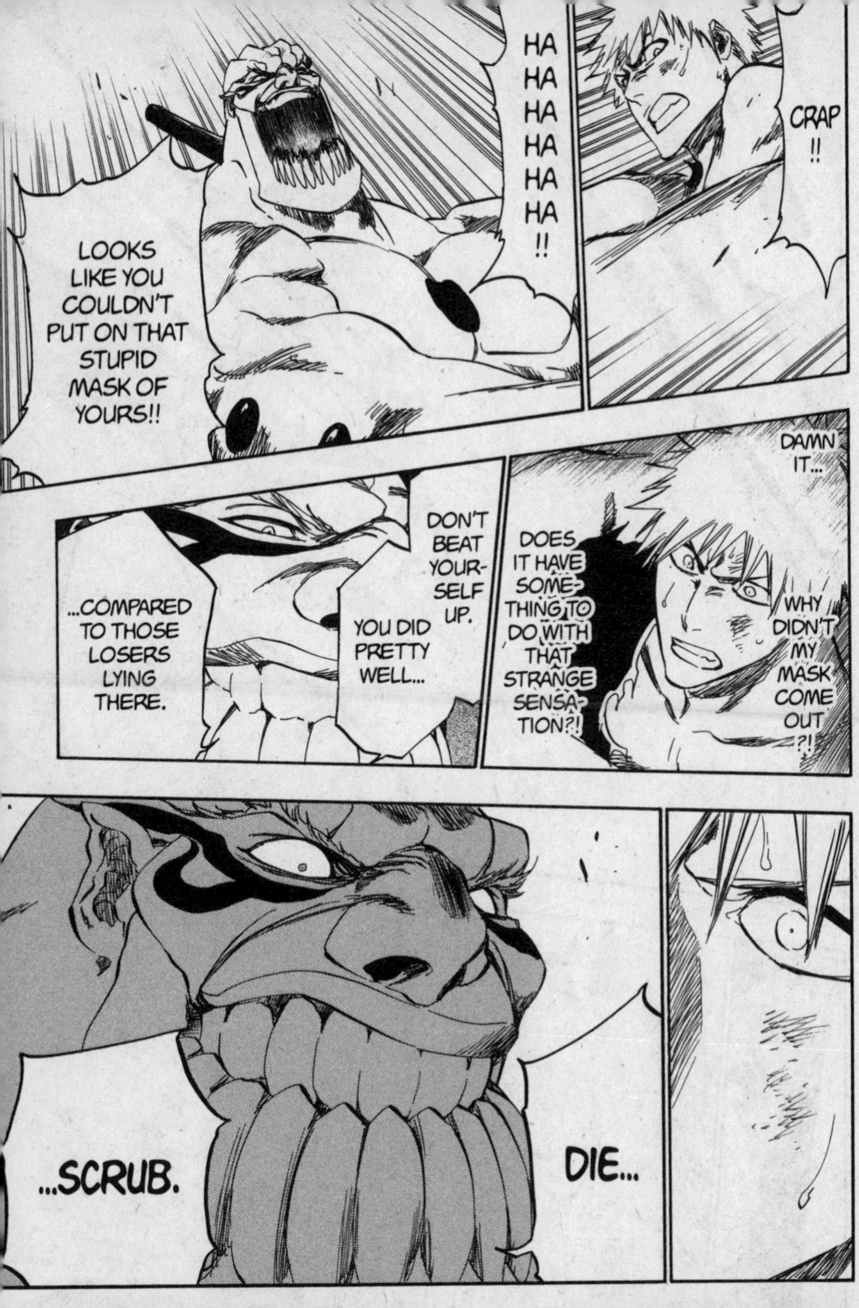
CRAP!!
HA HA HA HA HA HA!!
LOOKS LIKE YOU COULDN'T PUT ON THAT STUPID MASK OF YOURS!!
DAMN IT...
WHY DIDN'T MY MASK COME OUT?!
DOES IT HAVE SOME-THING TO DO WITH THAT STRANGE SENSA-TION?!
DON'T BEAT YOUR-SELF UP.
YOU DID PRETTY WELL...
...COMPARED TO THOSE LOSERS LYING THERE.
DIE...
...SCRUB.

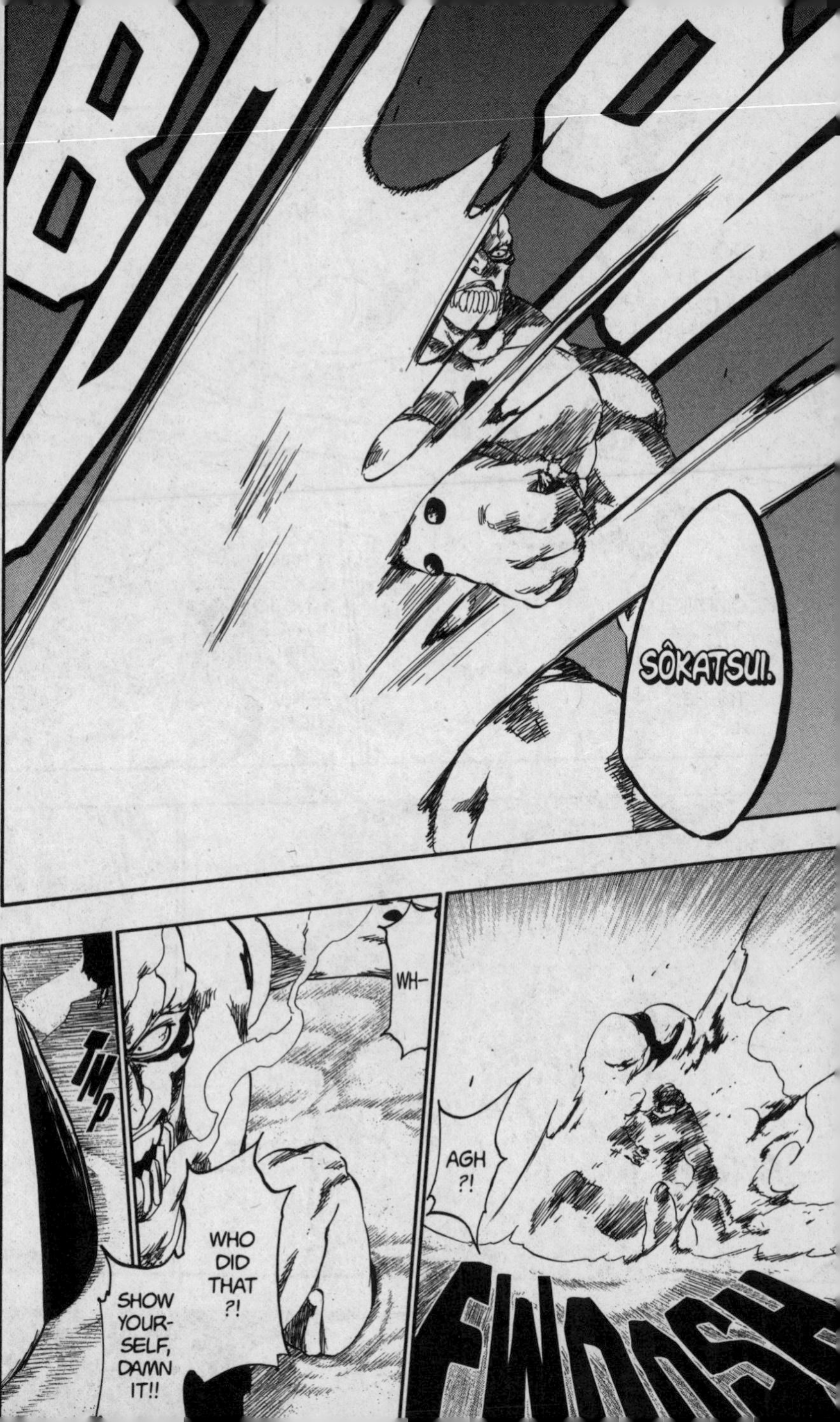
SÔKATSUI!.
AGH ?!
WH-
WHO DID THAT ?!
SHOW YOUR-SELF, DAMN IT!!
TMP

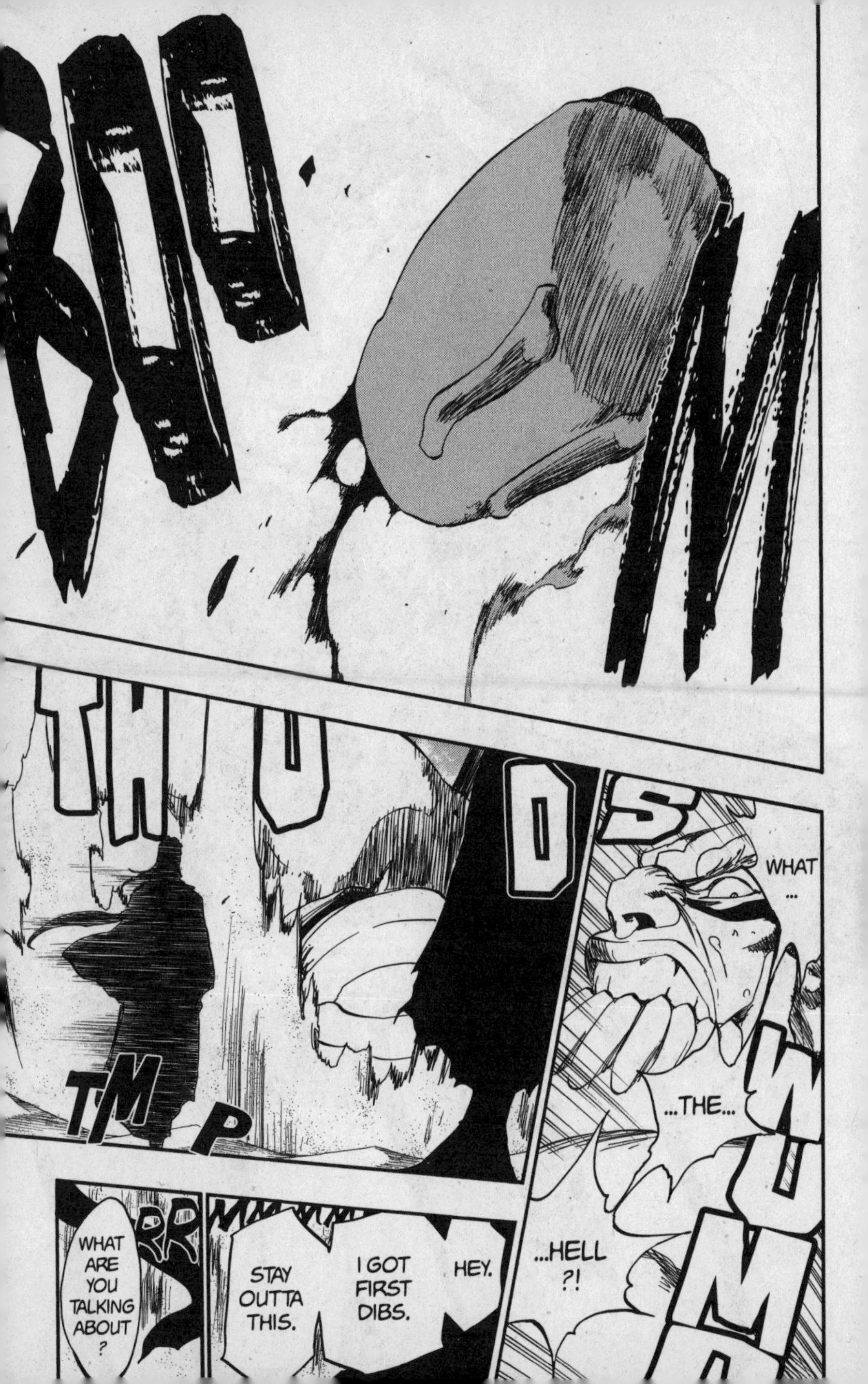
BOOM
WHAT ...
...THE...
...HELL ?!
THUDS
TMP
HEY.
I GOT FIRST DIBS.
STAY OUTTA THIS.
WHAT ARE YOU TALKING ABOUT ?

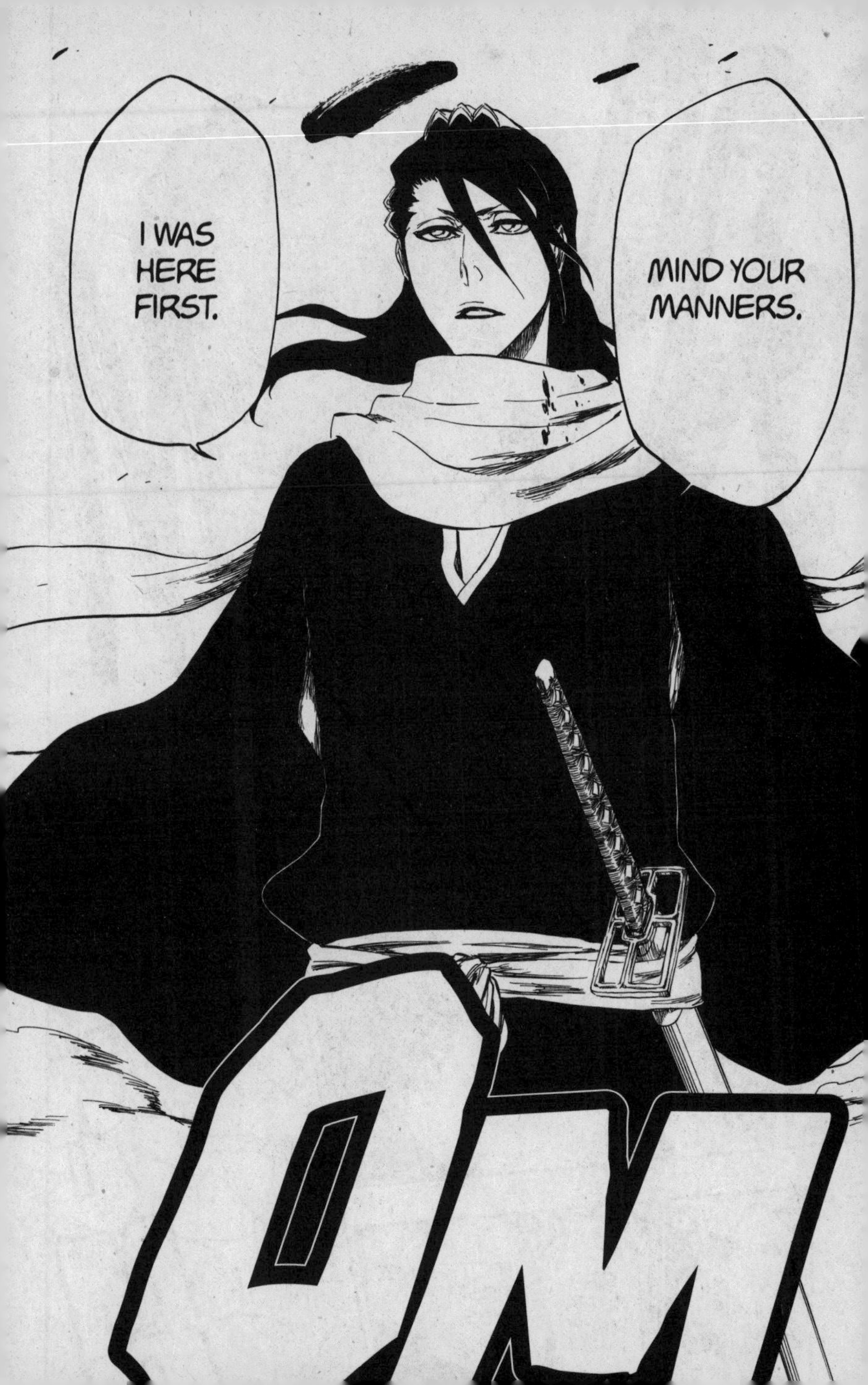
MIND YOUR MANNERS.
I WAS HERE FIRST.

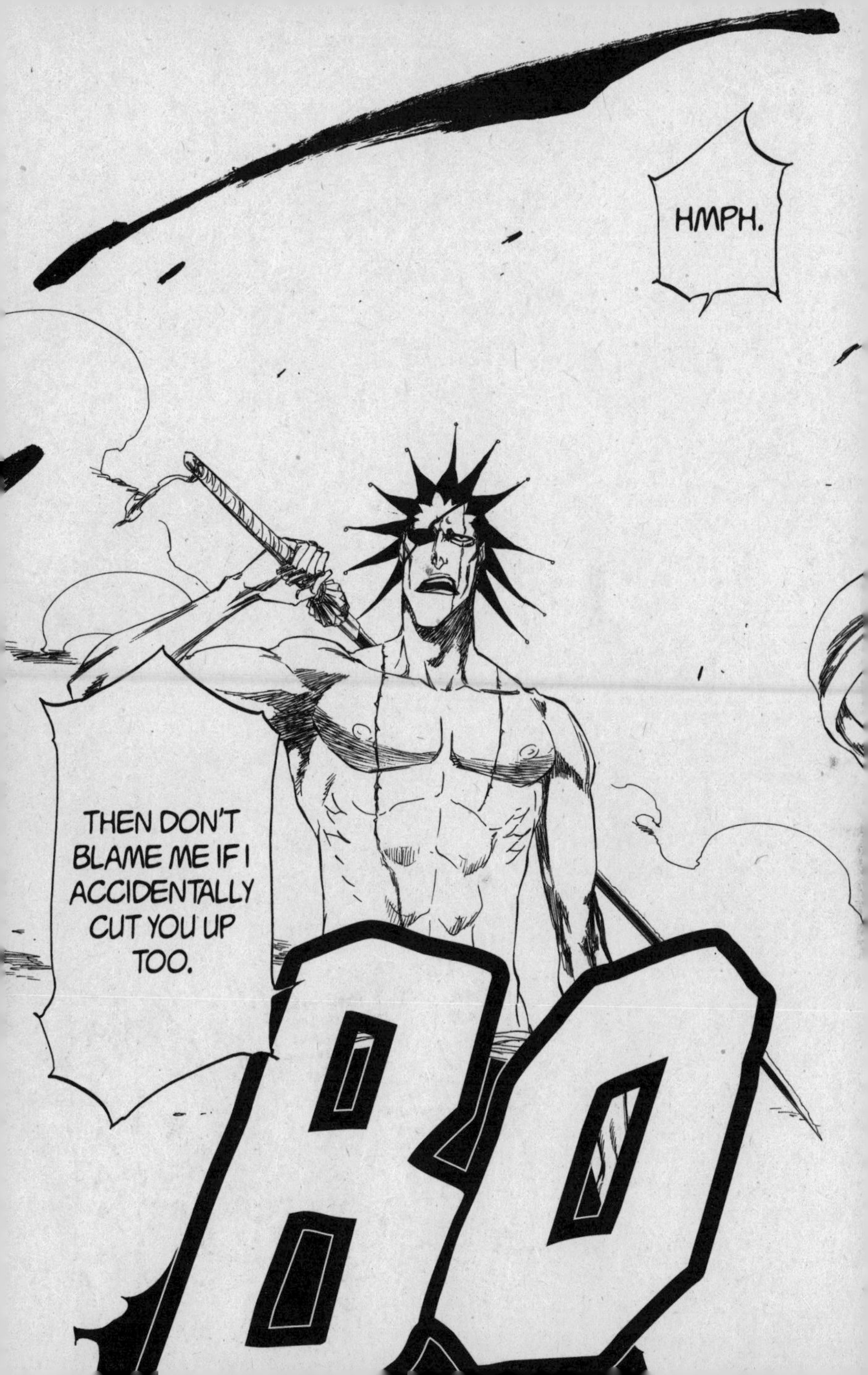
HMPH.
THEN DON'T BLAME ME IF I ACCIDENTALLY CUT YOU UP TOO.
BO

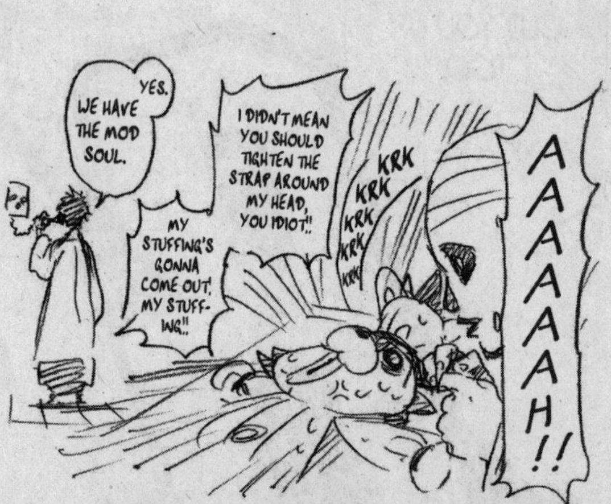
AAAAAAH!!
KRK KRK KRK KRK KRK
I DIDN'T MEAN YOU SHOULD TIGHTEN THE STRAP AROUND MY HEAD, YOU IDIOT!!
YES. WE HAVE THE MOD SOUL.
MY STUFFING'S GONNA COME OUT! MY STUFF-ING!!

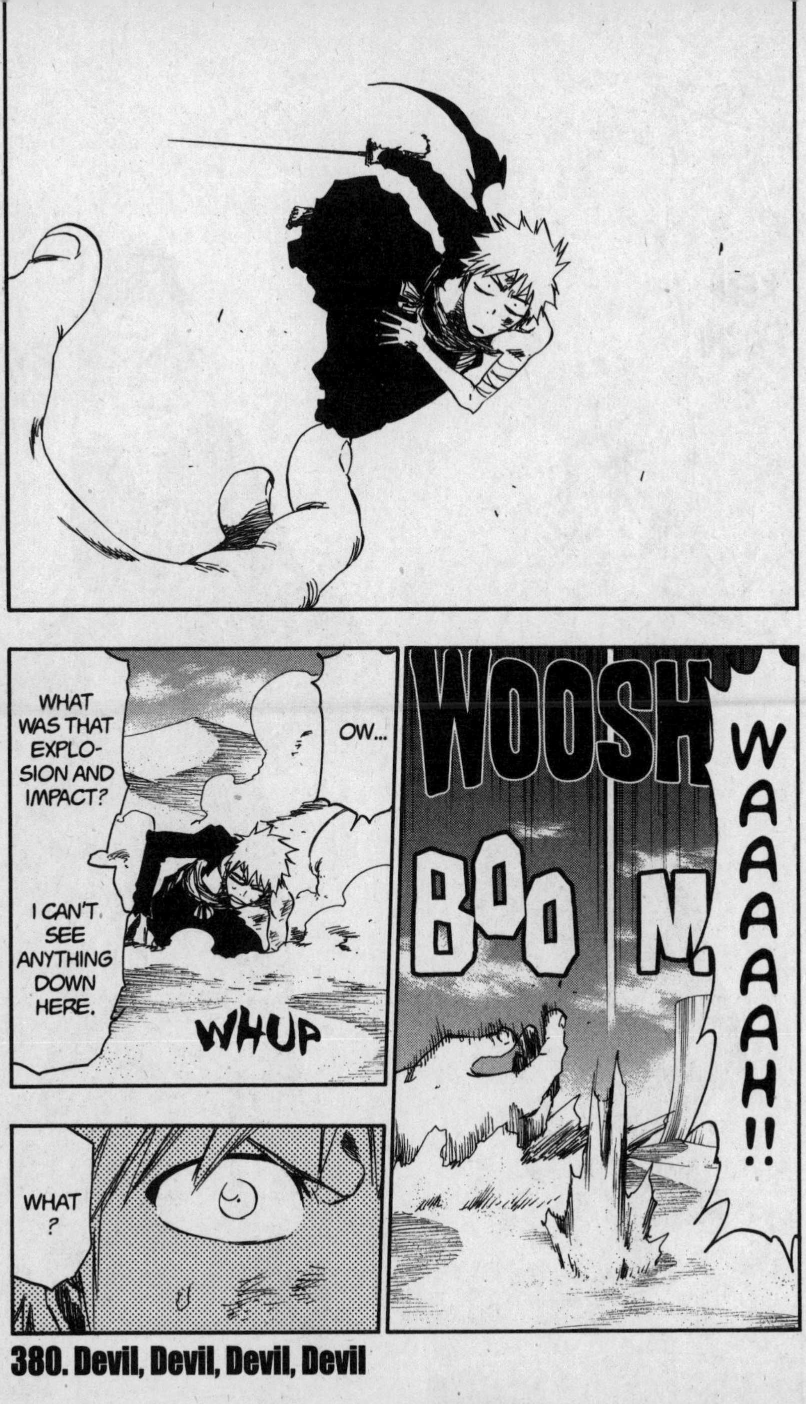
WOOSH
BOOM.
WAAAAAH!!
OW...
WHAT WAS THAT EXPLOSION AND IMPACT?
I CAN'T SEE ANYTHING DOWN HERE.
WHUP
WHAT?

380. Devil, Devil, Devil, Devil

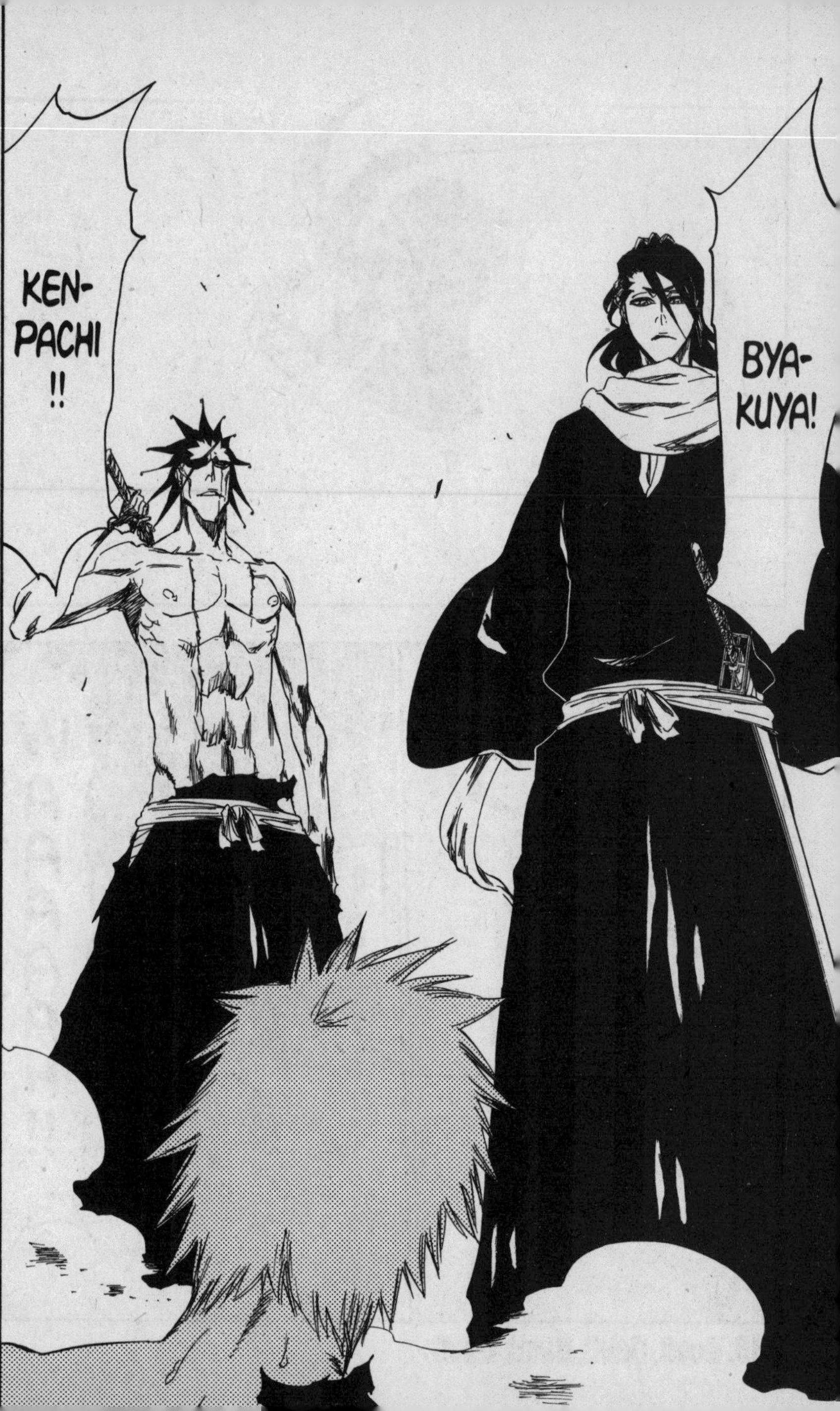
BYA-KUYA!
KEN-PACHI !!

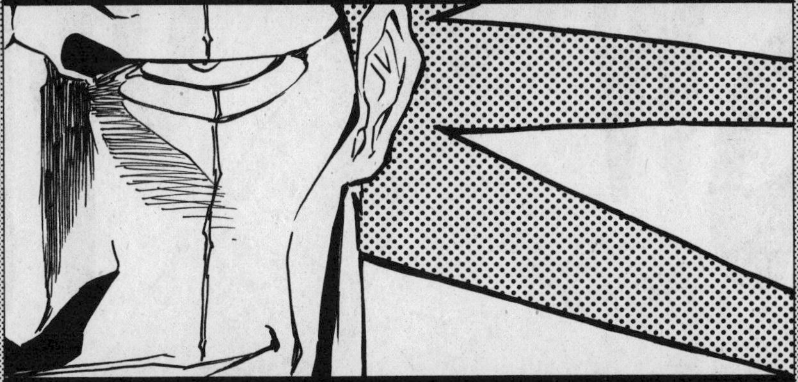

BLEACH380.

Devil, Devil, Devil, Devil

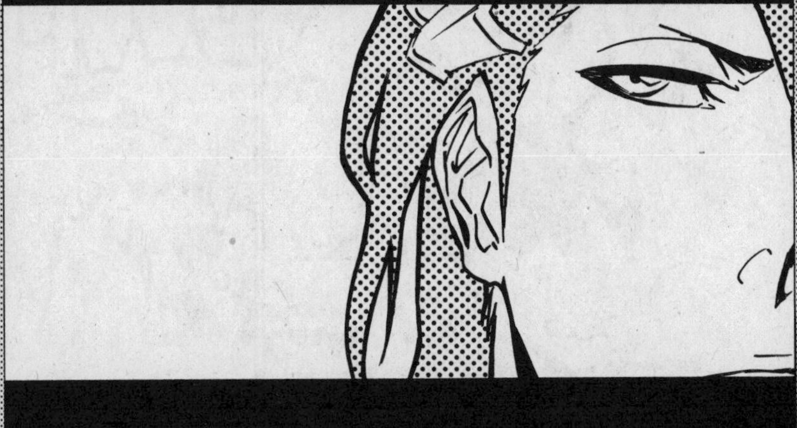

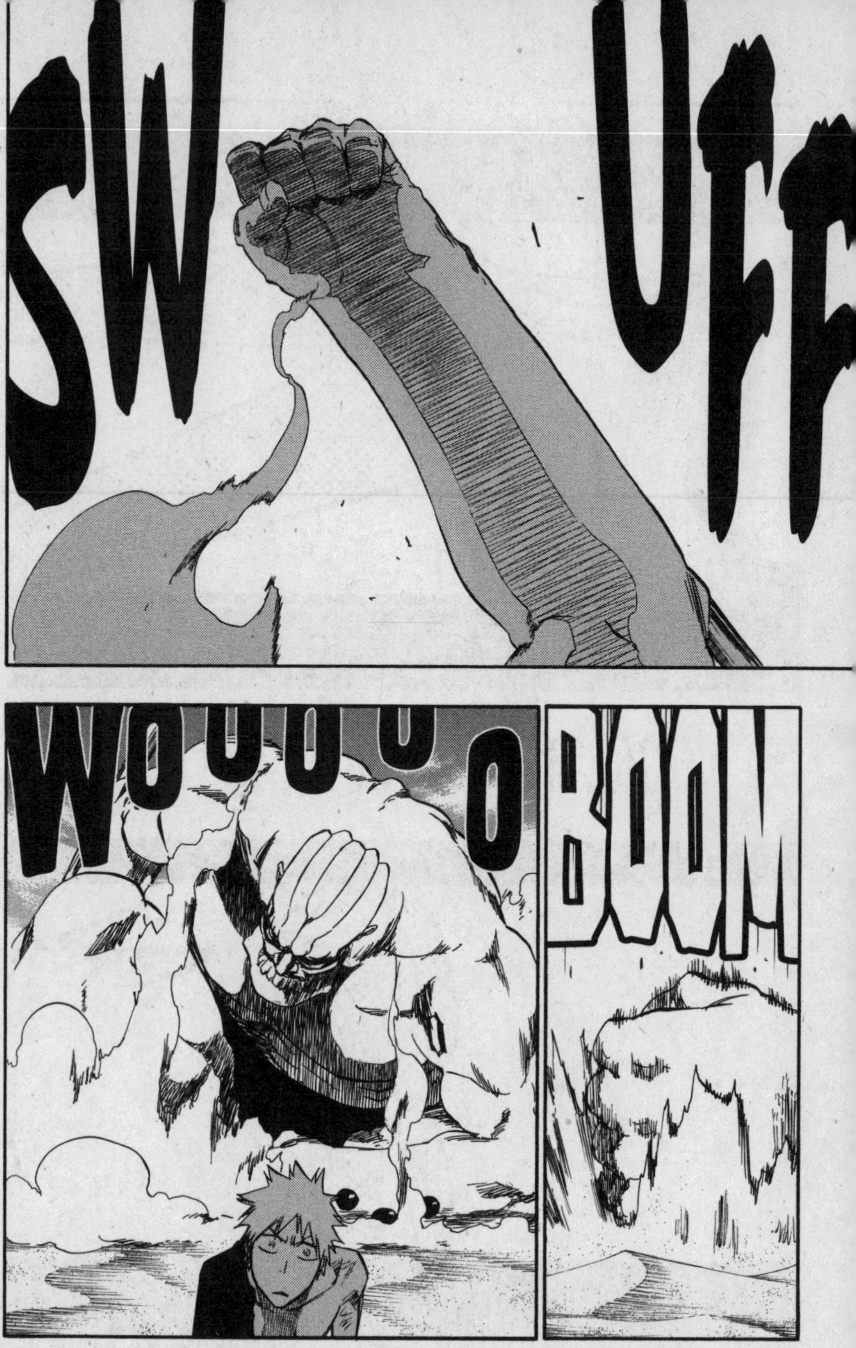
SWUFF
BOOM
WOOOOO

READ THIS WAY

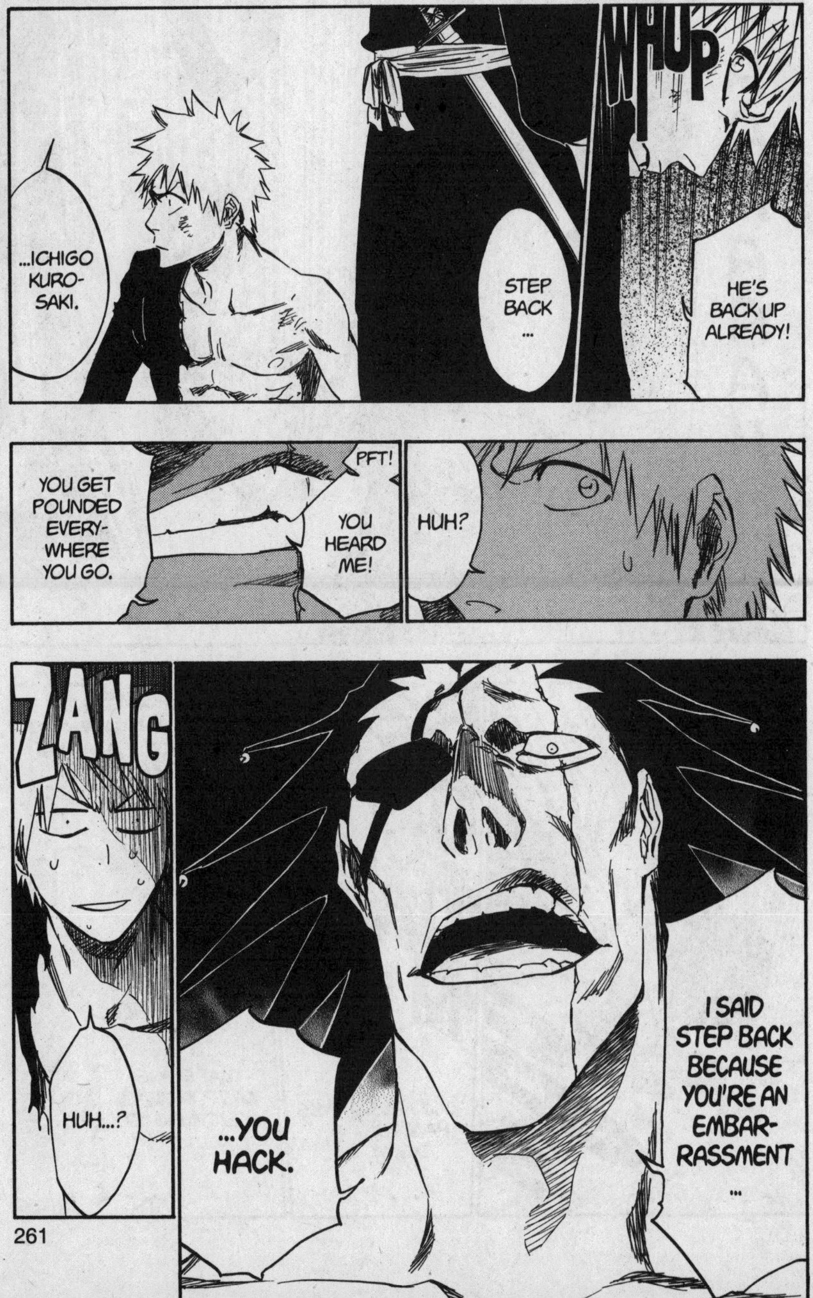
WHUP
HE'S BACK UP ALREADY!
STEP BACK ...
...ICHIGO KURO-SAKI.
HUH?
PFT!
YOU HEARD ME!
YOU GET POUNDED EVERY-WHERE YOU GO.
I SAID STEP BACK BECAUSE YOU'RE AN EMBAR-RASSMENT ...
...YOU HACK.
ZANG
HUH...?

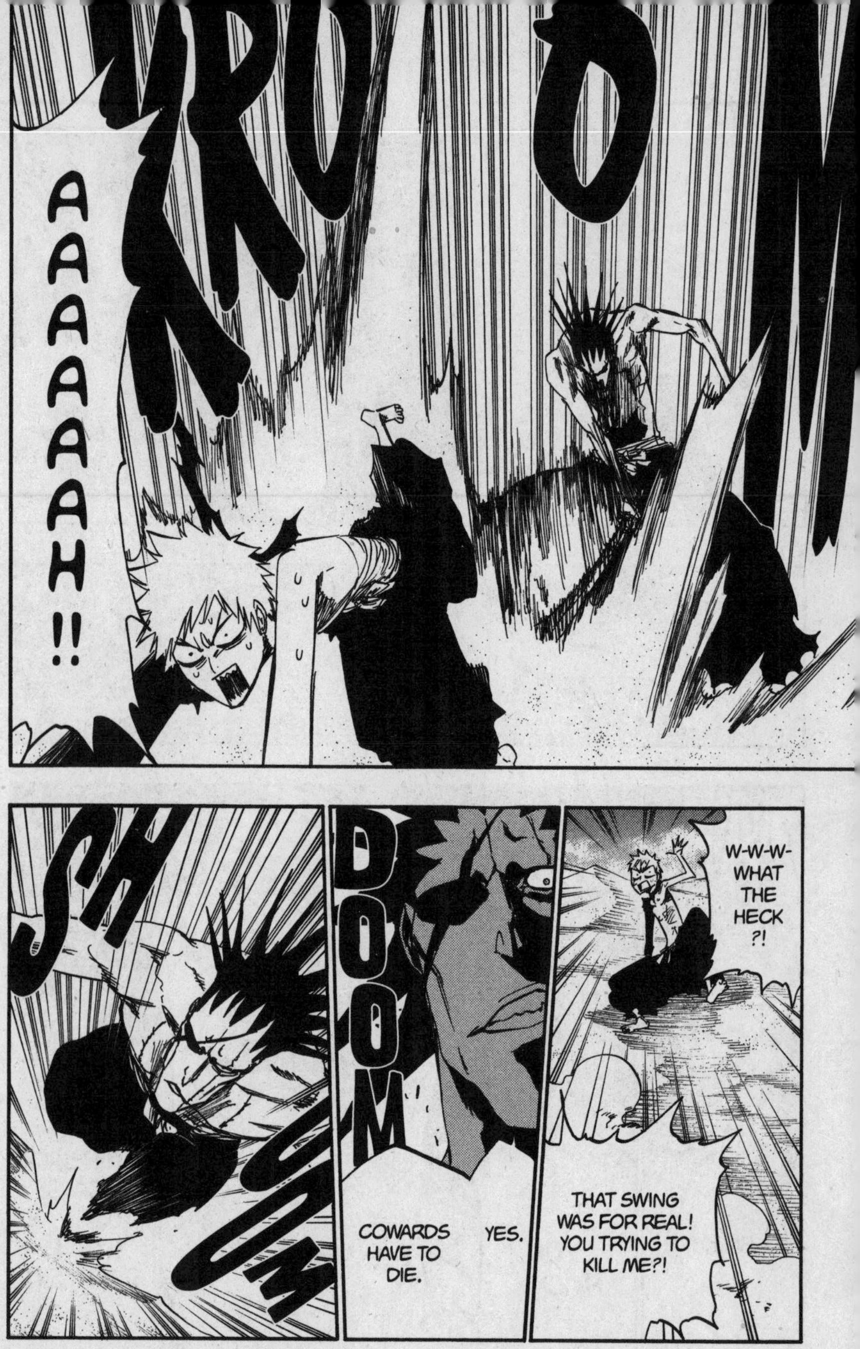
AAAAAAAH!!
W-W-W-WHAT THE HECK ?!
THAT SWING WAS FOR REAL! YOU TRYING TO KILL ME?!
DOOOM
YES.
COWARDS HAVE TO DIE.

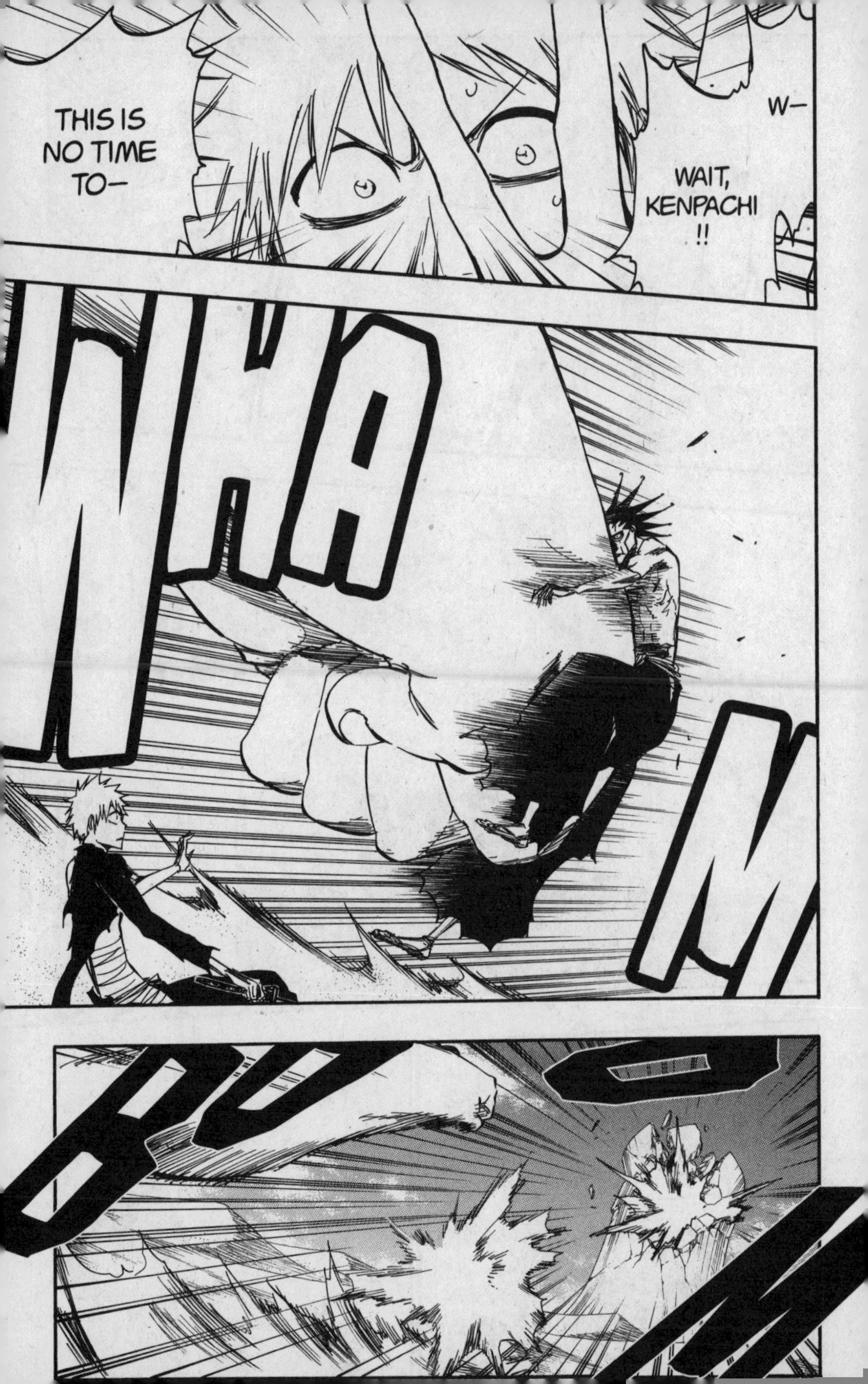
W—
WAIT, KENPACHI !!
THIS IS NO TIME TO—
WHAM

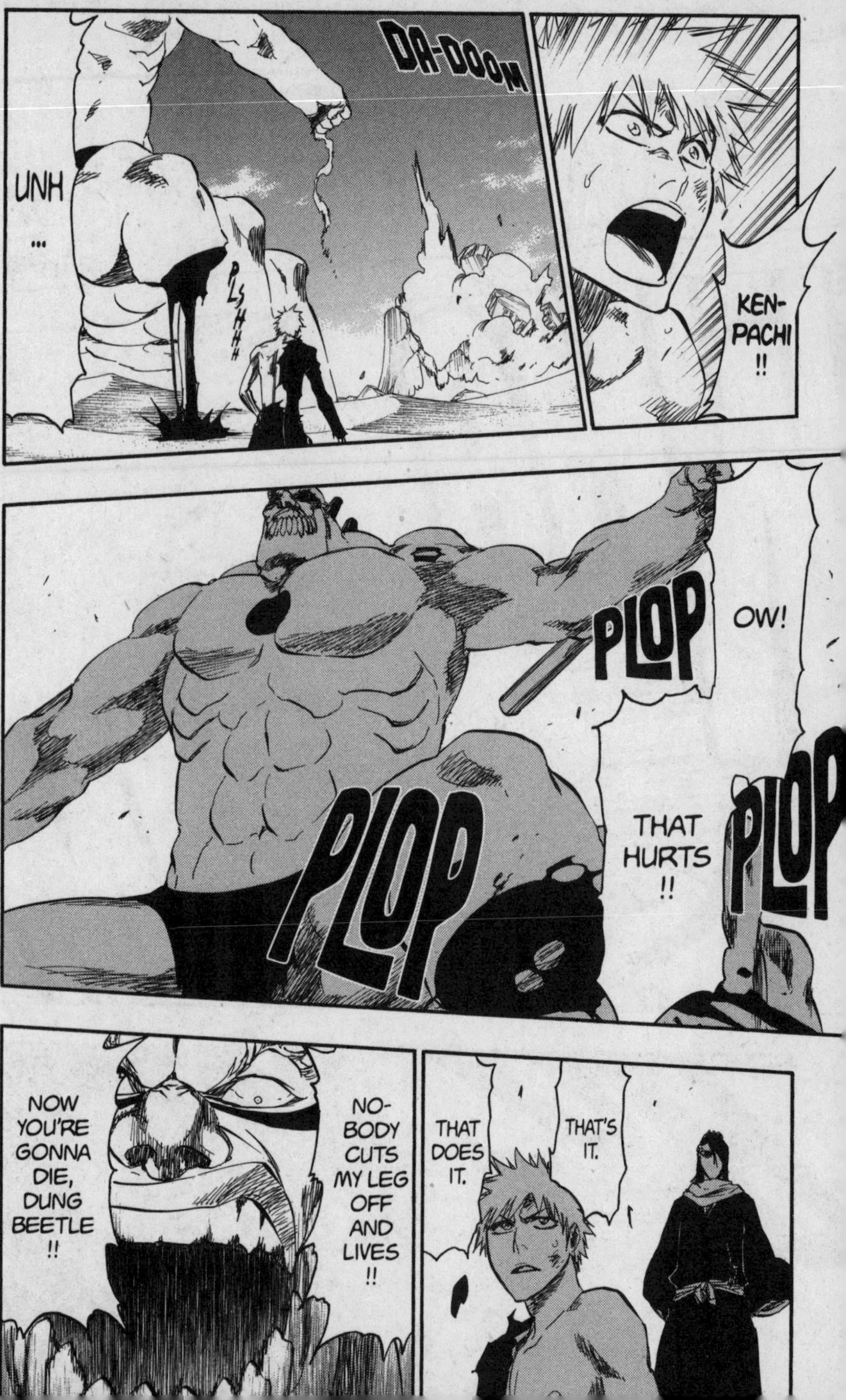
KEN-PACHI !!
DA-DOOM
PLSHHH
UNH ...
OW!
PLOP
PLOP
THAT HURTS !!
PLOP
THAT'S IT.
THAT DOES IT.
NO-BODY CUTS MY LEG OFF AND LIVES !!
NOW YOU'RE GONNA DIE, DUNG BEETLE !!

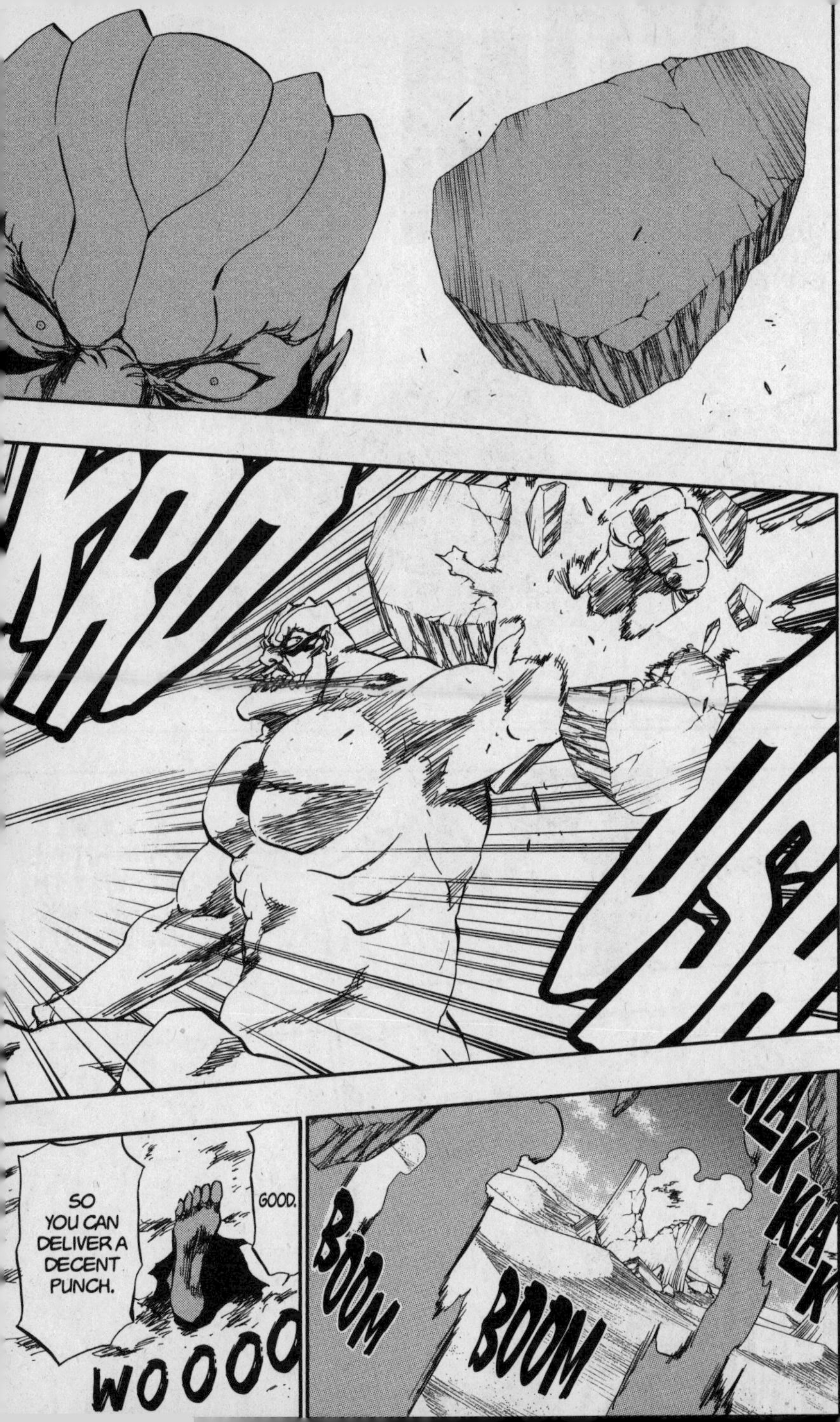
KLAK KLAK
BOOM
BOOM
SO YOU CAN DELIVER A DECENT PUNCH.
GOOD.
WOOOO

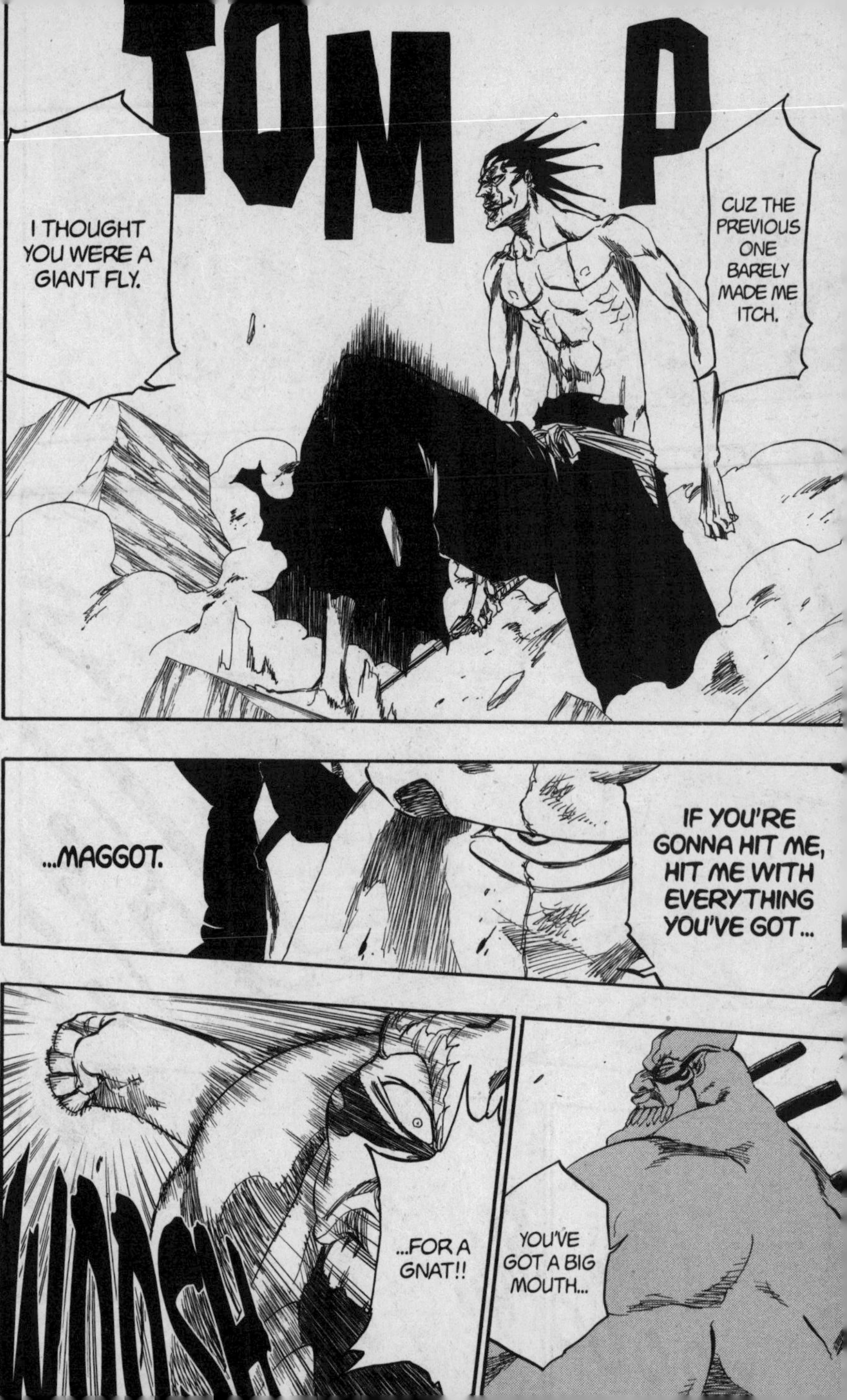
TOMP
CUZ THE PREVIOUS ONE BARELY MADE ME ITCH.
I THOUGHT YOU WERE A GIANT FLY.
IF YOU'RE GONNA HIT ME, HIT ME WITH EVERYTHING YOU'VE GOT...
...MAGGOT.
YOU'VE GOT A BIG MOUTH...
...FOR A GNAT!!
WOOSH

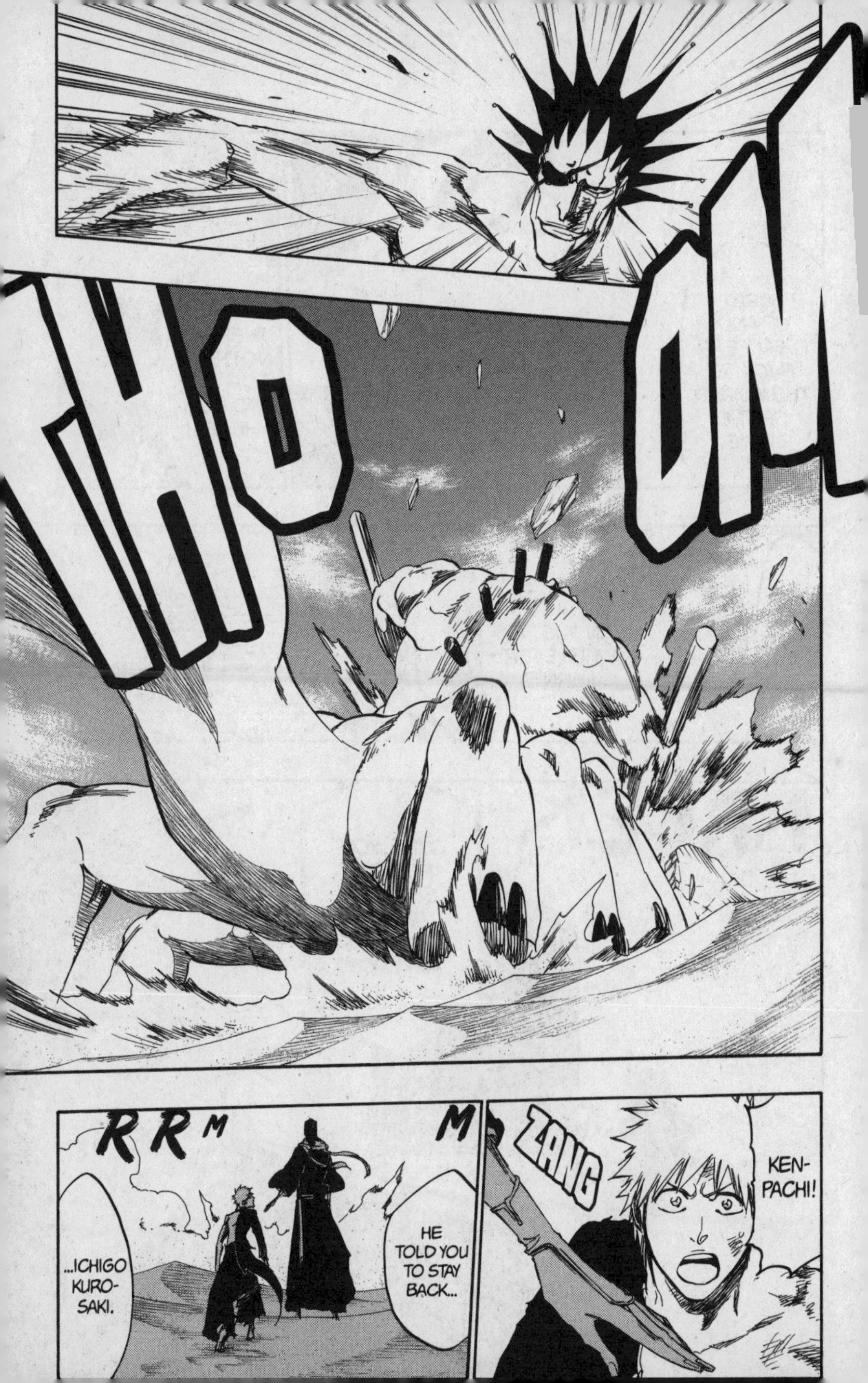
THOOM
ZANG
KEN-PACHI!
RRMM
HE TOLD YOU TO STAY BACK...
...ICHIGO KURO-SAKI.

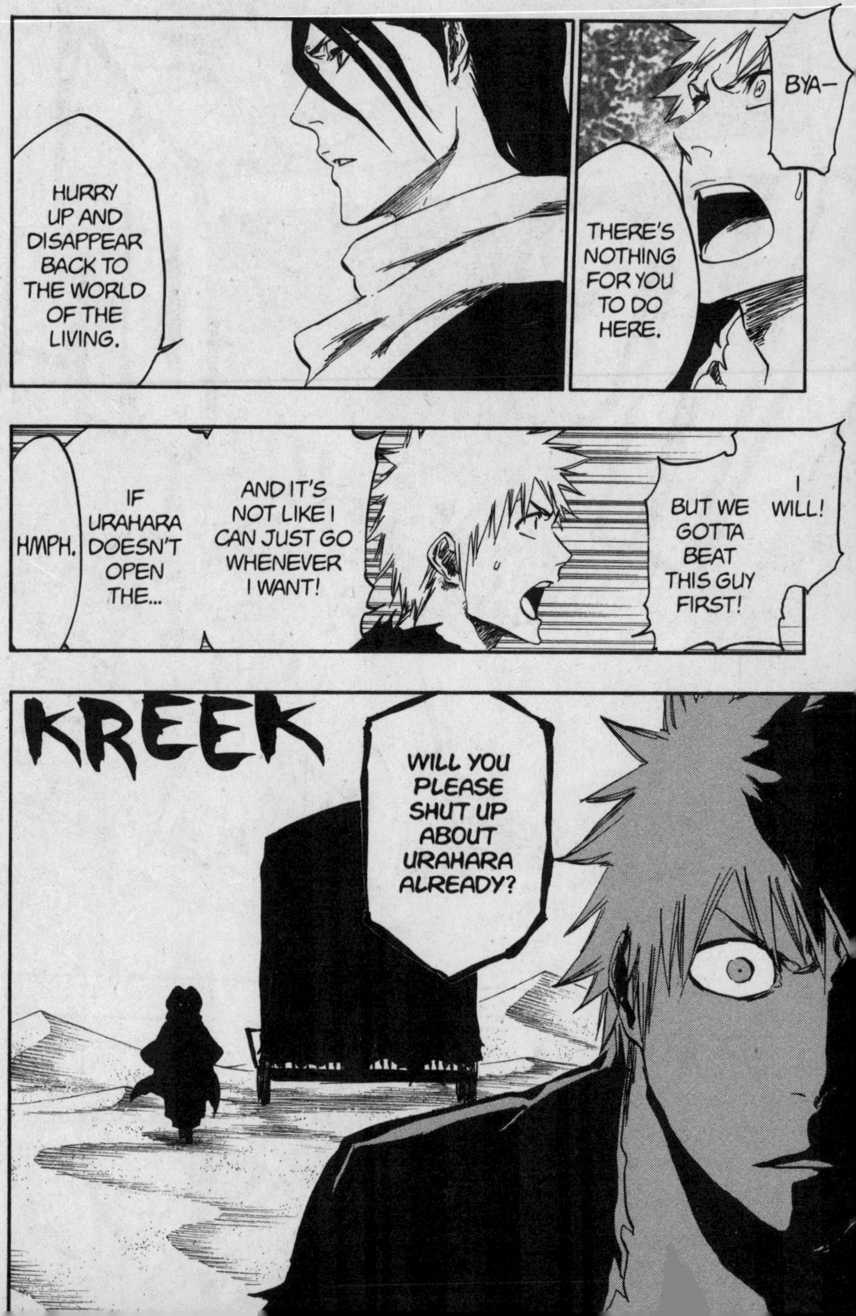
BYA—
THERE'S NOTHING FOR YOU TO DO HERE.
HURRY UP AND DISAPPEAR BACK TO THE WORLD OF THE LIVING.
I WILL!
BUT WE GOTTA BEAT THIS GUY FIRST!
AND IT'S NOT LIKE I CAN JUST GO WHENEVER I WANT!
IF URAHARA DOESN'T OPEN THE...
HMPH.
WILL YOU PLEASE SHUT UP ABOUT URAHARA ALREADY?
KREEK

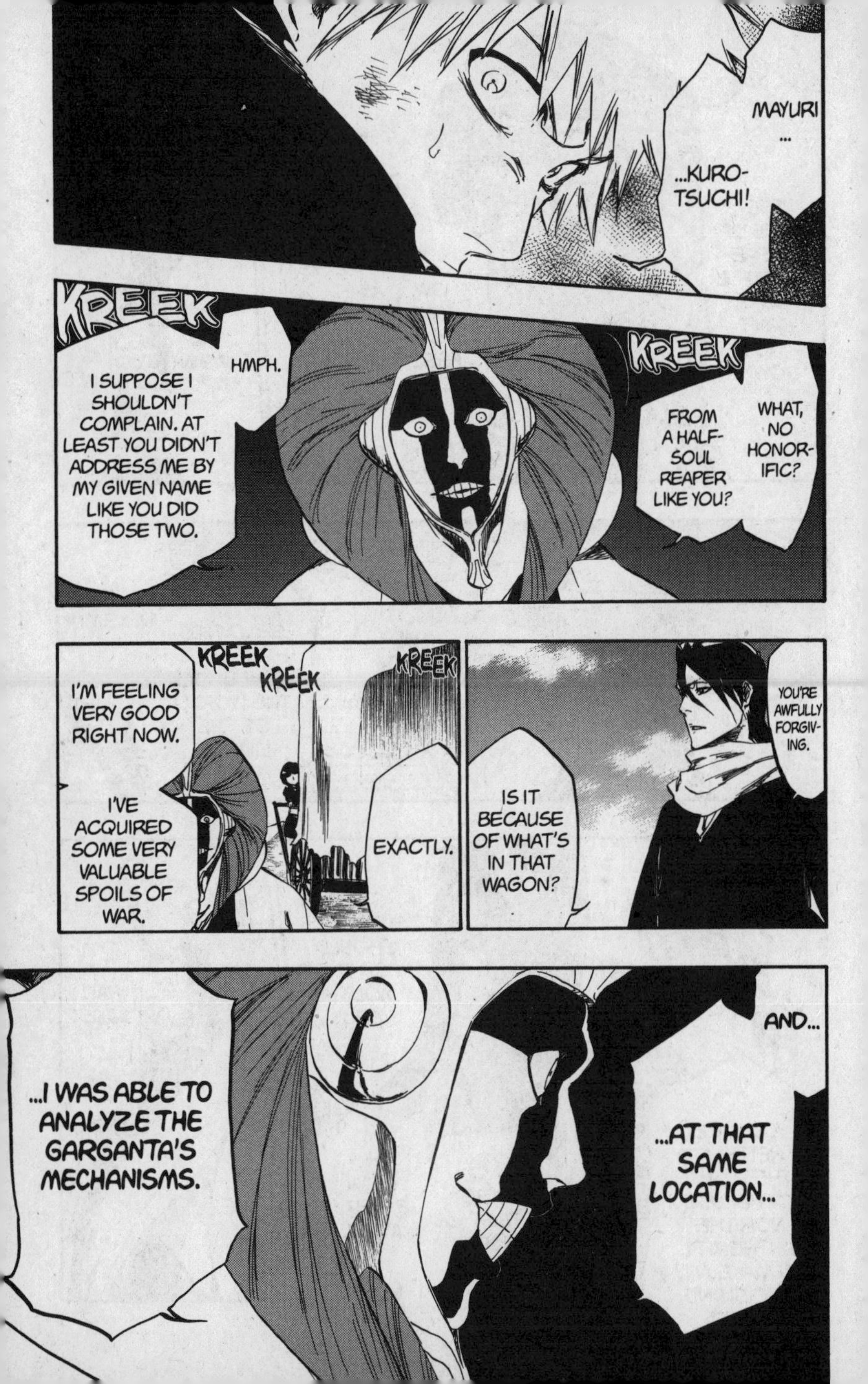
MAYURI ...
...KURO-TSUCHI!
KREEK
WHAT, NO HONORIFIC?
FROM A HALF-SOUL REAPER LIKE YOU?
KREEK
HMPH.
I SUPPOSE I SHOULDN'T COMPLAIN. AT LEAST YOU DIDN'T ADDRESS ME BY MY GIVEN NAME LIKE YOU DID THOSE TWO.
YOU'RE AWFULLY FORGIV-ING.
IS IT BECAUSE OF WHAT'S IN THAT WAGON?
KREEK
EXACTLY.
KREEK
KREEK
I'M FEELING VERY GOOD RIGHT NOW.
I'VE ACQUIRED SOME VERY VALUABLE SPOILS OF WAR.
AND...
...AT THAT SAME LOCATION...
...I WAS ABLE TO ANALYZE THE GARGANTA'S MECHANISMS.

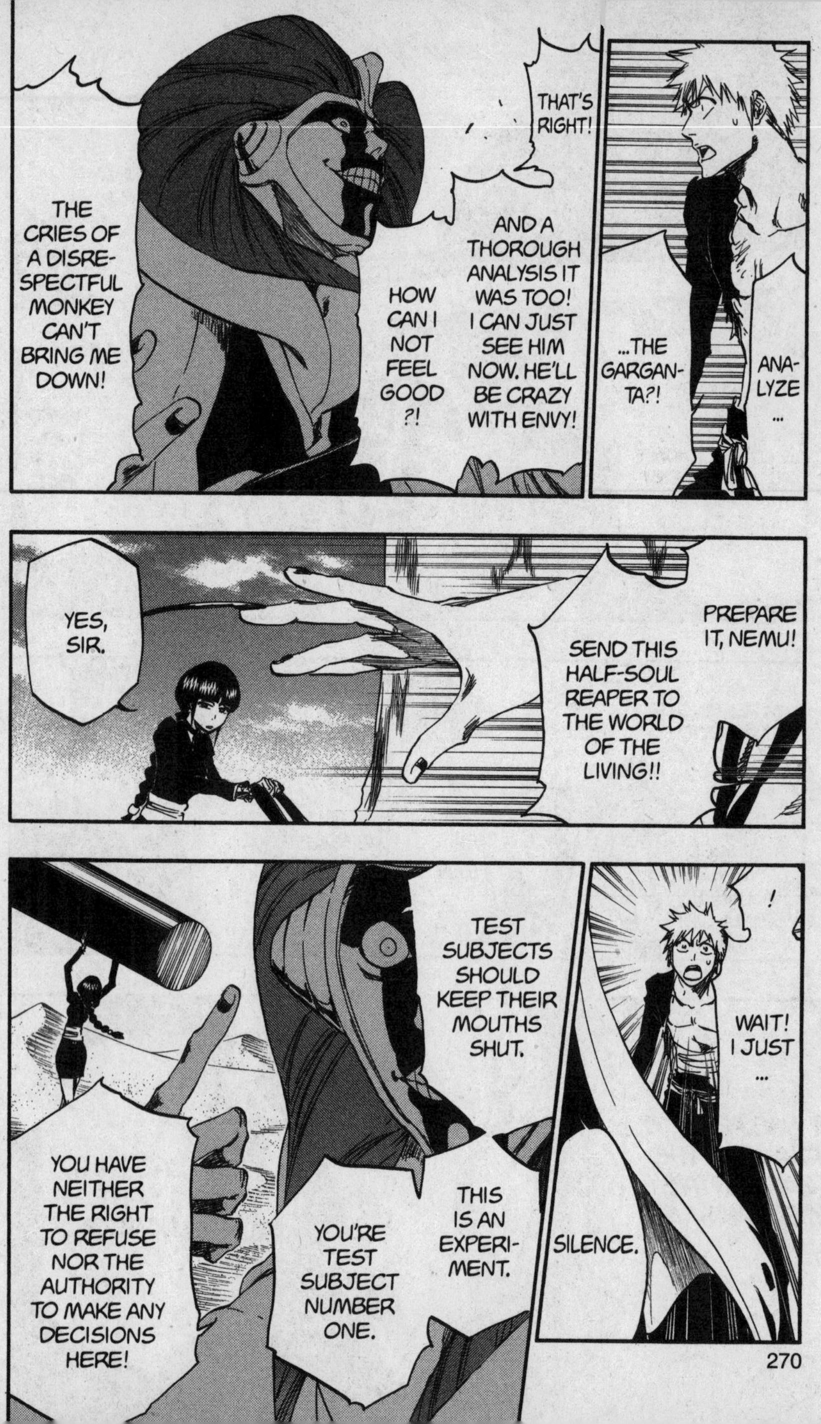

ANA-LYZE...
...THE GARGAN-TA?!
THAT'S RIGHT!
AND A THOROUGH ANALYSIS IT WAS TOO! I CAN JUST SEE HIM NOW. HE'LL BE CRAZY WITH ENVY!
HOW CAN I NOT FEEL GOOD?!
THE CRIES OF A DISRE-SPECTFUL MONKEY CAN'T BRING ME DOWN!
PREPARE IT, NEMU!
SEND THIS HALF-SOUL REAPER TO THE WORLD OF THE LIVING!!
YES, SIR.
!
WAIT! I JUST...
SILENCE.
TEST SUBJECTS SHOULD KEEP THEIR MOUTHS SHUT.
THIS IS AN EXPERI-MENT.
YOU'RE TEST SUBJECT NUMBER ONE.
YOU HAVE NEITHER THE RIGHT TO REFUSE NOR THE AUTHORITY TO MAKE ANY DECISIONS HERE!

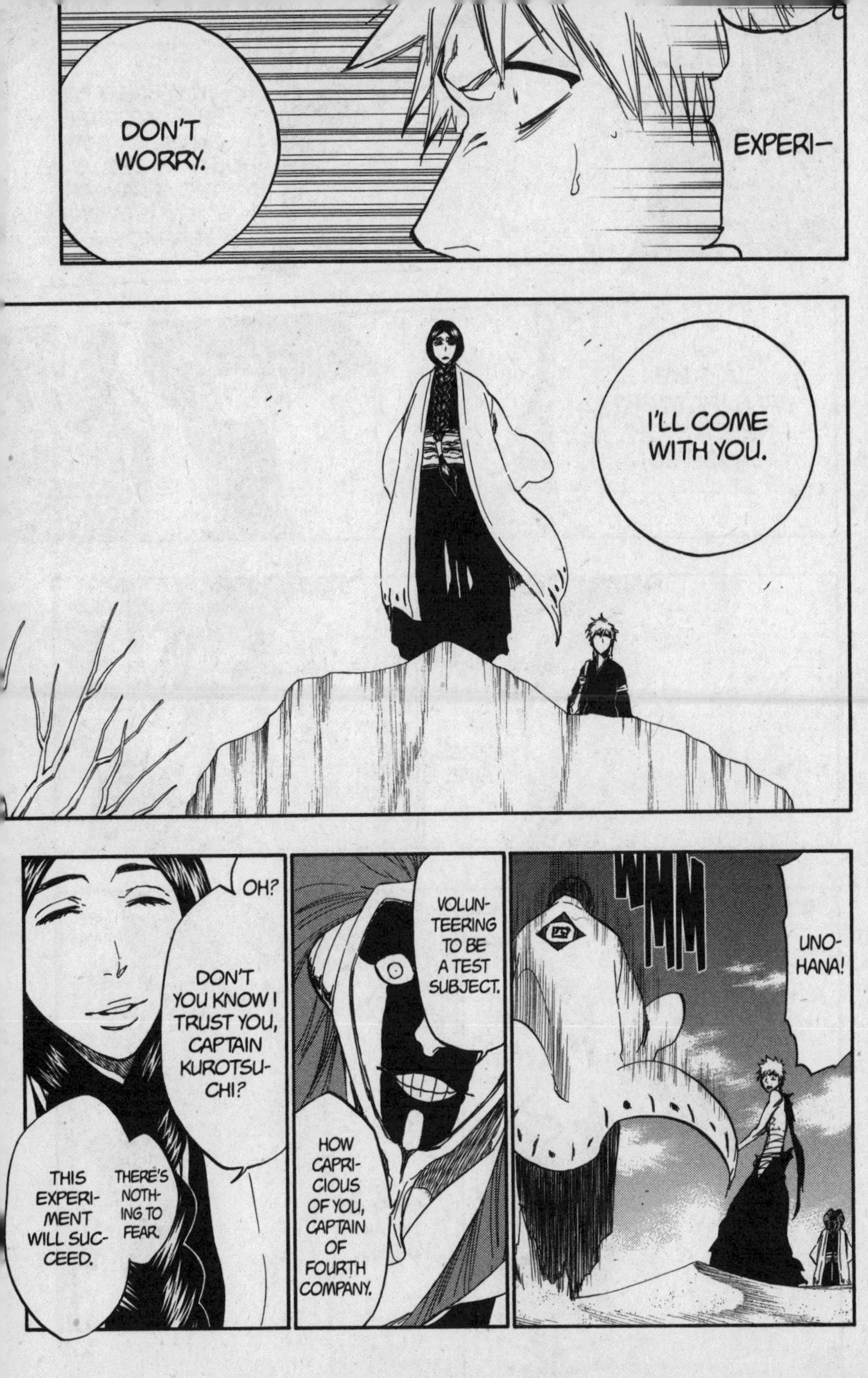
EXPERI-
DON'T WORRY.
I'LL COME WITH YOU.
WMM
UNO-HANA!
VOLUN-TEERING TO BE A TEST SUBJECT.
HOW CAPRI-CIOUS OF YOU, CAPTAIN OF FOURTH COMPANY.
OH?
DON'T YOU KNOW I TRUST YOU, CAPTAIN KUROTSU-CHI?
THERE'S NOTH-ING TO FEAR.
THIS EXPERI-MENT WILL SUC-CEED.

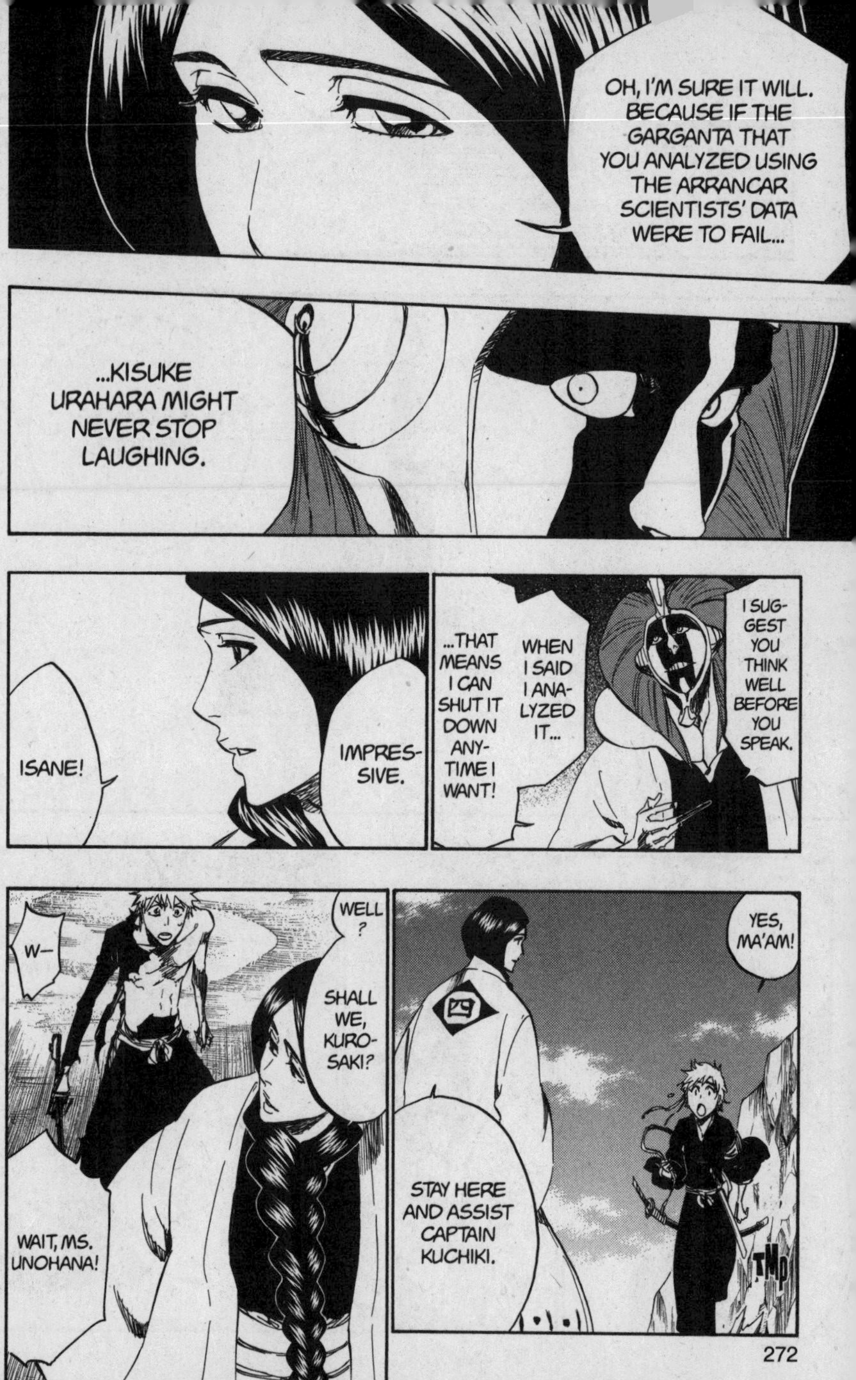
OH, I'M SURE IT WILL. BECAUSE IF THE GARGANTA THAT YOU ANALYZED USING THE ARRANCAR SCIENTISTS' DATA WERE TO FAIL...
...KISUKE URAHARA MIGHT NEVER STOP LAUGHING.
I SUGGEST YOU THINK WELL BEFORE YOU SPEAK.
WHEN I SAID I ANALYZED IT...
...THAT MEANS I CAN SHUT IT DOWN ANYTIME I WANT!
IMPRESSIVE.
ISANE!
YES, MA'AM!
STAY HERE AND ASSIST CAPTAIN KUCHIKI.
TMP
WELL?
SHALL WE, KUROSAKI?
W—
WAIT, MS. UNOHANA!

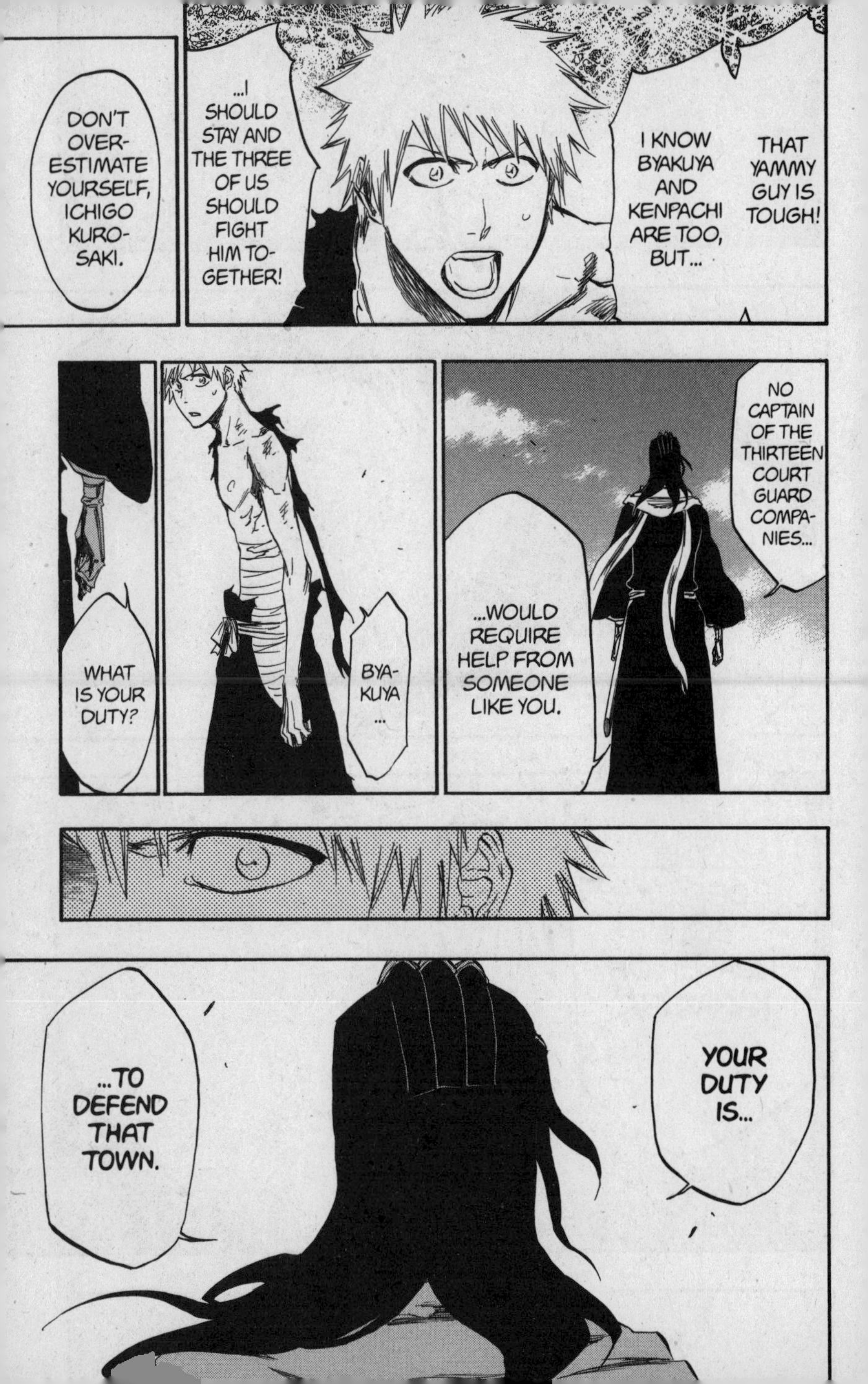
THAT YAMMY GUY IS TOUGH!
I KNOW BYAKUYA AND KENPACHI ARE TOO, BUT...
...I SHOULD STAY AND THE THREE OF US SHOULD FIGHT HIM TOGETHER!
DON'T OVERESTIMATE YOURSELF, ICHIGO KUROSAKI.
NO CAPTAIN OF THE THIRTEEN COURT GUARD COMPANIES...
...WOULD REQUIRE HELP FROM SOMEONE LIKE YOU.
BYAKUYA...
WHAT IS YOUR DUTY?
YOUR DUTY IS...
...TO DEFEND THAT TOWN.

GO.

YOU ARE...

...THE DEPUTY SOUL REAPER OF KARAKURA.

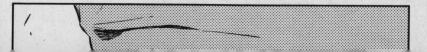

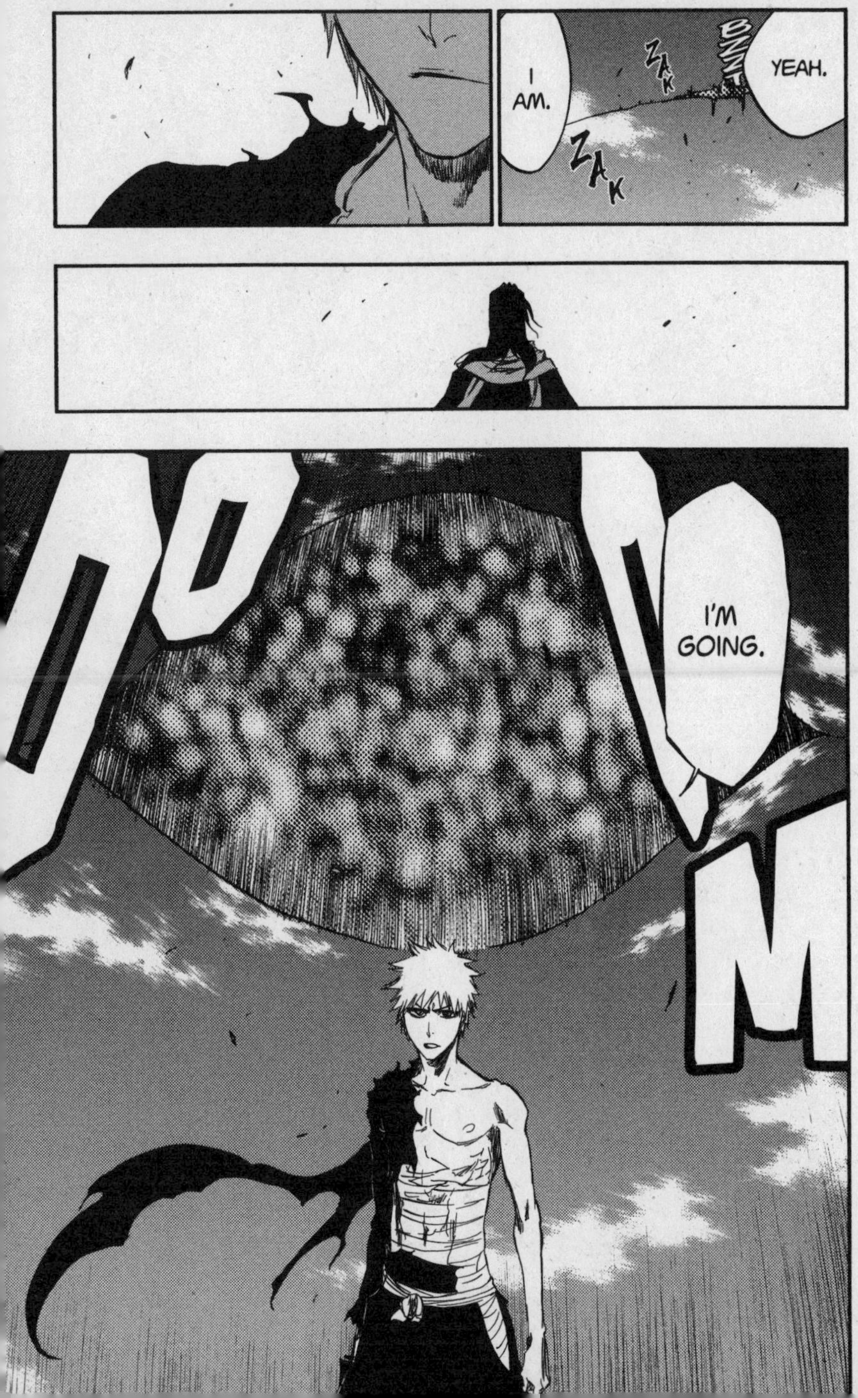
YEAH.
BZZT
ZAK
I AM.
ZAK
DOOM
I'M GOING.

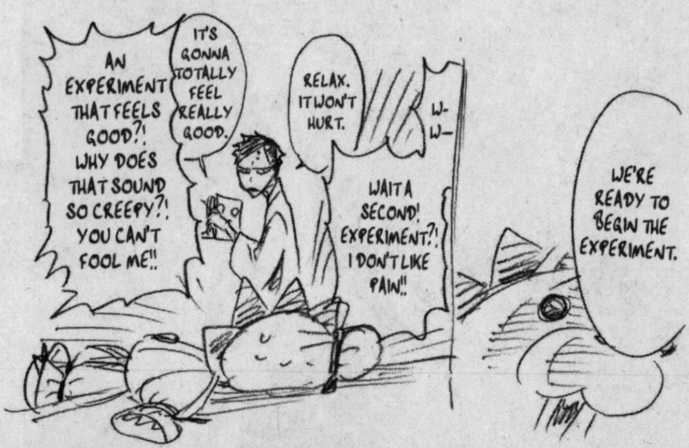
WE'RE READY TO BEGIN THE EXPERIMENT.
W- W—
WAIT A SECOND! EXPERIMENT?! I DON'T LIKE PAIN!!
RELAX. IT WON'T HURT.
IT'S GONNA TOTALLY FEEL REALLY GOOD.
AN EXPERIMENT THAT FEELS GOOD?! WHY DOES THAT SOUND SO CREEPY?! YOU CAN'T FOOL ME!!

381. Words Just Don't Like You

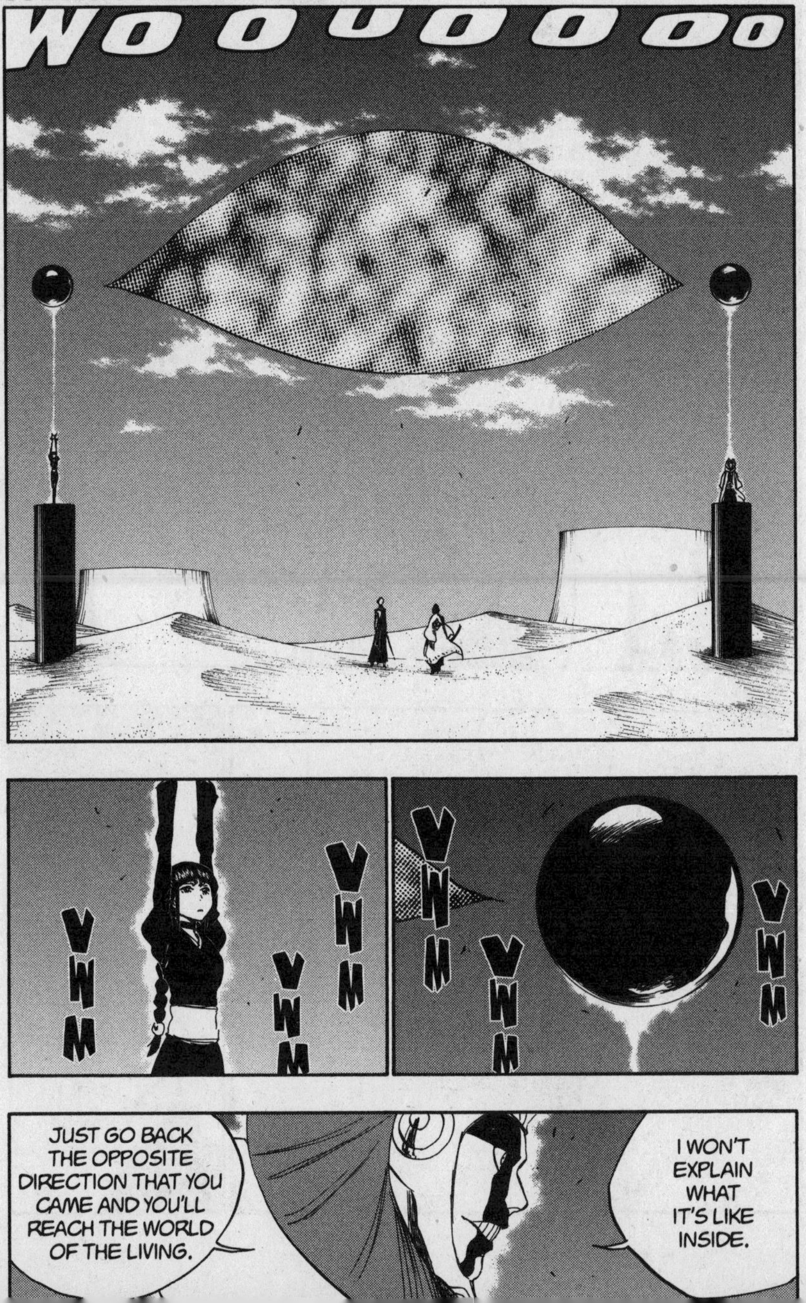
WOOOOOOO
VWM
VWM
VWM
VWM
VWM
VWM
I WON'T EXPLAIN WHAT IT'S LIKE INSIDE.
JUST GO BACK THE OPPOSITE DIRECTION THAT YOU CAME AND YOU'LL REACH THE WORLD OF THE LIVING.

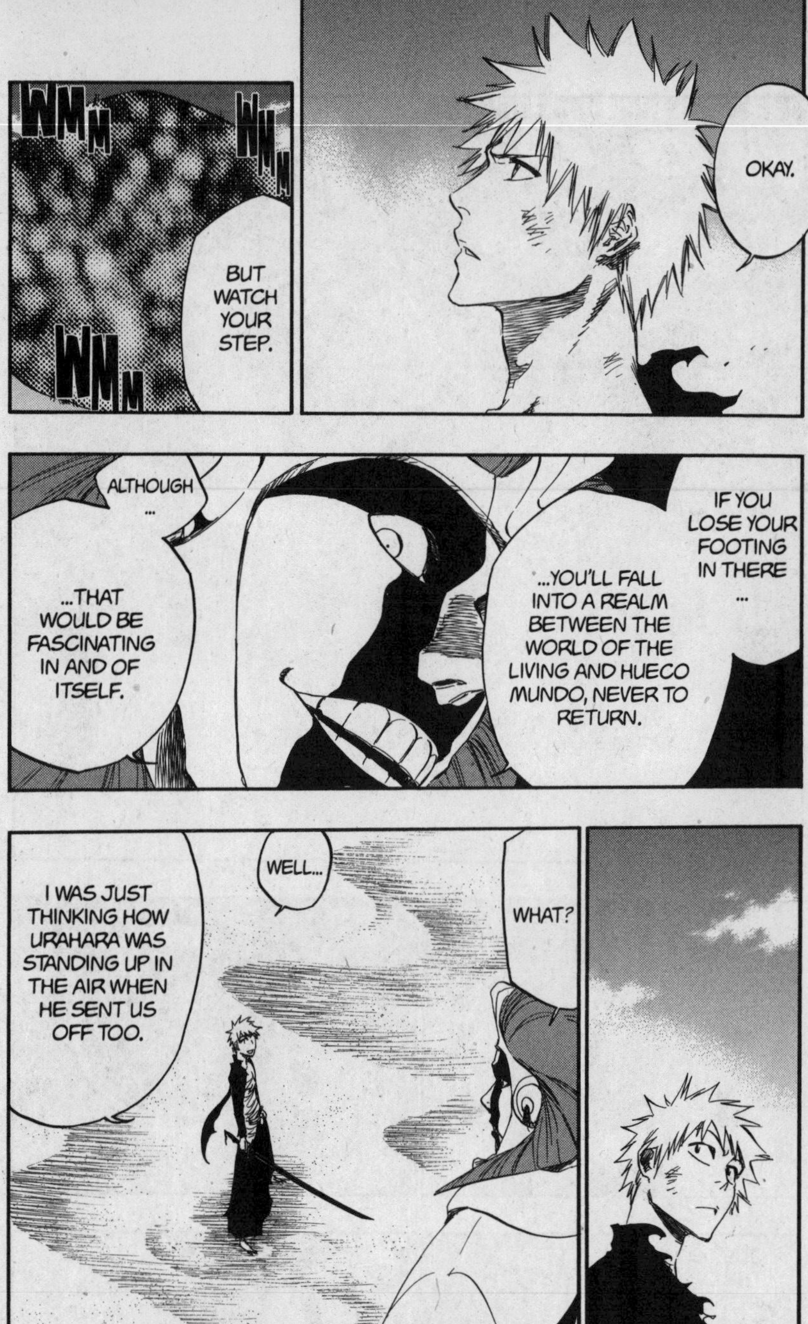
OKAY.
WMM
WMM
BUT WATCH YOUR STEP.
WMM
IF YOU LOSE YOUR FOOTING IN THERE ...
...YOU'LL FALL INTO A REALM BETWEEN THE WORLD OF THE LIVING AND HUECO MUNDO, NEVER TO RETURN.
ALTHOUGH ...
...THAT WOULD BE FASCINATING IN AND OF ITSELF.
WHAT?
WELL...
I WAS JUST THINKING HOW URAHARA WAS STANDING UP IN THE AIR WHEN HE SENT US OFF TOO.

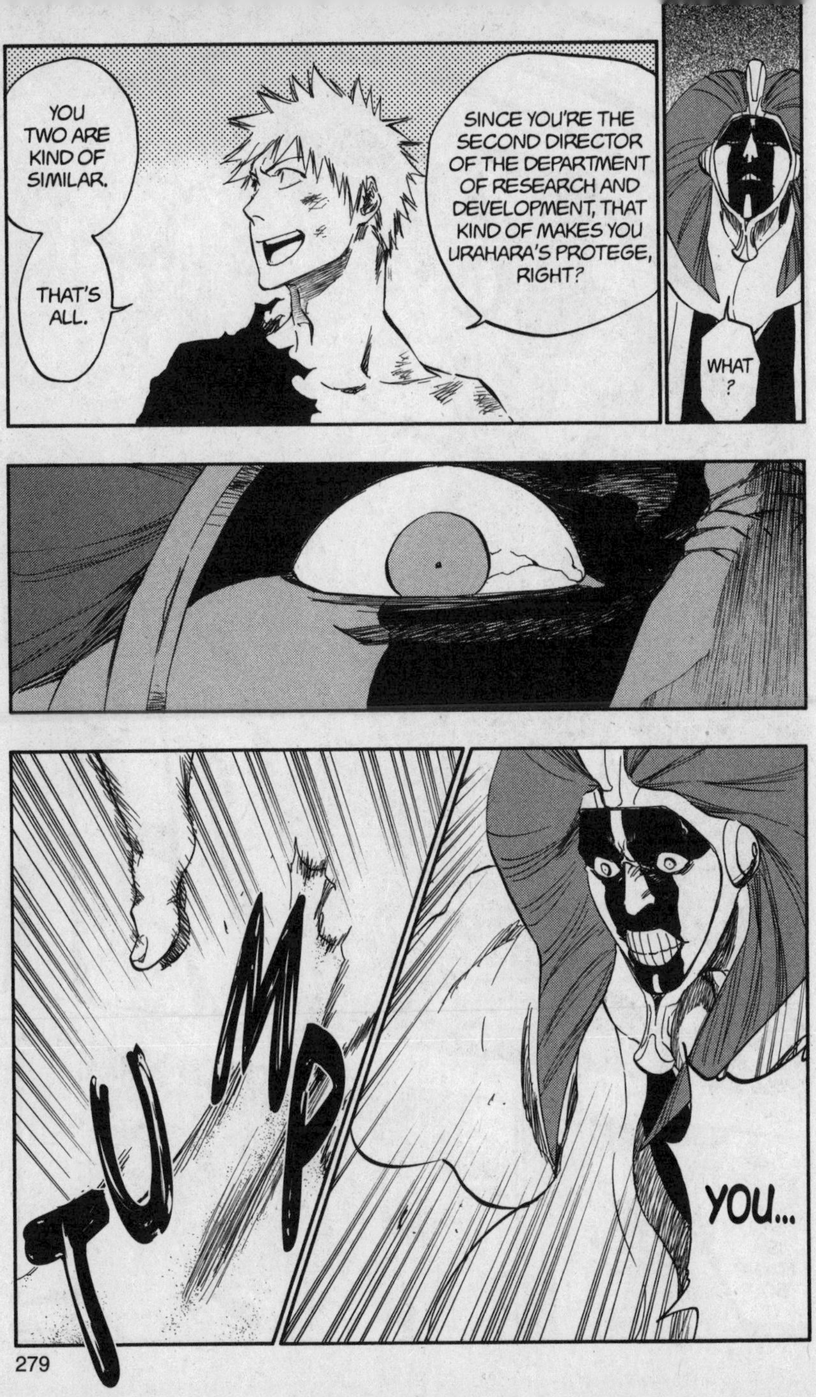
WHAT?
SINCE YOU'RE THE SECOND DIRECTOR OF THE DEPARTMENT OF RESEARCH AND DEVELOPMENT, THAT KIND OF MAKES YOU URAHARA'S PROTEGE, RIGHT?
YOU TWO ARE KIND OF SIMILAR.
THAT'S ALL.
YOU...
TUMP

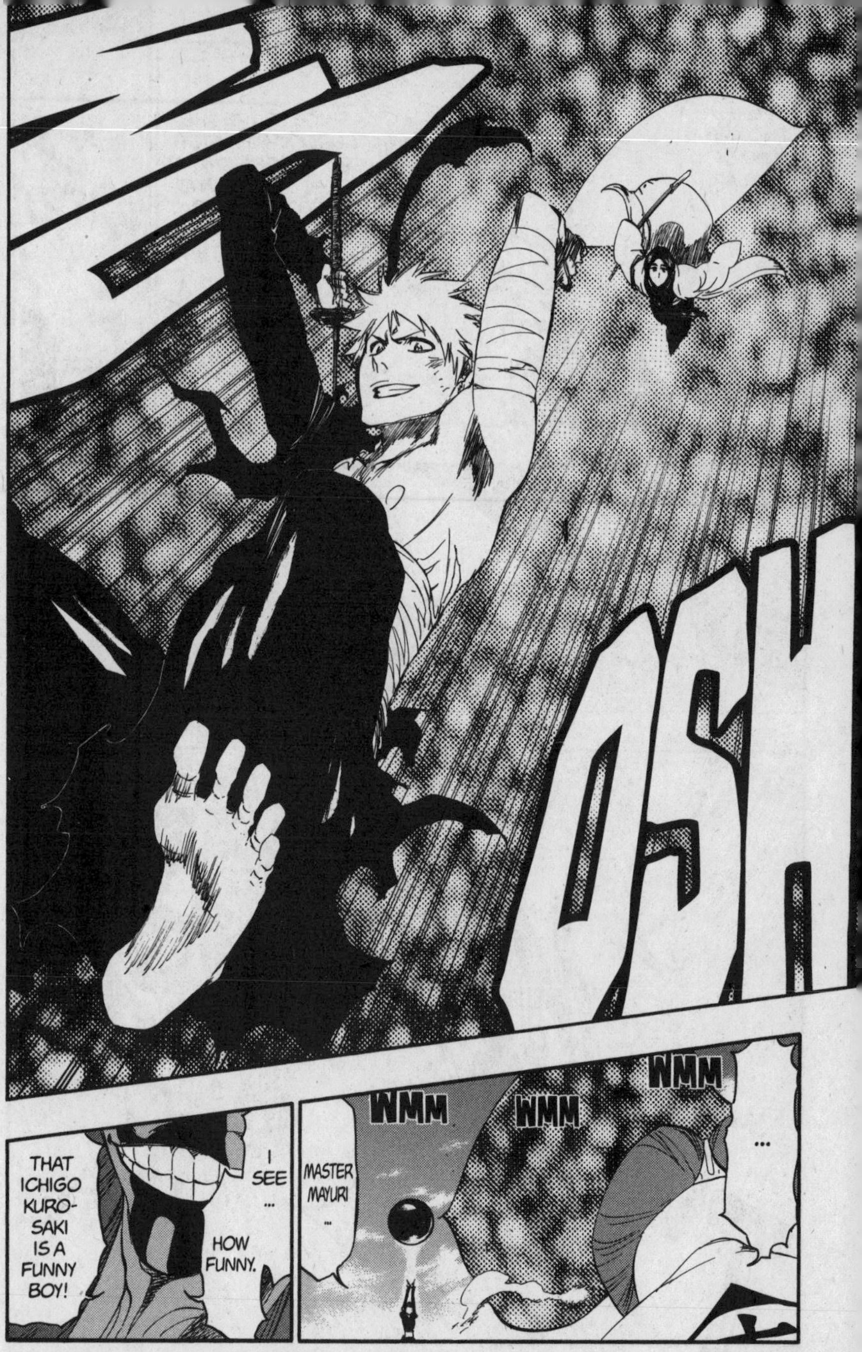
OSH
WMM
...
WMM
WMM
MASTER MAYURI ...
I SEE ...
HOW FUNNY.
THAT ICHIGO KUROSAKI IS A FUNNY BOY!

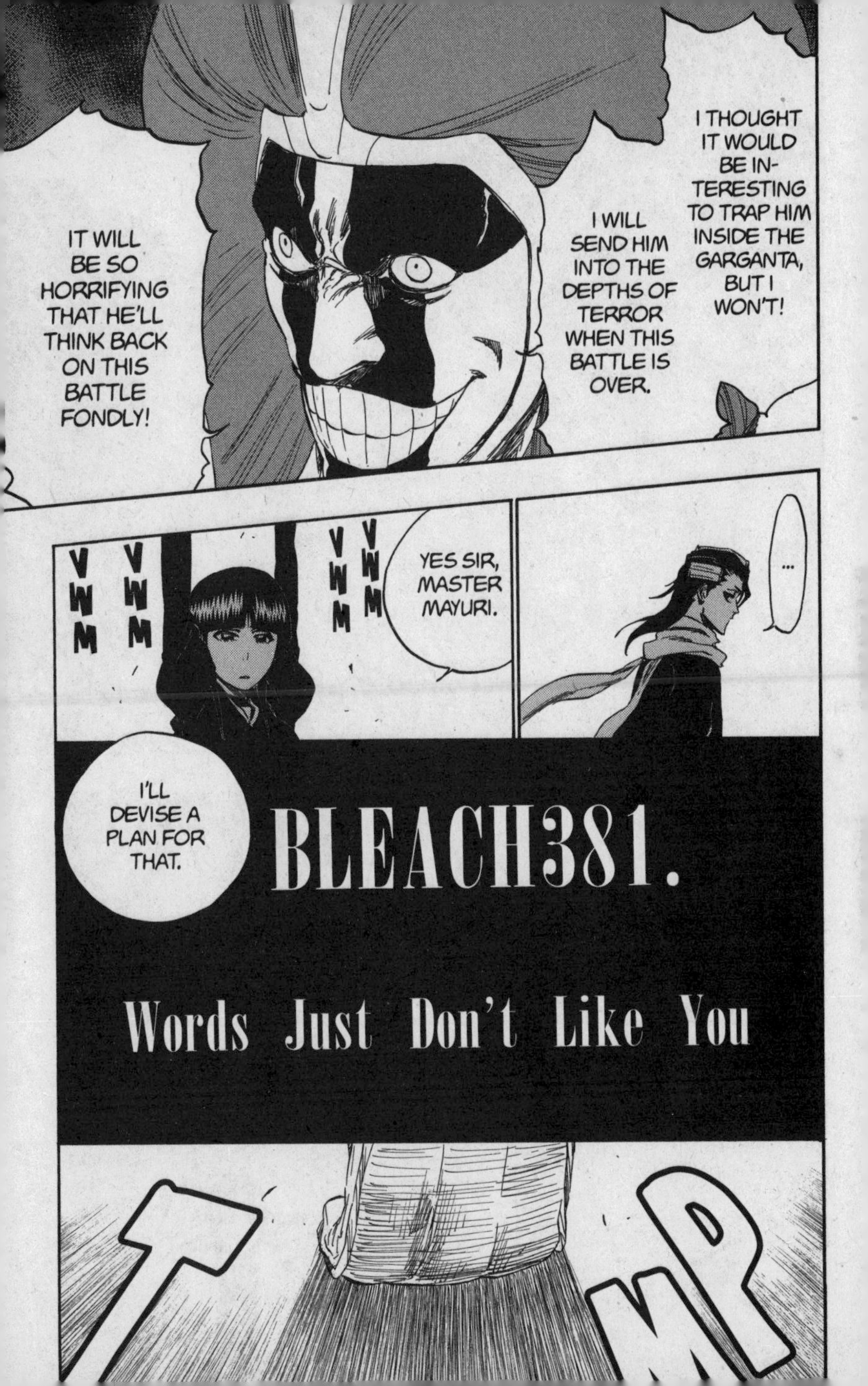
I THOUGHT IT WOULD BE IN-TERESTING TO TRAP HIM INSIDE THE GARGANTA, BUT I WON'T!
I WILL SEND HIM INTO THE DEPTHS OF TERROR WHEN THIS BATTLE IS OVER.
IT WILL BE SO HORRIFYING THAT HE'LL THINK BACK ON THIS BATTLE FONDLY!
...
YES SIR, MASTER MAYURI.
VWM VWM
VWM VWM
I'LL DEVISE A PLAN FOR THAT.
BLEACH381.
Words Just Don't Like You
TMP

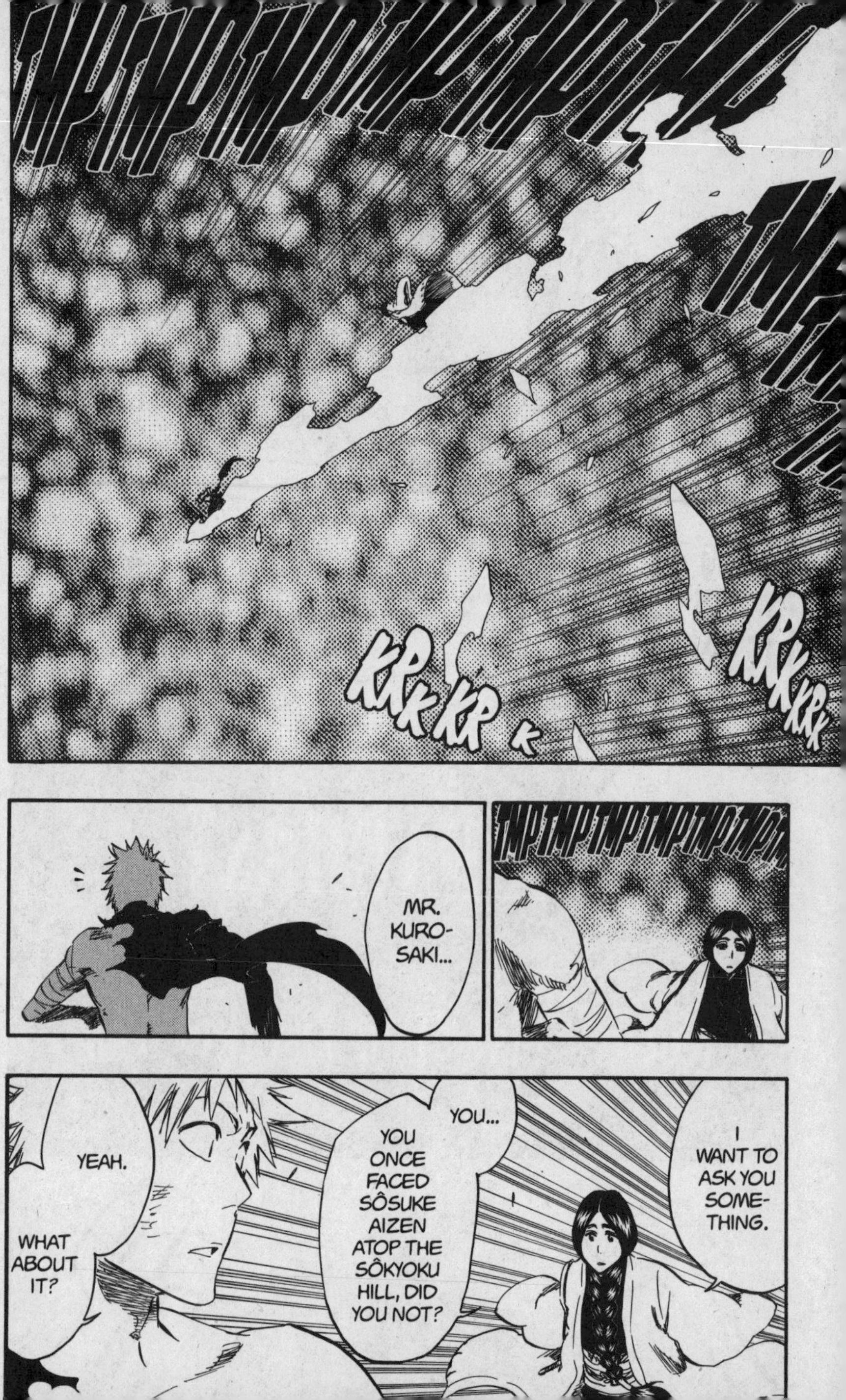
KRK KR K
TMP TMP TMP TMP TMP TMP
MR. KURO-SAKI...
I WANT TO ASK YOU SOME-THING.
YOU...
YOU ONCE FACED SÔSUKE AIZEN ATOP THE SÔKYOKU HILL, DID YOU NOT?
YEAH.
WHAT ABOUT IT?

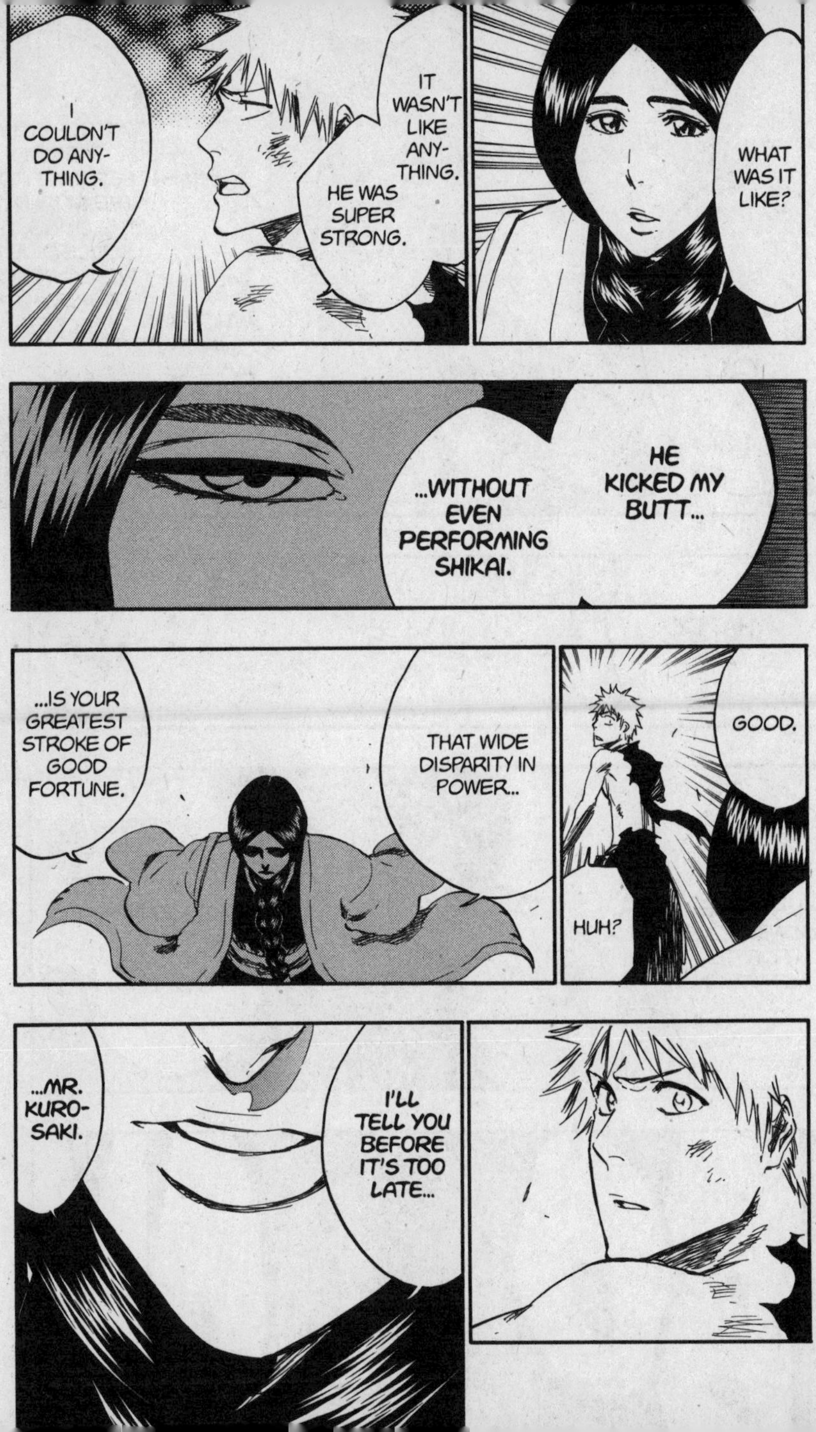
WHAT WAS IT LIKE?
IT WASN'T LIKE ANYTHING.
HE WAS SUPER STRONG.
I COULDN'T DO ANYTHING.
HE KICKED MY BUTT...
...WITHOUT EVEN PERFORMING SHIKAI.
GOOD.
HUH?
THAT WIDE DISPARITY IN POWER...
...IS YOUR GREATEST STROKE OF GOOD FORTUNE.
I'LL TELL YOU BEFORE IT'S TOO LATE...
...MR. KUROSAKI.

AT THIS POINT, THE ONLY PERSON FROM THE WORLD OF THE LIVING, THE SOUL SOCIETY, HUECO MUNDO OR ANYWHERE ELSE...

...WHO CAN CONFRONT SÔSUKE AIZEN...

...IS PROBABLY YOU.

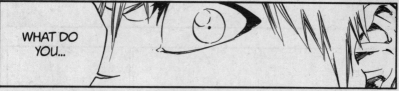

WHAT DO YOU...

I WILL TELL YOU...

...HIS ZANPAKU-TÔ KYÔKA SUIGETSU'S ABILITY...

...AND THE CONDITIONS FOR ITS ACTIVATION.

BOOM

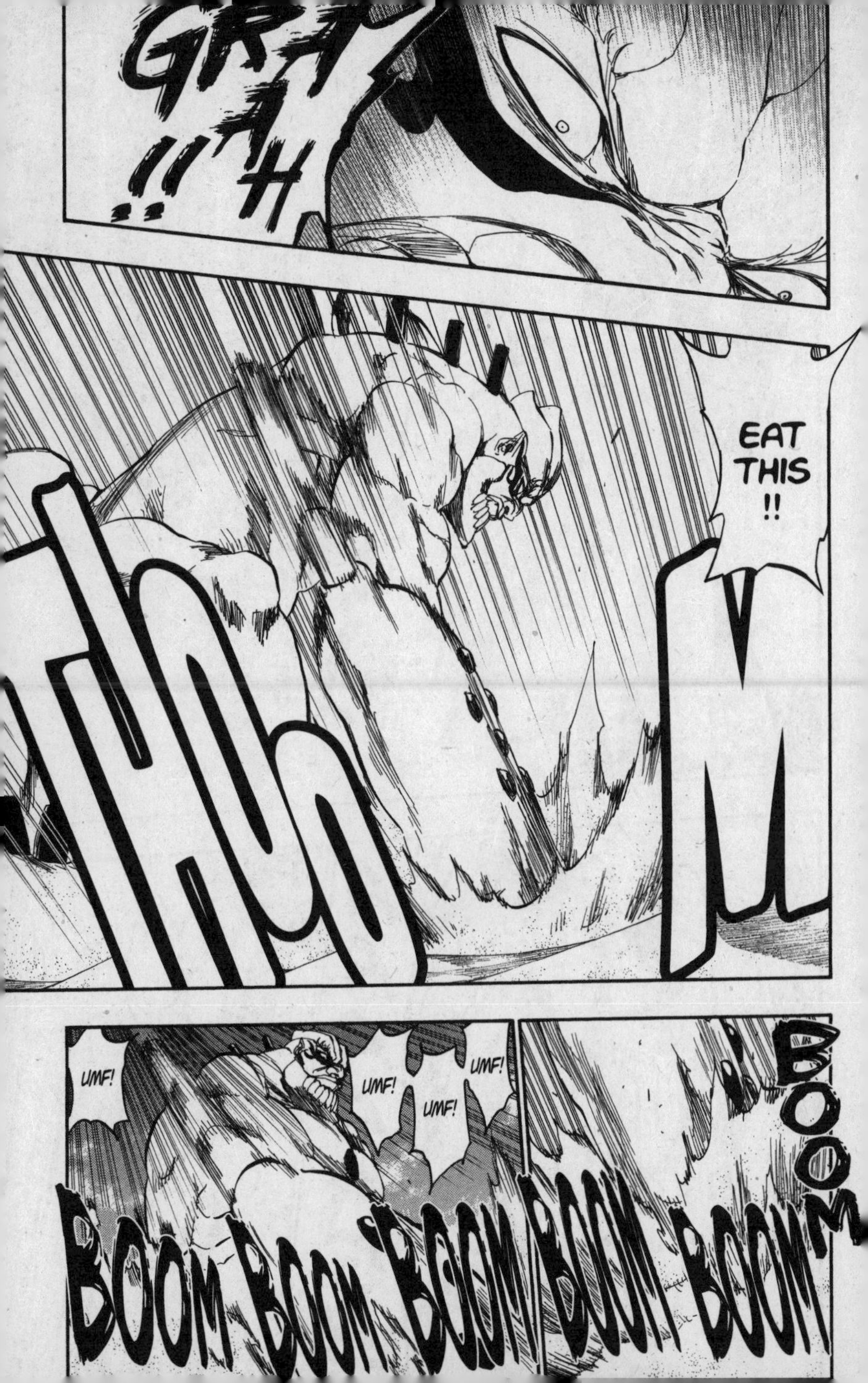
GRAAH!!
EAT THIS!!
HOOM
BOOOM
UMF!
UMF!
UMF!
UMF!
BOOM BOOM BOOM BOOM BOOM

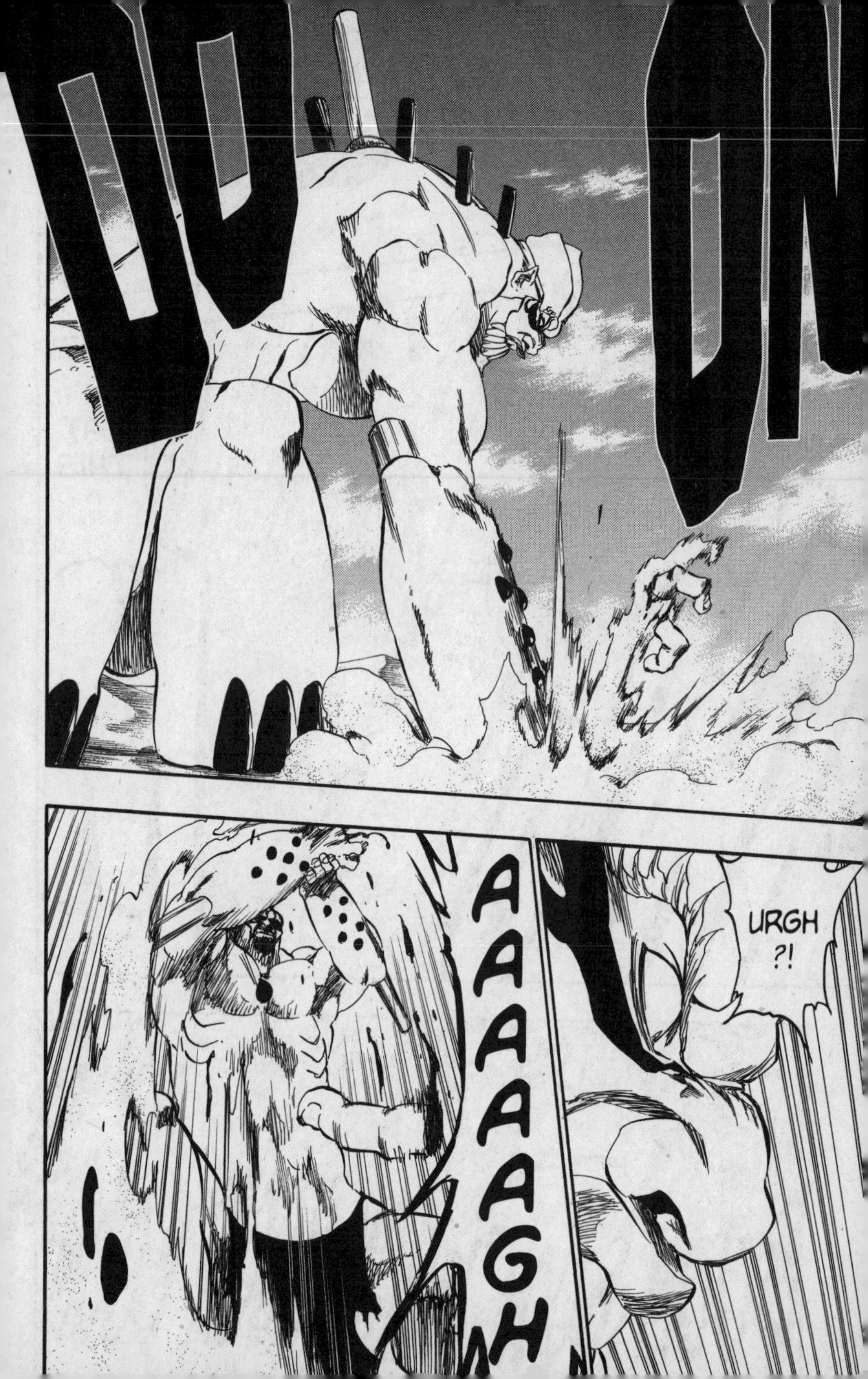
URGH ?!
AAAAAGH

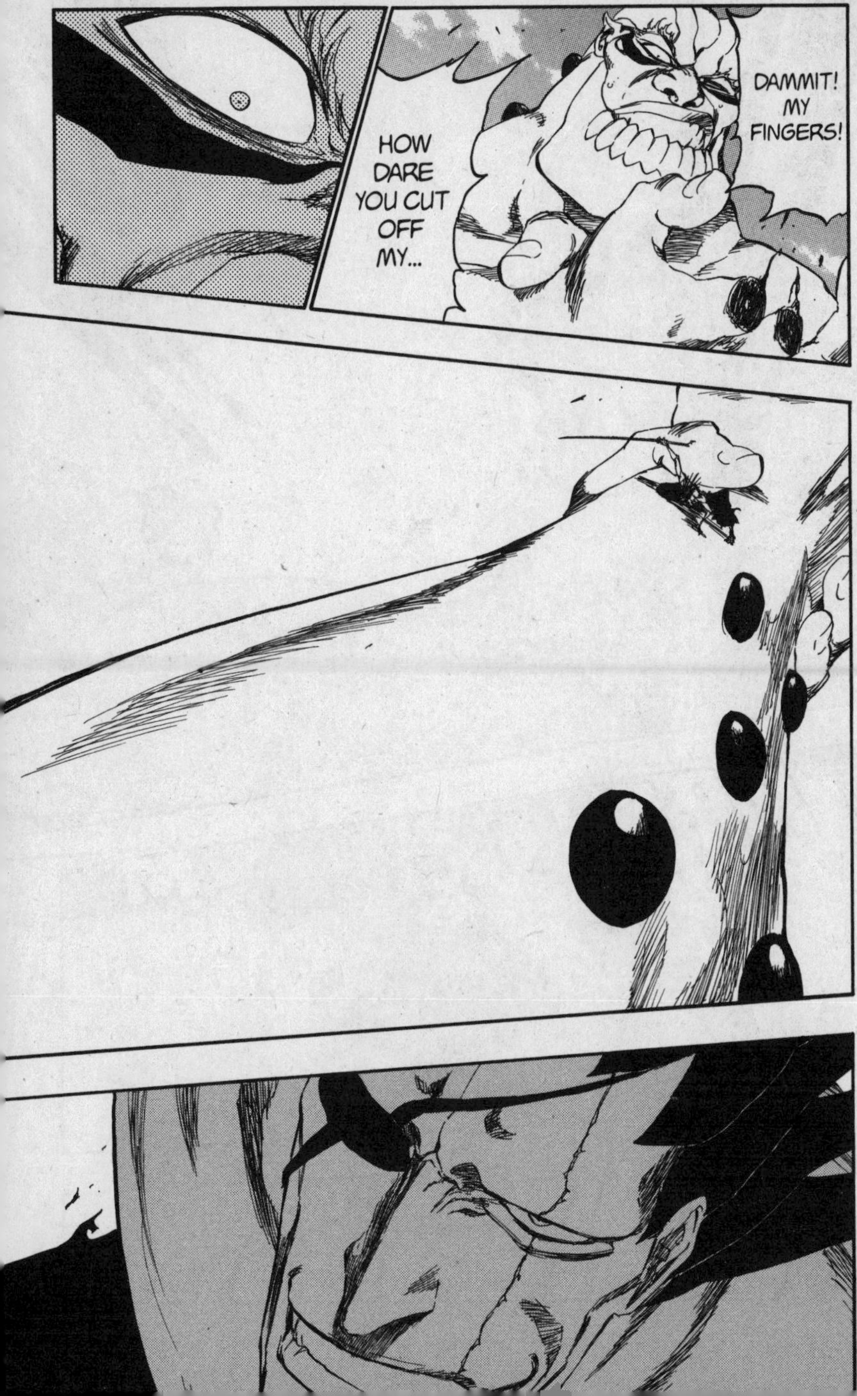
DAMMIT! MY FINGERS!
HOW DARE YOU CUT OFF MY...

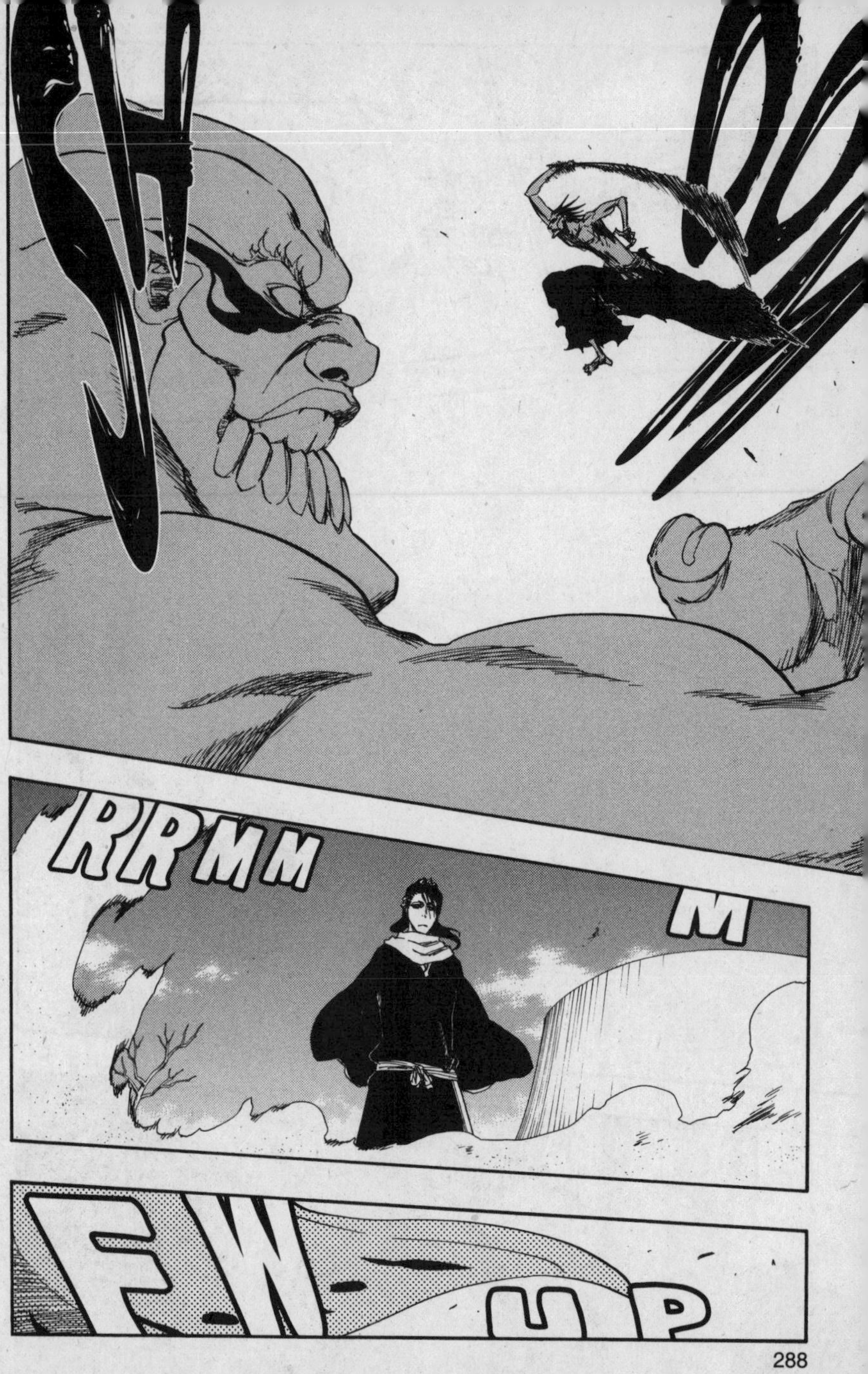
RRMM
M
FWUP

READ THIS WAY

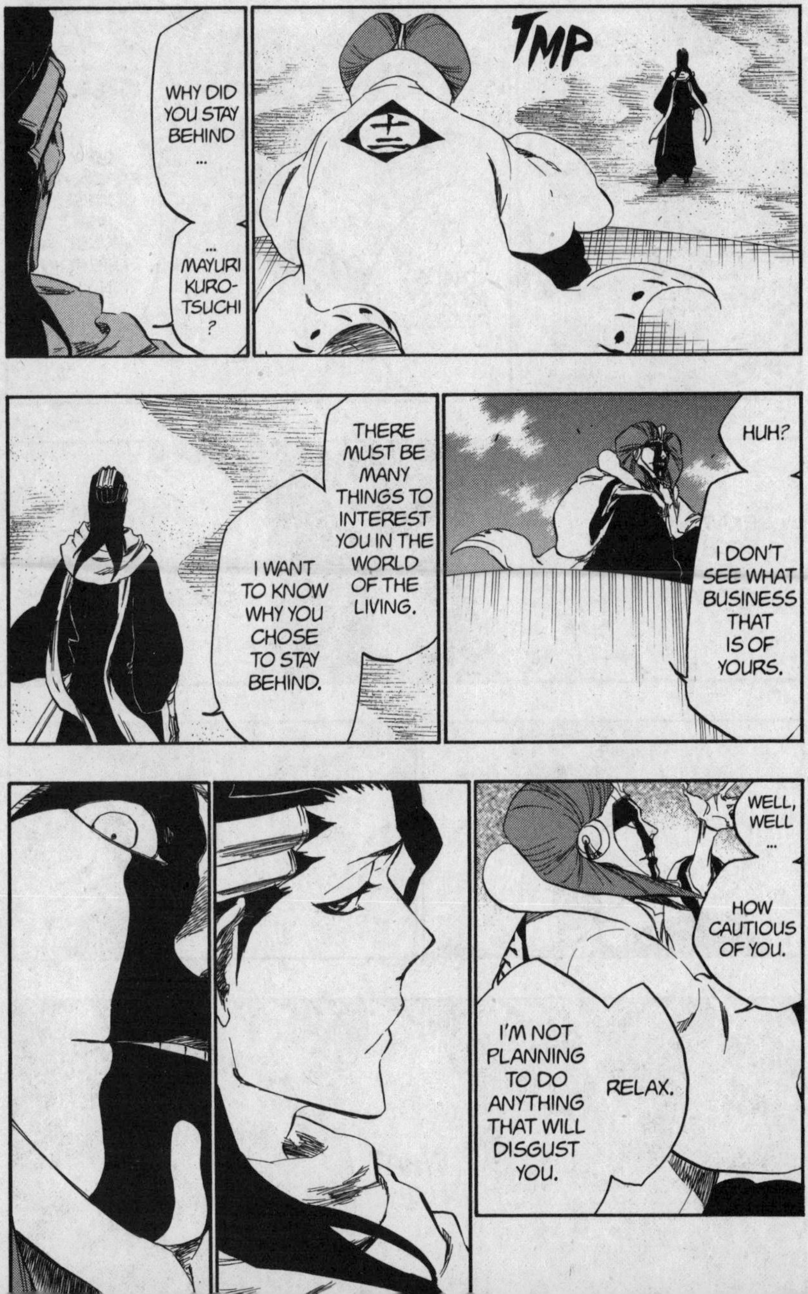
TMP
WHY DID YOU STAY BEHIND ...
... MAYURI KURO-TSUCHI ?
HUH?
I DON'T SEE WHAT BUSINESS THAT IS OF YOURS.
THERE MUST BE MANY THINGS TO INTEREST YOU IN THE WORLD OF THE LIVING.
I WANT TO KNOW WHY YOU CHOSE TO STAY BEHIND.
WELL, WELL ...
HOW CAUTIOUS OF YOU.
RELAX.
I'M NOT PLANNING TO DO ANYTHING THAT WILL DISGUST YOU.

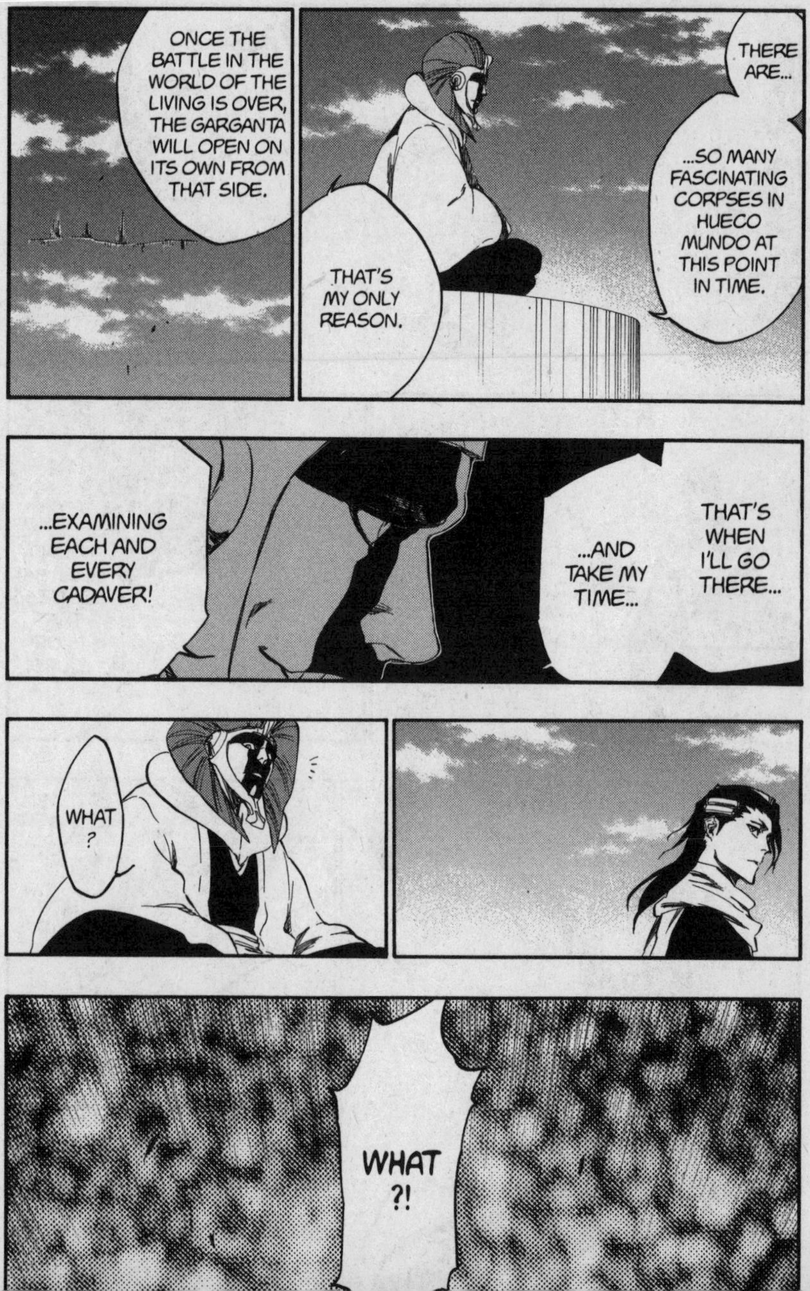
THERE ARE...
...SO MANY FASCINATING CORPSES IN HUECO MUNDO AT THIS POINT IN TIME.
THAT'S MY ONLY REASON.
ONCE THE BATTLE IN THE WORLD OF THE LIVING IS OVER, THE GARGANTA WILL OPEN ON ITS OWN FROM THAT SIDE.
THAT'S WHEN I'LL GO THERE...
...AND TAKE MY TIME...
...EXAMINING EACH AND EVERY CADAVER!
WHAT?
WHAT?!

READ THIS WAY

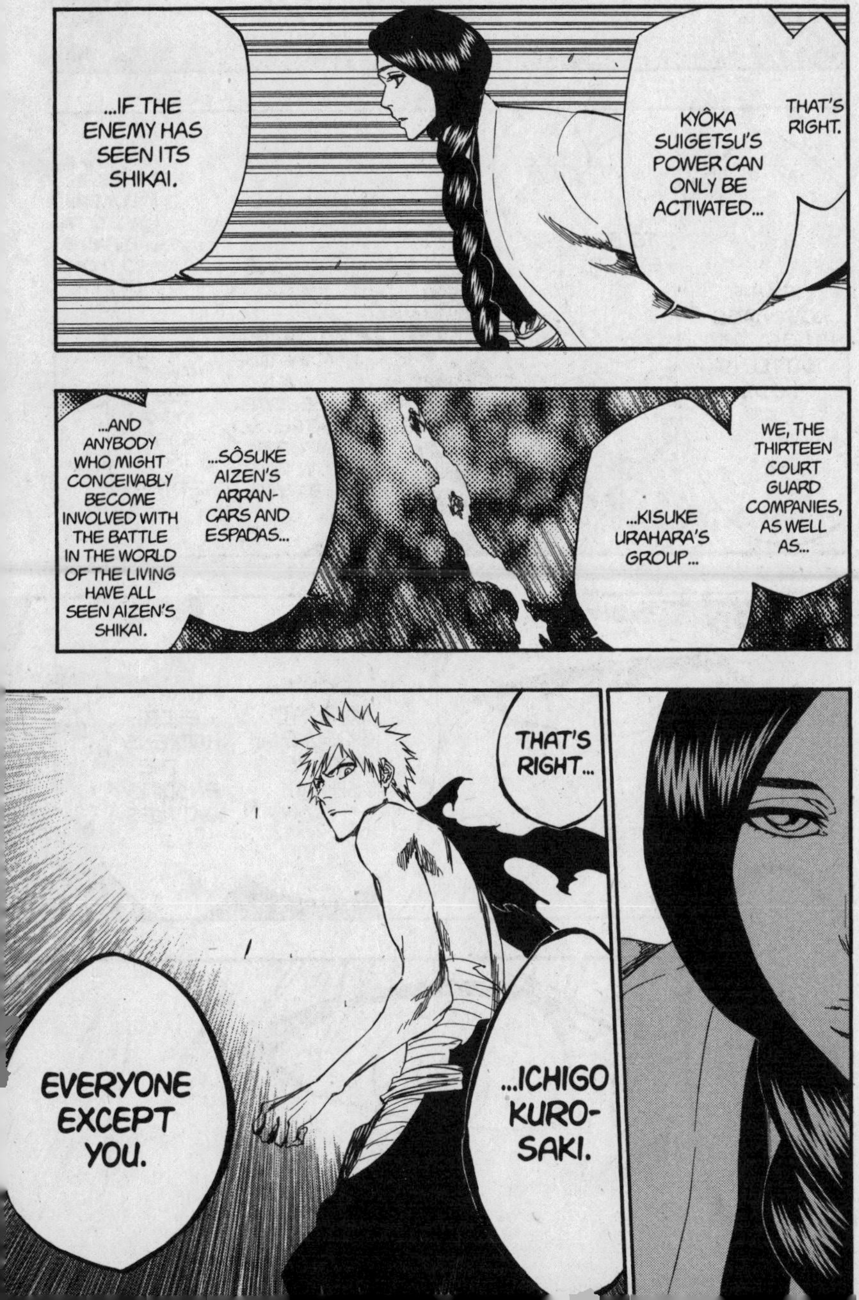
THAT'S RIGHT.
KYÔKA SUIGETSU'S POWER CAN ONLY BE ACTIVATED...
...IF THE ENEMY HAS SEEN ITS SHIKAI.
WE, THE THIRTEEN COURT GUARD COMPANIES, AS WELL AS...
...KISUKE URAHARA'S GROUP...
...SÔSUKE AIZEN'S ARRANCARS AND ESPADAS...
...AND ANYBODY WHO MIGHT CONCEIVABLY BECOME INVOLVED WITH THE BATTLE IN THE WORLD OF THE LIVING HAVE ALL SEEN AIZEN'S SHIKAI.
THAT'S RIGHT...
...ICHIGO KUROSAKI.
EVERYONE EXCEPT YOU.

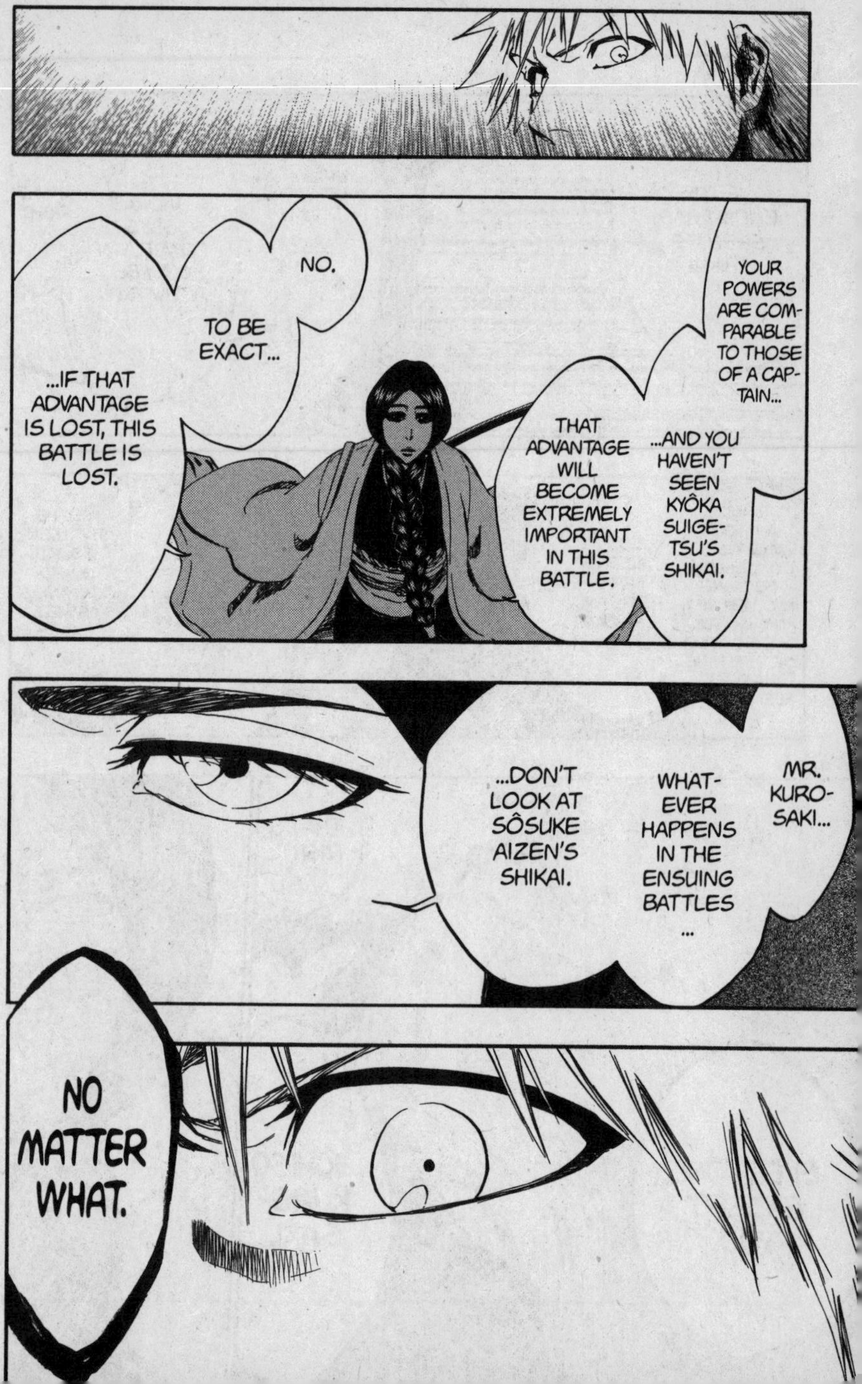
YOUR POWERS ARE COMPARABLE TO THOSE OF A CAPTAIN...
...AND YOU HAVEN'T SEEN KYÔKA SUIGETSU'S SHIKAI.
THAT ADVANTAGE WILL BECOME EXTREMELY IMPORTANT IN THIS BATTLE.
NO.
TO BE EXACT...
...IF THAT ADVANTAGE IS LOST, THIS BATTLE IS LOST.
MR. KUROSAKI...
WHATEVER HAPPENS IN THE ENSUING BATTLES...
...DON'T LOOK AT SÔSUKE AIZEN'S SHIKAI.
NO MATTER WHAT.

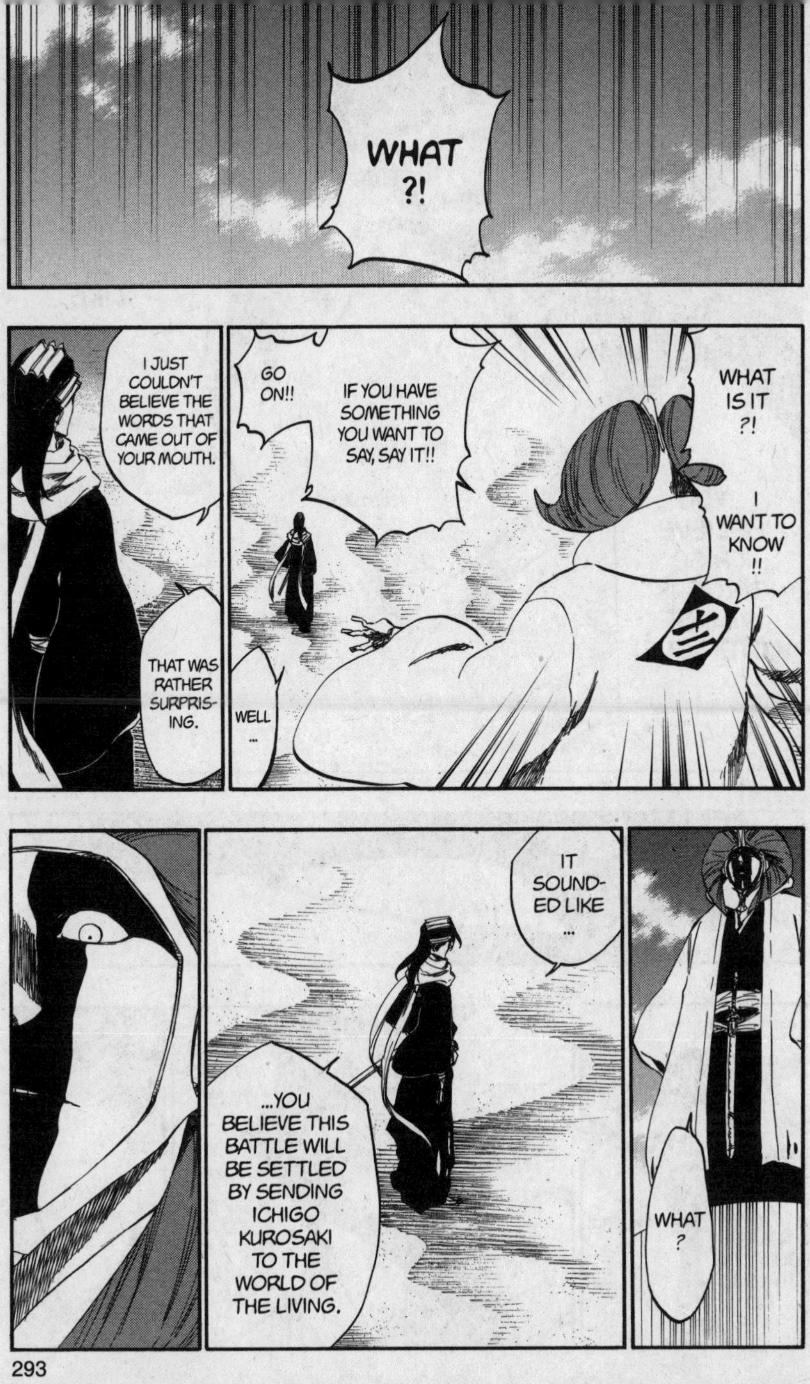
WHAT ?!
WHAT IS IT ?!
I WANT TO KNOW !!
IF YOU HAVE SOMETHING YOU WANT TO SAY, SAY IT!!
GO ON!!
WELL ...
I JUST COULDN'T BELIEVE THE WORDS THAT CAME OUT OF YOUR MOUTH.
THAT WAS RATHER SURPRIS-ING.
WHAT ?
IT SOUND-ED LIKE ...
...YOU BELIEVE THIS BATTLE WILL BE SETTLED BY SENDING ICHIGO KUROSAKI TO THE WORLD OF THE LIVING.

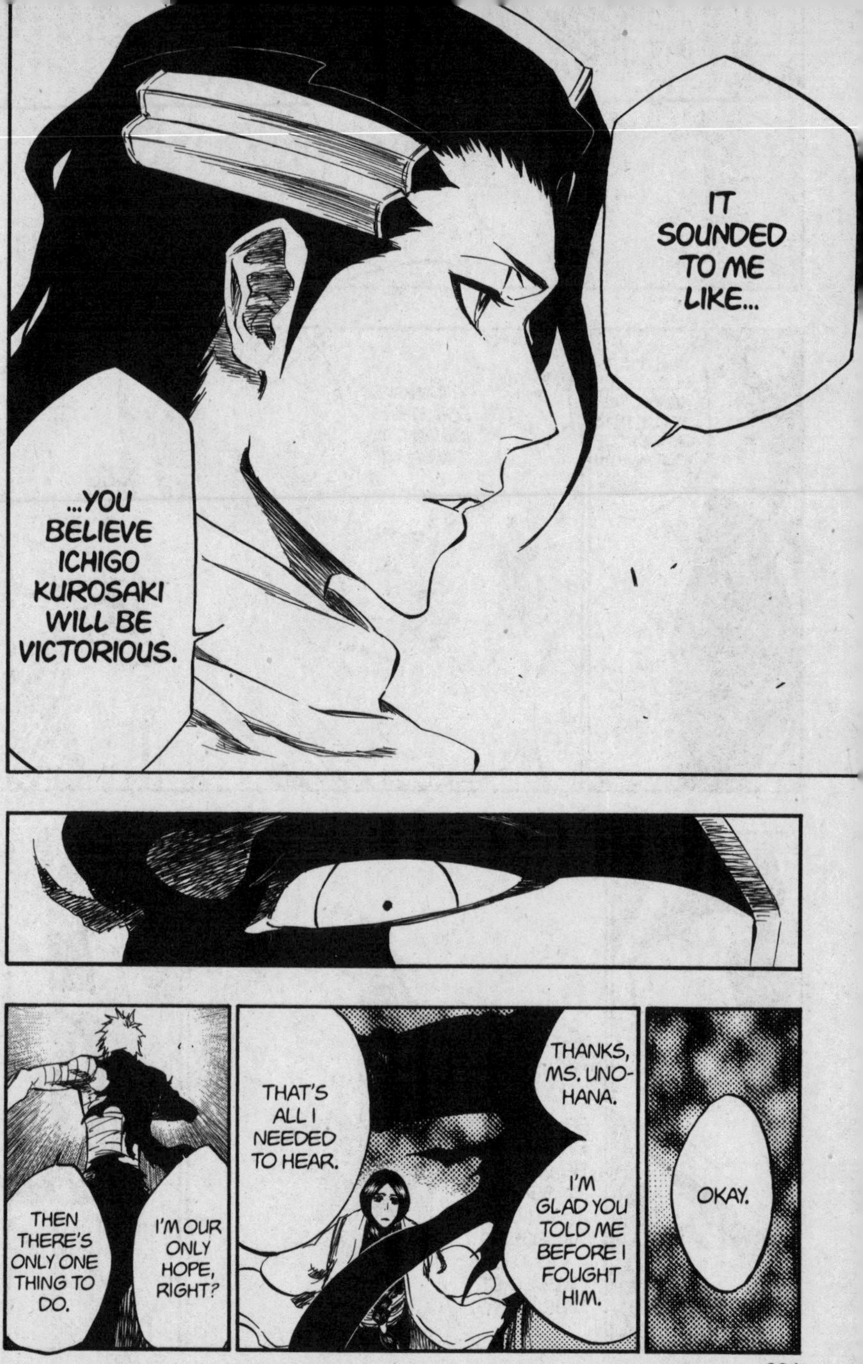
IT SOUNDED TO ME LIKE...
...YOU BELIEVE ICHIGO KUROSAKI WILL BE VICTORIOUS.
OKAY.
THANKS, MS. UNO-HANA.
I'M GLAD YOU TOLD ME BEFORE I FOUGHT HIM.
THAT'S ALL I NEEDED TO HEAR.
I'M OUR ONLY HOPE, RIGHT?
THEN THERE'S ONLY ONE THING TO DO.

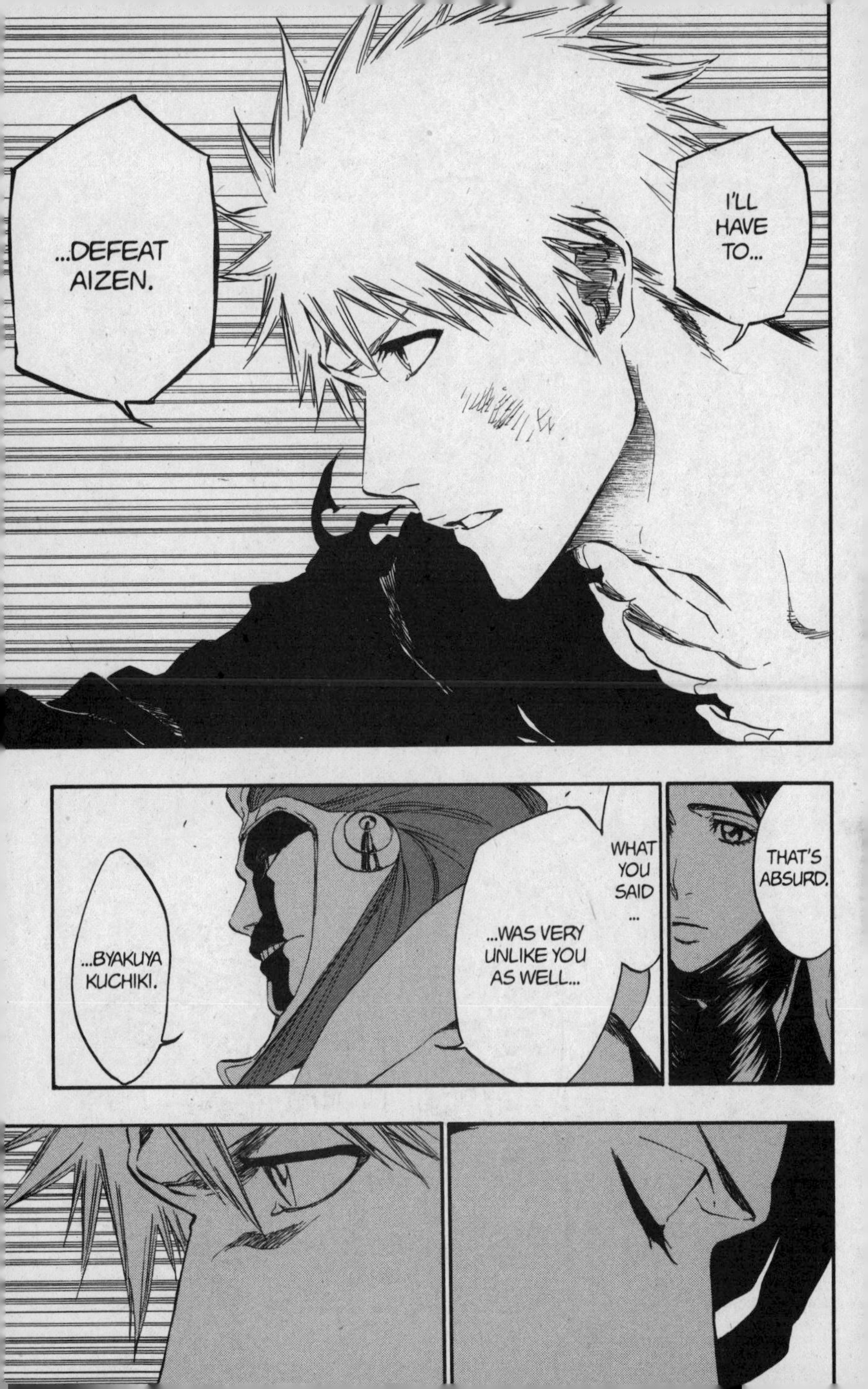
I'LL HAVE TO...
...DEFEAT AIZEN.
THAT'S ABSURD.
WHAT YOU SAID ...
...WAS VERY UNLIKE YOU AS WELL...
...BYAKUYA KUCHIKI.

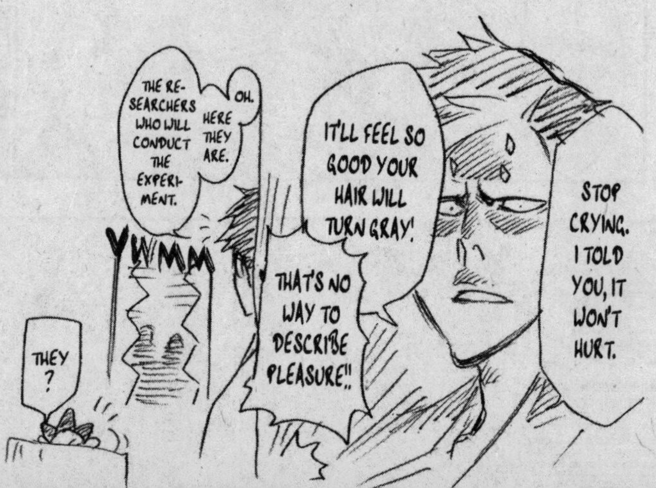
STOP CRYING. I TOLD YOU, IT WON'T HURT.
IT'LL FEEL SO GOOD YOUR HAIR WILL TURN GRAY!
THAT'S NO WAY TO DESCRIBE PLEASURE!!
OH. HERE THEY ARE.
THE RE-SEARCHERS WHO WILL CONDUCT THE EXPERI-MENT.
VWMM
THEY?

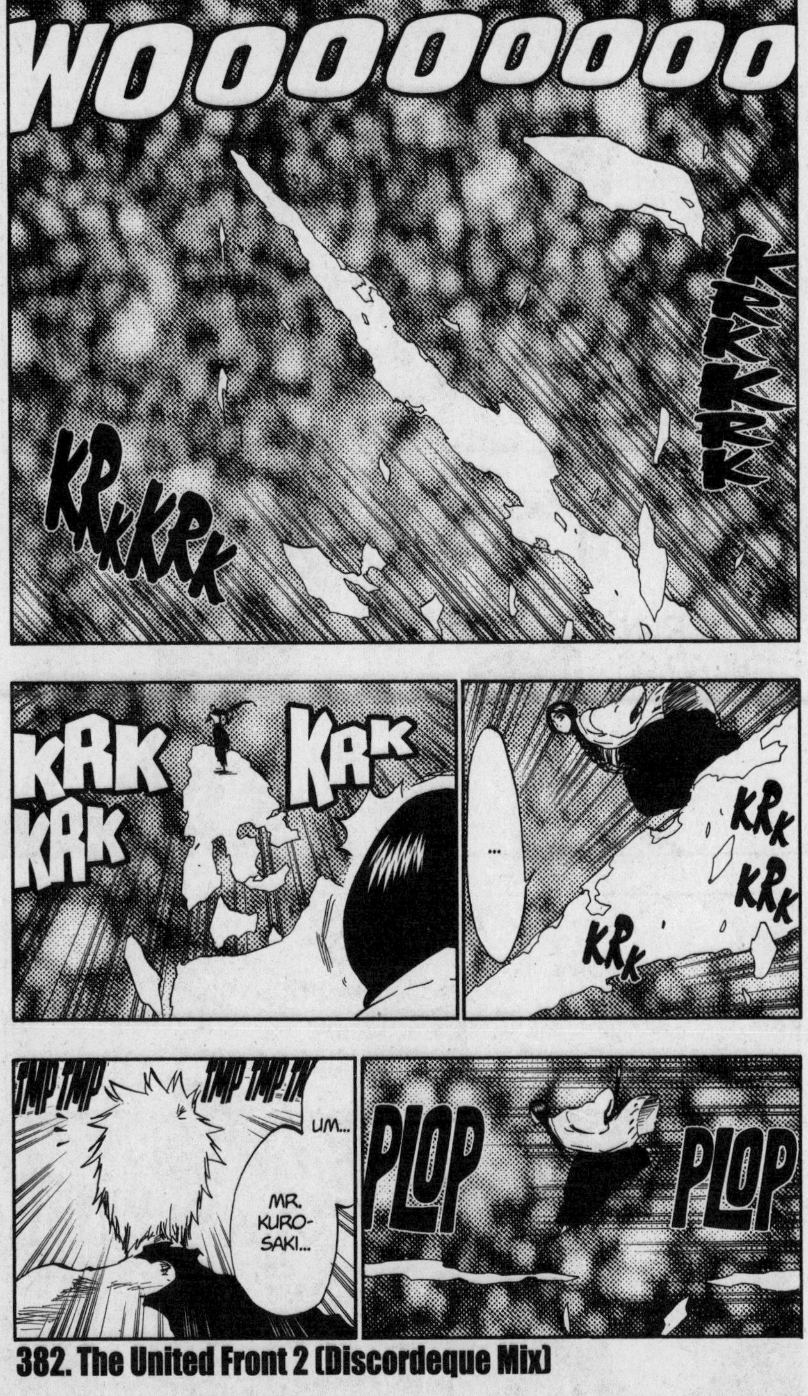
WOOOOOOOOO
KRKKRK
KRKKRK
...
KRK
KRK
KRK
KRK
KRK
KRK
PLOP
PLOP
TMP TMP
TMP TMP TK
UM...
MR. KURO-SAKI...

382. The United Front 2 (Discordeque Mix)

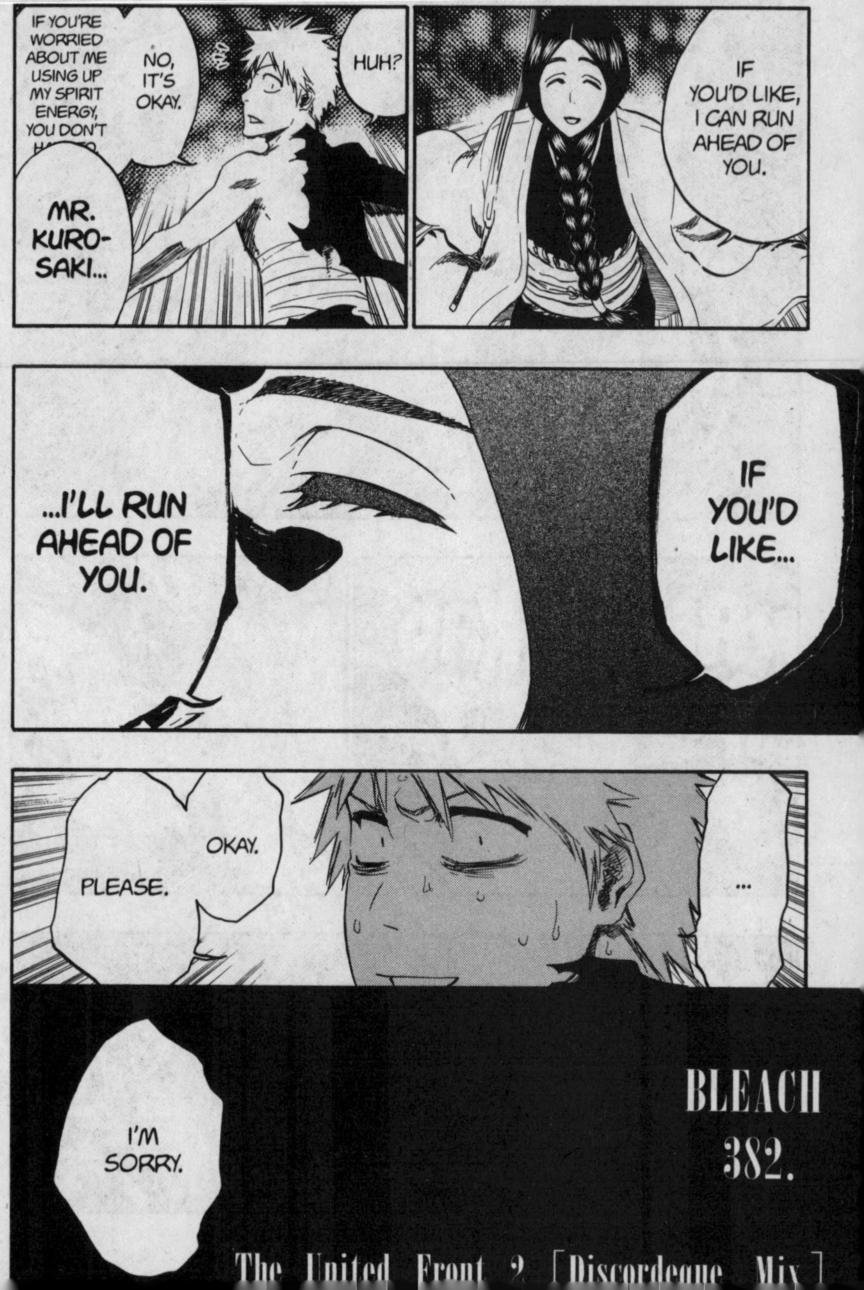
IF YOU'D LIKE, I CAN RUN AHEAD OF YOU.
HUH?
NO, IT'S OKAY.
IF YOU'RE WORRIED ABOUT ME USING UP MY SPIRIT ENERGY, YOU DON'T
MR. KURO-SAKI...
IF YOU'D LIKE...
...I'LL RUN AHEAD OF YOU.
...
OKAY.
PLEASE.
I'M SORRY.
BLEACH 382.
The United Front 2 「Discordeque Mix」

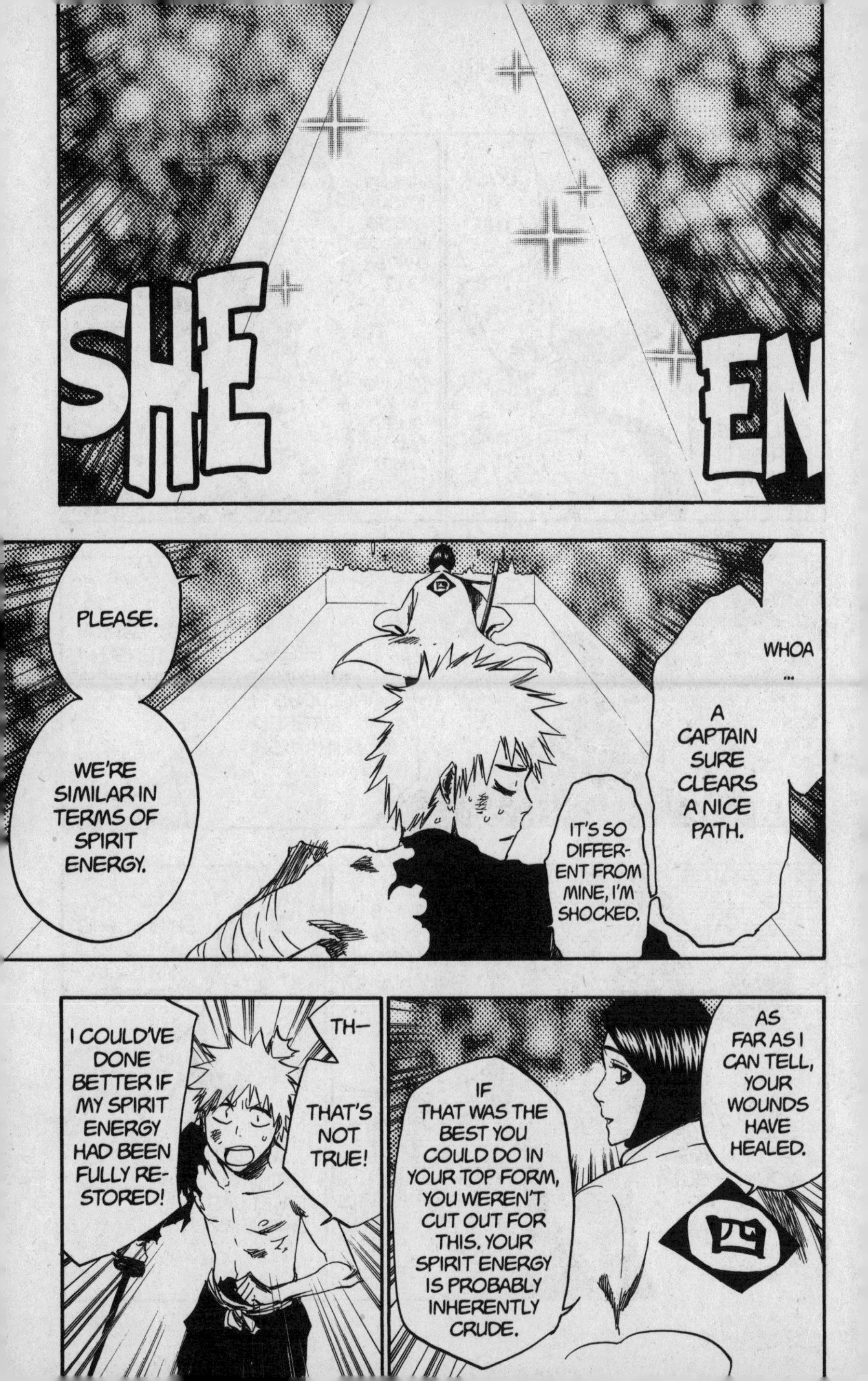
SHE EN
WHOA ... A CAPTAIN SURE CLEARS A NICE PATH.
IT'S SO DIFFERENT FROM MINE, I'M SHOCKED.
PLEASE.
WE'RE SIMILAR IN TERMS OF SPIRIT ENERGY.
AS FAR AS I CAN TELL, YOUR WOUNDS HAVE HEALED.
IF THAT WAS THE BEST YOU COULD DO IN YOUR TOP FORM, YOU WEREN'T CUT OUT FOR THIS. YOUR SPIRIT ENERGY IS PROBABLY INHERENTLY CRUDE.
TH—
THAT'S NOT TRUE!
I COULD'VE DONE BETTER IF MY SPIRIT ENERGY HAD BEEN FULLY RESTORED!

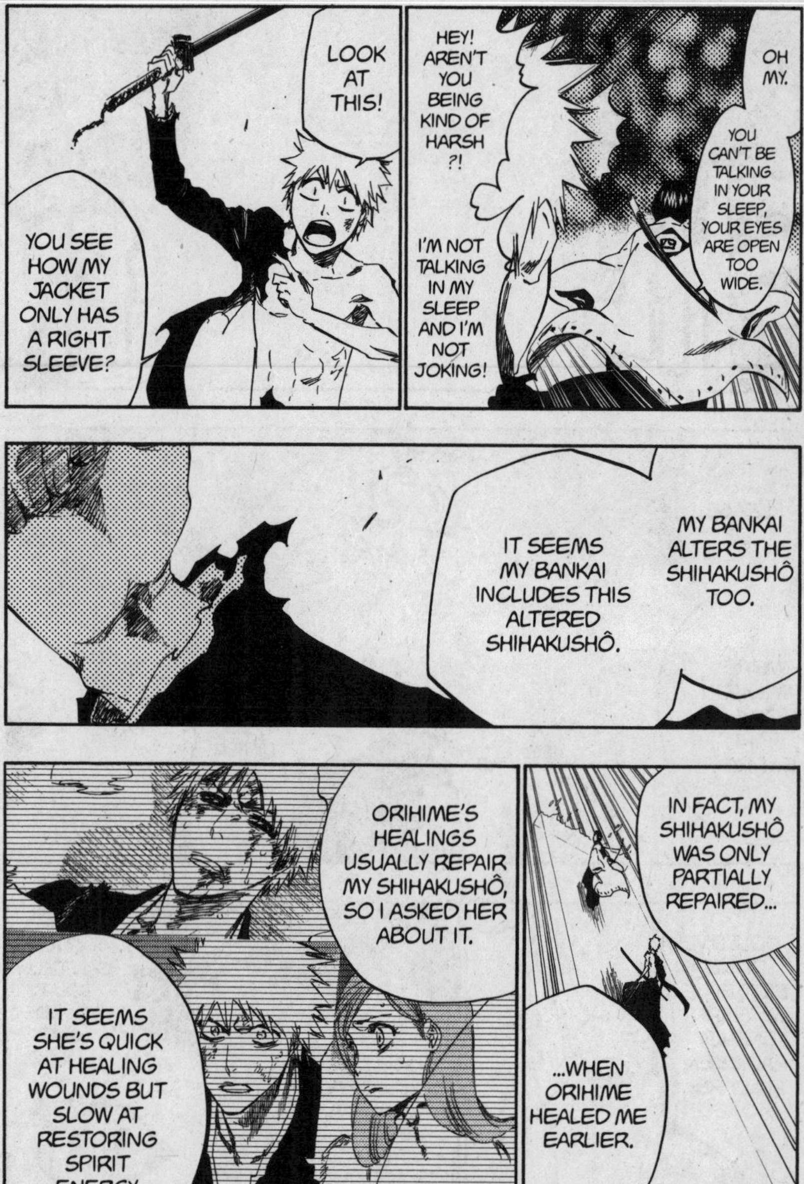
OH MY.
YOU CAN'T BE TALKING IN YOUR SLEEP, YOUR EYES ARE OPEN TOO WIDE.
HEY! AREN'T YOU BEING KIND OF HARSH ?!
I'M NOT TALKING IN MY SLEEP AND I'M NOT JOKING!
LOOK AT THIS!
YOU SEE HOW MY JACKET ONLY HAS A RIGHT SLEEVE?
MY BANKAI ALTERS THE SHIHAKUSHÔ TOO.
IT SEEMS MY BANKAI INCLUDES THIS ALTERED SHIHAKUSHÔ.
IN FACT, MY SHIHAKUSHÔ WAS ONLY PARTIALLY REPAIRED...
...WHEN ORIHIME HEALED ME EARLIER.
ORIHIME'S HEALINGS USUALLY REPAIR MY SHIHAKUSHÔ, SO I ASKED HER ABOUT IT.
IT SEEMS SHE'S QUICK AT HEALING WOUNDS BUT SLOW AT RESTORING SPIRIT ENERGY.

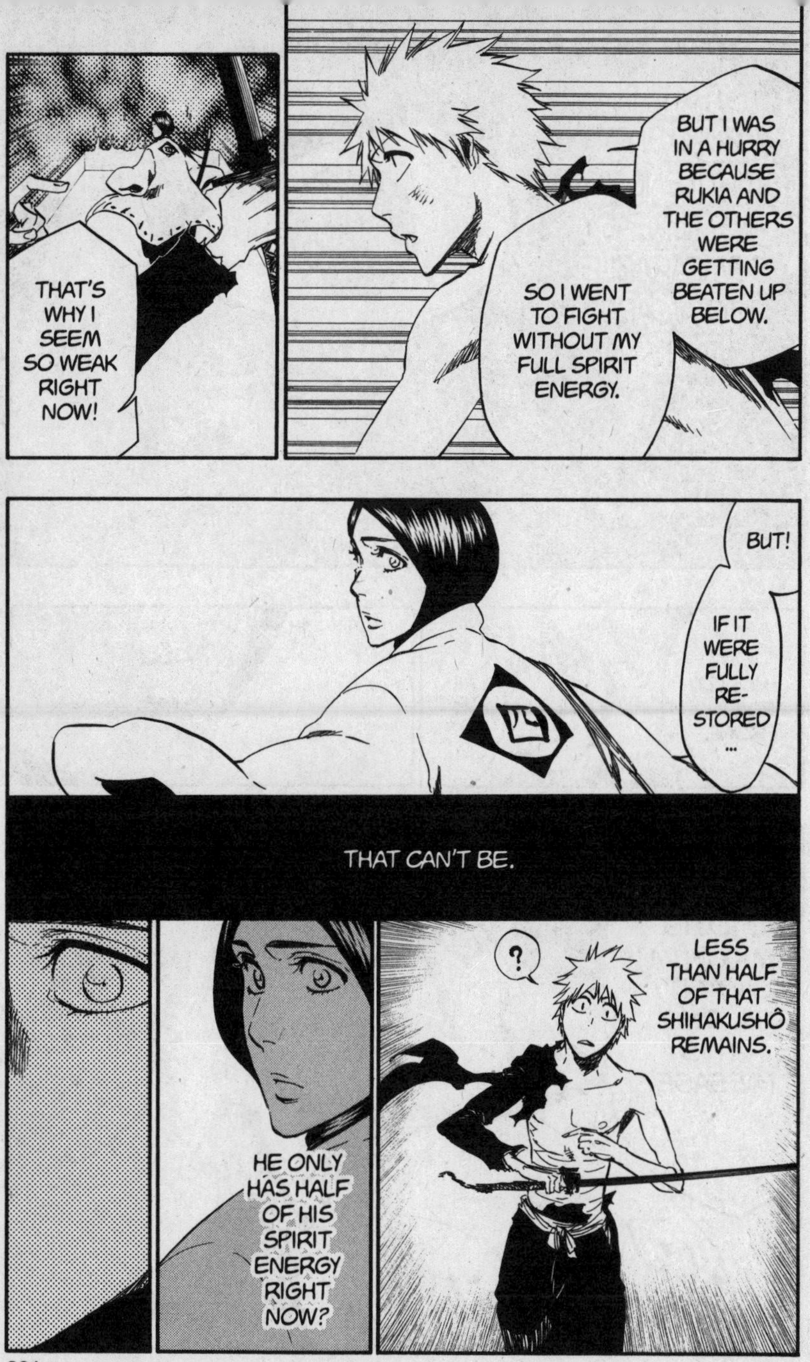

BUT I WAS IN A HURRY BECAUSE RUKIA AND THE OTHERS WERE GETTING BEATEN UP BELOW.
SO I WENT TO FIGHT WITHOUT MY FULL SPIRIT ENERGY.
THAT'S WHY I SEEM SO WEAK RIGHT NOW!
BUT!
IF IT WERE FULLY RE-STORED ...
THAT CAN'T BE.
?
LESS THAN HALF OF THAT SHIHAKUSHÔ REMAINS.
HE ONLY HAS HALF OF HIS SPIRIT ENERGY RIGHT NOW?

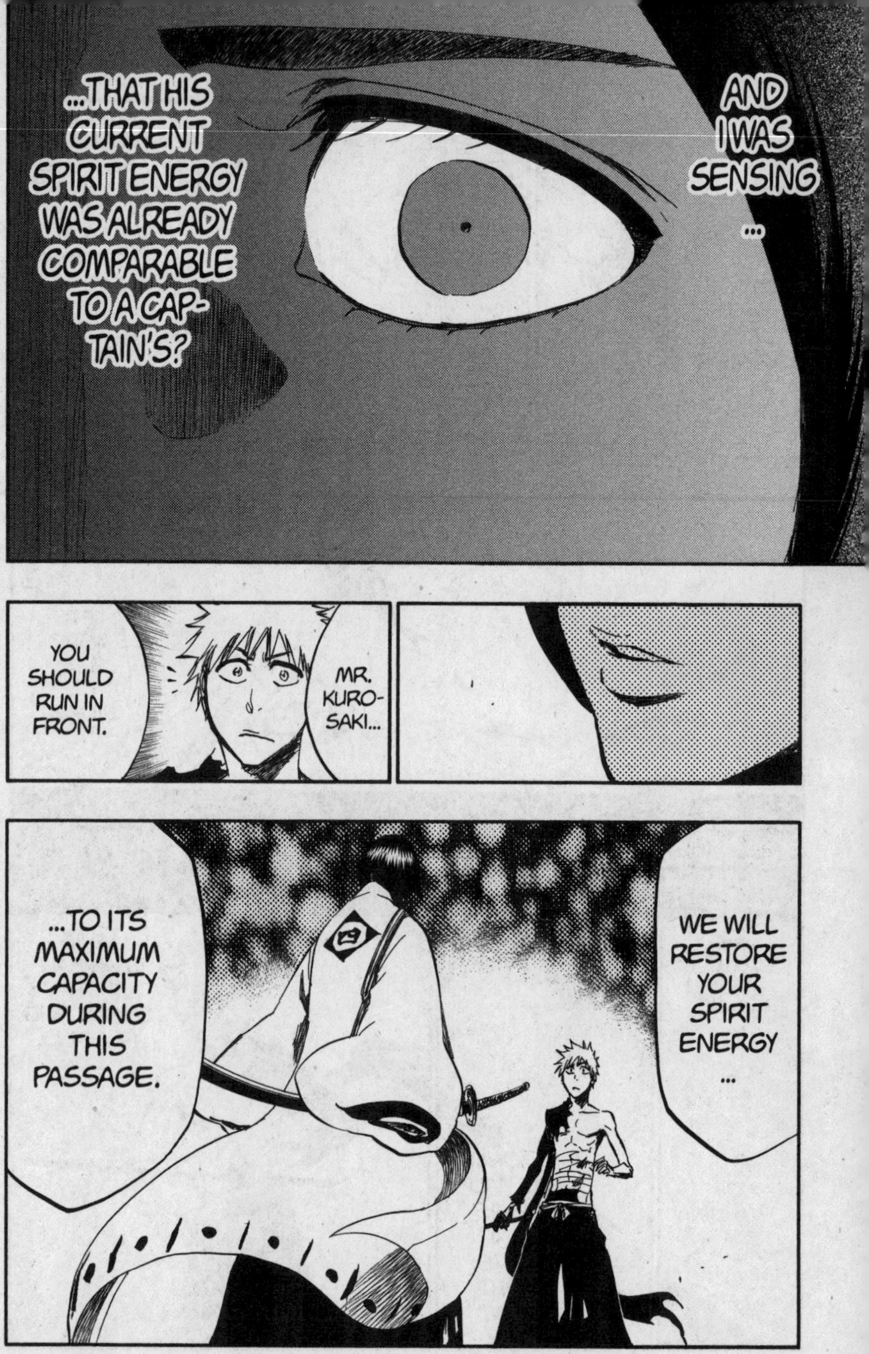
AND I WAS SENSING ...
...THAT HIS CURRENT SPIRIT ENERGY WAS ALREADY COMPARABLE TO A CAP-TAIN'S?
MR. KURO-SAKI...
YOU SHOULD RUN IN FRONT.
WE WILL RESTORE YOUR SPIRIT ENERGY ...
...TO ITS MAXIMUM CAPACITY DURING THIS PASSAGE.

READ THIS WAY

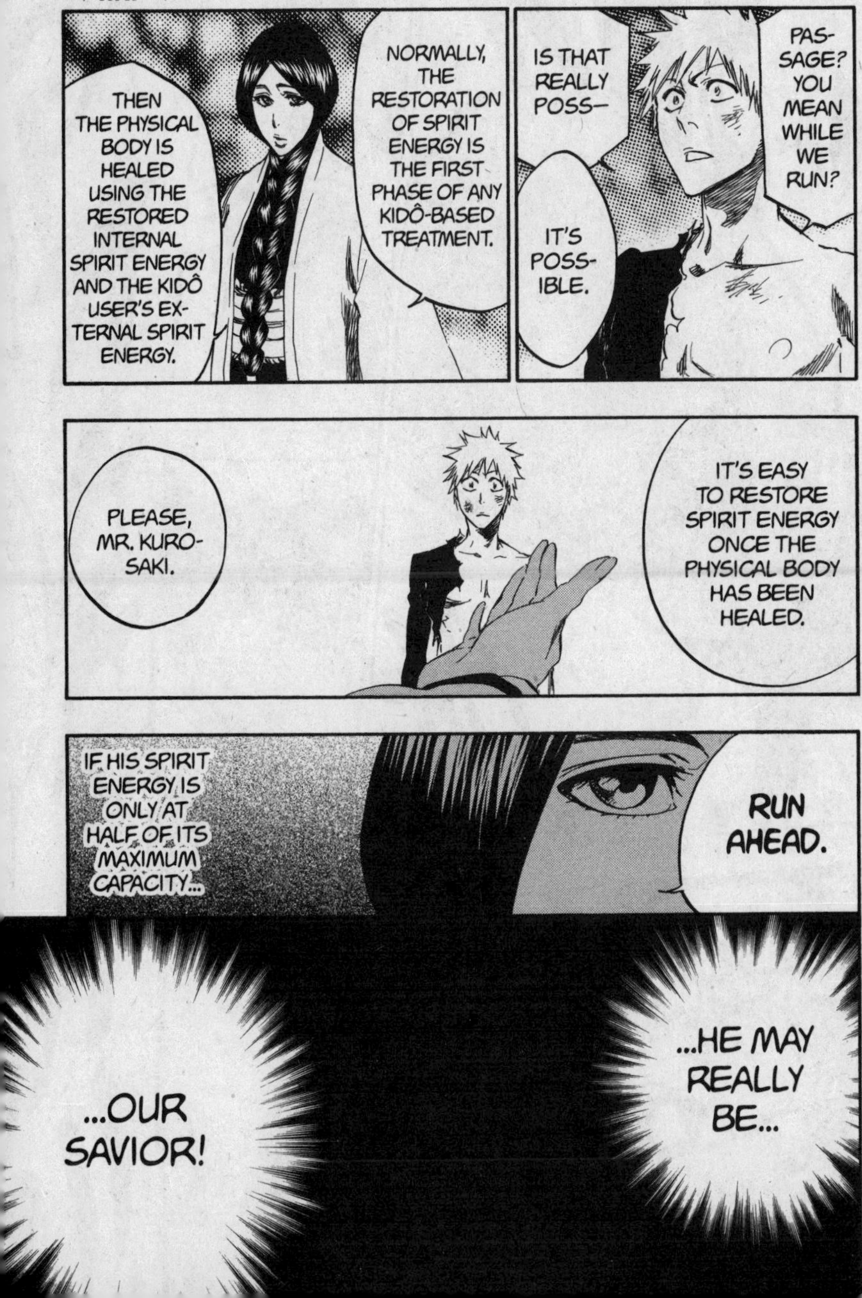

PAS-SAGE? YOU MEAN WHILE WE RUN?
IS THAT REALLY POSS—
IT'S POSS-IBLE.
NORMALLY, THE RESTORATION OF SPIRIT ENERGY IS THE FIRST PHASE OF ANY KIDÔ-BASED TREATMENT.
THEN THE PHYSICAL BODY IS HEALED USING THE RESTORED INTERNAL SPIRIT ENERGY AND THE KIDÔ USER'S EX-TERNAL SPIRIT ENERGY.
IT'S EASY TO RESTORE SPIRIT ENERGY ONCE THE PHYSICAL BODY HAS BEEN HEALED.
PLEASE, MR. KURO-SAKI.
RUN AHEAD.
IF HIS SPIRIT ENERGY IS ONLY AT HALF OF ITS MAXIMUM CAPACITY...
...HE MAY REALLY BE...
...OUR SAVIOR!

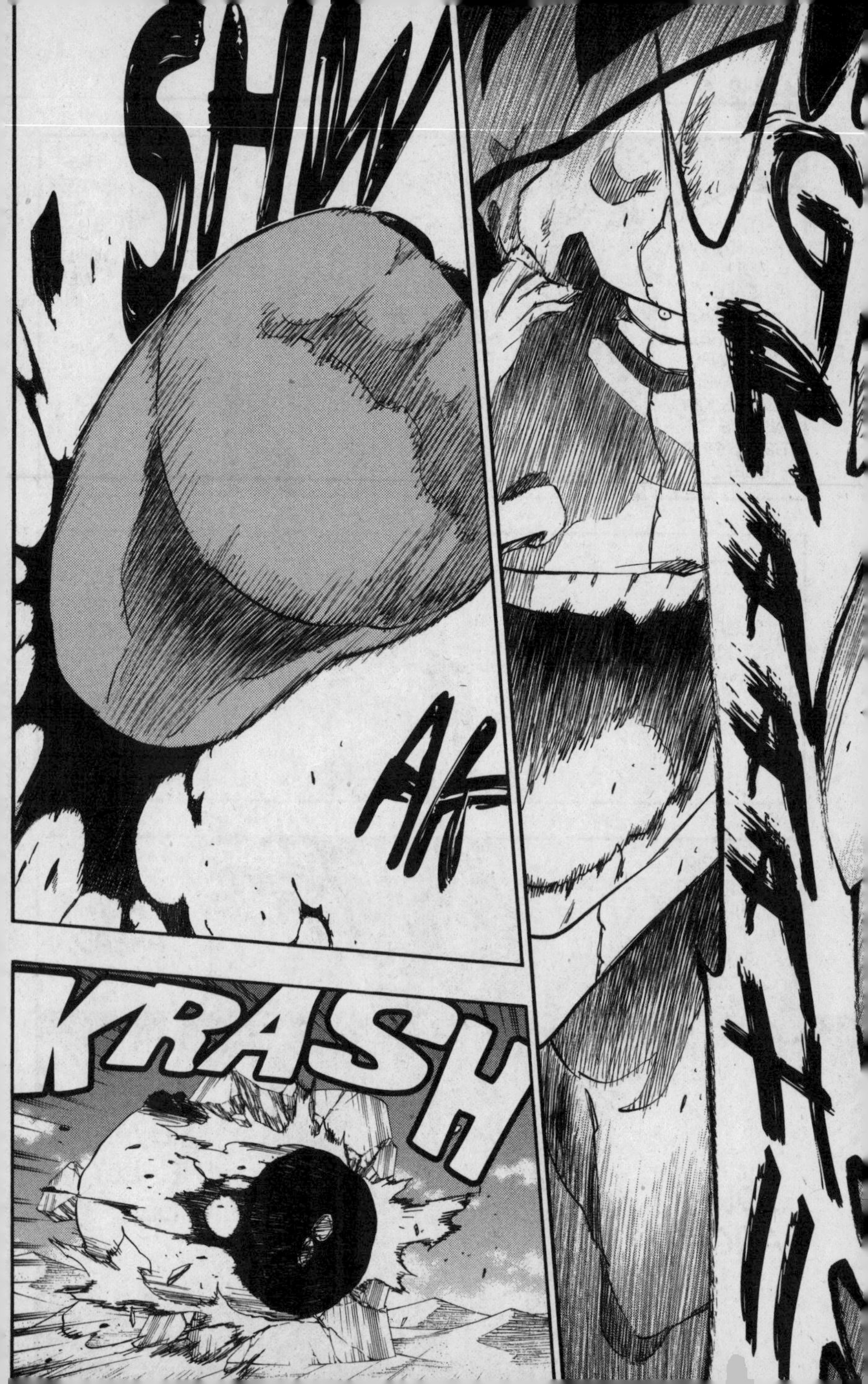
AH
KRASH

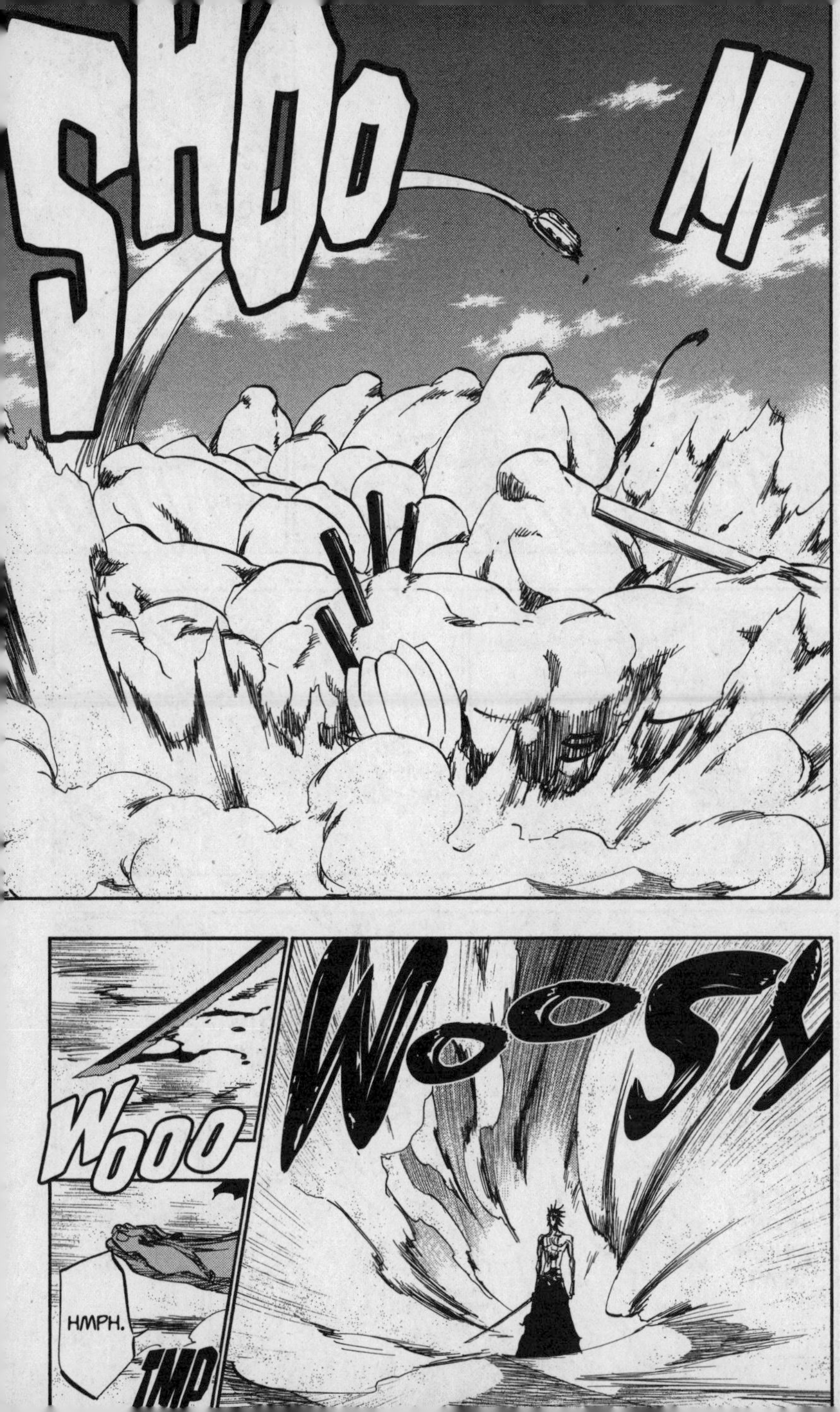
SHOOM
WOOOSH
WOOO
HMPH.
TMP

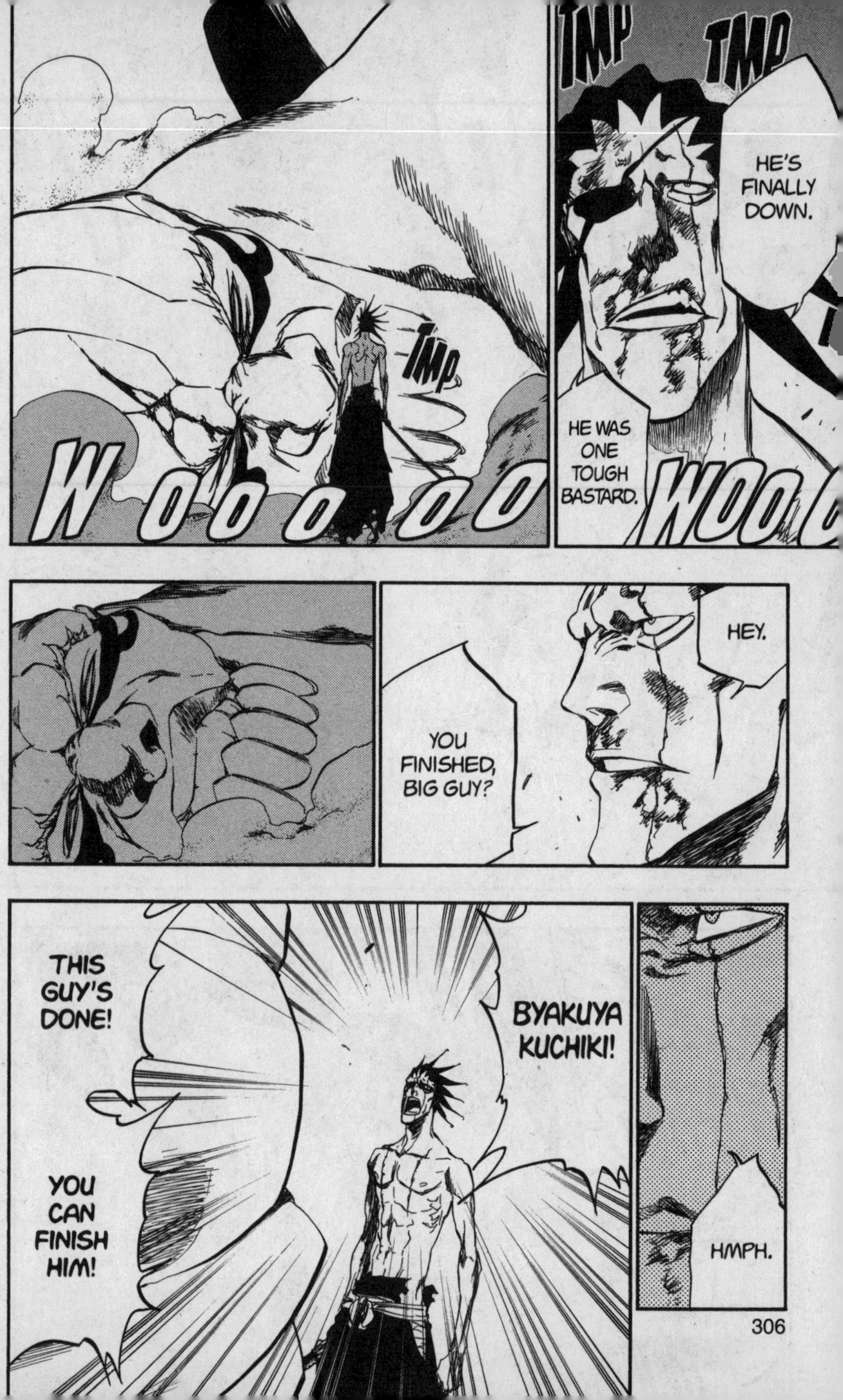
TMP
TMP
HE'S FINALLY DOWN.
HE WAS ONE TOUGH BASTARD.
WOOO
TMP
WOOOOOO
HEY.
YOU FINISHED, BIG GUY?
HMPH.
BYAKUYA KUCHIKI!
THIS GUY'S DONE!
YOU CAN FINISH HIM!

READ THIS WAY

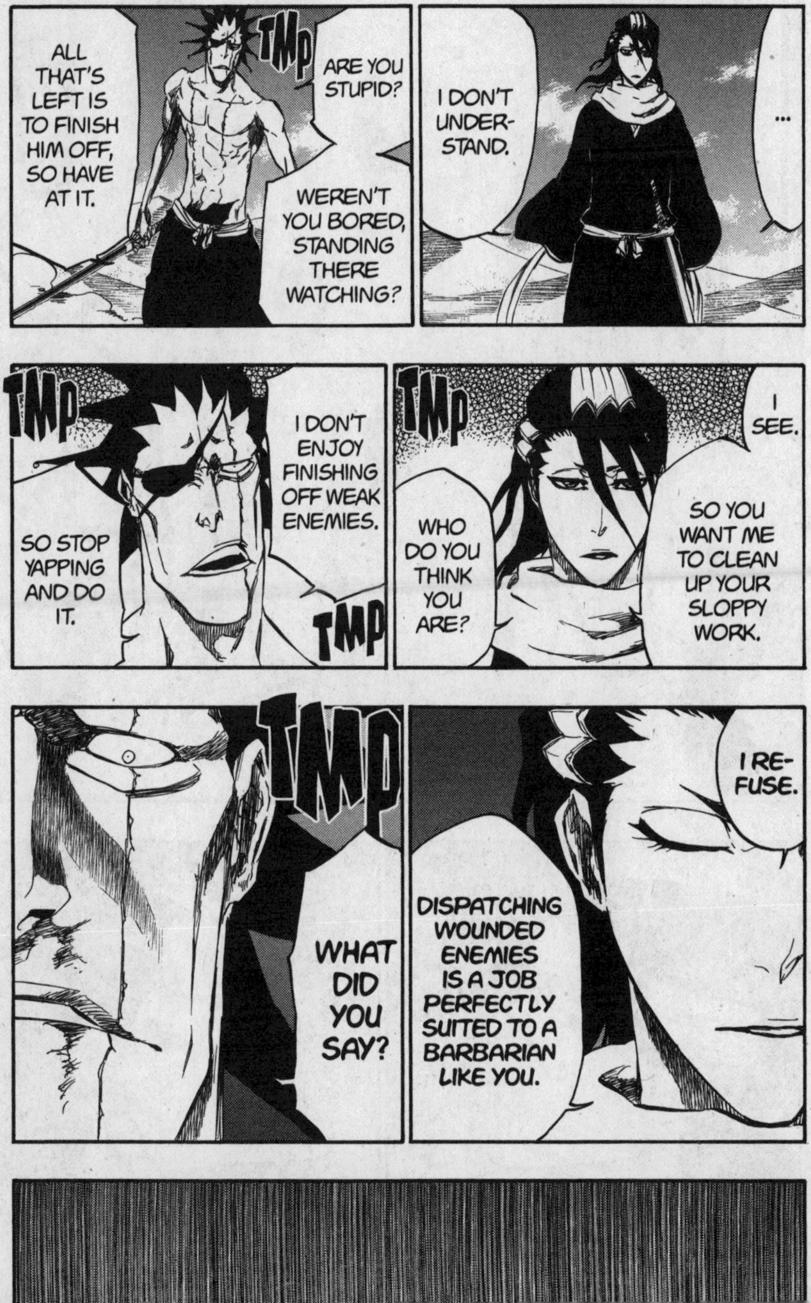
...
I DON'T UNDERSTAND.
TMP
ARE YOU STUPID?
ALL THAT'S LEFT IS TO FINISH HIM OFF, SO HAVE AT IT.
WEREN'T YOU BORED, STANDING THERE WATCHING?
I SEE.
TMP
SO YOU WANT ME TO CLEAN UP YOUR SLOPPY WORK.
WHO DO YOU THINK YOU ARE?
I DON'T ENJOY FINISHING OFF WEAK ENEMIES.
TMP
SO STOP YAPPING AND DO IT.
TMP
I RE-FUSE.
DISPATCHING WOUNDED ENEMIES IS A JOB PERFECTLY SUITED TO A BARBARIAN LIKE YOU.
TMP
WHAT DID YOU SAY?

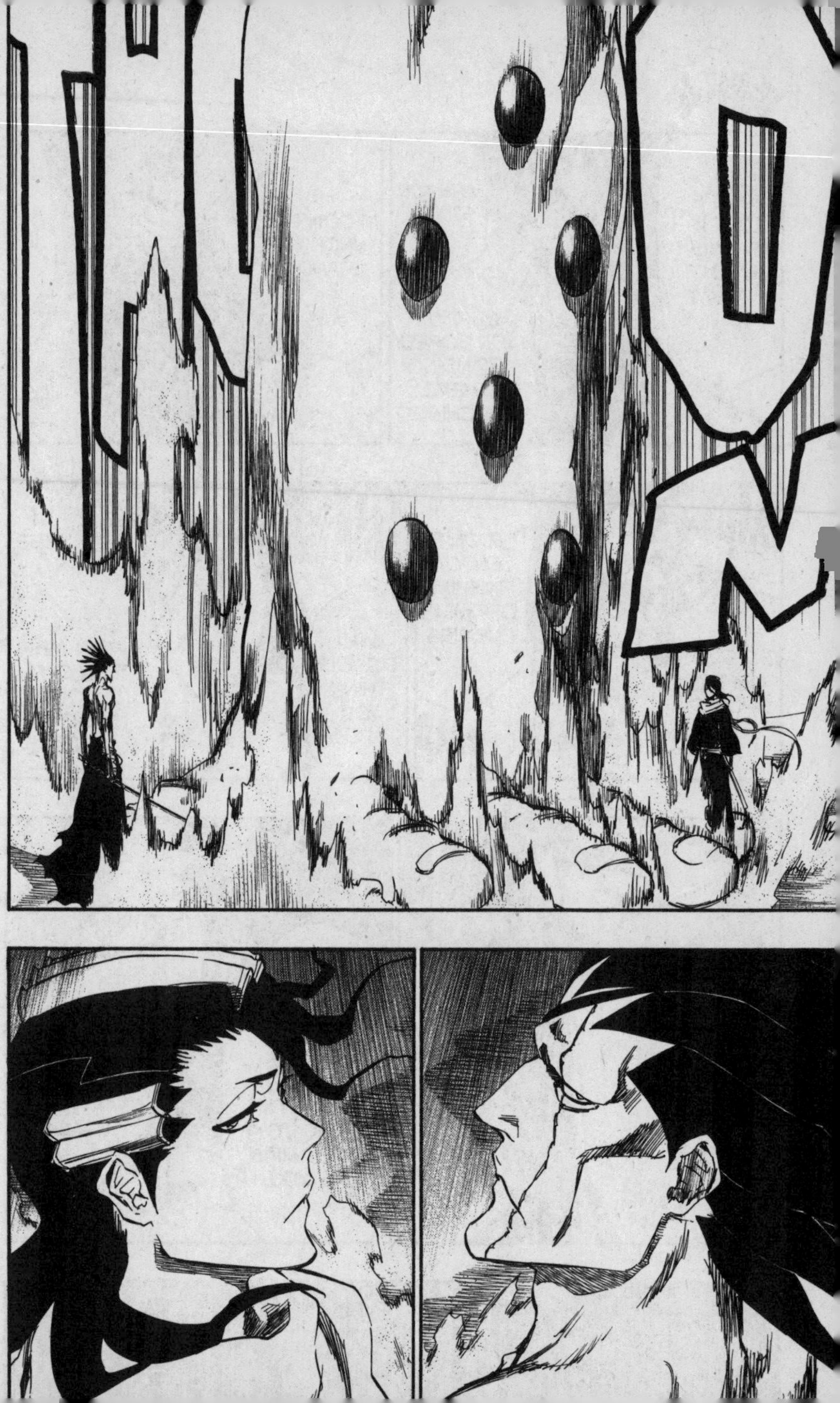

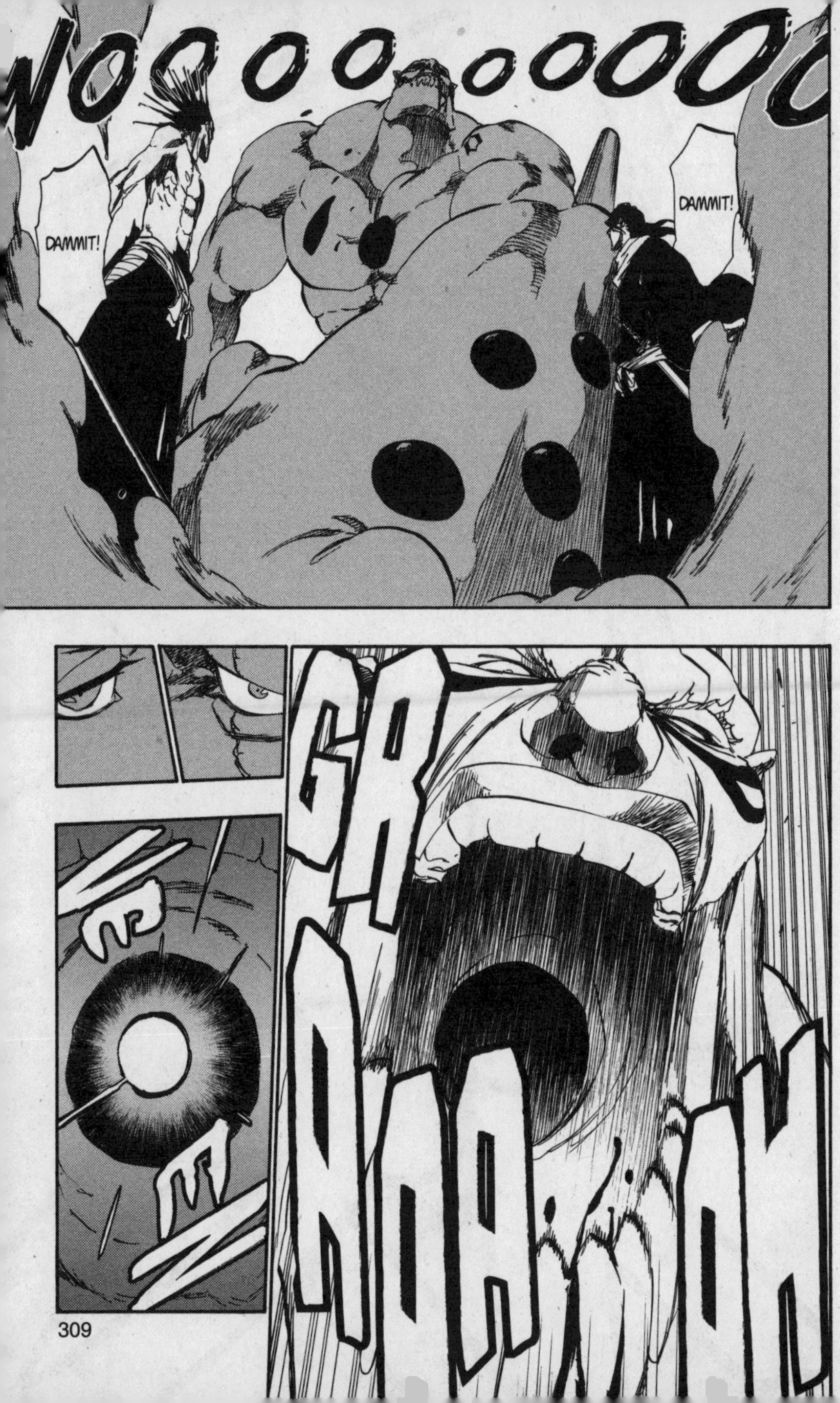
WOOOOOOOOOO
DAMMIT!
DAMMIT!
GRRAAAAAH

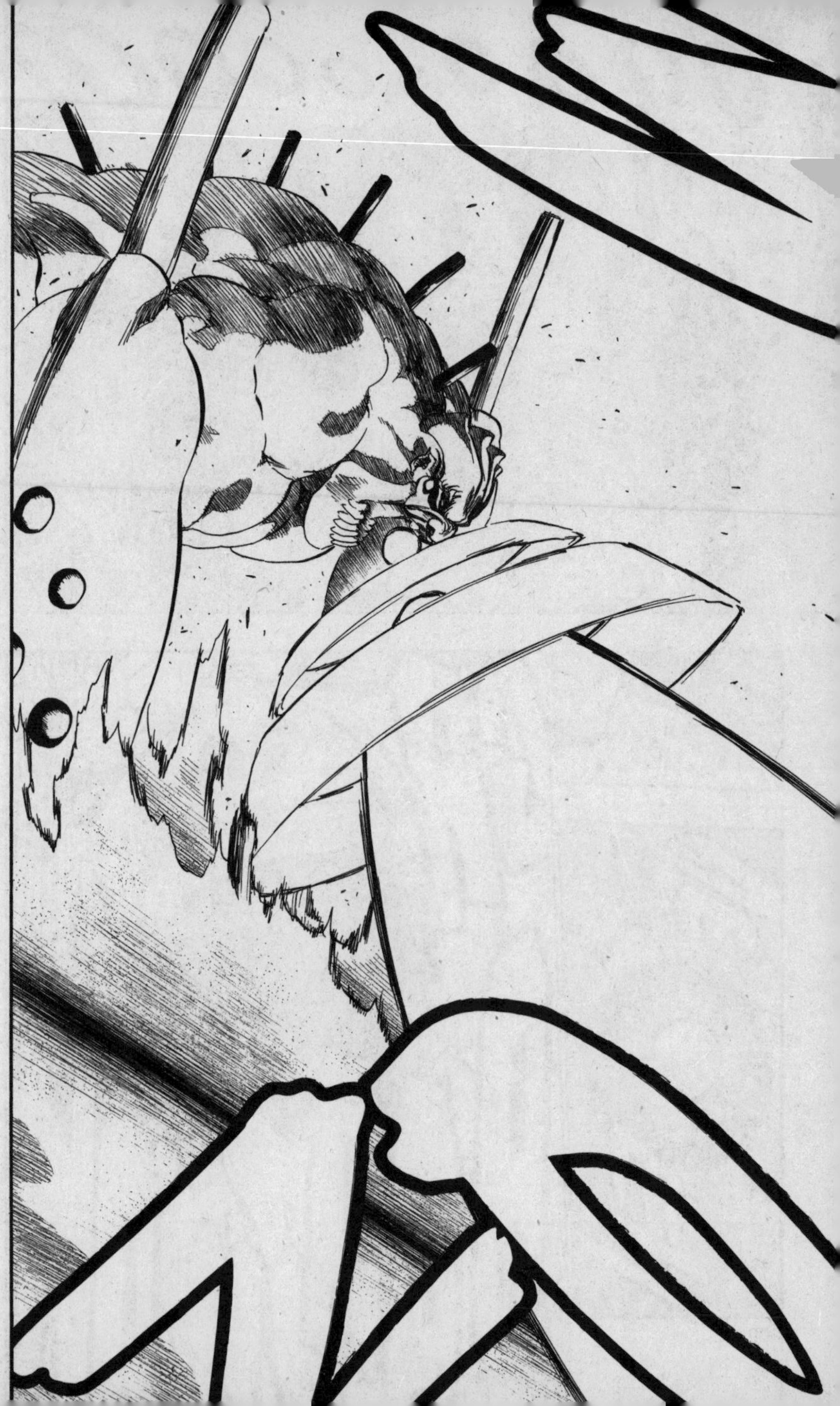

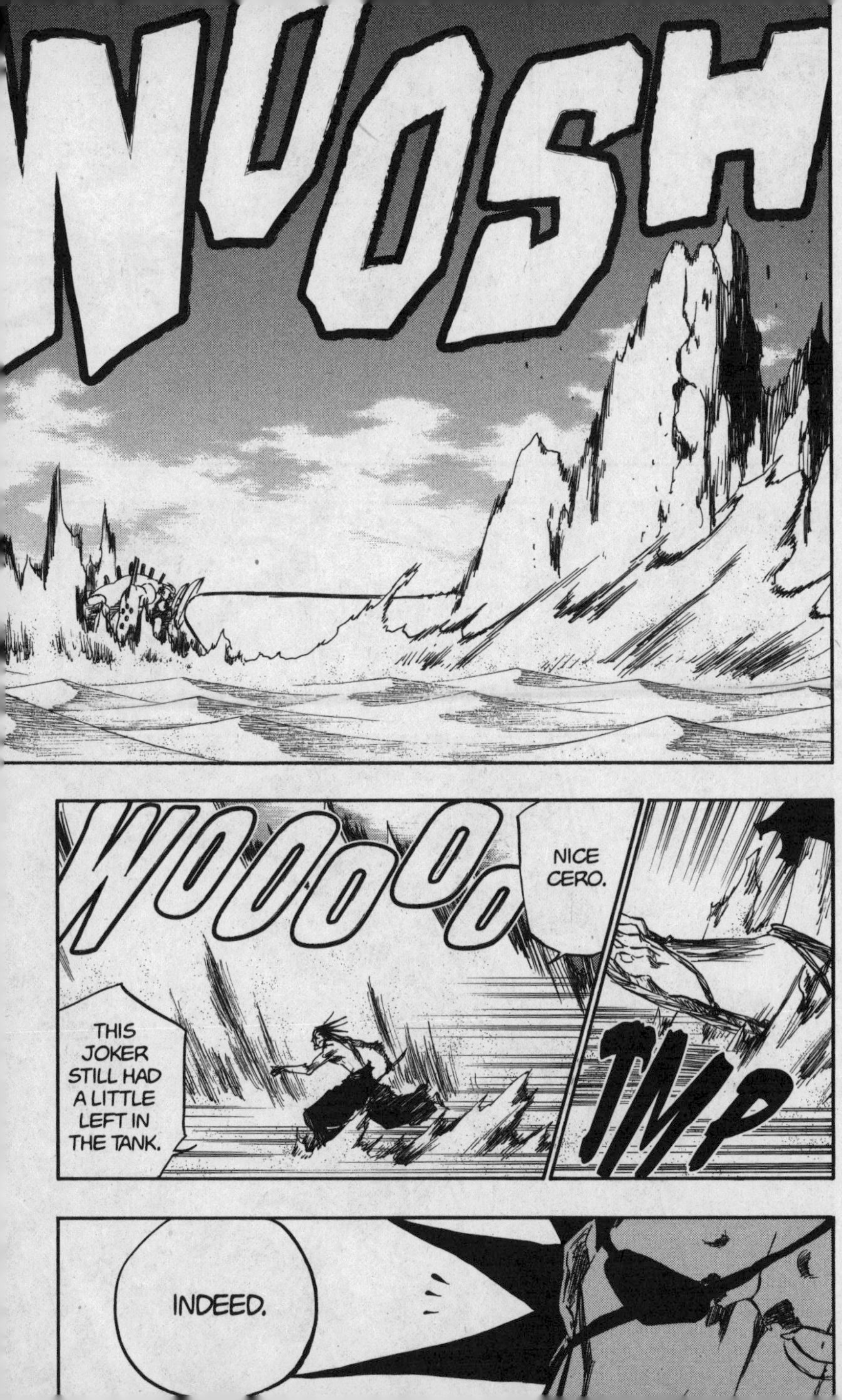
WHOOSH
TMP
WOOOOO
NICE CERO.
THIS JOKER STILL HAD A LITTLE LEFT IN THE TANK.
INDEED.

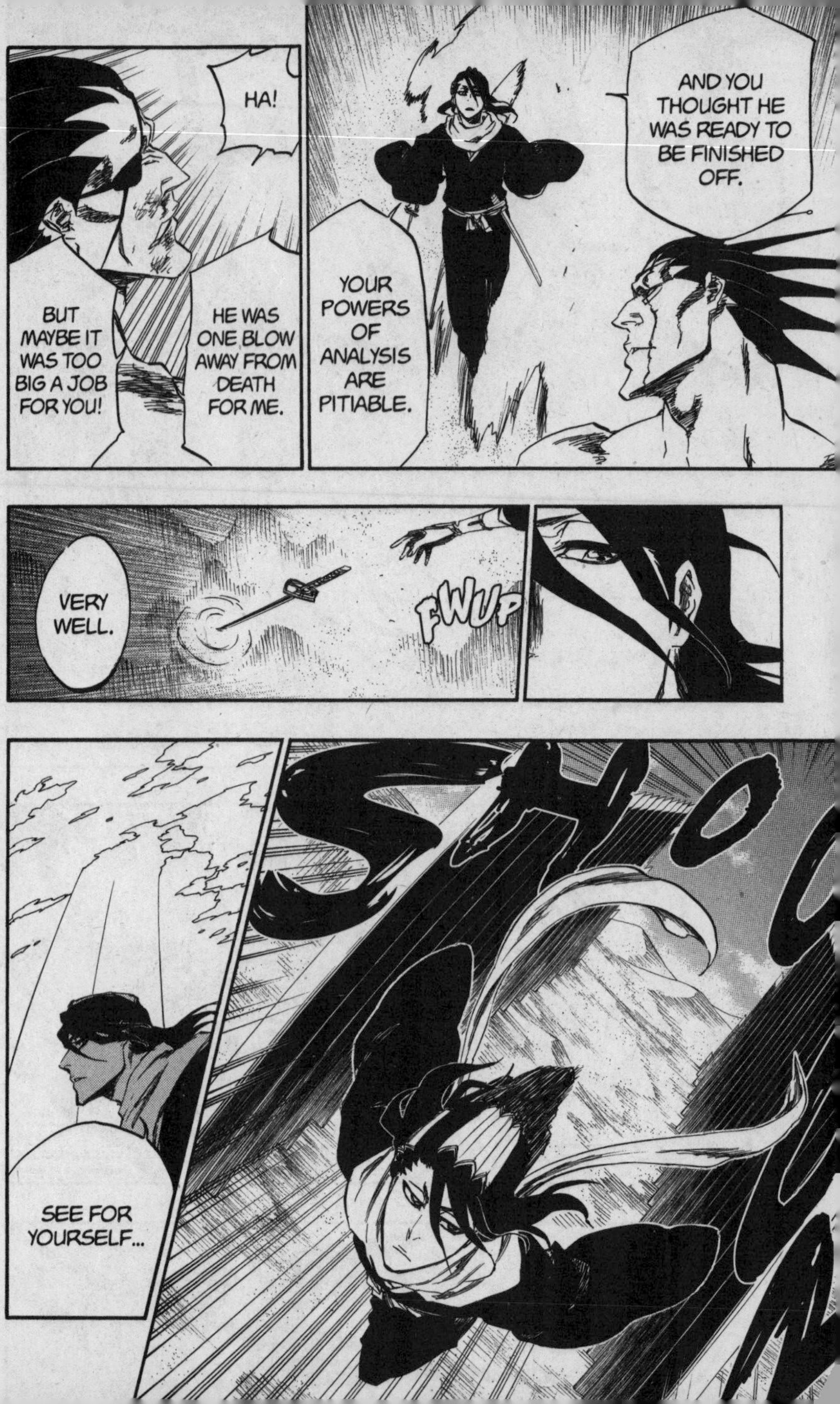
AND YOU THOUGHT HE WAS READY TO BE FINISHED OFF.
YOUR POWERS OF ANALYSIS ARE PITIABLE.
HA!
HE WAS ONE BLOW AWAY FROM DEATH FOR ME.
BUT MAYBE IT WAS TOO BIG A JOB FOR YOU!
FWUP
VERY WELL.
SEE FOR YOURSELF...

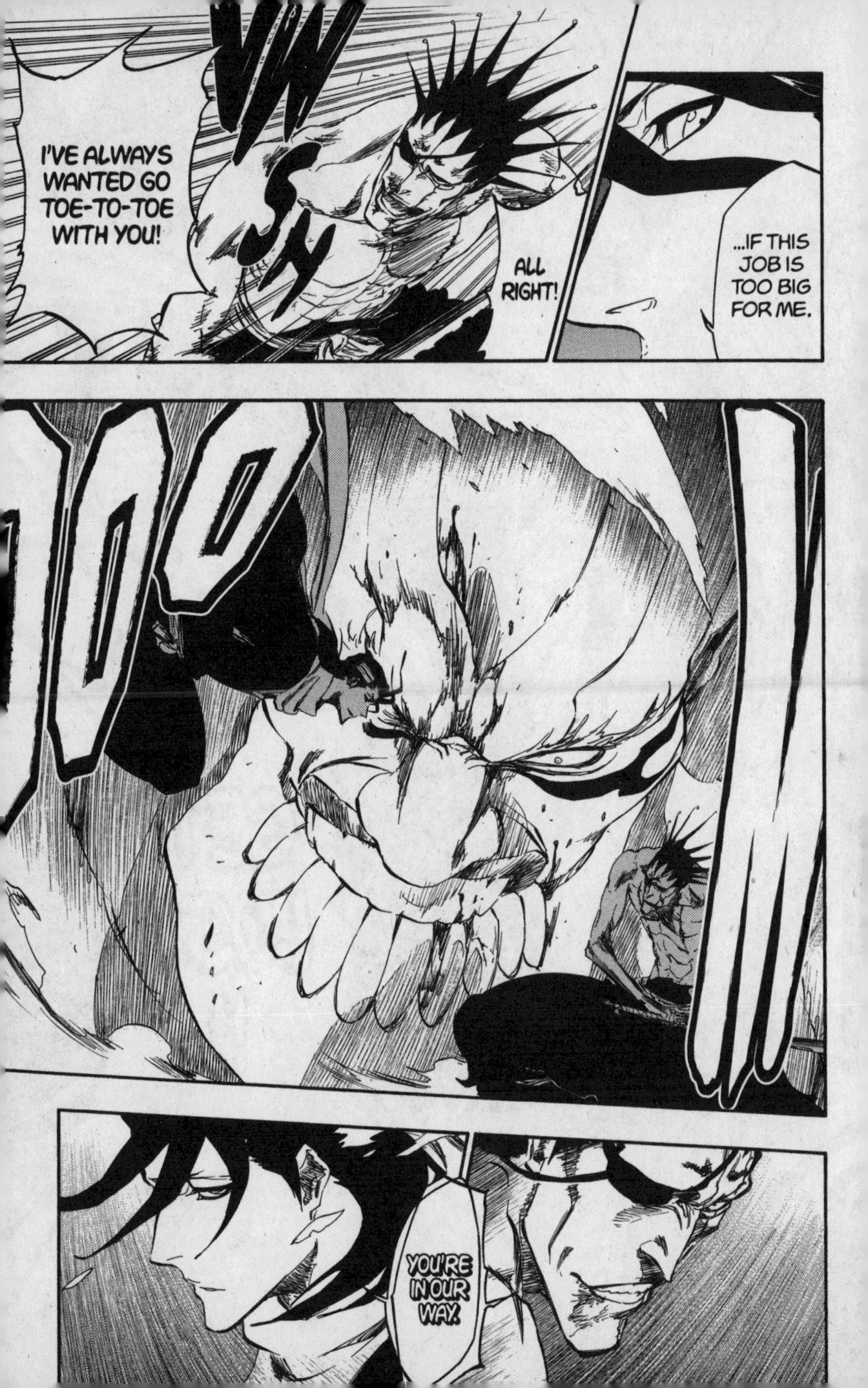
...IF THIS JOB IS TOO BIG FOR ME.
ALL RIGHT!
I'VE ALWAYS WANTED GO TOE-TO-TOE WITH YOU!
YOU'RE IN OUR WAY.

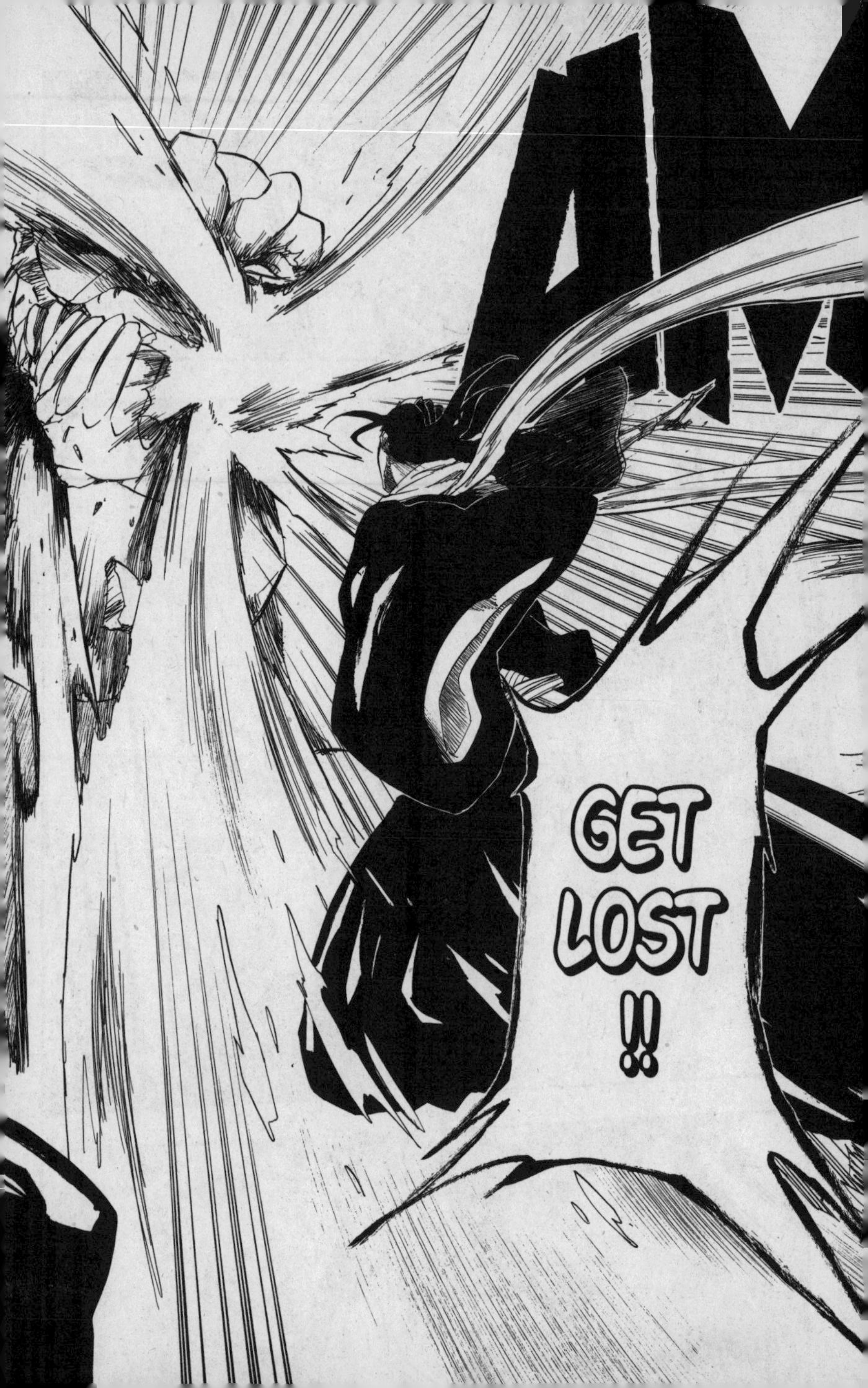
GET LOST!!

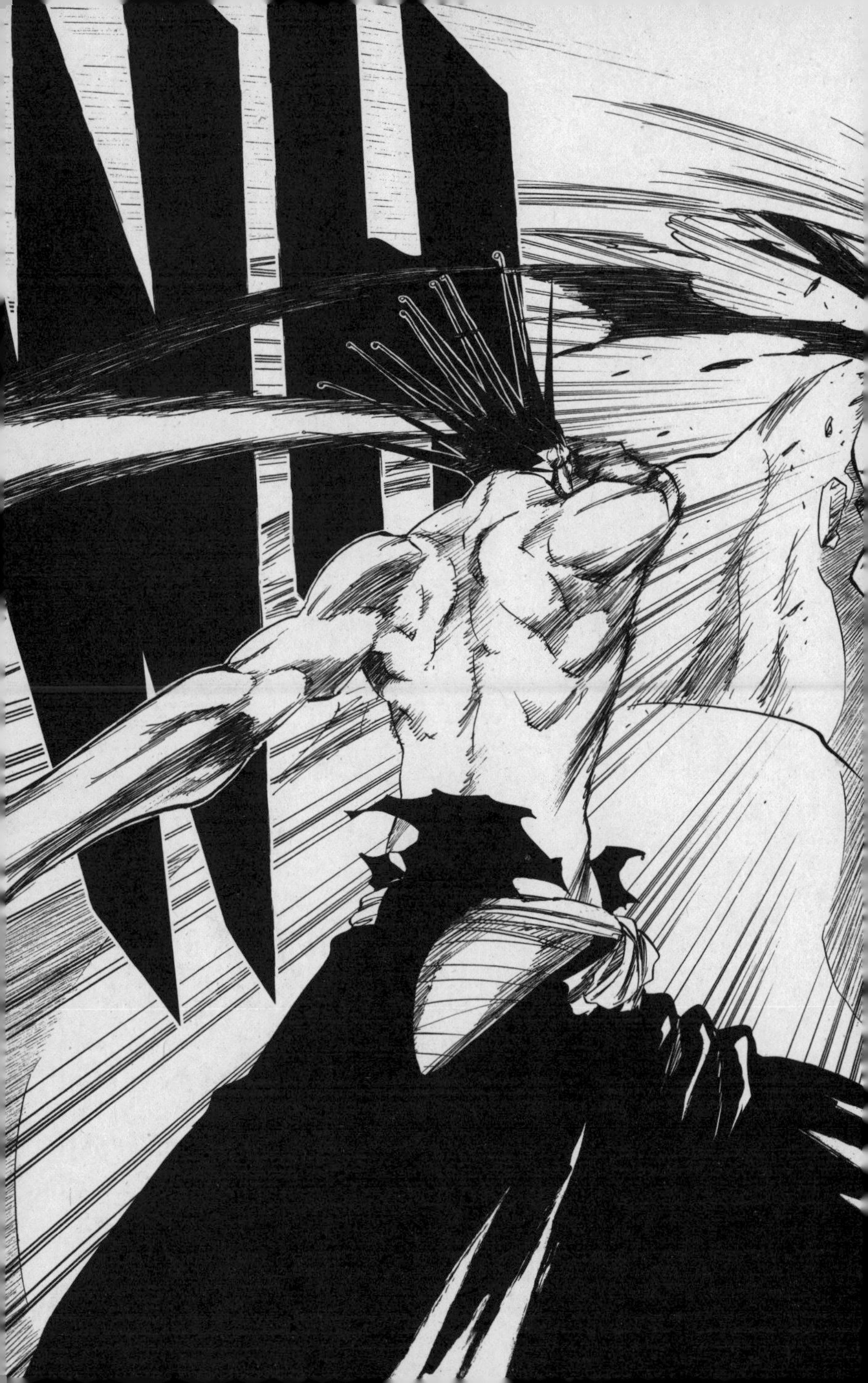

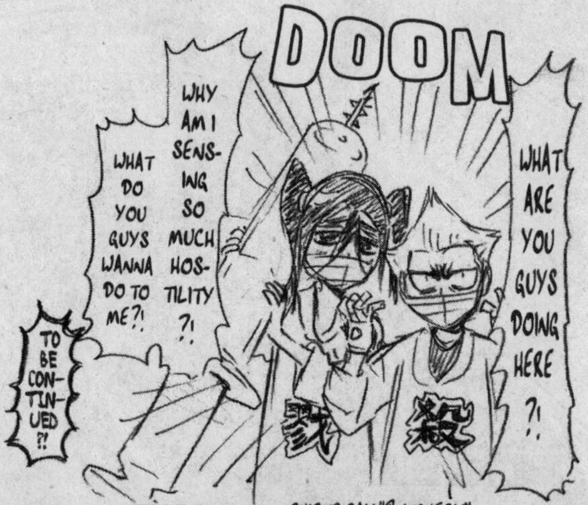
DOOM
WHAT ARE YOU GUYS DOING HERE?!
WHY AM I SENSING SO MUCH HOSTILITY?!
WHAT DO YOU GUYS WANNA DO TO ME?!
TO BE CONTINUED?!
*SHIRTS SAY "BUTCHERY"

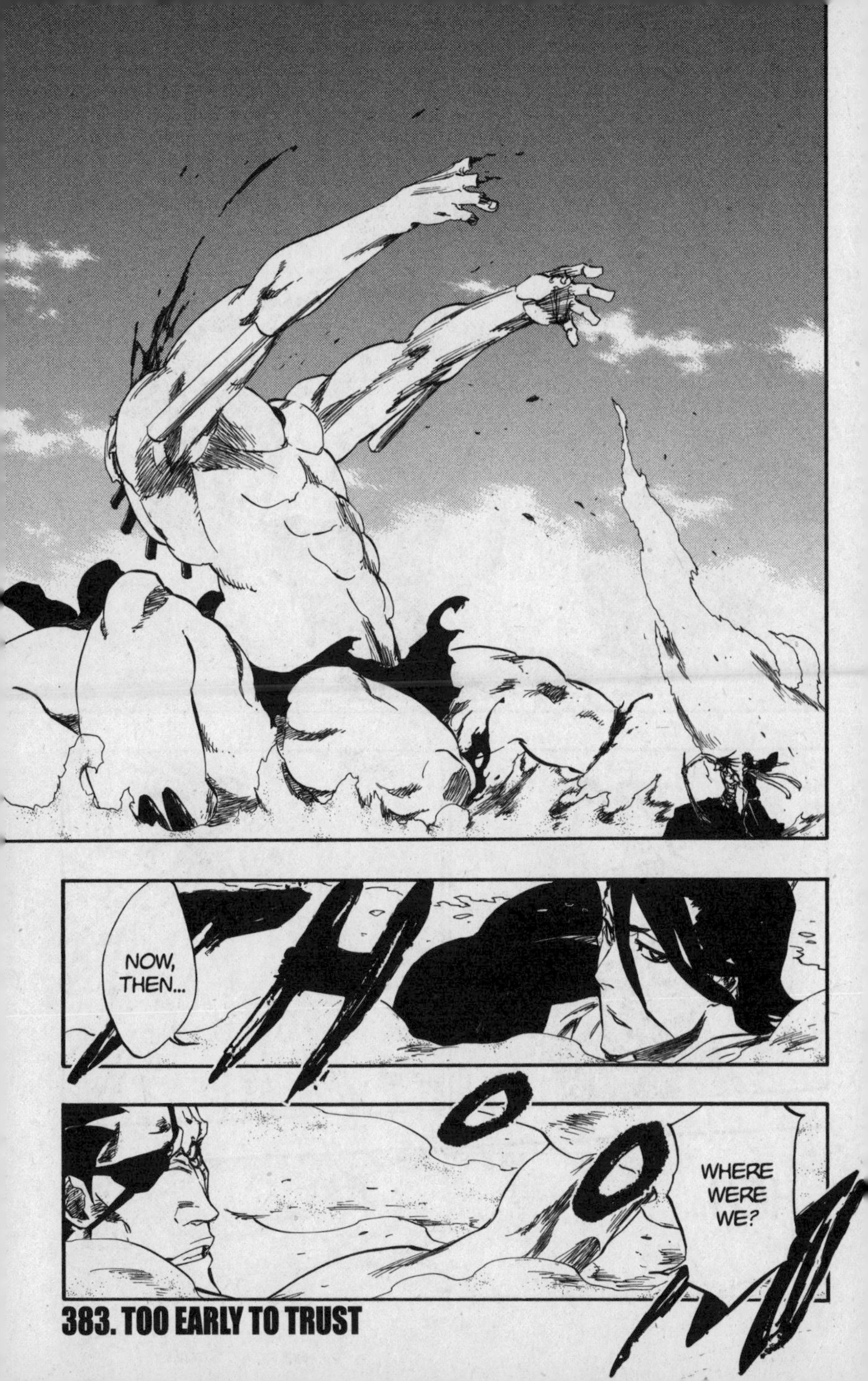
NOW, THEN...
WHERE WERE WE?

383. TOO EARLY TO TRUST

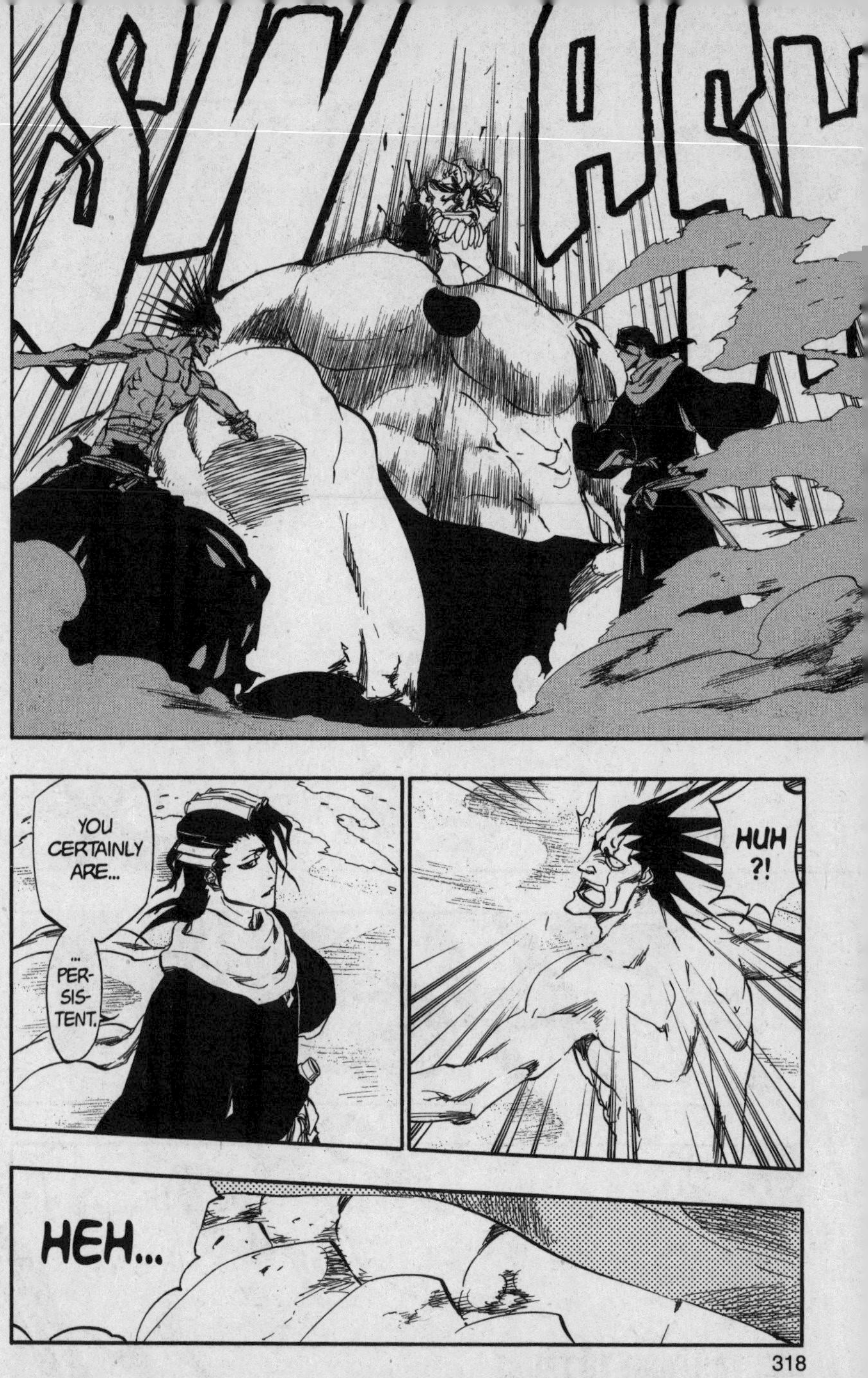
HUH ?!
YOU CERTAINLY ARE...
...PER-SIS-TENT.
HEH...

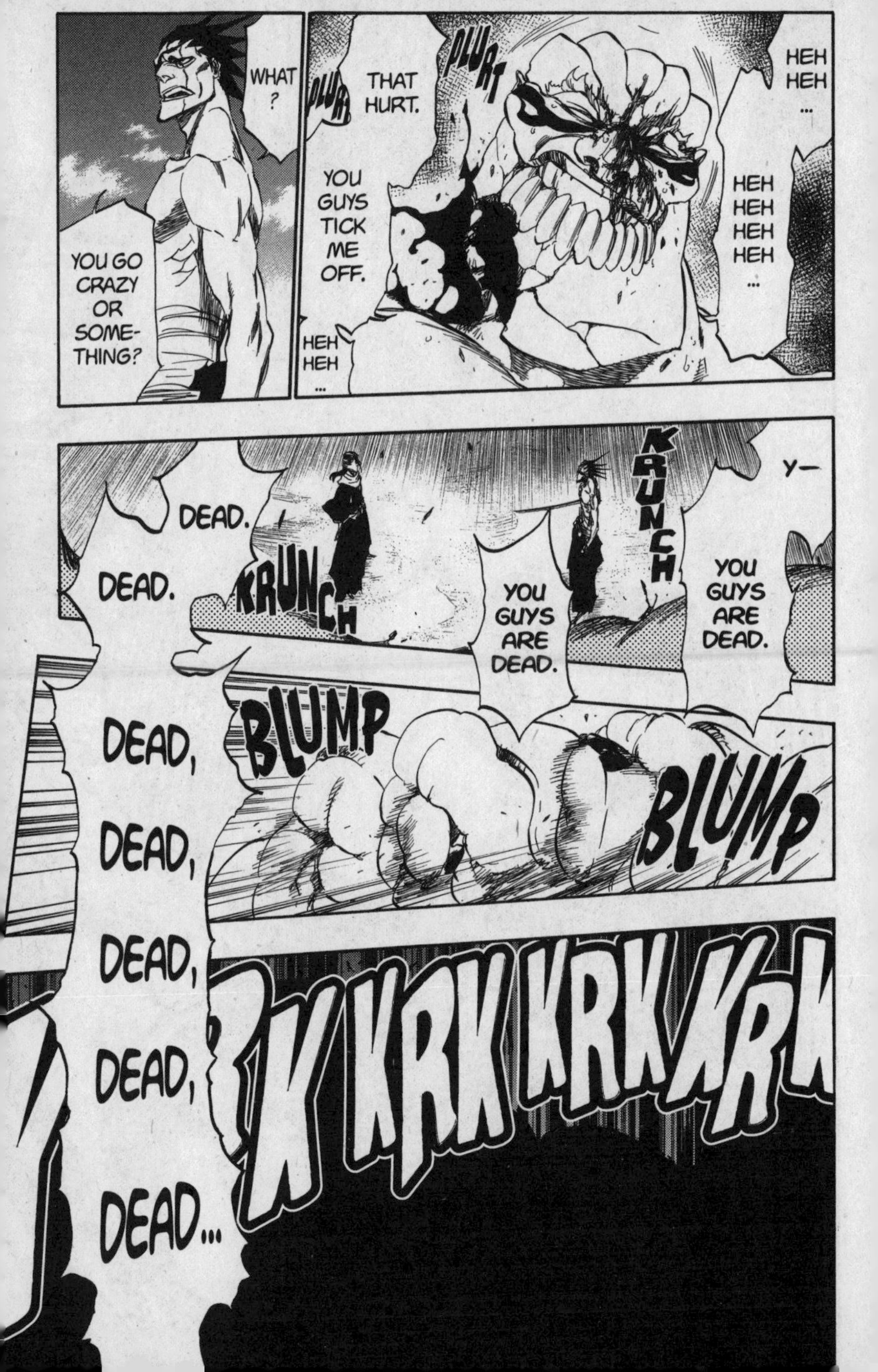
HEH HEH ...
HEH HEH HEH HEH ...
PLURT
THAT HURT.
PLURT
YOU GUYS TICK ME OFF.
HEH HEH ...
WHAT ?
YOU GO CRAZY OR SOME-THING?
Y—
KRUNCH
YOU GUYS ARE DEAD.
YOU GUYS ARE DEAD.
KRUNCH
DEAD.
DEAD.
BLUMP
BLUMP
DEAD,
DEAD,
DEAD,
DEAD,
DEAD...
KRK KRK KRK KRK

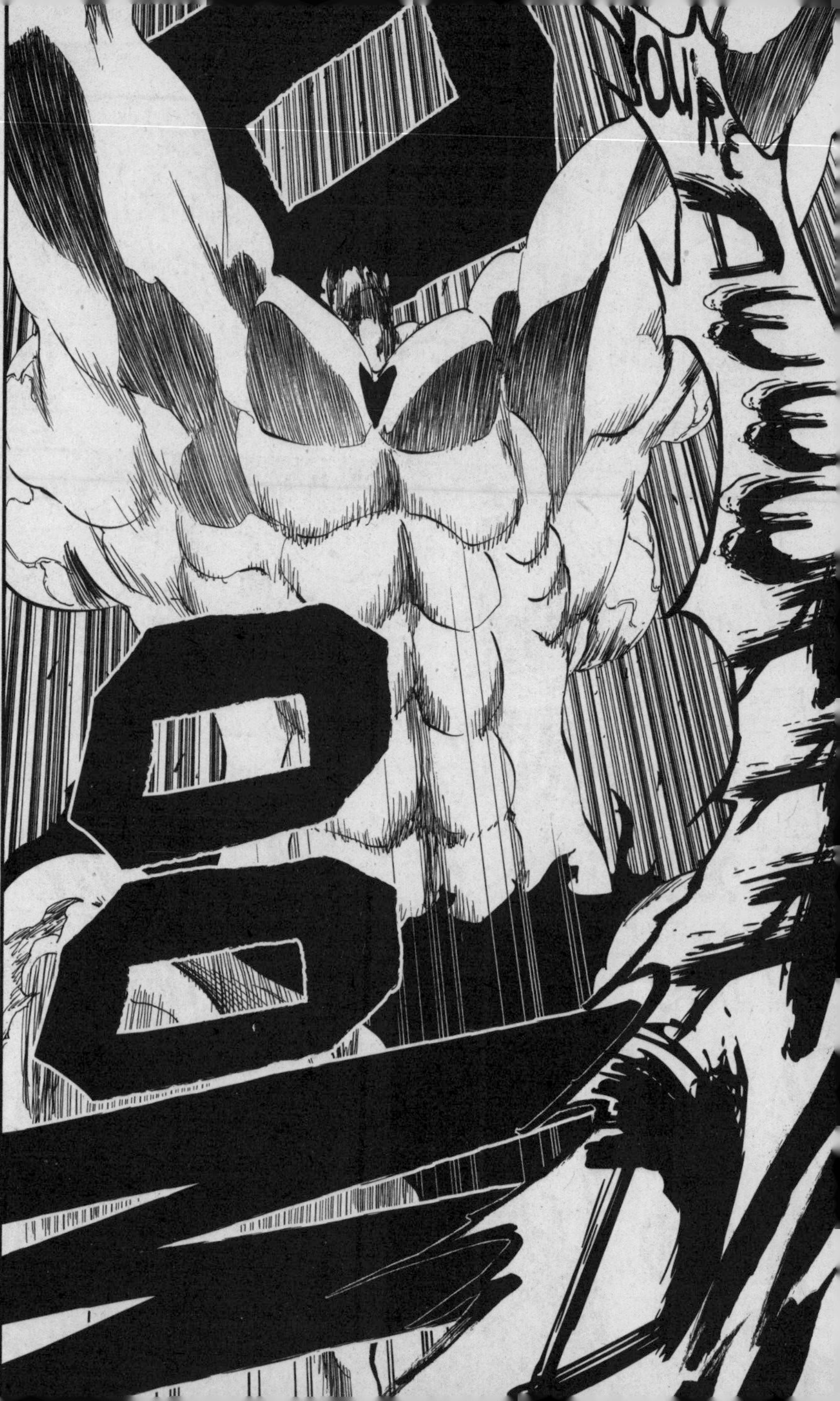
YOU'RE

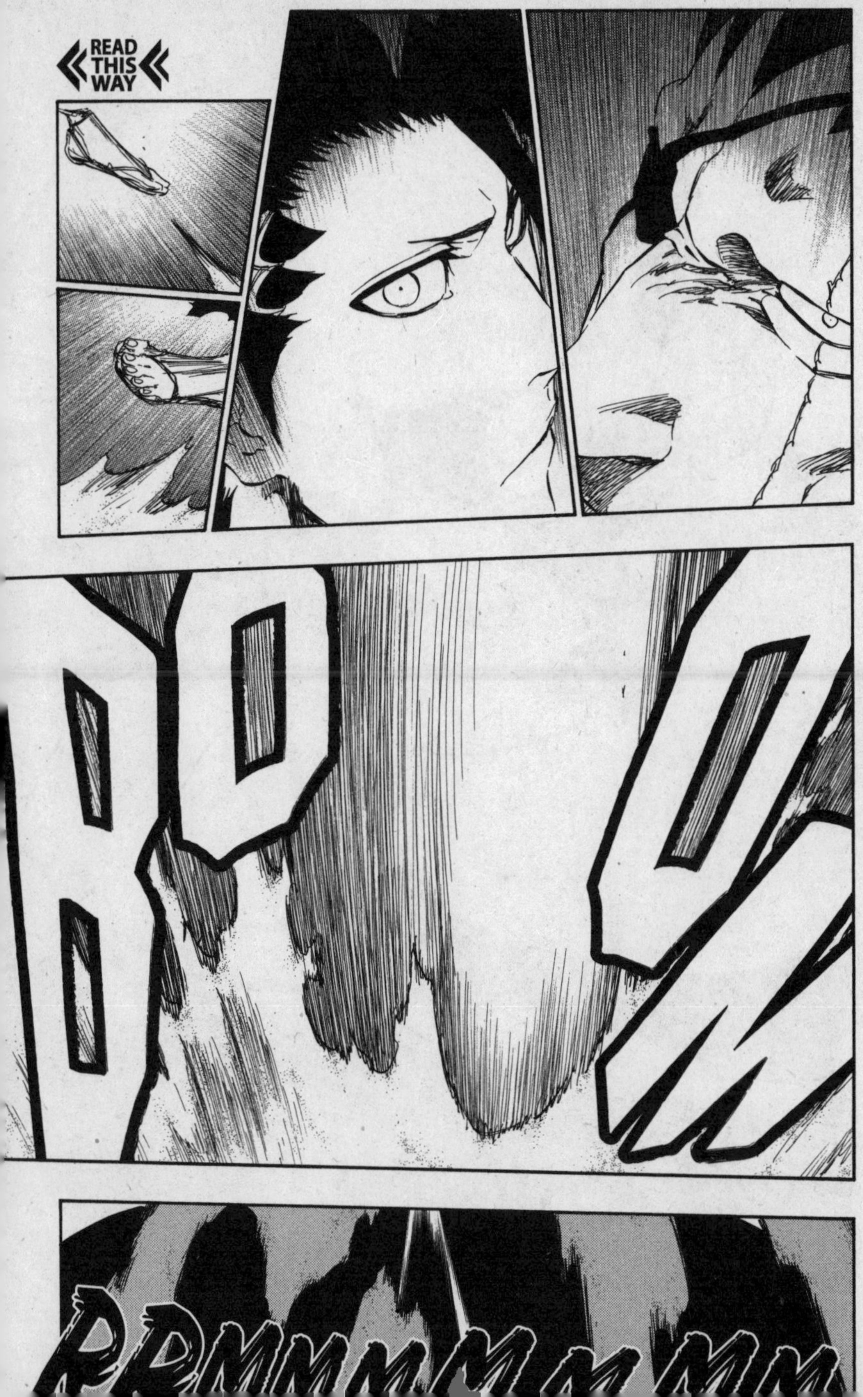
READ THIS WAY

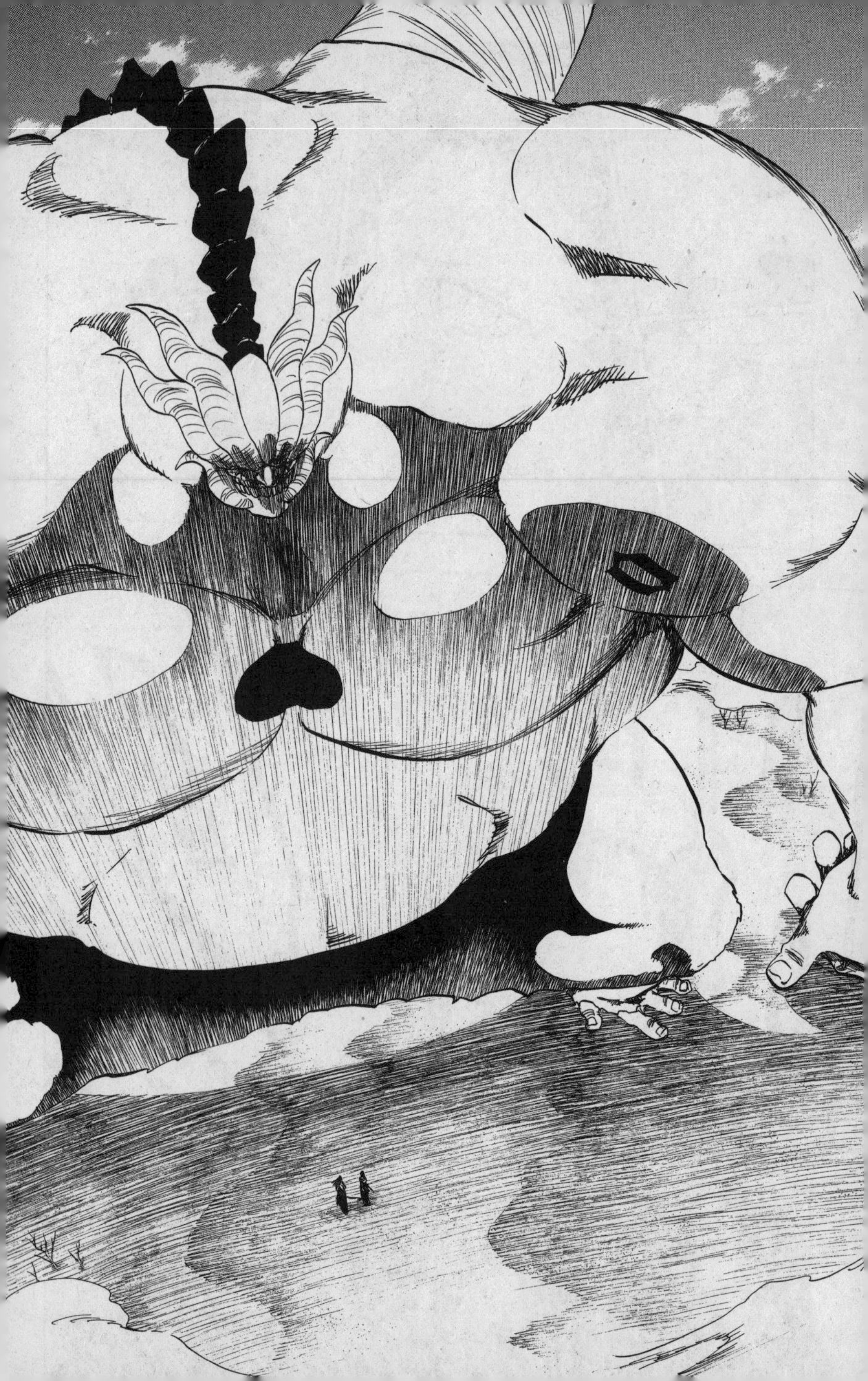

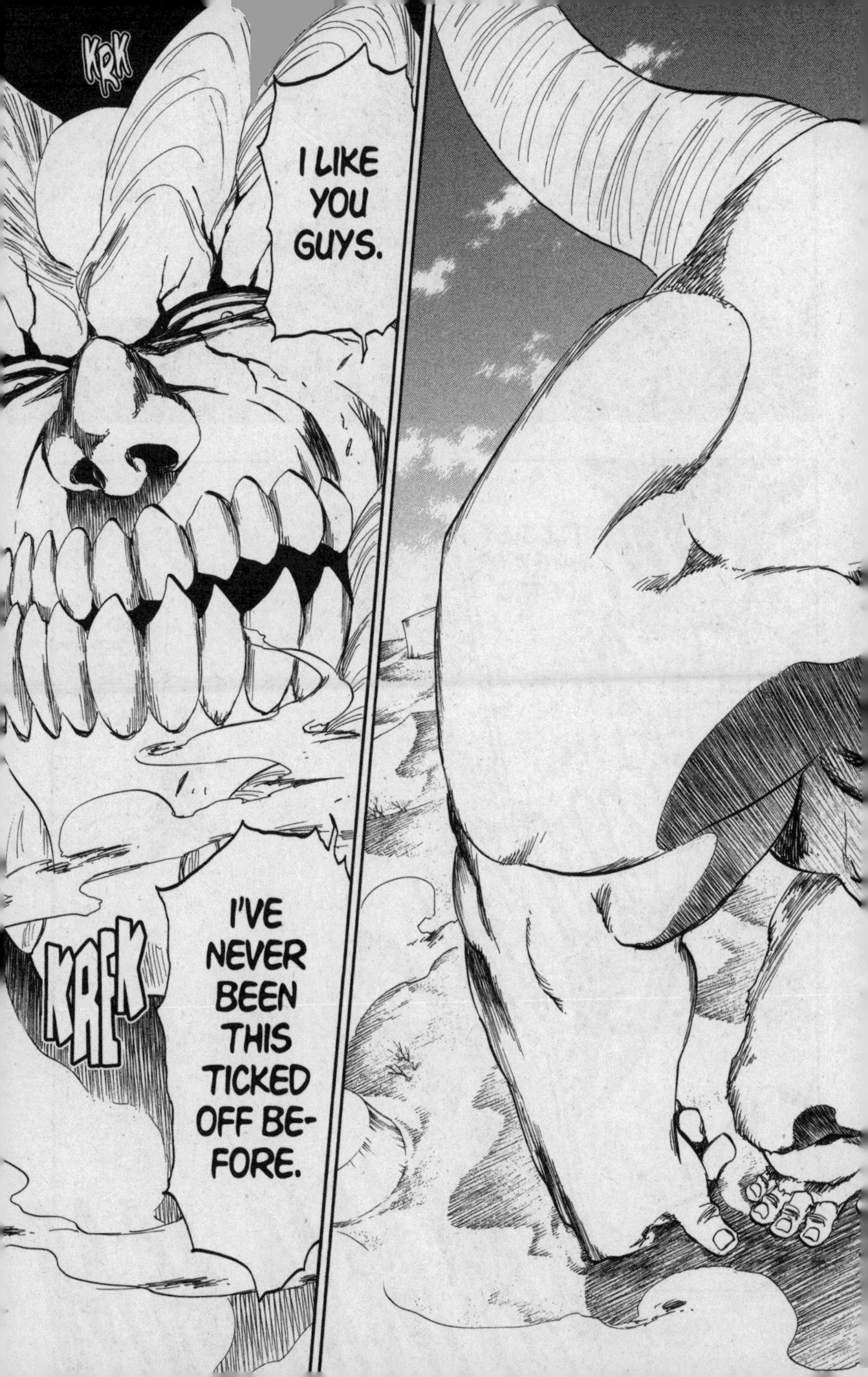
KRK
I LIKE YOU GUYS.
KRK
I'VE NEVER BEEN THIS TICKED OFF BEFORE.

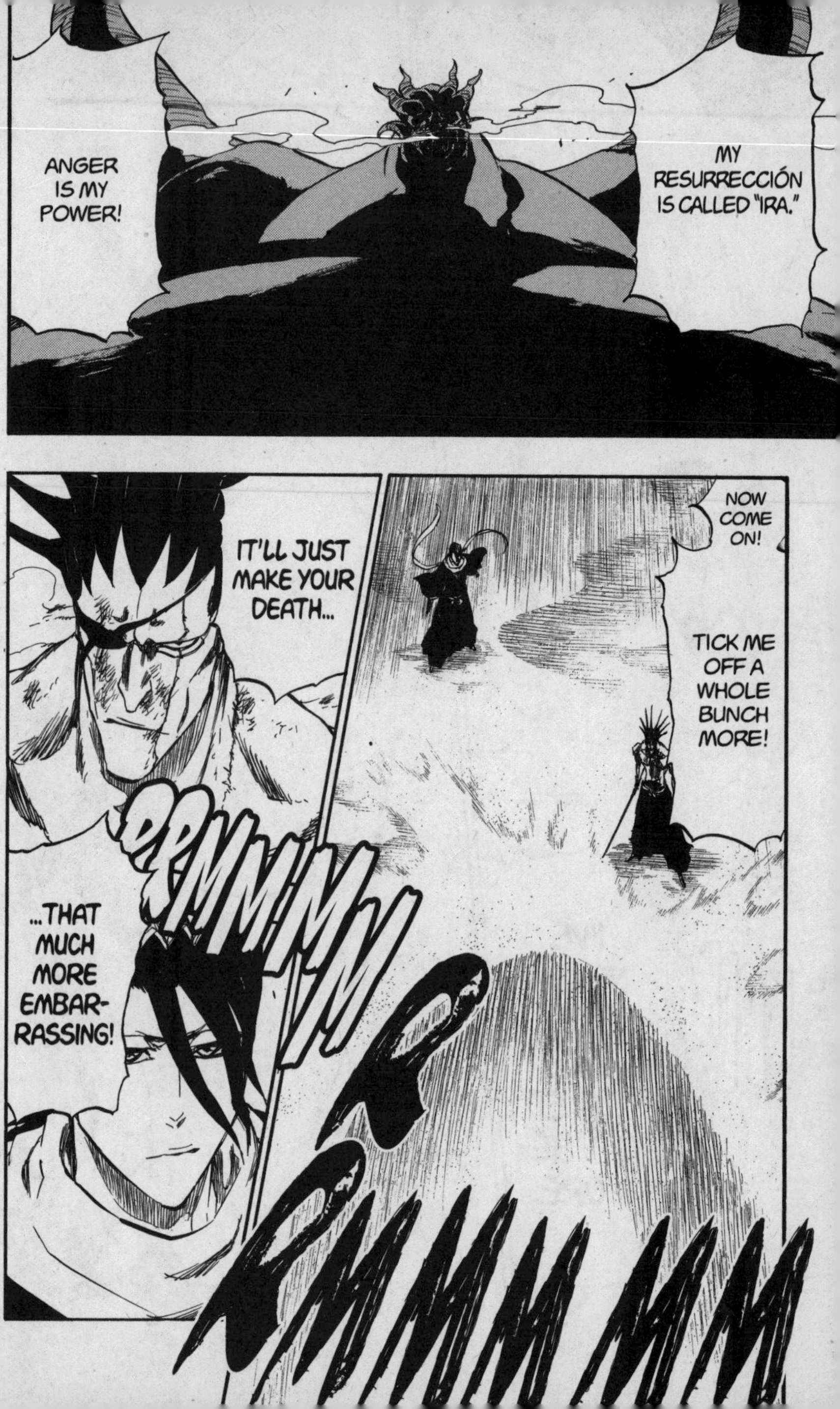
MY RESURRECCIÓN IS CALLED "IRA."
ANGER IS MY POWER!
NOW COME ON!
TICK ME OFF A WHOLE BUNCH MORE!
IT'LL JUST MAKE YOUR DEATH...
...THAT MUCH MORE EMBARRASSING!

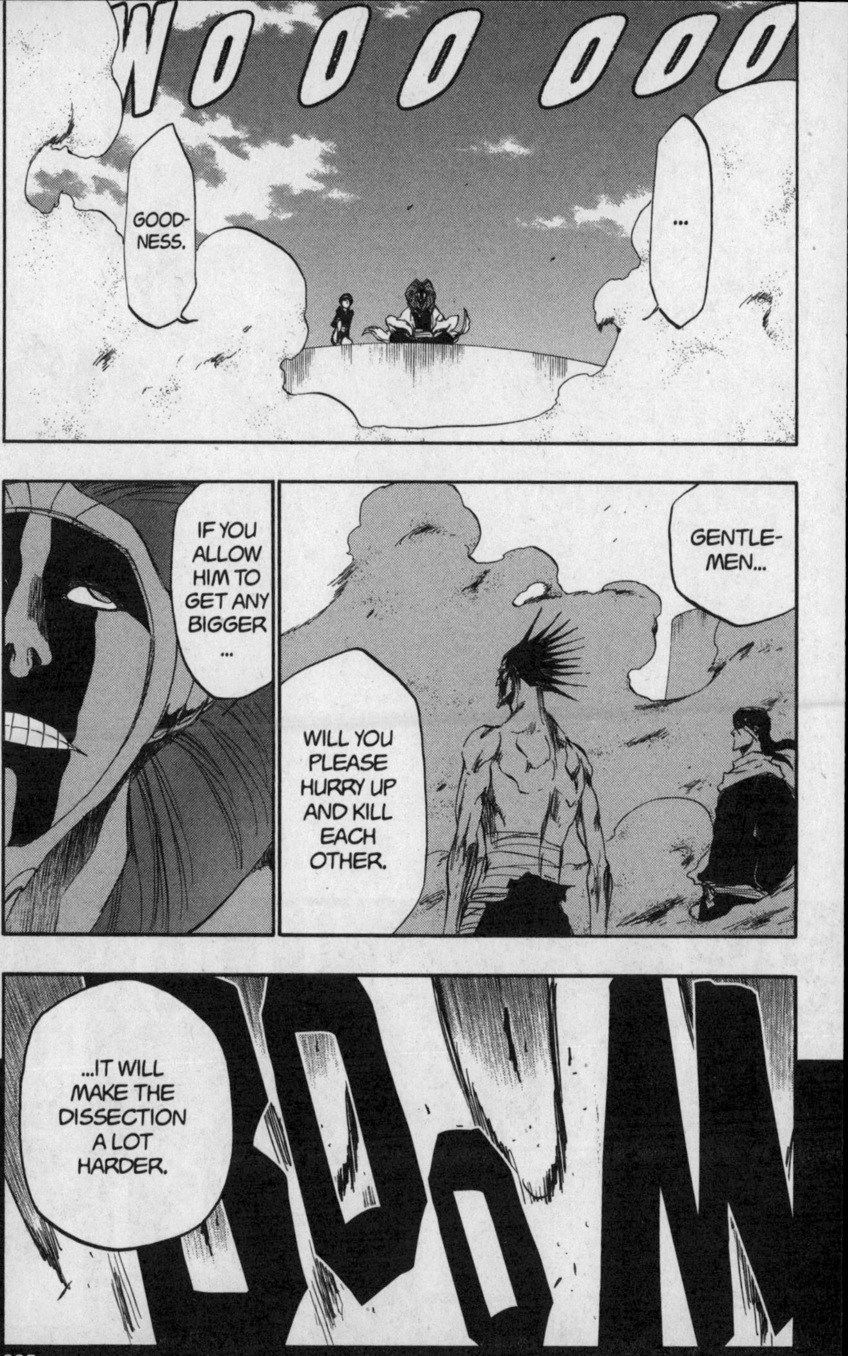
WOOOOOO
...
GOOD-NESS.
GENTLE-MEN...
WILL YOU PLEASE HURRY UP AND KILL EACH OTHER.
IF YOU ALLOW HIM TO GET ANY BIGGER ...
...IT WILL MAKE THE DISSECTION A LOT HARDER.

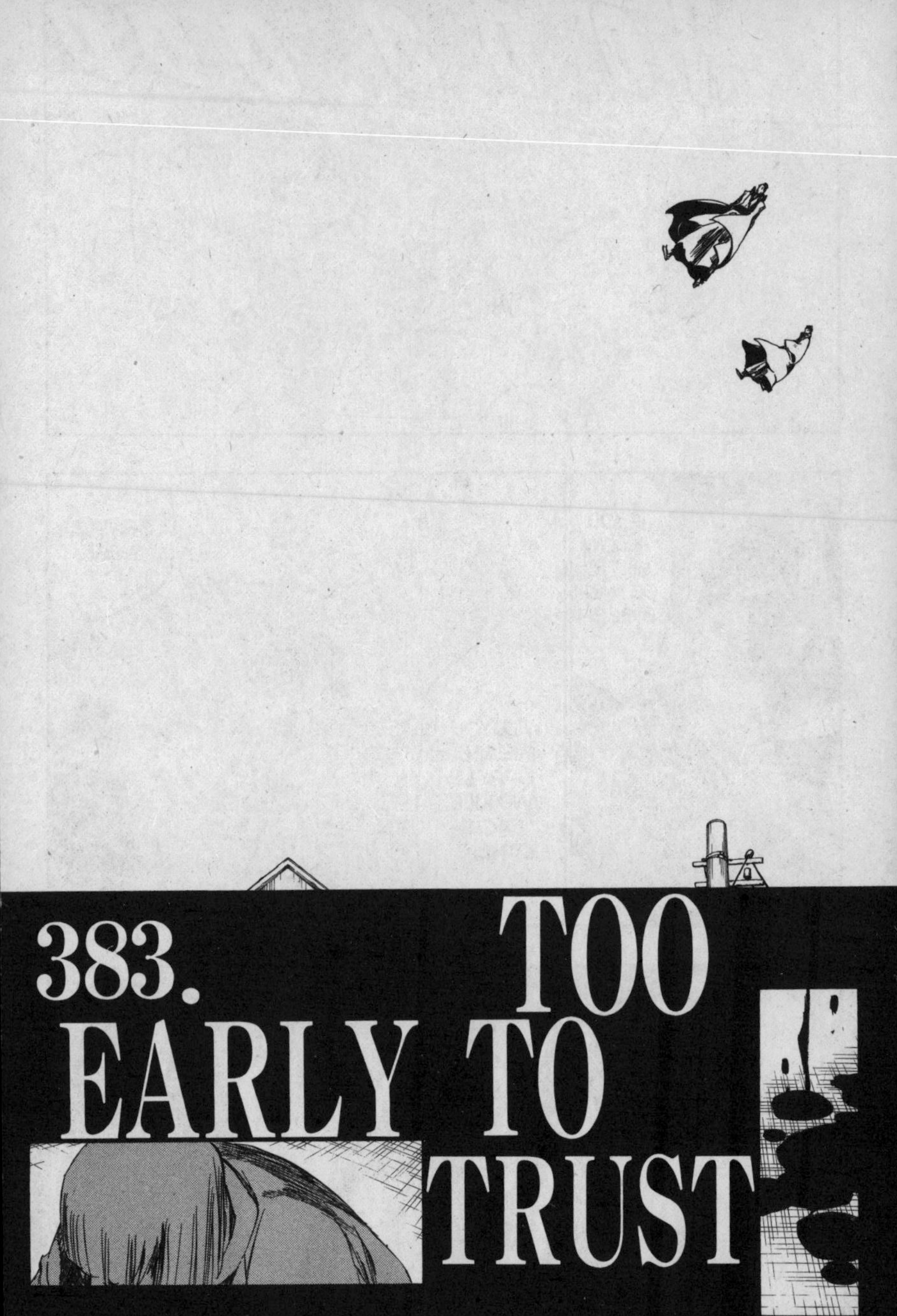
383.
TOO
EARLY TO
TRUST

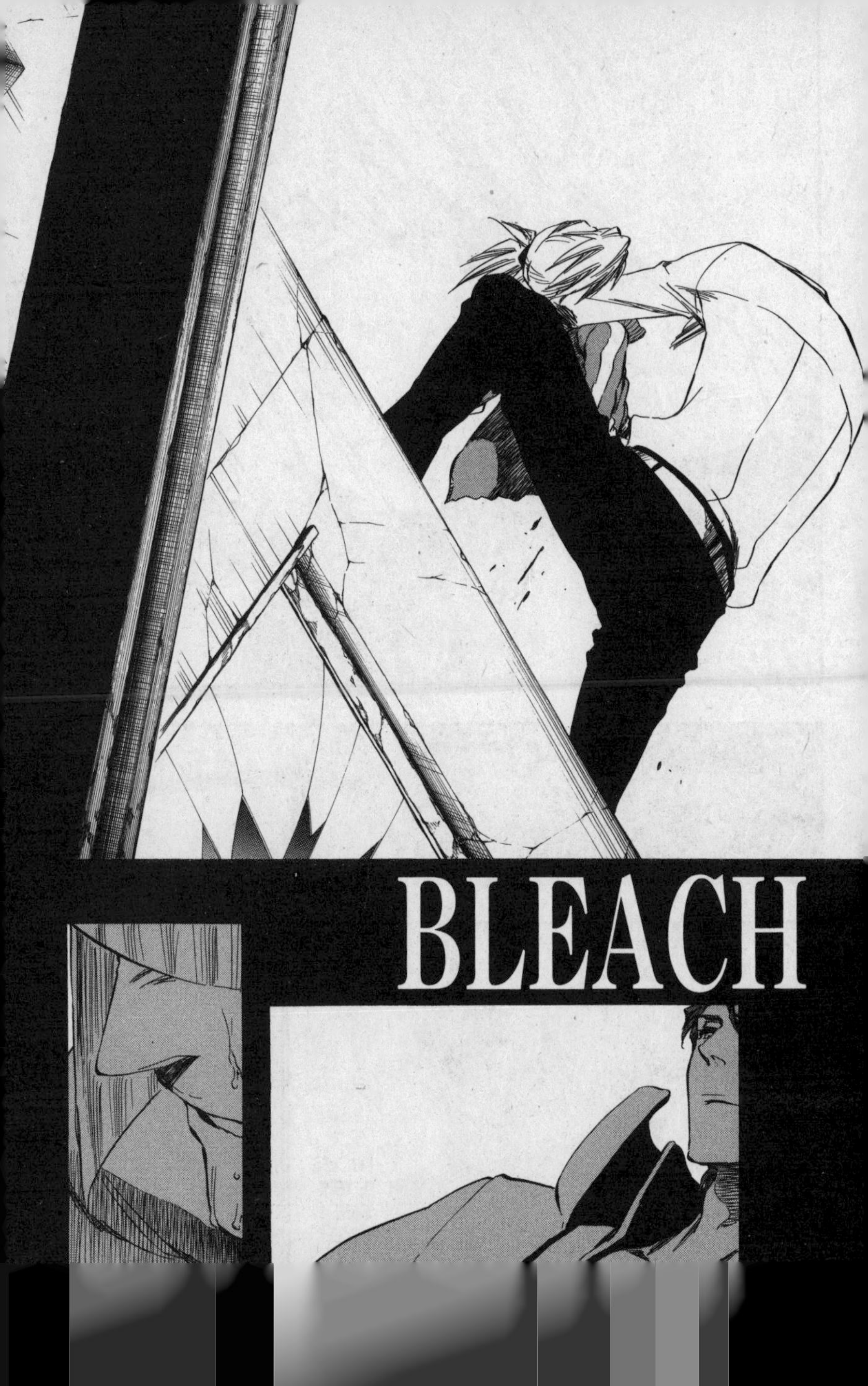
BLEACH

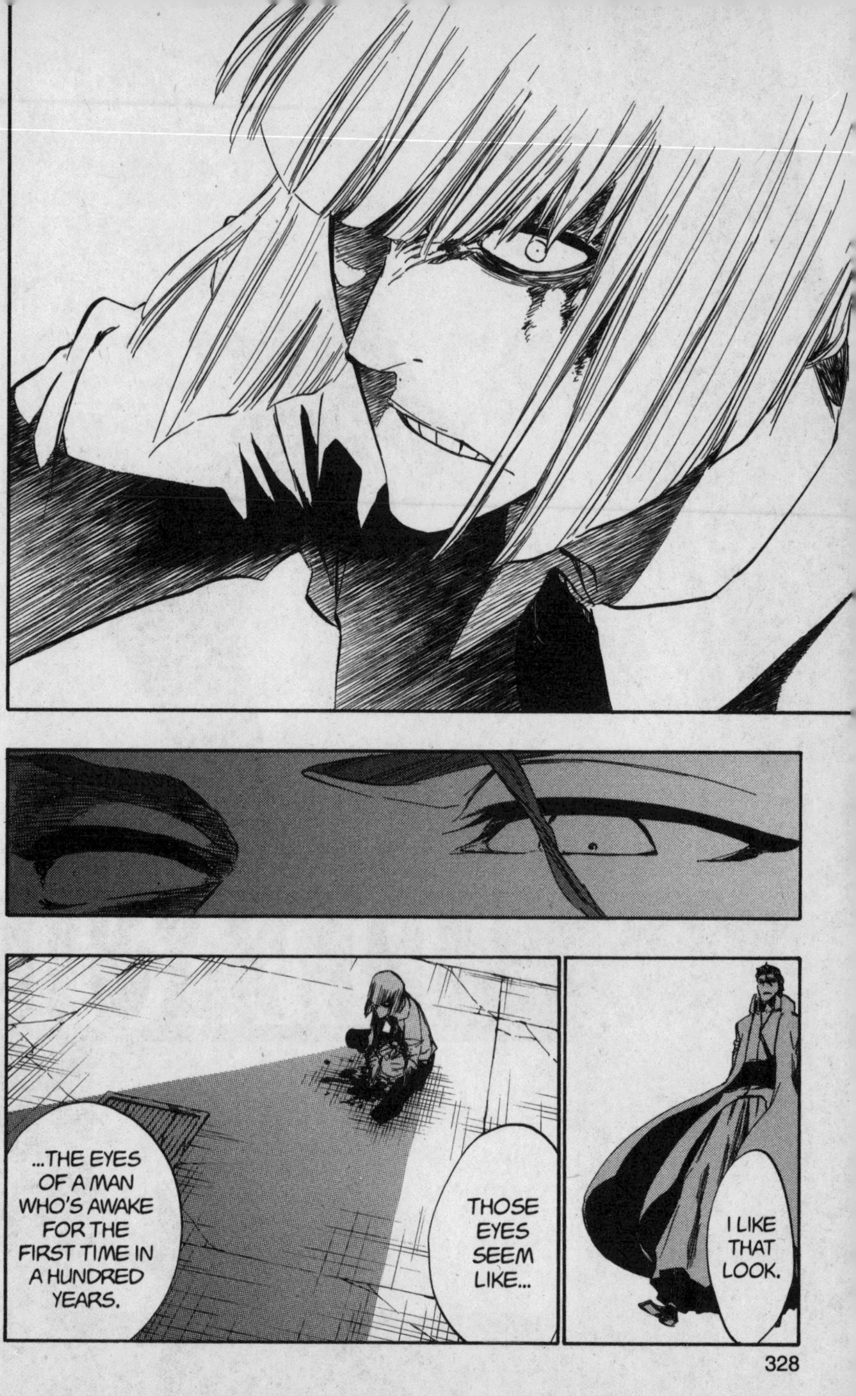
I LIKE THAT LOOK.
THOSE EYES SEEM LIKE...
...THE EYES OF A MAN WHO'S AWAKE FOR THE FIRST TIME IN A HUNDRED YEARS.

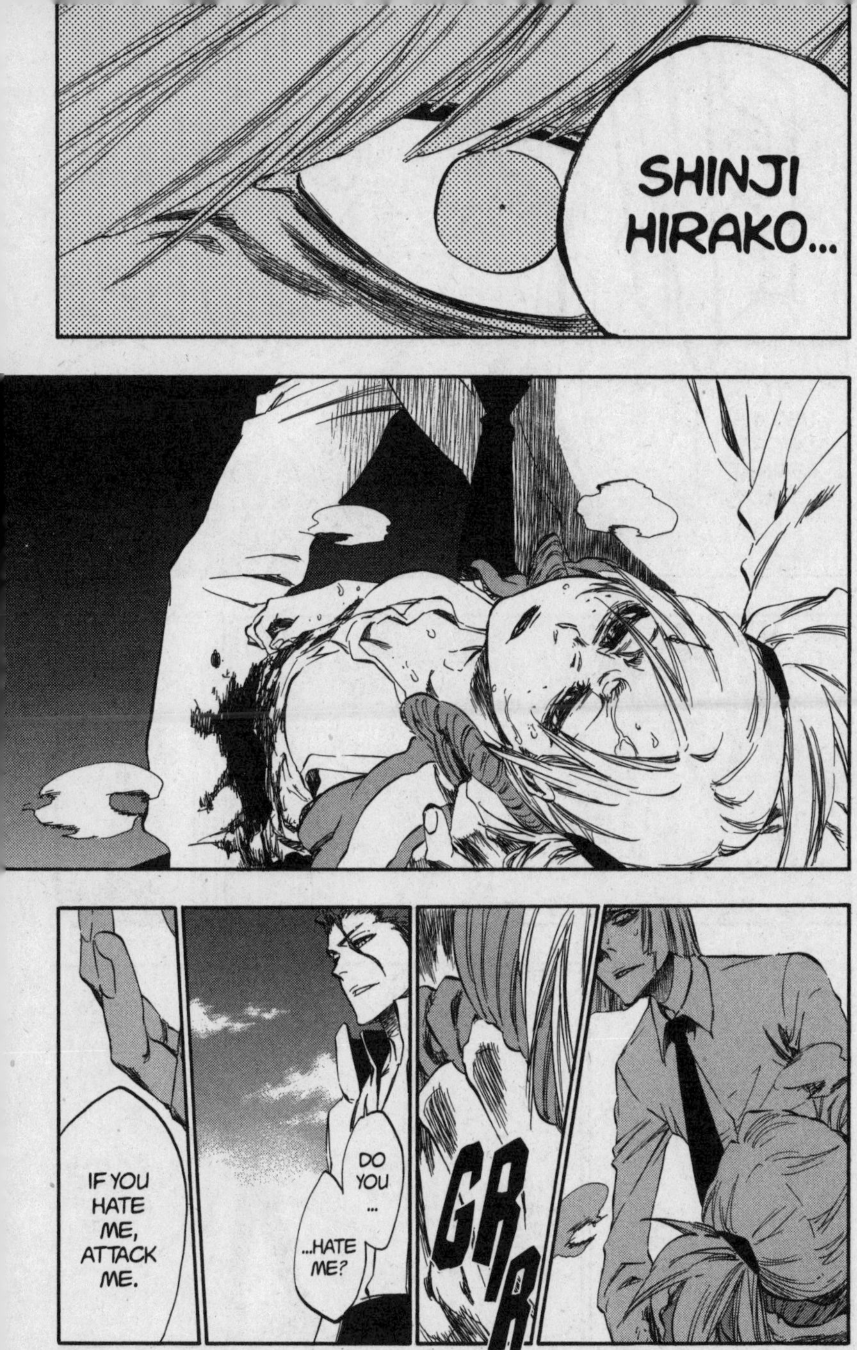
SHINJI HIRAKO...
GRR
DO YOU...
...HATE ME?
IF YOU HATE ME, ATTACK ME.

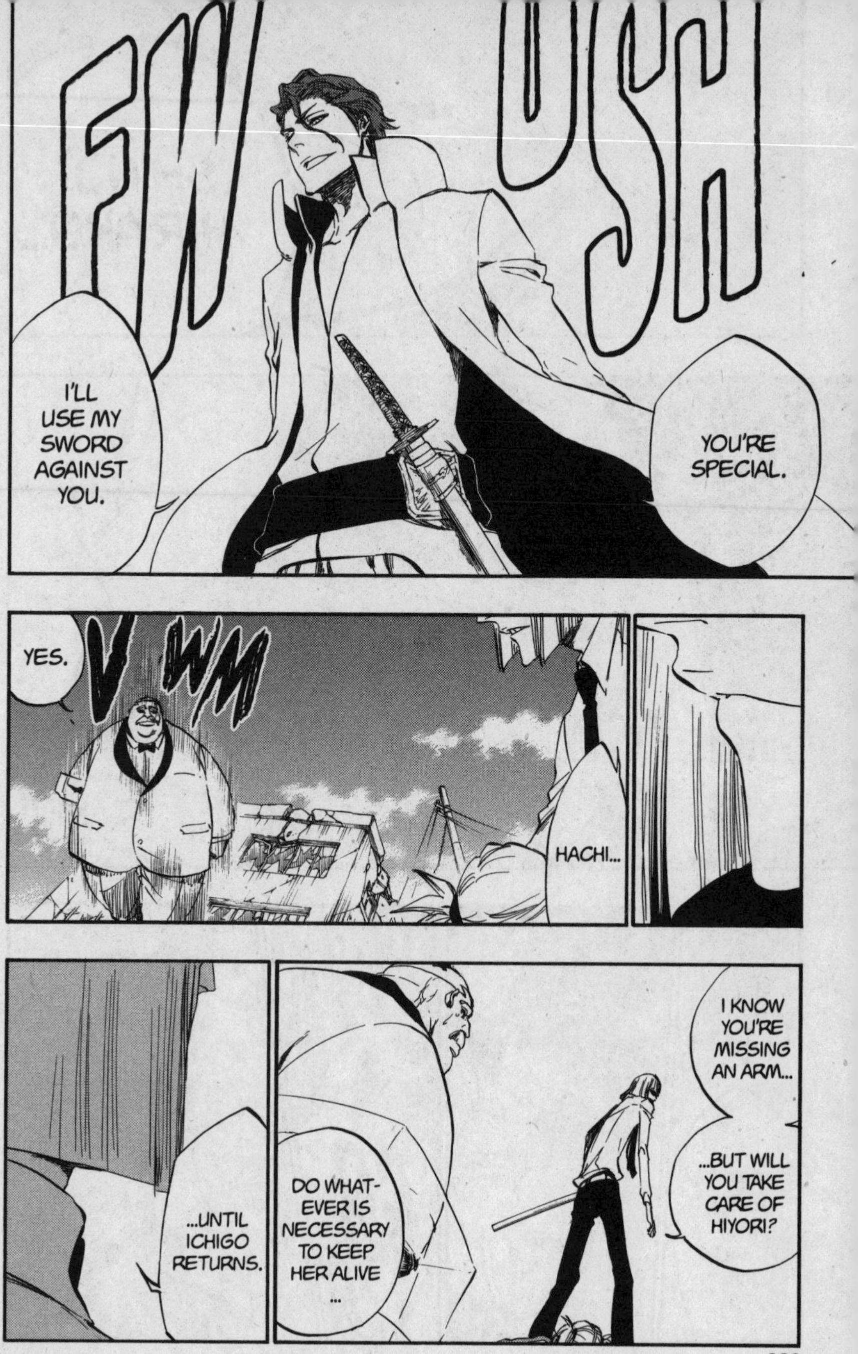
FWUSH
YOU'RE SPECIAL.
I'LL USE MY SWORD AGAINST YOU.
HACHI...
VWM
YES.
I KNOW YOU'RE MISSING AN ARM...
...BUT WILL YOU TAKE CARE OF HIYORI?
DO WHATEVER IS NECESSARY TO KEEP HER ALIVE...
...UNTIL ICHIGO RETURNS.

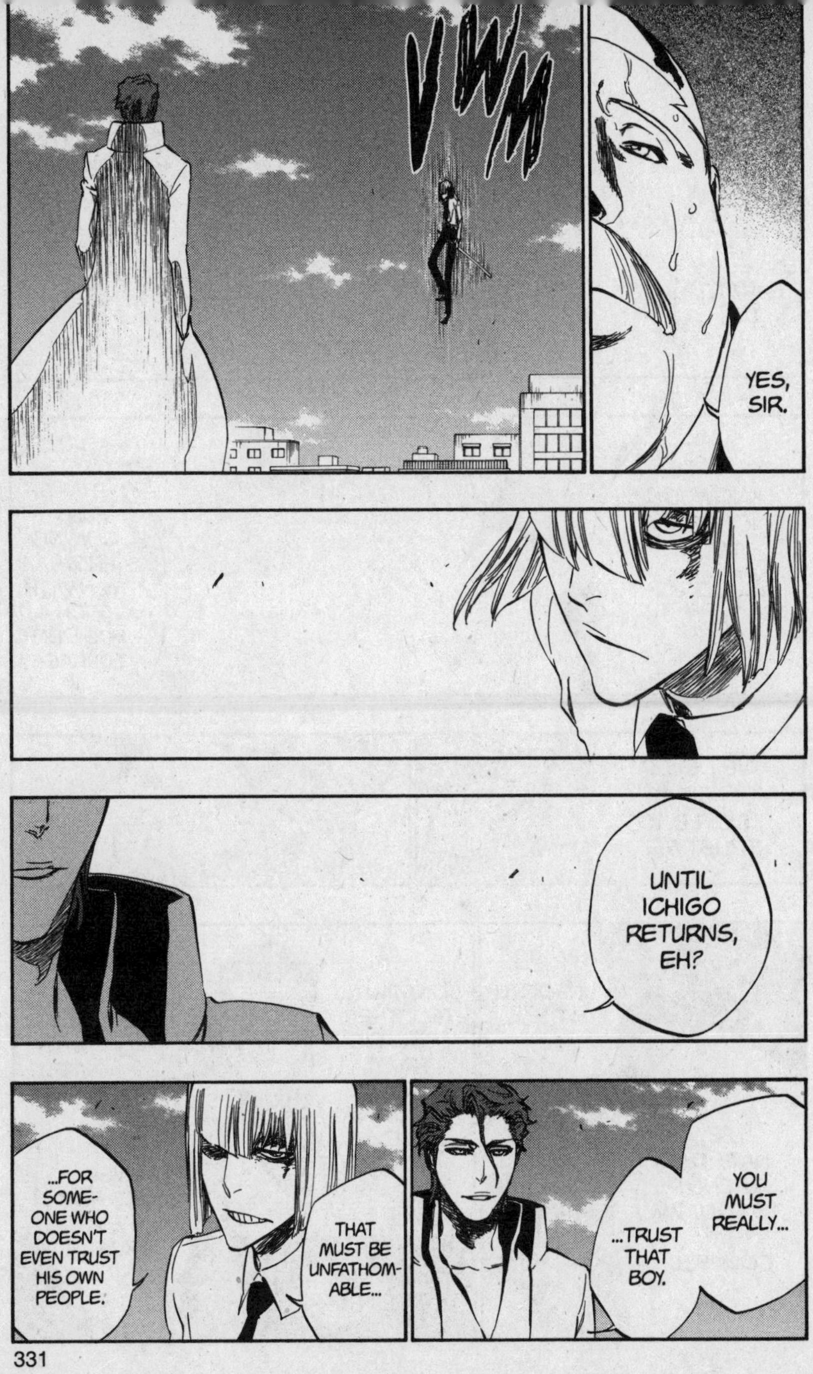
YES, SIR.
VWM
UNTIL ICHIGO RETURNS, EH?
YOU MUST REALLY...
...TRUST THAT BOY.
THAT MUST BE UNFATHOMABLE...
...FOR SOMEONE WHO DOESN'T EVEN TRUST HIS OWN PEOPLE.

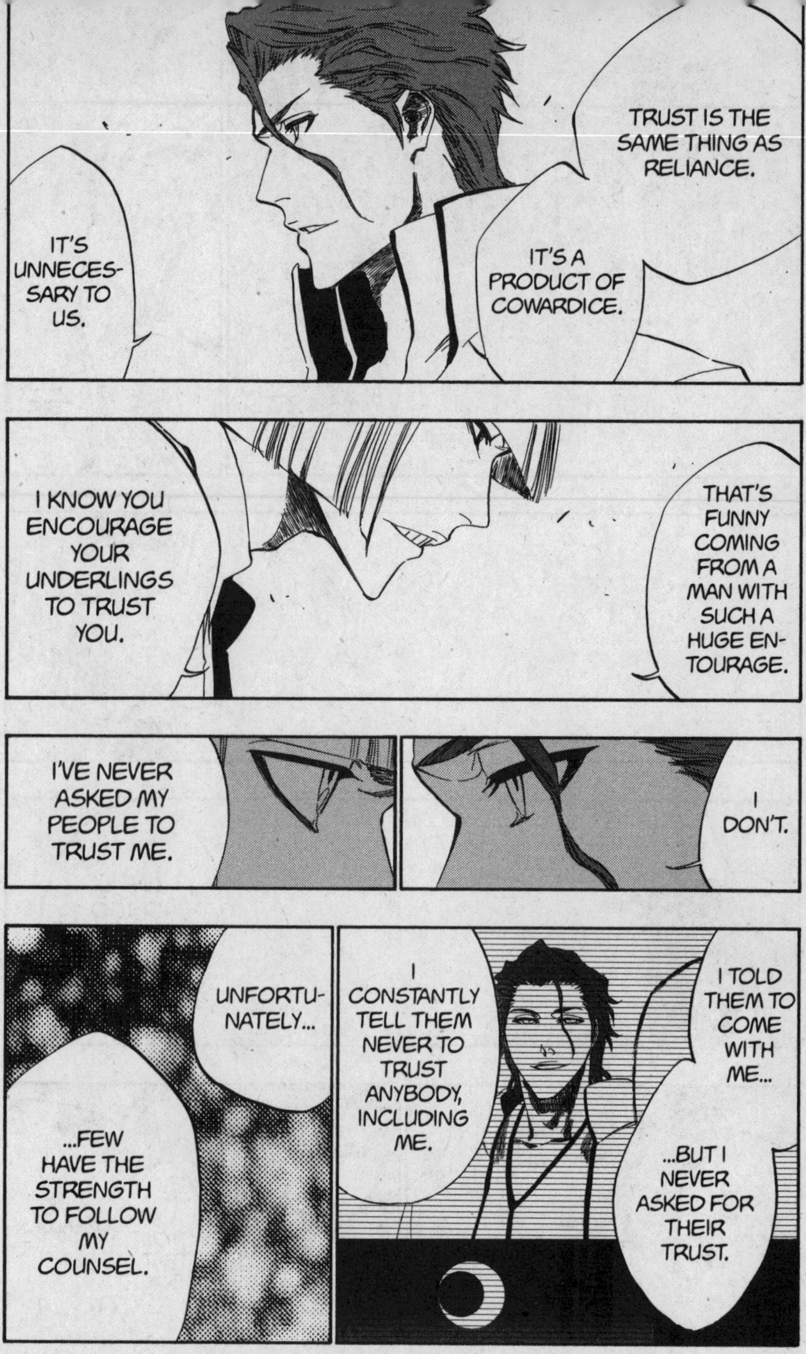
TRUST IS THE SAME THING AS RELIANCE.
IT'S A PRODUCT OF COWARDICE.
IT'S UNNECESSARY TO US.
THAT'S FUNNY COMING FROM A MAN WITH SUCH A HUGE ENTOURAGE.
I KNOW YOU ENCOURAGE YOUR UNDERLINGS TO TRUST YOU.
I DON'T.
I'VE NEVER ASKED MY PEOPLE TO TRUST ME.
I TOLD THEM TO COME WITH ME...
...BUT I NEVER ASKED FOR THEIR TRUST.
I CONSTANTLY TELL THEM NEVER TO TRUST ANYBODY, INCLUDING ME.
UNFORTUNATELY...
...FEW HAVE THE STRENGTH TO FOLLOW MY COUNSEL.

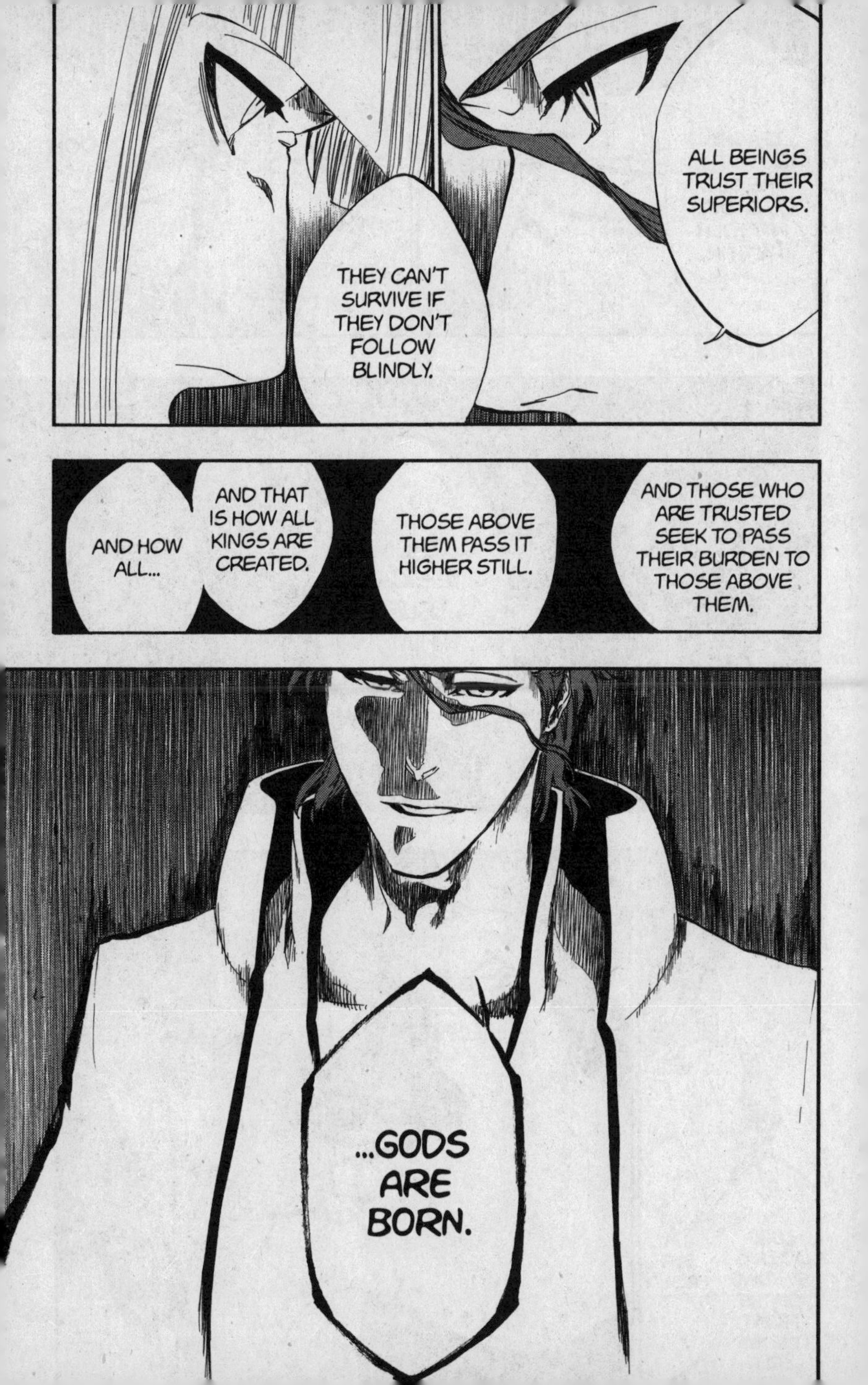
ALL BEINGS TRUST THEIR SUPERIORS.
THEY CAN'T SURVIVE IF THEY DON'T FOLLOW BLINDLY.
AND THOSE WHO ARE TRUSTED SEEK TO PASS THEIR BURDEN TO THOSE ABOVE THEM.
THOSE ABOVE THEM PASS IT HIGHER STILL.
AND THAT IS HOW ALL KINGS ARE CREATED.
AND HOW ALL...
...GODS ARE BORN.

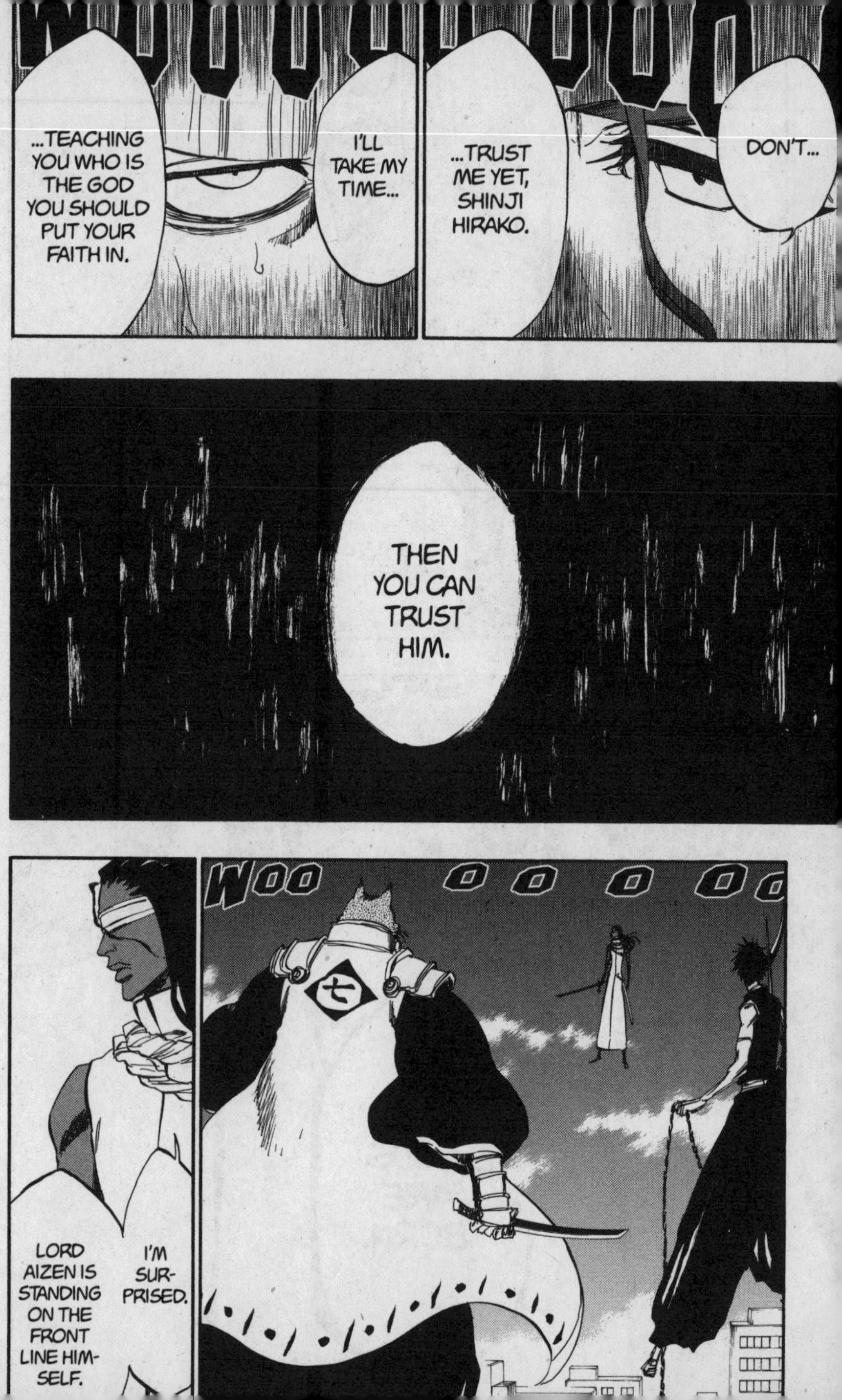
DON'T...
...TRUST ME YET, SHINJI HIRAKO.
I'LL TAKE MY TIME...
...TEACHING YOU WHO IS THE GOD YOU SHOULD PUT YOUR FAITH IN.
THEN YOU CAN TRUST HIM.
WOOOOOOOO
I'M SUR-PRISED.
LORD AIZEN IS STANDING ON THE FRONT LINE HIM-SELF.

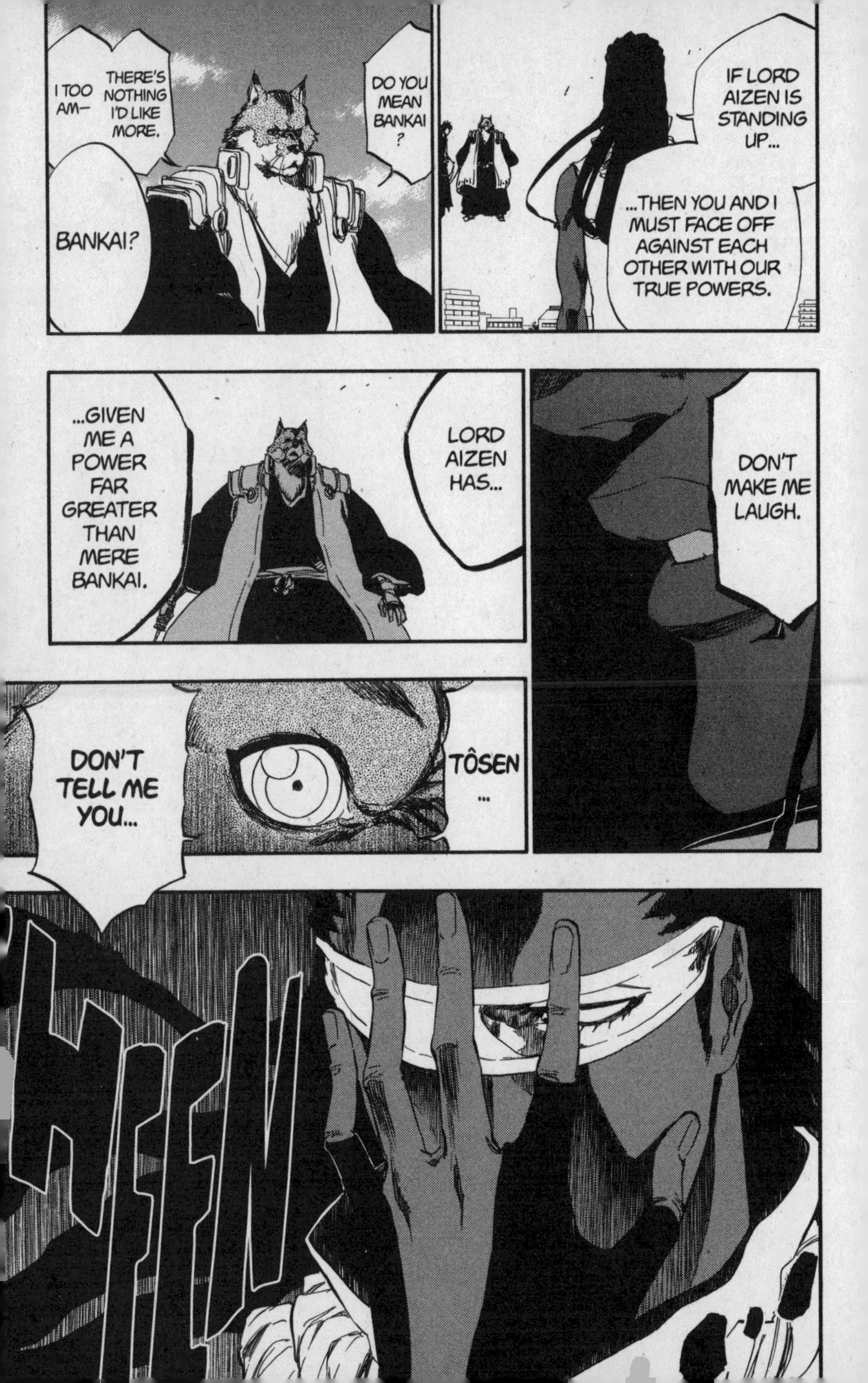
IF LORD AIZEN IS STANDING UP...
...THEN YOU AND I MUST FACE OFF AGAINST EACH OTHER WITH OUR TRUE POWERS.
DO YOU MEAN BANKAI?
THERE'S NOTHING I'D LIKE MORE.
I TOO AM—
BANKAI?
DON'T MAKE ME LAUGH.
LORD AIZEN HAS...
...GIVEN ME A POWER FAR GREATER THAN MERE BANKAI.
TÔSEN...
DON'T TELL ME YOU...

384. Can't Fear Your Own Sword

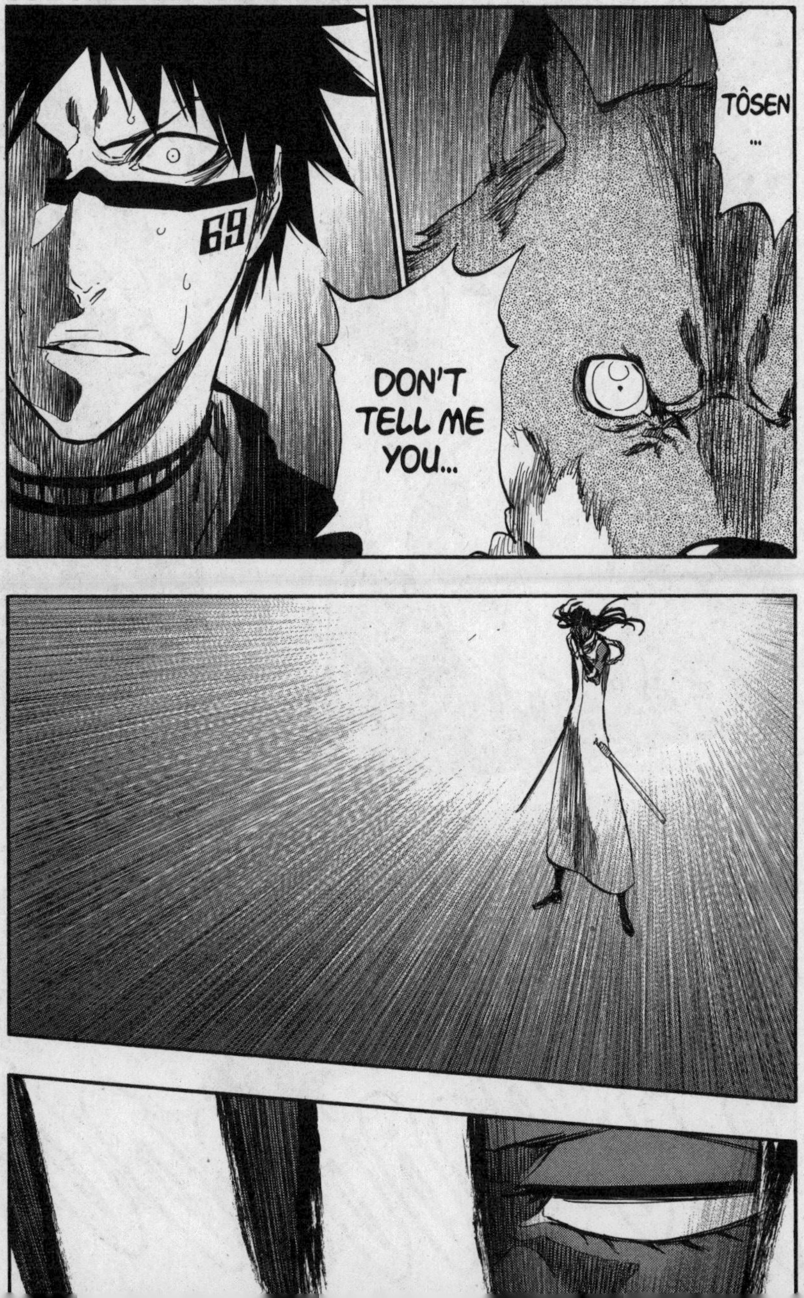
TÔSEN ...
DON'T TELL ME YOU...

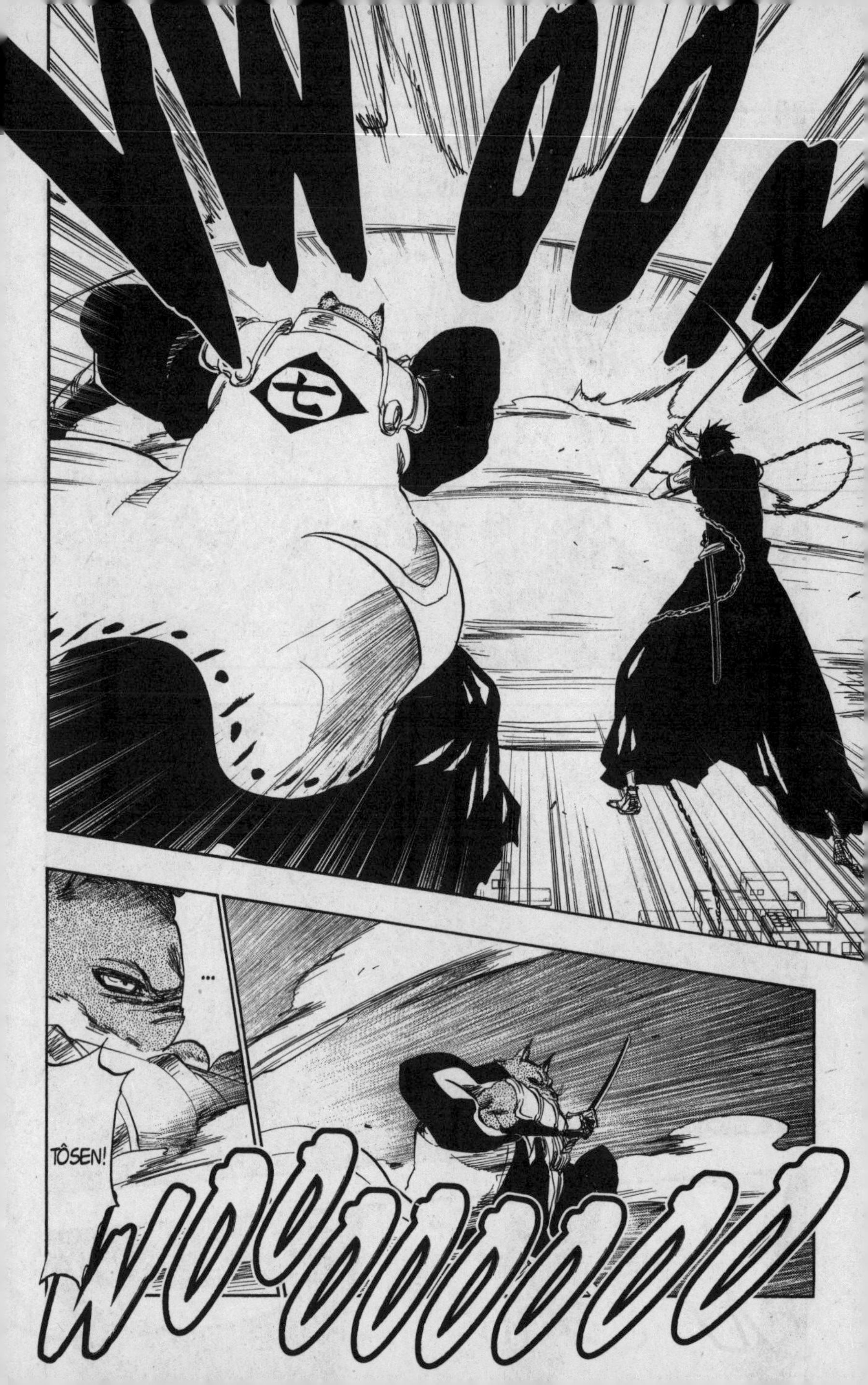
WHOOM
...
TÔSEN!

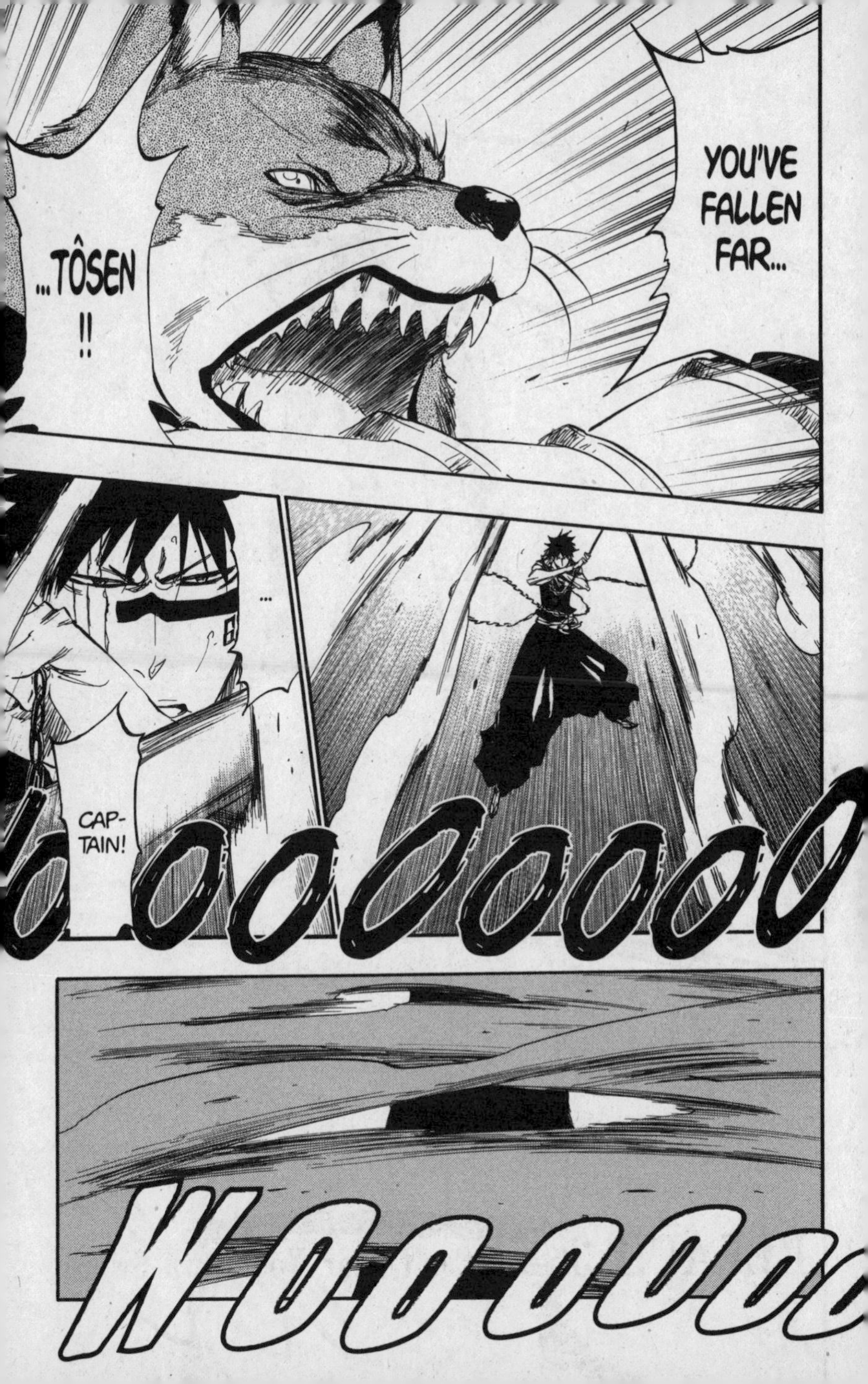
YOU'VE FALLEN FAR...
...TÔSEN !!
...
CAP-TAIN!
OOOOOOOO
WOOOOOO

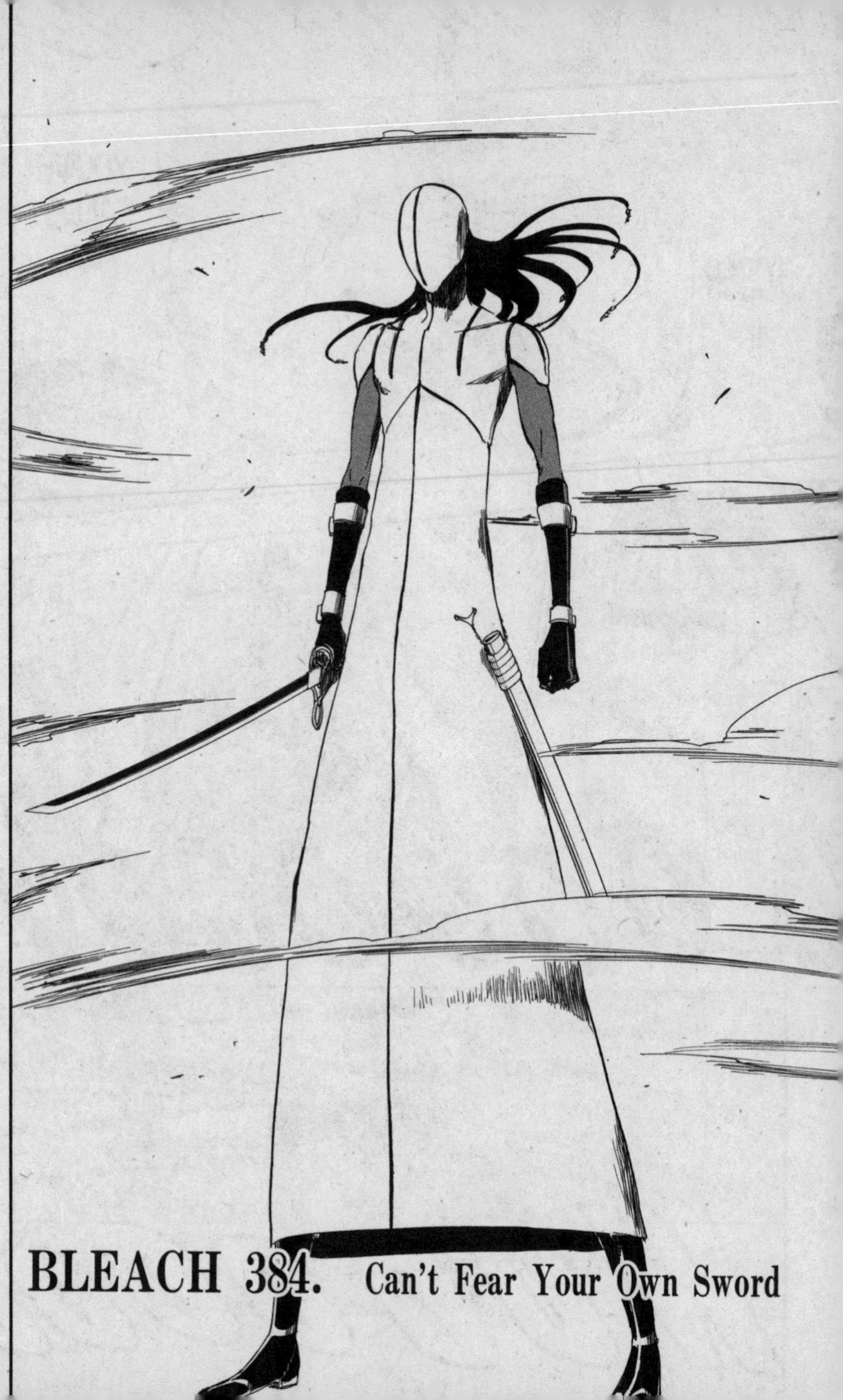
BLEACH 384. Can't Fear Your Own Sword

KREK

...HOLLOW-
FICATION,
CAPTAIN
TÔSEN
?!

IS
THAT
...

...

HOL-
LOW-
FY...

WHY?

IT
IS.

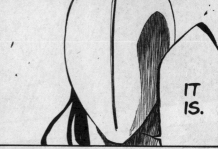

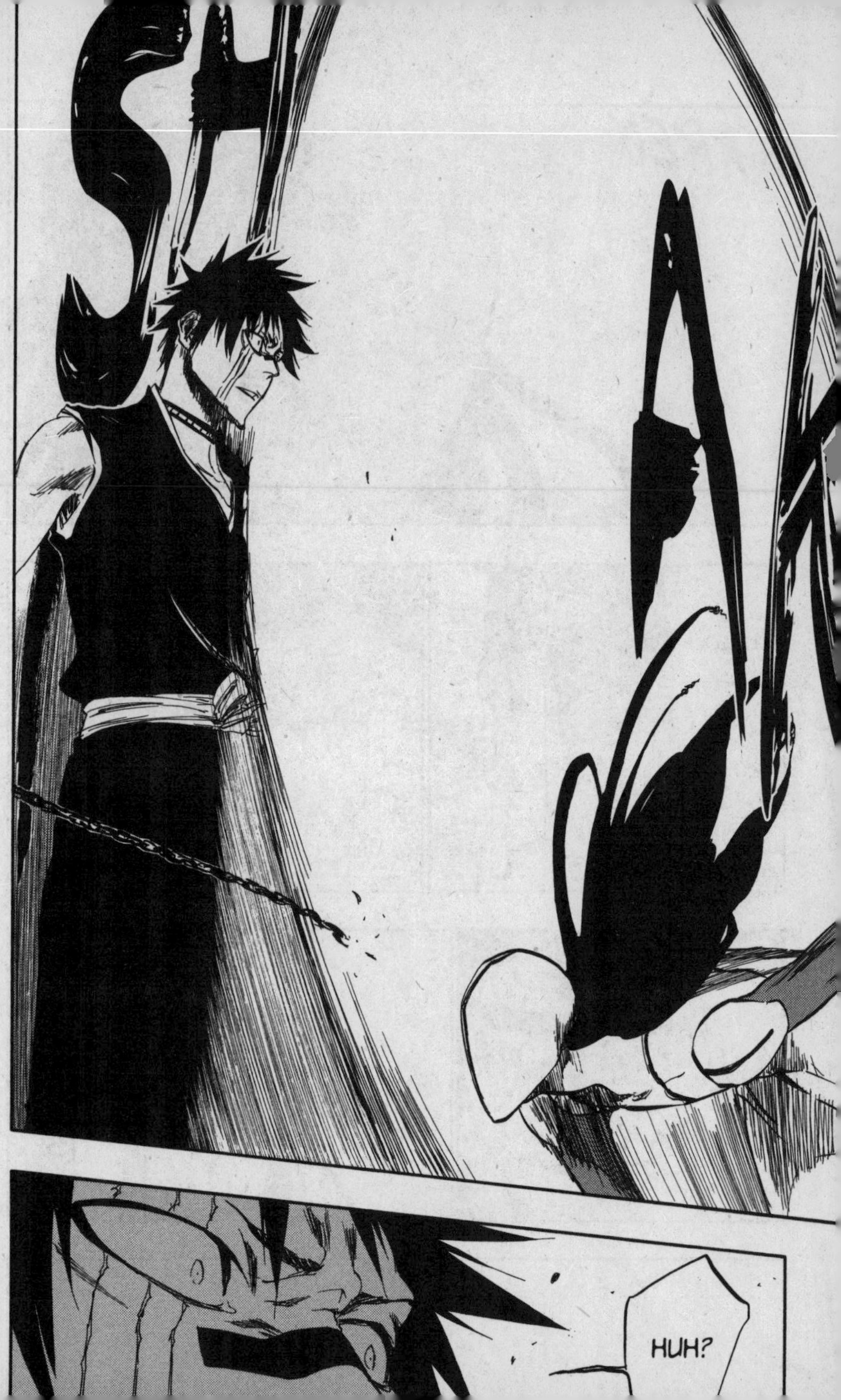
HUH?

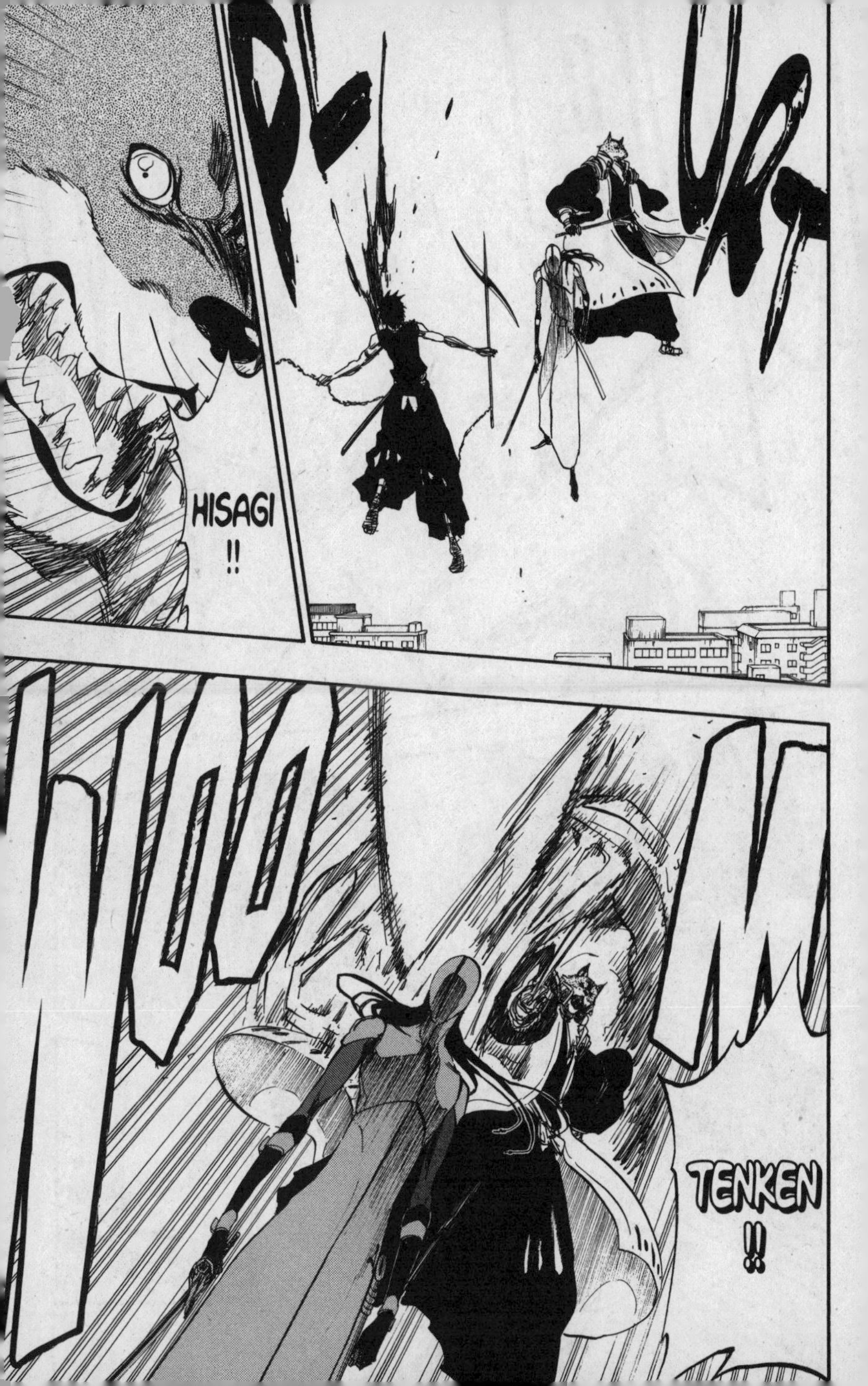
HISAGI !!
TENKEN !!

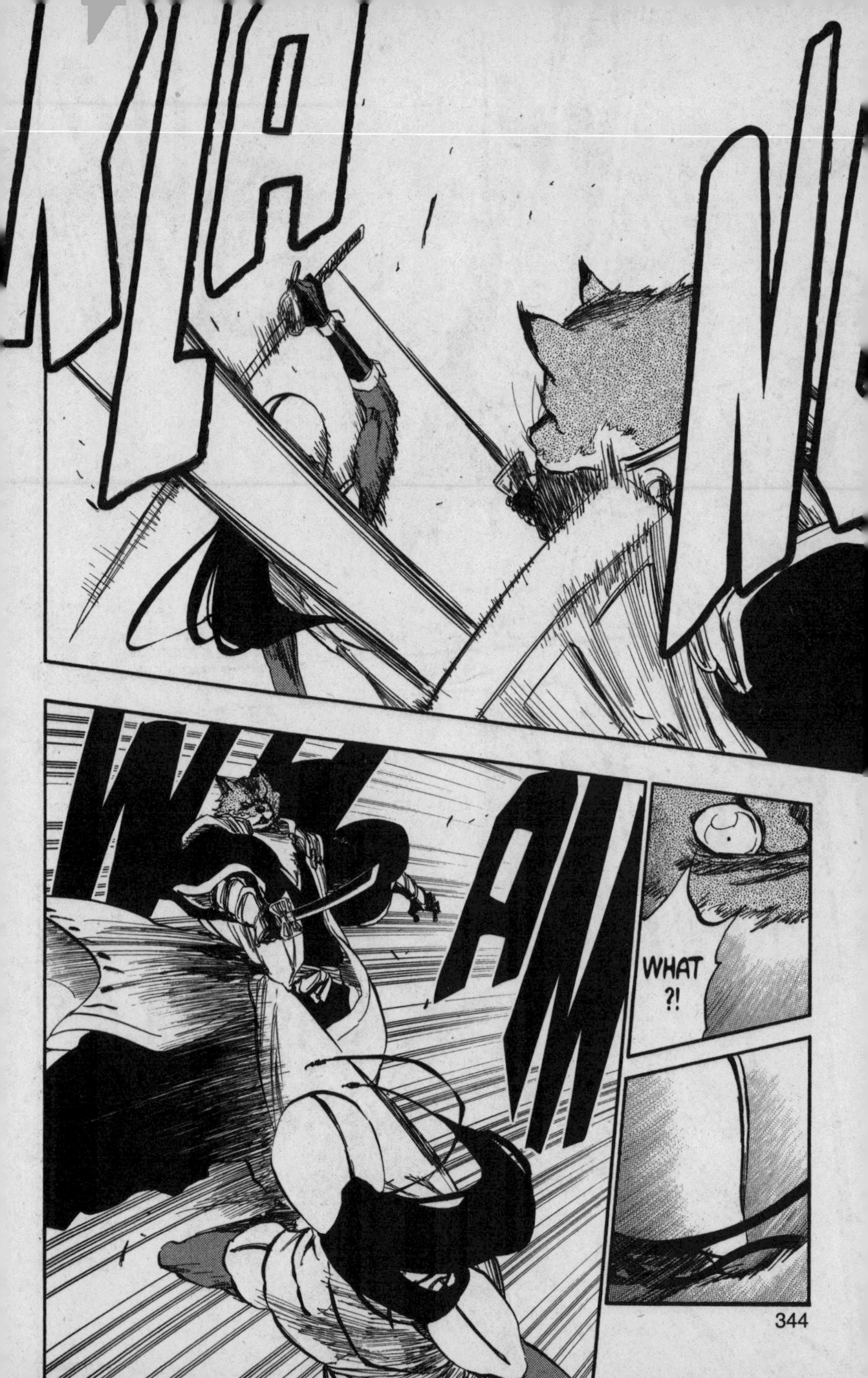
WHAM
WHAT ?!
WHAM

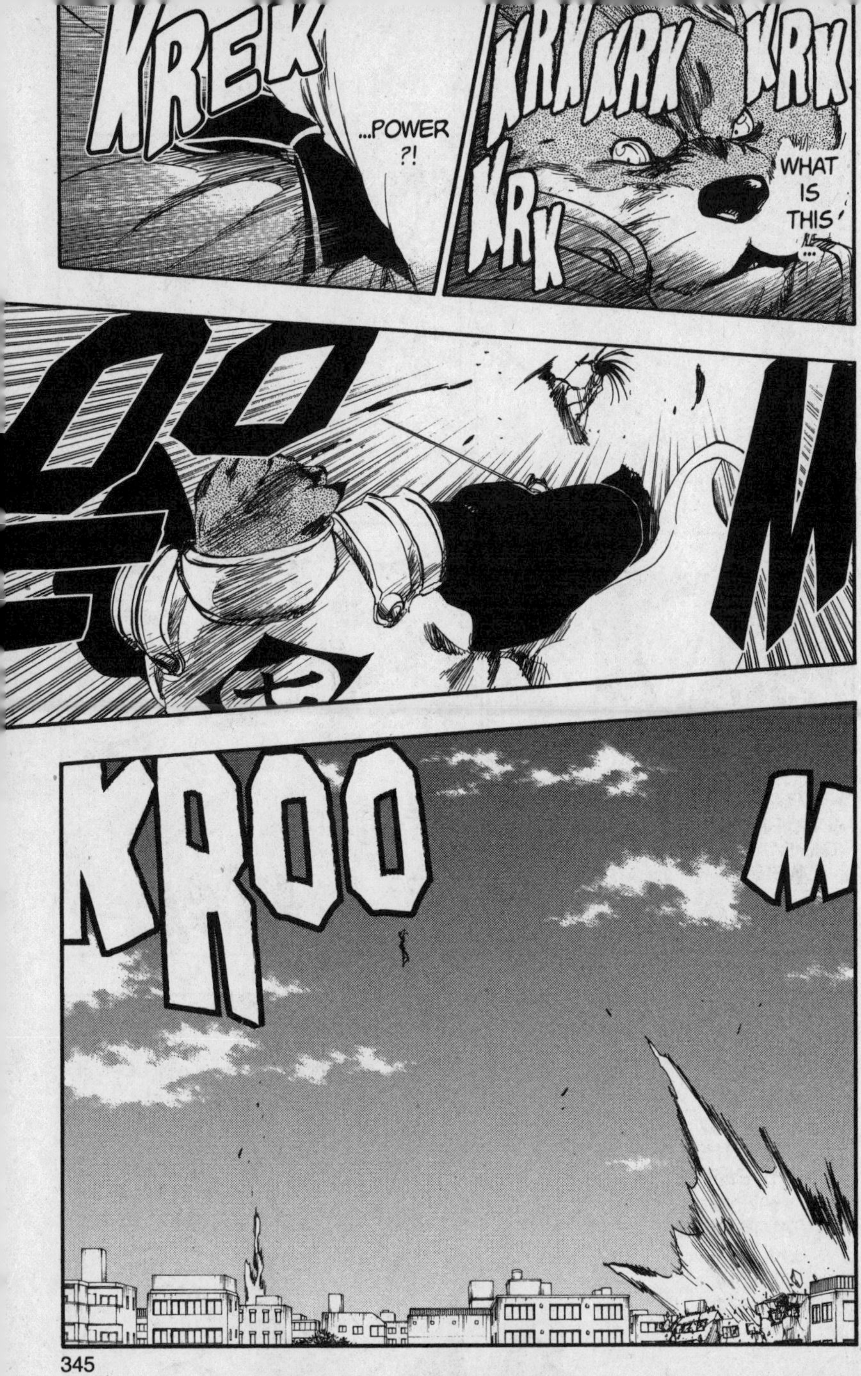
KRN KRK KRK
KRK
WHAT IS THIS...
KREK
...POWER ?!
KROOM

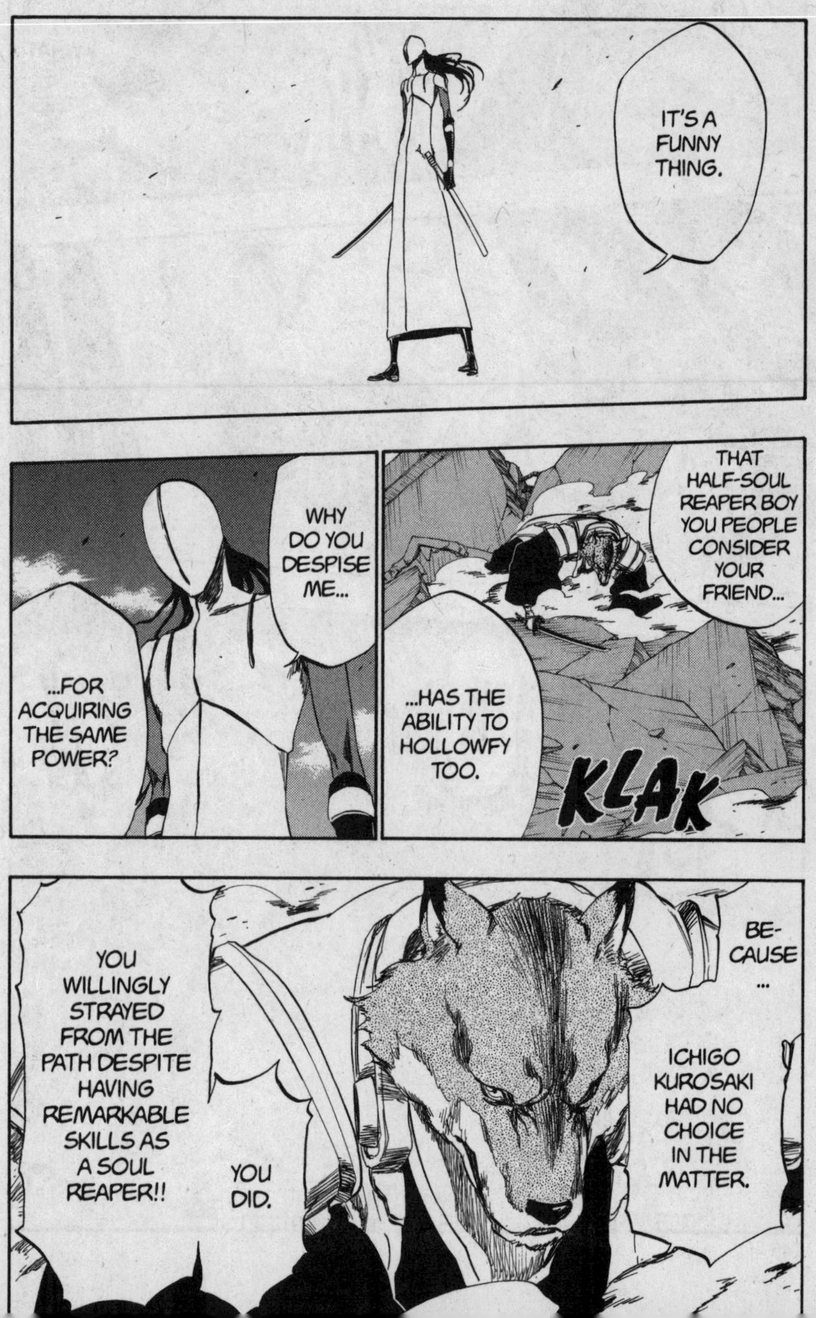
IT'S A FUNNY THING.
THAT HALF-SOUL REAPER BOY YOU PEOPLE CONSIDER YOUR FRIEND...
...HAS THE ABILITY TO HOLLOWFY TOO.
KLAK
WHY DO YOU DESPISE ME...
...FOR ACQUIRING THE SAME POWER?
BE-CAUSE...
ICHIGO KUROSAKI HAD NO CHOICE IN THE MATTER.
YOU DID.
YOU WILLINGLY STRAYED FROM THE PATH DESPITE HAVING REMARKABLE SKILLS AS A SOUL REAPER!!

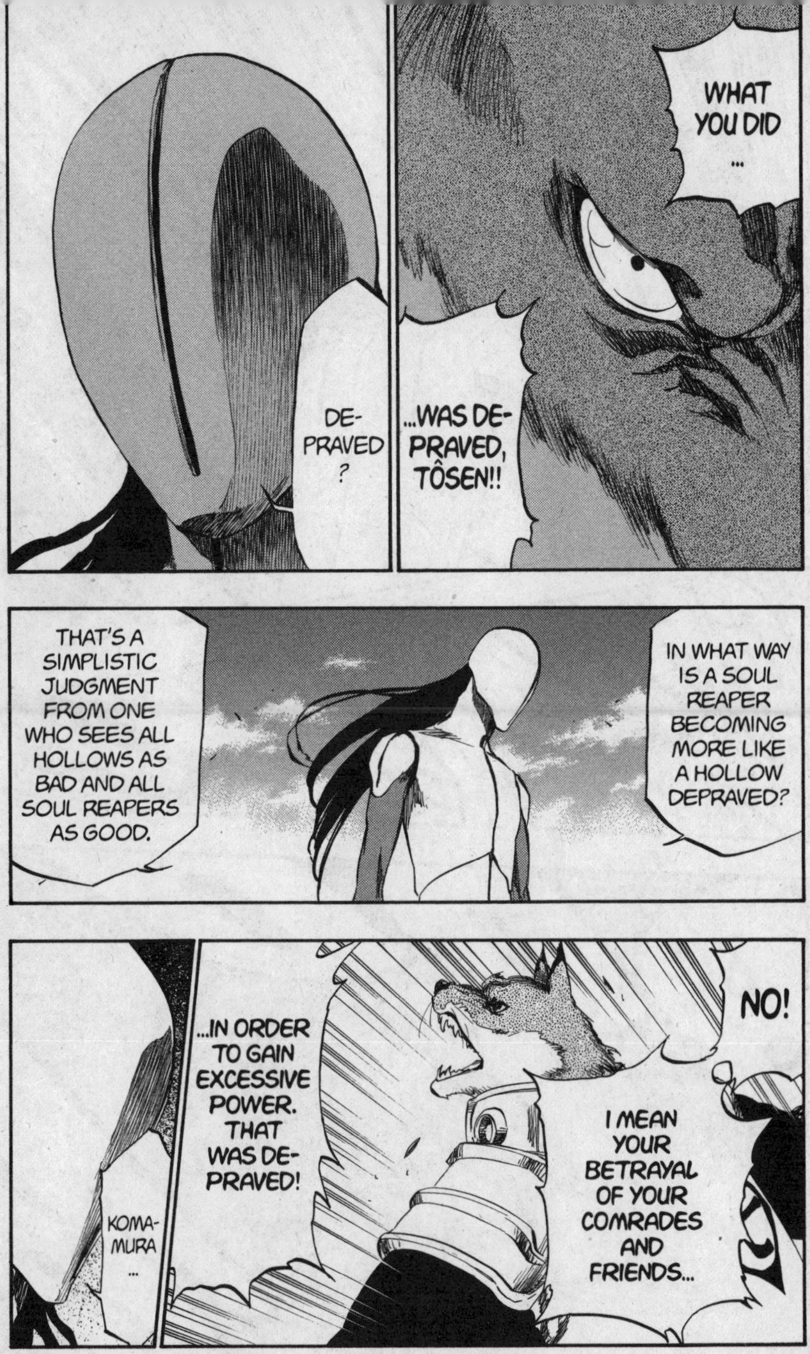
WHAT YOU DID ...
...WAS DEPRAVED, TÔSEN!!
DEPRAVED ?
IN WHAT WAY IS A SOUL REAPER BECOMING MORE LIKE A HOLLOW DEPRAVED?
THAT'S A SIMPLISTIC JUDGMENT FROM ONE WHO SEES ALL HOLLOWS AS BAD AND ALL SOUL REAPERS AS GOOD.
NO!
I MEAN YOUR BETRAYAL OF YOUR COMRADES AND FRIENDS...
...IN ORDER TO GAIN EXCESSIVE POWER. THAT WAS DEPRAVED!
KOMAMURA ...

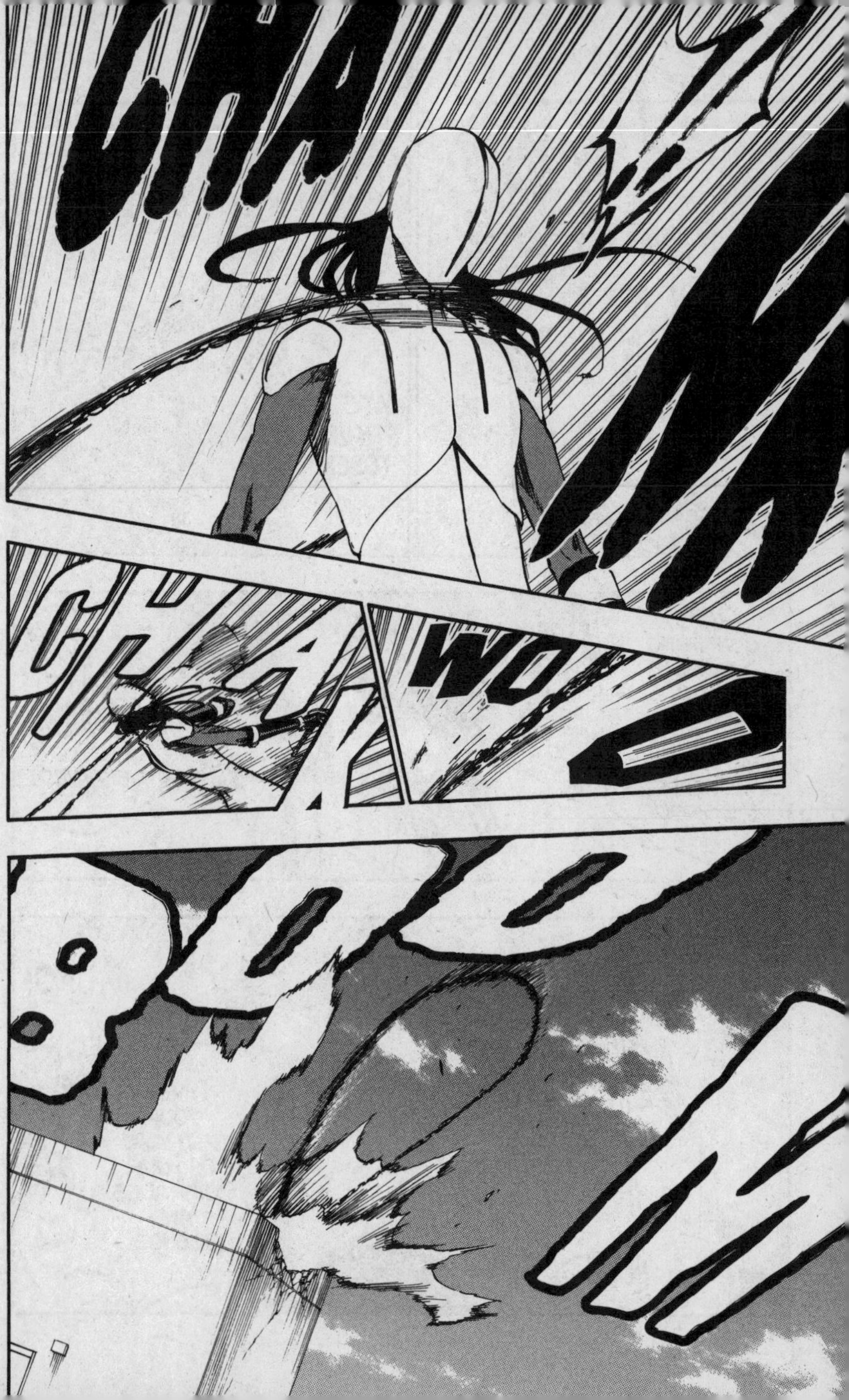
CHA
WO
CHA

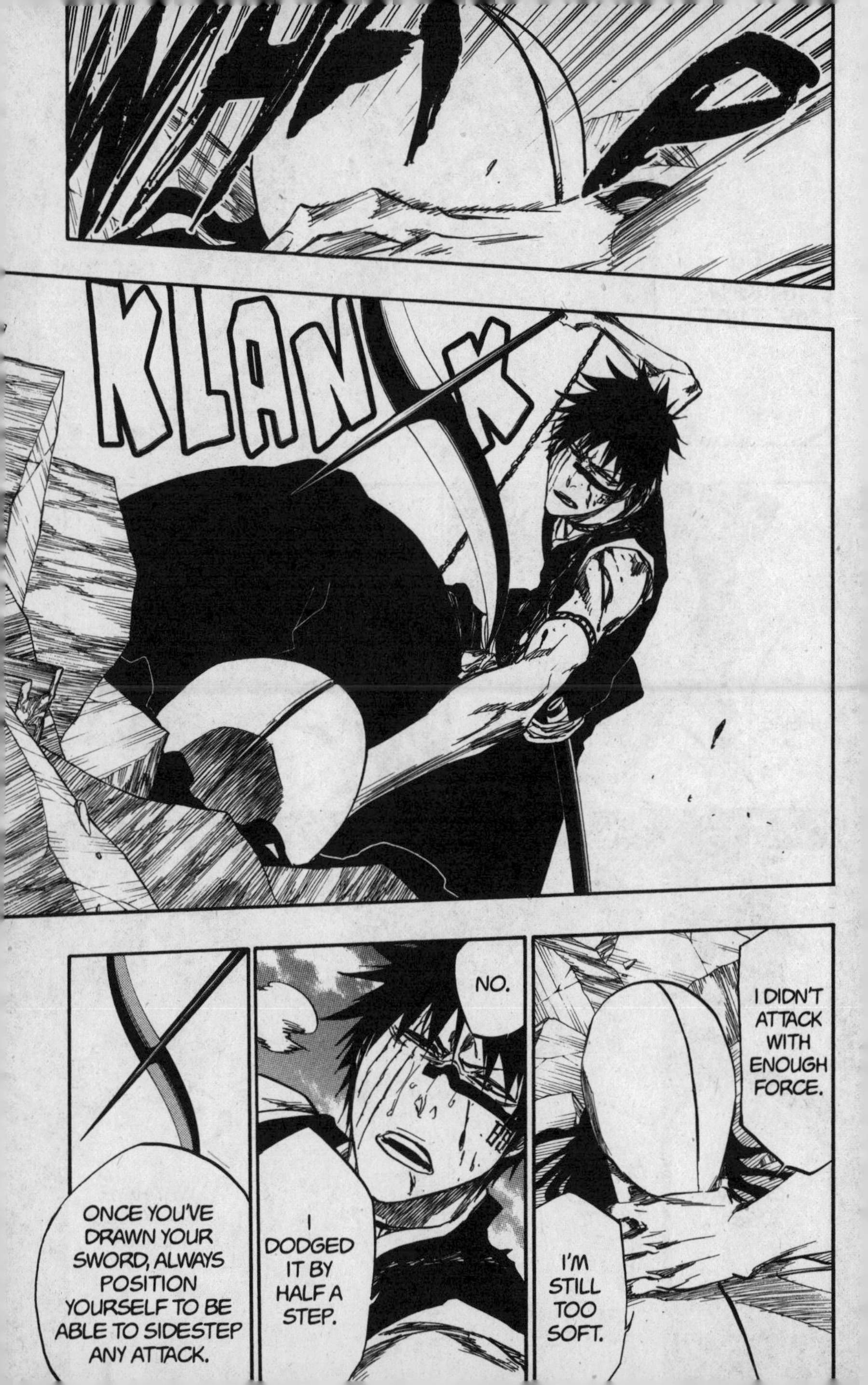
WHAP
KLANK
I DIDN'T ATTACK WITH ENOUGH FORCE.
I'M STILL TOO SOFT.
NO.
I DODGED IT BY HALF A STEP.
ONCE YOU'VE DRAWN YOUR SWORD, ALWAYS POSITION YOURSELF TO BE ABLE TO SIDESTEP ANY ATTACK.

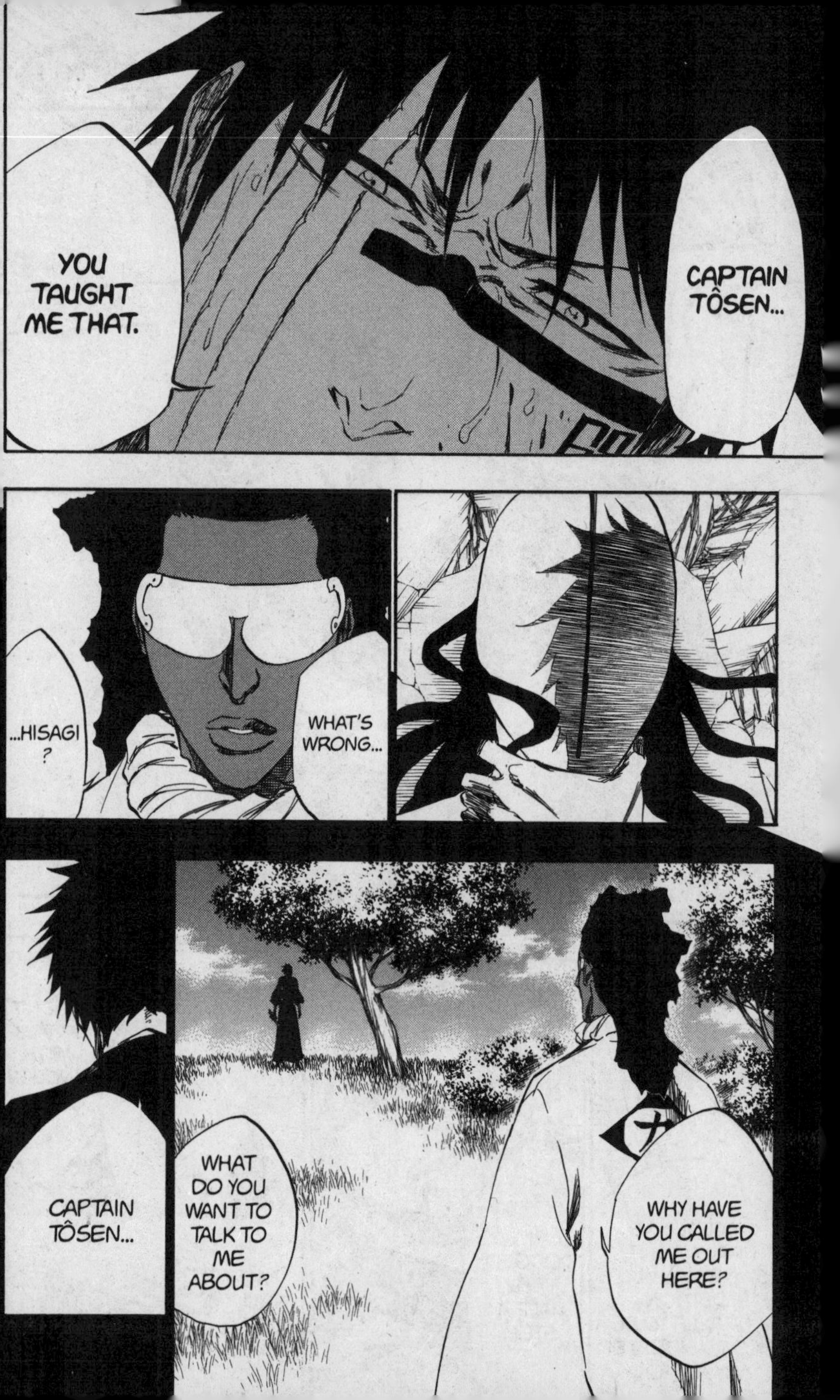
CAPTAIN TÔSEN...
YOU TAUGHT ME THAT.
WHAT'S WRONG...
...HISAGI?
WHY HAVE YOU CALLED ME OUT HERE?
WHAT DO YOU WANT TO TALK TO ME ABOUT?
CAPTAIN TÔSEN...

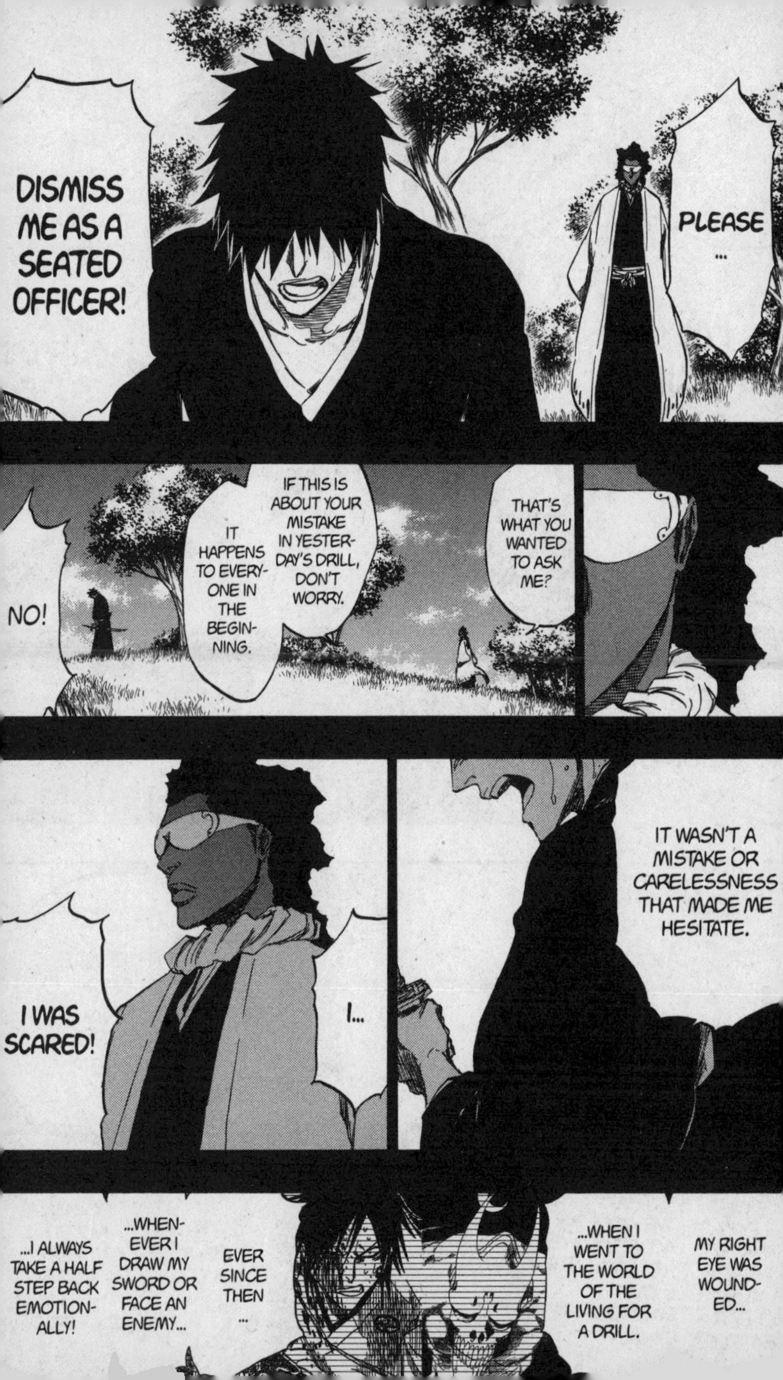
PLEASE ...
DISMISS ME AS A SEATED OFFICER!
THAT'S WHAT YOU WANTED TO ASK ME?
IF THIS IS ABOUT YOUR MISTAKE IN YESTERDAY'S DRILL, DON'T WORRY.
IT HAPPENS TO EVERYONE IN THE BEGINNING.
NO!
IT WASN'T A MISTAKE OR CARELESSNESS THAT MADE ME HESITATE.
I...
I WAS SCARED!
MY RIGHT EYE WAS WOUNDED...
...WHEN I WENT TO THE WORLD OF THE LIVING FOR A DRILL.
EVER SINCE THEN ...
...WHENEVER I DRAW MY SWORD OR FACE AN ENEMY...
...I ALWAYS TAKE A HALF STEP BACK EMOTIONALLY!

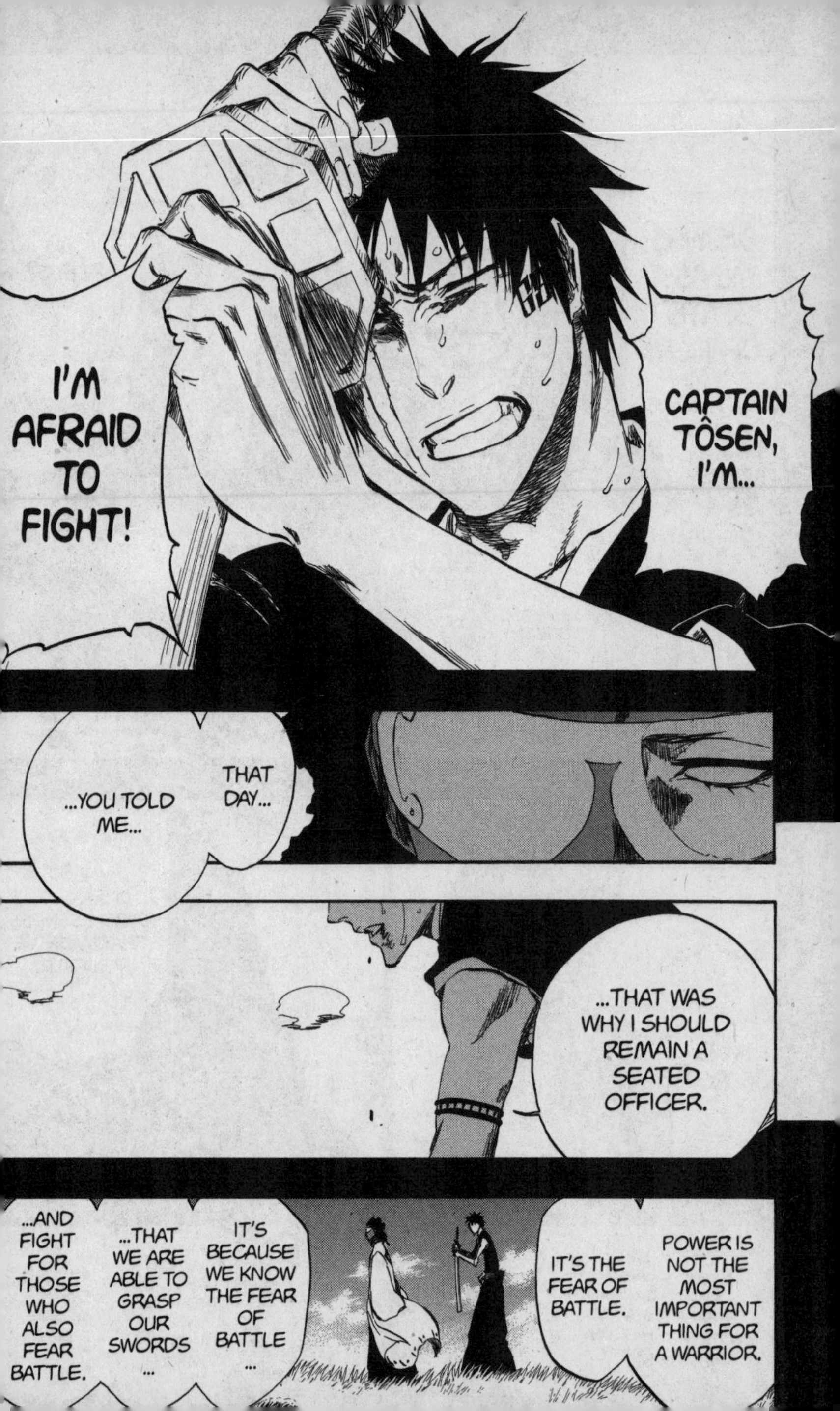
CAPTAIN TÔSEN, I'M...
I'M AFRAID TO FIGHT!
THAT DAY...
...YOU TOLD ME...
...THAT WAS WHY I SHOULD REMAIN A SEATED OFFICER.
POWER IS NOT THE MOST IMPORTANT THING FOR A WARRIOR.
IT'S THE FEAR OF BATTLE.
IT'S BECAUSE WE KNOW THE FEAR OF BATTLE...
...THAT WE ARE ABLE TO GRASP OUR SWORDS...
...AND FIGHT FOR THOSE WHO ALSO FEAR BATTLE.

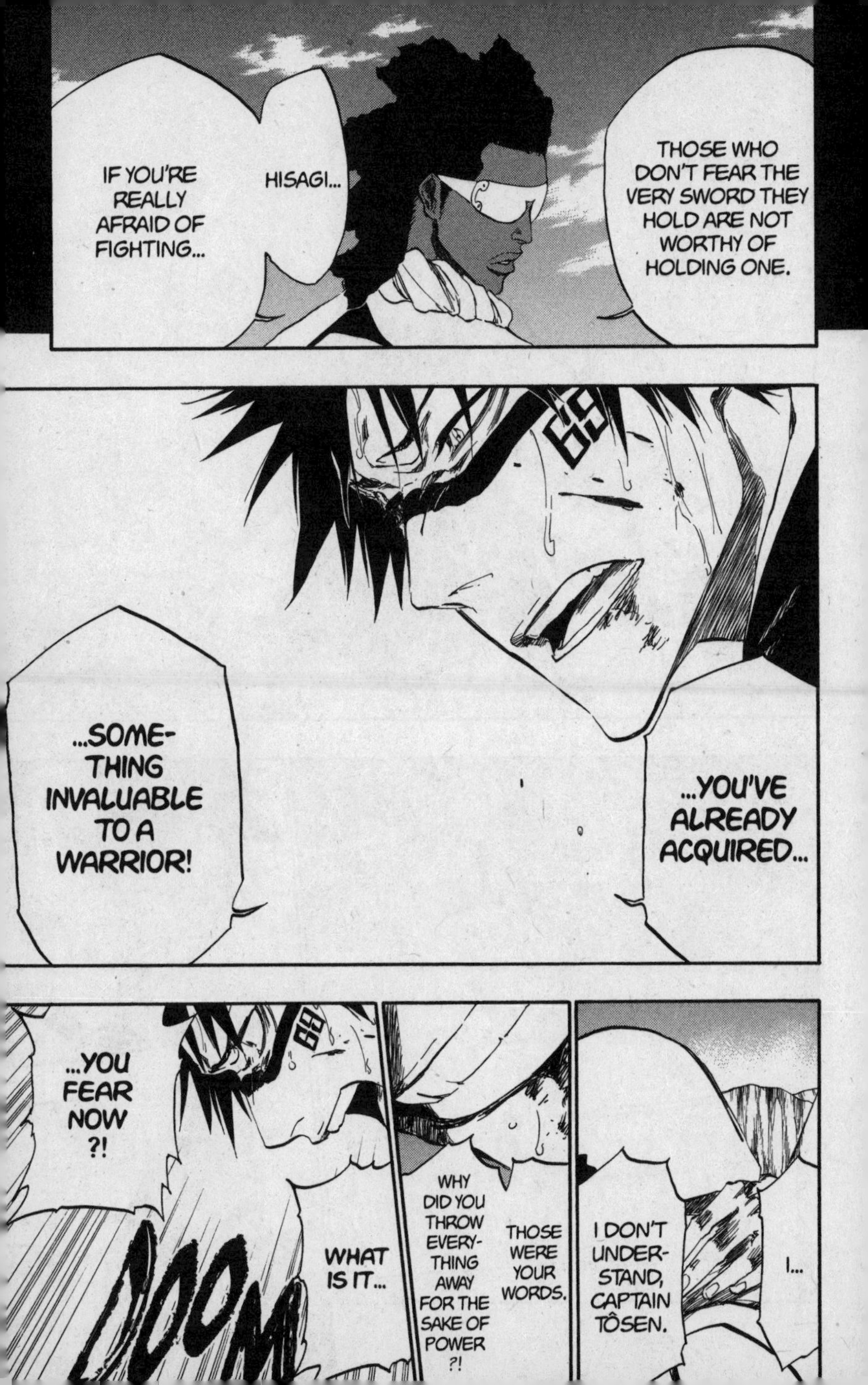
THOSE WHO DON'T FEAR THE VERY SWORD THEY HOLD ARE NOT WORTHY OF HOLDING ONE.
HISAGI...
IF YOU'RE REALLY AFRAID OF FIGHTING...
...YOU'VE ALREADY ACQUIRED...
...SOME-THING INVALUABLE TO A WARRIOR!
I...
I DON'T UNDER-STAND, CAPTAIN TÔSEN.
THOSE WERE YOUR WORDS.
WHY DID YOU THROW EVERY-THING AWAY FOR THE SAKE OF POWER ?!
WHAT IS IT...
...YOU FEAR NOW ?!
DOOM

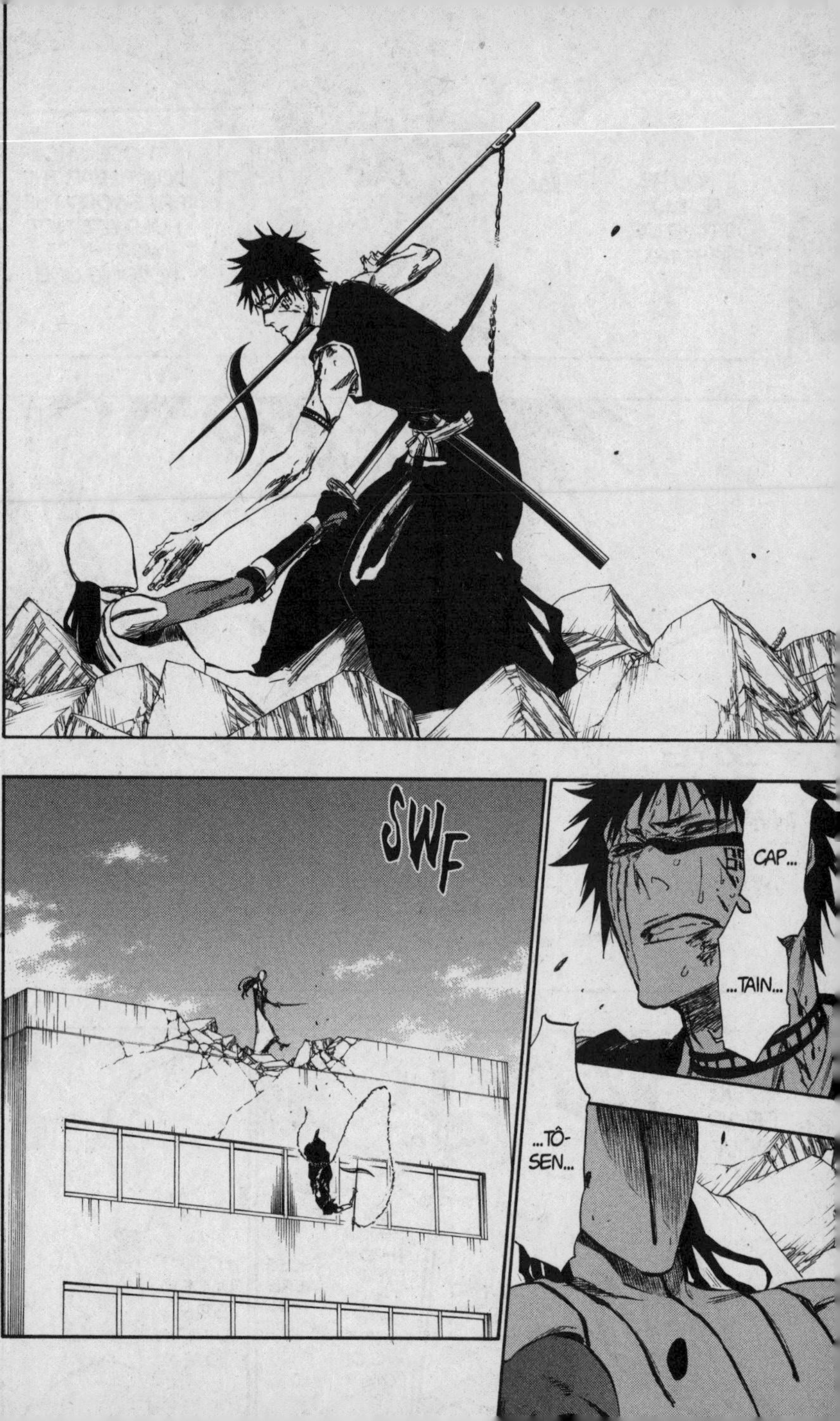
CAP...
...TAIN...
...TÔ-SEN...
SWF

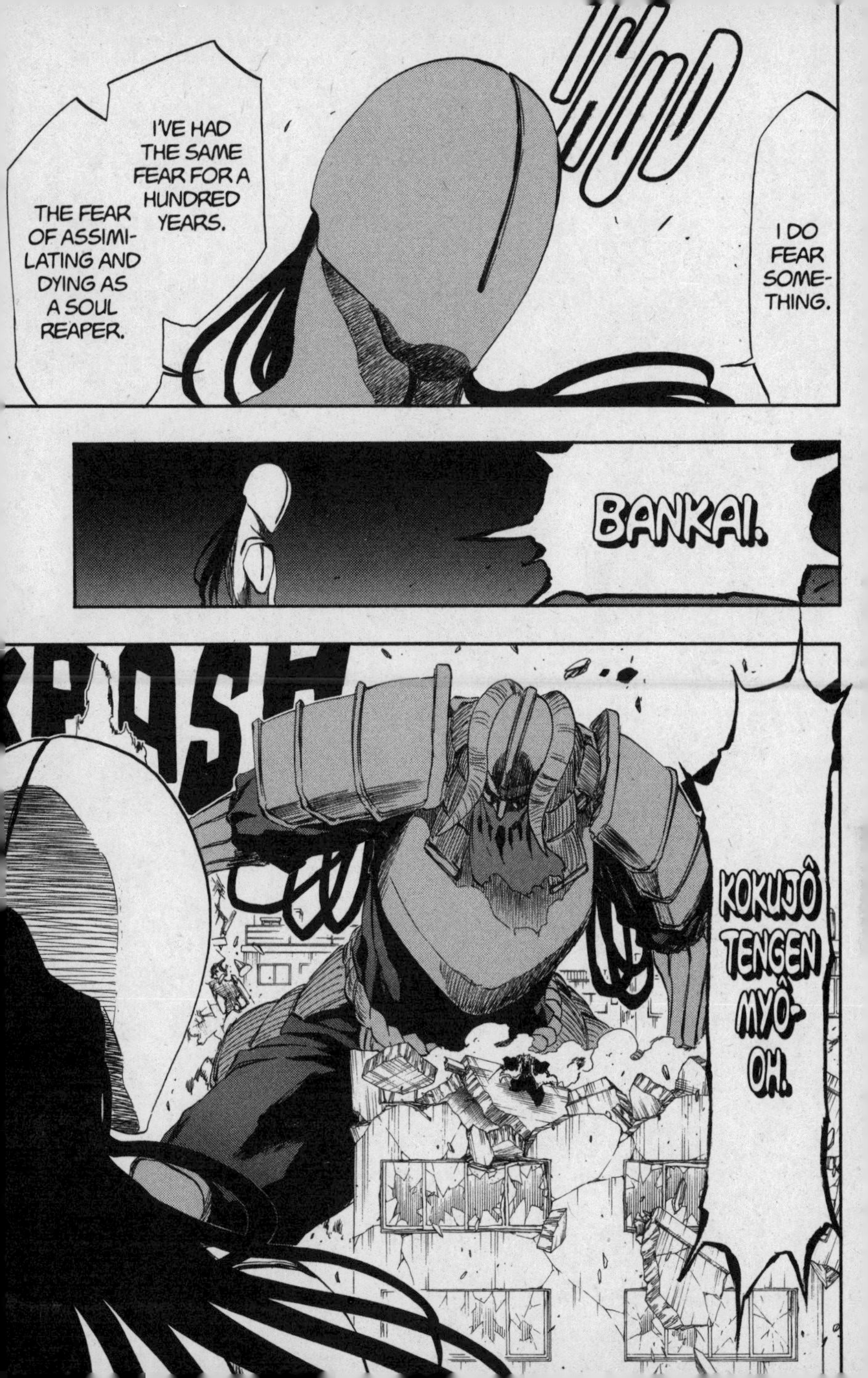
I DO FEAR SOME-THING.
I'VE HAD THE SAME FEAR FOR A HUNDRED YEARS.
THE FEAR OF ASSIMI-LATING AND DYING AS A SOUL REAPER.
BANKAI.
KOKUJÔ TENGEN MYÔ-OH.

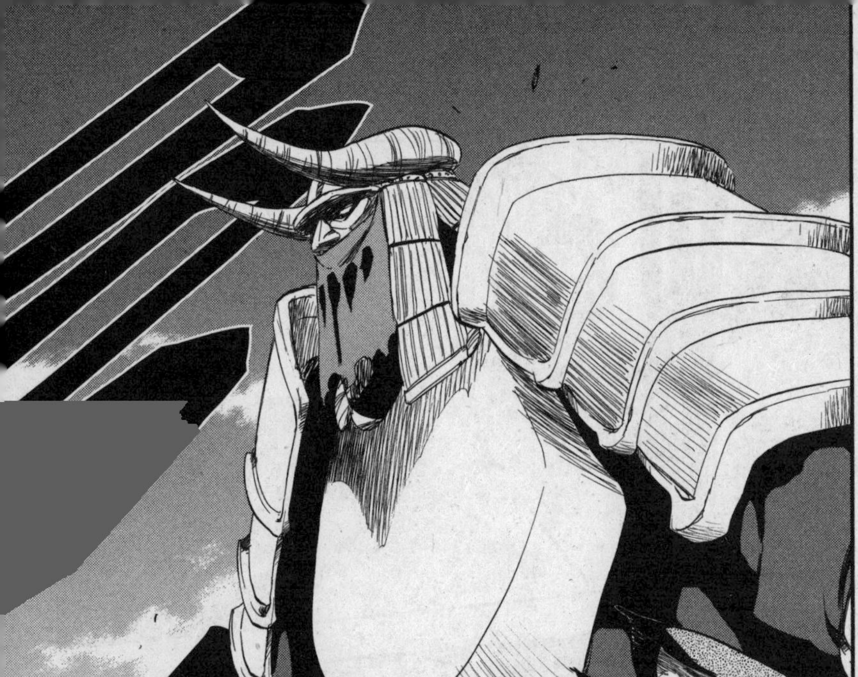

385. Vice It

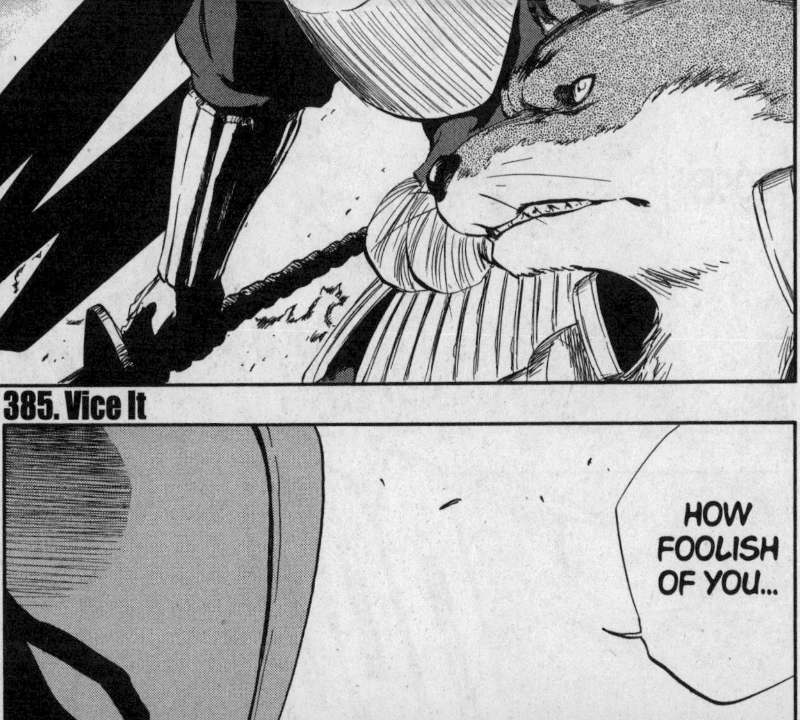
HOW FOOLISH OF YOU...

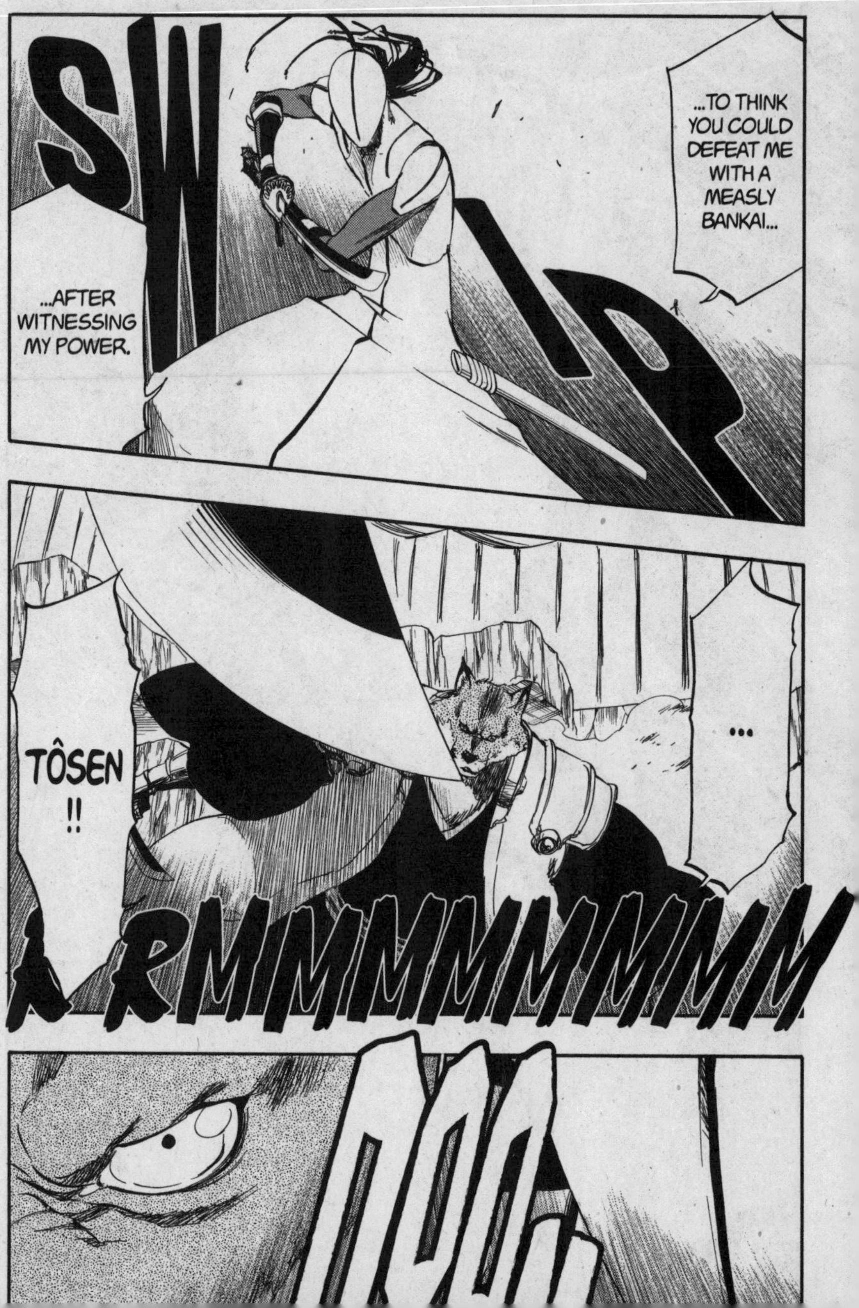

...TO THINK YOU COULD DEFEAT ME WITH A MEASLY BANKAI...
SWIP
...AFTER WITNESSING MY POWER.
...
TÔSEN !!
RMMMMMMMMM

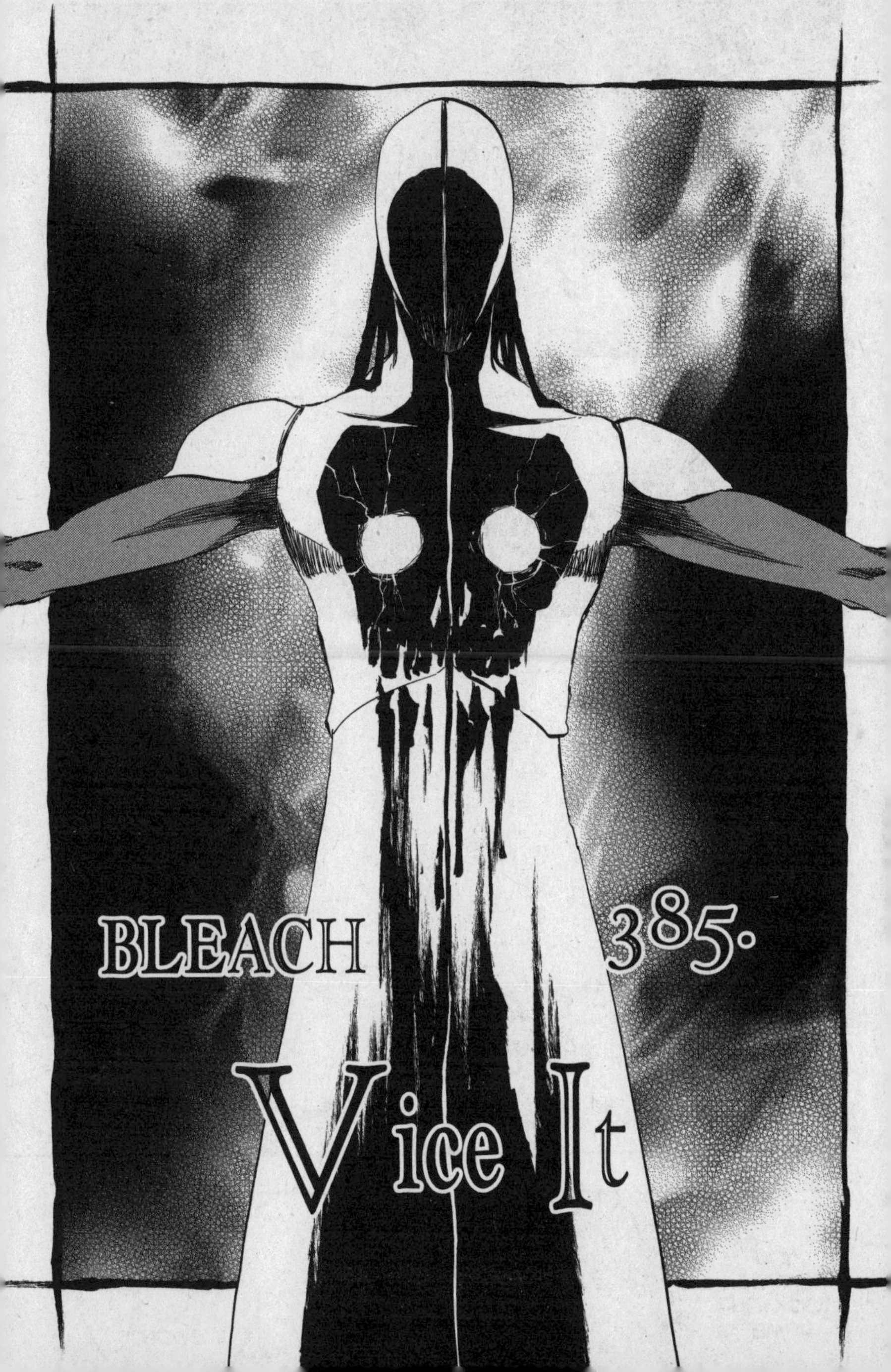
BLEACH 385.
Vice It

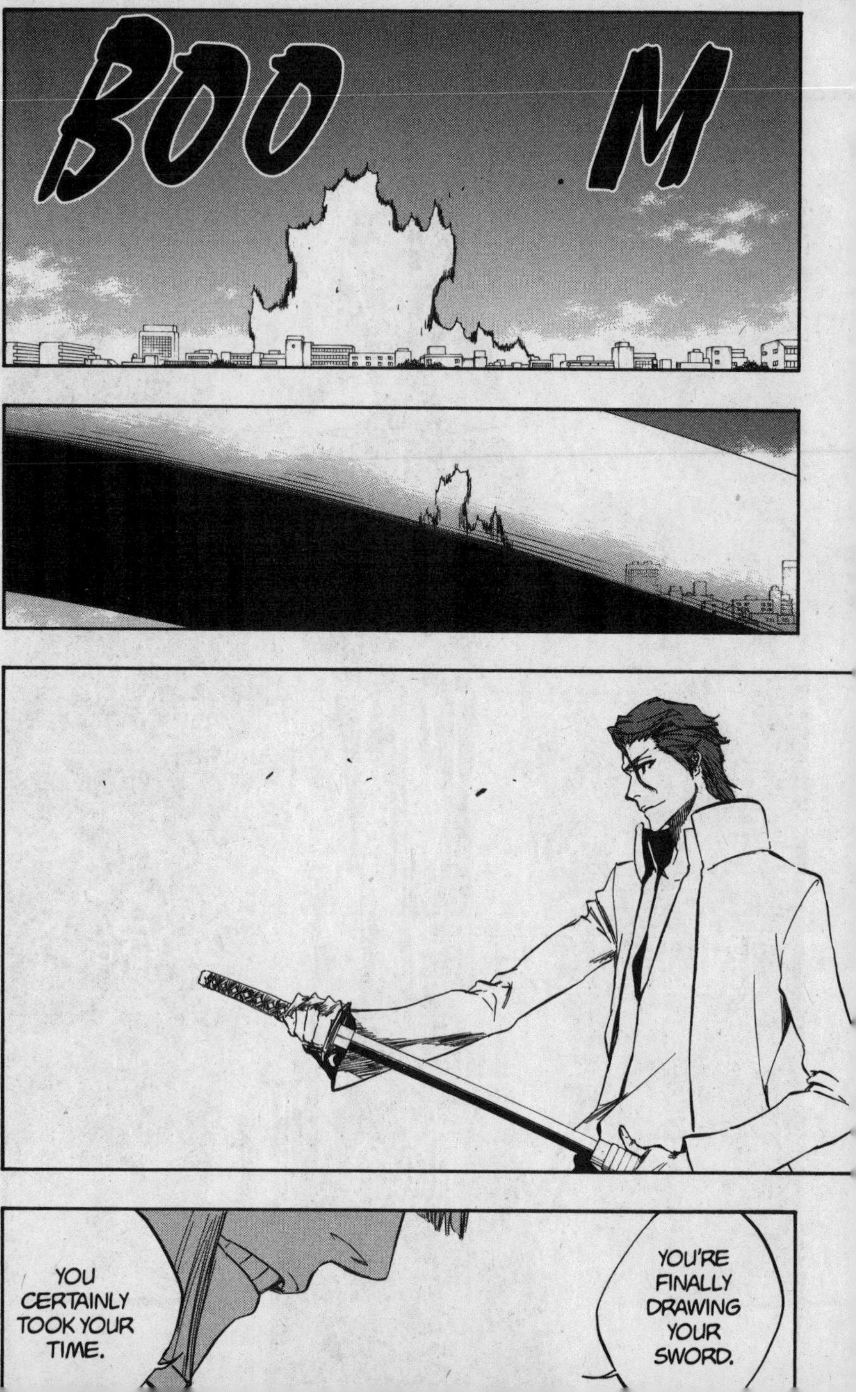
BOOM
YOU'RE FINALLY DRAWING YOUR SWORD.
YOU CERTAINLY TOOK YOUR TIME.

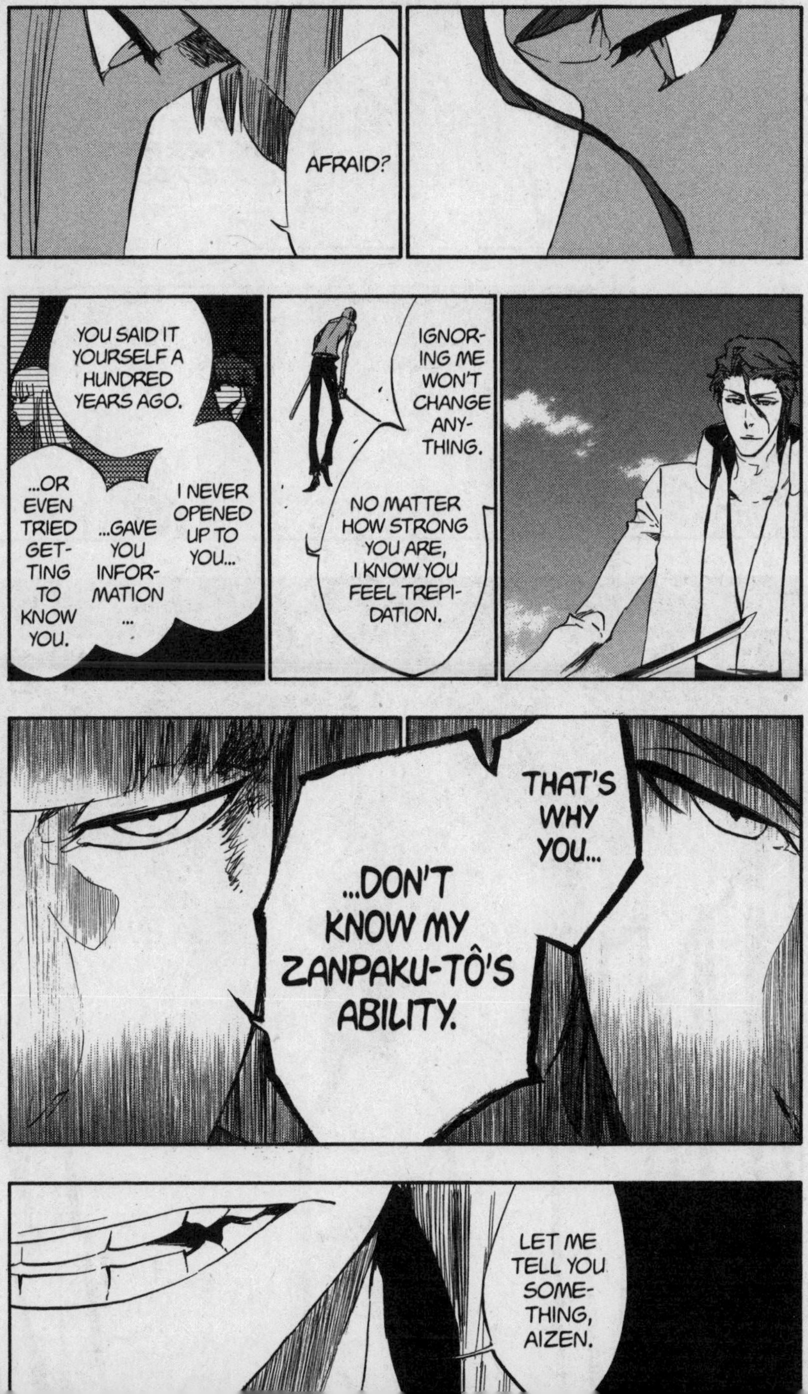
AFRAID?
IGNORING ME WON'T CHANGE ANYTHING.
NO MATTER HOW STRONG YOU ARE, I KNOW YOU FEEL TREPIDATION.
YOU SAID IT YOURSELF A HUNDRED YEARS AGO.
I NEVER OPENED UP TO YOU...
...GAVE YOU INFORMATION...
...OR EVEN TRIED GETTING TO KNOW YOU.
THAT'S WHY YOU...
...DON'T KNOW MY ZANPAKU-TÔ'S ABILITY.
LET ME TELL YOU SOMETHING, AIZEN.

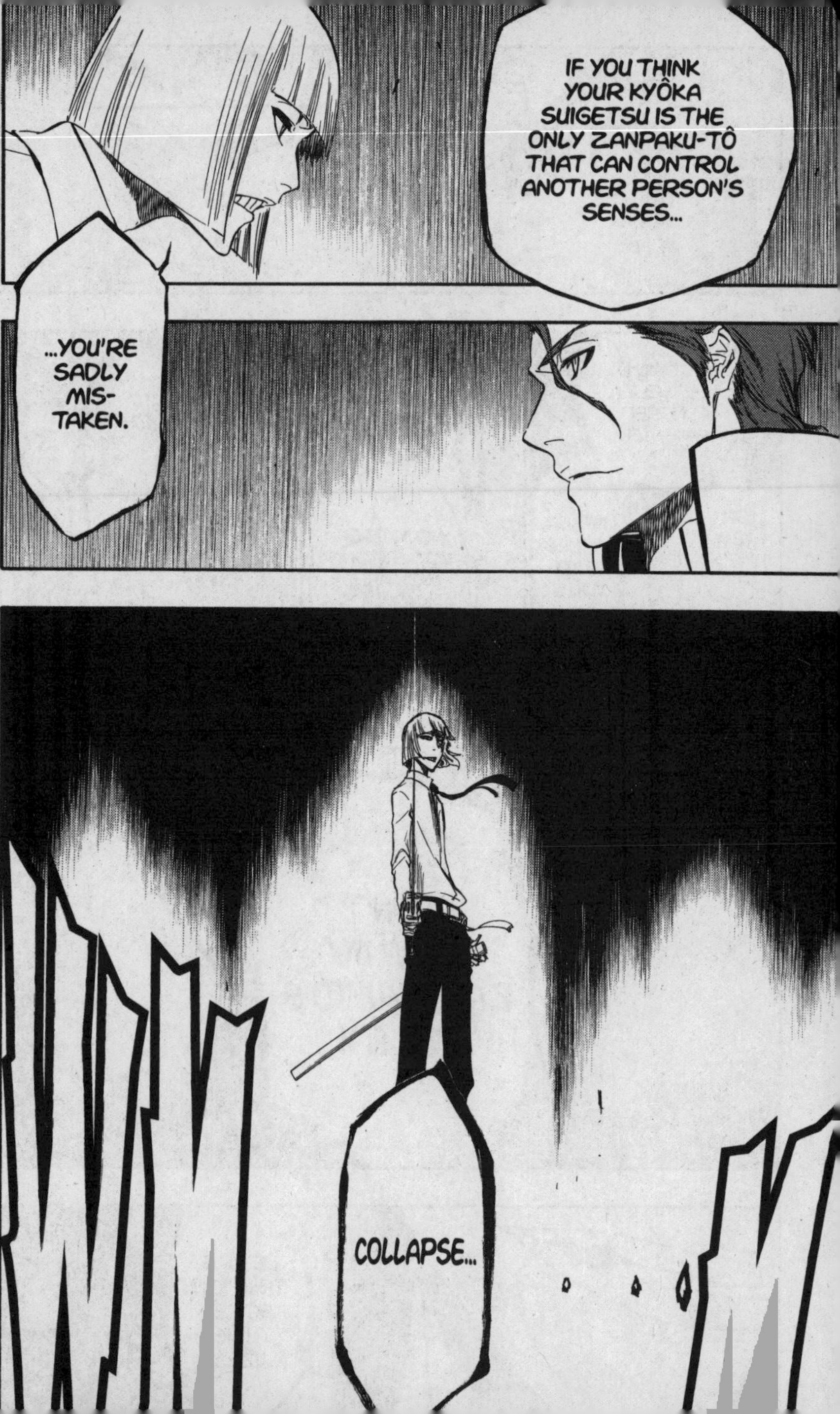
IF YOU THINK YOUR KYÔKA SUIGETSU IS THE ONLY ZANPAKU-TÔ THAT CAN CONTROL ANOTHER PERSON'S SENSES...
...YOU'RE SADLY MIS-TAKEN.
COLLAPSE...

...SAKA-NADE.
(COUNTER STROKE)

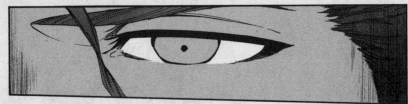

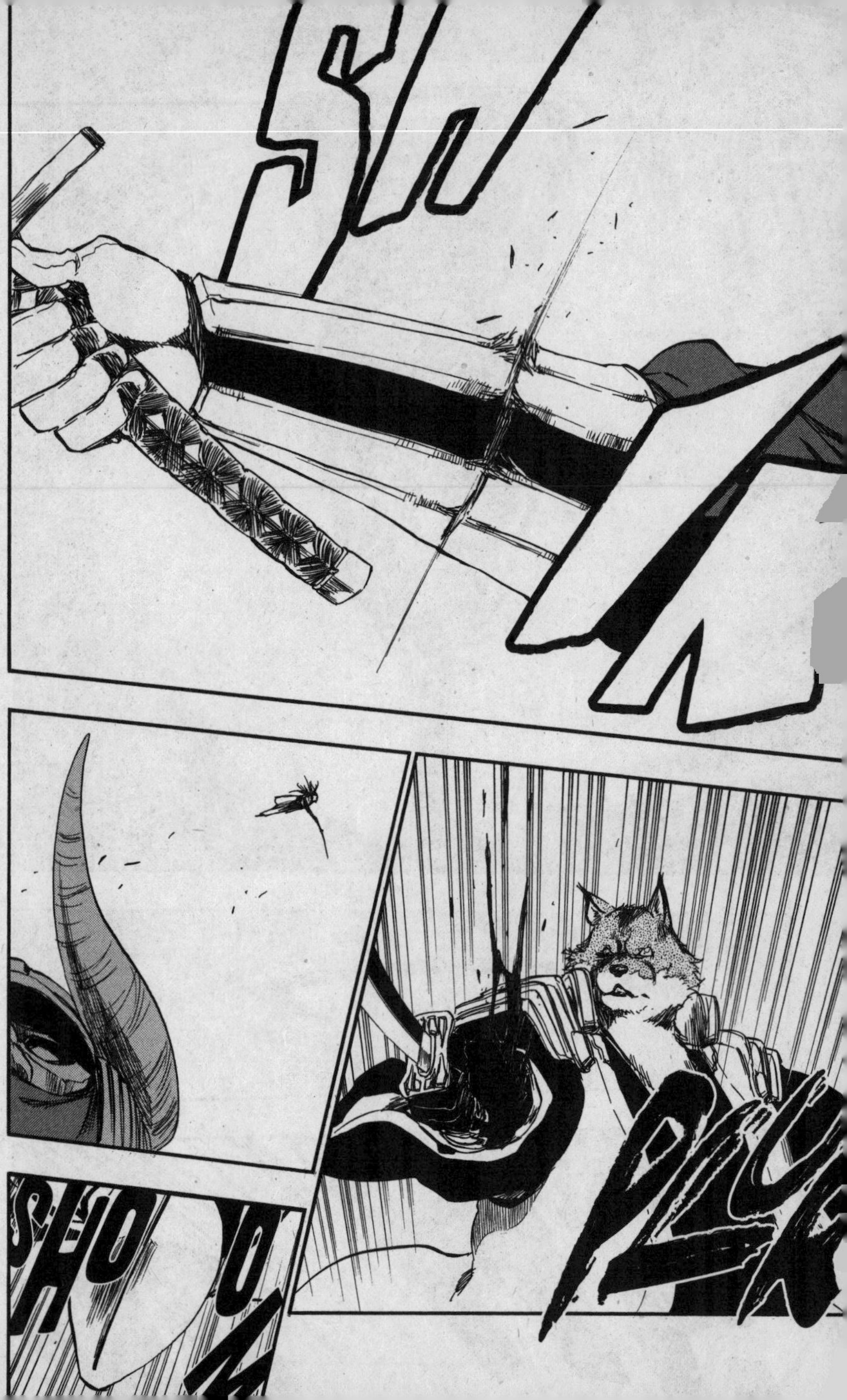
SHOOM

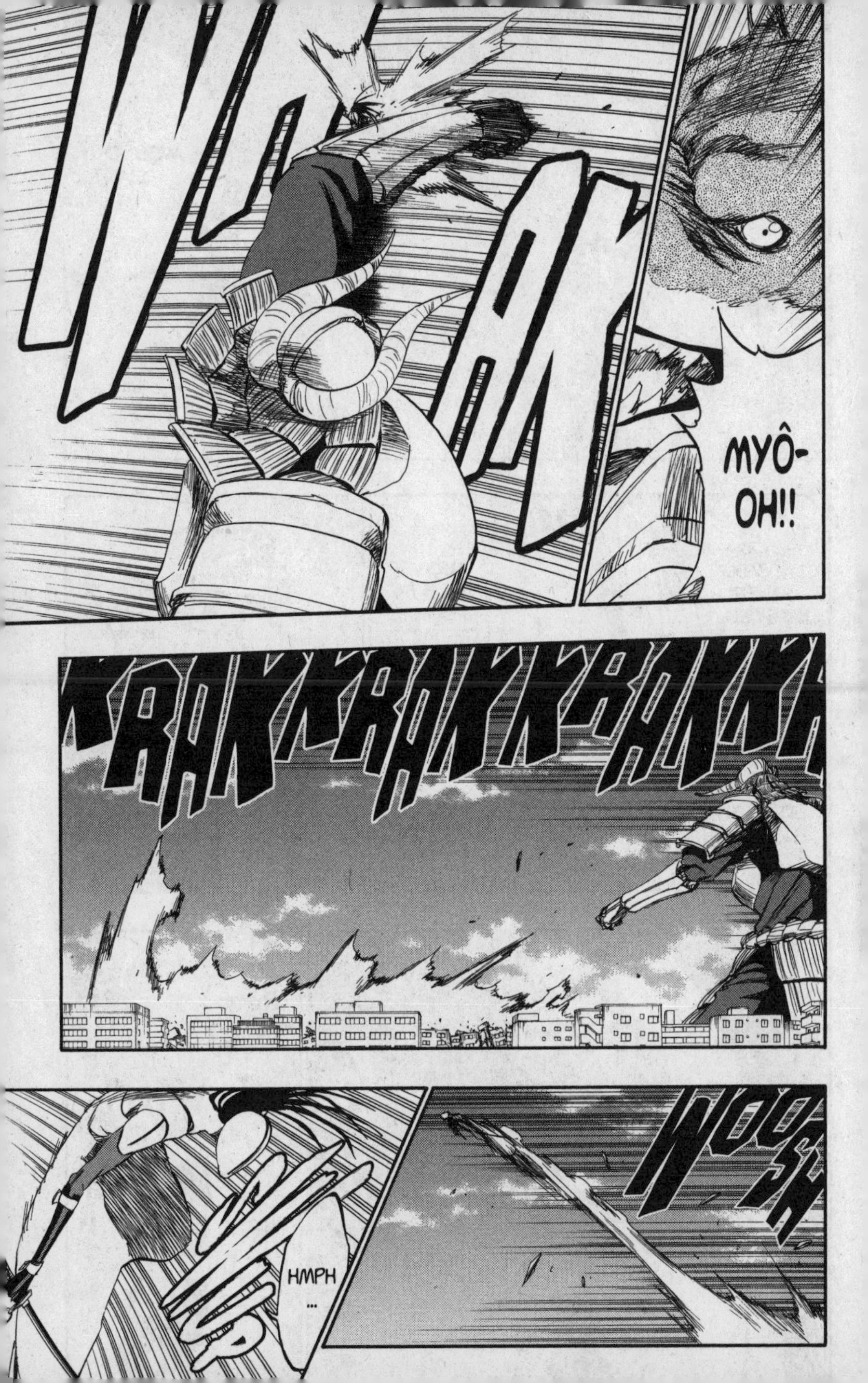
MYÔ-
OH!!
WOOSH
HMPH
...

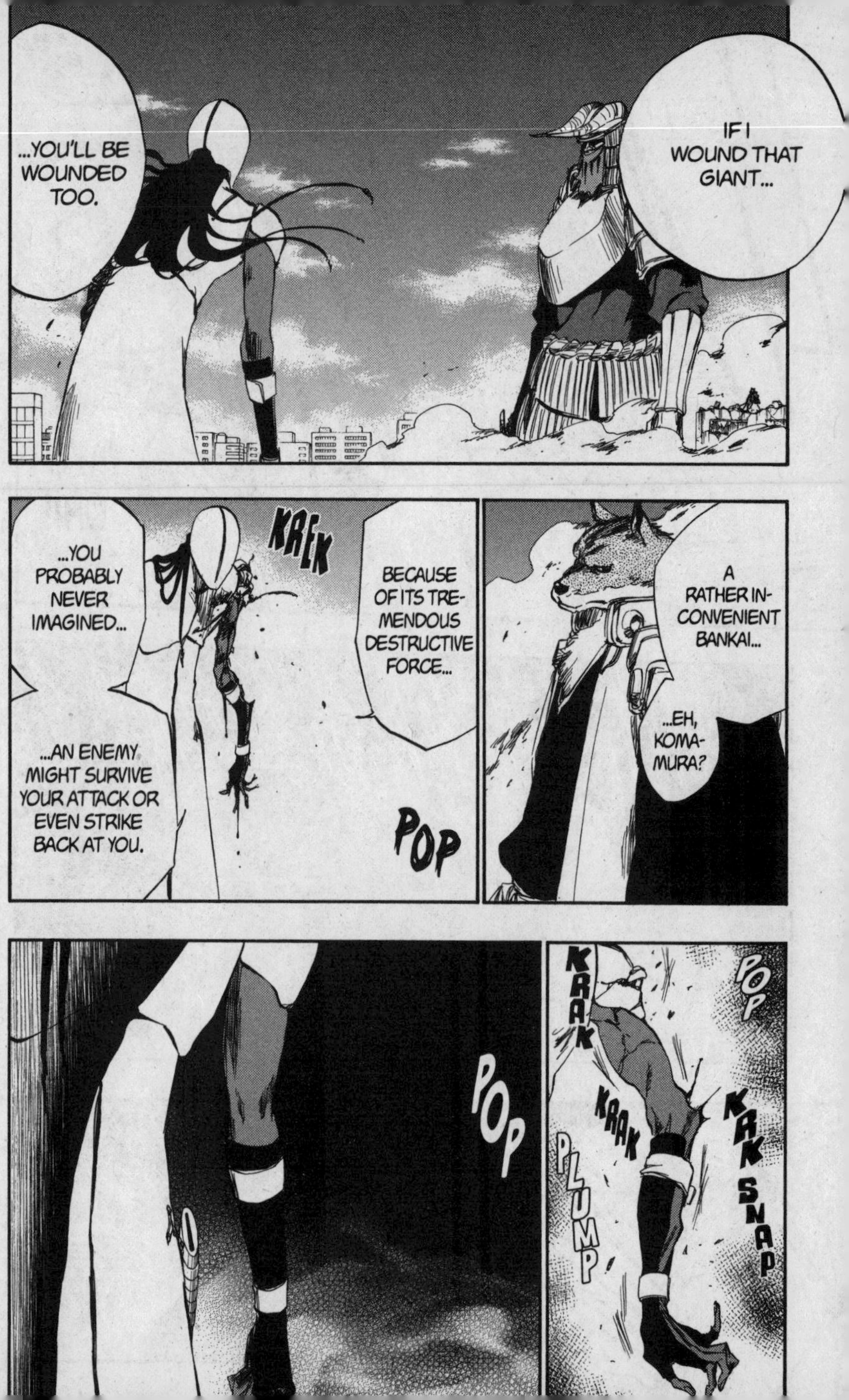
IF I WOUND THAT GIANT...
...YOU'LL BE WOUNDED TOO.
A RATHER INCONVENIENT BANKAI...
...EH, KOMAMURA?
BECAUSE OF ITS TREMENDOUS DESTRUCTIVE FORCE...
KREK
...YOU PROBABLY NEVER IMAGINED...
...AN ENEMY MIGHT SURVIVE YOUR ATTACK OR EVEN STRIKE BACK AT YOU.
POP
POP
KRAK
KRAAK
KRAK
SNAP
PLUMP
POP

READ THIS WAY

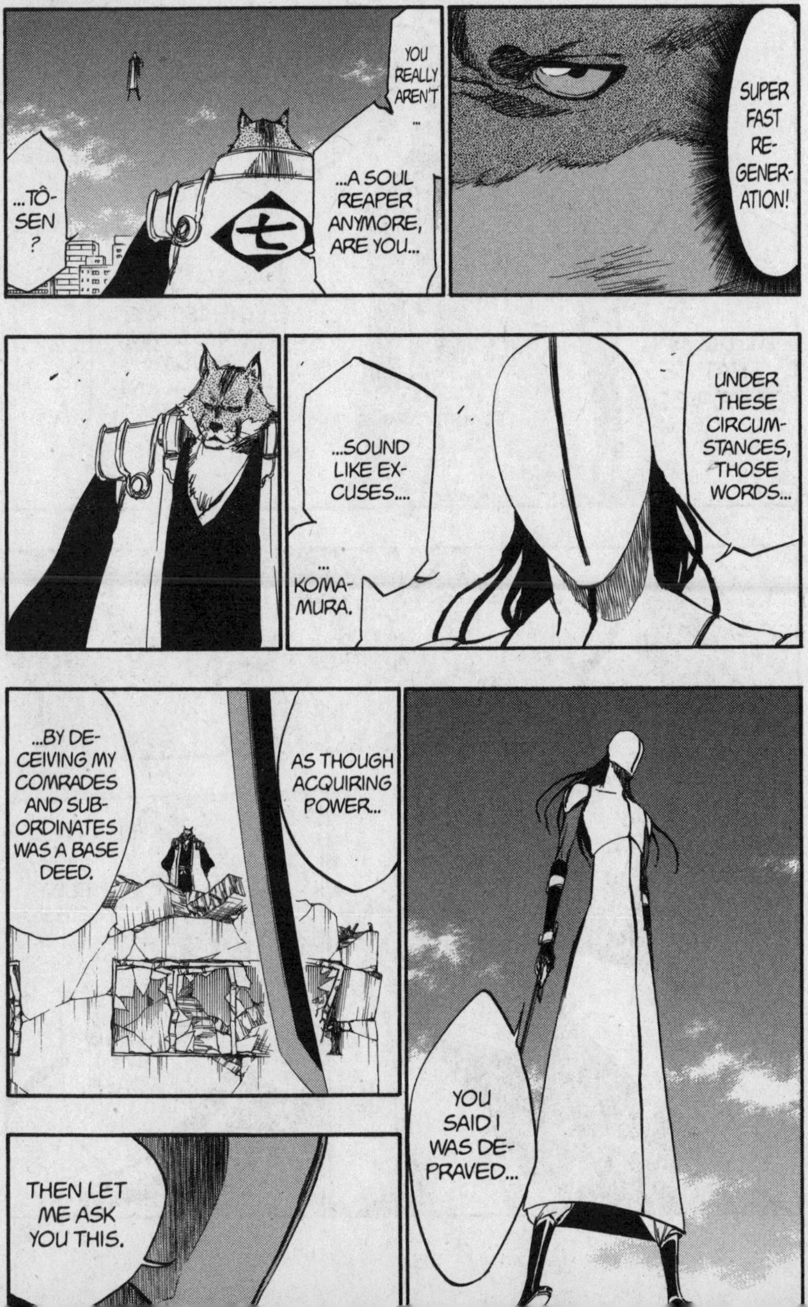
SUPER FAST REGENERATION!
YOU REALLY AREN'T ...
...A SOUL REAPER ANYMORE, ARE YOU...
...TÔSEN?
UNDER THESE CIRCUMSTANCES, THOSE WORDS...
...SOUND LIKE EXCUSES....
...KOMAMURA.
YOU SAID I WAS DEPRAVED...
AS THOUGH ACQUIRING POWER...
...BY DECEIVING MY COMRADES AND SUBORDINATES WAS A BASE DEED.
THEN LET ME ASK YOU THIS.

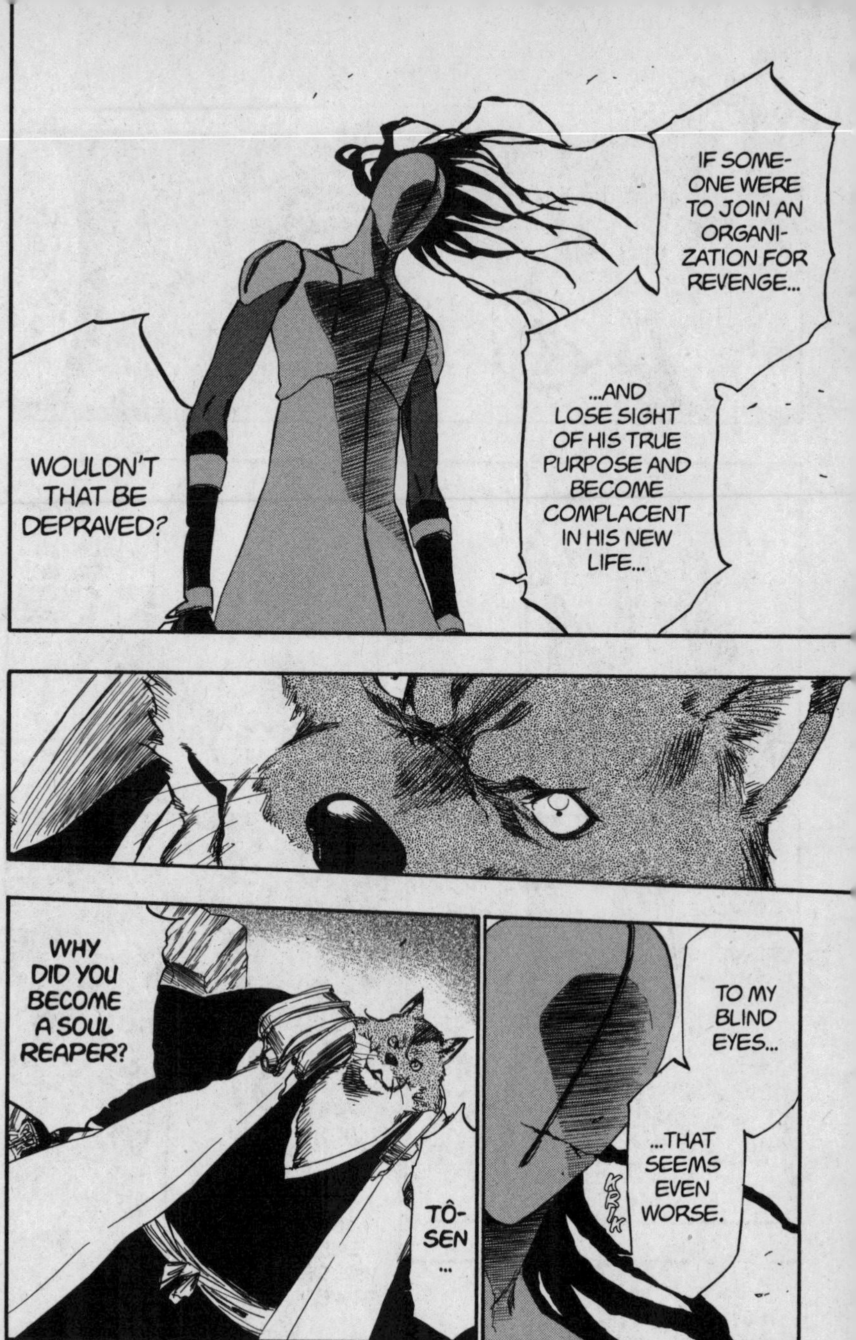
IF SOMEONE WERE TO JOIN AN ORGANIZATION FOR REVENGE...
...AND LOSE SIGHT OF HIS TRUE PURPOSE AND BECOME COMPLACENT IN HIS NEW LIFE...
WOULDN'T THAT BE DEPRAVED?
TO MY BLIND EYES...
...THAT SEEMS EVEN WORSE.
KRIK
WHY DID YOU BECOME A SOUL REAPER?
TÔSEN...

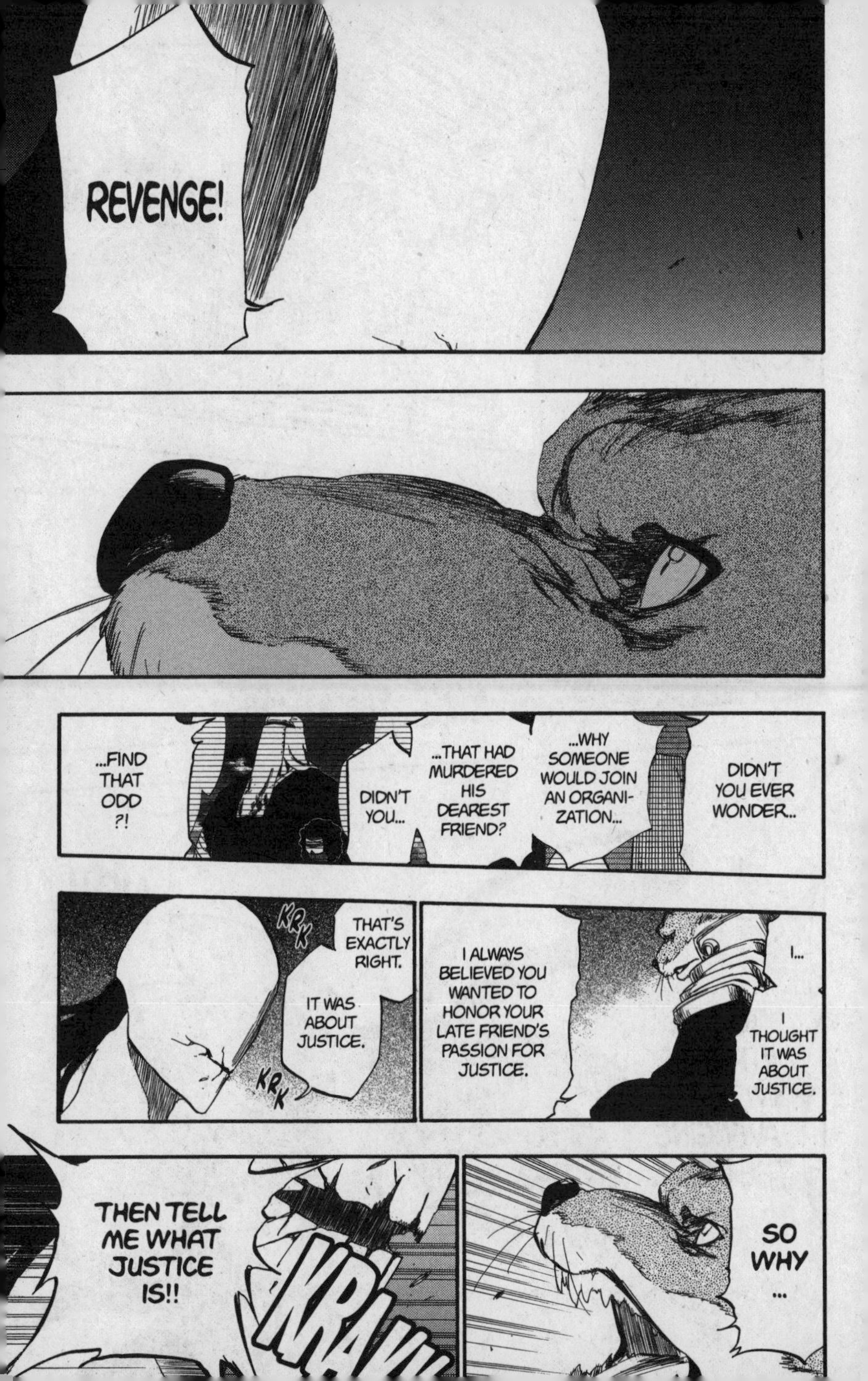
REVENGE!
DIDN'T YOU EVER WONDER...
...WHY SOMEONE WOULD JOIN AN ORGANIZATION...
...THAT HAD MURDERED HIS DEAREST FRIEND?
DIDN'T YOU...
...FIND THAT ODD?!
I...
I THOUGHT IT WAS ABOUT JUSTICE.
I ALWAYS BELIEVED YOU WANTED TO HONOR YOUR LATE FRIEND'S PASSION FOR JUSTICE.
KRK
THAT'S EXACTLY RIGHT.
IT WAS ABOUT JUSTICE.
KRK
SO WHY...
THEN TELL ME WHAT JUSTICE IS!!

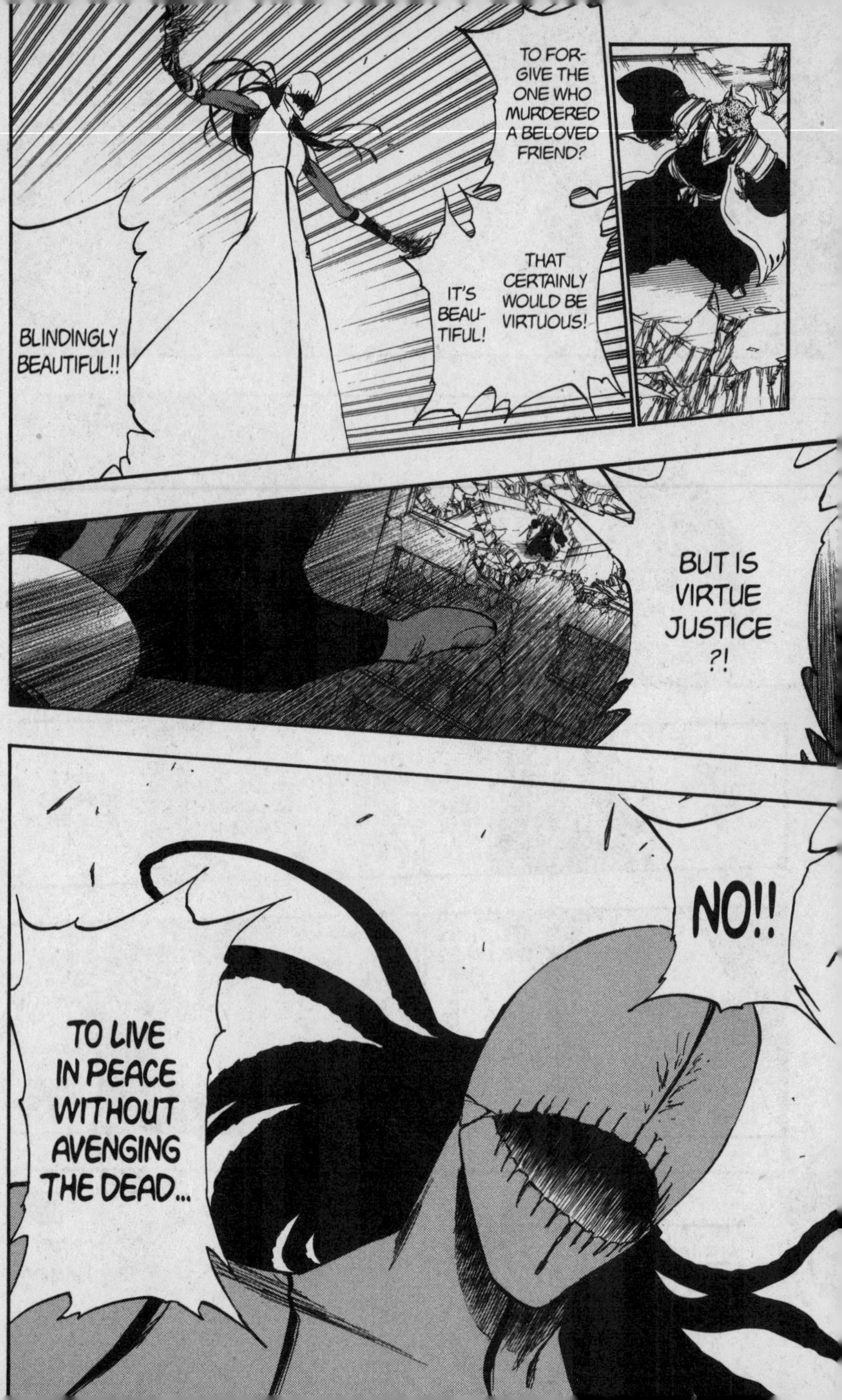
TO FORGIVE THE ONE WHO MURDERED A BELOVED FRIEND?
THAT CERTAINLY WOULD BE VIRTUOUS!
IT'S BEAUTIFUL!
BLINDINGLY BEAUTIFUL!!
BUT IS VIRTUE JUSTICE ?!
NO!!
TO LIVE IN PEACE WITHOUT AVENGING THE DEAD...

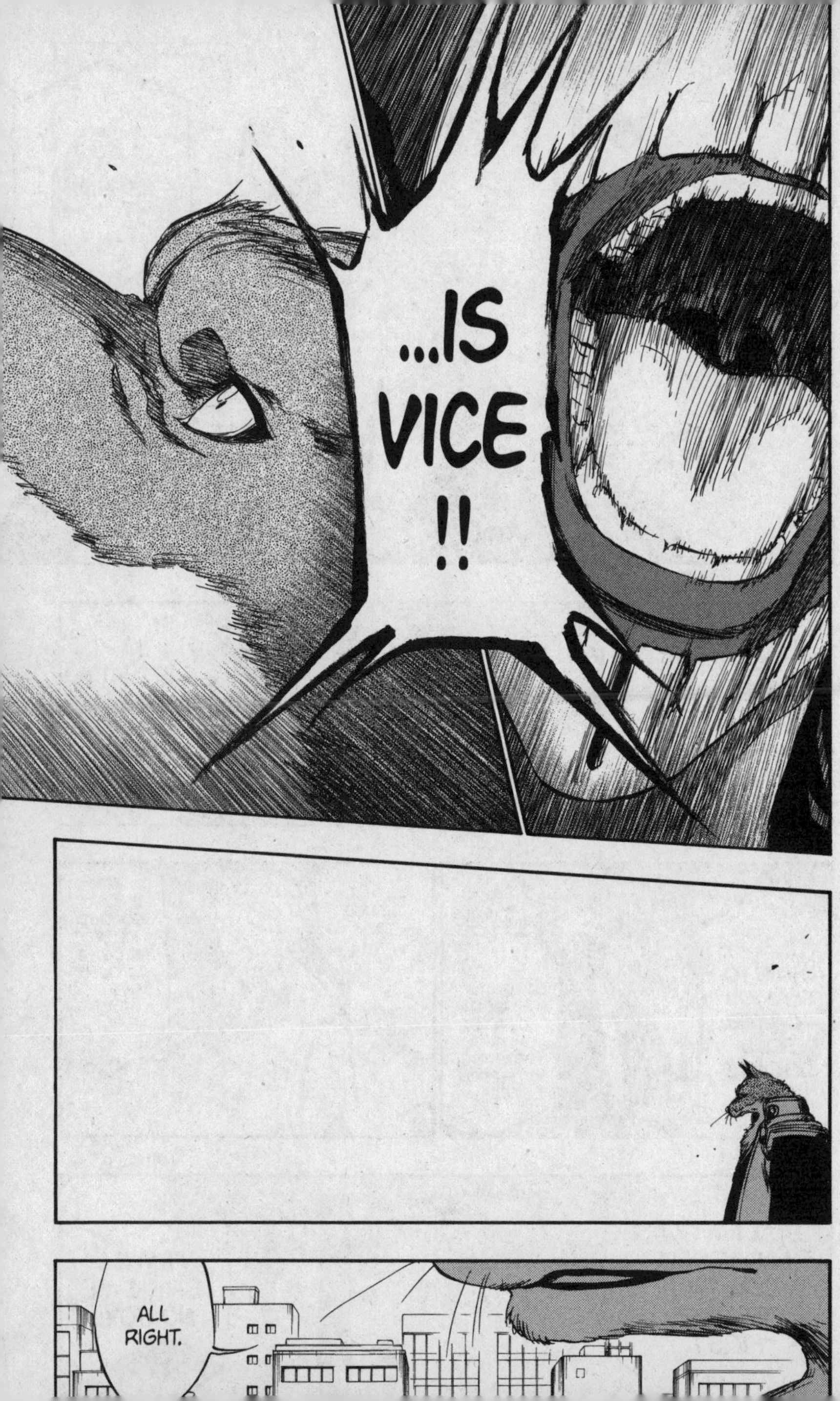
...IS VICE !!
ALL RIGHT.

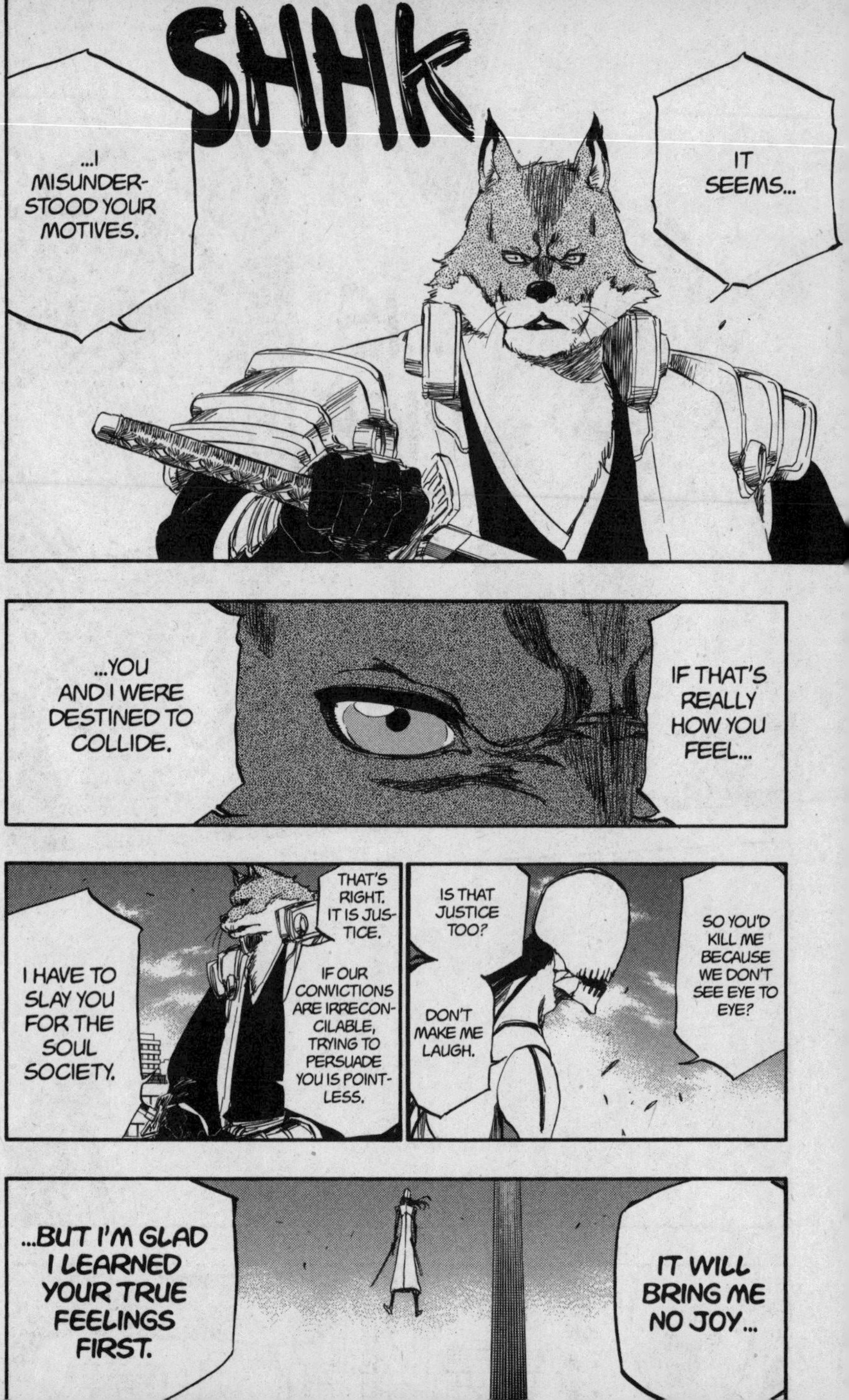
SHHK
IT SEEMS...
...I MISUNDERSTOOD YOUR MOTIVES.
IF THAT'S REALLY HOW YOU FEEL...
...YOU AND I WERE DESTINED TO COLLIDE.
SO YOU'D KILL ME BECAUSE WE DON'T SEE EYE TO EYE?
IS THAT JUSTICE TOO?
DON'T MAKE ME LAUGH.
THAT'S RIGHT. IT IS JUSTICE.
IF OUR CONVICTIONS ARE IRRECONCILABLE, TRYING TO PERSUADE YOU IS POINTLESS.
I HAVE TO SLAY YOU FOR THE SOUL SOCIETY.
IT WILL BRING ME NO JOY...
...BUT I'M GLAD I LEARNED YOUR TRUE FEELINGS FIRST.

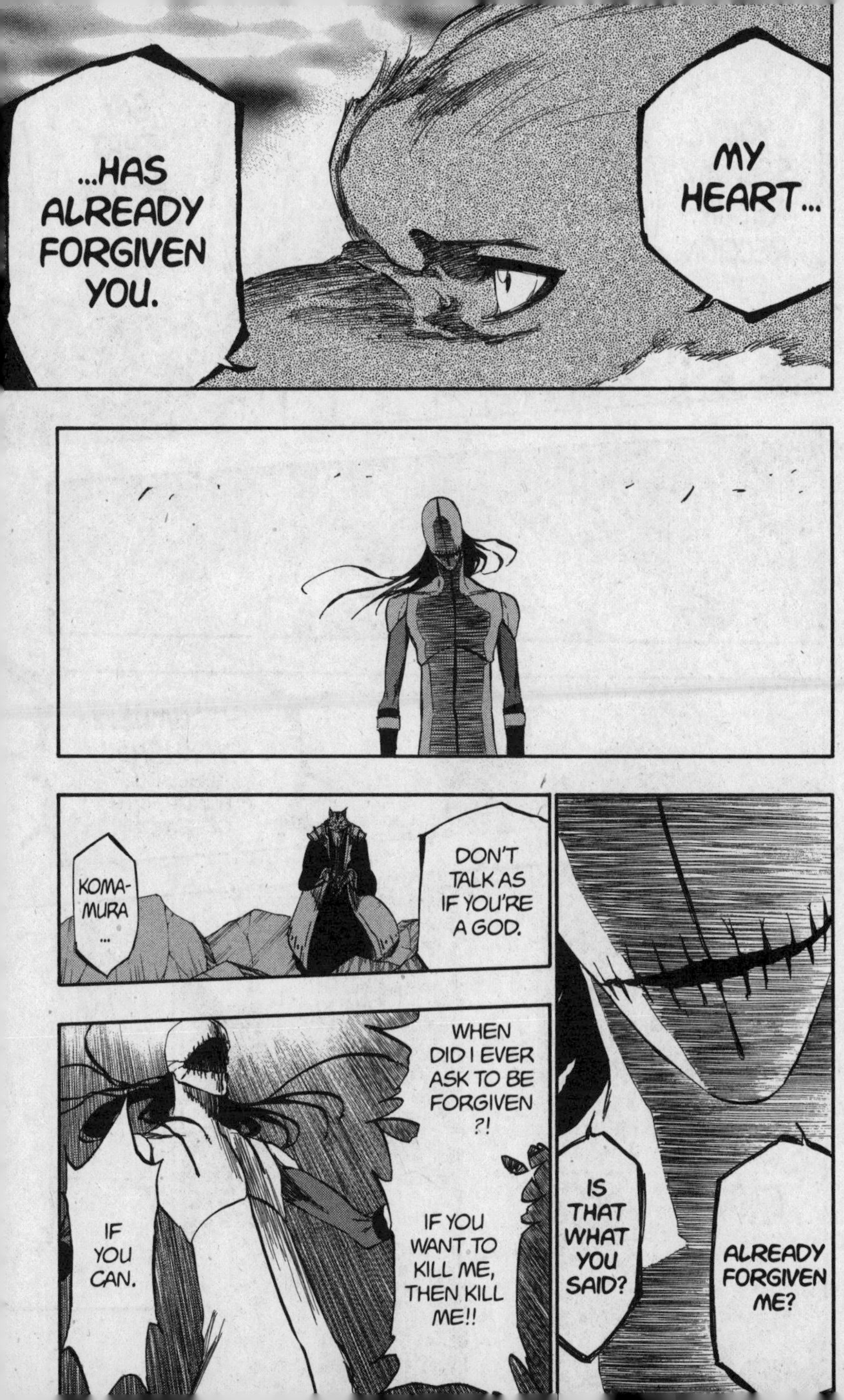
MY HEART...
...HAS ALREADY FORGIVEN YOU.
ALREADY FORGIVEN ME?
IS THAT WHAT YOU SAID?
DON'T TALK AS IF YOU'RE A GOD.
KOMAMURA...
WHEN DID I EVER ASK TO BE FORGIVEN?!
IF YOU WANT TO KILL ME, THEN KILL ME!!
IF YOU CAN.

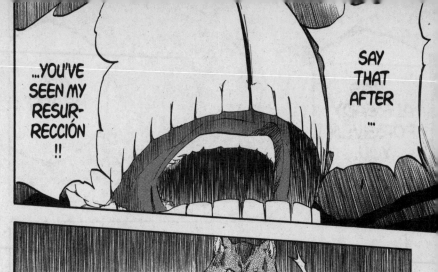

SAY THAT AFTER...

...YOU'VE SEEN MY RESUR-RECCIÓN!!

SUZUMUSHI HYAKUSHIKI. (BELL BUG HUNDREDTH CEREMONY)

GRILLAR GRILLO. (CRAZED CRICKET)

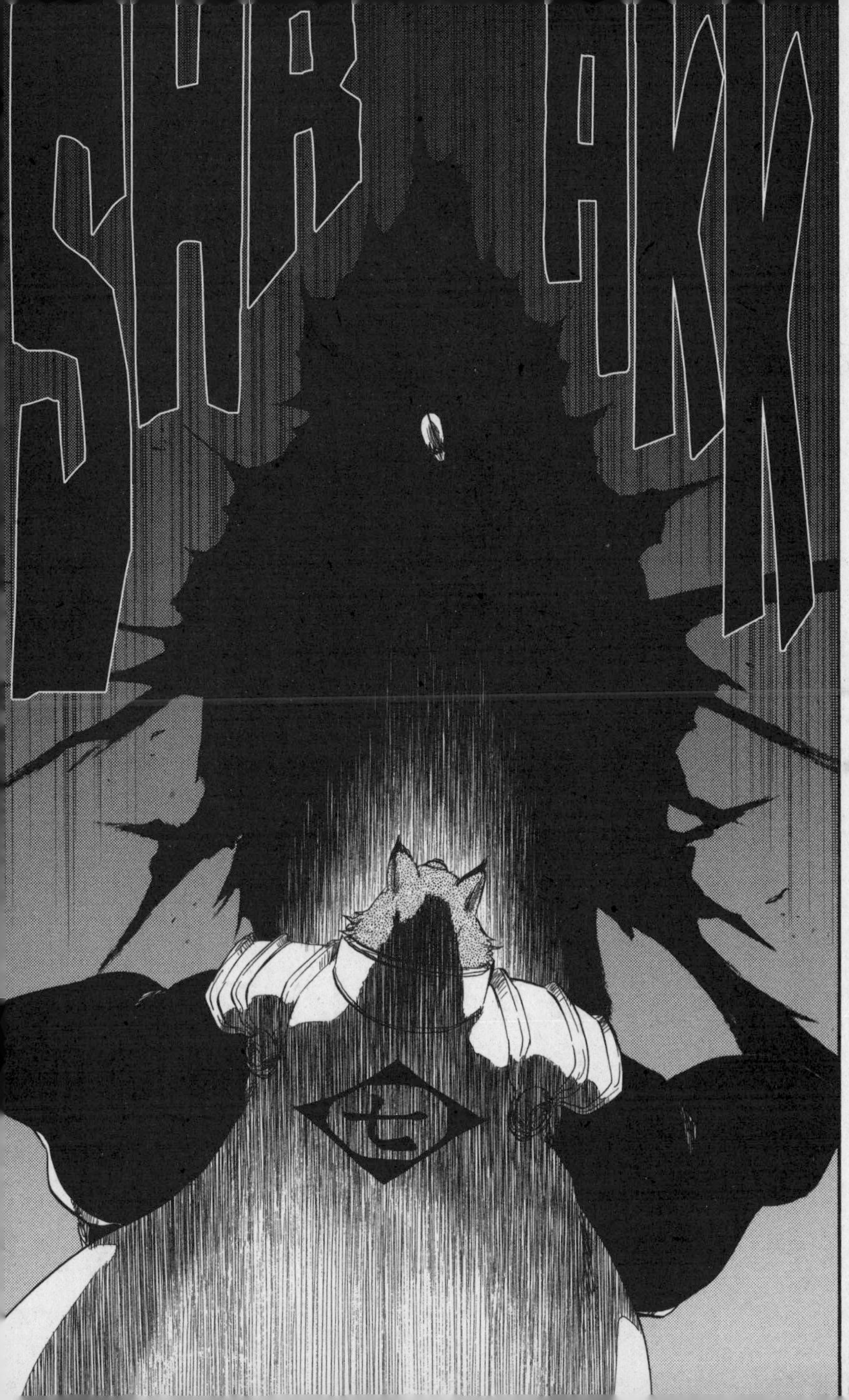
SHRAKK

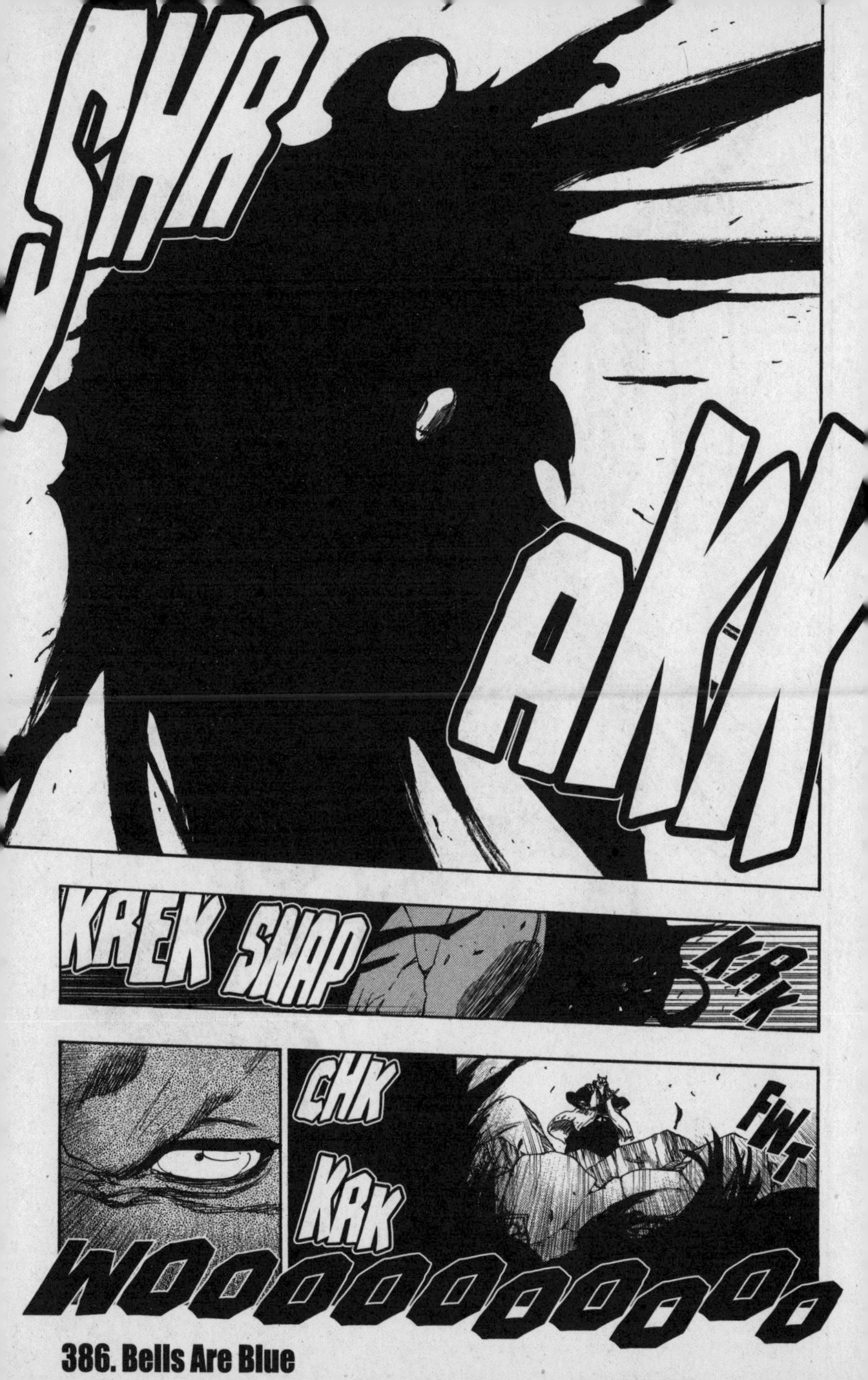
SHR
AKK
KRK
SNAP
KREK
FWT
CHK
KRK
WOOOOOOOOOO

386. Bells Are Blue

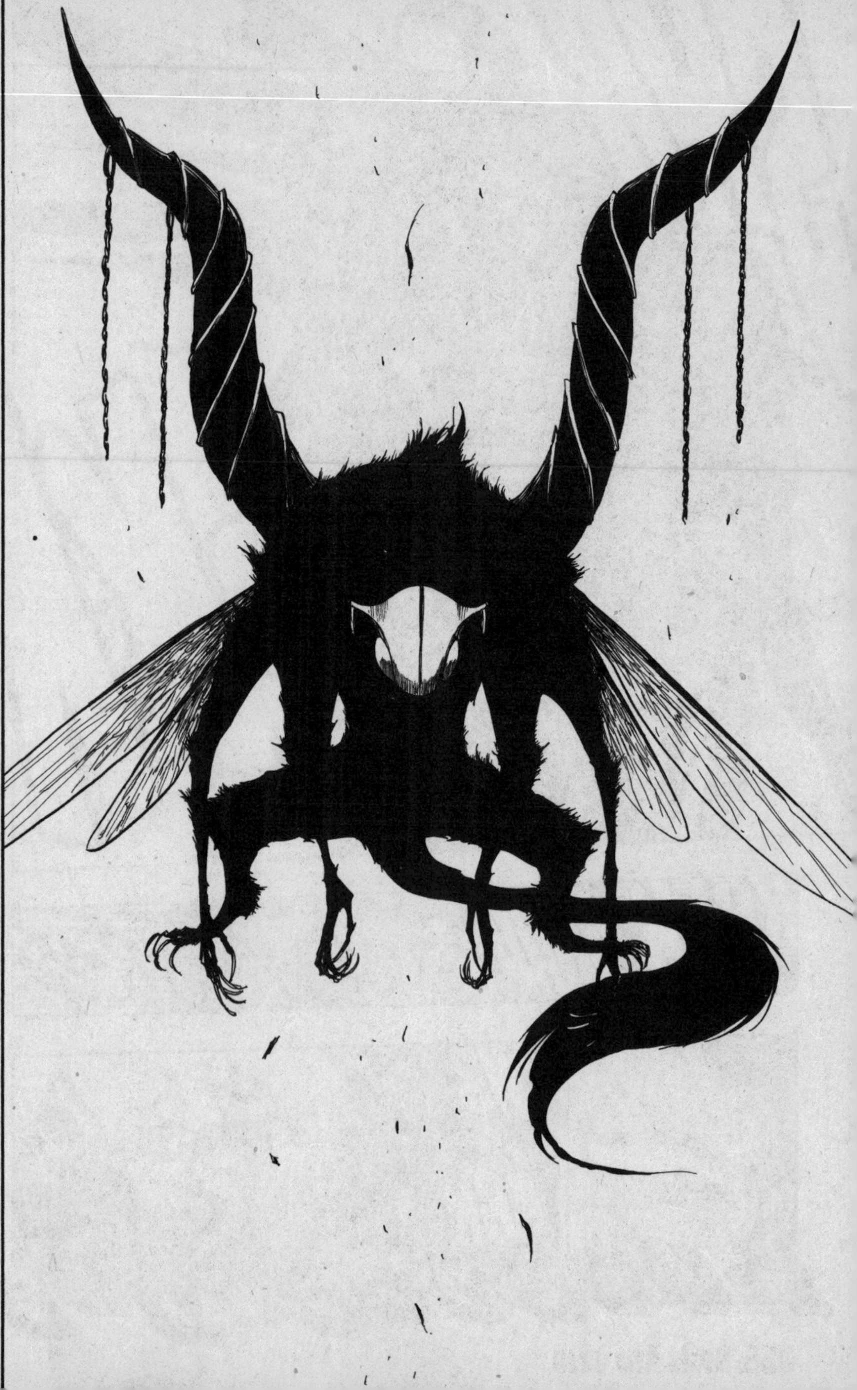

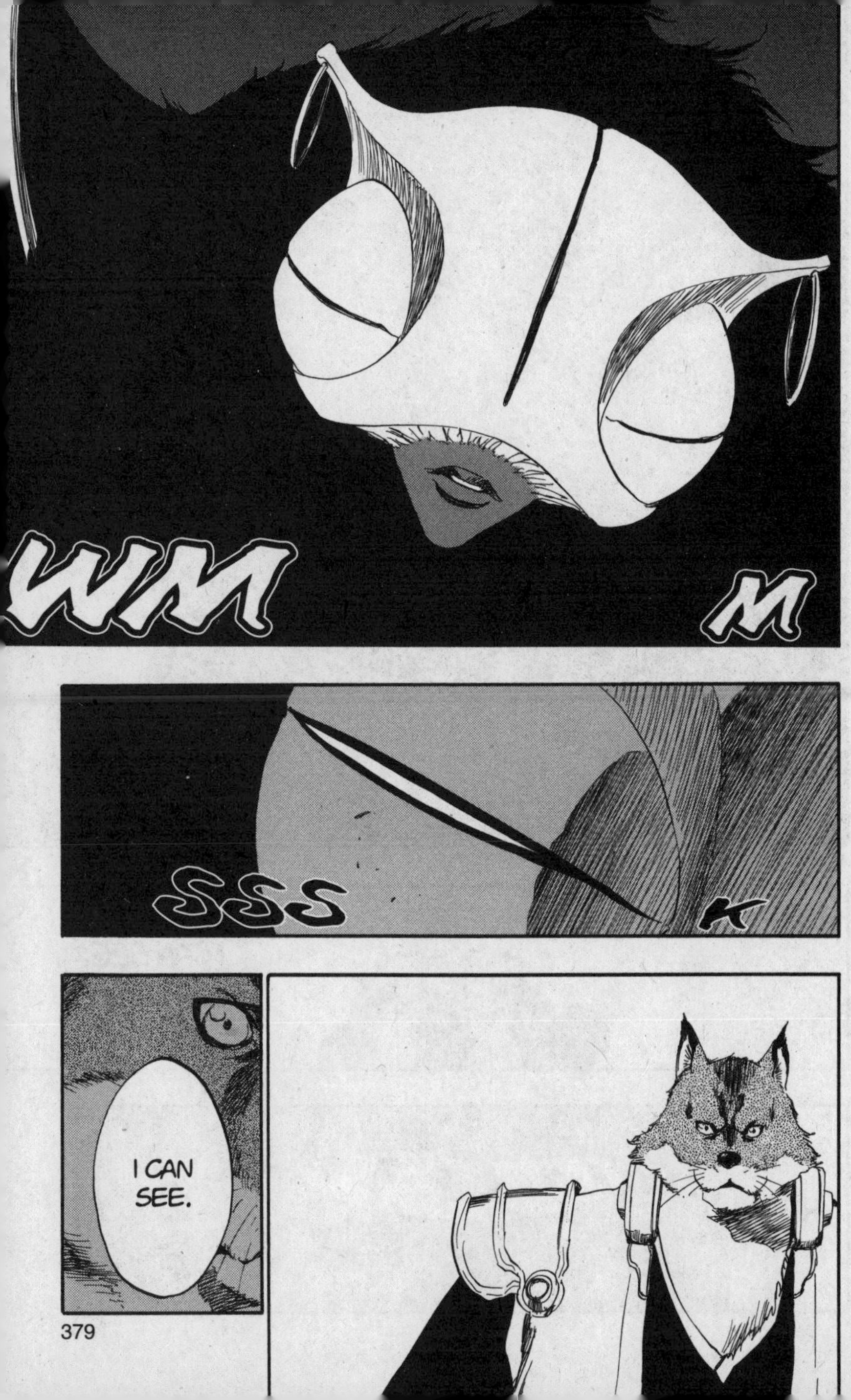
WM
M
SSS
K
I CAN SEE.

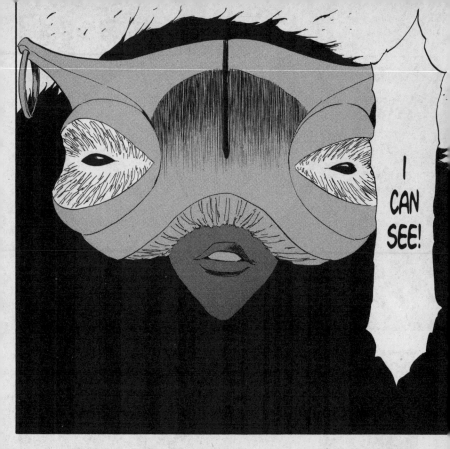

I CAN SEE!

I CAN SEE, KOMAMURA!!

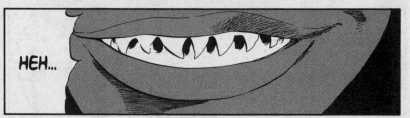

HEH...

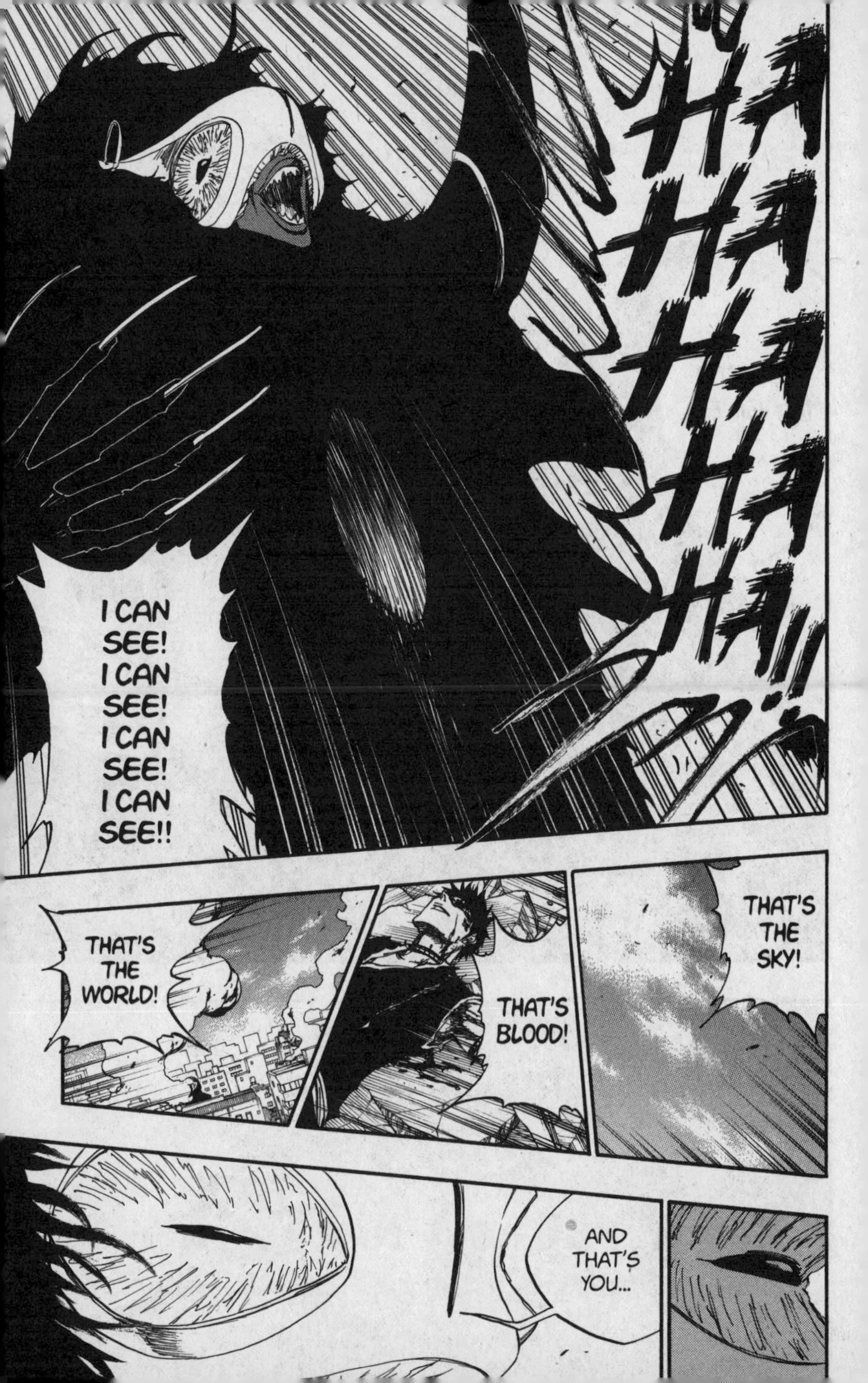
I CAN SEE! I CAN SEE! I CAN SEE! I CAN SEE!!
THAT'S THE SKY!
THAT'S BLOOD!
THAT'S THE WORLD!
AND THAT'S YOU...

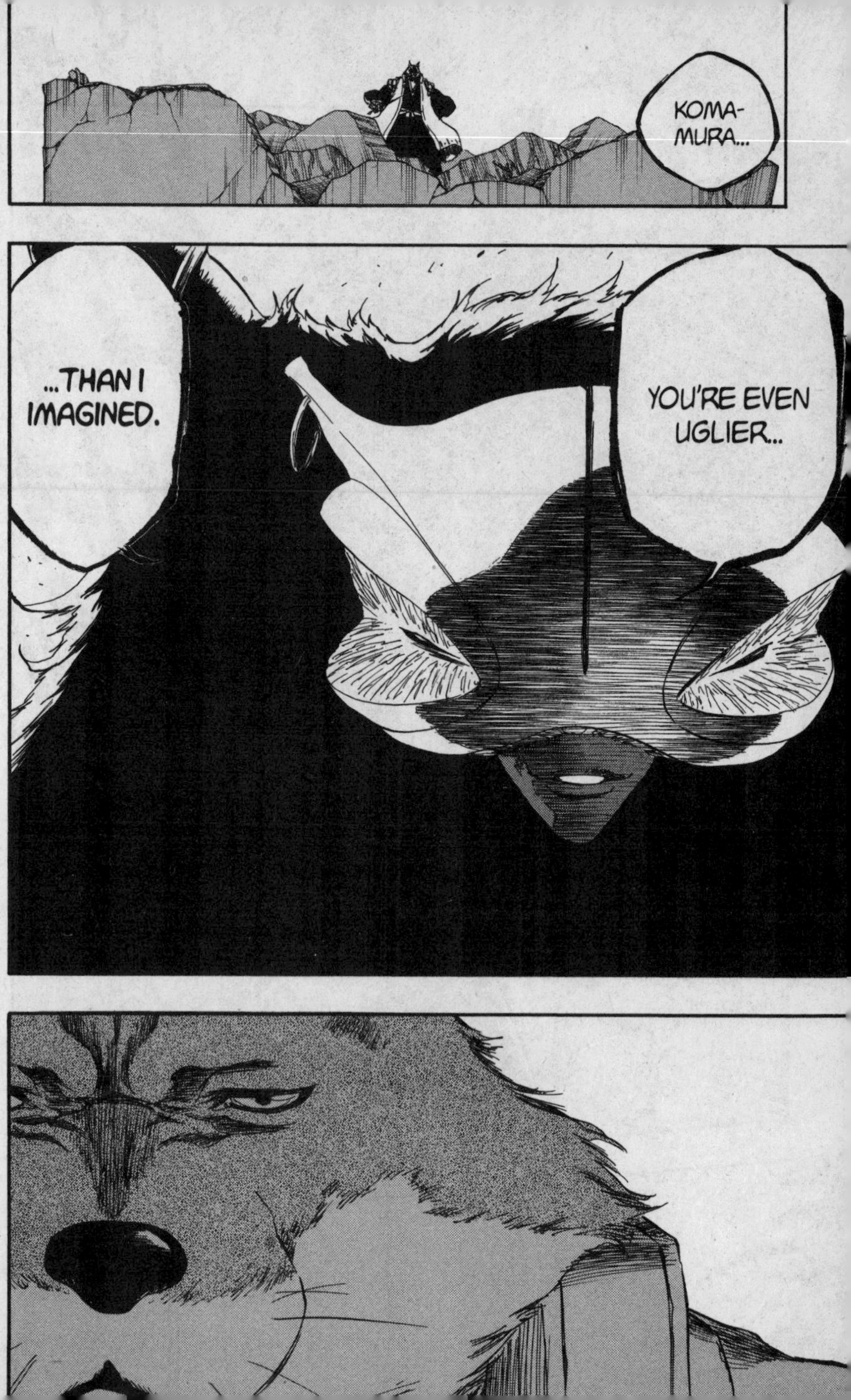
KOMA-
MURA...
YOU'RE EVEN UGLIER...
...THAN I IMAGINED.

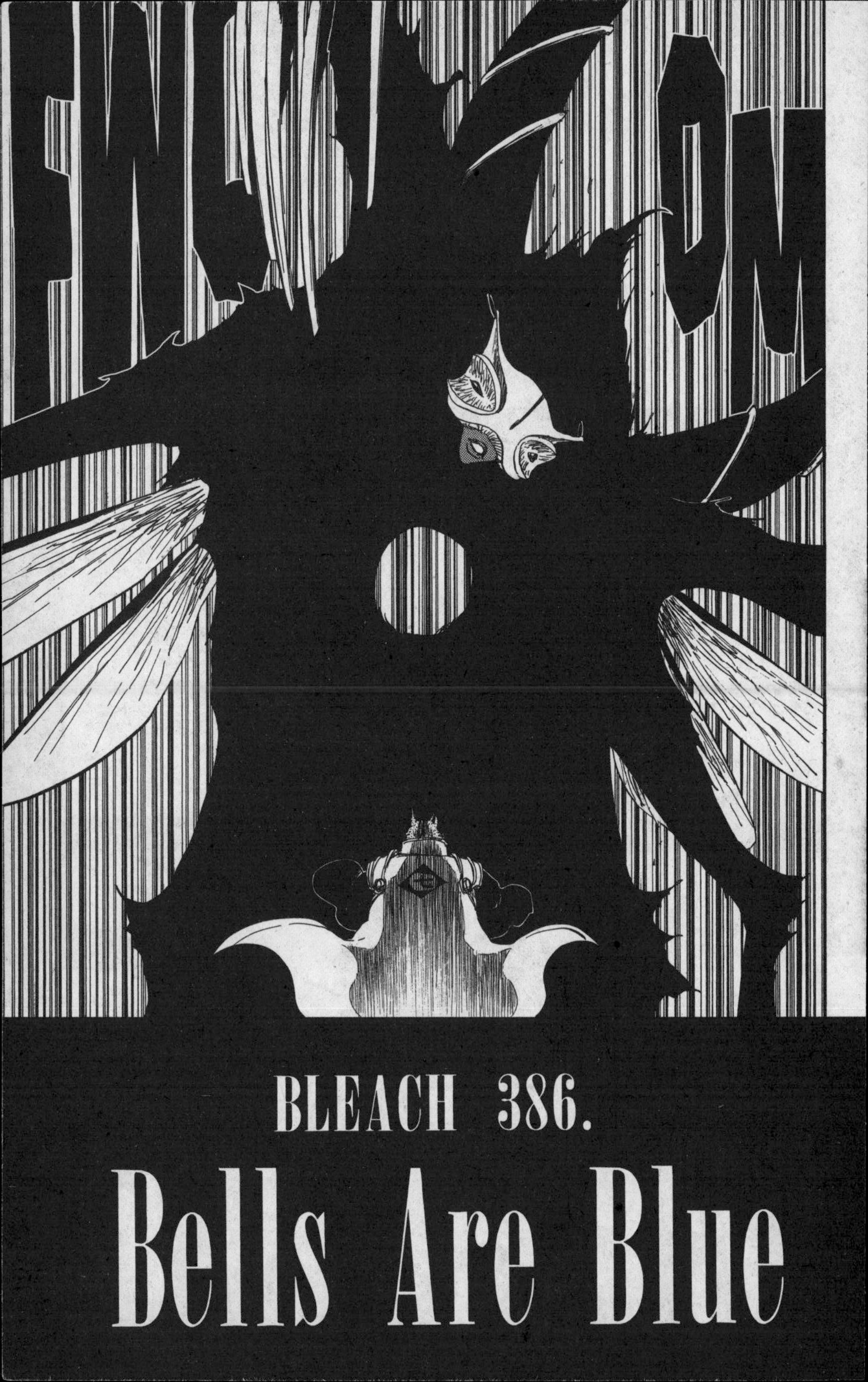

BLEACH 386.

Bells Are Blue

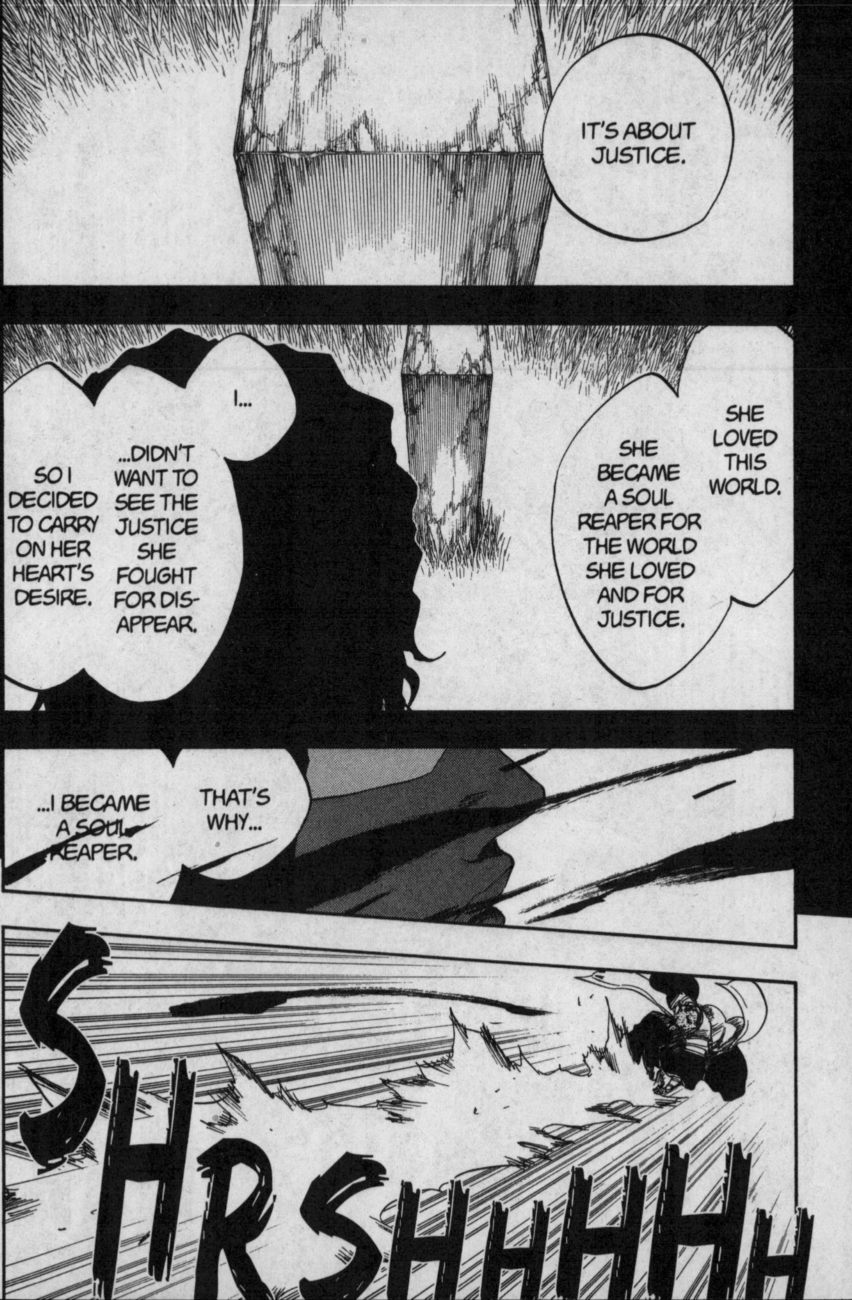
IT'S ABOUT JUSTICE.
SHE LOVED THIS WORLD.
SHE BECAME A SOUL REAPER FOR THE WORLD SHE LOVED AND FOR JUSTICE.
I...
...DIDN'T WANT TO SEE THE JUSTICE SHE FOUGHT FOR DIS-APPEAR.
SO I DECIDED TO CARRY ON HER HEART'S DESIRE.
THAT'S WHY...
...I BECAME A SOUL REAPER.
SHRSHHHHH

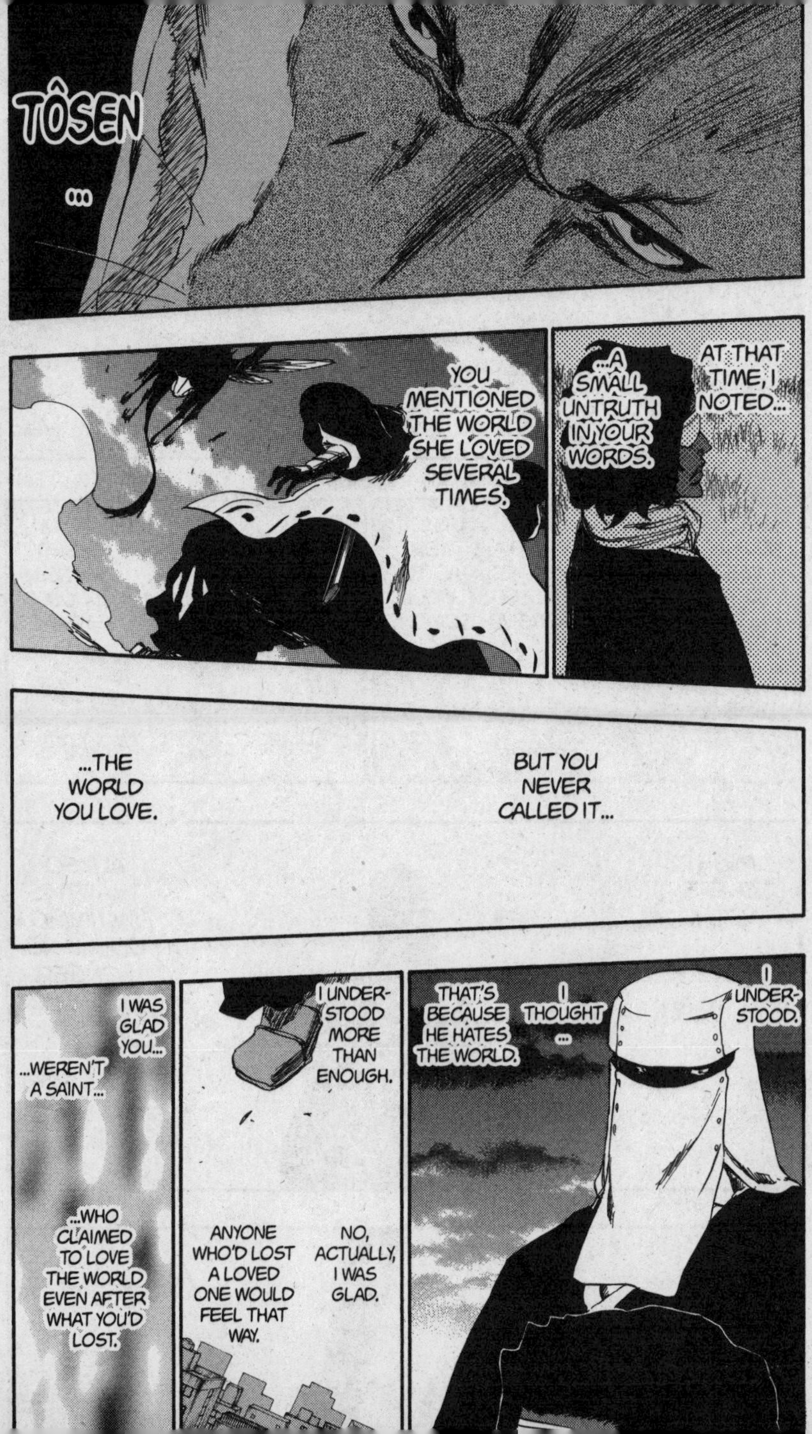
TÔSEN
...
AT THAT TIME, I NOTED...
...A SMALL UNTRUTH IN YOUR WORDS.
YOU MENTIONED THE WORLD SHE LOVED SEVERAL TIMES.
BUT YOU NEVER CALLED IT...
...THE WORLD YOU LOVE.
I UNDERSTOOD.
I THOUGHT...
THAT'S BECAUSE HE HATES THE WORLD.
I UNDERSTOOD MORE THAN ENOUGH.
NO, ACTUALLY, I WAS GLAD.
ANYONE WHO'D LOST A LOVED ONE WOULD FEEL THAT WAY.
I WAS GLAD YOU...
...WEREN'T A SAINT...
...WHO CLAIMED TO LOVE THE WORLD EVEN AFTER WHAT YOU'D LOST.

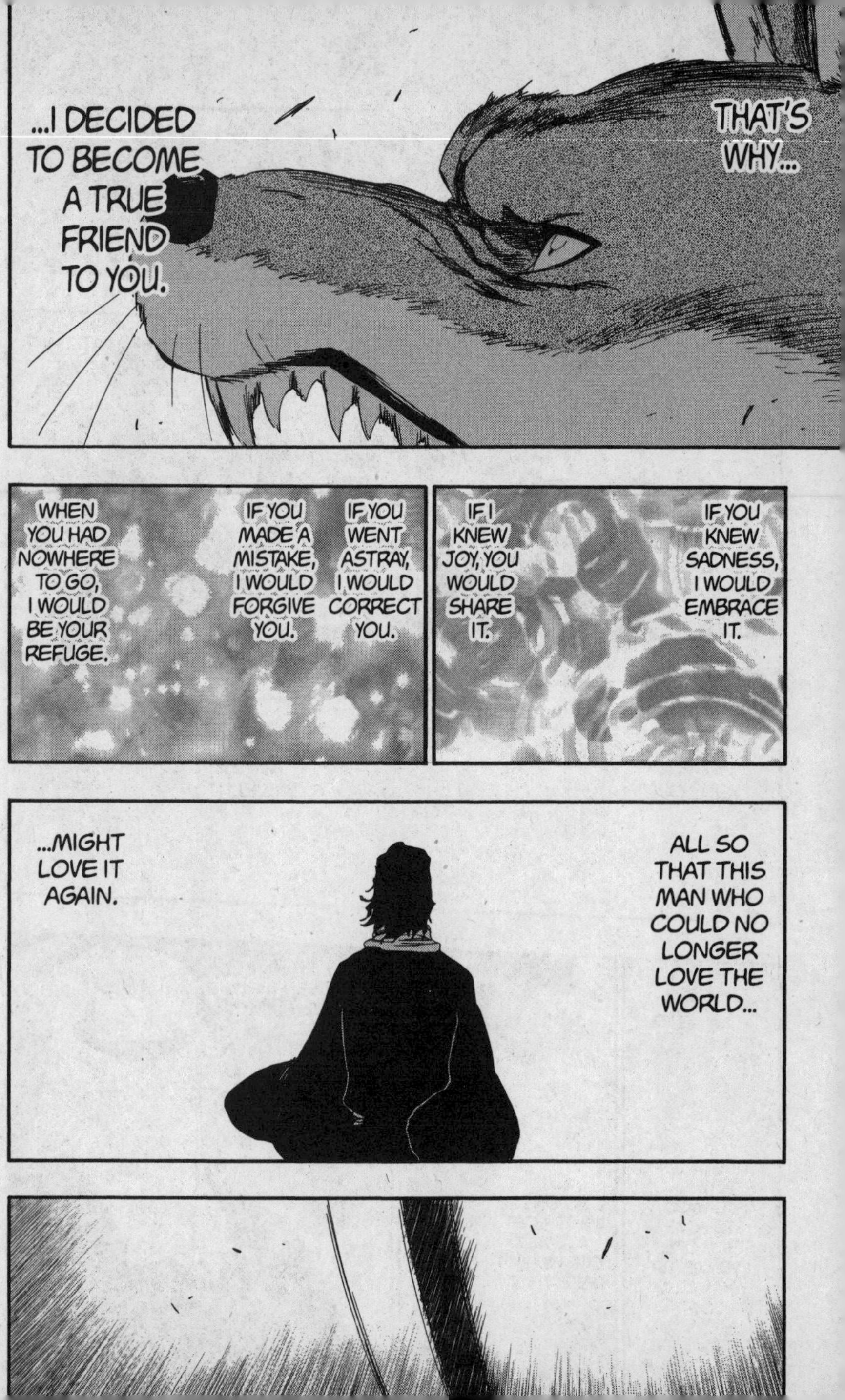
THAT'S WHY...
...I DECIDED TO BECOME A TRUE FRIEND TO YOU.
IF YOU KNEW SADNESS, I WOULD EMBRACE IT.
IF I KNEW JOY, YOU WOULD SHARE IT.
IF YOU WENT ASTRAY, I WOULD CORRECT YOU.
IF YOU MADE A MISTAKE, I WOULD FORGIVE YOU.
WHEN YOU HAD NOWHERE TO GO, I WOULD BE YOUR REFUGE.
ALL SO THAT THIS MAN WHO COULD NO LONGER LOVE THE WORLD...
...MIGHT LOVE IT AGAIN.

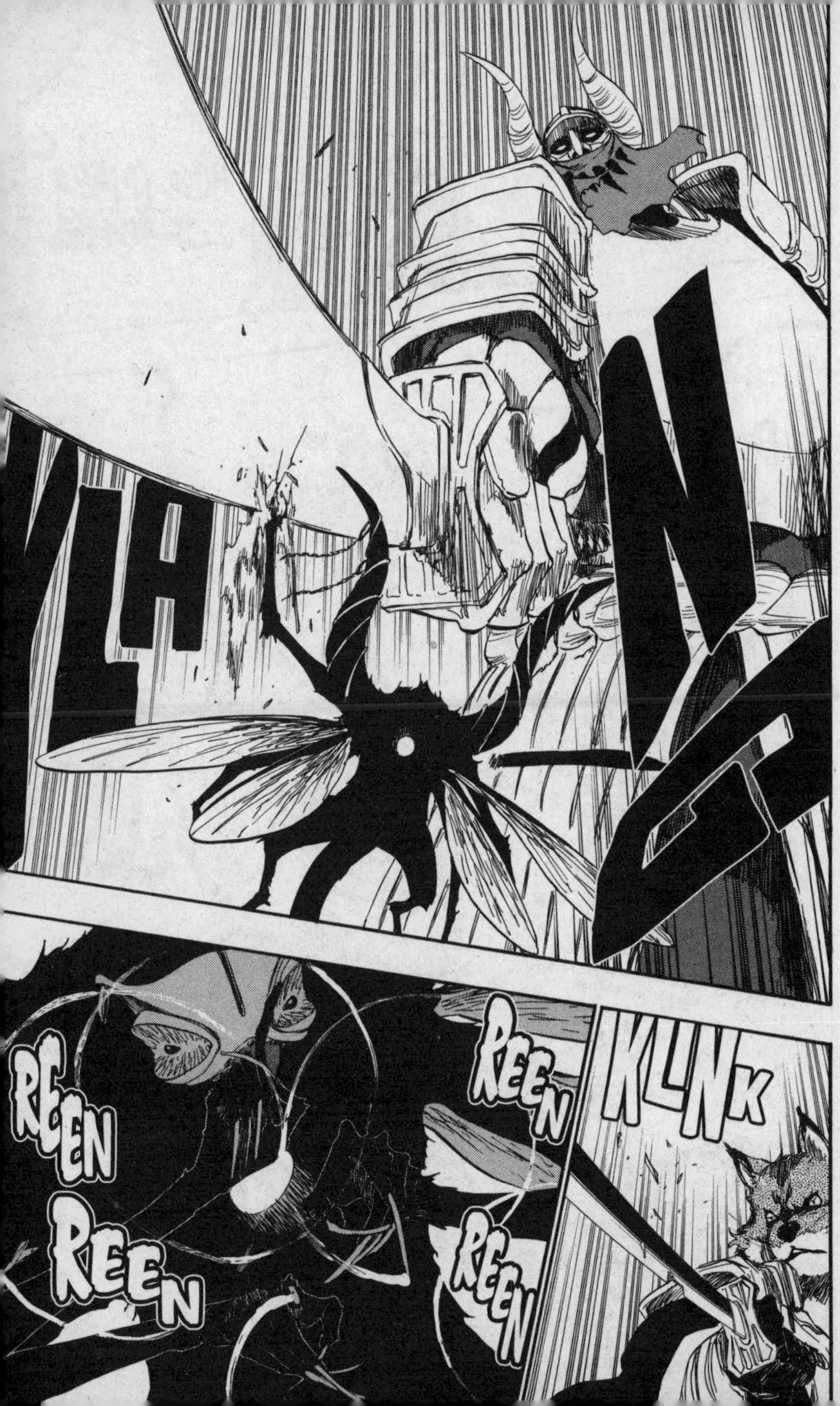
KLINK
REEN
REEN
REEN
REEN

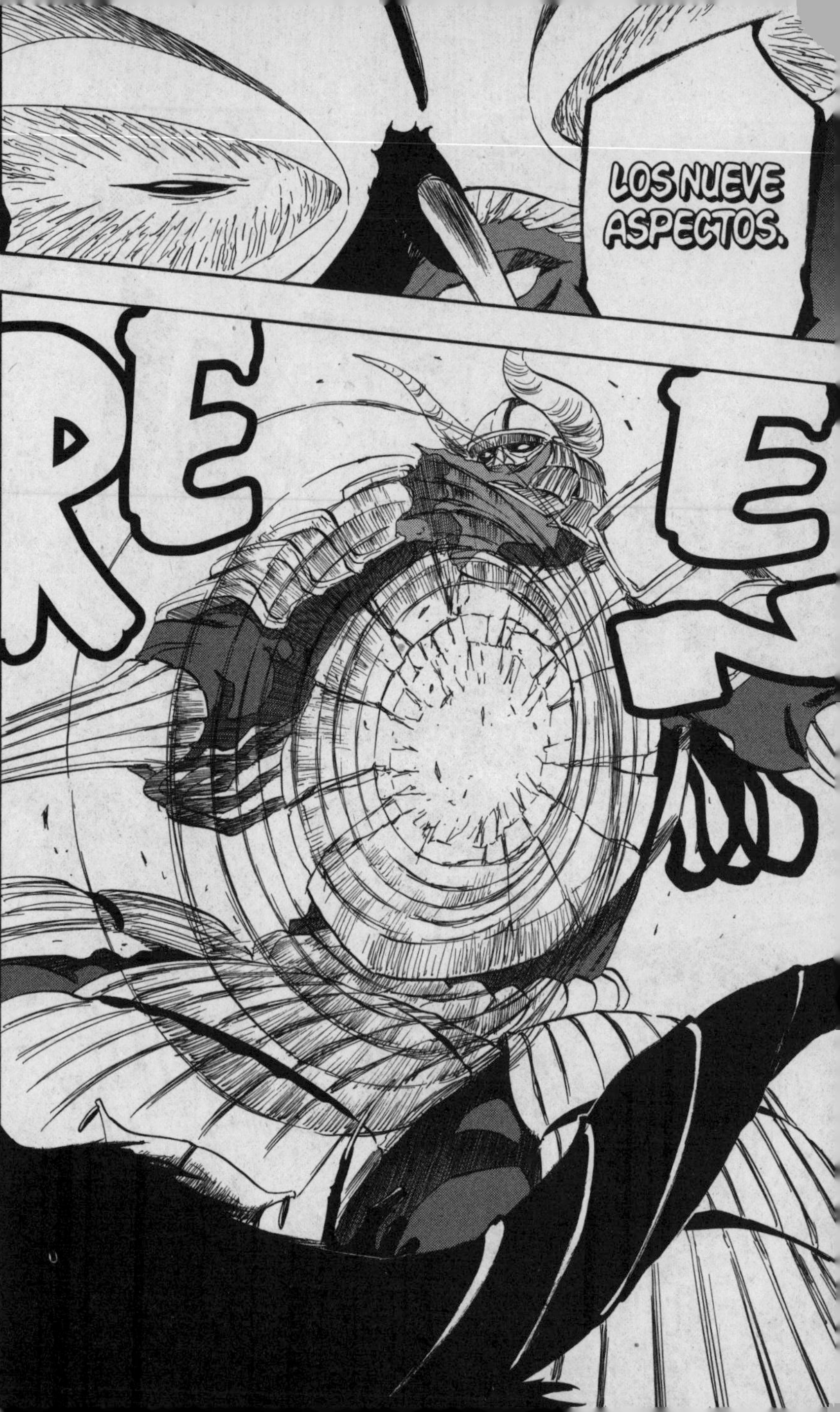
LOS NUEVE ASPECTOS.

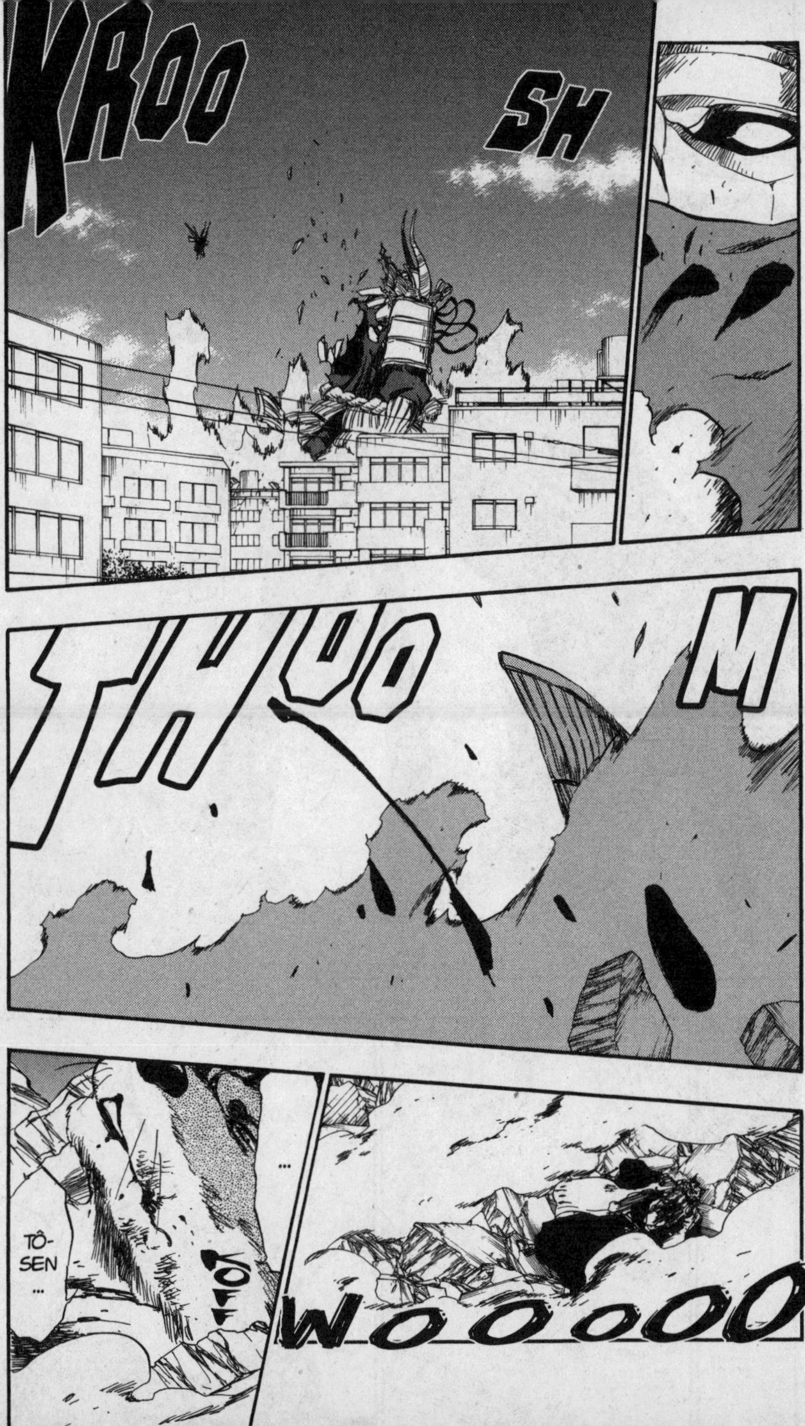
KROOSH
THOOM
WOOOOOO
...
TÔSEN ...

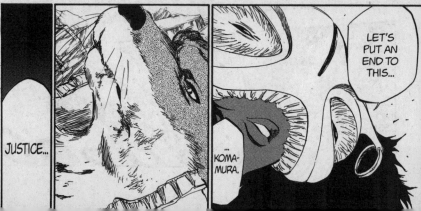

JUSTICE...

...KOMA-
MURA.

LET'S
PUT AN
END TO
THIS...

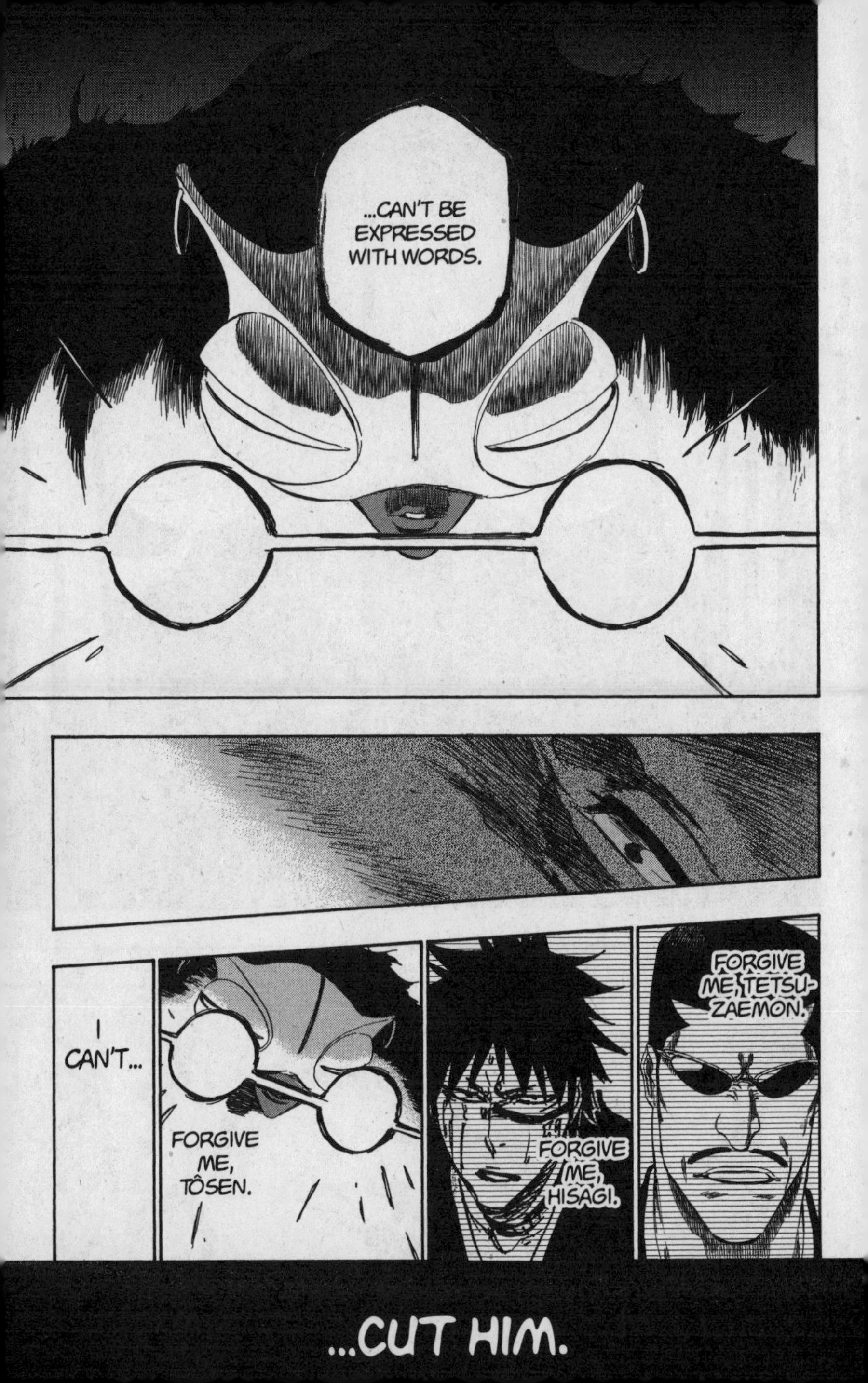
...CAN'T BE EXPRESSED WITH WORDS.
FORGIVE ME, TETSUZAEMON.
FORGIVE ME, HISAGI.
I CAN'T...
FORGIVE ME, TÔSEN.
...CUT HIM.

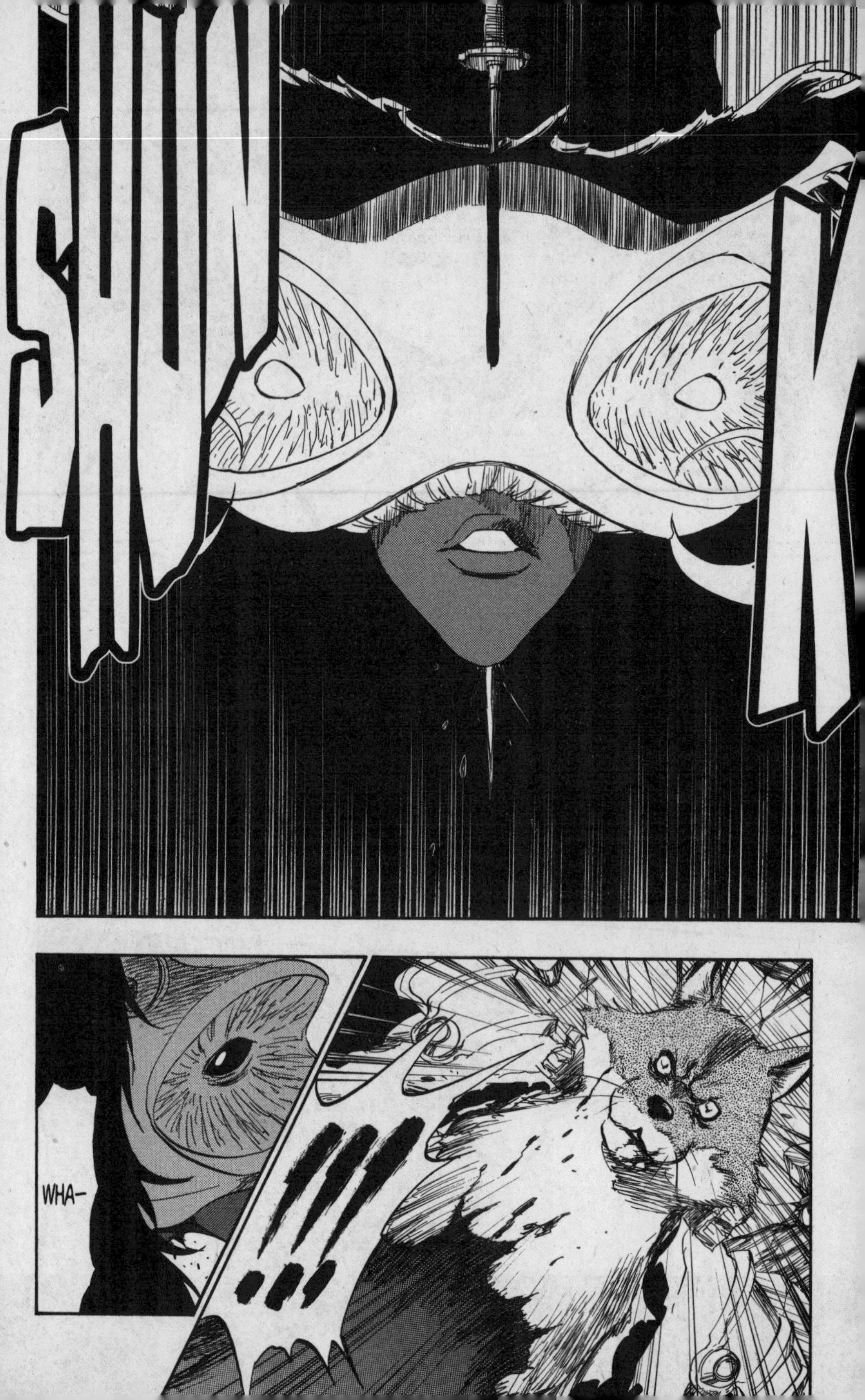
SHUNK
!!!
WHA-

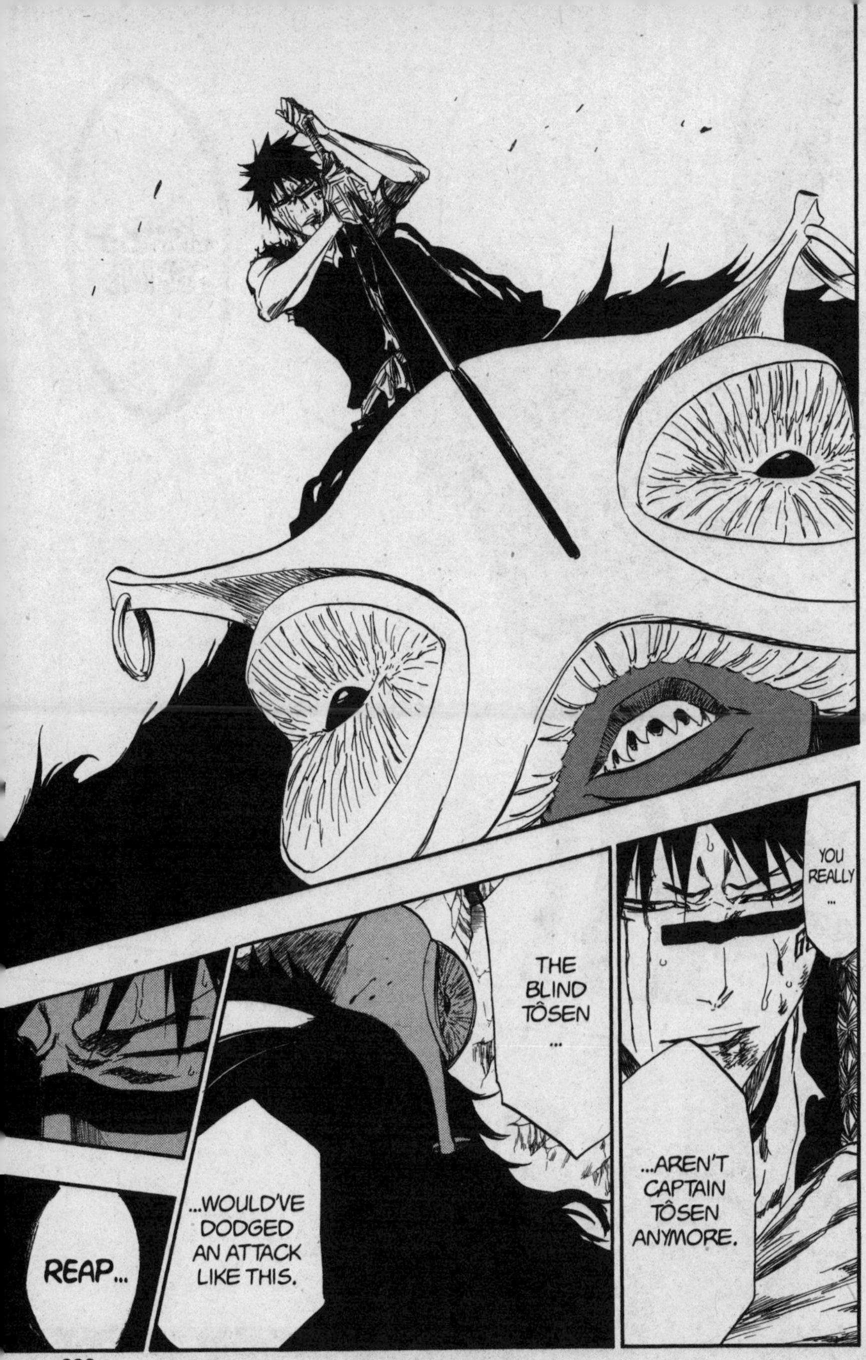
YOU REALLY ...
...AREN'T CAPTAIN TÔSEN ANYMORE.
THE BLIND TÔSEN ...
...WOULD'VE DODGED AN ATTACK LIKE THIS.
REAP...

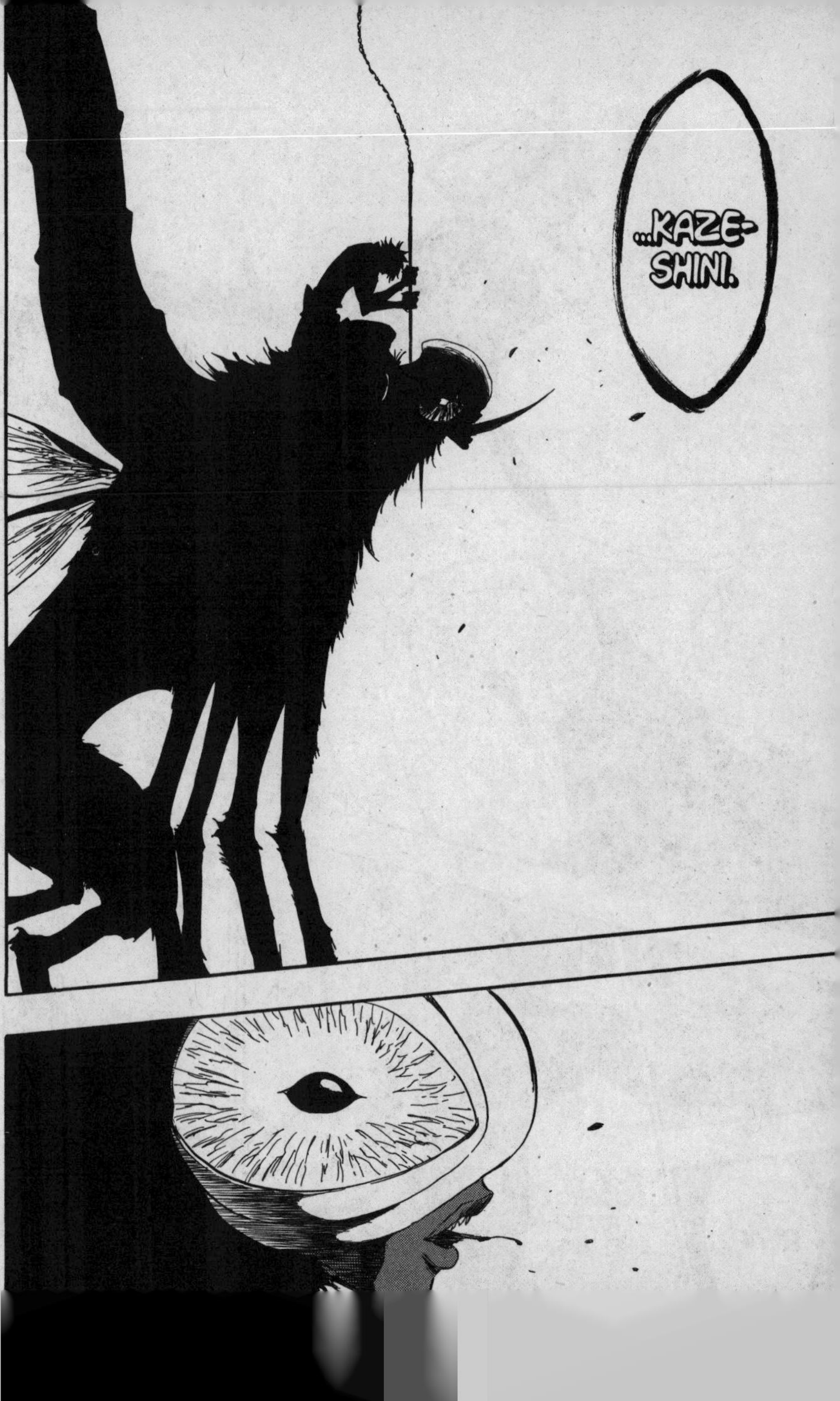
...KAZE-SHINI.

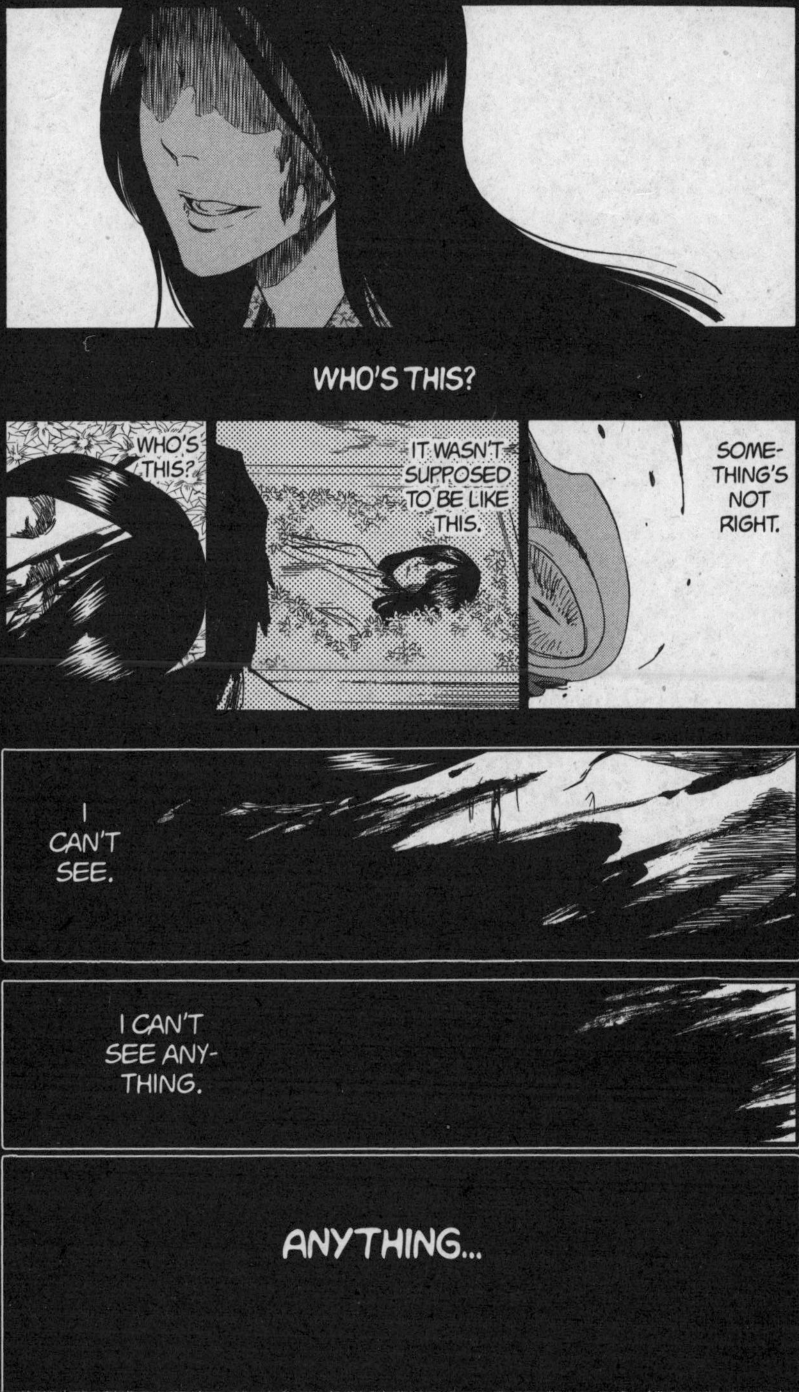
WHO'S THIS?
SOME-THING'S NOT RIGHT.
IT WASN'T SUPPOSED TO BE LIKE THIS.
WHO'S THIS?
I CAN'T SEE.
I CAN'T SEE ANY-THING.
ANYTHING...

A hotpot dinner I'd planned with some friends around New Year's got pushed back to February because I was busy, then to March because I was getting ready to move, then to April because I was actually making the move. As I write this, April is almost over.

I wonder if my friends would be willing to come eat a hotpot dinner in early summer...?

-Tite Kubo, 2010

Do not live bowing down.
Die standing up.

BLEACH45 THE BURNOUT INFERNO

STARS AND

平子真子
Shinji Hirako

Tôshirô Hitsugaya

黒崎一護

Ichigo Kurosaki

★ plot

When high school student Ichigo Kurosaki meets Soul Reaper Rukia Kuchiki his life is changed forever. Soon Ichigo is a soul-cleansing Soul Reaper too, and he finds himself having adventures, as well as problems, that he never would have imagined. Now Ichigo and his friends must stop renegade Soul Reaper Aizen and his army of Arrancars from destroying the Soul Society and wiping out Karakura as well.

After a fierce battle in Las Noches to save Orihime, Ichigo heads to Karakura Town for the final battle! But a coalition of the Thirteen Court Guard Companies and the Visoreds seems unable to defeat Aizen's minions. After a deadly duel, Komamura finds himself at Tôsen's mercy. But the finishing blow is preempted when Hisagi's sword pierces Tôsen's head!

BLEACH ALL

藍染惣右介

Sôsuke Aizen

狛村左陣

Sajin Komamura

Genryusai Shigekuni Yamamoto

山本元柳斎重國

STORIES

BLEACH45

THE BURNOUT INFERNO

Contents

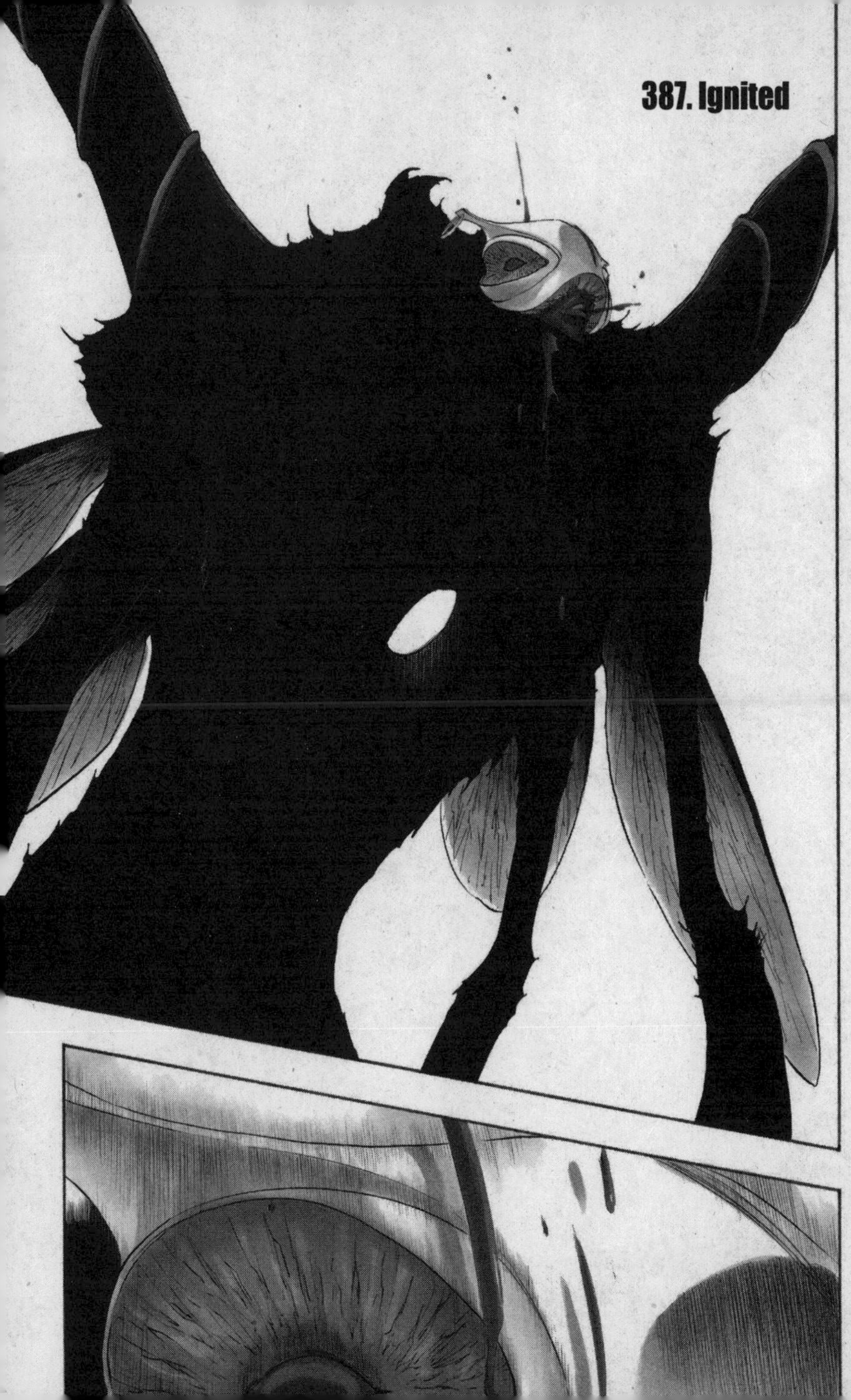
387. Ignited

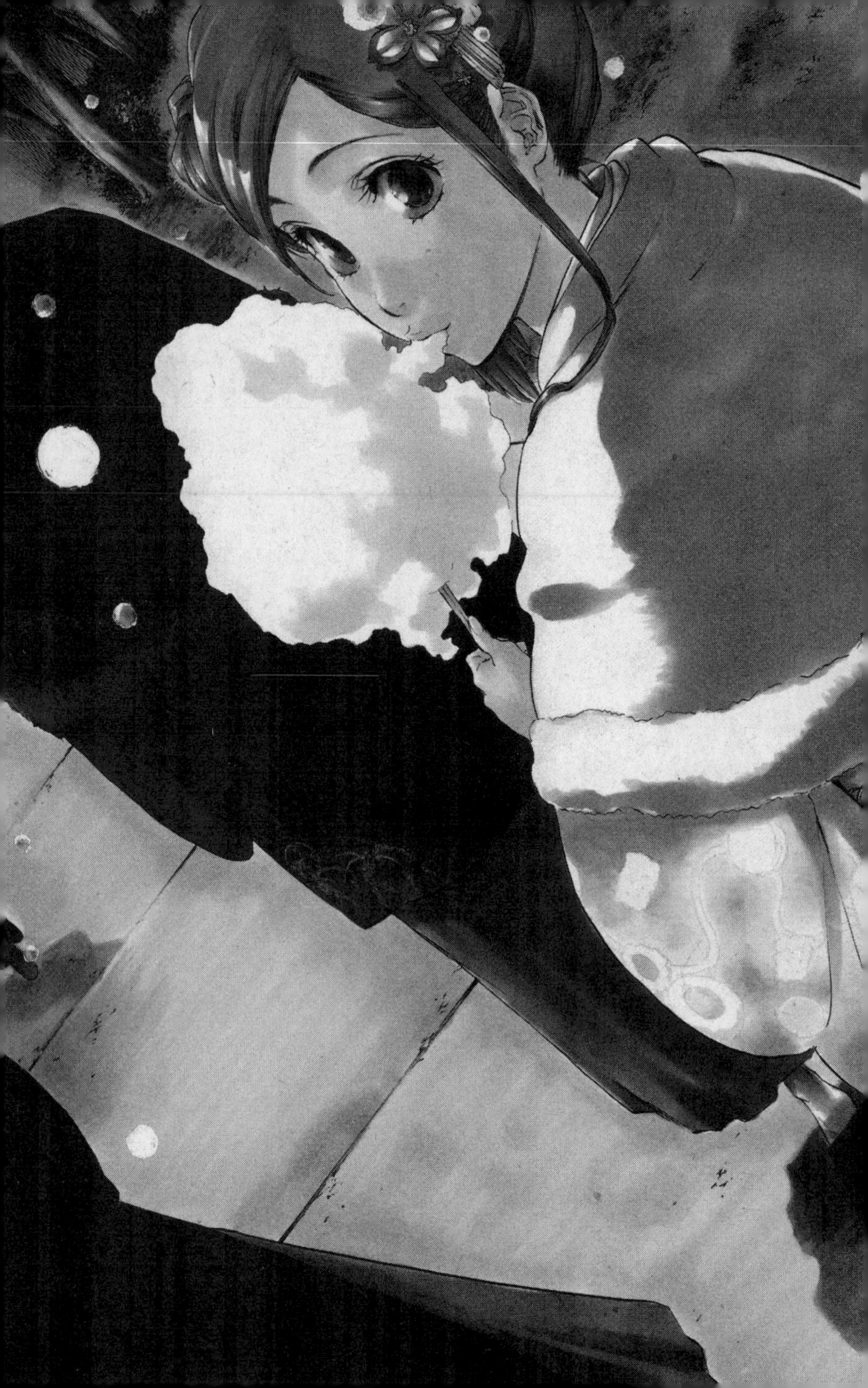

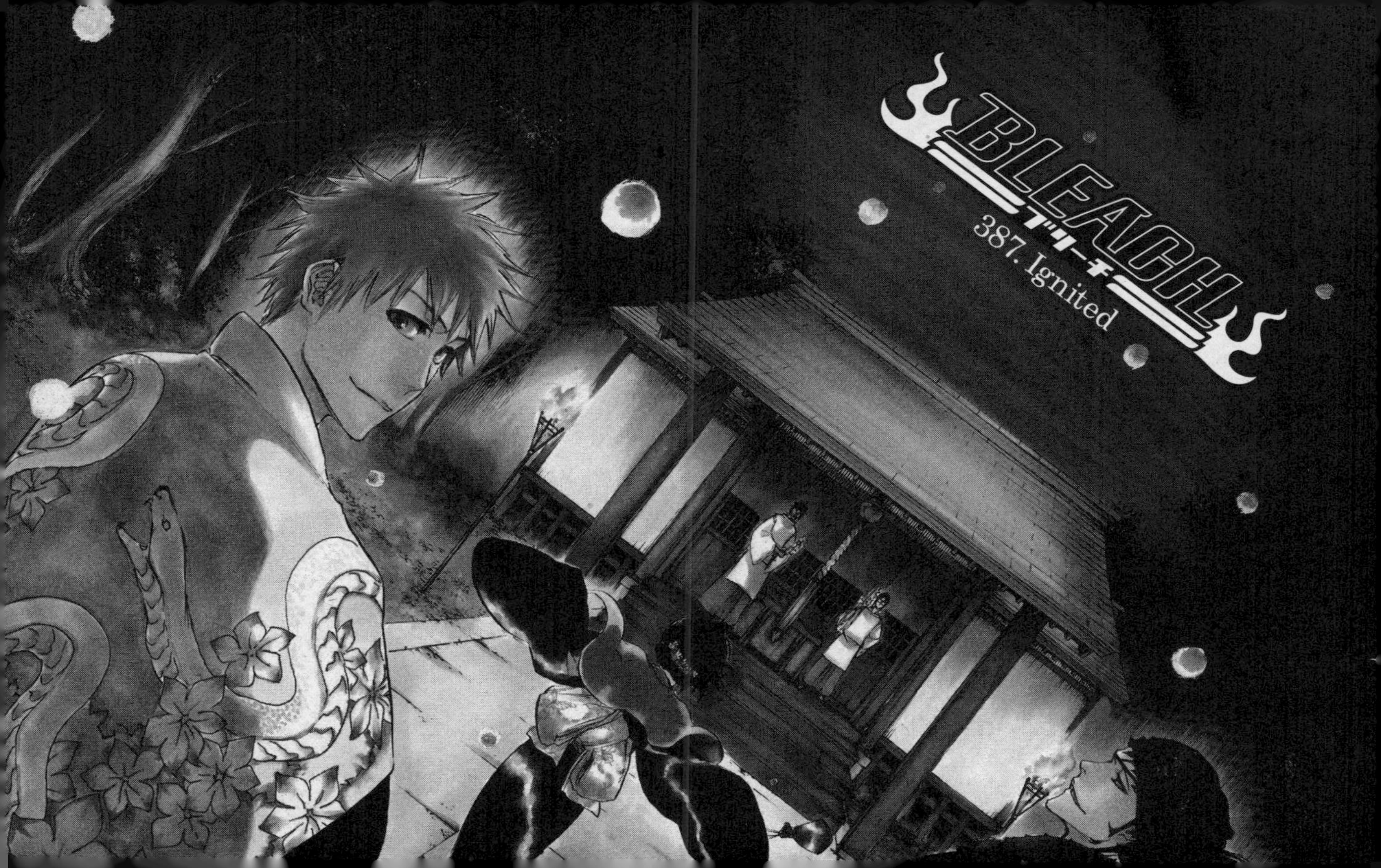
BLEACH
ブリーチ
387. Ignited

BLEACH
ブリーチ

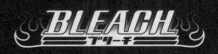

READ THIS WAY

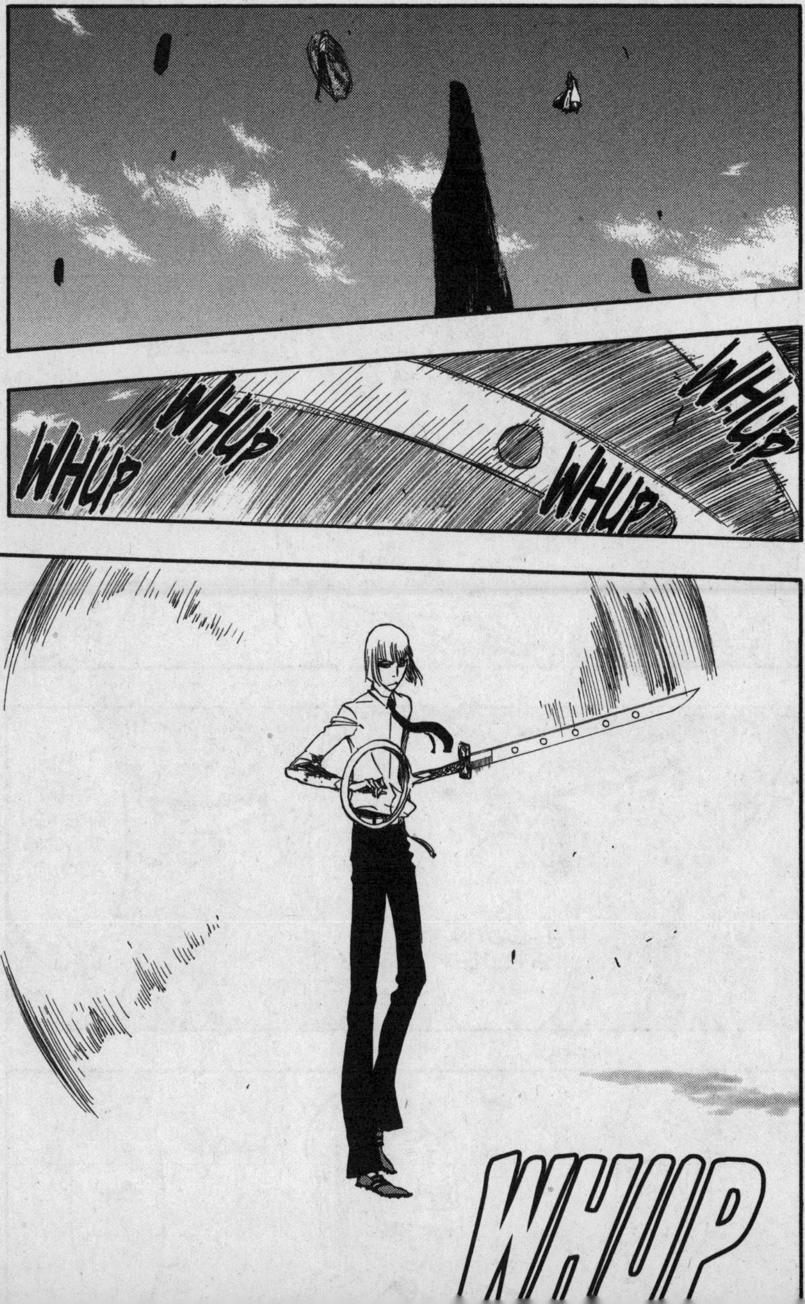
WHUP
WHUP
WHUP
WHUP
WHUP

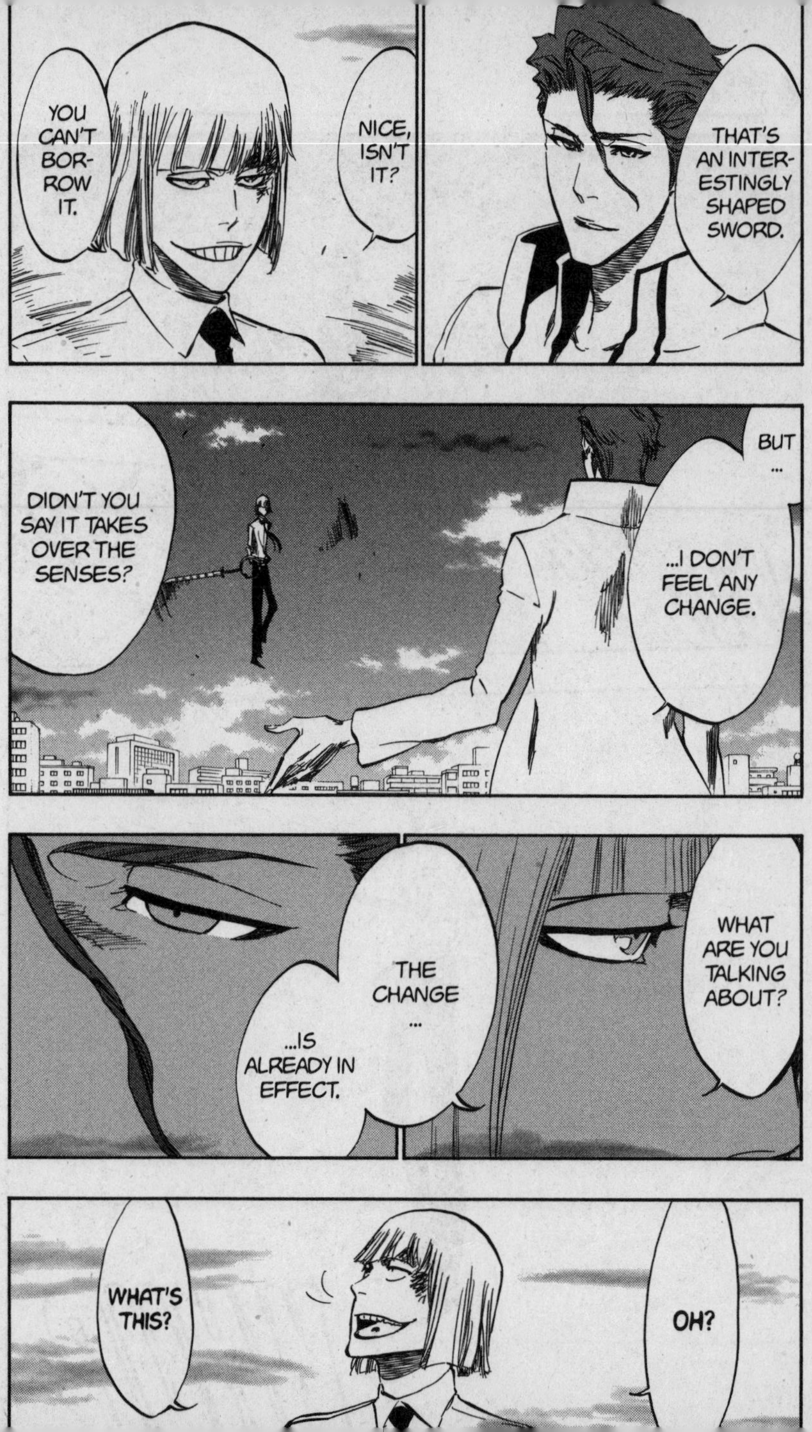
THAT'S AN INTERESTINGLY SHAPED SWORD.
NICE, ISN'T IT?
YOU CAN'T BORROW IT.
BUT ...
...I DON'T FEEL ANY CHANGE.
DIDN'T YOU SAY IT TAKES OVER THE SENSES?
WHAT ARE YOU TALKING ABOUT?
THE CHANGE ...
...IS ALREADY IN EFFECT.
OH?
WHAT'S THIS?

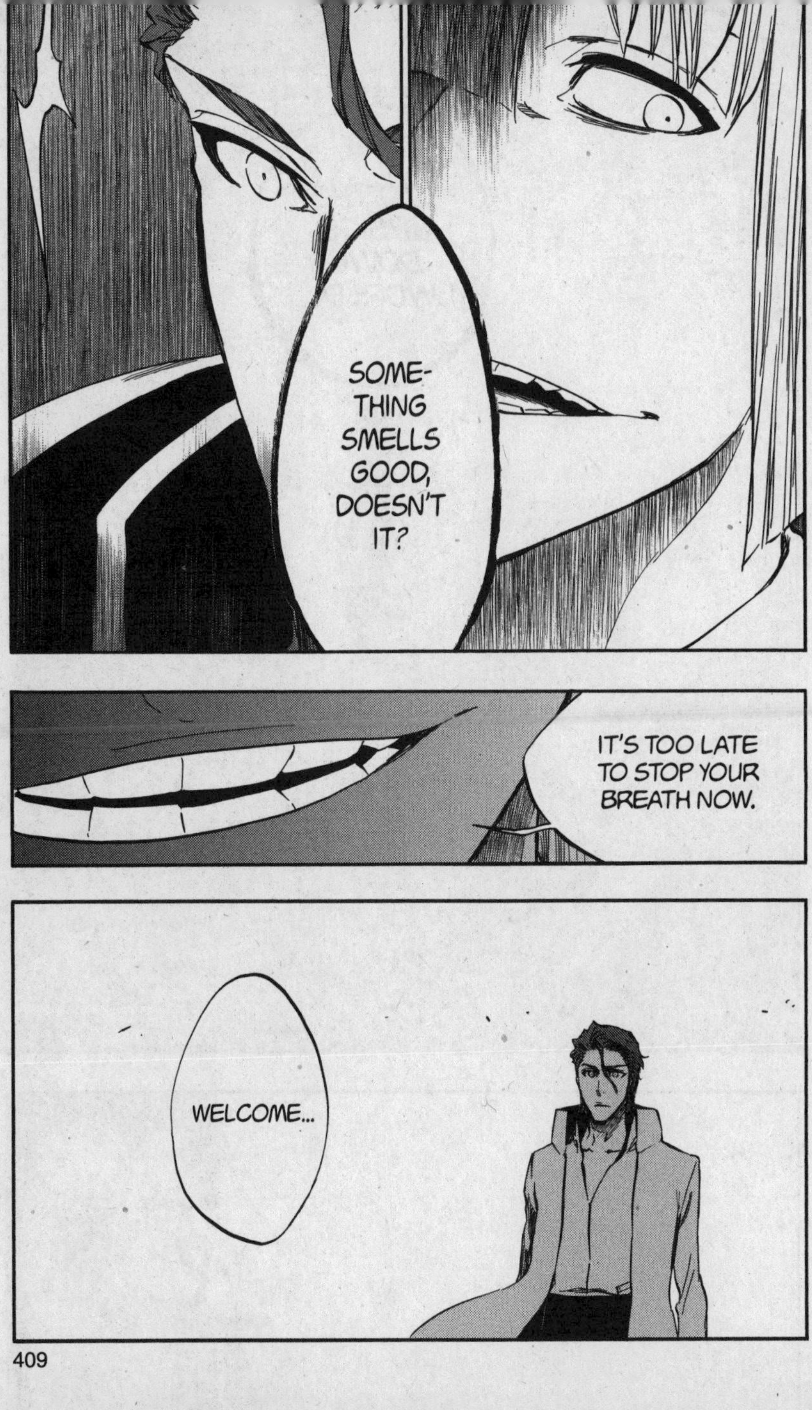
SOME-THING SMELLS GOOD, DOESN'T IT?
IT'S TOO LATE TO STOP YOUR BREATH NOW.
WELCOME...

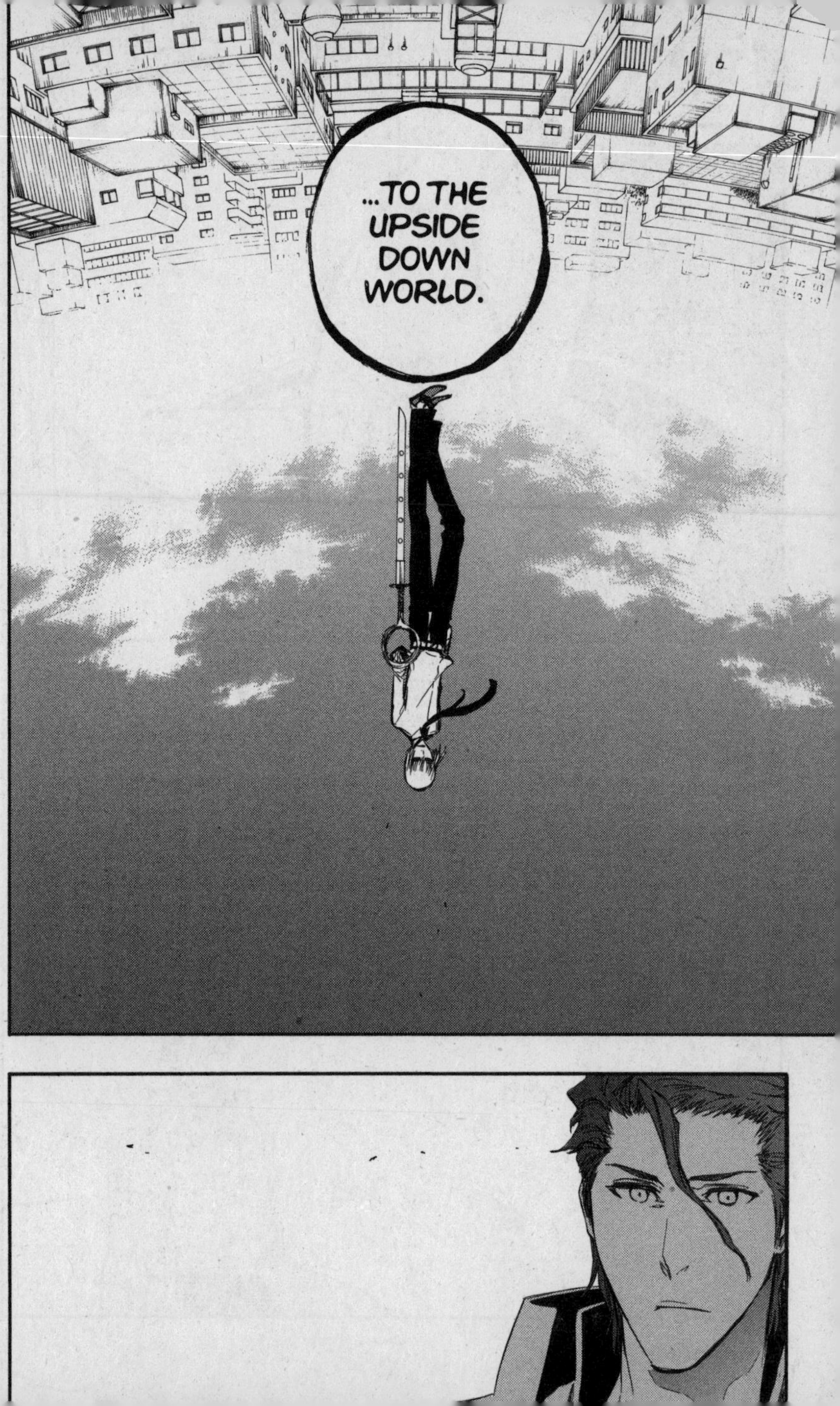
...TO THE UPSIDE DOWN WORLD.

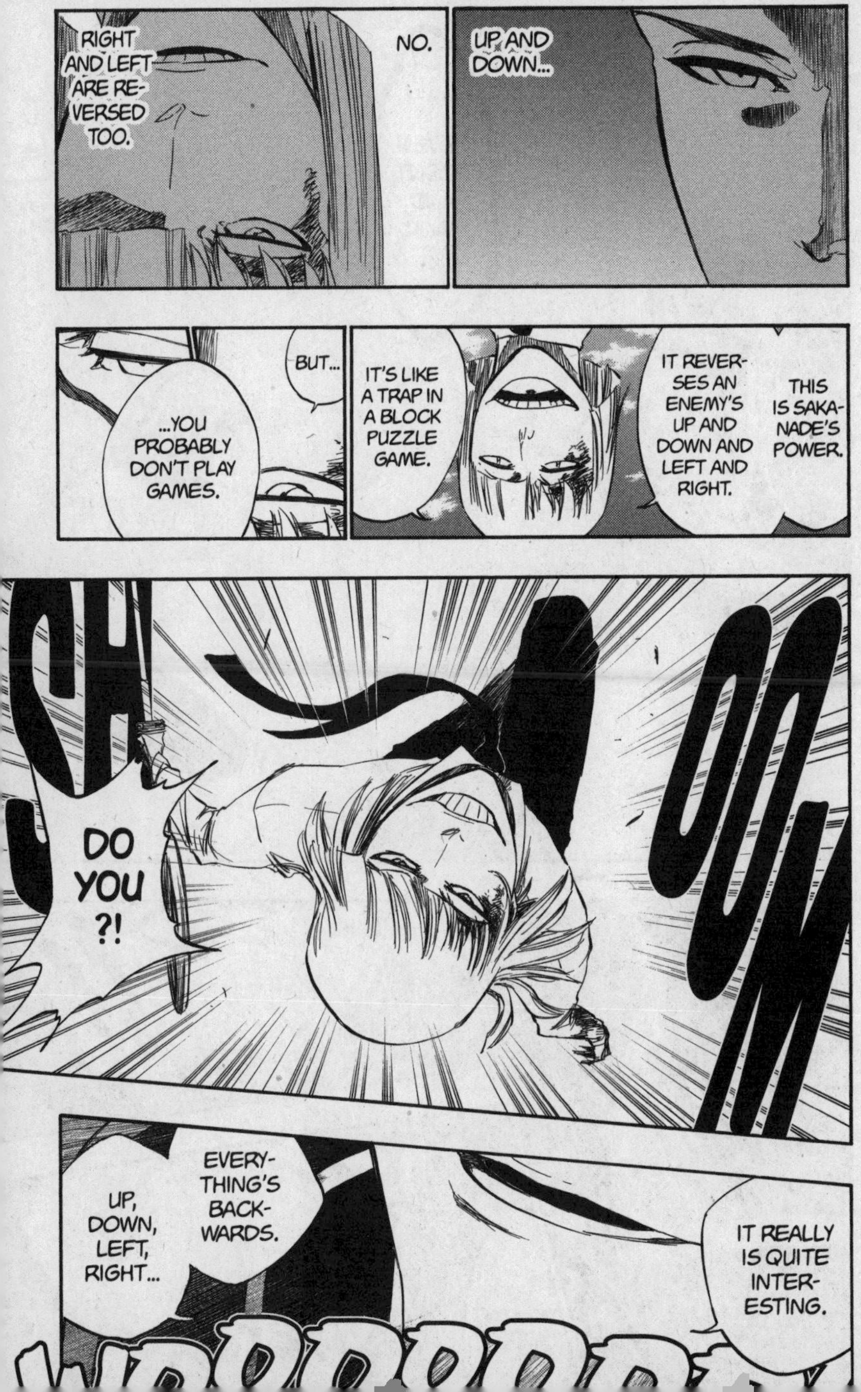
UP AND DOWN...
NO.
RIGHT AND LEFT ARE REVERSED TOO.
THIS IS SAKANADE'S POWER.
IT REVERSES AN ENEMY'S UP AND DOWN AND LEFT AND RIGHT.
IT'S LIKE A TRAP IN A BLOCK PUZZLE GAME.
BUT...
...YOU PROBABLY DON'T PLAY GAMES.
DO YOU?!
IT REALLY IS QUITE INTERESTING.
EVERYTHING'S BACKWARDS.
UP, DOWN, LEFT, RIGHT...

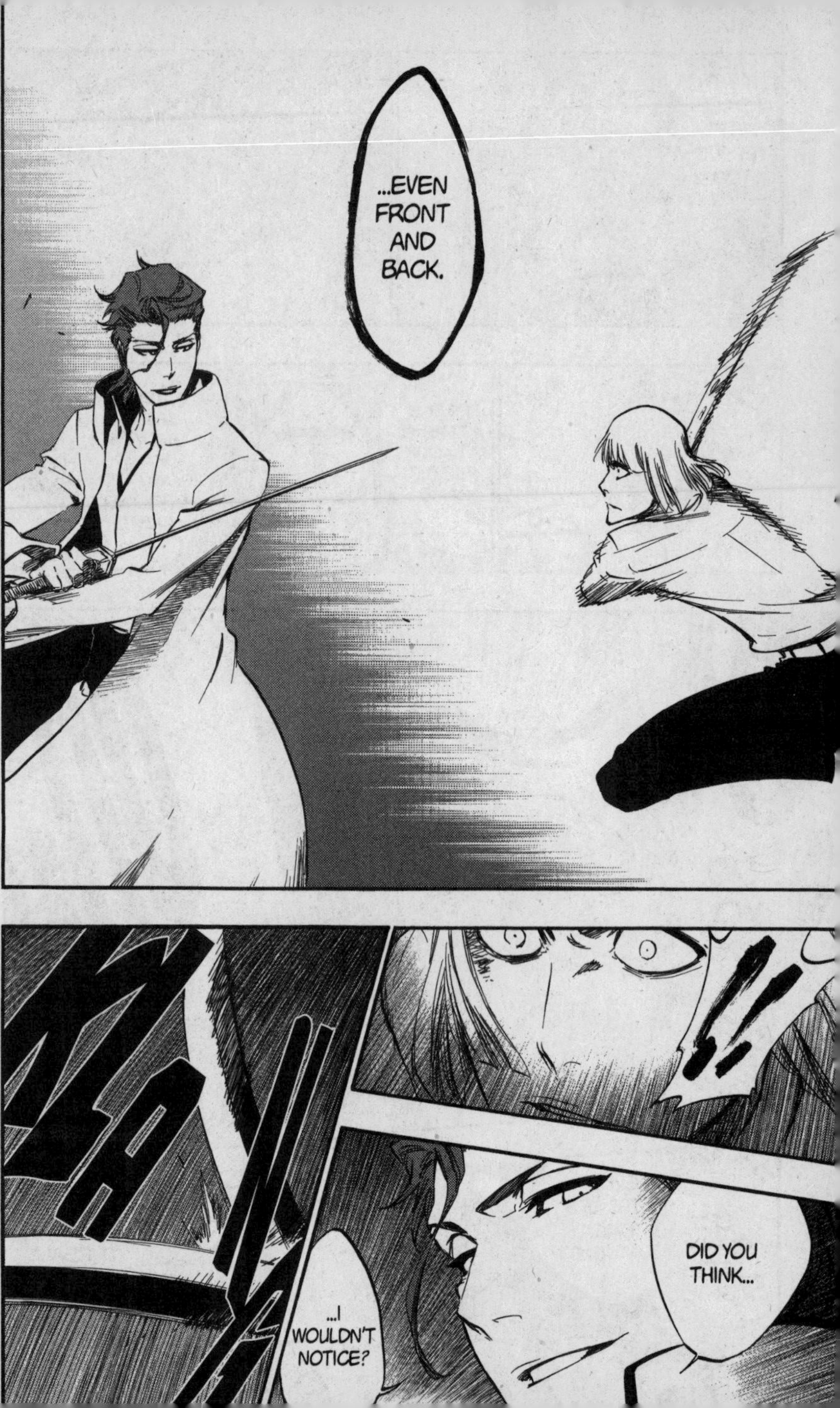
...EVEN FRONT AND BACK.
DID YOU THINK...
...I WOULDN'T NOTICE?

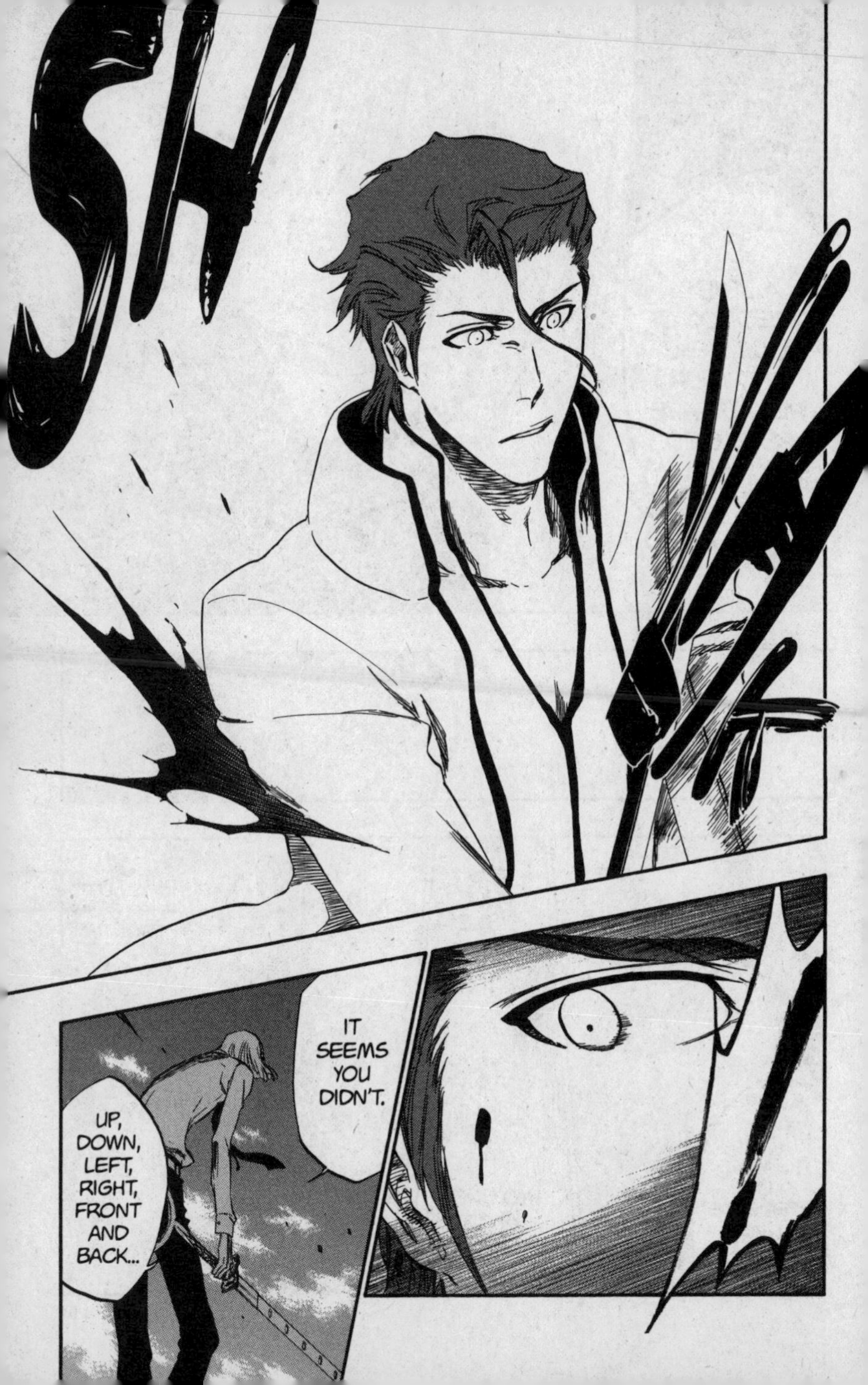
SH
IT SEEMS YOU DIDN'T.
UP, DOWN, LEFT, RIGHT, FRONT AND BACK...

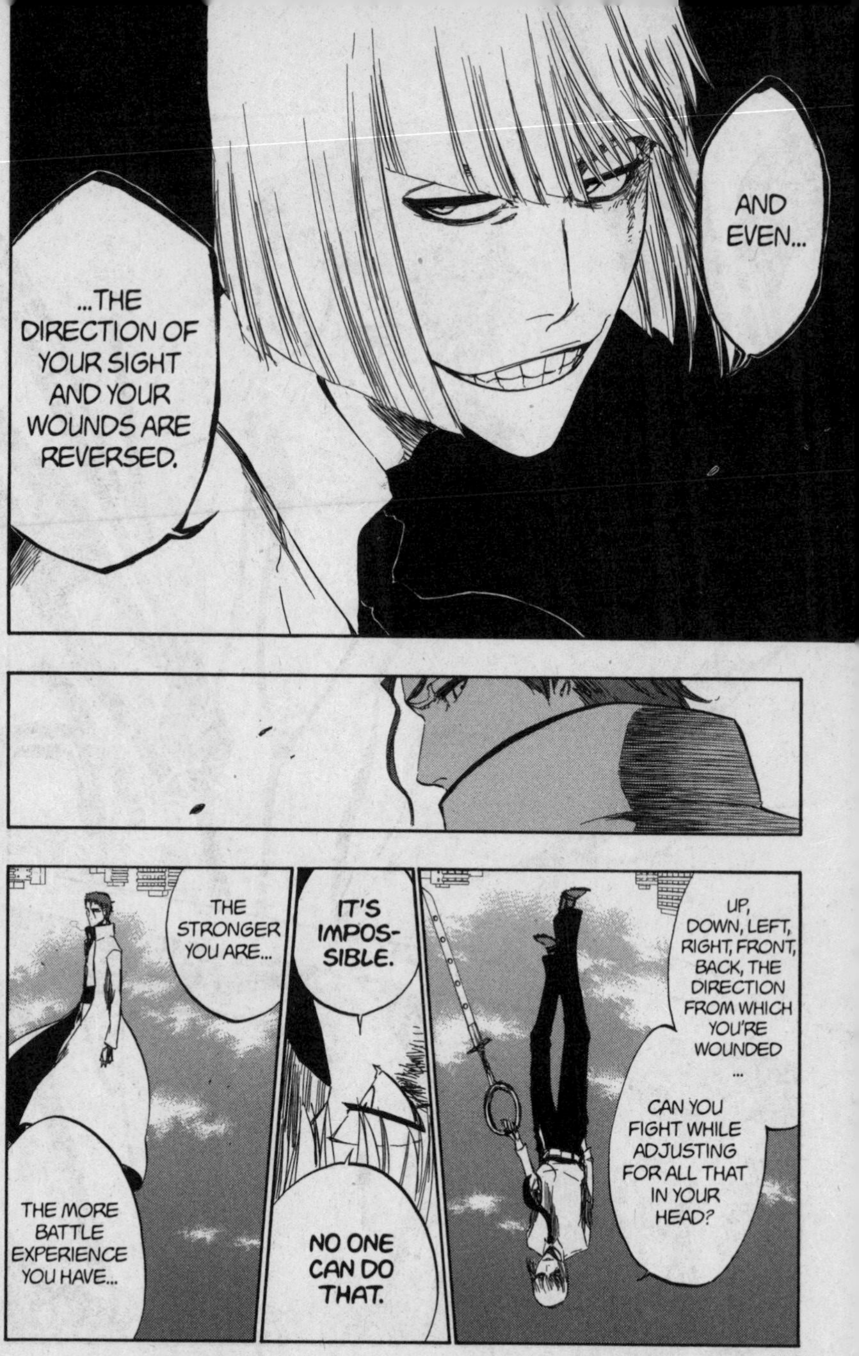
AND EVEN...
...THE DIRECTION OF YOUR SIGHT AND YOUR WOUNDS ARE REVERSED.
UP, DOWN, LEFT, RIGHT, FRONT, BACK, THE DIRECTION FROM WHICH YOU'RE WOUNDED ...
CAN YOU FIGHT WHILE ADJUSTING FOR ALL THAT IN YOUR HEAD?
IT'S IMPOSSIBLE.
NO ONE CAN DO THAT.
THE STRONGER YOU ARE...
THE MORE BATTLE EXPERIENCE YOU HAVE...

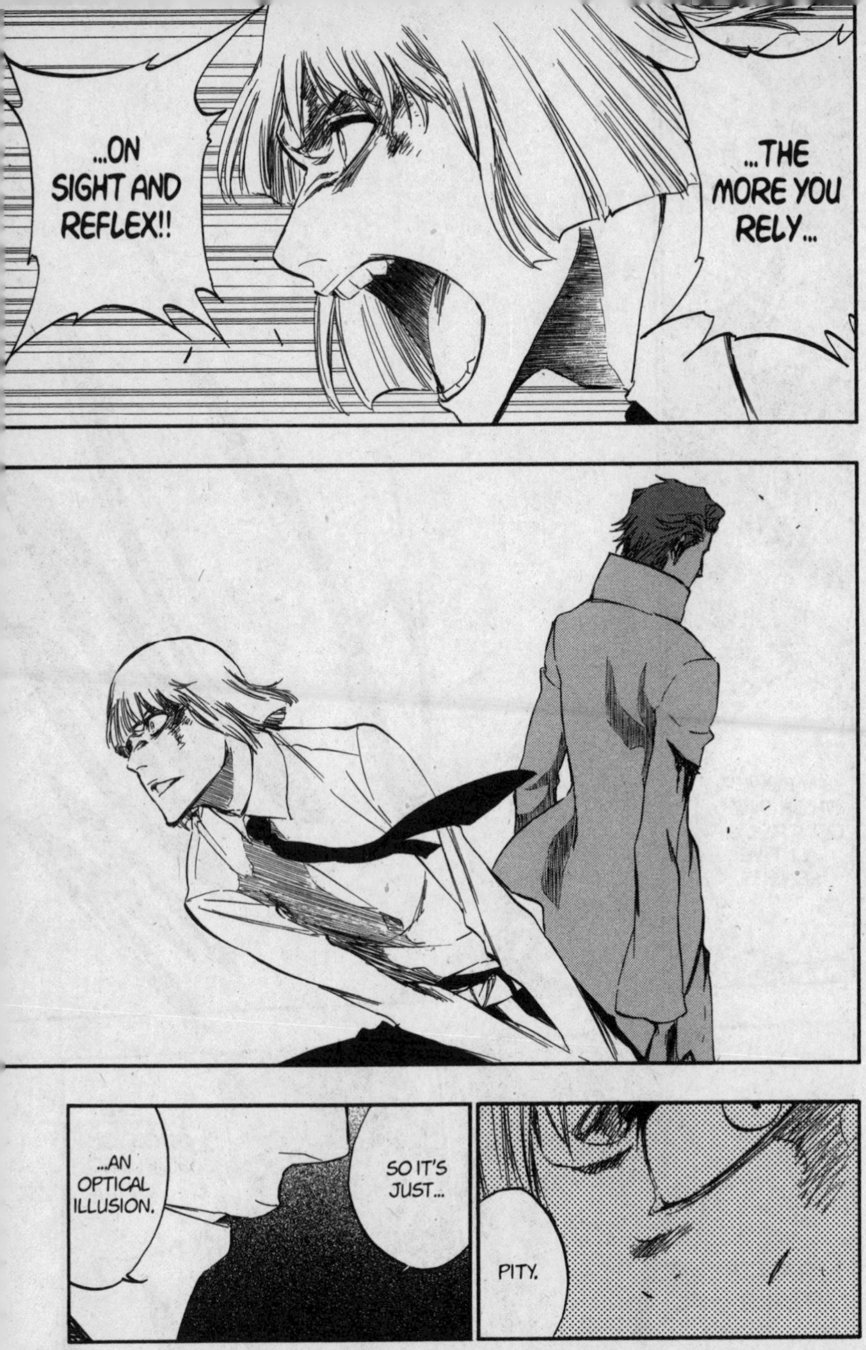
...THE MORE YOU RELY...
...ON SIGHT AND REFLEX!!
PITY.
SO IT'S JUST...
...AN OPTICAL ILLUSION.

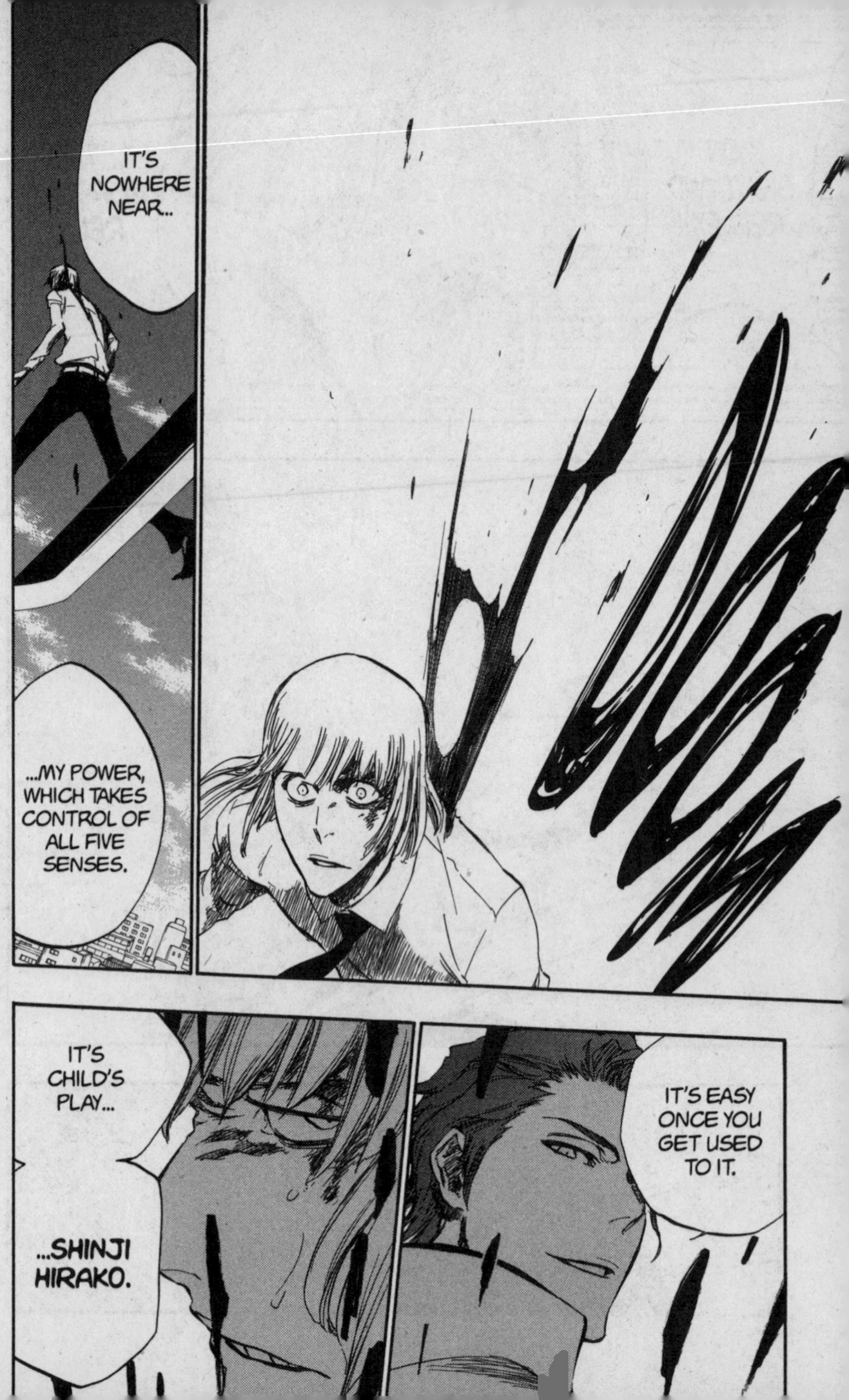
IT'S NOWHERE NEAR...
...MY POWER, WHICH TAKES CONTROL OF ALL FIVE SENSES.
IT'S EASY ONCE YOU GET USED TO IT.
IT'S CHILD'S PLAY...
...SHINJI HIRAKO.

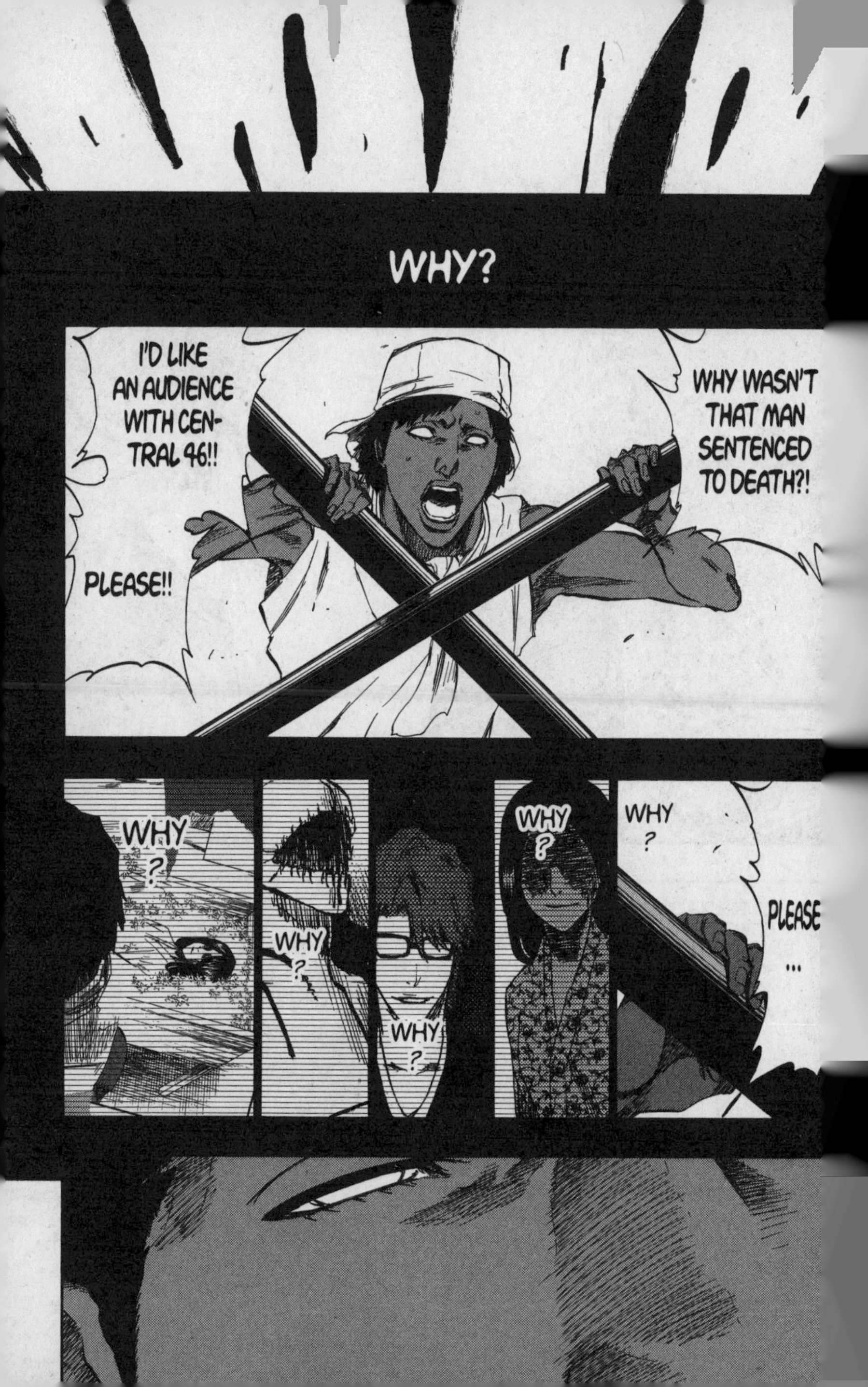
WHY?
WHY WASN'T THAT MAN SENTENCED TO DEATH?!
I'D LIKE AN AUDIENCE WITH CEN-TRAL 46!!
PLEASE!!
WHY ?
PLEASE ...
WHY ?
WHY ?
WHY ?
WHY ?

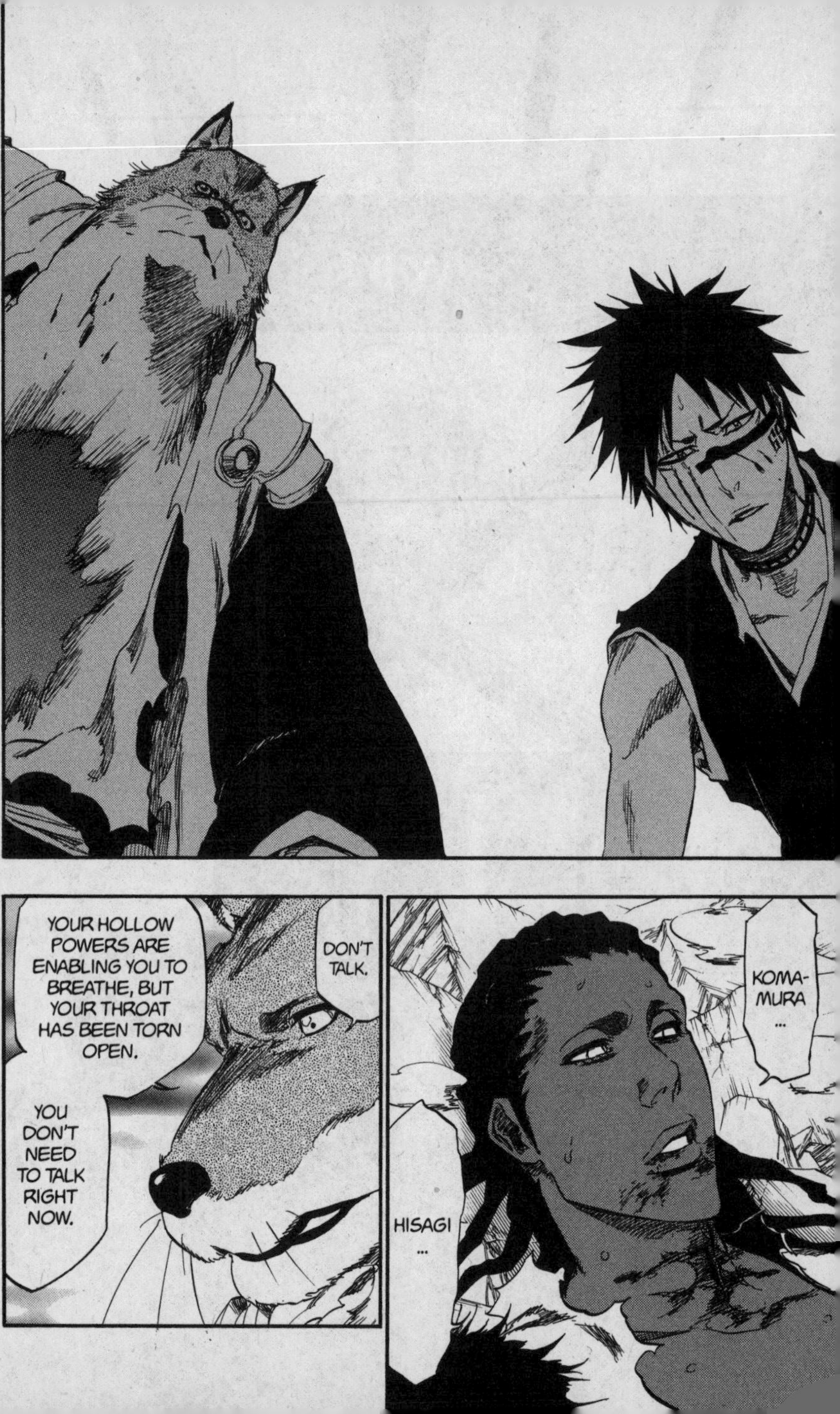
KOMAMURA...
HISAGI...
DON'T TALK.
YOUR HOLLOW POWERS ARE ENABLING YOU TO BREATHE, BUT YOUR THROAT HAS BEEN TORN OPEN.
YOU DON'T NEED TO TALK RIGHT NOW.

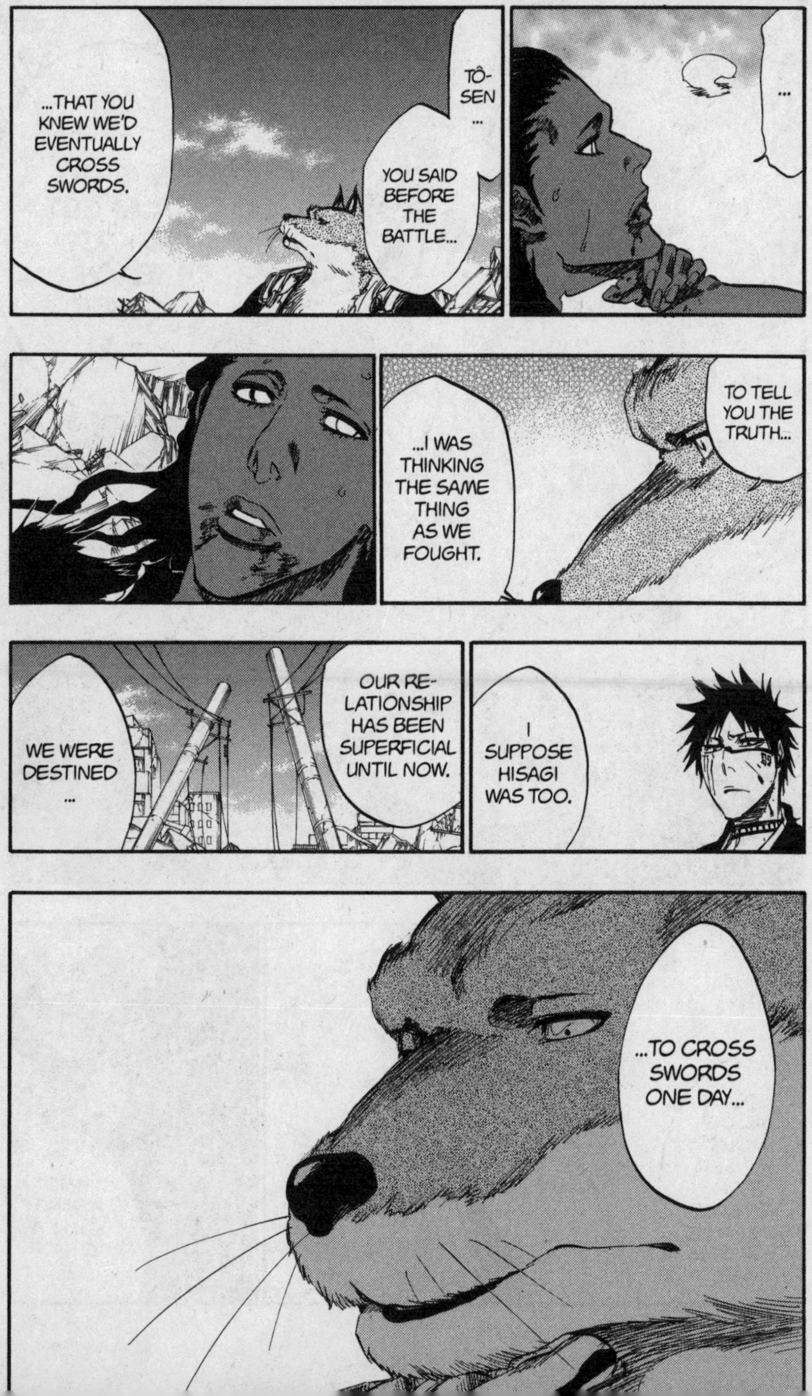
...
TÔ-SEN ...
YOU SAID BEFORE THE BATTLE...
...THAT YOU KNEW WE'D EVENTUALLY CROSS SWORDS.
TO TELL YOU THE TRUTH...
...I WAS THINKING THE SAME THING AS WE FOUGHT.
I SUPPOSE HISAGI WAS TOO.
OUR RE-LATIONSHIP HAS BEEN SUPERFICIAL UNTIL NOW.
WE WERE DESTINED ...
...TO CROSS SWORDS ONE DAY...

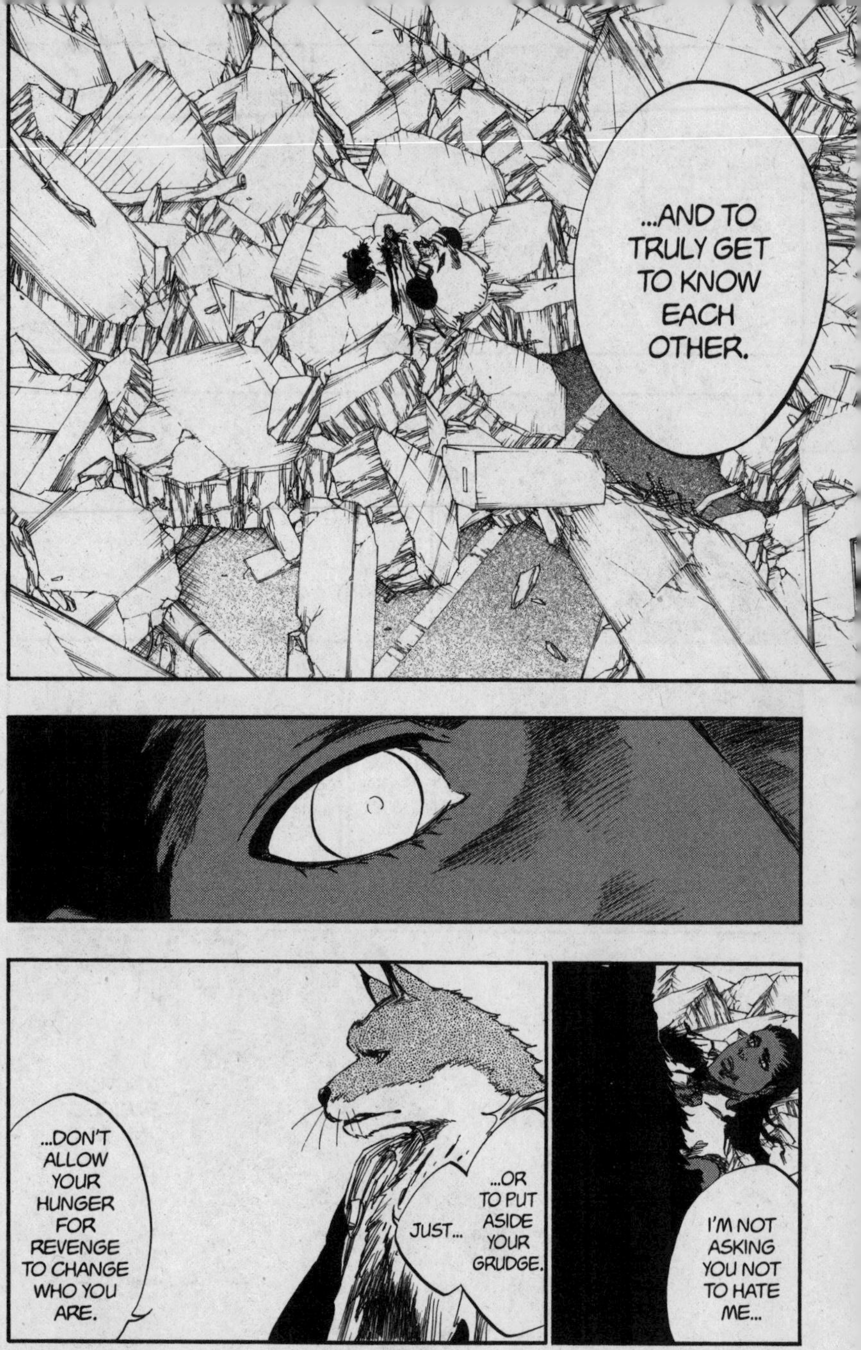
...AND TO TRULY GET TO KNOW EACH OTHER.
I'M NOT ASKING YOU NOT TO HATE ME...
...OR TO PUT ASIDE YOUR GRUDGE.
JUST...
...DON'T ALLOW YOUR HUNGER FOR REVENGE TO CHANGE WHO YOU ARE.

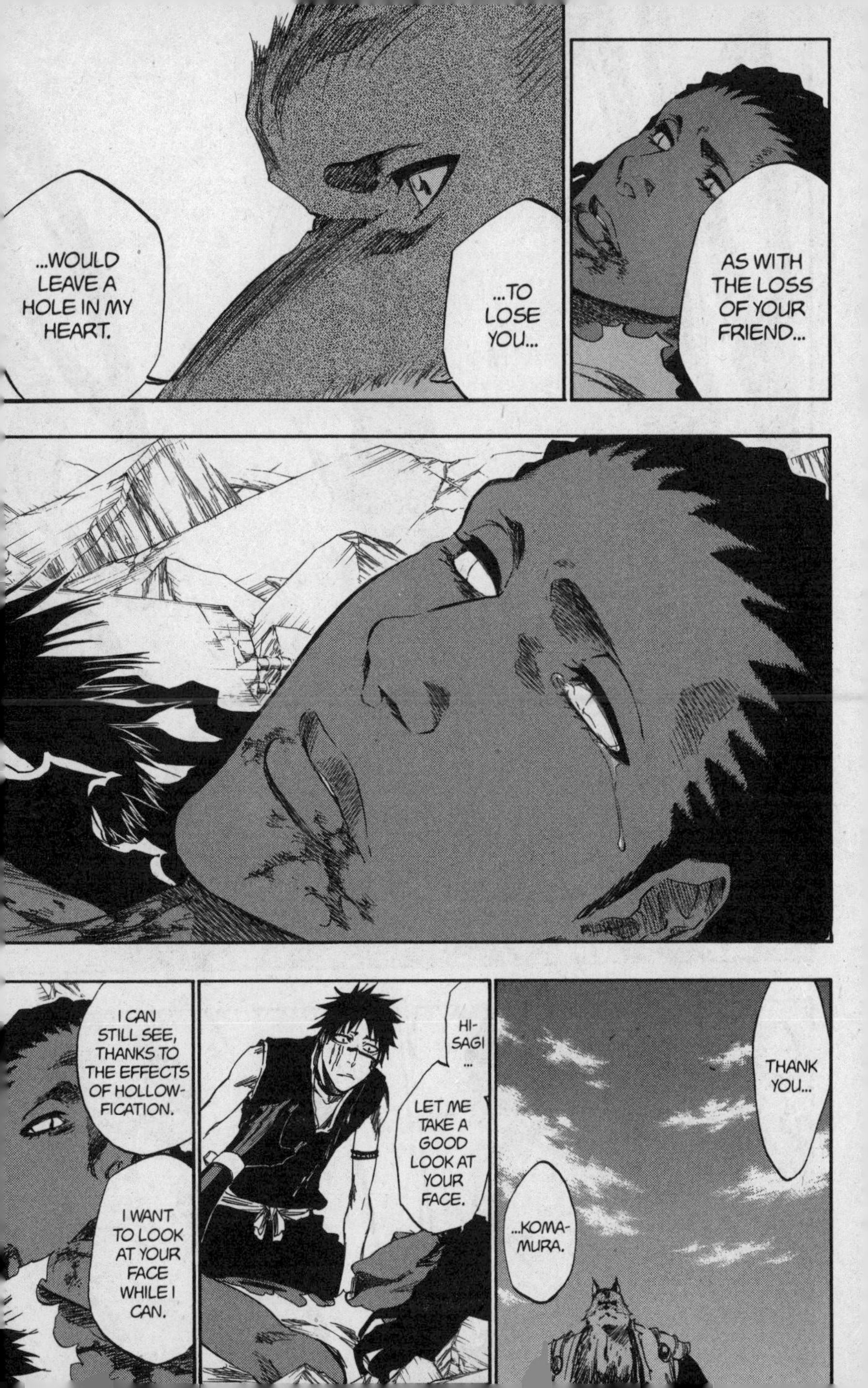
AS WITH THE LOSS OF YOUR FRIEND...
...TO LOSE YOU...
...WOULD LEAVE A HOLE IN MY HEART.
THANK YOU...
...KOMAMURA.
HISAGI...
LET ME TAKE A GOOD LOOK AT YOUR FACE.
I CAN STILL SEE, THANKS TO THE EFFECTS OF HOLLOWFICATION.
I WANT TO LOOK AT YOUR FACE WHILE I CAN.

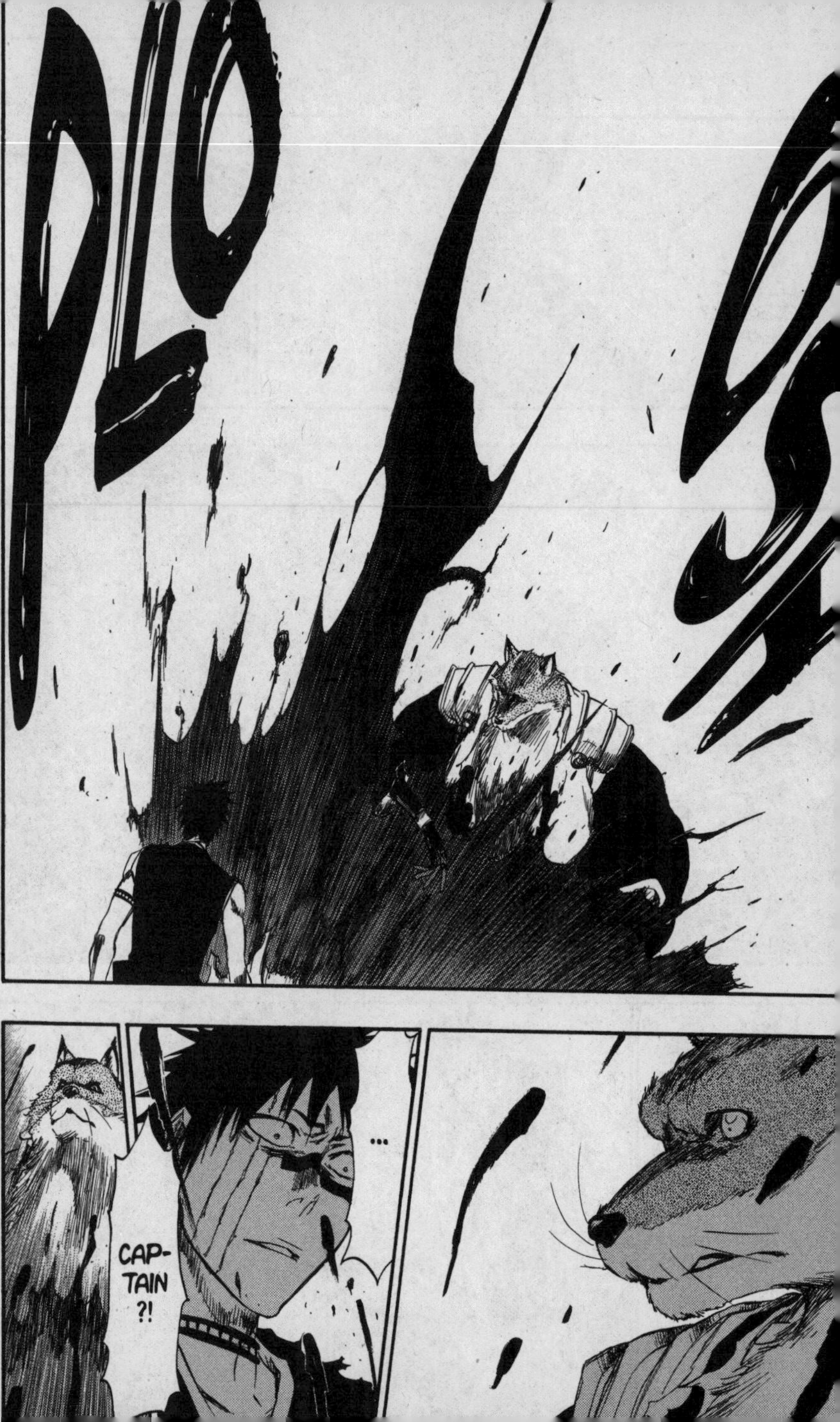
...
CAP-
TAIN
?!

CAP-
TAIN
!!

AIZEN
!!

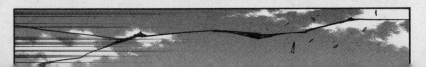

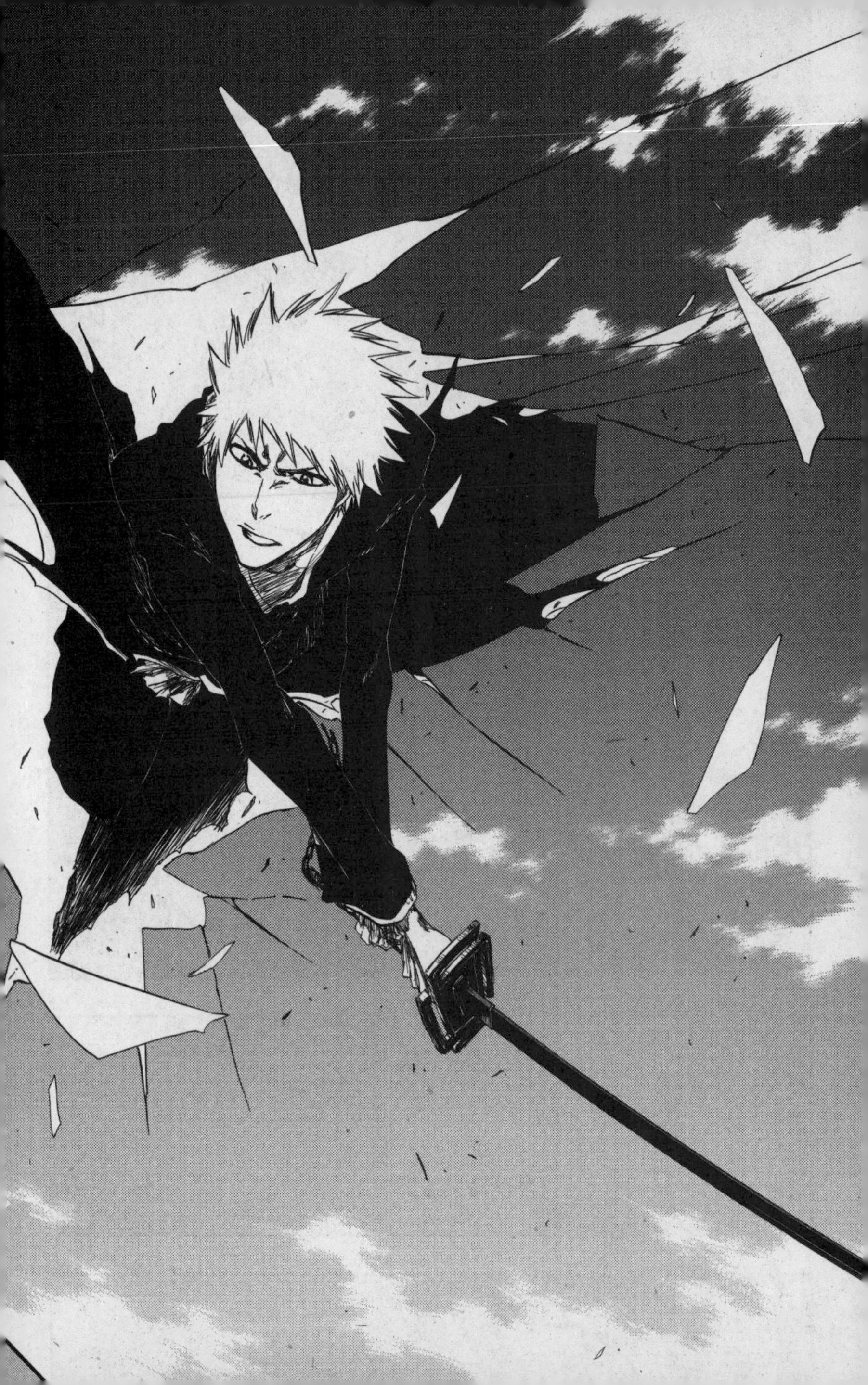

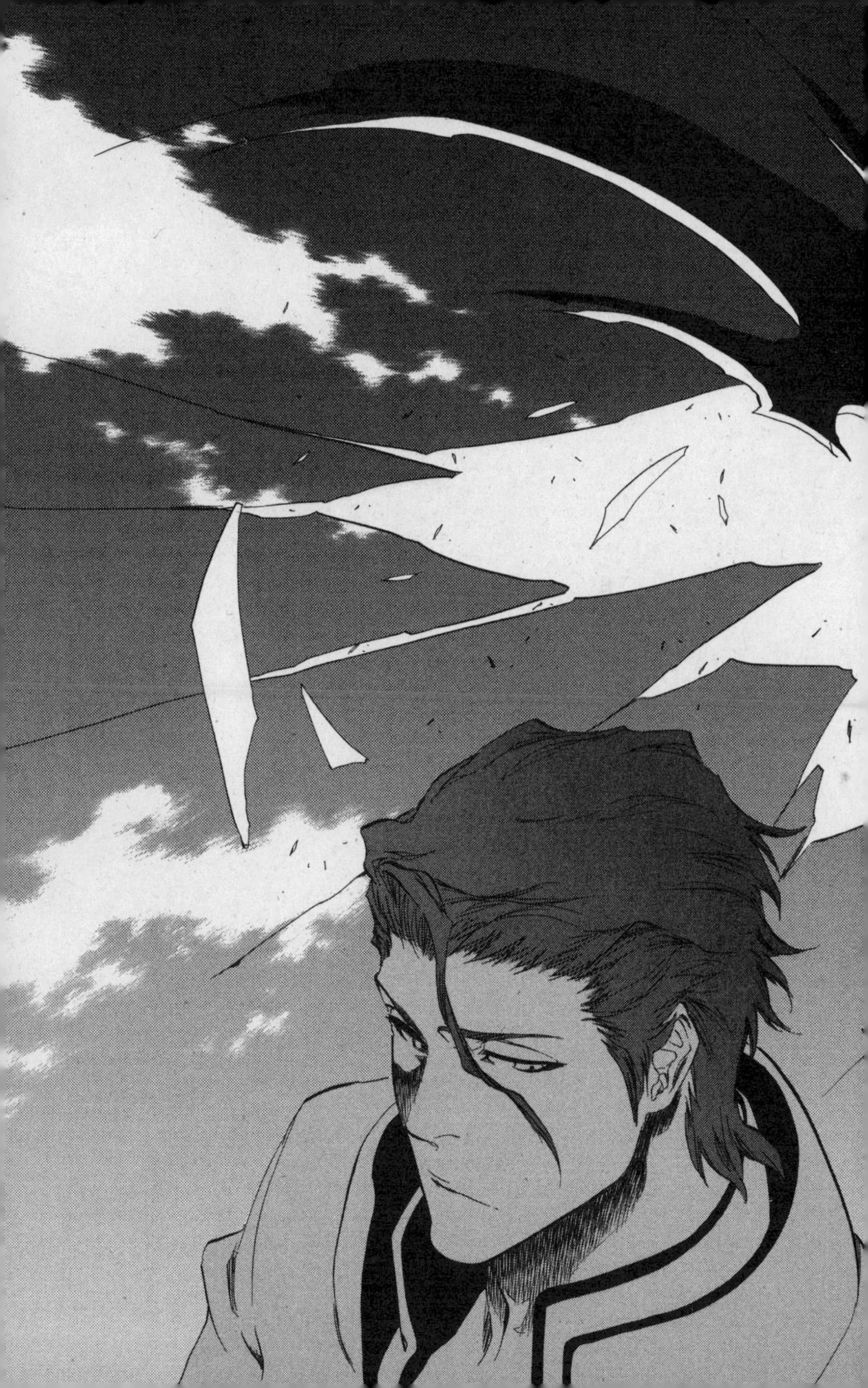

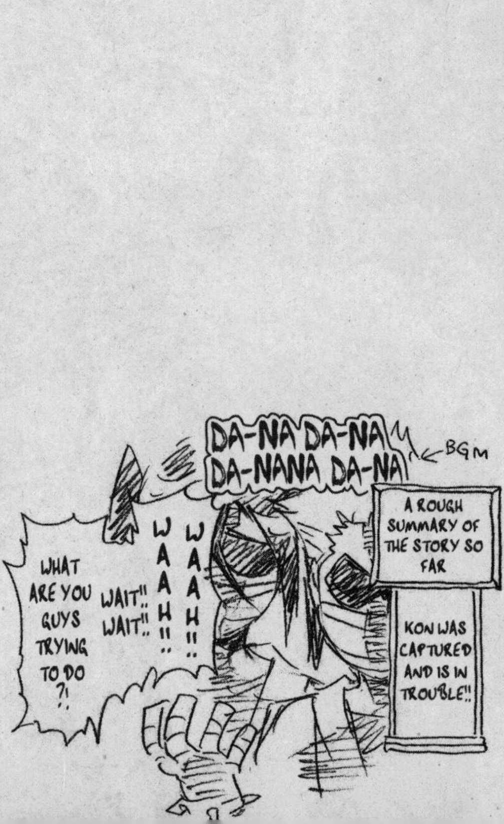
A ROUGH SUMMARY OF THE STORY SO FAR
KON WAS CAPTURED AND IS IN TROUBLE!!
BGM
DA-NA DA-NA DA-NANA DA-NA
WAAAH!!
WAAAH!!
WAIT!! WAIT!!
WHAT ARE YOU GUYS TRYING TO DO?!

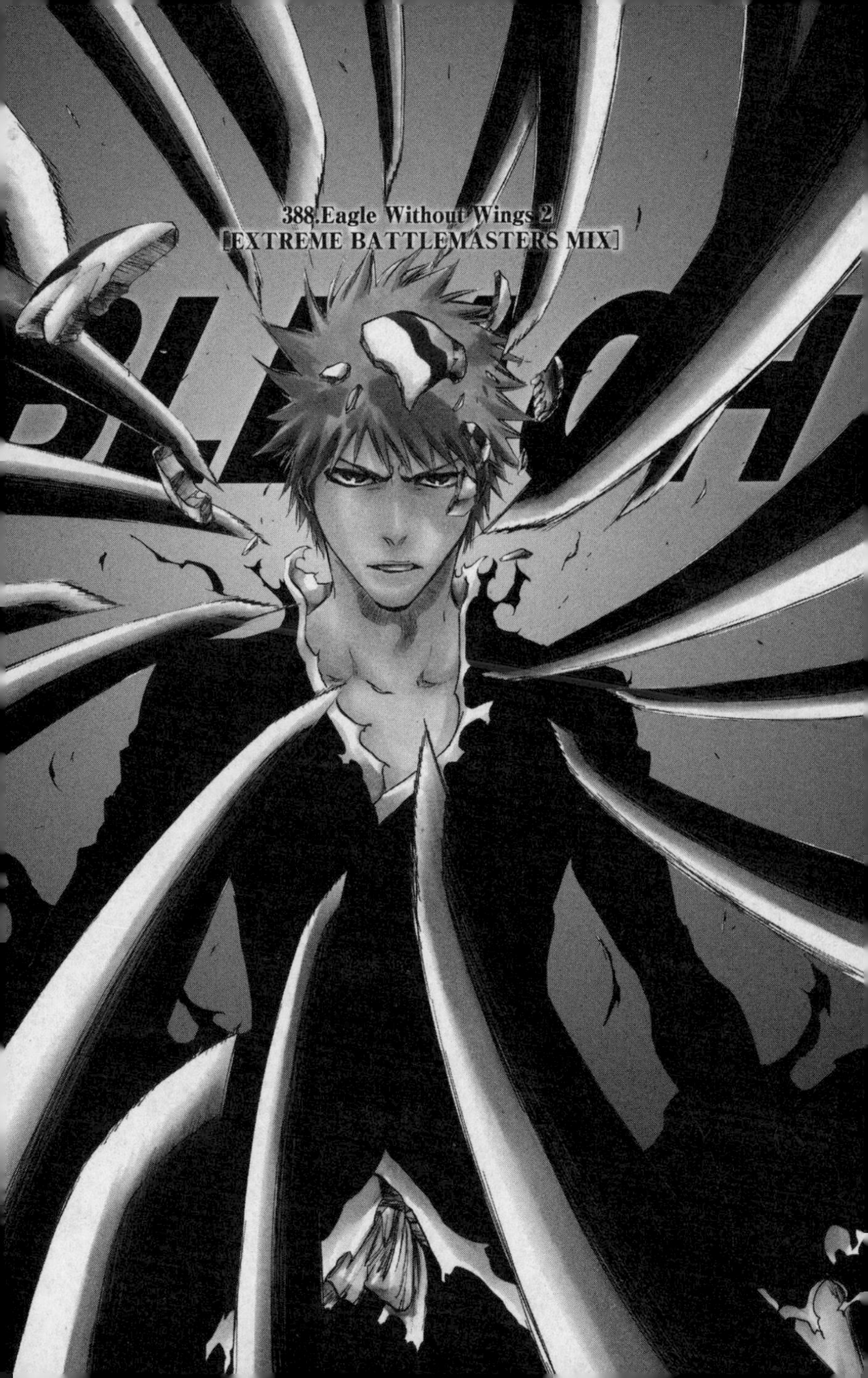
388.Eagle Without Wings 2
[EXTREME BATTLEMASTERS MIX]
BLEACH

BLEACH

ブリーチ

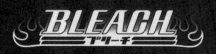

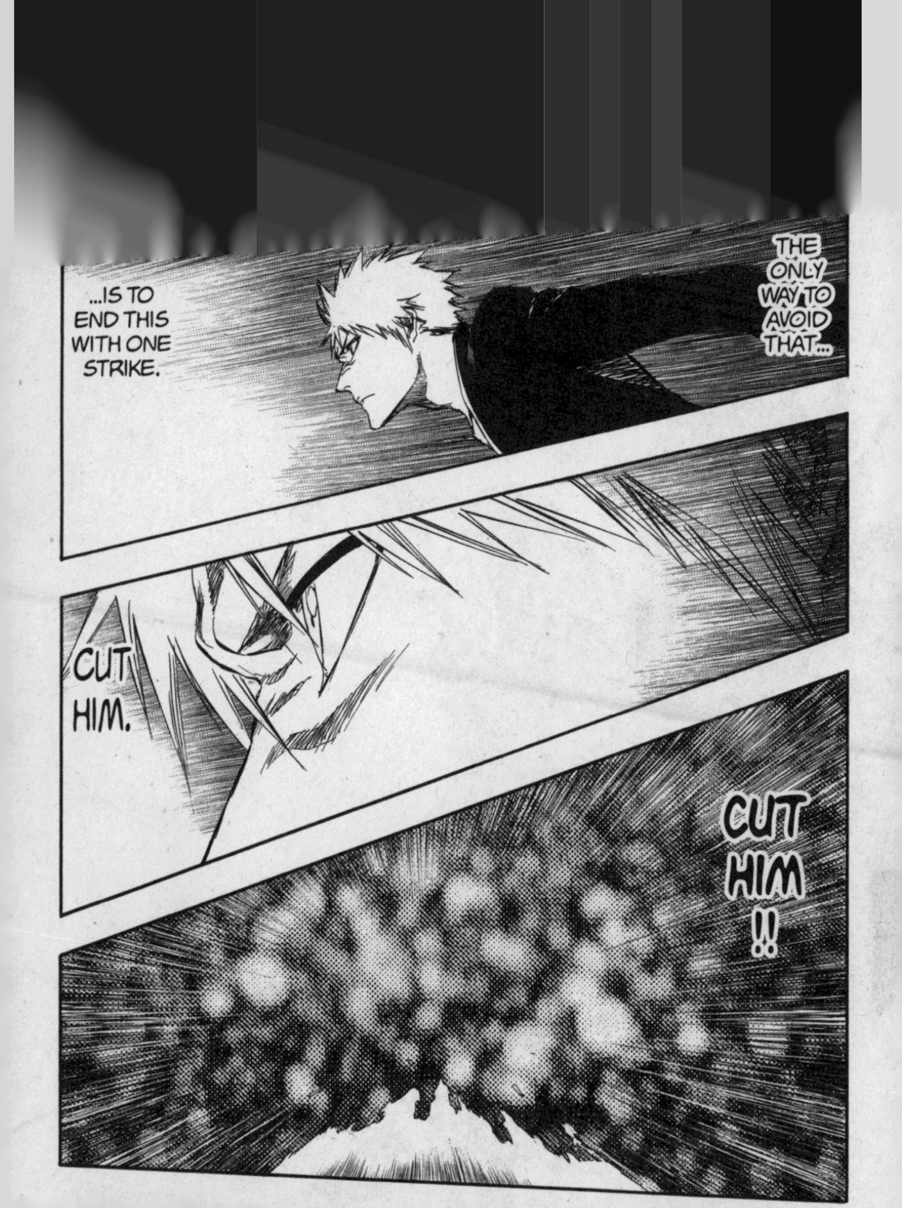
THE ONLY WAY TO AVOID THAT...
...IS TO END THIS WITH ONE STRIKE.
CUT HIM.
CUT HIM!!

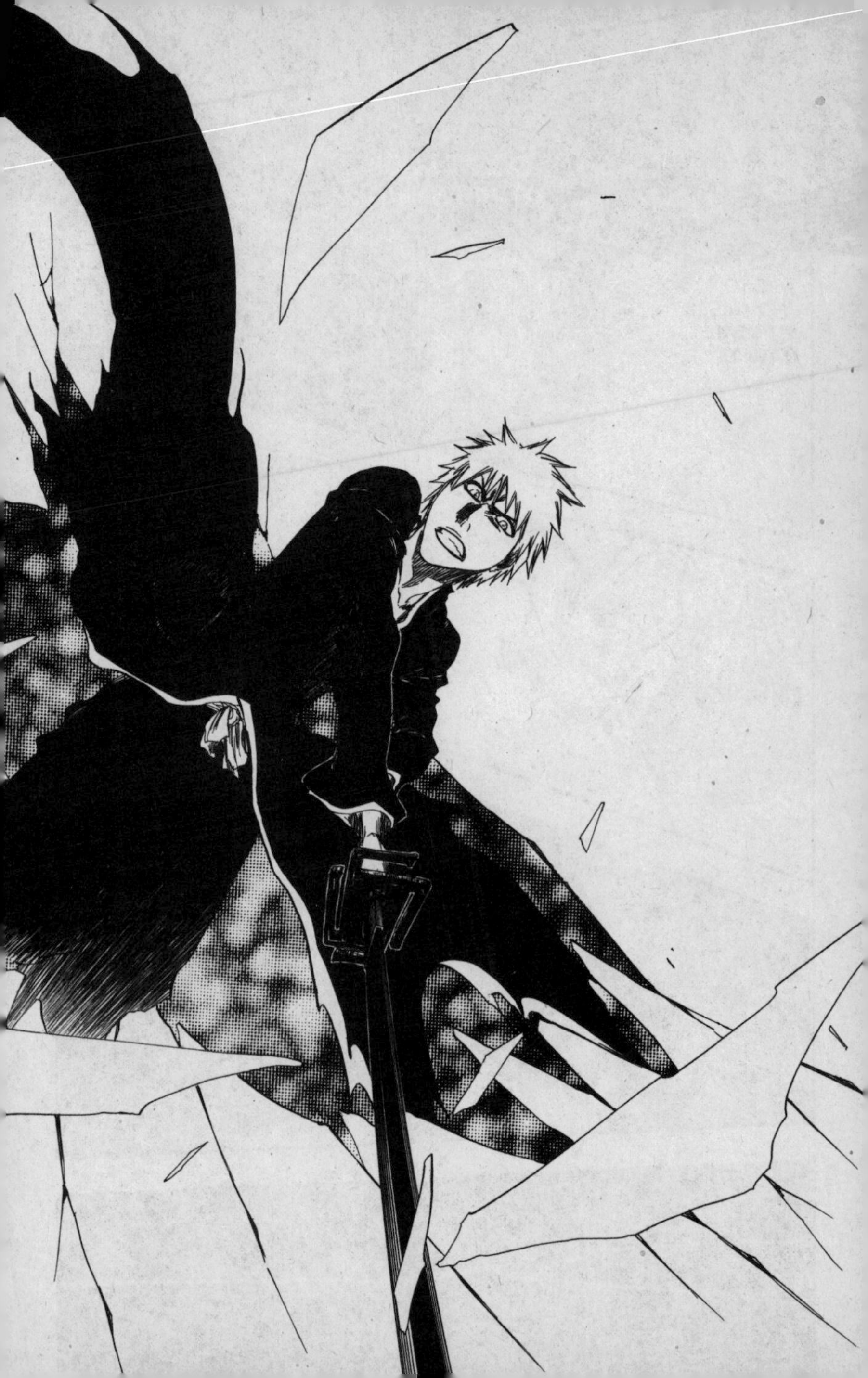

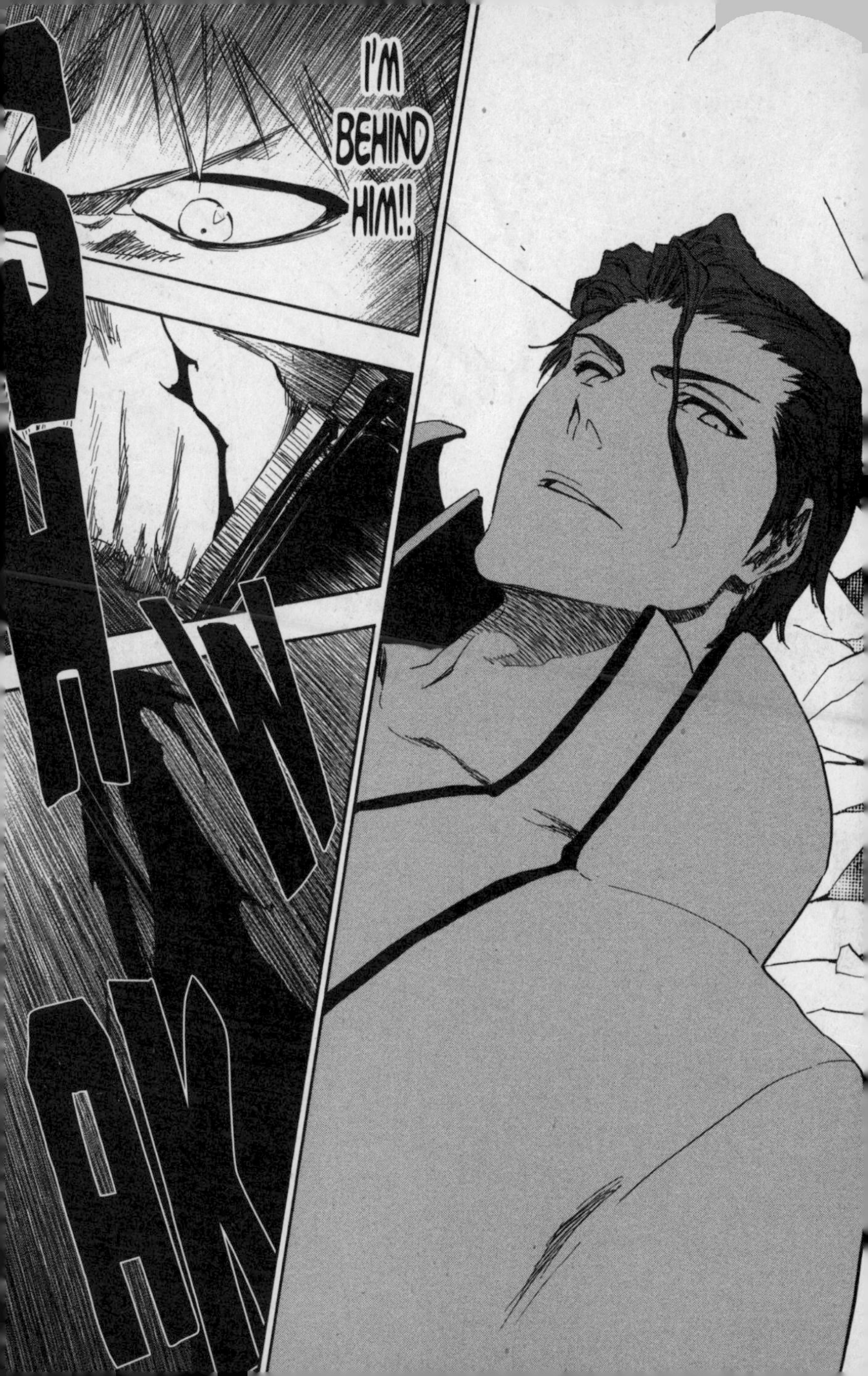
I'M BEHIND HIM!!

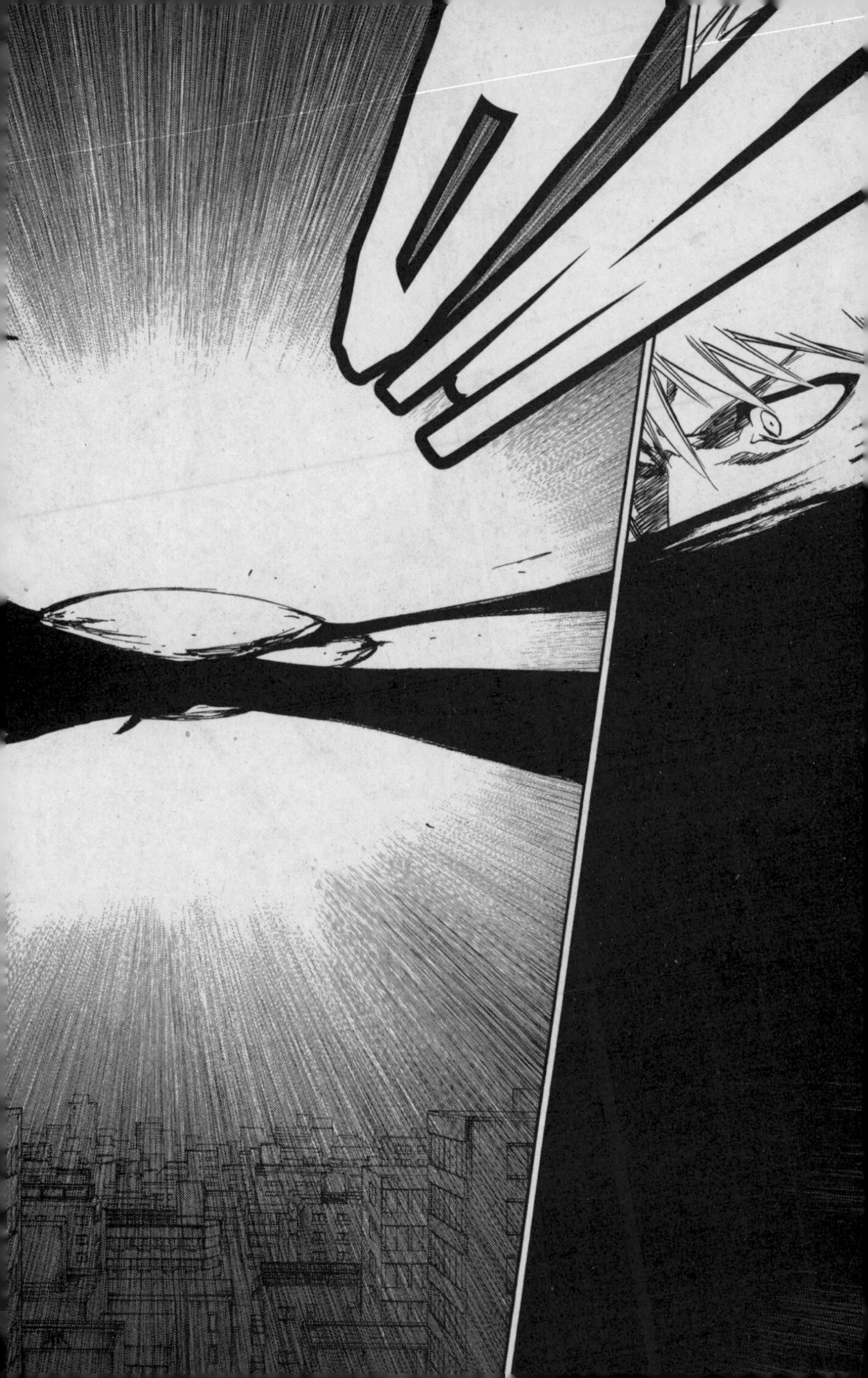

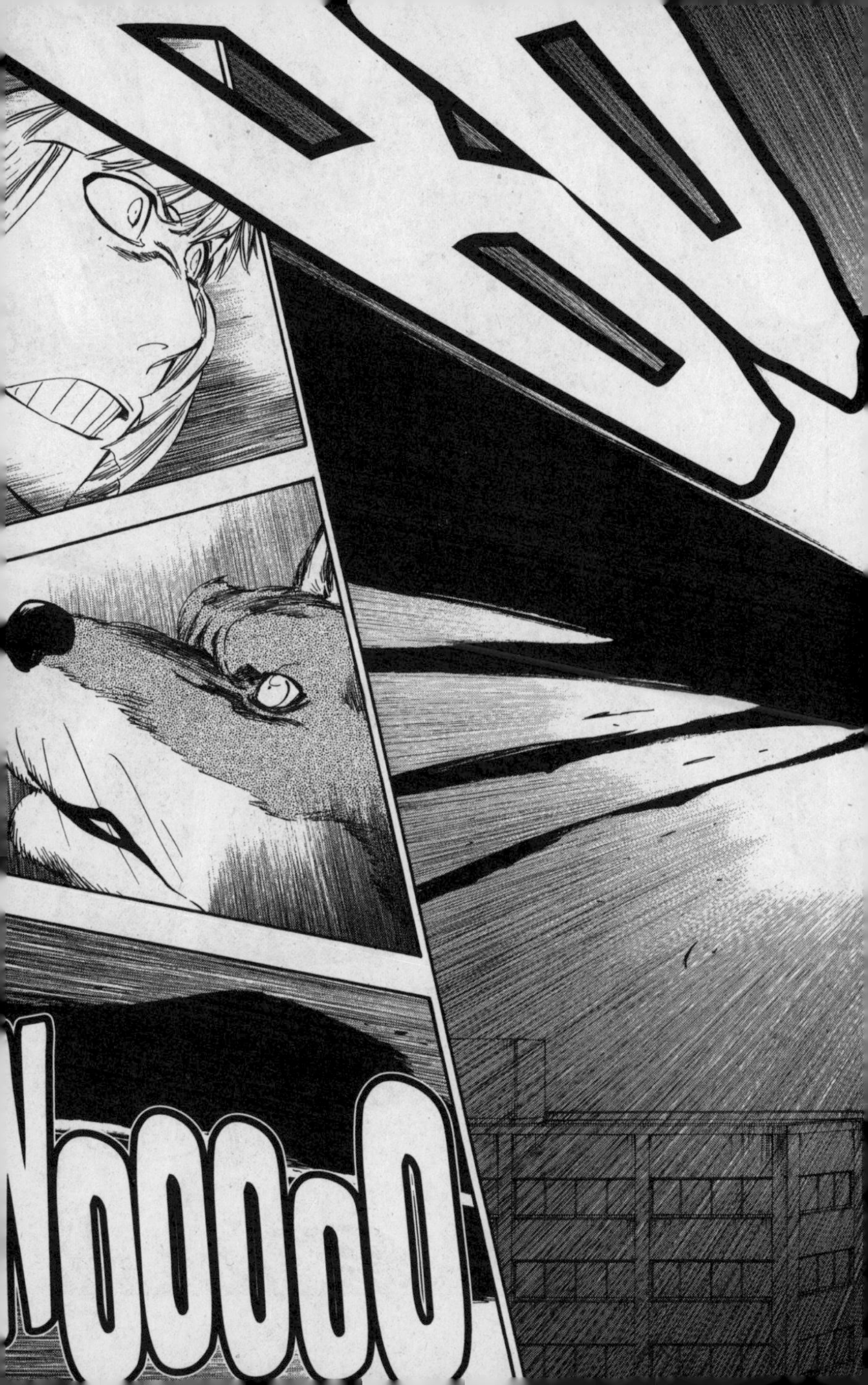
NOOOOO

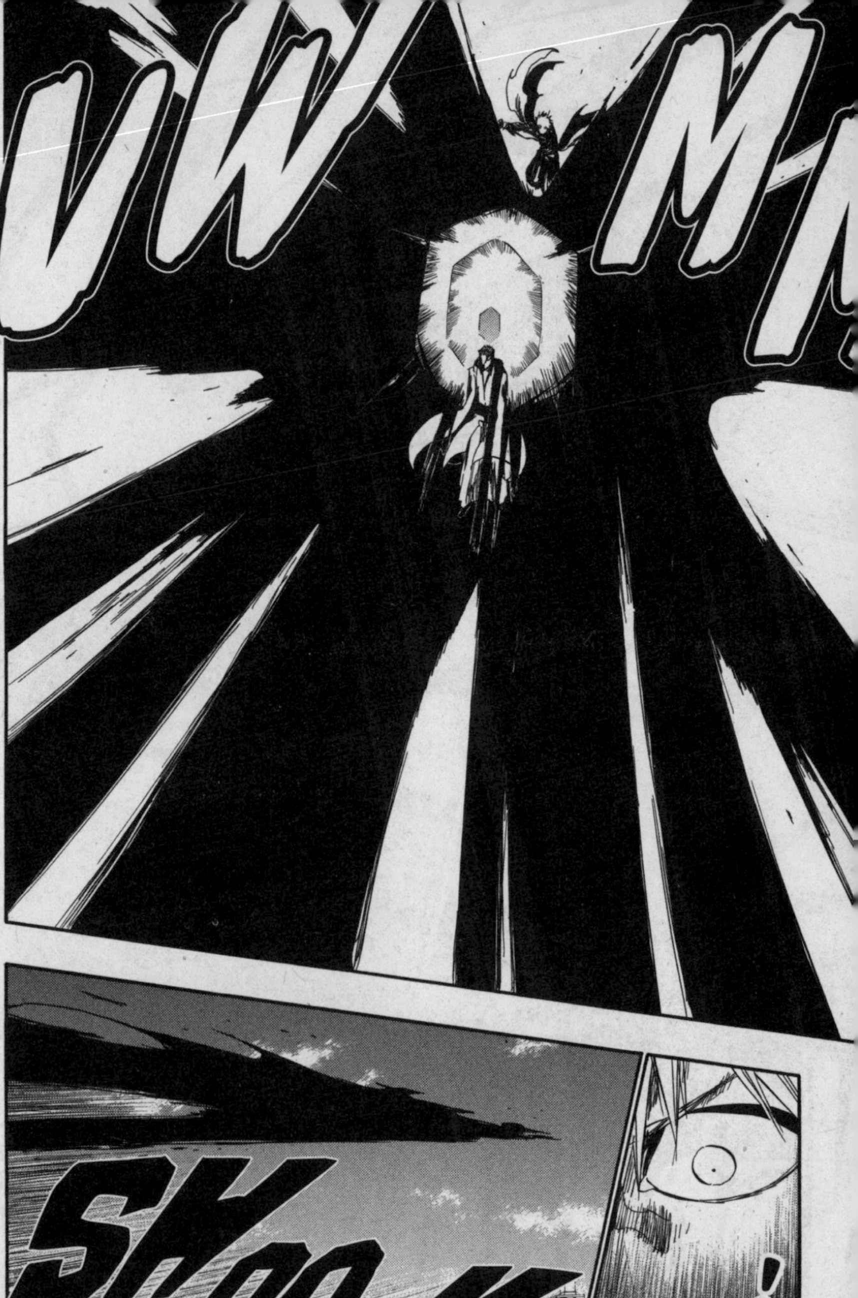
VWM
!
SHOOM

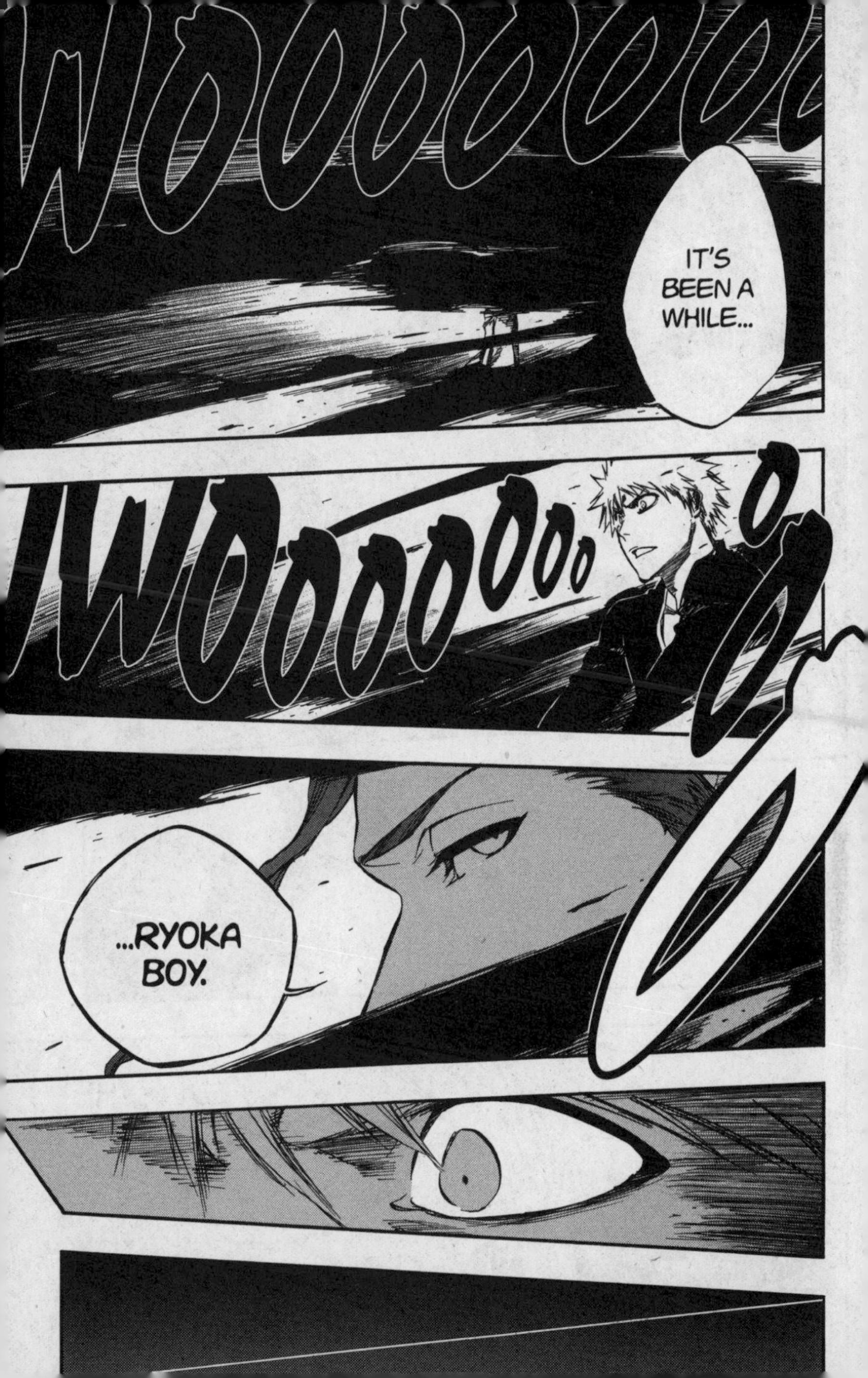
IT'S BEEN A WHILE...
...RYOKA BOY.

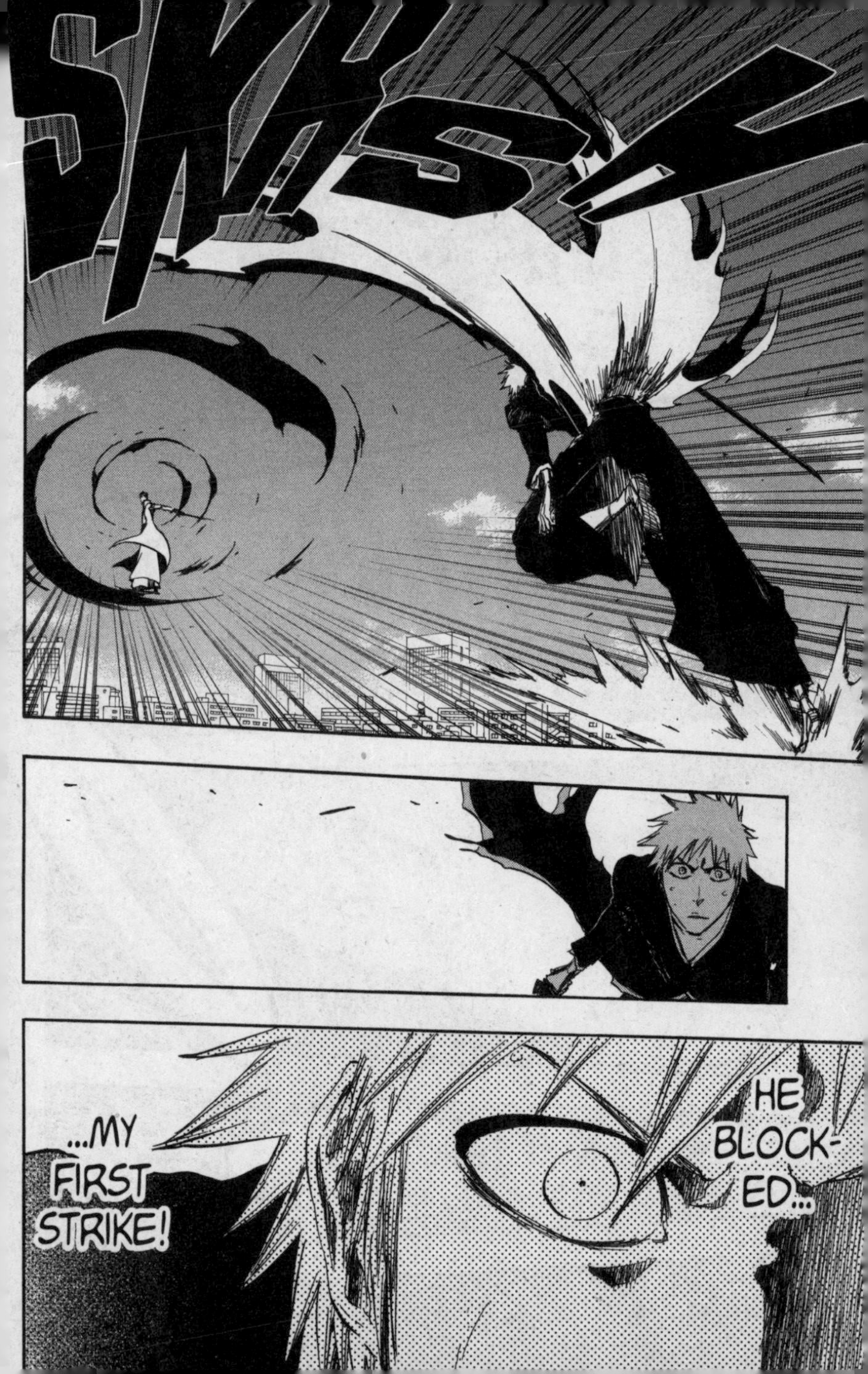
HE BLOCKED...
...MY FIRST STRIKE!

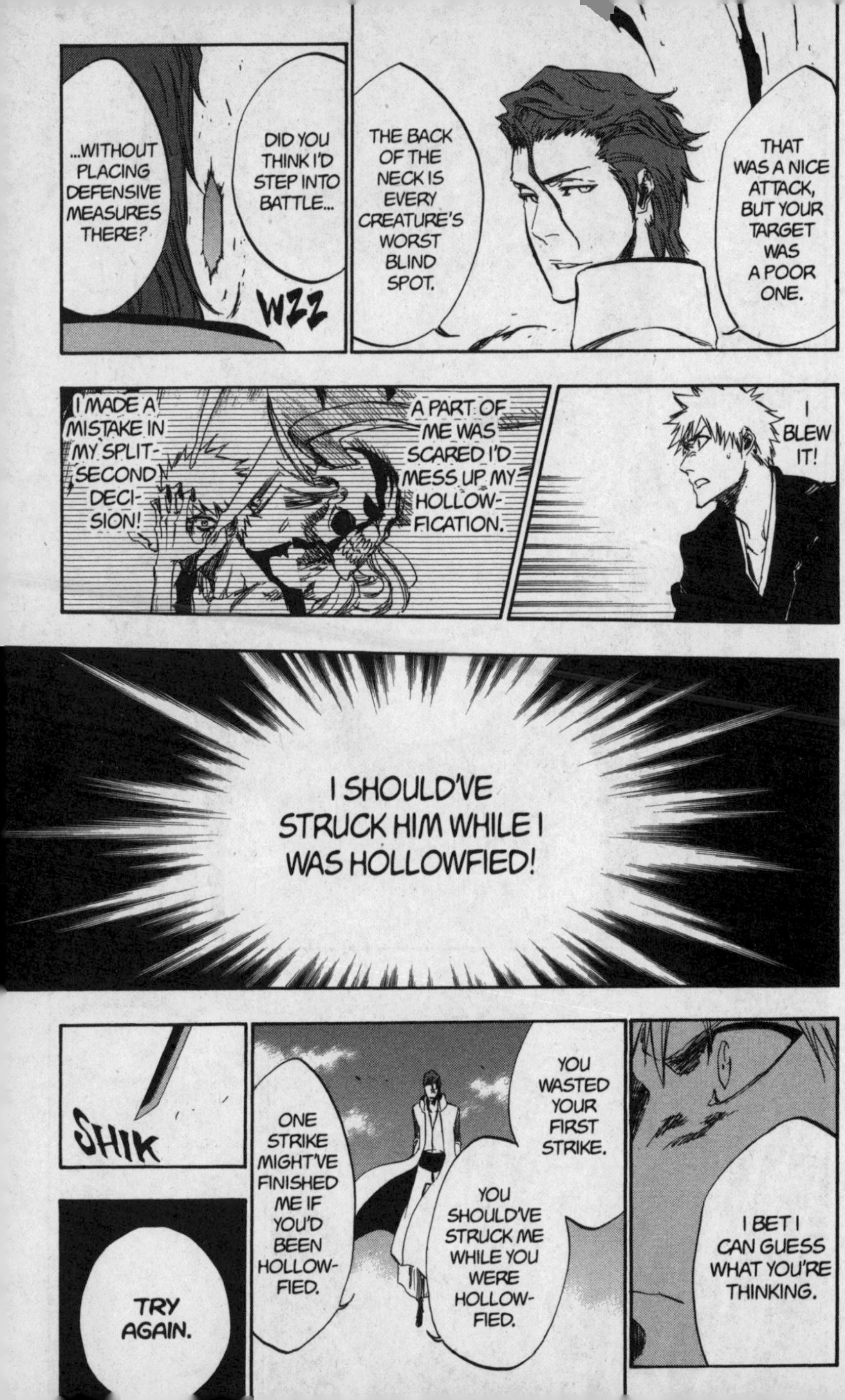
THAT WAS A NICE ATTACK, BUT YOUR TARGET WAS A POOR ONE.
THE BACK OF THE NECK IS EVERY CREATURE'S WORST BLIND SPOT.
DID YOU THINK I'D STEP INTO BATTLE...
...WITHOUT PLACING DEFENSIVE MEASURES THERE?
WZZ
I BLEW IT!
A PART OF ME WAS SCARED I'D MESS UP MY HOLLOW-FICATION.
I MADE A MISTAKE IN MY SPLIT-SECOND DECI-SION!
I SHOULD'VE STRUCK HIM WHILE I WAS HOLLOWFIED!
I BET I CAN GUESS WHAT YOU'RE THINKING.
YOU WASTED YOUR FIRST STRIKE.
YOU SHOULD'VE STRUCK ME WHILE YOU WERE HOLLOW-FIED.
ONE STRIKE MIGHT'VE FINISHED ME IF YOU'D BEEN HOLLOW-FIED.
SHIK
TRY AGAIN.

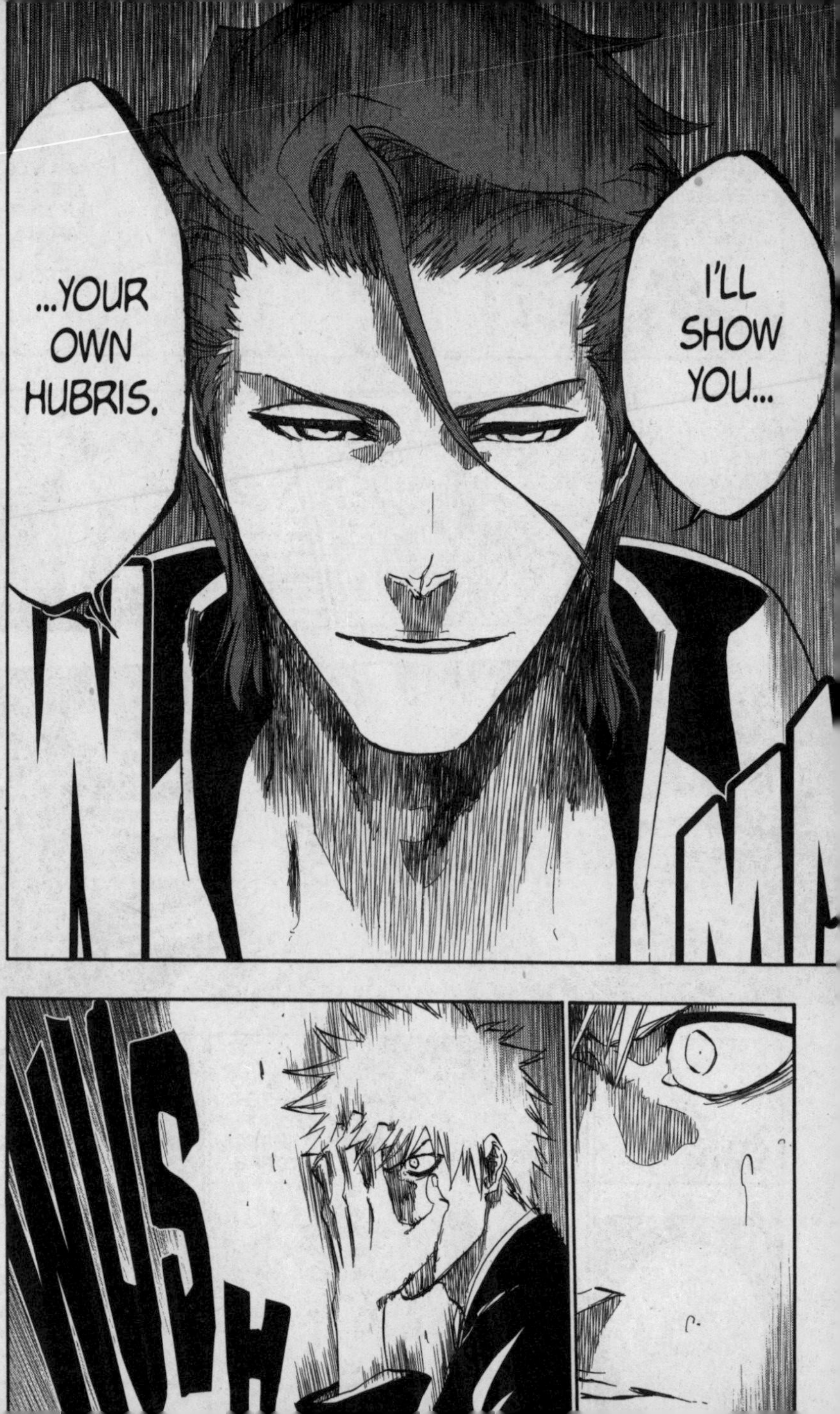
I'LL SHOW YOU...
...YOUR OWN HUBRIS.

READ THIS WAY

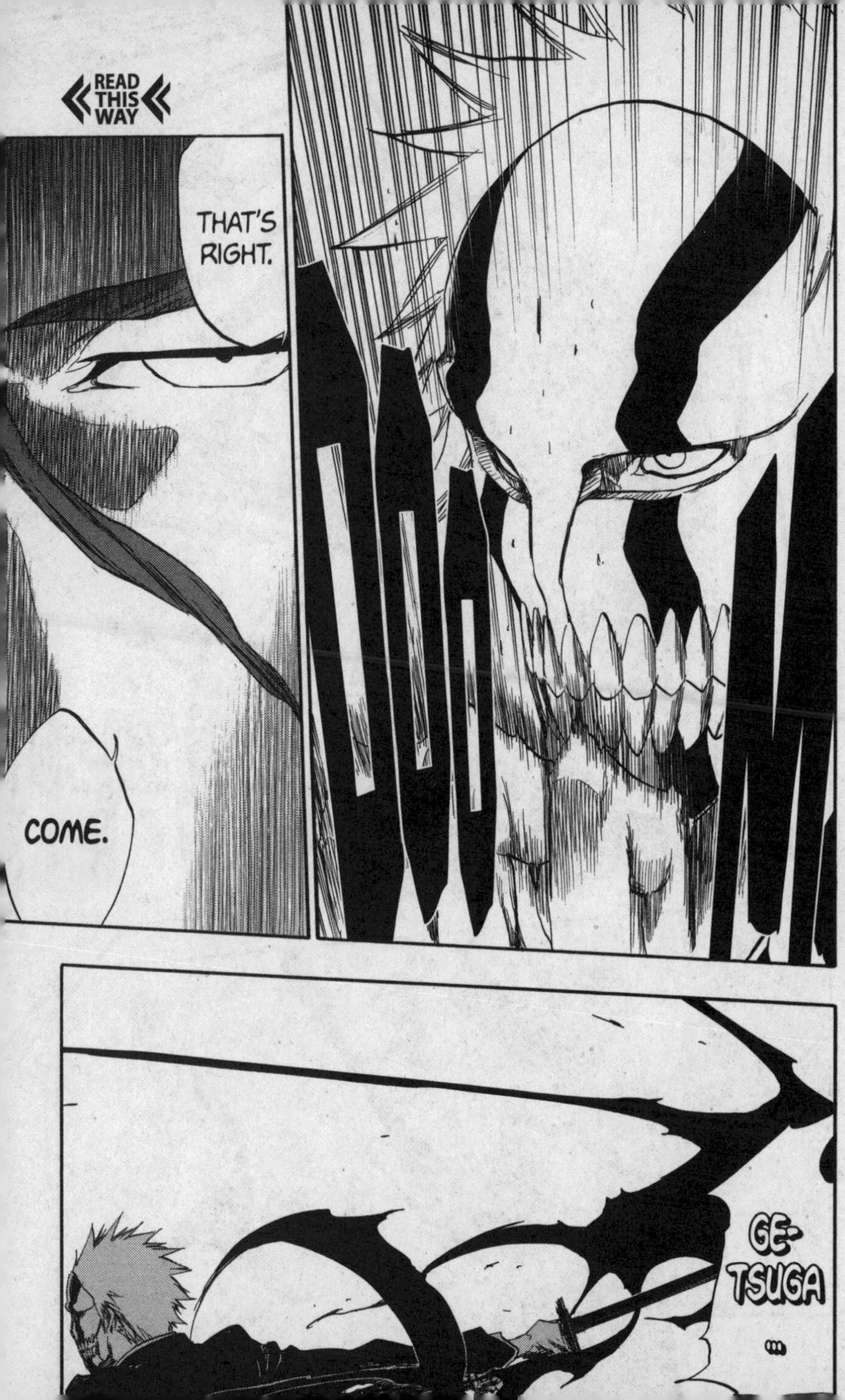
THAT'S RIGHT.
COME.
GE-TSUGA...

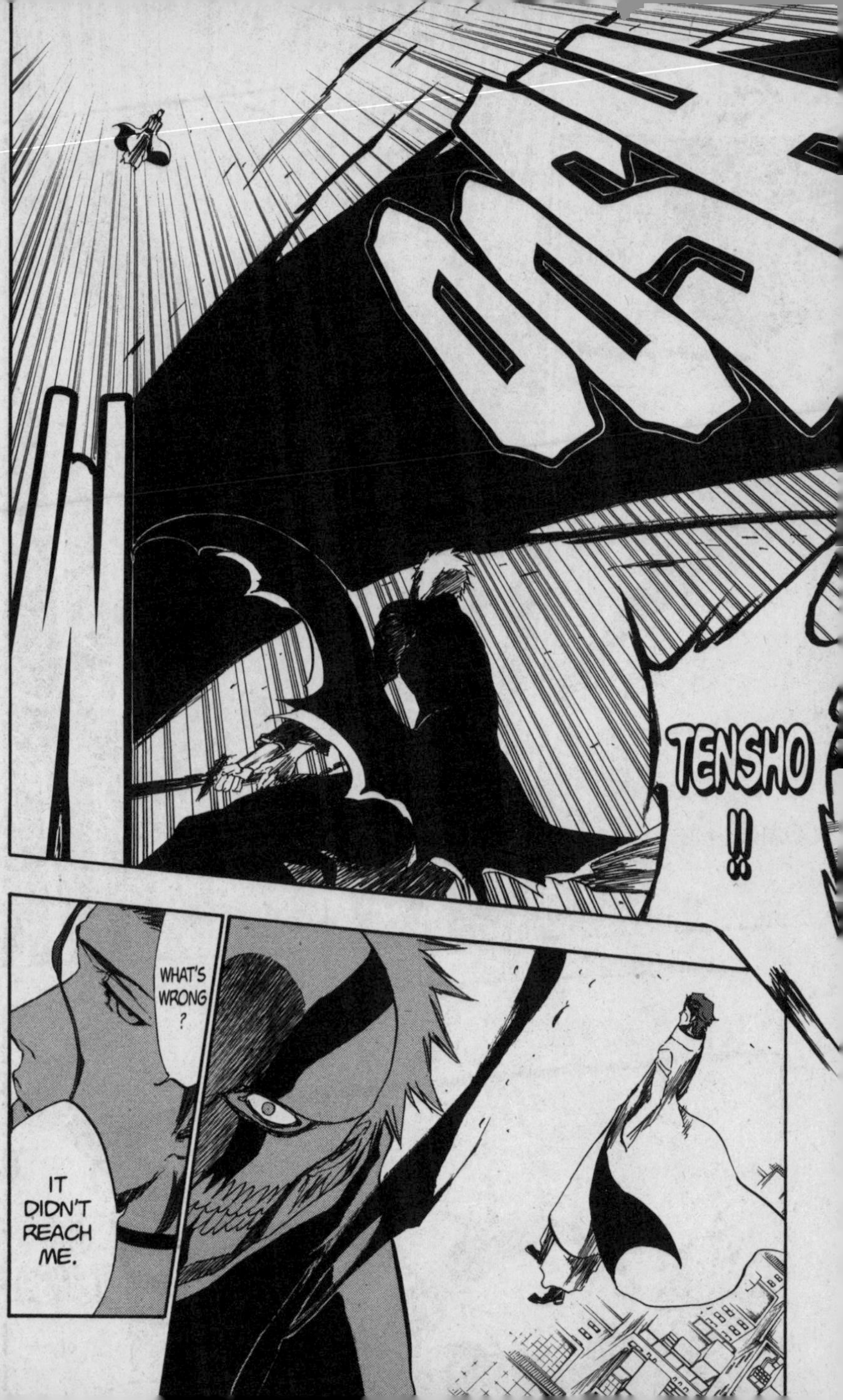
TENSHO !!
WHAT'S WRONG ?
IT DIDN'T REACH ME.

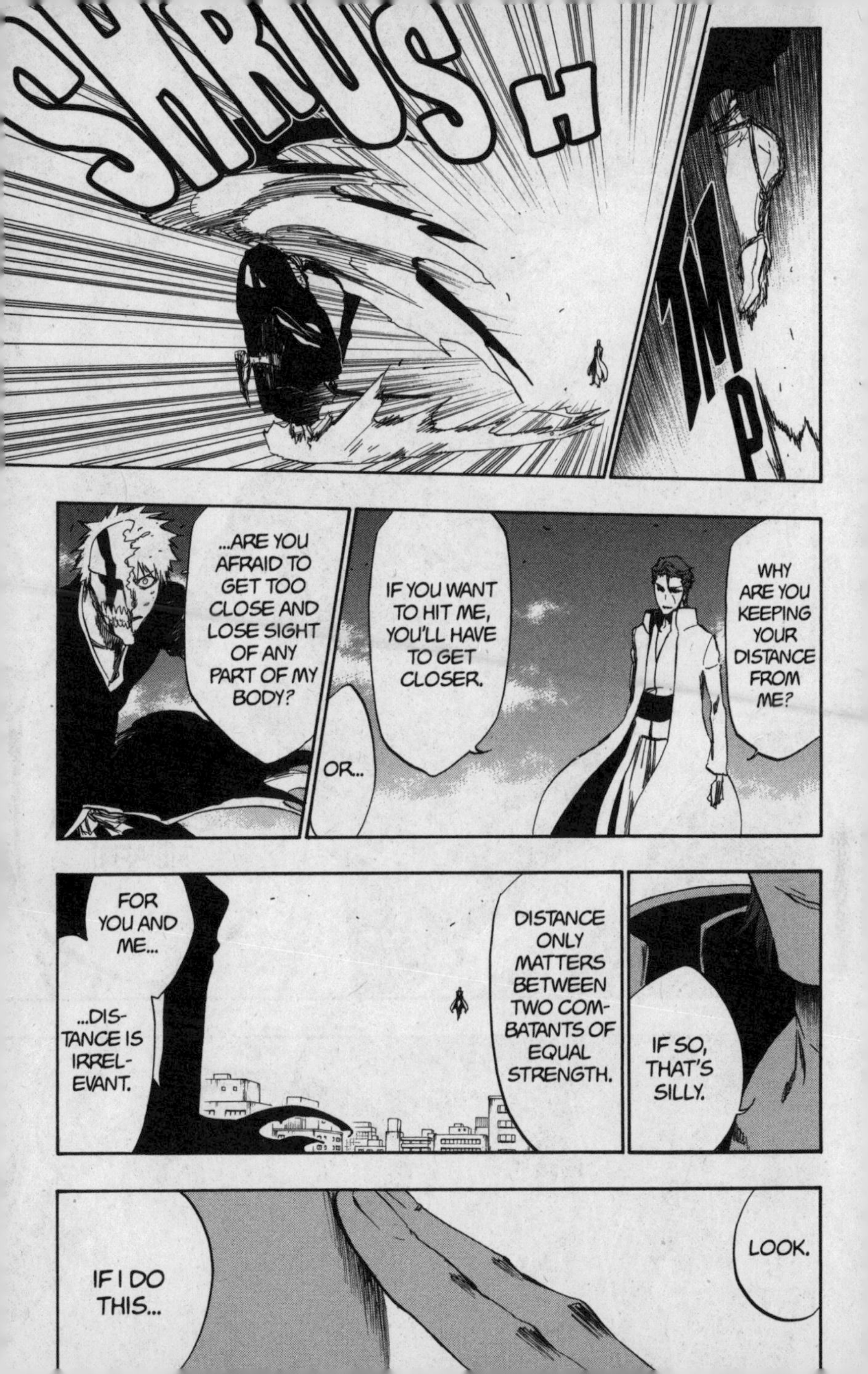
SHRUSH
WHY ARE YOU KEEPING YOUR DISTANCE FROM ME?
IF YOU WANT TO HIT ME, YOU'LL HAVE TO GET CLOSER.
OR...
...ARE YOU AFRAID TO GET TOO CLOSE AND LOSE SIGHT OF ANY PART OF MY BODY?
IF SO, THAT'S SILLY.
DISTANCE ONLY MATTERS BETWEEN TWO COMBATANTS OF EQUAL STRENGTH.
FOR YOU AND ME...
...DISTANCE IS IRRELEVANT.
LOOK.
IF I DO THIS...

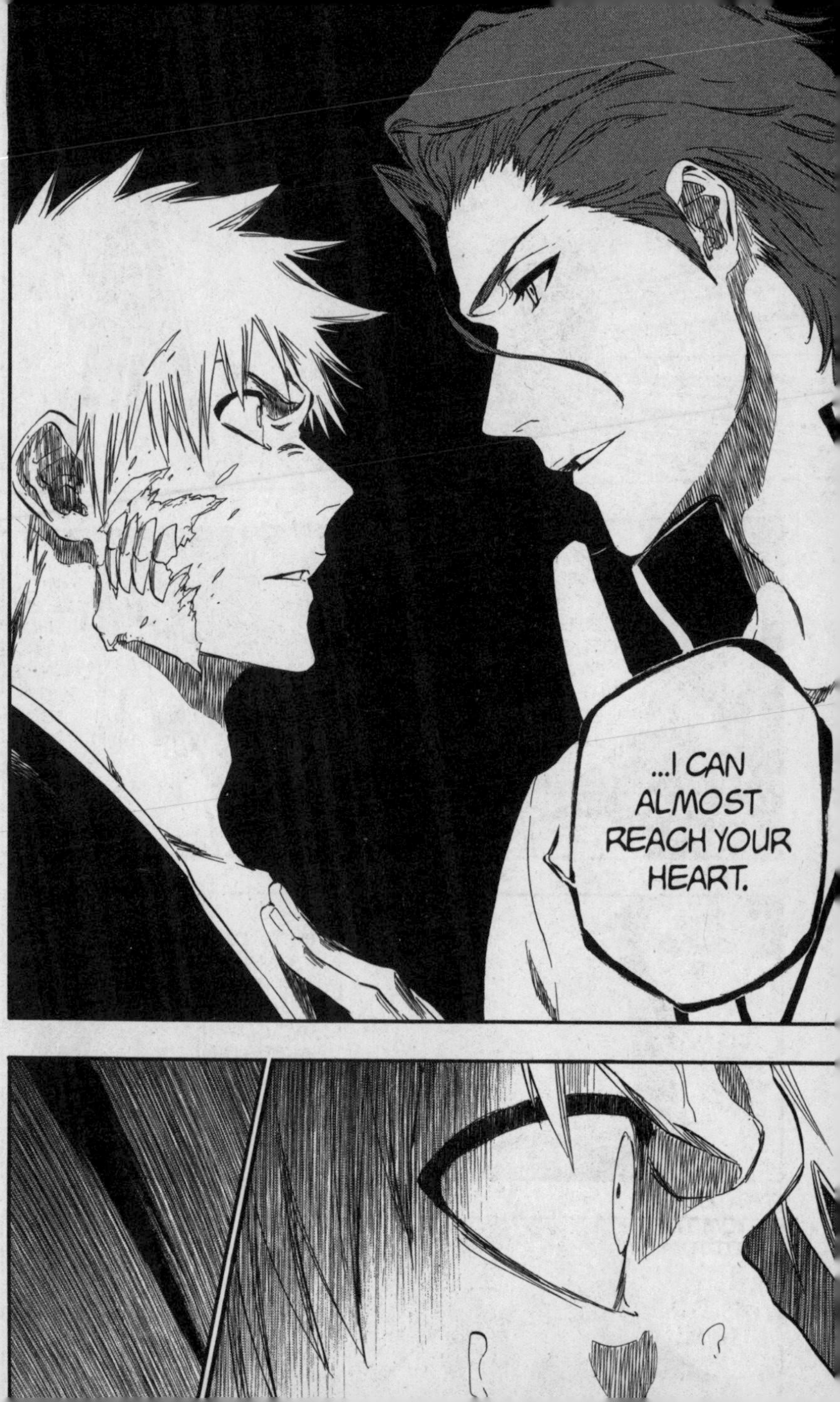
...I CAN ALMOST REACH YOUR HEART.

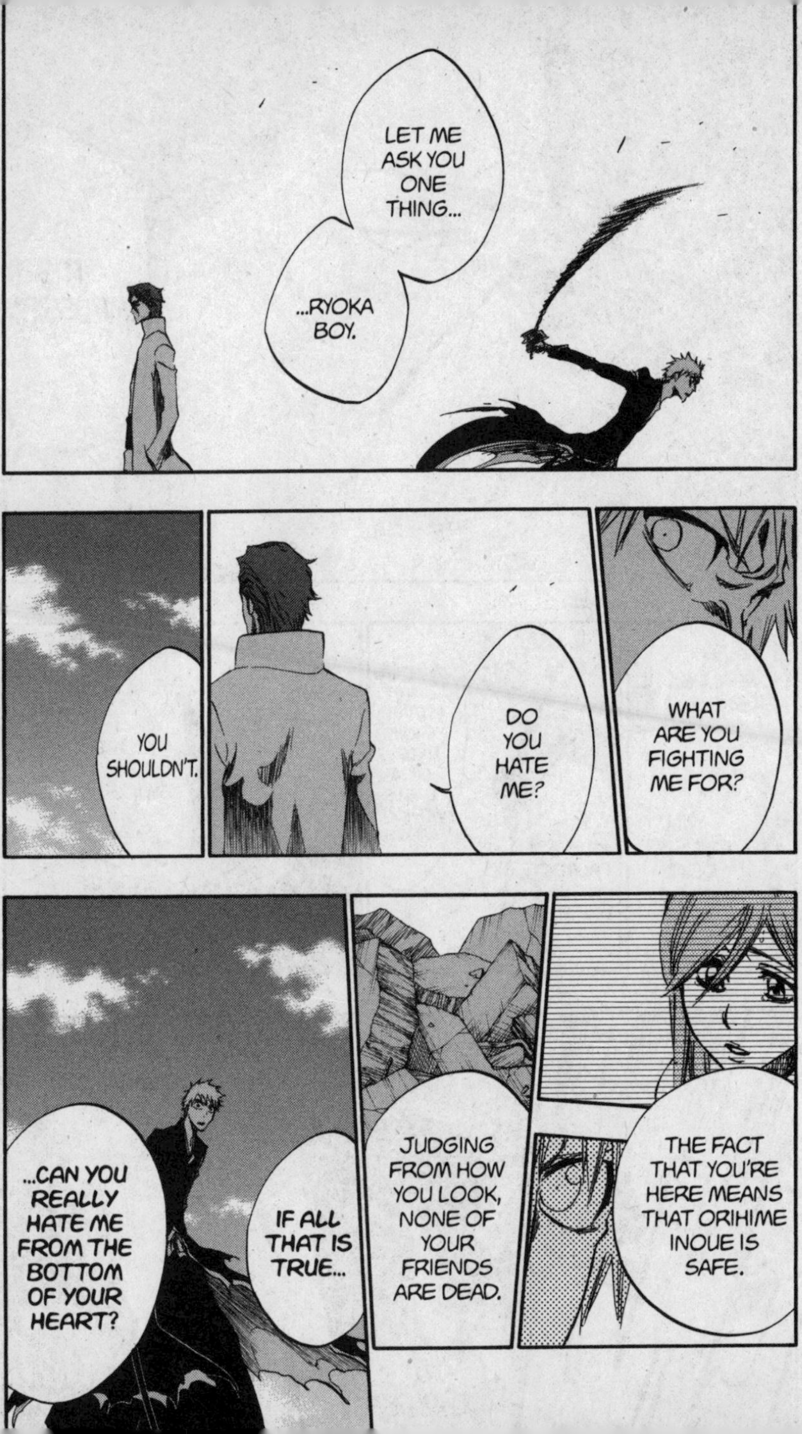
LET ME ASK YOU ONE THING...
...RYOKA BOY.
WHAT ARE YOU FIGHTING ME FOR?
DO YOU HATE ME?
YOU SHOULDN'T.
THE FACT THAT YOU'RE HERE MEANS THAT ORIHIME INOUE IS SAFE.
JUDGING FROM HOW YOU LOOK, NONE OF YOUR FRIENDS ARE DEAD.
IF ALL THAT IS TRUE...
...CAN YOU REALLY HATE ME FROM THE BOTTOM OF YOUR HEART?

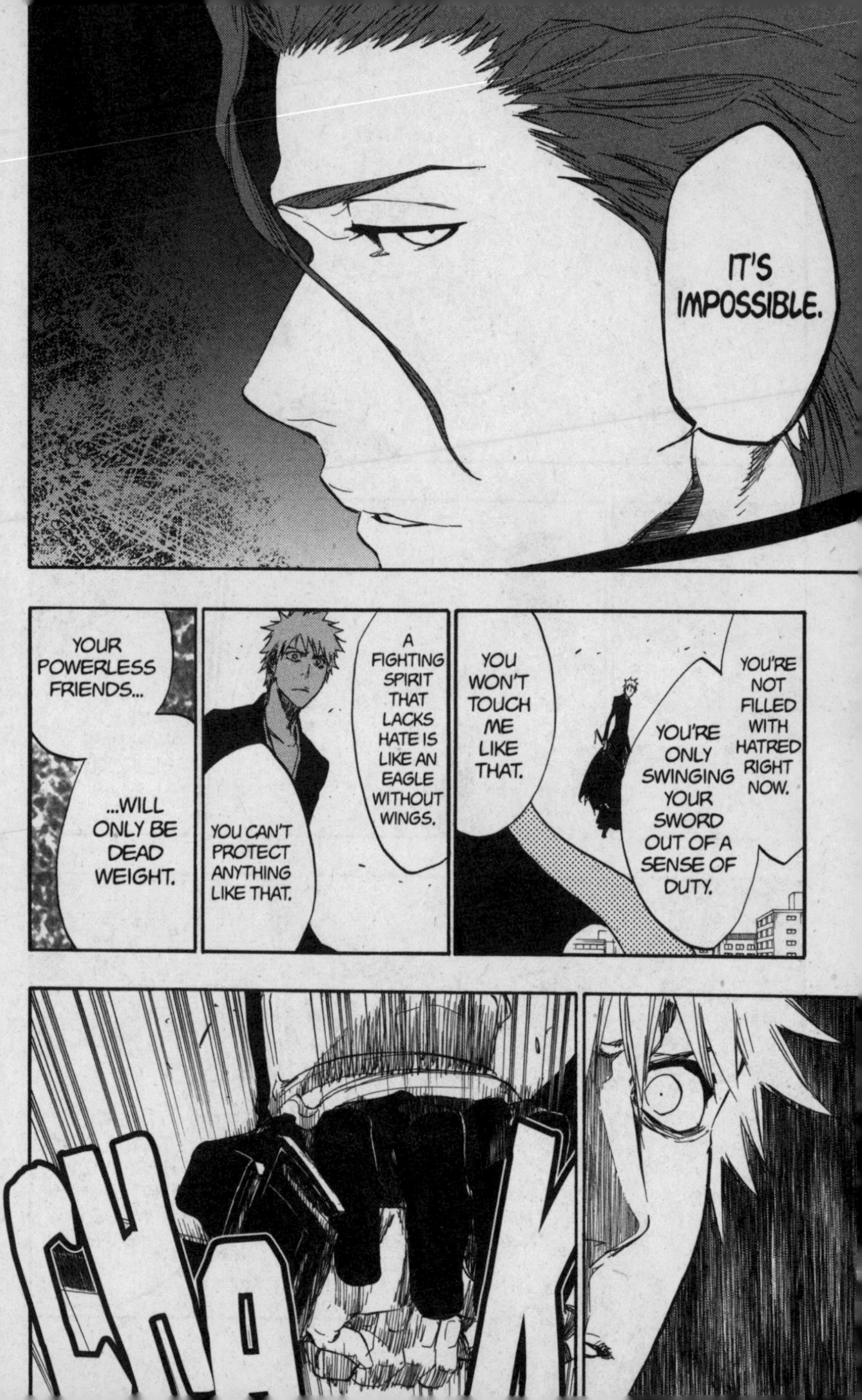
IT'S IMPOSSIBLE.
YOU'RE NOT FILLED WITH HATRED RIGHT NOW.
YOU'RE ONLY SWINGING YOUR SWORD OUT OF A SENSE OF DUTY.
YOU WON'T TOUCH ME LIKE THAT.
A FIGHTING SPIRIT THAT LACKS HATE IS LIKE AN EAGLE WITHOUT WINGS.
YOU CAN'T PROTECT ANYTHING LIKE THAT.
YOUR POWERLESS FRIENDS...
...WILL ONLY BE DEAD WEIGHT.
CHA

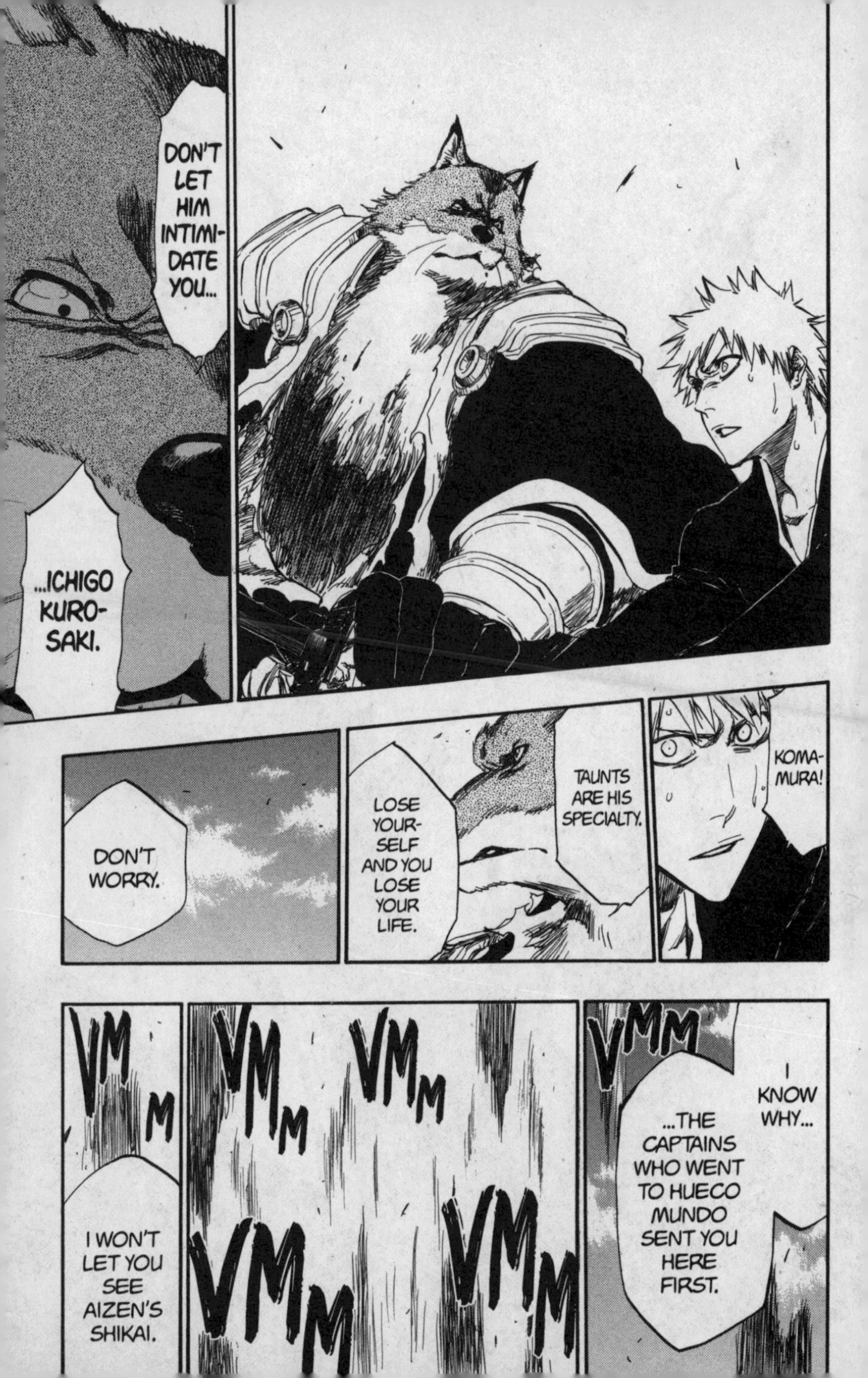
DON'T LET HIM INTIMI-DATE YOU...
...ICHIGO KURO-SAKI.
KOMA-MURA!
TAUNTS ARE HIS SPECIALTY.
LOSE YOUR-SELF AND YOU LOSE YOUR LIFE.
DON'T WORRY.
VMM
I KNOW WHY...
...THE CAPTAINS WHO WENT TO HUECO MUNDO SENT YOU HERE FIRST.
VMM
VMMM
VMMM
VMMM
VMM
I WON'T LET YOU SEE AIZEN'S SHIKAI.

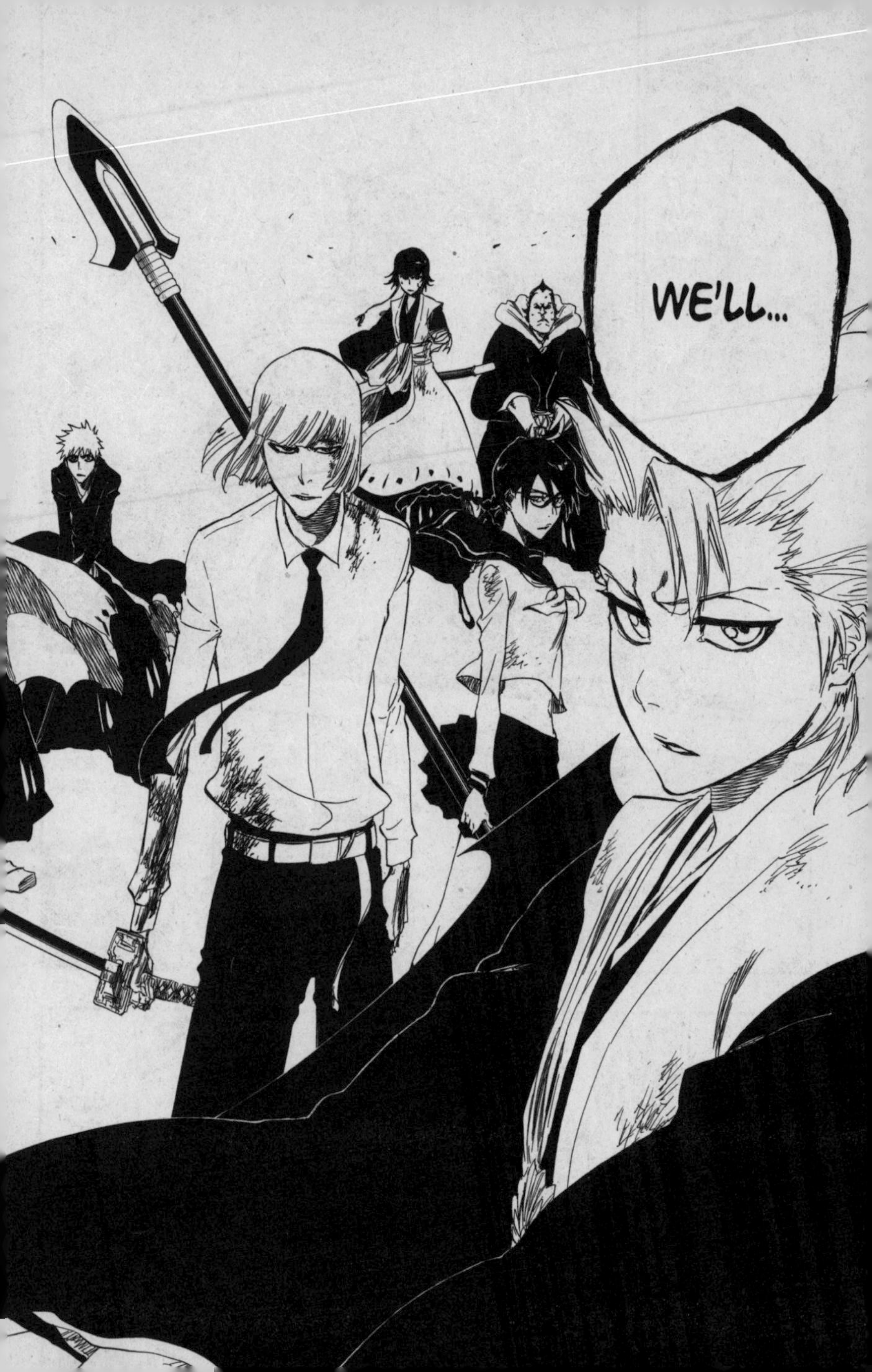
WE'LL...

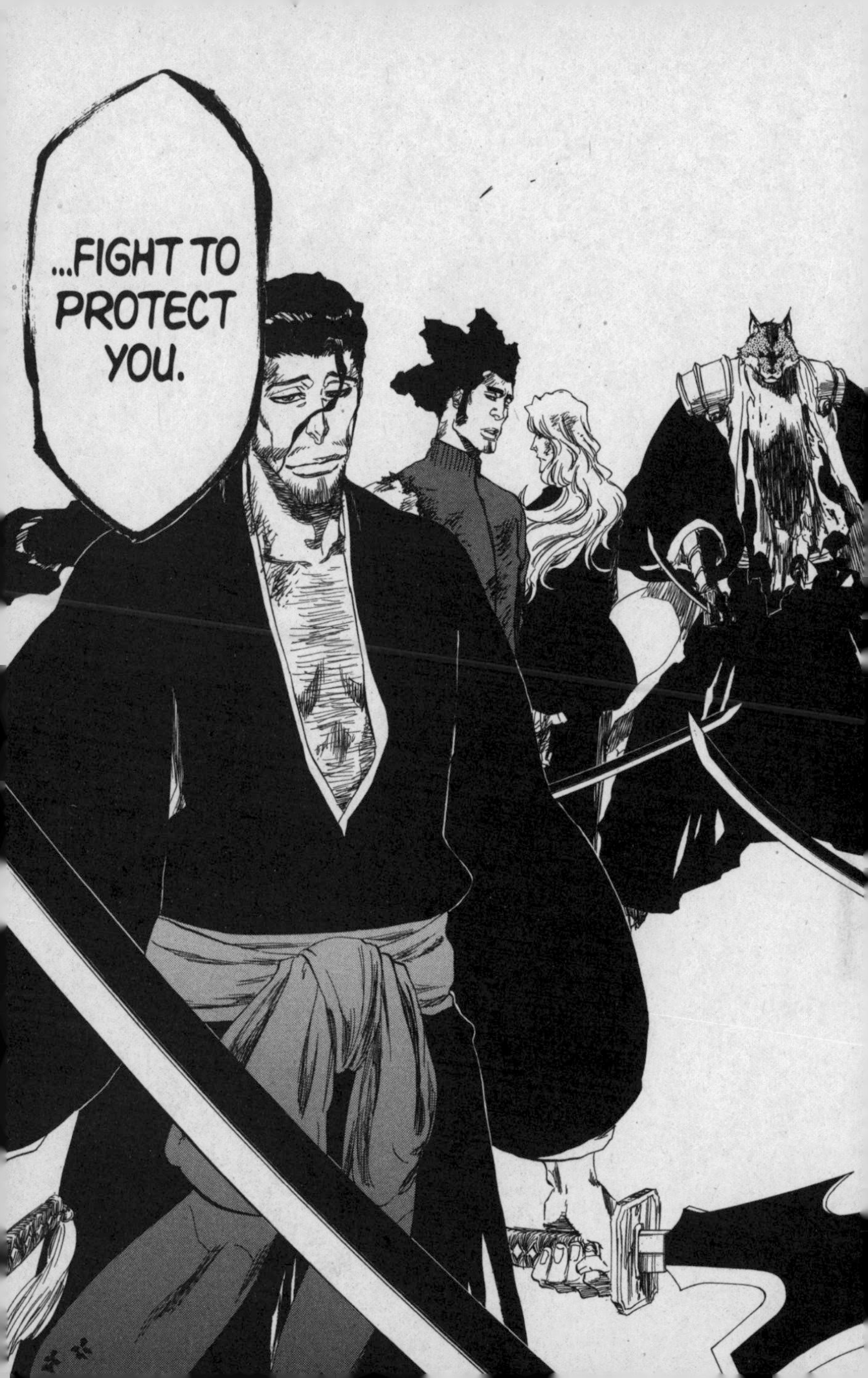
...FIGHT TO PROTECT YOU.

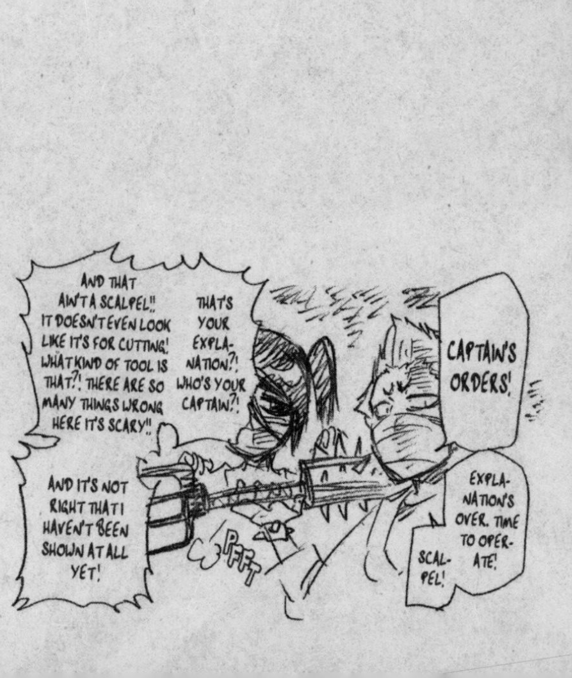
CAPTAIN'S ORDERS!
EXPLANATION'S OVER. TIME TO OPERATE!
SCALPEL!
THAT'S YOUR EXPLANATION?! WHO'S YOUR CAPTAIN?!
AND THAT AIN'T A SCALPEL!! IT DOESN'T EVEN LOOK LIKE IT'S FOR CUTTING! WHAT KIND OF TOOL IS THAT?! THERE ARE SO MANY THINGS WRONG HERE IT'S SCARY!!
PFFFT
AND IT'S NOT RIGHT THAT I HAVEN'T BEEN SHOWN AT ALL YET!

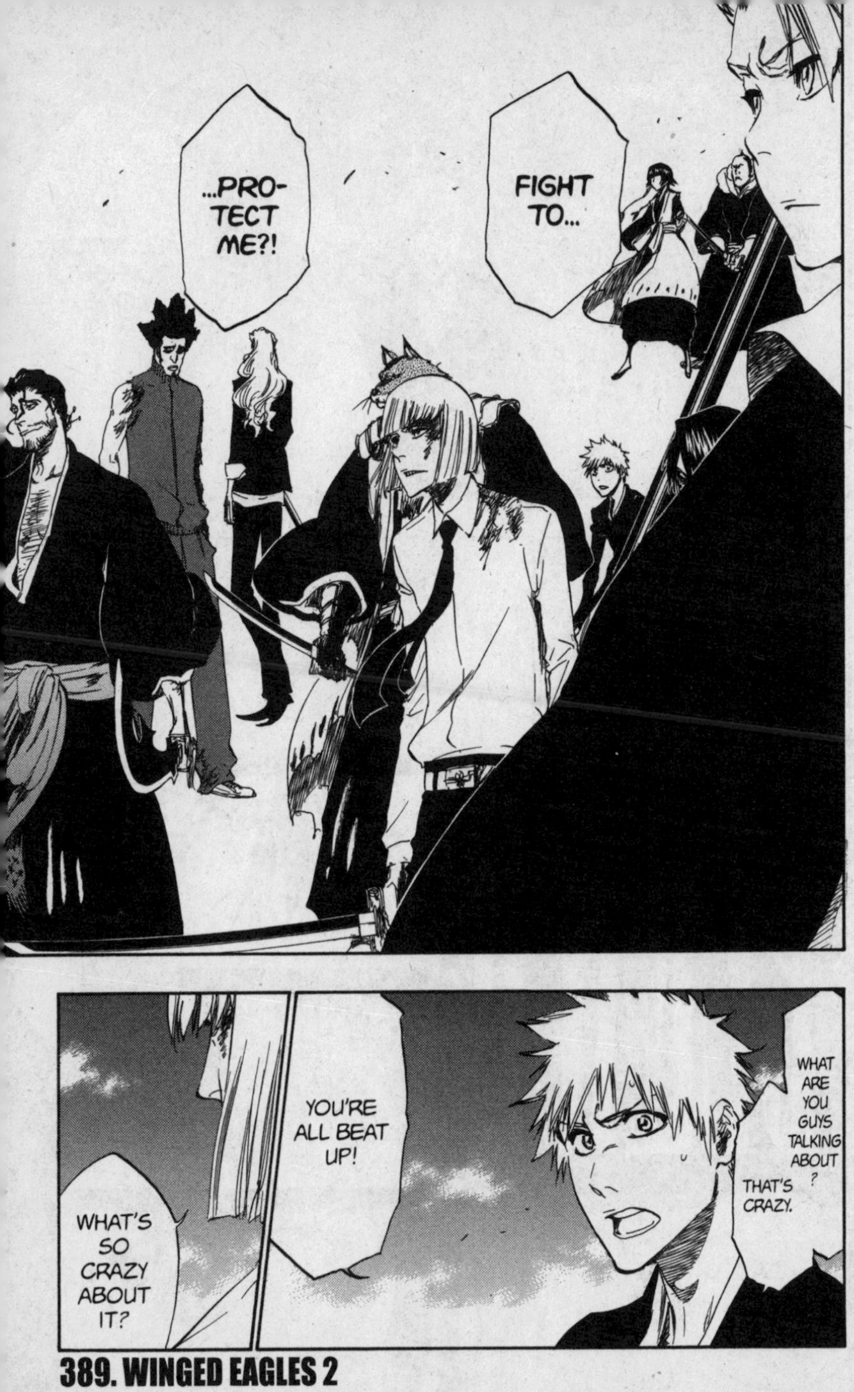
FIGHT TO...
...PRO-TECT ME?!
WHAT ARE YOU GUYS TALKING ABOUT?
THAT'S CRAZY.
YOU'RE ALL BEAT UP!
WHAT'S SO CRAZY ABOUT IT?

389. WINGED EAGLES 2

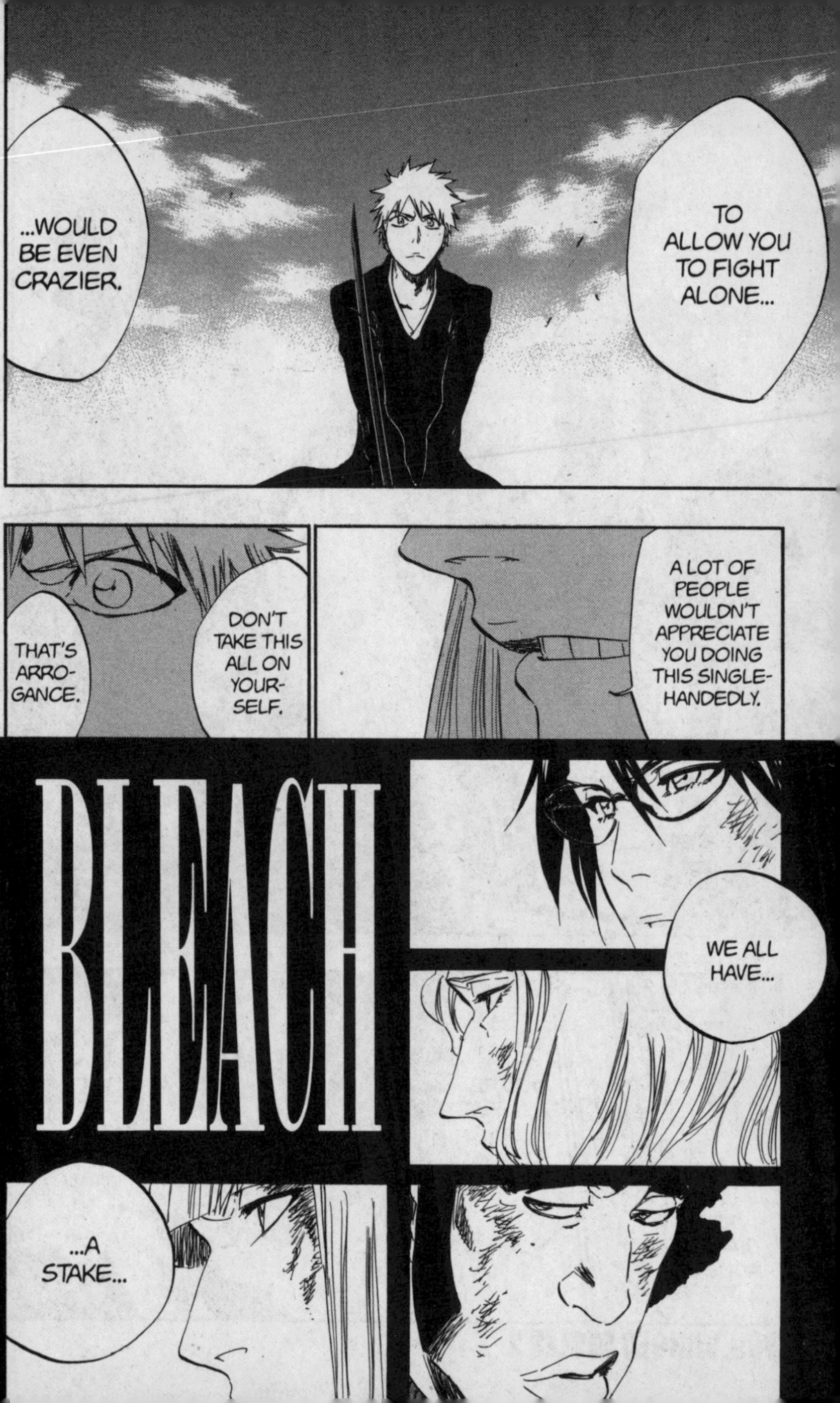
TO ALLOW YOU TO FIGHT ALONE...
...WOULD BE EVEN CRAZIER.
A LOT OF PEOPLE WOULDN'T APPRECIATE YOU DOING THIS SINGLE-HANDEDLY.
DON'T TAKE THIS ALL ON YOURSELF.
THAT'S ARROGANCE.
WE ALL HAVE...
BLEACH
...A STAKE...

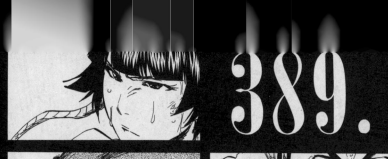

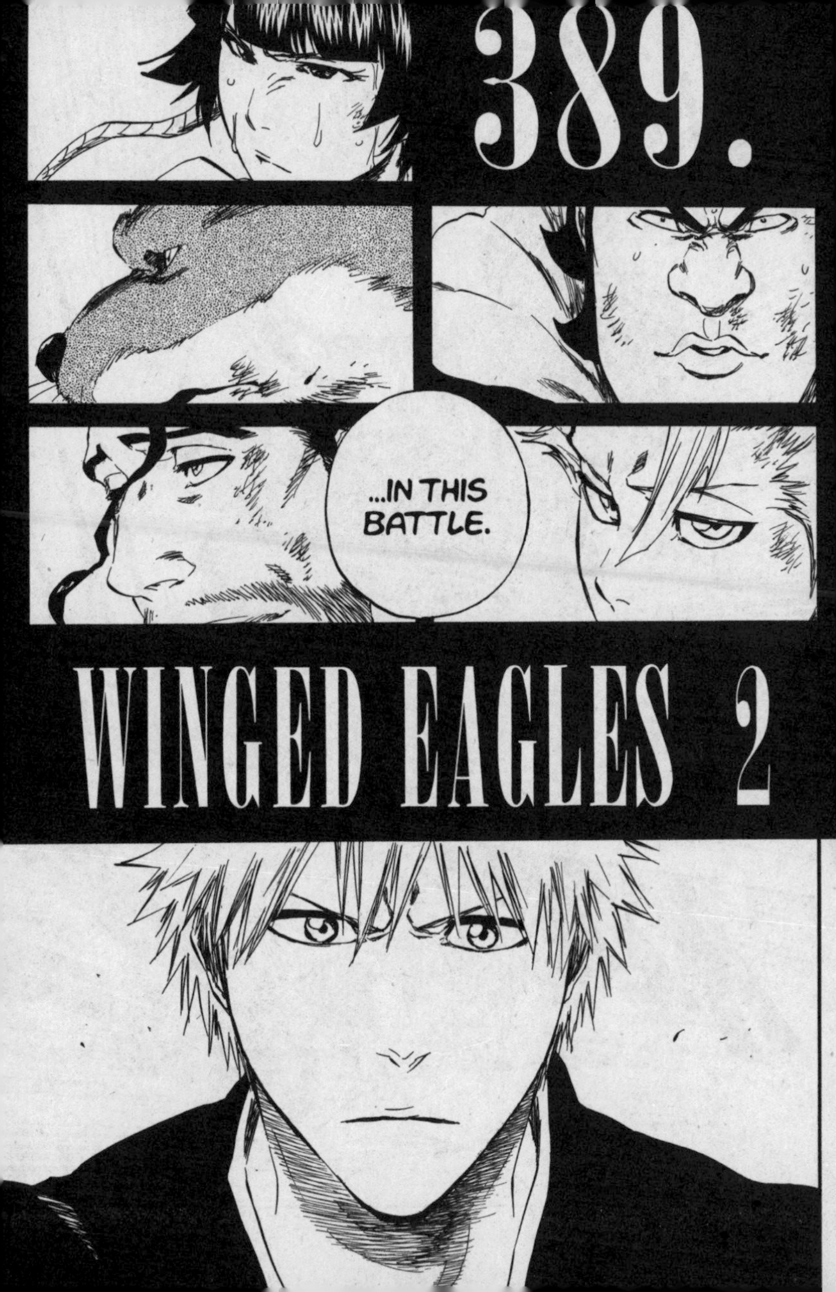
389.
...IN THIS BATTLE.
WINGED EAGLES 2

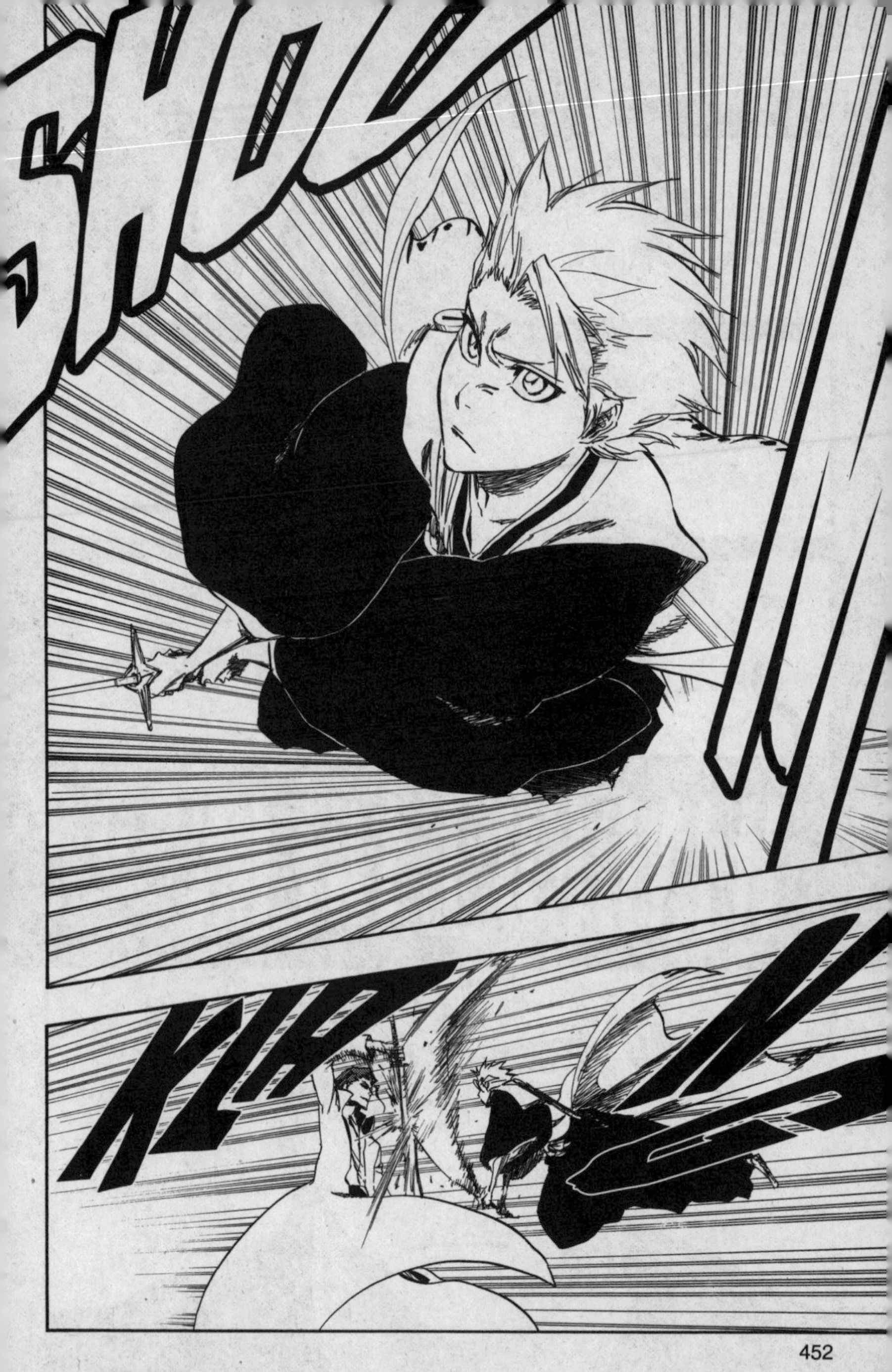

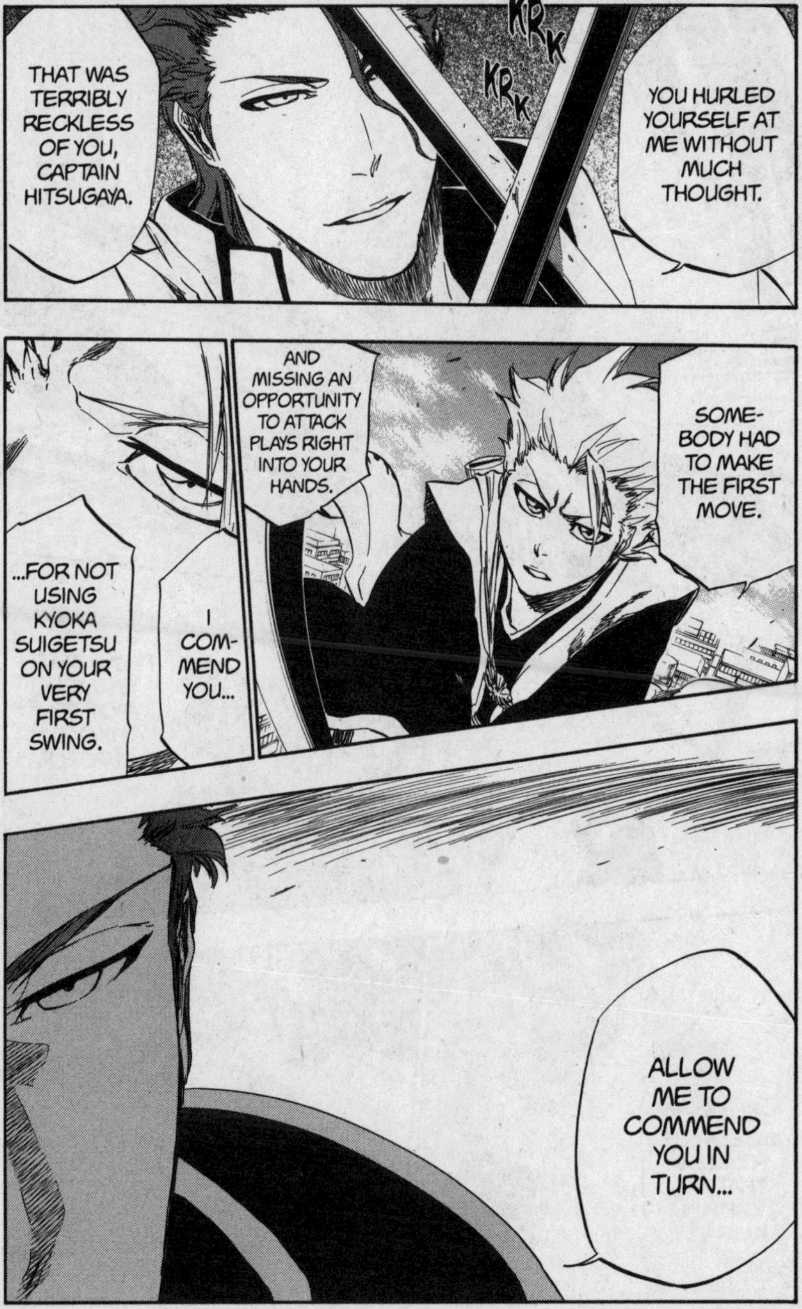
YOU HURLED YOURSELF AT ME WITHOUT MUCH THOUGHT.
KRK
KRK
THAT WAS TERRIBLY RECKLESS OF YOU, CAPTAIN HITSUGAYA.
SOME-BODY HAD TO MAKE THE FIRST MOVE.
AND MISSING AN OPPORTUNITY TO ATTACK PLAYS RIGHT INTO YOUR HANDS.
I COM-MEND YOU...
...FOR NOT USING KYOKA SUIGETSU ON YOUR VERY FIRST SWING.
ALLOW ME TO COMMEND YOU IN TURN...

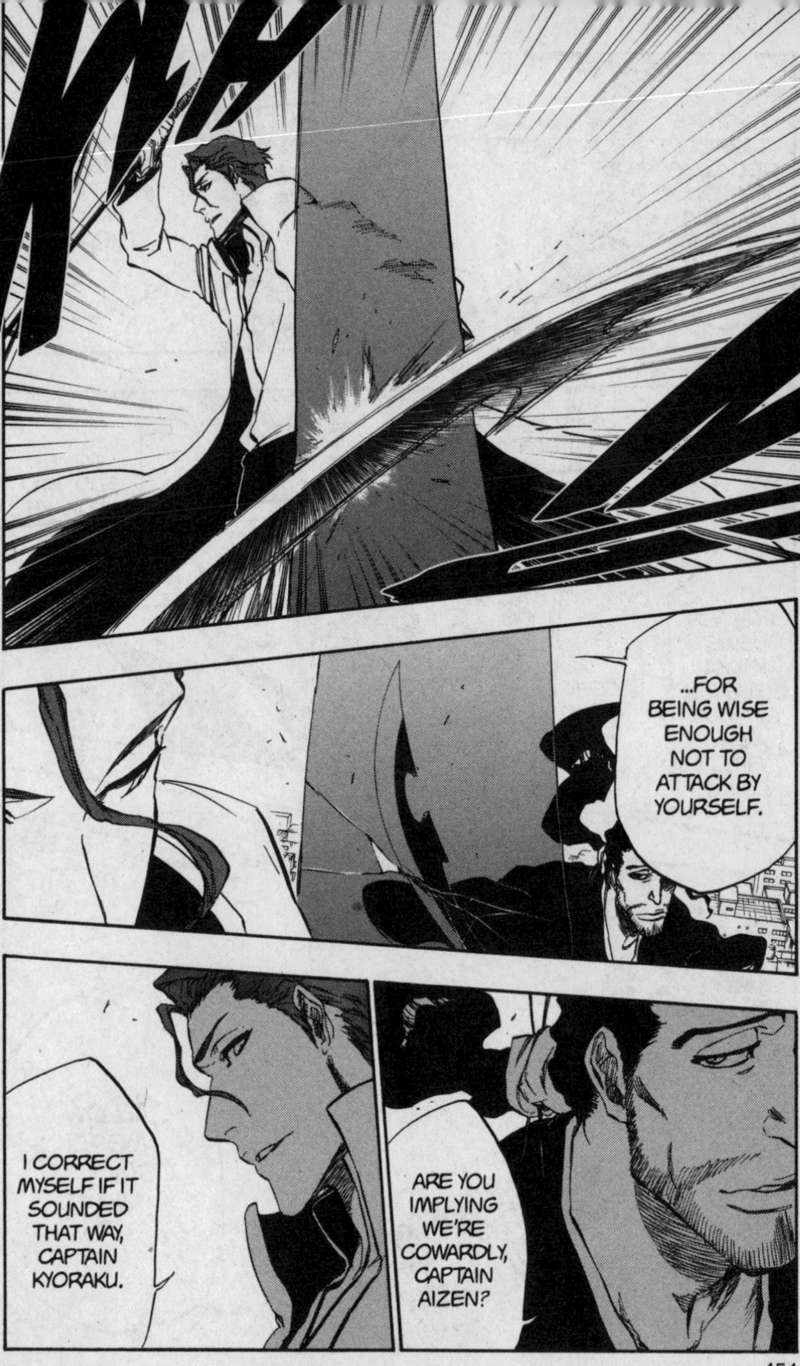
...FOR BEING WISE ENOUGH NOT TO ATTACK BY YOURSELF.
ARE YOU IMPLYING WE'RE COWARDLY, CAPTAIN AIZEN?
I CORRECT MYSELF IF IT SOUNDED THAT WAY, CAPTAIN KYORAKU.

READ THIS WAY

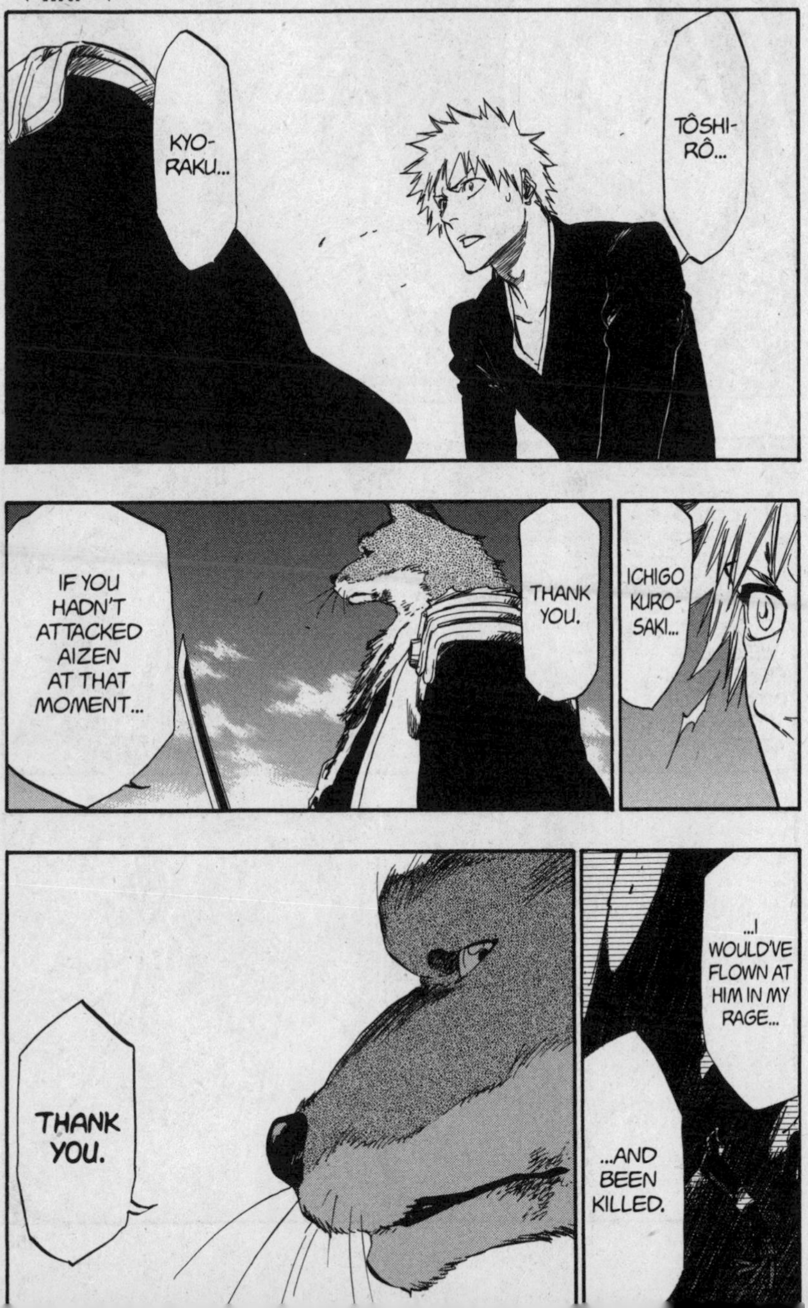
TÔSHIRÔ...
KYORAKU...
ICHIGO KUROSAKI...
THANK YOU.
IF YOU HADN'T ATTACKED AIZEN AT THAT MOMENT...
...I WOULD'VE FLOWN AT HIM IN MY RAGE...
...AND BEEN KILLED.
THANK YOU.

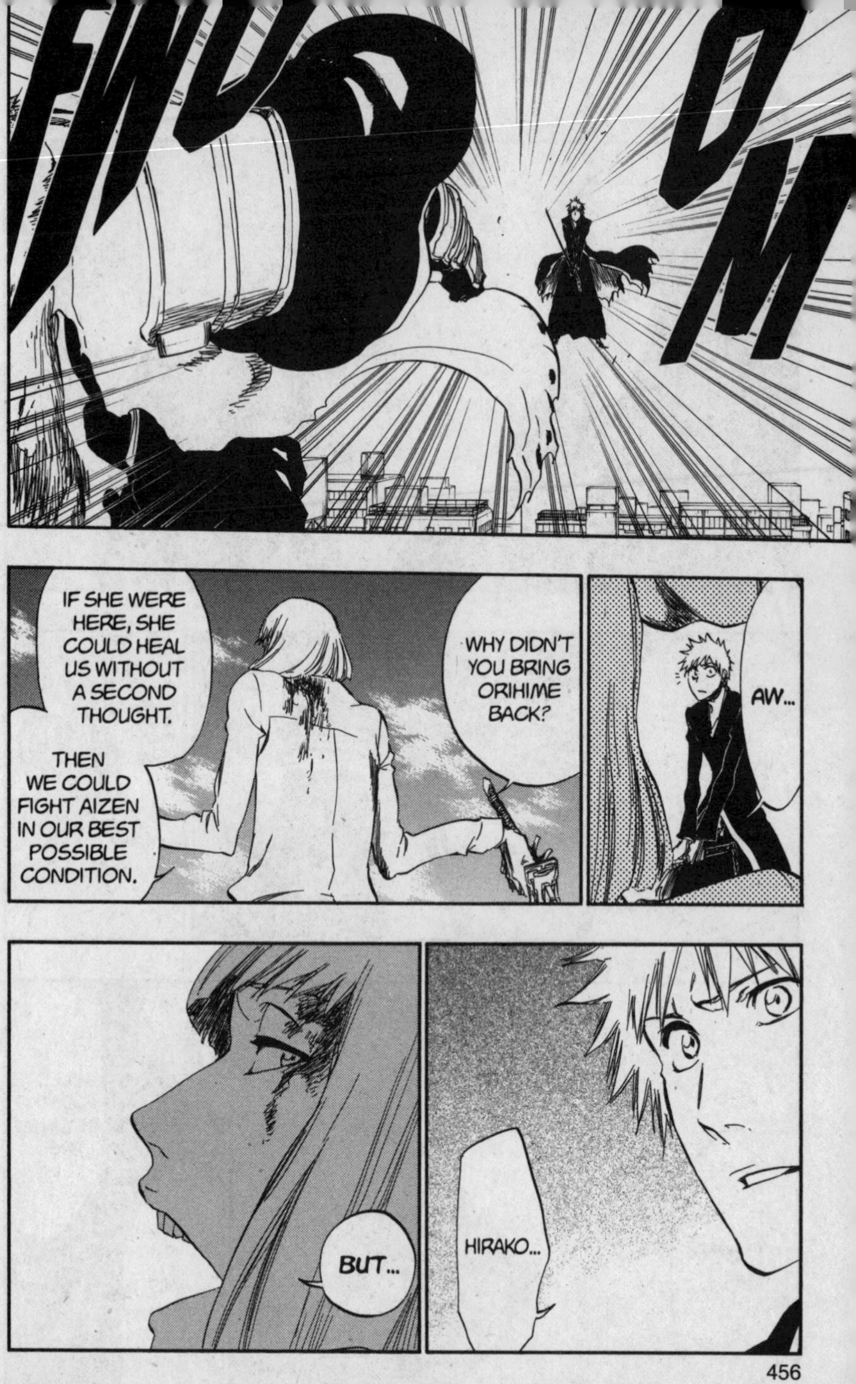
AW...
WHY DIDN'T YOU BRING ORIHIME BACK?
IF SHE WERE HERE, SHE COULD HEAL US WITHOUT A SECOND THOUGHT.
THEN WE COULD FIGHT AIZEN IN OUR BEST POSSIBLE CONDITION.
HIRAKO...
BUT...

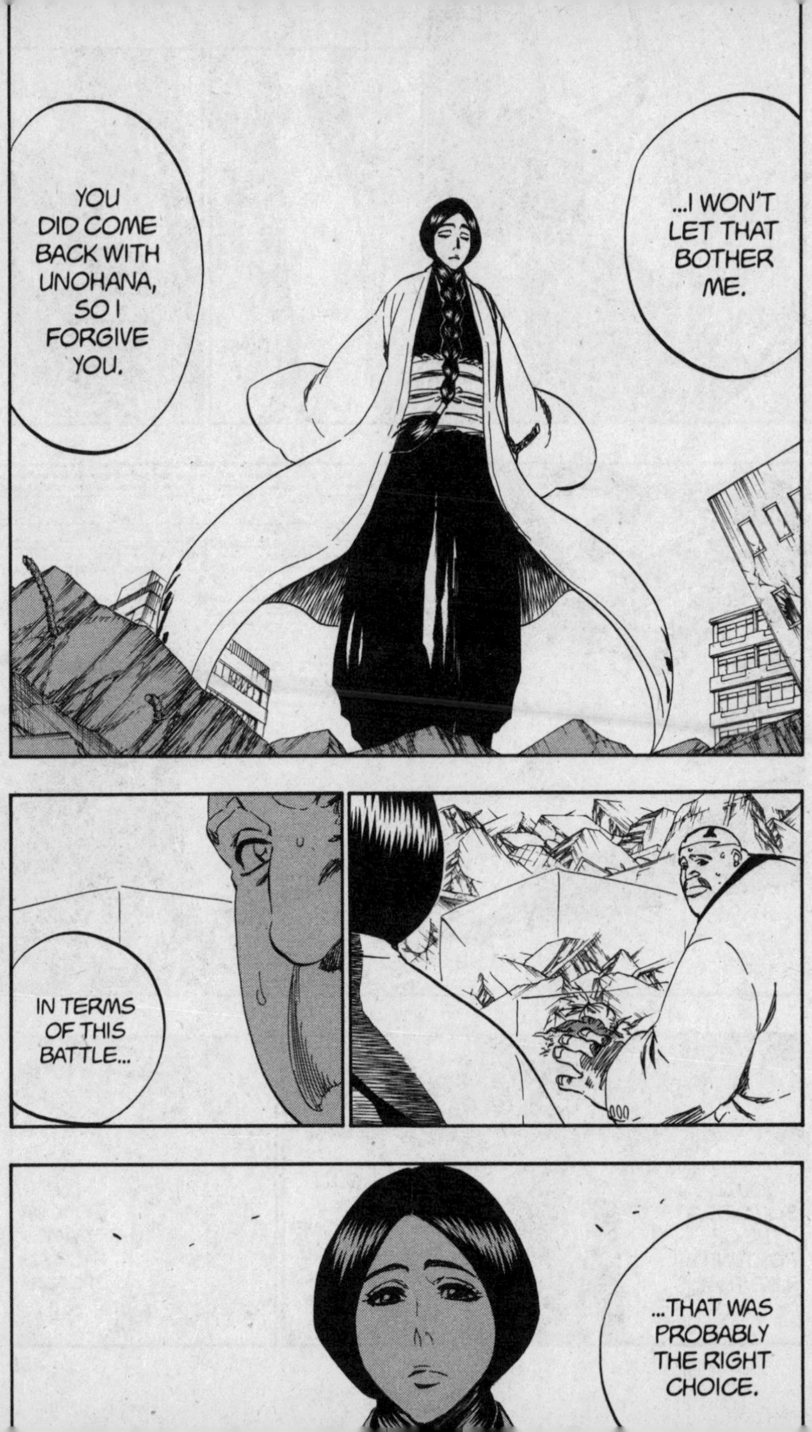
...I WON'T LET THAT BOTHER ME.
YOU DID COME BACK WITH UNOHANA, SO I FORGIVE YOU.
IN TERMS OF THIS BATTLE...
...THAT WAS PROBABLY THE RIGHT CHOICE.

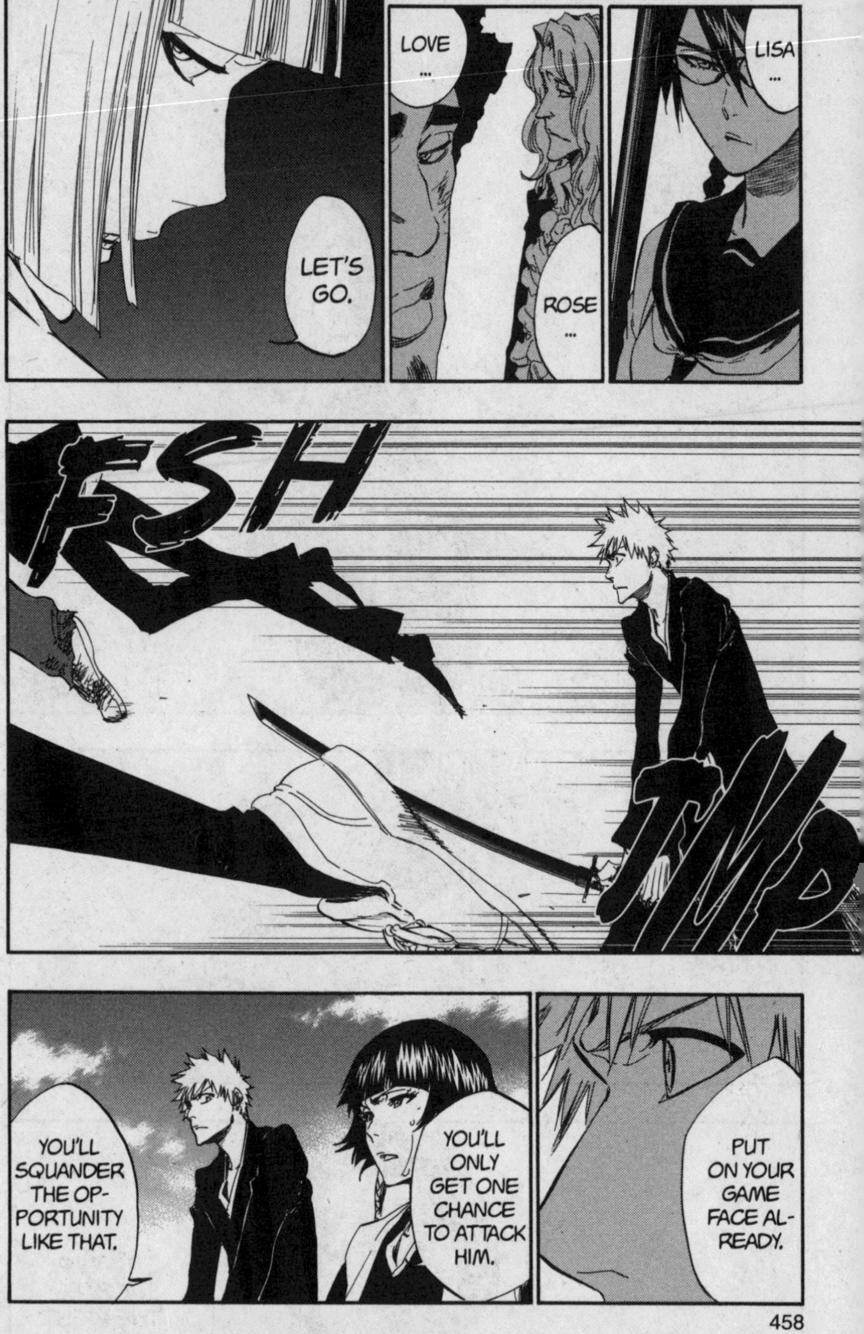
LISA ...
LOVE ...
ROSE ...
LET'S GO.
FSH
TMP
PUT ON YOUR GAME FACE AL-READY.
YOU'LL ONLY GET ONE CHANCE TO ATTACK HIM.
YOU'LL SQUANDER THE OP-PORTUNITY LIKE THAT.

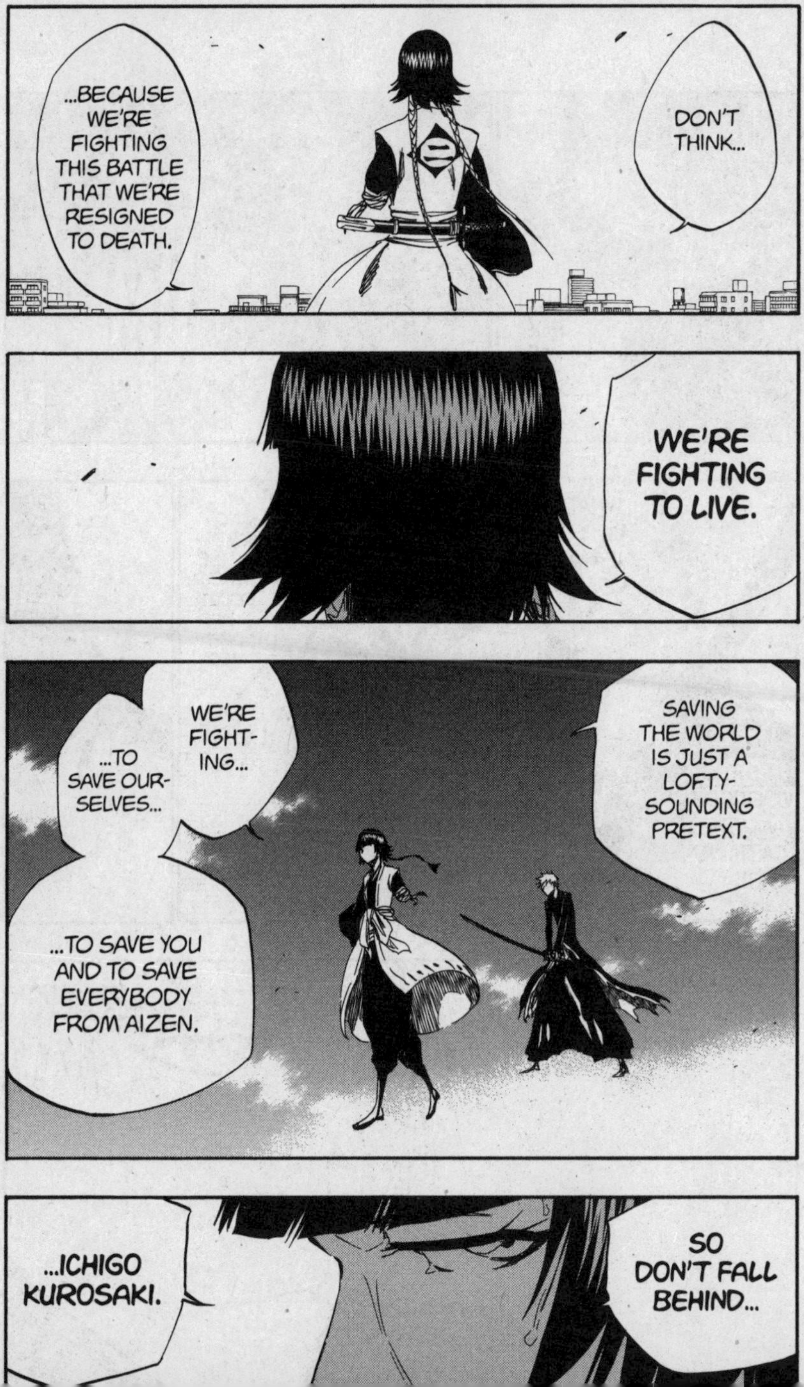

DON'T THINK...
...BECAUSE WE'RE FIGHTING THIS BATTLE THAT WE'RE RESIGNED TO DEATH.
WE'RE FIGHTING TO LIVE.
SAVING THE WORLD IS JUST A LOFTY-SOUNDING PRETEXT.
WE'RE FIGHTING...
...TO SAVE OURSELVES...
...TO SAVE YOU AND TO SAVE EVERYBODY FROM AIZEN.
SO DON'T FALL BEHIND...
...ICHIGO KUROSAKI.

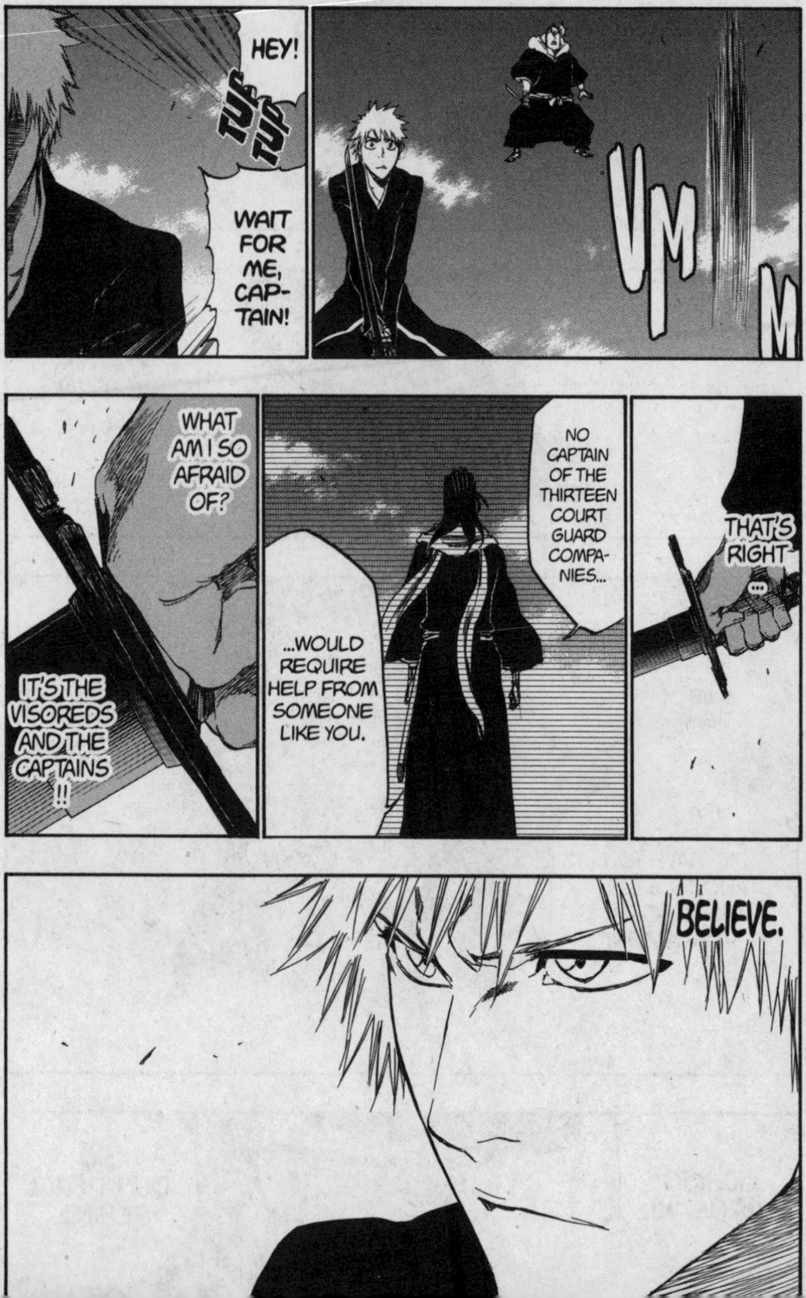
VMM
HEY!
TUP TUP
WAIT FOR ME, CAPTAIN!
THAT'S RIGHT...
NO CAPTAIN OF THE THIRTEEN COURT GUARD COMPANIES...
...WOULD REQUIRE HELP FROM SOMEONE LIKE YOU.
WHAT AM I SO AFRAID OF?
IT'S THE VISOREDS AND THE CAPTAINS!!
BELIEVE.

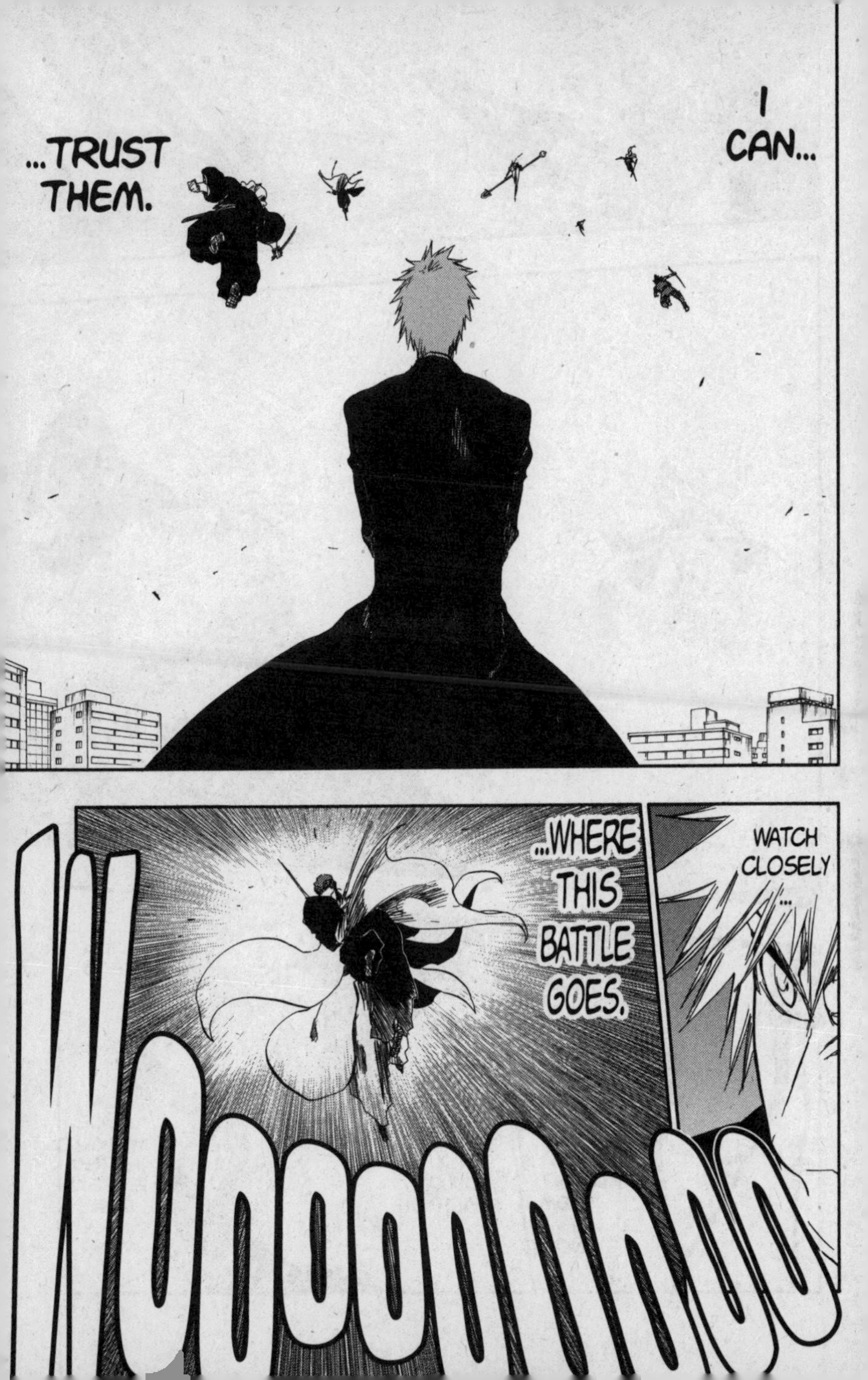
I CAN...
...TRUST THEM.
WATCH CLOSELY...
...WHERE THIS BATTLE GOES.

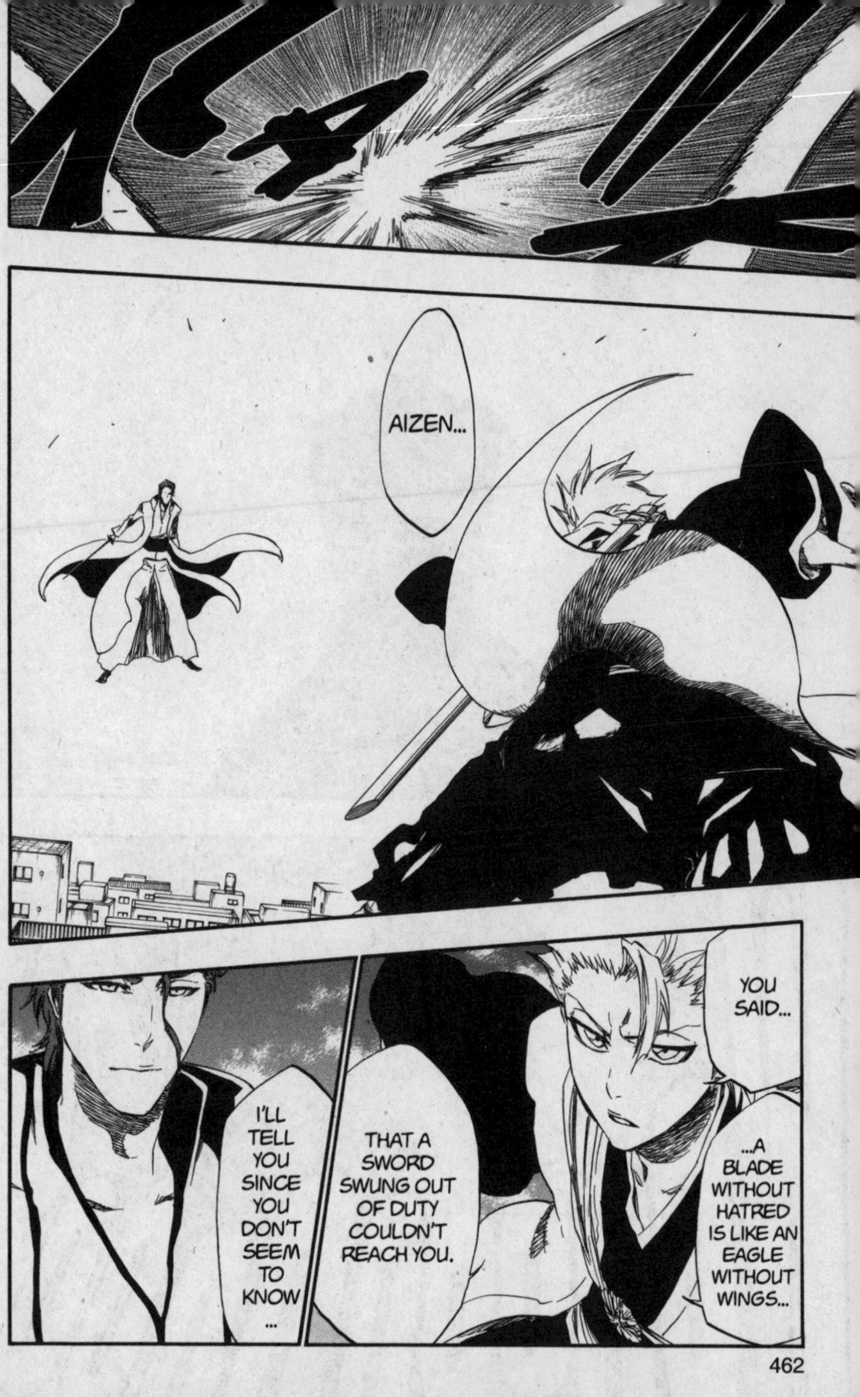
AIZEN...
YOU SAID...
...A BLADE WITHOUT HATRED IS LIKE AN EAGLE WITHOUT WINGS...
THAT A SWORD SWUNG OUT OF DUTY COULDN'T REACH YOU.
I'LL TELL YOU SINCE YOU DON'T SEEM TO KNOW...

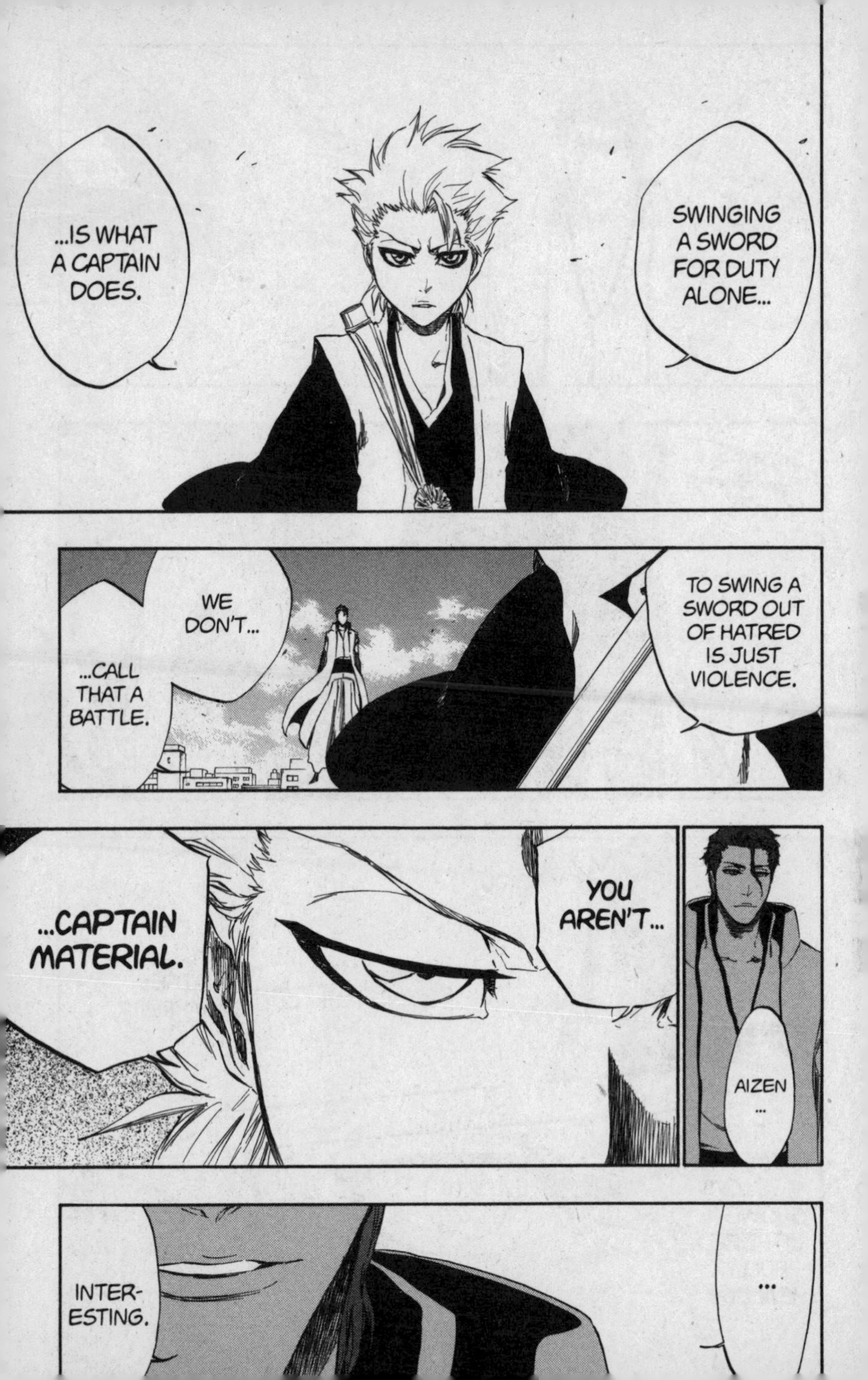
SWINGING A SWORD FOR DUTY ALONE...
...IS WHAT A CAPTAIN DOES.
TO SWING A SWORD OUT OF HATRED IS JUST VIOLENCE.
WE DON'T...
...CALL THAT A BATTLE.
AIZEN ...
YOU AREN'T...
...CAPTAIN MATERIAL.
...
INTER-ESTING.

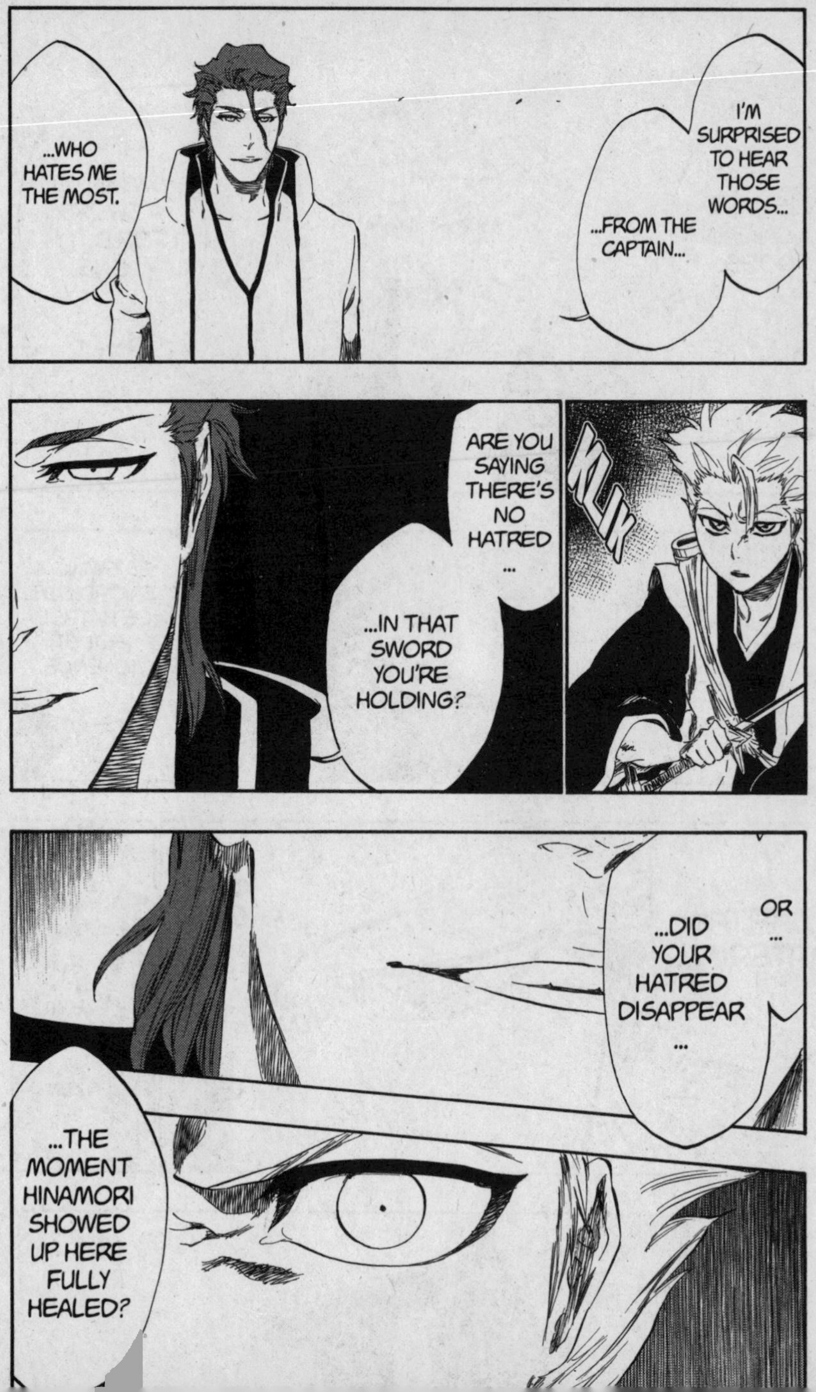
I'M SURPRISED TO HEAR THOSE WORDS...
...FROM THE CAPTAIN...
...WHO HATES ME THE MOST.
KLIK
ARE YOU SAYING THERE'S NO HATRED ...
...IN THAT SWORD YOU'RE HOLDING?
OR ...
...DID YOUR HATRED DISAPPEAR ...
...THE MOMENT HINAMORI SHOWED UP HERE FULLY HEALED?

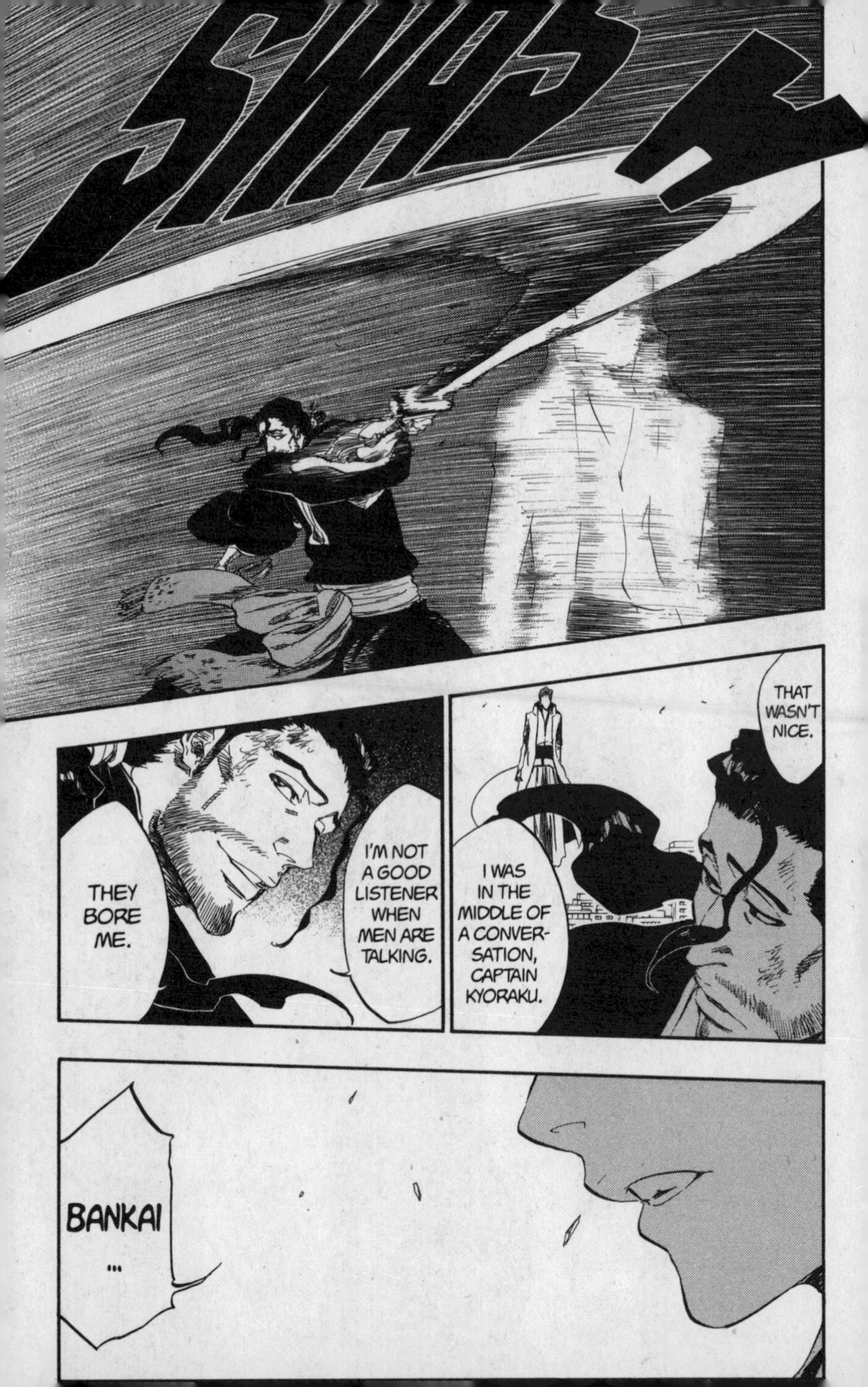
THAT WASN'T NICE.
I WAS IN THE MIDDLE OF A CONVERSATION, CAPTAIN KYORAKU.
I'M NOT A GOOD LISTENER WHEN MEN ARE TALKING.
THEY BORE ME.
BANKAI ...

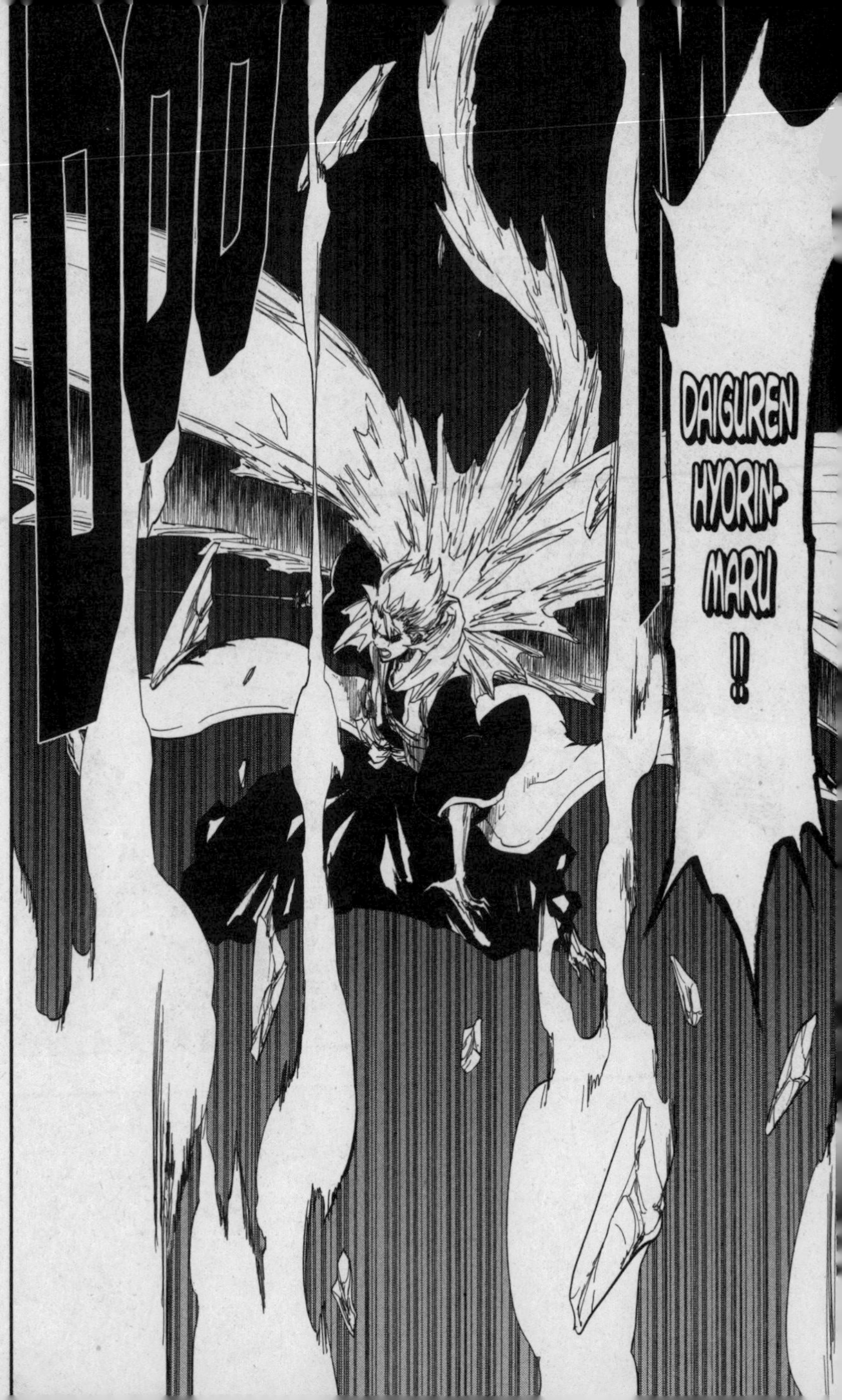
DAIGUREN HYORIN-MARU !!

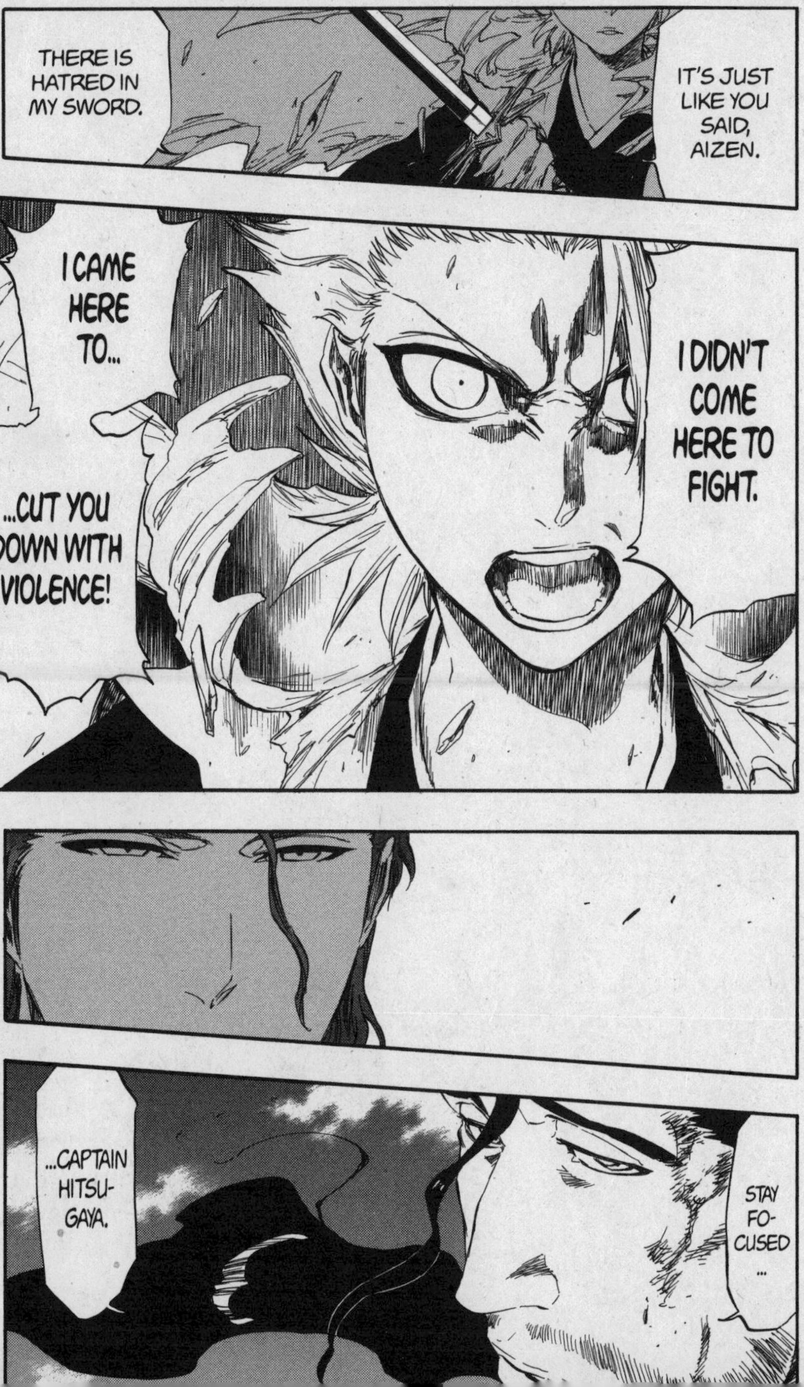
IT'S JUST LIKE YOU SAID, AIZEN.
THERE IS HATRED IN MY SWORD.
I DIDN'T COME HERE TO FIGHT.
I CAME HERE TO...
...CUT YOU DOWN WITH VIOLENCE!
STAY FO-CUSED...
...CAPTAIN HITSU-GAYA.

TUP
TUP
TUP
HOLD ON! YOU'RE SERIOUSLY GONNA OPERATE ON ME?! WHAT FOR?!
INFORMED CONSENT, PLEASE!!
GASP!! I'M BEING SHOWN!! Y-YES!!
HEH HEH HEH...
YOU SEEM TO BE IN SOME TROUBLE, KON.
TUP

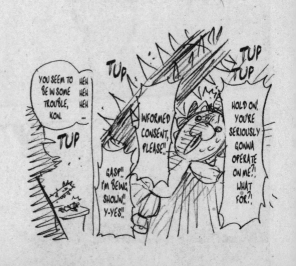

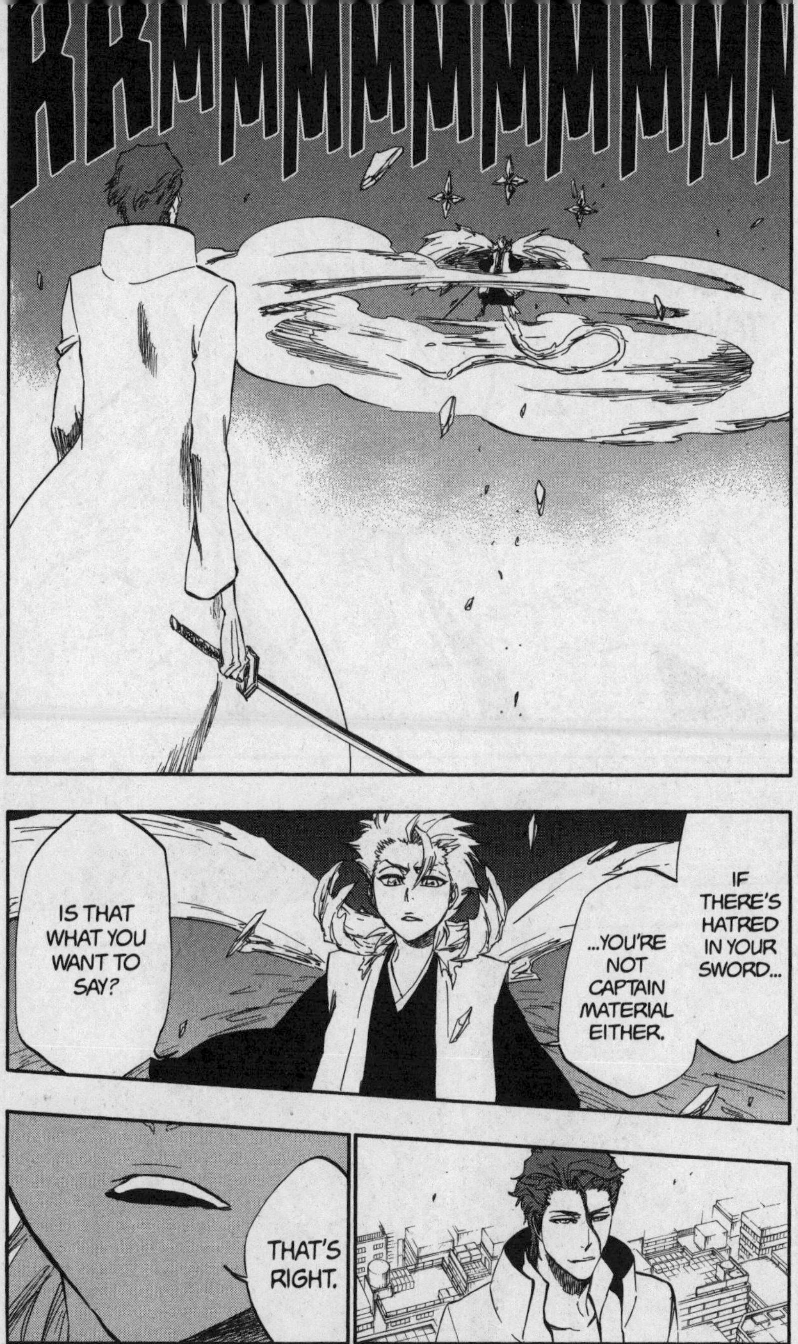
KKMMMMMMMMMMMN
IF THERE'S HATRED IN YOUR SWORD...
...YOU'RE NOT CAPTAIN MATERIAL EITHER.
IS THAT WHAT YOU WANT TO SAY?
THAT'S RIGHT.

390. BEYOND THE DEATH UNDERSTANDING

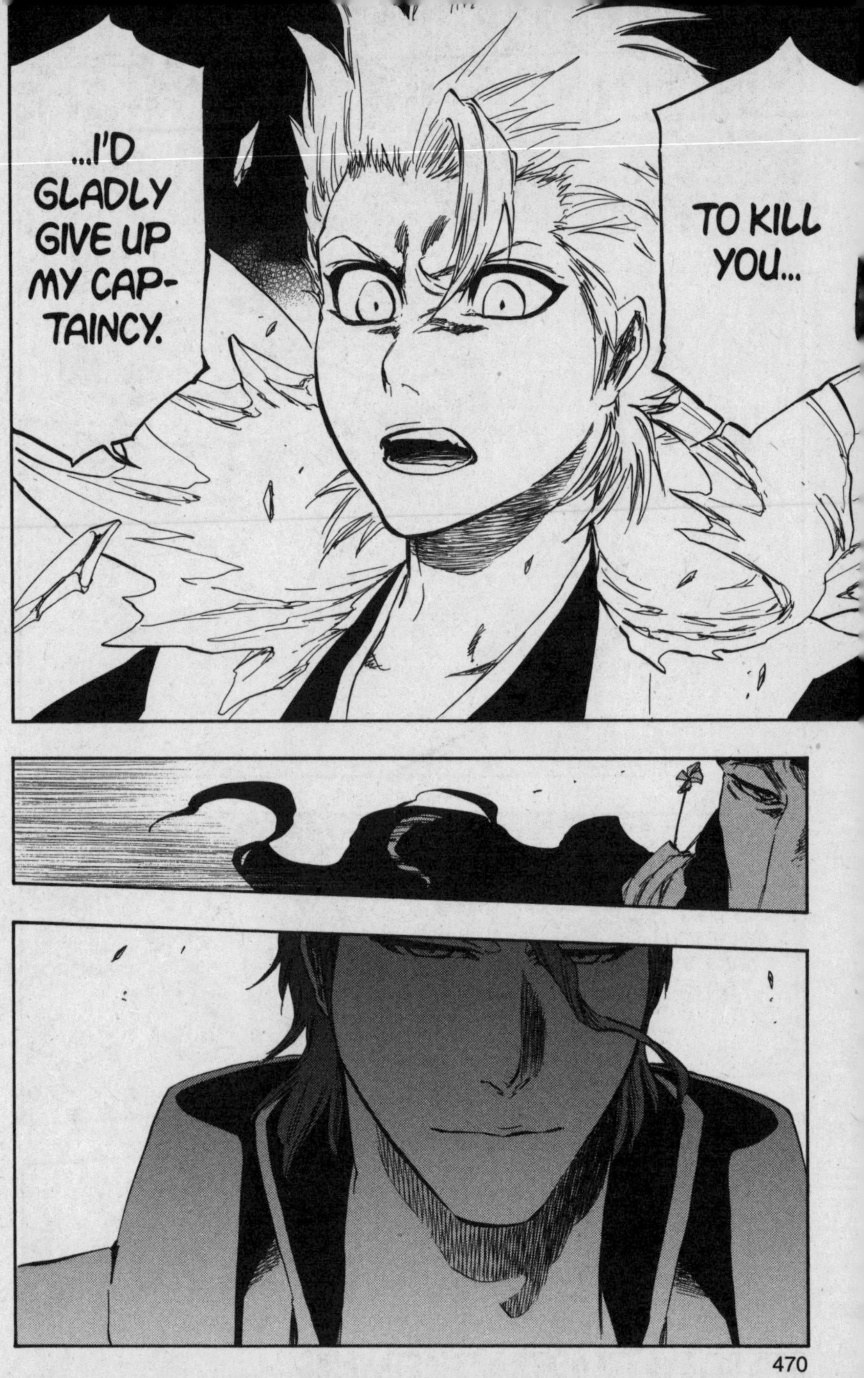
TO KILL YOU...
...I'D GLADLY GIVE UP MY CAP-TAINCY.

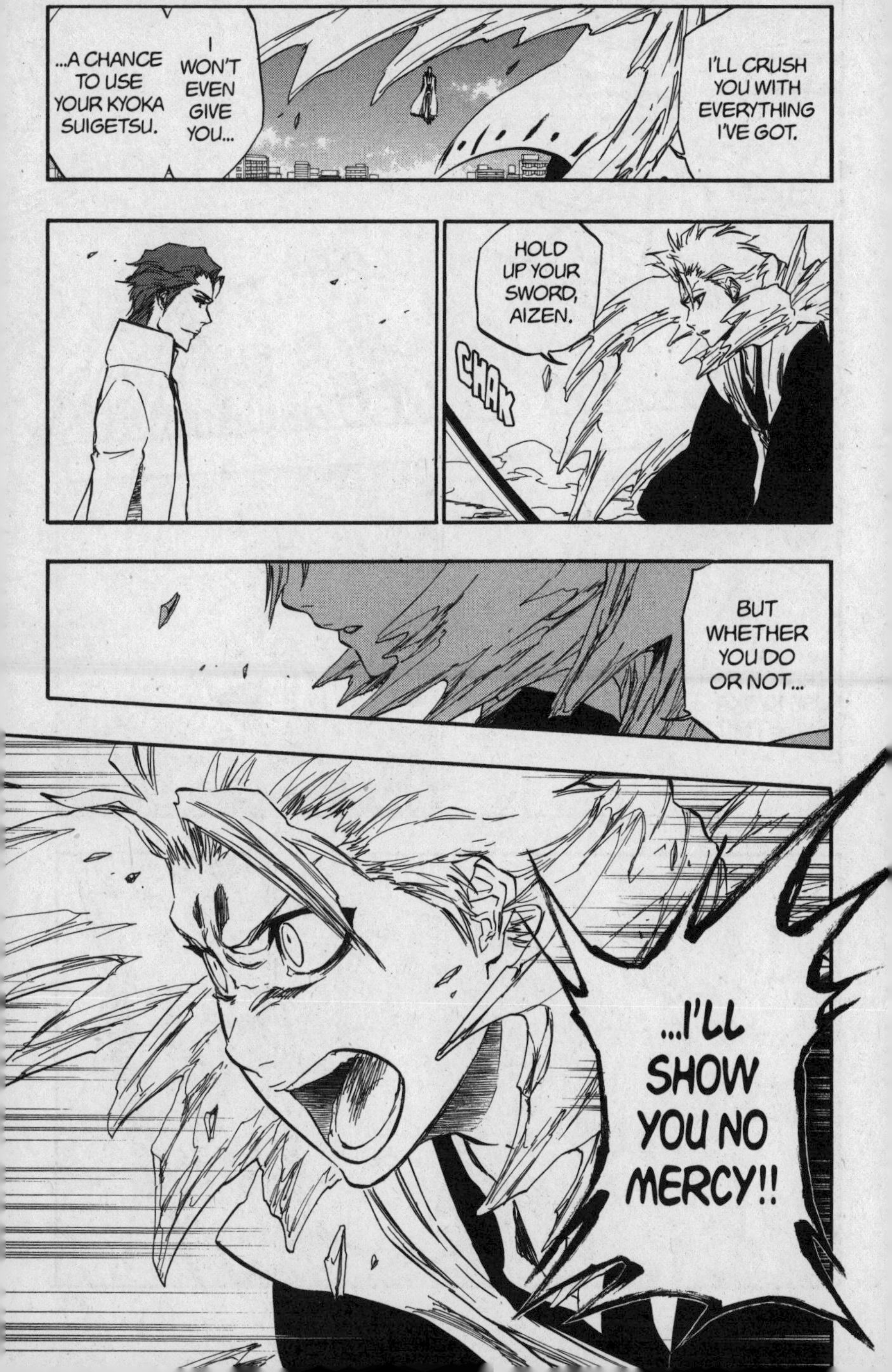
I'LL CRUSH YOU WITH EVERYTHING I'VE GOT.
I WON'T EVEN GIVE YOU...
...A CHANCE TO USE YOUR KYOKA SUIGETSU.
HOLD UP YOUR SWORD, AIZEN.
CHAK
BUT WHETHER YOU DO OR NOT...
...I'LL SHOW YOU NO MERCY!!

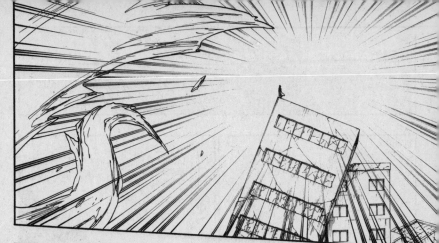

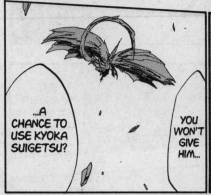

YOU WON'T GIVE HIM...
...A CHANCE TO USE KYOKA SUIGETSU?
OH BOY.

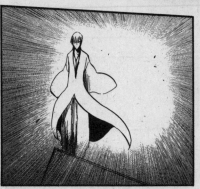

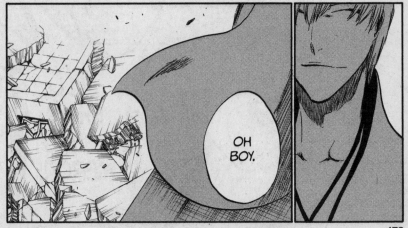

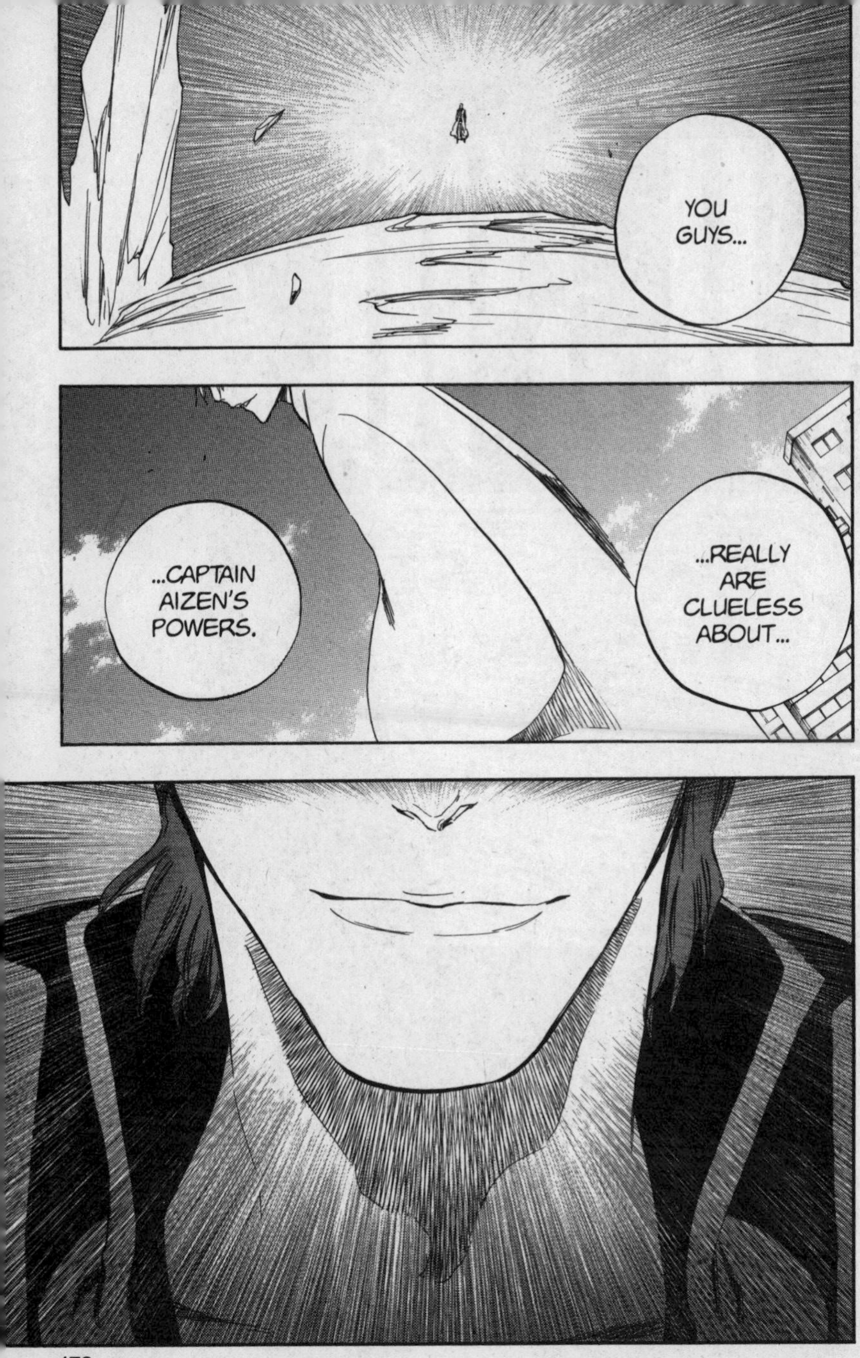
YOU GUYS...
...REALLY ARE CLUELESS ABOUT...
...CAPTAIN AIZEN'S POWERS.

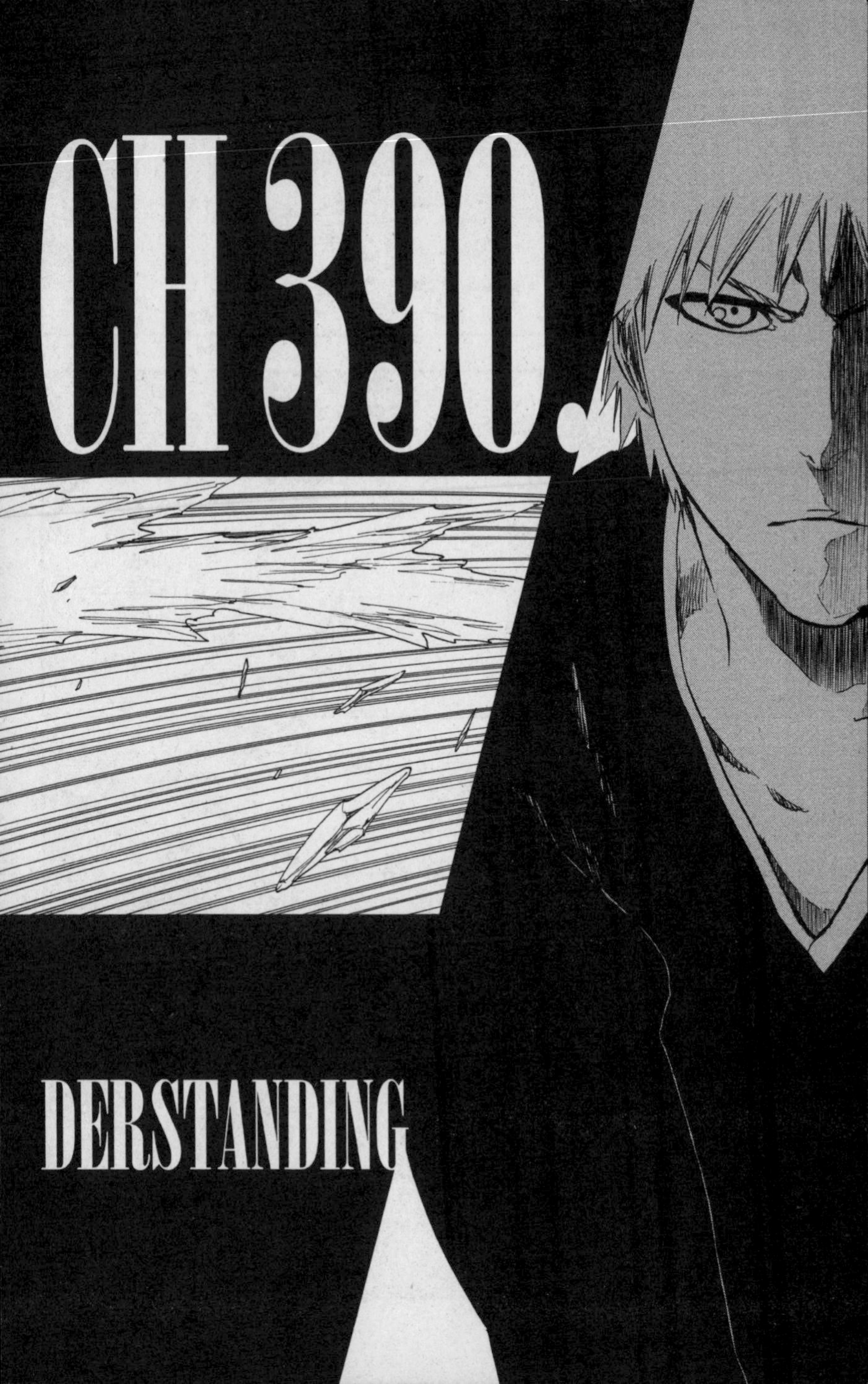
CH 390.
DERSTANDING

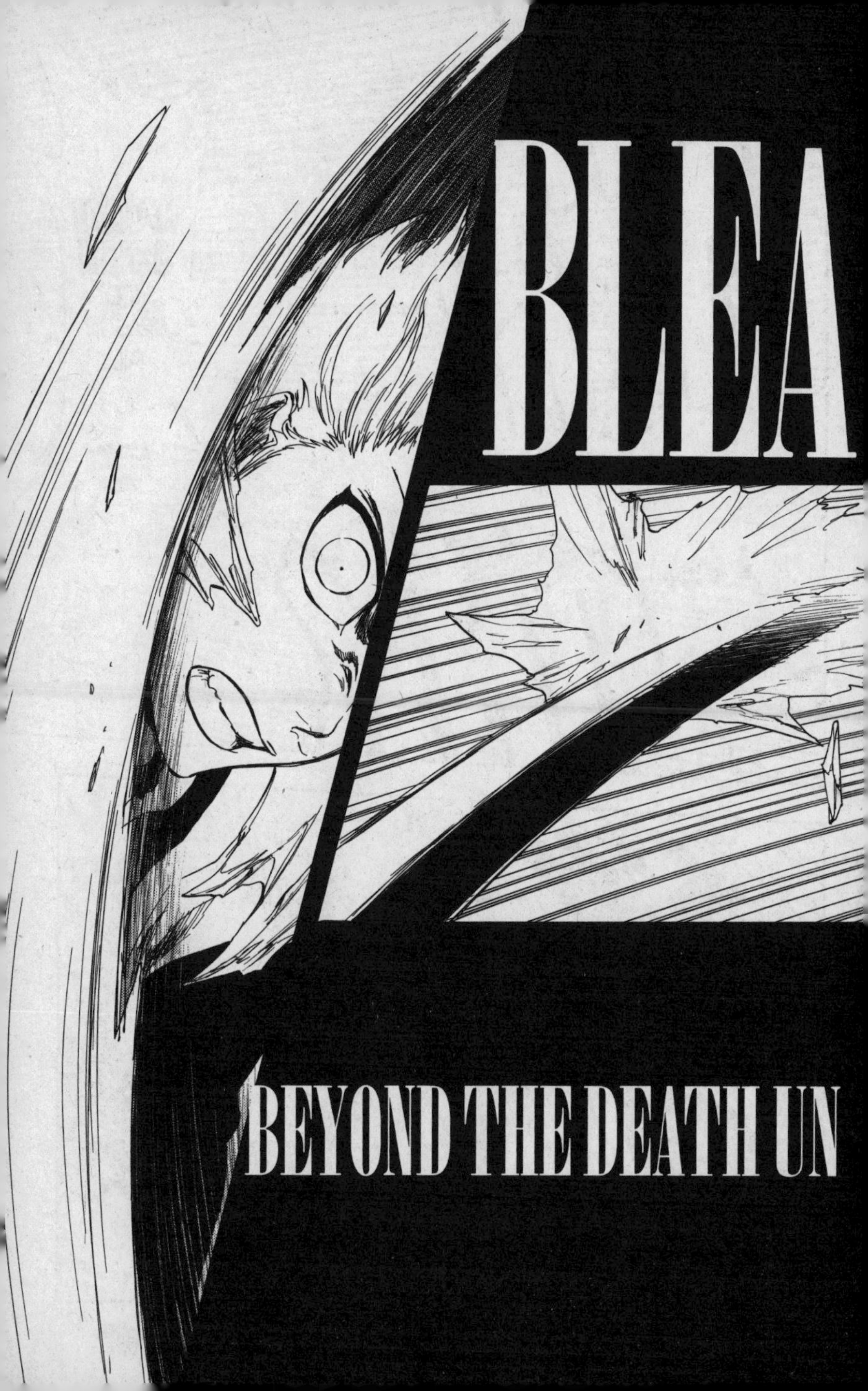
BLEA
BEYOND THE DEATH UN

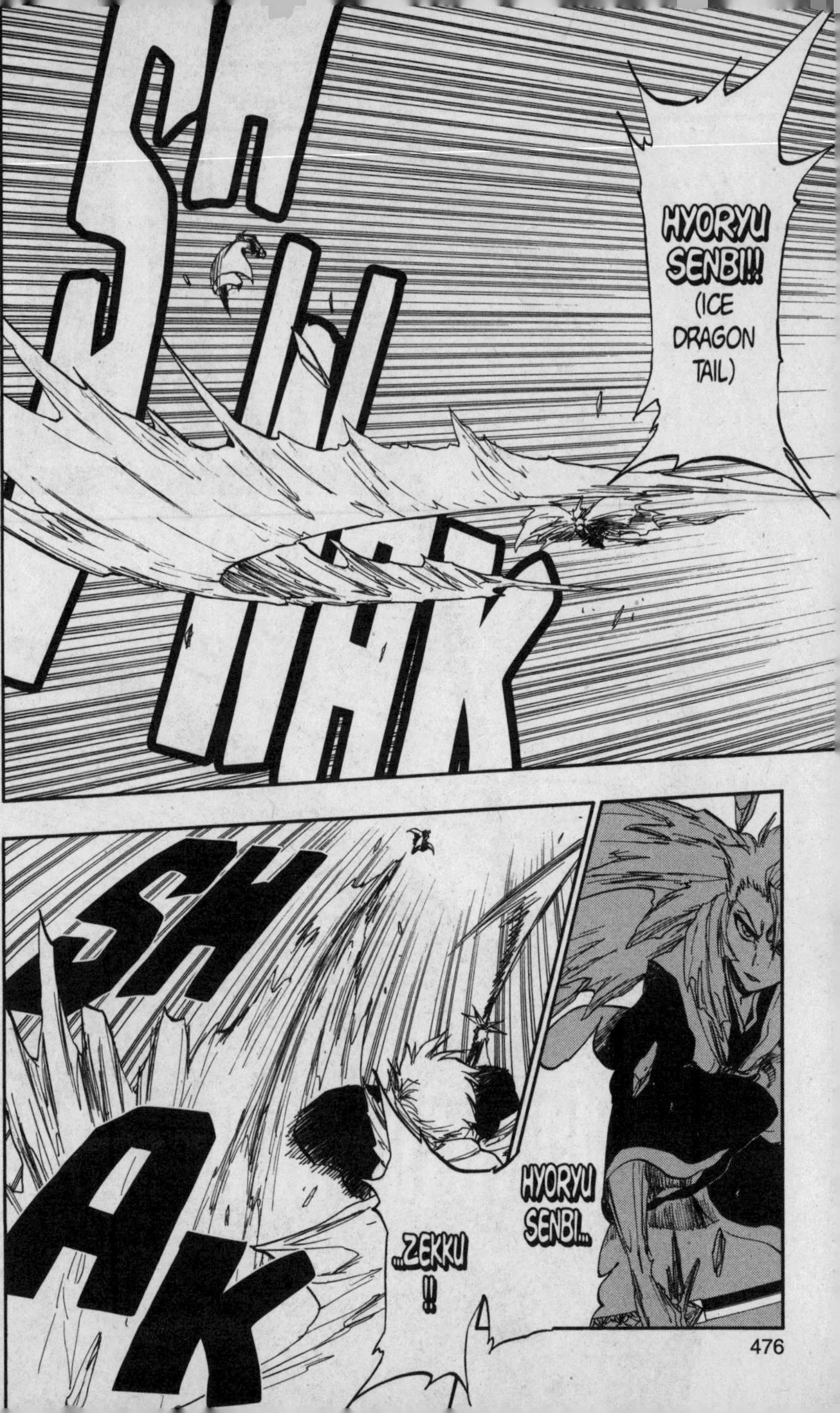
HYORYU SENBI!! (ICE DRAGON TAIL)
HYORYU SENBI...
...ZEKKU!!
SHAK

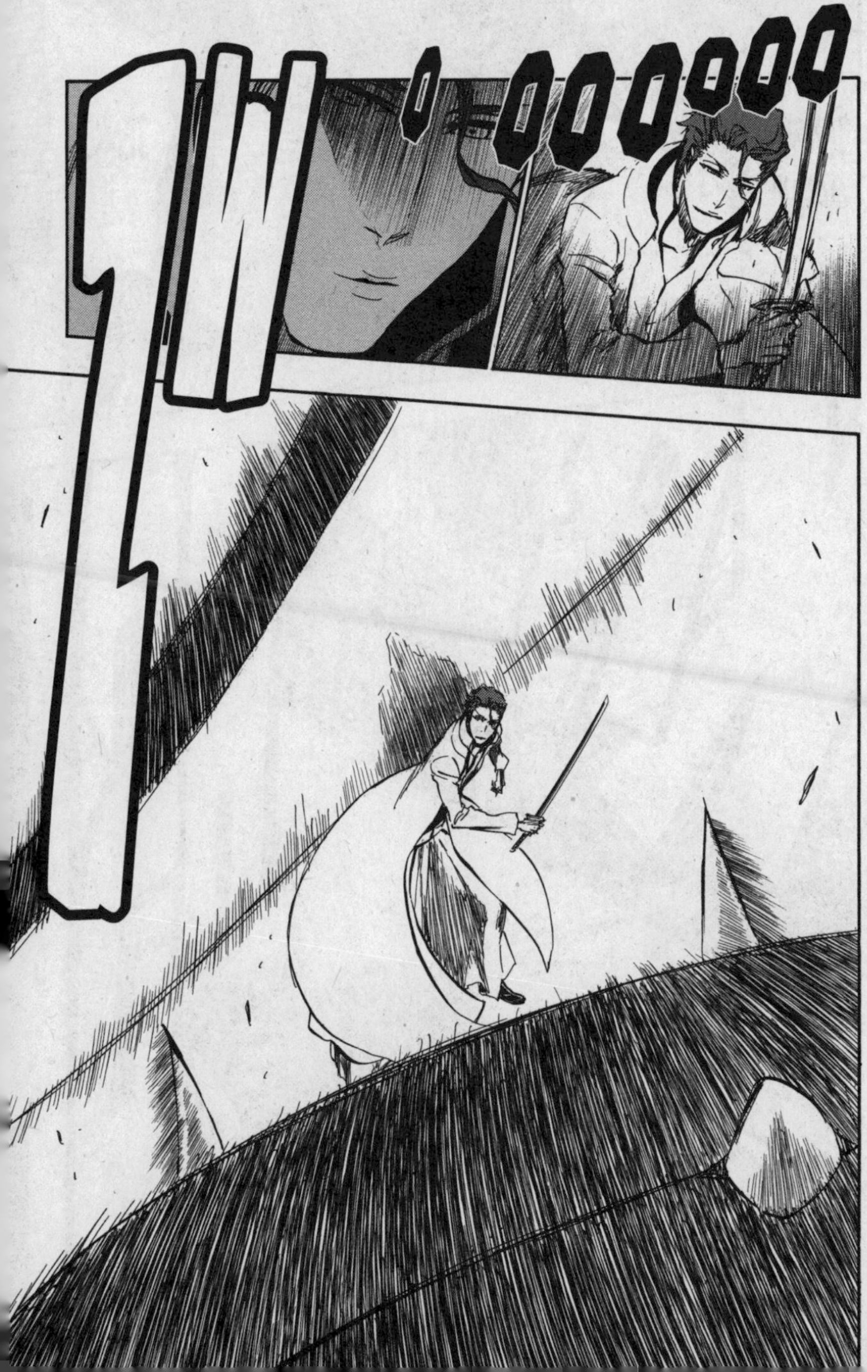
ZWOOOOOOO

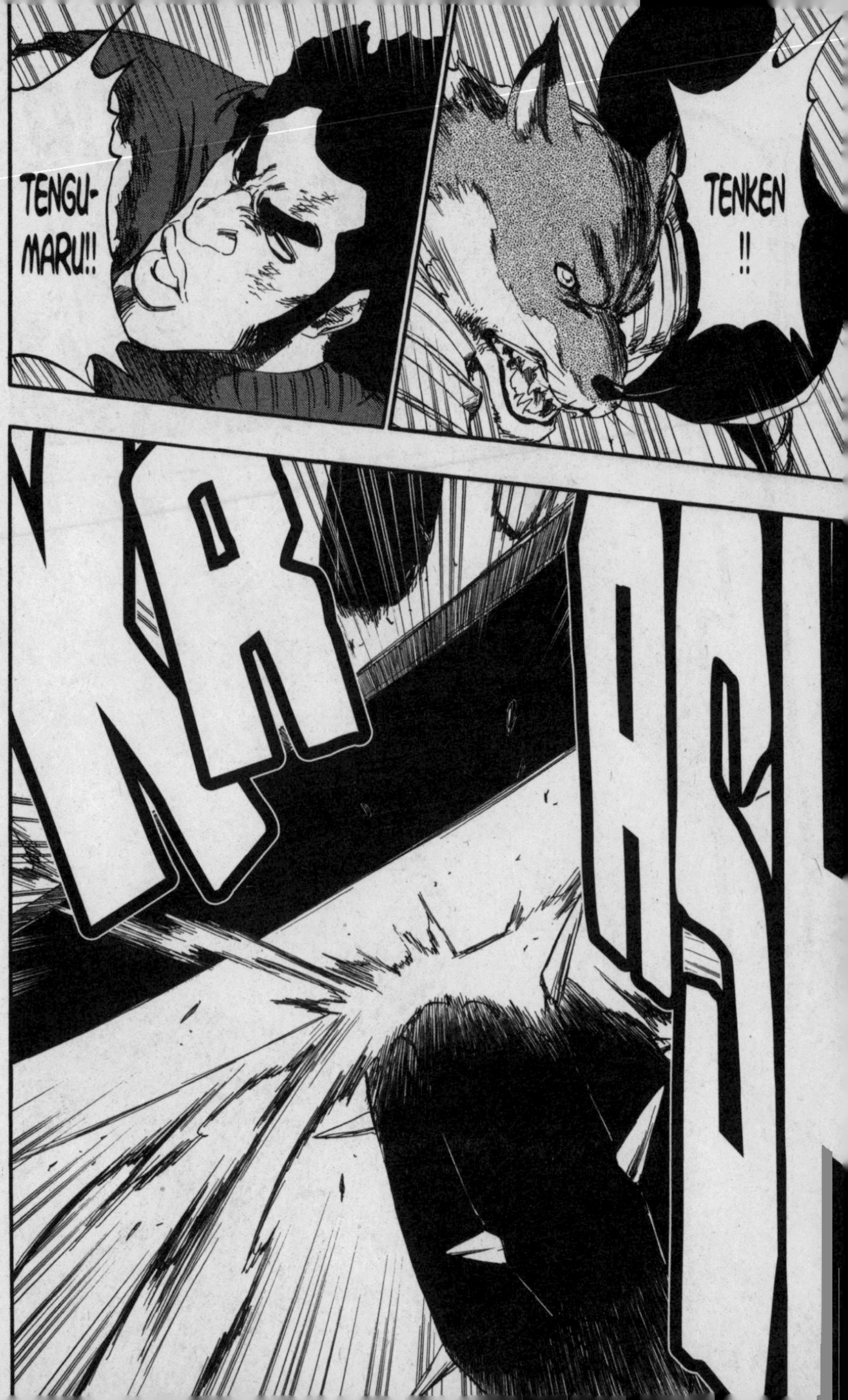
TENKEN !!
TENGU-MARU!!

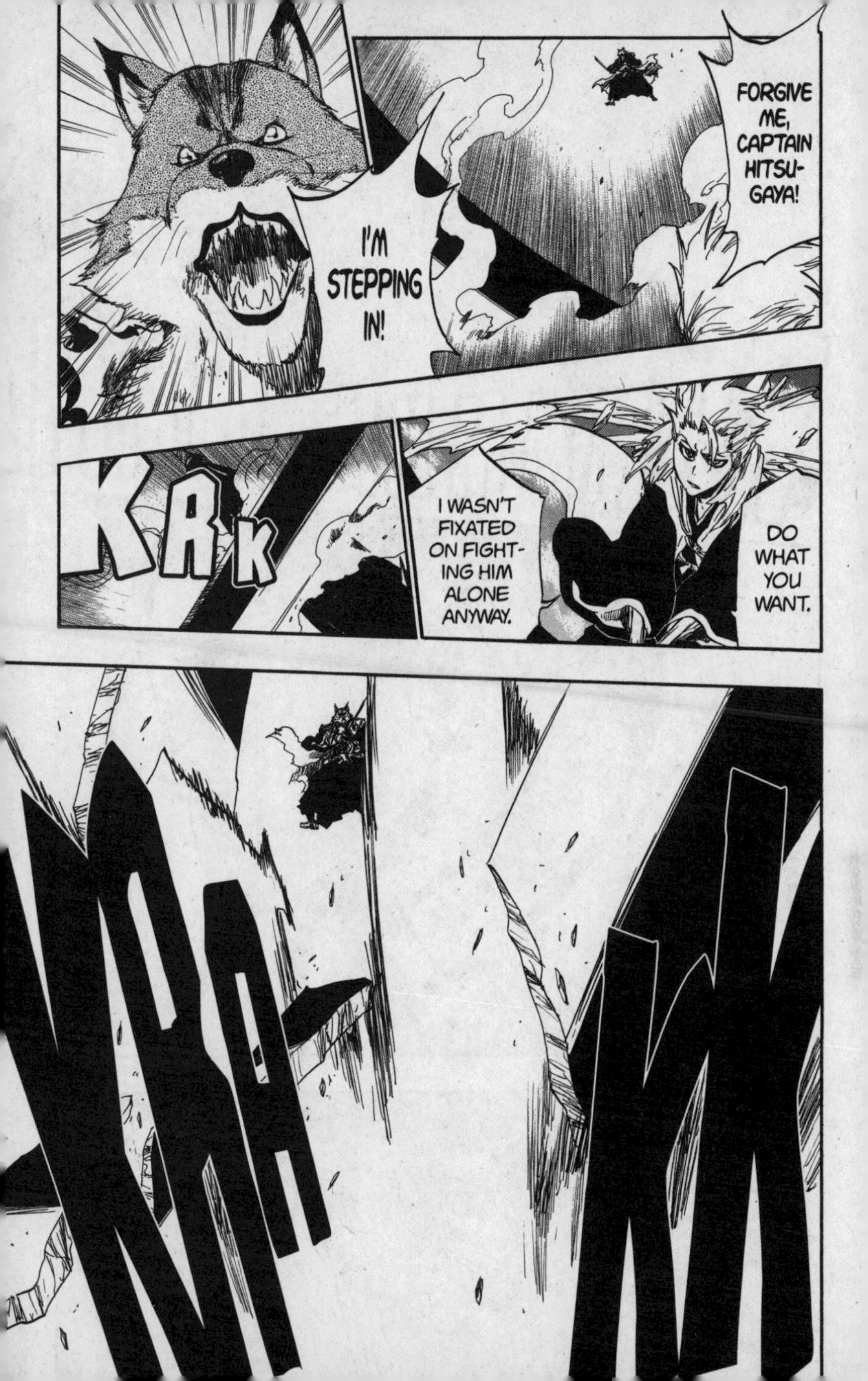
FORGIVE ME, CAPTAIN HITSU-GAYA!
I'M STEPPING IN!
DO WHAT YOU WANT.
I WASN'T FIXATED ON FIGHT-ING HIM ALONE ANYWAY.
KRAK

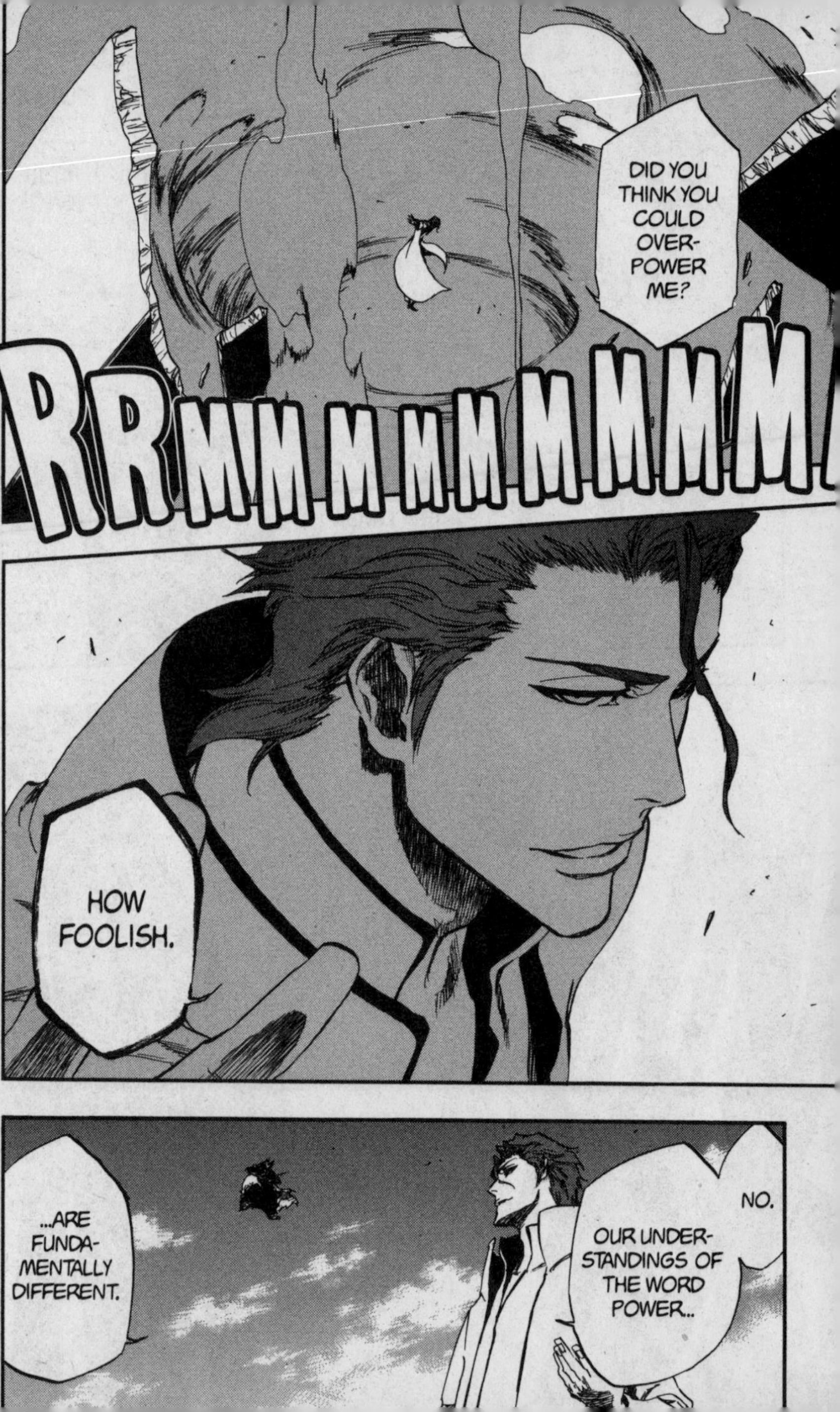
DID YOU THINK YOU COULD OVER-POWER ME?
RRMMMMMMMMMMM
HOW FOOLISH.
NO.
OUR UNDER-STANDINGS OF THE WORD POWER...
...ARE FUNDA-MENTALLY DIFFERENT.

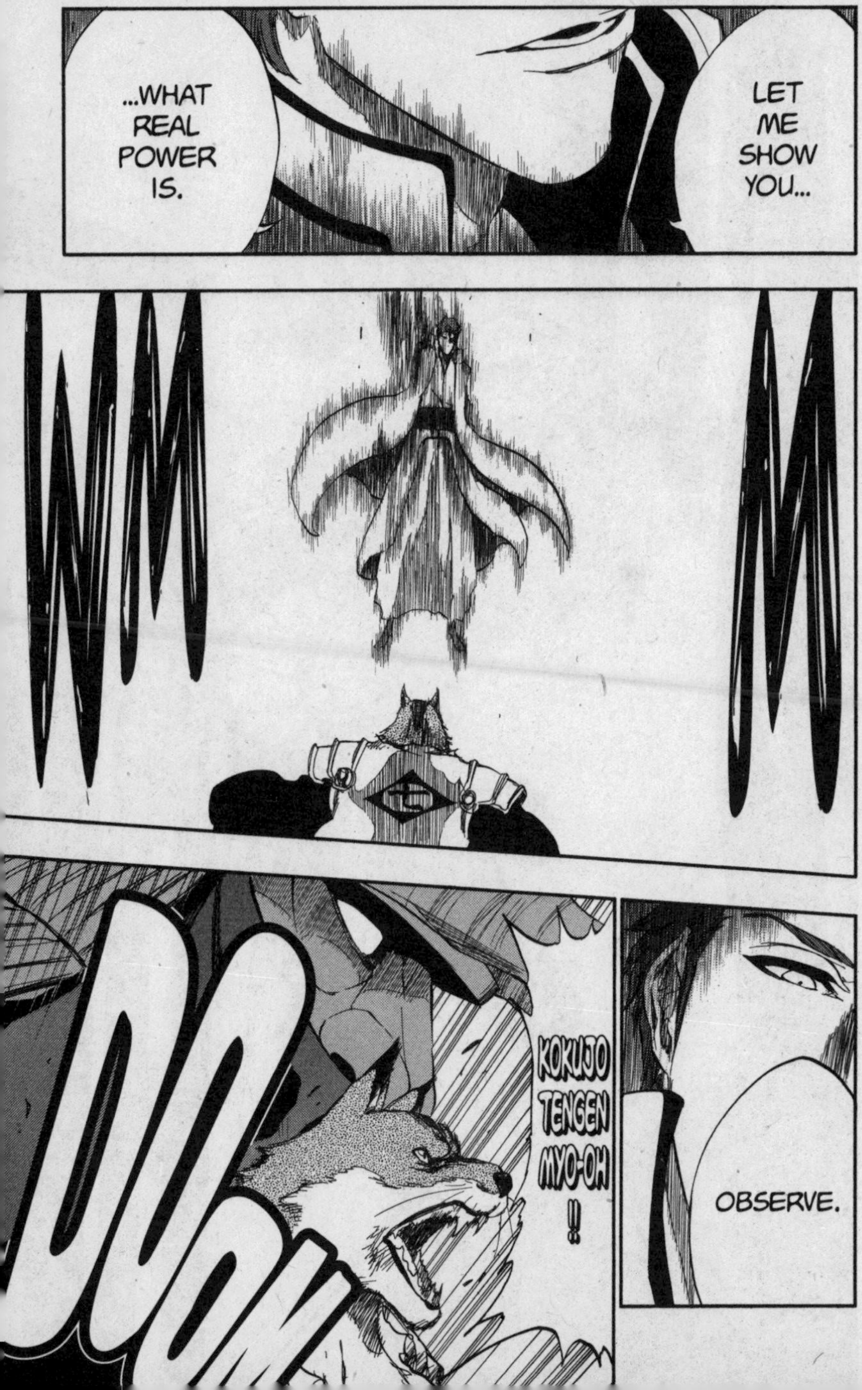
LET ME SHOW YOU...
...WHAT REAL POWER IS.
OBSERVE.
KOKUJO TENGEN MYO-OH!!

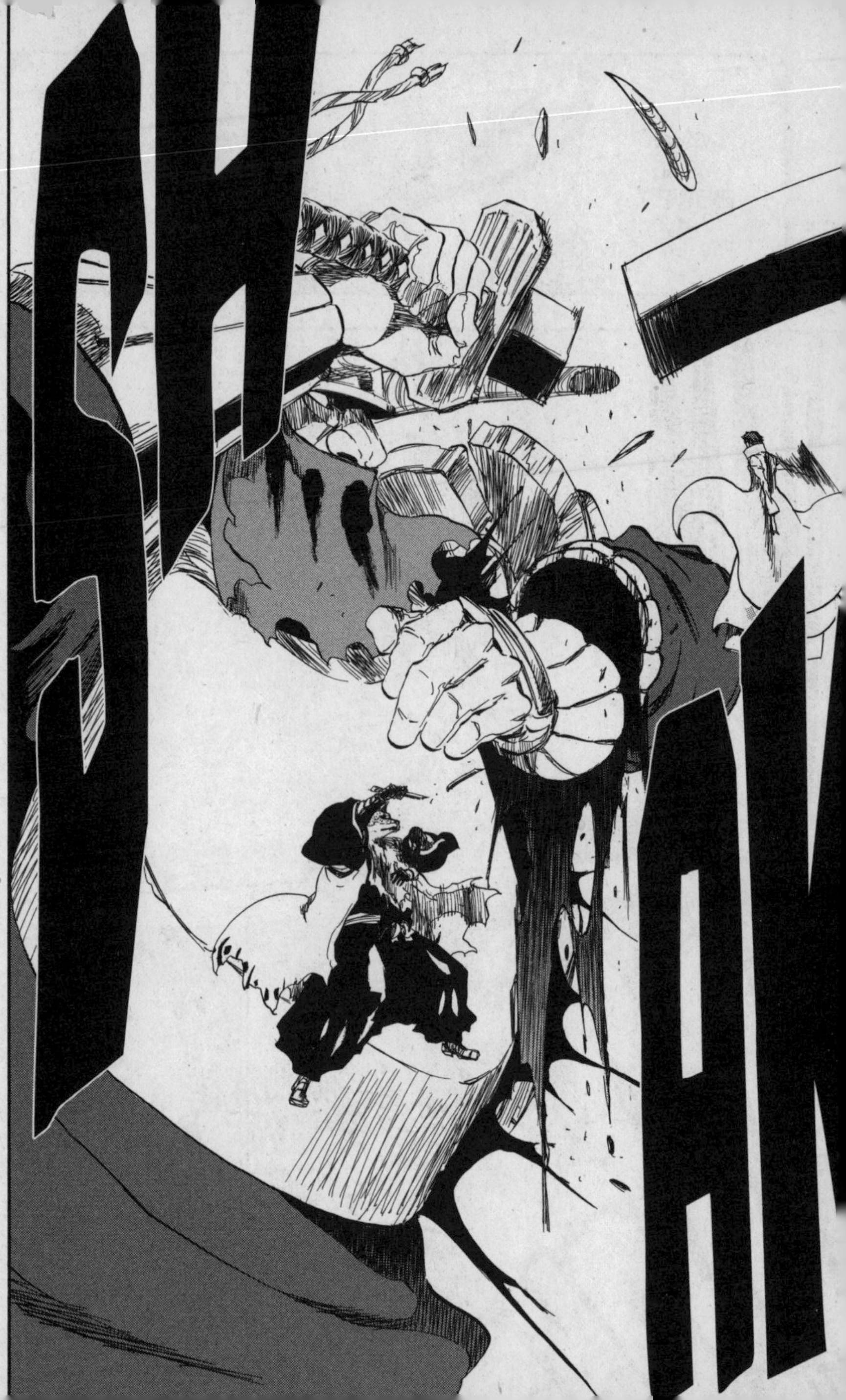
SCH
AK

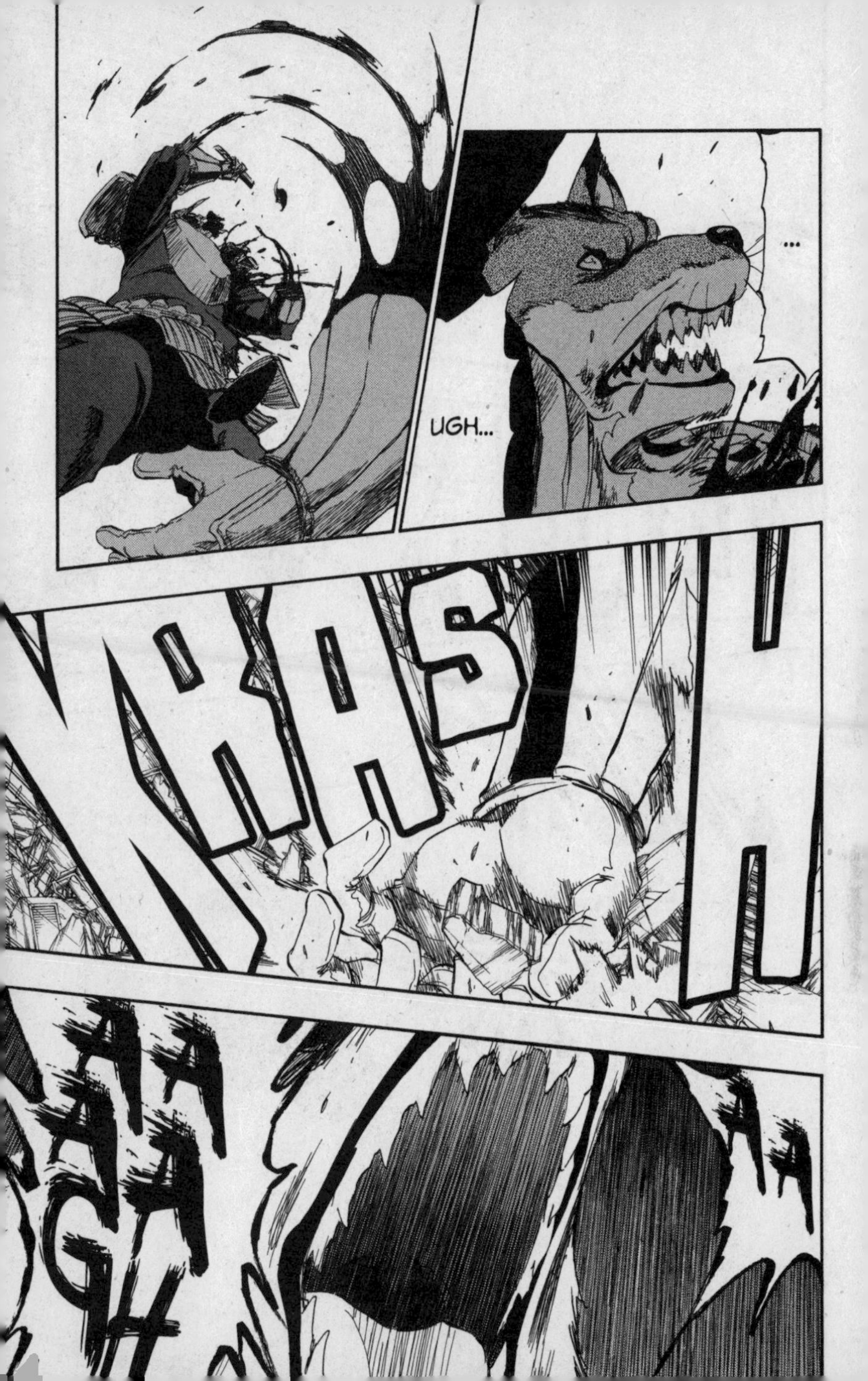
...
UGH...
KRASH

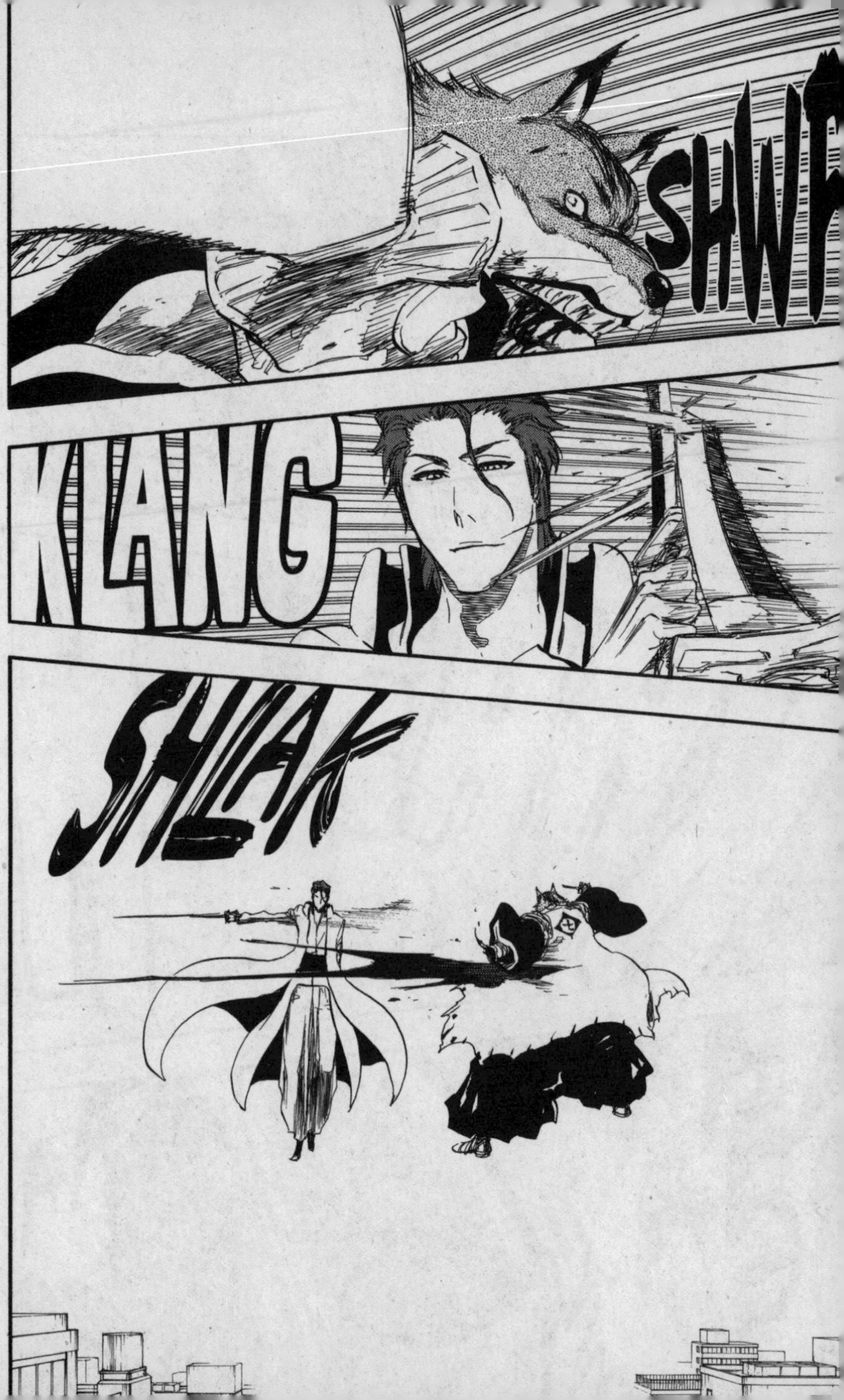
SHWF
KLANG
SHLAK

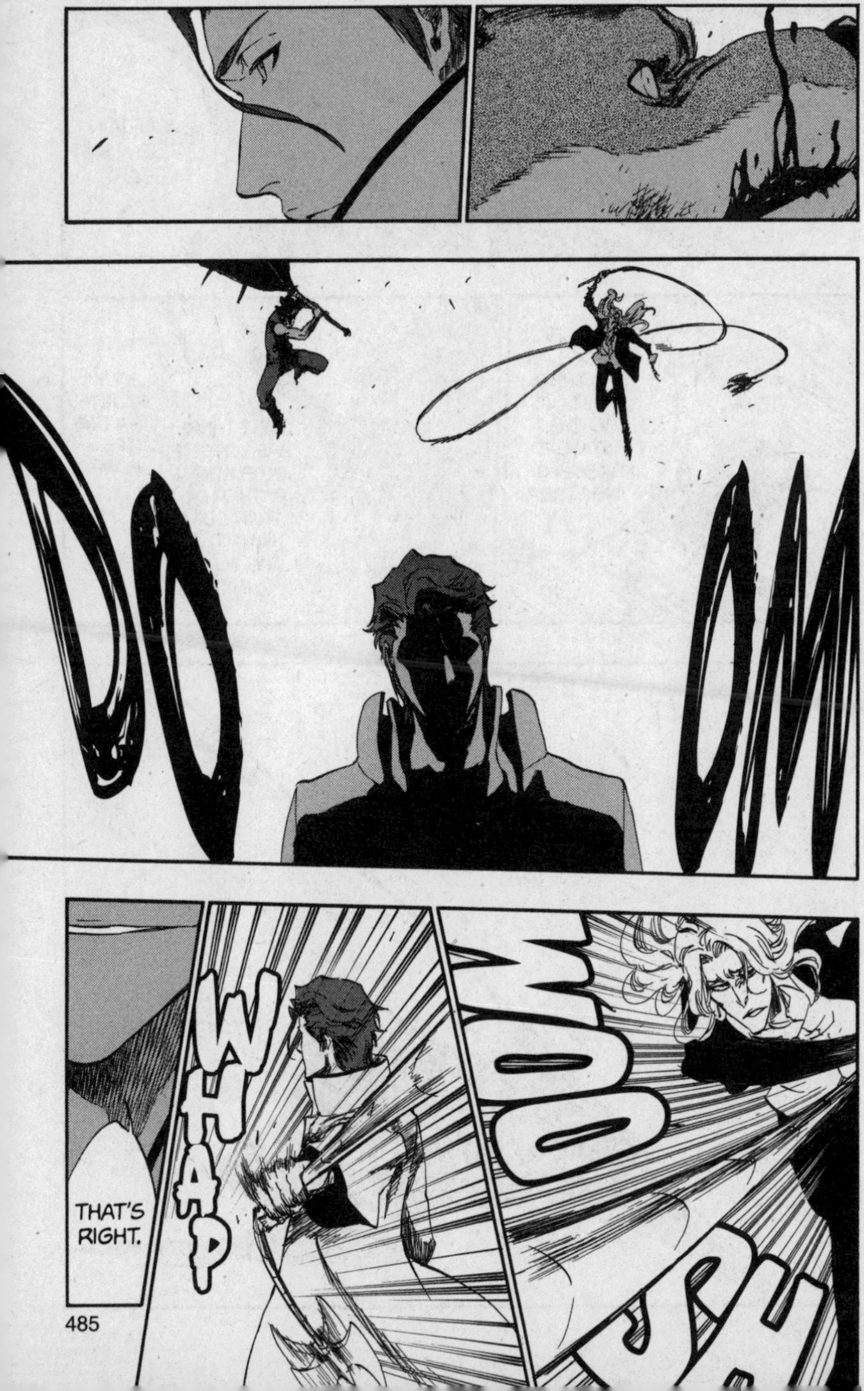
DOOM
WOO
WHAP
THAT'S RIGHT.

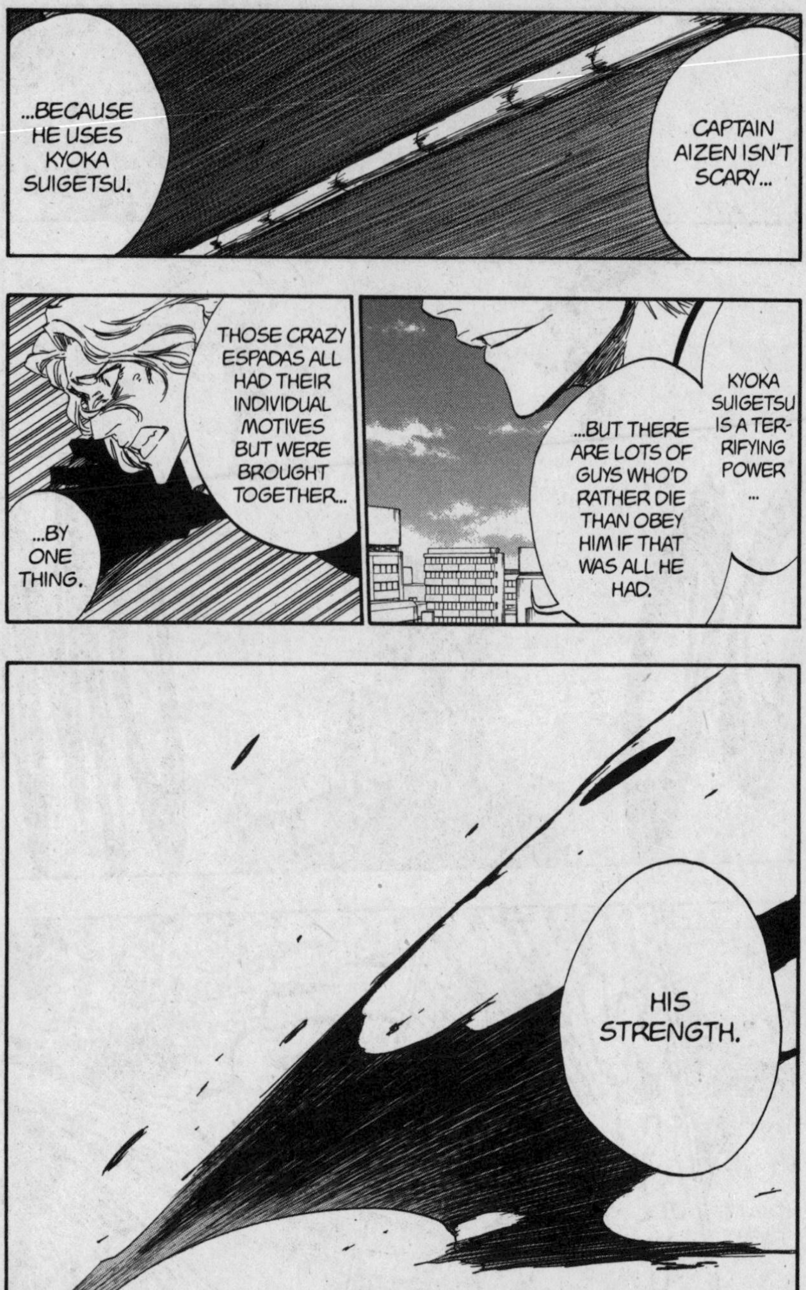
CAPTAIN AIZEN ISN'T SCARY...
...BECAUSE HE USES KYOKA SUIGETSU.
KYOKA SUIGETSU IS A TERRIFYING POWER...
...BUT THERE ARE LOTS OF GUYS WHO'D RATHER DIE THAN OBEY HIM IF THAT WAS ALL HE HAD.
THOSE CRAZY ESPADAS ALL HAD THEIR INDIVIDUAL MOTIVES BUT WERE BROUGHT TOGETHER...
...BY ONE THING.
HIS STRENGTH.

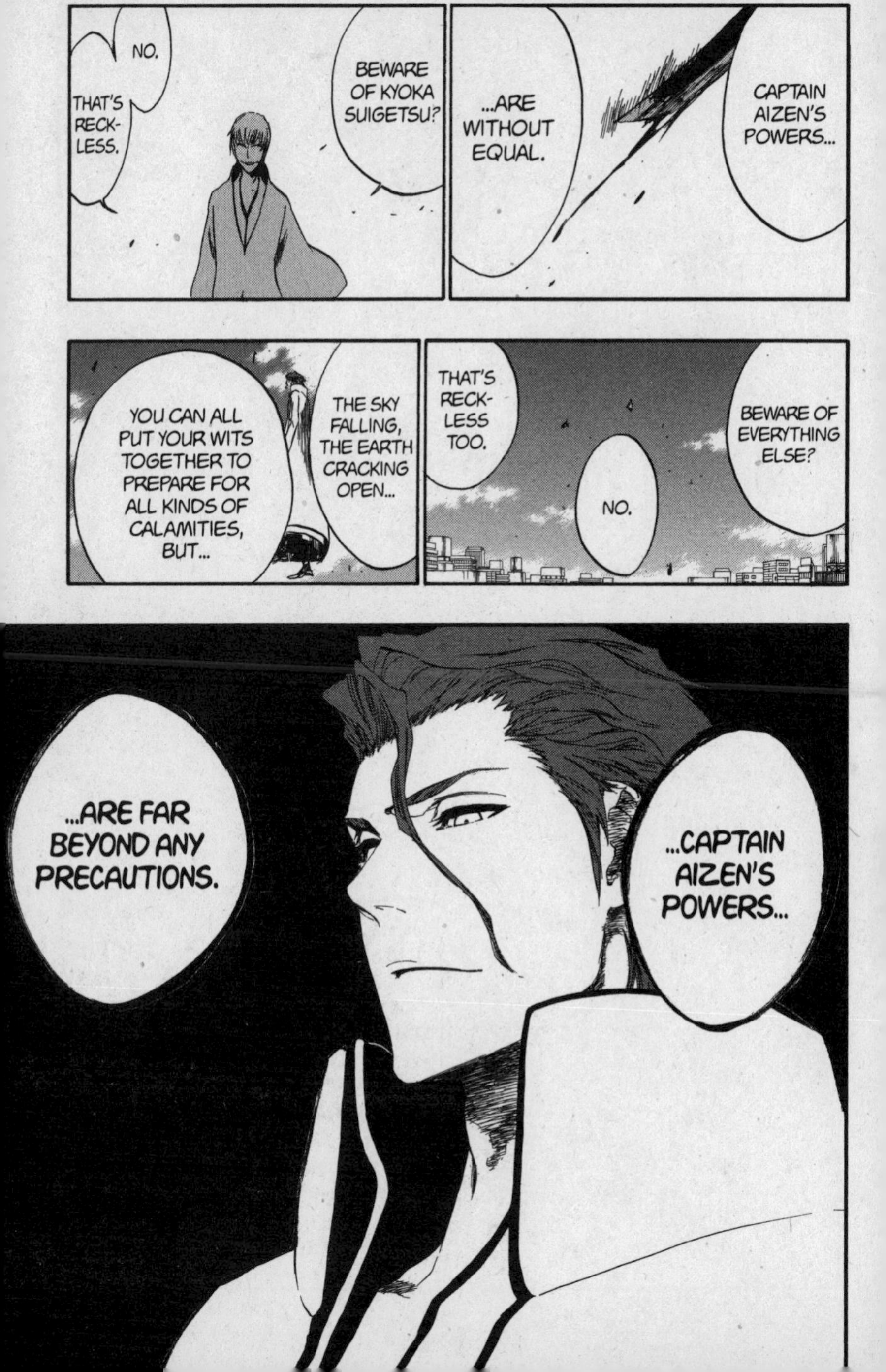
CAPTAIN AIZEN'S POWERS...
...ARE WITHOUT EQUAL.
BEWARE OF KYOKA SUIGETSU?
NO.
THAT'S RECK-LESS.
BEWARE OF EVERYTHING ELSE?
NO.
THAT'S RECK-LESS TOO.
THE SKY FALLING, THE EARTH CRACKING OPEN...
YOU CAN ALL PUT YOUR WITS TOGETHER TO PREPARE FOR ALL KINDS OF CALAMITIES, BUT...
...CAPTAIN AIZEN'S POWERS...
...ARE FAR BEYOND ANY PRECAUTIONS.

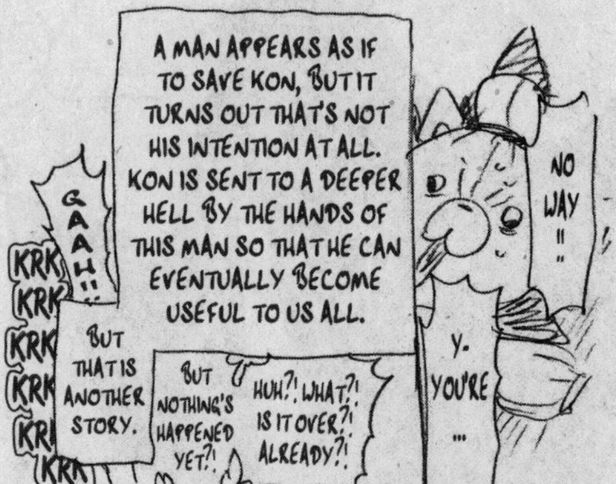
NO WAY!!
A MAN APPEARS AS IF TO SAVE KON, BUT IT TURNS OUT THAT'S NOT HIS INTENTION AT ALL. KON IS SENT TO A DEEPER HELL BY THE HANDS OF THIS MAN SO THAT HE CAN EVENTUALLY BECOME USEFUL TO US ALL.
Y. YOU'RE...
HUH?! WHAT?! IS IT OVER?! ALREADY?!
BUT NOTHING'S HAPPENED YET?!
GAAAH!!
BUT THAT IS ANOTHER STORY.
KRK KRK KRK KRK KRK KRK

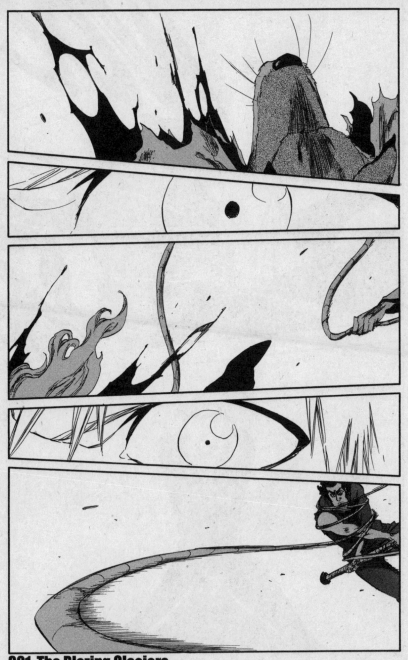

391. The Blazing Glaciers

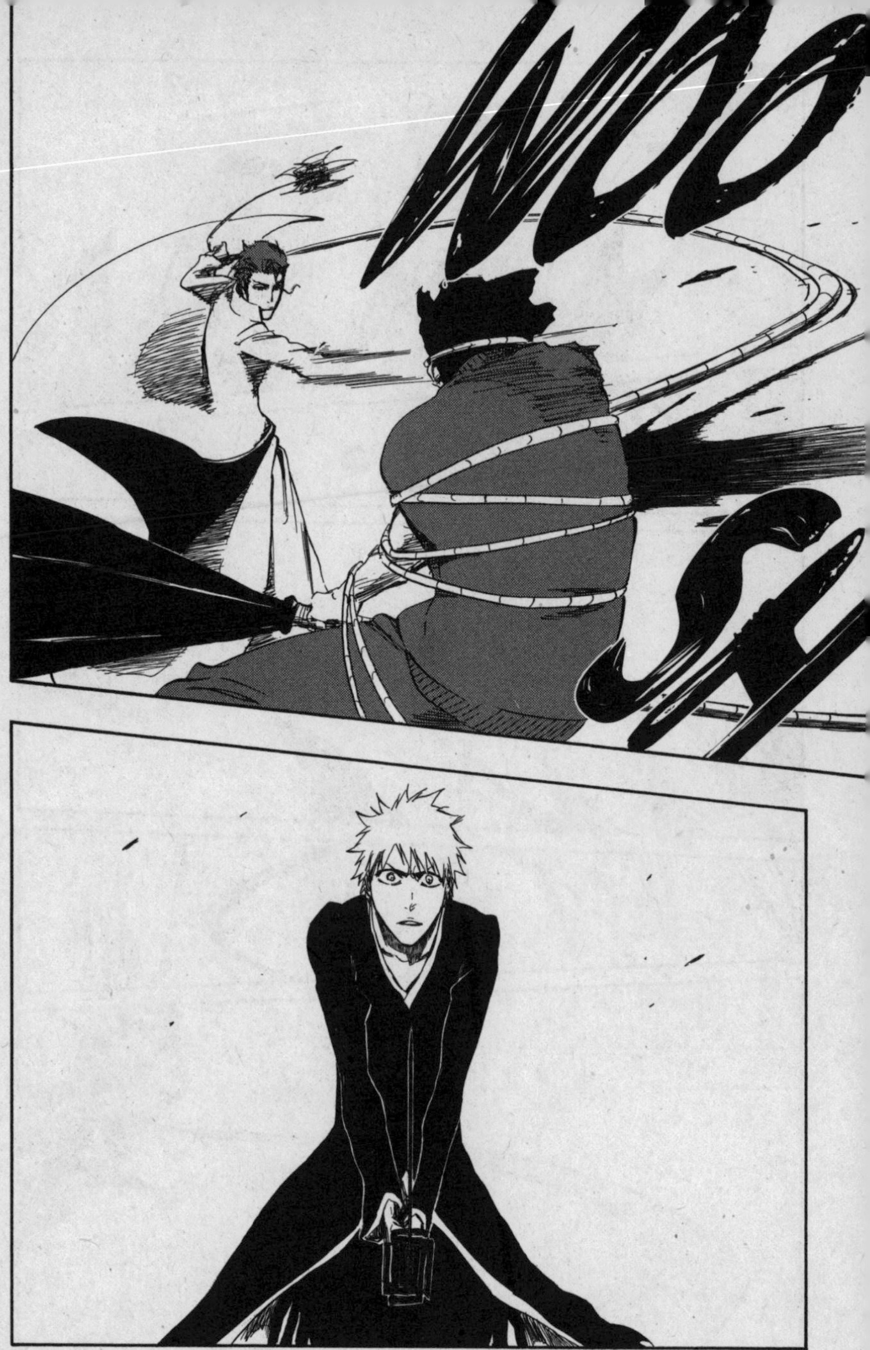
WOOSH

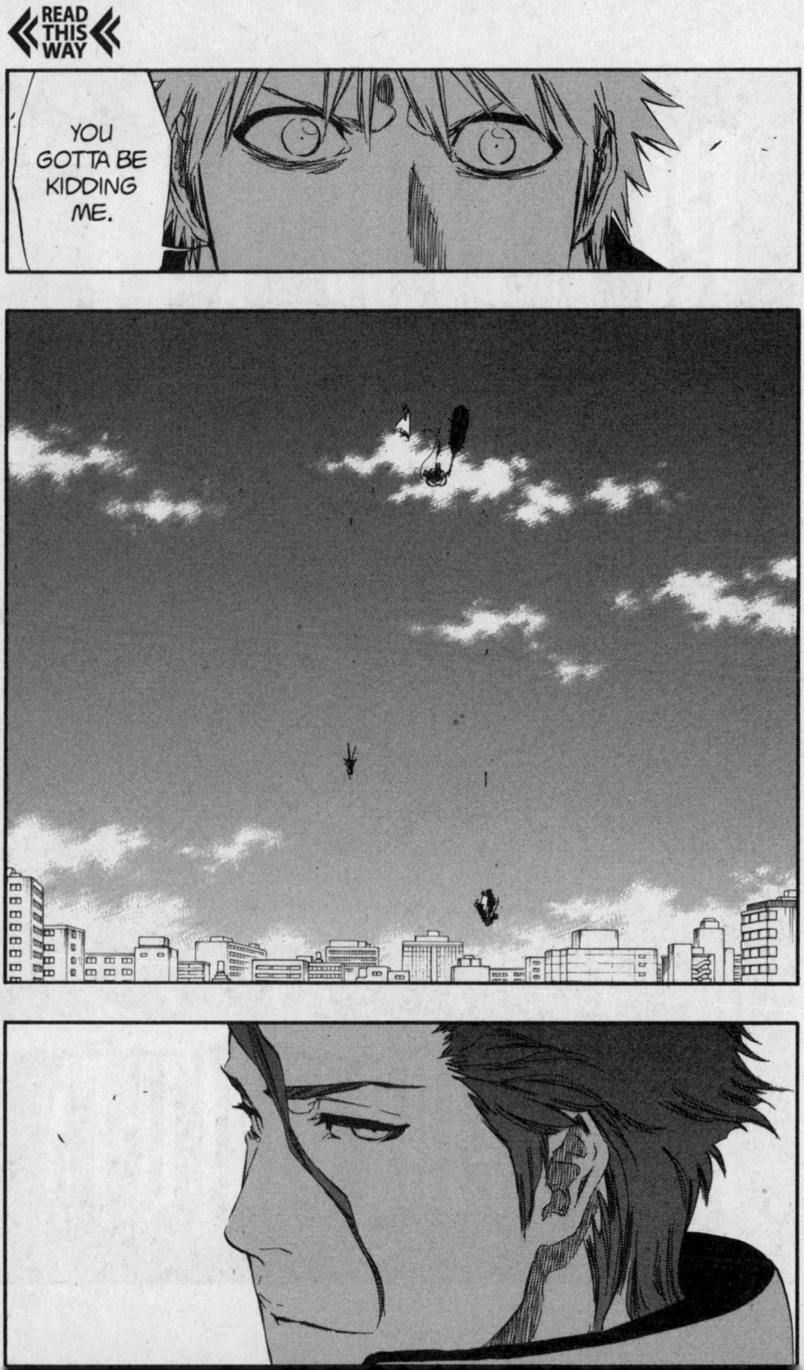
READ THIS WAY
YOU GOTTA BE KIDDING ME.

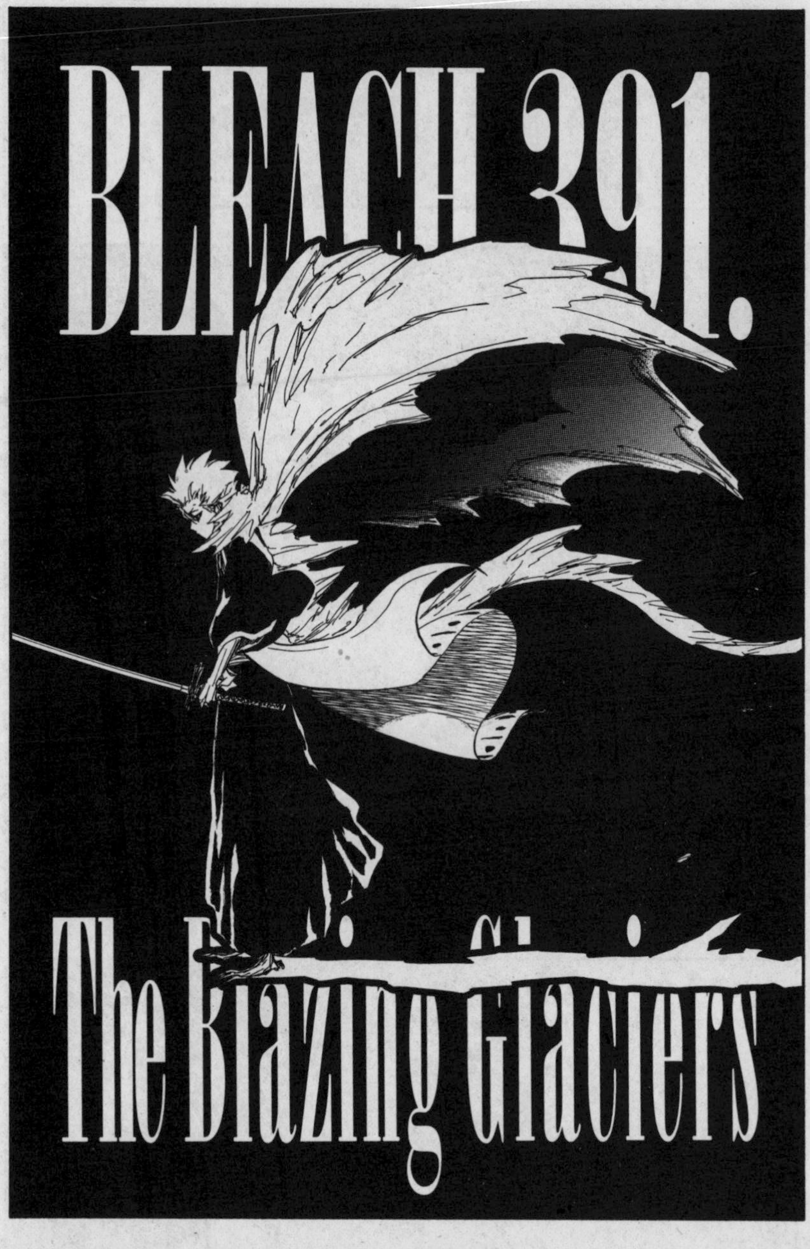
BLEACH 391.
The Blazing Glaciers

READ THIS WAY

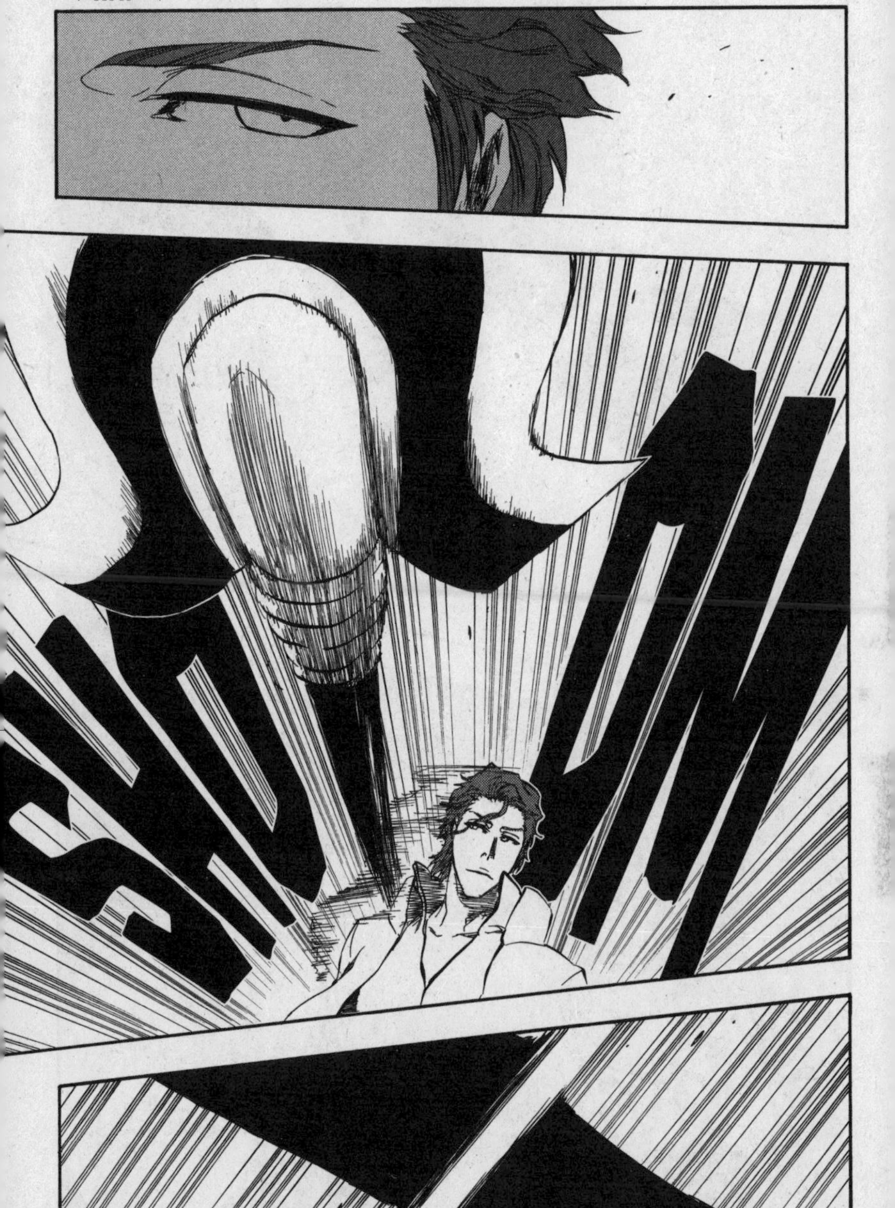

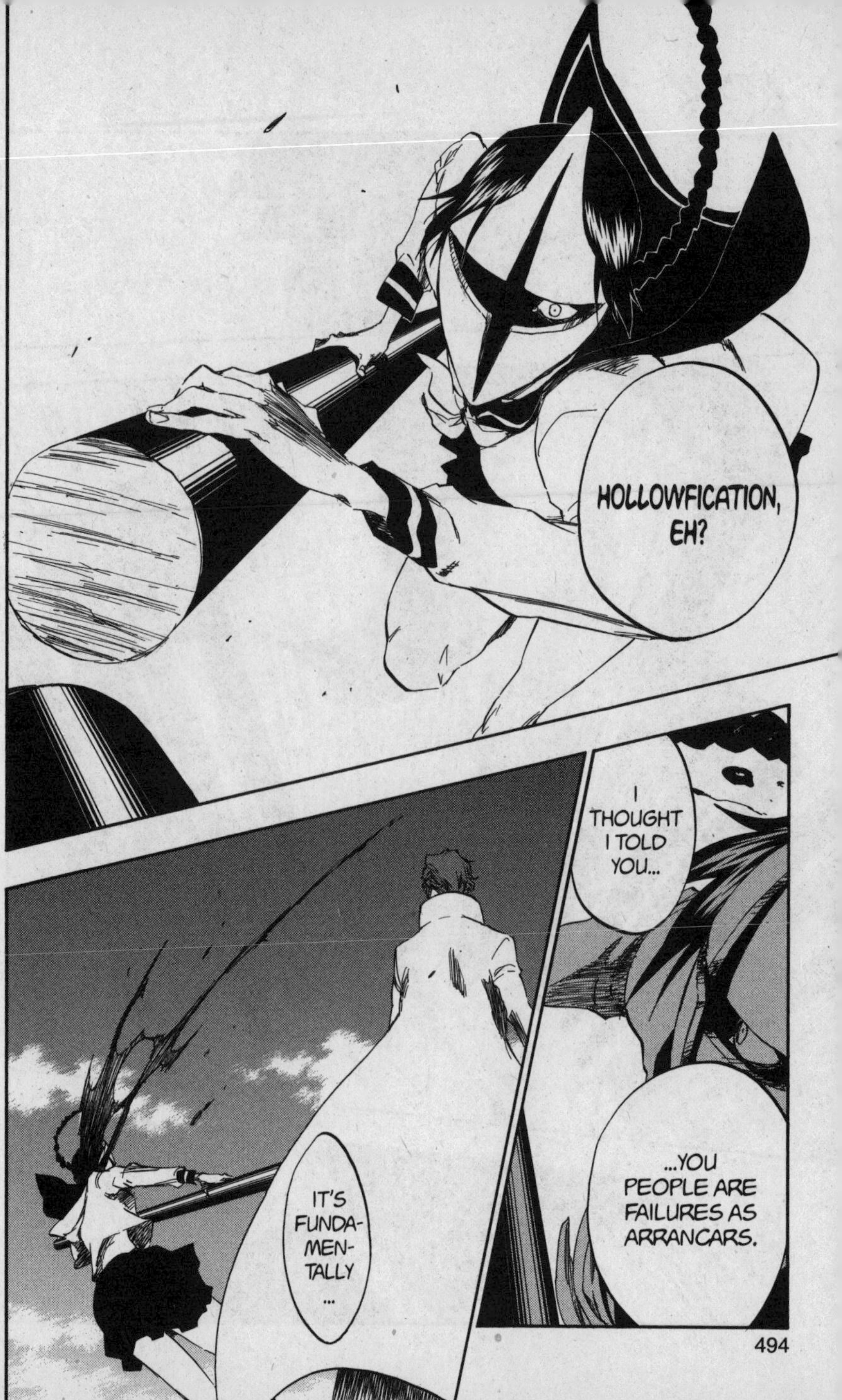
HOLLOWFICATION, EH?
I THOUGHT I TOLD YOU...
...YOU PEOPLE ARE FAILURES AS ARRANCARS.
IT'S FUNDA-MEN-TALLY ...

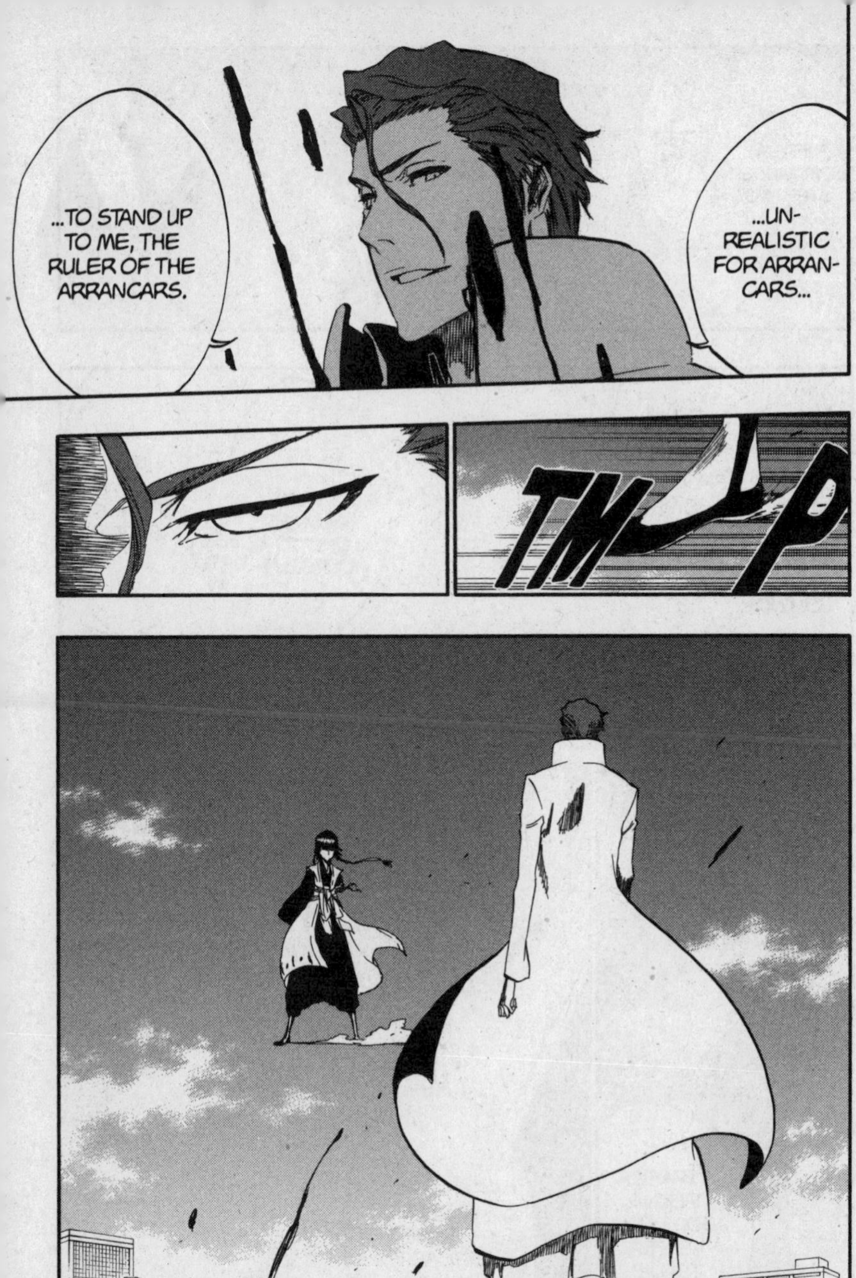
...UN-REALISTIC FOR ARRAN-CARS...
...TO STAND UP TO ME, THE RULER OF THE ARRANCARS.
TMP

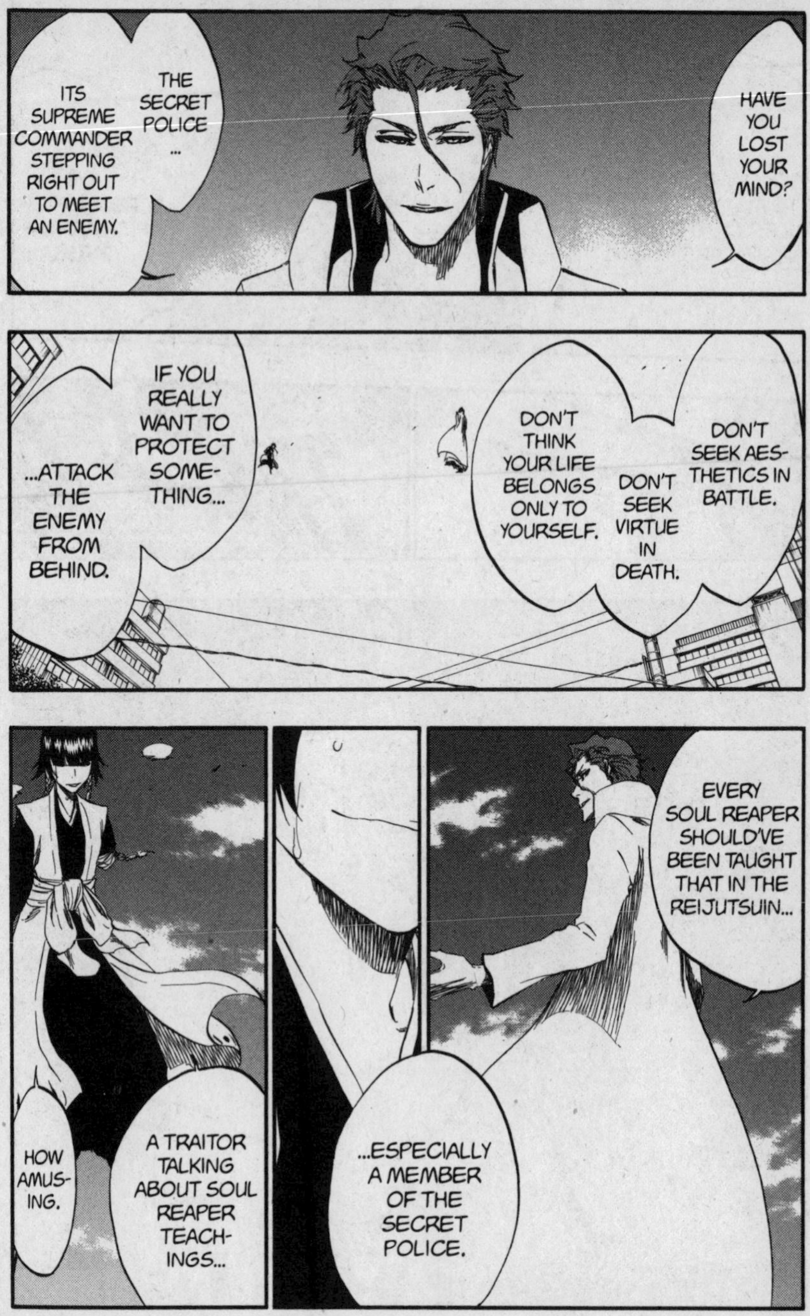
HAVE YOU LOST YOUR MIND?
THE SECRET POLICE...
ITS SUPREME COMMANDER STEPPING RIGHT OUT TO MEET AN ENEMY.
DON'T SEEK AESTHETICS IN BATTLE.
DON'T SEEK VIRTUE IN DEATH.
DON'T THINK YOUR LIFE BELONGS ONLY TO YOURSELF.
IF YOU REALLY WANT TO PROTECT SOMETHING...
...ATTACK THE ENEMY FROM BEHIND.
EVERY SOUL REAPER SHOULD'VE BEEN TAUGHT THAT IN THE REIJUTSUIN...
...ESPECIALLY A MEMBER OF THE SECRET POLICE.
A TRAITOR TALKING ABOUT SOUL REAPER TEACHINGS...
HOW AMUSING.

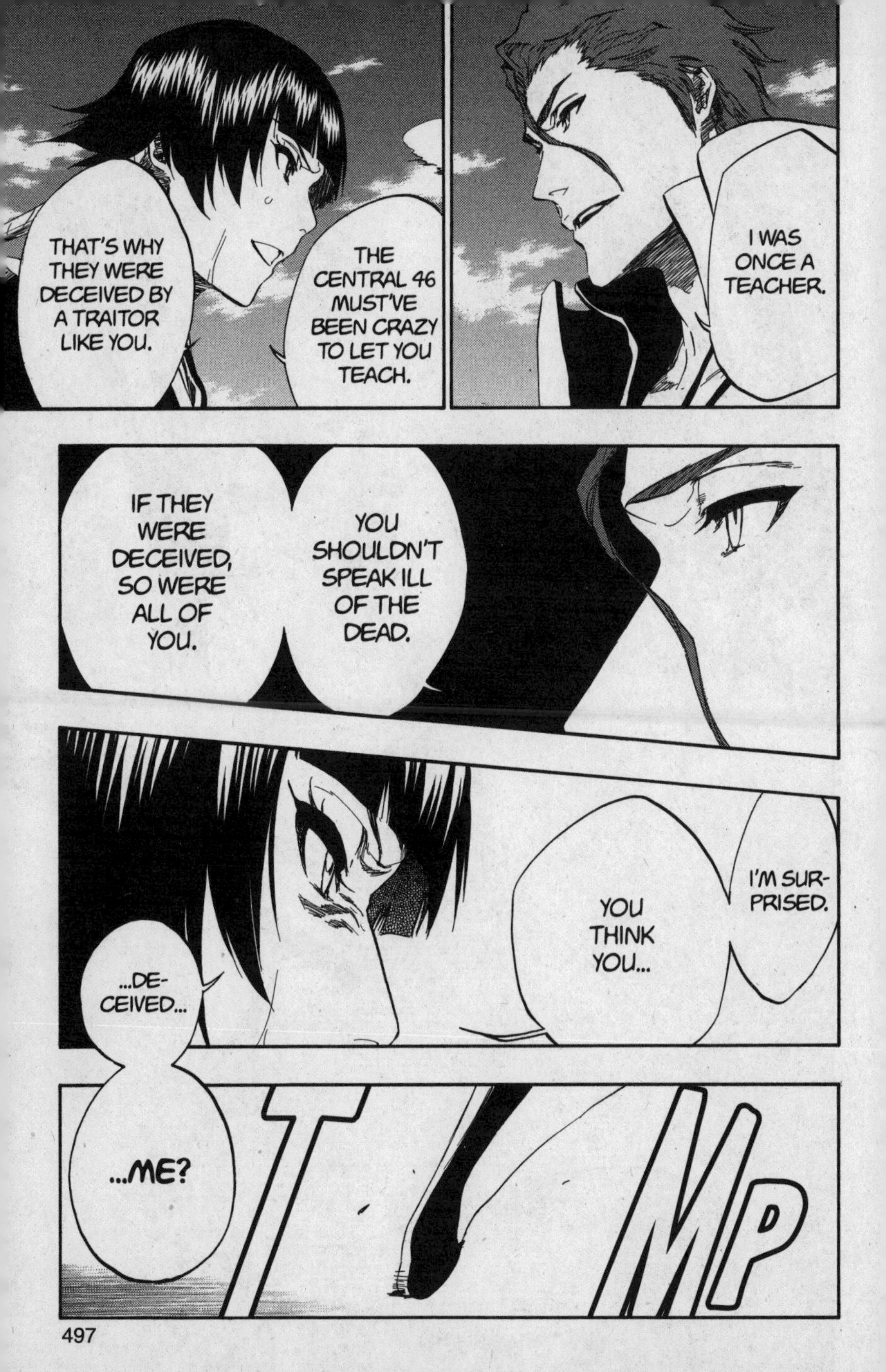
I WAS ONCE A TEACHER.
THE CENTRAL 46 MUST'VE BEEN CRAZY TO LET YOU TEACH.
THAT'S WHY THEY WERE DECEIVED BY A TRAITOR LIKE YOU.
YOU SHOULDN'T SPEAK ILL OF THE DEAD.
IF THEY WERE DECEIVED, SO WERE ALL OF YOU.
I'M SUR-PRISED.
YOU THINK YOU...
...DE-CEIVED...
TMP
...ME?

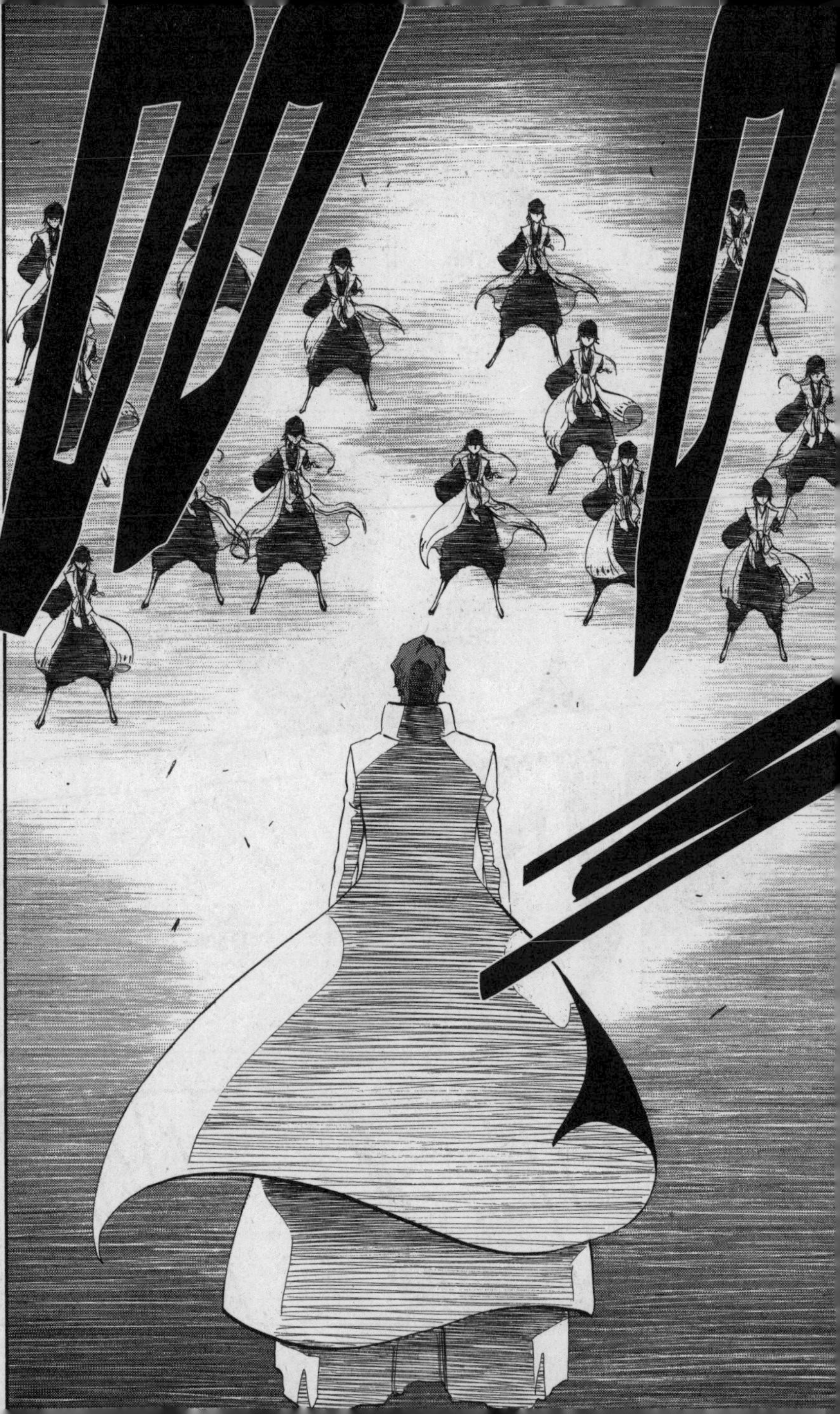

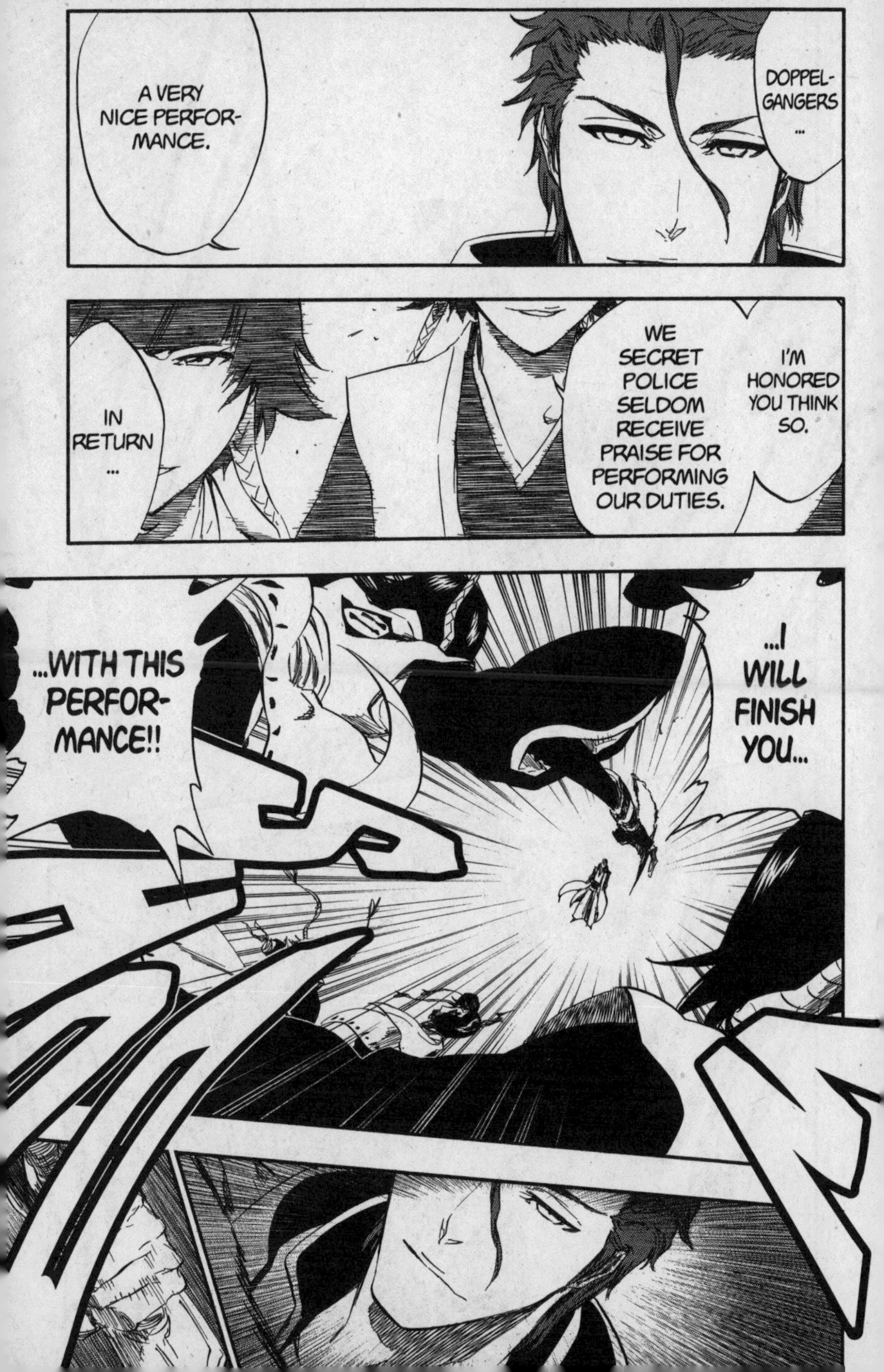
DOPPELGANGERS...
A VERY NICE PERFORMANCE.
I'M HONORED YOU THINK SO.
WE SECRET POLICE SELDOM RECEIVE PRAISE FOR PERFORMING OUR DUTIES.
IN RETURN...
...I WILL FINISH YOU...
...WITH THIS PERFORMANCE!!

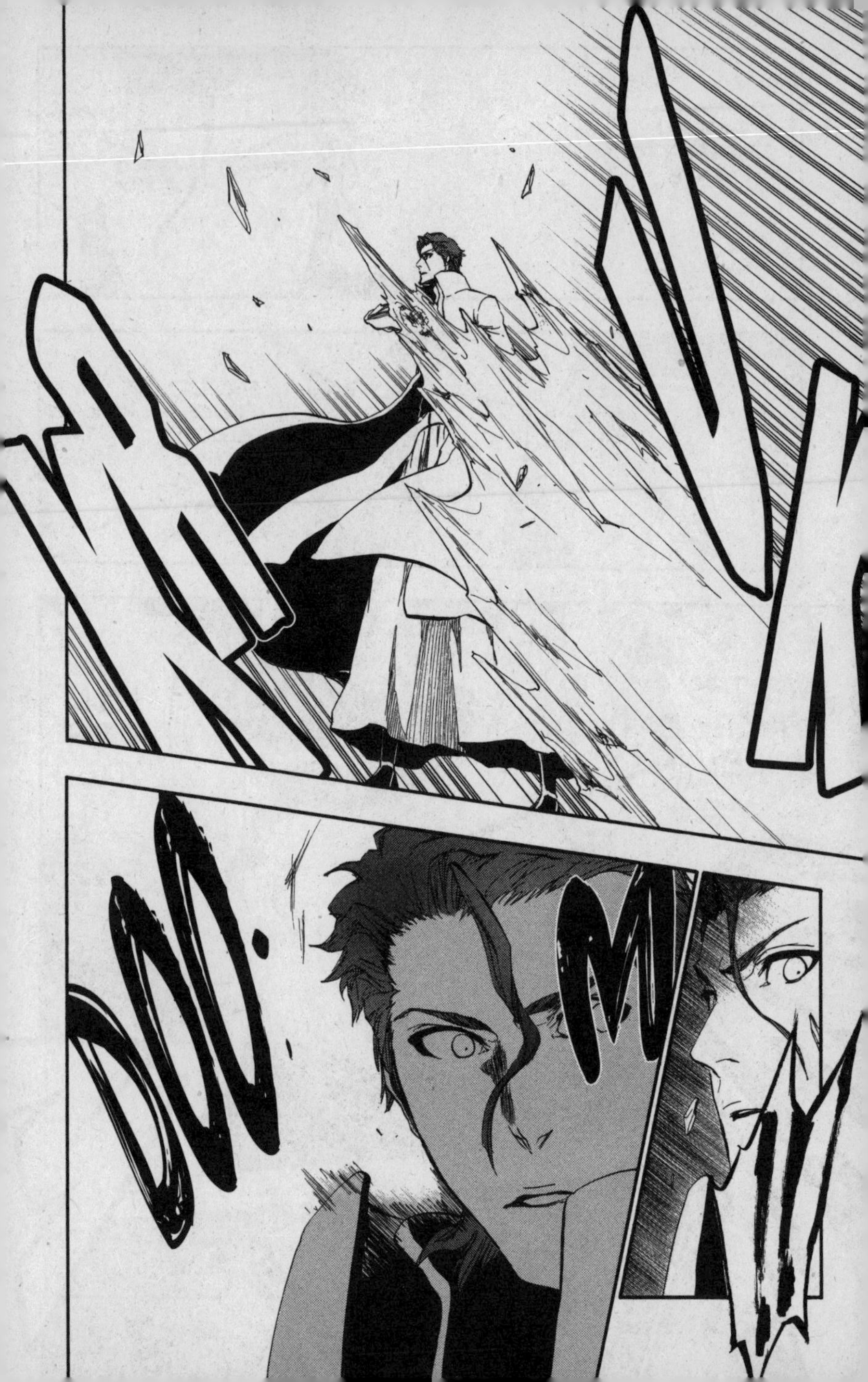

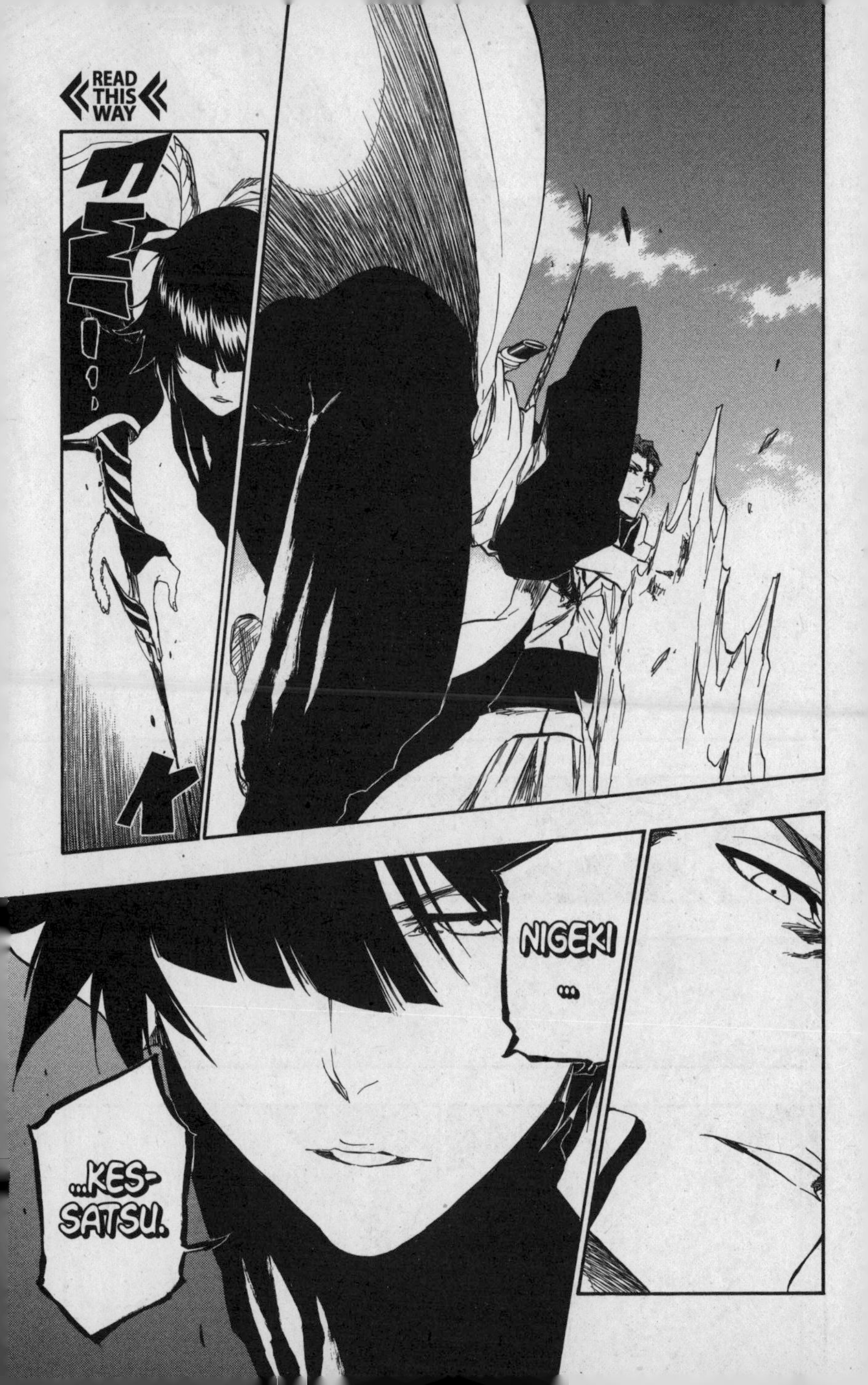
READ THIS WAY
FWM...!!
K
NIGEKI
...
...KES-
SATSU.

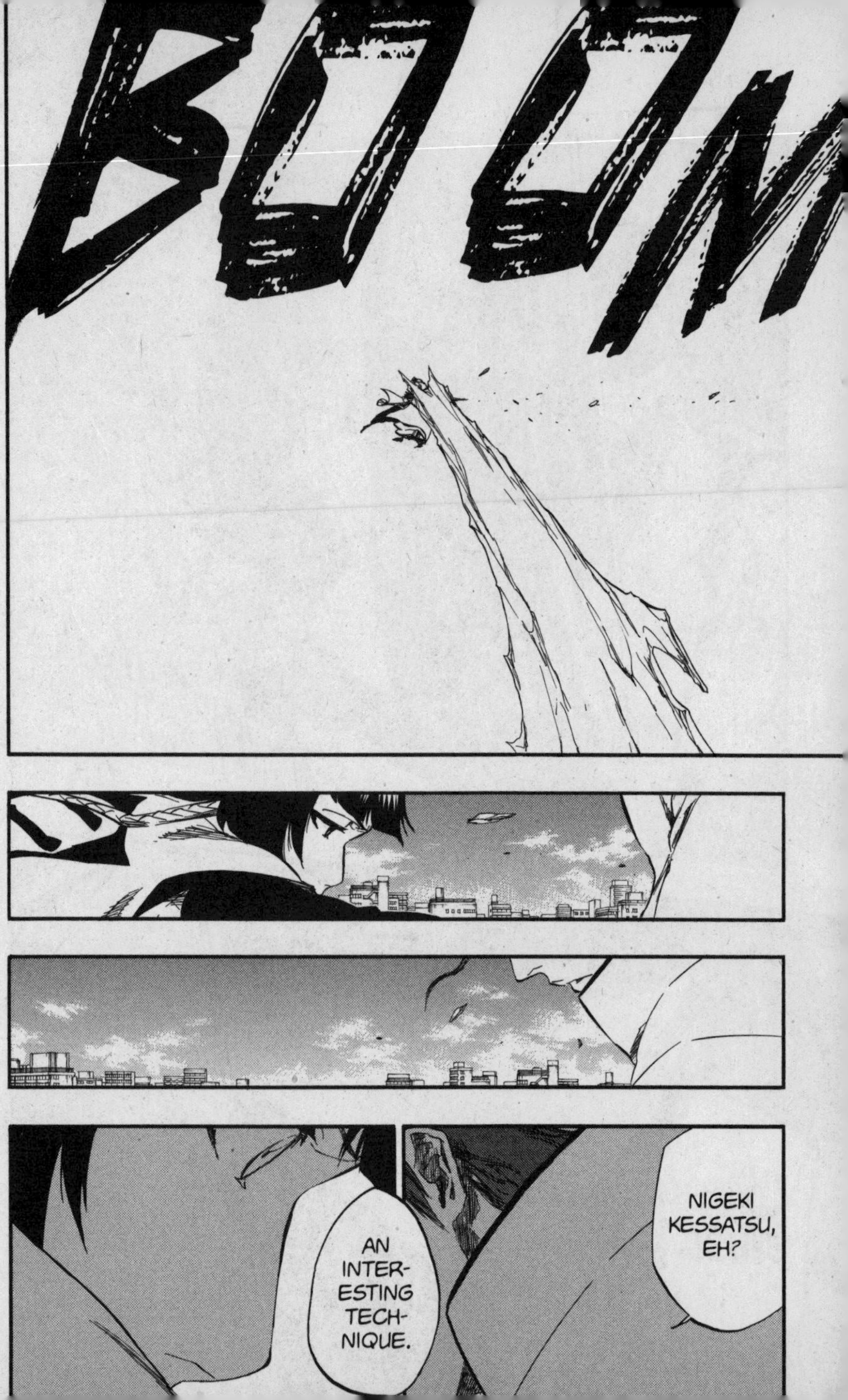
BOOM
NIGEKI KESSATSU, EH?
AN INTER-ESTING TECH-NIQUE.

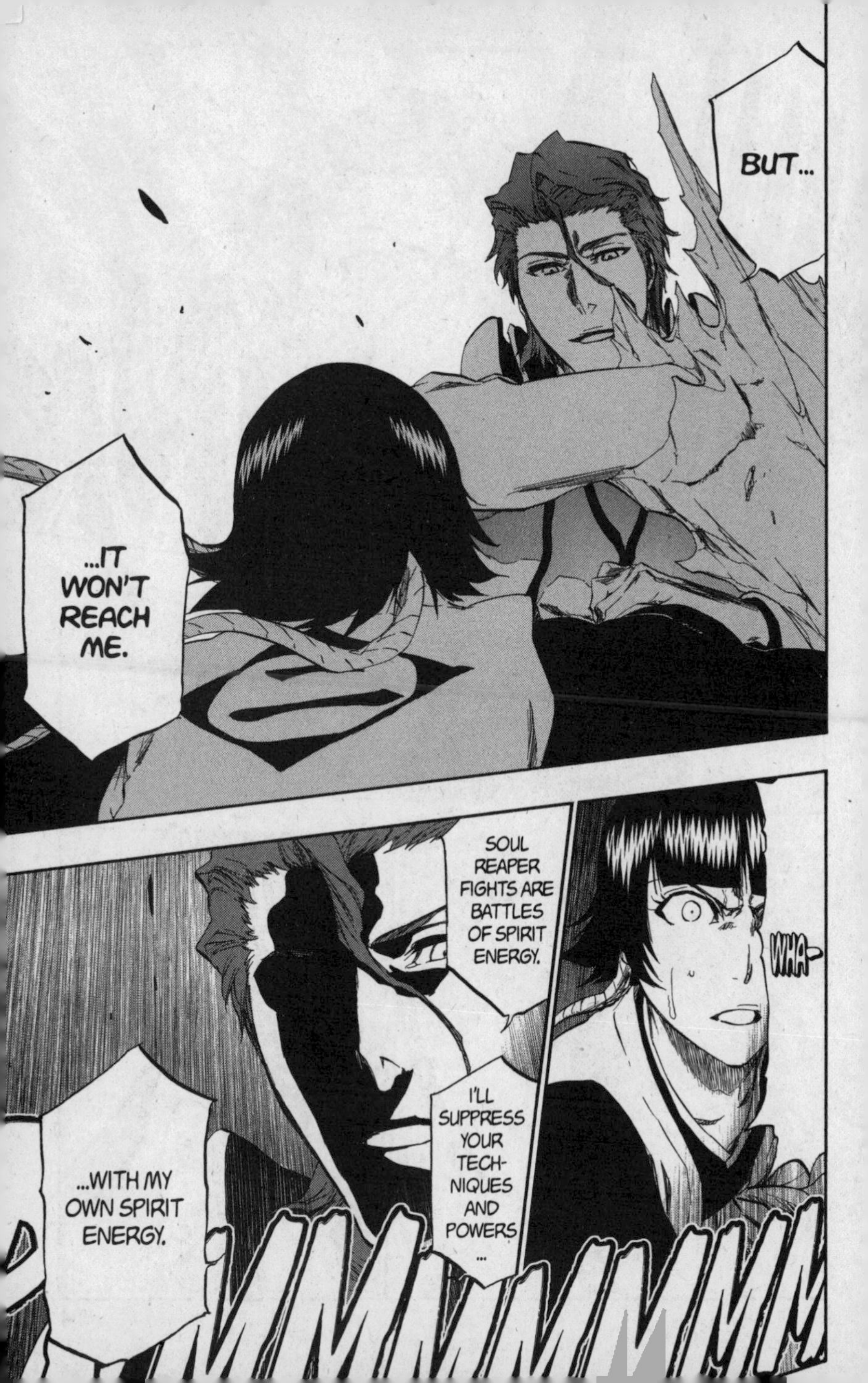
BUT...
...IT WON'T REACH ME.
WHA-
SOUL REAPER FIGHTS ARE BATTLES OF SPIRIT ENERGY.
I'LL SUPPRESS YOUR TECH-NIQUES AND POWERS...
...WITH MY OWN SPIRIT ENERGY.

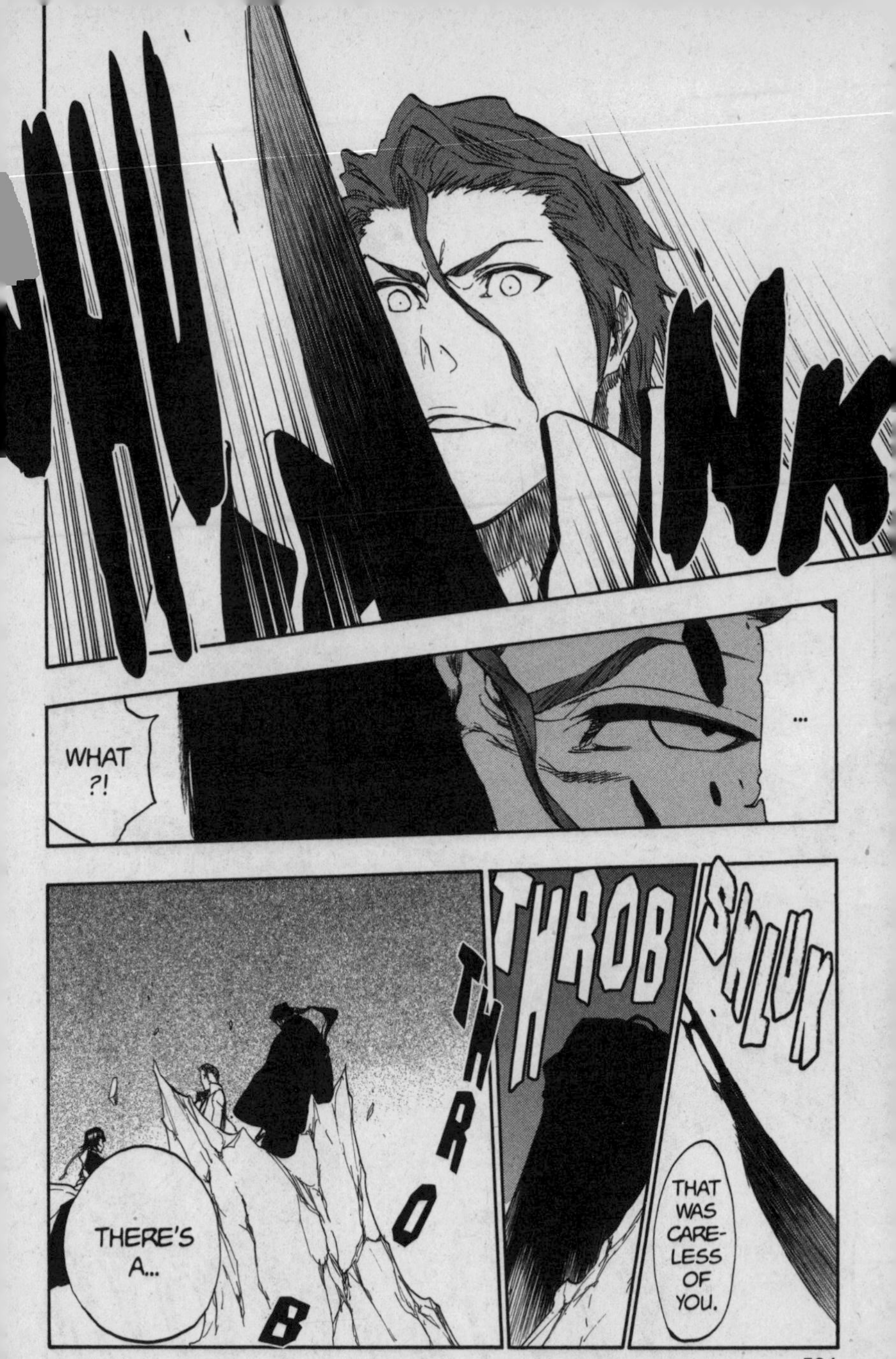
...
WHAT ?!
SHLUK
THAT WAS CARE-LESS OF YOU.
THROB
THROB
THERE'S A...

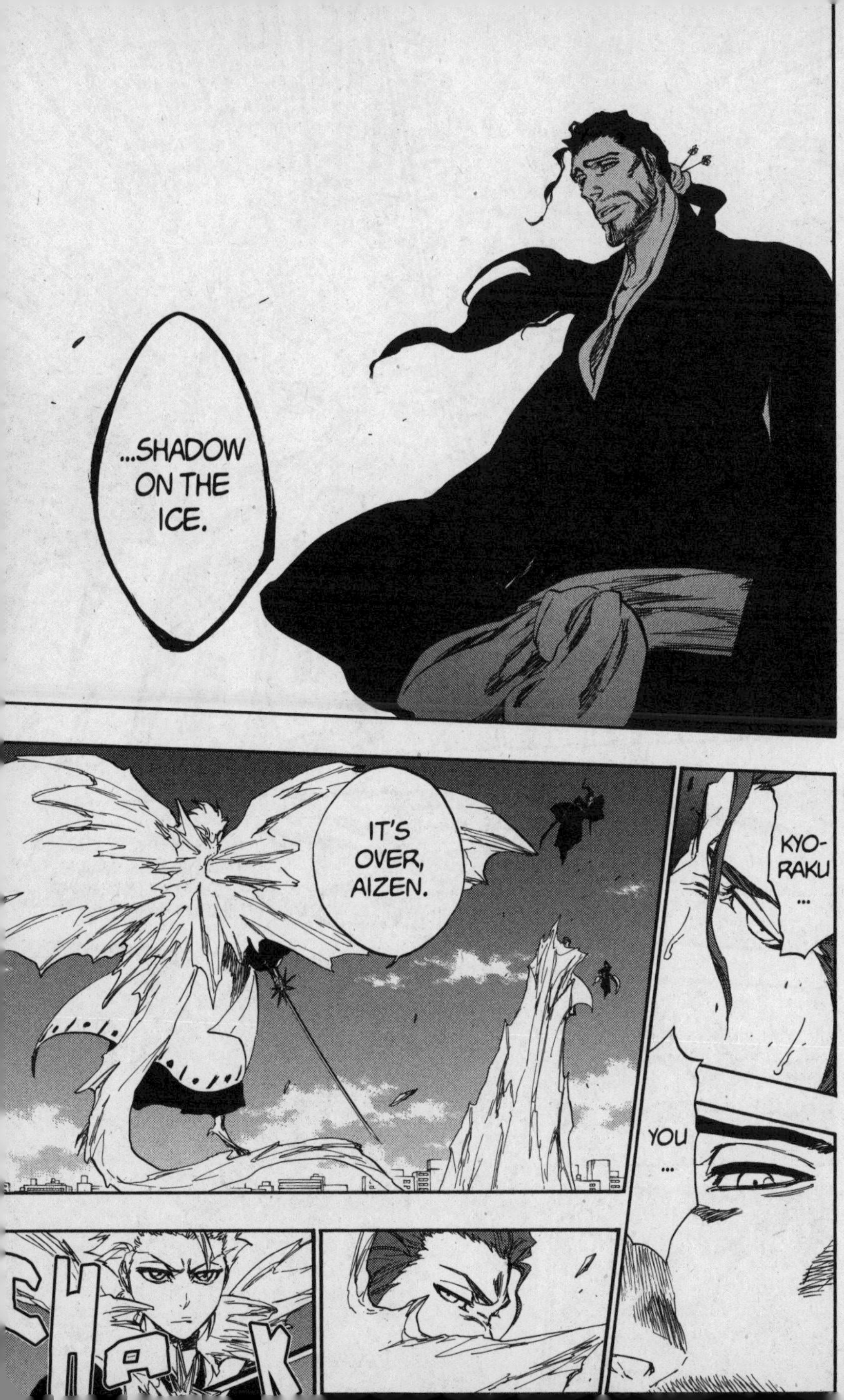
...SHADOW ON THE ICE.
KYO-RAKU ...
YOU ...
IT'S OVER, AIZEN.
CHAK

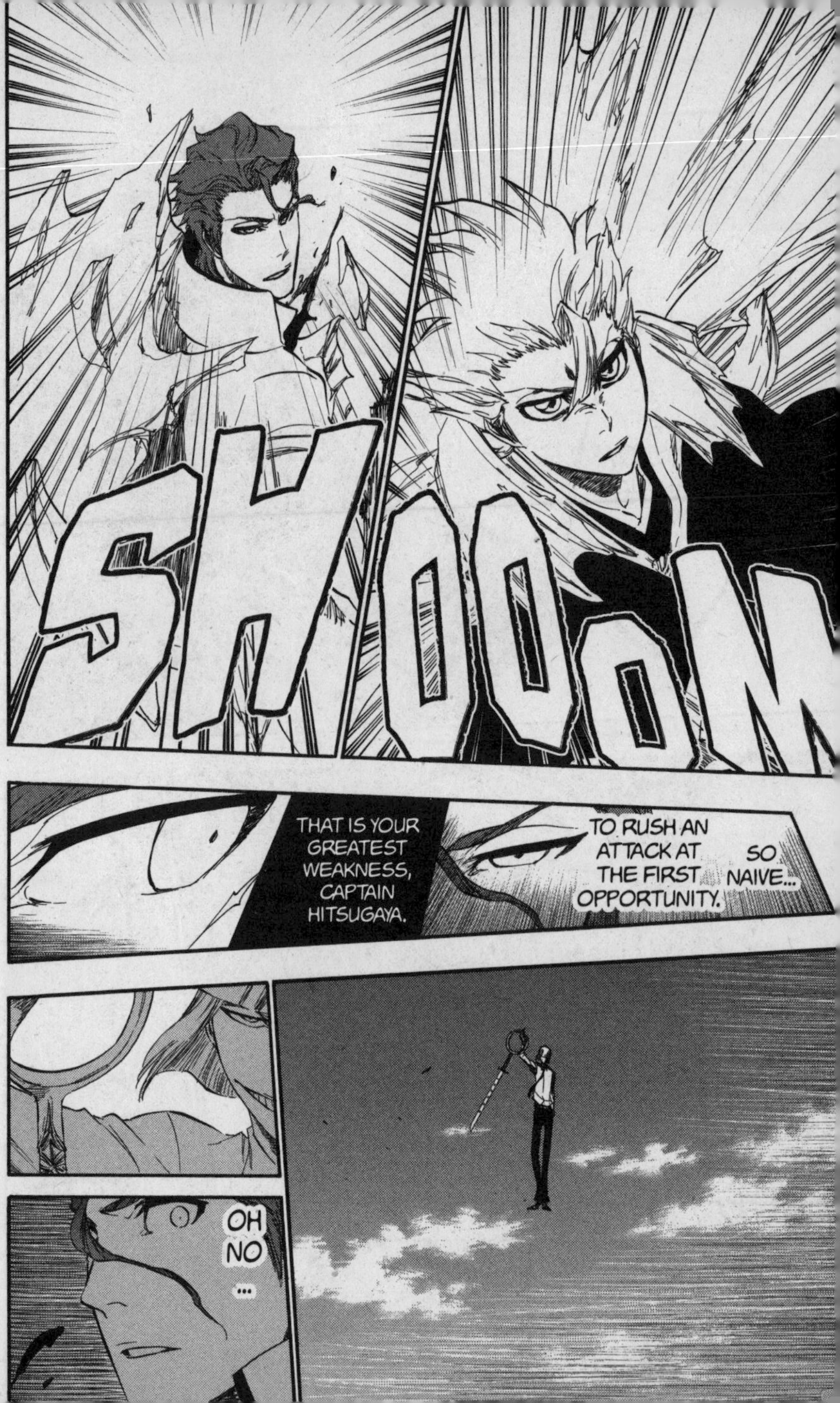
SHOOOM
SO NAIVE...
TO RUSH AN ATTACK AT THE FIRST OPPORTUNITY.
THAT IS YOUR GREATEST WEAKNESS, CAPTAIN HITSUGAYA.
OH NO ...

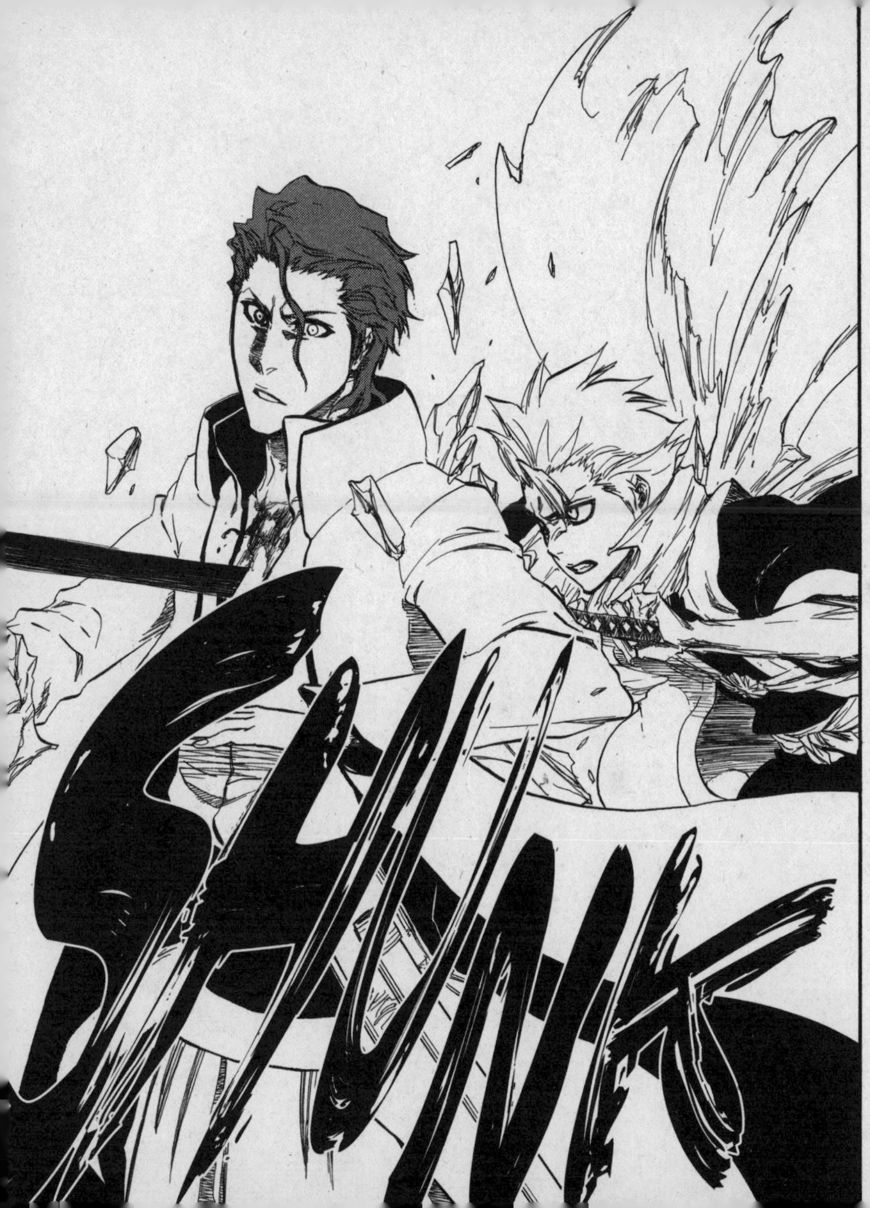
SHUNK

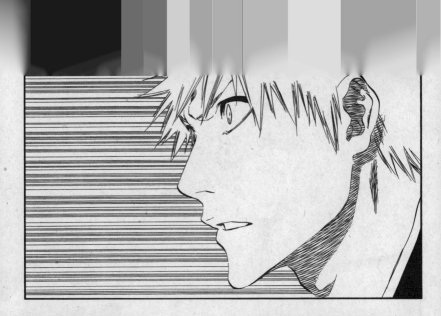

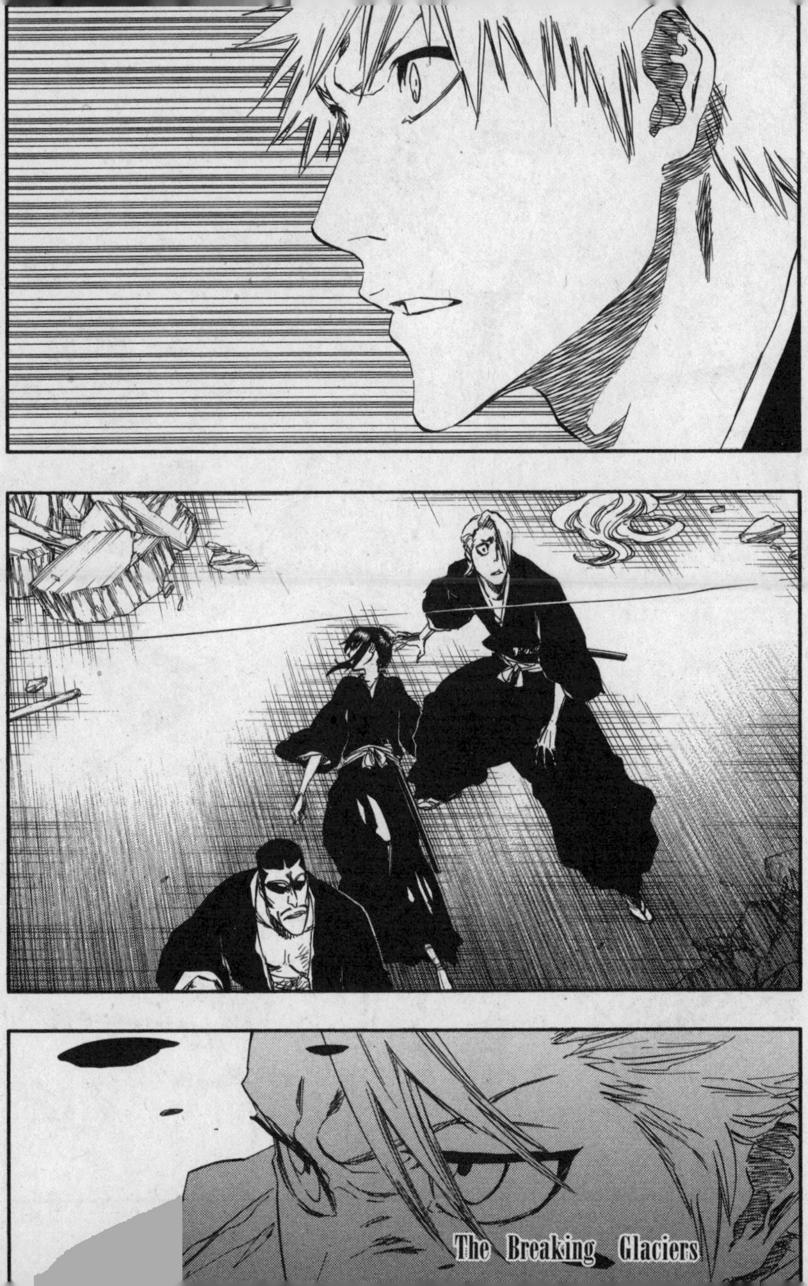
The Breaking Glaciers

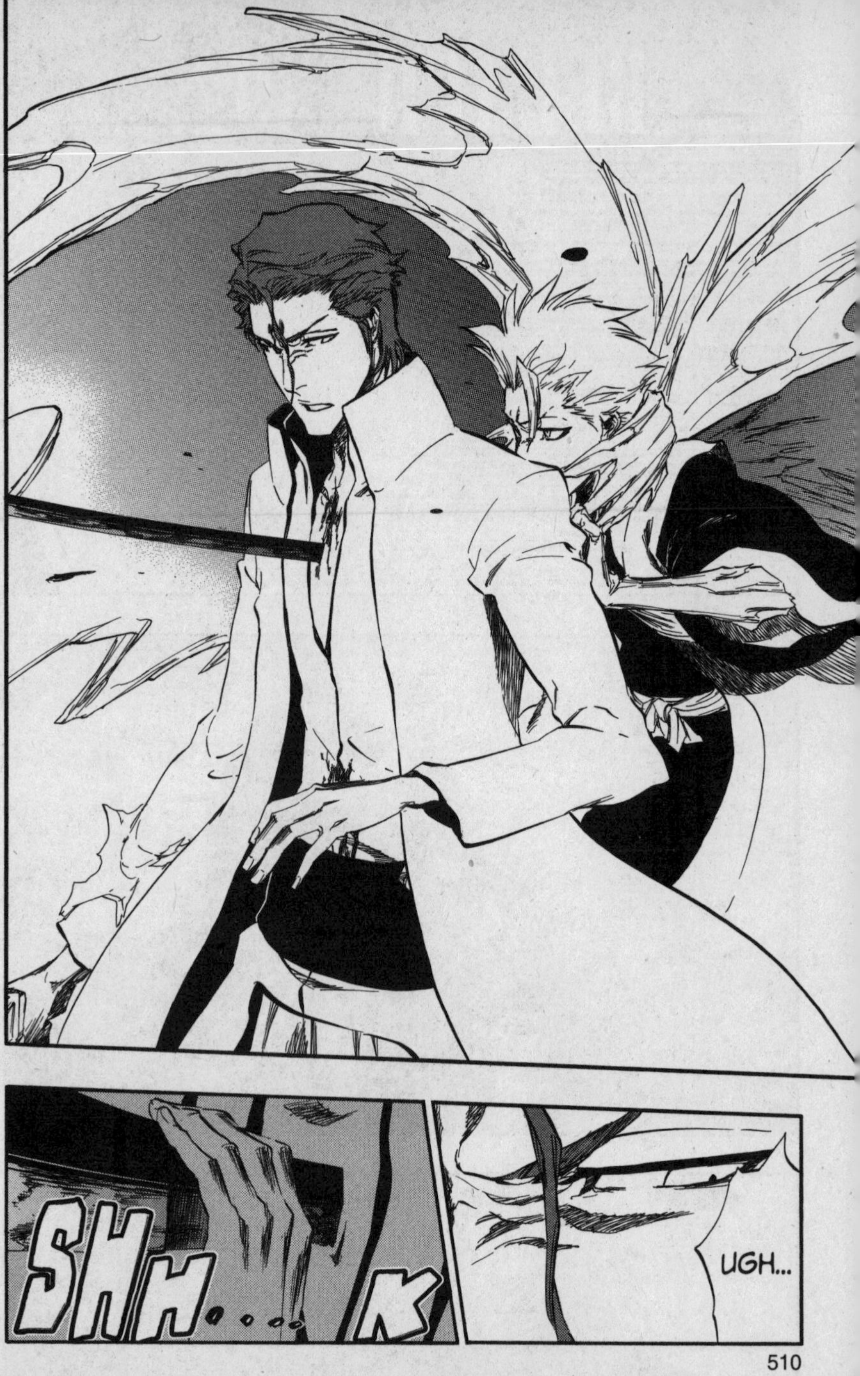
UGH...
SHH...K

READ THIS WAY

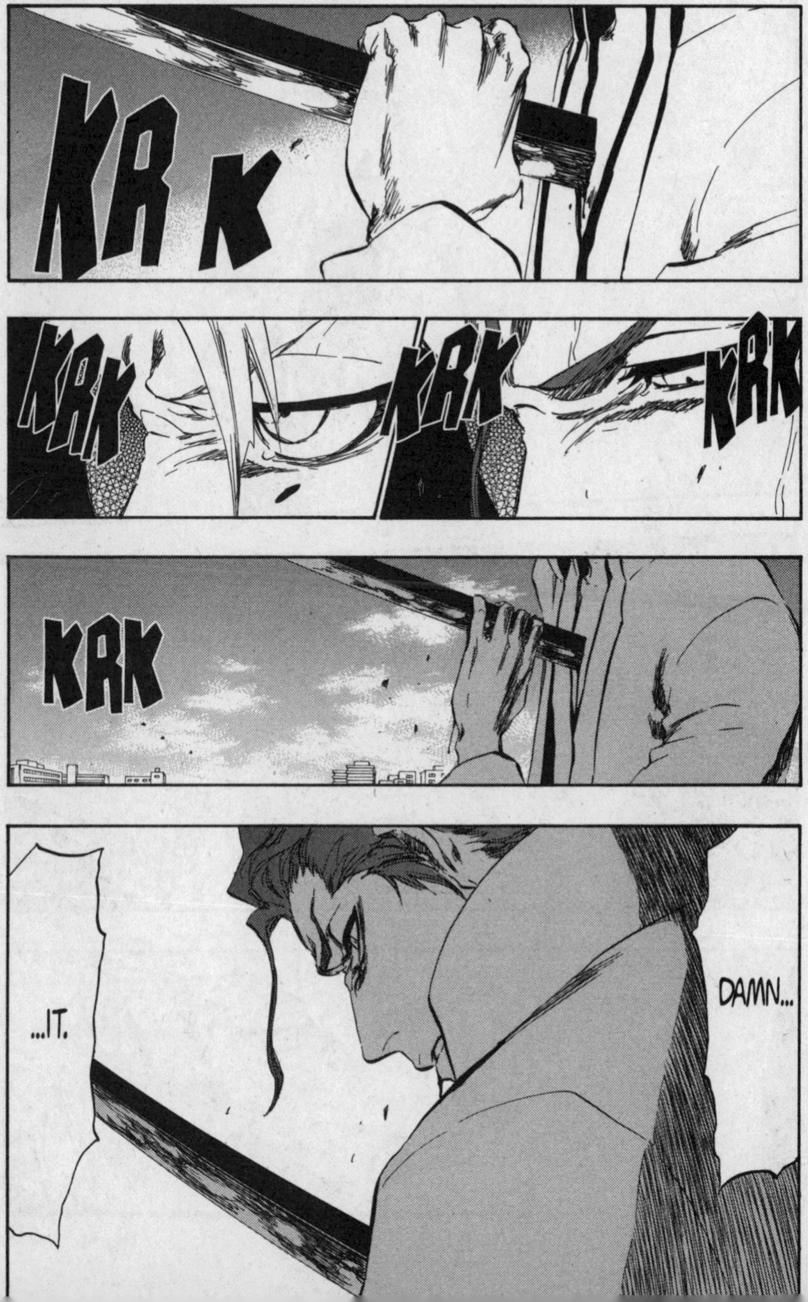
KRK
KRK
KRK
KRK
KRK
DAMN...
...IT.

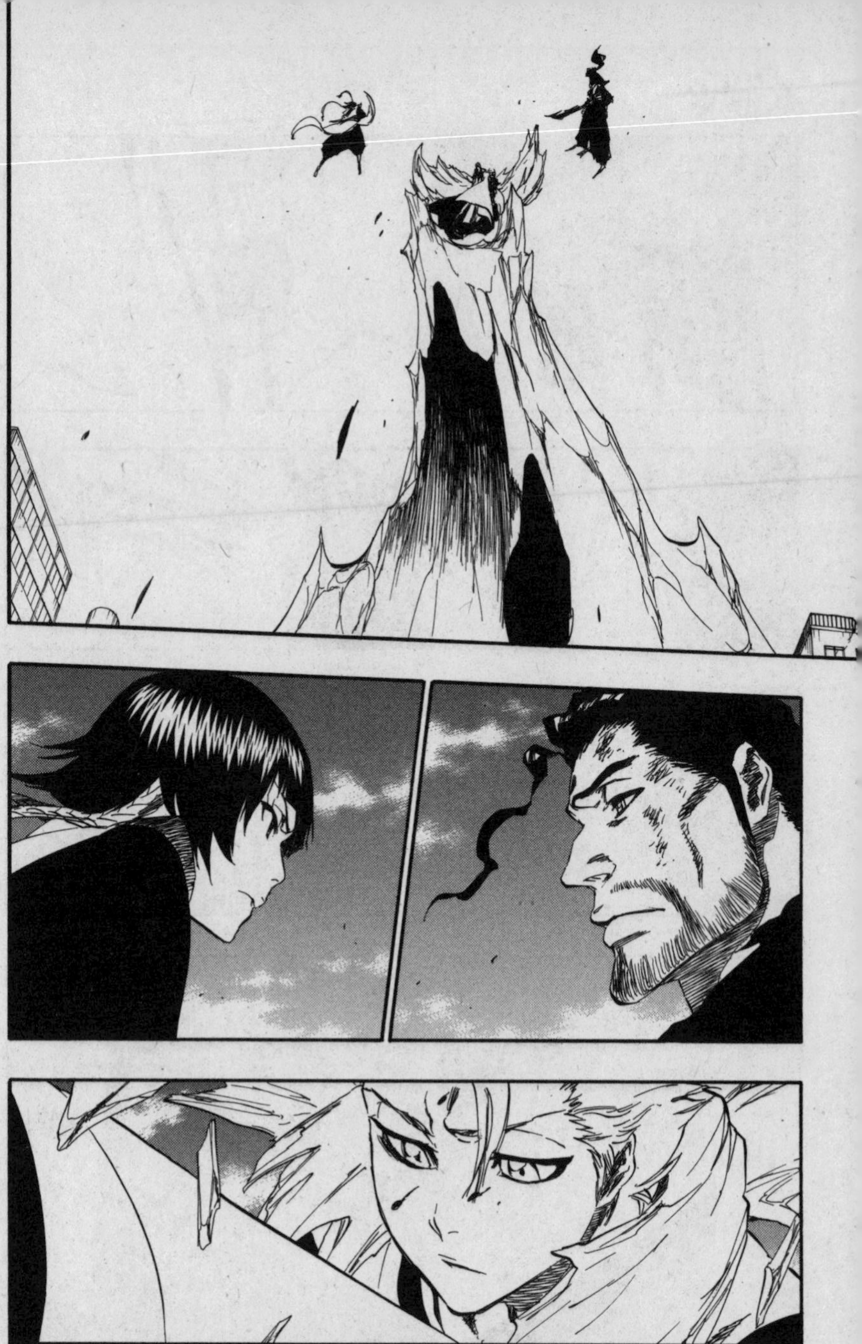

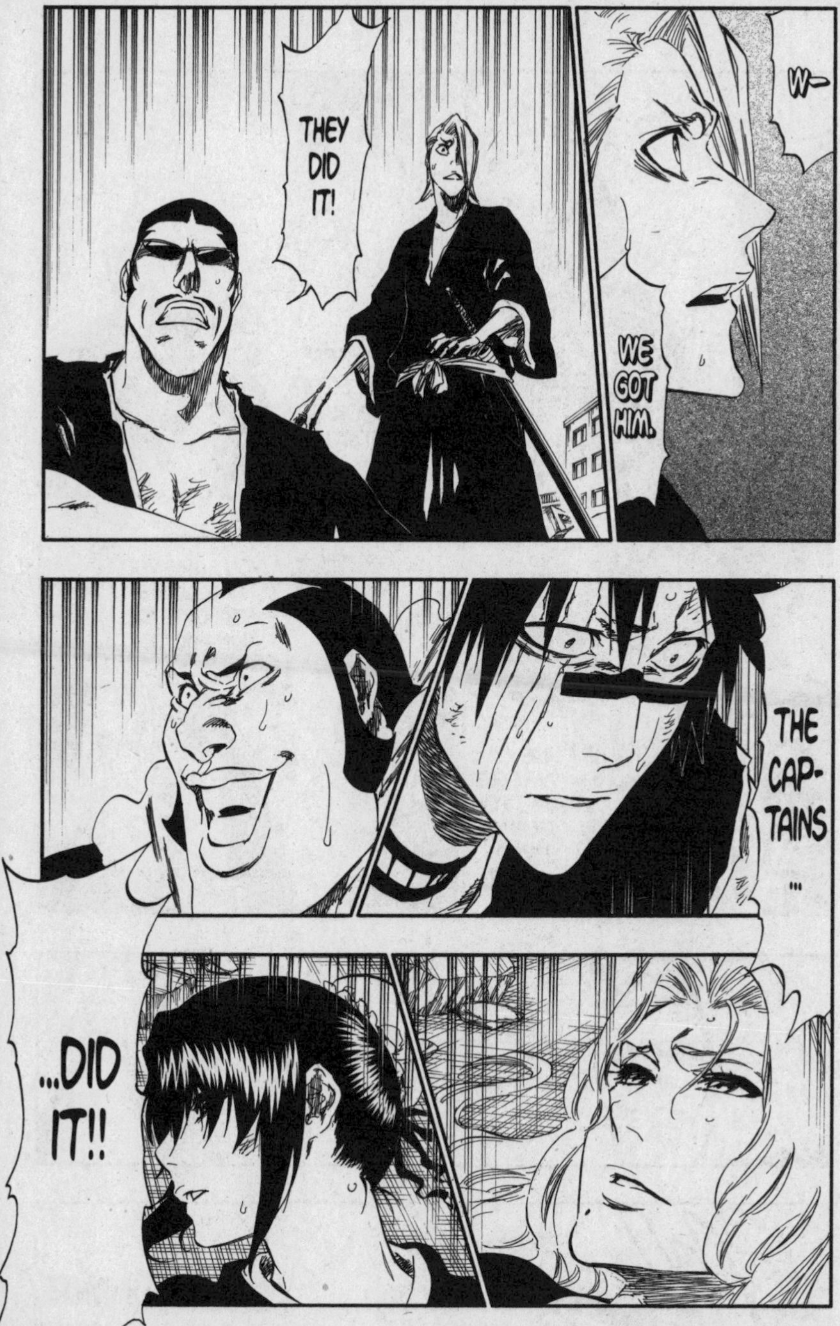
W-
WE GOT HIM.
THEY DID IT!
THE CAP-TAINS...
...DID IT!!

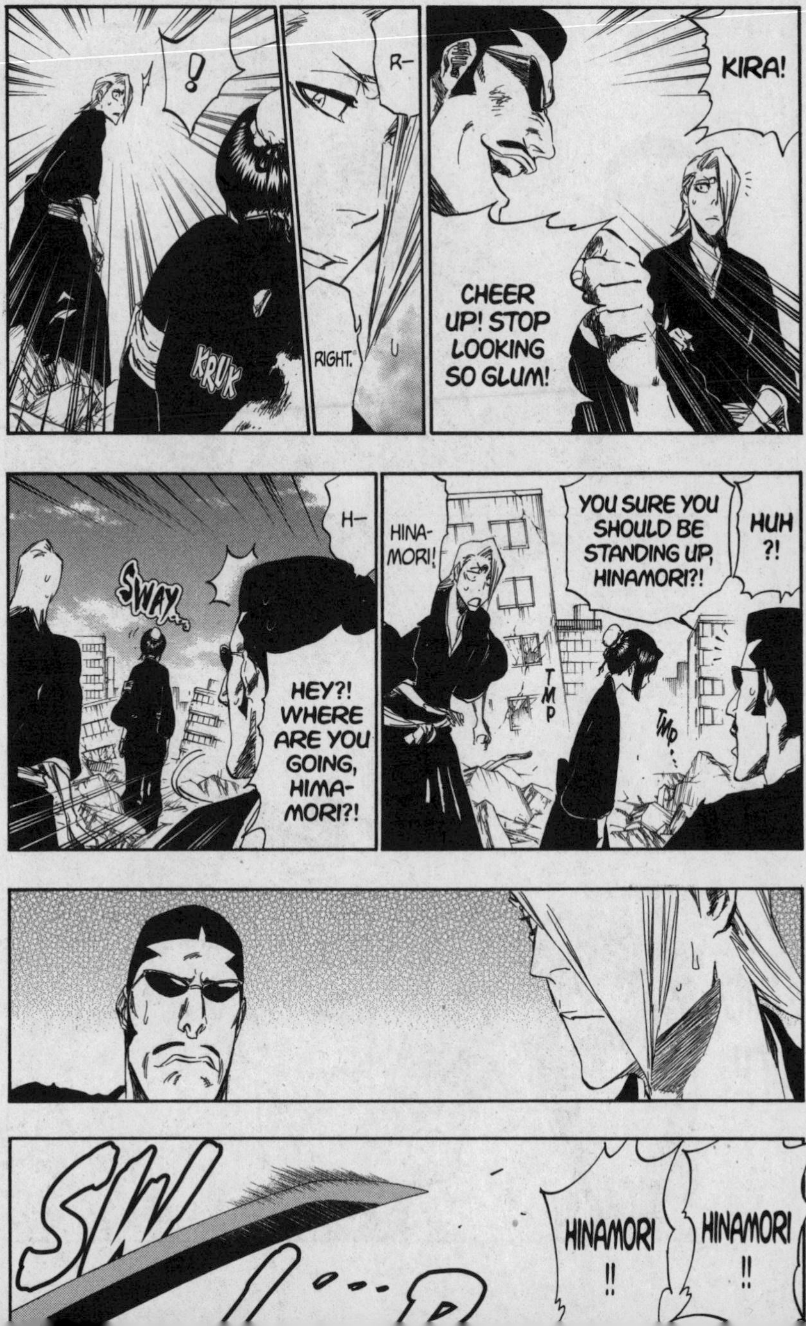
KIRA!
CHEER UP! STOP LOOKING SO GLUM!
R—
RIGHT.
!
KRUK
HUH ?!
YOU SURE YOU SHOULD BE STANDING UP, HINAMORI?!
HINA-MORI!
TMP
TMP...
H—
SWAY...
HEY?! WHERE ARE YOU GOING, HIMA-MORI?!
HINAMORI !!
HINAMORI !!
SW

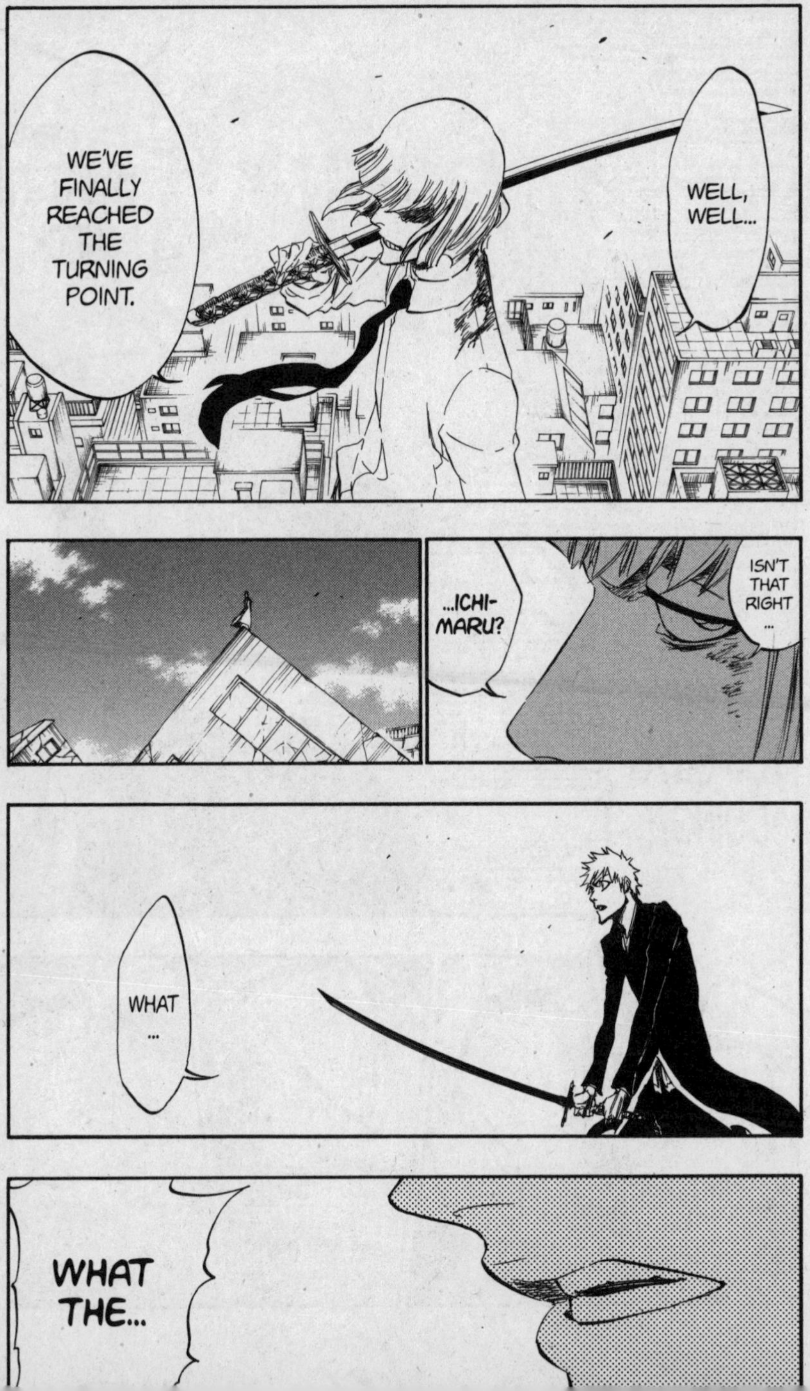
WELL, WELL...
WE'VE FINALLY REACHED THE TURNING POINT.
ISN'T THAT RIGHT ...
...ICHI-MARU?
WHAT ...
WHAT THE...

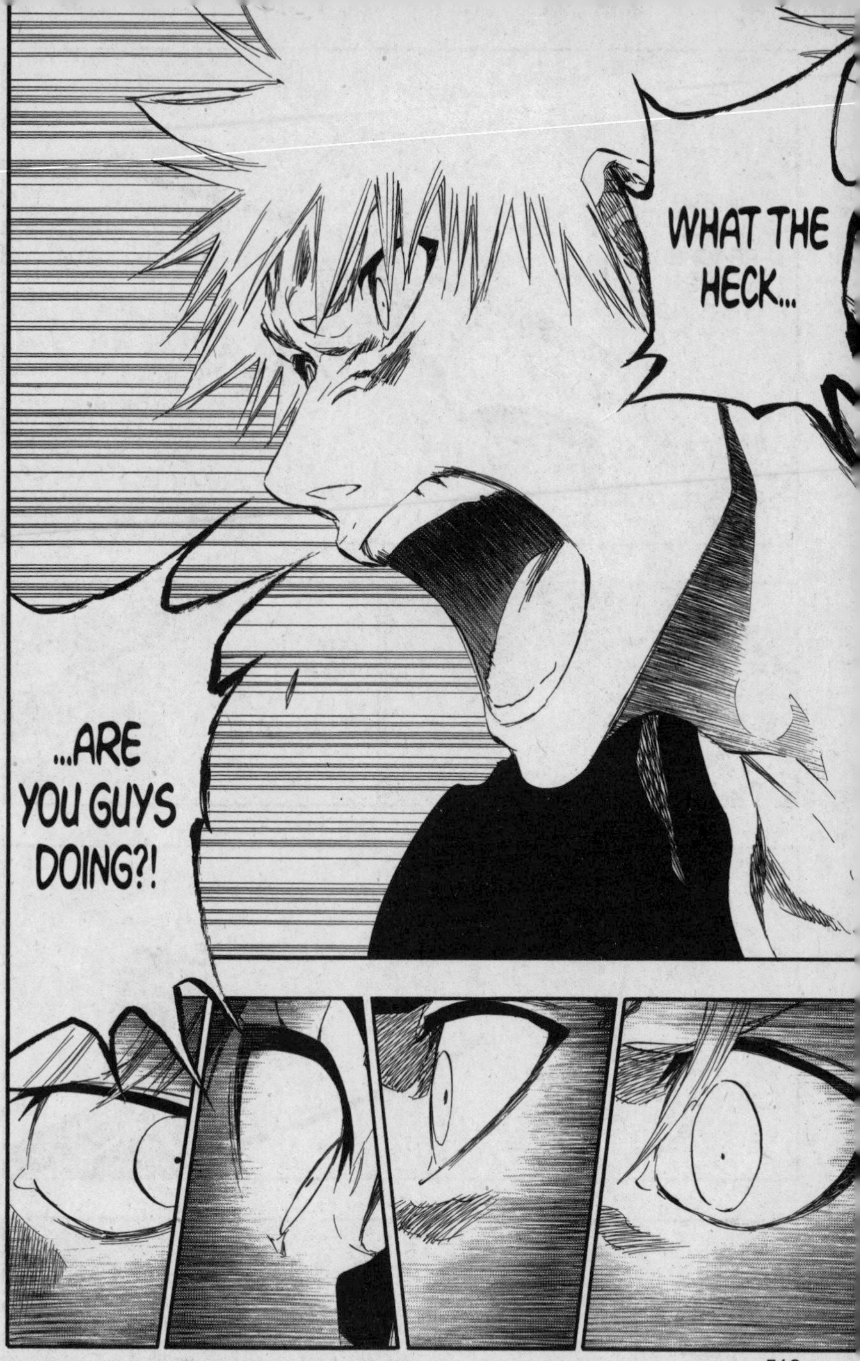
WHAT THE HECK...
...ARE YOU GUYS DOING?!

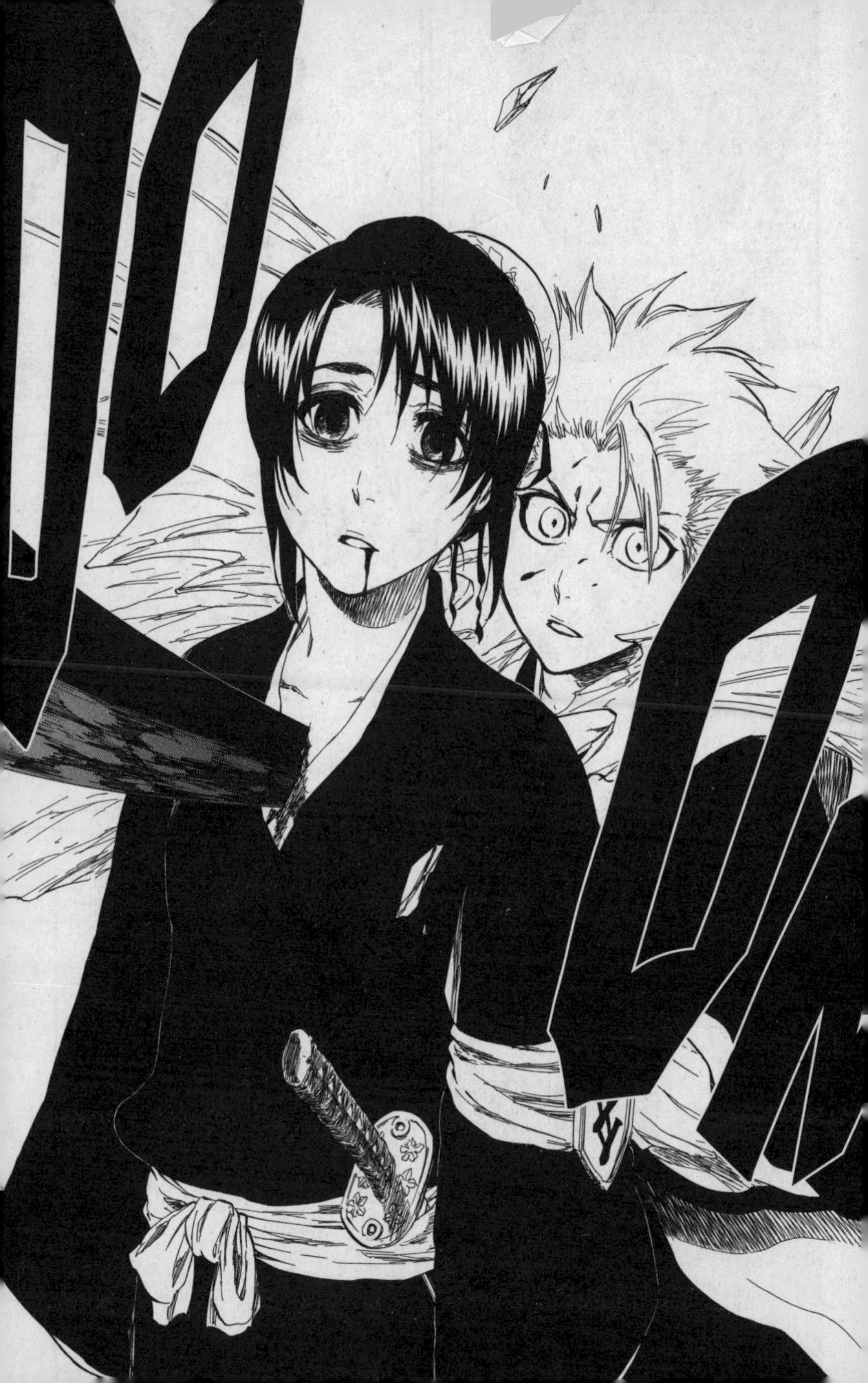

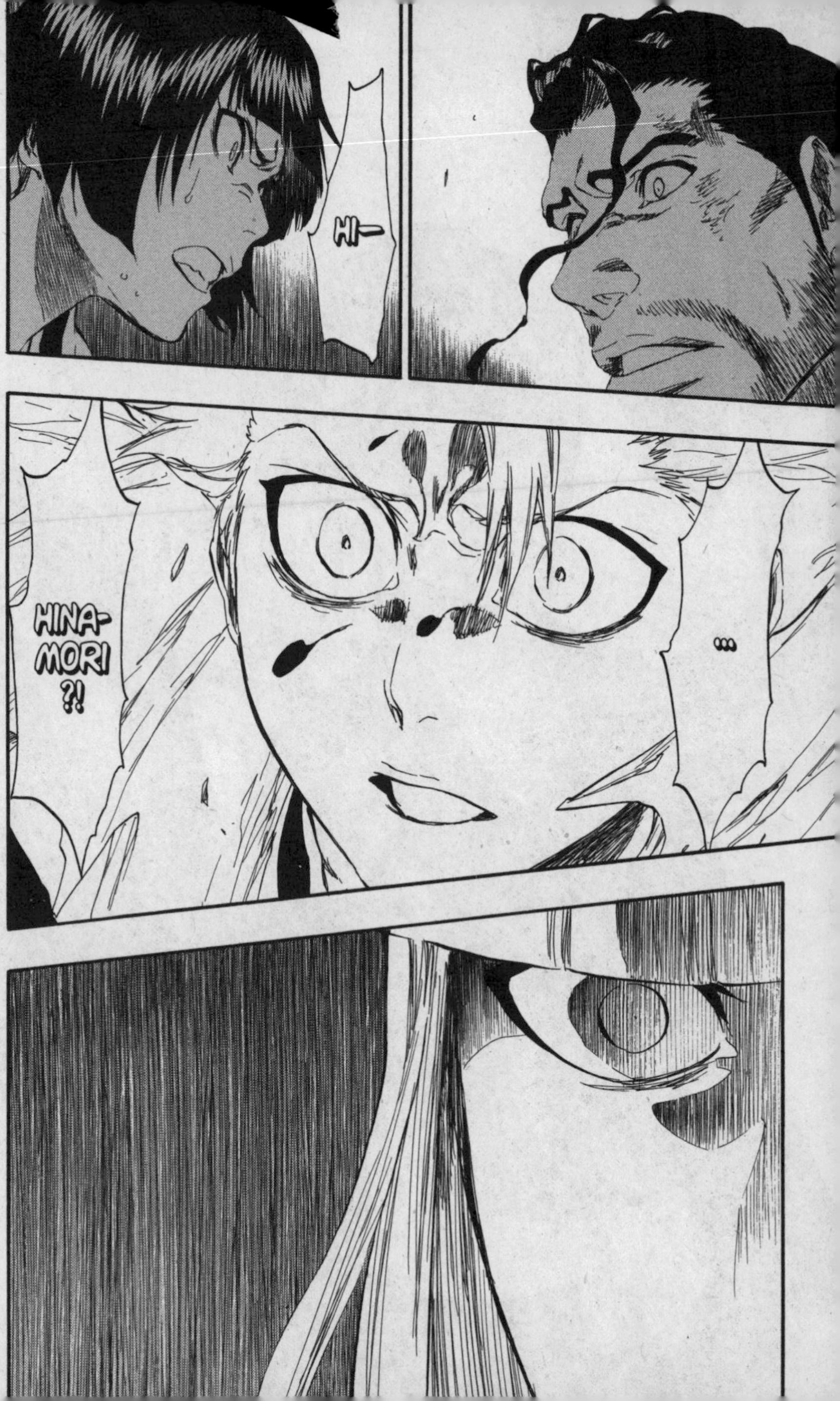
HI–
...
HINA-MORI ?!

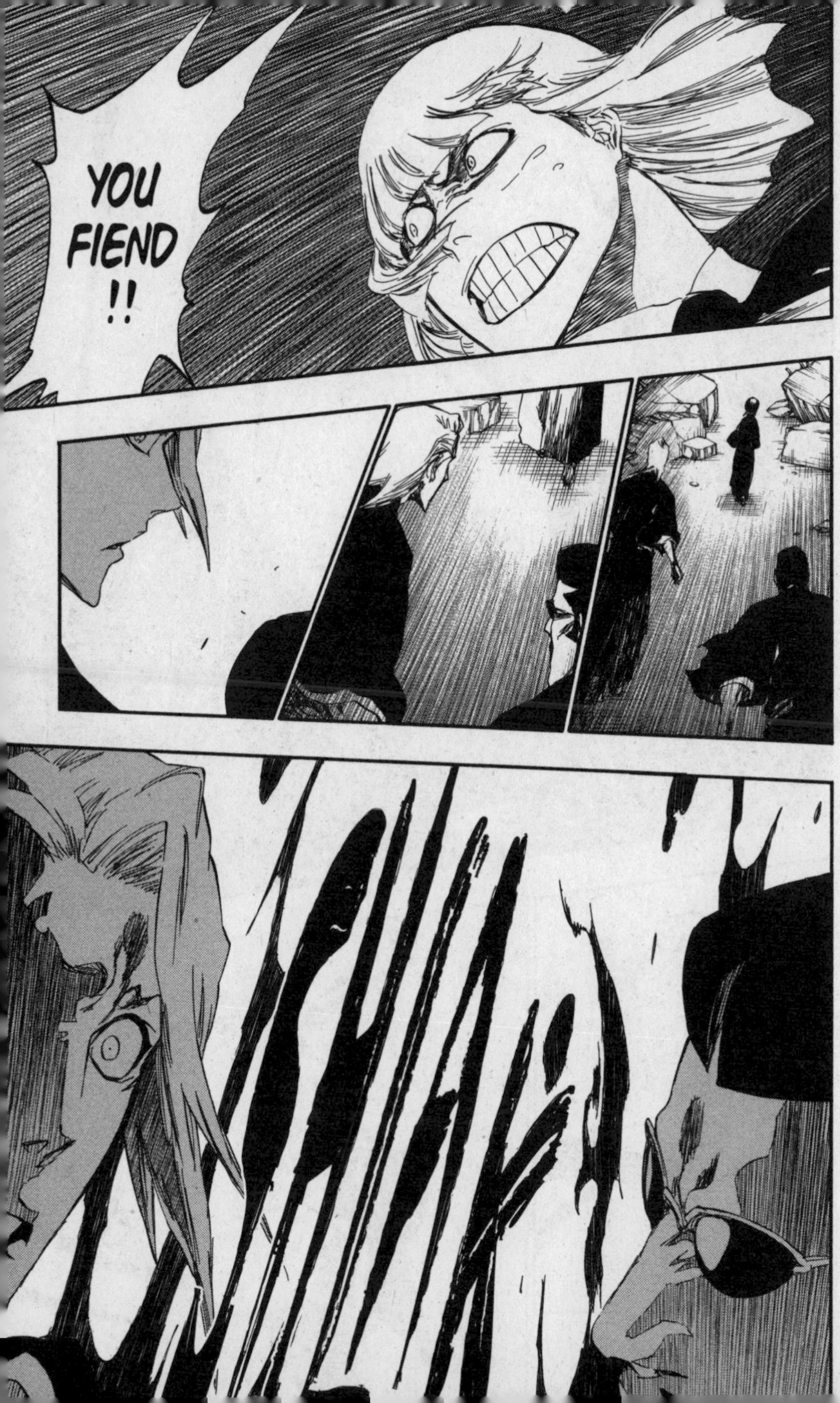
YOU FIEND !!

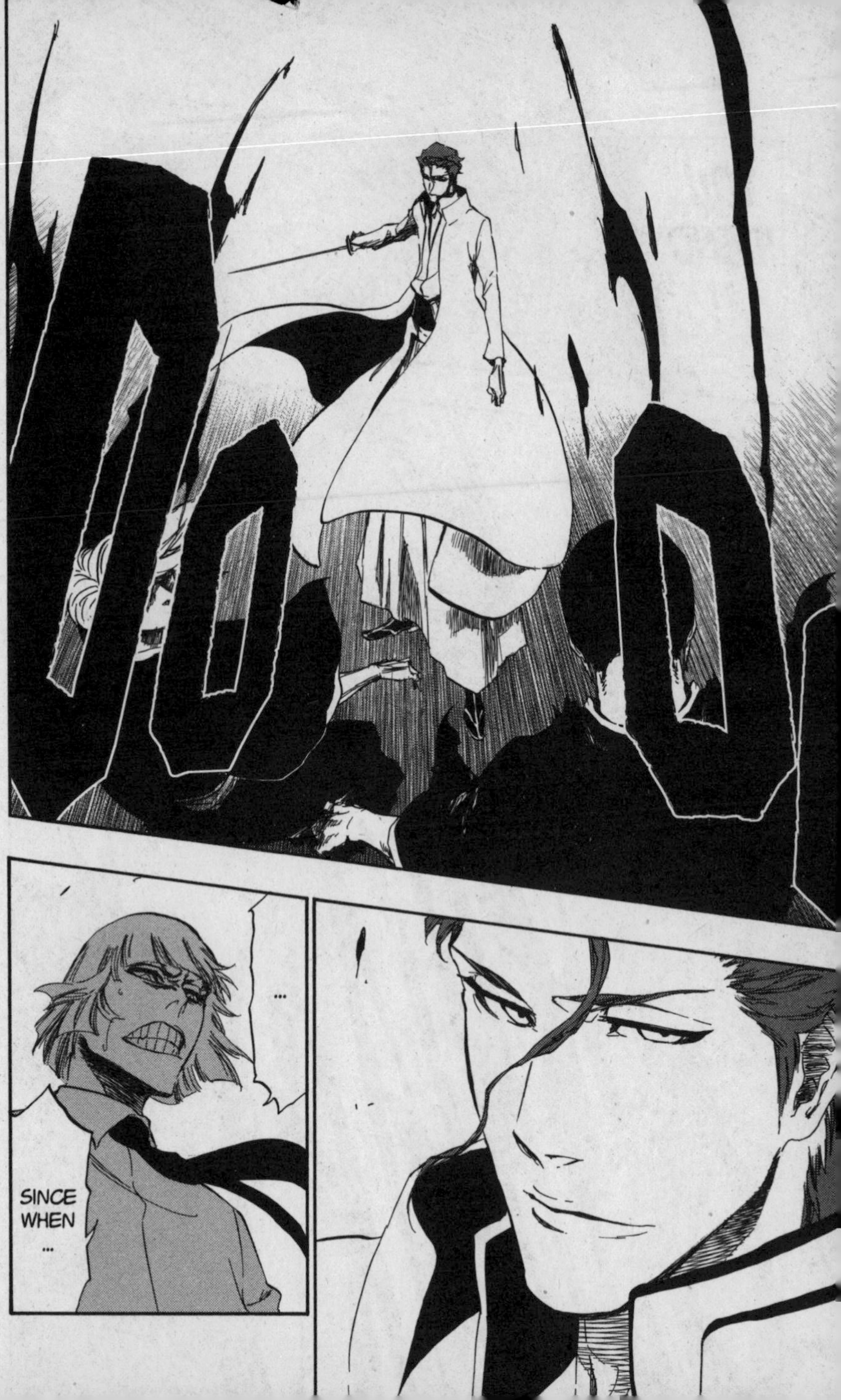
...
SINCE WHEN
...

READ THIS WAY

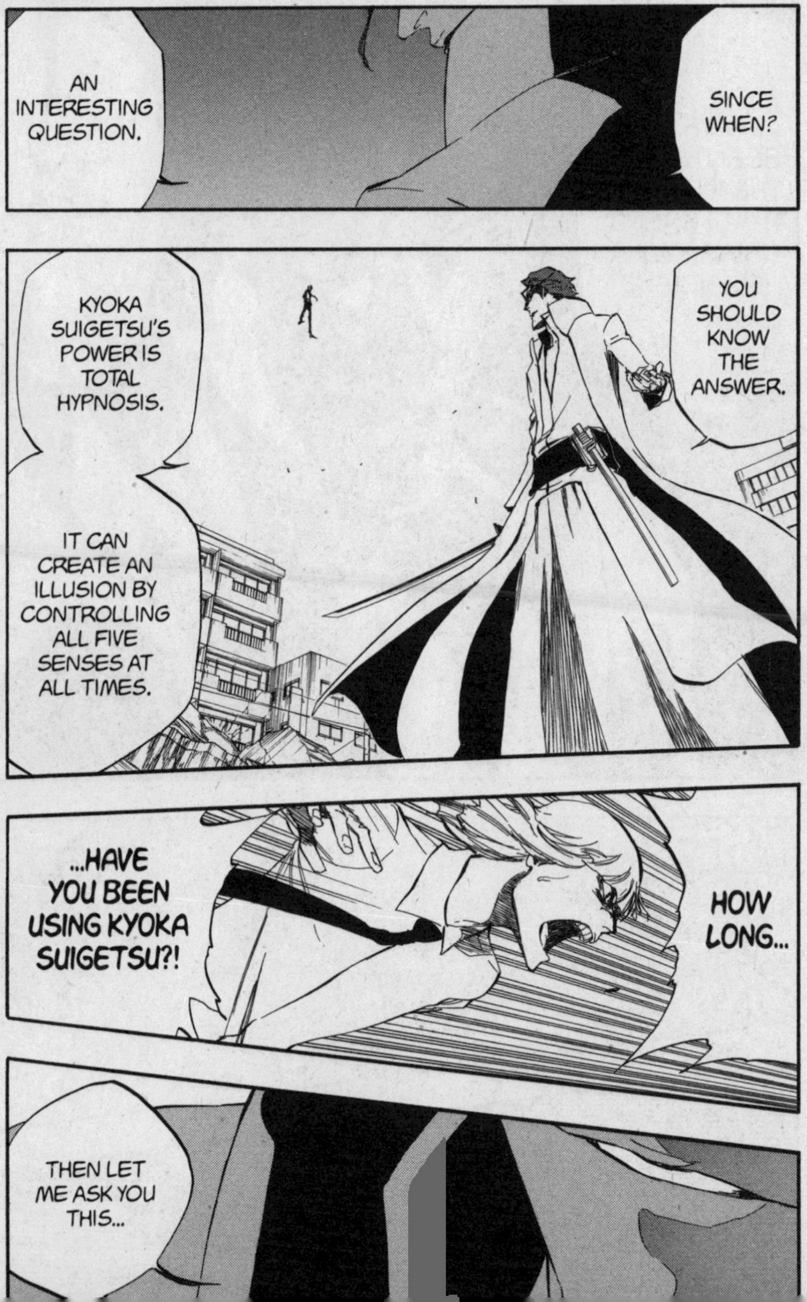
SINCE WHEN?
AN INTERESTING QUESTION.
YOU SHOULD KNOW THE ANSWER.
KYOKA SUIGETSU'S POWER IS TOTAL HYPNOSIS.
IT CAN CREATE AN ILLUSION BY CONTROLLING ALL FIVE SENSES AT ALL TIMES.
HOW LONG...
...HAVE YOU BEEN USING KYOKA SUIGETSU?!
THEN LET ME ASK YOU THIS...

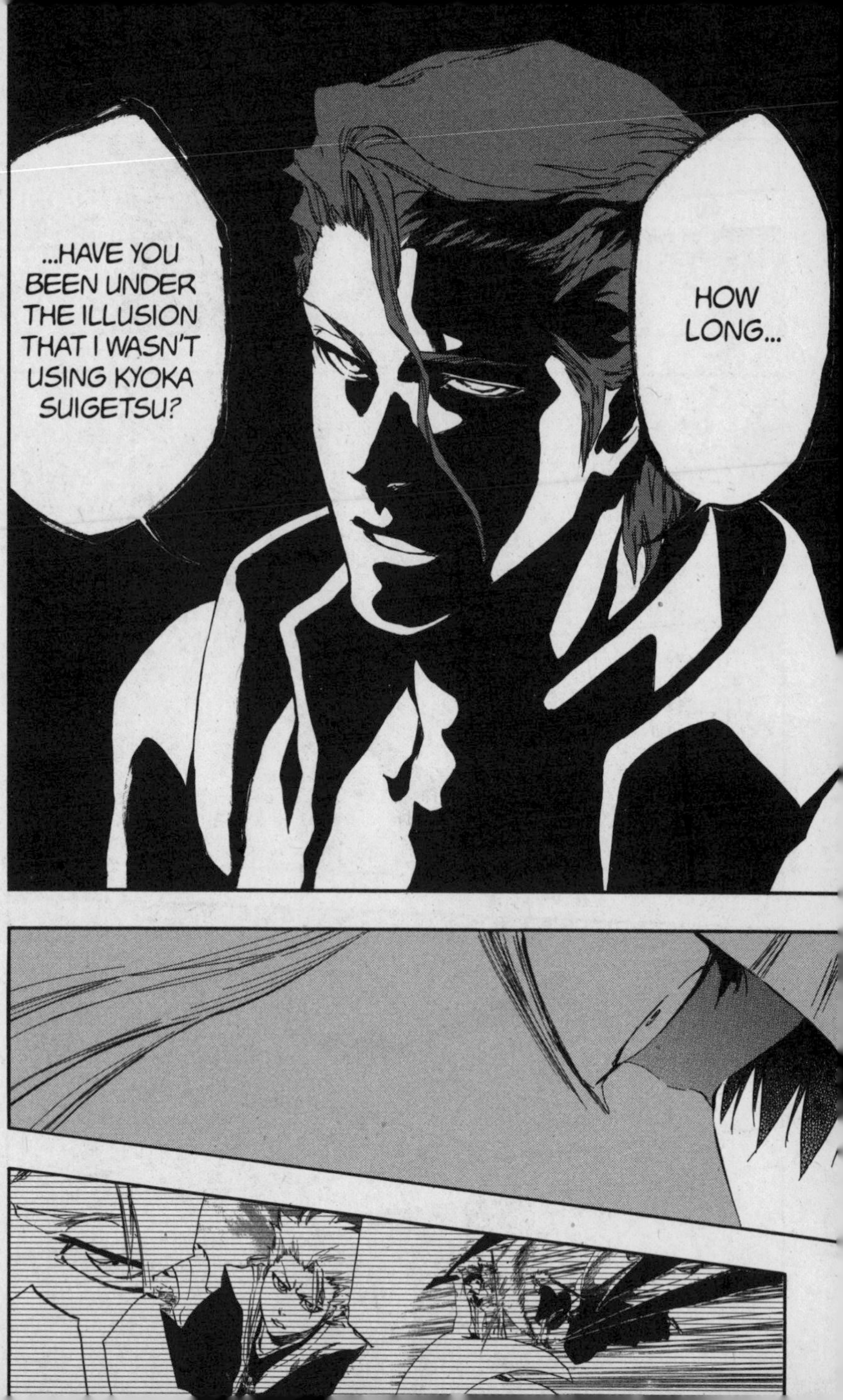
HOW LONG...
...HAVE YOU BEEN UNDER THE ILLUSION THAT I WASN'T USING KYOKA SUIGETSU?

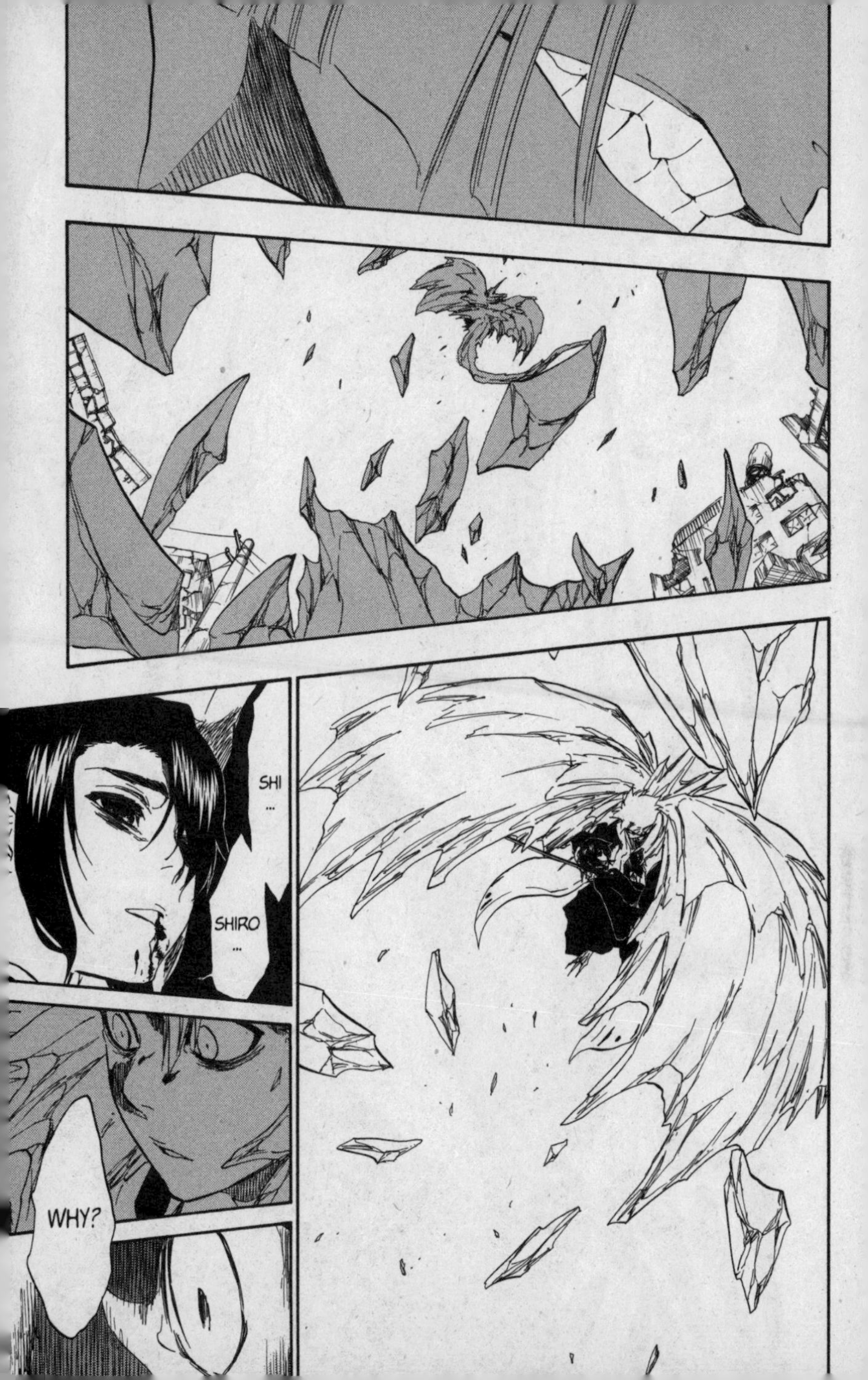
SHI ...
SHIRO ...
WHY?

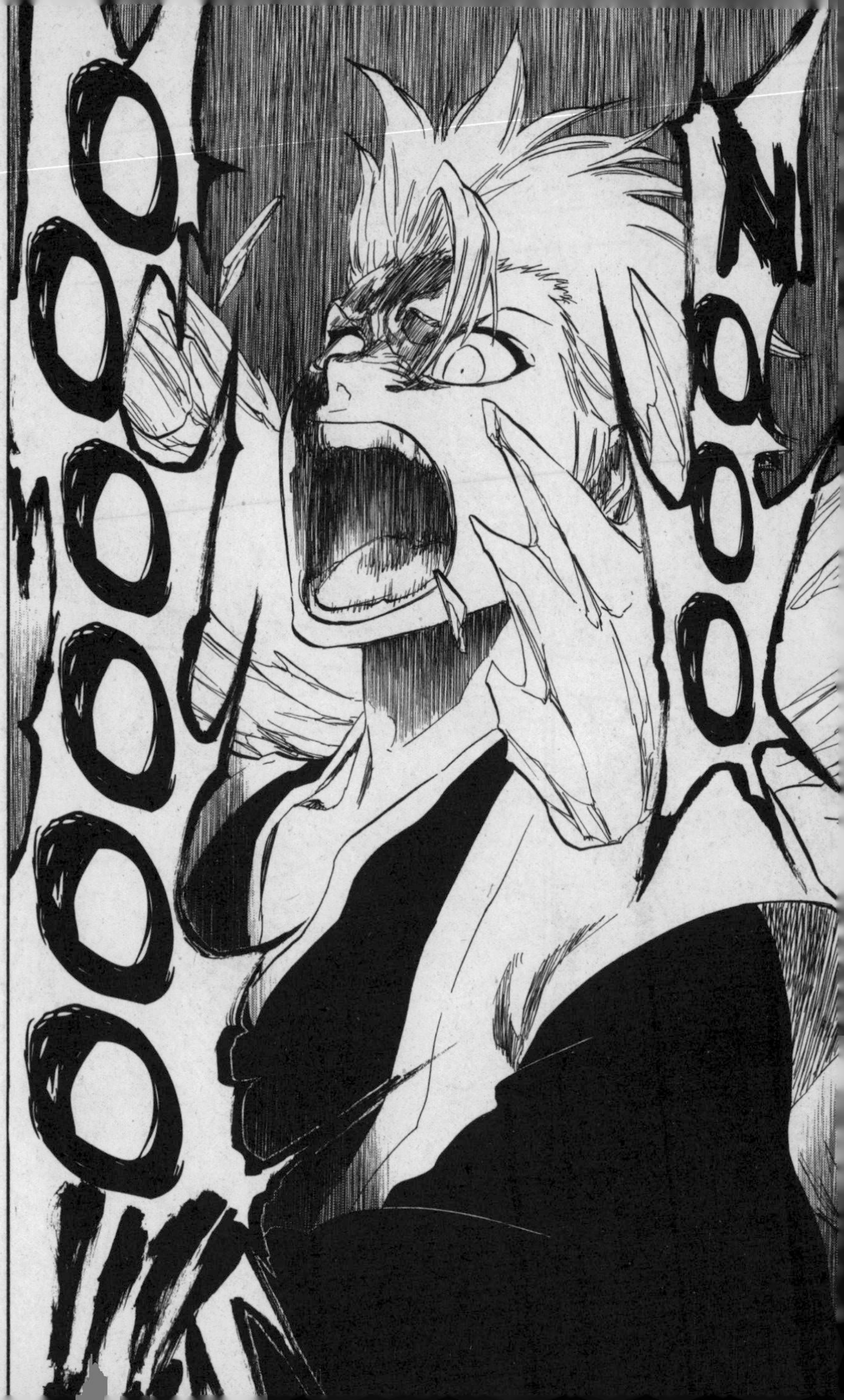
NOOOOO
NOOOOOOO!!

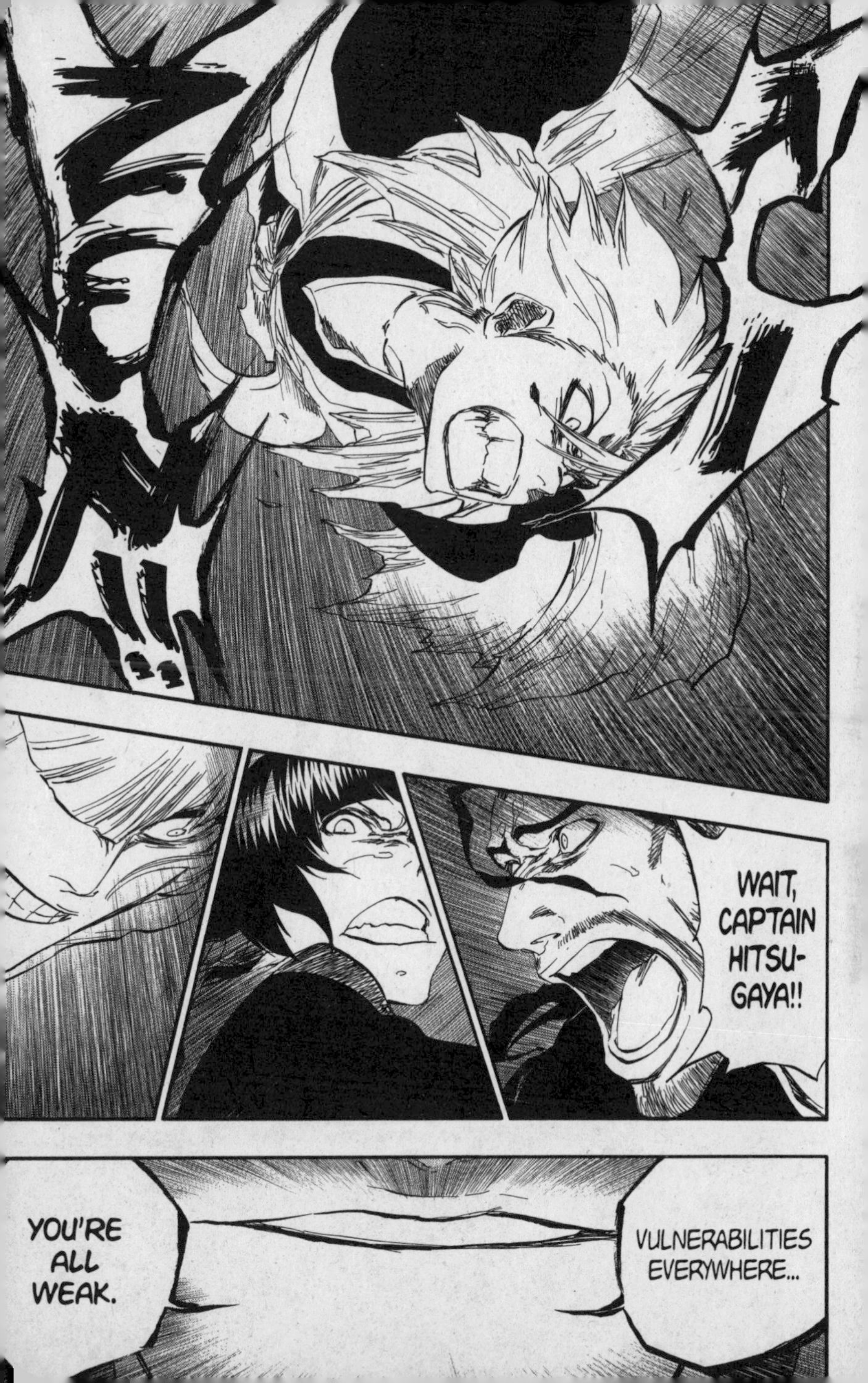
WAIT, CAPTAIN HITSU-GAYA!!
VULNERABILITIES EVERYWHERE...
YOU'RE ALL WEAK.

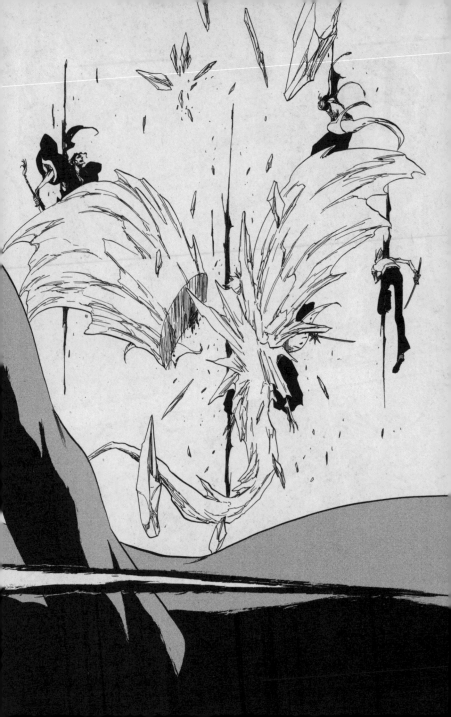

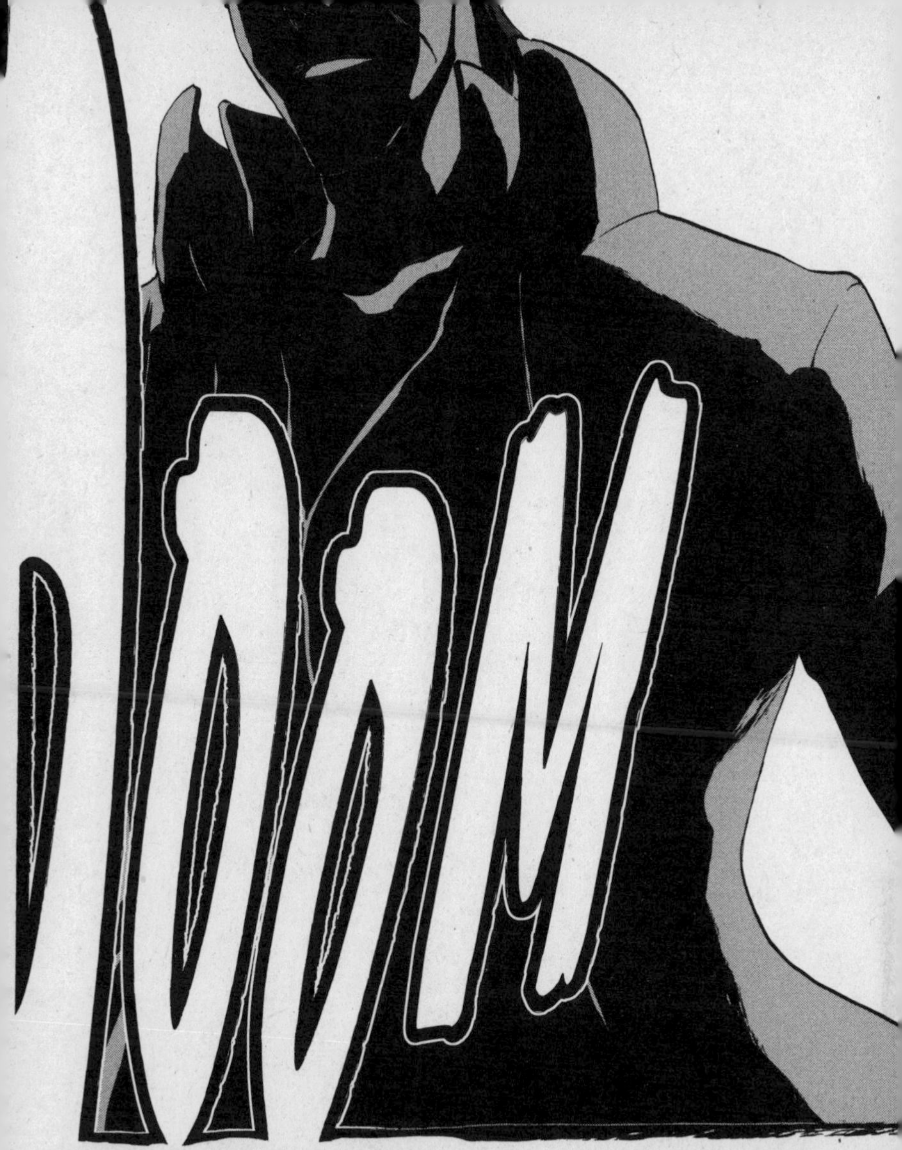

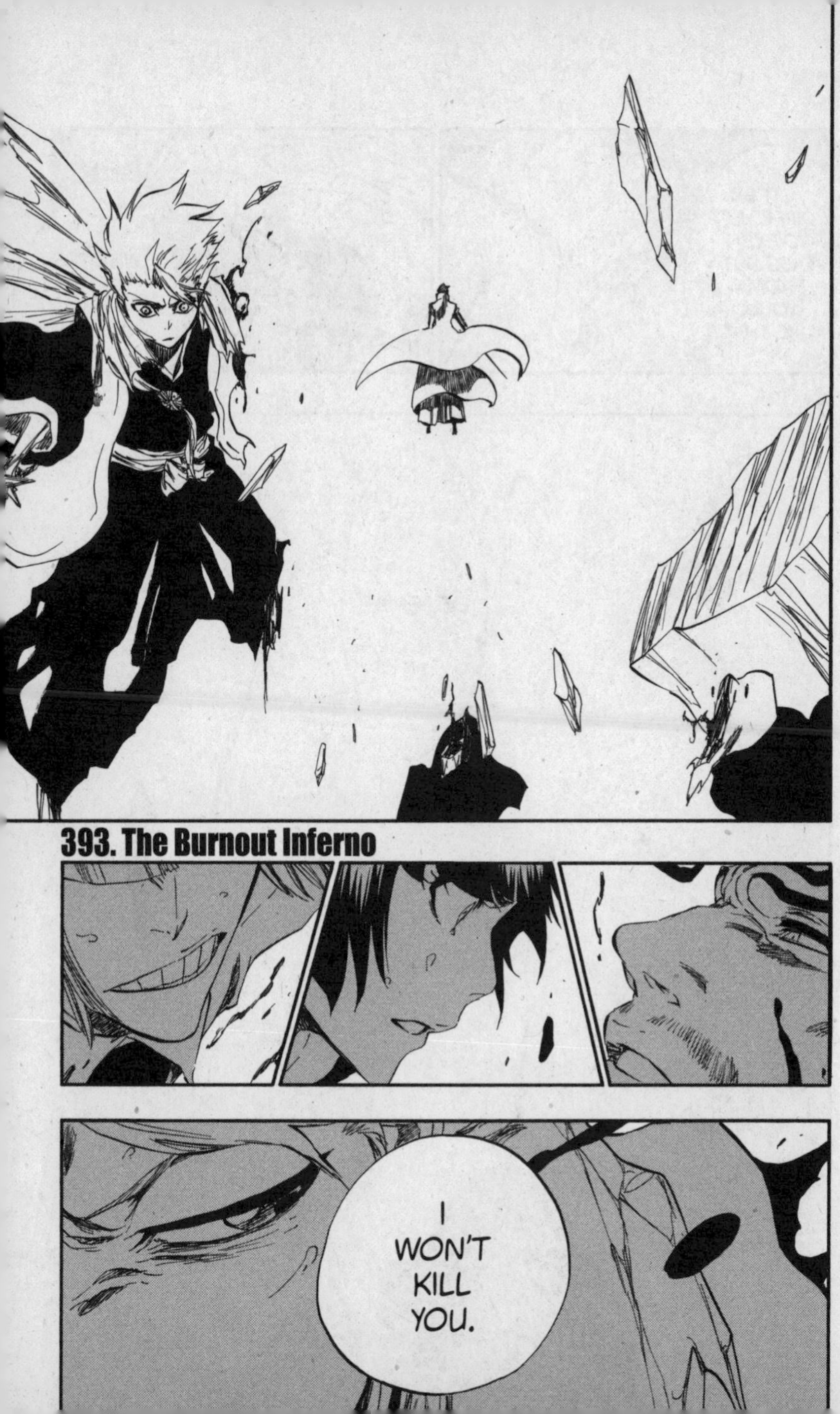
393. The Burnout Inferno
I WON'T KILL YOU.

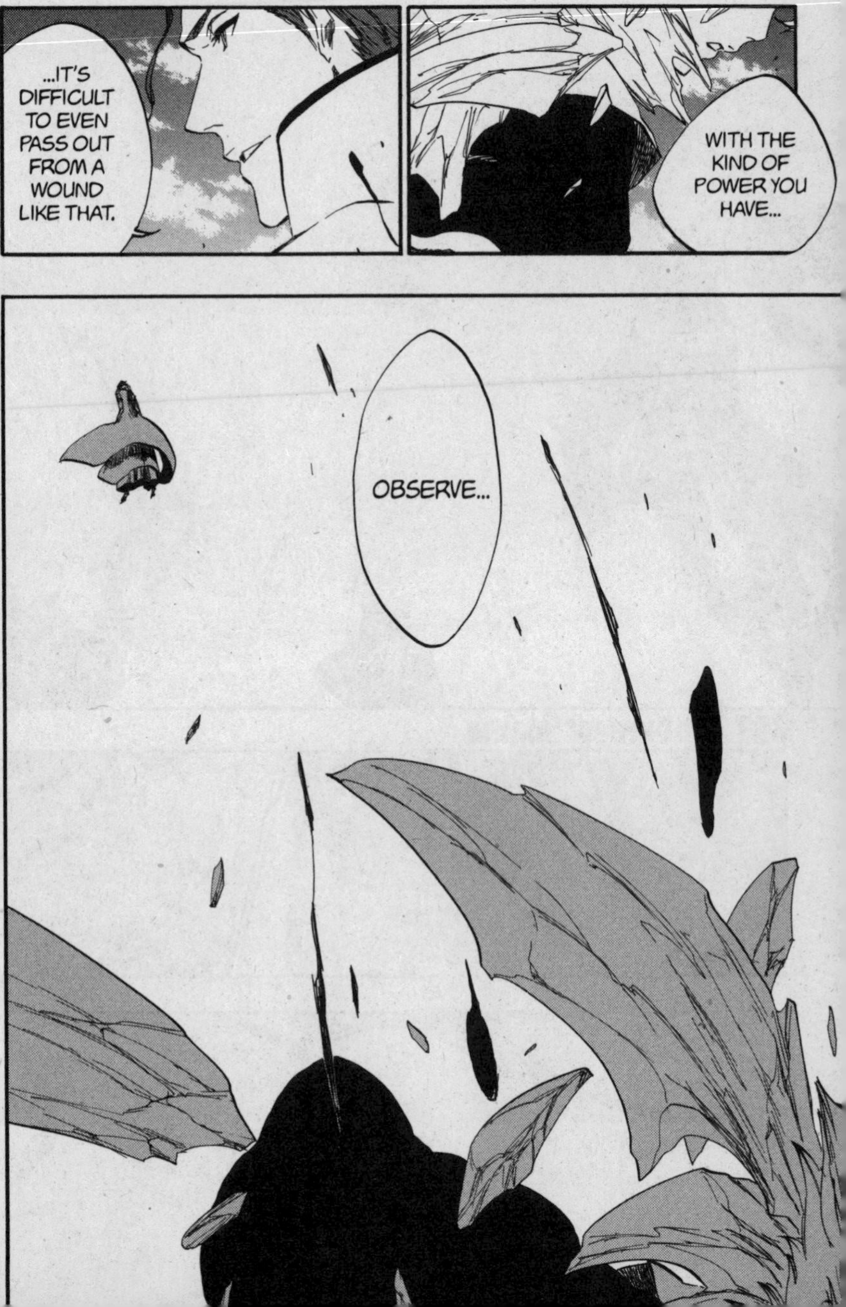
WITH THE KIND OF POWER YOU HAVE...
...IT'S DIFFICULT TO EVEN PASS OUT FROM A WOUND LIKE THAT.
OBSERVE...

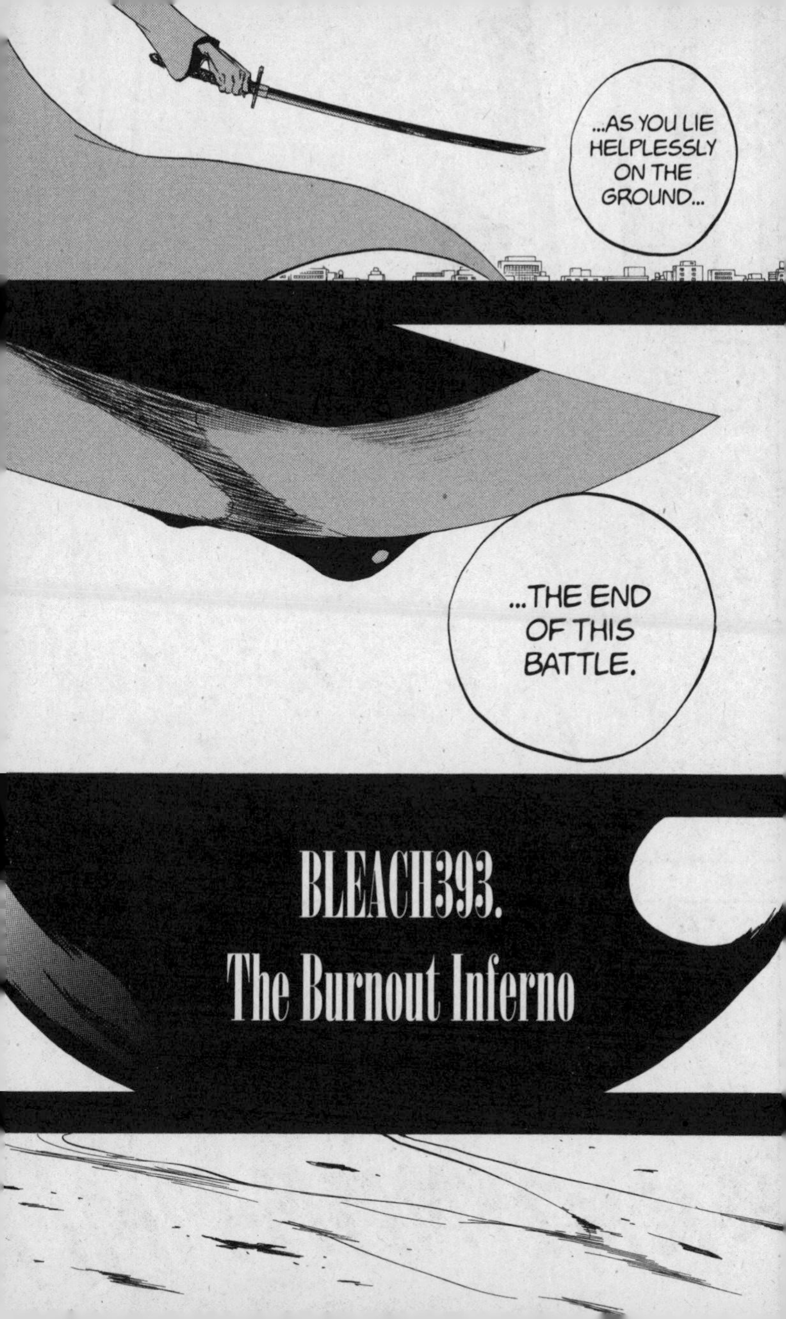
...AS YOU LIE HELPLESSLY ON THE GROUND...
...THE END OF THIS BATTLE.
BLEACH393.
The Burnout Inferno

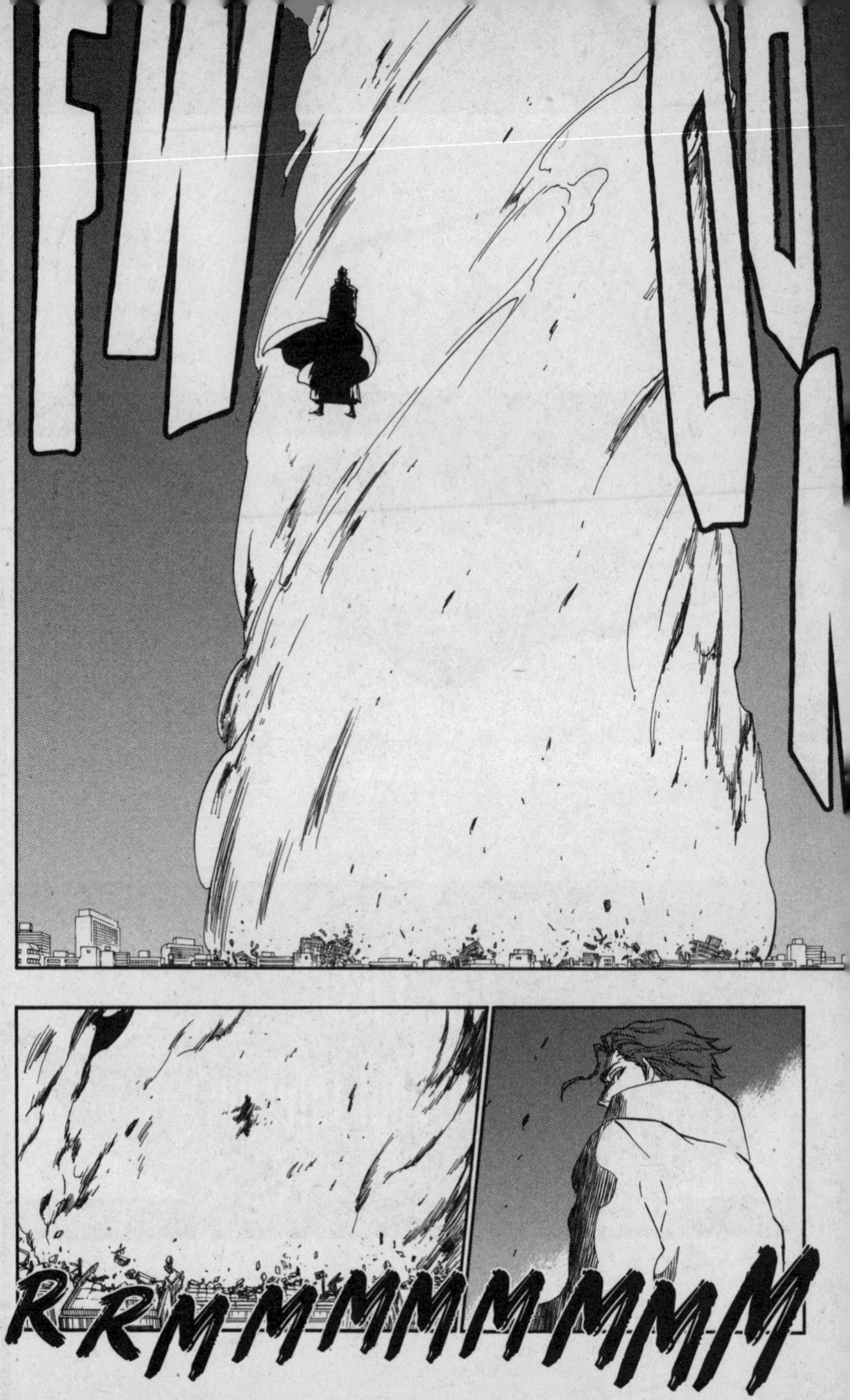
RRMMMMMMMMMMM

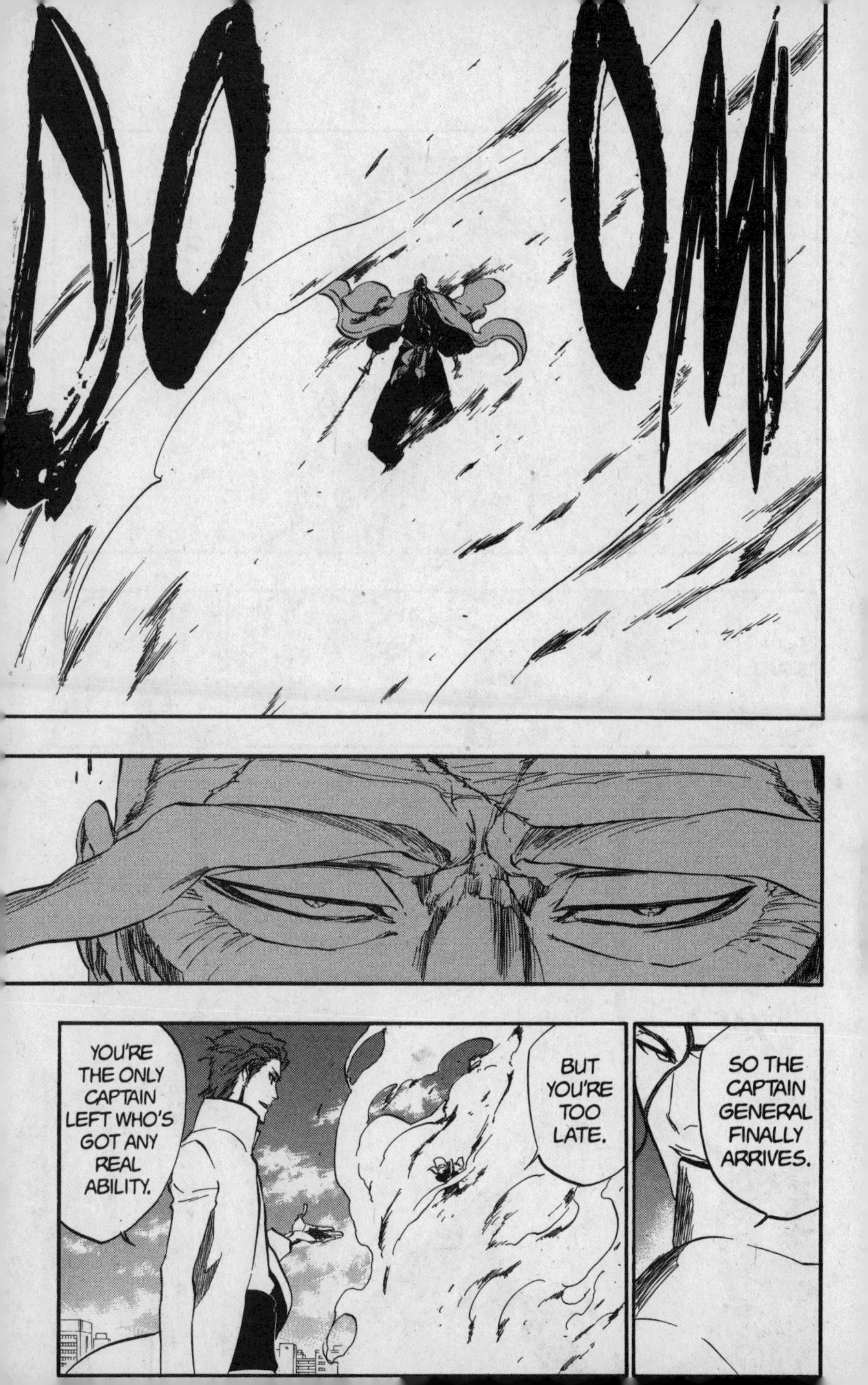
DOOM
SO THE CAPTAIN GENERAL FINALLY ARRIVES.
BUT YOU'RE TOO LATE.
YOU'RE THE ONLY CAPTAIN LEFT WHO'S GOT ANY REAL ABILITY.

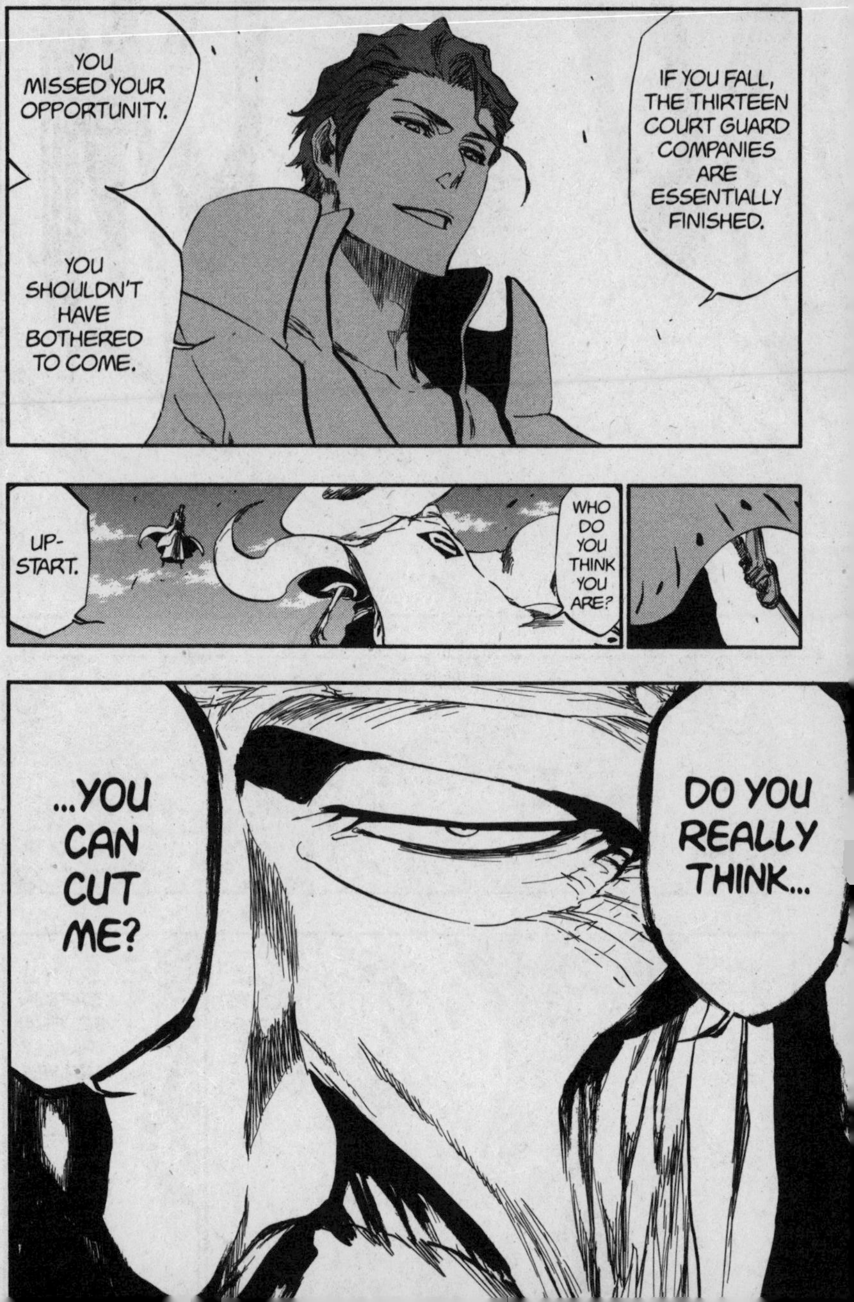
IF YOU FALL, THE THIRTEEN COURT GUARD COMPANIES ARE ESSENTIALLY FINISHED.
YOU MISSED YOUR OPPORTUNITY.
YOU SHOULDN'T HAVE BOTHERED TO COME.
WHO DO YOU THINK YOU ARE?
UP-START.
DO YOU REALLY THINK...
...YOU CAN CUT ME?

READ THIS WAY

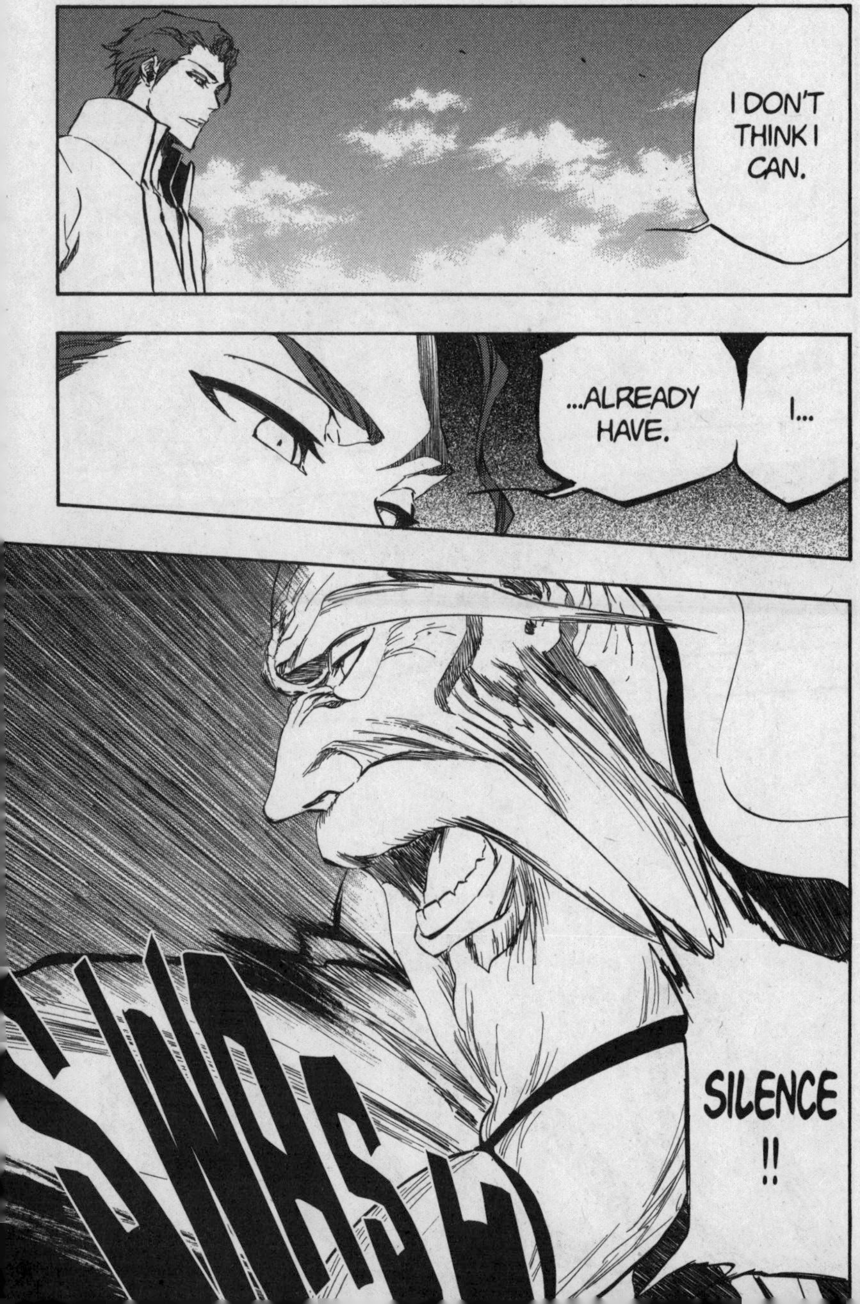
I DON'T THINK I CAN.
I...
...ALREADY HAVE.
SILENCE !!

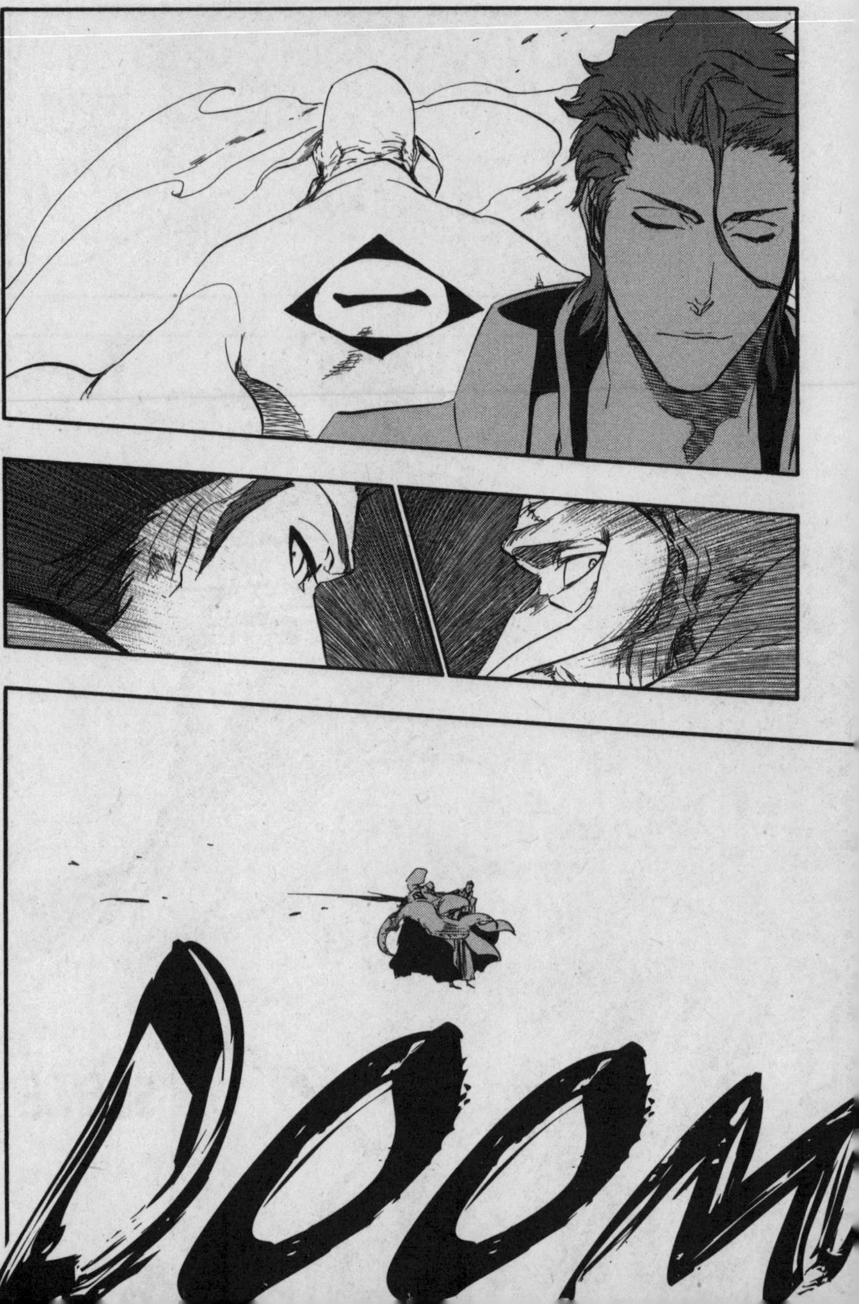
DOOM

READ THIS WAY

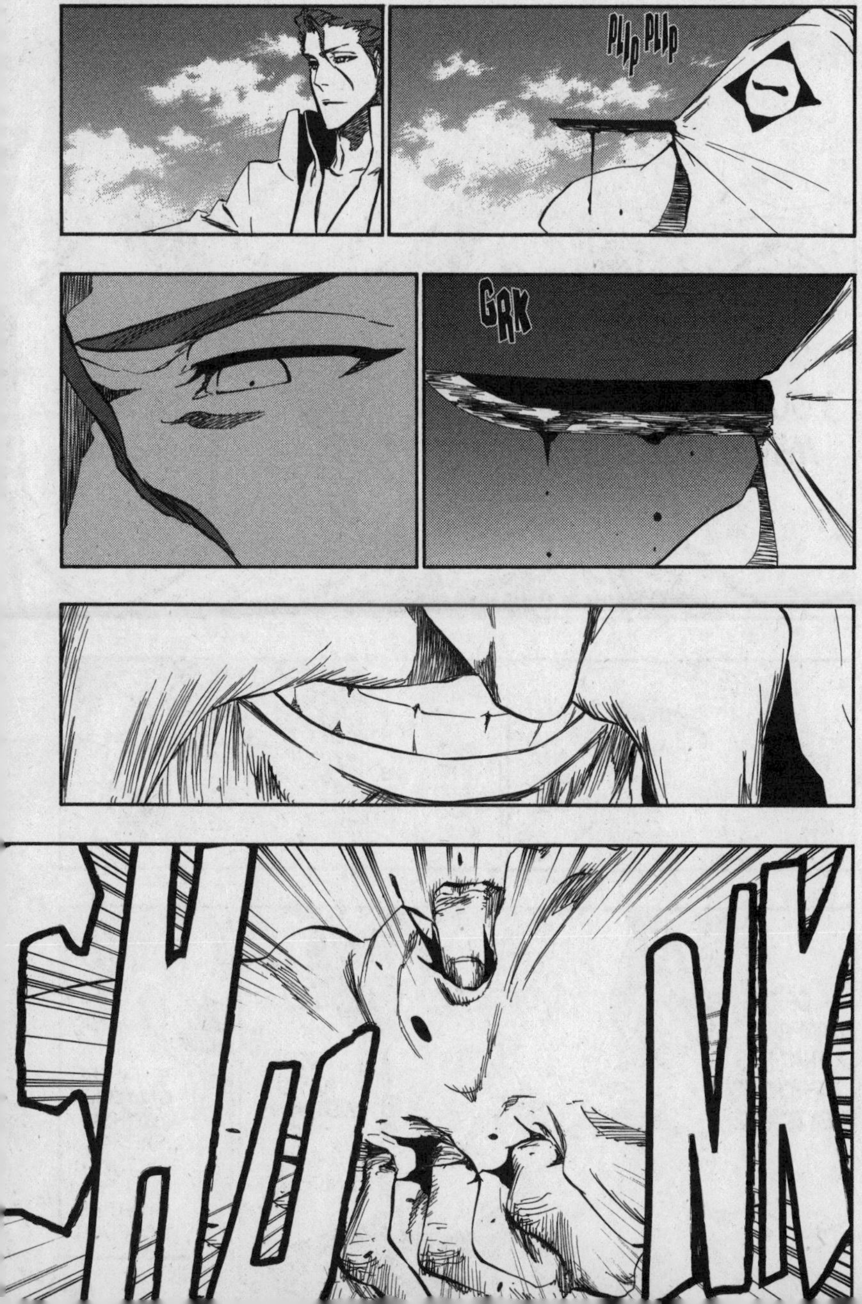
PLIP PLIP
GRK

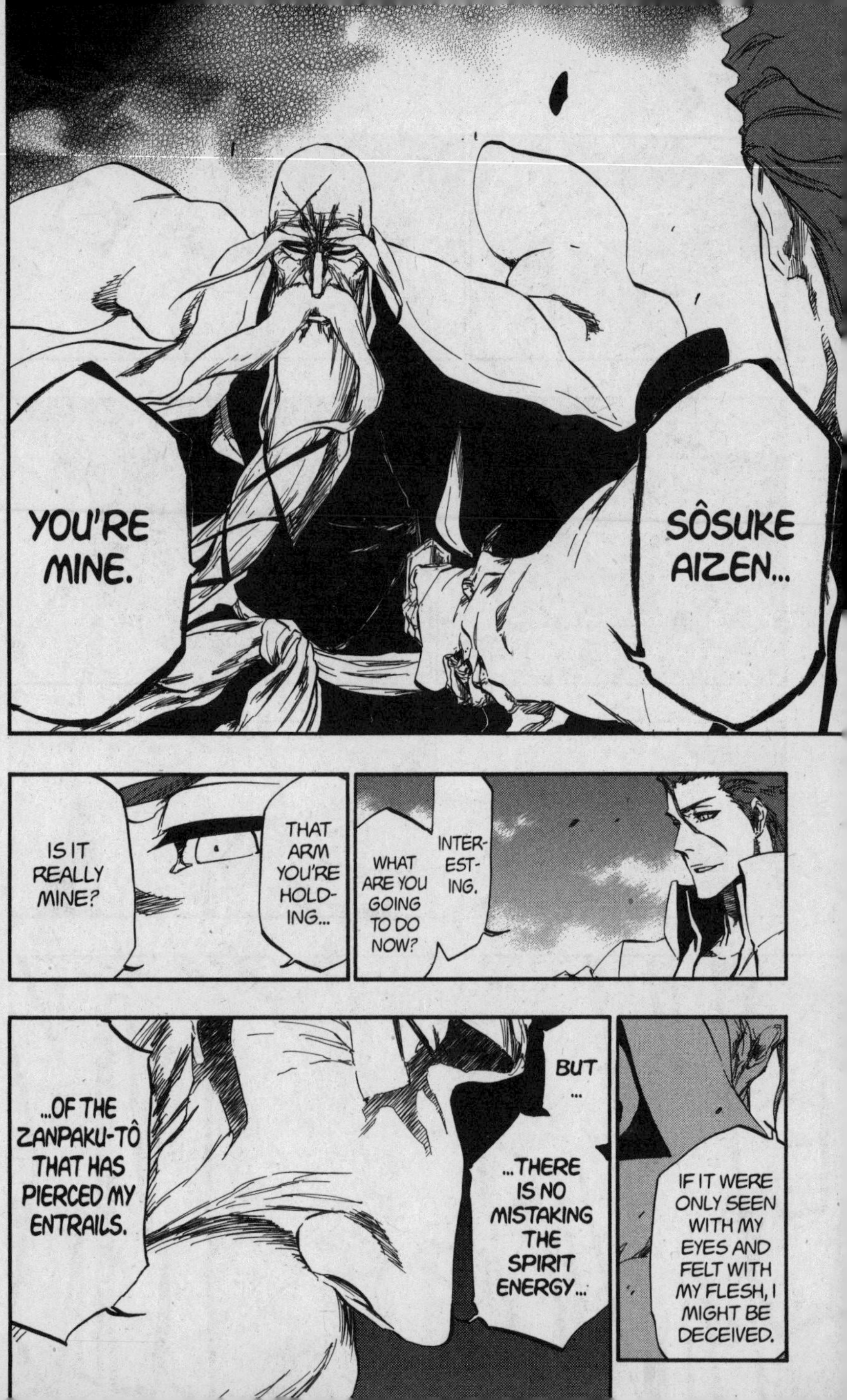
SÔSUKE AIZEN...
YOU'RE MINE.
INTER-EST-ING.
WHAT ARE YOU GOING TO DO NOW?
THAT ARM YOU'RE HOLD-ING...
IS IT REALLY MINE?
IF IT WERE ONLY SEEN WITH MY EYES AND FELT WITH MY FLESH, I MIGHT BE DECEIVED.
BUT...
...THERE IS NO MISTAKING THE SPIRIT ENERGY...
...OF THE ZANPAKU-TÔ THAT HAS PIERCED MY ENTRAILS.

READ THIS WAY

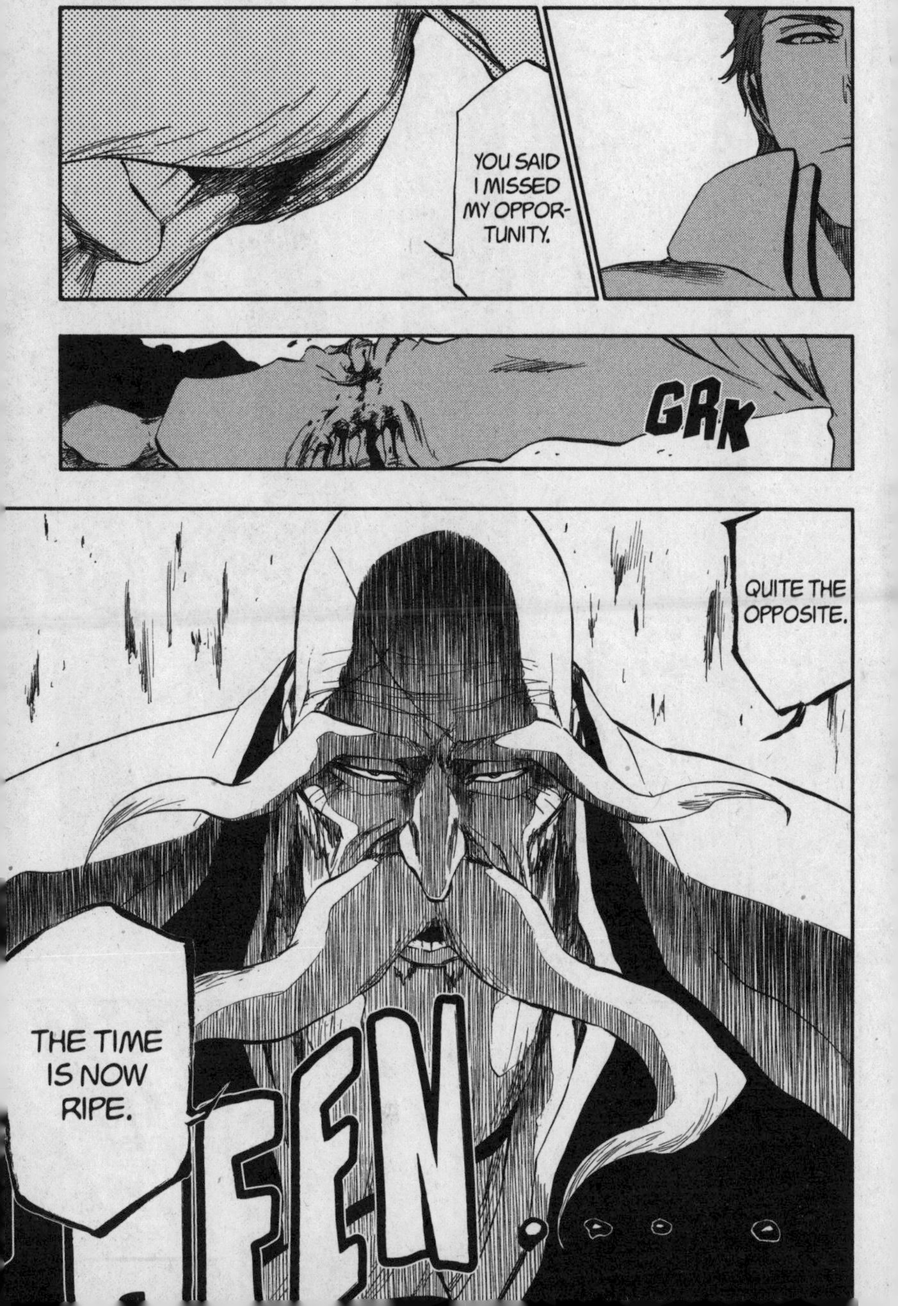
YOU SAID I MISSED MY OPPOR-TUNITY.
GRK
QUITE THE OPPOSITE.
THE TIME IS NOW RIPE.
FEN

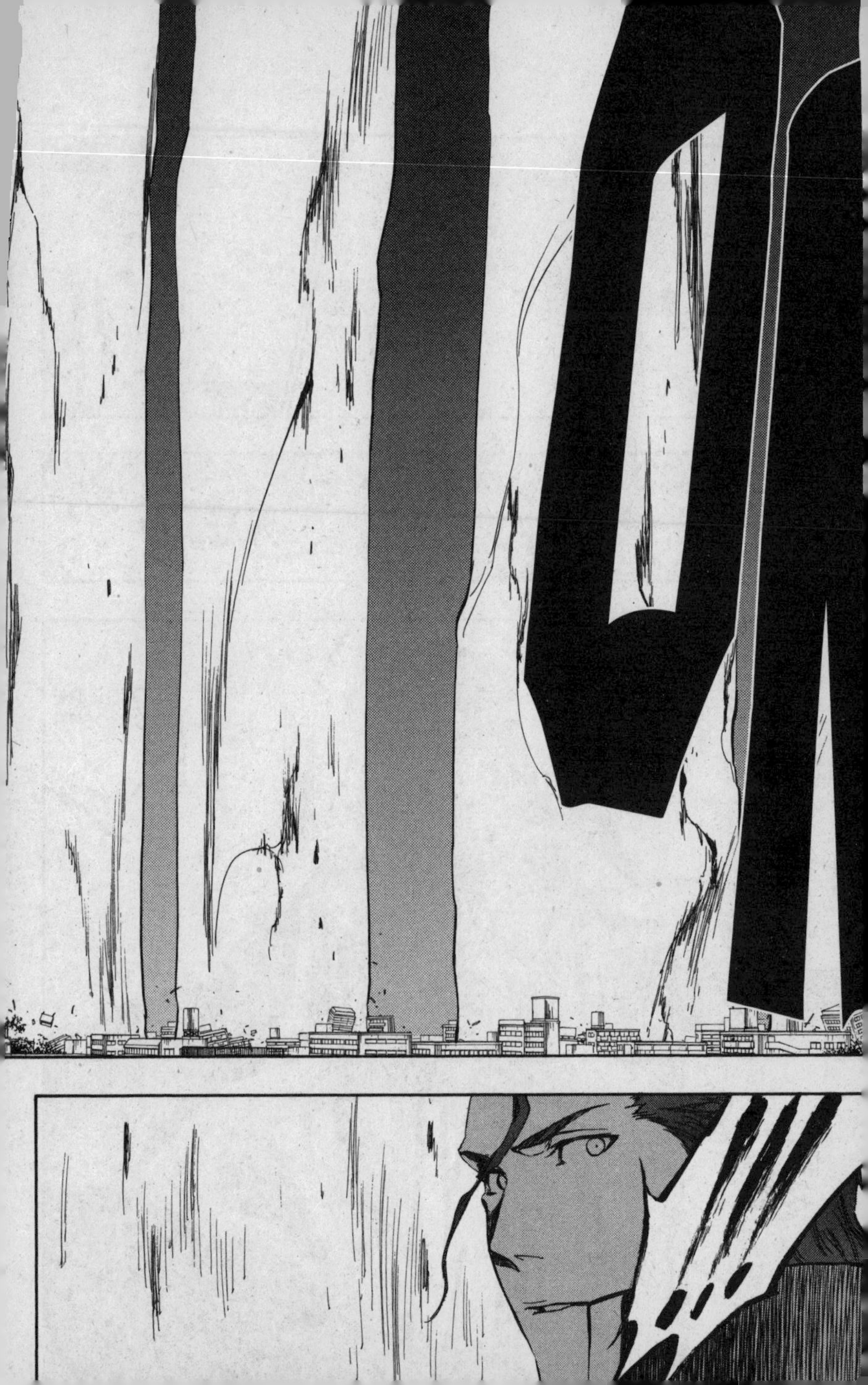

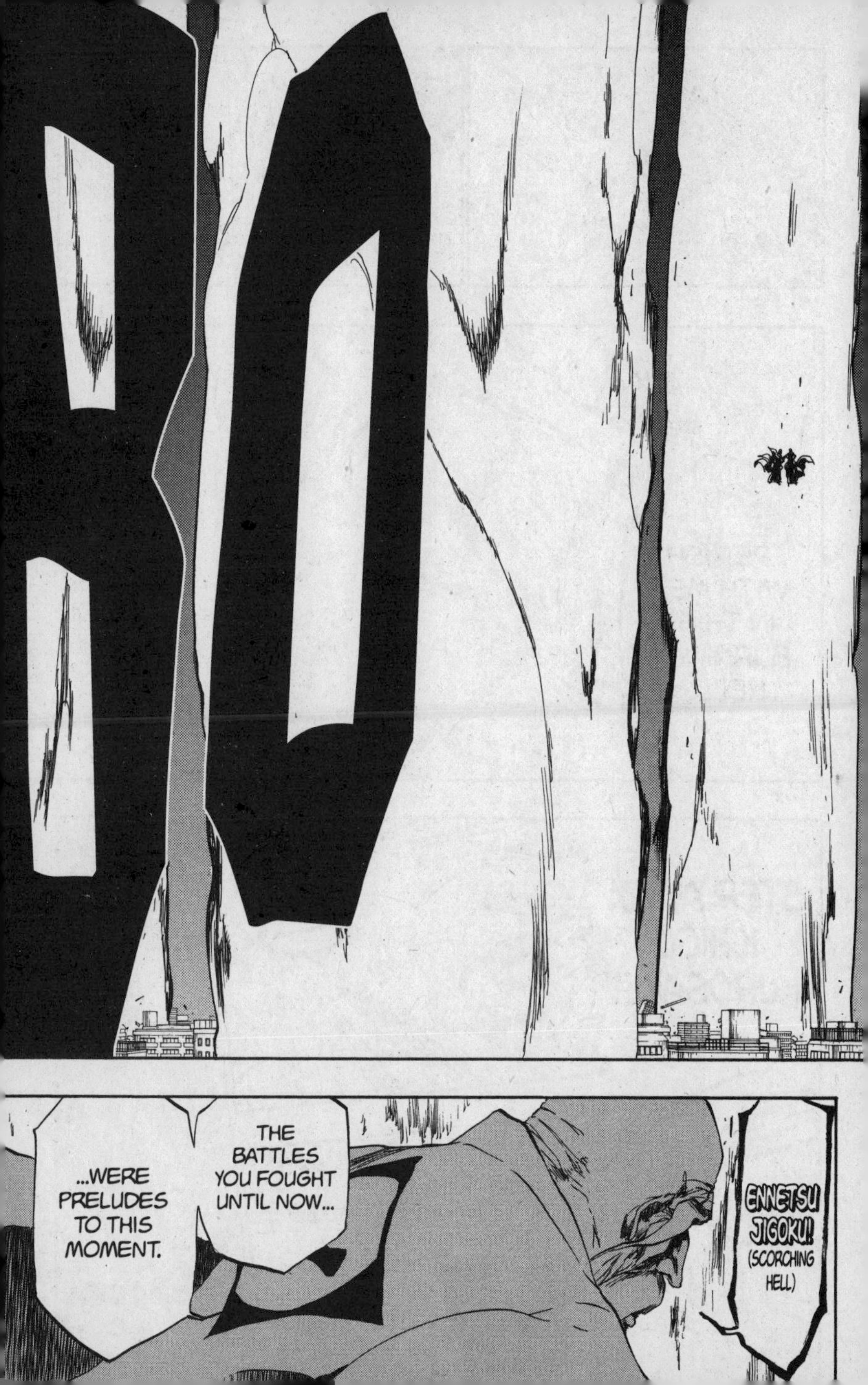
ENNETSU JIGOKU!! (SCORCHING HELL)
THE BATTLES YOU FOUGHT UNTIL NOW...
...WERE PRELUDES TO THIS MOMENT.

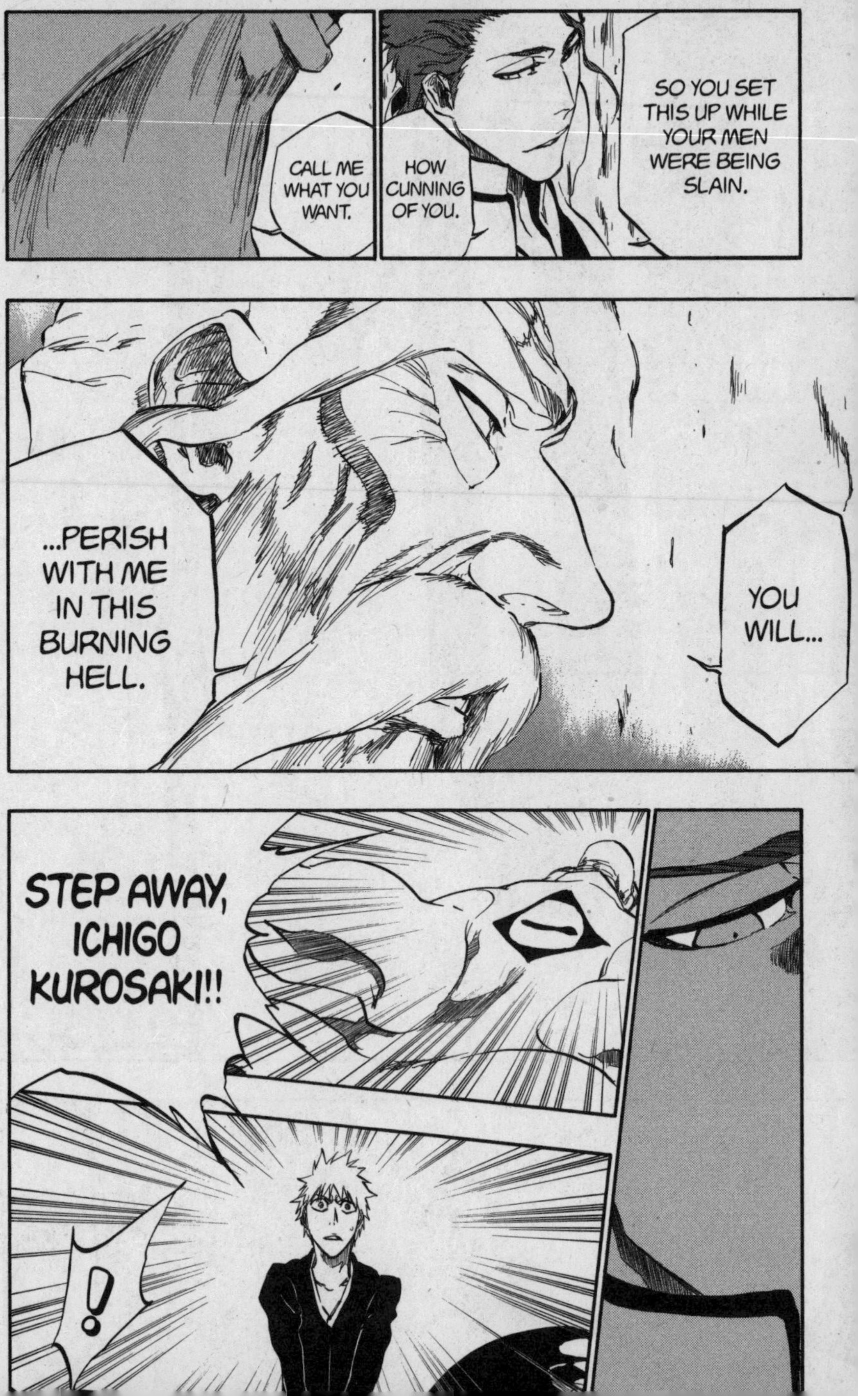
SO YOU SET THIS UP WHILE YOUR MEN WERE BEING SLAIN.
HOW CUNNING OF YOU.
CALL ME WHAT YOU WANT.
YOU WILL...
...PERISH WITH ME IN THIS BURNING HELL.
STEP AWAY, ICHIGO KUROSAKI!!
!

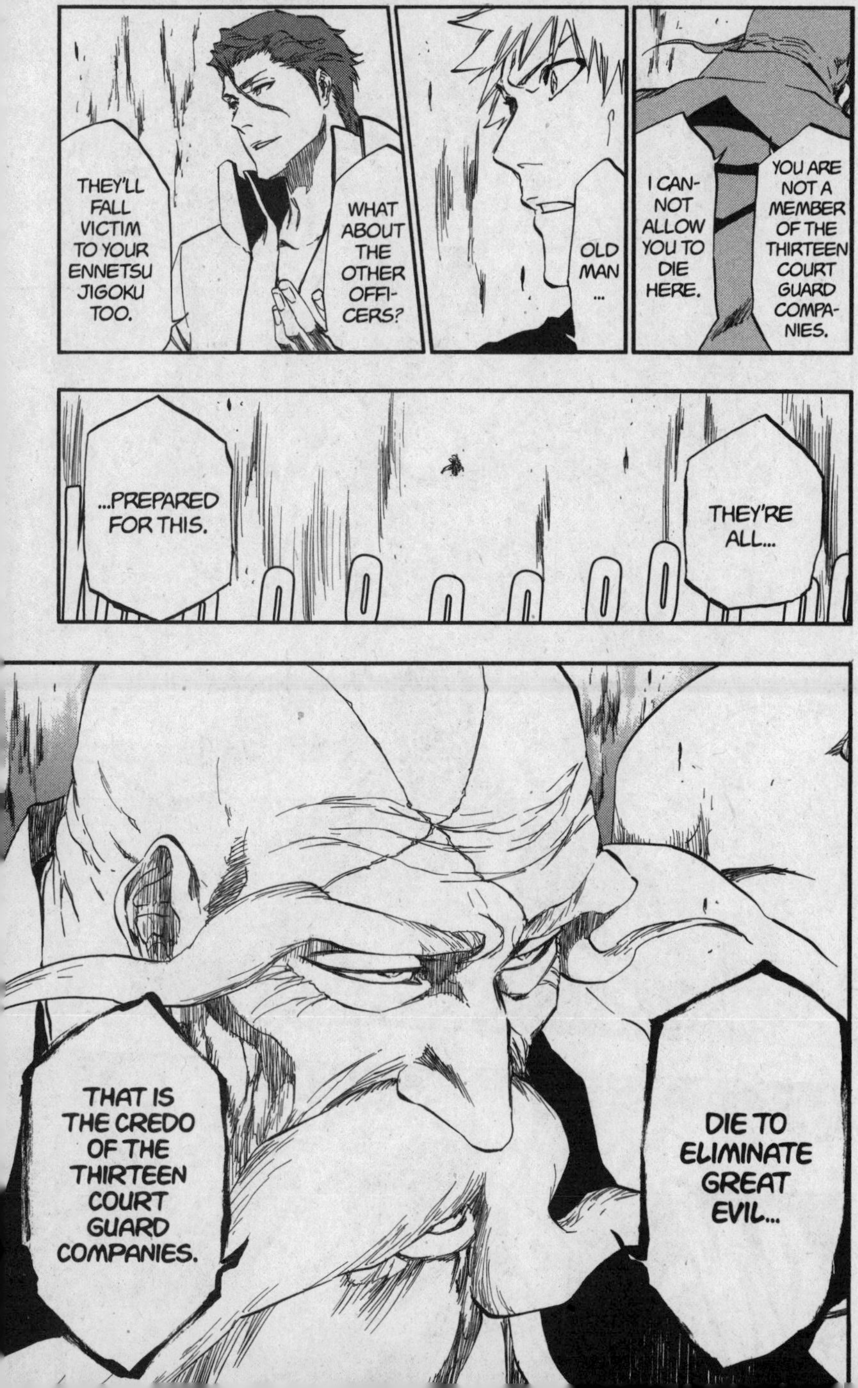
YOU ARE NOT A MEMBER OF THE THIRTEEN COURT GUARD COMPANIES.
I CANNOT ALLOW YOU TO DIE HERE.
OLD MAN...
WHAT ABOUT THE OTHER OFFICERS?
THEY'LL FALL VICTIM TO YOUR ENNETSU JIGOKU TOO.
THEY'RE ALL...
...PREPARED FOR THIS.
DIE TO ELIMINATE GREAT EVIL...
THAT IS THE CREDO OF THE THIRTEEN COURT GUARD COMPANIES.

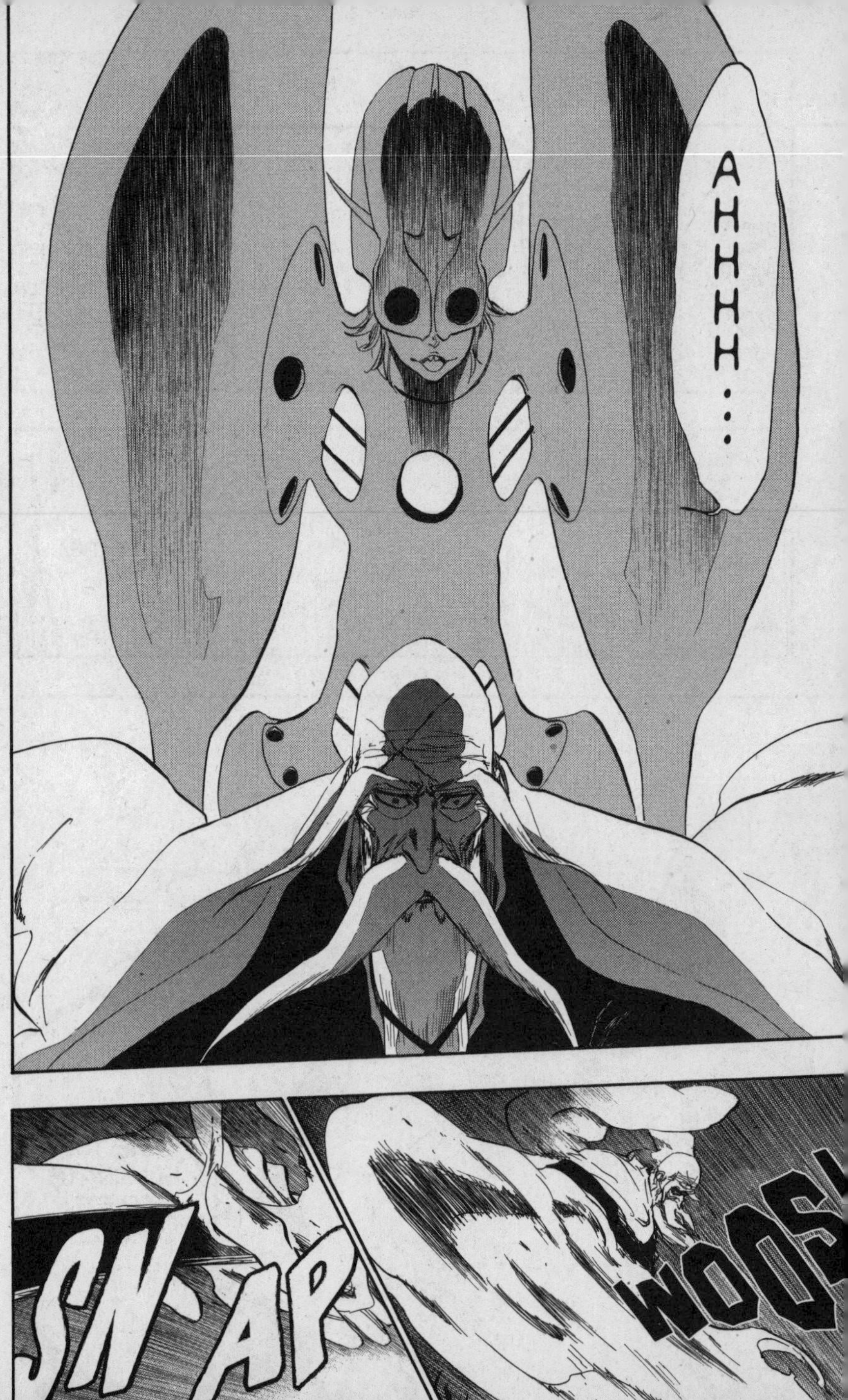
AHHHH...
WOOS
SNAP

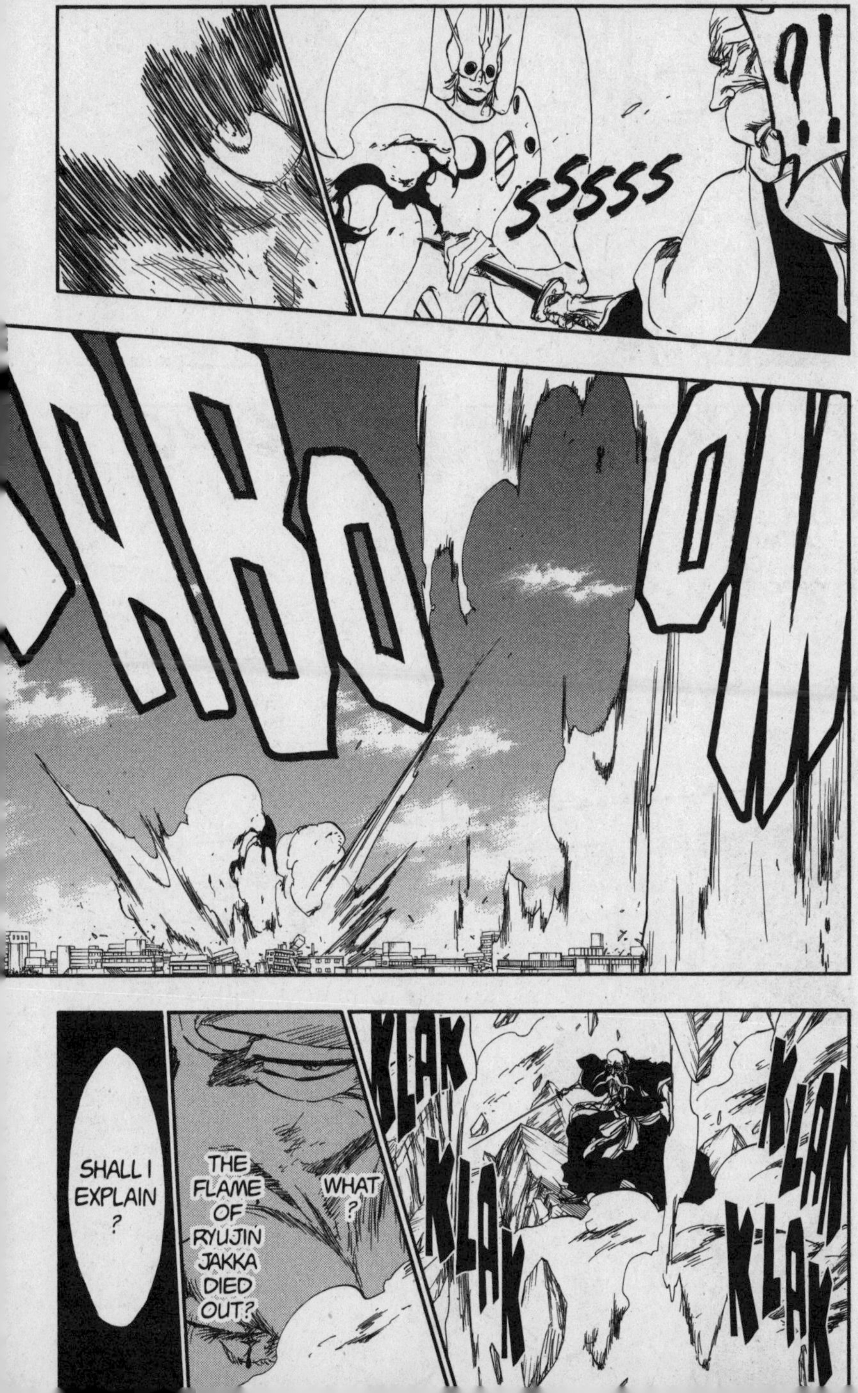
?!
SSSSS
KLAK KLAK
KLAK KLAK
WHAT?
THE FLAME OF RYUJIN JAKKA DIED OUT?
SHALL I EXPLAIN?

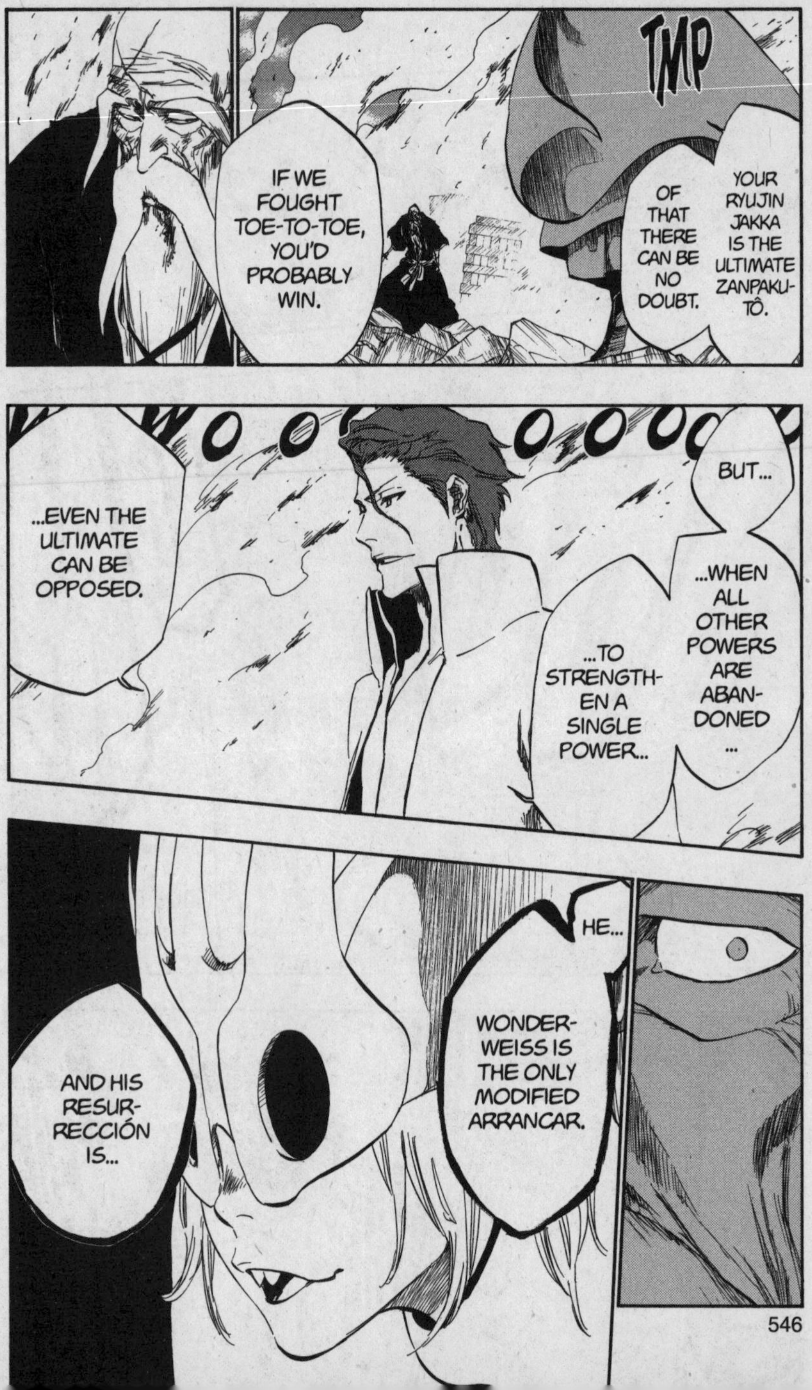
TMP
YOUR RYUJIN JAKKA IS THE ULTIMATE ZANPAKU-TÔ.
OF THAT THERE CAN BE NO DOUBT.
IF WE FOUGHT TOE-TO-TOE, YOU'D PROBABLY WIN.
WOOOOOO
BUT...
...WHEN ALL OTHER POWERS ARE ABAN-DONED...
...TO STRENGTH-EN A SINGLE POWER...
...EVEN THE ULTIMATE CAN BE OPPOSED.
HE...
WONDER-WEISS IS THE ONLY MODIFIED ARRANCAR.
AND HIS RESUR-RECCIÓN IS...

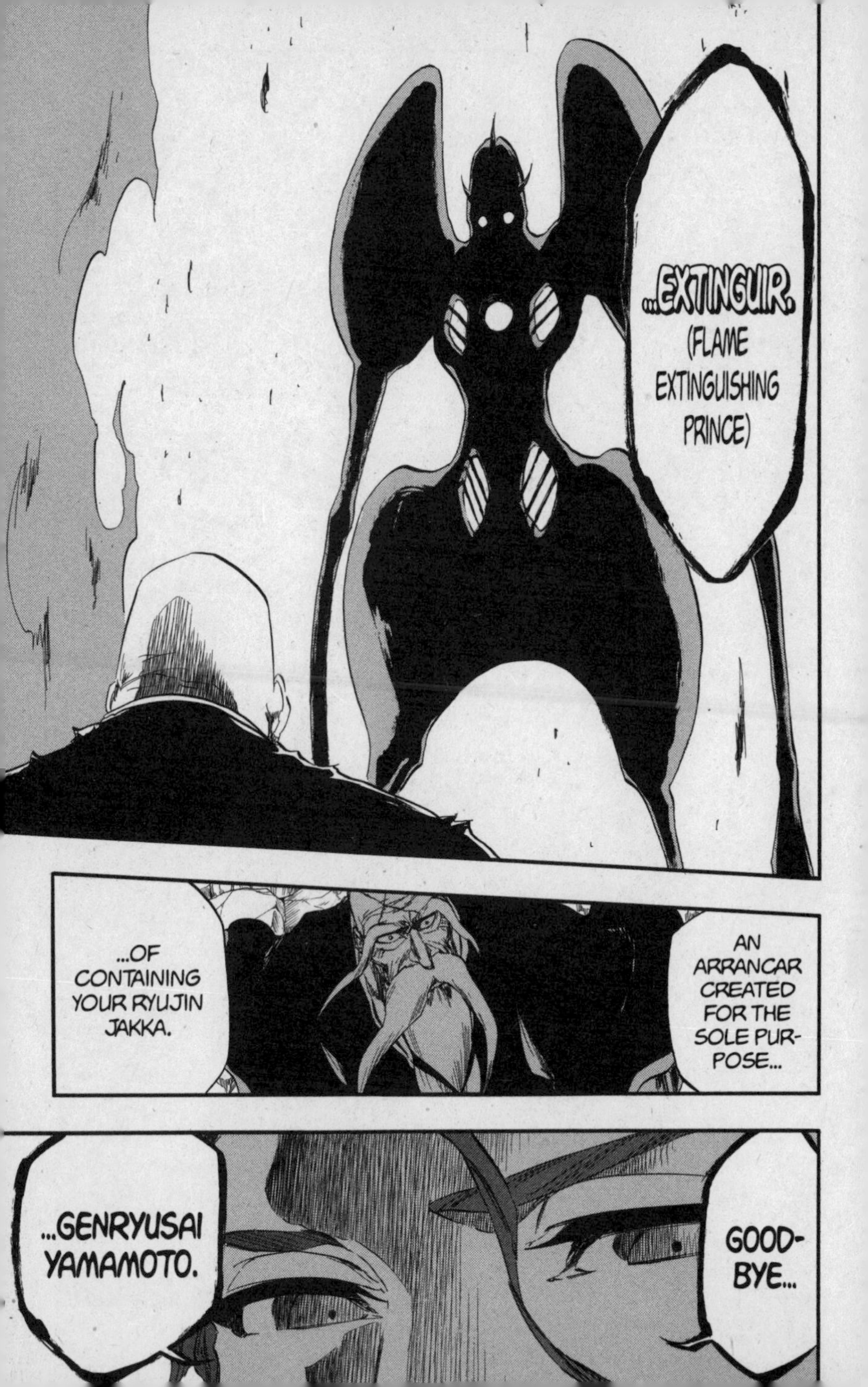
...EXTINGUIR. (FLAME EXTINGUISHING PRINCE)
AN ARRANCAR CREATED FOR THE SOLE PURPOSE...
...OF CONTAINING YOUR RYUJIN JAKKA.
GOOD-BYE...
...GENRYUSAI YAMAMOTO.

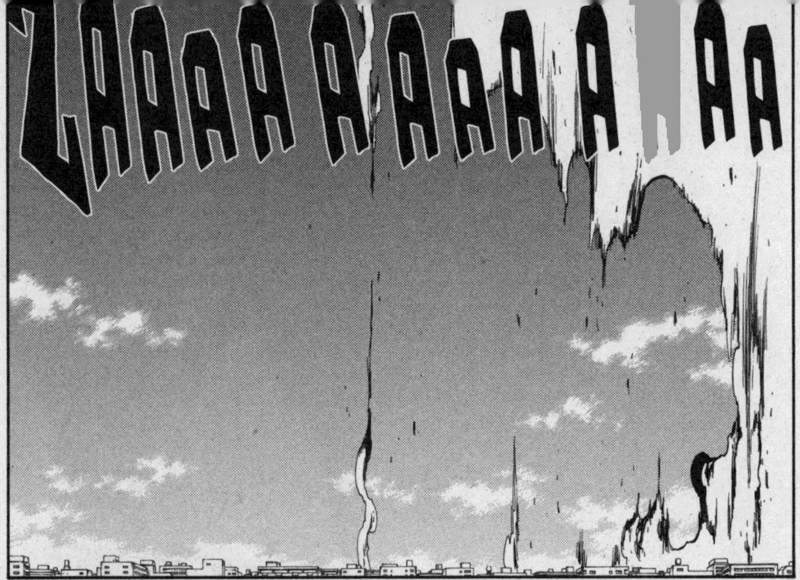
LAAAAAAAAAAA

394. The Burnout Inferno 2

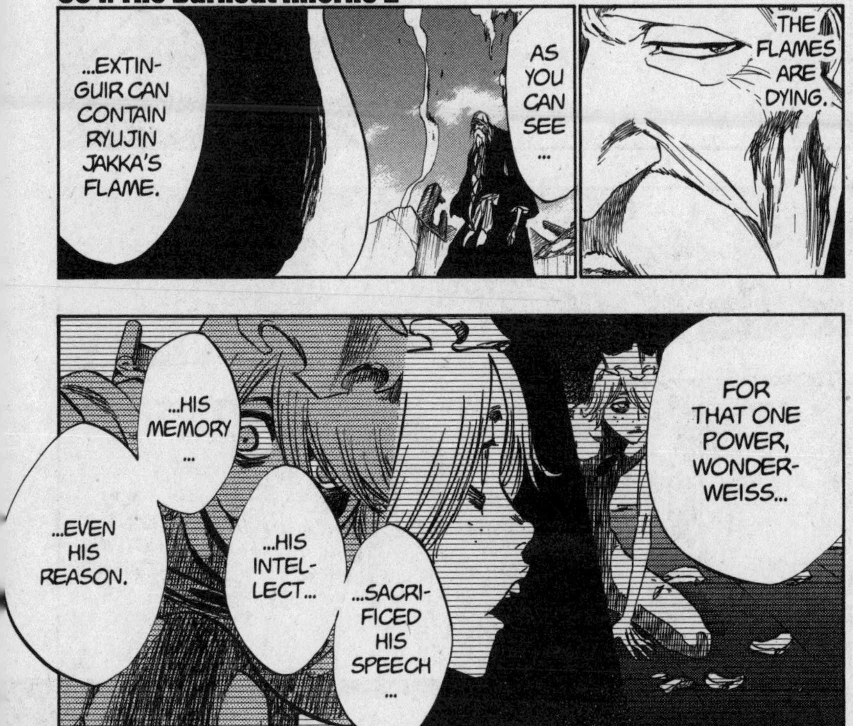
THE FLAMES ARE DYING.
AS YOU CAN SEE ...
...EXTINGUIR CAN CONTAIN RYUJIN JAKKA'S FLAME.
FOR THAT ONE POWER, WONDERWEISS...
...SACRIFICED HIS SPEECH ...
...HIS INTELLECT...
...HIS MEMORY ...
...EVEN HIS REASON.

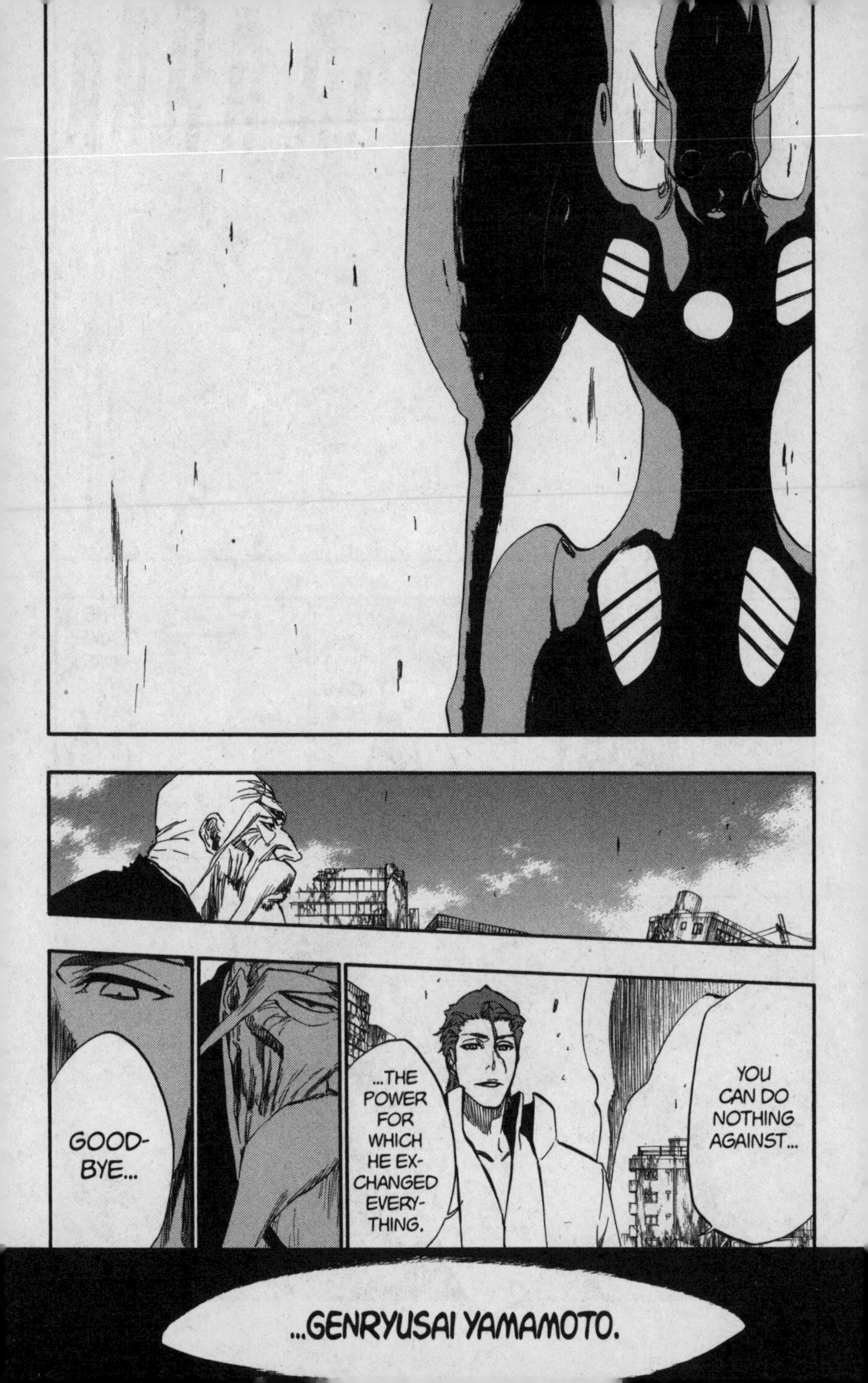
YOU CAN DO NOTHING AGAINST...
...THE POWER FOR WHICH HE EXCHANGED EVERYTHING.
GOOD-BYE...
...GENRYUSAI YAMAMOTO.

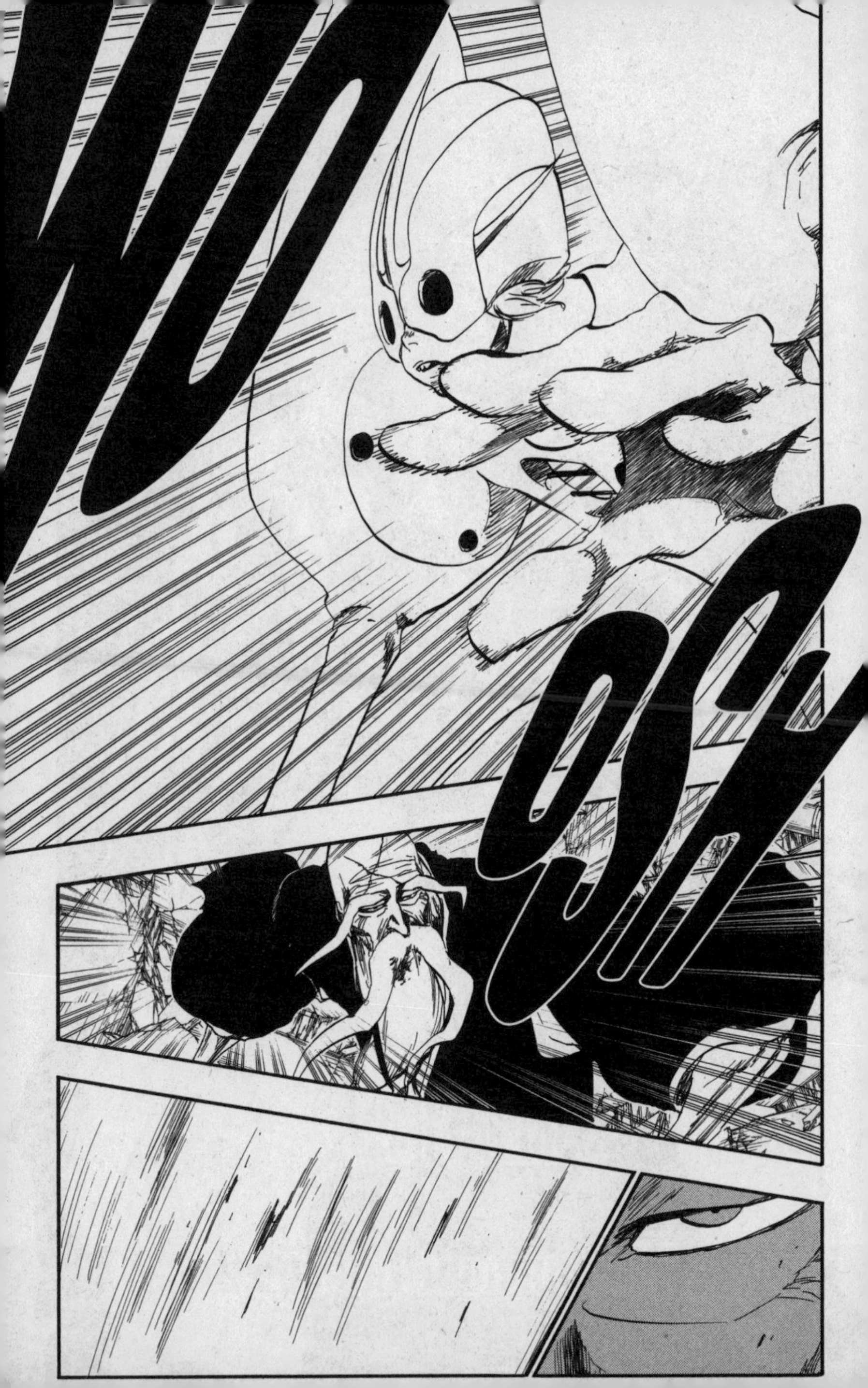

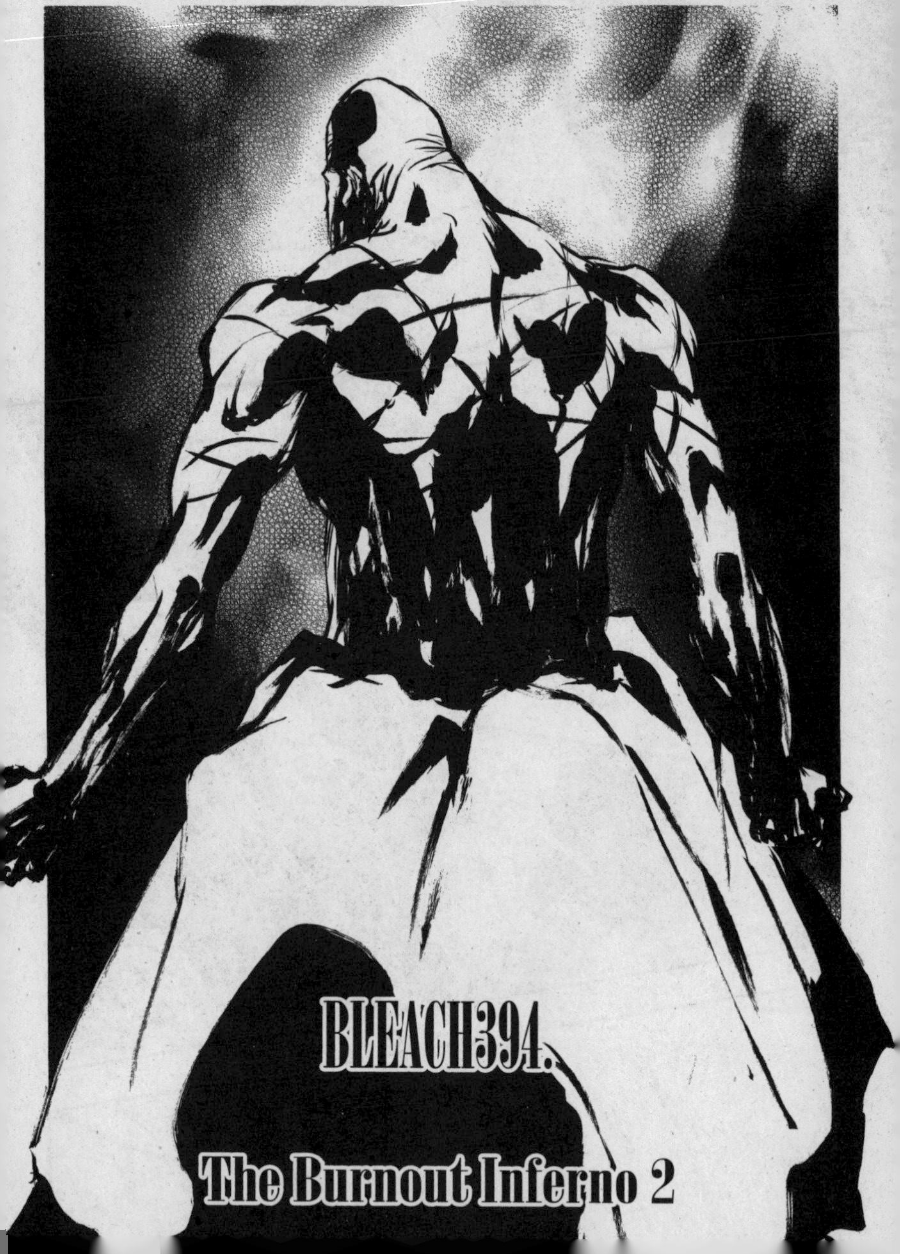
BLEACH394.
The Burnout Inferno 2

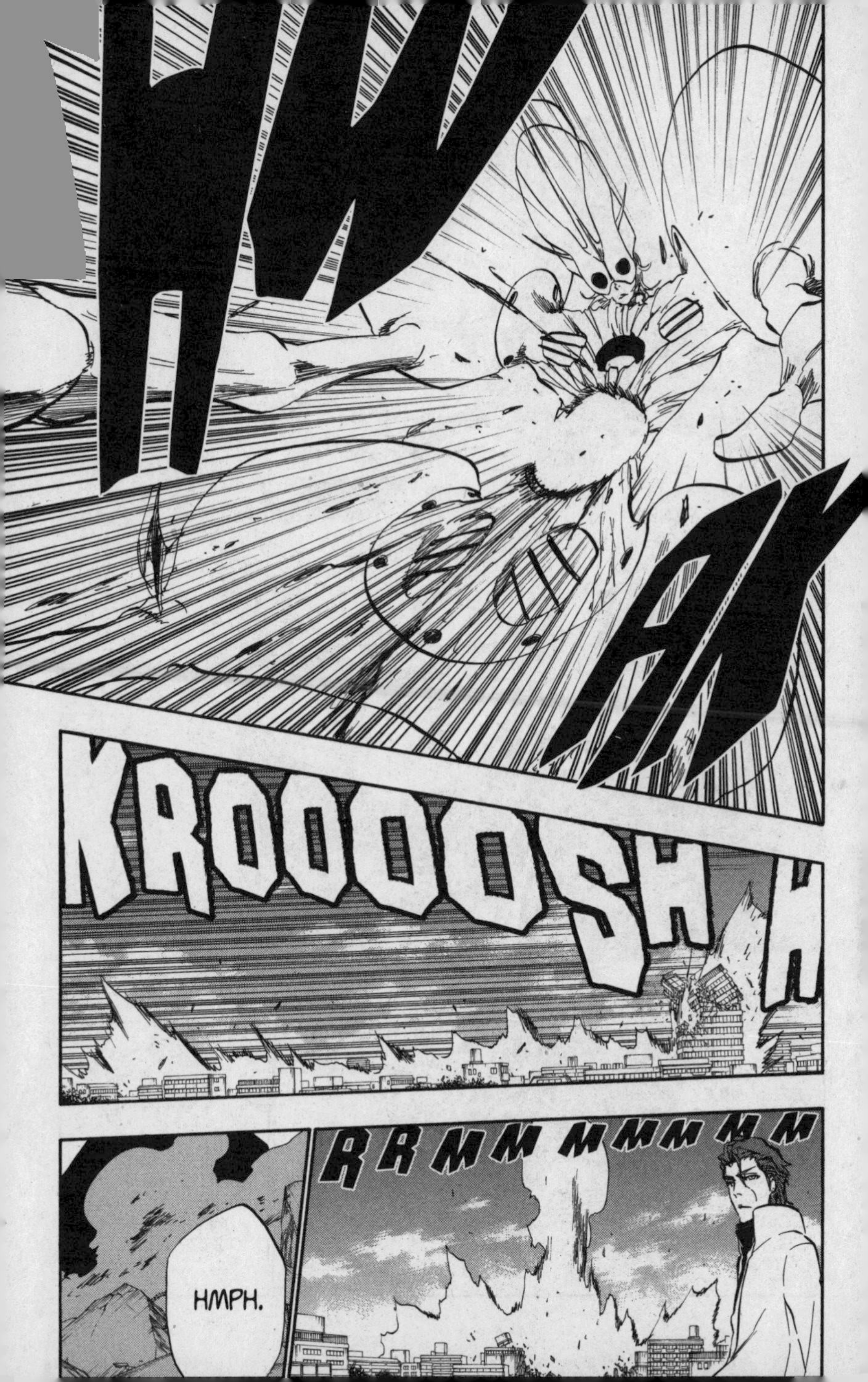
KROOOOSH
RRMMMMMMM
HMPH.

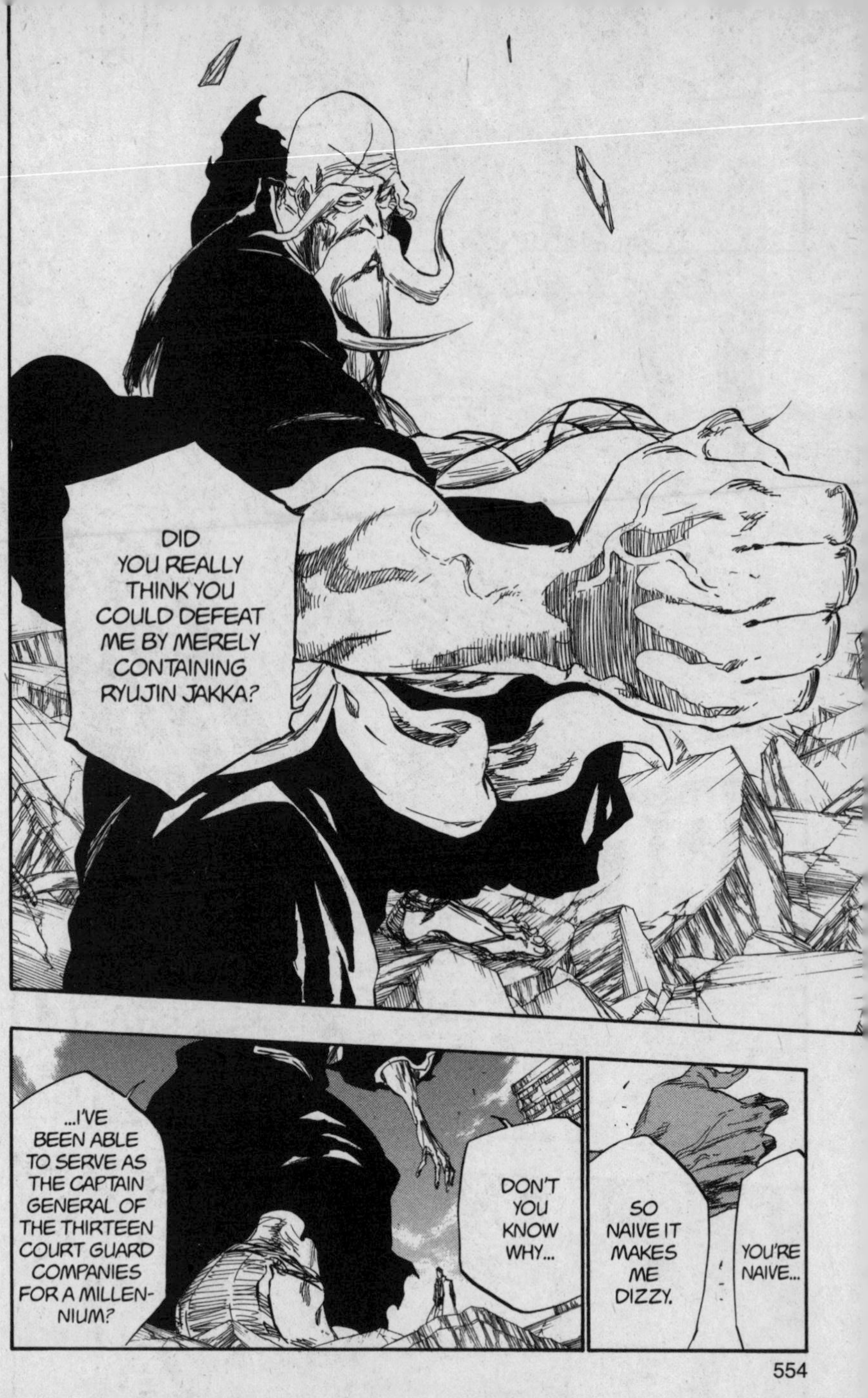
DID YOU REALLY THINK YOU COULD DEFEAT ME BY MERELY CONTAINING RYUJIN JAKKA?
YOU'RE NAIVE...
SO NAIVE IT MAKES ME DIZZY.
DON'T YOU KNOW WHY...
...I'VE BEEN ABLE TO SERVE AS THE CAPTAIN GENERAL OF THE THIRTEEN COURT GUARD COMPANIES FOR A MILLENNIUM?

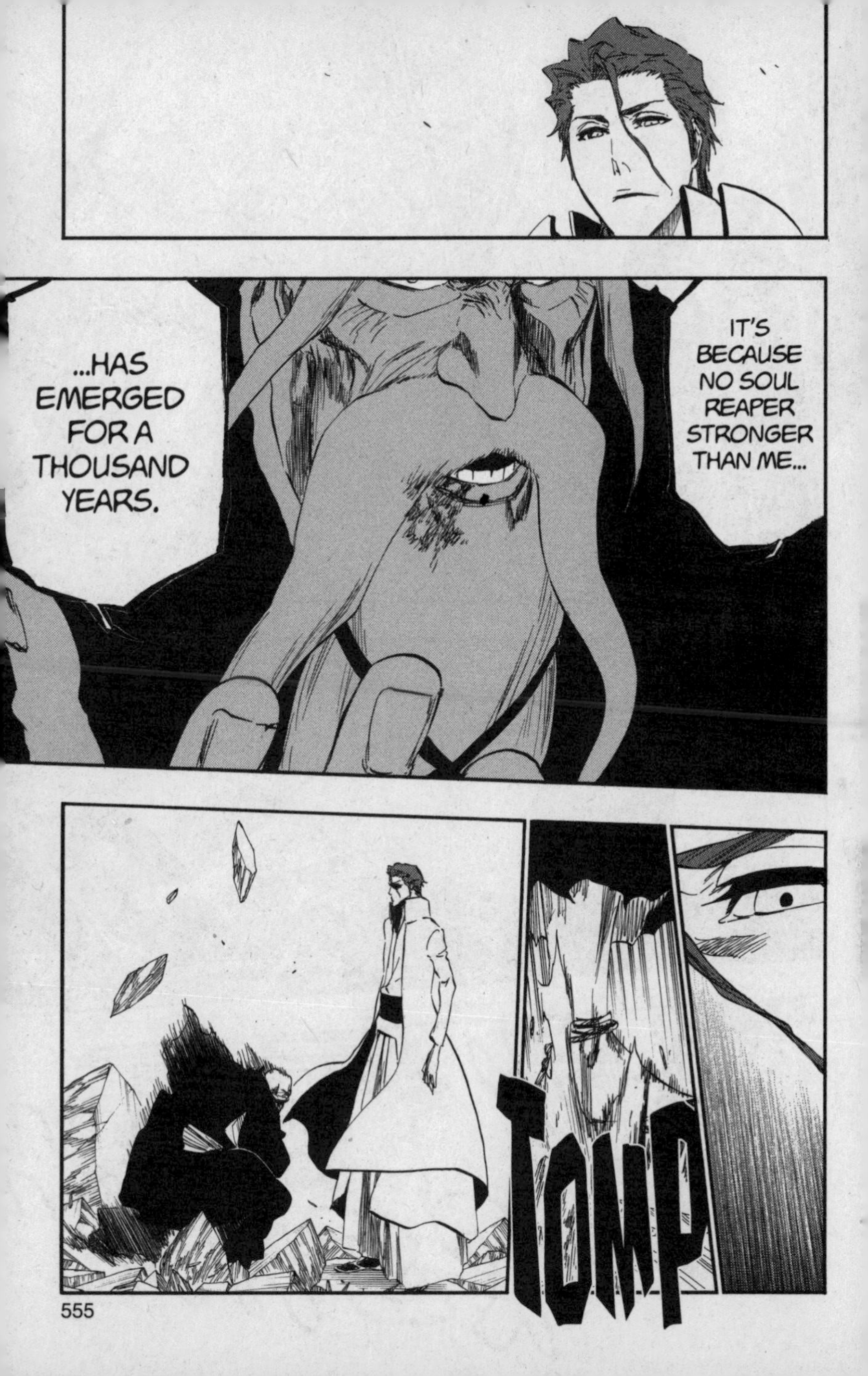
IT'S BECAUSE NO SOUL REAPER STRONGER THAN ME...
...HAS EMERGED FOR A THOUSAND YEARS.
TOMP

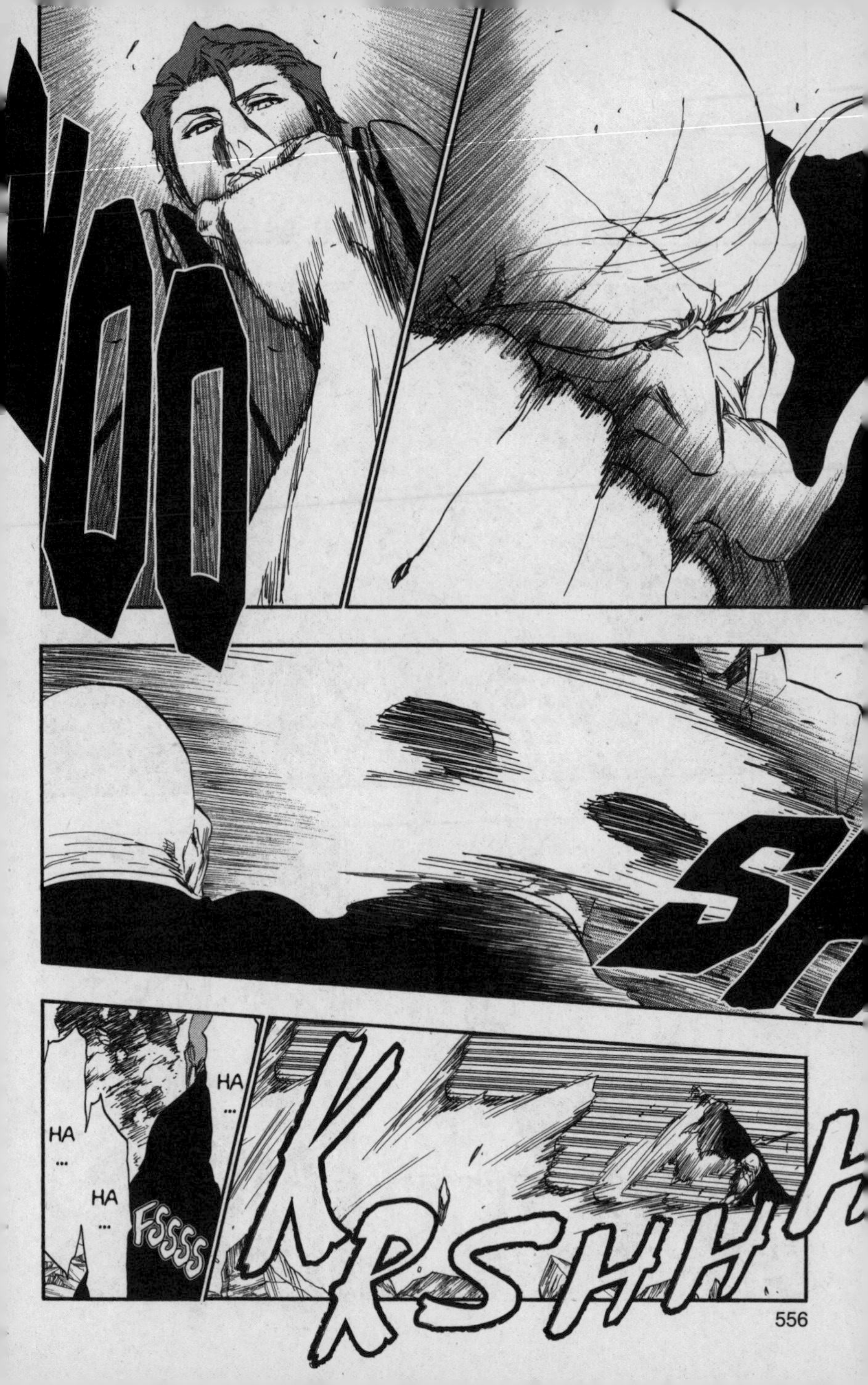
KRSHH
HA
...
HA
...
HA
...
FSSSS

READ THIS WAY

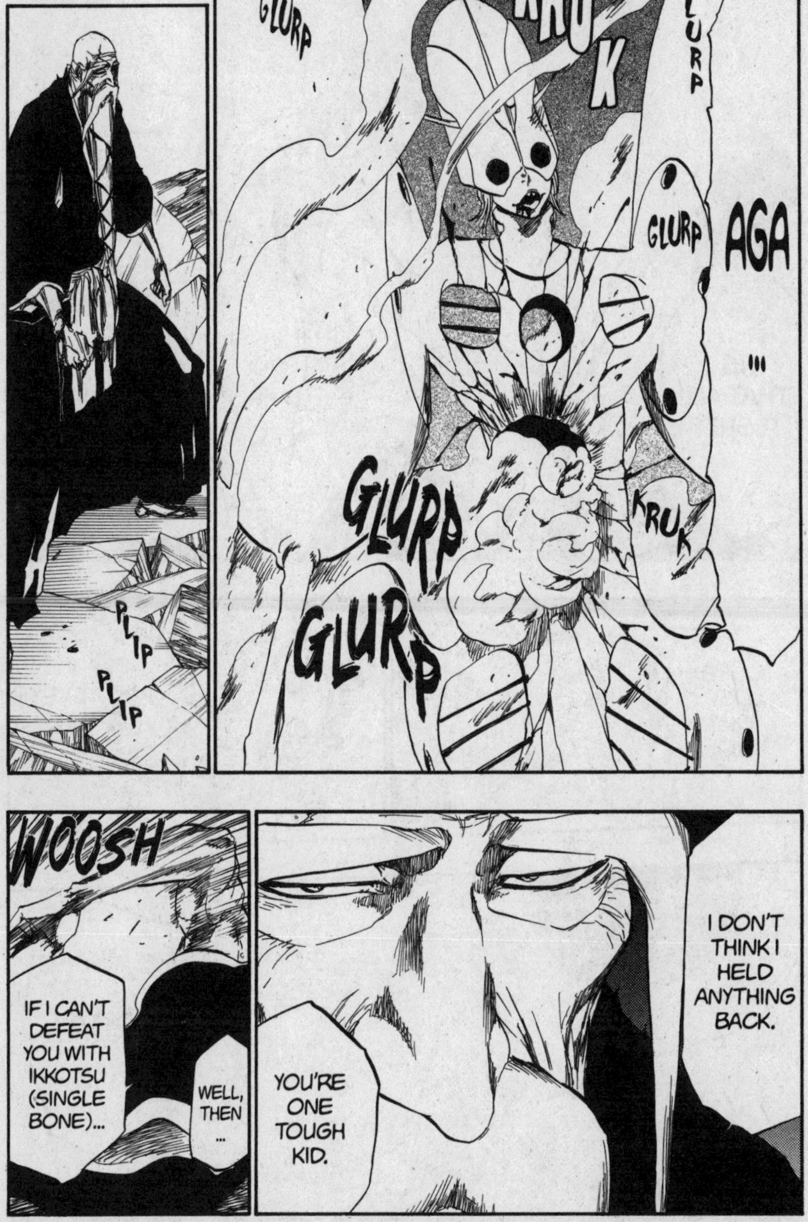
GLURP
KRUK
GLURP
AGA
...
GLURP
KRUK
GLURP
GLURP
PLIP
PLIP
I DON'T THINK I HELD ANYTHING BACK.
YOU'RE ONE TOUGH KID.
WOOSH
IF I CAN'T DEFEAT YOU WITH IKKOTSU (SINGLE BONE)...
WELL, THEN ...

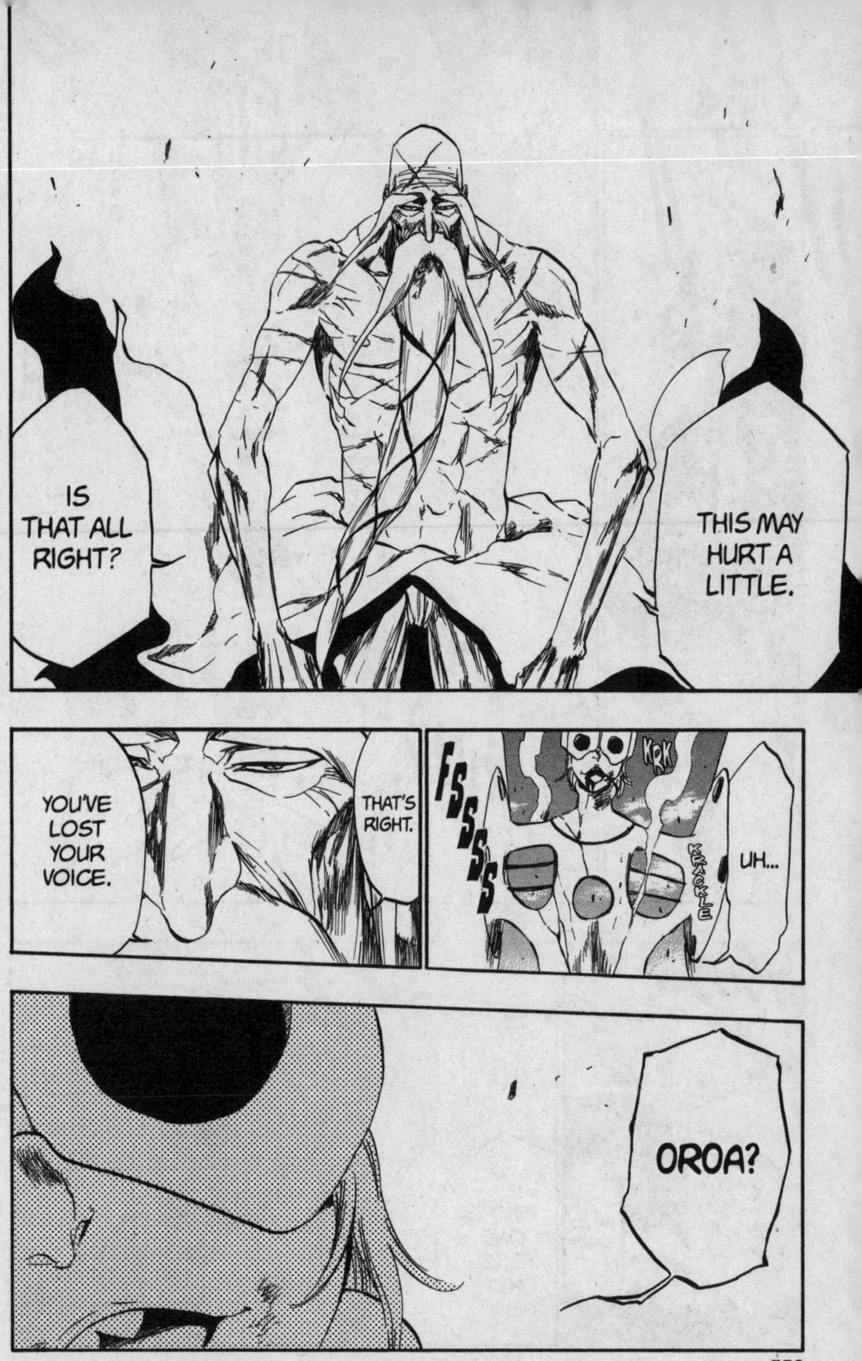
THIS MAY HURT A LITTLE.
IS THAT ALL RIGHT?
KRK
UH...
KRACKLE
FSSSS
THAT'S RIGHT.
YOU'VE LOST YOUR VOICE.
OROA?

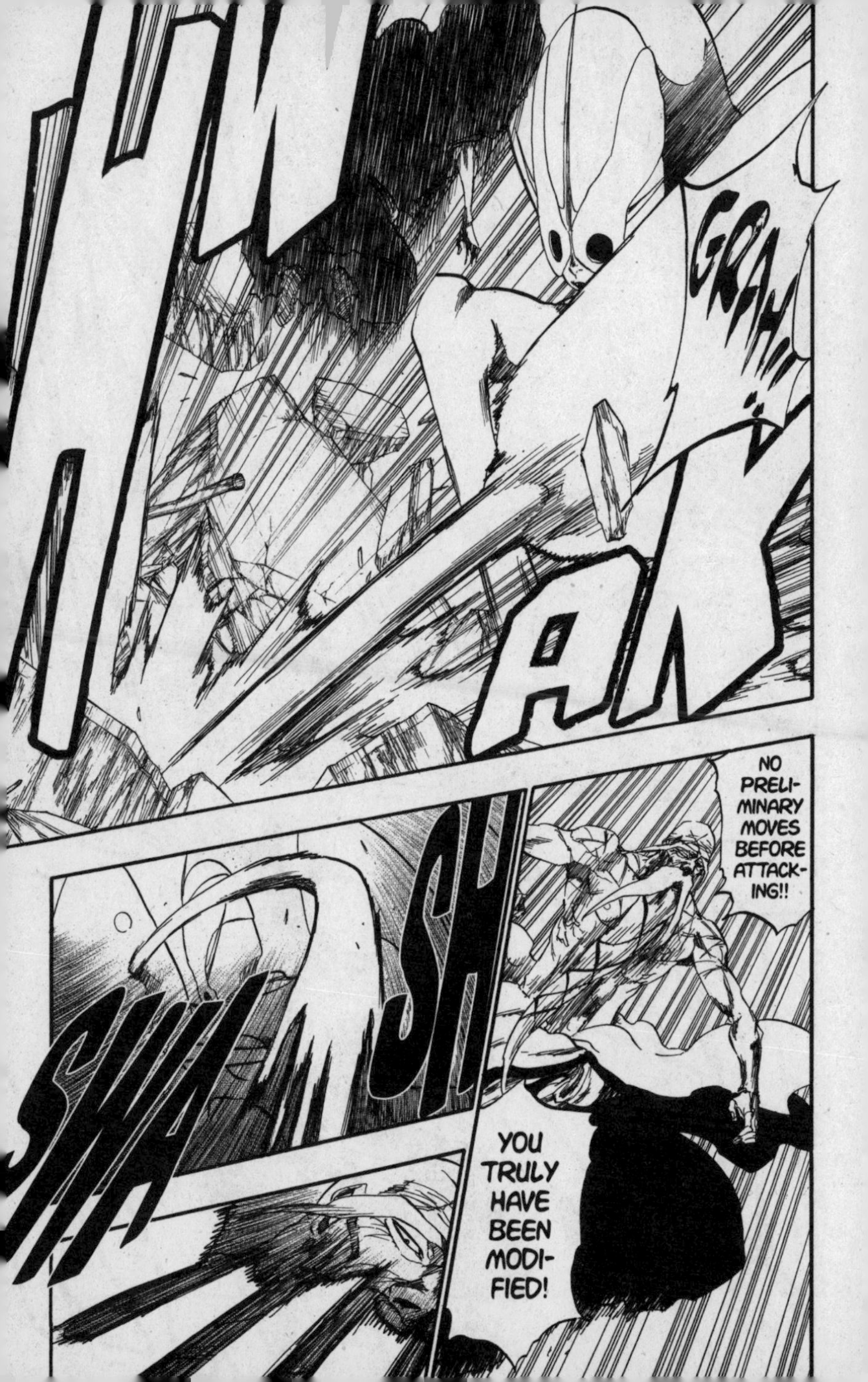
GRAH!!
NO PRELIMINARY MOVES BEFORE ATTACKING!!
YOU TRULY HAVE BEEN MODIFIED!

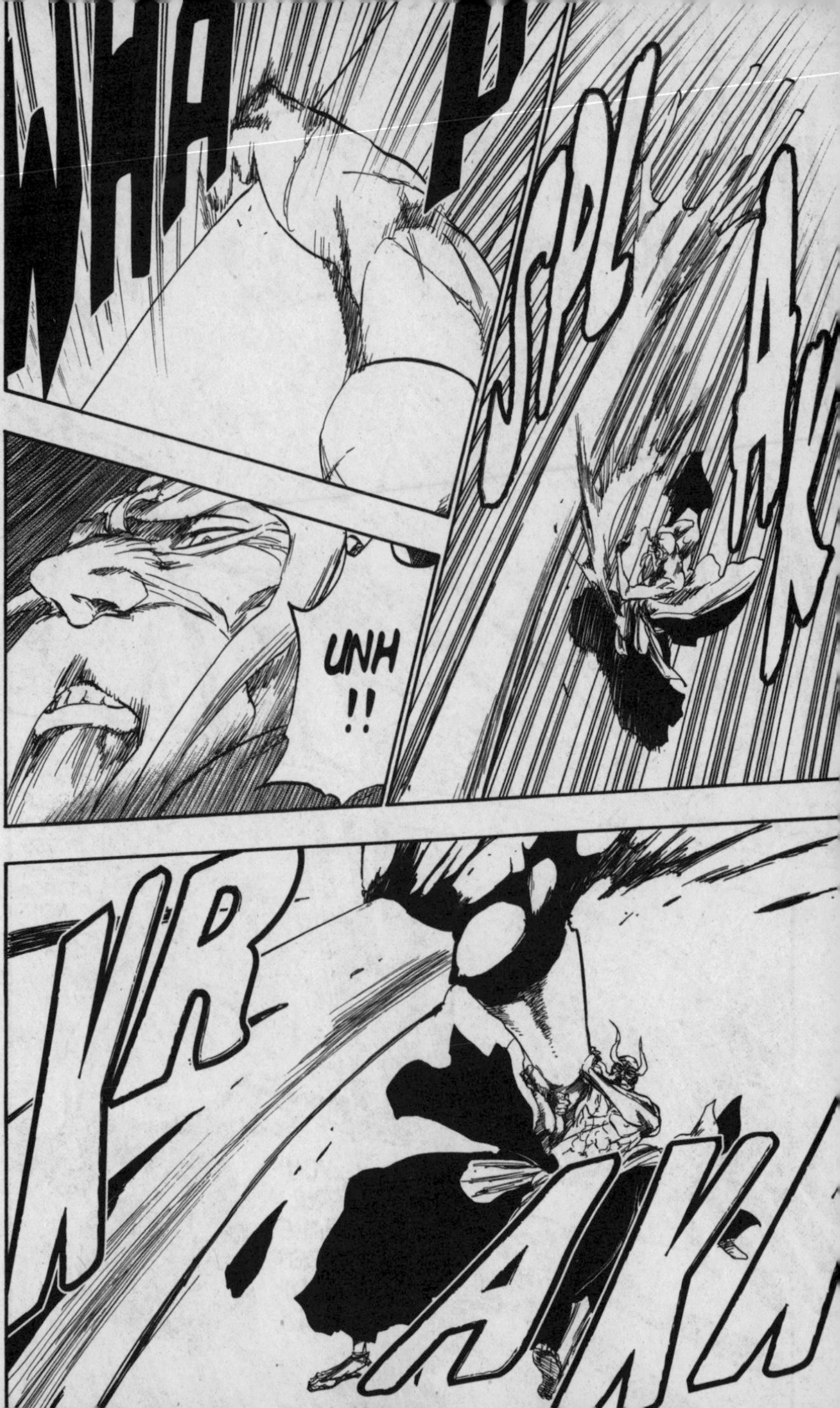
WHAP
UNH!!

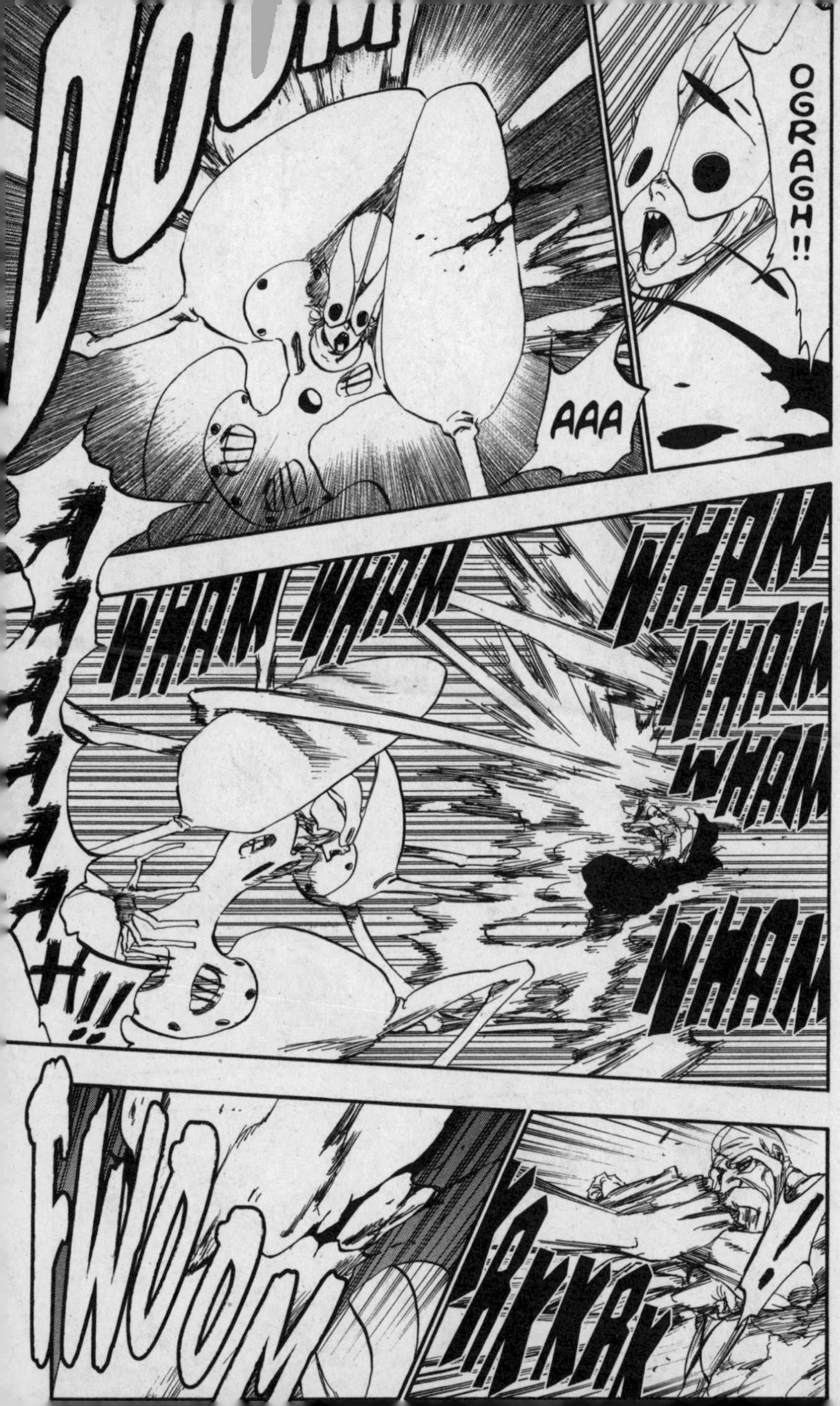
OGRAGH!!
AAA
WHAM
WHAM
WHAM
WHAM
WHAM WHAM
AAAAAAAH!!

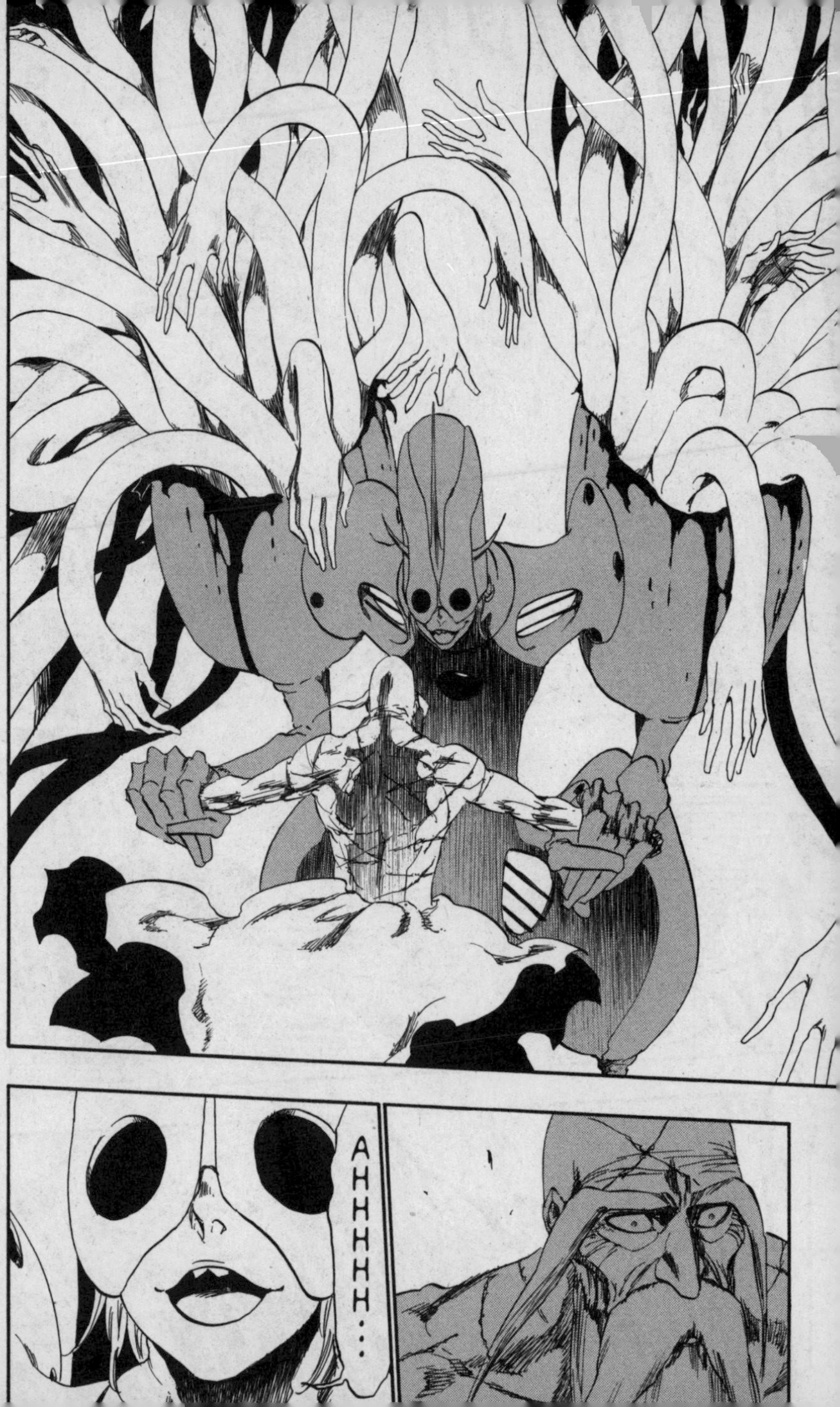
AHHHHH...

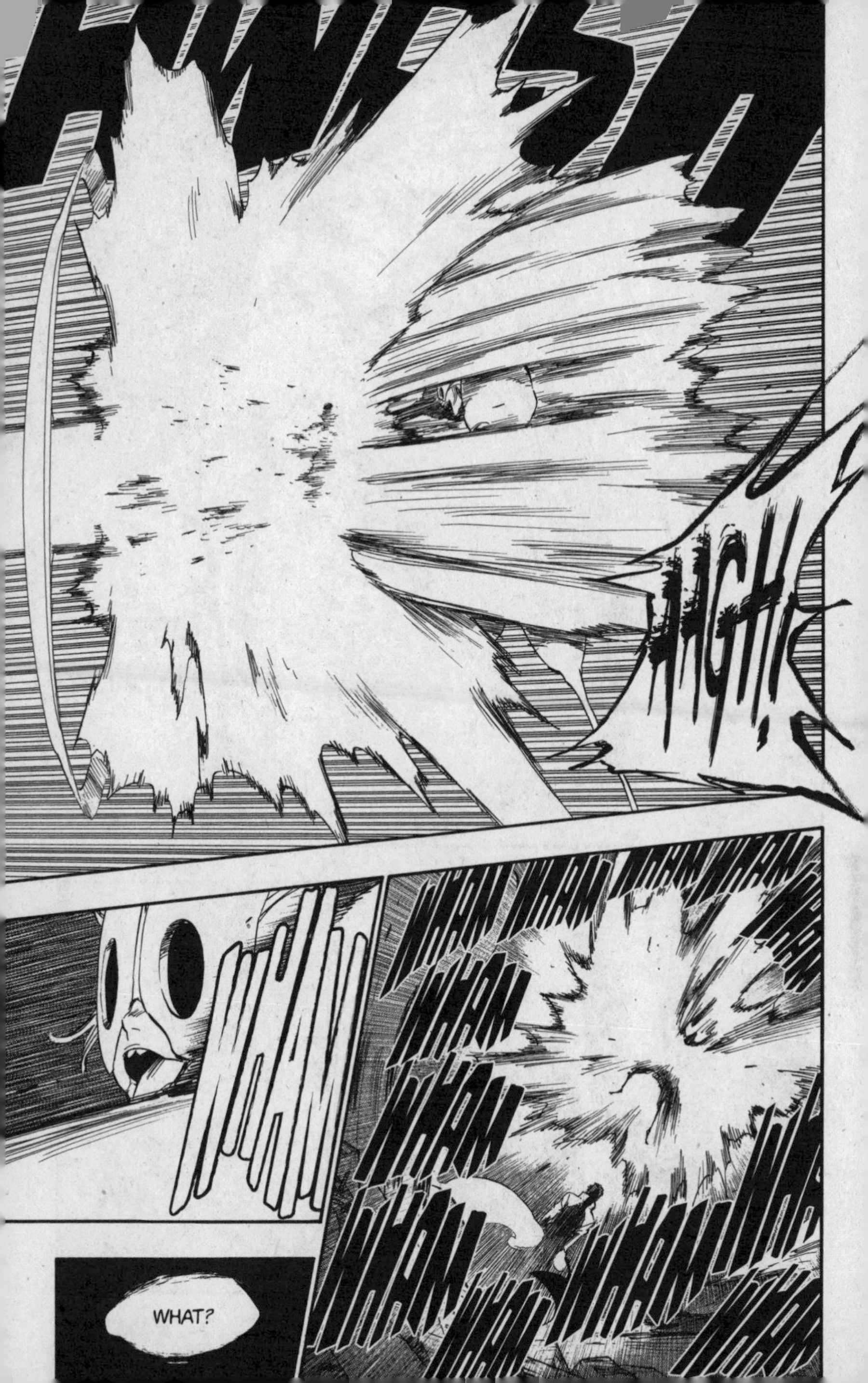
AAGH!!
WHAM WHAM WHAM WHAM
WHAM
WHAT?

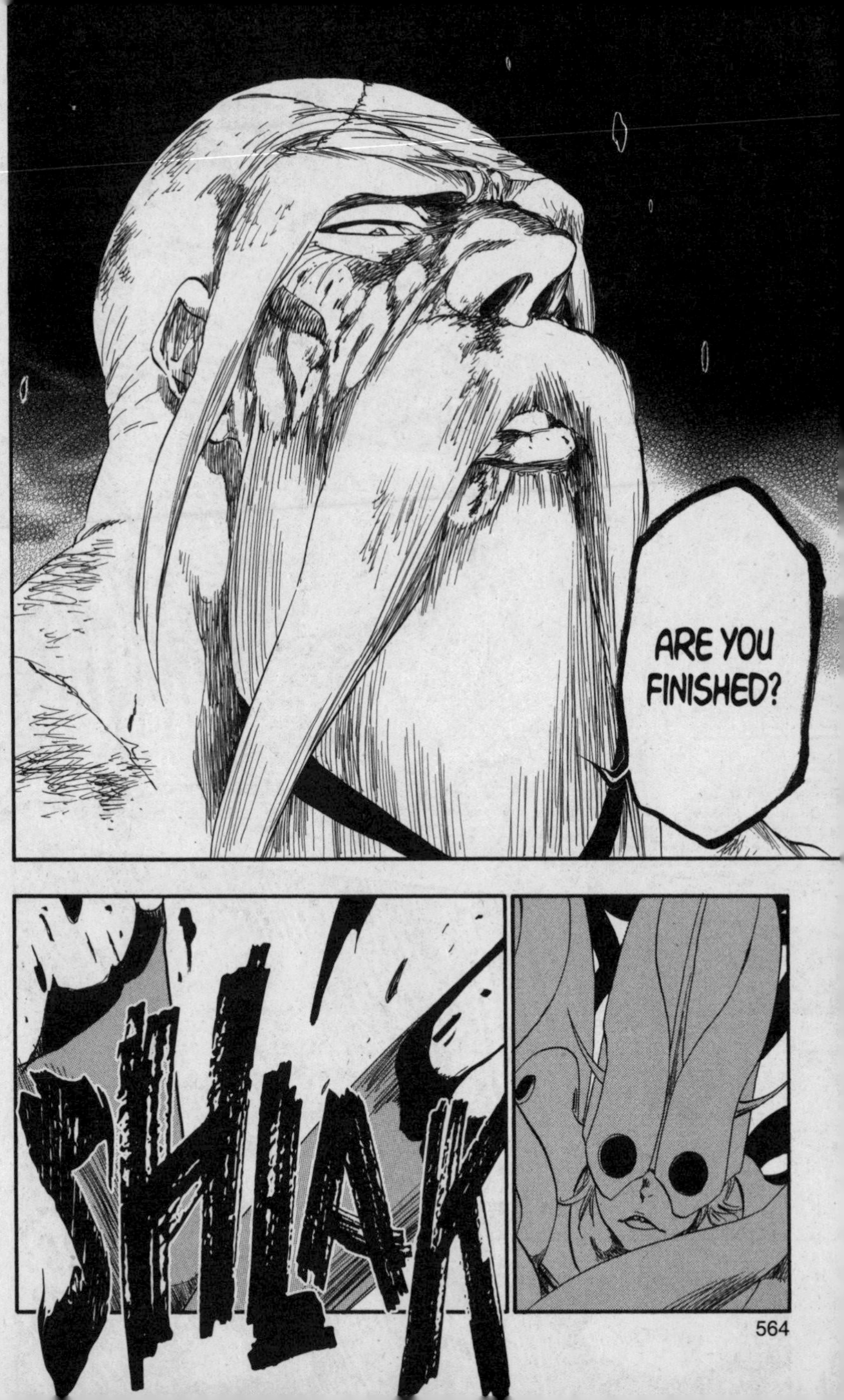
ARE YOU FINISHED?
SHLAK

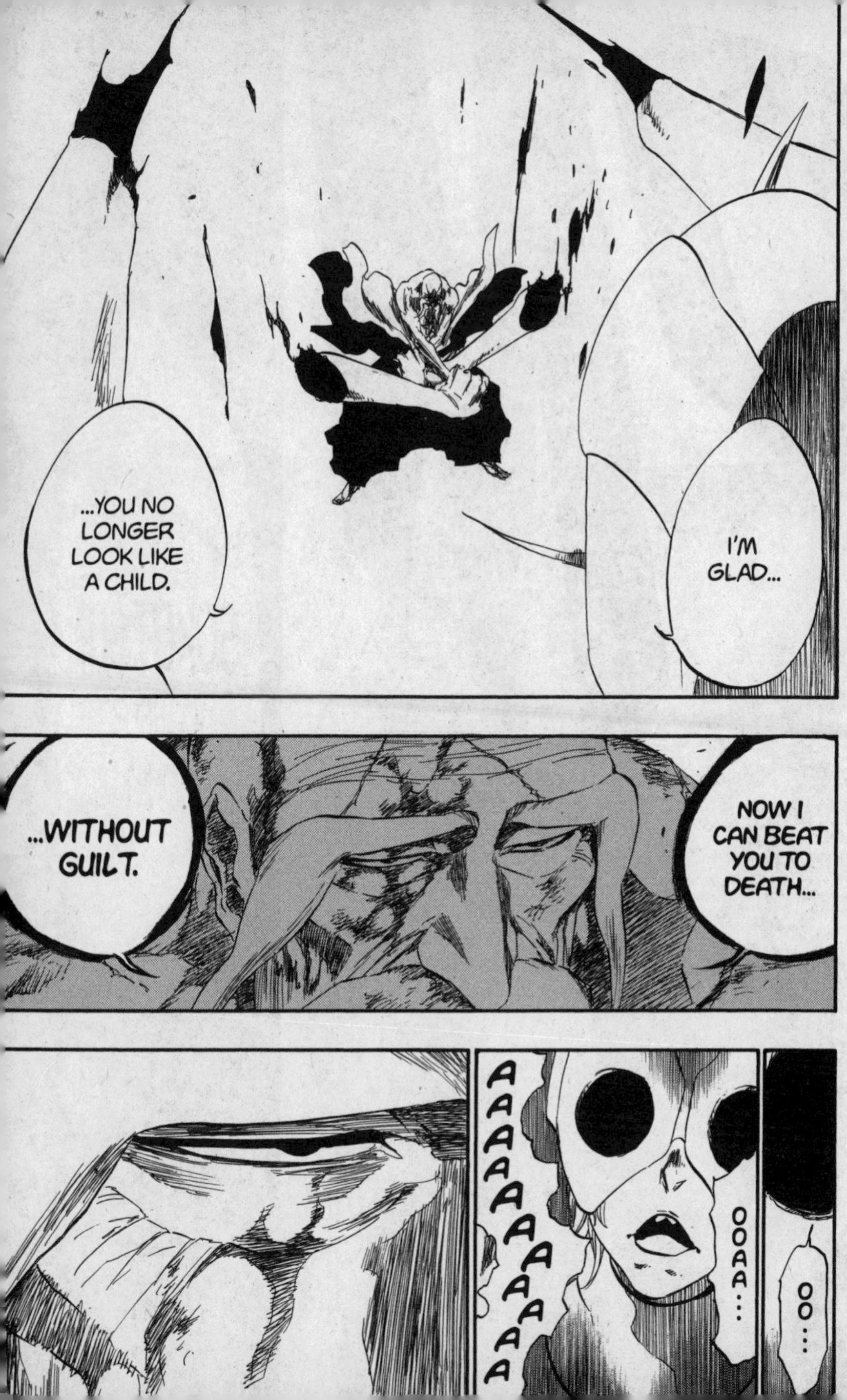

I'M GLAD...
...YOU NO LONGER LOOK LIKE A CHILD.
NOW I CAN BEAT YOU TO DEATH...
...WITHOUT GUILT.
OO...
OOAAA...
AAAAAAAAAAAAAA

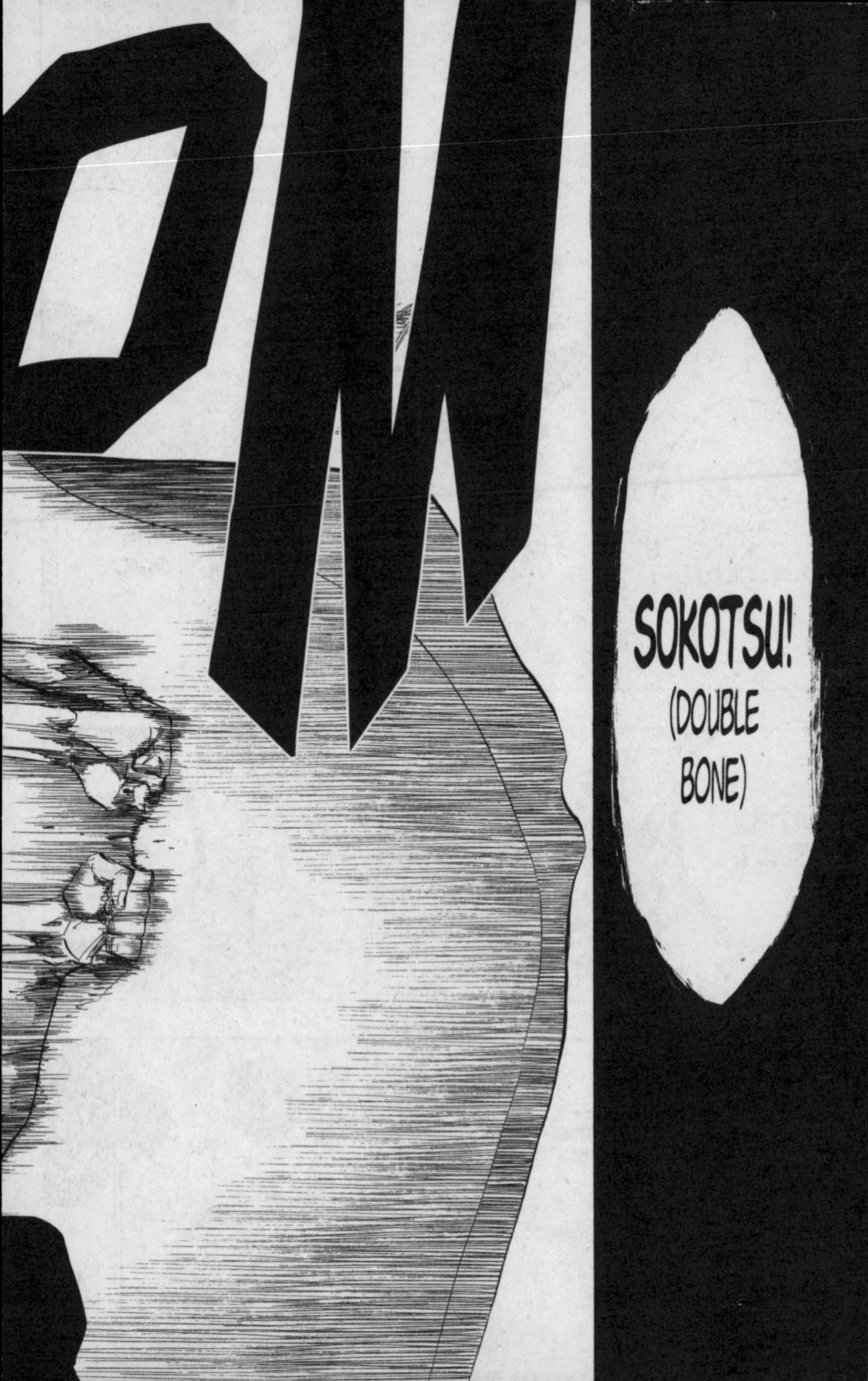
SOKOTSU! (DOUBLE BONE)

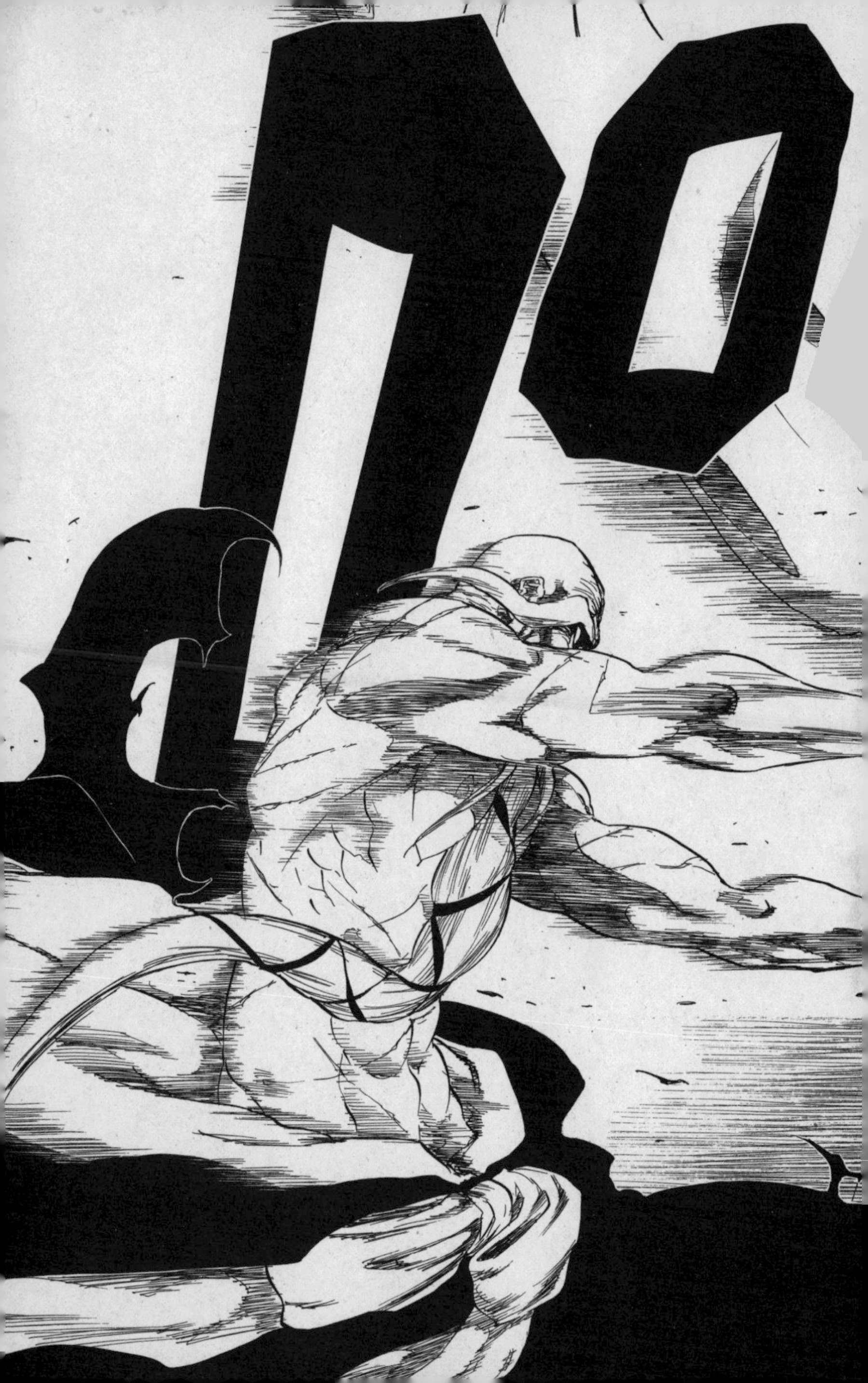
DO

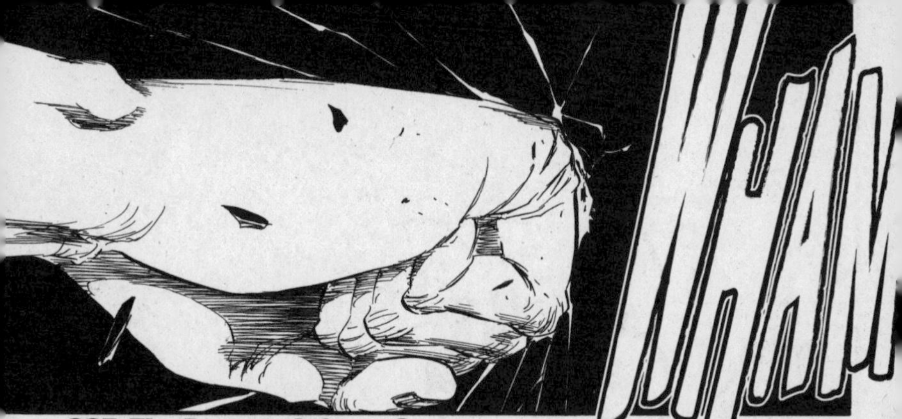
WHAM

395. The Burnout Inferno 3

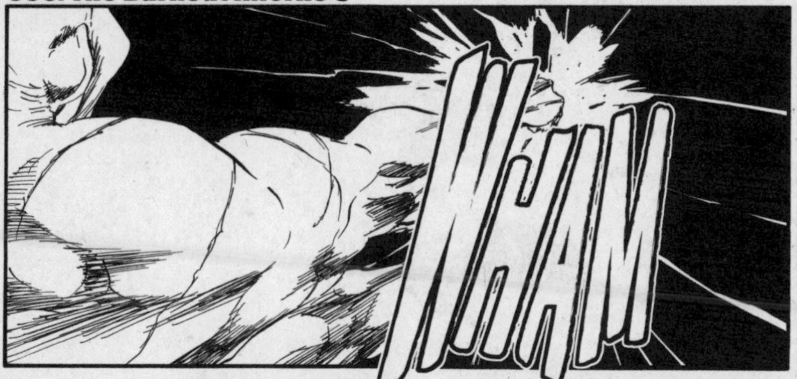
WHAM

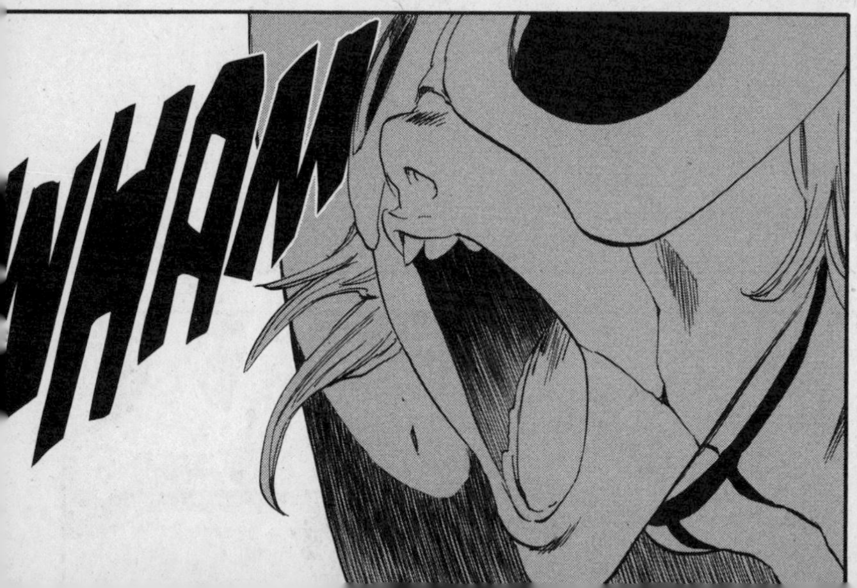
WHAM

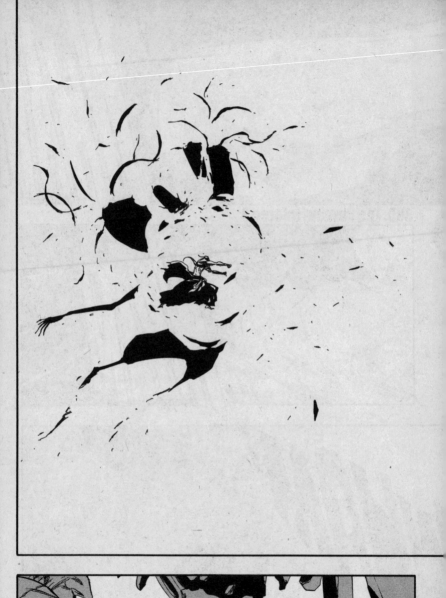

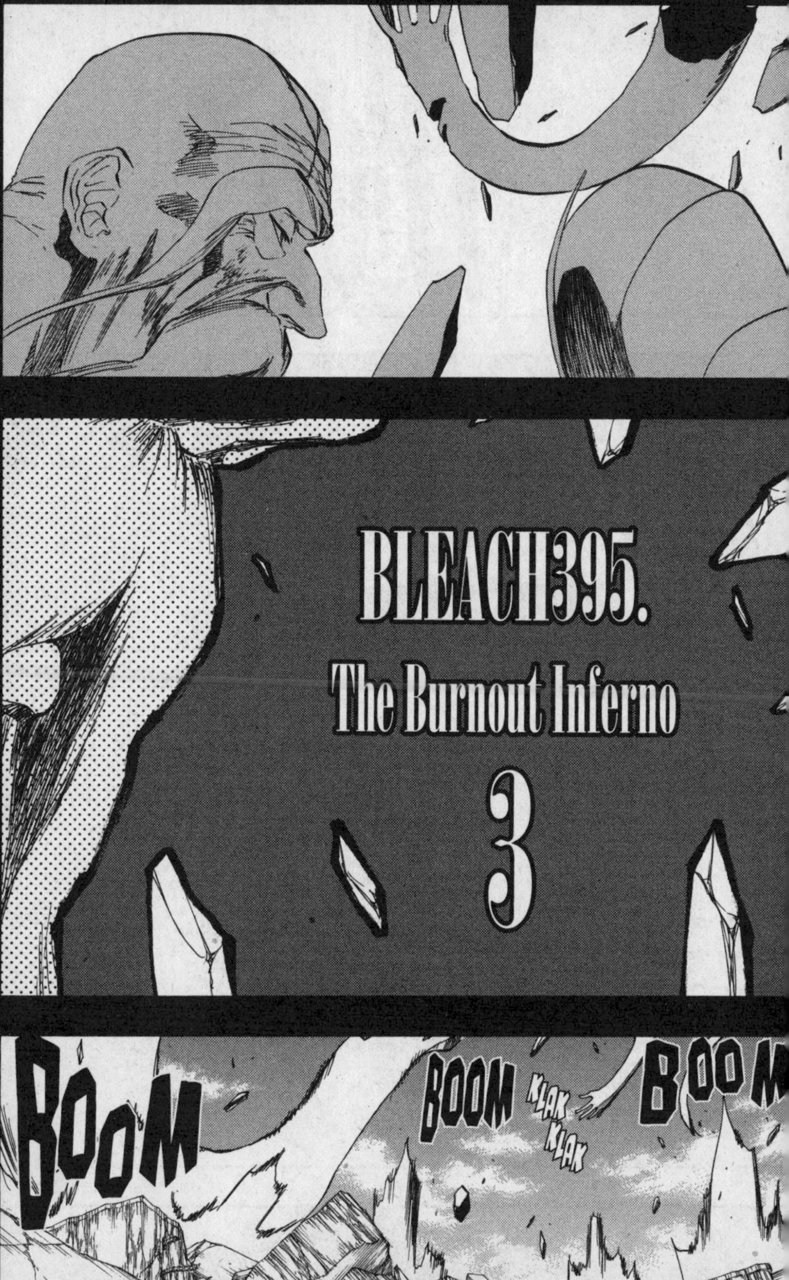
BLEACH395.
The Burnout Inferno
3
BOOM
BOOM
KLAK KLAK
BOOM

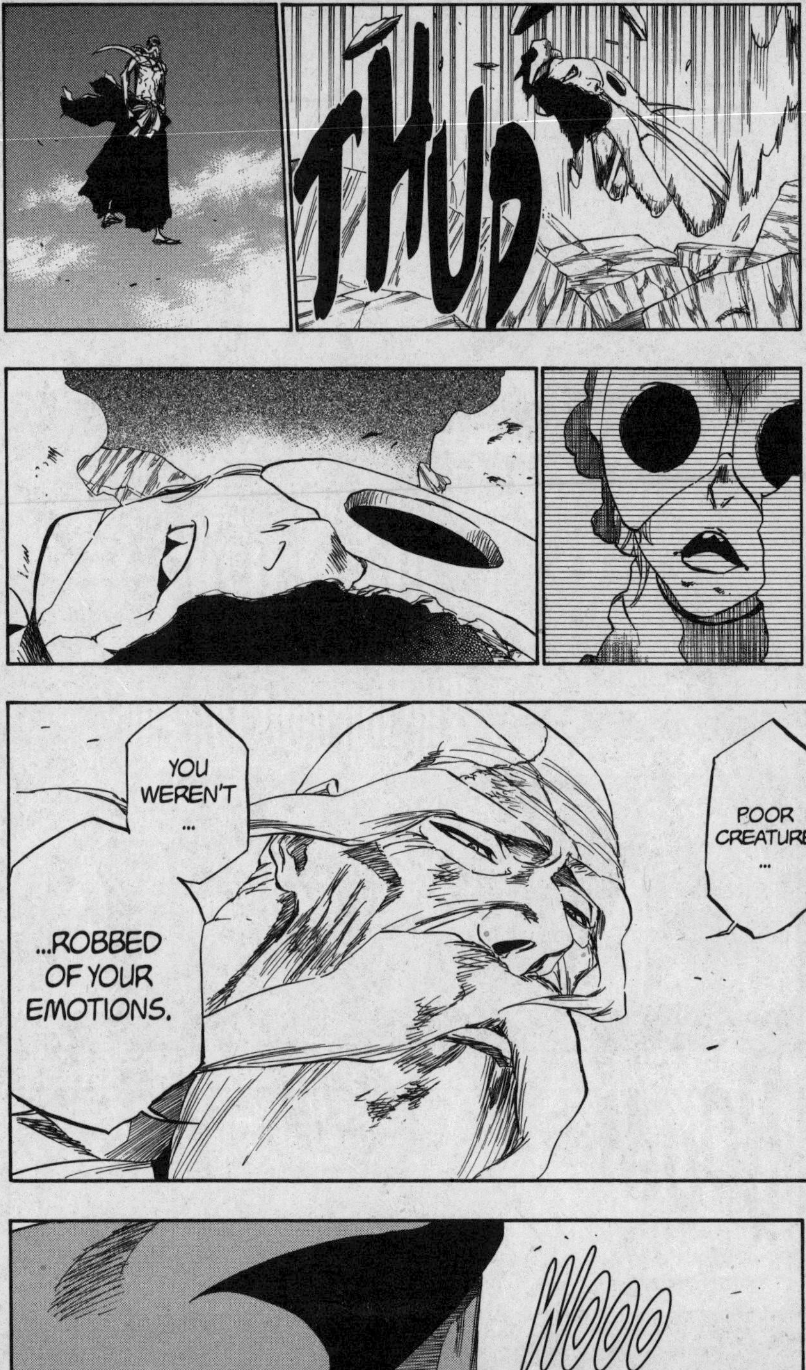
THUD
POOR CREATURE...
YOU WEREN'T...
...ROBBED OF YOUR EMOTIONS.
WOOO

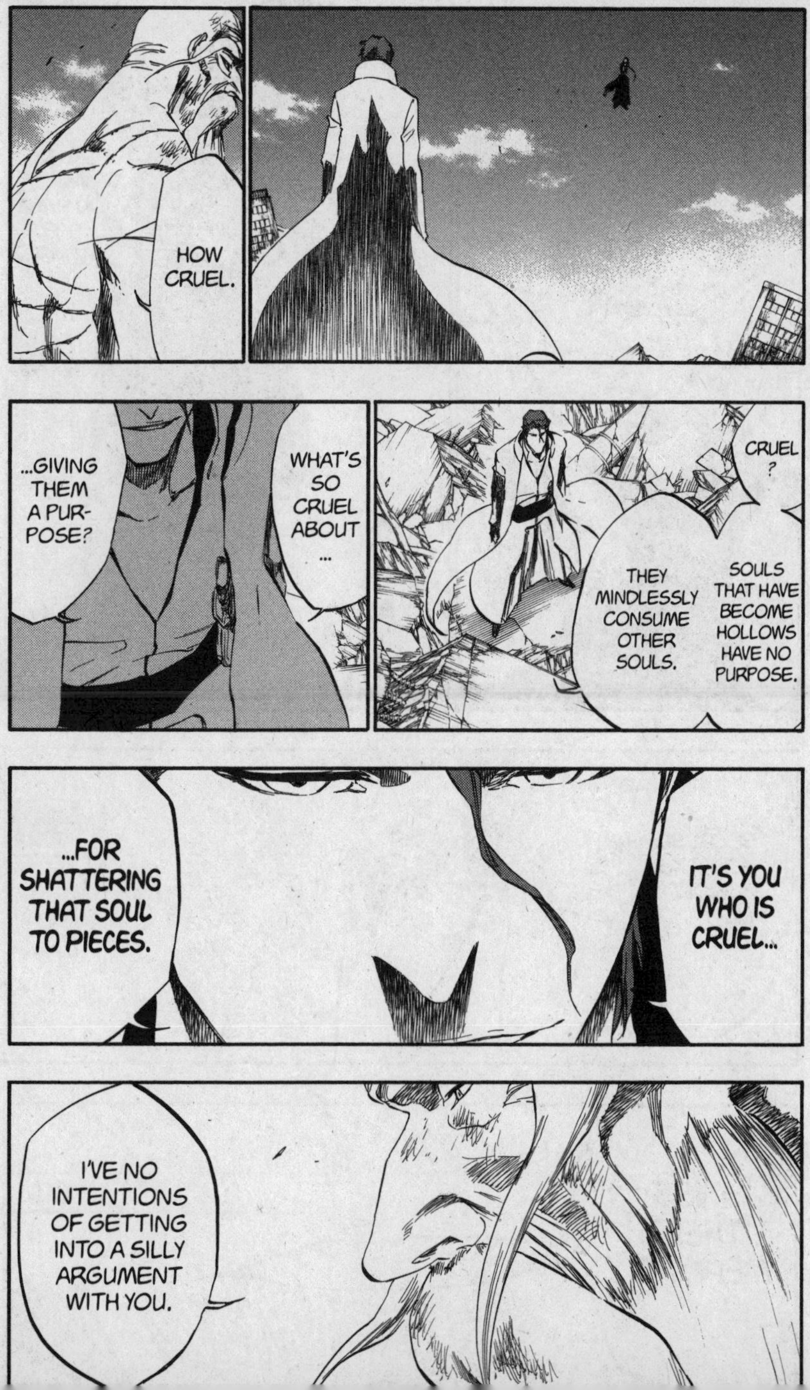
HOW CRUEL.
CRUEL?
SOULS THAT HAVE BECOME HOLLOWS HAVE NO PURPOSE.
THEY MINDLESSLY CONSUME OTHER SOULS.
WHAT'S SO CRUEL ABOUT ...
...GIVING THEM A PURPOSE?
IT'S YOU WHO IS CRUEL...
...FOR SHATTERING THAT SOUL TO PIECES.
I'VE NO INTENTIONS OF GETTING INTO A SILLY ARGUMENT WITH YOU.

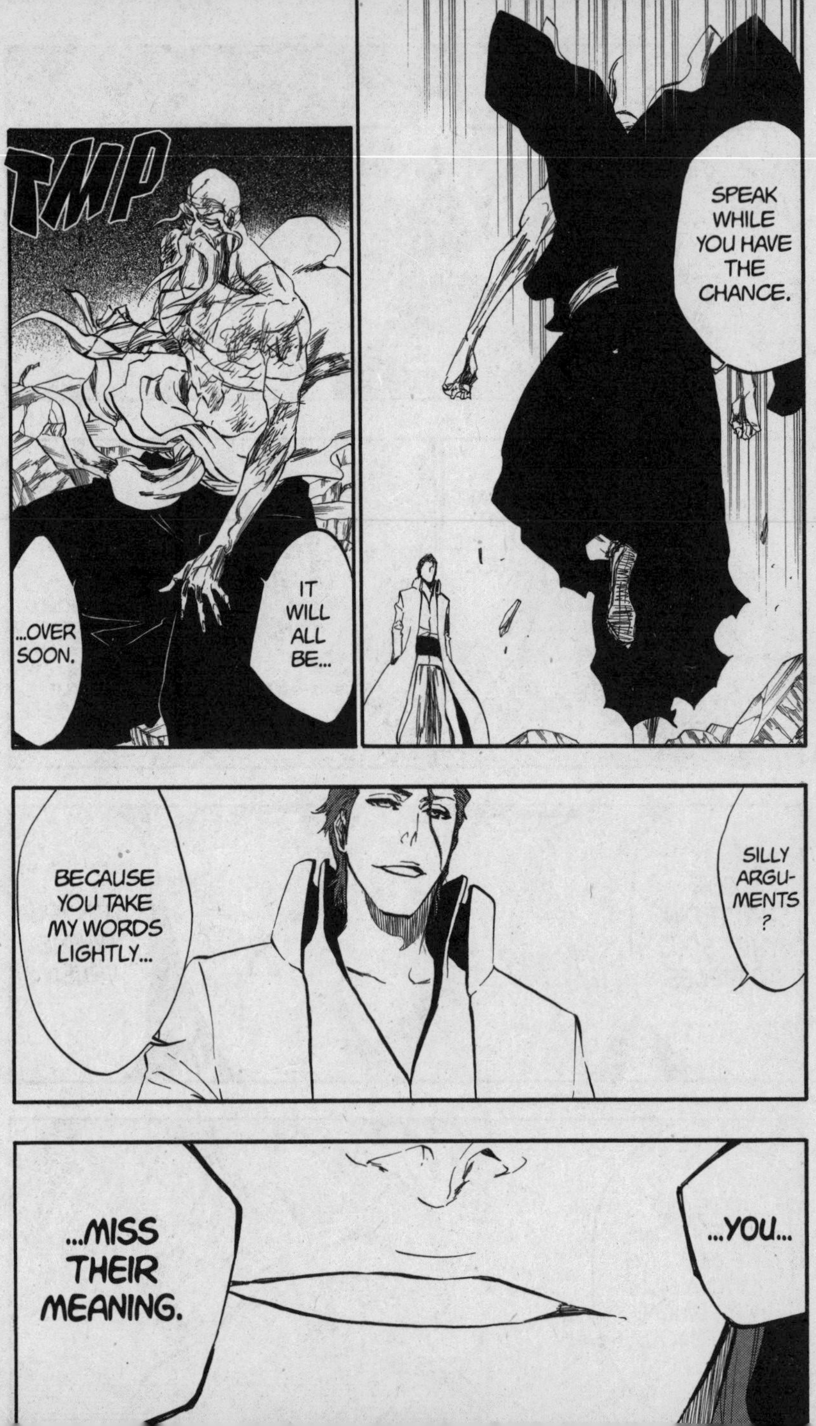
SPEAK WHILE YOU HAVE THE CHANCE.
TMP
IT WILL ALL BE...
...OVER SOON.
SILLY ARGU-MENTS?
BECAUSE YOU TAKE MY WORDS LIGHTLY...
...YOU...
...MISS THEIR MEANING.

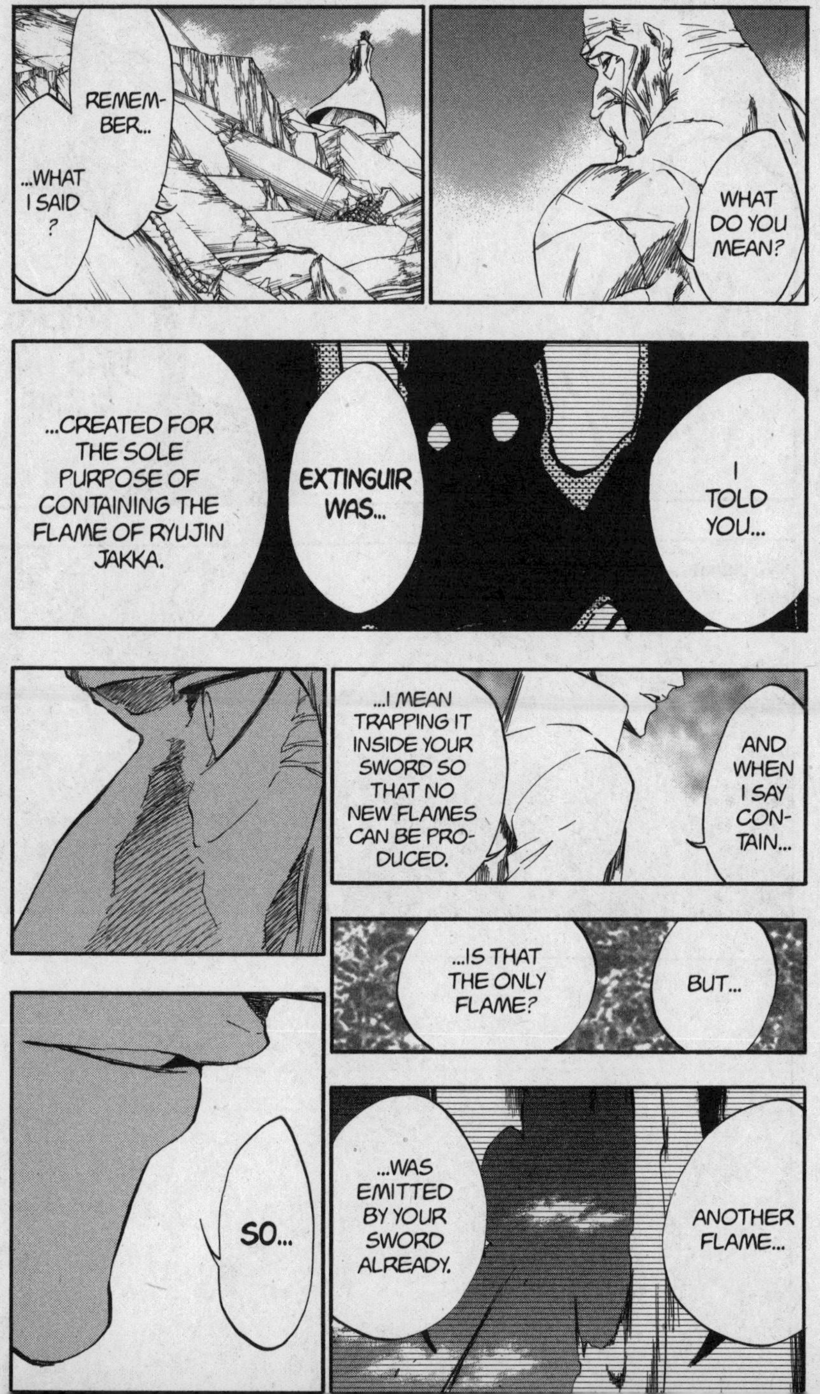
WHAT DO YOU MEAN?
REMEMBER... ...WHAT I SAID?
I TOLD YOU...
EXTINGUIR WAS...
...CREATED FOR THE SOLE PURPOSE OF CONTAINING THE FLAME OF RYUJIN JAKKA.
AND WHEN I SAY CONTAIN...
...I MEAN TRAPPING IT INSIDE YOUR SWORD SO THAT NO NEW FLAMES CAN BE PRODUCED.
BUT...
...IS THAT THE ONLY FLAME?
ANOTHER FLAME...
...WAS EMITTED BY YOUR SWORD ALREADY.
SO...

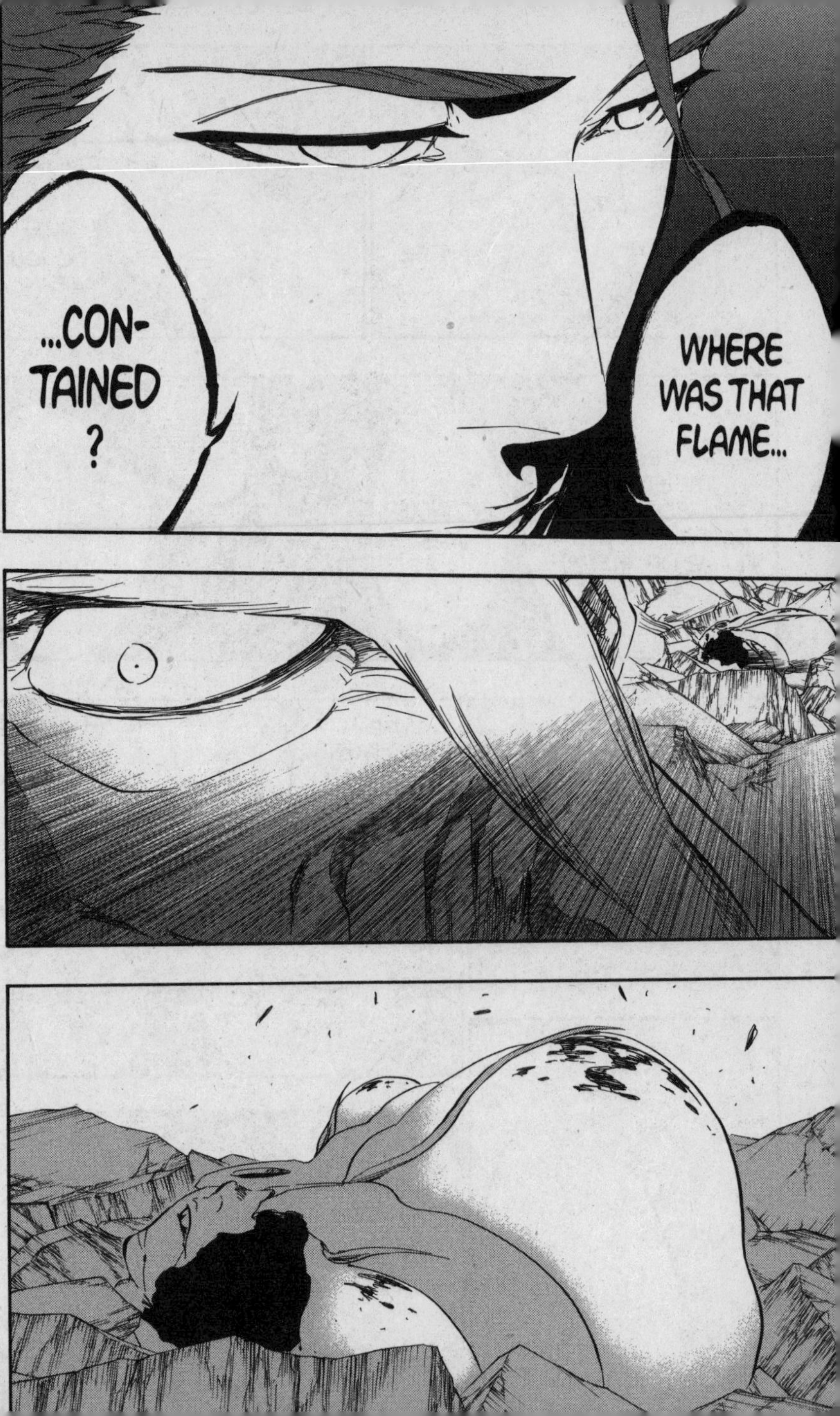
WHERE WAS THAT FLAME...
...CON-TAINED?

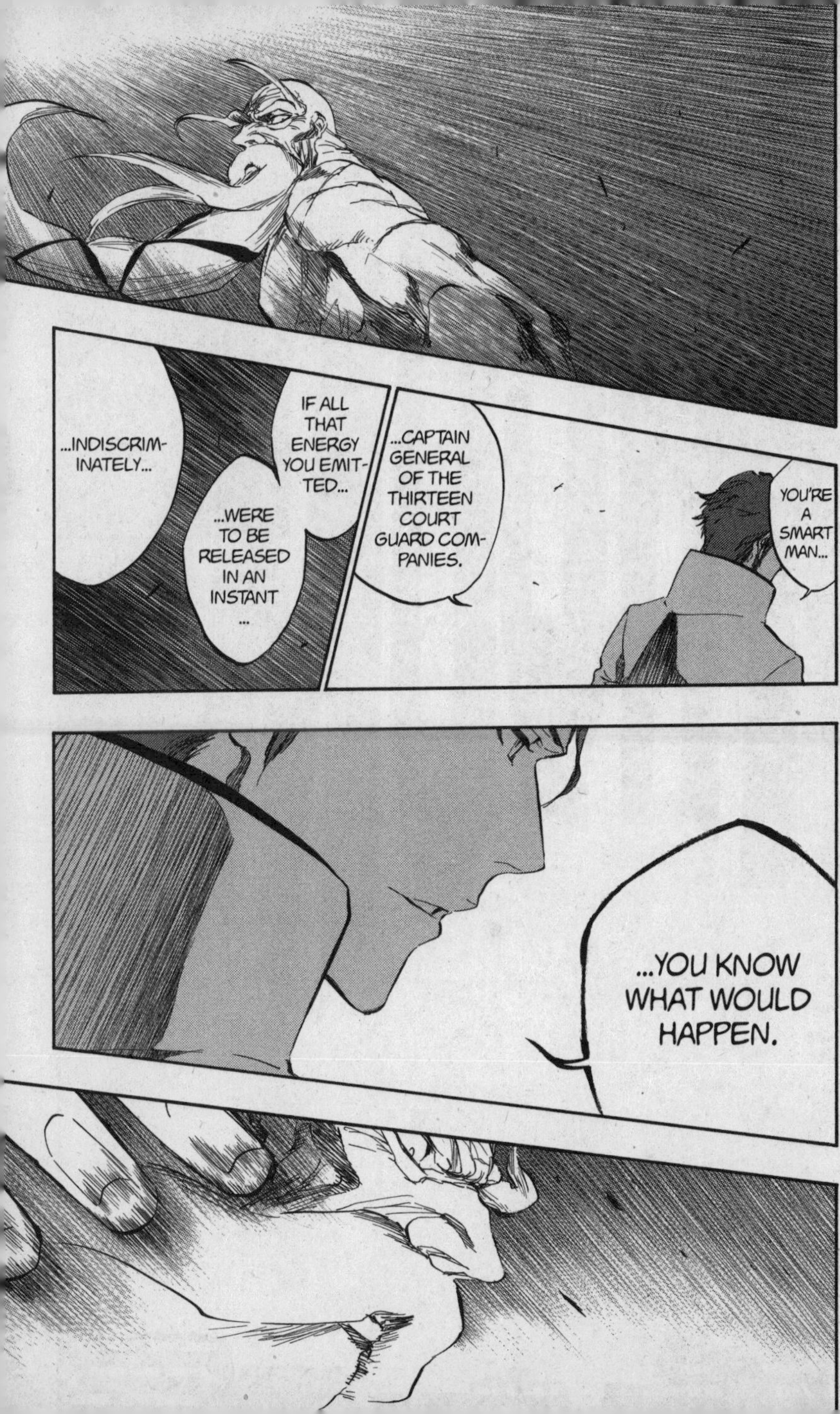
YOU'RE A SMART MAN...
...CAPTAIN GENERAL OF THE THIRTEEN COURT GUARD COMPANIES.
IF ALL THAT ENERGY YOU EMITTED...
...WERE TO BE RELEASED IN AN INSTANT...
...INDISCRIMINATELY...
...YOU KNOW WHAT WOULD HAPPEN.

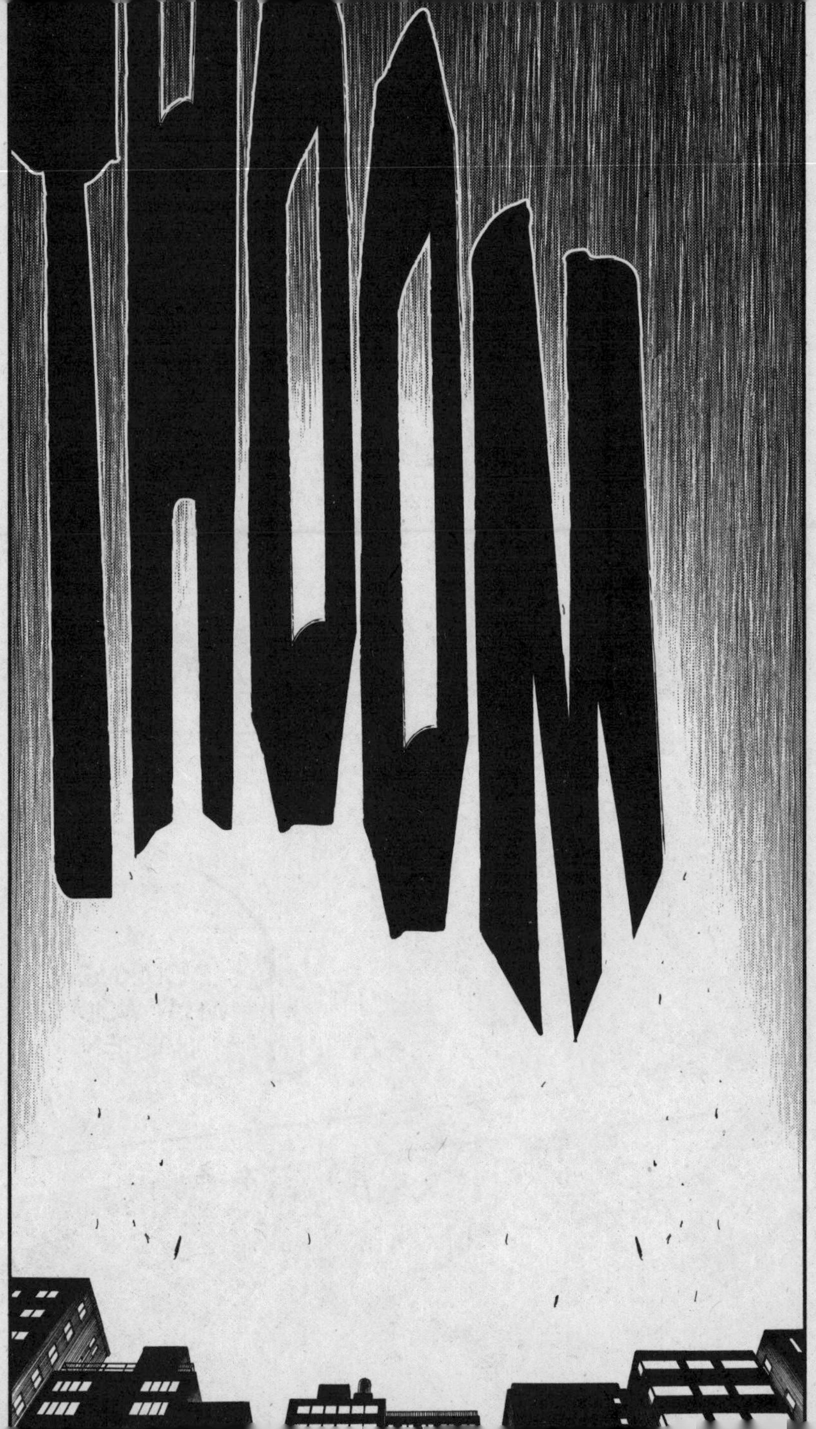
THOOM

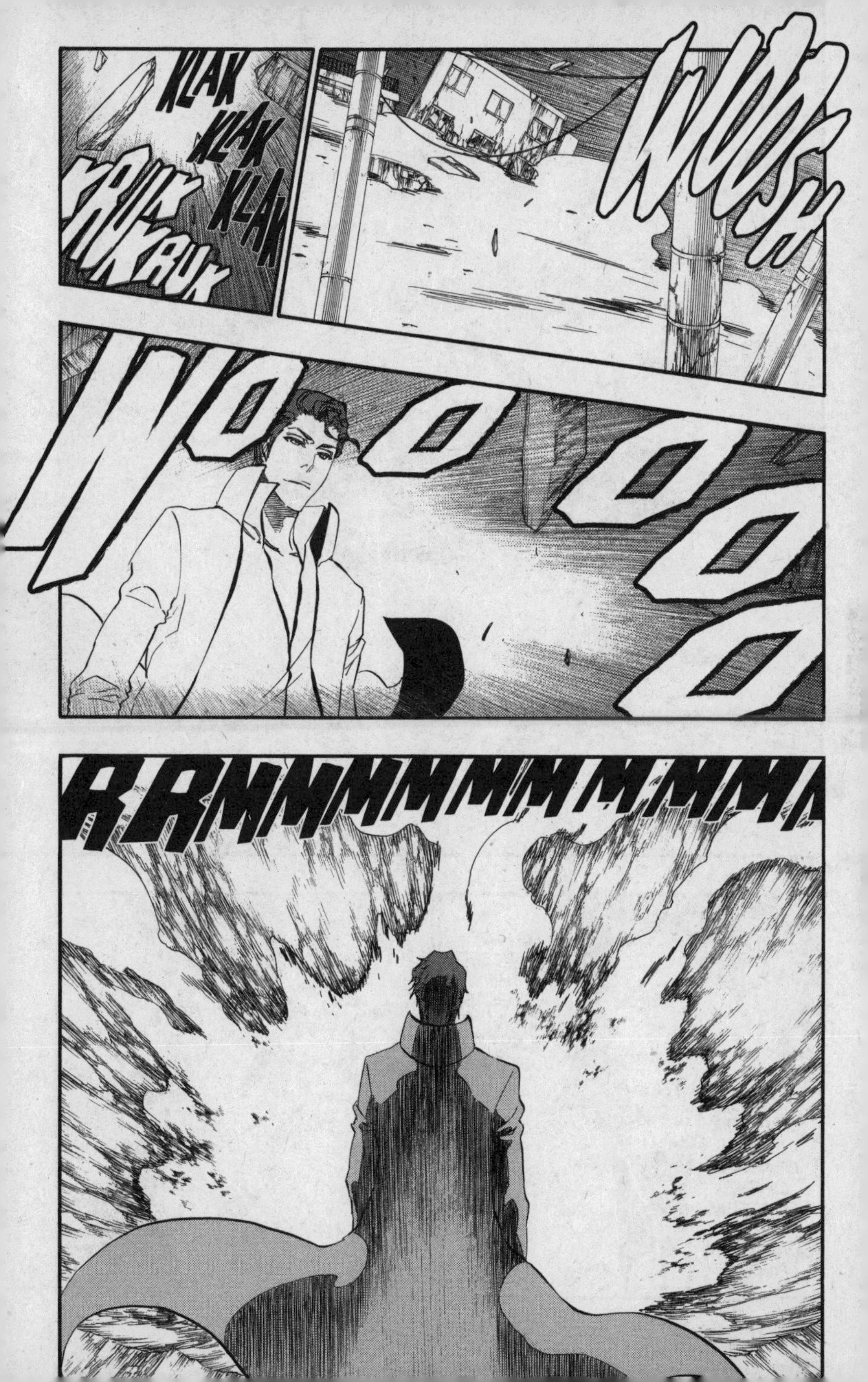
WUUSH
KLAK
KLAK
KLAK
KRUK KRUK
WOOOOOOO
RRMMMMMMMMMMM

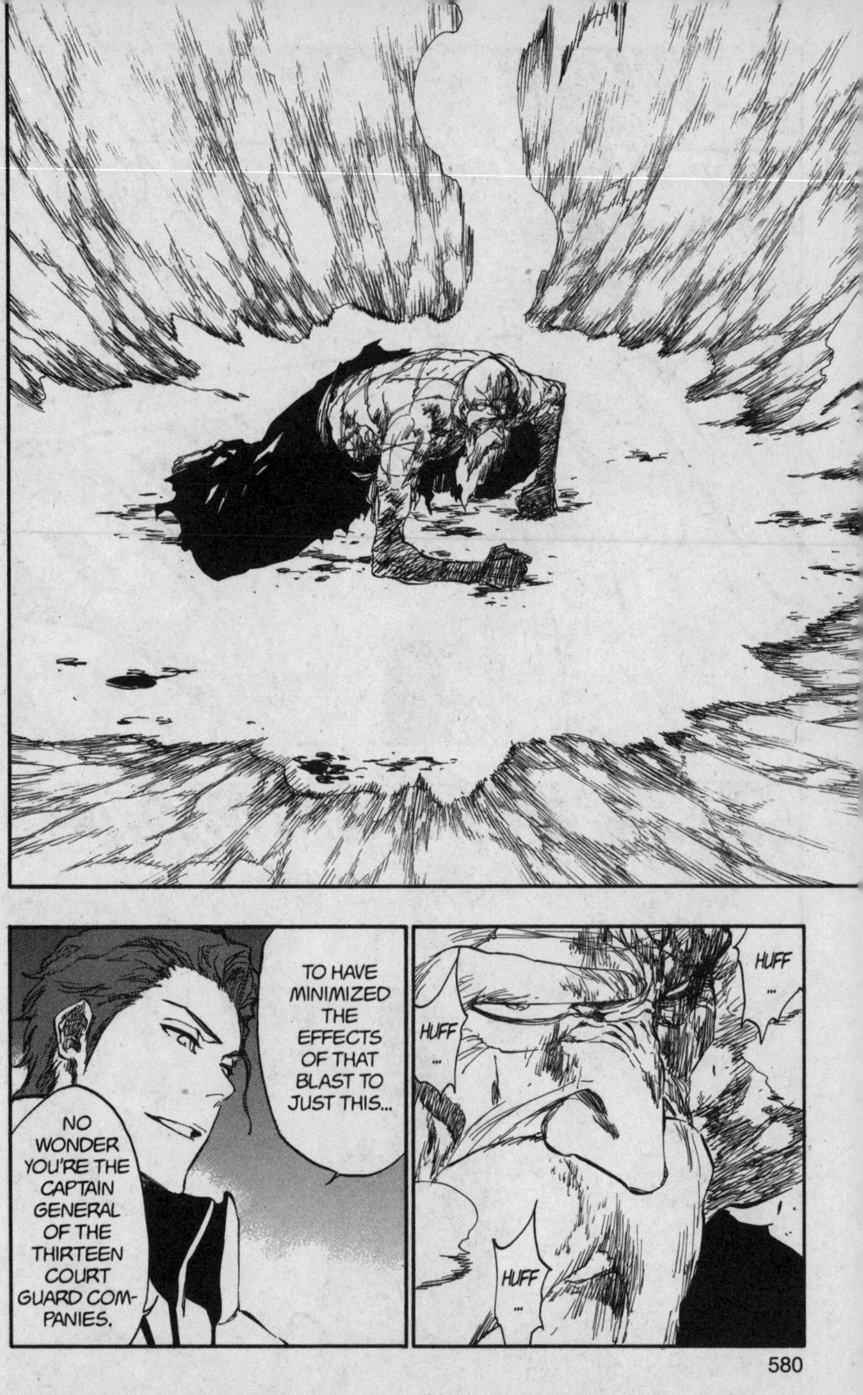
HUFF ...
HUFF ...
HUFF ...
TO HAVE MINIMIZED THE EFFECTS OF THAT BLAST TO JUST THIS...
NO WONDER YOU'RE THE CAPTAIN GENERAL OF THE THIRTEEN COURT GUARD COMPANIES.

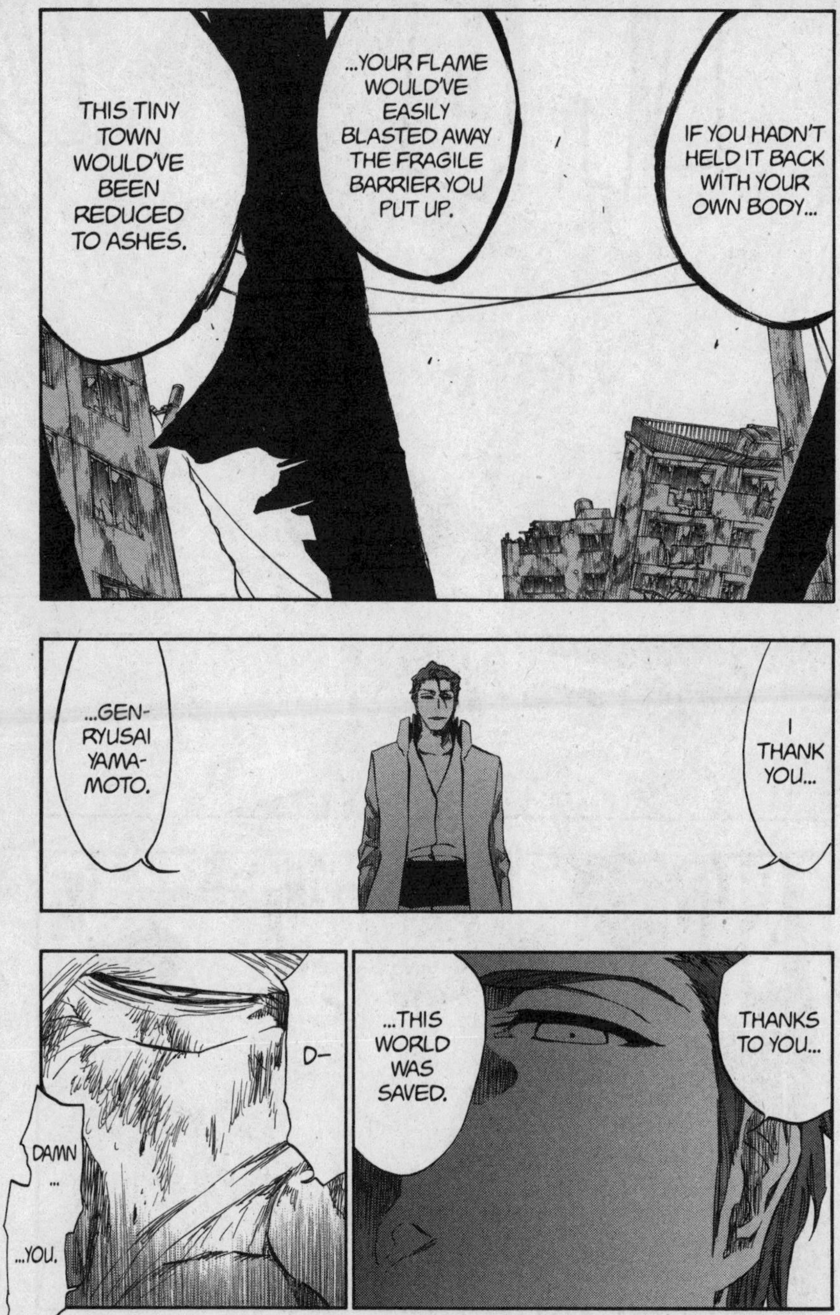
IF YOU HADN'T HELD IT BACK WITH YOUR OWN BODY...
...YOUR FLAME WOULD'VE EASILY BLASTED AWAY THE FRAGILE BARRIER YOU PUT UP.
THIS TINY TOWN WOULD'VE BEEN REDUCED TO ASHES.
I THANK YOU...
...GENRYUSAI YAMAMOTO.
THANKS TO YOU...
...THIS WORLD WAS SAVED.
D-
DAMN ... ...YOU.

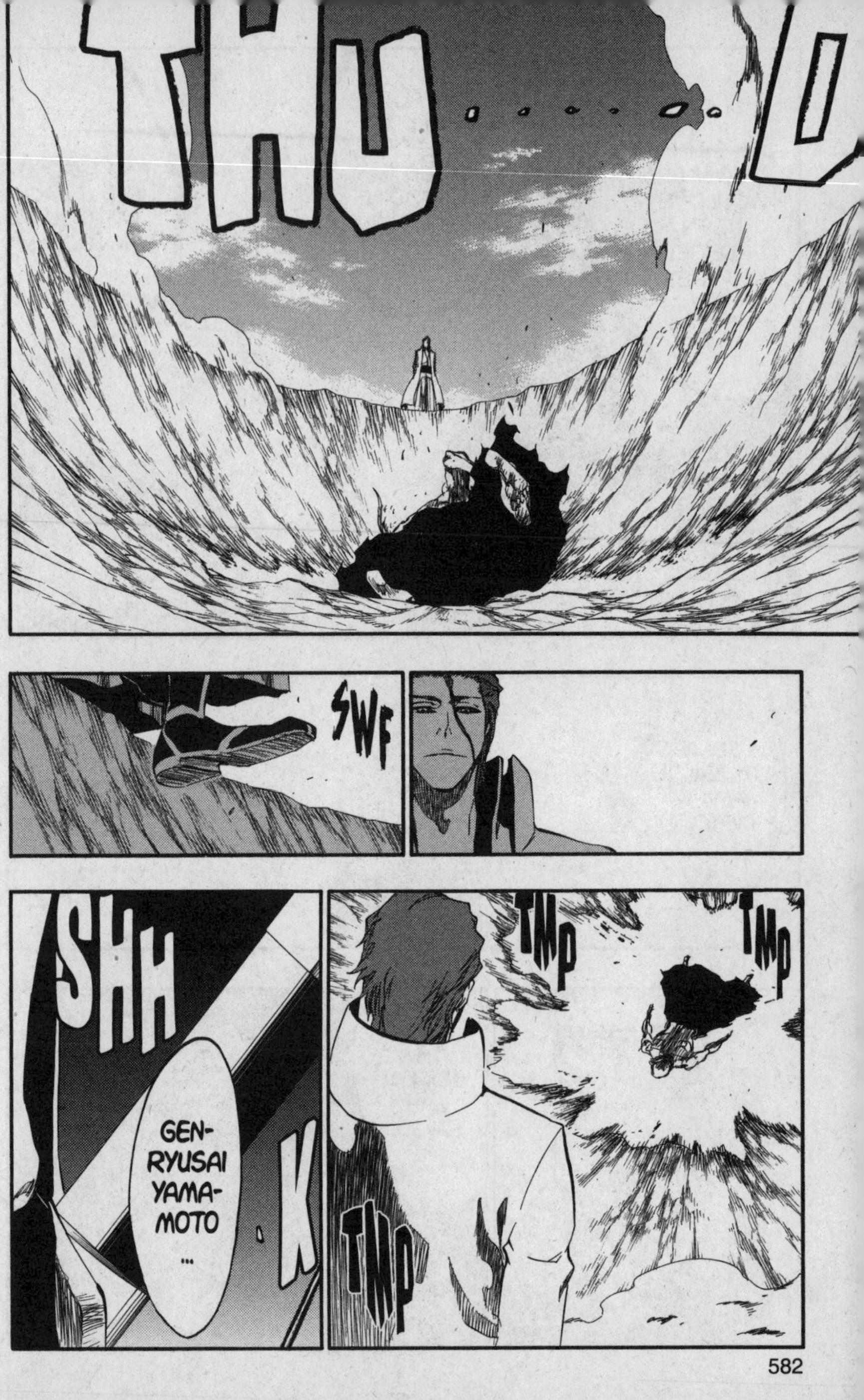
THU......D
SWF
TMP
TMP
TMP
SHH
GEN-RYUSAI YAMAMOTO...
K

READ THIS WAY

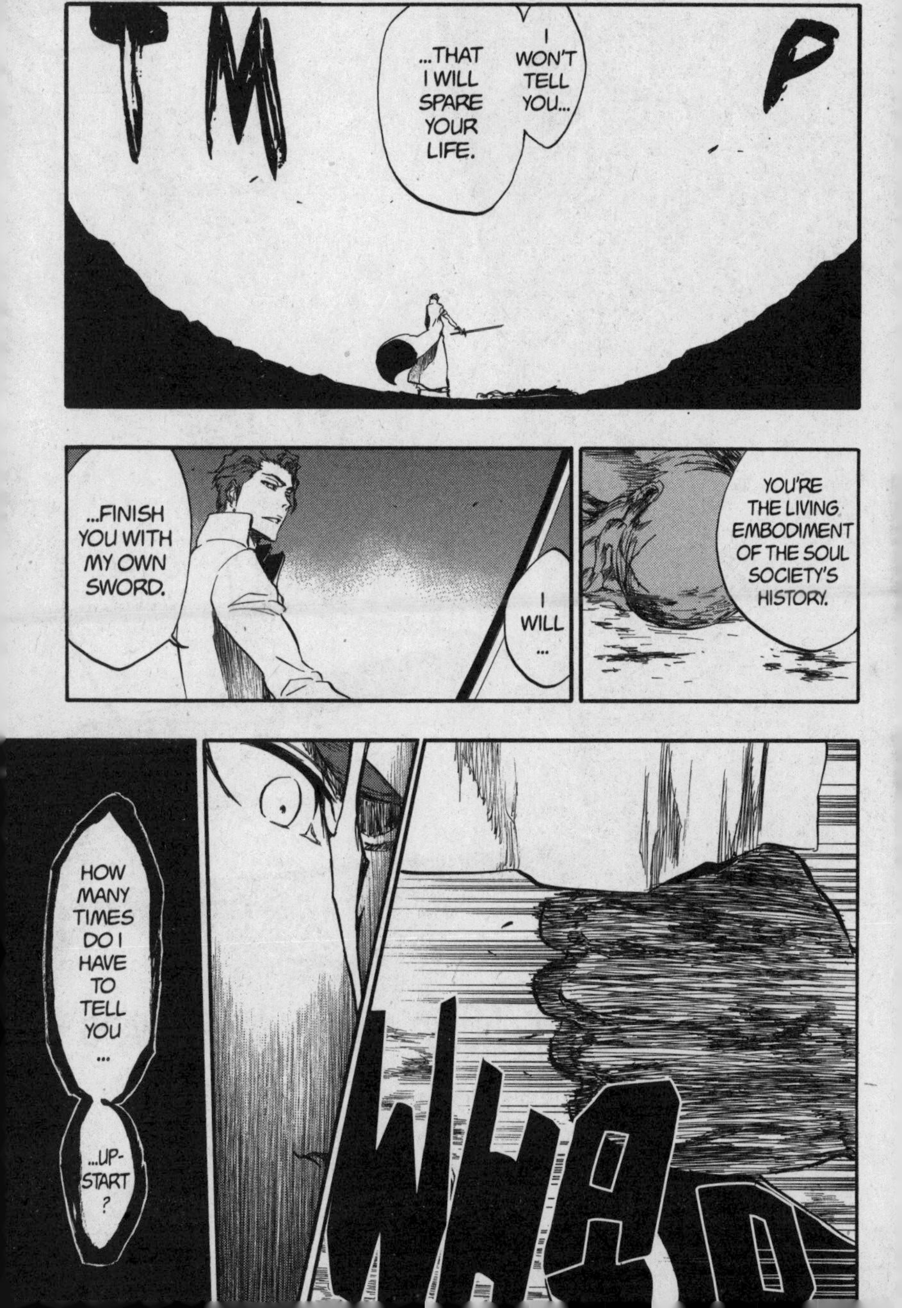
TMP
I WON'T TELL YOU...
...THAT I WILL SPARE YOUR LIFE.
YOU'RE THE LIVING EMBODIMENT OF THE SOUL SOCIETY'S HISTORY.
I WILL ...
...FINISH YOU WITH MY OWN SWORD.
HOW MANY TIMES DO I HAVE TO TELL YOU ...
...UP-START ?
WHAD

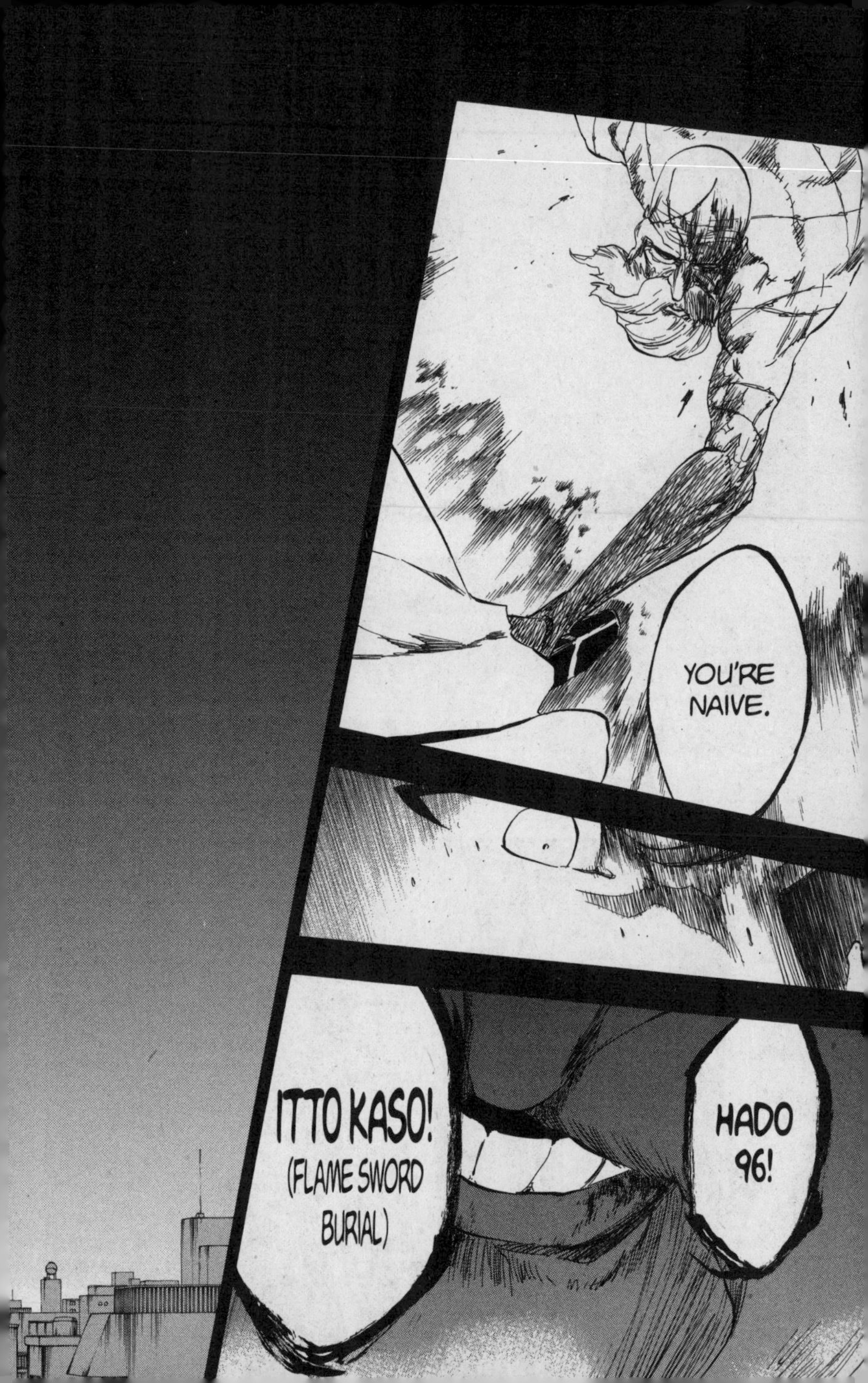
YOU'RE NAIVE.
HADO 96!
ITTO KASO!
(FLAME SWORD BURIAL)

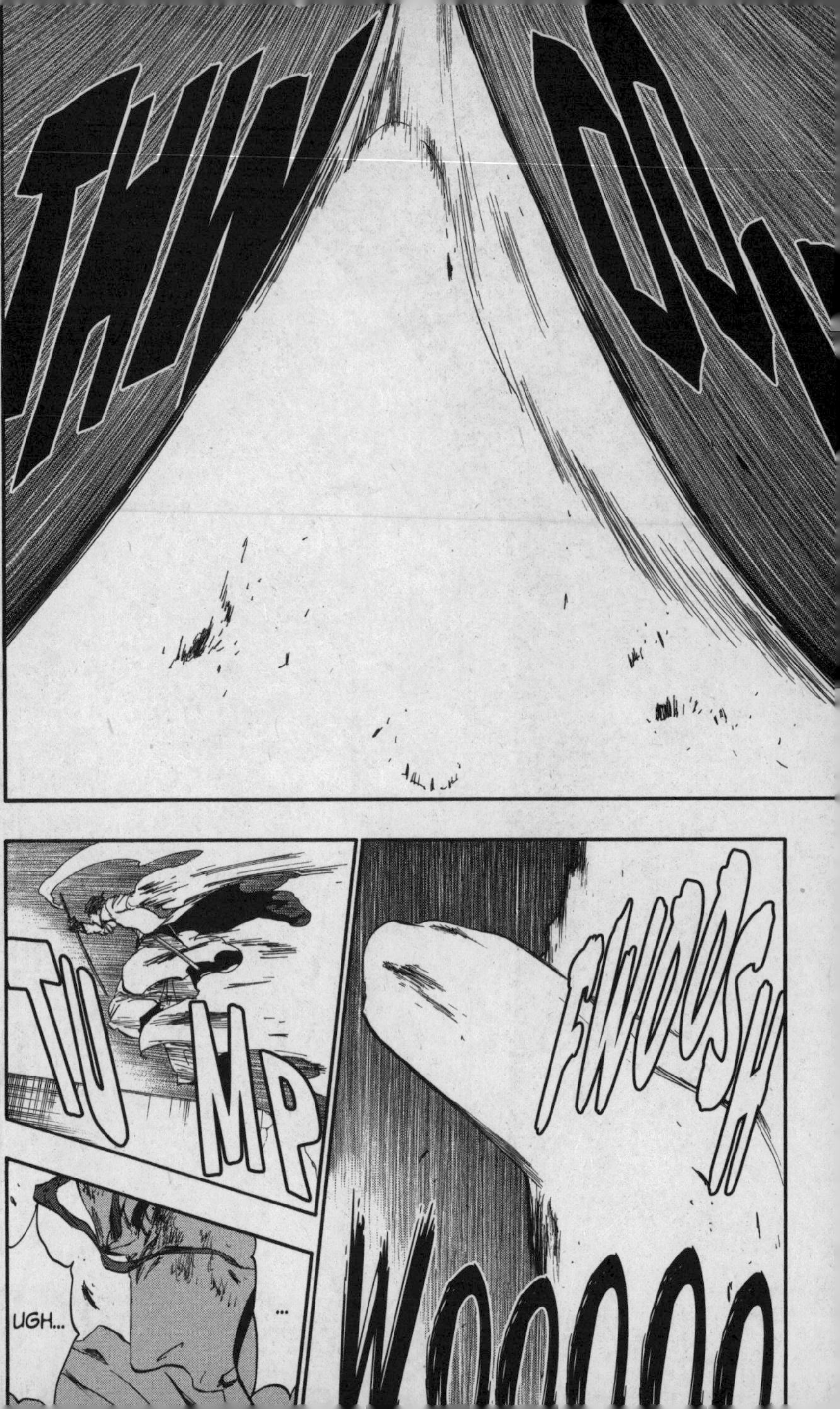
FWOOSH
WOOOOO
THUMP
...
UGH...

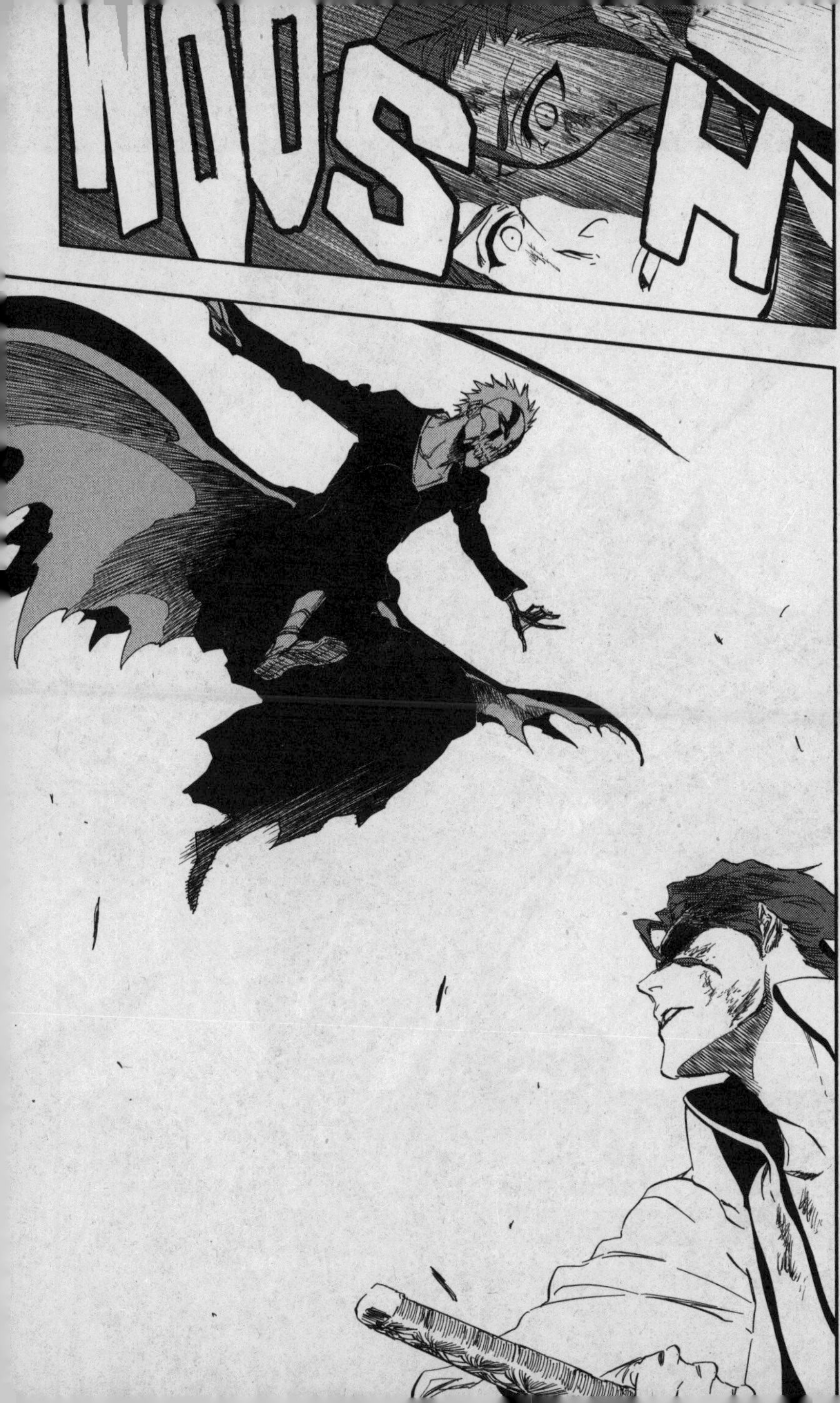

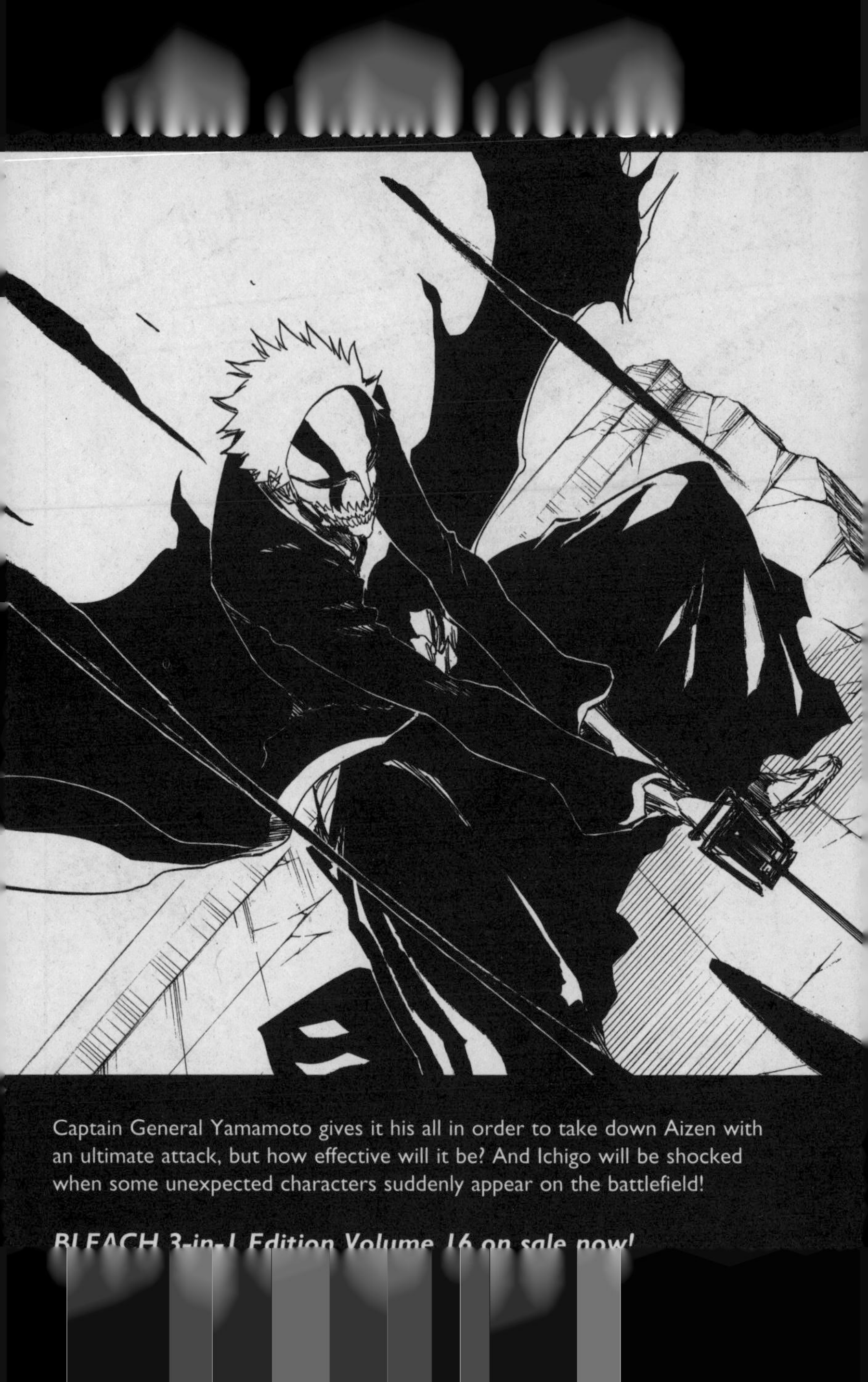

Captain General Yamamoto gives it his all in order to take down Aizen with an ultimate attack, but how effective will it be? And Ichigo will be shocked when some unexpected characters suddenly appear on the battlefield!

BLEACH 3-in-1 Edition Volume 16 on sale now!

Black ✤ Clover

STORY & ART BY YŪKI TABATA

Asta is a young boy who dreams of becoming the greatest mage in the kingdom. Only one problem—he can't use any magic! Luckily for Asta, he receives the incredibly rare five-leaf clover grimoire that gives him the power of anti-magic. Can someone who can't use magic really become the Wizard King? One thing's for sure—Asta will never give up!

SHONEN JUMP

VIZ media
www.viz.com

NARUTO

Story and Art by
Masashi Kishimoto

Naruto is determined to become the greatest ninja ever!

Twelve years ago the Village Hidden in the Leaves was attacked by a fearsome threat. A nine-tailed fox spirit claimed the life of the village leader, the Hokage, and many others. Today, the village is at peace and a troublemaking kid named Naruto is struggling to graduate from Ninja Academy. His goal may be to become the next Hokage, but his true destiny will be much more complicated. The adventure begins now!

WORLD'S BEST SELLING MANGA!

SHONEN JUMP

www.shonenjump.com   www.viz.com

You're Reading in the Wrong Direction!!

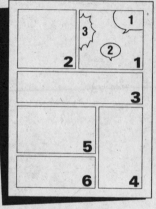

Whoops! Guess what? You're starting at the wrong end of the comic!

...It's true! In keeping with the original Japanese format, **Bleach** is meant to be read from right to left, starting in the upper-right corner.

Unlike English, which is read from left to right, Japanese is read from right to left, meaning that action, sound effects and word-balloon order are completely reversed... something which can make readers unfamiliar with Japanese feel pretty backwards themselves. For this reason, manga or Japanese comics published in the U.S. in English have sometimes been published "flopped"—that is, printed in exact reverse order, as though seen from the other side of a mirror.

By flopping pages, U.S. publishers can avoid confusing readers, but the compromise is not without its downside. For one thing, a character in a flopped manga series who once wore in the original Japanese version a T-shirt emblazoned with "M A Y" (as in "the merry month of") now wears one which reads "Y A M"! Additionally, many manga creators in Japan are themselves unhappy with the process, as some feel the mirror-imaging of their art skews their original intentions.

We are proud to bring you Tite Kubo's **Bleach** in the original unflopped format. For now, though, turn to the other side of the book and let the adventure begin...!

—Editor